The MOVING PICTURE BOY

The
MOVING
PICTURE
BOY

An International Encyclopaedia
from 1895 to 1995

JOHN HOLMSTROM

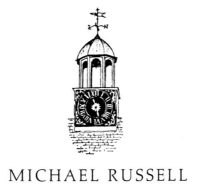

MICHAEL RUSSELL

© John Holmstrom 1996

First published in Great Britain 1996
by Michael Russell (Publishing) Ltd
Wilby Hall, Wilby, Norwich NR16 2JP

Typeset in Palatino
Printed and bound in Great Britain
by Biddles Ltd, Guildford and King's Lynn

Designed by Humphrey Stone

ISBN 0 85955 178 4

Contents

Foreword

In its 'featured' entries, this book is arranged not alphabetically but chronologically, to convey the history of the cinema and the way it has reflected social conditions and priorities in different countries at any given moment. At its end, the alphabetical index of names will include not only 'featured' ones but about 1,500 others who have played leads or memorable roles.

I have defined 'boy' as meaning, in show-biz terms, a male child whose voice has not yet broken, but who is old enough to learn lines. So there are few babies, and not many teenagers. I have made one or two allowances at the upper end, but only when the subject's 'boyishness' was convincing. In general the children in this book are between, say, 5 and 14.

Each entry will consist of name, nationality, date and place of birth where known, some biographical and descriptive notes and a filmography – even if it's only one title.

The nationality given (see p.8 for abbreviations) may not be that of the subject's birth if he migrated and if all or most of his films were made elsewhere. But this will emerge from his entry. Both his birthplace and films will be assumed to belong to 'his' country unless otherwise stated.

If the years fall within the 20th century, the initial '19' is omitted in the list of films, thus saving space and focusing on the vital digits.

A boy's filmography is often preceded by a note of later films he appeared in as an adult. These will not usually be credited to him in the indices, and will only appear if an authentic child actor is also involved. Thus the index entry for *Life Begins for Andy Hardy* will refer you to Bobby Winkler but not to its over-age star, Mickey Rooney.

If a boy actor's name, mentioned in another boy's entry, is followed by a diamond – ◊ – it indicates that he too has a featured entry. (See Boy Film Actors listing, p. 399.)

I finally abandoned, as too cluttering, the differentiation between full-length and short films, and between TV films and those made for the cinema. But only a selection of TV films is offered.

Titles in the filmographies are always given in the original language (where known), with an English translation (where possible) in brackets after it, except where the meaning is obvious even to non-linguists. We also add certain nonliteral English-language release titles. If these were well-known in the USA or Britain, they may also appear (cross-referenced) in the index.

Titles lengthened by whimsical appendages will be referred to by their accepted shorter form: thus *Le testament d'Orphée*, not *Le testament d'Orphée, ou Ne me demandez pas pourquoi*.

I have only put provisional or working titles in the index where these are not easily found elsewhere. Many reference books such as the Hollywood Film Archive's *Film Buff's Bible* (1972, ed. D. Richard Bauer) have useful lists of such titles. Probably the best and widest-ranging of all is the British Film Institute's *Catalogue of Stills, Posters and Designs* (1982, ed. Markku Salmi).

In choosing between two possible dates, either for a birth or a film, I have almost always opted for the earlier. If the birthdate is too early, its owner will no doubt tell me. If the film date precedes its premiere (usually the touchstone for film dating) it may give a truer indication of the year in which the film was shot. This would not apply, however, in the early years of the century, when films were often edited at breakneck speed and screened within weeks of their shooting.

For ease of finding within each year of a filmography, I have arranged films in alphabetical order, not in order of completion or premiere.

In the biographical notes, I have shown little interest in companies, contracts or salaries; nor in the 'sports and hobbies' so beloved of most previous kidologists. If the child was interested in astrology, pig-sticking or crocodile-breeding, I shall probably mention it. Swimming, riding or stamp-collecting, however, will not merit inclusion.

Nor do I go much into private lives, except in cases of drama or fatality. (It did seem rather extraordinary of Marc Best, writing nearly three years after Bobby Driscoll's well-publicised death, not even to mention that he was dead, let alone in what miserable circumstances.) Whether the subject married, or got divorced, or didn't, is none of our business.

On the rare occasions when I am so uncharitable as to say that little So-and-So was a little so-and-so, the tense is to be noted: I refer to his long-gone screen persona, not to his present well-loved and upstanding self.

TRANSLITERATION

Working on radio as a newsreader and music presenter, I became aware of the futility of international systems of transliteration as guides to *pronunciation*, which should after all be one of its basic functions. A transliteration has failed if it needs to be re-translated into a phonetic spelling, and to avoid this each language (or group of languages) should really have its own transliteration of Russian, Arabic, Chinese, Japanese and so on.

I am too ignorant of Oriental languages to attempt an 'English transliteration' of most of these, but as the Russian cinema bulks large in this book I have profited from the wise counsel of my friend Dmitri Makarov – who among other kindnesses has performed the heroic task of scanning the whole vast Soviet Film Catalogue for boy actors of the past and synopses of their films.

Dmitri admitted that no satisfactory or consistent system of transliteration from Russian had yet been devised – none that was simple enough not to need endless 'interpreting' – and agreed that it was worth my floating a purely pragmatic system of my own.

Many of the Russian vowels are preceded by a slight 'y' sound: thus a name apparently spelt Lebedev could transliterate as 'Lyebyedyef'. Unfortunately this not only looks grotesque, but could be misconstrued by an average English reader as 'Lie-by-dife'. The problem is less acute, happily, with the other vowels, where it's pretty clear that the 'y' is used consonantally. With 'e', though, I am using the 'y' only at the beginning of a word or name ('Yevgeni'), or to separate two vowels ('Alekseyev').

In tandem with the reservation of 'y' for consonantal purposes, I shall be rendering all the subtly complex endings previously rendered as '-y', '-iy', '-ij', '-īī', etcetera, simply as '-i'. Since I am also abandoning the old-established, French-inspired 'tch' for the simpler 'ch' – as in 'church' – it follows that Tchaikovsky now becomes Chaikovski: a shock to the system, I know, but surely one we can adjust to. (We are already perfectly happy with Chekhov.)

In addition, I'm proposing a novelty which I think will be a genuine help to pronunciation. When a final '-ov' or '-ëv' is, as quite often, *stressed*, I'm changing the 'v' to an eye-catching 'ff', to remind one of similarly stressed phrases like 'push *off*'. Thus: Malenkov but Khrushchoff, Andropov but Gorbachoff.

The vowel in a final '-ov' will have the same lack of weight and colour as the last 'o' in Jackson or Robertson. Nearly all unstressed vowels in Russian are colourless and neutral.

'Ch' as in 'church' I have mentioned. Of the other transliterated consonants, 'kh' is a guttural sound as in the Scottish 'loch', and 'zh' is like the 's' in 'measure'.

Acknowledgements

My first and greatest thanks must go to the British Film Institute and its staff, for the generous help they have given me, both over research in the reference and stills libraries and in the wonderful range of films, of all nations and periods, shown at the National Film Theatre. I owe a particular debt to Gillian Hartnoll, Michelle Snapes and Bridget Kinally for their forbearance of my seemingly endless delvings, and to the sadly missed John Gillett for his encyclopaedic knowledge and his unrivalled, lovingly compiled seasons of foreign films.

I want to thank many foreign archives and institutes for their kindness, with special mention of Sam Gill and all those at the Academy of Motion Picture Arts and Sciences in Beverly Hills. Also to the Museum of Modern Art (New York), the Cinémathèque Française, the Museo Nazionale del Cinema (Turin), Westdeutscher Rundfunk and, in their various national film archives, to Abas Hoxha (Albania), Meg Labrum (Australia), Milka Staykova and Nicholas Kaftandjieff (Bulgaria), Janus Barfoed (Denmark), Constanze Pollatschek, Helga Belach and Herbert Wiemer (Germany), Theodoros Adamopoulos (Greece), Adam Tóth (Hungary), P.K.Nair (India), Marica Marcellino (Italy), Akira Shimizu (Japan), Mariana Olteanu (Romania), Dolores Devesa (Spain), Bengt Forslund (Sweden), Leonid Kozloff, the late Mark Strochkov and the film studios of Georgia, Latvia and Lithuania (USSR, as was), and Zoran Sinobad (Yugoslavia, ditto).

Additional help with photographs has been given by the New York State University Library at Purchase, and with translations by members of the BBC Overseas Service – most particularly the late John Newman (Japanese), Shakuntala Chandan (Hindi) and Teresa Javorska (Czech) – and by the unbeatable staff of the BBC Pronunciation Unit.

I thank the great film production companies of the world – on my own behalf and that of the international children's charity Intercare, to whom this book's royalties are going – for their generous forbearance over my use of their stills. (Sadly, permission has been refused by Disney and Paramount, which has caused a few gaps in post-1940 American illustrations.) Special generosity has been shown in Britain by the Rank Organisation, Romulus and the Children's Film Foundation. If I have failed to contact any owners of copyright, I ask for your understanding, and hope that you will approve the book's purpose.

There are two scholars I'd like to single out for their immense kindness in providing me with information on just about anything in European cinema: Geoffrey Donaldson of Rotterdam and Hanns-Georg Rodek of Schwenningen. They have been towers of strength over a long period, as has Markku Salmi of the BFI, that peerless identifier of stills and hoarder of movie credits. More recently I have had great help from the American masters of the birth-and-death, Bill Doyle and the much-missed Bob Evans.

I've had expert and unstinting guidance on the cinema of their own countries from Peter Clauhs and Herbert Holba (Austria), Euchariste Paulhus (Canada), Wang Rui (China), Zdeněk Stabla (Czechoslovakia), Marguerite Engberg and Court Helmer (Denmark), Markku Salmi (Finland), Raymond Chirat and Roger Icart (France), Aldo Bernardini and Vittorio Martinelli (Italy) and Gösta Werner (Sweden), together with four good men who have died in the last few years: Wadim Berestowski (Poland), Istvan Csurgay (Hungary), Peter Hagemann (Germany) and Jean Mitry (France).

Among many friends (some also departed) who have contributed information, inspiration, photographs, suggestions or sheer hard work are Kevin Brownlow, Ginevra de Csipkay, Jon Curle, Timothy d'Arch Smith, Lee Donlin, Chris Edmonds, Ander Gunn, Jerry Jones, Elisabeth Julius-Berneis, Dick Kelly, Dmitri Makarov, Werner Mohr, Carsten Niemann, Liam O'Leary, Raef Payne, Garth Pedler, Malcolm Pleasants, David Robinson, Ken Sephton, Jacques Simonot, Chris Symonds, Bob Villard and Tony White.

Finally, and far from least, let me thank all those ex-boy-actors — and their directors and families — who have answered my questions and questionnaires with such patience and good humour, and without whom, it can safely be asserted, none of this would have happened.

Introduction

My first visit to the cinema was not a success. Instead of smiling and sobbing with *National Velvet* or *Lassie Come Home* – those came later – I was taken by a maiden aunt to see some gory epic, of which the only image that stays with me is the sweating, close-up face of somebody being either crucified or burnt at the stake. (Since I seem to recall flames but not thorns, it may have been the latter.) What this did to my psyche is unsure, but at the time I watched in horrified silence, stoically assuming that it was a foretaste of the adult life that awaited me, and that I had better get used to the idea.

Green gills on returning home may have convinced my elders that the lesson was premature, for I never went out with that particular aunt again and the pabulum thereafter was of a 'family' nature: the full-length Disney cartoons, some harmless swashbuckling with Errol Flynn, films featuring Roddy McDowall as a sensitive but plucky boy who shamed me, or Anne Revere as a calm, rock-like mother quite unlike my own.

Saturday-night entertainments at boarding school meanwhile introduced me to the comedies of Will Hay and the Hulberts, potted British history of the *Tudor Rose* and *Sixty Glorious Years* variety, empire-building parables like *The Four Feathers* and *King Solomon's Mines*. As adult role-model, however, I took not Ronald Colman nor Ralph Richardson but the absent-mindedly tetchy Michael Wilding, whom I still find admirable. My favourite comic, I blush to admit, was Arthur Askey.

The children didn't make a great impression on me, apart from McDowall, Margaret O'Brien (very much the tiny *grande dame*) and Butch Jenkins (a freckled id of sloth). I came in for some middle-period Shirley Temple, but she was altogether too bright and bossy for my taste, besides being disqualified by sex from any serious identification. Mickey Rooney was too bumptious and too far advanced into the vale of teens.

Child actors soon ceased to interest me, anyway. My own concerns were now with 'adult' subjects: romantic partners, artistic and professional qualms, tests of moral and physical courage. These in turn gave way to social issues and exotic settings, as the world of foreign cinema was explored. (America had not counted as foreign, having already been so assimilated into our culture.) France, Russia, Italy, Germany and Sweden took turns in enriching my internal scenery.

In the course of this cinematic education, I encountered foreign child actors for the first time — seeming, in their only half-followed lingo, twice as real and interesting as the Anglo-Saxons I had hitherto known. *Gorki's Childhood, Nous les gosses, Bicycle Thieves, Germany Year Zero, Shoeshine, Le visiteur*, and later *Jeux interdits* and the Apu trilogy from India revealed spunky, stoical kids with little or no accretion of directorial sugar or sanctimony. Foreign tongues may, of course, have flattered their owners — to my ears — by the mere absence of Hollywood cuteness or British primness, but these children were acting in a way I hadn't seen enough of before: with their eyes, their bodies, their very spirits sometimes.

What did flatter them, in a sense, was the quality of the films they were acting in. It was hardly fair to compare the relatively bland 'family film' of the late Thirties and early Forties with the angry blaze of emotion and talent that burst from the embers of World War Two. In retrospect, the 'family film' had its own nobility — often misplaced or rose-tinted, but deep-rooted too. One kind of cinema was complemented by the other, and perhaps ultimately sterile without it.

Many of the foreign kids had another advantage: they were not professional actors but first-time-out amateurs, chosen because they looked right for a part and seemed to have the intelligence, sensitivity and above all the malleability that the director needed. In most cases they made few or no further screen appearances. The ones that built up careers as children were usually those who already had training and stage experience, but also the adaptability to move with the times and their own changing frames.

It was hereabouts, I suppose, that the phenomenon of child acting began to interest me as a subject: the simultaneous naturalness and unnaturalness of the pursuit, and its built-in pathos, since the gift almost always seemed to evaporate with adolescence, or at least would need to be consciously relearnt; the awful anticlimax of such 'discontinued' children's lives, the depths of disappointment from which only the toughest could hope to clamber.

Although many children are natural and exuberant actors — or at least performers — the very concept of a Child Star strikes us now as more than a little repulsive. We think on the one hand of a pampered, conceited and petulant moppet, surrounded by an adoring (if secretly loathing) cohort of adult minions — agents, press-men, dressers, secretaries, tutors; and on the other the exploiters (not excluding parents) living off each small monster, milking every last dollar from it while they can, before the bloom fades, childish cuteness sprouts into gawky self-consciousness, and another drained, disoriented adolescent is flung out on to the studio scrapheap.

Press agents throughout the decades have insisted, almost desperately, that their particular star-child — despite the studio-centred life, the adult company, the bright lights and the razzmatazz — was just an ordinary kid once the day's work was done, never happier than with his train-set or her dolls, helping Mom in the kitchen or enjoying a rough-and-tumble with the local boys. No one was fooled.

With some happy exceptions, the Child Star *was* a rather wretched creature, both spoiled and overworked, arrogant and bewildered, hopelessly cut off from ordinary people and an ordinary childhood. During the heyday of the phenomenon — say from 1910 to 1940 — the successful ones worked almost continuously, while the less successful trained, auditioned and fought for those secondary parts which would at least keep their parents and agents in reasonable comfort and might, God willing, lead to a lucky break and a place in the Big League.

Their way of life couldn't by any stretch of the imagination be called natural for a child. By and large they were hothouse plants, and not always very attractive ones. But whatever silly things the small performers may be required to do, they themselves will normally have been chosen for possessing more than average looks, intelligence or personality. True, there are examples of children representing merely pretty dolls for adults to drool, swoon or agonise over, but these 'moppets' (the awful word for once seems apt) seldom had a long shelf-life.

The Child Star was, almost by definition, a product of the capitalist system — notably of the USA, whose films reached every corner of the film-going world, even the early Soviet Union. Not only was a receptive public needed to take the child to its great warm heart, recognise it with pleasure in story after story, laugh and cry with it, but also a high-powered and highly skilful advertising industry to market the child as a world-wide product, make it a household name and face. If none of the moppets was merchandised quite as relentlessly as a Mickey Mouse or a Snoopy, there were innumerable Coogan, Temple and Cooper ephemera: dolls, clocks, colouring books and toffee-tins. (Just as the anxious face of E. T. adorned more recent chocolate-boxes.)

Other major film-making nations created their own child stars, on a modester scale, often hailed as Britain's/France's/Schleswig-Holstein's Jackie Coogan or Shirley Temple. But they only promoted them half-heartedly even at home, as if resigned to the triumph of their Hollywood rivals, and made few and abortive efforts to export their films.

As if exemplifying the adage that children should be seen but not heard, the silent period really was the golden age of child film actors. France had her Bébé, Bout de Zan, Simone Genevois and Jean Forest, Germany her Loni Nest and Waldemar Pottier, and the USSR had a whole throng of featured kids. But despite their appeal, only the earliest of these, such as Bébé (known in the USA as 'Jimmie', in Germany as 'Bubi', and so on), made much impression abroad.

Partly from antipathy and partly from realism, I am very sparing with the word 'star', which to me means one who plays a whole string of leading roles, and whose next film is eagerly awaited. Once full-length films became the norm, there were only three major child stars — Coogan, Temple and Cooper — and only a handful of children, since 1940, who played more than one or two starring roles. Mark Lester was a star for about five years after *Oliver!*, but not a very fascinating one for those short on maternal instincts. Ricky Schroder has been a star in recent times, but much of his work has only been seen on television, and though it's no longer reasonable to exclude TV films and even series from a study like this – they are all recorded on some film-like medium, which has at least as good a chance of survival as old-style film stock – they inevitably *seem* more ephemeral.

At the dawn of the cinema there were no stars, and even when the public began recognising favourites these remained shrouded in anonymity – 'The Biograph Girl', 'The Kalem Cowboy', and so on – probably, in the main, for contractual reasons. (Theatre proprietors would not have been best pleased to think that their principal assets were wearing themselves out all day at the studios, before clocking in half dead for the live show.) It wasn't till 1909 that players began to be credited: at first just the leading two or three names, then gradually more.

The subjects of some of the early child movies were bizarre in the extreme, often based on sentimental music-hall ballads or poems. One called *Papa's Letter* - filmed at least twice before 1914 – was a favourite party-piece of the novelist G. B. Stern. This is how it went.

A little boy watches his widowed mother writing a letter, and asks if they could send one to Daddy in heaven. He's told that letters don't go that far. Hearing the postman approaching, he then sticks a stamp on his own forehead and asks if *he* can be a letter. The reply is still negative. So the child runs out into the road to look for a box and attempt to post himself. At which point, by sheer bad luck, 'a pair of maddened horses', having broken free from a carriage, hurtle round the corner and trample the little fantasist into the dust:

> Dark the mark upon his forehead,
> Where the cruel hoof had trod.
> He was stamped and gone to heaven:
> Papa's Letter was with God!

Which rivals the newspaper headline glimpsed in the 1980 masterpiece *Airplane!*: 'Boy trapped in refrigerator eats own foot.'

One of my first tasks, which took many months, was to scan microfilm, from 1909 to 1920, of the American trade weekly *Moving Picture World*, a hefty item of more than 100 pages aimed partly at exhibitors and partly at cinema-goers. (Or kinema-goers. The terms 'film' and 'movie' had not yet been settled on, and films were still 'photoplays', while a screenwriter was a 'scenarioist'.) The sheer productivity of the early film industry was terrifying: the combined efforts of the competing companies were turning out nearly 100 new films every week – mostly short ones, it's true, but beginning to get longer. Two-reelers (about 20 minutes) started appearing in 1911 or so, and the first four-reeler in early 1914. This was D. W. Griffith's *Judith of Bethulia*, soon to be eclipsed in size by his vast *Birth of a Nation* and *Intolerance*.

It was a fascinatingly alien world to me, peopled by rubes (gullible rustics), simps (simpletons), wimps (the word has now made a welcome comeback), milquetoasts and pantywaists (varieties of effete gentlemen) and yeggs (burglars or safebreakers). There was much emphasis on the hilarious smelliness of Limburger cheese. Popular characters bore names like Lord Helpus, Musty Suffer, Svengarlic, Kneeland Pray, Roy L. Flush and Colonel Heeza Liar.

The humour was, you might say, crude, though even I was startled by a 1913 Pathe film called *The Hairy Ainus*, which I took for a spelling mistake before learning with some relief that it referred to the Ainu, a shaggy Japanese tribe.

Child actors were present in abundance: adorable little girls bringing estranged parents together again, generous rich boys showing charity to the poor, defiant poor boys whupping rich ones for mocking their shabby clothes, pathetic match-girls, gallant drummer-boys, pranksters and tragic victims of both sexes.

Each of the studios had its resident company, including two or three children (often of company players). Yale Boss and Andy Clark were Edison's leading boys, Paul Kelly and Kenneth Casey were with Vitagraph, Judson Melford with Kalem, Roy Hauck with Thanhouser, Roy Clark with Selig. Some, like Leland Benham of Thanhouser, were usually teamed with little girls: in his case with Marie Eline and Helen Badgley.

France and Italy were ahead of the USA with 'personalised' kid series: Pathé's 'Bébé' comedies (with Anatole Mary) began in 1910, to which Cines launched its rival Cinessino (Eraldo Giunchi) in the same year, and Eclair's 'Willy' series (Willie Sanders) followed in 1912. It wasn't till the end of 1913 that Edison launched its 'Adventures of Andy' (Andy Clark), to be followed by Vitagraph's Sonny Jim (Bobby Connelly), Keystone's Little Billy (Paul Jacobs) and Universal's curious 'comedy-travelogues' featuring Matty Roubert.

The girls, meanwhile, were having a boring time, largely confined to domestic settings and soulful or sweetly-smiling roles. Only the occasional tomboy like Mary McAllister escaped much into the knockabout open-air world. It was a period when men had all the interesting jobs, and when boys left school earlier and started fending for themselves in quite ambitious ways. Most of the little girls of the screen, at this stage, were just 'pretty darlings' – something their worst enemies couldn't have said of the most successful boys. But there were exceptions: Gertie Messinger and Violet Radcliffe, in the 'Kiddie Comedies' (1915-18) of Chester and Sidney Franklin, were a total delight.

By the 1920s the emancipation of women had filtered down to child-level, and girls like Baby Peggy Montgomery were real personalities, in a rather more true-to-life sense than Shirley Temple a decade later. The admirable Mitzi Green and Jane Withers, overshadowed by Temple, were the liberated successors to Baby Peggy.

When I started hunting for vanished film children I saw it – in my fathomless ignorance – as a six-month jaunt, covering a few dozen of either sex. After a few weeks I became aware that there were hundreds, if not thousands, of interesting kids, and that it was going to be impossible to accommodate them within a single handlable volume. Should I therefore confine myself to a particular area of film history, temporal or geographical? But this conflicted with my original basic idea, which had been to juxtapose the film kids of widely different countries at precise moments in time.

Another thing began to emerge: almost all the little girls of the cinema were poorly documented, and most had vanished into the mists of time — largely because so many had married and changed their names, and would need extensive sleuthing to track down. I wasn't going to have the time. Some, like Madge Evans and Virginia Lee Corbin, had continued their careers into adulthood, and some had been well covered by writers like Marc Best and Richard Lamparski (whose *Whatever Became Of . . .?* books are essential reading for students of acting history).

Had I been based in America, I might have traced a sufficient number of girls to justify their inclusion in the present book. As it was, it seemed best to give them a leisurely volume of their own, and get the boys on the road first.

A second volume will also give me a chance to append Addenda and Corrigenda to the contents of Vol. 1, since I count on the ex-boy-actors and their relatives and friends to supply much information I have failed to find, and to correct my inevitable errors. This has been a vast trawl through the shoals of cinematic sprats, covering a century, in just about all the film-making countries of the world: the depth of research has been, to put it mildly, uneven.

So, inevitably, has the degree of cooperation received from archives in far-flung countries I couldn't afford to visit in person. Some have been enchanting and efficient; others promised marvels but produced little, and all I've been able to do is list some of their films involving boy actors. The Russians (whom I did visit) fell quite silent after an early surge; the Indians claimed their film titles were untranslatable.

I haven't, needless to say, seen all the films I list. No one has. Many are lost or untraceable — 'out-of-date' films were scrapped ruthlessly before the cinema developed a sense of history, and even now archives are notoriously cagey about their holdings, often afraid to betray the indirect crook'd ways by which they acquired their treasures, or the 'confidential' nature of bequests.

My listing, vast as it is, can't hope to be complete, but I think I have got most of the best films into it as well as some of the worst. And the selection of 'featured' boys is of course a personal one, but should include nearly all the notables as well as a few surprises. As David Patrick put it, in his preface to *Chambers's Biographical Dictionary*: 'Omissions there must be: the omitted will readily detect them.'

Many 'facts' I have simply taken on trust where I found them, in old periodicals or the yearbooks of foreign film industries: and while I have approached all these with a healthy pinch of salt — and considerable scepticism about dates of birth — I shall undoubtedly have swallowed and regurgitated some fibs and errors. This is a pioneering work, an attempt to drag forgotten faces and reputations back into the light before the dust of oblivion covers them beyond recall. If I had waited till I was sure of every fact, it would never have appeared.

Corrigenda are the breath of a scholar's life, but Addenda are even better. Dates and places of birth, credits omitted, subsequent careers: I long to hear from anyone who can supply them.

As I continued my researches, I began to see the four archetypes of the boy actor as the Angel, the Hero, the Clown and the Pug. Almost every boy fell into one or more of these categories. Only the Angel — soulful, passive, beautiful, suffering, 'smiling through' — defied adulteration, and perhaps for this reason was the least interesting. The Hero (active, resourceful, plucky, determined) blended well with the Clown (quick, spry, larky, droll) or the Pug (slow, brave, dogged). The negative side of these stereotypes was, for the Angel, insipidity; for the Hero, conventionality; for the Clown, silliness; and for the Pug, aggressiveness.

Other sub-types, such as Snake and Victim, sometimes came into play: an angel/snake, for instance, would be as intriguing as he was rare: Jackie Searl, perhaps, even on occasion John Moulder-Brown. And Mark Lester was the inevitable angel/victim, just as Coogan was angel/clown and Cooper was hero/pug.

A child actor's chance of being remembered depends largely on luck. If he was in films with now forgotten stars or directors, his chance of resurrection — on TV, for instance — is almost nil: programmers like famous names. But I hope this book will revive some little reputations, and may even lead to some of their films being rediscovered and shown again.

Even where the films are lost, it's worth recovering the titles: part of the poetry of their era. Consider: *The Abysmal Brute; The Hard-Boiled Canary; Half Shot at Sunrise; The Knickerbocker Buckaroo; Chartroose Caboose; Dogalog; Gasoloons; Feudin' Rhythm; Roarin' Lead; Fig Leaves; Three Kids and a Queen; A Bore of a Boy; The Primal Law; The Reverse Be My Lot; The Radio Hound; The Social Ghost; A Pullman Nightmare; Jeepers Creepers; Grabbing Grabbers; Pink Gods; Joe and Ethel Turp Call on the President* . . . not forgetting what may have been the world's most self-defeating title — *It Wasn't Poison After All!*

The mere names are often fine enough. Bubbles Noisom has earned an entry of his own, but I'm proud too to have listed talents as diverse as Bobby Fuehrer, Antik Kim and Janusz Wawrzyszczyk.

National Abbreviations

AC	Algeria	Fl	Finland	NZ	New Zealand
AL	Albania	FR	France	PA	Panama
AR	Argentina	GB	United Kingdom	PE	Peru
AT	Austria	GE	Germany, except 1945-90	PH	Philippines
AU	Australia	GR	Greece	PK	Pakistan
BE	Belgium	HK	Hong Kong	PL	Poland
BF	Burkina Faso	HU	Hungary	PR	Puerto Rico
BG	Bulgaria	ID	Indonesia	PT	Portugal
BO	Bolivia	IE	Ireland	RO	Romania
BR	Brazil	IL	Israel	SE	Sweden
CA	Canada	IN	India	SG	Singapore
CH	Switzerland	IR	Iran	SN	Senegal
CL	Chile	Is	Iceland	SU	U.S.S.R.
CN	China	IT	Italy	TH	Thailand
CO	Colombia	JP	Japan	TN	Tunisia
CR	Costa Rica	KN	N Korea	TR	Turkey
CS	Czechoslovakia	KS	S Korea	TW	Taiwan
CU	Cuba	LB	Lebanon	US	U.S.A.
CY	Cyprus	LK	Sri Lanka	UY	Uruguay
DD	Germany (East)	LU	Luxemburg	VE	Venezuela
DE	Germany (West)	MA	Morocco	VN	N Vietnam
DK	Denmark	ML	Mali	VS	S Vietnam
DZ	Algeria	MX	Mexico	YU	Yugoslavia
EG	Egypt	NL	Netherlands	ZA	South Africa
ES	Spain	NO	Norway	ZM	Zambia

François Clerc (left) at the receiving end of the screen's first prank. Le petit Duval (right) puts his foot down.

Alan Williamson (left) raises the dust in Our New Errand Boy.

le petit Duval

FRANCE

b: circa 1881

The clever Louis Lumière – a manufacturer of photographic products in Lyon – didn't quite invent the movie camera: that was Thomas Edison in 1889. But Edison's Kinetoscope was only a kind of peep-show, and Lumière had the wit to devise its necessary adjunct, the film projector.

In his first public show, in Paris at the end of 1895, he offered tiny home movies and one or two documentary snippets: a train arriving at a railway station (the audience flinched as it steamed towards them), workers leaving the Lumière factory. There was also a half-minute joke (rather a venerable one) called *L'arroseur arrosé*, or *Le jardinier et le petit espiègle*. The little rascal in question was thus the screen's first child actor, perpetrator of the screen's first prank.

Assisting a gardener who is watering the flowers, the gardener's boy slyly puts his foot on the hosepipe. The flow of water stops, the gardener peers into the nozzle to see what can be blocking it, the boy withdraws his foot, the gardener is drenched, the laughing boy is scragged.

In medium shot, as in most early movies before the heyday of the close-up, we get no clear impression of the rascal's face. But this crop-headed, skinny kid in shirt-sleeves and corduroys already offers a potent image of the Labouring Lad as well as of the Mischief-Maker and Menace.

The gardener's boy was played by a young apprentice from the Lumière factory in Lyon. With a less common name than Duval, he might even have been traceable. The gardener (a genuine one) was another Lumière employee, François Clerc.

1895 L'arroseur arrosé (The waterer watered)

Alan Williamson

BRITAIN

b: 3 Feb 1886
d: 3 May 1952

James Williamson, a pioneer of British cinema, produced and directed films in Brighton between 1897 and 1909 (after which he devoted himself exclusively to the manufacture and merchandising of film and photographic materials and equipment). He soon began to evolve his own grammar of movie-making, and his *Fire!* of 1901, for instance, depends largely on cross-cutting for its tension. In 1902 he sold his chemist's shop and started full-time production at the Wilbury studios.

His sons Alan, Tom, Stuart and Colin became Britain's first juvenile 'household faces'. In the Two Naughty Boys films, Alan's co-star was kid brother Colin – and it needs pointing out that the 'spoons' in question were not items of cutlery but young people engaged in 'spooning' or making love. The titles make exhaustingly clear the pranksomeness of this strand of the early cinema.

1898 Two Naughty Boys Upsetting
       the Spoons
     Two Naughty Boys Sprinkling
       the Spoons
     Two Naughty Boys Teasing
       the Cobbler
1901 Teasing Grandpa
     Those Troublesome Boys
1905 Our New Errand Boy

Bobby Harron as a young man

Bobby Harron

USA

b: 24 Apr 1893 (New York)
d: 1 Sep 1920 (New York)

Bobby Harron and Jack Smith ◇ (Jack Pickford) were the first two boy film stars to develop into young adult ones. Pickford died at 36, Harron at 27 – after a 'gunshot accident' in a hotel bedroom. Some said it was suicide, but no note was left. His younger brother Johnnie (1903-39), forgotten as a child actor – though making a brief appearance as the 'boy with the barrel' in D.W. Griffith's *Hearts of the World* (18) – succeeded Bobby as a popular juvenile lead in the 1920s, but faded with the coming of sound, and lived the same short span as Pickford.

Bobby, less conventionally handsome than Johnnie, had a pleasant Irish face with a wide forehead and sharp chin, and small dark eyes which could be merry but also terribly sad. He obviously touched the heart of Griffith, who met him at the Biograph studios in New York in 1908, a year or two after he had graduated from odd-job boy to 13-year-old bit player in one- or two-reelers. The bits grew bigger

over the next few years – Griffith usually directing – and included some leads. After four secondary roles in *Birth of a Nation*, Griffith promoted him to star in *Intolerance* and *Hearts of the World*. By 1920 Robert Harron was planning to branch out into production, and then – bang.

Was it suicide? The pressures on the stars of early movies, with their manic rate of production, was certainly appalling. Harron had been upset that Richard Barthelmess seemed to have supplanted him as leading man in Griffith's films; when he died, he had been preparing for the premiere of his new film, whose preview had not gone well. On the other hand, who would choose to shoot himself in the *lung*? The answer may well have been depression, plus a shaking hand.

The director Victor Heerman, who had known him well, was convinced it was an accident. Harron was a devout Catholic, and suicide would have been a mortal sin. The loaded pistol, Harron said, had been taken away from a depressed friend who seemed in a suicidal mood. He had wrapped it in some trousers in a suitcase, and forgotten it. (But does one really forget a loaded pistol? And why hadn't he unloaded it?) Then, while he was unpacking, it had 'dropped to the floor and fired'.

The Harron family, it must be said, was peculiarly accident-prone. Bobby's sister Tessie died at 19, during the 1918 'flu epidemic in Hollywood, and his successful actor brother John suddenly in 1939, in his mid-thirties. The body of his 65-year-old father, John Harron, Senior, was found burning in an incinerator behind his own petrol station on South Broadway in October 1930: the coroner's verdict, rather oddly, was suicide, but the family believed it was murder during robbery.

07 Doctor Sinkum
08 At the French Ball
　 Bobby's Kodak
　 The Boy Detective
　 The Helping Hand
　 The Test of Friendship
　 The Valet's Wife

Jack Smith (later Jack Pickford)

USA

b: 18 Aug 1896 (Toronto)
d: 3 Jan 1933 (Paris)

John Charles Smith was the youngest of three early-orphaned siblings. His sister Gladys, the eldest, was put into show business at a tender age as 'Baby Gladys', and some years later became transformed into Mary Pickford, the irrepressible, rosebud-mouthed superstar of the Teens and Twenties.

When Mary was signed up by Biograph in 1909, Jack – already an experienced stage trouper – followed her, as he did seven years later when she accepted an astronomic offer to move from Famous Players to First National. Her stipulation was that if they took her, they took him too. By this time, though, he was well known in his own right after a stream of teenage roles.

Jack had a sensitive oval face, and brown hair which fell becomingly forward unless brilliantined. According to need, he smiled

Jack Pickford (né Smith) – aged 20 – as the 1917 Tom Sawyer.

impishly or suffered beautifully, and was a much-loved juvenile lead right up to the late Twenties. He was a highly-strung creature, and led a rackety life not untouched by tragedy. In 1920 his first wife, the actress Olive Thomas, poisoned herself in Paris, dying in the same hospital where Jack himself was to die thirteen years later, after a nervous collapse. An earlier influenza attack had weakened his heart.

It's hard to assess the limits of his career as a 'boy actor', since he didn't make his first film till he was 13, and created the screen's first notable Tom Sawyer when he was nearly 21! (The film – with Robert Gordon as Huck, George Hackathorne as Sid and Antrim Short ◇ as Joe Harper – is more like a whimsical documentary on the young unemployed.) But Jack Pickford was unquestionably a charmer.

10 All on Account of the Milk
    A Child's Stratagem
    The Cloister's Touch
    Examination Day at School
    Gold Is Not All
    Happy Jack, a Hero
    The Iconoclast
    The Kid
    The Modern Prodigal
    The Musketeers of Pig Alley
    Over Silent Paths
    When We Were in Our Teens
    White Roses
11 The Aggressor
    Artful Kate
    A Boy of the Revolution
    The Convict's Heart
    A Dog's Tale
    A Dream
    The Fisher Maid
    For Her Brother's Sake
    The House That Jack Built
    In Old Madrid
    In the Sultan's Garden
    Little Nell's Tobacco
    The Lost Necklace
    A Manly Man
    The Message in the Bottle
    Sisters
    The Speed Demon
    The Stuff Heroes Are Made Of
    Their First Misunderstanding

Erik Crone

DENMARK

b: 14 Sep 1896
d: 4 Apr 1971

A handsome, serious boy in emotional stories on stage and screen, Erik Crone left most of the Danish larking to his contemporaries Cai Voigt ◇ and Casper Petersen. His intelligence and professionalism was exemplary: he responded perfectly to direction and performed like an equal with adult actors. And, wrote the critic Hermann Bang, 'he died beautifully'.

In a stage play Erik was called upon to speak four languages, and hardly turned a hair. But sometimes the challenges were more physical. In one film he had to crash a car into a tree, and in another he was strapped to the fuselage of an airborne plane – all for 5.25 kroner a day.

When only 19, Erik Crone became a director of Baltisk Film, and later formed his own newsreel company.

10 Livets storme (Life's storms)
    Mordet i Bakerstreet
      (Murder in Baker Street)
    Den nye huslærer (The new tutor)
11 Ekspeditricen (The shop-girl)
    Hævnen er sød (Revenge is sweet)
    Jernbanens datter
      (Daughter of the railway)
12 Bedstemoders vuggevise
      (Grandma's lullaby)

Philip Tannura

USA

b: 28 Mar 1897 (New York)
d: 7 Dec 1973

Phil Tannura was a successful child actor on stage and screen in the years before World War One – he was in further films in 1917-18 – and worked as stills photographer and cameraman for Edison before serving in the US Signal Corps. After the war he was cameraman for Paramount and Pathe, and later opened a London studio for Paramount. In the early 1930s he joined London Films, and for some years worked on British productions before moving back to the USA. In the 1950s and 1960s he was mainly a TV cameraman. His son Phil junior followed him in the same career.

11 The Awakening of John Bond
12 Hogan's Alley
    The Little Bride of Heaven
    Rowdy and His New Pal
    The Stolen Nickel

Robert Tansey

USA

b: 28 Jne 1897 (Brooklyn, N.Y.)
d: 17 Jne 1951 (Hollywood)

Robert Emmett Tansey was the eldest of three acting brothers (see also John ◇ and Sheridan ◇), the offspring of stage parents. Their father was the comedian John Tansey, and their mother the character actress Emma Purcell, who herself had performed as a child.

Robert appeared on stage from the age of four, but he had only a year or so of major roles in movies before adolescence intervened. He was back on the screen by the time he was 20, and in 1930 he and John together wrote, directed and edited a film called *Romance of the West*. Robert returned to direct several more movies in the last decade of his life.

11 For the Queen
12 Hazel Kirke

Cai Voigt

DENMARK

b: circa 1897

Voigt (his first name usually given the uncommon C rather than K) was a wry, agile comedian with a whimsical manner: the grotesque *Rulleskøjterne* would have suited Buster Keaton. He had a busy young stage career, and after filming during the day was sometimes known to appear in three different theatres during the evening.

Voigt went on to act as an adult.

Cai Voigt

Joris Ivens

HOLLAND

b: 18 Nov 1898 (Nijmegen)
d: 28 Jne 1989 (Paris)

In 1911 a cowboys-and-Indians 'home movie' called *The Wigwam* was scripted and directed, at the age of twelve, by the future great socialist-internationalist documentary film-maker, born Georg Henri Anton Ivens. It was the logical brainchild of a camera-mad family: his grandfather had been a photographic pioneer in Holland, and his father, C.A.P. Ivens, owned a chain of camera shops.

More or less the whole family appeared in this schoolboy extravaganza, which actually got rather good reviews when it was shown to an Amateur Photographers' Society meeting in Amsterdam in December 1915. They credit the direction to C.A.P. Ivens, but Joris firmly stated in later years that *he* had directed it as well as having written and starred in it.

Kenneth Casey

USA

b: 10 Jan 1899 (New York)
d: 10 Aug 1965 (New York)

Around 1912 there were two 'Vitagraph Boys': Paul Kelly ◊ was strong, silent and modestly plucky, while Kenneth Casey was the prankster, with dark bobbed hair and an ambiguous expression. He was often teamed in impish comedies with Vitagraph's little girl star, Adele de Garde, and had considerable musical gifts, being adept on the piano, violin and cornet to name but three. He also composed songs, including an immodest tribute to himself called 'The Moving Picture Boy', which he sang in vaudeville:

Just because I am the Moving
  Picture Boy,
That is why I'm everybody's
  love and joy.

Vitagraph's enigmatic imp Kenneth Casey

Every time my face is flashed
  upon the screen
They say: 'Oh, he's the sweetest
  thing we've ever seen.'. . .

In 1913 Casey and Vitagraph parted company; he had been with them for nearly five years. His ambition now was to appear in vaudeville, but current US law classed him as too young for this, so he crossed the Atlantic and successfully toured British and South African music-halls instead. At the end of 1914 he returned to the States, and the following February, having reached the required age of 16, made his American stage debut as 'the Vitagraph boy' at Hammerstein's Victoria Theater, offering an act that besides its many instrumental delights was enriched by 'Scotch jokes, and an English coster song'.

Kenneth Casey's screen appearances henceforth were scant: but he was seen, for instance, in *The Model* (15) and *The Adventure* (20). The composing and song-writing blossomed, though, and he even had a hand in the well-loved 'Sweet Georgia Brown'. He had his own publishing firm, and at one time his own orchestra, with whom he played on vaudeville and radio and in the recording studio. (He had by now added the trumpet to his personal armoury.)

Another child actor of the same name was in circulation, though not noticeably in movies, in the 1930s: it may have been Kenneth Casey, Junior. But Kenneth I stuck with popular music, and in due course proclaimed his Republican allegiance with a 'President Eisenhower March'.

Roy Royston

BRITAIN

b: 5 Apr 1899 (Mill Hill, London)
d: 7 Oct 1976 (Kingston-upon-Thames)

Sympathisers with the harassed clergyman in John Gilling's *Plague of the Zombies* of 1965, as the hands and arms of the undead sprout like daffodils through the hallowed loam of his churchyard, may not realise that this had once been a blithe boy star of British knockabout comedy. But Roy Royston (born Roy

Charles Crowden, though no relation to the admirable Graham Crowden of recent British comedies) had half a century earlier enjoyed two or three hectic years as the kid hero of the films of Lewis Fitzhamon, usually in partnership with his sister Marie.

Roy made his stage debut in December 1910, at the Haymarket Theatre, London, as Tyltyl in a revival of Maeterlinck's *Blue Bird*. From 1912, movies took priority for a while, but for the rest of his long career he kept the two strands in tandem.

Besides abundant stage work, Royston appeared sporadically in British films for the rest of his life: they included *One Summer's Day* (17), *Mr Wu* (19), *The Magistrate* (21), *Just for a Song* (30), *The Big Splash* (35), *Conquest of the Air* (40) and of course *The Plague of the Zombies* (65).

During World War Two – doubtless influenced by his flying film, *Conquest of the Air* – he served in the RAF, reaching the rank of squadron leader.

Roy's younger brother GERALD ROYSTON also appeared in a handful of films, including a 1914 version of *Little Lord Fauntleroy* where he took over the name part from the originally scheduled child star Joan Morgan. (She was to become a leading actress of the early 1920s and a successful novelist and playwright, still very much alive and well in 1996.)

Vitagraph's straightforward Kelly

Paul Kelly

USA

b: 9 Aug 1899 (Brooklyn, N.Y.)
d: 6 Nov 1956 (Beverly Hills, Cal.)

The granite-jawed tough guy of scores of movies from the Twenties to the Fifties – sometimes a cop, sometimes a robber – came from a poor Irish family which had the luck to live opposite the Vitagraph studios in New York. They used to lease out their furniture to the company for use in one-reelers. Eventually they leased out their seven-year-old son, and the slim and personable Paul showed star quality. In no time he was up on the posters as 'Chick Kelly, the Vitagraph Boy', and earning much more than a kitchen dresser.

Between movies, he did stage work in stock companies, played Shakespeare in Robert Mantell's troupe, and even took juvenile leads on Broadway, including an early incarnation of Booth Tarkington's 'Penrod'. (See Wesley Barry ◊ *et al.*) He played 'The Good Little Devil' on stage with Mary Pickford.

Always an impressive figure, and a role-image for young American manhood, Kelly was involved in 1918 in a bizarre 'moral hygiene' film called *Fit to Fight*, aimed at the armed forces and dealing with 'the terrible effect of certain diseases', to which a patriotic cast gave its services free'and in which our hero can be seen looking suitably worried. (An even more blush-provoking example of this genre, *The Solitary Sin*, decorates the career of the square-jawed Gordon Griffith ◇.)

Probably the worst thing that happened to Paul Kelly in real life was his two-year jail sentence in 1927 for the manslaughter of the actor Ray Raymond, whom he had thumped rather too hard in a fight over Raymond's wife, the actress Dorothy MacKaye. She was also sent to San Quentin for concealing facts about the fight – which may not, in fact, have been the whole cause of Raymond's death. (A touching account of the case can be found in the second of Kenneth Anger's ◇ indispensable though often repulsive 'Hollywood Babylon' volumes.)

Kelly used his 'lost years' sensibly in preparing for return to a now talking cinema – the change had come at precisely this moment of history. His career resumed almost as if it had never left off, bygones were bygones,and for the next 25 years he seldom stopped working and was a familiar and reassuring face to filmgoers. He was the hero of the 1942 serial *The Secret Code*, and the 1947 thriller *Fear in the Night*. He and Dorothy were married in 1931, and remained a devoted couple till her death in a car accident.

08 A Good Little Devil
11 Jimmie's Job
12 Billy's Burglar
    Captain Barnacle's Waif
    An Expensive Shine
    How Millie Became an Actress
    A Juvenile Love Affair
13 Counselor Bobby
    Cutey Tries Reporting
    The Feudists
    Heartsease
    The Mouse and the Lion
14 Buddy's Downfall
    Buddy's First Call

Lillian's Dilemma
The Man That Might Have Been
The Reformation of the Gang

Otto Reinwald

GERMANY

b: 23 Aug 1899 (Konstanz)
d: 1969

With his classic features and wavy blond hair, Otto Reinwald – 'the Crown Prince of Film' – could have been the perfect Death-in-Venice *garçon fatal*: but far from lounging around in decorative attitudes, his film character was usually daring and practical, no stranger to heroic adventures. In Benjamin Christensen's *The Mysterious X*, for instance, he risked many deaths in finding evidence to clear the wronged name of his father, arriving in split-second time to halt the firing-squad.

Christensen later remembered Otto as 'an exceptionally nice, attractive boy, more beautiful than talented'. He also recalled his conquering a dread of water to plunge into the harbour at Elsinore – a display of real courage and impeccable professionalism.

Not obvious heroes: Otto Reinwald and friend in
Det hemmelighedsfulde X

Otto was the only boy of four siblings; his sisters Grete (born 1902) and Hanni (1903-78) both made considerable movie careers as children and young adults. They all appeared as a family vaudeville act in Berlin, managed by their father, and it was while playing in Denmark that they were introduced to Christensen.

Reinwald continued in movies – with many leading roles – for most of the next two decades, until 1932. Ten years later he reappeared as an *Aufnahmeleiter* or production manager, and continued in this new career for the rest of his working life, with only one further credit as an actor – in *Unternehmen Edelweiss* (1954).

13 Der Film von der Königin Luise
    (The Queen Louisa film)
    Det hemmelighedsfulde X
    (The mysterious X – DK)
    Ein Sommernachtstraum in unserer Zeit
    (A modern Midsummer Night's Dream)
14 Die Geschichte der stillen Mühle
    (The story of the silent mill)
    Im Schützengraben (In the trench)
15 Filmens Datter (Daughter of the film – DK)
    Fluch der Schönheit (Curse of beauty)
    Katastrofen i Kattegat
    (Disaster in the Kattegat – DK)
    Pengenes magt (Power of money – DK)
    Proletardrengen
    (The working-class boy – DK)
    Der zwölfjährige Kriegsheld
    (The 12-year-old war hero)

Yale Boss

USA

b: 18 Oct 1899 (Utica, N.Y.)
d: 16 Nov 1977 (Augusta, Georgia)

Fair and flop-haired, Yale Boss ('Yale' an anglicisation of his Swiss grandmother's maiden name) was perhaps the best-loved of all America's early film children. He was a better-looking Mickey Rooney ◇, usually cast in cheeky parts but perfectly capable of dignified pathos. He could 'provoke shouts of laughter or cause unbidden tears to flow', and was prodigal in 'little touches which would only be expected of actors of great experience'. His sisters Matilda and Frances also acted,

Edison's Yale Boss as a teenager

though apparently with less power.

In 1907 he had a leading role in a Broadway musical called 'Top of the World', and his first screen appearance was directed by D.W.Griffith for Biograph. After a brief move to Thanhouser, he settled with Edison in 1911, on a five-year contract at $25 per week. During this period he played in a constant stream of two-reelers. His total tally is said to have been more than 300 titles, of which we print a mere few dozen. He was best known latterly as the office boy in the series *Dolly of the Dailies*.

At this point Boss took a two-year break from acting, in order to 'complete his education'. In December 1916 'Moving Picture World' heralded his return to the studios: 'As a boy he earned wide popularity among film patrons by his cleverness and his engaging personality'.

In 1917 he had leads in *The Half-Back* and in *Knights of the Square Table* (with Andy Clark ◇ and Paul Kelly ◇ also in the cast), but over the following three years he only averaged earnings of eight dollars a week. His career faded out – his last featured part seems to have been in *Souls For Sale* (23) – and after leaving the movies he was at various times a clerk with the US Shipping Board, a book-keeper with an ice company, a pencil manufacturer, a private detective, a bricklayer, a salesman and a motor mechanic.

In this last capacity Yale Boss worked for the Georgia Power Company throughout the 1930s and until enlisting in the US Navy during World War Two. After the war he bought a piece of land and built his own garage and service station. Also, in 1948, he became the proud father of twin boys.

09 His First Commission
I Did It, Mama
10 The Actor's Children
11 April Fool
At the Threshold of Life
Bob and Rowdy
A Cure for Crime
Edna's Imprisonment
For the Queen
An Island Comedy
Josh and Cindy's Wedding Trip
The Little Girl Next Door
Papa's Sweetheart
A Personal Affair
The Question Mark
The Ransom of Red Chief
Rowdy and His New Pal
A Sane Fourth of July
Santa Claus and the Clubman
Stage-Struck Lizzie
The Story of the Indian Ledge
Tommy's Geography Lesson
Trading His Mother
Uncle Hiram's List
The Unfinished Letter
Winnie's Dance
The Yarn of the 'Nancy Bell'
12 The Artist and the Brain Specialist
Bobby's Dream
Bobby's Long Trousers
The Boy and the Girl
The 'Cub' Reporter
Curing the Office Boy
Hogan's Alley
How Bobby Joined the Circus
How the Boys Fought the Indians
The Little Artist of the Market
The Little Delicatessen Store
Lucky Dog
Max and Maurice
Mr Pickwick's Predicament
Mother Goose in a Sixteenth Century Theater
Revenge is Sweet
The Stolen Nickel
The Sunset Gun

The Totville Eye
What Happened to Mary *(series)*
The Winking Parson
13 All on Account of a Portrait
Archie and the Bell-Boy
Aunt Elsa's Visit
Boy Wanted
The Dream Fairy
Enoch and Ezra's First Smoke
He Swore Off Smoking
How a Horseshoe Upset a Happy Family
The Inventor's Sketch
The Janitor's Quiet Life
A Mistake in Judgment
Mr Newcombe's Necktie
The Office Boy's Birthday
The Title Cure
The Two Merchants
Within the Enemy's Lines
A Youthful Knight
14 Andy Goes on the Stage
Dolly of the Dailies *(serial)*
The Ghost of Mother Eve
How Bobbie Called Her Bluff
The Janitor's Flirtation
Molly the Drummer Boy
Shorty
A Tale of Old Tucson
The Temple of Moloch
15 Cartoons in a Seminary
The House of Fear
The Ivory Snuff Box
The Man Who Vanished

Alfred Willmore
(Micheál Mac Liammóir)

IRELAND

b: 25 Oct 1899 (Cork)
d: 6 Mar 1978 (Dublin)

Alfred Willmore, the child's real name, was only discarded in the 1920s for the more romantic Gaelic pseudonym of Micheál Mac Liammóir. He grew into a flamboyant, narcissistic creature of the old theatre, and his few later film appearances were collectors' pieces. The best-known was his Iago in Welles's 1952 *Othello*, a film whose production he described in his highly entertaining book 'Put Money in Thy Purse'.

Like another great theatrical monster, Emlyn Williams, Mac Liammóir was best known latterly for his one-man recitals. He appeared as Oscar Wilde and other Irish worthies, straining the texts through a larynx kippered in cigar smoke, histrionically brightening and dimming his hooded eyes to denote passion or ravaged grief.

To see him as pathetic Micah Dow in *The Little Minister* of 1915 would be a rare treat, if anyone could find it.

11 Henry VIII (GB)
14 Enoch Arden (GB)
15 The Little Minister (GB)

Collier at seven

Buster Collier

USA

b: 12 Feb 00 (New York)
d: 5 Feb 87 (San Francisco)

Dark-haired Buster, or Willie, was the son of the actor and playwright William Collier (1866-1944). From 1908 he made frequent appearances on the New York stage, usually with his father, which probably accounts for the lack of film work before he landed an unrefusable star role in *The Bugle Call*.

While in the play 'Take My Advice' in New Orleans in 1911, he had to appear in court as a 'delinquent child' when his employers were accused of violating the child labour laws. It was a role he relished: rising to the occasion like a trouper, he charmed the judge with his poise in giving evidence.

Throughout the Twenties (with some 60 films) and the early Thirties he was an important juvenile lead, with slightly the air of a pocket Valentino; later he became a film executive. At the dawn of the talkies he tested unsuccessfully for the title role in *The Jazz Singer*, after George Jessel had walked out and Eddie Cantor turned it down.

As his acting career declined, he was consoled by becoming 'one of the foremost fishers for swordfish on the Pacific coast'.

16 The Bugle Call
   Going Straight
17 Tom Sawyer

Albert Hackett

USA

b: 16 Feb 00 (New York)
d: 16 Mar 95

Albert and his younger brother Raymond◇ were sons of the actress Florence Hackett (1882-1954), but no relation to Buddy Hackett (born 1924, as Leonard Hacker) or to Joan Hackett (1942-83). From 1904 both brothers were appearing on stage and screen, and they did so for some twenty more years. (Though Albert as a child had once disgraced himself on stage by chewing gum when supposed to be dead.) Their main film work was for Lubin.

As a man Albert turned to screen writing, and in partnership with his wife Frances Goodrich (1891-1984) produced some of the most accomplished scenarios of the Thirties and Forties, notably for the *Thin Man* films, *Rose Marie*, *The Firefly*, *Lady in the Dark*, *It's a Wonderful Life* and *The Virginian*.

12 Just Pretending
13 Annie Rowley's Fortune
   The School Principal
15 Black Fear
   The House Party

RAYMOND HACKETT, Albert's fair-haired younger brother, was born in New York 15 July 1902 and died in Los Angeles 7 July 1958. He was on stage from the age of four and in movies before he was ten.

Raymond Hackett became a handsome and popular leading man in the films of the Twenties and the first few years of the talkies; thereafter he worked mainly on the stage. In 1936 he married Blanche Sweet, another star of the silent era and seven years his senior.

12 A Child's Devotion
   Little Boy Blue
13 Annie Rowley's Fortune
   Longing for a Mother
14 The Price of a Ruby
   The Shadow of Tragedy
15 The Ringtailed Rhinoceros
   A Siren of Corsica

Short as a teenager

Antrim Short

USA

b: 11 Jly 00 (Cincinnati, Ohio)
d: 24 Nov 72 (Los Angeles)

Mark Antrim Short – who matched his surname, but was also fair and square, and good-looking in a pugnacious sort of way – was brought up in an acting family, with successful acting parents (Mr and Mrs Lewis Short, who can both be seen with him in *There's No Place Like Home*), and an elder and a younger acting sister (Florence and Gertrude). Antrim first trod the boards at six, and made his screen debut in 1912 with Biograph.

He had star roles in *The Yellow Dog* (18) and *Please Get Married* (19), and from now until the early Thirties was in constant demand. Then, as his acting career petered out, he got involved in the early stages of the Screen Actors' Guild, and in 1937 became head of its claim department.

In 1940 he was a casting director for Central Casting, and later for Samuel Goldwyn, Republic and Universal. In 1947 he went into management partnership, and then established his own agency.

13 Bobby's Baby
14 Jess of the Mountain Country
    John Barleycorn
    Where the Trail Divides
15 The Cry of the First-Born
    The Gambler of the West
    Jack Chanty
16 Alone in the World
    Corporal Billy's Comeback
    The Flirt
    Nancy's Birthright
    There's No Place Like Home

Gone west young man

Judson Melford

USA

b: circa 1900

Judson was the son of actor-director George Melford (1889-1961), and in December 1910 travelled west with his parents and sister in Kalem's first California company. He stayed there till 1914 when his father was succeeded by J.W.Horne.

10 The Touch of a Child's Hand
11 Daniel Boone's Bravery
    On the War Path
    Rescue from the Desert
12 The Driver of the Deadwood Coach
    The Power of a Hymn
    The Runaways

Wolfgang Zilzer

GERMANY

b: 20 Jan 01 (Cincinnati, Ohio)

Son of a Hungarian-Jewish immigrant – the actor Max Zilzer – Wolfgang was born in Cincinnati within six months of Antrim Short $^\diamond$. But his mother died a year or two later, and his father returned to Germany in 1905. The six-year-old Wolfgang made his stage debut in Berlin in a production of Ibsen's 'Enemy of the People', but was in no films before 1915.

Young Zilzer continued to act tirelessly in Germany throughout the Twenties (also in one or two Czech films) and until 1933, when he emigrated to his former home, the USA. After acting at the German Theater in New York he was recruited by Hollywood, and appeared in many movies of the late Thirties and early Forties, such as *Ninotchka* and *To Be Or Not To Be*.

In the mid-1960s he changed his professional name to Paul Andor, and appeared as late as 1979 in *A Private Life*.

15 Der Barbier von Filmersdorf
    (The barber of Filmville)
    Überlistet (Outwitted)

Roy Hauck

USA

b: circa 1901

Roy made his stage debut at the age of seven. All his early films were for Thanhouser, but at the end of 1914 he moved to Arrow. He was quite a small Hauck, standing only 5'3" in his socks in 1916.

14 Bobby's Plot
    A Gentleman for a Day
    Guilty or Not Guilty
    Her Big Brother
    The Million Dollar Mystery
    The Tin Soldier and the Doll
15 Right Off the Bat
16 Gloria's Romance (*serial*)

Eric Desmond
(Reginald Sheffield)

BRITAIN/USA

b: 18 Feb 01 (London)
d: 8 Dec 57 (Pacific Palisades, Cal.)

Matthew Reginald Sheffield Cassan came from a family with a strong sense of pedigree. He claimed direct descent on his father's side from the 17th-century soldier, poet and courtier John Sheffield, 1st Duke of Buckingham, and on his mother's side from Benjamin Franklin. Hopes of a transatlantic dynasty were not, as it turned out, to be wholly disappointed.

The sturdy, curly-haired little boy was discovered by the British director, producer and inventor Cecil Hepworth, and appeared as Reggie Sheffield in what is said to have been his debut film, *Lieutenant Pie's Love Story*. In August 1913 he changed his screen name to Eric Desmond (after the Earls of Desmond?) but appeared on the London stage the following month, in a Charles Hawtrey farce, as Reginald Sheffield. It was as Eric Desmond, though, that he continued busily to perform for Hepworth until 1915, when he became a war evacuee to the USA and appeared in his first American film – as Reginald Sheffield. All very confusing.

Father of Tarzan's Boy: Eric Desmond (Reggie Sheffield).

Curt Bois

GERMANY

b: 5 Apr 01 (Berlin)
d: 25 Dec 91 (Berlin)

Bois made his stage debut at the age of six. There even survives a 1908 gramophone record of the little Curt, as 'Wunderkind Heinerle' in Leo Fall's operetta 'Der fidele Bauer', singing a duet with his unfortunate mother (Grete Dierkes) in which he nags for toys she can't afford. The operetta was subsequently filmed, and commemorated on postcards.

Between 1914 and 1920, Curt Bois toured with the Drawing Room Humorist Revue, but kept on acting in plays and films – with star roles in *Der Jüngling aus der Konfektion* (26) and *Der Fürst von Pappenheim* (27). In 1933, like Wolfgang Zilzer ◇, he left Germany, progressing via Vienna, Paris and London to the USA.

He made his Broadway debut in 1935, and became even more of a Hollywood indispensable than Zilzer, from *Tovarich* and *Gold Diggers in Paris* to *Cover Girl* and *The Great Sinner*. He could be a slippery waiter, a camp sophisticate or a quivering drunk, he could (as in *Casablanca*) be a pickpocket.

Bois returned to Germany in 1950. He played Gogol's 'Government Inspector'

In 1939 a sturdy, curly-haired little boy called Johnny Sheffield ◇ burst into the Hollywood jungle wearing nothing but a loincloth, but otherwise looking the spitting image of pre-1914 Eric Desmond. Needless to say, this was the evacuee's son, and the evacuee himself had made a very useful Hollywood career as a debonair, aristocratic character actor – one which he kept going right up to his death in 1957. He played President Grant in *Centennial Summer* (46).

It hadn't, though, lived up to the hopes of one who had played the hero of *David Copperfield* both as a child (in 1913) and as a man (in 1923). The boy David in Thanhouser's 1911 *David Copperfield*, incidentally, was played by one of the company's female stars, Flora Foster.

Heinerle Lied.
Gar nix is mir dann zu viel
Für mein Buberl, Heinerl du.
Wenn ich's Geld erst habn tu'!

Grete Dierkes.
DER FIDELE BAUER.
Elite Berlin phot.
33197/4.

*Curt Bois (with Grete Dierkes) on stage in
'Der fidele Bauer'*

in East Berlin, and two years later, with the
Berliner Ensemble, created the role of Puntila – the rich master who is only humane
when drunk – in Brecht's 'Herr Puntila und
sein Knecht Matti'. (He repeated his performance in 1955, in Cavalcanti's Austrian
film version of the play.)

He also directed a film of his own, *Ein
Polterabend* (DD 55). Thereafter, his career
continued in West Germany, with much
stage work, notably his Malvolio in a
'Twelfth Night' directed by Fritz Kortner.
He was still acting as late as 1987, in Wim
Wenders's film *Der Himmel über Berlin*.

In 1981 Curt Bois published his
memoirs, 'Zu wahr, um schön zu sein'
(Too true to be good). He had been a true
delight.

08 Der fidele Bauer (The merry peasant)
09 Klebolin klebt alles
   (Sticko sticks everything)
   Der kleine Detektiv (The little detective)
   Mutterliebe: Bauernhof und Grafen-
     schloss
     (Mother-love in farm and castle)
12 Des Pfarrers Töchterlein
   (The parson's little daughter)
13 Das Geschenk des Inders (The Indian's gift)

Paul Willis

USA

b: 9 Apr 01 (Chicago)

Paul G. Willis had an anxious little face
which hardly suggested humour or
heroism, beyond that of an ambitious
bank clerk. But he had manly leads in *Little
Kaintuck* and *The Little Lumberjack*.

In 1919 a rather over-age Willis played
Dickon in *The Secret Garden*. He continued
in films till the mid-Twenties.

13 Little Kaintuck
14 The Poor Folks' Boy
15 Could a Man Do More?
   The Indian Trapper's Vindication
   The Little Lumberjack
   The Little Matchmakers
   The Little Soldier Man
16 The Fall of a Nation

Fridtjof von Kaulbach

GERMANY/DENMARK

b: 26 May 01
d: 12 Sep 68

This lanky scion of a famous Munich
family of painters was christened after his
godfather, the Arctic explorer Fridtjof
Nansen. He was altogether well-
connected: his mother was the exotic
Danish dancer Tilly Kaulbach, and when
she remarried he acquired as stepfather
George Schnéevoigt, who directed his
early Danish films. His sister Ebba also
acted.

The boy excelled in dramatic or poetic
roles, and they were nearly always leading ones; comedy was seldom attempted,
though it must often have threatened.

13 Klein Svend und seine Mutter
   (Little Svend and his mother – GE)
   Stærkere end dynamit
   (Stronger than dynamite – DK)
   Under galgen (Beneath the gallows – DK)
15 De mystiske Z-Stråler
   (The mysterious Z-rays – DK)
16 Mysteriet på Duncan Slot
   (The mystery at Castle Duncan – DK)

John Tansey

USA

b: 8 Oct 01 (New York)
d: 28 Apr 71 (N. Hollywood)

The first of Robert Tansey's ◇ younger
brothers was described by a reviewer as

The intrepid Fridtjof von Kaulbach (right) confronts cosmic espionage in De mystike Z-Stråler

'the sweetest, dearest, brightest and most genuine child . . . Little John Tansey has a glowing, exquisite face, a sense of humor and a pretty tenderness which all go to make him the marvel kid of Broadway.' That was in 1909, in a play called 'This Woman and This Man'.

John, who started acting even younger than Robert, was widely regarded as the paragon not merely of Tanseys but of all American boy actors. He, Gladys Egan and Adele de Garde were the first noted (and named) children in the Biograph company.

John Tansey continued to act on stage and screen throughout the Silent period – *The Heart of a Girl* (18), *Little Miss Hoover* (18), *Trouping with Ellen* (24), *The Sky Rider* (28), *Silent Sentinel* (29), *Romance of the West* (30) – and he was the star as well as co-author and co-director of *Romance of the West*.

In 1934, to inject a jarring note, his wife (also a writer) divorced him on grounds of cruelty.

08 The Redman and the Child
09 And a Little Child Shall Lead Them
15 Black Fear
16 Broken Chains

Brothers Robert and Sheridan soldiered on, keeping the Tansey flag flying in Hollywood for another decade or so. Robert latterly became a busy and successful director.

SHERIDAN (or Sherry), youngest of the Tansey boys, was born around 1905. His acting career – usually in Westerns – stretched at least from 1916 to 1939, for instance in *The Steadfast Heart* (23), *Fools' Highway* (24), *Fast Fightin'* (25), *The Fighting Boob* (26), *Code of the Cow Country* (27), *The Obligin' Buckaroo* (27), *Silver on the Sage* (39).

16 The Foolish Virgin
   A Lucky Gold Piece
17 The Little Duchess
   The Runaway
18 Conquered Hearts
   The Power and the Glory
19 The Two Brides
20 Over the Hill to the Poorhouse
   Uncle Sam of Freedom Ridge

Harold Goodwin

USA

b: 1 Dec 02 (Peoria, Illinois)
d: 12 Jly 87

Lean, manly Harold Goodwin – not to be confused with the later British character actor – was in movies from the age of seven, but got his best parts from twelve onwards. He had the title role in *Mike's Elopement*, and rode alongside W.S. Hart in *The Silent Man*.

Goodwin's career lasted for several decades, but his heyday was the Twenties, when he was a popular young leading man, with star roles in *Oliver Twist, Jr.* (21), *Burning Words* (23) and many other films. He was in *All Quiet on the Western Front* (31), *Hallelujah I'm a Bum* (33), *Hollywood Parade* (39), and so on.

10 Heart o' the Hills
15 As in Days of Old
   The Ever-Living Isles
   The Little Orphans
   Mike's Elopement
   The Noon Hour
   Old Heidelberg
16 Dad's Outlaws
17 The Sawdust Ring
   The Silent Man

Ronald Cricks

BRITAIN

b: circa 1902

'Master Ronald' – full name announced as Ronald Howard Cricks – was the son of George Cricks (of the London production company of Cricks and Martin) and was featured in several of their films.

One *Reginald* Howard Cricks was born in West Ham in 1902 – no Cricks having apparently been born in Britain in the years 1896-1901. Some were registered (mostly in London) between 1902 and 1908, but no Ronald. Was Master Ronald really Master Reginald?

13 A Newsboy's Christmas Dream
14 A Daughter of France

Eduardo Notari

ITALY

b: 1 Jan 03 (Naples)
d: 1986

As five-year-old 'Bebè', Eduardo was the screen mascot of the Neapolitan company Dora Films, whose output was written and directed by his remarkable mother, Elvira Coda (1875-1944) and photographed by his father, Nicola Notari (1875-1955). Dora was very much a family firm, and 'Bebè' would appear in hand-coloured public relations flashes on screen, saying 'Please, no smoking', 'Kindly remove your hat' or 'Thank you, and come again'.

Later, Eduardo – no longer 'Bebè' but 'Gennariello' – threw his tiny weight behind the Italian struggle to annexe Libya, in a jingoistic war-game for Dora.

(At about this time, the far bigger Ambrosio company launched its highly successful little-girl star, MARIA BAY, known in almost all her ten films between 1911 and 1914 as 'Firulì'. Like 'Bébé' Mary ◇ and Willie Sanders ◇, she became an apache, a policeman, a housemaid or a doctor, winning the lottery or meeting a snowman.)

Dora films were rooted in working-class culture, and from dramas of passion and honour they turned after the war to 'sceneggiate', dramatisations of popular songs. A typical patriotic tear-jerker, *L'Italia s'è desta*, in which Notari starred as a young man of 24, shows poor Gennariello returning from the Great War, having had both his arms amputated. He can't raise his hat to salute the flag as it passes: so the flag salutes him.

A final Gennariello film, *Napoli, terra d'amore*, with our hero running a jazz-band à la Mickey Rooney, was a huge flop. With the coming of sound, the Fascists found excuses to ban dialect films in the interests of 'national culture', and Dora closed down. Eduardo Notari went to Rome and became a businessman. Half a century later he was still at the head of Dora Distributors.

12 La guerra italo-libica tra scugnizzi
   napoletani
   (The war between Italy and Libya as
   fought by Neapolitan urchins)
17 Mandolinata a mare
   (Mandolin concert at sea)

A Broth of a Boy: *Andy concocts a message*

Andy Clark

USA

b: Mar 03 (New York)
d: 16 Nov 60 (New Rochelle, N.Y.)

Edison's homely comic kid, overlapping
with Yale Boss ◊ and then taking over
from him, established his renown through
the series of twelve one-reelers, *The Adventures of Andy*.

   After five years of intense and popular
activity Andy Clark took a rest. But later
he returned to the screen, playing a jockey
in two films of the mid- Twenties, and was
seen again in 1930 in *Hit the Deck*. He also
became an assistant director.

12 Bobby's Long Trousers
   How the Boys Fought the Indians
   Mother Goose in a Sixteenth
   Century Theater
13 Archie and the Bell-Boy
   Enoch and Ezra's First Smoke
   Greedy George
   It Wasn't Poison After All
   Mr Newcombe's Necktie
14 'The Adventures of Andy'
   (Andy Gets a Job; Andy Plays Hero;
   Andy Goes on the Stage; Andy the
   Actor; Andy and the Hypnotist; Andy

Plays Cupid; Andy Goes a-Pirating;
   Andy Has a Toothache; Andy Learns to
   Swim; Getting Andy's Goat; Andy and
   the Redskins; Andy Falls in Love)
   The Drama of Heyville
   Making a Convert
   The New Partner
   One Touch of Nature
   Quarantined
   Those Clever Kid Comedies
15 A Broth of a Boy
   Cartoons in the Kitchen
   Snap Shots
   A Tribute to Mother
16 Blind Man's Buff
   The Trail of Chance
17 The Apple-Tree Girl
   Gallegher
   The Great Bradley Mystery
   Knights of the Square Table

Lewis Sargent

USA

b: 19 Aug 03 (Los Angeles)
d: 19 Nov 70 (Los Angeles)

Lewis was one of the older members of
the Franklin brothers' 'Kiddie' troupe,
playing mature roles like Ben Gunn in
Treasure Island. But at 15 he became
the cinema's first convincing Huck Finn.
(Robert Gordon in the 1917 *Tom Sawyer*
and the 1918 *Huck and Tom* had been far
too old, as had Jack Pickford's ◊ Tom.)

The Huck Finn of 1919: Lewis Sargent

*Sargent (left) with his 1919 Tom Sawyer
(Gordon Griffith)*

   His boyhood over, the rangy, athletic
Sargent acted busily throughout the
Twenties and Thirties. He was in *Anne of
Green Gables, Nurse Marjorie* and *The Soul
of Youth* (all 20), *Just Around the Corner*
(21), and the following year in the Jackie
Coogan *Oliver Twist*, but only as Noah
Claypole. Also in 1922 he starred in a
series of 'Lewis Sargent Comedies' for
Universal.

   In 1927 he was the hero of a two-
reeler boxing series called *The Fighting
Fool*, and in 1928 of a series of twelve
Racing Blood stories. In *Crashing Broadway*
(33) he was billed as 'Louis Sargent', but
this was probably a printer's error. He was
seen in *New Adventures of Tarzan* (35) and
Tarzan and the Green Goddess (37) before
drifting out of the movies.

17 Aladdin and the Wonderful Lamp
   Treasure Island
18 Ace High
   Ali Baba and the Forty Thieves
   All Woman
   The Coming of the Law
   Fan Fan
   Six Shooter Andy
19 The Heart of Youth
   Huckleberry Finn
   Miss Adventure

Ermanno Roveri

ITALY

b: 5 Oct 03 (Milan)
d: 28 Dec 68 (Milan)

The dark, sweet-natured Roveri worked chiefly with the Turin company Gloria, then with Cines, Ambrosio, Silentium and Lombardo. Following his popularity as Gloria's resident imp 'Frugolino', he reached his height of early fame in 1915-16 as the hero of some of the 'Cuore' ('Hearts') tales of Edmondo De Amicis. Another Gloria boy with leads in the series was Luigi Petrungaro ◇.

'Cuore' (1886) is, or was, the central Italian schoolboy classic, a sort of diary taking its reader through the school year, interspersed with heart-rending stories of friendship and patriotic heroism. It has been repeatedly filmed in whole or in part, most recently by Luigi Comencini.

After some teenage roles in films in 1920-21, Roveri turned largely to the theatre, and became a well-known comic actor during the Twenties. From 1931 to 1934 he was a leading light of the 'Za-Bum' reviews, and subsequently formed his own company. But he was still seen in such films as *Aldebaran* (35), *Re di dinari* (36), *Nina, non far la stupida* (37), *Due milioni per un sorriso* (39) and *Una famiglia*

All at sea: Ermanno Roveri in Naufragio

impossibile (40). Later in life he performed mainly on TV and radio.

The Italian Film Lexicon describes him as an intelligent and flexible actor, and a brilliant mimic.

13 Io mi chiamo Frugolino
    (My name is Frugolino)
14 Buon Natale! (Merry Christmas!)
   Frugolino sguattero
    (Frugolino the scullery boy)
   Il piccolo cerinaio (The little match-seller)
   Il portafoglio rosso (The red notebook)
15 L'infermiere di Tatà (Daddy's male-nurse)
   La piccola vedetta lombarda
    (The little Lombard lookout)
   Il piccolo patriota padovano
    (The little Paduan patriot)
   Il piccolo scrivano fiorentino
    (The little Florentine scrivener)
   Il tamburino sardo
    (The Sardinian drummer-boy)
16 Christus
   Dagli Appennini alle Ande
    (From Apennines to Andes)
   Naufragio (Shipwreck)
   Sangue romagnolo (Blood of Romagna)
   Valor civile (Civil courage)
17 La felicità (Happiness)
18 Ercole (Hercules)
19 Bruscolo (Titch)
   Un segreto nel chiostro
    (A secret in the cloister)

Roy Clark

USA

b: circa 1903

The namesake of today's jolly country-and-westerner was for several years the star male kid of the Selig Polyscope Company. Even in black-and-white he was clearly red-haired (hence the lead in *Brick Top*) and he was still small enough in 1918 to be referred to as a 'little boy' in *A Woman's Fool*.

Roy was serious, freckly and wholly masculine — which made all the more curious his casting as seven-year-old Percy Putnam, the redeemed hero of *Sissybelle*. Percy is 'the pampered darling of a wealthy mother, who fails to see the manly side of things or discern the yearnings in the restless heart of a boy. . . .

Roy Clark, Selig's boy star, in 1914

She has him cabined in the nursery, playing with dolls, just like his little sister, so that he will not become contaminated by the naughty boys in the neighbouring streets.' (They are the ones who have dubbed him 'Sissybelle'.)

His father and the family doctor, however, drive Percy out into the back alley to learn 'the manly art of self-defense, and some other things meant for a boy.'.

Though it's not explained what these might be, the dogged insistence on manliness is one of the most boring features of early (and even middle) American cinema.

12 The Lake of Dreams
   The Little Indian Martyr
   Me and Bill
   A Waif of the Sea
13 Grandaddy's Boy
   His Sister
   A Little Hero
   Love Before Ten
   Movin' Pitchers
   The Noisy Six
   The Probationer
   Sissybelle
   The Tattle Battle
   Venus and Adonis
   When the Circus Came to Town
14 At the Transfer Corner
   The Cop on the Beat

Luigi Petrungaro

ITALY

b: 10 Feb 04 (Seminare, R.C.)

As a child, Luigi – whose father, Guido, was a stage and screen actor – played in many films made in Turin by Savoia and Gloria. He shared heroic roles with Ermanno Roveri◇ in Gloria's *Cuore* series.

Petrungaro as the hero of Il tamburino sardo

From 1920 Petrungaro trained as a ballet dancer; from the mid-Twenties till the end of the Forties he was a light comedy actor. Then he left the profession and had an office job till his retirement in 1964.

Indispensable: Lindau-Schulz, the great detective's aide

Rolf Lindau-Schulz

GERMANY

b: 21 Aug 04 (Thale, Harz mountains)
d: 27 Jly 69 (Santa Monica, Cal.)

Rolf's mother, the writer Margarethe Lindau-Schulz, scripted the first film he appeared in. He was signed up on a three-year contract by the detective star Stuart Webbs (1885-1936, RN Ernst Reicher) as his junior sidekick, and appeared in more than twenty Webbs thrillers – such as *Ein rätselhafter Blick* – in 1917-19. He got two more big roles in 1922, in *Das Spielzeug einer Dirne* and *Firnenrausch*, and dropped the Schulz.

It doesn't seem to have brought him luck. His entry in Mühsam and Jacobson's 1926 'Lexicon des Filmes' is graced with 34 lines of doggerel called 'Mein Lebenslauf' (My Life Story). It's a pathetic tirade against the blindness of German producers – who, he says, prefer to employ British or American actors, anything except the home-grown talent which luxuriates all around them:

'Where are the teenagers?' everyone
says,
Slamming the studio doors in their
face.

For Rolf Lindau the doors seem to have remained closed.

Fernand Mertens

BELGIUM

b: 25 Dec 04 (Brussels)
d: 2 Nov 70 (Paris)

A Christmas baby of theatrical parents, the future Fernand Gravey (or Gravet) had everything going for him. His father, Charles-Léopold Mertens, was director of a Brussels theatre, where his mother (*née* Gravey) also acted. Before his screen

Fernand Mertens – the future Fernand Gravey – in Het meisje uit de bloemenvelden

23

debut at the age of six, he had often appeared on stage – for instance with the great Mounet-Sully in 'Oedipus'.

In December 1914 he was evacuated to London, and was a contemporary of the future Field-Marshal Montgomery at St Paul's School, Hammersmith. The fluent English he acquired was to serve him well in British and American films of the mid-Thirties, such as *Bitter Sweet, The King and the Chorus Girl* and *The Great Waltz*. He was decorated for gallantry in World War Two.

Several of his childhood films were directed by Alfred Machin, father of 'Clo-Clo' Machin ◇.

12 Sans famille (No relations)
13 Un épisode de Waterloo
   (Waterloo episode)
   Monsieur Beulemeester, garde civique
   (Monsieur Beulemeester, civil guard)
   Saida a enlevé Manneken Pis
   (Saida has kidnapped Manneken Pis)
   30 ans, ou la vie d'un joueur
   (30 years, or a gambler's life)
14 Het meisje uit de bloemenvelden
   (The girl from the tulip-fields –
   NL/BE/FR)

Junior Carnahan

USA

b: 1904 (Pittsburgh)

Handsome Thomas B. Carnahan acted as a child for Biograph, Vitagraph, Kinemacolor, Metro, Pathe, Fox and Thanhouser, to name but a few. From 1911 he was a celebrated figure, in a small way, on the New York stage, then undergoing a vogue for 'Children's Theater' – children playing adult roles. He played Dick Deadeye in an all-kid production of 'HMS Pinafore', but later specialised in 'old man' roles. In 1914, however, he played Cedric Fauntleroy in Toronto. An uncritical critic called him 'a master mimic, a remarkable beauty, a child marvel'.

On film, 'Junior' Carnahan had the lead in Kinemacolor's *Jack and the Beanstalk*, and in *Chris and the Wonderful Lamp* acted

A lad 'n' his double: Carnahan in Chris and the Wonderful Lamp

opposite himself in double image. Twenty years later, as plain Thomas Carnahan, he was still acting on stage, a serious, good-looking leading man.

13 In the Shadow
   The Late Mr Jones
15 Doctor Rameau
   An Enemy to Society
16 The Sex Lure
17 Chris and the Wonderful Lamp
18 Uncle Tom's Cabin

Floored: Russell McDermott yields to the charms of Mary McAllister in Sadie Goes to Heaven

Russell McDermott

USA

b: circa 1904

Russell was an amusing brunet who was sometimes teamed with the tomboy Mary McAllister. He had one of the decade's shortest titles and two of its longest.

17 The Fable of the Back-Trackers from
   the Hot Sidewalks
   The Fable of the Toilsome Ascent and
   the Shining Table Land
   Pants
   Sadie Goes to Heaven
   Young Mother Hubbard

Danny Reulos

FRANCE

b: circa 1904

Danny was the small brother-in-law of (hold tight) the elder brother of the fantastical pioneer movie-maker Georges Méliès.

In an extremely large nutshell: Danny's sister, Hortense Reulos, had married the middle-aged Gaston Méliès, who was later to manage the American branch of the family movie firm, and to direct a few films in the States himself. These included a junior Western called *The Cowboy Kid* (1912), with elderly Gaston's eight-year-old brother-in-law in the title role.

Danny's own elder brother, Lucien Reulos, was an early movie-camera designer and a collaborator of Georges Méliès. Probably only Ivy Compton-Burnett could have done justice to this monkey-puzzle of a family tree.

Maurice Touzé

FRANCE

b: 7 Feb 05 (Asnières, Paris)

A likeable dark boy with sleepily drooping eyelids, Maurice Touzé made both stage and screen debuts around 1914. In 1919, Visio Films bought rights on the stories of Alfred Machard, 'le romancier des gosses', and Touzé starred in the four opening films of the series, directed by Adrien Caillard. He was partnered more than once by the enchanting Simone Genevois, the future Joan of Arc of 1927.

He went on to play leads in *La Belle Nivernaise* (1923) and *Peau de Pêche* (1929).

15 Le fils d'un autre (Another man's son)
19 Popaul et Virginie
   Poucette, ou le plus petit détective
   du monde

A fine romance: Maurice Touzé and la petite Crétot in Popaul et Virginie

(Thumbscrew, the world's smallest detective)
20 Un million dans un main d'enfant
   (A million in a child's hand)
   Le syndicat des fessés
   (The spanked boys' union)

Ernest Butterworth

BRITAIN/USA

b: 8 May 05 (Lancashire, England)
d: 2 May 86 (North Hollywood)

This Lancashire exile had a pleasingly open, honest face. His father, equally Ernest (1876-1950), had been an actor too, and his brothers Frank and Joe◇ both graced the screen, but not much beyond their late teens.

11 The Little Cripple
13 A Child's Influence
15 The Kingdom of Nosyland
16 It Can't Be True
17 The Crab
18 Selfish Yates
   Tad's Swimming Hole
   Thief or Angel
19 The Luck of the Irish
20 A Beggar in Purple
   The Lord Loves the Irish
21 Her Mad Bargain
   The Love Special

Edouard Trebaol

USA

b: 20 May 05 (Hollywood)

The French immigrant Trebaol family included fifteen offspring, nearly all of whom did film work. Eddie, the eldest boy, stocky and cocky, first caught the public eye as Johnny Jones's◇ country cousin in the 'Edgar' series. But he became still better known for his spirited Artful Dodger to the Oliver of Jackie Coogan◇.

Two of Eddie's younger brothers, the lanky Yves (b: 6 Aug 06) and the curly François (b: 17 Jne 10) joined him in *Honest Hutch*, by which time they had been acting for four or five years. François can also be seen in *Breaking Into Society* (23).

c.18 Ruth's Millions
20 'Edgar' series
   Honest Hutch
   The Penalty
21 Oliver Twist

Anatole 'Bébé' Mary

FRANCE

b: 18 Jly 05 (Paris)
d: 6 Oct 74 (Plan-de-Cuques, Marseille)

Anatole Clement Mary (later Abélard), a skittish and charming infant, was the nephew of the popular novelist and playwright Jules Mary. He began performing on stage as 'Bébé' at the age of three. At five he was spotted and signed up by the great Louis Feuillade (1873-1925), who was to achieve the height of his powers between 1913 and 1918 in the bizarre serial adventures of *Fantômas*, *Les vampires*, *Judex* and *Tih-Minh*.

In 1910 Pathé starred the infant in three whimsical shorts: *Tom Pouce*, *Le petit Roi de Rome* and *La lettre au petit Jésus*. The response was enthusiastic, so they launched Feuillade's first series of 'Bébé' comedies, featuring the same mischievous child. He became a worldwide favourite – known as 'Bubi' in Germany, 'Jimmie' in the USA, and so on.

From now on every film carried his screen name. The titles in the first series were 'Baby eats his soup', 'Baby in Morocco', 'Baby isn't afraid of burglars', 'Baby's cure', 'Baby cheats', 'Baby the apache', 'Baby smokes', 'Baby turns black', 'Baby goes fishing' and 'Baby's discovery'.

Babies – or tots at any rate – suddenly became big business, and a rash of tiny stars broke out across the cinema sky. A little Liverpudlian, Willie Sanders◇, was signed up by Eclair on the strength of two British shorts, and was built up with some success as a French-based rival to Pathé's 'Bébé'. Back in England, the Clarendon company launched 'Daddy's Didums', while Italy came up with Eraldo Giunchi◇, and in due course the USA produced Bobby Connelly◇, Paul Jacobs◇ and other tot comics. (Though the versatile

The great 'Bébé'(Anatole Mary, centre) senses the end of an era in Bébé adopte un petit frère, *with Marcel Levesque (right).*

Connelly was rather more.) No serious rival emerged in the other Continental countries.

In later series 'Bébé' was to appear as flirt, moralist, millionaire, philanthropist, hypnotist, conjuror, insurance salesman, king, tramp, Hercules, socialist, sleep-walker, peacemaker, judge and gardener. He would go deaf, go sick, get drunk, suffer from neurasthenia, find a wife for his uncle, protect his sister, punish his father, take up ju-jitsu, archery and spiritualism, pretend to drown himself, fall in with a donkey, a satyr, a financier and Napoleon. Bébé got around.

He got around outside the studios too. In 1913, for instance, he and his seven-year-old sister accepted a month's engage-ment at the Royal Orpheum Theatre, Budapest.

The fourth series of 1913-14 was directed by Gambard, for Gaumont. The reason for the change of company and director was that Feuillade and Pathé had finally lost patience with the increasingly spoilt and insufferable Bébé and his ex-ploitative parents, and shown them the door. Into the prodigy's shoes stepped the sprightly René Poyen $^\diamond$ – 'Bout de Zan'.

There were no further 'Bébé' films after the Gambard series, but our hero was far from finished. Having taken a couple of years off to complete his studies, he returned to the stage (he was in Lucien Guitry's company between 1916 and 1919), and then branched out into sporting activities, notably boxing (he fought under the name of Kid René). Then he tried the music-halls (as René Duclos), and ended up farming in French North Africa.

In 1934 the screen beckoned again, and back he came with yet another name: René Dary. This time it was for good. The tough little ex-pug, who had never lacked charm and panache, became a big B-movie star – a sort of poor man's Gabin – in the late Thirties and right through the Forties. Towards 1950 he was an Administrative Producer (for instance with C.I.C.C.) and then Director-General of Eclectic Films. He also acquired a share in a company that made unbreakable glass. He even wrote a novel, 'Express 407'.

In spite of these distractions, he still found time to act. He could be seen, for instance, in *Touchez pas au grisbi* (1953), and as late as 1966 had a star role in *Le feu de Dieu*. René Dary acted almost up to his death.

10 La lettre au petit Jésus
   (A letter to baby Jesus)
   Le petit Roi de Rome
   (The little King of Rome)
   Tom Pouce (Tom Thumb)
   First 'Bébé' series *(10 shorts)*
11 Second 'Bébé' series *(33 shorts)*
   Le bracelet de la marquise
   (The marchioness's bracelet)
   La fille du juge d'instruction
   (The examining magistrate's
   daughter)
12 Third 'Bébé' series *(33 shorts)*
   Le Petit Poucet (Tom Thumb)
   Haut les mains (Hands up)
13-14 Fourth 'Bébé' series *(28 shorts)*

Leland Benham

USA

b: 20 Sep 05 (Boston)
d: 26 Sep 76

Leland was very much 'the Thanhouser boy' from his seventh to eleventh years. His father, Harry Benham (1886-1969) was a Thanhouser star, together with his mother, Ethyle Cook (1880-1949) and kid sister Dorothy. He was generally teamed, though, with one or both of two other little girls: Marie Eline ('the Thanhouser Kid') and Helen Badgley ('The Thanhouser Kidlet'). From 1916 Leland and family left to work for other companies.

He was an intelligent, grown-up-looking child, and presumably a useful mimic, since in June 1915 he won third prize in a Charlie Chaplin impersonation contest at a Chaplin night at Murray's restaurant, New York.

12 Cross Your Heart
   The Cry of the Children
   The Greatest of These is Charity
   In a Garden
   The Ladder of Life
   The Making of an American
   On Probation
13 The Children's Conspiracy
   The Clothes Line Quarrel
   The Heart of a Child

The Benham family: Leland with parents Harry and Ethyle and sister Dorothy.

Jack and the Bean Stalk
King René's Daughter
A Pullman Nightmare
14 Coals of Fire
The Desert Tribesman
A Dog's Good Deed
Guilty or Not Guilty
His Reward
In Peril's Path
A Mohammedan Conspiracy
The Skating Master
The Success of Selfishness
15 Big Brother Bill
Bud Blossom
Do Unto Others
Fairies and Witches
Helen Intervenes
Just 'Kids'
The Little Captain of the Scouts
Milestones of Life
A Perplexing Pickle Puzzle
The Refugee
The Spirit of Audubon
The Two-Cent Mystery
Which Shall It Be?
16 Papa by Proxy
The Path of Happiness
17 Four Seasons
Over the Hill
The Victim

Renato Visca

ITALY

b: 1905 (Rome)

Renato came from a Roman theatre family which specialised in 19th-century demotic dramas as a 'Compagnia Dialettale'. He

began working for the Cines film company around the age of five.

Among his earliest films, from 1910, were *I due macchinisti* (The two mechanics), *La finestra illuminata* (The lighted window) and *Rataplan*.

In *Cajus Julius Caesar* he played Brutus as a boy, and in *Christus* someone even more eminent at a junior phase. In *Fabiola* he was the boy saint Tarcisius. He had a humbler role in *Romanza di un cane povero*, whose hero was a spirited poodle called Cheri.

Renato's career continued to flourish. After *Sinfonia pastorale, La bottegha dell' antiquario, I tre amanti* and *La cicala e la formica* (all 1921), he had his first film lead in *Il segreto della grotta azzurra* (The secret of the blue cave, 1922).

The following year he confirmed his star status, with an important part in Mario Volpe's *Il grido dell' aquila* (The eagle's cry – generally held to be the first Fascist film) and leads in *Jolly* (Mario Camerini's first film, a circus story co-starring Diomira Jacobini; Visca was a balloonist) and *Sirena* (an attempt at a sound film, made in Naples with real singers).

Visca's three remaining roles were all starring ones: in 1927 *El moroso de la nona* and *Kip tebbi* (filmed by Camerini in Tripoli – the title is Libyan for 'As you like it') and in 1928 *Valle santa*, with Tina Xeo. But at this point, while firmly at the top, he retired from acting and took over the family firm.

12 Cajus Giulius Caesar (Caius Julius Caesar)
14 Il portafoglio rosso (The red notebook)
16 Christus
    Giovanni Episcopo
    Romanza di un cane povero
    (Romance of a poor dog)
17 Carnevalesca (Carnival)
18 Fabiola
    La tentata (A woman tempted)
19 L'attentato (The attack)

Esben Lykke-Seest

NORWAY

b: 10 Jly 05 (West Akershus)
d: 8 Feb 88

Blond, leggy Esben, son of the novelist Peter Lykke-Seest, had the central role in *Historien om en gut*. He was sufficiently impressive to be offered a Hollywood film, but his father turned the offer down.

Esben went on to become managing director of British Petroleum in Norway.

19 Æresgjesten (The guest of honour)
    Historien om en gut (A boy's story)

Bhalchandra Phalke

INDIA

b: circa 1905

Balchandra, son of Dhundiraj Govind Phalke (1870-1944), the great pioneer of Indian cinema, played in his father's first film.

12 Raja Harishchandra

Balchandra's younger brother Nilkanth also had a vital role in their father's *Birth of Shree Krishna* of 1918.

Burwell Hamrick

USA

b: 1906
d: 21 Sep 70 (Hollywood)

Burwell Filson Hamrick – 'Chick', as he was known – had a busy film career from his tenth year or earlier, besides acting in stock at Universal City. In the autumn of 1917 he felt confident enough to take an expensive solo ad in Moving Picture World, with a cheeky photo and the legend 'Yes, I'm that kid you saw at the movie'.

The gamble paid off, and though never a star Hamrick was in steady employment until his mid-teens at least, acting with Mary Pickford among others. He had modest featured parts in one or two more films: *The Face Between* (22), *Through a Glass Window* (22), *Rouged Lips* (23). Later on he became a film set designer.

16 Bobby and the Roses
    Jimmie Straightened Out
    Polly Put the Kettle On

The Pursuing Vengeance
The Romance of Billy Goat Hill
17 The Devil-Stone
John Ermine of the Yellowstone
The Little Pirate
18 First Aid
The Heritage
How Could You Jean?
A Law Unto Herself
19 The Brute Breaker
20 Black Beauty
Seeds of Vengeance
Shore Acres
Smoldering Embers

Fabien Haziza

FRANCE

b: 1906 (Oran, Algeria)

His father was a teacher in Algeria. When
they moved to Paris, Fabien won a child
beauty prize and followed his sister Gilberte into the movies. In *Judex* he played
the hero as a boy; *Travail* was based on
Zola.

Although *Romain Kalbris* was subtitled
'le roman d'un enfant' Haziza, now nearly
16, played the lead. He continued to act,
for instance in 1925 as the beastly elder
brother in *Poil de Carotte*, and as a quite
harmless brother of Gance's Napoleon.

17 Judex
19 Travail (Labour)
20 Loin du foyer (Far from home)
21 Gigolette
Les parias de l'amour (Love's pariahs)
La pocharde (The inebriate woman)
22 Romain Kalbris

Fabien Haziza (right) as the boy Judex

Merveille du Mersey: Willie Sanders

Willie Sanders

BRITAIN/FRANCE

b: 1906 (Liverpool)

Looking for a kid rival to Pathé's all-
conquering 'Bébé' Mary◇, the Eclair
studio surprisingly seized upon a curly-
haired urchin from Merseyside, who had
already made a hit in two Hepworth films,
particularly as an infant boxer in *The Man
to Beat Jack Johnson*.

Before British producers signed him up,
Eclair offered five-year-old Sanders, 'the
Liverpool boy wrestler' – whose talents
also included skating, fencing and the
violin – a three-year contract. They then
launched him on a series of '*Willy*' comedies (there were to be 71 in all) mostly
directed by Joseph Faivre and Victorin
Jasset.

As 'Willy' – besides another boxing
match, this time with Bombardier Wells –
he looked after his sick uncle, played
truant from school, sampled his first cigar,
tried dining without paying, became by
turns a skating instructor, a ghost, a
gymnast and a painter.

It sounds exhausting, but 'le petit William' achieved considerable international
popularity. In Germany, the Illustrierte
Kino-Woche described him as 'the great

little comic'. A melodiously roguish sentence bears grim promise of more pranks
in the offing: 'Eine lustige Idee entsteht im
krausen Kopf des hübschen Bübchens'. (A
jolly idea is born in the handsome laddie's
curly head.)

Unlike the careers of 'Bébé' and 'Bout
de Zan', Willie Sanders's ended in early
childhood. Presumably this was partly due
to the outbreak of war and Willie's return
to Britain, partly to the flooding of
the British market with the flourishing
American kid comedies, to say nothing of
his former rivals in France. But although
Willie had undoubted looks and cockiness,
there was something a bit mechanical
about his tricks, and he hadn't the charm
or charisma of the Parisians.

10 Little Willie's Adventures with a Tramp
The Man to Beat Jack Johnson
12-14 'Willy' comedies

Maurice Mathieu

FRANCE

b: circa 1906

'Le petit Mathieu' had already filmed
for Feuillade in France, before going to
Holland in 1911 with the Alfred Machin
company. He was in at least three of the
'Hollandsche Films' Machin shot at
Volendam for distribution by Pathé.

12 La hantise (The obsession)
Het lijden van de scheepsjongen
(The cabin-boy's torment – NL/FR)
De molens die juichen en weenen
(The mills rejoice and weep – NL/FR)
La peinture et les cochons
(Painting and pigs – NL/FR)

Eraldo Giunchi

ITALY

b: circa 1906

Eraldo's mother was Lea Giunchi, a
leading actress of the dominant Roman
company Cines. (No one seems quite sure
who his father was: perhaps the clown
Natale Guillaume.)

From the age of about four he starred, as 'Cinessino', in a series of little comedies designed to rival those of Pathé's 'Bébé'. (See Anatole Mary ◇.) In this he had dealings with a ballerina, Grandpa's pipe and a gramophone, imitated the French film hero Fantômas, and so on. *Il sogno patriotico di Cinessino* was a bit of upbeat propaganda hastily filmed on Italy's entry into the war.

Eraldo Giunchi appeared once or twice more, now under his own name, but only in minor roles.

10-13 'Cinessino' films
    (Cinessino e la ballerina; C. e la pipa del
      nonno; C. ha fortuna; C. imita
      Fantômas; C. salvatore; C. e il
      grammofono)
13 Non far piangere la bambina
    (Don't make the baby cry)
15 Il sogno patriotico di Cinessino
    (Cinessino's patriotic dream)

George Hupp

USA

b: circa 1906

The gentle-looking fair-haired George, whose best leads were in *Pie* and *Paradise Garden,* was not wholly without macho appeal, as is shown by a study of him and a little-girl contemporary performing an energetic 'Apache dance' – a happily lost art-form which involved a great deal of flinging about of the female partner.

16 Irma in Wonderland
    Naked Hearts
    Pie
    Us Kids
17 The Cricket
    The Little Orphan
    Paradise Garden
    The Plow Woman
18 The Kaiser, the Beast of Berlin
    The Lure of Luxury

Matty Roubert

USA

b: 22 Jan 07 (New York)
d: 17 May 73 (Honolulu)

Matty Roubert

Occasionally billed as 'Matty Rupert', he was the son of William L. Roubert, who was to direct him in some of his most shamelessly 'promotional' outings, such as *The Waif, Heritage* and the *Romances of Youth* series. But he had already had five years' experience after a debut in the 1910 Vitagraph *Uncle Tom's Cabin*, claimed as America's first three-reel film.

During 1912-13 he was featured by the Powers company as 'Master Matty' (usually with their little girl star, 'Baby Early'; the pair were to renew the partnership for Warners in 1915). In 1914 the footloose moppet was working with Universal as the star of their *Universal Boy* series. Among other studios he graced were Biograph, Edison, Pathe and Famous Players.

The Universal Boy, a series of ten shorts, was described as 'comedy-travelogue'. In it, Matty met many celebrities of the day, including Colonel Roosevelt, Oscar Hammerstein, the Secretary for War, the Cornell rowing crew and the leader of the Boy Scouts of America. (Jackie Coogan ◇ was to trump this a few years later by notching up, in real life, the League of Nations and the Pope.) More democratically, Matty was filmed with newsboys,

dockers, baseball players, life-savers and fishermen, and with puzzled immigrants on Ellis Island.

Matty was a dark, handsome child with a rosy face, 'snapping hazel eyes' and a sometimes rather sensual, world-weary, Parisian expression. In his prime he sported a pageboy bob in the Buster Brown manner. He had leading roles in *Driftwood* (1916) and *Parentage* (1917). A reviewer of the latter commented on 'the amount of poise, the fine repose' in his face, though in fact Matty played a mean character. *The Waif* and *Heritage* were both gutter-to-glory sagas of child stardom, expressly tailored as theatrical showcases for little Roubert. (In *The Waif* he displayed himself as Sherlock Holmes, Fagin – and Sarah Bernhardt playing La Tosca.)

Matty Roubert continued a modest career for the next 25 years or so. But he was never again a star.

10 Uncle Tom's Cabin
12 The Coming Generation
    The Leg and the Legacy
    The Skeleton
13 Mammy's Chile
    A Man's Awakening
    Snow White
    When Dolly Died
14 John Barleycorn
    The Universal Boy (series)
    Vasco, the Vampire
15 A Bachelor's Christmas
    The Five Senses
    Her New Yob
    The Scarlet Mark
    The Waif
16 The Big Sister
    Blind Man's Buff
    Driftwood
17 Parentage
20 Heritage
    Romances of Youth (series)
23 For You My Boy
    The Stolen Child

Joseph 'Chip' Monahan

USA

b: 16 May 07 (New York)

The darkly handsome Joseph A. Monahan, Junior, has been allotted various birthdates, ranging between 1904 and 1908. He became known as 'Chip' from the title of his first important film. The subsequent *Chip's Carmen* – or 'Burlesque on Burlesque' – was a kid version of Chaplin's existing parody. Young Joseph played Don José to the Carmen of his sister Mary.

Later, as a 'screen and presentation star', Chip re-emerged as Joseph A. McKenna.

15 A Chip Off the Old Block
   Chip's Elopement
16 Chip's Backyard Barnstormers
   Chip's Carmen
   Chip's Movie Company
   Chip's Rivals
   A Diamond from the Pie
   For Sale, a Daddy
   The World War in Kidland
17 The 'Lincoln' Cycle
18 Peter Ibbetson
21 Silver Wings

Thomas Carr

USA

b: 4 Jly 07 (Philadelphia)

Thomas was the third son of the screen's great 'motherly' actress Mary Carr, and younger brother of Johnny ◇ and Stephen ◇. He appeared in movies from 1910, initially for the long-established Lubin company.

Thomas Carr continued as actor till the late Thirties, when he joined Republic, doing various script and production jobs before directing his first film, *Santa Fe Saddlemates*, in 1945. Thereafter he directed mainly Westerns, for cinema and TV (including the *Rawhide* series). *The Tall Stranger* (57) was one of his finest.

12 Buster's Dream
14 Little Breeches
17 The Barrier
18 Virtuous Wives
19 Through the Toils
20 The Idol Dancer
   Over the Hill to the Poorhouse
   Velvet Fingers
   The White Bottle

Thomas's two elder brothers, Johnny and Stephen, had both started acting in films at about the same time.

JOHNNY CARR – born circa 1904, died 27 Nov 56 – had his biggest success as 'Skinnay' in *Boy Scouts to the Rescue* (18), and it led to his own spin-off series the following year.

Johnny's acting career lasted for a time, in films like *The Kentuckians* (21), *The Go-Getter* (23) and *The Earth Woman* (26).

15 The Great Divide
   The House of Fear
   The Stowaway
17 The Barrier
   Over the Hill
   Polly of the Circus
18 Boy Scouts to the Rescue
19 'Skinnay' comedies
   (Fotygraft Gallery; New Folks in Town;
   A Rainy day; Skinnay, School and
   Scandal; S'prise Party 'n' Ever'thing;
   When a Feller Needs a Friend)

The middle brother, STEPHEN CARR – born circa 1905, died 20 May 86 – appeared in several movies from 1912 onwards. Later, though he tried his hand at directing, it never took over his career, as with young brother Thomas. Stephen spent half a century acting in movies, e.g. *Little Old New York* (23), *Hell's Angels* (30), the *Superman* serial (49) and *Crooked River* (58).

12 Buster's Dream
15 The Great Divide
   The House of Fear
   The Stowaway
17 The Barrier
   Polly of the Circus
18 Boy Scouts to the Rescue
   Little Miss No-Account
   The Littlest Scout
   The Mating
   The Song of the Soul
   The Street of Seven Stars
   To the Highest Bidder
19 'Skinnay' series
20 The Key to Power
   Over the Hill to the Poorhouse
   The Restless Sex
   Roaring Oaks

Gordon Griffith

USA

b: 4 Jly 07 (Chicago)
d: 12 Dec 58 (Hollywood)

This athletic fellow entered the movies around 1913. With Paul Jacobs ◇, he became one of the leading 'Keystone Kids', and was in several of Chaplin's 1914 comedies. Like Wesley Barry ◇ (whose *Penrod* he would later appear in) he had kid parts in the 'Ham and Bud' series.

Gordon was no tender flower. Under the headline 'A Little Too Much Realism', a 1914 reporter penned a vivid account of the filming of a rough-and-tumble in *Little Sunset*. In this baseball story, the eponymous hero 'licks the Apaches' former bat-boy in a fair fight, and becomes bat-boy himself. Unfortunately, the boy chosen for the defeat didn't want to be licked, and furthermore he didn't propose to be licked as long as his two fists held out. Gordon Griffith, who plays "Little Sunset", had no intention of being downed either, especially as the play demanded that he win out. The fight did not go according to schedule. . . . Holding the boys apart by main strength, Mr Bosworth explained that it was only make-believe. "But I kin lick him easy!" howled the other boy. "Can't either!" yelled Sunset, and they were at it again. . . .'

Griffith could claim to have been the screen's first Tarzan – several minutes ahead of Elmo Lincoln – in *Tarzan of the Apes* in 1918. 'Gordon Griffith,' wrote a critic, 'a youthful actor of uncommon gifts, impersonates Tarzan as a boy. He is a fit subject for a sculptor, as he climbs through the trees in the company of the apes, his naked body showing its grace of line in every move.' The same could hardly be said of the grotesquely barrel-chested Lincoln. Gordon swung again two years later in the serial *Son of Tarzan*.

He would soon be seen as Tom Sawyer in the 1920 *Huckleberry Finn*, but meanwhile must have swallowed hard before signing up for a moral propaganda film of 1919, which did not belie its title: *The*

Solitary Sin. This was 'a study of sexual abuses on the part of young men, through neglect on the part of their parents. It follows the careers of three boys. One was taken in hand by his father, while still very young, and profited by learning the secrets of nature and sex. The other boys were allowed to grow up in ignorance; one contracts syphilis and is not allowed to marry, the other goes insane from self-abuse.'

It is a relief to hear that Gordon was the one 'taken in hand by his father' in the nick of time. (The other, less fortunate principals were left tactfully uncredited.) One imagines that masturbation had a lean year or two following this hair-raising sermon.

Jungle Trail of the Son of Tarzan, released in 1923, was simply a cut-down version of the 1920 *Son of Tarzan*. Griffith had another lead in *The Street of Tears* (24), and went on acting till the mid-Thirties. Then he moved into assistant directing and producing with various companies.

Above left: *Tarzan, boy of letters.*
Below left: *Traces of beastliness: Gordon Griffith with T. Dempsey Tabler and Karla Schramm in* Son of Tarzan

Naked Hearts
The Other Woman
A Son of Neptune
Storming the Trenches
Two Mothers
17 Like Babes in the Wood
The Price of Silence
18 Hitting the High Spots
The Romance of Tarzan
Tarzan of the Apes
The Yellow Dog
19 Cupid Forecloses
Huckleberry Finn
The Solitary Sin
Under the Top
20 The Kentucky Colonel
Penrod (released 1922)
Son of Tarzan (serial)
To Please One Woman
21 Peck's Bad Boy
That Something
The Village Blacksmith
22 Catch My Smoke
More To Be Pitied Than Scorned
23 Main Street

Francis Marion

USA

b: 22 Jly 07 (Omaha, Nebraska)

Having spent most of his childhood in
Louisville, Kentucky, Francis – unrelated
to Don 'John Henry' Marion ◇ – moved
with his mother to Los Angeles after his
father's death. One of her friends was
Constance Collier, who recommended the
boy to D.W.Griffith. They both made
their screen debut in Macbeth.

Francis continued to act for a few more
years, and in 1927 had a star role in The
Wreck of the Hesperus.

16 Macbeth
17 The Clash of Steel
Mary from America
The Rented Man
18 Hearts of the World
The Legion of Death
19 The World and Its Woman
21 Little Lord Fauntleroy
22 The Kingdom Within
Up and Going
23 Why Women Remarry

Wesley Barry

USA

b: 10 Aug 07 (Los Angeles)

Mickey Rooney's ◇ predecessor as Boy
of the People was also red-haired, but
skinnier and more elfish, the son of a
grocer. He was discovered by Marshall
Neilan, who was to direct some of his
best films. Neilan later described him as
'a natural born artist', and supervised his
education with extreme thoroughness.
He introduced six-year-old Wesley Barry
into the Ham and Bud series, with the
comic duo of Lloyd V. Hamilton and Bud
Duncan.

Barry was an instant hit, and over the
next few years became well known to
filmgoers. He appeared in six of Mary
Pickford's movies, beginning with The
Foundling and ending with Daddy Long
Legs (where he was memorable as a small
orphan with a drink problem). In that same
post-war year, 1919, he was seen in The
Unpardonable Sin as 'George Washington
Sticker, an American Boy Scout from
Kansas, but temporarily in Belgium'.
'If any boy actor', wrote a critic, 'ever
succeeded in making more out of a part
than Wesley does out of Sticker, neither
the screen nor the stage has any record of
the event.'

His popularity can be gauged by the fact
that in 1920 an impostor tried to cash in
on it: a boy called Sidney Ward Scott was
touted around by his father on a 'Wesley
Barry personal appearance' tour. To com-
plaints that he was insufficiently freckled,
the Scotts replied that these were only
painted on for the camera. Other natural
accidents couldn't be so easily foreseen
('Pseudo Wesley Barry Runs Into Real
Wesley Barry's Grandma and Runs Away'
– headline in 'Moving Picture World'),
and when the Scotts tried the bluff again
in Detroit, Marshall Neilan got wind of it
and called the police.

During 1920 Wesley got his first incon-
trovertible lead in the title role of Penrod, a feature-length kid film based on
the 1914 Booth Tarkington best-seller.
Penrod, for the benefit of non-American
readers, was the American forerunner of
Richmal Crompton's William, who saw
the light eight years later – a creature
of wild imagination and grandiose
stratagems, from the ruins of which, by a
mixture of luck and bluster, he emerges
unscathed. Subsequent screen Penrods
included Ben Alexander ◇, Leon Janney ◇
and Billy Mauch ◇.

Checkered careers: Wesley Barry (left) and Mary Pickford in Daddy Long Legs

Above: *Wesley, roadhog*

Right: *Wesley, aesthete*

Wesley Barry's *Penrod* wasn't in fact released until 1922, by which time he had had another lead in *Dinty* – an earlier role writ larger.

Though he retained his impishness, the teens eventually crept up on Wesley Barry. He married in 1926, but remained a popular screen teenager for several more years. As late as 1934 he was playing a Huck-Finnish role in *The Life of Vergie Winters*, and Ford among others employed him in the 1930s. His last featured role was in *Rocky* (48).

After World War Two, he produced and/or directed a few B movies, and at one stage had his own company, Genie Productions. He produced 70 of the 113 *Wild Bill Hickok* TV half-hours for Broidy Productions, in which he was a partner.

Messinger in 1920

Buddy Messinger

USA

b: 26 Oct 07 (San Francisco)
d: 25 Oct 65 (Hollywood)

Melvin Joe Messinger was a great bruiser of a boy, inclining to fat though not in the Arbuckle or Joe Cobb ◇ class. He and his comelier sister Gertie sprang to fame around their ninth year in the Kiddie Comedies which the Franklin brothers, Chester and Sidney, turned out for Fox between 1915 and 1918. These delightfully robust romances, with the children taking adult parts and the larger girls sometimes donning moustaches and playing dashing gentlemen, had very much the air of end-of-term school entertainments and often used the traditional pantomime stories.

While Gertie – who had a delicious sense of comedy – played heroines or floozies, her big brother was naturally cut out for bullying or villainous roles. (Though when they needed a Giant, for *Jack and the Beanstalk*, the Franklins engaged an enormous adult, Jim Tarvers, to make the children look even tinier by comparison.) Buddy could be superbly malevolent, or just touchingly thick. He would have enjoyed playing Long John Silver in the 1917 *Treasure Island*: but the part went to the barnstorming Violet Radcliffe!

After the Franklin series ended, he remained in great demand, and was seen as the hulking bane of Johnny Jones ◇ in the *Edgar* comedies and of Ben Alexander ◇ in *Penrod and Sam*.

His teenage role in *Trifling with Honor* was a juicy one, and in 1924 he himself became the star of a series of comedy shorts with titles like *Boyhood Days*, *Sunny Gym* and *Buddy at the Bat*. Though he gradually ceased to be a household name, he remained a valuable Hollywood heavy and kept his career going for another twenty years. He also toured in vaudeville as a pianist-comedian.

16 Fighting Joe
   Gloriana
   The Street Urchin
17 Aladdin and His Wonderful Lamp
   The Babes in the Woods
   The Brownies
   Jack and the Beanstalk
   The Mikado
   Pinafore
   Treasure Island
   Two Little Imps Doing Their Bit
18 Ali Baba and the Forty Thieves
   Fan Fan
   Six Shooter Andy
19 The Hoodlum
   The Luck of the Irish

20 'Edgar' comedies
21 The Old Nest
   The Old Swimmin' Hole
22 The Flirt
   A Front Page Story
   Shadows
   When Love Comes
23 The Abysmal Brute
   Penrod and Sam
   Trifling With Honor
   The Turmoil

Johnny Jones
(Edward Peil, Jr.)

USA

b: 18 Nov 07 (Beloit, Wisconsin)
d: 7 Nov 62 (San Andreas, Cal.)

Charles Edward Peil, a vigorous, keep-fit boy with rather bulging blue-grey eyes, was the son of actors. His father, Edward J. Peil (1888-1958), was a beefy and often menacing stalwart of thrillers and Westerns – he played, for instance, 'Evil Eye' in D.W. Griffith's *Broken Blossoms* – while his mother, Etta Raynor, was a more graceful performer.

Though young Charlie had graced the boards at six months, and been in films

Actor-manager: Johnny Jones (left) attempts to dominate Lucille Ricksen in Edgar's Hamlet

with Constance Talmadge (several times) and Mary Pickford (once), besides non-starring roles with the Franklin Kiddies, his identity was kept a strict secret – presumably in the interests of 'real, typical American boy-next-door quality' – when he was chosen to play *Edgar*, hero of some stories written specially for Goldwyn by Booth Tarkington of 'Penrod' fame. (Author also, incidentally, in 1918, of 'The Magnificent Ambersons'.)

Edgar is very much a rehash of Penrod – the 'good bad boy' with an over-lively imagination – and Charles Peil became plain Johnny Jones for the duration of these twelve two-reelers and some time after. (Confusingly, Edgar's kid brother Charlie was played by Charlie's kid sister Virginia.)

Changing his screen name to Edward Peil, Jr., Charles/Johnny remained in movies till the 1930s.

18 The Walls of Jericho
19 Salomy Jane
   The Shepherd of the Hills
20-21 The Adventures and Emotions
   of Edgar Pomeroy (series)
   (Edgar and Teacher's Pet; E.'s Hamlet; E.'s
   Jonah Day; E. Takes the Cake; E.'s Sunday
   Courtship; E. Camps Out; E.'s Little Saw;
   Get-Rich-Quick Edgar; E. the Explorer; E.'s
   Country Cousin; E.'s Feast Day; E. the
   Detective.)
21 The Old Nest
22 Broadcasting Night Life in Hollywood
   Makin' Movies
   Stung
   Supply and Demand

Sydney Wood

BRITAIN

b: 1907

18 The Great Impostor
19 The Power of Right
   The Warrior Strain
20 David and Jonathan
   The Dawn of Truth
   The Ever-Open Door
   The Flame
   Her Benny
21 The Double Event

Alfred Idström

FINLAND

b: circa 1907

Olli's Apprenticeship was an almost instant screen version, by Teuvo Puro, of a new book by the popular children's author Anni Swan. (She had written it as a cautionary tale for her own exuberant child.

After a rumpus with his rich parents, Olli, the four-year-old son of the manor – played in this phase by Sirkka Puro, the director's little daughter – runs away, survives some adventures and takes ship to Sweden, where he is given shelter by a kindly cobbler.

Some eight years pass, and Olli (now played by Alfred Idström) stows away on a boat back to Turku. There he holes up with another kindly cobbler until some louse frames him for a theft. He is sent to a reformatory, but rescued. Eventually he returns to his parents, who had long given him up for dead.

Some of Jackie Coogan's ◊ films had stories no better than this. Idström was a nice kid, but no Coogan.

20 Ollin oppivuodet (Olli's apprenticeship)

Ben Grauer

USA

b: 2 Jne 08 (Staten Island, N.Y.)
d: 31 May 77 (New York)

Benjamin Franklin Grauer (with that handle, how could the kid go wrong?) was the son of a civil engineer, surveyor and antique dealer. He was known as plain Ben, or Bunny, and enjoyed ten years on stage and screen, between 1915 and 1925.

In 1930 Grauer joined NBC as an announcer and interviewer, and from then until his retirement in 1973 was their 'all-round man': sometimes news-man, reporter, sports commentator, actor, chairman and host. His was described as 'the most authoritative voice in the world'.

18 The Caillaux Case
   Neighbors
19 Break the News to Mother
   The Hidden Truth
   The Mad Woman
20 The Idol Dancer
21 Annabel Lee
22 My Friend, the Devil
   The Town That Forgot God
23 Does It Pay?

Jean Rauzéna

FRANCE

b: June 1908 (Pantin, Paris)
d: 30 Mar 70 (Paris)

Jean was the younger brother of the actor Fernand Rauzéna (1900-76). Speaking of his 'proud and majestic' performance as the Roi de Rome in *L'agonie des aigles*, and

Jean Rauzéna in Un bon petit diable

his marvellously expressive face, critics hailed him as a great actor of the future. He played an admirably frisky lead in *Un bon petit diable* the following year.

He went on to appear as a Jewish teenager in *La terre promise* (25), and as Louis Bonaparte in Gance's *Napoléon* (26). In the Thirties he worked almost entirely in the theatre, and later he became France's foremost *'bruiteur'*, or special effects man, in cinema and radio.

22 L'agonie des aigles (The eagles' agony)
   L'île sans nom (The nameless island)
   Pasteur
   Les Roquevillard
23 Un bon petit diable (A good little devil)

Milton Berlinger

USA

b: 12 Jly 08 (New York)

Young Berlinger – later the comedian Milton Berle – had sprung to local fame at the age of five as a Chaplin impersonator, then toured in vaudeville with his sister. He was on the New York stage at 12, and was in one or two more youthful films, such as *Lena Rivers* (25) and *Sparrows* (26), plus a handful of screen appearances in the Thirties and Forties, before he became a popular favourite on television, 'Uncle Miltie'.

14 The Perils of Pauline
   Tillie's Punctured Romance
16 Easy Street
17 Little Brother
20 Birthright
   Humoresque
   The Mark of Zorro
22 Divorce Coupons

Arthur Redden

USA

b: 17 Jly 08 (Boston, Mass.)

19 The Mayor
   The Other Half
   The Pointing Finger
   The Solitary Sin
   The Way of the Strong

20 The Road to Divorce
   Smiling All the Way
   The Third Generation

René Poyen ('Bout de Zan')

FRANCE

b: 5 Oct 08 (Paris)

'Bout de Zan' (literally 'bit of liquorice') was three years younger than 'Bébé' Mary ◇, his small predecessor at Pathé. 'Bébé' was already a national figure when, towards the end of his second series of shorts, the director Feuillade planted a powerful cuckoo in the Pathé nest.

'Bébé' had been the mischievous darling of a middle-class screen family, lording it unchallenged. With the introduction in 1912 (in *Bébé adopte un petit frère* and *Bébé, Bout de Zan et le voleur*) of a street-wise urchin who was better-looking than 'Bébé' and a natural comic, the star's tiny nose must have been put firmly out of joint. One would like to have been a fly on the wall as this lilliputian *All About Eve* drama simmered at the Pathé studios.

It was known that Feuillade had had about enough of 'Bébé', with his prima donna airs and his insufferable parents; but he couldn't possibly dump such a valuable commodity till he had found a successor whom the public demonstrably preferred. Little René Poyen looked just the job, and delivered the goods: he got even more laughs than 'Bébé'. In 1913 Feuillade directed the first 'Bout de Zan' series for Pathé, and 'Bébé' moved over to Gaumont.

There were to be 62 'Bout de Zan' shorts over the next two years, and like those of 'Bébé' and 'Willy' they won an international audience. (In the U.S. and Britain he was billed as 'Tiny Tim'.)

In the course of them, he fell in with a tramp, a chimney-cleaner, a lion, a fisherman and a mannequin, to name but a few. After August 1914 he met a *poilu*, a *boche* and a spy. He became a boxer, a pacifist, a grocer, a street singer, a male nurse. He also performed in vaudeville, stole an

Mighty mouse: 'Bout de Zan' (René Poyen) circa 1913

elephant, attempted suicide, attended a masked ball, had jaundice, wrote his memoirs, overheard a crime on the telephone, found a torpedo and – of course – tried to join the army.

Little Poyen had enormous elegance and charm. With a pint-sized version of the dark, witty handsomeness of (say) Daniel Gélin 30 years later, he soon acquired total command of the double-take, the gallant flourishes of a gutter dandy, the sly wink at the audience. When in due course he became 'Réglisse' (liquorice again), sidekick of the patrician sleuth and wrong-righter Judex, you felt as much confidence in his resourcefulness as in his master's. He also acquired a girl-friend, the tiny Olinda Mano.

But he wasn't merely clever. The fact that the great Feuillade was still directing him in 1924 speaks volumes for his amiability and professionalism. After 1920 he dropped the cognomen and acted simply as René Poyen. He had briefly, through a contractual dispute over the use of the name 'Bout de Zan', been billed as 'Pique-Puce' (Flea-Cracker), a pun on Picpus.

With the approach of adolescence he began to look, and act, strangely like Jean-Pierre Léaud ◇, future hero of *Les quatre cents coups* and the sequels in which he incarnated the young François Truffaut, alias Antoine Doinel. René found himself a screen mate in a droll little pudding of a girl called 'Bouboule' who doggily worshipped him in *Le gamin de Paris* and elsewhere.

Even in this phase of Poyen's career, normally a deadly one for boy actors, Cinématographie Française called his playing 'habile, discret, naturel, agréable et fin' – as comprehensive a seal of approval as a screen teenager can ever have had.

(The 'Ursus' of the 1919 film is, oddly enough, not a bear but an elephant.)

In 1924 he appeared in *Lucette*, *L'orphelin de Paris*, *Pierrot-Pierrette* and *Romanetti*, and in 1925 in *Les murailles de silence*.

These last two films were not directed by Feuillade, who died in 1925. Like Léaud without his Truffaut, René Poyen must have felt utterly bereft, and there is no record of his appearing in any other film

until 1932. Then he crops up in an early talkie called *Clochard*. So, oddly enough, does a certain 'Bout de Zan' in one called *Le bidon d'or*.

By 1967, our resilient hero was director of a rubber factory in Paris. Is the mighty mouse still alive, in his eighties? No one in the film world seems to know.

12 Bébé adopte un petit frère
    (Bébé adopts a little brother)
    Bébé, Bout de Zan et le voleur
    (Bébé, Bout de Zan and the burglar)
13 First 'Bout de Zan' series (*26 shorts*)
14 Second 'Bout de Zan' series (*19 shorts*)
    L'enfant de la roulotte (The caravan kid)
    L'intègre (The upright man)
15 Third 'Bout de Zan' series (*17 shorts*)
    Les vampires (*serial*)
16 C'est pour les orphelins
    (It's for the orphans)
    Judex (*serial*)
    Nouvelles aventures de Judex (*serial*)
17 La nouvelle mission de Judex (*serial*)
19 Ursus
20 Les deux gamines (Two saucy girls)
    La proie (The prey)
23 La fille bien gardée
    (The well-protected girl)
    Le gamin de Paris (The Parisian urchin)
    La gosseline (That little girl)

Roswell Johnson

USA

b: 1908 (New York)

'Buster' Johnson, son of a Lubin camera-man, was in many Lubin movies from 1911. 'Moving Picture World' described him as 'an unusually handsome blonde, well built and as robust as a fawn'. Not so robust, though, as his contrasting 'heavy', Brooks McCloskey, who loured on him in the 'Buster' films. Brooks was the son of Lawrence S. McCloskey, a Lubin screen-writer. They liked to keep things in-house at Lubin.

'Buster', said a lady journalist, 'plays girls or boys with equal intelligence, and the more mischief required in the role the better.'

12 A Bachelor's Waterloo
    Buster and the Cannibals
    Buster and the Gypsies
    Buster and the Pirates
    Buster in Nodland
    Buster's Dream
    The Kiddies' Christmas
    Little Boy Blue
    'Twixt Love and Ambition
13 His First Experience
    Tamandra, the Gypsy
16 Grouchy

Franco Capelli

ITALY

b: circa 1908

He was the son of the actor and director Dante Capelli, and grandson of the 19th-century actor Enrico Capelli (1828-1908), the greatest Hamlet and Othello of his period in Italy. Franco had the lead in three cheap but popular films directed by his father in 1920 for Piemonte-Film, then played further leads for Ambrosio (*Il giro del mondo*, though a great success, was their last film before bankruptcy) and for Tiziano. Nearly all his work was for northern Italian companies.

14 Peppeniello
15-19 (other films for Gloria)

Phone-trapping: Edouard Mathé (left) as Judex's brother, René Poyen as Réglisse

20 La scogliera della morte (The reef of death)
   Lo scoiattolo del mare (The sea squirrel)
   Lo strano viaggio di Pim Popò
      (Pim Popo's strange journey)
21 Il giro del mondo di un birichino
      (A scamp goes round the world)
   Biribì, il piccolo poliziotto di Parigi
      (Biribi, the little Paris policeman)

Also around this time were born two junior acrobats, 'Arnold' and 'Patatà', both of whom were to die in their teens. These little daredevils were a major attraction of a troupe led by Luciano Albertini, who later starred as 'Sansone' or 'Sansonia' in Italian and German films.

ARNOLD (whose real name is unknown) first appeared on the screen in 1917, and was a regular in the *Lilliput* series for Albertini Films between 1919 and 1921. He died in the mid-1920s. So – in October 1926, of septicaemia – did Aldo Mezzanotte, known as PATATA and Arnold's partner with the Albertinis. He was seen in the 1921 films *Der König der Manege*, *Die eiserne Faust* and *Die Todesleiter*.

Charley Jackson

USA

b: circa 1908

14 Boy
16 The Heart of a Hero
17 A Son of Democracy (from Benjamin
      Chapin's *Lincoln* cycle)
18 Cecilia of the Pink Roses
   The Love Net
   The Power and the Glory
   Snug Harbor
   To Him That Hath
   Vengeance
   Wives of Men
   The Yellow Ticket
21 The Black Panther's Cub
22 For His Sake

Willie Johnson

USA

b: circa 1908

Willie's father was the actor Tefft Johnson,

who directed the *Sonny Boy* films and played Sonny Boy's father. Willie may also, in 1915, have been the 'Billy Johnson' teamed with Bobby Connelly ◇ in *The Faith of Sonny Jim*.

16 Sonny Boy at the Bat
   Sonny Boy at the Dog Show
   Sonny Boy in School Days
17 The Courage of Silence

Tibi Lubinsky in Prinz und Bettelknabe, *with A. D. Weisse as Lord Chancellor*

Tibi Lubinsky

HUNGARY/AUSTRIA

b: circa 1908

Tibor Lubinszky, as he was spelt in his Hungarian days, was probably the leading European boy actor (in straight roles) before the arrival of Martin Herzberg ◇. After 1920 he worked mainly in Austria and Germany, sometimes for his fellow-Hungarian Sandor (later Alexander) Korda. His sister Manci also filmed.

Die Geheimnisse von London was a newly filmed version of *Oliver Twist*. An earlier 'Prince and Pauper' made by Edison had Cecil Spooner (female) in the title roles.

17 A tüz (The fire – HU)
18 Erdekházasság
      (Marriage of convenience – HU)
   A kis Lord (Little Lord Fauntleroy – HU)
19 Twist Oliver (Oliver Twist – HU)

20 A csodagyerek (The child prodigy – HU)
   Draghfy Eva (Eva Draghfy – HU)
   Die Geheimnisse von London
      (Mysteries of London – GE/AT)
   Prinz und Bettelknabe
      (The prince and the pauper – AT)
21 Bobby auf der Fährte
      (Bobby on the ferry – AT)
22 Herren der Meere (Lords of the sea – AT)
   Lukrezia Borgia (GE)
   Revanche (A debt repaid – GE)
   Versunkene Welten (Sunken worlds – AT)
23 Az egyhuszasos leany
      (A girl for two farthings – HU)
24 Um ein Königskind (The royal child)

Maurice Thompson

BRITAIN

b: circa 1908

Maurice was a lean, intense boy. One critic, reviewing *Froggy's Little Brother*, called him 'one of the greatest child actors the screen has yet found', but another remarked: 'His vocabulary of gestures and expressions is rather limited.' W.P. Kellino engaged him for *Rob Roy*, but used him instead in *A Soul's Awakening*.

21 The Fifth Form at St Dominic's
   Froggy's Little Brother
22 Long Odds
   The Peacemaker
   A Soul's Awakening

Limited vocabulary: Maurice Thompson in Froggy's Little Brother

Friends in adversity: Bobby Connelly and Miriam Battista in the 1920 Humoresque

Bobby Connelly

USA

b: 4 Apr 09 (Brooklyn, N.Y.)
d: 5 Jly 22 (Lynbrook, N.Y.)

Robert Joseph Connelly entered films, for Kalem, at the age of three. From July 1913 he (alongside his younger sister Helen) worked for Vitagraph, and he became one of their most valuable stars, especially through his *Sonny Jim* and *Bobby* series. After 1918 he moved to other studios.

'Moving Picture World' called him 'a superior and natural little actor that many would be pleased to grab out of the picture and hug-up.' 'To say he is cute,' a later critic wrote, 'is not to do the little gentleman justice: he is finished. . . . He has the most remarkably obedient fountain of tears that the screen exhibits. He stirs the emotions of the theatregoer.'

This homely, plumpish, round-eyed child – somewhat like Britain's Vincent Winter ◇ of 40 years later – had a talent for pathos. He could supply his full quota of boyish pranks, though. As Sonny Jim he visited the North Pole, the Circus and the Mardi Gras, became a Little Captive and a Cave Dweller, had a First Love Affair and faced the Bear Facts.

Soon after his 13th birthday poor Bobby was, indeed, finished – dying of bronchitis and (perhaps fittingly) an enlarged heart. He had been one of the best-loved of all the early cinema's child actors.

12 The Country Kid
13 Bunny's Mistake
   The Carpenter
   Goodness Gracious
   Love's Sunset
   Street Singers
14 The Crutch
   The Drudge
   Goodbye Summer
   The Idler
   The Little Captain
   The Portrait
14-15 'Sonny Jim' series *(21 one-reelers)*
15 A Case of Eugenics
   Easy Money
   Following the Scent
   The Hand of God
   How Cissy Made Good
   The Island of Regeneration
   Old Good-for-Nothin'
   The Patriot
   The Prince in Disguise
   The Professor's Romance
   The Third Party
   The Tigress
   To Cherish and Protect
   The Turn of the Road
   The Writing on the Wall
16 Britton of the Seventh
   Fathers of Men
   From Out of the Past
   Her Bad Quarter of an Hour
   The Law Decides
   The Man Behind the Curtain
   A Prince in a Pawnshop
   The Rookie
   Salvation Joan
   The Suspect
17 'Bobby' series *(15 one-reelers)*
   The Bottom of the Well
   The Discounters of Money
   Her Right to Live
   Intrigue
   Womanhood, the Glory of the Nation
18 Gas Logic
   Out of a Clear Sky
   The Seal of Silence *(serial)*
   A Youthful Affair
19 Reclaimed: the Struggle for a Soul
   Between Love and Hate
   The Unpardonable Sin
   What Love Forgives
20 A Child for Sale
   The Flapper
   Humoresque
   Other Men's Shoes
21 The Old Oaken Bucket
22 A Wide-Open Town
   Wildness of Youth

Nicolas Roudenko

FRANCE

b: 1 May 09 (Nice)
d: 23 Aug 76 (Paris)

No one knows why Abel Gance's 'little Napoleon' is billed on the great film as 'Wladimir Roudenko'. Wladimir was neither his name nor his father's, and he doesn't seem to have acted under it on any other occasion.

He was the son of Russians who emigrated to France soon after the turn of the century, and who both served with the French Army during World War One. His father left his mother, and Nicolas had a childhood of much unhappiness and privation. He found himself in acting, which involved so much truancy from school that he never sat an exam. He began film work around 1921 with Marcel l'Herbier.

'Masters and pupils', says a caption in *Napoléon*, 'felt the same antipathy for this proud, fierce child who lived in a kind of savage isolation.'

It does indeed take a little time to warm to Roudenko, who is wholly without winsomeness. His eyes are glassy, his nose beaky, his mouth narrow and snapping. His rare smiles are like icicles. It's not till you see him with his caged pet and *alter ego*, the mountain eagle – emblem and symbol of Napoleon throughout the film – that you realise the perfect match. This is the complete eaglet, armed with a man's will.

We first meet him out in the snow, marshalling his side in the educational snowball battle (one of Gance's most famous *tours de force*) organising sorties and taking

Little Napoleon (Nicolas Roudenko) and his eagle (Michel)

revenge on treacherous opponents who, like Cocteau's Dargelos, put stones in their snowballs. His two principal tormentors later get their own back by releasing his eagle into a blizzard.

Napoleon confronts and takes on his entire dormitory, and a wild pillow-fight prefigures *Zéro de conduite* in a storm of feathers, the screen splitting into four, then nine struggling images. Finally the little spitfire is overpowered by the staff, dragged away and flung out into the snow. There he crouches on a cannon, while his only human friend, the school cook, creeps out and puts a cloak round his shoulders and a hat on his head. As Napoleon sits staring wretchedly into the darkness, his eagle returns to him.

The passion this puny little Russian brought to his incarnation of France's national hero is so powerful, it knocks you sideways. It is the greatest child performance of the silent screen, and one of the most moving in all cinema.

In *André Cornélis* (based on a novel by Paul Bourget) he had a role of similar intensity – though more traditionally filmed – as a boy who, Hamlet-like, vows vengeance on his father's murderer, and grows up to find it is his stepfather he must kill. *Mateo Falcone*, shot in Corsica by William Delafontaine, was a pioneering colour venture of which little evidence survives.

With adolescence, Nicolas's brief, thrilling career fizzled out. The arrival of the talkies swept Gance's masterpiece into oblivion, and Nicolas refused even to talk about his acting in later years. He never married, and worked as technician with Thomson's. He died of cancer at the age of 67, and is buried in the Russian cemetery at Sainte-Geneviève des Bois. If he could have lived just a few years longer, till Kevin Brownlow's devoted reconstruction of *Napoléon* brought it to triumphant life again, he would have been hailed by cheering audiences wherever the film was screened.

25 Napoléon
27 André Cornélis
28 Mateo Falcone

GEORGES HENIN (b: 22 Nov 13), the sly boy who as Eugène de Beauharnais pleads for the return of his father's sword, and later eavesdrops on Napoleon's wooing of Josephine, had a small part the following year in Dreyer's *La passion de Jeanne d'Arc*. Having thus appeared in two of the world's greatest films, Georges wisely retired and became a commercial artist.

Gösta Alexandersson

SWEDEN

b: 16 Oct 09 (Stockholm)
d: 17 Mar 88

Gösta became famous as the country boy 'Anderssonskans Kalle', hero of a classic Swedish children's book.

22 Amatörfilmen (The amateur film)
   Anderssonskans Kalle
    (The Anderssons' Kalle)
23 Anderssonskans Kalle på nya upptag
   (New adventures of the
    Anderssons' Kalle)
   Friaren från landsvägen
    (Proposal on the highroad)
25 Skeppargatan 40 (40 Skipper Street)

Alexandersson as Kalle

True Boardman, Jr.

USA

b: 28 Oct 09 (Seattle)

Both his parents were well-known actors,

Son of Stingaree: True Boardman, Jr., in 1923

and his grandmother a playwright. His father (who died in 1918, aged only 36, basically of overwork) was famous as 'Stingaree', the chivalrous, monocled, violin-playing but steel-fisted hero of two film series during World War One. His mother, Virginia Eames (1889-1971), who after her husband's death acted as Virginia True Boardman, was a familiar mother-figure in late silent films and early talkies. (She did not, as stated in an otherwise admirable American catalogue, play the lead in *Michael O'Halloran!*)

True Junior, a handsome but slightly harassed-looking blond, made his debut at 15 months in a Selig film starring William Desmond. He had featured roles in 'Bronco Billy' and 'Hazards of Helen' films.

In spite of his 1923 success as the hero of Gene Stratton Porter's soppy story of a heroic newsboy, True Junior seems to have made no further screen appearances as a child, though he can be seen in early talkies like *Scareheads* (31), *The Sign of the Cross* (32) and *The Speed Reporter* (32). But later in the Thirties he began writing for radio, then for films and TV.

15 A Boy at the Throttle
   The Girl Who Dared
18 Shoulder Arms
   Uncle Tom's Cabin
19 Daddy Long Legs
   Deliverance
20 A Woman Who Understood
22 The Flirt
23 Michael O'Halloran

True Boardman's granddaughter Liza Gerritsen became a fine child actress.

Palle Brunius

SWEDEN

b: 5 Nov 09 (Stockholm)

Paul Gomer Brunius, blond son of the Swedish director John W. Brunius (1884-1937) played the hero-as-boy in his pastoral drama *Synnöve Solbakken*: a face of tragic, petulant beauty with a sullen mouth, a short nose and huge seething blue eyes.

Palle was in two more films as a child, then re-emerged as a teen-ager in his father's *Karl XII* (25) and after a further pause in *Havets melodi* (34).

19 Synnöve Solbakken
20 Ombytta roller (Changing roles)
   Trollsländar (Dragonflies)

Lauritz Falk

SWEDEN

b: 16 Nov 09 (Brussels)
d: 1966

Per Lindberg's *Norrtullsligan* is a refreshingly unusual silent movie about four young women who share an apartment, and their working lives in Stockholm offices: it combines warmth and wit with a healthy tang of early feminism. The only male who comes well out of it is the central girl's kid brother. (She works to keep him at boarding school.) Young Lauritz is a delight, with an amused, expressive face and a wicked upward slant to the eyebrows. He also sports a fascinating period coiffure.

Falk built himself a fine acting career and was in some 40 Swedish films between 1936 and 1972, including Christian-Jaque's *Singoalla* (SE/FR 49) and Mai Zetterling's *Nattlek* (66). He also directed, in 1944, two films of his own: *Lev farligt* and *Vändkorset*. Between 1953 and 1955 he made several appearances in the American TV series *Foreign Intrigue*.

23 Norrtullsligan (The Norrtull Gang)

Falk and the working girls (l. to r.: Renée Björling, Tora Teje and Inger Tidblad) in Norrtullsligan

Raymond Lee

USA

b: 1909
d: 26 Jun 74 (Canoga Park, Cal.)

Though he never had a star role, Raymond moved in distinguished circles. After being employed by D.W. Griffith and the Franklin brothers, he worked repeatedly with Chaplin and Jackie Coogan ◇.

16 Intolerance
17 Aladdin and His Wonderful Lamp
   Jack and the Beanstalk
18 Six Shooter Andy
19 Ali Baba and the Forty Thieves
   A Day's Pleasure
21 The Kid
   No Woman Knows
23 Long Live the King
   The Pilgrim
24 Abraham Lincoln
   Bread

Maury Steuart

USA

b: 1909

Maurice Steuart, Jr. had not only parents who were actors, but two younger sisters (Loel and Eldean) who followed him successfully into the business. His pretty, curly head sometimes led him, as was the custom of the day, into screen transvestism. After one such appearance a newspaper reported: 'Maury has no objection to missives of appreciation either of his work or his good looks, but he has the most deep-rooted antipathy to being called a "girl" and receiving "mash notes" from love-sick little boys.'

   His 1912 debut was under the direction of D.W. Griffith.

12 A Child's Remorse
14 Rip Van Winkle
15 Bondwomen
   A Child in Judgment
   Evidence
   The Moth and the Flame
   A Poor Relation
   Under the Gaslight
   Vanity Fair

16 The Awakening of Helena Ritchie
   Gloria's Romance (serial)
   Ruth's Remarkable Reception
   The Stolen Triumph
17 Bridges Burned
   Sleeping Fires
18 A Successful Adventure
   The Way to a Man's Heart
20 Dangerous Paradise
   The Flapper

Willi Allen

GERMANY

b: circa 1909

About the time 'Sunshine Sammy' Morrison ◇ came on the scene in America, the German cinema produced a popular little black boy of its own. Usually he was in marginal roles, as hotel buttons or the like, and often he was burdened with names like 'Piccanini' or 'Cioccolattino', but this cheerful kid kept smiling and dashing about. Once in a while, as in *Der kleine Muck*, he had a cast-iron, copper-bottomed star part, and grabbed it. He also acted in foreign films, notably as sidekick of the titan Maciste in Italy and Battling Siki in France.

   The great Gerhard Lamprecht, incidentally, in his 'Catalogue of the German Silent Cinema', identifies as Willi Allen a near-teenage black page-boy in the 1914 film *Paragraph 80, Absatz II*. Yet subsequent photographs of Willi make this impossible, and Lamprecht himself is still referring to him as 'child' in 1923.

20 Die Geheimnisse von New York
   (Mysteries of New York)
   Kakadu und Kiebitz
   Maciste contra la morte
   (Maciste versus Death – IT)
   Il viaggio di Maciste
   (Maciste's journey – IT)
   Il testamento di Maciste
   (Maciste's testament – IT)
   Nachtgestalten (Shapes of the night)
   Ratten der Grossstadt (Rats of the big city)
   Sein letzter Trick (His last trick)
21 Die drei Tanten (The three aunts)
   Der heilige Hass (Holy hatred)
   Der kleine Muck (Little Muck)
22 Der blinde Passagier (The blind passenger)

Man sollte es nicht für möglich halten
   (You wouldn't believe it possible)
   Die Schuhe einer schönen Frau
   (A lovely woman's shoes)
23 Der Kaufmann von Venedig
   (The Merchant of Venice)
   Knock-Out (FR)
   Nanon
24 Aus eigener Kraft (By your own strength)
25 Der König und die kleinen Mädchen
   (The king and the little girls)
27 Meine Tante – deine Tante
   (My aunt and yours)

Western Union always delivers: Johnny Fox, Jr., in The Midnight Message

Johnny Fox

USA

b: circa 1909

'An unattractive freckled youth with decidedly crude manners,' wrote an ungenerous reviewer in 1926. 'His performance makes up in energy, however, what it lacks in charm.' A later judge, while allowing that the red-haired Fox was no oil-painting, remarked on his 'alert features and look of candour'.

   John Fox, Jr., a less subtle successor to Wesley Barry ◇, had apparently been a timid little boy, who learned confidence from acting. He made a forceful impression in *One Glorious Day* as an aggressive spirit called Ek, who enters with entertaining results into the body of a mild Professor (Will Rogers); and was notable in 1923 as a banjo-strumming kid in *The Covered Wagon*. His best juvenile part, though, was as the Western Union messenger hero of *The Midnight Message*.

Johnny Fox continued in movies till the end of the silent period, with at least one more leading part in 1928 as the hero of (naturally) *Freckles*. Then he took to screen writing, on films like *The Trail of the Lonesome Pine* (36) and *The Little Shepherd of Kingdom Come* (61).

18 Why America Will Win
20 The City Sparrow
 A Cumberland Romance
 What's Your Hurry?
21 No Woman Knows
 Peck's Bad Boy
22 One Glorious Day
 The Radio Hound
 Too Much Wife
23 Blow Your Own Horn
 The Covered Wagon
 Crooked Alley
 The Extra Man
 Hollywood
24 Do It Now
 Jack o' Clubs
 The Passing of Wolf MacLean
 When a Man's a Man
25 Contraband
 Don't
 Friendly Enemies
 The Lady
 The Pony Express
 Speed Mad
 The Unwritten Law
26 The Bar-C Mystery
 Laddie
 The Midnight Message
 The Speeding Venus
 The Sporting Lover

Peter Eysoldt

GERMANY

b: 1 Apr 10 (Berlin)
d: 4 Nov 85 (Munich)

His father was the painter Benno Berneis, his mother the fine actress Gertrud

Peter Eysoldt, 1918

Eysoldt, who appeared with him in *Mutter, dein Kind ruft* and *Ich hatt' einen Kameraden*. Peter inherited Gertrud's strong, attractive face. The critic Herbert Ihering found him excellent on stage (for instance as Ptolemy in 'Caesar and Cleopatra') but rather stagey on screen.

Mutter, dein Kind ruft, incidentally, was the first screen version of the Stefan Zweig story later filmed as *Brennendes Geheimnis* or *Burning Secret*, with remarkable performances by Hans-Joachim Schaufuss ◊ (33) and David Eberts (88).

In 1933 Peter appeared at Erika Mann's 'Peppermill' cabaret in Munich, but soon afterwards left Germany for America, where he became – under his proper name of Peter Berneis – a distinguished screenwriter: *The Hunchback of Notre Dame* (39), *Portrait of Jennie* (48) and *The Glass Menagerie* (50) were among his scripts.

In 1953 Berneis returned to West Germany, and not only wrote further screenplays but directed three films. He lived by turns in Munich and Beverly Hills.

23 Mutter, dein Kind ruft
  (Mother, your child is calling)
24 Ich hatt' einen Kameraden
  (Once I had a comrade)
  Die Puppe vom Lunapark
  (The Luna Park doll)
  Die Schmuggler von Bernina
  (The smugglers of Bernina)

Lewis Shaw

BRITAIN

b: 6 May 10 (London)
d: 13 Jly 87 (London)

His father was a schoolmaster and lecturer, and Lewis had no dramatic training before he was chosen to appear in A.A.Milne's play 'Success' at the Haymarket Theatre, London, in June 1923. His father's career then took him to France for a couple of years, during which he was chosen for leading parts in films directed by Louis Mercanton and Georges Monca.

In Mercanton's *Les deux gosses* he not only acted opposite France's leading boy actor of the period, Jean Forest ◊, but with the director's tiny son Jean Mercanton ◊, who in his turn was to become a popular screen performer. (Lewis was professionally known in France as 'Leslie Shaw' because the French could not decide whether to pronounce him 'Louis' or 'Léviss'.) It was a considerable honour for an English boy to be chosen to portray Rémi, hero of Hector Malot's oft-filmed *Sans famille*, the saga of a foundling's travels with an itinerant entertainer and his performing dogs.

Having returned home, Lewis Shaw worked a good deal on the London stage, and in 1929-30 toured Australia and New Zealand in 'Young Woodley' and 'Journey's End'. He continued to act in British films, as a whimsical and charming juvenile lead of the Thirties.

After distinguished service in World War Two, however, he retired, joining the management of the casting directory, 'Spotlight'. In later life he and his wife Betty lived mainly on an Italian island, but he was just starting to resume his acting

Lewis Shaw (right) has designs on Marjorie Hume's handbag, to buy medicine for Jean Forest (left) in Les deux gosses

career – superb cameos on British TV – when his final illness was diagnosed.

24 Les deux gosses (The two boys – FR: *serial*)
25 Sans famille (No relations – FR: *serial*)
   Confessions (GB)

Winston Miller

USA

b: 22 Jne 10 (St Louis, Mo.)

When his boyhood career was over, Miller continued acting for a time, but in the mid-Thirties turned prolifically to screenwriting. Among his best work are the screenplays for *My Darling Clementine*, *Run For Cover* and *Tension at Table Rock*.

22 The Power of a Lie
23 The Light That Failed
   The Love Piker
   The Little Church Around the Corner
24 The Iron Horse
   Secrets
25 Kentucky Pride
   Man and Maid
   Stella Dallas

Joseph Depew

USA

b: 11 Jly 10 (Harrison, N.J.)
d: 30 Oct 88 (Escondido, Cal.)

Born of thespian parents, and sometimes spelt with a big P in the middle, Depew was busy on stage and screen from the age of five. He had his biggest chance as the eleven-year-old hero of *Timothy's Quest*, Kate Douglas Wiggin's popular sentimental story of 1892.

After one or two more appearances in his late teens, Joseph Depew disappears from sight, to re-emerge after World War Two as an assistant director in Hollywood. Later he became a successful TV director, on shows like *The Beverly Hillbillies*.

21 Clay Dollars
   Dream Street
22 The Broken Silence
   Timothy's Quest
23 The Daring Years
   Jacqueline, or Blazing Barriers
   The Steadfast Heart

24 The Fifth Horseman
   Grit
   Icebound
   The Law and the Lady
25 The Swan

Paul Jacobs

USA

b: 31 Jly 10 (Laclede, Idaho)

When he was seven months old, his parents moved to Los Angeles, settling determinedly next to a movie studio. From 1913 he played for Keystone (with Gordon Griffith ◇), Universal (the Sterling Kid Comedies, with Olive Johnson and tough-guy Violet Radcliffe) and, from 1915, with the Franklin child troupe. After a while he became better known (and usually billed) as Billy Jacobs, from his much-loved characterisation as 'Little Billy' in many comedies of 1914.

Paul was largely trained by the comedian Ford Sterling, who often starred with him for Keystone. He was small for his age, and at four passed for two, a fiction encouraged by his promoters.

A chubby child with golden curls and an 'irresistible smile', he was not without artistic pretensions, insisting on cameras turning even while he rehearsed at Keystone. But the public regarded him as 'the best little scream ever', and lapped up his jolly pranks:

Billy smiled his 'Billy grin'
When he spied the jelly tin....

He had reason to smile. By 1916 Paul/Billy had joined Lasky and was earning $10,000 a year. He had purchased his own car, and paid a chauffeur out of his salary to drive him to work in it. The chauffeur's memoirs would have made rich reading.

13 Across the Alley
   Billy Dodges Bills
   His Sister's Kids
   The Horse Thief
   Our Children
   The Rogues' Gallery
   Teddy Tetzlaff and Earl Cooper,
     Speed Kings

Kindly leave the stage: Paul Jacobs as Little Billy

Willie Minds the Dog
14 A Backyard Theater
The Battle
A Beach Romance
Billy's Charge
Billy's Riot
Bowery Boys
The Broken Doll
Carman's Romance
It's a Boy
Kid Auto Races at Venice
Kids
Little Billy's City Cousin
Little Billy's Strategy
Little Billy's Triumph
Lost in the Studio
A Race for Life
Those Country Kids
15 Her Filmland Hero
Lizzie's Watery Grave
Olive's Love Affair
Olive's Pet
16 Ambrose's Cup of Woe
The Clown
The Garden of Allah
The Heart of Nora Flynn
His Lying Heart
The House with the Golden Windows
Little Billy's School Days
The Valiants of Virginia

17 Cactus Nell
Lost, a C(r)ook
The Primrose Ring
Thirst
Those Without Sin
The Tides of Barnegat
Unconquered

18 A Hoosier Romance
Little Orphant Annie

Paul's young cousin JOEY JACOBS also filmed with Keystone.

Adolf Branald

CZECHOSLOVAKIA

b: 4 Oct 10 (Prague)

Adolf Karel, son of stage director Richard Branald, was the first notable boy actor of the Czech screen, with a face that could be droll or sensitive.

After devoting his young adult days largely to the theatre, plus a spell as a railway employee, Karel Branald – by now less keen on the name Adolf – emerged as one of Czechoslovakia's leading postwar novelists. Two of his first successes concerned railway workers' resistance to the Nazis. His first film scenario was a version of his book 'Dedeček automobil'.

18 Alois vyhral los (Alois wins the lottery)
Československy Jekišek (A Czech Jekyll)
22 Komptoiristka (The shop-girl)
Venoušek a Stazička
(Little Vaclav and little Anastasia)
25 Hraběnka z Podskali (The Countess of Podskal)

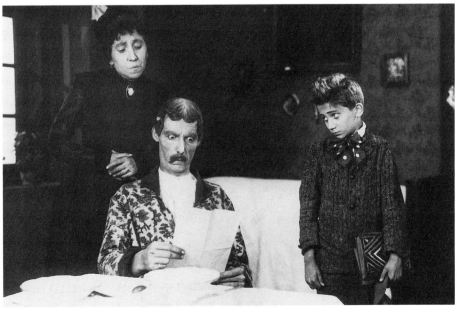

Bad news for little Vaclav: Adolf Branald (right) in Venoušek a Stazička

Life with a working mother: Russell Thaw and Evelyn Nesbit in The Woman Who Gave

Per Stensgård

DENMARK

b: 1910

This tiny creature made his screen debut at the age of three months, and scored a hit at 2½ as 'little Ole', a comic child chimneysweep, in *Den sorte familie*. He had a starring role in *Arvingen til Skjoldborg*, written and co-directed by his father, and wasn't big enough to protest at having to play a little girl in *Enken*.

Russell Thaw

USA

b: 25 Oct 10

Master Russell William Thaw was less an actor than a charity appeal. His mother was the once-celebrated beauty Evelyn Nesbit (1884-1967), a former chorus-girl and model. She had become a national figure in 1906, when her wealthy husband, Harry Thaw, shot her lover, the prestigious architect Stanford White, on the roof terrace of the Madison Square Garden, a grandiose New York building which White himself had designed.

Russell, a subsequent child by Thaw after his release from jail, appeared with Evelyn in a series of tear-jerking movies which exploited her notoriety while projecting her as a noble Magdalen martyred by the gutter press. Critics were sarcastic about the fading beauty 'trying with such talent as she possesses to pick up a good living for herself and child. Fate,' continued Moving Picture World, 'has buffeted Miss Nesbit about with sufficient uncharitableness to restrain any impulse to hand her another "wallop". She bears a fixed expression of determination to bear the abuse the scenarioist has heaped upon her, with a calm and fixed purpose to get the six reels over with.'

Evelyn's titles are magnificently self-indulgent. A born survivor, she was to live to a ripe old age, and to see herself portrayed by Joan Collins in *The Girl in the Red Velvet Swing* (1955), though not by Elizabeth McGovern in the 1981 *Ragtime*, based on E.L.Doctorow's novel in which she plays a leading role.

Interestingly enough, her Dance Instructor in *Ragtime* is played by Donald O'Connor ◇ – and Stanford White (briefly) by Norman Mailer.

Zheng Xiaoqiu

CHINA

b: 1910 (Shanghai)

Xiaoqiu, elder son of the pioneer Chinese film director and actor Zheng Zhengqiu, had star roles from the outset. He continued into his later teens and mid-twenties with leads in *Kong gu lan* (26), *Ti xiao yinyuan* (32), *Chun chan* (33) and *Zi mei hua* (34) among others.

In 1934 he also began to direct, with *Ruozhe, ni de mingzi shi nüren* (48) and *Li yuan ying lie* (49) among his biggest successes. After 1952 he turned to directing scientific and educational films – more than forty to date.

Jerry Devine

USA

b: circa 1910

It was tempting to identify Jerry with the much-loved character actor Andy Devine (1905-77) – born Jeremiah Schwartz – but the boy actor appears to be about five years too young.

Jerry Devine, whose father was an actor in the 1920s, appeared in some fifty films as a child, and was seen in a few talkies such as *The Mad Game* (33). In the late 1930s he began turning out radio scripts, first comedy and later crime. He did a nine-year stint as writer and director of 'This Is Your FBI'.

He wrote two Broadway shows, 'The Amorous Flea' and 'Never Live Over a Pretzel Factory' (1963), and his autobiographical play 'Children of the Wind' was premiered in Chicago in 1973.

20 Over the Hill to the Poorhouse
21 Clay Dollars
   Hush Money
   Remorseless Love
22 The Headless Horseman
   Sherlock Holmes
   A Wide-Open Town
23 The Custard Cup
   Potash and Perlmutter
   The Steadfast Heart
24 Damaged Hearts
   Tongues of Flame

Kai Heimann

DENMARK

b: circa 1910

Dark little Kai played pampered noble or hounded beggar-child, and even became convincingly Japanese for *Troen, der frelser*. His best and liveliest roles were in *En moderne landevejsridder* and *Solskinbørnene*.

He was offered terms by Hollywood, it's said, but Nordisk Film wouldn't let him go.

14 Guldhørnene (Golden horns)
16 Troen, der frelser (Troen the rescuer)

17 Maharajahens yndlingshustru
   (The Maharajah's favourite wife)
   En moderne landevejsridder
   (An up-to-date tramp)
   Solskinbørnene (The sunshine children)

Newton House

USA

b: 10 Jan 11 (Holly, Colorado)
d: 23 Jly 87

Another cowboy kid, presumably grandson of an earlier Newton House, 'actor and cattleman' (1865-1948). Billed as 'the champion kid rider of the world', he starred, with his fiery horse Marky, in a string of two-reelers for Universal in 1927-28.

Newton House continued acting till at least 1935, in *Devil Dogs of the Air*. His younger siblings Donald, Dorothy and Jimmy followed him into the acting profession, but with less success.

24 Not One to Spare
   The Ridin' Kid from Powder River
   The Spirit of the USA
25 Little Annie Rooney
   Shattered Lives
26 The Buckaroo Kid
27 Clearing the Trail
   The Red Warning
   Riding Gold
   The Ridin' Whirlwind
28 Buckskin Days
   The Danger Trail
   The Fighting Kid
   The Ride for Help
   Ropin' Romance
   A Son of the Frontier
   Untamed
   Winged Hoofs

A possible elder brother, CHANDLER HOUSE, born around 1903, had a lead in *The Father* (15), plus small parts the following year in Griffith's *Intolerance* and Walsh's *Pillars of Society*, and a further role in *The Little Orphan* (17). He went on to be a movie cameraman.

Martin Herzberg.

Martin Herzberg

GERMANY/DENMARK

b: 15 Jan 11 (Berlin)

The dark, androgynous glamour of Martin Fritz Herzberg enraptured all beholders, notably the Danish director A.W.Sandberg, who discovered Martin in Germany and took him to Denmark to play classic roles in *Anna Karenina, Great Expectations* and *David Copperfield*.

When he appeared in *The Blackguard*, even the British succumbed. A reviewer in Bioscope described the 14-year-old Martin as 'a youth of exceptional physical beauty, and an ideal subject for the duly appreciative cameraman'. The French were more measured in their praise. Ciné-Miroir reckoned him just about Jackie Coogan's ◊ equal in dramatic scenes, but nowhere near him in 'fantaisie et vivacité'.

Martin's biggest hit was as the young David Copperfield. The great Frederik Jensen, who played his father, regarded him as a natural actor, and spoke of his wonderful sad eyes in the scene of parting.

Herzberg was a crippled boy violinist in *Wienerbarnet*: no less than four of his films have to do with fiddling. (Esther Kjær Jensen, who played young Estelle to his young Pip in *Great Expectations*, also remembered him as a brilliant cardsharper – but only out of fun. His nature seems to have been as sweet as his looks.)

His career continued in classics like *Maria Stuart* (27) and teenage subjects like *Primanerliebe* (27), *Die Siebzehnjährigen* (28), *Die Halbwüchsigen* (29), and ended with a lead in *Väter und Söhne* (30).

In 1931 Herzberg went to live in the Canary Islands with the Danish camera-man Christen Jørgensen. Herzberg himself began earning money as a portrait photo-grapher, and did some work in Spanish films. Eventually, in 1959, he married a German fashion designer and had a son.

18 Jugendliebe (Youthful love)
19 Das Geheimnis von Schloss Holloway
    (The mystery of Holloway Castle)
    Die Sühne der Martha Rex
    (The atonement of Martha Rex)
20 Die Benefiz-Vorstellung der Vier Teufel
    (The Four Devils' benefit performance)
21 Lasse Mansson fra Skaane
    (Lasse Mansson from Skaane – DK)
22 Anna Karenina (DK)
    David Copperfield (DK)
    Der Halunkengeiger (The crooked fiddler)
    Den sidste dans (The last dance – DK)
    Store forventninger
    (Great Expectations – DK)
23 Alles für Geld (Anything for money)
    Komödianten des Lebens (Life's mummers)
    Die Magyarenfürstin
    (The Magyar princess)
    Paganini
24 Carlos und Elisabeth
    Kan kvinder fejler?
    (Can women do wrong? – DK)
    Wienerbarnet (The child of Vienna – DK)
25 The Blackguard (GB)
    Die Prinzessin und der Geiger
    (The princess and the fiddler)

Mickey Brantford

BRITAIN

b: 26 Mar 11 (Brixton, London)

Mickey's real name is said to have been Comerford, though the English Registry of Births and Deaths has no trace of a Michael Comerford (or Brantford) having been born in London around 1911. His parents were the actors Bert and Aggie

Mickey Brantford and Mary Odette in Not for Sale

Brantford, and his sister (also Aggie, b: 14 Jan 1915) followed him into movie work. Mickey was a brown-haired boy with an oval, slightly mask-like face. He was also, for what it's worth, a gifted middle-distance runner.

As a young adult, between 1927 and 1939, Mickey was in about thirty films. He played the sleuth's sidekick, Tinker, in the *Sexton Blake* series of 1928, had the lead in *Suspense* (30), and was in *Jew Süss* (34) and *The Phantom Light* (35), besides lighter offerings like *Mr Cohen Takes a Walk* (35).

17 The Man the Army Made
21 The Glorious Adventure

22 'Famous Poems by George Sims' series
    (The Lights o' London; The Road to
    Heaven; Sal Grogan's Face)
    The Game of Life
    The Sporting Instinct
23 Conscripts of Misfortune
    A Gamble with Hearts
    The Knockout
    The Rest Cure
    This Freedom
24 Claude Duval
    Holloway's Treasure
    The Mating of Marcus
    Not For Sale
25 Afraid of Love
26 Mare Nostrum (US)
    'Marriage License?' (US)
    Second to None
    Triumph of the Rat

Baby Peggy Montgomery takes a shine to Spec O'Donnell in The Darling of New York

Walter 'Spec' O'Donnell

USA

b: 9 Apr 11 (Fresno, Cal.)
d: 14 Oct 86 (Woodland Hills)

'Spec' O'Donnell, though red-haired and freckled – the son of non-theatrical parents – was by no means an All-American redhead of the bronco-busting, Buzz Barton ◇ type. To call 'Spec' homely would imply that your home was in grave need of repair. Beady little eyes peering out over a disastrous profile gave the impression of some shy, decrepit jungle creature flushed from its lair.

Usually he played the foolish, good-natured buddy or butt; occasionally, with some enjoyment (as in *Sparrows*), a real, downright brute. In *Little Annie Rooney*, though, he was very touching as Mary Pickford's loyal henchperson.

He became quite a celebrity in the mid-Twenties – at least locally, as 'Madera's one and only movie actor'. A special company was formed to make two-reelers starring him, and Douglas Fairbanks is said to have called him the greatest child star of the day.

He was presumably nicknamed 'Spec' because he was speckled (i.e. freckled), but unless he himself inspired the dubbing

of others, the name may have already been specific to O'Donnells, as Nobby to Clarks and Chalky to Whites. In a 1926 film, *The Speeding Venus*, Johnny Fox ◇ played a character called 'Speck O'Donnell', and there was another as late as *Heaven Only Knows* (47).

Spec continued in innumerable movies for the next forty years or so, often in short comedies with Andy Clyde, Leon Errol, Laurel and Hardy and – most memorably – the Jewish comic Max Davidson. He can be seen in *Strangers on a Train* (51), *Has Anybody Seen My Gal?* (52) and apparently as late as *Convoy* (78).

23 Children of Dust
    The Country Kid
    The Darling of New York
    Little Johnny Jones
    Main Street
24 The Foolish Virgin
25 The Devil's Cargo
    The Dressmaker from Paris
    Headlines
    Little Annie Rooney
    The Price of Success
    Tomorrow's Love
26 Hard Boiled
    Old Ironsides
    Private Izzy Murphy
    Sparrows

Ben Alexander

USA

b: 26 May 11 (Goldfield, Nev.)
d: 5 Jly 69 (Hollywood)

'The freckled expounder and interpreter of a child's soul, to whom nice little Jackie Coogan and all the other studious Baedekers of child psychology must bow the knee. . . . Incredible artistry.' Such was the verdict of Germany's *Filmwoche*, in 1924, on the playing of Nicholas Benton Alexander III, better known as Ben or Benny. (But, later, Nick to his friends.)

His first public appearance was on the cover of a rose catalogue, his second as Cupid in *Each Pearl a Tear*; and after two years in the movies he won the world's heart as 'the littlest brother' in Griffith's World War One epic *Hearts of the World*, jealously sticking his six-year-old tongue out at his brother's girl friend. Ben Alexander began as a cuddlesome, strikingly Aryan infant, sleepy and sensual in a Robert Mitchumish way, gradually becoming more aquiline as adolescence approached.

He was the screen's second 'Penrod', handsomer than Wesley Barry ◇ had been, more passionate than puckish.

Though never a star again – the real magic left him with the onset of puberty, and he became, in his own words, purely a commercial actor – the handsome Alexander continued to get good secondary roles during the Twenties and early Thirties. (He was, for instance, one of the young Germans in *All Quiet on the Western Front*, and Lew Ayres, its hero, became his closest real-life friend.) At first his roles were decent and idealistic, then turned caddish or worse in films like *Are These Our Children?* and *This Day and Age*: he complained that he was fast becoming 'the screen's youngest Dracula'.

In 1935, however, he began working as a presenter for several NBC radio

A difficult letter: Ben Alexander, circa 1923

Cupid joins the colours: Ben Alexander, 1918

programmes, culminating in the Sunday-night 'Signal Carnival' from 1936 to 1939. This left his weekdays free, and Ben went back to Stanford to complete his education, abandoning his original ambition of medicine in favour of Business Administration. Later he diversified from acting into commerce, and ended up owning a large Hollywood motel, two gas stations, a car dealership and some mortuaries.

After naval service in World War Two, Ben Alexander moved from radio to TV, and was only lured back to acting by his friend Jack Webb, whose tubby sidekick he became in the TV series 'Dragnet' (52-59). A few years later he himself became the star of another series, 'Felony Squad' (66-69). There was no time for more.

16 Big Tremaine
   Each Pearl a Tear
   Macbeth
17 The Little American
   A Romance of the Redwoods

What Money Can't Buy
18 The Heart of Rachel
   Hearts of the World
   The Lady of the Dugout
   Little Orphant Annie
   The One Woman
   The Turn in the Road
19 Battle of Youth
   The Better Wife
   The Hushed Hour
   Josselyn's Wife
   The Mayor of Filbert
   Tangled Threads
   The White Heather
20 The Family Honor
   Fighting Job
   The Luck of Geraldine Laird
   The Notorious Mrs Sands
   Through Eyes of Men
   The Triflers
   The Whiphand
21 The Heart Line
   The Sky Pilot
22 In the Name of the Law
23 Boy of Mine
   Jealous Husbands
   Penrod and Sam

24 Juvenile Comedies *(series)*
    A Self-Made Failure
25 Flaming Love
    Frivolous Sal
    Pampered Youth
    The Shining Adventure
26 The Highbinders
    Scotty of the Scouts *(serial)*

Francis Carpenter

USA

b: 9 Jly 11 (Glenwood Springs, Col.)

This wide-eyed, curly-haired blond –
whose real name was Francis Willburn
Keef – was a leading star of the Franklin
brothers' 'Kiddie Pictures' troupe of miniature mummers. When he climbed up a
beanstalk, emoting madly, the vegetable
scarcely shook. He perished piteously, as
Master Macduff, in the Beerbohm Tree
Macbeth of 1916.

  In 1920 he was signed up by Famous
Players-Lasky, but the best of his career
was over. All washed up at twelve!

15 The Baby
    The Commanding Officer
    Dirty Face Dan
    Hearts and Flowers
    Let Katy Do It
    Old Heidelberg

Make my day, Giant. Francis Carpenter in
Jack and the Beanstalk

16 The Children in the House
    The Defenders
    Going Straight
    Gretchen the Greenhorn
    Intolerance
    The Little School Ma'am
    Macbeth
    Martha's Vindication
    The Patriot
    A Sister of Six
17 Aladdin and the Wonderful Lamp
    Ali Baba and the Forty Thieves
    The Babes in the Woods
    The Brownies
    Jack and the Beanstalk
    The Mikado
    Pinafore
    Treasure Island
18 Fan Fan
    The Girl with the Champagne Eyes
    Les Misérables
    True Blue
19 The Forbidden Room
21 The Infamous Miss Revell
    Rip Van Winkle
23 The Lone Star Ranger

Ettore Casarotti

ITALY

b: 22 Oct 11 (Sao Paolo, Brazil)

His mother, Carmen Casarotti, was
a secondary character actress for the
Ambrosio company of Turin; she played
the hero's wife, for instance, in the *Frico*
series. She suggested Ettore for the role of
the small child in Eleonora Duse's *Cenere*.

  The beginning of the Twenties brought
crisis to Ambrosio, and at the start of
1922 they dismissed all their artists.
Therafter, young Ettore earned some
useful lire posing for postcards, and in his
late teens – a year or two after the death
of Valentino – he came second in an
all-European competition to find 'a new
Valentino'. (Another Italian, Alberto
Rabagliati, came first.)

  It led to nothing. After posing for a few
more postcards, the distinguished youth
became a commercial salesman. In later
years Casarotti would weep, remember-
ing his glorious childhood with Ambrosio.
Real life had proved a sad let-down.

Casarotti assumes priority in Marzy

16 Cenere (Ashes)
17 Fiacre N.13 (Cab No.13)
    Marzy nel vasto mondo
      (Marzy in the great wide world)
    L'orfana del ghetto
      (The orphan girl of the ghetto)
    Il pescatore del Rhone
      (The fisherman of the Rhone)
19 La cantoniera N.13 (Signal-girl 13)
    La gibigianna (The popinjay)
    Il medico delle pazze
      (The madwomen's doctor)
    Smorfie di Pulcinella (Pulcinella's grimaces)
20 La farfalla della morte
      (The butterfly of death)
    Lacrime del popolo (A people's tears)
    La ruota del falco (The falcon's wheel)
    Terra (Earth)
    Zavorra umana (Human dregs)

Georgie Stone

USA

b: 1911

The date of birth is dubious – he may
have been born earlier, and certainly *looks*
older than his Franklin Kiddy co-star
Francis Carpenter ◇.

  Georgie shouldn't be confused, at any
rate, with George E. Stone (1903-67), who
started playing reptilian crooks around
1927. He looks a solid, serious little boy,
and *Ali Baba* was his first appearance with
the Franklin tots.

  In 1920 he was chosen as W.S.Hart's
mini-cowboy sidekick in *Just Pals*, and the

51

Teacher's pet: George Stone with Dorothy Gish in The Little Schoolma'am

following year played the star's younger son when Hart had a rare non-Western role in *The Whistle* (seeking retribution for the death of his older boy in an industrial accident).

15 The Ash Can
   Dirty Face Dan
   The Doll House Mystery
   For Love of Mary Ellen
   The Game of Three
   The Kid Magicians
   Let Katy Do It
   The Little Cupids
   Little Dick's First Case
   The Little Life Guard
   The Rivals
   The Right to Live
   The Runaways
   The Straw Man
   A Ten Cent Adventure
16 The Children in the House
   Children of the Feud
   The Defenders
   Going Straight
   Gretchen the Greenhorn
   The Gun Fighter
   Jim Bludso
   The Little Schoolma'am
   Martha's Vindication
   The Patriot
   A Sister of Six
   Two Waifs
17 Ali Baba and the Forty Thieves
   Cheerful Givers
   In Slumberland
   Sudden Jim
   Wild Sumac
18 An Even Break
   The Gypsy Trail

   Six Shooter Andy
   Till I Come Back to You
19 The Jungle Trail
   The Poppy Girl's Husband
   The Speed Maniac
20 Fighting Cressy
   Just Pals
   Rio Grande
   The Scoffer
   Seeds of Vengeance
21 Desperate Trails
   Jackie
   Penny of Top Hill Trail
   The Sin of Martha Queed
   The Whistle
   White and Unmarried
23 The Fourth Musketeer

Joe Butterworth

USA

b: circa 1911

The dark and personable Joe was probably, but not certainly, a kid brother of Ernest and Frank. With a scowl as fine as Billy Gray's ◇ thirty years later, he had leads in *Heroes of the Street*, in Ben Alexander's ◇ *Penrod and Sam* (as Sam) and the title role in *The Good Bad Boy*. He was one of Mary Pickford's knickerbockered tormentors in *Little Annie Rooney*.

Joe continued for another year or two, in *Born to the West* (26), *The Earth Woman* (26), *Arizona Bound* (27), *Three's a Crowd* (27). Then he scowled and went away.

20 A Woman Who Understood
22 Heroes of the Street
23 Penrod and Sam
24 Black Lightning
   Geared to Go
   The Good Bad Boy
   Little Robinson Crusoe
   North of Nevada
25 Little Annie Rooney
   The Narrow Street

Joe Butterworth (left) with Ben Alexander and Gladys Brockwell in Penrod and Sam

Teddy Gordon Craig

BRITAIN

b: circa 1911

Not to be confused with the great Gordon Craig's son Edward Arthur, later the designer Edward Carrick. (Who, oddly enough, remembered posing with Ellen Terry in tests for the 1917 film *Her Greatest Performance*.)

There was also a London cinema owner called Gordon Craig around this time, and Teddy was probably his son.

18 Consequences
19 The Double Life of Mr Alfred Burton
20 A Bachelor Husband
 The Breed of the Treshams
 The Money Moon
 True Tilda
 Uncle Dick's Darling
21 Dick's Fairy
 The Door That Has No Key
 The Headmaster
 Roses in the Dust
23 Miriam Rozella

Jørgen Schønberg

DENMARK

b: circa 1911

Olaf Fønss, who starred opposite Jørgen in his big role of Little Teddy, declared that the child would soon have become a millionaire in Hollywood. In Denmark, however, Jørgen earned 10 kroner a day, plus a rocking-horse when the film was ·completed.

14 Ansigtet (The face)
 Lille Teddy (Little Teddy)
15 Det stjaalne ansigt (The steel face)
16 Lykken (Fortune)
 Bajaderens hævn (The bayadere's revenge)

Yura Zimin

USSR

b: circa 1911

After playing a homeless boy in *The Hot Gang*, Yura's last two roles were major.

Fedkina pravda is a touching story of friendship between boys of different backgrounds: but when their pranks lead to trouble, the little bourgeois Tolya (Marik Maya) always contrives to offload the blame on to proletarian Fedka (Zimin). In a boating accident, Fedka dies saving Tolya.

In *Kashtanka*, based on a Chekhov story, 'Little Chestnut' is a dog, lost and found again by Fedya (Zimin keeping almost the same name).

24 Tyoplaya kompaniya (The Hot Gang)
25 Fedkina pravda (Fedka's truth)
26 Kashtanka (Little Chestnut)

Frankie Lee

USA

b: 1 Jne 12 (Gunnison, Colorado)
d: 19 Apr 68

Frankie, the elder brother of Davey Lee ◇ (Jolson's Sonny Boy), had cloudily soulful blue eyes with a faint look of Leslie Caron. He was one of the favourite 'straight' boy actors of the American silent cinema. His father later wrote dialogue for the talkies.

16 Grouches and Smiles
 Her Greatest Story
 Her Husband's Faith
 Her Husband's Honor
 The Right to be Happy
 A Romance of Billy Goat Hill
 The Shriveled Soul
 Sins of Her Parent
 The Woman Who Dared
17 The Bronze Bride
 By Speshul Delivery
 Durand of the Bad Lands
 The Field of Honor
 God's Crucible
 Little Mariana's Triumph
 North of Fifty-Three
 One Touch of Sin
 The Soul of Satan
 Two Little Imps Doing Their Bit
18 Boss of the Lazy Y
 Cheating the Public
 Her Fling
 Quicksand
 The Sheriff's Son
 Vive la France
19 Bonds of Love
 Ching
 Daddy Long Legs
 The Law of Man
 The Miracle Man
 Rough Riding Romance
 The Westerners

Mending ways: Frankie Lee and Bessie Love in The Swamp

Frankie Lee in The Poverty of Riches

20 Bunty Pulls the Strings
Judy of Rogues' Harbor
Moon Madness
Nurse Marjorie
An Old Fashioned Boy
The Sin of Martha Queed
21 A Certain Rich Man
The Foolish Matrons
Godless Men
His Mother's People
The Killer
The Other Woman
The Poverty of Riches
The Primal Law
Shame
The Swamp
22 Borderland
Call from the Wild
Deserted at the Altar
Flaming Hearts
Heart's Haven
The Hero
The Scrapper
Shattered Idols
The Third Alarm
While Justice Waits
23 The Age of Desire
The Barefoot Boy

Children of Dust
The Flame of Life
Robin Hood, Jr.
The Unknown Purple
24 Poisoned Paradise
25 Code of the West
The Golden Strain

Elmo Billings

USA

b: 24 Jne 12 (California)
d: 6 Feb 64 (Los Angeles)

Elmo (possibly a screen name purloined from Elmo Lincoln, the screen's first Tarzan) was a freckled redhead who was in early 'Our Gang' comedies. His real name may have been Bennie or Richard Billings.

In *Two Wagons* – Will Rogers' parody of *The Covered Wagon* – Elmo took the Johnny Fox ◇ role, but armed with a saxophone instead of a banjo, and a chocolate bar instead of a quid of tobacco.

In the 1950s Elmo Billings became a film editor and laboratory technician for RKO and Paramount.

23 Two Wagons – Both Covered
24 Driftwood
Flames of Desire
Locked Doors

Triumph
The Woman on the Jury
25 The Golden Bed
His Secretary
The Midnight Flyer
The Monster
The Shining Adventure
What Fools Men
26 The Auction Block
Dance Madness
The Johnstown Flood
Take It From Me
There You Are!
27 It
Tumbling River
28 How to Handle Women

Jean Forest

FRANCE

b: 27 Sep 12 (Paris)
d: 27 Mar 80

The dark, sleek-haired Forest eventually had the looks of a matinee idol (though a sensitive and charming one), but there was nothing smooth about his first characterisation as 'The Mouse' in Jacques Feyder's *Crainquebille*, based on the Anatole France story of an old vegetable-seller befriended by a guttersnipe.

His next for Feyder, *Visages d'enfants*,

Elmo Billings (right) holds off Glenn Tryon in How to Handle Women

Almost too clean: Jean Forest yearns for the simple life in Gribiche

urchin who is adopted by a rich American lady (Rosay) but pines for his mother. By an even weirder coincidence, his real-life mother died at this point, and he really was adopted by Rosay – a fate which would have been envied by many Parisian orphans.

Gribiche, his last film for Feyder, shows Jean Forest in his finest colours: graceful, frisky, humorous and sad by turns. He had already shared the lead in the serial *Les deux gosses* for Louis Mercanton, and henceforth he worked for other directors, with three more leading roles before childhood ended.

After a pause for puberty, Forest returned in *Une femme a menti* (1930, the French version of *The Lady Lies*) and in the title role of *Etienne* (32). After two 1935 films, *Tovarich* and *La route impériale*, his last appearance was as the apostle John in Duvivier's *Golgotha* of 1936.

Two years later he began a career in radio, where he became a distinguished writer: two of his scripts, *Une larme du Diable* (51) and *La composition de calcul* (56) won Prix Italia awards. His son Jean-François later worked in TV.

22 Crainquebille
23 Visages d'enfants (Children's faces – CH)
24 Les deux gosses (The two boys – *serial)*
   Jocaste
25 Gribiche
   Jack
27 Les coeurs héroïques (Heroic hearts)

Peter Dear

BRITAIN

b: September 1912

Peter made his London stage debut in December 1925, and began a long career. In 1928 he lengthened his name to Dearing for professional purposes, and in 1936 began directing plays.

In the 1950s he went to the U.S. as Professor of Drama at Rollins University, Florida, and in October 1957 was appointed artistic director of the Grand Theatre in London, Ontario.

took him deeper. It was a bitterly truthful study of the resentment of a little Swiss boy, still mourning his mother, who is abruptly presented with an unsympathetic stepmother and stepsister. Eleven-year-old Jean was remarkable in it, a tiny figure simmering with grief and rage.

He had been spotted, a couple of years earlier, by Feyder and his wife Françoise Rosay in the Place du Tertre, where the Forests lived. Feyder persuaded the parents to give him guardianship of the boy, who was thus removed from his working-class surroundings and transplanted into an atmosphere of middle-class culture. The situation is weirdly echoed in the 1925 film *Gribiche* (directed by Feyder) in which Jean plays a Paris

Peter Dear

Coy Watson, Jr.

USA

b: 16 Nov 12 (Los Angeles)

He was christened James Caughey Watson, Jr. – but his casting-director father had already tired of having his middle name pronounced 'Coffee', and simplified it to 'Coy', with some approximation to the Irish original.

Young Coy was acting, as best he could, from the age of one, and was to be followed, after a few years' pause, by eight siblings: Gloria, Louise, Harry◇, Billy◇, Delmar◇, Garry, Bobs◇ and Vivian. (Seven of these can be seen together in the 1935 film *Life Begins at Forty*, with the older girls as teenagers and Bobs barely five. Photograph on p. 105.) They were all born in the same house in Berkeley Avenue, Edendale, two blocks from Mack Sennett's studio on Glendale Boulevard.

Coy Junior, the most conventionally good-looking of the boys, was sandy-haired, with a longish, freckled but quite dignified face which he could do funny things with. In *Fig Leaves* (26) he played a 'Stone Age newsboy', and in *Buttons* (27) – as 'Brutus, the Captain's tiger' – he is an ocean liner pageboy very conscious of his seniority to Jackie Coogan◇.

Coy continued acting into the early sound era – for instance *Blue Skies* (29), *Nix On Dames* (29), *Puttin' On the Ritz* (30), *Sidewalks of New York* (32). He was then persuaded by his uncle George, a well-known news photographer, to turn to the camera instead.

Coy achieved much distinction in this new role, and after World War Two his five younger brothers, by now also skilled photographers, joined him in the found- ing of a commercial studio, Six Watson Brothers Photography, Inc. He had already, in 1949, launched the first 'Hollywood TV Newsreel'.

More Watson coverage later.

Ernie Morrison

USA

b: 20 Dec 12 (New Orleans)
d: 24 Jly 89 (Lynwood, Cal.)

The happy, wiry Frederick Ernest Morrison, later known as 'Sunshine Sammy', began filming at the age of three in a somewhat roundabout fashion. His father, a brilliant cook, was lured from his

Brutus (Coy Watson, Jr., left) entertains doubts about Jackie Coogan in Buttons

Sunshine Sammy mocks the young lovers (Johnny Downs and Mary Kornman) in Our Gang's The Champeen *(1923)*

post with a wealthy New Orleans family by a yet better offer in Los Angeles. He fell in with film studio people (as Richard Lamparski relates), and on hearing that a little black boy was needed for a short featuring the Pathe moppet Baby Marie Osborne, took along the next-door neighbour's son. The latter proved hopeless, so next day Mr Morrison took along his own Ernie.

Morrison Junior leapt wholeheartedly into the spirit of the thing and smiled like an angel. From 1917-19 he partnered Marie Osborne dozens of times, and seems to have been the first American negro child to be credited by name — not that this saved him from being called, variously, 'little Sambo', 'Rastus', 'Snowball', 'the diminutive Nubian', 'the frolicsome pickaninny', etcetera. (There was not a lot of Black Power around in those days.) In France he was known simply as 'l'Afrique'.

During 1919-20 Ernie was featured in many short comedies with Snub Pollard. Hal Roach, who had taken to him greatly, starred him in *The Pickaninny* (21). It was to have been the first in a series of 'Sunshine Sammy' one-reelers, but white distributors didn't see it as spelling home run. However, Roach signed Ernie up as a founder-member of 'Our Gang', and he was in 28 'Gang' films, from 1922-24.

In a few of the early ones he was called 'Booker T. Bacon' or 'Sorghum', before they settled once and for all on 'Sunshine Sammy'. One of his memorably named roles was 'Washington Joffre Foch Pershing Johnson' in *The Old Maid's Baby*. He acted with Harold Lloyd in *Get Out and Get Under*, and with Wesley Barry ◊ in *Penrod*.

Apart from a 1929 appearance in *Steppin' Along*, the tap-dancing Ernie subsequently concentrated on stage work. Managed by his father (something of a business wizard,

who already owned a grocery chain and was a large candy wholesaler) he now began several years of vaudeville appearances, as 'the Sepia Star of Our Gang Comedies'. Later he formed a band called 'Sunshine Sammy and His Hollywood Syncopators', and in the mid-Forties danced (as a temporary member of the Step Brothers) in *Shine On, Harvest Moon* and *Greenwich Village*. He was the jive-talker 'Scruno' in the *East Side Kids* series.

Ernie Morrison quit show business around 1950 and went to work as a quality control inspector in the aerospace industry in Los Angeles, quietly proud at having once been the first black million-aire movie-actor. He made guest appearances in TV comedy series like 'Good Times' and 'The Jeffersons'.

Grab the Ghost
Insulting the Sultan
Live and Learn
A London Bobby
Money to Burn
Park Your Car
Penrod (*released 1922*)
Red Hot Hottentots
Rock-a-Bye Baby
Shoot on Sight
Speed to Spare
Trotting Through Turkey
Waltz Me Around
You're Pinched
21 Late Lodgers
The Pickaninny
22 Haunted Spooks
Number, Please
'Our Gang' (*6 shorts*)
23 'Our Gang' (*15 shorts*)
24 'Our Gang' (*7 shorts*)

Brown in The Lady Lies

Tom Brown

USA

b: 13 Jan 13 (New York)
d: 3 Jne 90 (Los Angeles)

The parents of this square-jawed, blue-eyed child, Harry Brown and Marie Francis, were both theatre actors, and Thomas Edward Brown first faced the footlights as a babe in his mother's arms. At two he became a national face advertising Arrow Collars, and later was 'The Buick Boy'.

In 1924, after training at the Professional Children's School, he landed his first film role as the pathetic urchin Shocky in *The Hoosier Schoolmaster*. The following year Tom appeared on the New York stage in the Gleason comedy 'Is Zat So?', and in 'Neighbors' (26). He was already quite a veteran of radio.

In 1929, aged 16, he had a good role in *The Lady Lies*, and his tough but innocent looks soon made him a popular teenage star in films like *Fast Companions* (role-model to Mickey Rooney ◇), *Hell's Highway* and *Tom Brown of Culver* (all 1932, and the title of the last one merely a happy coincidence). He went on to be Tyrone Power's brother in *In Old Chicago* (38) and Wallace Beery's son in *Sergeant Madden* (39). Brown remained in such parts till World War Two and even after it, latterly essaying a less angelic image in *The Pay-Off* (42), *The House on 92nd Street* (45) and *Ringside* (49).

He was recalled to the U.S. Army for service in Korea, rising to lieutenant-colonel, and when that was over resumed his acting career, though now mainly on TV. He had leading roles in the 'Gunsmoke' and 'General Hospital' series.

24 The Hoosier Schoolmaster
25 The Wrongdoers
26 Sons of the Legion
That Old Gang of Mine

Billy 'Red' Jones

USA

b: 9 Feb 13

William Charles Jones was a fine example of the heroic pug. The flaming hair which provided his cognomen streamed wildly back from a square, freckled face dominated by defiant blue eyes. 'For freckles, he can't be beat', boasted his entry in the casting directories without much fear of disagreement. 'Original and clever — no waste of time or film,' it added pragmatically.

When he was ten or so, Red Jones made background appearances with 'Our Gang'.

Billy [Red] Jones

He deserved better, and on completing *The Circus*, Chaplin praised him wryly as the only actor who had ever 'broken' him in a scene. Among the orphans of Mary Pickford's *Sparrows*, Red was the crippled boy.

23 Slow as Lightning
25 The Ancient Mariner
The Bandit's Baby
Dark Angel
The Lure of the Wild
Range Buzzards
The Road to Yesterday
Thunder Mountain
26 The Sap
Sparrows
27 The Final Extra
A Harp in Hock
The Missing Link
Sky High Saunders
Three Miles Up
28 The Circus
The Hound of Silver Creek
The Phantom Flyer

Bobby Gordon

USA

b: 21 Aug 13 (Pittsburgh)

Cheeky Bobby Gordon, who could also be strikingly effective in soulful parts, should not be confused with the much older Robert Gordon (1895-1971, real name Robert Gordon Duncan) who

Jewish flyweight: Bobby Gordon in His People *with his parents, Rosa Rosanova and Rudolph Schildkraut*

played Huck in the 1917 *Tom Sawyer*.

Nine-year-old Bobby was spotted at a prizefight by the director William Beaudine, looking for a Jewish boy to play the hated Maurice Levy in *Penrod and Sam*. (Racial caricatures are a depressing feature of Booth Tarkington's otherwise likeable 'Penrod' books, and have undoubtedly assisted them into oblivion. One would rather not recall the names of the little black brothers: Herman and Verman.)

Bobby had many more Jewish parts to play – in *The Cohens and Kellys* and *The Jazz Singer*, for instance – but seldom such demeaning ones. His biggest parts were in *Lazy Lightning* (with the cowboy star Art Acord) and in *A Race For Life* (with Rin Tin Tin).

Bobby Gordon stayed in the business until World War Two.

23 The Country Kid
   Penrod and Sam
24 The Good Bad Boy
   The Sign of the Cactus

25 The Happy Warrior
   His People
26 The Cohens and Kellys
   Lazy Lightning
27 The Fortune Hunter
   The Jazz Singer
   Mountains of Manhattan
   Sinews of Steel
   What Every Girl Should Know
28 A Race for Life

Martijntje de Vries

HOLLAND

b: 18 Sep 13 (Amsterdam)
d: 30 Apr 43 (Sobibor, Poland)

Martijn Henri de Vries was the grandson of one of Holland's best-loved actresses, Esther de Boer-van Rijk. He and his elder sister Hesje (born 22 Jly 09) were both in *Koningin Elisabeth's Dochter* – both playing the royal daughter of the title at different stages of early childhood.

Five years later Martijntje had a far more significant part in *De leugen van Pierrot* (not released till 1922), and it looked as if the director Maurits Binger was going to develop him as a boy star to play opposite his budding little girl star Renée Spiljar (born 29 Jan 13). But about this time Binger joined forces at his Hollandia studios with the English director Bernard Doxat-Pratt: Doxat-Pratt had a photogenic little son called Norman ◊, two years younger than Martijntje . . . and so it went. Norman became 'the new Jackie Coogan'.

Martijntje seems never to have acted again. Tragically, he was to perish in Sobibor concentration camp, aged 29.

15 Koningin Elisabeth's dochter (Queen Elisabeth's daughter)
20 De leugen van Pierrot (Pierrot's lie)

Maurice Murphy

USA

b: 3 Oct 13 (Seattle)
d: 23 Nov 78 (Los Angeles)

Maurice was the younger brother of Jack Murphy, who was born in 1912 and also acted as a boy. (Jack played John in *Peter Pan*, and was in *Stella Dallas* among other films.) Both Murphys had solid, plumpish Irish good looks.

Martijntje de Vries

Maurice Murphy in The Flesh and the Devil

Maurice continued to act as a young man. After filming in *The College Coquette*, *The Spirit of Youth* and *The Three Outcasts* in 1929, he was one of the young German recruits in *All Quiet on the Western Front* (30), then appeared in *Seas Beneath* (31) and with Jackie Cooper ◇ in *When a Feller Needs a Friend* (32).

His later films included *Pilgrimage* (33), *The Crusades* (35), the serial *Tailspin Tommy* (36), *Tovarich* (37), *The Reluctant Dragon* (41) and *Destination Tokyo* (44).

23 The Self-Made Wife
24 The Last Man on Earth
   Peter Pan
25 The Home Maker
   Stella Dallas
   Thank You
26 Beau Geste
   Flesh and the Devil
27 The American
   The Call of the Heart
   The Stolen Bride
   The Shepherd of the Hills
28 Alias the Deacon
   The Michigan Kid

Johnny Downs

USA

b: 10 Oct 13 (Brooklyn, N.Y.C.)
d: 6 June 94 (Coronado, California)

At ten, John Morey Downs was already looking like a college boy, and didn't change too much during the next forty years. His 1923 'Our Gang' debut (in *The Champeen*, see p.57) was a bit-part only, and it was two more years before he was recalled to Gang service as a regular, playing one of the maturer kids – sometimes a bully, though his nature was too nice for this to be wholly convincing.

Approaching 14, Johnny left the Gang and appeared in 'proper films', not all of them light-hearted. His agonised ascent of a steep and seemingly endless staircase in Vidor's *The Crowd*, on hearing of his father's heart attack, is one of the classic images of the silent cinema.

Soon Downs was old enough to play real college-boy parts, and as he had a pleasant singing voice he was in a whole string of musicals in the mid-Thirties. When college boys went out of fashion in Hollywood things got leaner, so he turned to vaudeville and then TV.

Apart from a few unmemorable film roles in the Fifties (for instance *The Caddy* and other Martin and Lewis frolics) his cinema career was over. He now settled contentedly to his new role as TV host, and between 1954 and 1971 fronted a kids' show called 'The Magic Key'.

Johnny Downs, circa 1926

23 'Our Gang' (*1 short*)
25 'Our Gang' (*9 shorts*)
26 'Our Gang' (*10 shorts*)
27 'Our Gang' (*3 shorts*)
   The Crowd
   Jesse James
   Outlaws of Red River
   Valley of the Giants
29 The Trail of '98

Leon Holmes

USA

b: 26 Nov 13 (San Francisco)

His real name was Leon Sederholm. He was a strange, moon-faced boy with dark flopping hair and slithering eyes who could play Jewish comic roles, full-blooded sentiment (like his young violinist in *Frisco Sally Levy*) or unnerving grotesques (like his lunatic boy in *The King of Kings*). He seems to have begun filming around 1922.

Holmes continued to appear in movies – *Sidewalks of New York* (32), *Guilty Parents* (34), *Union Pacific* (39) – at least until World War Two.

25 Getting 'Em Right
   The Happy Warrior
   Hogan's Alley
   A Man of Nerve
   A Woman Named Lou
26 April Fool
   The Block Signal
   The Flying Horseman
   Hungry Arms
   Meet the Prince
   Out of the Storm
   Poker Faces
   Redheads Preferred
   Sunshine of Paradise Alley
   That Model from Paris
   Vindicated
27 The Final Chapter
   Frisco Sally Levy
   The Jazz Singer
   The King of Kings
   Out All Night
   The Shamrock and the Rose
28 'Fox Rascals' series
   Freckles
   The Latest from Paris
29 The Dummy
   Woman from Hell

Pontius Pilate (Victor Varconi, left) takes a firm line with the Possessed Boy (Leon Holmes)
in The King of Kings

Ferko Szecsi

HUNGARY

b: 1913
d: circa 1968

The round-faced Ferko was a spirited child, sometimes teamed with the younger and more angelic Gida Lázár ◇. He could be all sunny charm, as Little Lord Fauntleroy; he could also be slimy, as the traitor Gereb in *The Boys of Paul Street*. (The hero, Nemecsek, was played by Gyuri Faragó.)

After World War Two, Szecsi became a producer for Hungarian Radio. He made at least one more film appearance, in *Zöldar* (65).

17 A gyanu (Suspicion)
   Három hét (Three weeks)
   A kétlelkü asszony
      (The woman with two souls)
   A koldusgróf (The beggar Count)
   Egy krajczár története
      (The story of a kreutzer)
   A nagyur (The big gentleman)
   A tüz (The fire)

20 Gyermeksziv (Heart of a child)
   Lengyelvér (Polish blood)
   Névtelen vár (Castle without a name)
21 Christoph Columbus (GE)
   Elnémult harangok (The bells fall silent)

A megfagyott gyermek (The frozen child)
22 A kis lord (Little Lord Fauntleroy)
   Meseország (Fairyland)
23 A három árva (The three orphans)
   Leánybecsület (A maiden's honour)
24 Az örszem (The sentry)
   A Pál utcai fiuk (The Paul Street boys)
25 Soll man heiraten?
      (Should one marry? – GE)

Newton Hall

USA

b: circa 1913

The fair-haired Newton Hall tended to play rather gentlemanly (not to say prissy) little boys. Inevitably, he was Georgie Bassett in the 'Penrod' films.

20 Burning Daylight
   Dinty
   The Forbidden Thing
   Penrod
22 At the Sign of the Jack o' Lantern
23 Children of Dust
   Penrod and Sam
24 Abraham Lincoln
   A Girl of the Limberlost
25 The Business of Love
   Stella Dallas
26 My Old Dutch

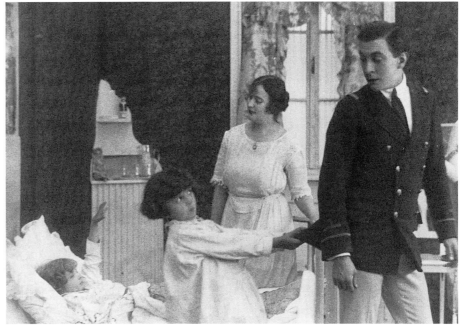

Ferko Szecsi (one from left) arrests an officer in Gyermeksiv. *Reclining, extreme left, Gida Lázár*

With piebald friend, André Heuzé as the 1925 Poil de Carotte

André Heuzé

FRANCE

b: circa 1913

The screen's first 'Poil de Carotte' may have been André Heuzé *junior* – son of the film-writer, director and journalist André Heuzé (1880-1942), friend and collaborator of Louis Feuillade among others.

Jules Renard's 1894 novel, with its portrait of a rustic child misunderstood by his father and persecuted to the point of suicide by an appalling stepmother and a slob of an elder brother, provided France's boy actors with a classic role in theatre and cinema adaptations. It has been filmed four times for the cinema, and Duvivier's 1925 version was the first of them. (His 1932 sound remake, with Robert Lynen ◇ as Carrots, is the best-known, and it was shot again in 1951 with the overripe Christian Simon ◇ and in 1973 with the overweight François Cohn.)

Heuzé is more spirited and skittish than his successors, but all the more piteous in his final despair. The film itself, with memorable adult performances and a sharp, fresh feel of the open air, deserves to be seen as often as Duvivier's other fine rendering.

25 Poil de Carotte (Carrots)
26 Le diable au coeur (Devil in the heart)
27 La grande épreuve (The big test)
28 Graine au vent (Seed in the wind)
29 Les sables mouvants (Shifting sands)

Gustl Stark-Gstettenbaur

GERMANY

b: 1 Mar 14 (Straubing, Bavaria)

August Ludwig Gstettenbaur, a cabinet-maker's son, was a jolly, lusty boy with a flair for acrobatics and a gift for imitating animals as well as humans. By the time he was ten he had won local fame as a gymnast, and when he was 13 his trainer, Joe Stark, became his manager and took him to Berlin. Gustl's father died in 1928, and Stark adopted the boy, who added his name to the front of his own for professional purposes.

In Berlin he appeared as an acrobat and entertainer in cabaret, and was spotted by the famous actor Eugen Klöpfer, who cast him as Falstaff's Page in 'Henry IV' at the Lessing-Theater. Carl Zuckmeyer wrote a children's play, 'Kakadu-Kakada', specially for him, and in 1930, after many Berlin shows, he created the role of the Page-Boy in Erik Charell's 'Im Weissen Rössl' (White Horse Inn), which he played for 17 months. During its run he had a Hollywood offer, but Charell wouldn't release him.

Gustl had a real actor's face, precociously sly and subtle. His first film appearance was in Fritz Lang's *Spione*, where he had little to do but demonstrate his gymnastic powers with a startling back-flip. Leading parts were to follow in *Der Piccolo vom Goldenen Löwen, Der Kampf der Tertia, Die Räuberbande, Wolga-Wolga* (devoted servant to the rebel Stenka Razin) and – for Lang again – *Frau im Mond*. This was the last of his 18 silent film appearances, and a memorable one as a stowaway on a moon rocket.

Gustl Gstettenbaur – he eventually dropped the 'Stark' – remained a popular juvenile lead throughout the Thirties and beyond, usually playing the role of a healthy, humorous country lad. His 1931 films included *Elisabeth von Österreich, Im Banne der Berge, Die Königin einer Nacht,*

Gustl in Wolga-Wolga

Kyritz-Pyritz, Schuberts Frühlingstraum and *Der Storch streikt*; the following year came *Das Geheimnis um Johann Orth, Mädchen zum Heiraten* and *Strich durch die Rechnung*. And there were to be nearly 100 more. Among the later ones were *Der laufende Berg* (41), *Die heimliche Bräute* (44) and the Franco-Italian co-production *La vache et le prisonnier* (60).

After the war Gustl and his wife (the revue artist Gracie Schenk, with whom he often toured in their own show) left the ruins of their house behind in Berlin, and moved back to his old home town, Hindelang in Bavaria.

There, in the Allgäu, the pair of them ran the wine-restaurant Bei Gustl.

27 Luther
    Spione (Spies)
28 Der Kampf der Tertia
        (The battle of the Third Form)
    Der Piccolo vom Goldenen Löwen
        (The page-boy at the Golden Lion)
    Die Räuberbande (The robber band)
    Wolga-Wolga (Volga, Volga)
29 Frau im Mond (Woman in the moon)
    Die Herrin und ihr Knecht
        (The lady and her squire)
    Karl Valentin, der Sonderling
        (The strange Karl Valentin)
30 Delikatessen
    Dolly macht Karriere (Dolly the career girl)
    Kohlhiesels Töchter
        (Kohlhiesel's daughters)
    Die Marquise von Pompadour
    Wien, du Stadt der Lieder
        (Vienna, city of song)
    Die zärtlichen Verwandten
        (The tender kinsfolk)

Roby Guichard

FRANCE

b: 9 Apr 14 (Lyon)

Until his locks were shorn in 1925 – to play an English boy in *La flamme* – blue-eyed Robert was able to portray handsome girls, as he did when playing the heroine as a child in *Le comte Kostia*. (It was no fun, he said, being brutalised by Conrad Veidt; he carried the bruises for three weeks.)

Roby Guichard, 1925

Roby made his screen debut in *Mon p'tit*, and in *Les vacances* co-starred with two of France's best little girls, Olinda Mano and Bouboule. He spoke appreciatively of them both, and of Yvette Langlais, his junior partner in *L'abbé Constantin*. Clearly he was something of a ladies' man. More portentously, he was also the immature prophet Elijah in *La terre promise*.

Reviewing Roby's *Titi* in 1926, the critic of Cinéa praised his 'magnificent ease, authority, wit and sensitivity' – not bad for a 13-year-old.

22 La bouquetière des innocents
        (The flower-girl of the innocent)
    Mon p'tit (My kid)
    Le Noël du père Lathuille
        (Father Lathuille's Christmas)
    Les mystères de Paris (Secrets of Paris)
23 Le cousin Pons (Cousin Pons)
    Mon oncle Benjamin (My Uncle Benjamin)
    Violettes impériales (Imperial violets)
24 Le comte Kostia (Count Kostya)
    Les vacances (The holidays)
25 L'abbé Constantin (Father Constantine)
    La flamme (The flame)
    Sans famille (No relations)
    La terre promise (The promised land)
26 L'île enchantée (The magic island)
    Titi premier, roi des gosses
        (Titi I, King of the Kids)
27 Ames d'enfants (Children's souls)
28 L'équipage (The crew)
    Le film du Poilu (The Poilu's film)

Hans Peter Peterhans

GERMANY

b: 19 May 1914

This quasi-palindromic child star was graceful and distinguished-looking, and probably son of the actor Josef Peterhans, who was with him in at least two of these films. (There was also a Carl Peterhans.)

He was 'the little Duke' in person, and also the controversial son of the manor (his mother was a servant-girl) in *Grieshuus*, a historical melodrama based on a story by Theodor Storm and boasting some of the most impressive sets of its time.

An actor called Hans Peterhans appeared in the 1932 film *Theodor Körner*. A briefer palindrome, but it may have been Hans Peter.

23 Wilhelm Tell
24 Deutsche Helden in schwerer Zeit
        (German heroes in hard times)
    Der kleine Herzog (The little Duke)
25 Der Wilderer (The poacher)
    Zur Chronik von Grieshuus
        (The Grey House chronicles)

The little master (Hans Peter Peterhans) supported by his grandfather (Rudolf Rittner) in Zur Chronik von Grieshuus

Bourgeois romance: Pražský in Dvě matky

Béda Pražský

CZECHOSLOVAKIA

b: 15 Jne 14
d: 6 Aug 75

Czechoslovakia's first male screen moppet (Adolf Branald ◇ was definitely an *actor*) was not, it seems, the son of director Přemysl Pražský. In the 1930 film he was billed as 'Béda Pražský-Bardon'.

19 Láska je utrpením (Love is suffering)
20 Dvě matky (Two mothers)
   Sněženky (Snowdrops)
22 O velkou cenu (For the Grand Prix)
23 Pepánek Nezdara (No-hope Joey)
29 Pražské švadlenky (Dressmakers of Prague)
30 Vendelínův očistec a ráj
      (Vendelin's purgatory and paradise)

Mickey Daniels

USA

b: 25 Aug 14 (Rock Springs, Wyoming)

The original freckled boy of 'Our Gang', tough, boot-faced Mickey Daniels, was actually christened Richard – and indeed was billed as 'Richard Daniels, Jr.' until the end of 1923. (His father, Richard Daniels, Sr., was an actor who also appeared in some early Gang comedies.) The boy's face really was his fortune: he had only to grin goofily or glower through his thicket of freckles to become irresistible.

Mickey had started his film career in 1918 with Universal. Hal Roach initially signed him up with 'Our Gang' at a salary of $37.50 per week, but two years later this had risen to $175. He outgrew the Gang in 1926, but returned for a few guest appearances in the 1930s.

During 1930-32 he played one of the leads in Roach's high school comedy series *The Boy Friends*, and he continued to appear in films up to 1941. After the war he left the business and became a construction engineer.

22 Doctor Jack
   Her Night of Nights

Mickey Daniels hits out in Giants vs. Yanks
(Our Gang, 1923)

   The Little Minister
   My Wild Irish Rose
   'Our Gang' *(4 shorts)*
23 Safety Last!
   'Our Gang' *(15)*
24 Girl Shy
   The White Sheep
   'Our Gang' *(12)*
25 'Our Gang' *(12)*
26 'Our Gang' *(6)*
28 On to Reno

Pat Moore with Mrs Wallace Reid in Broken Laws

Pat Moore

USA

b: 20 Oct 14 (Weston-super-Mare, GB)

Pat (real name said to be Terrence) was a son of the Irish actress Norah Moore, a leading lady at the Gaiety Theatre. His younger brother Micky ◇ acted too, and so to a lesser extent did their elder brother Brian.

In his early twenties Pat Moore was in *The Crusades* (35), playing the Earl of Leicester's squire.

16 Heart of a Fool
18 The Seal of Silence *(serial)*
   The Squaw Man
   Woman's Weapons
19 Fires of Fate
   Forbidden Fire
   His Divorced Wife
   Luck in Pawn
   Out of the Dust
   Prairie Gold
   A Prisoner for Life
   A Rogue's Romance
   Sahara
   The Sleeping Lion
20 Madame X

Jackie Coogan

USA

b: 26 Oct 14 (Los Angeles)
d: 1 Mar 84 (Santa Monica, Cal.)

Certainly the greatest child superstar of the silent period, and only equalled by Shirley Temple after the coming of sound, Jackie was born if not in a trunk, at least with the roar of greasepaint loud about him. At a perilously early age he was crawling on to the vaudeville stage in his parents' comedy act, and soon became an established and adored part of it.

When he was four, the fateful encounter with Charlie Chaplin took place. Chaplin saw him in a revue at the Orpheum Theatre in Los Angeles, and went round to meet him. Among Jackie's first words to the great man (by Chaplin's account) were: 'I am a prestidigitator who works in a world of legerdemain' – whereupon Chaplin, duly dumbfounded, exclaimed to Coogan *père*: 'This is the most remarkable person I have ever met.' The story sounds too good to be true, but whatever really was said, Chaplin put Jackie straight into his next comedy, *A Day's Pleasure*, and a year later gave him the co-starring title role in his first full-length film, *The Kid*. (It was actually shot in 1920.)

Coogan's cloth-capped, baggy-panted version of the Chaplin tramp persona, plus his beauty and his astonishing gift for comedy and pathos, left the world groggy

Jackie Coogan in Daddy

with admiration. *The Kid* was a brilliant film and none of the subsequent Coogan vehicles had anything like its quality, nor anyone of Chaplin's calibre for him to act with. But he was, undeniably, a marvel of grace and sauciness, with his pageboy bob and taunting brown eyes that would have made him an ideal screen kid brother for Louise Brooks, had anyone had the wit to bring them together.

Jackie Coogan as Tom Sawyer, Mitzi Green as Becky

His *Kid* success led to extensive merchandising: by September 1921 'Bioscope' was describing the 'Evripoze' Coogan doll that every child would want to play with and take to bed. The age of the T-shirt had not yet arrived, but there were Coogan caps, games and match-holders. Almost overnight, Jackie was one of the most famous people in the United States – and beyond.

His follow-up vehicle was based on the popular 'Bad Boy' stories of G.W.Peck. Again he wore a cloth cap (though a less decrepit one) and again wowed the nation. In 1921 he got down to the smiles and tears as an immigrant orphan in *My Boy* with Claude Gillingwater, then in *Trouble* was teamed with Wallace Beery (as Jackie Cooper ◇ was later to be), and finally played a very under-sized *Oliver Twist*.

Three more successful vehicles came the following year: Jackie was being wisely promoted, and not worked into the ground. In 1924 he had two movie commitments, in one of which Ouida's *A Dog of Flanders* found itself retitled *A Boy of Flanders* – no nonsense about who was the star here. But he also toured America and Europe to raise money by selling 'Mercy Bonds' for an orphans' fund. He was received in Geneva by the League of Nations, and in Rome by Pope Pius XI, who awarded him the Gold Cross of the Order of Jerusalem. It's a pre-echo of the charitable efforts of sportsmen and pop-stars of our day, but some people then found the razzmatazz faintly disgusting in however good a cause.

In 1925 he again made only two films, partnered in both by Max Davidson as a Jewish ragpicker. He was said to be planning a return to the stage, and studying the role of Hamlet, no less, with the playwright David Belasco. (Sad that the show never hit the road, or should one say the fan.)

When he turned 12, Jackie's official 'little boyhood' ended with a ceremonial shearing of the locks which had adorned him as guttersnipe and prince, and the landmark was commemorated in *Johnny Get Your Hair Cut*. The new sporty image was launched with his performance as a jockey, and clean-cut Coogan then starred as a page-boy on an ocean liner and as a brave little Civil War bugler. They were respectfully received, but some of the magic seemed, Samson-like, to have departed with the hair.

Whether through boredom, weariness or diminishing returns, the decision was made to give the boy a break from filming.

During a 3-year withdrawal from the studios, Jackie visited Britain with his father, and they appeared at the London Palladium in November 1928 in a sketch called 'Presenting His Dad'. When they returned to the States the following year, there began to be talk of a comeback, and if he couldn't play the Prince of Denmark, it was felt that he might well incarnate a more homebred national hero. Late in 1930 – after a guest appearance, as himself, in *Free and Easy* – his *Tom Sawyer* reached the screen and was well liked. Ten months later *Huckleberry Finn* followed – and that really was the end of Jackie Coogan's boyhood.

The well-known sequel was sad and ugly. Over his decade or so of stardom, Jackie's earnings of something like four million dollars had been paid, pending his 21st birthday, into a company controlled by his parents. But on 4 May 1935, just before the pay-out was due, his father was killed in a car crash; so were three passengers, including his ex-Huck, Junior Durkin. Jackie escaped with injuries. In the shock and grief of the aftermath (for he adored his father) he didn't like to ask about his money.

With somewhat unseemly haste, Mrs Coogan remarried (this is when he really *should* have played Hamlet) and references to financial matters were brushed aside. Jackie, in his turn, married a starlet called Betty Grable, and found he needed the money. His mother and stepfather declined to release it. Eventually, in 1938, Jackie was obliged to sue them for his capital. But by that time they had spent most of it, and the law suit ate up much of the remainder. All that was left for the former prince of the silver screen, once settlement had been reached, was some 6% or so of his hard-earned fortune. Coogan and Grable split up.

The whole business had been so monstrous, and public sympathy was so strong, that a new law was drafted and passed in California called the Child Actors' Bill, obliging a child's earnings to be kept in trust till majority, safe from the depredations of even the nearest and supposedly dearest. It was updated in 1986, but is still thought of as the Coogan Bill.

Jackie didn't fade away. True, he only had one adult leading role (*Home on the Range*, 1935) and a scattering of minor ones in the Thirties and Forties. But finally, fat and bald and with only the great brown eyes to remind one of his lost youth, he re-emerged from World War Two as a useful player of crooks and grotesques. He is probably best remembered as the repulsive Uncle Fester in TV's 'Addams Family' series.

But, more sympathetically, he can be seen in a fine 1982 film called *The Escape Artist*, which stars a fascinating boy actor, Griffin O'Neal ◇, almost exactly 50 years his junior. Crumpled old Jackie plays the harassed proprietor of a magic goods and tricks shop – a prestidigitator in a world of legerdemain.

17 Skinner's Baby
19 A Day's Pleasure
21 The Kid
     My Boy
     Peck's Bad Boy
22 Oliver Twist
     Trouble
23 Circus Days
     Daddy
     Long Live the King
24 A Boy of Flanders
     Little Robinson Crusoe
25 Old Clothes
     The Rag Man
27 The Bugle Call
     Buttons
     Johnny Get Your Hair Cut

Buzz Barton

USA

b: 5 Nov 14 (Gallatin, Texas)
d: 20 Nov 80 (St Louis)

The Boy Rider, The Bantam Cowboy, The Fightin' Redhead, The Freckled Rascal – Buzz Barton's film titles tell it all. (His real name was Billie Lamarr.) He was the archetypal junior cowboy of the closing years of the silent cinema. If it hadn't been silent, he'd have made a lot of noise – ridin', roarin', ropin' and fightin' till the cows came home.

He was generally the protagonist, his own boy, not a sidekick like his younger contemporary Frankie Darro ◇. His russet hair bristled, his honest blue eyes glared defiance, he whooped exultantly. He was so completely the prairie rider that his name passed into the folk memory. Buzz Barton air-rifles were sold. (And a decade or so later the Buzz-name was attached to another boy rider of the screen, Robert Henry ◇.)

Barton had been raised on a ranch, and at 12 won the title of Champion Trick Rider and Fancy Rider. In 1926, performing in a show at Cheyenne, Wyoming, he was spotted by a scout from FBO, and soon afterwards was launched in *The Boy Rider*.

From the 1931 serial *The Lone Defender* onward, Buzz Barton rode, shot and fought steadily through the Thirties, but no longer a prodigy, just a cowboy among others. He didn't return to the saddle after World War Two, not in front of a camera anyway. An unrecognisable Buzz Barton is the train conductor in *In the Heat of the Night* in 1967.

27 The Boy Rider
     The Slingshot Kid
28 The Bantam Cowboy
     The Fightin' Redhead
     The Lariat Kid
     The Little Buckaroo
     Orphan of the Sage
     The Pinto Kid
     Rough Ridin' Red
     Wizard of the Saddle
     Young Whirlwind
29 The Freckled Rascal
     The Little Savage
     Pals of the Prairie
     The Vagabond Cub
30 Canyon Hawks

Breezy Eason, Jr.

USA

b: 19 Nov 14 (California)
d: 25 Oct 21 (Hollywood)

Reaves Barnes Eason was the little son of the director William Reeves Eason (1886-1956), who in his early days almost always spelt his name Reaves, and who was later responsible for the terrifying chariot race in the 1926 *Ben Hur*.

Breezy Junior (his mother was the

Unsaddled: Buzz Barton and admirer

Road clear to Paradise: Breezy Eason, Jr.

actress Jimsy Mayo) was being built into a tiny Western star, 'Universal's Littlest Cowboy', when the unthinkable happened: aged only six, he was crushed by a truck on one of his father's sets.

Harry Carey, who had starred with him in *The Fox* and written a part specially for him, held Breezy's hand as he died in hospital. 'The wonder child of the screen,' wrote a columnist, leaving no tear un-jerked, 'went west with a grin on his face and his little fists clenched.'

16 Gold and the Woman
   Patches
18 Nine-Tenths of the Law
19 Back from the Dead
   The Cowboy and the Kid
   The Texas Kid
   The Thunderbolt
20 Blue Streak McCoy
   A Nose in a Book
   Out of the Sky

Pink Tights
Two Kinds of Love
21 The Fox

Waldemar Pottier

GERMANY

b: 30 Dec 14 (Berlin)

His parents were the actors Ernst Jacobi and Jeannette Pottier, and he has at various times been known as Pottier-Jacobi or Jacobi-Pottier. Waldemar appeared on stage from the age of two, and in films from four, acting with some of the greatest names of his day: Moissi, Jannings, Veidt, Pola Negri, Elisabeth Bergner.

He was not such an exotic creature as his German predecessor, Martin Herzberg ◇, but a thoughtful, intelligent and spirited performer much liked by the critics. Two of his best parts were in *Karusellen* (as a circus boy having knives thrown at him) and in *Das edle Blut* (as a sensitive boy in a military school). In *Aus der Jugendzeit* and *Zwei Kinder* he was teamed with the popular little girl star of the time, Loni Nest.

Under the Nazis, Waldemar's career was hampered by the possession of a Jewish grandmother: the obscene professional permits of the time required evidence of three unblemished Aryan generations. Between 1931 and 1939 he got virtually no work, but had a small part in the 1950 American film *The Big Lift*, and from 1952 made several films for DEFA in East Berlin.

18 Erborgtes Glück (Borrowed happiness)
19 Menschen (Humans)
20 Ich – bin – du (I am you)
   Der Leidensweg der Inge Krafft
      (Inge Krafft's path of sorrow)
21 Die Ehrenschuld (The debt of honour)
   Grausige Nächte (Nights of horror)
   Das Weib des Pharao (Pharaoh's wife)
22 Die Finsternis ist ihr Eigentum
      (Darkness is hers)
   Marie Antoinette
23 Die arme Sünderin (The poor sinner)
   Karusellen (SE – The roundabout)

Pottier in Pirandello's 'Man, Beast and Virtue'

Waldemar Pottier ponders, without much enthusiasm, a life on the ocean wave.

24 Aus der Jugendzeit klingt ein Lied
    (A song from days of youth)
    Strandgut (Flotsam)
    Zwei Kinder (Two children)
25 Die Anne-Liese von Dessau
    (Anne-Lise of Dessau)
    Husarenfieber (Hussar fever)
    Um Recht und Ehre (For right and honour)
27 Das edle Blut (Noble blood)

Mickey Bennett

USA

b: 1914 (Victoria, B.C., Canada)
d: 6 Sep 50 (Hollywood)

Michael Charles Bennett was not a pretty sight, with a scrubby head and pale, slightly bulging eyes. By the time he was 11, he looked like a punch-drunk Irish bruiser with the beginnings of a double chin. But his worst enemies could not have called him a sissy, and he had distinct comic gifts, as many directors discovered. He could also convey dour integrity.

Facing Bobby Gordon◇, he provided the junior Irish element in *The Cohens and Kellys*, and was W.C.Fields's awful son in *It's the Old Army Game* (the role taken by Tommy Bupp◇ in the near-remake, *It's a Gift*). Other juicy parts, with more human

content, came in *Big Brother, Babe Comes Home* (a baseball story starring Babe Ruth in person) and *A Boy of the Streets*.

Mickey Bennett continued to appear in films of the Thirties, and was later employed as an assistant director.

22 The Man Who Played God
    Reported Missing
23 Big Brother
    The Empty Cradle
    The Last Moment
    Loyal Lives
    Marriage Morals
24 The New School Teacher
    Second Youth
25 Big Pal
26 The Cohens and Kellys
    Grabbing Grabbers
    Honesty – the Best Policy
    It's the Old Army Game
    There Ain't No Santa Claus
27 Babe Comes Home
    A Boy of the Streets
    Slaves of Beauty
    The Sting of Stings
    Women Love Diamonds

Mickey Bennett with Babe Ruth in Babe Comes Home

28 The Ghost Talks
    The Head of the Family
    Papa's Vacation
    Tillie's Punctured Romance
    United States Smith
    The Vanishing West *(serial)*
29 The Dummy
    Footlights and Fools
30 Father's Son
    Strictly Modern
    Swing High

Shura Zavyaloff

USSR

b: circa 1914

His debut was as Mishka, a newspaper boy causing chaos at the headquarters of the White Russian general Yudenich.

In his two 1928 films and *Adres Lenina*, Shura and another boy, Borya Litkin◇, are teamed together playing characters with their own first names: 'Shura' (a worker's son) and 'Borya' (a doctor's son). *Zolotoi myod* is a happy drama of the conversion of vagabond boys into communal bee-keepers.

What is less happy is that virtually all Shura's films, like so many early Soviet ones, are now believed lost.

He stayed in the movies, but his adult profession turned out not to be that of actor but of cameraman.

25 Mishka protiv Yudenicha
    (Mishka versus Yudenich)
26 Volzhskiye buntari (Volga rebels)
28 Joi i Druzhok (Joy and Buddy)
    Zolotoi myod (Golden honey)
29 Adres Lenina (Lenin's address)
    Doroga v mir (Road to the world)

Dick Winslow

USA

b: 25 Mar 15 (Jennings, Louisiana)
d: 7 Feb 91 (North Hollywood)

Richard Winslow Johnson was a graceful, witty and versatile boy, well fitted to sustain a 60-year career in the cinema. Five

Johnson siblings, including elder brother Kenneth, helped him support his parents.

Dick Winslow really never stopped acting. His countless films were to include *Tom Sawyer* (30, as brother Sid), *Sarah and Son* (30), *Seed* (31), *Tom Brown of Culver* (32), *Mutiny on the Bounty* (35), and later on *My Reputation* (46), *The Benny Goodman Story* (55), *The Errand Boy* (62), *Airport* (69), *Funny Lady* (75), *Movie Movie* (78) and *First Monday in October* (81).

Airport was a singularly apt check-in for Dick, since a mainstay of his employment between 1957 and 1962 had been as in-flight pianist-singer on 'champagne flights' between Los Angeles and Las Vegas. He was also an entertainer at Disneyland.

21 My Boy
24 Not One to Spare
26 Trumpin' Trouble
27 Judgment of the Hills
   Range Courage
   Special Delivery
28 Avalanche
29 Love, Live and Laugh
   Marianne
   Sweetie
   The Virginian
   Wonder of Women

Gida Lázár

HUNGARY

b: 26 Aug 15 (Budapest)

Gida's mother was a famous actress, his father a bank-clerk. The angelic-looking child started filming when he was nearly five, and became a firm favourite in Hungary, often in tandem with the slightly older Ferko Szecsi ◇. He also acted in the theatre: roles as dissimilar as Falstaff's Page and Little Eyolf.

Lázár returned to filming in his teens, notably in *Nászut a vilag köröl*, one of the very first Hungarian talkies.

On stage, he became a National Theatre player in 1937, but was dismissed in 1945 because he wouldn't join the Communist Party. Later he worked with the State Puppet Theatre.

20 Gyermeksziv (Heart of a child)

Gida Lázár

21 Elnémult harangok (The bells fall silent)
22 Meseország (Fairyland)
   Pi-Pa-Po (GE)
23 A lélek órása (The watchmaker of souls)
24 Holnap kezdödik az élet
   (Life begins tomorrow)
   Frauen, die nicht lieben dürfen
   (Women forbidden to love – GE)
25 Die Königsgrenadiere
   (The king's grenadiers – GE)

Yura Chernishoff

USSR

b: circa 1915

26 Svezhi veter (Fresh wind)
27 Lesnoi chelovek (Man from the forest)
28 Besprizorniye (Vagabond boys)
   Za stenoi (Beyond the wall)
30 Ikh ulitsa (Their street)

Borya Litkin

USSR

b: circa 1915

Borya was the posher screen buddy of Shura Zavyaloff ◇. He continued to appear as 'Borka' or 'Boris' in two subsequent films, which suggests public recognition. Nearly all his child roles were leading ones.

He was involved with Arctic fishing in *Severnaya lyuboff* and with bee-keeping in *Zolotoi myod*. In *Adres Lenina* he and Shura gave a facelift to Lenin's former home in Leningrad.

While Zavyaloff became a cameraman, Litkin later became a sound engineer in films.

27 Severnaya lyuboff (Northern love)
28 Joi i Druzhok (Joy and Buddy)
   Zolotoi myod (Golden honey)
29 Adres Lenina (Lenin's house)
30 Lyagavi (The sneak)

Vasya Lyudvinski

USSR

b: circa 1915

An exemplary boy, Lyudvinski at least twice played the part of a pioneer (boy scout), and at least twice under his own name of Vasya: he was 'Vasya the reformer', and in *Besprizorniye* had the leading role of 'Vasya, an old drunkard's son'. The biggest of his other roles was in *Marika*.

In *Marika* he is a street cigarette-seller, with pioneer and police connections, who saves a peasant girl from the clutches of a gang of thieves. *Vasya – reformator* is a satirical comedy from the era of Lenin's New Economic Policy: the resourceful young Vasya (Lyudvinski) exposes the sham miracles of a rogue priest, who has converted his church into a cinema! In *Taras Shevchenko* he undergoes appalling traumas and privations as the doubly orphaned child of a serf family – later to grow into an artist.

After 1931 Lyudvinski seems to have made only one further appearance: a minor role in the 1938 film *Morskoi post* (Naval station).

25 Marika
26 Bukhta smerti (The bay of death)
   P.K.P./Pilsudski kupil Petluri
   (Pilsudski buys Petlura)
   Spartak (Spartacus)
   Svezhi veter (Fresh wind)
   Taras Shevchenko
   Vasya – reformator (Vasya the reformer)
   V kogtyakh sovetskoi vlasti
   (In the grip of Soviet power)
27 Cherevichki (The slippers)
28 Besprizorniye (Vagabond boys)
   Za stenoi (Beyond the wall)
31 Volchi khutor (Village of wolves)

Robert Parrish

USA

b: 4 Jan 16 (Columbus, Georgia)
d: 4 Dec 95 (Long Island, NY)

Bob Parrish is featured here not because he was an important child actor (which he wasn't) nor because he later became a fine director (which he did), but because he has written, in 'Growing Up In Hollywood', incomparably the most entertaining of all movie kid memoirs. (And he is not to be confused with James Robert Parish, who wrote a book on 'Great Child Stars'.)

The Parrish family – with boys Gordon and Robert and girls Beverly and Helen – moved from Georgia to Hollywood in 1926. Robert already cherished a dream of being a director (with megaphone) since accompanying his mother to *Broken Bossoms* (the L wasn't lit up that day) and forming the opinion that all the world's movies were directed by a man called D.W.Griffith. (When he was cast as a newsboy in *City Lights*, Bob asked Chaplin to point Griffith out to him.)

He and two other boys engaged in *The Divine Lady* had their view of Admiral Nelson revolutionised by the 'Kiss me, Hardy' story, and affected to believe that they were surrounded by a shipload of fairies. 'We swished around with our hands on our hips, lips pursed, and our powder monkeys' rags flowing in the sea breeze.' To which their elderly tutor at last snapped 'Cut out all this fag crap'.

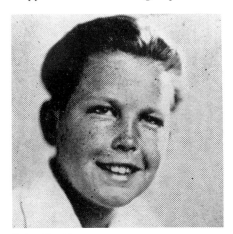

Robert Parrish, 1927

Don't expect to see much of Robert Parrish in most of these assignments: he was largely a 'bits and lines' kid. In *City Lights* he's the peashooting newsboy who grabs Chaplin's cane. (The taller, blonder one is Austen Jewell.)

His book describes marvellously how he graduated from child actor to bit player, then assistant, then sound editor – working throughout his career, on and off, with the alarming John Ford – before achieving his ambition to direct. The anecdotes throughout are masterly, with a particularly heart-warming one for anyone who ever wanted to be sick over Dick Powell.

27 Yale vs. Harvard ('OG')
28 The Divine Lady
   Four Sons
   Mother Machree
   Riley the Cop
29 The Iron Mask
   Men Without Women
   The Racketeer
30 All Quiet on the Western Front
   The Big Trail
   The Right to Love
   Up the River
31 Annabelle's Affairs
   City Lights
   Penrod and Sam

Junior Coghlan torments Elinor Fair in The Yankee Clipper

Junior Coghlan

USA

b: 15 Mar 16 (New Haven, Connecticut)

This cheerful, brown-eyed Irish-American was just about the most likeable boy actor of the late silent screen. His father, Frank Coghlan, Sr., was a doctor, and his mother, Katherine, an actress. In early childhood he earned good money as a model, then followed his mother's profession to considerable effect. He hit the screen at the age of three, at $3 a day.

Though Frank Junior could look sad and waifish if business required, he was irrepressibly optimistic by nature, and when the leading roles began to come they were of an active, self-reliant nature. In *Let 'Er Go, Gallegher* he was an orphaned newsboy with his own furnished flat (an abandoned taxicab), who became the sidekick of an investigative journalist. Other rewarding parts came in *Rubber Tires*, *The Yankee Clipper* (as a stowaway) and *Marked Money*.

Sometimes, foreshadowing Mickey Rooney's ◊ persona of the mid-Thirties, he would be the rough street kid cast

Junior Coghlan with Bessie Love in Rubber Tires

23 years, initially as a Naval Aviator and latterly as a Public Affairs Officer, proving an invaluable link between the Navy and Hollywood producers.

Around the time of his retirement (in 1965, at the rank of Lieutenant Commander) he had a little role in *The Sand Pebbles*, and since then has combined public relations work in Los Angeles with dozens of appearances on film and TV – in recent years as 'spokesman' for Curtis Mathes TV in their commercials.

opposite the posh one, as he was with Philippe DeLacy ◇ in the military-school setting of *Square Shoulders*. The chemistry was perfect.

The 1931 Penrod was Leon Janney ◇, and Frank Coghlan (as Junior was now beginning to be called) was his Sam. The homely potato-faced boy was growing into a personable youth, and his child career was over. He was in the 1932 serial *Last of the Mohicans*, and played the four-year-old Shirley Temple's elder brother in a series called 'Frolics of Youth'. He often cropped up in supporting parts in films of the Thirties, sometimes as a jockey (for he was a skilled rider), sometimes

as gang leader in opposition to the Dead End Kids.

Then, just as his career was fading, came a lucky break: the still eager and innocent-looking Frank was cast in the leading role of radio reporter Billy Batson (for whom the invocation of 'Shazam' worked wonders) in *The Adventures of Captain Marvel*. Launched in 1941, it was one of the most popular of all big-screen serials. Coghlan was Mickey Rooney's buddy in *Men of Boys Town* (40) and many of the *Andy Hardy* films.

Having clocked up more than 300 screen appearances, he joined the U.S. Navy during World War Two, and stayed for

Norman Doxat-Pratt

BRITAIN/HOLLAND

b: 1 Jne 16 (London)
d: 18 Sep 82 (London)

He was the younger son of Bernard Doxat-Pratt, who co-directed several films in Haarlem for the Hollandia company founded by Maurits Binger in 1912. Norman appeared in several, and by 1922 was being billed as 'another Jackie

Alfredo Hurtado ('Pitusin')

SPAIN

b: 6 Dec 17 (Madrid)
d: 1965

When he was five, Alfredo Hurtado Franco enrolled at a film-acting school in Madrid run by the actress Flora Rosini. His mother then wrote and produced a modest little film to earn money and show off the child's evident skills. This led to the part in *La medalla del torero*.

Alfredo, known from his debut as 'Pitusin' ('Pretty Little Thing'), became Spain's first child star, 'el Chiquitin español' (the Spanish 'Kid', after Coogan). When not busy filming, he would give poetry and guitar recitals.

Inevitably, 'Pitusin' Hurtado was chosen to incarnate for the screen the 'Little Guide of Tormes', said to be the first child protagonist in world fiction. As Christopher Morgan has pointed out, the Lazarillo is both hero and narrator of the anonymous picaresque novel published in Spain in 1554.

Hurtado continued to act in films till his early twenties. From 1940 he became assistant to several leading directors such as Florian Rey, Ladislao Vajda and Antonio Roman, and in the 1950s directed two or three modest films of his own.

23 La buenaventura de Pitusin
     (Pitusin's good luck)
24 Los granujos (The urchins)
   La medalla del torero
     (The bull-fighter's medal)
25 La revoltosa (The wild girl)
   El lazarillo de Tormes
     (The little guide from Tormes)
   La chavala (The lass)
   Amapola
26 Malvaloca
   El pilluelo de Madrid
     (The scamp of Madrid)
27 En la tierra del sol (In the land of the sun)
28 Agustina de Aragon
   Corazones sin rumbo
     (Aimless hearts – ES/GE/FR)
31 Sombras de circo (Shadows of the circus)

'Mimmo' circa 1924

Mimmo Palermi

ITALY

b: 1917
d: August 1925

Filippo, 'Mimmo' to his friends, was the son of Amleto Palermi (1889-1941), a leading Italian director throughout the Twenties and Thirties. He was a handsome little boy, in the manner of Jackie Coogan◇, and his adoring father directed all three of his films. In the first, *Paradiso*, Mimmo had the star part, as a lost boy in search of his parents, and the public fell for him in a big way.

Alas, Mimmo was to see paradise all too soon. In the summer of 1925 he contracted pneumonia. Complications set in, and the family doctor said he must have a blood transfusion at once, at home, as they couldn't get him into a hospital and most clinics were shut during the holidays. Amleto Palermi himself raced around Rome searching for a bottle of plasma. At last he was promised that a male nurse would arrive with one, the last in town. The door-bell rang, and Palermi opened it, shouting 'Quick, please, quick!' The man leapt for the stairs, but tripped

halfway up: the bottle flew from his sweating hands and smashed against the wall. Mimmo died next day.

The film historian Vittorio Martinelli, who told me this pathetic story – and to whose enormous kindness I'm indebted for virtually all my information on the Italian silent cinema – says that all three of Mimmo's films are now lost, and the only surviving evidence of this little ghost is one or two photographs and appreciative press reviews.

23 Paradiso (Paradise)
24 La freccia nel cuore (Arrow in the heart)
   La via del peccato (The street of sin)

Andy Shuford

USA

b: 1917 (Helena, Arkansas)

William Shuford acted under his father's name of Andy. He was a lithe, freckled, outdoor boy and a brilliant rider; but he also had narrow, 'skinny' eyes which after a while made him an invaluable player of 'mean' parts – for instance as a foe of Jackie Cooper◇ in *When a Feller Needs a Friend*. In most of his films of 1931-32, though, he is co-starring with cowboy Bill Cody (grandson of 'Wild Bill') in the 'Bill and Andy' series.

Shuford left the movies when he was 18, and enlisted in the Air Force. He served for many years, and won the British DFC during World War Two.

26 The Fourth Commandment
   Slow Down
   The Winning of Barbara Worth
27 The Bush Leaguer
   Fast and Furious
   It
   The Missing Link
   Open Range
   The Society Architect
   The Wreck of the Hesperus
28 Buck Privates
30 The Big Trail
   The Divorcee
   Moby Dick
31 Dugan of the Bad Lands
   The Easiest Way
   The Great Meadow

Headin' for Trouble
The Montana Kid
Oklahoma Jim
A Rider of the Plains
Ten Cents a Dance
32 The Champ
Ghost City
Land of Wanted Men
Law of the North
Mason of the Mounted
Texas Pioneers
When a Feller Needs a Friend

Buck Black

USA

b: circa 1917

Briefly, in 1928, Buck advertised himself as 'Bret Black' – which may or may not have been his actual name. He was a likeable, toothy brunet with a gift for pathos when his Western duties permitted, for he was another hard-ridin' kid and a valued 'little pal' of silent cowboys such as Ken Maynard. He also had a couple of outings (as Bret) with 'Our Gang'.

23 Big Dan
Snowdrift
The Spanish Dancer
You Can't Get Away With It
24 Checkers
Crossed Trails
Empty Hearts
A Girl of the Limberlost

Buck Black, circa 1928

Heavy mouse: Emile Genevois (left) with Tramel in Crainquebille

Gold Heels
Idle Tongues
The Last Man on Earth
Not One to Spare
Walk Right In
25 As No Man Has Loved
The Bad Lands
The Bandit Tamer
Big Pal
The Bloodhound
Durand of the Bad Lands
Lights of Old Broadway
The Man That Never Smiled
Rough Going
The Trouble Buster
26 Born to Battle
Eyes of the Night
A Regular Scout
Senor Daredevil
27 Hills of Peril
The Silent Avenger
Ten Years Old ('OG')
28 Russ Farrell, Aviator *(series)*
29 Noisy Noises ('OG')
30 Personality

Emile Genevois

USA

b: 1 Jan 18 (Barlin, Pas de Calais)

Pudgy, brown-eyed Genevois is almost too mature for our study, but creeps under the net for having played two important roles in his fifteenth year: 'the Mouse' in the remake of *Crainquebille*, and Gavroche (a rather well-fed one) in the 1933 *Les misérables*. At this age he just about punched his weight.

He was working as a page-boy for Pathé, producers of *Les misérables*, when he was spotted, invited to audition, and outstripped hundreds of other would-be Gavroches. The film's star, Harry Baur, nicknamed him 'le Môme' (the Kid).

Genevois had several more parts in 1934, and was such a useful type that he seldom stopped working until the 1970s at least. Once the youthful bounce had left him, he settled for playing weak, good-natured slobs. He can be seen in such famous films as *La bête humaine, Nous les gosses, Quai de Grenelle* and *Casque d'Or*.

33 Crainquebille
Les misérables (The poor and wretched)

A word here about the role of 'Gavroche', the heroic guttersnipe who dies at the barricades in Victor Hugo's *Misérables*. This has been the most-filmed of French classics, and because the chapters involving Gavroche have a patriotic, revolutionary character, he is quite as emotionally central to French popular culture as are

Tom Sawyer and Huck Finn to America, and certainly more than Oliver Twist, Tom Brown and Jim Hawkins to Britain. In Italy, the patriotic stories (such as 'The Sardinian Drummer-Boy' and 'The Little Lombard Scout') in Edmondo De Amicis' old schoolboy favourite 'Cuore' carry a similar charge of populist emotion.

It's interesting that while France and Italy have successfully enshrined this kind of naïve, flag-waving nobility in a beloved book, neither Britain, Germany nor the United States – all great 'fighting' nations with a powerful tradition of patriotic brain-washing – seem to have managed an equivalent. Nor, Huck Finn apart, have they produced much by way of a proletarian child hero: Sawyer, Twist and Brown are middle-class, and even the humble Hawkins is beyond doubt upwardly mobile.

The USA, of course, had its traumatic Civil War, with toughly humane Yankees pitted against wrong-but-romantic Confeds: and boy actors as different as Jackie Coogan ◇, Billy Mauch ◇, Spanky McFarland ◇, Orley Lindgren ◇, Kevin Corcoran ◇ and Kurt Russell ◇ starred gallantly in Civil War stories. But this was a creepy kind of patriotism.

In Britain, few of the once-popular adventure stories of Marryat, Ballantyne and Henty seem to have been filmed, and in Germany, sadly, the most obviously 'heroic' boy icons emerged in hortatory films of the Nazi period, like Hitlerjunge Quex and *Kadetten*.

Among early Gavroches, CHARLES BADIOLE is outstanding in Henri Fescourt's 1925 film: a lean dog of a boy, about 13, with a cool, humorous air and an extraordinarily relaxed grace outside the scenes of violent action. Emile Genevois in 1933 is, as noted, more pawky; and the Fox version of 1935 simply omitted Gavroche.

In an Italian *Miserabili* of 1947, RINALDO SMORDONI ◇ (the younger of the boys in *Sciuscia*) was the heroic gamin; as was BOBBY HYATT ◇ in the Fox remake of 1952, and in 1957 and 1958, in French co-productions, CHRISTIAN FOURCADE ◇ (of *Little Boy Lost*) and JIMMY URBAIN ◇ (who

went on to become a famous dancer).

But perhaps the ideal Gavroche, seen in a Franco-British TV film of 1978, was DEXTER FLETCHER ◇. Hugo would have approved of this valiant starveling.

Norman 'Chubby' Chaney

USA

b: 18 Jan 18 (Baltimore)
d: 29 May 36 (Baltimore)

The amiable Norman Chaney succeeded Joe Cobb ◇ in late 1929 as the resident fatso of 'Our Gang', though they had overlapped for Joe's last few outings on the cusp between silents and talkies. Norman had emerged as winner from a reported 20,000 contestants for the honour. But though smaller than Joe, he was only a couple of months younger, and (as was sadly to emerge) not nearly so robust. Joe was short and spherical, but his features were at least in proportion, whereas Norman's were tiny and seemed cramped into a grim, unhappy mask on the front of his head.

Hal Roach's writers and directors found it funny to cast 'Chubby' as a furious lover or something equally grotesque. The child did his best to be a miniature Sidney Greenstreet, but it was more painful than amusing to watch. The cult of the child fatso was one of the early cinema's least pleasing sidelines. Buddy Messinger ◇ was no problem – he was simply beefy and well-nourished, protected by his comic sense – but lard specialists like Lincoln Stedman, Albert Schaefer and Tommy Hicks were used as butts, often cruelly so.

Norman Chaney sweated and puffed through two years and 18 shorts with 'Our Gang' before he in turn was shown the door. He never acted again. When he joined the Gang he had weighed 113 pounds, and over the next five or six years this swelled to nearly 300. He was not merely obese: he was diagnosed as having a serious glandular defect, and when he was eighteen it killed him. By the time he died poor Chubby had almost wasted away.

'Pop' Ordell as Fatty Finn in The Kid Stakes

Robin Ordell

AUSTRALIA

b: 19 Jan 18
d: 13 Aug 42

Robin ('Pop') Ordell was the son of the popular writer and comedian Athol Dowe, who worked under the name of Tal Ordell. He was born Robert Dowe, and was later known as Robert Athol Buntine. His sole, but considerable, claim to cinematic fame was for having starred in *The Kid Stakes*, Australia's first kid film (his father directing), which was based on one of Australia's best-loved comic strips, the creation of Syd Phillips. (It ran from 1923 to 1977.)

Robin, though no more than plump, incarnated the strip's hero, 'Fatty Finn', in this admirably grubby story of a donkey-race, surrounded by familiars like 'Bruiser Murphy', 'Seasy', 'Headlights Hogan', 'Shooey Shugg' and 'Master Algie Snoops'. (An unsuccessful remake appeared in 1980, with Ben Oxenbould as Fatty.)

In adult life Robert Buntine became a radio announcer. In August 1942, serving as a Flight Sergeant with the Royal Australian Air Force, he was shot down over the Mediterranean. His name is on the war memorial at Valetta in Malta.

27 The Kid Stakes

Sweet music: Jackie Condon (right) with 'Wheezer' Hutchins

Jackie Condon

USA

b: 24 Mar 18 (Los Angeles)
d: 13 Oct 77 (Inglewood)

John Michael 'Dusterhead' Condon, a child of almost supernatural charm and sauciness, was best known as the tousled ingénu of 'Our Gang' – one of its 1922 founder-members.

However, Jackie had been more or less a hambone even in swaddling clothes, and according to the Picture Show Annual of 1930 'was known for some time as the youngest female impersonator on the screen'. Presumably this had to be stopped, and a male impersonator, Mary Pickford, took the lead in the 1921 *Fauntleroy*.

According to Maltin and Bann, Jackie's subsequent show business career came to nothing, in spite of his looks and repeated attempts at comeback, and in the 1970s he was working with Rockwell International in Los Angeles, alongside the Gang's first 'fatty', Joe Cobb ◇. This seems to dispose of an attractive counter-rumour, that he had made a career in the Navy and become an admiral.

19 Daddy Long Legs
   The Hoodlum
20 Pollyanna
21 'Hallroom Boys' comedies
   Little Lord Fauntleroy
   Love Light
22 The Bride-To-Be
   Penrod
   'Our Gang' *(6 shorts)*
23 'Our Gang' *(15)*
   Jus' Passin' Through
   Speed the Swede
24-29 'Our Gang' *(57 more)*

Kenneth Rive

GERMANY/BRITAIN

b: 26 Jly 18

Dark-haired Kenny Rive (sometimes spelt Rieve) grew up bilingual, with a British father – who worked at the UFA studios from the 1920s – and a German mother.

He had a glamorous costume role in *Emerald of the East* as a kidnapped Indian child prince, carried off by rebels to their tribal home in the hills. Kenneth's father was one of the cameramen in this British film directed by its star, Jean de Kuharski.

As a personable boy-next-door he continued his acting career until the mid-Thirties, appearing for instance in *Der Zigeunerbaron* (35, The Gipsy Baron). Then he and his family left Nazi Germany and moved to England.

Kenneth Rive with Joshua Kean in Emerald of the East

After World War Two Kenneth Rive became an important London distributor of foreign cinema with his firm, Gala Films.

27 Das Geheimnis des Abbé X
   (The secret of the Abbé X – GE)
   Prinz Louis Ferdinand (GE)
28 Emerald of the East (GB)
29 A Knight in London (GB)
30 Der weisse Teufel (The white devil – GE)
31 Ihre Hoheit befiehlt
   (Her Highness commands – GE)
   Lügen auf Rügen (Lies on Rügen – GE)
32 Husarenliebe (Hussar love – GE)
   Rasputin (GE)

Stefan Rogulski

POLAND

b: 27 Aug 18 (Warsaw)

Stefan (or Zbyszek) Rogulski was a fair, gentle, romantic-looking boy, the son of a tailor. At the age of eight he enrolled at a ballet school in Warsaw, which he attended for five years. Then he was given the lead in *Janko muzykant*, based on a novel by Henryk Sienkiewicz (1846-1916) about a young street-musician. He had an important part in *Głos serca* the same year, but his other best chance came in 1932, in Aleksander Ford's *Legion ulicy*, a salty

Stefan Rogulski in the title role of Janko muzykant

and realistic drama of street gangs.

Rogulski went on to play teenage roles in stage plays like Rostand's 'L'homme que j'ai tué' and Wedekind's 'Frühlings Erwachen'. But World War Two and its convulsions in Poland put paid to the rest of his career, and his sons Krzysztof and Jerzy (who both had ambitions as actors) later emigrated to France.

30 Janko muzykant (Janko the musician)
   Głos serca (Voice of the heart)
31 Dziesięciu z Pawiaka
   (The Ten from Pawiak)
32 Legion ulicy (Legion of the streets)

The leading boy in *Legion ulicy* was played by the extraordinary TADEUSZ FIJEWSKI (1911-78). If he hadn't been nearly sixteen when he made his first film, Fijewski would certainly have had a major entry in this book, since he not only went on to be one of Poland's leading actors, but continued to play 'juvenile' parts until his late thirties! He was a slight, blond, elfish lad, somewhat in the Jean-Louis Barrault mould, more convincing as 'the eternal student' than as a grubby schoolboy.

Frankie Darro

USA

b: 22 Dec 18 (Chicago)
d: 25 Dec 76 (Huntington Beach, Cal.)

Frankie's real name was Johnson. His parents were vaudevilleans, and with the get-up-and-go attitude typical of theatrical babies of the period he lost no time in getting into the family act in Chicago. (Frank Johnson, Senior, was in young Frankie's first film, *Judgment of the Storm*, in which the tot performs 'an acrobatic dance'.)

He went on to become one of the most active, as well as acrobatic, of all screen children, and in more than twenty Westerns between 1925 and 1929 he was the kid sidekick of cowboy star Tom Tyler. But he also played in very different kinds of film: in sentimental drama or, for instance, as Harry Langdon as a boy in *Long Pants*.

Frankie Darro in The Circus Kid

His work-rate was prodigious – by 1930 he claimed to have been in 'fifty Western pictures and several hundred others'. No wonder he sometimes had a harassed air.

If Darro's claim is to be believed, even our vast list represents less than half of his output. He continued in his teens to work busily – sometimes as a jockey (using his ridin' skills), sometimes as a delinquent (with his seen-it-all look, which can't by then have needed much practice). He did fine work in *Wild Boys of the Road* (33), *No Greater Glory* (34) and *Little Men* (35).

He was in several more serials, such as *The Wolf Dog* (33), *Burn 'Em Up Barnes* (34), *Phantom Empire* (35) and *Junior G-Men of the Air* (42). He provided the voice of Lampwick in Disney's *Pinocchio* (40), and can still be seen in a few films of the Fifties and Sixties, like *Pat and Mike* (52) and *The Carpetbaggers* (64).

23 Judgment of the Storm
24 Half-a-Dollar Bill
   Racing for Life
   Roaring Rails
   The Signal Tower
   Women and Gold
25 Confessions of a Queen
   The Cowboy Musketeer
   Fearless Lover
   Fighting the Flames
   Her Husband's Secret
   The Lady

Darro and Eddie Dowling in The Rainbow Man

Let's Go, Gallagher
The People versus Nancy Preston
Phantom Express
So Big
Wandering Footsteps
The Wyoming Wildcat
26 The Arizona Streak
The Carnival Girl
The Cowboy Cop
Flaming Waters
Hearts and Spangles
The Masquerade Bandit
Out of the West
Red Hot Hoofs
The Thrill Hunter
Tom and His Pals
Wild to Go
27 Born to Battle
Cyclone of the Range
The Desert Pirate
The Flesh and the Devil
Flying U Ranch
Her Father Said No

Judgment of the Hills
Lightning Lariats
Long Pants
Moulders of Men
Tom's Gang
28 The Avenging Rider
The Battling Buckaroo
The Circus Kid
The Eagle's Talons
Hearts and Hoofs
Little Mickey Grogan
Mystery Valley
Phantom of the Range
The Road to Eldorado
Terror
Terror Mountain
The Texas Tornado
Tyrant of Red Gulch
When the Law Rides
29 Gun Law
Idaho Red
The Pride of Pawnee
The Rainbow Man

The Red Sword
Trail of the Horse Thieves
30 Blaze o' Glory
31 The Lightning Warrior *(serial)*
The Mad Genius
Public Enemy
The Sin of Madelon Claudet
The Vanishing Legion *(serial)*
32 Amateur Daddy
Cheyenne Cyclone
The Devil Horse *(serial)*
Three on a Match
Way Back Home

Hans Joachim Schaufuss

GERMANY

b: 28 Dec 18
d: 27 Oct 41 (Mikhailovska, nr Orel)

Three months before the charming hero of the 1931 *Emil and the Detectives* was shot down over Ireland, Emil's ally and fixer, Gustav with the horn, had fallen on the Eastern front. Hitler was proving an effective Herod for these innocents.

Hans Joachim was the son of the well-known actor Hans Hermann Schaufuss (1893-1982): both of them appear in *Die Töchter Ihrer Exzellenz*. The boy, small for his age, had an earnest, intelligent, faintly dishevelled air which was very endearing. He could play comedy and quite intense drama. (He's superb as the son used by a seducer to approach his mother in *Brennendes Geheimnis*.) And he could bustle and organise as he did in *Emil*.

Schaufuss continued to act until 1939, and would surely have made a fine career. Like poor Rolf Wenkhaus ◇, he deserved better than such a useless death.

31 Emil und die Detektive
32 Was sagt Onkel Emil dazu
    (What does Uncle Emil say?)
Der weisse Dämon (The white demon)
33 Brennendes Geheimnis (Burning secret)
Gretel zieht das grosse Los
    (Gretel wins the lottery)
Der Zarewitsch (The Tsarevich)
34 Annette im Paradies (Annette in Paradise)
Nischt geht über die Gemütlichkeit
    (Good nature is essential)
Die Töchter Ihrer Excellenz
    (Your Excellency's daughters)

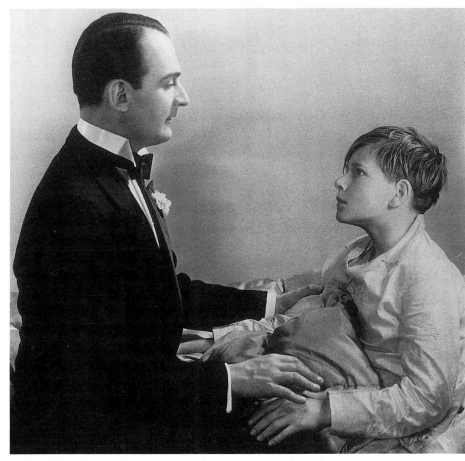

Falling idol: Willi Forst and Hans Joachim Schaufuss in Brennendes Geheimnis

Donald Haines

USA

b: 1918

Donald was a sandy-haired, freckled lad who radiated unassuming good nature. Somehow he found himself appearing in slapstick shorts of the late 1920s – in roles as unlikely as a knockabout Fauntleroy – and even starring in a series called the 'Smitty' comedies, in which Jackie Searl ◊ Eugene Jackson ◊ and George Ernest ◊ were also featured in their tenderer years.

Between 1930 and 1933 he was seen sporadically in second-rank roles with 'Our Gang', and continued until the end of his teens in such films as *Little Miss Nobody* (36), *Boys Town* (38), *Down on the Farm* (38), *Kidnapped* (38), *Three Comrades* (38), *Never Say Die* (39), *Sergeant Madden* (39), *East Side Kids* (40) and *That Gang of Mine* (40).

30 'Our Gang' *(5 shorts)*
31 Newly Rich
   'Our Gang' *(5 shorts)*
   Skippy
32 'Our Gang' *(5 shorts)*
   When a Feller Needs a Friend
33 'Our Gang' *(1 short)*
34 The Band Plays On
   Little Man, What Now?
   Manhattan Melodrama
   No Greater Glory
35 Straight from the Heart
   A Tale of Two Cities
   The Winning Ticket

Dean Reisner (Dinky Dean)

USA

b: 1918

Dean – who appeared as 'Dinky Dean' in his best-known role, as the child in Chaplin's *Pilgrim* – was the son of the actor/director Charles (Chuck) Reisner, who appeared as a heavy in several Chaplin films. (He was the Criminal in *The Pilgrim*.) Dean was also sometimes known as Charles Reisner, Junior, and to add to the confusion both he and his father were often billed as Riesner.

From 1948 Dean turned his hand to directing, script-writing and lesser off-camera work in films.

21 Peck's Bad Boy
22 A Ladies' Man
23 Hollywood
   The Pilgrim
   A Prince of a King
29 Square Shoulders

Russell Francis Griffin

USA

b: circa 1918

With a snub nose and rather bulging eyes, the child Griffin resembled an enraged pekinese, and was obvious brat material.

22 Beyond the Rainbow
   Sure Fire Flint
23 Jacqueline, or Blazing Barriers
   Lawful Larceny
   Marriage Morals
   Three o'Clock in the Morning
   You Are Guilty
24 The Average Woman
   The New School Teacher
25 The Man Who Found Himself
   The Pearl of Love

'André Rolane'

FRANCE

b: circa 1918

There is quite a bit of chat in French cine-magazines of the period about the dear little boy who appears in *Le petit Jacques* (23) and *Les deux gosses* (24). In 1925 it is announced that he will be in an Italian production called *The Blind Woman of Pompeii*.

When it appears, in 1926, the little boy turns out to be played by a little girl called Andrée Rolane, who looks a year or so older than André when we last saw him.

She goes on to play (most memorably) Cosette as a child in *Les misérables*, and the heroine of a kiddie-weepie called *Les larmes de Colette*.

There are various articles about her, even interviews. Not one of them mentions the existence of a male sibling with near-identical name. (Would any parents really let themselves in for such inevitable confusions?) Finally, in one of the interviews, Andrée comes right out and admits that she played *Le petit Jacques* in 1923 . . . .

Exit André, I think.

Hans Richter

GERMANY

b: 12 Jan 19 (Berlin)

The only survivor among the principals of the 1931 *Emil and the Detectives* (even Inge Landgut, the pertly wholesome Pony Hütchen, and more recently the German voice of Miss Elly in 'Dallas', has sadly now left us) is the ginger-haired, snub-nosed, freckle-faced Hans Richter. As 'the Flying Stag', he once hurtled through the Berlin streets on a sort of foot-propelled skateboard with shaft and handlebars (what in those days was meant by a scooter), pausing only to utter stern Red Indian greetings.

He should not be confused with a famous surrealist film-maker of the same name (1888-1976), let alone with a famous orchestral conductor (1843-1916).

Hans Richter, like Wenkhaus◇ and Schaufuss◇, hadn't acted before *Emil*, but he has seldom stopped since it. His cheeky face adorned countless films of the early Thirties, often as page or lift-boy. (He was the thieving, 'unpatriotic' Communist boy in *Hitlerjunge Quex*.) In his late teens he began to fill out, and his insolent presence took a fleshier form.

For a time it seemed that Richter might have large ambitions. In 1936, when he was rehearsing for *Traumulus* with Emil Jannings, the magazine 'Filmwoche' called him 'the teenage Jannings' and clearly reckoned him a serious actor of the future.

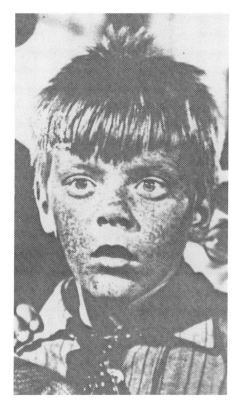

Hans Richter as the Flying Stag in Emil und die Detektive

He studied with Albert Florath after the war, but though he became a well-known comedian, the serious roles never quite came to him, in the cinema at least. The Flying Stag settled into middle age as a well-rounded character actor who could be genial or unpleasant with equal ease.

On the stage, though, he had wider opportunities, playing in Shakespeare, Molière, Büchner and Brecht among others. With his wife and son Richter successfully launched a summer theatre festival in the small town of Heppenheim, near Heidelberg.

31 Emil und die Detektive
32 Das Blaue vom Himmel (Sky blue)
33 Drei blaue Jungs – ein blondes Mädel
　　(Three blue boys and one blonde girl)
　　Die Fahrt ins Grüne
　　(Journey into the countryside)
　　Hände aus dem Dunkel
　　(Hands from the darkness)
　　Hitlerjunge Quex (Hitler Youth Quex)
　　Keine Angst vor Liebe
　　(No worry about love)
　　Der Page vom Dalmasse-Hotel
　　(The page from the Hotel Dalmasse)

　　Seine erste Liebe (His first love)
34 Abenteuer eines jungen Herrn in Polen
　　(A young gentleman's adventure
　　in Poland)
　　Abenteuer im Südexpress
　　(Adventure on the Southern Express)
　　Das Blumenmädchen vom Grand-Hotel
　　(The flower-girl at the Grand Hotel)
　　Die englische Heirat
　　(The English wedding)
　　Früchtchen (Fruitlet – AT)
　　Liebe dumme Mama (Dear silly Mama)
　　Peter, Paul und Nanette
　　Der schwarze Walfisch
　　(The black whale)
　　Wenn ein Mädel Hochzeit macht
　　(When a girl gets married)

Bruce Guerin

USA

b: 18 Jan 19 (Los Angeles)

Little Bruce, who excelled in portrayals of 'woebegone urchins', is best remembered now as the grubby tot in *The Salvation Hunters*, a somewhat phoney essay in social realism with which Josef 'von' Sternberg launched himself on the Hollywood scene. The tot, it must be said, was more real than the film – grave, droll, completely unsentimental, and with a disconcerting look of the star, George K. Arthur.

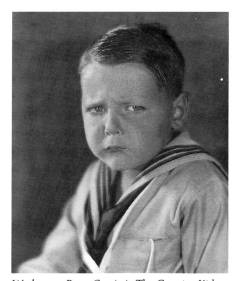

Woebegone: Bruce Guerin in The Country Kid

Bruce's sister Marjorie (about five years his senior) had worked for D.W.Griffith in her swaddling days, and in 1915 took the title role in the Franklin brothers' first 'kiddie picture', *The Baby*.

22 The Bachelor Daddy
   Kindred of the Dust
   Love in the Dark
   The Woman He Loved
23 The Age of Desire
   Brass
   The Country Kid
   Drifting
24 Lover's Lane
   The Man Who Smiled
   Revelation
25 The Parasite
   The Salvation Hunters
   Under the Rouge

Desmond Tester

BRITAIN

b: 17 Feb 19 (Ealing, London)

With a disorderly quiff of red hair, a homely face in which bluff good nature struggled with diffidence, and the weird middle-class accent of early English talkies (he was in fact educated at the posh Highgate School in London), Desmond Tester was Britain's leading boy actor of the mid-Thirties, and though he didn't make all that many youthful films, had some very important parts.

He had made his stage debut at the Duchess Theatre, London, in December 1931, as the page in 'The Merry Wives of Windsor', and a year or so later created the title role in a stage version of 'Emil and the Detectives'. (When it was filmed in 1935, the younger and less characterful John Williams was the hero.)

After a secondary part in *Midshipman Easy*, 1936 was Tester's annus mirabilis, playing sidekick to Maurice Chevalier in *The Beloved Vagabond*, the boy king Edward VI in *Tudor Rose* (his 1936 head looking frankly absurd emerging from 1547 gear), and – unforgettably – as Sylvia Sidney's schoolboy son blown up on the London bus by Oscar Homolka's

Quiffy: Desmond Tester as Edward VI in Tudor Rose

bomb in *Sabotage*. (It is one of Hitchcock's wickedest tricks that up to the very last moment one doesn't believe this can actually happen.)

A few years after the end of World War Two, the amiable Tester emigrated to Australia, where he became well-known on TV as host of a children's show called 'Channel Ninepins', and as a principal comic in the long-running serial 'The Kaper Cops' (1959-65). More recently he has appeared in films as various as *Barry McKenzie Holds His Own* (74) and *Wild Duck* (84).

34 Night Club Queen
35 Midshipman Easy
36 The Beloved Vagabond
   Sabotage
   Tudor Rose
37 Non-Stop New York
38 The Drum
   An Englishman's Home

Mickey McBan

USA

b: 27 Feb 19 (Spokane, Washington)

He was the fair-haired, blue-eyed son of British theatrical parents, and was getting good screen parts by the time he was four. In personality Mickey was mid-way between Jackie Cooper ◇ and John Howard Davies ◇: mousier than the one, spunkier than the other, with an amused, reassuring expression. He was delightful as 'Slightly', smallest of the Lost Boys, in the 1924 *Peter Pan*.

By the end of the silent era, at the age of ten, he was one of Hollywood's leading boy actors, full of character, yet he failed to carry his career on into the realm of sound. His best roles were in *The Return of Peter Grimm*, *Sorrell and Son* and the part-talkie *Father and Son*, his final picture.

Perhaps the very ordinariness that made him so castable as a boy weighed against him in later roles – yet, since all were agreed on his talent, this seems unlikely unless he suffered from ill health or had an unusually awkward voice.

23 Daytime Wives
   The Man Who Won
   Poor Men's Wives
   The Temple of Venus
24 The Dawn of a Tomorrow
   Hot Water
   Not a Drum Was Heard
   Peter Pan
   The Thief of Bagdad
   Untamed Youth
25 The Circle
   The Clodhopper
   The Freshman
   A High Jinx
   The Splendid Crime
   The Splendid Road
   The Unholy Three
26 Beau Geste
   Helen and Warren *(serial)*
   The Return of Peter Grimm
   Somebody's Mother
27 Quality Street
   Sorrell and Son
   The Way of All Flesh
   What Every Girl Should Know
   When a Dog Loves
29 Father and Son

Sorrell and son: H.B. Warner and Mickey McBan

Bruyninckx as De Witte

Jefke Bruyninckx

BELGIUM

b: 13 Aug 19 (Duffel)

Around his fourteenth year, in a country which has never made many films (its Flemish-speakers are catered for by Holland, French-speakers by France), Jozef Bruyninckx was plucked from obscurity — on account of his lean, rebellious looks,

intelligence and blond hair — to play the lead in *De Witte*.

This was one of the first Flemish talkies and certainly the most successful: it remained popular with generations of children till its remake 45 years later. The original comedy of poor village life, which Ernest Claes based on his own childhood

and the people of his own village of Zichem, had itself been a perennial best-seller and gone into 120 editions. 'Whitey', the hero, is a sort of accident-prone Huck Finn.

A 14-year-old in pre-television Belgium wasn't going to have many more child roles come his way, and Jef Bruyninckx didn't. But he was to make a career in show business all the same. Between 1941 and 1953 he graduated from film editor to assistant director; then he directed *De Klucht van de brave Moordenaar* (55), and three years later *Vrijzegel met 40 Kinderen*.

34 De Witte (Whitey)
35 Uilenspiegel leeft nog (Eulenspiegel lives)

Billy Butts

USA

b: 8 Sep 19 (Dallas, Texas)

Among Mary Pickford's nestful of orphaned and homeless kids in *Sparrows*, the only one who actually looked like a sparrow was William Charles Allen Butts. He had that tiny, indomitable quality plus, it's true, the sort of pathetic trustfulness a real sparrow would scorn.

Billy Butts supported by Fred Thomson in The Tough Guys

Billy was the child of non-theatrical parents, but was acting in films by the age of four and kept at it for another decade, a well-liked and heart-melting face. Around 1927 he appeared in a couple of 'Our Gang' shorts, and also took over from Jackie Morgan ◇ as the son of the house in the popular 'Gumps' series, for its last year or so. But he was best suited to outdoor alliances with screen cowboys.

By the early Thirties the sparrow-look had gone. Billy Butts was now just an ordinary, pleasant, rather stolid boy with sandy hair.

24 The Clean Heart
   The Girl Expert
   My Mamie Rose
   Rough and Ready
26 The Canadian
   The Flying Horseman
   Lone Hand Saunders
   Sparrows
   The Tough Guy
   The Two-Gun Man
   Uncle Tom's Uncle ('OG')
27 The Gumps *(series)*
   The Land Beyond the Law
   The Last Outlaw
   The Mysterious Rider
   Tired Business Men
   Women Love Diamonds
28 The Black Ace
   None But the Brave
   Taking a Chance
   Wild West Romance
29 Alias Jimmy Valentine
   The Lone Star Ranger
   The Virginian
30 The Medicine Man
31 Are These Our Children?
   Newly Rich
   Young Sinners
32 Lady and Gent
   The Night of June 13
33 Scarlet River

Serge Grave

FRANCE

b: 21 Sep 19 (Paris)

If Serge Grave, perhaps the best French boy actor of the 1930s, had started making films as young as Billy Butts ◇, he would have notched up a whole pageful.

Serge Grave with Robert Lynen (left) in Sans famille

As it is, starting at 14, he didn't do badly, with three big leads in 1936: as Claudinet (the Lewis Shaw ◇ part) in the talkie remake of *Les deux gosses*, as Lebrac in *La guerre des gosses* (itself remade in 1963 as *La guerre des boutons*, its proper title) and as Asticot, opposite Maurice Chevalier, in *Le vagabond bien-aimé* (the part taken by Desmond Tester ◇ in the British version). He also played the villain-as-a-boy in Guitry's *Roman d'un tricheur*.

He was now 16 – young for his age, but with a late-developing tendency to shoot up, and the beginnings of an aquiline nose. By contrast with the homely Tester, Grave was ardent, romantic and patrician, like a fledgling Gérard Philipe.

Two years later, aged nearly 19, Serge Grave was still playing a schoolboy in *Les disparus de Saint-Agil*, and doing it with some grace, but there was a strong sense of knobbly knees. By 1941 he was a prisoner of war in German hands. When peace arrived, he resumed his career and had youthful roles in several films – but not many after 1950.

He retired in favour of a career in schools television.

34 Hôtel du Libre-Echange (Free Trade Hotel)

   Sans famille (No relations)
   Zouzou
35 Debout, là-dedans! (Stand up in there!)
   L'équipage (The crew)
   J'aime toutes les femmes (I love all women)
   Jérôme Perreau
   Les parents terribles (Awful parents)
36 Les deux gamines (The two girls)
   Les deux gosses (The two boys)
   Les grands (The big boys)
   La guerre des gosses (The kids' war)
   La loupiote (The wee girl)
   Mon père avait raison
     (My father was right)
   Le roman d'un tricheur
     (The story of a cheat)
   Le vagabond bien-aimé
     (The beloved vagabond)

Gogi Ratiani

USSR

b: 1919 (Svaneti Mestya)
d: 1941

This Georgian boy is probably the only Soviet child actor to have given his name to a film – indeed two films. (Stalin soon decided that such cult of personality should start and finish at the top.) Gogi was discovered by the great Georgian director Kote Mardzhanishvili, who cast him in the stage play 'Samanishvili's Stepmother' before building a story round him.

Cult of personality: Gogi Ratiani in Gogi Ratiani

His eponymous film – set in the seething revolutionary Georgia of 1905 – tells of a schoolboy friendship between Gogi and Kiko (Sh. Dadeshkeliani), both gifted caricaturists of their teachers. In an earthquake, Gogi's parents are killed; Kiko, severely injured, is rescued by his buddy but removed to hospital in Tiflis.

Gogi follows, lives rough, sleeps in dustbins, finds work as a shoeshine boy and shelter with a concierge. Kiko, both arms amputated, comes to live with them and learns to draw with his left foot. (Dadeshkeliani anticipating Daniel Day-Lewis.) In a strange happy ending, both boys enter art school.

In the follow-up film of 1928, Gogi and three other boys (including Dadeshkeliani) constructed a home-made aeroplane; but it hadn't the convincing drama and emotion of the first story.

Before his early death the brilliant young Ratiani held a senior post in an ethnographic museum.

27 Gogi Ratiani
   Dva shaluna (The two pranksters)
28 Elisso
   Gogi – otvazhni lyotchik
      (Gogi the fearless pilot)

Bajar Batto

INDIA

b: circa 1919

29 Gopal Krishna
30 Rani Saheba (Her Majesty the Queen)
32 Maya Machchindra

Louis Lefebvre

FRANCE

b: circa 1919

'For one of the leads /in *Zéro de conduite*/ Vigo had selected a boy who lived near him, whom he had met in the Parc Montsouris. Louis Lefebvre, who plays Georges Caussat, was the terror of the district, an odd but delightful urchin. He had a gift for telling fantastic stories that

'Je vous dis merde.' Gérard de Bédarieux (right) repulses Léon Larive in Zéro de conduite

took place at the bottom of the sea or on the moon. Herrings, sardines and whales were the heroes. Under a tough exterior, he was very sensitive, and liked to be on his own.' (From an article in 'Cinéma 1951', by Henri Storck and P.E.Sales-Gomes)

Jean Vigo's famously anarchic film, with its quality of a dream that has elements of both the funny and the sinister, was actually banned in France, between 1933 and 1945, for 'anti-French' subversiveness. Among its quartet of trouble-makers was Gérard de Bédarieux as the androgynous but rebellious Tabart, who refuses to be fondled by the masters – 'Je vous dis merde' – but, like his later counterpart in Lindsay Anderson's *If . . . .*, accepts the embraces of a loyal comrade. Coco Golstein was Tabart's lover Druel, and Gilbert Pruchon was the school cook's son Colin, alias 'Haricot fils'. ('Colin' also means, in French, the coalfish or green pollack, so it's a suitably nourishing name.)

There is extraordinary confusion about the names in *Zéro de conduite* – real as well as fictional. A recent 'complete Vigo' in paperback, with full texts and credits,

refers to Tabart as 'Tabard' and Druel as 'Bruel', mistakes which had already appeared elsewhere, though they don't tally with the film's own credits. Lefebvre is spelt in two different ways, and the player of 'Bruel' appears as Coco Golstein in the text, but as 'Constantin Kelber' in the credits.

As I have also seen the version 'Constantin Goldsteinkehler', it may be that 'Coco Golstein' – the spelling on the film itself – was the garbled abbreviation of a double-barrelled name whose second half was either Kehler or Kelber. If the excellent Coco is still around, I hope he will clear the matter up for us, once and for all.

Louis Lefebvre was chosen again by Jean Vigo for his only other feature film, the glorious *L'Atalante*, a poetic comedy about life on a Seine barge. Lefebvre was a hard-pressed cabin-boy, having to live with Michel Simon among life's other hazards. Raymond Durgnat wrote aptly of his 'thick mischievous eyes, like an apprentice satyr's'.

33 Zéro de conduite (Nought for conduct)
34 L'Atalante (The Atalanta)

Jürgen Ohlsen

GERMANY

b: circa 1919

One of the few amusing things about the Third Reich was the trouble it had in finding the right 'image' to project to the German people and the wider world. The fact that Josef Goebbels had a club foot and looked like one of the cruder anti-semitic caricatures in Der Stürmer (and that a leading Nazi was called Rosen-berg) was awkward. So were the party's problems with heroes: the first famous Nazi 'martyr', Horst Wessel, was known to be a pimping thug.

In a nation teeming with blond, blue-eyed children, it's similarly ironic that the great boy-icon of the Nazi cinema was played by a boy with a Danish surname. (Later, when they wanted a 'perfect German boy' for propaganda films in the 1940s, they chose the Swedish-born Gunnar Möller. One would almost have thought they were exercising posi-tive discrimination in favour of racial minorities – blond ones, of course.)

Hitlerjunge Quex (from a book of the same name) was based on a real-life killing which had shocked Berlin a year earlier. A 12-year-old schoolboy called Herbert Norkus, out in the streets at dawn stick-ing up posters for a forthcoming Nazi

Militant: Jürgen Ohlsen as Quex

Between two fires: Ohlsen with Claus Clausen (left) and Heinrich George in Hitlerjunge Quex

meeting, was viciously set upon, knifed and left to die by a group of Communist roughs. Goebbels instantly spotted the propaganda potential of a boy martyr: he made a moving oration over Herbert's grave and hailed him as a model for the idealistic youth of Germany.

The Nazi cinema badly needed a success after the flop of its first 'emblematic' film, *S.A. Mann Brand*, earlier in 1933, from which all but the already converted stayed away in droves, and which was generally considered fatuous. *Hitlerjunge Quex* was to be another matter: based on a true case which lingered in the national memory, and directed by the expert Hans Steinhoff.

Who was to play 'Quex'? (This, short for 'Quecksilber' – quicksilver, from his tire-less zeal for the Party – was the nickname of the film's young hero, Heini Völker, poor Norkus's reincarnation.) A teenage actor called Hermann Braun was picked for the part, but fell ill just as filming started and was replaced, with glamorous mystery, by a boy billed simply as 'ein Hitlerjunge', though referred to by those in the know as 'Jürgen'.

This was Jürgen Ohlsen, a boy a year or two younger than Braun, who had

been spotted sunbathing by the Wannsee. He was suitably blond and handsome, but with a disarmingly gentle, innocent air which was a propagandist's god-send. He had never acted, but played his scenes with expressive simplicity. Even in his H.J. uniform he looked the perfect sacrificial lamb. (Still photographers had a job producing the defiantly heroic image which ended up on the posters.)

Jürgen Ohlsen appeared a couple of years later, under his own name, in one more film: *Wunder des Fliegens*, in which he played a teenage glider pilot. He sur-vived World War Two (unlike the hap-less Hermann Braun) and was last heard of living in Austria.

33 Hitlerjunge Quex (Hitler Youth Quex)
35 Wunder des Fliegens (The miracle of flight)

George Breakston

USA

b: 22 Jan 20 (Paris)
d: 21 May 73 (Paris)

Although George's father was American, his mother was French, and France was

George Breakston as Young Pip in Great Expectations

zone, and didn't return to acting when it was over. Instead, he took to writing and directing for television and the cinema, usually choosing exotic or open-air subjects, as in *The Scarlet Spear* (54) and the TV series 'African Patrol' and 'Jungle Boy'. He also directed the fine British boy actor Frazer McIntosh ◇ in two films of the mid-Sixties.

34 Great Expectations
   It Happened One Night
   Mrs Wiggs of the Cabbage Patch
   No Greater Glory
   Successful Failure
35 The Dark Angel
   Life Returns
   The Return of Peter Grimm
36 Boulder Dam
   Second Wife
   Small Town Girl

Hughie Green

BRITAIN

b: 2 Feb 20 (London)

Hugh Green had a Scottish-Canadian father and an Irish mother, and spent much of his childhood in Canada. But perhaps a

where he came into the world and left it. The Breakstons moved to America when he was seven, and he began getting radio and stage work in New York and Los Angeles, long before his debut in films.

This frail, fair-haired boy, with cloudy blue eyes and a cowlick, inspired affection and protectiveness in the manner, later, of Claude Jarman ◇, John Howard Davies ◇ and Mark Lester ◇. He was doubly touching when being heroic, notably in *No Greater Glory*, the first American version of Ferenc Molnar's popular 1907 novel *A Pál utcai fiúk* (The Boys of Paul Street), which had already been filmed in Hungary in 1924, and would be again in 1968.

Dying gloriously of pneumonia contracted in a desperate exploit against the opposing gang (leader, Frankie Darro ◇), and with Jimmy Butler ◇ and Donald Haines ◇ among the grateful comrades gathered round his bedside, little George is a figure of admirable pathos. He tapped the vein again in *Great Expectations* (as Young Pip), *Mrs Wiggs of the Cabbage Patch* and *The Return of Peter Grimm*.

As a teenager, George played Mickey Rooney's ◇ friend Breezy in some of the *Andy Hardy* films, and had small parts in *Swanee River* (39) and *The Grapes of Wrath* (40).

During World War Two he was a military cameraman in the Pacific battle

Hughie Green (centre) as Midshipman Easy. To left of him, Desmond Tester, with Robert Adams as the cook.

more powerful influence on his future life was the fact that he had as godfather the great comic Harry Tate. On his return to London the boy saw Tate in action at many a music-hall, and absorbed tricks of comedy timing from him. (Film survives from the mid-Thirties of godfather and godson performing a sketch together.)

By the time he was 14 he had his own radio show ('Hughie Green and His Gang') and made his entry into movies, first in *Little Friend* with Nova Pilbeam and then in the title role of *Midshipman Easy*, a wholly delightful version of a once-famous boys' adventure by Captain Marryat which marked the solo directorial debut of Carol Reed. (Uncle Harry also has a featured part.) Hughie creates a tactless and absent-minded hero of enormous, blundering charm – a bizarre cross, if it can be imagined, between Mickey Rooney ◇ and Ernest Thesiger.

Green wasn't much seen in films after this, though he crops up in the 1940 *Tom Brown's Schooldays*. He did war service in the Royal Canadian Air Force, and during the Fifties and Sixties became a popular presenter of quiz and talent shows, such as 'Double Your Money' and 'Opportunity Knocks' on British TV. By this time his charm had coarsened to a sort of ogling archness that was painful to those of a sensitive disposition.

34 Little Friend
35 Big Ben Calling
      Midshipman Easy

Douglas Haig

USA

b: 9 Mar 20 (New Orleans)

Placid, pleasant-looking Douglas Patrick Haig was in films from the age of two, continuing strongly into the era of talkies.

25 Dynamite's Daughter
26 The Scarlet Letter
      The Strong Man
27 Fireman Save My Child
      The Gingham Girl
      Wings
28 The Family Group

Sugaring the pill: Douglas Haig with Emil Jannings in Sins of the Fathers

      Fools for Luck
      Sins of the Fathers
      The Street of Sin
29 Betrayal
      Welcome Danger
30 Caught Short
31 The Cisco Kid
      Skippy
32 Attorney for the Defense
33 The Return of Casey Jones
      That's My Boy
35 Man's Best Friend

Jean Mercanton

FRANCE

b: 17 May 20 (Marseille)
d: 4 Nov 47 (Paris)

Hughie Green ◇ was lucky to have Harry Tate for a godfather: Jean Mercanton had Sarah Bernhardt for a godmother. He also had one of France's leading film directors, Louis Mercanton, for father, and made his screen debut, at the age of 17 days, in the arms of another legendary French actress, Réjane. (The film, *Miarka*, was her last; she died the same year.)

Forbearing to push his luck, Jean stayed in the nursery for the next four years, before appearing as a tot in Louis Mercanton's serial *Les deux gosses*, which starred Lewis Shaw ◇ and Jean Forest ◇. By the late 1920s the career of this dark-eyed blond child was well under way, usually

but not always working for his father. (*Toute sa vie*, incidentally, was the French version of *Sarah and Son*.)

While directing *Passionnément*, Jean's father, Louis Mercanton, died, and it was three years before the boy appeared on screen again – in a film suitably entitled *Les grands* (The big boys), for Jean was now rising 16. His career, it turned out, was far from finished. Without quite being star material, the personable youth was much in demand for the next ten years, with important roles in *Le petit chose* and *Trois de Saint-Cyr* (38), and the lead in the unfinished *Air pur* of 1939, aborted at outbreak of war.

After a further dozen or so films, Jean Mercanton had another lead in *Désarroi* (46). Then, late in 1947, ill luck dealt its last card: on November 4 he died, a victim of the current polio epidemic.

20 Miarka, la fille à l'ourse
        (Miarka and the she-bear)
24 Les deux gosses (The two boys)
26 La petite bonne du Palace
        (The maid at the Palace)
27 Croquette
      Le passager (The passenger)
28 Vénus
29 Le mystère de la Villa Rose

Jean Mercanton, circa 1926

(The mystery of the Villa Rose)
30 A mi-chemin du ciel (Halfway to heaven)
L'arlésienne (The girl from Arles)
L'enfant de l'amour (The child of love)
La lettre (The letter)
Toute sa vie (All her life)
31 Une idée de génie (A brilliant idea)
Il est charmant (He is charming)
Marions-nous (Let's get married)
Le meeting
Ohé! Ohé! (Hi! Hi!)
Princesse, à vos ordres
  (At your service, Princess)
Les rois mages (The Magi)
Sur le tas de sable (On the sand-heap)
32 Avec l'assurance (With the insurance)
Cognasse (Mr Quince)
La femme poisson (The woman-fish)
Monsieur Albert
Les rivaux de la piste (Rivals of the track)
Stupéfiants (Narcotics)
33 Passionnément (Passionately)

Jackie Searl

USA

b: 7 Jly 20 (Anaheim, California)

In an age of clever kids, Jackie Searl was one of the cleverest. He started his professional career on radio at the age of three, and became well known on a Los Angeles children's programme in the mid-Twenties, chattering away as 'Orange County Buddy'. He made his film debut at six, and got a lead, with Donald Haines ◇, in a forgotten series called the 'Smitty' comedies; but, cleverness apart, there was no sign that this was to be a child actor out of the main stream.

Then, around his tenth birthday, Searl was cast as Sid – the hero's mean, sneaky kid brother – in the Jackie Coogan ◇ *Tom Sawyer*. In fact, it was an unequal contest, with the great Coogan past his childhood prime and Searl just entering his own: the junior monster's glee in treachery was exhilarating to watch, and almost stole the film. Paramount smartly put him on contract.

From this moment Jackie realised that there could be fame and wealth in being unlovable. His shrewd little face gleaming with spite, he was seen in a series of films,

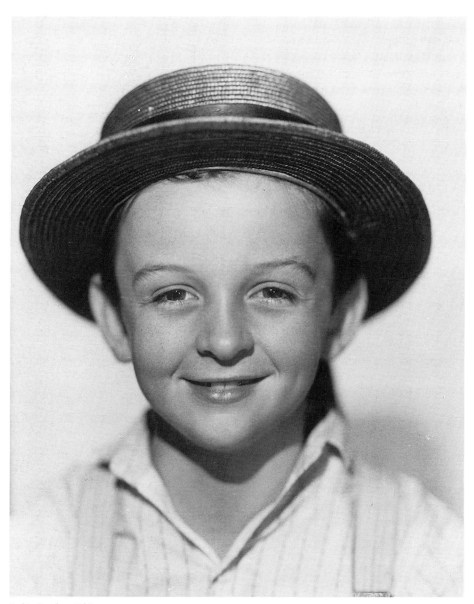

Jackie Searl as Sid Sawyer

pitted against the 'good-hearted toughs' of the period – Jackie Cooper ◇, Mickey Rooney ◇, Jane Withers. They would be allowed to rout him in the end (since good is supposed to triumph over evil), but not before he had inflicted considerable psychological damage along the way. Searl became known as 'The Snitching Sissy', 'The Sandbox Attila', 'The Kid Everybody Wants to Spank' – and it suited him just fine.

He had occasional holidays from meanness: he was, for instance, the wounded son of an Irish cop, adopted by a Jewish antique dealer, in *Hearts of Humanity*, and a memorable Dormouse in the 1933 *Alice in Wonderland*. But what his public still loved most of all was to see the pretty little features twist into a snarl or a sneer.

Now well into his teens, Searl (occasion-ally misspelt Searle) continued to enlarge his gallery of meanies, snurges and smart alecs. He was, naturally, the false claimant in the 1936 *Little Lord Fauntleroy*; he was again a rival (amorous, this time) of Jackie Cooper in *That Certain Age* (38), for the affections of Deanna Durbin; he was in famous comedies like *My Little Chickadee* (40) and *The Paleface* (48). He can sometimes be seen as a dubious customer propping up a Western bar. But the parts dwindled, and by the Sixties he was semi-retired and devoting most of his energies to business, though he appeared now and then on TV.

Allen 'Farina' Hoskins

USA

b: 9 Aug 20 (Boston, Mass.)
d: 26 Jly 80 (Oakland, California)

The first thing to say about 'Farina' (named after a breakfast cereal) is that despite those terrible braids and ribbons he had one of the most beautiful faces of any of the world's child actors – a perfect oval with enchantingly gentle, humorous eyes and a smile that could melt mountains. We can only regret that all too often in 'Our Gang' he was required to weep

Sky high fly: a well-guarded 'Farina' Hoskins

(which he did with virtuoso facility) or goggle in craven fear. Acting had little dignity for a black performer in those dear, deadly days.

When he was still a baby his family moved to Los Angeles, and before he was two Hal Roach's spies, possibly tipped off by Ernie Morrison ◇, had spotted him and gathered him in for the master's approval. Little did the child know it, but he was to be with the Gang for ten years and 106 comedy shorts – the all-time in-Gang record. Roach developed a particular admiration and affection for him, and he was one of only three Gang stalwarts to be

retained after the arrival of sound. (The other two being Mary Ann Jackson and 'Wheezer' Hutchins ◇.)

Thanks to his bizarre coiffure, and the fact that he wore a dress and had a name ending with 'a', it was generally assumed by the public that Farina was a girl. (Not just demeaned but unsexed.) Then after a year or two the garb became recognisably masculine, and in spite of the spring-loaded coils of hair Farina was acknowledged as a chap.

His last appearance as a Gang regular was in the spring of 1931, though (with Mickey Daniels ◇, Mary Kornman and

Farina as emcee of The Voice of Hollywood

Joe Cobb ◇) he made a guest comeback in *Fish Hooky* in 1933. Later that year he and other Gangers also took part in a charity short called *The Stolen Jools,* and in No.13 of the 'Voice of Hollywood' one-reelers he was Master of Ceremonies.

Apart from a split-second materialisation in *After the Thin Man* (36), this was about the end of Allen Hoskins' movie career. He and his sister Jannie (who had sometimes been seen as 'Mango' in the Gang comedies) took a vaudeville act around the States.

After World War Two service in the South Pacific, Hoskins studied drama and got qualifications, but no jobs – even with

Hal Roach. Eventually, disillusioned, he left the scenes of his triumphs and moved north to Alameda, near San Francisco. There, with a loving wife and six children, he built a new and valuable career working with psychologically disturbed and mentally retarded people. 'Farina' was as sweet a guy as he always looked.

22-31 'Our Gang' comedies' *(105)*
32 You Said a Mouthful
33 Fish Hooky ('OG')
   The Life of Jimmy Dolan
   The Mayor of Hell
   The Stolen Jools
35 Reckless

Derek Blomfield

BRITAIN

b: 31 Aug 20 (London)
d: 21 Jly 64 (Brittany)

His father was a doctor, his mother, Rosamond Sheila Lehmann, was not the novelist. His best part was in *Turn of the Tide,* as a boy in a Yorkshire fishing village: doing a brave stab at a Yorkshire accent, he is hugely likeable. His role in *Emil* is not a leading one.

Blomfield continued to act until his early death; but he was hampered by a painfully nervous smile, and tended to get landed with 'jolly decent' parts.

32 Love On Wheels
35 Emil and the Detectives
   Turn of the Tide
36 Shipmates o' Mine
   Wedding Group

Derek Blomfield with J. Fisher White in The Turn of the Tide

Horst Teetzmann

GERMANY

b: 30 Aug 20

Teetzmann, an upstanding blond with a faint touch of Mickey Rooney ◇, claimed to speak perfect English because he had worked for MGM in Hollywood. (Nature of work unspecified.)

The 1935 *Weisse Hölle vom Piz Palü* was the expanded, talkie version of Arnold Fanck's 1929 mountaineering classic.

Horst Teetzmann continued busily throughout the Thirties, and was in one or two important pieces like *Zu neuen Ufern* (37); but much of his work was in short comedies or in dubbing of American films.

34 Mausi (Mousie)
   La Paloma
   Die rosarote Brille
     (Rose-coloured spectacles)
35 Anekdoten um den alten Fritz
     (Stories about Old Fritz)
   Familie Schimek (The Schimeks)
   Hilde Petersen postlagernd
     (Hilde Petersen, poste restante)
   Stützen der Gesellschaft (Pillars of Society)
   Die weisse Hölle vom Piz Palü
     (The white hell of Piz Palü)

Mickey Rooney

USA

b: 23 Sep 20 (Brooklyn, N.Y.C.)

Joseph Yule, Jr. – for so he was born – came of yeoman vaudeville stock, and at 11 months was carried on stage in best traditional style. At two he had become part of the Yules' act, and at four he went to seek his fortune in Hollywood, where the first part he landed was that of a midget. (Rooney has never been large, and it is safe to assume that at four he was even less so.) He auditioned for a job with 'Our Gang', but Hal Roach wasn't much taken with him.

A year later things really started to move. A series was being planned, based on the cartoon kid 'Mickey McGuire' from the comic strip 'Toonerville Folks'. Five-

Better than one: Stymie Beard (left) shares a barrel with Farina

year-old Joe Junior got the lead, and celebrated by ditching his own name and simply becoming, for professional purposes, Mickey McGuire. The larger-than-life character, brash and bossy, suited him to a T. Wearing a fractured bowler hat, he ruled over a gang including such picturesque personnel as Stinky Davis, Hambone Johnson, Katink', and Teeth McDuff. There was also the Kid Brudder, plus a token girl (Tomboy Taylor) and a token gnome (Billy Barty ◇).

From *Mickey's Battle* in 1927 to *Mickey's Holiday* in 1932, the series ran to a total of 33 two-reelers before he quit to pursue a wider career. (It tottered on briefly without him, then collapsed.) Since the name McGuire went with the job, he needed to find a new one. Mickey Looney? suggested someone, perhaps with a Chinese accent. So Mickey Rooney he became.

His first good part as an independent was in a racetrack drama called *Fast Companions*, starring (as a jockey) the former boy actor Tom Brown ◇; Mickey showed he was a real person, not just the sassy automaton of the past few years. His air of a streetwise piglet stood him in good stead in the louche urban surroundings of early crime talkies, and he was equally at home in the worlds of the stage (*Broadway to Hollywood*) or the circus (*The Big Cage*). He was a natural comic – and he could act.

By the mid-Thirties Mickey Rooney's was a 'household face' to Americans. He also caught the eye of a distinguished Austrian exile, the director Max Reinhardt, who audaciously cast him as Puck in an open-air production of 'A Midsummer Night's Dream'.

In 1935 this evolved into a spectacular film, with Mickey still in the part which by

ABOVE: *Mickey Rooney in* Fast Companions
BELOW: *with Clyde Beatty in* The Big Cage

now was second nature to him. Tiny horns peeping through the blond locks, armed with nothing but a furry loincloth and a manic giggle, his is an amazing creation. He describes weird vocal arabesques – relishing the text almost too well – snorts and gambols with uninhibited grace. There is something authentically wild about him. True, the giggle is overdone and he is often exhausting, but no doubt Puck would be exhausting. As a mocking urchin-sprite, certainly, Rooney is unbeatable, taunting the baffled quartet of lovers with cooing or belligerent voices.

He was the younger brother in a film version of Eugene O'Neill's *Ah, Wilderness!* (he would be the elder brother in *Summer Holiday*, the musical remake of 1948); and in 1937, as good-hearted New York bootblack Dick in *Little Lord Fauntleroy*, was teamed for the first time with his antithesis, the cool, fastidious Briton, Freddie Bartholomew ◇.

The Devil Is a Sissy (retitled by the British – who could not bear rude words – *The Devil Takes the Count*) in fact came after *Fauntleroy*, reprising in a modern setting the chalk-and-cheese relationship with Bartholomew which had been so effective in Victorian dress. They were to meet again in 1937 in *Captains Courageous*, and in 1938 in *Lord Jeff*.

At this point, with diminutive Rooney coming up to his 16th birthday, about to assume for the first time (in *A Family Affair*) the persona of Andy Hardy, and to team up for the first time (in *Thoroughbreds Don't Cry*) with Judy Garland, we had better concede that he is now a teenager and no longer a child. He will steadily get tubbier – and so will Garland – during their nine films together. The Andy Hardies will puff on till 1946, with an ill-judged resurrection in 1958 (*Andy Hardy Comes Home*, in which Mickey's son Teddy makes his film bow).

And Mickey's golden reputation – in 1938 he was given a special Academy Award for 'bringing to the screen the spirit and personification of youth' – will become sadly tarnished, as his talent coarsens into cliche. 'By his own admission,' wrote David Shipman, 'Rooney was bumptious and big-headed at this time . . . . Qualities which had sat well on him as a youngster now began to look like aggressiveness; and he was the same off-screen as on, which meant that he had enemies.'

Rooney was not stupid, though, and had the ability to learn from his mistakes. In the Fifties and Sixties he carved himself out a solid new career as a character actor – not all fury and self-indulgence now, but at last some realism and some hard-won reticence. He is still there, past 70 and looking good, a rubbery, reassuring little Hollywood landmark.

26 Not To Be Trusted
27 Orchids and Ermine
27-32 'Mickey McGuire' comedies
32 The Beast of the City
   Fast Companions
   High Speed
   My Pal the King
   Sin's Pay Day
33 The Big Cage
   The Big Chance
   Broadway to Hollywood
   The Chief
   The Life of Jimmy Dolan
   The Lost Jungle *(serial)*
   Officer Thirteen
   The World Changes
34 Beloved
   Blind Date
   Chained
   Death on the Diamond
   Half a Sinner
   Hide-Out
   I Like It That Way
   The Lost Jungle
   The Love Birds
   Manhattan Melodrama
   Upperworld
35 Ah, Wilderness!
   The County Chairman
   The Healer
   A Midsummer Night's Dream
   Reckless
   Riffraff
36 The Devil Is a Sissy
   Down the Stretch
   Little Lord Fauntleroy

RIGHT: *Billy Kent Schaffer with Viola Dana in* The Ice Flood

Billy Kent Schaeffer

USA

b: 26 Sep 20

An appealing fair-haired child who resembled a baggy-eyed Ricky Schroder ◇, little Schaeffer was – like his rather similar predecessor Walter Wilkinson ◇ – mainly employed in open-air action dramas.

A Billy Schaeffer is credited in the 1937 film *As Good As Married* – perhaps a one-off comeback.

25 The Home Maker
   The Man Without a Conscience
26 The Arizona Sweepstakes
   The Ice Flood
   Lost at Sea
   The Truthful Sex
27 The Enemy
   Hills of Kentucky
   Simple Sis
28 Warming Up
   The Wind

Ronnie Hepworth

BRITAIN

b: 1920 (Italy)

Ronnie and his younger brothers Henry and John – who all acted in British films of the mid-Thirties – were great-nephews of the famous Sir Charles Hawtrey (1858-1923).

Ronnie, a brown-eyed version of William (James) Fox ◇ in the next generation, had the same tousled prep-school charm, though he was much too posh for the accordion-playing hero of his biggest hit, *Danny Boy*. This shamelessly sentimental story was to be remade a mere seven years later with the slightly younger Grant Tyler ◇.

33 Channel Crossing
   Dick Turpin
34 Danny Boy
   Grand Prix
36 Cock o' the North
   Conquest of the Air

Ronnie's blond younger brothers (who followed him at intervals of about a year apiece) were with him in *Channel Crossing* and *Dick Turpin*, and without him in *Men of Yesterday* (37).

HENRY HEPWORTH was also in *The Broken Rosary* (34), *The City of Beautiful Nonsense* (34) and *Housemaster* (38); while the round-faced JOHN HEPWORTH had quite a big role in *Land Without Music* (36) and a near-invisible one in Britain's first Technicolor feature, *Wings of the Morning* (37).

Dorothy Dickson and Ronnie Hepworth in Danny Boy

Bobby Burns

GERMANY

b: circa 1920 (Berlin)

Not to be confused with the American comic Bob Burns (1893-1956), plump little Bobby – real name Robert Müller – was the only native boy actor apart from Gustl Stark-Gstettenbaur ◇ well known enough to be featured in a German series of film fan postcards in early 1930. He was

also described, fatuously, as 'the world's youngest film-star'. The American reviewer in 'Variety', for one, was unimpressed by his talents.

28 Hotelgeheimnisse (Hotel secrets)
   Mary Lou
   Mein Herz ist eine Jazzband
      (My heart is a jazz band)
29 Bobby, der Benzinjunge
      (Bobby the petrol kid)
   Giftgas (Poison gas)
30 Der weisse Teufel (The white devil)

Frankie Thomas

USA

b: 9 Apr 21 (New York)

His parents (Frank M. Thomas and Mona Bruns) were both actors, and Frank Junior was carried on stage at nine months, thereby beating Mickey Rooney ◇. He nearly beat him to something with farther-reaching consequences: he was originally cast to play Andy Hardy in *A Family*

Affair, and was only replaced by Rooney at the last minute.

This blue-eyed boy, with wavy blond hair, had an expression of such indolent sensuality that it's a miracle he could bestir himself to do any seriously committed acting. That he could, however, is attested by his work in five Broadway plays during the early Thirties. He got particularly glowing notices in 1934 for his performance in 'Wednesday's Child'. Unusually – for stage actors tend to be thrust aside on such occasions – when RKO decided to film it, in the same year, they did so with Frankie.

The raves were repeated, and the following year he had the lead in a remake of Ouida's story *A Dog of Flanders*. He was also tested for the title role in MGM's *David Copperfield*, but the British-bred Freddie Bartholomew ◇ not surprisingly got it. Frankie Thomas had come late to Hollywood, and he was nearly 15 when he got a plum part in the Universal serial *Tim Tyler's Luck*.

O.P. Heggie and Frankie Thomas in A Dog of Flanders

For some time hereafter his screen realm was that of adolescence, delinquent or otherwise: *Boys Town, Little Tough Guys in Society, The Angels Wash Their Faces, Code of the Streets*. At the very end of the Thirties he at least found respectability and a solid job as boy friend of a girl detective (former child star Bonita Granville) in the *Nancy Drew* films, and with Kay Francis in *Always In My Heart* (42).

After World War Two he had the title role, on TV and radio simultaneously, in the sci-fi series 'Tom Corbett, Space Cadet' (1950-55). Then he turned to TV writing ('My True Story') and producing ('Four Star Theater'). He is now retired from show business, but instead a famous expert on bridge.

34 Wednesday's Child
35 A Dog of Flanders
37 Tim Tyler's Luck *(serial)*

Robert Lynen

FRANCE

b: 24 May 21 (Jura)
d: 1 Apr 44 (Karlsruhe, Germany)

Though both Robert's parents were artistic, neither was of the cinema: his father was a painter, his mother a former singer of American extraction.

The boy was a strange selection, on the face of it, to portray 'Carrots', the tragically misunderstood hero of Jules Renard's story, in its first sound version in 1932. (The director, Duvivier, had already made a successful silent one seven years earlier.) He had no previous acting experience, and his dreamy, poetic air didn't suggest the mischievousness that was a necessary part of Poil de Carotte's makeup. But, with the scenario tailored to fit his very different temperament, and Alexandre Tansman's music to create a haunting atmosphere, the frail, skinny Lynen, peering through a mist of freckles, is unforgettable.

Overnight, Robert became France's favourite child. The public longed to see him rescued from rural misery: very well then, he should become a boy king (*Le petit roi*), and have royalty thrust on him again a few years later (*L'éducation du prince*). But he should also continue from time to time to embrace poverty (*Sans famille, Le petit chose*).

Lynen really was a star. He was neither good-looking, nor cute, nor funny, nor even particularly boyish. On the contrary, he was a pale, delicate creature (without benefit of freckles) with a soft, rather feminine profile. But there was sweetness and intelligence and a kind of gallantry

Robert Lynen, the 1932 'Poil de Carotte'.

about him that touched all hearts.

Of his eight remaining films, one was Duvivier's famous *Un carnet de bal* (37), and there were to be two more star roles in 1938, in *L'éducation du prince* and *Le petit chose*. He was also featured in *Mollenard* (37), *Le fraudeur* (37) and *La vie est magnifique* (38). But the shadows were gathering around Robert Lynen. In 1937 his unstable father had killed himself by jumping from a fifth-floor window; and in September 1939 France went to war.

Lynen was in two more films: *Espoirs* (40) and *Cap au large* (42). The latter had been filmed in the Zone Libre, and on February 7, 1943, soon after its completion, he was arrested by German security agents and charged with being a Resistance fighter. He was imprisoned at Marseilles, then moved to Fresnes and finally across the border to Karlsruhe, where he was executed on April Fool's Day, 1944. Heroes don't always look like heroes.

A year earlier, as it happened, Robert's father in *Poil de Carotte*, the great Harry Baur, had died after being arrested and tortured by the Germans.

32 Poil de Carotte (Carrots)
33 Le petit roi (The little king)
34 Sans famille (No relations)
35 Son autre amour (His other love)
36 La belle équipe (The great team)
   L'homme du jour (Man of the day)

Henkie Klein

HOLLAND

b: 1 Jne 21 (Amsterdam)

The boy's real name, like his father's, was Heinrich Kleinmann. Heinrich Senior was a Dutch film distributor who moved to Germany in the early Twenties and began to direct films under the name of Henk Kleinman (dropping his final N). But he was consumptive, and could only complete a handful of films, some of them featuring his small son. The boy had a quaint, sad face, and was promoted as 'the Dutch Jackie Coogan', though his career was inevitably too slender to merit the claim.

Henkie Klein in Droomkoninkje

Only his first two films could be said to have starred Henkie. *Amsterdam* was really a documentary, with a couple of acted scenes, and the talkie *Hollands jeugd* was left unfinished for lack of funds. Henk senior was obliged to move back to Germany a second time, and work in the documentary section of UFA.

The boy received an offer to go to Hollywood, but his father would have been too frail to make the journey, and his mother wanted to stay with him, so nothing could be done. Henkie returned to Holland after the War, and sold photographic goods at Schiphol Airport.

25 Stille Nacht, heilige Nacht
   (Silent night, holy night – GE)
26 Droomkoninkje
   (Little dream king – NL/GE)
28 Amsterdam (NL)
30 Zeemansvrouwen (Sailors' wives – NL)
34 Hollands jeugd (Dutch youth – NL)

Harry Watson

USA

b: 31 Aug 1921 (Los Angeles)

The second of six Watson brothers who prospered in Hollywood throughout the Twenties and Thirties – Coy ◊, Harry, Billy ◊, Delmar ◊, Garry and Bobs ◊ – was plump and jolly. He can be seen tormenting W.C. Fields in *The Barber Shop*, then tormented by Fred Astaire in *A Damsel in Distress*, and as the second lead with Billy Mauch ◊ in *Penrod and Sam*. (What was less evident in *The Barber Shop* was that he was helpfully carrying Fields's gin supply hidden in a prop.)

The younger Watsons, 1935: Harry at no. 3

In his mid-teens, Harry continued in *Kid-napped* (38), *Little Miss Broadway* (38) and, with three other Watsons, in *Mr Smith Goes to Washington* (39). After World War Two, he joined his five brothers in the family photographic studio, and was also in demand as a newspaper and TV photographer.

Jackie Cooper

USA

b: 15 Sep 21 (Los Angeles)

His name has been variously rendered as (1) John Cooper, Junior, (2) John Cooperman, Junior and (3) James Bigelow. His father, at any rate – who left home when Jackie was two – acted in silent film comedies as Jack Cooper; his mother, Mabel Bigelow, was a professional pianist, later a secretary at 20th Century Fox; and his uncle was the prolific director Norman Taurog. So there was no lack of screen pedigree.

Taurog, who had himself been a boy actor, was busy around 1925 directing Lloyd Hamilton's two-reel comedies, and cast his characterful nephew in some of them, billing him (this does not get easier) as Leonard Cooper. Jackie – as we shall

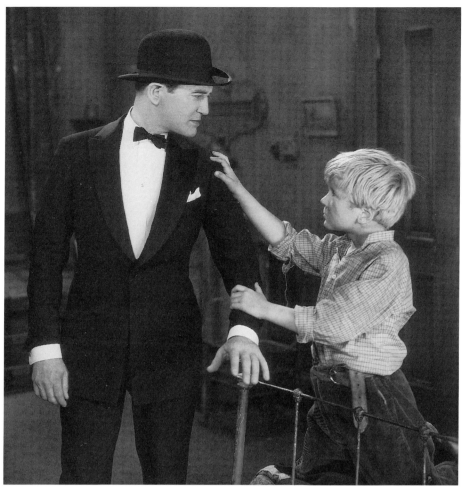

Jackie Cooper with Richard Dix in Young Donovan's Kid

continue to call him – also appeared with the comedian Bobby Clark.

In 1929 he graduated to feature films (not his uncle's) and also became a leading member of 'Our Gang', with whom he remained till 1931 and his break into the big time with *Skippy* and its sequel, *Sooky*. Both were directed by Taurog, and both also featured Jackie Coogan's kid brother Robert ◇. Between them came *The Champ*, directed by King Vidor.

Skippy, which won Cooper an Academy Award nomination, was a huge popular hit, and until the mid-Thirties he was big box-office – in fact he and Shirley Temple were to be the screen's last child superstars. No later child has approached their universal acclaim.

Unlike Temple, Cooper had neither beauty of face nor of voice. He achieved what he did solely through personality

and talent. His tough, vehement ten-year-old manner was endearingly comic, and when he jerked the tears (as he was doing even, now and then, with 'Our Gang') he did so with genuine pathos and a certain tact – not the maudlin barnstorming which Rooney would sometimes lay on. With an 'Aw, gee . . .' the defiant face would begin to melt, the lower lip stick out still further, and he would weep like a man. The world wept with him.

His four-time partnership with Wallace Beery (from *The Champ* to *Treasure Island* and *O'Shaughnessy's Boy*) was an inspired pairing of rough diamonds – often, as in *The Bowery*, almost like a married relationship, with tantrums, jealousies, stormings-out and tearful reconciliations. (There are even 'infidelities': on one occasion Jackie storms out and shacks up with George Raft instead.) When disreputable Beery totters home after a late night out, Cooper the home-maker is virtually waiting behind the door with frying-pan poised. It's a funny and tender parody of the real thing, though to imply it's *not* real is to underestimate it.

By 1936 Cooper was becoming too big to be cute, but his popularity lasted through the Thirties, with characteristic leads in *Boy of the Streets* (37), *Gangster's Boy* (38) and the serial *Scouts to the Rescue* (39). Also in 1939 he played Henry Aldrich in *What a Life*, when Clifford Goldsmith's successful Broadway play was filmed, and again in *Life With Henry* in 1941. Thereafter, Jimmy Lydon took over the role for the nine remaining 'Henry Aldrich' movies.

In the late Forties, having returned from the war, Jackie was reunited with both Coogan brothers ◇ in the dismal comedies *Kilroy Was Here* and *French Leave*. These depressed him so much that for a decade or so he devoted himself to the stage, including a nation-wide tour with 'Mr Roberts'. Then in 1955 he got the chance to direct and star in a TV sitcom called 'The People's Choice' (sharing the limelight with a 'talking' basset-hound called Cleo). It ran for three years, and he

followed it up with 'Hennessy' (a further three years), in which he was a Navy doctor.

He directed his first feature film, *Stand Up and Be Counted*, in 1972, and occasionally appears as an actor in the cinema — for instance in *Chosen Survivors* (74) and the *Superman* films — or on TV. Jackie Cooper is still very much in business.

29 Sunnyside Up
Three Live Ghosts
Fox Movietone Follies of 1929
'Our Gang' *(4 shorts)*
30 'Our Gang' *(8)*
31 'Our Gang' *(3)*
The Champ
Jackie Cooper's Christmas Party
Skippy
Sooky
Young Donovan's Kid
32 Divorce in the Family
When a Feller Needs a Friend
33 The Bowery
Broadway to Hollywood
Lost
34 Lone Cowboy
Peck's Bad Boy
Treasure Island
35 Dinky
O'Shaughnessy's Boy
36 The Devil is a Sissy
Tough Guy

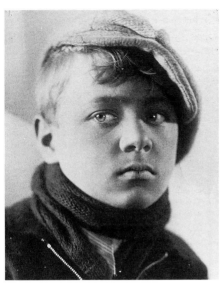

Hallberg, the 1934 'Anderssonskans Kalle'.

Nils Hallberg

SWEDEN

b: 18 Sep 21 (Stockholm)

Nils Hallberg's career started at the top, when he played Sweden's equivalent of Tom Sawyer, the village boy Kalle (hero of a long-popular children's book).

For the next half-century or so Hallberg seldom stopped working: he had been in another 90 films by 1972. He's probably best remembered as 'Freddy Sjöström' in the Hillman series, made between 1958 and 1963. He has also directed in the theatre.

34 Anderssonskans Kalle
(The Anderssons' Kalle)
35 Flickornas Alfred (Their darling Alfred)
Grabbarna i 57:an (The kids at No. 57)
36 Fröken blir piga (From Miss to maid)
Stackars miljonärer (Poor millionaires)
37 Lyckliga Vestköping (Lucky Vestköping)

Jimmy Butler

USA

b: 24 Sep 21
d: 18 Feb 45 (France)

Butler was dark, square-faced, manly, and not the most exciting of performers. Because of his intelligence and solid merits

Jackie Cooper (centre) in Dinky. *One from left, George Ernest; on right, Sidney Miller*

he made a useful career, but he was temperamentally incapable of bringing off a star part and was wisely never given one. He could supply decent pathos or rational enthusiasm.

After a dozen or so more films in his later teens, including *Boys Town* and *Shopworn Angel* (both 1938), Jimmy Butler was one of the few American ex-child-actors to be killed in action in World War Two.

31 The Bad Sister
33 Beloved
   Only Yesterday
34 I'll Fix It
   Manhattan Melodrama
   Mrs Wiggs of the Cabbage Patch
   No Greater Glory
   Romance in Manhattan
35 The Awakening of Jim Burke
   The Dark Angel
   Dinky
   Laddie
   When a Man's a Man
37 Battle of Greed
   The County Fair
   Stella Dallas
   Wells Fargo

David Durand

USA

b: 29 Sep 21 (Los Angeles)

The dark, handsome David Durrant (his real name) first achieved fame as a radio prodigy known as 'Little Boy Blue'. One of his earliest ventures into screen work was with 'Our Gang' (in *Uncle Tom's Uncle*), but it didn't lead to Gang membership. This didn't matter. Durand, a better-looking Frankie Darro ◇, did very well indeed.

Like Frankie Thomas ◇ (who had the lead in *Wednesday's Child*), Dave Durand later joined Hollywood's's teenage pool of urban delinquency: *Angels With Dirty Faces, A Criminal Is Born, Streets of New York* and *Boys' Reformatory* will do for 1938-39 starters. And though the personable youth was sometimes allowed to represent sterling qualities *(Scouts to the Rescue; Kirk of the Campus; Naval Academy)* it still

Exit bumping: David Durand with Charles Winninger in Bad Sister

didn't add up to the sort of career such a gifted boy had had a right to expect.

One of his last featured acting roles was in *Million Dollar Kid* (44).

Durand in Viva Villa!

26 Uncle Tom's Uncle ('OG')
27 Get Your Man
28 Tropic Madness
29 Innocents of Paris
   The Song of Love
30 Jazz Cinderella
   Ladies Love Brutes
   Live and Learn
31 Bad Sister
   Rich Man's Folly
   The Spy
32 Forbidden Company
   Probation
   Robinson Crusoe and Son
   Silver Dollar
33 Cradle Song
   The Great Jasper
   Jennie Gerhardt
   The Life of Jimmy Dolan
   Son of the Border
34 As the Earth Turns
   The Band Plays On
   Hat, Coat and Glove
   Little Men
   Wednesday's Child
   Viva Villa!

George Ernest

USA

b: 20 Nov 21 (Pittsfield, Mass.)

The importance of George's being Ernest is obvious when you consider that his real (Danish) surname was Hjørth, which might have choked the average movie-goer. He had wavy fairish hair and an amiable, unmemorable, long-jawed face. The Hjørths had moved to California when George was two and he got his first film experience three years later.

Like so many others, he had a trial outing or two with 'Our Gang' (in 1931) without becoming a regular. He became a familiar film kid in the mid-Thirties, particularly as the middle son in the 'Jones Family' series. (The smallest Jones boy was BILLY MAHAN ◇, who didn't appear in many non-Jones pictures.)

The Joneses pressed on till 1940, and George Ernest with them. He was in *Stardust on the Sage* (42), but then the war caught up with him, and he didn't return to the screen after it.

George Ernest in Too Many Parents

Claude Machin

FRANCE

b: 1921

Claude, or 'Clo-Clo' as he was always called, was a late child of the versatile director Alfred Machin (1877-1929). Machin was famous at the start and end of his career for his wild-life photography. To begin with he had filmed big-game hunting, but latterly preferred to train and work with live animals.

Fair-haired Clo-Clo, who had appeared in Machin's movies from a tender age, became in the last two before his father's death a sort of tiny white (non-lethal) hunter, friend rather than killer of the jungle beasts. Some of these were faked – a huge snake for instance – but most were real, and Clo-Clo was genuinely at ease with them. When his particular pet, the chimpanzee Auguste, died, Clo-Clo is said to have wept for a week. But he also had human companionship in the jungle films, in the shape of a little black boy of his own age called 'Colibri' (Humming-Bird).

Before editing had finished on the last film – also known as *Robinson Junior* – Alfred Machin suddenly died, and Clo-Clo's career came to an end. Apart from the 1928 co-production, directed by Guido Brignone (though Machin scripted it), he had only worked for his father.

Freddie Burke Frederick

USA

b: 13 Jan 22 (San Francisco)
d: 31 Jan 86 (Glendale, Cal.)

This fair, solemn, broad-browed child was unrelated to Pauline Frederick (with whom he appeared in *Evidence*). He was in movies from the age of one, in Joe Rock comedies, and then in Mack Sennett's 'Smith Family' series. In 1928 he played the hero's little son in King Vidor's faintly repulsive masterpiece *The Crowd*.

For his performance in *Evidence*, the following year, he amassed some of the most glowing reviews a child actor can ever

Clo-Clo Machin with 'Colibri' (left) and serpent in Black and White

Freddy Frederick and Conway Tearle in Evidence

have had. 'He is a gallant, mannerly, intelligent, good looking little fellow,' wrote the Chicago Tribune, 'with the poise of an ambassador quaintly sitting on the shoulders of the genuine simplicity of childhood. He is completely real, understandable and appealing.'

'His understanding of dramatic situations is almost unbelievable,' said one columnist; 'winsome yet manly,' gasped another. The Philadelphia Inquirer reckoned him a leading contender for Jackie Coogan's ◇ crown; the 'Chicago Daily Times' called him 'the sensation of the picture', and 'Motion Picture News' judged him 'adorable . . . a profusion of work will come tumbling his way.'

And so, for a time, it did.

In 1933, aged eleven and rich in experience, Master Frederick should have been in his pomp, the terrible teens only on a far horizon: yet no more significant parts seem to have come his way, though

he was still advertising himself in the trade directories, somewhat forlornly, in 1937. It can't have been his voice, since this had been specifically praised in his early talkies. What went wrong?

26 Fangs of Justice
   Fast Freight
28 The Crowd
   The Latest from Paris
   Marry the Girl
29 Blue Skies
   Evidence
   Mamba
   New Year's Eve
30 Jazz Cinderella
   Ladies Love Brutes
   Let Us Be Gay
   Mothers Cry
   Redemption
   Second Wife
   Viennese Nights
   Wall Street
31 The Spy
   Up for Murder
33 The Iron Master

Helle Winther

SWEDEN

b: 31 Mar 22 (Trelleborg)

As urchin or office boy, the comically doleful little Helle was a valued face in Swedish films of the Thirties. (Like England's David Hannaford ◇ later.)

31 Brokiga blad (Miscellany)
32 Ett skepp kommer lastet
   (A ship and its cargo)
   Skråköpings Rundradio inviges
   (Radio Skråköping takes the air)
   Svarta rosor (Black roses)
33 Bomans pojke (Boman's boy)
35 Tjocka släkten (Close relatives)
36 Kvartetten som sprängdes
   (The quartet that split up)
37 Än leva de gamla gudar
   (The old gods live still)
   En flicka kommer till stan
   (A girl comes to the city)
38 Svensson ordnar allt (Leave it to Svensson)

Winther in Tjocka släkten

Eric Pavitt

BRITAIN

b: 7 Jly 22 (Poplar, London)

Eric was a dark, handsome boy who came from a theatrical family, both his parents and two sisters treading the boards.

In *Strip, Strip, Hooray!* he was with Freddie Bartholomew ◇ (nearly two years

Eric Pavitt educates Will Hay in Dandy Dick

his junior) before the latter crossed the
Atlantic to become Hollywood's little
Englishman. Probably his best part came
in *My Friend the King*, one of Michael
Powell's very earliest films, which Powell
also scripted. Eric played a sailor-suited
boy King, befriended by a taxi-driver
(Jerry Verno).

He also had leads in *The Bells of St
Mary's, Stamboul* and *Children of the Fog*,
and scenes with Will Hay in *Dandy Dick.*
More humbly, he was a member of the
Buggins family in *Radio Parade.*

Until the war caught him up, Pavitt
continued to appear in films such as *The
Lion Has Wings* (39) and *Gestapo* (1940).
He didn't persevere as an actor when
it was over, but kept links with show business and ended his career as a location
manager for Thames Television.

28 The Bells of St Mary's
     Warned Off
29 Auld Lang Syne

30 The Black Hand Gang
     Greek Street
31 My Friend the King
     Stamboul
32 Reunion
     Strip, Strip, Hooray!
33 Radio Parade
34 My Old Dutch
     Paris Plane
     Sing As We Go
35 Can You Hear Me, Mother?
     Children of the Fog
     Dandy Dick
     Get Off My Foot
36 Faithful
     Find the Lady
     The Lonely Road
     Queen of Hearts
     Radio Lover
37 Dangerous Fingers

Kaoru Ito

JAPAN

b: 29 Jly 22 (Tokyo)

34 Alupusu taisho (Alpine master)
35 Otome gokoro sannin shimai
     (Three pure-hearted sisters)
     Tsumayo bara no yoni
     (Wife! Be like a rose)
     Itazura kozo (Naughty young priest)
     Enoken no Kondo Isamu
     (Enoken's Isamu Kondo)

Later films included *Chushingura* (39), *Seishun
yakyu nikki* (39), *Moyuru ozora* (40) and *Hawaii
maley oki kaisen* (42).

Eldon Gorst

BRITAIN

b: 14 Aug 22 (Scheveningen, Holland)
d: 2 Mar 50 (Los Angeles)

His father — a remarkable personality
with a passionate sense of justice — had
begun adult life as an actor, but marriage
convinced him of the need for a more reliable income and he entered the consular
service: thus it was that Eldon was born in
Holland.

After some stage experience in England
– 'A Midsummer Night's Dream', 'Where
the Rainbow Ends' – he was chosen to
play Tom Tulliver (James Mason) as a boy
in *The Mill on the Floss*, and then got a
leading part in *The Big Fella*, as a gen-
teel runaway who is given shelter by a
friendly black seaman (Paul Robeson).

Eldon – billed as 'Eldon Grant' in the
latter film – was small for his age. He had
enormous self-possession and an impish
charm which he used ruthlessly on the
great singer.

His only other screen appearance in
Britain was as a teenager in *Goodbye, Mr
Chips* (39). After his beloved father's
untimely death, his mother married a
Hungarian and the family was overtaken
by the war. The two boys succeeded in
leaving Hungary, and Eldon went to the
USA, where he joined the Royal Canadian
Air Force.

After the war, he did his best to make
a living, while keeping his mother and
sisters in Budapest supplied with food par-
cels. He was in 'Leave Her to Heaven' on
the Broadway stage (40, with Ruth

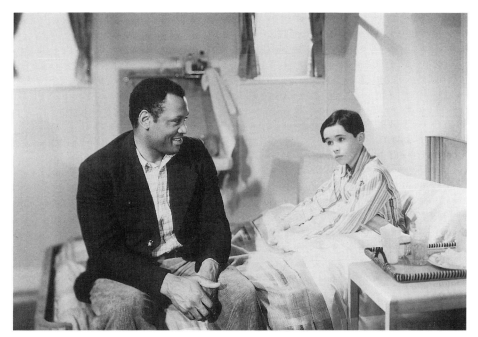

Paul Robeson and Eldon Gorst in The Big Fella

Chatterton) and in the film *The Exile* (48, with Douglas Fairbanks, Jr.). With plans of marriage, he developed a skill in cabinet-making to supplement his modest income as an actor.

Then, just as this new venture had begun to prosper, he was the innocent party in a car crash, and sustained a head injury which seriously affected his ability to concentrate and memorise. Nothing seemed left, and eventually, in despair at the ruin of his hopes, the unlucky Eldon Gorst shot himself.

37 The Big Fella
   The Mill on the Floss

Hans Fehér

AUSTRIA

b: 14 Sep 22 (Vienna)
d: 1 Apr 58 (Los Angeles)

Hans's mother was the actress Magda Sonja, his father the director Friedrich Fehér. (Fehér's real name was Weiss. He was born in 1889, studied in Vienna, acted in Germany, was director of Vienna's Renaissance-Theater 1924-25, and emigrated to Britain in 1933.)

The boy's three films were all directed by his father, the first two being triple co-productions. (In the Czech versions he was billed as 'Jeníček Fehér'. His actual name was Johann Anton Weiss.) He was a dumpy, agreeably ordinary-looking child with no great histrionic pretensions, but was fluent in Czech, German, French and English, and was said to have learned to walk the tightrope in less than a week.

In *The Robber Symphony*, a whimsical extravaganza based on a story by Anton Kuh, Hans played Giannino, the child of a

Hans Fehér in The Robber Symphony

family of strolling players who fall in with some picturesque and not-too-frightening robbers. His mother played his mother, and his father, as well as directing, conducted 'the Concordia Symphony Orchestra' in his own score. *Robber Symphony* – some of it filmed 15,000 feet up Mont Blanc – is a weird period piece which deserves an occasional airing.

After three unrewarding years in Britain, the Fehérs moved on to the USA, arriving in Los Angeles in December 1936. Friedrich eventually found paltry work directing 'soundies' – tiny cinema samplers of pop-video length, featuring bands and soloists of the time. After the war he returned to Germany, and died in Stuttgart in 1950.

Young Hans, who became a Las Vegas croupier, didn't long outlive his father.

30 Když struny lkají /Ihr Junge
      (When strings weep/Her boy –
      CS/AT/GE)
32 Štvaní lidé /Gehetzte Menschen
      (Hunted men – CS/AT/GE)
36 The Robber Symphony (GB)

Marcel Mouloudji

FRANCE

b: 16 Sep 22 (Paris)
d: 14 Jne 94

Son of an Algerian Kabyle, the amiable Marcel had plenty of film work as a boy, notably in *La guerre des gosses* (the first film version of Louis Pergaud's 'La guerre des boutons') and the school-based comedy-thriller *Les disparus de Saint-Agil*. In 1936 he was a junior member of the 'Groupe Octobre', which played in factories to audiences of striking workers.

He continued a popular French actor for the next two decades – soon dropping his first name and being billed simply as Mouloudji – in such films as *L'enfer des anges* (39), *Adieu Léonard* (43), *Boule de Suif* (45), *Les jeux sont faits* (47), *Nous sommes tous des assassins* (52) and *Rafles sur la ville* (58). From his teens onwards, though, he began to win equal celebrity as a popular

Mouloudji (left) with Serge Grave in La guerre des gosses

famous Meglin school for child actors. (The 1934 technicolor short *Show Kids* was a showcase for their products.) He appeared on Broadway in 'Tomorrow and Tomorrow' before it was filmed.

He is most often seen nowadays as the Tsarevich in *Rasputin and the Empress*.

31 Ambassador Bill
32 Rasputin and the Empress
   Strange Interlude
   Tomorrow and Tomorrow
33 The Bowery
   Broadway to Hollywood
   Bureau of Missing Persons
   The Stranger's Return
   Today We Live
34 I Give My Love
   Little Men
   No Greater Glory
   Show Kids
   You Can't Buy Everything

Clive Baxter

BRITAIN

b: 1922 (London)
d: 22 Aug 78

Clive, a handsome, serious-looking brunet – the perfect Young Gentleman – was fine for instance in the opening scenes of *The Four Feathers*. He continued to act as a young adult, with featured parts in *The Guinea Pig* (49) and *Lady Godiva Rides Again* (51).

35 Two Hearts in Harmony
37 School for Husbands
   Young and Innocent
39 The Four Feathers
41 The Ghost of St Michael's
   Ships With Wings

recording star. His first singing lead on screen was in *Tout chante autour de moi* (54).

Mouloudji also published several novels.

36 La guerre des gosses (War of the kids)
   Jenny
   Ménilmontant
37 A Venise, une nuit (One night in Venice)
   Claudine à l'école (Claudine at school)
   Mirages
38 Les disparus de Saint-Agil
      (Lost boys of Saint-Agil)
   L'entraîneuse (The lady trainer)
   Les Gaietés de l'Exposition
      (Exhibition Follies)

Tad Alexander

USA

b: 29 Dec 22 (Lexington, Nebraska)

It's a pity that this personable, brown-eyed, curly-haired boy, with intelligence to match his looks, and a pleasing name that weds the demotic with the imperial, hadn't the spark of genius to go with these advantages.

His family had moved to Los Angeles when he was a mere toddler. He was educated there, and also attended the

Ethel Barrymore and Tad Alexander in Rasputin and the Empress

Willie Kerr with John Longden in The Silence of Dean Maitland

Willie Kerr

AUSTRALIA

b: 1922 (Cape Town, South Africa)

Willie, a child of theatrical parents, was on stage from 10 weeks. He toured, and had his own act in 'tent shows'. He began broadcasting in Sydney ('the Child Discovery from Wagga Wagga'), and toured Australia in an all-boy show. He made his legitimate stage debut in Melbourne in 1931.

His role in *Harmony Row* was as 'Leonard, a precocious boy soprano', but in the 1934 film he played the tragic hero's blind son.

In 1947 Bill Kerr left Australia and moved to Britain, where he became well known as a character actor in films – such as *The Dam Busters* (55) and *The Shiralee* (57) – but most of all as the phlegmatic 'Bill' in the radio series 'Hancock's Half Hour'. Later he returned to his home country and became a sturdy pillar of the Australian acting establishment, with notable roles in *Gallipoli* (81), *Dusty* (82), *The Year of Living Dangerously* (82), *Vigil* (84), and in many TV series.

33 Harmony Row
34 The Silence of Dean Maitland

Syova Makutonin

USSR

b: circa 1922

The interesting Syova – occasionally spelt Mukotinin – was the hero of three belated silent fantasies directed by M. Stepanov in the mid-1930s.

Sami gryazni presents Syova as a filth-monster of homeric proportions. If you bath him, the tub clogs up; wash him in the river and pollution sets in. Animals and birds flee him at sight. But finally he is transformed into a model of sweetness and cleanliness, loved by all.

In his next film Syova is given a pet monkey which creates havoc in the house and has to be unloaded. In the third, visiting the zoo, he throws a bit of broken glass into a bear's feeding trough, and later has nightmares about the beast in agony. (Though in fact it is unscathed.)

The oriental adventure *Ai-Gul*, starring the splendidly named boy ANTIK KIM, only

found a supporting role for Syova.

34 Sami gryazni (The dirtiest boy)
35 Pro obezyanku (About a little monkey)
   Steklyanni zavtrak (Glass for breakfast)
36 Ai-Gul

'Mircha'

FRANCE/AUSTRIA

b: circa 1922

34 Le scandale (Scandal – FR)
35 Bout de chou (Little pet – FR)
36 Der kleine Kavalier
   (The little cavalier – AT/HU)

Shahu Modak

INDIA

b: circa 1922

Shahu was said to be the first child star of the Indian talkies.

32 Shyam Sunder (Lord Krishna)
   The Prince and the Pauper
33 Bulbule Punjab (Nightingale of Punjab)
34 Nand Ke Lala
   Seva Sadan
36 Honhar (One who promises)

Mario Artese

ITALY

b: 10 Jan 23

Curly blond urchin.

38 Piccoli naufraghi (Little castaways)
40 Piccolo alpino (Boy of the Alps)
   Gli ultimi della strada (Lowest of the low)
42 La battaglia (The battle)

Jackie Moran

USA

b: 26 Jan 23 (Mattoon, Illinois)
d: 20 Sep 90 (Greenfield, Mass.)

His father was a successful lawyer (a state prosecutor, in fact) and his mother had musical leanings. Jackie, the younger of two boys, had a fine voice that won him solo status in the local church choir, and a handsome face that won him advertising jobs for Coca-Cola and the like. With the promise of a screen test extracted from a timely meeting with Mary Pickford, his family moved to Los Angeles: he had his screen test, and it led to nothing.

Behind the smiling, stalwart exterior, Jackie had a sensitive nature that found all the show-biz ingratiation distasteful and embarrassing. He was also a terrible worrier, and with good reason. After a stage performance at last won him – in *Valiant Is the Word for Carrie*, one of the world's most gruesome titles – a film part which brought success, his father gave up the law and became his rather incompetent manager. Now Jackie had to support the family, and it made his life a nightmare, as he told Richard Lamparski. (Whose 'Whatever Happened To . . .?' books are essential reading for their interviews with former film actors.)

He was a too-civilised Huck in the 1937 *Tom Sawyer*, and valiant was the word for his attempt to bring conviction to *Michael O'Halloran*, as the saintly newsboy.

In 1939 Jackie had more fun as Buster Crabbe's space sidekick in the ineffable *Buck Rogers* serial, besides *Everybody's*

Jackie Moran, circa 1937

Hobby, *Meet Doctor Christian*, *The Spirit of Culver* and a minuscule appearance in *Gone With the Wind*. His 1940 credits were *Anne of Windy Poplars*, *The Haunted House* and *Tomboy*.

In the late 1940s, after about twenty more parts, Jack Moran, with undisguised relief, quit the scene. Over the next three decades he ran a liquor business, wrote scripts for the scandalous Russ Meyer, sold newspapers and did medical work. He was a man without illusions.

36 And So They Were Married
   Any Man's Wife
   Valiant Is the Word for Carrie
37 The Adventures of Tom Sawyer
   Michael O'Halloran
   Outcast
38 Arson Racket Squad
   Barefoot Boy
   Mad About Music
   Mother Carey's Chickens

Bobby Rietti

BRITAIN

b: 8 Feb 23 (London)

Robert Rietty – as he now spells himself – is the son of the Italian-Jewish actor and director Victor Rietti (1888-1963).

He first worked in films in 1932. In 1935 he had the title role in a London version of 'Poil de Carotte' at the Fortune Theatre, and the following year played Jonathan (opposite Elisabeth Bergner) in J.M.Barrie's 'The Boy David' at His Majesty's.

In the British *Emil and the Detectives* this highly intelligent child was the bespectacled 'Professor'.

After World War Two, Rietty continued his acting career – he can be seen, for instance, as Jeremy Spenser's◇ watchdog in *Prelude to Fame* (50) – and, with his usefully international air, in *The Italian Job* (69) and *Never Say Never Again* (83). But his work as playwright, broadcaster and translator has been even more valuable. In 1960 he was appointed Cavaliere al Merito for his services to the Italian drama.

33 Heads We Go
34 Happy
   My Song Goes Round the World
   The Private Life of Don Juan
35 Children of the Fog
   Emil and the Detectives
   The Scarlet Pimpernel

Nand Buyl

BELGIUM

b: 12 Feb 23 (Antwerp)

Fernand Buyl (more usually Nand or Nandje) was the younger Belgian contemporary of Jefke Bruyninckx◇, and worked with him in Flemish-language films of the Thirties.

Buyl continued to act for some time, then turned to stage production. He finally became Director of the Flemish Theatre in Brussels.

34 De Witte (Whitey)
35 Alleen voor U (Just for you)
36 Uilenspiegel leeft nog (Eulenspiegel lives!)
37 Havenmusiek (Music of the port)
38 Drie flinke kerels (Three rough types)

Yakov Segel

USSR

b: 10 Mar 23 (Rostov-on-Don)

His first film appearance was as Robert Grant in a version of Jules Verne's 'Les enfants du capitaine Grant'.

Yakov Segel in Deti Kapitana Granta

After World War Two, Segel returned to the cinema, and in 1954 completed the director's course at VGIK. He subsequently directed several films, including *Pervi den mira* (59, The first day of peace) and *Razbudite Mukhina!* (65, Wake Mukhin up!).

In 1980 he was named an Honoured Artist of the People.

36 Deti Kapitana Granta
(Captain Grant's Children)

Bobby Jordan

USA

b: 1 Apr 23 (New York)
d: 10 Sep 65 (Los Angeles)

He did modelling work from the age of three. Five or six years later he got into show business: vaudeville, radio and finally (around 1933) the movies. He had played in 'Dead End' on the New York stage, and went to Hollywood to repeat his role.

For the next few years Bobby Jordan – youngest of the 'Dead End Kids' – was a Hollywood fixture as a cheerful low-life teenager, the lank lock flopping over one eye. Occasionally, as in *Military Academy* (40) or the serial *Adventures of the Flying Cadets* (43), he was required to smarten himself up a bit, but on the whole he remained Basic Scruff.

Ceasing to be obviously juvenile, he faded gradually from the scene, and died in his early forties. One of his last named parts was in *News Hounds* (47).

34 Kid Millions
37 Dead End
38 Angels With Dirty Faces
Crime School
My Bill
Reformatory
A Slight Case of Murder

Gene Reynolds

USA

b: 14 Apr 23 (Cleveland, Ohio)

Eugene Reynolds Blumenthal – for it is he – was a wildly romantic-looking boy, with the features of a matinee idol and expressive, intelligent brown eyes. If a youngster with artistic or idealistic leanings was called for in a movie of the late Thirties, Reynolds was your choice. He was a dead ringer for Tyrone Power (and actually grew into him in the 1938 film *In Old Chicago*) but without old Ty's air of honest bafflement.

He began at two with some modelling, took the stage (in Detroit) at six, then began to do radio work. The road led inexorably to screen tests in Hollywood, and a debut in *Too Many Parents*. MGM had him under contract from 1938.

Gene had some more good parts in 1940, in *Gallant Sons, The Mortal Storm* and *Santa Fe Trail*, and in the 1942 serial *Junior G-Men of the Air*. Then, when war embroiled the USA, he served with the Navy. Once it was over he resumed his acting career, but without any conviction that it was what he wanted to do. He had parts in *The Big Cat* (49), *The Country Girl* (54) and *Diane* (55).

After working in television he got the chance to write and direct, and it was this that eventually led to his most priceless contribution to the popular culture of our times. He became producer (and sometimes writer or director) of TV's 'M*A*S*H' series, with its magnificent complexity of response and richness of repartee.

36 Libeled Lady
Sins of Man
Thank You, Jeeves!
Too Many Parents
37 The Californian
Captains Courageous
Madame X
Thunder Trail
38 Boys Town
The Crowd Roars
In Old Chicago
Love Finds Andy Hardy
Men With Wings
Of Human Hearts
39 Bad Little Angel
The Flying Irishman
The Spirit of Culver
They Shall Have Music

Gene Reynolds with William Gargan in The Crowd Roars

Madden, 1927

Jerry Madden

USA

b: 29 Jne 23 (Los Angeles)

Malcolm Edward Madden, an extrovert redhead, was only two when he got a contract from Fox. He decided fairly early in life – after starring in and as *Jerry the Giant* – that he preferred to be known as Jerry. His stardom was as brief as it was precocious: in spite of a featured role alongside Tom Mix in *The Last Trail*, by the 1930s he was just a supporting kid among many.

About 40 years later the name of Jerry Madden re-surfaced as co-producer of the TV series 'Alice'.

25 The Heart Breaker
26 The Blue Eagle
    Jerry the Giant
    Napoleon, Junior
    The Unknown Soldier
27 A Dog's Pal
    The Gay Retreat
    Gun Gospel
    The Haunted Ship
    The Last Trail
    A Wolf in Cheap Clothing
28 Carmen
29 Marching On
    Sound Your A
35 Dr. Socrates
36 Bullets or Ballots
37 Penrod and Sam

Sherwood Bailey

USA

b: 6 Aug 23
d: 6 Aug 87 (Newport Beach, Cal.)

Sherwood V. Bailey joined the roster at 'Our Gang' in the summer of 1931, a tough, freckled, square-faced redhead who oddly enough got featured, to begin with, not as a tough but as a spoiled momma's boy, smart-ass and goodie-goodie. It suited oddly, too, with the Gang nickname he was given: 'Spud', which sounds like a tough after all.

The fact that the Gang never quite decided how to use Sherwood probably accounted for the fact that they released him after nine films. He went on to a thriving five years of better and tougher roles elsewhere. The boy was a natural bruiser, and valued as such.

After one or two more appearances – for instance in *Young Tom Edison* (40) – Bailey disappeared from the movie scene. In adult life he became a respected civil engineer, and died on his 64th birthday.

29 Joyland
    Summer Saps
31 'Our Gang' *(3 shorts)*
32 'Our Gang' *(6)*

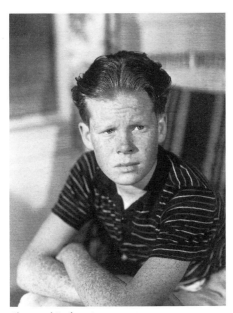

Sherwood Bailey, circa 1938

33 The Big Stampede
    The Mysterious Rider
35 The Loud Speaker
    Paddy O'Day
36 The Devil Is a Sissy
    The Plainsman
    Too Many Parents
37 Girl Loves Boy
    Quality Street
    Quick Money
    Shall We Dance?
38 Angels With Dirty Faces
    Having Wonderful Time
    King of the Underworld
    Reformatory

Lawford in Poor Old Bill

Peter Lawford

BRITAIN/USA

b: 7 Sep 23 (India)
d: 24 Dec 84 (Los Angeles)

Born Peter Sydney Vaughn Aylen, this future member of Hollywood's 'Rat Pack' must have suffered hideous trauma in the womb: his pregnant mother had to watch his cuckolded father elaborately blow his brains out in front of her. Peter became the stepson of Lieutenant-General Sir Sydney Lawford (1866-1953). He was intended to follow 'Swanky Syd' into the Army, but from tenderest years showed a deplorable leaning towards the theatre.

Little Peter's first recorded engagement was back in Britain, in *Poor Old Bill*. In a featured part he charmed everyone, and was compared – inevitably – to Jackie Coogan ◇. In 1937 the Lawfords settled in California, and after a modest sampler in *Lord Jeff*, Peter Lawford launched his adult film career in the 1940s. (Oddly enough, so did the retired Sir Sydney.)

Lawford's attempt to be the new Cary Grant was doomed to failure, with neither the talent nor the scripts to support it. He was a pleasant, debonair, unmemorable star in a dwindling line of films.

31 A Gentleman of Paris (GB)
   Poor Old Bill (GB)
38 Lord Jeff (US)

Mickey Rentschler with Grant Withers and hound in Radio Patrol

Mickey Rentschler

USA

b: 6 Oct 23 (Detroit)

Milton Edward Rentschler, the son of German-speaking parents, first came to prominence in childhood as a bird-call imitator on radio. He was a strong, handsome, rather scornful-looking boy.

Rentschler played Joe Harper in *Tom Sawyer*, and again in *Huckleberry Finn* the following year. He was in *I Married a Witch* (42), and continued at least until *The Redhead from Manhattan* (54).

33 His Private Secretary
34 The Brand of Hate
   Kid Millions
   A Modern Hero
35 Black Fury
   Hot Off the Press
   The Scarlet Letter
36 Follow Your Heart
   Jailbreak
   Sins of Man
37 The Adventures of Tom Sawyer
   Radio Patrol *(serial)*
38 The Adventures of Huckleberry Finn
   Boys Town
   The Crowd Roars
   The Devil's Party
   Peck's Bad Boy with the Circus

Tomio Aoki ('Tokkan-Kozo')

JAPAN

b: 7 Oct 23 (Yokohama)

This amazing boy, with the troubled forehead and narrow, wary eyes of a bruiser, was the great Yasujiro Ozu's favourite child actor of the early Thirties and was featured in dozens of his films. When he was young his parents divorced, and he spent the rest of his childhood with his mother. She ran a bar popular with actors from the Shochiku studios, and there the charismatic Tomio was spotted.

His apparently doggy, doughy face was capable of minute shifts of emotion. The exasperated relationship with his boozy father in *Passing Fancy* is incredibly moving, culminating in a scene where the contrite father allows the boy to hit him repeatedly. Tomio was marvellous as the younger brother in *I Was Born, But . . .*, outscoring his elder in the hunger-strike that follows their rebellion against adult hypocrisy and boot-licking.

Tomio would weep for grief or shame, never for mere pain. He was a wonderful striker of mocking or defiant poses, limbs at traditionally insulting angles. After his 1929 lead he was usually billed simply as 'Tokkan-Kozo'. He also acted in a few of Mikio Naruse's early films.

In the 1940s Tomio Aoki formed a company of travelling actors. His later films were *Ginza no onna* (55), *Biruma no tategoto* (56 – The Burmese harp), *Bakumatsu taiyoden* (57), *Nianchan* (59), *Buta to gunkan* (61), *Kuroba no taiyo* (68) and *Kareinaru ichizoku* (74).

In 1971 he became managing director of International Television Enterprise.

29 Kaishain seikatsu (An office-worker's life)
   Tokkan kozo (Naughty boy)
   Zenbu seishin ijo ari (Everyone's mad)
30 Ara! Sono shunkan yo! (That's just when!)
   Ara! Tairyo dane (What a catch!)
   Ashi ni sawatta koun
      (Luck touched my legs)
   Entotsu otoko (Man on a chimney)
   Fukeiki jidai (Age of depression)
   Iroke dango soudouki
      (Story of a wild passion)
   Ishikawa Goemon no hoji
      (Ishikawa Goemon's memorial service)
   Kaishain kubiyoke senjutsu
      (The company-man strategy)
   Koi no shakkin gurui no senjutsu
      (Money for love)
   Ogotte chodaiyo! (Give me a treat)
   Rakudai wa shita keredo (I flunked, but...)
   Umi no koshinkyoku (A march at sea)
   Yometori konki kurabe
      (Wives need patience)
31 Bofuu no bara (Rose in the storm)
   Danjo oshikurabe
      (Strong men, strong women)
   Hige no chikara (Moustache power)
   Kiken shingo (Danger signal)
   Machi no rumpen (Tramp in the street)
   Namida no aikyomono
      (Tears of happiness)
   Onna wa tsuyokute hitorimono
      (Woman is strong and independent)

Tomio Aoki (left) with Hideo Sugawara (centre) and Tatsu Saito in Umarete wa mita keredo. . .

Onna wa tsuyokute yowai mono
(Woman is both strong and weak)
Otto yo naze nakuka
(Why does the husband weep?)
Watashi no Papasan Mama ga suki
(Daddy loves Mummy)
32 Aozora ni naku (Crying to the blue sky)
Chokoreto garu (Chocolate girl)
Eraku nare (Get wise)
Kawaii gokesan (The pretty widow)
Onna wa nete mate
(Going to sleep without a woman)
Umarete wa mita keredo (I was born, but...)
33 Awatemono no Kumasan (Kumasan panics)
Dekigokoro (Passing fancy)
Okusama no moryoku (Violent wives)
Otoko yamome no Gansan
(Gansan the widower)
Taihen na otome (Virgin extraordinary)
34 Genkanban to ojosan
(The porter and the lady)
Koshi no nuketa onna
(A woman out of joint)
Namerareta aitsu (A disrespectful fellow)
Ukigusa monogatari
(Story of floating weeds)
35 Boya banzai (Three cheers for Boya)
Hakoiri musume (An innocent maid)
Hanamuko no negoto
(The bridegroom talks in his sleep)
Kare to kanojo to shonentachi
(He, she and the boys)
Konoko sutezareba
(If I don't get rid of the child)
Tokyo no yado (An inn in Tokyo)

36 Hitori musuko (The only son)
37 Hanagata senshu (A star athlete)
Kaze no naka no kodomo
(Children in the wind)
Shukujo wa nani o wasuretaka
(What did the lady forget?)

Malcolm 'Big Boy' Sabiston

USA

b: 4 Nov 23

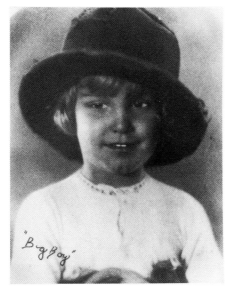

'Big Boy' Sabiston

There's some confusion about the name of this infant star: Maltin and Bann call him 'Malcolm Sebastian', and his real name is said to have been 'Malcolm Williams'. Oddly enough the well-known heavy, Guinn 'Big Boy' Williams (1907-62), also acted as a child – for instance in the 1919 film *Almost a Husband*.

Young Malcolm, a brown-eyed blond of considerable poise, started his career in *Three Weeks* – his age at the time – but reached his apogee in the 'Big Boy' comedies of 1927-29, which are all the films listed below under those years.

24 Bread
Three Weeks
26 My Kid
27 Shamrock Alley
She's a Boy
28 Angel Eyes
Chilly Days
Come to Papa
The Gloom Chaser
Hot Luck
Kid Hayseed
Navy Beans
No Fare
29 Fixer
Ginger Snaps
Helter Skelter
Joy Tonic
31 The Phantom

Johnny Singer

BRITAIN

b: 4 Dec 23 (Hastings)
d: 7 Jly 87 (Tunbridge Wells)

Johnny Singer's was a ubiquitous face in British films of the Thirties: often the cheeky office junior or bossy little pageboy who would get quick laughs when the plot was flagging. In *Tudor Rose* he has a split-second appearance on the edge of a crowd. He does nothing but throw his cap in the air and shout 'Long live the Queen!' – but nearly every 1936 filmgoer in Britain would have recognised him with affection.

Sometimes, though – as in *My Old Dutch, Something Always Happens* or *This Green Hell* – he had a real leading role and grabbed it.

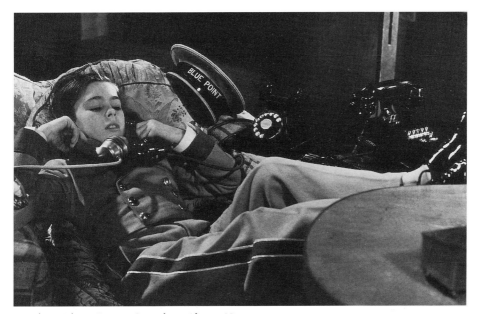

Busy lines: Johnny Singer in Something Always Happens

Johnny's first recorded public appearance was in miniature white tie and tails, winning a fancy dress competition and then conducting a brass band near Northampton. Two years later, he was billed at a Gala Novelty Dance in London as 'Little John Singer of Kine-Variety and Talking Picture Fame, direct from the Criterion Restaurant...the World's Youngest Cabaret Star'. He danced, he sang, he did impressions. He was also a famously quick learner of lines.

By the mid-Thirties he was regularly described as 'the British Mickey Rooney', and in January 1940 he and Celia Lipton re-enacted the Rooney and Garland roles in a radio version of 'Babes in Arms'. They also sang with the Henry Hall Band. By this time Johnny had appeared in about 100 films.

He continued to act, sometimes with the little Mancunian film company – taking the romantic lead in 1942 in *Somewhere in Camp*. He was a sailor in *In Which We Serve* (42) and in *The Cruel Sea* (53). But five years of war had intervened, in which – as a soldier – John Singer had taken part in the Allied invasion of Europe, done duty in Palestine, and been demobbed in 1947 with the rank of Captain.

It wasn't easy to build an acting career again, and in due course he turned to script-writing, notably (in partnership with John Warren) for the TV comedian Dick Emery, who also starred in the spin-off film *Ooh – You Are Awful* (72). After Warren's death, Singer's son Steven became his co-writer.

Singer with Ian Hunter in Something Always Happens

Billy Watson

USA

b: 25 Dec 23 (Los Angeles)

Billy was the third and brightest-eyed of the Watson boys — younger than Coy Jr.[◇] and Harry[◇], older than Delmar[◇], Garry and Bobs[◇]. Usually perky, he had to be pathetic as Micah Dow in *The Little Minister*, and held his own surprisingly well with Katharine Hepburn.

Billy continued to act. In 1938 he was in *The Adventures of Huckleberry Finn*, *In Old Chicago* and *Kidnapped*, and in the following year in *Mr Smith Goes to Washington*, *Stanley and Livingstone* and *Young Mr Lincoln*: all prestige films. But he began to switch his professional interest to photography.

Billy Watson as Micah Dow in The Little Minister

In 1958 he joined with his five brothers in the founding of a photographic studio in Los Angeles, though he didn't quite abandon his earlier career. He is the only one of the Watsons still acting — a regular, for instance, in ABC TV's 'General Hospital'.

Jean Bara

FRANCE

b: 1923

Little Jean had an amused air of worldly sophistication, a nursery hint of white tie and tails. In *Boule de gomme* he had a high old time playing a child actor who always laughs when he should be crying and vice versa.

Bara continued at least into his mid-teens, with *Ceux de demain* (38) and *Les trois tambours* (39).

Jean Bara in Il était une fois

Antonín Jedlička

CZECHOSLOVAKIA

b: 1923

Antonín, who looked like a broken-nosed Terry Kilburn[◇], was a popular child actor who continued into adult life, for instance in *Taňa a dva pistolníci* (67).

Antonín (left) and Vladimír Jedlička in To byl český muzikant

Antonín's blond kid brother Vladimír Jedlička, some five years younger, was also seen in Antonín's two 1940 films, as well as in *Ulička v raji (Little road to Paradise*, CS/AT 36) and *Cestou křizovou* (The way of the cross, 38).

Bobby Nelson

USA

b: 1923 (California)

Bobby was one of the youngest and busiest of the screen's mini-horsemen, and successfully survived the switch to talkies. He partnered famous cowboys like Hoot Gibson and Tom Tyler. Most of his early films, and the thirteen 'Pioneer Kid' two-reelers of 1929-30, were directed by his father, Jack Nelson. Many were for the Sennett and Educational studios.

Swathed in leopardskin, Bobby was tiny brother-in-law-to-be to the lantern-jawed athlete and stuntman Frank Merrill in the 15-episode Tarzan serial of 1928, which Jack Nelson helped to direct. (See p. 497.) Most of the child's other films were Westerns, but in the Dickie Moore° *Oliver Twist* of 1933 he appeared as a no less undersized Noah Claypole.

26 Beyond the Rockies
   The Border Whirlwind
   The Fighting Boob
   Hair Trigger Baxter
   The Valley of Bravery
27 Bulldog Pluck
   The Life of an Actress
   Sunshine of Paradise Alley
28 The Cheer Leader
   Tarzan the Mighty (serial)
29 A Boy and a Bad Man
   Dangerous Days
   The Kid Comes Through
   Orphan of the Wagon Trails
   Waif of the Wilderness
30 Alias the Bandit
   The Battling Kid
   The Danger Claim
   The Last Stand
   The Pony Express Kid
   The Post of Honor
   Roaring Ranch
   Six-Gun Justice
   Son of Courage

Bobby Nelson, circa 1933

   The Texan
   Two-Fisted Justice
31 The Dogalog
   Spell of the Circus (serial)
   Two Gun Caballero
32 The Boiling Point
   Daring Danger
   Partners
   A Scarlet Weekend
33 The Cowboy Counsellor
   King of the Arena
   Oliver Twist
   On Your Guard
34 Black Fury
   The Way of the West
35 The Cowboy and the Bandit
   The Crimson Trail
   Cyclone of the Saddle
   The Ghost Rider
   Rough Riding Rangers
   Texan Terrors
   The Throwback
36 Captured in Chinatown

   The Drunkard
   Thunderbolt
   Valley of the Lawless
37 Boothill Brigade
   The Gambling Terror
   Gun Lords of Stirrup Basin
   The Red Rope

Igor But and Boris Runge

USSR

b: circa 1923

These two young Russians won instant fame in the Soviet Union in *A Lone White Sail*, directed by Vladimir Legoshin. (The title quotes from Lermontov: 'A lonely sail gleams white against a haze of blue'.) It was the first filming of Valentin Katayev's gloriously evocative book, packed with details of the games Russian boys of the pre-revolutionary period played with brass buttons and cigarette packets, and the most popular soft drinks.

The story is set at the time of the 1905 uprisings: tough little Gavrik (But) and his fisherman grandfather give shelter to a hunted rebel sailor from the *Potemkin*, and Gavrik's liberal-bourgeois buddy Petya (Runge) is drawn into the resulting drama.

The defiant and humorous IGOR BUT had been featured as 'Rizhik' (Ginger) in the 1935 film, in which three boys at an orphanage, inspired perhaps by *Gogi — otvazhni lyotchik*, build their own aeroplane and after a hazardous flight gate-crash (more or less literally) a public reception for the Russian air ace V.S. Molokov. But's performance earned him the role of Gavrik.

35 Po sledam geroya (In a hero's footsteps)
36 Beleyet parus odinoki (A lone white sail)
40 Vesenni potok (Torrent of spring)

The sensitive, likeable BORIS RUNGE had another leading role, after *A Lone White Sail*, in *Lichnoye delo* (A private matter, 39), and was featured again in 1942 in the ninth edition of *Boyevoi kinosbornik* (Battle Cine-Magazine). He continued to make occasional film appearances, and became an actor at the Moscow Theatre of Satire.

Boris Runge (left) and Igor But in Beleyet parus odinoki

Lenya Fesechko

USSR

b: circa 1923

The burly Lenya played two important title roles in films directed by Alexei Maslyukov, but had no other featured part.

36 Karl Brunner
38 Mitka Lelyuk

Finn Mannu

DENMARK

b: circa 1923 (Madeira)

Finn was the 'millionaire' hero of his only film. He also played Oliver Twist on the Copenhagen stage, but didn't persist as an actor. More practically, he became a waiter, and later emigrated to the USA, where he continued his career in the hotel business.

36 Millionærdrengen (The boy millionaire)

François Rodon

FRANCE

b: circa 1923

Rodon was an endearingly dozy-looking boy who had featured parts in *Pasteur* and several other films of the later Thirties.

35 Le chant de l'amour (The song of love)
   Les mystères de Paris (Secrets of Paris)
   Pasteur
36 Le coupable (The guilty man)
   Jacques et Jacotte
   Ménilmontant
37 Ma petite marquise (My little marchioness)
38 Faisons du cinéma (Let's make a movie)
   Grand-père (Grandad)
40 Notre-Dame de la Mouise
   (Our Lady of Poverty)

Roger Daniel

USA

b: 3 Jan 24 (Akron, Ohio)

Roger, the son of Irish-American parents, was an orphan at six. He played the piano and guitar, but his chief asset was an open, sensitive face. He was in fact a strikingly handsome fellow, with flashing eyes and romantic hair – a sort of brunet version of Wally Albright ◇.

Typical leads came in *Boy Slaves*, as the most soulful of the juvenile workers exploited by a turpentine factory, and in

Roger Daniel (right) with Adolphe Menjou in King of the Turf

123

King of the Turf as a racehorse-crazy kid who becomes a groom and then a winning jockey for Adolphe Menjou.

In his later teens Daniel was in *Her First Romance* (41), *Life Begins for Andy Hardy* (41), *We've Never Been Licked* (43), and in 1946 featured in two *Joe Palooka* films. This was paltry reward for one who should have become a Burbank Byron. In due course he left acting and became a sound recordist.

37 Hollywood Round-Up
38 Lord Jeff
   Reformatory
39 Boy Slaves
   King of the Turf

Hideo Sugawara

JAPAN

b: 3 Jan 24 (Hakodate)

Hideo began filming with the Shochiku studio, and was – although three months his junior – Tomio Aoki's ◊ serious elder brother in one of Yasujiro Ozu's most famous films, *I Was Born, But. . . .* (He remade it in 1959 as *Ohayo*/Good Morning).

I Was Born, But. . . . is a subtle, hilarious but often painful comedy about status and dignity, power and humiliation. Two little boys find their likeable father turning before their eyes into a contemptible figure of fun, as they watch a home movie in which he clowns around to amuse his boss. When he explains that he has to abase himself if they want to eat, they protest by going on hunger strike. Compromise is reached in the end, but not before a lot of rueful truths have emerged. Hideo Sugawara, hardly less than Aoki, is tremendous.

30 Chichi (Father)
31 Tokyo no gassho (Tokyo chorus)
32 Umarete wa mita keredo
      (I was born, but....)
   Aozora ni naku (Crying to the blue sky)
33 Aniki (Elder brother)
35 Jikatsu suru onna (Independent woman)
39 Machi no hanauri musume
      (The flower girl)

Gentle hint: 'Snookums' McKeen in Christmas Cheer

Lawrence McKeen

USA

b: Jan 1924
d: 2 Apr 33 (Los Angeles)

This highly successful and impish baby, of an Irish family, sprang to fame with the filming, from 1926, of George McManus' popular comic strip 'The Newly-Weds'. With a bizarre unicorn twist of hair, he incarnated 'Baby Snookums' in such episodes as *Snookums' Tooth*, *Snookums Disappears* and *Snookums Cleans Up*, and achieved sufficient eminence to be received at the White House by President Coolidge.

At the age of four, de-unicorned and re-named, Lawrence McKeen progressed to his own 'Sunny Jim' series (1929-30).

Alas, at eight the poor ex-Snookums died of blood poisoning.

26-28 'The Newlyweds and Their
         Baby' *(series)*
29 Baby Talks
   Christmas Cheer
   Mush Again
   No Boy Wanted
30 Brother for Sale
   She's a He

Over-reacting: Sinclair in Five Little Peppers

Ronald Sinclair

NEW ZEALAND/USA

b: 21 Jan 24 (Dunedin, New Zealand)
d: 22 Nov 92 (Los Angeles)

The aristocratic Sinclair had a New Zealand father and a British mother; his real name was Richard Arthur Hould. Having made a modest four-year-old stage debut as an elf, he found himself in 1933 acting with Sybil Thorndike at a Dunedin theatre.

Billed as 'Ra Hould', he had the main child part in *Down On the Farm*, New Zealand's first talkie. Then, on Miss Thorndike's advice, his parents took him not to England (their original idea) to further his movie ambitions, but to Hollywood. It worked, and he got a part in *Beloved Enemy*.

At the end of 1937, for *Thoroughbreds Don't Cry* (a film with Rooney and Judy Garland), he changed his performing name from Ra Hould to Ronald Sinclair. It did no harm. Nor did playing Young Scrooge in *A Christmas Carol*. The outrageously handsome youth continued to thrive.

Three more 'Little Peppers' films absorbed Sinclair's energies in 1940; he was also in *That Hamilton Woman* (41) and *Desperate Journey* (42). The other Pepper

boys were Charles Peck (the rich boy in *Dead End*), Tommy Bond ◇ ('Butch' from 'Our Gang') and Jimmy Leake.

After World War Two Ronald Sinclair abandoned acting and learnt the craft of film editor, which he practised for the next 25 years. Films he worked on included – for Roger Corman – *The Premature*

Burial, *The Raven* and, oddly enough, another *Tower of London*.

35 Down on the Farm (NZ)
36 Beloved Enemy
37 Boots and Saddles
   Dangerous Holiday
   A Doctor's Diary
   Thoroughbreds Don't Cry
38 A Christmas Carol
39 Five Little Peppers and How They Grew
   The Light That Failed
   They Made Me a Criminal
   Tower of London

Sabu Dastagir

INDIA/BRITAIN/USA

b: 27 Jan 24 (Karapur, nr. Mysore)
d: 2 Dec 63 (Chatsworth, Los Angeles)

His birthplace was the Karapur jungle, 45 miles from Mysore in Southern India. His father, Sheik Ibrahim, a Mohammedan, was a mahout, or elephant-driver, for the Maharajah of Mysore, and Sabu was brought up among the elephants. (After his father's death, the Maharajah granted him a pension of 2 rupees a month.)

Robert Flaherty, shooting location

Ronald Sinclair (right) with Mickey Rooney in Thoroughbreds Don't Cry

Sabu in Elephant Boy

scenes in preparation for *Elephant Boy*, saw the fearless twelve-year-old riding an elephant, and within 24 hours, with the aid of an interpreter (Sabu spoke no English), had signed him up for the lead.

When the boy – billed simply as 'Sabu' in his films — was in due course sent to London to pursue his education, he picked up English with remarkable speed, and within a year was going to school with boys of his own age.

His first visit to the USA – for a personal appearance tour to publicise *The Drum* – was in 1938. He returned to England to film *The Thief of Bagdad* (40), but after the outbreak of war shooting had to be completed in the States.

This time he stayed for good, and most of his seventeen remaining films were made there: *The Jungle Book* (42), *Arabian Nights* (42), *Man-Eater of Kumaon* (48), *Song of India* (49), *Jaguar* (56) and so on. But there were also excursions, for instance to Britain for *Black Narcissus* (46) and *The End of the River* (47), or to Italy for *Buongiorno elefante* (52) and *Il tesoro del Bengalo* (53). Suddenly, just after making *A Tiger Walks* (US 63) and eight weeks before his fortieth birthday, Sabu died of a heart attack.

37 Elephant Boy
38 The Drum

Wolfgang Kieling

GERMANY

b: 16 Mar 24 (Berlin)
d: 7 Oct 85 (Hamburg)

Little Wolfgang had a froggy face and the voice of an angel. He was singing on the radio as early as 1930, though most of the wonderful records he made for Electrola weren't released until 1939. His repertoire included folk songs and children's songs (often in comical Disneyish arrangements), but also Bach, Mozart and Schubert. The voice was so sweet and sprightly, and so childlike even at 13 or 14 – unlike the ripe, bosomy tones of Ernest Lough or Aled Jones – that these will remain among the most precious of all treble recordings.

It was inevitable that such an endearing little boy should be invited to act, and he did so with the expected talent – not pretty or heroic enough to land leading children's roles in German films of the time, but a useful presence that could be sceptical or sad. His intelligence kept him in demand as a dubber of foreign movies: it fell to him to supply the voice of Freddy Bartholomew ◇, for instance, in at least four of his leads.

Kieling continued to act, and studied drama with Albert Florath and Hilde Körber, until his call-up in 1942. (In 1940 he had been a production assistant to Veit Harlan, who had directed him in three of his early films.) He was wounded on the Eastern front in October 1943, returned to active service about a year later, and was then captured by the Russians, who held him prisoner till 1949.

Making up for lost years, he energetically resumed his career, on stage and in the cinema, both in East and West Germany. The little angel-frog had become a stocky, powerful, often menacing personality. He was superbly bitter as an NCO in the East German war film *Betrogen bis zum jüngsten Tag* (57), and in the theatre — where he interpreted many classic parts – a memorable Othello. In 1966 he was the dogged security officer in Hitchcock's *Torn Curtain*, whom Paul Newman finds so horribly hard to kill; two years later he played Inspector van der Valk in the British film *The Amsterdam Affair*. He won the TV award of the German Academy of Performing Arts in 1974 for his performance as a transvestite in the play *Im Reservat*.

He was a temperamental man with many problems, and his private life was touched by tragedy with the suicide of his first

Wolfgang Kieling, 1940

wife. When he died of cancer in 1985, he was one of the most admired and loved of German actors. Some of his boyhood recordings were played, to poignant effect, at his funeral.

36 Guten Abend, gute Nacht
    (Good evening, good night)
    Maria, die Magd (Maria the maid)
37 Heimweh (Homesickness)
    Hier irrt Schiller (Schiller is wrong)
    Die Kreutzersonate (The Kreutzer Sonata)
38 Frauen für Golden Hill
    (Women for Golden Hill)
    Gute Reise, Herr Meyer
    (Bon voyage, Herr Meyer)
    Klimbusch macht Wochenende
    (Klimbusch's week-end)
    Schatten über St Pauli
    (Shadow over St Pauli)
    Träume sind Schäume
    (Dreams are only bubbles)
39 Die Reise nach Tilsit (The journey to Tilsit)

Freddie Bartholomew

BRITAIN/USA

b: 28 Mar 24 (London)
d: 23 Jan 92 (Sarasota, Florida)

Frederick Llewellyn was the son of a British soldier with Welsh connections, but instead of being brought up by his parents in London he was entrusted to the care of grandparents in Warminster, Wiltshire. He was a poised, intelligent child who blossomed under the admiration he gained from reciting poems and stories at local events. His maiden aunt, Millicent Bartholomew, saw hopes of glory in him, with herself as his king-maker. His indifferent parents made her his guardian. So he became the actor, 'Freddie Bartholomew'.

In 1930 Aunt Cissie (on her grander days, 'Myllicent') heard of a British film being shot near Warminster. She got Freddie a part in it, and it led to another a year later. She decided to take him back to London to study at the Italia Conti drama school. There, he was among the boys introduced to George Cukor and David O. Selznick, on the lookout for a possible 'young David Copperfield' for MGM's

Freddie Bartholomew in the British film Fascination

projected foray into Dickens; but British regulations about children acting abroad frustrated their hopes of borrowing him or any other young Briton. Louis B. Mayer, back home, was rooting for the too-old and anyhow unsuitable Jackie Cooper◇.

Aunt Cissie, a female Patton or Montgomery, saw a way to break through the impasse. In 1934 she took ten-year-old Freddie on 'a little visit' to the United States, just to widen his horizons; and, 'out of politeness', she rang MGM to ask how they were getting on in their hunt for a young Copperfield. The rest, as they say, is history. Within the twelvemonth Freddie was exchanging small-talk with W.C.Fields and lolling in the arms of Greta Garbo. This was better than church socials in Wiltshire!

In a funny way it may have been easier for American audiences to like Bartholo-mew than it was (and is) for the British, unaided by the charm of the exotic. To a Briton, Freddie – even in the nursery – always suggested a little magistrate, a little accountant, a little bishop: a little almost anything that was not the noisy, dirty human boy. True, he had intelligence and tact, and he could convey pain. One couldn't help admiring him, but couldn't often love him. I agree with nearly all critics that his best performance by a mile

was in *Captains Courageous*, where his priggishness was deservedly battered, and he ended as something like a man. But in *Little Lord Fauntleroy*, for instance, Ricky Schroder◇ would later act him into a cocked hat, by sheer *joie de vivre* and force of feeling.

Fauntleroy and *Captains* were two of the five films in which Mickey Rooney◇ would be pitted against Bartholomew: the rough and rowdy against the smooth and discreet. It worked beautifully.

When he was 14, and had earned himself (and Aunt Cissie) a mountain of dollars, his British parents took them to law to try – against Freddie's wishes – to dissolve her guardianship. After endless appeals and counter-appeals, they failed. But this, and another legal battle with MGM over his contract, eroded most of the mountain.

By 15, Bartholomew was not only shooting up but beginning to sprout an aquiline nose of William Powellesque proportions, which finally put paid to 'boyish' parts, since his personality had never been truly boyish anyway.

He continued to get work: in 1939 *Spirit of Culver* and *Two Bright Boys*, in 1940 *Swiss Family Robinson* and *Tom Brown's Schooldays* (in which James Lydon played Tom, and Freddie was his friend East), in 1941 *Naval Academy*, in 1942 *A Yank at Eton* and *Cadets On Parade*. But he was a declining asset, and there would be only four more films.

After the last, *St Benny the Dip* (51), he became a TV host, then a TV director, and finally an advertising executive. Young Freddie was nobody's fool.

31 Fascination (GB)
32 Lily Christine (GB)
    Strip, Strip, Hooray! (GB)
35 Anna Karenina
    David Copperfield
    Professional Soldier
36 The Devil is a Sissy
    Little Lord Fauntleroy
    Lloyds of London
37 Captains Courageous
38 Kidnapped
    Listen, Darling
    Lord Jeff

Bartholomew, with W.C. Fields as Micawber, in the 1935 David Copperfield

Billy and Bobby Mauch

USA

b: 6 Jly 24 (Peoria, Illinois)

Of the famous Mauch twins (pronounced somewhere between Maak and Mawk), Billy was the 'elder', *i.e.* saw daylight first. He was also the one that officially had their first movie lead – I stress 'officially'.

They were obviously a strong and glamorous pair, and once out of diapers began to make a name in their locality as singing and dancing identicals. In 1932 their mother got modelling work for them in New York.

The Mauchs also began to broadcast – though radio seems rather a waste of twinship – and were heard by Warner Brothers. Once Warners saw what they looked like, they cast Billy to play Fredric March (pronounced March) as a boy in *Anthony Adverse*. It was a very good . . . match.

The theory was that Bobby was to act as Billy's stand-in – for unimportant, non-speaking shots, or in case of indisposition. Once the film was safely in the can, however, they revealed to its director, Mervyn Le Roy, that they had been taking turns in the lead throughout, confident that no-one would notice. (The only way you *could* tell them apart was by throwing a ball at one of them or asking him to sign an autograph: Billy is left-handed, Bobby right-handed. But no doubt the twins had thought of this too, and put in a lot of practice with their 'wrong' hands.)

They are said to have played the same trick throughout *The White Angel*, where Billy was cast as a drummer-boy befriended in the Crimea by Florence Nightingale.

Unconvinced, Warners offered a contract to Billy alone. 'But Mrs Mauch,' reported Richard Lamparski after interviewing the duo many years later, 'insisted that they both be signed. When

Warners demurred she threatened to sign Bobby to a rival studio. They were both placed under contract at $350 a week each, with an added $150 a week for Mrs Mauch as their guardian'. Full marks to the Mauchs.

With both twins now on the payroll, Warners decided they had better get their money's worth. Mark Twain's *The Prince and the Pauper* was an obvious subject – and they made a classy job of it, with fine music by Erich Korngold and rich costumery. Then Billy alone was cast as the hero in the another version of Booth Tarkington's second 'Penrod' book, *Penrod and Sam*. (Sam was Harry Watson ◇ – it couldn't very well be Bobby Mauch, who really does seem to have confined himself to stand-ins this time.)

The object of the strategy became clear when, with some violence to the Tarkington canon, Penrod was cloned into twins, producing endless scope for hilarious confusion, and jobs for both Mauchs in two more comedies. The series could have run and run, but thank goodness it didn't. The twins were nice, cheerful, personable boys. Great comics they were not.

The brothers made one more twin-exploiting feature together – *Double Trouble* (41) – before doing war service with the Air Force. There seemed unlikely to be a resurgence of twin films afterwards, so Bob Mauch turned to film and TV editing.

Billy was in a few more films: *That Hagen Girl* (47), *The Street With No Name* (48), *Roseanna McCoy* (49), *Bedtime For Bonzo* (51), *People Will Talk* (51). Then he too decided enough was enough and became a sound editor for his old firm, Warners.

36 Anthony Adverse
   The White Angel
37 Penrod and Sam
   The Prince and the Pauper
38 Penrod and His Twin Brother
   Penrod's Double Trouble

The Mauches — which way round? — in The Prince and the Pauper

Vladimír Salač (right) with Antonín Jedlička in Madla zpiva Evropě

Vladimír Salač

CZECHOSLOVAKIA

b: 14 Jly 24

Vladimír Salač was a suave, smooth, poised boy — a kind of blond middle-european Freddie Bartholomew ◇ — but didn't hit his stride till he was fourteen.

In 1939 he seldom stopped working, and kept up the pace in 1940 with *Adam a Eva, Druha směna, Dva tydny štěsti, Madla zpiva Evropě* and *Prosim, pane Profesore!*

With more films in 1941, Salač became a leading Czech juvenile, and continued after the war.

38 Škola, základ života
    (School prepares you for life)
39 Cesta do hlubin studakovy duše
    (Journey to the depths of a
    student's soul)
    Humoreska (Humoresque)
    Příklady tahnou (The power of example)
    Studujeme za školou
    (We study for the school)
    Ted' zas my (Here we are again)
    Tulak Macoun (Macoun the tramp)
    Ulice zpiva (The street is singing)
    Venoušek a Stazička
    (Little Vaclav and little Anastasia)

Lee Van Atta

USA

b: 22 Jly 24 (San Francisco)

This flop-haired blond was sometimes an amusing ninny, but a resourceful action-boy in the serials.

36 Fury
    Second Wife
    Too Many Parents
    Undersea Kingdom *(serial)*
37 Captains Courageous
    Dick Tracy *(serial)*
39 The Affairs of Annabel

Raj Kapoor

INDIA

b: 14 Oct 24 (Peshawar)
d: 2 Jne 88 (New Delhi)

Ranbirraj Kapoor was the son of another leading film actor and producer, Prithvi Raj Kapoor (1906-1972), and brother of two other actors, Shashi ◇ and Shammi Kapoor. His own first recorded appearance was at the age of seven, in *The Toy Cart.*

From around his twentieth year, in films

Kid's brother: Robert Coogan (p.130)

like *Neel kamal* (47) and *Awara* (51), he began to win popularity throughout the sub-continent, and even established his own character-type, though not a wholly original one. To quote Ephraim Katz: 'He typically plays a Chaplinesque "little fellow" who overcomes great odds with the fervour of conviction.' He ended as an idolised, if overweight, superstar.

From 1948 he also produced his own films, and eventually succeeded his father as head of the powerful Kapoor dynasty.

32 The Toy Cart
35 Inqilab (Revolution)
39 Bari didi (Elder sister)

Robert Coogan

USA

b: 13 Dec 24 (Glendale, Cal.)
d: 12 May 78

More than a decade after Jackie Coogan's ◇ first screen triumphs, his kid brother Robert Anthony, in a 'Kid'-style cloth cap, was given the role of a cute little pest in Jackie Cooper's ◇ *Skippy*, and again in *Sooky*. Everyone – that is to say the rasher critics – prophesied that he would be greater than his brother. In spite of two more films the following year, he definitely wasn't.

Eventually Robert Coogan reappeared, with some other ex-kid-stars like Spanky McFarland ◇, in *Johnny Doughboy* (42), and later in some of the Bowery Boys and Joe Palooka films. After *Third of a Man* (63) he did little more screen work.

31 Skippy
   Sooky
32 The Miracle Man
   Sky Bride

Sammy McKim

USA

b: 20 Dec 24 (Seattle)

Sammy, with his square, freckled face and snub nose, was a hard-riding Western boy well known in the late Thirties for his spirited participation in several serials and the films of the 'Three Mesquiteers'. (His younger brother Harry 'Jeep' McKim was also a busy child actor in the early Forties.)

Sam, however, was an artist as well as actor and rider. In 1940, not yet sixteen, he had some cartoons published in the Hollywood Citizen-News, and after Army service during World War Two combined part-time acting – *The Hucksters* (47), *Flamingo Road* (49) – with four years of study (advertising and illustration) at the Los Angeles Art Center. Then he returned to the colours for 17 months in Korea. Released in 1952 as a first lieutenant, he resumed study, this time at the Chouinard Art Institute, now and then

Say It With Songs: *Al Jolson and Davey Lee*

mixing in an acting assignment: *Above and Beyond* (52), *The Bigamist* (53).

Finally, declining a part offered by John Ford in *The Long Gray Line*, he joined the art department of 20th Century Fox, and later became an animator at the Disney studios, where he was still able to make an occasional appearance before the cameras: *Nikki* (61), *The Gnome-Mobile* (67).

35 Annie Oakley
   This Is the Life
36 Country Gentlemen
   The Plough and the Stars
37 The Game That Kills
   Gunsmoke Ranch
   Heart of the Rockies
   Hit the Saddle
   Mama Runs Wild
   The Painted Stallion (serial)
   The Trigger Trio
38 Call the Mesquiteers
   The Great Adventures of Wild Bill Hickok
     (serial)
   Hunted Men
   The Lone Ranger (serial)
   The Old Barn Dance
   Red River Range
   Reformatory
39 Flying G-Men (serial)

The New Frontier
The Night Riders
Rovin' Tumbleweeds
Western Caravans
40 Hi-Yo Silver!
   Laddie
   Little Men
   Rocky Mountain Rangers
   Texas Terrors

Ge Zuozhi

CHINA

b: circa 1924 (Hong Kong)

Zuozhi had a Chinese mother but a Spanish father, who remarried after the mother's death. The desolate boy acquired the name of 'Wild Child', and *Heixin fu* told of his own experiences. He starred again two years later in *Mitu de gaoyang*, directed by Tsai Chusheng.

In 1937 he returned to Hong Kong and, in the sad words of the Beijing scholar Wang Rui – the source of almost all my material on the Chinese cinema – 'became homeless and wandered along until death'.

34 Heixin fu (Evil-hearted)
36 Mitu de gaoyang (Stray kids)

Davey Lee

USA

b: 29 Dec 24 (Hollywood)

Frankie Lee's ◇ younger brother saw in the dawn of the talkies, in *The Singing Fool*, on Al Jolson's knee. But his first 'all-talking' film was *Say It With Songs*, released in August 1929.

Davey was a pretty little fellow, but without Frankie's talent, and tended to be a rather passive recipient of screen-parental love. At least in *Frozen River* he had the more stimulating company of Rin-Tin-Tin.

By the beginning of 1930 Davey was said to be earning the almost incredible sum of $3,000 a week. But he didn't like filming, and gave it up 'because his health was suffering' – or, according to a less

Ge Zuozhi in Mitu de gaoyang

poignant version of events, because his mother got an offer of $3,500 for him to make personal appearances in vaudeville.

28 Bellamy Trial
    The River Pirate
    The Singing Fool
29 Frozen River
    Say It With Songs
    Skin Deep
    Sonny Boy
30 The Squealer
32 Girl Crazy

Leonard Kibrick

USA

b: circa 1924

This first of two Kibricks (see also Sidney, 'the Woim' ◇) is said in his infancy to have won a Beautiful Baby competition in a Los Angeles newspaper. If so, it must have been downhill all the way thereafter, or the photograph was heavily doctored, or the judges were drunk, or bribed, or joking.

By the age of ten, at any rate, Len Kibrick, with a baleful freckled face under a grim bush of ginger hair, was a real milk-curdler, the natural successor to Spec O'Donnell ◇. This wasn't going to frighten 'Our Gang', though. They had room for that kind of thing.

After *Roxie Hart* (42) Leonard, like Sidney, followed his father into the scrap-metal business. He then became a successful contractor.

33 The Bowery
34 Kid Millions
    'Our Gang' *(4 shorts)*
35 Ah, Wilderness!
    'Our Gang' *(4)*
36 Dimples
37 Love Is News
38 Boys Town
    Just Around the Corner
    My Lucky Star
    Peck's Bad Boy with the Circus
39 Fisherman's Wharf
    It's a Wonderful World
    Jesse James
    Rose of Washington Square

(l. to r.:) Stymie Beard, Tommy Bond, Wally Albright and Leonard Kibrick in a 1934 Our Gang comedy

Stanley and Livingstone
Tail Spin
40 'Our Gang' *(1)*

Akira Oizumi

JAPAN

b: 1 Jan 25 (Tokyo)

Kaze no Matasaburo made him famous, though he had already been for three years with the Gekidan Toho children's theatre company.

In his twenties he appeared in *Yabure daiko* (49), *Mata au himade* (50), *Jiyu gakko* (51) and in *Saikaku ichidai onna* (52, known abroad as 'The life of Oharu'). In 1959 he was in Ozu's *Ohayo*. More recently he has been in great demand as a character actor.

40 Kaze no Matasaburo
    (Whirlwind Matasaburo)
41 Ai no ikko (A family of love)

Stymie Beard

USA

b: 1 Jan 25 (Los Angeles)
d: 8 Jan 81 (Los Angeles)

There was something especially impressive about Matthew Beard, Junior, in 'Our Gang'. The Gang's director Bob McGowan dubbed the five-year-old newcomer 'Stymie' because he was always in the way. The bowler hat oddly suited his grown-up, laid-back air; his shaven head was as severely practical as 'Farina' Hoskins's ◊ had been rococo; nothing flustered him. He was given many of the best lines and delivered them with beautiful, off-hand crispness. 'Move over there, white boy, you's crowdin' me' – a line attributed by Stymie (in *Dogs Is Dogs*) to ham addressing eggs – might have been his own motto.

After 350 little black boys had been interviewed as possible successors to the much-loved Farina, Matthew strolled in and was so obviously right for the Gang that McGowan didn't even bother to test him. Directorially, it was love at first sight. Matthew was given a five-year contract

'Stymie' with hair, partnering Bonita Granville in Beloved Brat

on the spot, and there were to be no regrets on either side. Beginning at $100 a week (as 'Hercules', soon revised to 'Stymie') and rising finally to $500, he was a complete success, and loved every minute of it.

Although his father, Matthew Beard, Sr., was a minister of religion, things weren't always sweetness and light in the family, and his parents split up when he was quite young. However, both had encouraged him to act from an early age, and he continued to see his father.

After leaving the Gang in 1935, Stymie stayed in movies – those of his later teens included *Stormy Weather* (43) and *Fallen Angel* (45) – but the rest of his life was clouded by an addiction to drugs, and the illness and petty crime this brought with it. He had been busted at 16 for a few puffs of marijuana, and sent to reformatory. It was here (according to the blues musician T-Bone Walker, who knew him well in later life) that Stymie was introduced by older boys to the heroin that really screwed him up. Some reformation.

Eventually Stymie went to the Synanon drug rehabilitation center in Santa Monica, and stayed there for seven years

until the curse was finally off him. Then he began to get back into show business, as lovable a figure as ever in TV shows of the 1970s and films like *Truck Turner* (74) and *The Buddy Holly Story* (78) – but, sadly, died after a stroke at the beginning of 1981.

27 Uncle Tom's Cabin
29 Hallelujah!
    Hearts in Dixie
    Mamba
    My Best Girl
    Show Boat
30 'Our Gang' *(2 shorts)*
31 'Our Gang' *(8)*
32 'Our Gang' *(9)*
33 'Our Gang' *(6)*
34 'Our Gang' *(8)*
    Kid Millions
35 'Our Gang' *(3)*
    Captain Blood
36 Rainbow on the River
37 Reunion in Rhythm ('OG')
    Slave Ship
38 Beloved Brat
    Jezebel
    Kentucky
    Two-Gun Man from Harlem
39 Swanee River
    Way Down South
40 Broken Strings
    The Return of Frank James

Billy Burrud

USA

b: 12 Jan 25 (Hollywood)
d: 11 Jly 90 (Sunset Beach, Los Angeles)

His father, Dick Burrud, produced silent travelogues, or 'Scenic Pictures', which were popular around 1920. Bill, a burly and soon rather jowly lad, made his debut at seven in a road show called 'Music in the Air', and became a useful 'kid next door' in movies of the late Thirties. (Though capable of energetic action too: he was Buck Jones' sidekick in *The Cowboy and the Kid*, a remake of John Ford's *Just Pals* of 1920.)

In his late teens, Bill was in *Hitler's Children* (43). After Navy service in World War Two, he went to the Harvard Business School. He started a weekly fishing programme on Santa Ana radio, then did travelogues for KTTV. Finally, in 1954, he set up his own company, Bill Burrud Productions, which turned out – in an updated version of his father's line – no less than 14 travel and adventure series for television, notably 'Animal World' and 'Animal Odyssey'. Burrud also campaigned nobly for the protection of endangered species.

He kept his own performing skills, as a host on numerous TV shows and series, as well as in live events. In 1977 he directed *Curse of the Mayan Temple*.

35 His Night Out
   Three Kids and a Queen
36 The Cowboy and the Kid
   Devil's Squadron
   The Magnificent Brute
   Postal Inspector
   Pride of the Marines
   Two in a Crowd
37 Captains Courageous
   Fair Warning
   Girl Overboard
   Idol of the Crowds
   It Happened in Hollywood
   The Man in Blue
   Once a Hero
38 The Night Hawk

Tommy Bupp

USA

b: 2 Feb 25 (Norfolk, Virginia)
d: 25 Dec 83

The elder of the two Bupps was sandy-haired and freckled, with a snub nose and a pleasantly acerbic quality: few could have called Tommy 'sweet', at least without regretting it. But he was a true enthusiast. Having made his first movie appearance at 14 months (in something called *Mating Time*), he claimed to have made 75 by the time he was five. Moreover, he had a habit of turning up in the crowds of films he wasn't even engaged for – he would rather be an extra than kicking his heels.

He was characteristically cast as a pest or a sceptical little tough: W.C.Fields's bratty son in *It's a Gift*, or Bobby Breen's ◇ wry ally in *Fisherman's Wharf*. (Fields obviously sensed a kindred spirit, since he called Tommy, two or three years later, into some of his radio sketches.) He appeared – or at least was credited – in just one 'Our Gang' film: *Hi'-Neighbor!* And he made some roarin' Westerns.

One of his biggest roles, oddly enough, was opposite Will Hay in the 1938 British comedy *Hey! Hey! U.S.A.!*

After *The Way of All Flesh*, in which he and Darryl Hickman ◇ played Akim Tamiroff's sons, the admirable Bupp Major had a role in *Naval Academy* (41), and not much more.

34 Babes in Toyland
   Chained
   A Girl of the Limberlost
   Hi'-Neighbor! (OG)
   It's a Gift
   Kid Millions
   Little Men
   The Man from Hell
35 Ah, Wilderness!
   Arizona Badmen
   Ginger
   The Hoosier Schoolmaster
   Life Returns
   Paddy O'Day
36 Conflict
   It Had to Happen
   The Longest Night
   Pepper
   Piccadilly Jim
   Roarin' Guns
   San Francisco
   Sutter's Gold
37 Captains Courageous

Our Father: Billy Burrud with Henry Armetta in Three Kids and a Queen

Tommy Bupp with Norman Foster in The Hoosier Schoolmaster

The Cherokee Strip
High, Wide and Handsome
Hittin' the Trail
Love is on the Air
Make a Wish
Make Way for Tomorrow
Over the Wall
Roarin' Lead
Tex Rides with the Boy Scouts
Tovarich
38 Blind Alibi
The Devil's Party
Hey! Hey! U.S.A.! (GB)
Hunted Men
Little Orphan Annie
Love, Honor and Behave
Nancy Drew – Detective
Reformatory
A Slight Case of Murder
Swing Your Lady
39 Beware Spooks!
Confessions of a Nazi Spy
Emergency Squad
Fisherman's Wharf
Hero for a Day
Indianapolis Speedway
Joe and Ethel Turp Call
on the President
Mr Smith Goes to Washington

Mystery Plane
No Place To Go
Off the Record
On Your Toes
Outside These Walls
They Asked For It
The Unexpected Father
When Tomorrow Comes
40 Brother Rat and a Baby
Saga of Death Valley
The Way of All Flesh

Loaded: Tommy Bupp in Hey! Hey! USA!

Dévényi in the 1936 Légy jó mindhalálig

László Dévényi

HUNGARY

b: 8 Feb 25 (Hegyeshalom)

This serious, brown-eyed boy was chosen to play the idealistic hero of Zsigmond Móricz's once-famous school novel 'Légy jó mindhalálig'. (Filmed again in 1960.)
   Dévényi continued to appear as an actor in his later teens: *Férfihüség* (42), *Majális* (43), *Gyanu* (44). Then he moved to the production side, and in the 1960s began scripting and directing scientific and documentary films.

36 Evforduló (Anniversary)
   Légy jó mindhalálig (Always be good)
   A méltóságos kisasszony
      (The honorable young lady)
38 Fekete gyémántok (Black diamonds)
39 Bors Istvan (Istvan Bors)
40 Sarajevo

Bobby 'Wheezer' Hutchins

USA

b: 29 Mar 25 (Tacoma, Washington)
d: 17 May 45

'Wheezer' was a cheerful little boy who was barely two when he joined 'Our Gang' in the Spring of 1927 as one of a host of infants featured in *Baby Brothers* – but he had already been in one or two of the current 'Buster Brown' comedies. His only known appearance in a full-length film was in *Exposed* (32).

spelt Klaus in latter years, as if to empha-
sise his solidarity with new-found Father-
land rather than with old, lost Father.)

Young Sierck, with his delicate looks,
tended to be cast as an 'artistic' child –
sometimes in a positive sense (he was the
young Chopin in *Preussische Liebesgeschichte*) and sometimes (as in the loathsome
Kopf hoch, Johannes!) needing to be taught
to conform for the greater good.

In *Streit um den Knaben Jo* – probably one
of the silliest films ever made, in which Lil
Dagover convinces herself that her son is
a changeling – he was cast opposite a
straightfoward blond with the resound-
ing name of EBERHARD ITZENPLITZ. Herr Itzenplitz (born 8 Nov 26), after appearing

Claus Detlef Sierck, circa 1939

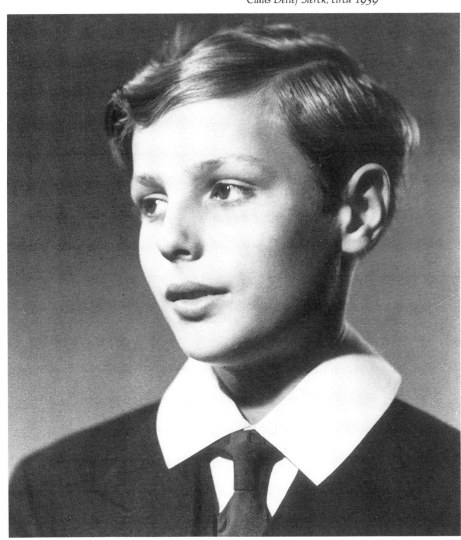

*David and Goliath: 'Wheezer' Hutchins defies
John Aassen in Our Gang's* Growing Pains
(1928)

Maltin and Bann, in their indispensable
guide to the Gang canon, describe him
aptly as an 'artless scene-stealer', and he
and 'Farina' Hoskins ◇ were the only two
principals to be retained when 'Our Gang'
switched to sound early in 1929. He
ended with a tally of 58 Gang titles.

After 'Wheezer' left the Gang in mid-
1933, at the age of eight, there is no
record of his having appeared before
movie cameras again. Twelve years later
he was killed in an accident at an army
training camp.

Claus Detlef Sierck

GERMANY

b: 30 Mar 25 (Berlin)
d: 6 Mar 44 (Novo Alexandrovka, Russia)

Claus Detlef Sierck, Junior, was the son of
the Danish-born director later known as
Douglas Sirk. The boy remained behind
when his father quit Germany in 1937,
and with his sensitive, aristocratic looks
became the *beau idéal* of German screen
youth – yet another non-native to fulfil
the role. (His first name was sometimes

in six more films in the early 1950s, became a distinguished director on TV.

Kadetten, based on an episode from the Seven Years' War, was not released till 1941 because of its anti-Russian sentiments, inconvenient in 1939. Its story of children from a military school, facing overwhelming Russian odds with death-defying heroism, persuaded countless German schoolboys of the sweetness and fitness of dying for their country, and prepared them for frozen graves in the East.

One of these boys was Claus Detlef Sierck.

35 Die Saat geht auf (The seed grows up)
37 Serenade
   Streit um den Knaben Jo
      (The struggle over young Jo)
38 Preussische Liebesgeschichte
      (Prussian love story)
   Schatten über St Pauli
      (Shadow over St Pauli)
   Verwehte Spuren (Lost traces)
39 Kadetten (Cadets)
   Das Recht auf Liebe (The right to love)
   Sehnsucht nach Afrika (Longing for Africa)
40 Aus erster Ehe (By the first marriage)
41 Kopf hoch, Johannes! (Chin up, Johannes!)
42 Der grosse König (The great King)

Tommy Kelly

USA

b: 6 Apr 25 (New York)

The 1938 Tom Sawyer was one of thirteen children of a poor Irish family in the Bronx. He was chosen as Tom out of 25,000 interviewed.

Freckled Tommy Kelly had three years of celebrity, but the parts grew less rewarding. After a few more films, such as *Double Date* (41), *Nice Girl* (41), *Mug Town* (43) and *The Magnificent Yankee* (50), he faded back into the crowd.

38 The Adventures of Tom Sawyer
   Peck's Bad Boy with the Circus
39 Gone with the Wind
   They Shall Have Music
40 Curtain Call
   Gallant Sons

Tommy Kelly (left), with Mickey Rentschler (centre) as Joe Harper, in The Adventures of Tom Sawyer

Irene
It's a Date
Military Academy

Rex Downing

USA

b: 21 Apr 25

Looking like a tougher Freddie Bartholomew◇, Rex Downing is now most often seen as the boy Heathcliff in *Wuthering Heights*. He doesn't have the looks of Olivier, but he has some of the fire, and makes a fine wildcat in the opening scenes.

He made a few appearances with 'Our Gang' early in his career, but only in a secondary capacity. His younger brother Barry also acted, sometimes in the same films.

Rex was in a few later films, such as *Blood and Sand* (41), *The Mayor of 44th Street* (42), *Gas House Kids* (46), *The Gangster* (47), *Call Northside 777* (47) and *He Walked By Night* (48).

35 'Our Gang' (3)
36 General Spanky
   Love on the Run
   'Our Gang' (4)
   Second Wife
37 Michael O'Halloran
   'Our Gang' (2)
38 The Arizona Wildcat
   The Black Bandit
   Bravest of the Brave
   The Man on the Rock
39 The Escape
   Mandrake the Magician
   Nurse Edith Cavell
   Wuthering Heights
40 Adventure in Diamonds

Heimo Haitto

FINLAND

b: 27 May 25 (Ruokolehti)

Unlike previous boy fiddlers of the screen, such as Martin Herzberg◇ and Leon Holmes◇ – who were lucky to be in action before the arrival of sound – Haitto was an actual child prodigy, following in the footsteps of Yehudi Menuhin. The

Soulful fiddler: Heimo Haitto in Pikku pelimanni

great Sibelius himself took the boy under his wing.

Pikku pelimanni had a fictional story, though it inevitably had some real-life input. Ten years later, material from it was used in something more nearly approaching a Haitto biopic, *Pikku pelimannista viulun kuninkaaksi* (From little fiddler to king of the violin).

In the meantime, in 1941, Haitto had had a featured spot in a Hollywood film which initially had the boring title *There's Magic in Music* – later changed to one which was certainly not boring, however bizarre: *The Hard-Boiled Canary*. He then settled and continued his musical career in the USA, and it wasn't till 1980 that he returned to live and work in Finland.

In 1985 a film called *Da capo* (FI/SE) was inspired by Haitto's life. It starred the Swedish boy violinist Jan Söderblom.

39 Pikku pelimanni (The little fiddler)
41 The Hard-Boiled Canary (US)

Marcel Krols

BELGIUM/HOLLAND

b: 10 Jly 25 (Wortel, Belgium)
d: 24 Dec 46

A stage play had been made from A. M. de Jong's popular novel *Merijntje Gijzen's*

jeugd, and de Jong himself had seen the ten-year-old Marcel Krols – sandy-haired, unglamorous, wholly believable – playing the title role in an amateur production. When the film was being set up, the author suggested Marcel to the producer.

Merijntje's younger brother Arjaan was played by KEES BRUSSE (b: 26 Feb 25, son of the writer M.J.Brusse).

Tragically, Krols died when he had just qualified as a teacher, and when his young wife was pregnant with a child he would never see.

36 Merijntje Gijzen's jeugd
(The youth of Merijntje Gijzen – NL)

Masao Hayama

JAPAN

b: 1 Aug 25 (Yokohama)

Masao – an intelligent boy used by both Ozu and Shimizu – had rather a heavy, elderly face and manner. He couldn't have played sprightly parts, and wasn't required to.

He continued acting in films till his mid-twenties: *Jigoku no kao* (47), *Gekido* (47), *Ware naki nurete* (47), *Norakura kaihin sodo* (48).

35 Jinsei no onimotsu (Burden of life)
Mashiroki Fuji no ne
(The white peak of Fuji)
Teiso mondo (Questions of chastity)
36 Hitori musuko (The only son)
Ofumi no hyoban (Popular Ofumi)

Masao Hayama (right) with Mitsuko Yoshikawa in Jinsei no onimotsu

37 Haha no shori (Mother's victory)
Kaze no naka no kodomo
(Children in the wind)
Kojo no tsuki (Moon over the ruins)
Shukujo wa nani o wasuretaka
(What did the lady forget?)
38 Kibo ni tatsu (Ever hopeful)
39 Kodomo no shiki (Four seasons of children)
41 Toda-ke no kyodai
(Siblings from the Toda family)

Donald O'Connor, circa 1938

Donald O'Connor

USA

b: 30 Aug 25 (Chicago)

His parents were originally circus performers: father an acrobat, mother a bareback rider and tightrope walker. Later they turned to the Theatre, with a family act of song, dance and acrobatics which earned them the title of 'The Royal Family of Vaudeville'. Donald used to be carried on to the stage to wave and gurgle at the audience from his infant wrappings until he was old enough to squeak a song and totter through a tiny dance. It can't have taken long, since at the age of one he is said to have danced a Black Bottom, and been tap-dancing at three. In the end he became one of the finest hoofers in the business.

With his pale, elfin eyes and saucy air, Donald was a natural for the movies. In *Melody For Two* he and two of his brothers did a vaudeville number, and he was then signed up by Paramount. (In *Tom Sawyer, Detective* he played Huck to the

O'Connor with Helen Twelvetrees in Unmarried

Tom of Billy Cook ◇, a boy who wasn't to rival O'Connor's subsequent career.)

A series of Universal musicals in the Forties (notably opposite Peggy Ryan) kept O'Connor in the popular eye, and in the Fifties he was six times partnered – rather less engagingly – by Francis, the Talking Mule. In the same decade, though, came some of his great dance-and-comedy performances: in *Singin' in the Rain* (52), *Call Me Madam* and *Walking My Baby Back Home* (53), *There's No Business Like Show Business* (54) and *Anything Goes* (56).

Finally he made his sporting but not quite adequate stab at portraying genius in *The Buster Keaton Story* (57). In a sense it demonstrated his limitations to O'Connor himself. After *That Funny Feeling* (65) he returned to vaudeville, and for years the cinema saw little of this admirable entertainer. Then he turned up in *Ragtime* (81) – as Evelyn Nesbit's dance teacher (see Russell Thaw ◇) – and in *Pandemonium* (82).

37 Melody for Two
38 Men with Wings
   Sing, You Sinners
   Sons of the Legion
   Tom Sawyer, Detective
39 Beau Geste
   Boy Trouble
   Death of a Champion
   Million Dollar Legs
   Night Work
   On Your Toes
   Unmarried

Wally Albright

USA

b: 3 Sep 25 (Burbank, Cal.)

That this curly blond with the bold, fine eyes may not have been quite so curly as everyone thought is revealed by Maltin and Bann, in their monumental guide to 'Our Gang', for whom Wally played leads during 1934. His rococo chevelure would wilt under the studio lights, and have to be revived between takes by the same curling-iron that had created it.

Walton Albright, Jr., began in the business as a babe, and acted busily throughout the Thirties. One of his most memorable roles – though a rather passive one – was as the terrified child in the lion cages in *Zoo in Budapest*. But after a nondescript debut in 'Our Gang' (*Choo-Choo!*, 32), he was featured two years later as the democratic rich boy Waldo in five of their best shorts. (Not to be confused with the later, bespectacled 'Waldo' of Darwood Kaye.)

He made only one or two adult movie appearances – his last recorded credit is in *The Wild One* (53). Then he left the profession, and prospered in other kinds of business – trucking and real estate. He also became a considerable sportsman, particularly with speedboats.

28 A Free Soul
   Going Ga-Ga
29 The Case of Lena Smith
   Scandal
   The Single Standard
   Thunder
   The Trespasser
   Wonder of Women
30 The Florodora Girl
   Song o' My Heart
   Vengeance
31 East Lynne
   Salvation Nell

Wally Albright and caged adult in Zoo in Budapest

Albright in King of the Sierras

Dickie Moore

USA

b: 12 Sep 25 (Los Angeles)

John Richard Moore's father was an Irish banker; his mother was of French stock. His screen debut came around his first birthday when he portrayed John Barrymore as a baby in *The Beloved Rogue* – after which he could be said never to have looked back, at least until the 1940s.

With his striking combination of very fair hair and very dark, intense eyes, the tiny Moore fluttered maternal hearts everywhere, and was featured as the screen baby of many a famous name in the early Thirties, notably of Marlene Dietrich in *Blonde Venus*. For eight films during 1932-33 he was a leading member of 'Our Gang' (and, piquantly, a particular buddy of Stymie Beard ◇). In 1933 he also played Oliver Twist.

By his mid-teens Dickie Moore's career was thinning out, though he was a well-liked lad and a few parts were found for him. In *Miss Annie Rooney* (42) he had the honour of giving Shirley Temple her first screen kiss – of a romantic nature – but it didn't take either of their acting careers much further.

After war service and a degree in journalism, Dick Moore was in a few more films like *Out of the Past* (47), *Killer Shark* (50) and *The Member of the Wedding* (53). Then, after acting and directing on the New York stage, he began to work for Actors Equity, editing their periodical and becoming for several years their Public Relations Counsel.

Later he moved into public relations on his own account, and published a fascinating autobiography called 'Twinkle, Twinkle, Little Star'. (Subtitled 'But Don't Have Sex or Take the Car'.)

Dickie Moore, circa 1935

Jean-Pierre Geffroy

FRANCE

b: 22 Sep 25 (Paris)

His father, Henri-Charles Geffroy (1895-1981), was a medical journalist who did much to popularise 'natural diet' in France, through many books and through his periodical 'La Vie Claire', which in turn led to the health food shops of the same name.

Out of some 2,000 young applicants, Jean-Pierre was chosen by the actor Gaston Modot — who had had a hand in the script — to play the leading role of Rozet in Louis Daquin's *Nous les gosses*, probably the most popular French children's film of all time. As it appeared in 1941, under the German occupation, this story of youthful solidarity was taken to the Parisian heart almost as a metaphor of survival.

It tells how an accident-prone boy kicks a football through an expensive

Jean-Pierre Geffroy as Rozet in Nous les gosses

school window, how his schoolmates raise the replacement money through fantastic commercial and artistic enterprise in the streets, how the money is then stolen by a pair of spivs, and how the kids get it back and bring them to justice. The story ends with a moving speech of congratulation from the headmaster – after which the same hapless boy propels a football through the brand-new window.

It's a film of lovely gags and lovely performances. Among some rather less honourable money-raising ploys (spraying mud on to the shoes of passing gentlemen to boost the boot-blacking, or posing as the starving children of a fake beggar) is a very thoughtful one: they all agree to donate their 'cinema money', but in case the parents ask what they have been to see, just one boy is deputed to go to the cinema and then retail the plot to the rest. Unfortunately he falls asleep in the middle of *La dame aux camélias* and wakes up again in the middle of the supporting cowboy film – with predictably charming results when one of his mates has to describe the plot to his elders.

Geffroy (wrongly credited on the film as 'Geoffroy') was 15 at the time of filming, but looks and sounds two years younger. He has a remarkable, streamlined face which recalls a Norman knight looking fiercely through his helmet, its power contrasting touchingly with the skinny body and the gentle, musical voice. He breathes utter desolation when the money vanishes and he, of all people, is suspected of pinching it.

Jean-Pierre's real-life parents, however, had a poor opinion of theatricals, and though he was allowed two more tiny film parts, there could be no question of pursuing an acting career. He married and settled down to help run the family health business. He is now an absurdly youthful grandfather – a tribute, presumably, to his father's dietary regime.

41 Nous les gosses (Us kids)
42 La belle aventure (The beautiful adventure)
   Le voile bleu (The blue veil)

Billy Barty

USA

b: 25 Oct 25 (Millsborough, Pa.)

In the history of the cinema, many midgets have played the parts of children. Billy Barty is the most eminent example of an actual child midget. He was the tiny blond fellow in the 'Mickey McGuire' series with the future Rooney °, the imp featured in *Gold Diggers of 1933* (the 'Pettin' in the Park' number) and in *Footlight Parade* ('Honeymoon Hotel' and 'Sittin' on the Back Fence'). In *A Midsummer Night's Dream* he was Mustardseed, and in *Nothing Sacred* the 'human dog'.

Oddly enough, Billy had also appeared on the French screen at the end of the 1920s, around the same time as 'Mickey McGuire', in a series called 'Théâtre de la Famille Roulotte' (Caravan Family Theatre), which featured the 'Troupe Macaque et Cie.' in short films like *Un auteur a succès* (A successful author), *Billy l'enfant terrible* (Frightful little Billy), *Emile est insupportable* (Emile is unbearable), *Mieux vaut star que jamais* (Better great than never), *Le torchon brûle chez les jocko* (Riot in the monkey-house) and *Les trois complices* (The three accomplices).

The rest of insupportable Billy's child career was in Hollywood.

While subject to modest growing pains, Billy Barty wasn't prominent for a time. But he re-surfaced in, for instance, *Pigmy Island* (50), *The Undead* (57), *Harum Scarum* (65) and, most notably, as the truculent tipster Abe Kusich in *The Day of the Locust* (75). Since then he has been seen more often, for instance in *Tough Guys* (86).

30 Follow the Swallow
31 Daddy Long Legs
   The Dog Doctor
   Goldie
   Monkey Business
   Over the Hill
31-32 'Mickey McGuire' series
33 Alice in Wonderland
   Footlight Parade
   Gold Diggers of 1933
   Out All Night

   Roman Scandals
34 The Gift of Gab
35 The Bride of Frankenstein
36 A Midsummer Night's Dream
37 Nothing Sacred

Pino Locchi

ITALY

b: 11 Nov 25 (Rome)

Pino was a boy with a plain, pleasant, squarish, intelligent face. He had a good part in his late teens in *Turbamento*, and continued acting for most of the next half-century.

31 L'ultima avventura (The final adventure)
32 Il natale di bebè (Baby's birthday)
   Sette giorni cento lire (Seven days, 100 lire)
   Zaganella e il cavaliere (Zaganella and the cavalier)
33 Camicia nera (Blackshirt)
   Il signore desidera (The gentleman wishes)
34 Il canale degli angeli (Angels' Canal)
35 Campo di maggio (May Field)
   Fiat voluntas dei (God's will be done)
   La luce del mondo (The light of the world)
38 Chi sei tu? (Who are you?)
   Fuochi d'artificio (Fireworks)
40 Gli ultimi della strada (Lowest of the low)

Douglas Scott

USA

b: 31 Dec 25 (Seattle)

His parents were British, with both Scots and French in the family genes; his grandfather, Isaac Scott, had been a famous brain specialist. They moved to Los Angeles when Douglas was three, and through a dancing school he attended he got a small part in a Fox film. In due course it led to a contract.

Douglas Scott didn't, it must be said, grow into one of Hollywood's more exciting child actors. He became a rather doughily handsome, heavy-chinned boy. But because he was intelligent and reliable, with striking eyes and a patrician manner, he got plenty of work. He's more acceptable as a supercilious meanie – in

Douglas Scott in Gus Edwards's Baby Follies

Wuthering Heights for instance – than as a cheerful or sensitive character.

Scott had one or two more films in his mid-teens – *Naval Academy* (41), *Get Hep to Love* (42) – but he didn't return to the screen after the War.

George Billings

USA

b: 1925

Not to be confused with the actor George A. Billings (1871-1934), who played Abraham Lincoln in the 1924 film. Sleek, fair and easy-going, young George was just about as unlike Lincoln as could be imagined – but his work-load can't have been much lighter.

He did occasional work with 'Our Gang', and in many shorts with comics like Charlie Chase, Leon Errol and Edgar Kennedy.

After two more films in 1941, and a return in *O.S.S.* (46), George did nothing much till *A Pocketful of Miracles* (61).

Vitya Kartashoff

USSR

b: circa 1925

The negative and prints of Eisenstein's aborted film *Bezhin Meadow*, remotely based on a Turgenev story, were destroyed during World War Two. All that survived, in the director's personal archive, were reference frames clipped out and put aside during editing.

The lost film was resurrected from these clippings by Naum Kleiman in the late 1960s, in an assemblage of marvellous still images which tell the story in half an hour. Some critics have felt that on the evidence of this 'potted' version, *Bezhin Meadow* might well have been Eisenstein's master-piece. (Those who find the Russian master a visual genius, but with a tendency to prolixity and ham, may actually be glad to have it in fat-free stills.)

The story tells of a brutal, reactionary old peasant who bitterly resents the New Age of rural reform, and above all its personification in his own schoolboy son Stepok, a mustard-keen Young Pioneer. In an appalling climax of rage, having been frustrated in his attempts to sabotage the collective harvest, he kills the boy.

Vitya Kartashoff, a slim, prancing sprite with a strange oval face and an aureole of spiky blond hair, creates a striking

Vitya Kartashoff in Bezhin lug

Communist angel-martyr. The critic Boris Shumyatski, in his devastating onslaught in Pravda in March 1937, accused Eisenstein of turning Stepok into a 'consecrated holy child' like a crucified Christ — and the cross is undeniably invoked in one image of the dying boy.

The real-life passion of young Kartashoff, the son of a Red Army driver, was in fact mathematics. (Pravda would have approved.) After war service he became a technician. He was seriously ill for a time, but was present in 1967 at the first showing of Kleiman's reconstruction.

37 Bezhin lug (Bezhin meadow)

Alyosha Lyarski

USSR

b: circa 1925
d: circa 1944

Mark Donskoi's trio of films based on Maxim Gorki's autobiographical trilogy, produced by the Moscow Children's Film Studio within a few years of the great writer's death, is one of the glories of the Russian cinema. Its first two parts, in which the dogged, puzzled Lyarski plays the hero, are unforgettable. (The older Young Gorki of *My Universities* is rather wet by comparison.)

Driven by poverty, Aleksei Peshkoff (Gorki's real name) and his widowed mother come to live with her parents in a provincial village. There he lives with, and works for, a hateful old grandfather — a monster of rage and avarice — lazy, scheming uncles and mean, sneaky little cousins. His only comforts, apart from his mother (but she soon goes away) are the extrovert young peasant who acts as the family's factotum (but he dies through an inane act of spite by the uncles) and his huge earth-mother of a Grandma (played with unique warmth and emotion by Massalitinova, like a sweet, wise, smiling old hippo — one of the world's great screen characterisations).

Young Aleksei sees greed, exploitation and injustice at close range, but he's not yet strong enough to fight it. For instance, one of the few people who is kind to him is an old man employed in a cloth-dyeing vat, in conditions that eventually cause him to lose his eyesight. Yet when his old friend is too blind to work and has to go out as a beggar, Aleksei shamefacedly avoids him. This kind of jolting truthfulness makes the film unforgettable.

Notable among the other boys in *Detstvo Gorkovo* are Igor Smirnoff as the little bedridden cripple Lyonya, indomitably sunny with his white mouse and his games, and the two weasely cousins (V.Khoroshenchikov and Y.Mamayev), plus the multi-ethnic gang of locals that Aleksei roams the fields with. Smirnoff appeared two years later in *Yakov Sverdloff* and in the Soviet youth classic *Timur i yevo komanda*. (See Livi Shchipachev ◊.)

Aleksei Lyarski, the enormously touching young Gorki, was killed in action during World War Two, joining Jimmy Butler ◊, Robert Lynen ◊, Robin Ordell ◊, Hans-Joachim Schaufuss ◊, Claus-Detlef Sierck ◊, Rolf Wenkhaus ◊ and others in the boy actors' Elysium.

38 Detstvo Gorkovo (Gorki's childhood)
   V lyudyakh (Out in the world)

Ernesto Velasquez

MEXICO

b: circa 1925

This boy warbler, once referred to as 'el Bobby Breen ◊ mexicano', had the lead in *La cancion del huerfano*, but this was his last film as a boy.

After a lapse of more than a decade,

Alyosha Lyarski in Detstvo Gorkovo, *with Igor Smirnoff (right) as Lyonya*

Ernesto Velazquez appeared in two or three films of the early Fifties, with a lead in *La niña Popoff* (51).

38 Alla en el Rancho Chico
     (Over at Boys' Ranch)
   Rosa de Xochomilco (Rose of Xochomilco)
   La china Hilaria (The girl Hilaria)
39 La cancion del huerfano
     (The orphan's song)

Jean Buquet

FRANCE

b: 18 Apr 26 (Paris)

The leader of the anti-Rozet faction in *Nous les gosses* was an aggressive, rather sneering 15-year-old (with faint touches of Jean Gabin and Farley Granger) who three years earlier had been a treacherous little wimp in *Les disparus de Saint Agil*. However he could, on occasion, be quite a dear.

In his late teens Buquet was in four more films: in 1942 *Les cadets de l'Océan* and *Fou d'amour*, in 1943 *Lucrèce* and *Le carrefour*. Then, in 1944, he volunteered for military service, and was in the liaison section of Leclerc's army during the final invasion of Germany. After the war he became a press reporter.

35 Bout de chou (Little pet)
   Debout, là-dedans! (Stand up in there!)
   Jérôme Perreau
36 L'appel du silence (The call of silence)
   La guerre des gosses (The kids' war)
37 Une femme sans importance
     (A woman of no importance)
   Ma petite marquise (My little marchioness)
   Orage (Storm)
   Soeurs d'armes (Sisters in arms)
38 Ceux de demain (Tomorrow's people)
   Les disparus de Saint-Agil
     (The lost boys of Saint-Agil)
   Remontons les Champs-Elysées
     (Let's go up the Champs-Elysées)
   Le révolté (The rebel)
   Le roman de Werther
     (The story of Werther)
39 La charrette fantôme (The phantom cart)
   Le duel
   L'enfer des anges (Angels' hell)
   Entente cordiale
   Les trois tambours (The three drummers)
40 De Mayerling à Sarajevo
     (From Mayerling to Sarajevo)
41 L'assassinat du Père Noël
     (The murder of Father Christmas)
   Nous les gosses (Us kids)
   Péchés de jeunesse (Sins of youth)

Delmar Watson, 1938

Delmar Watson

USA

b: 1 Jly 26 (Los Angeles)

Perhaps the busiest of all the Watson siblings, Delmar got cracking at the age of seven months in the 'Big Boy' shorts with Malcolm Sabiston ◇. His thespian ability can't have emerged too clearly in diapers, but he proved a live wire in later short subjects with Andy Clyde, 'Our Gang', Leon Errol and others.

Very much the brown-haired Irish lad in looks, Delmar was a spirited goat-boy Peter in Shirley Temple's *Heidi*, and one of four Watsons in *Mr Smith Goes to Washington*; he was said, quite believably, to have been in over 200 movies by 1938. Most of his roles were comic, but he had an occasional dramatic one, as in *Outside the Law*, and took it well.

Fair-haired GARRY (born 27 Sep 28), the next Watson after Delmar, also acted from a tender age, though not at quite such a furious rate as his elder brothers. And then came Bobs ◇.

After a young-adult movie appearance in *The Gas House Kids Go West* (47), Delmar Watson pursued a distinguished career as photographer, both for newspapers and as part of the 'Six Watsons'

Jean Buquet (left) with Jean-Pierre Geffroy in Nous les gosses

studio. Over the past 15 years he has published three photographic histories of Los Angeles and Hollywood.

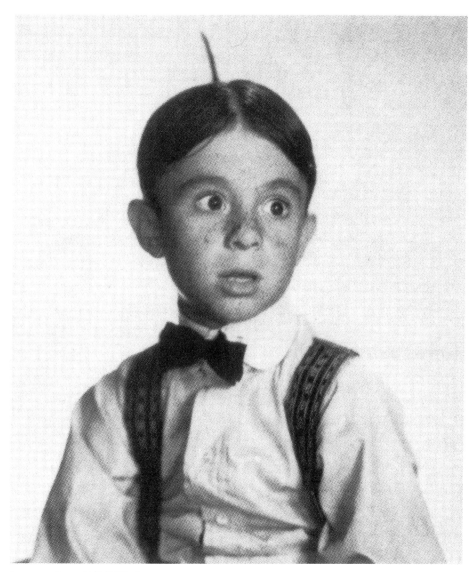

Insecure unicorn: 'Alfalfa' Switzer

Carl 'Alfalfa' Switzer

USA

b: 8 Aug 26 (Paris, Illinois)
d: 21 Jan 59 (Sepulveda, Cal.)

This 'squeaky-voiced master of the bug-eyed double-take', to quote Norman J. Zierold, was for many the crowning glory of 'Our Gang', if only because under the freckles, the centre parting and the grotesque over-confidence was a real and vulnerable child. His bossy pretensions were punctured often and deservedly, but there was sometimes a poignancy when they were: the edifice of self-esteem was so touchingly flimsy.

On the other hand Alfalfa's terrible singing concealed actual talent: he had, it seems, a beautiful natural voice, and began his career as a singer, accompanying himself on the mandolin. From the age of four he had joined his brother Harold in harmonious duets at local dos. Around the end of 1934, during a visit to their grandparents, the two boys dropped in on the Hal Roach studio, and in a calculated act of bravura mounted a hillbilly singsong in the 'Our Gang' cafeteria. It worked: within hours they had parts in a Gang comedy.

As 'Deadpan' or 'Slim', the fairer Harold stuck around and notched up 28 appearances over a five-year span. But Carl, as

145

'Alfalfa', became a big, big star – almost as big as the absurd character thought he was. The cowardly little dude with the unflattenable spike of hair (recalling 'Snookums' McKeen ◇ a decade earlier) and the almost unflattenable vanity swaggered and gulped his way through 60 Gang comedies with titles like *Rushin' Ballet, Bear Facts* or *Came the Brawn*. He never stayed long abashed when he made an ass of himself, and was graciously ready at any time to oblige his public by bursting into atonal song.

Alfalfa was allowed out of the Gang now and then to appear in short subjects with Charlie Chase and other comics. But in 1940 he was finally pensioned off, and next found fleeting prominence in a series called 'The Reg'lar Fellers'.

In 1942 Carl Switzer was in two shorts (*There's One Born Every Minute* and *Man or Mouse*) with the ten-year-old beginner Elizabeth Taylor. He was also seen in Bob Hope's *My Favorite Blonde, Mrs Wiggs of the Cabbage Patch* and two or three other films.

Over the next fifteen years, besides starring in *The Great Mike* (44) and in another series, *The Gas House Kids*, he pops up briefly at least 20 times, in films that include *The Human Comedy* (43), *Going My Way* (44), *It's a Wonderful Life* (46), *A Letter to Three Wives* (48), *Pat and Mike* (52), *Island in the Sky* (53), and *The High and the Mighty* (54).

In *Track of the Cat* (54) he played a 100-year-old man, but under the plastic wrinkles he still looked, and behaved, terribly young. In 1958 he got a really good part in *The Defiant Ones*, but it was to be his last.

Switzer's life began to get creepy. That same year, someone shot at him and wounded him, they never found out who or why. He had diversified into bartending, and acting as a bear-hunting guide. In 1959, in a quarrel with a former associate in the hunting business who, he claimed, owed him $50, our hero drew a knife on him and the man shot him dead. 'Justifiable homicide' was the verdict. The Bear Facts had caught up with Alfalfa.

35 'Our Gang' *(7 shorts)*
   Southern Exposure
36 'Our Gang' *(9)*
   Easy to Take
   General Spanky
   Kelly the Second
   Life Hesitates at 40
   Too Many Parents
37 'Our Gang' *(12)*
   Pick a Star
   Right in Your Lap
   Wild and Woolly
38 'Our Gang' *(13)*
   Scandal Street
39 'Our Gang' *(10)*
   Ice Follies of 1939
40 'Our Gang' *(9)*
   Barnyard Follies
   I Love You Again
41 The Reg'lar Fellers *(series)*

Billy Cook

USA

b: 13 Oct 26 (Menlo Park, Cal.)

The dark, solid Billy – whose birthday has also been given as November 25 – had a father who was a chemistry professor at Santa Clara University, and a journalist mother who dabbled in amateur dramatics at the Little Theatre in Palo Alto. When he was eleven she told him there was a nice part for a boy coming up soon, but he wasn't enthusiastic, and was only persuaded to try by the threat of a week's dish-washing if he didn't.

His stage debut led to work on radio, and this in turn to a film test. One of his first jobs was the title role in *Tom Sawyer, Detective*, with Donald O'Connor ◇ as his Huck.

38 The Arkansas Traveler
   Men with Wings
   Sons of the Legion
   Tom Sawyer, Detective
39 Beau Geste
   Disputed Passage
   Gone with the Wind
   I'm from Missouri
   Invitation to Happiness
40 The Blue Bird
   I Was an Adventuress
41 Naval Academy
42 The Major and the Minor

Tucker, 1936

Jerry Tucker

USA

b: 1 Nov 26 (Chicago)

Red-haired Jerry Schatz, the son of a boxing manager, performed on radio from the age of four. He was in seventeen 'Our Gang' comedies, from *Shiver My Timbers* in 1931 to *Three Men in a Tub* in 1938, sometimes identified as 'Percy' but never quite becoming a Gang regular. (Though he was in the Gang feature film, *General Spanky*.)

He was a tough boy, good at playing rich slobs, and got plenty of work outside the Gang, including a featured role in the 1938 *Dick Tracy* serial.

Jerry Tucker's movie career didn't go far into his teens. Education supervened. He was wounded while serving in World War Two, and afterwards became a communications engineer in New York.

31 Dr Jekyll and Mr Hyde
   Shiver My Timbers ('OG')
   Sooky
32 Blonde Venus
   The Miracle Man
   Newly Rich
   Prosperity

Tomorrow and Tomorrow
33 'Our Gang' *(2)*
Hello, Everybody!
Sitting Pretty
34 'Our Gang' *(4)*
35 'Our Gang' *(6)*
36 'Our Gang' *(2)*
Anything Goes
Captain January
Cavalcade of the West
General Spanky
37 Glove Taps ('OG')
Love in a Bungalow
Love Is On the Air
Penrod and Sam
Tovarich
Wells Fargo
38 Dick Tracy Returns *(serial)*
Federal Man Hunt
Maid's Night Out
Penrod and His Twin Brother
Penrod's Double Trouble
Reckless Living
Three Men in a Tub ('OG')

Buster Phelps

USA

b: 5 Nov 26 (Hollywood)
d: 10 Jan 83 (Los Angeles)

Silas Vernon Phelps, Jr. – more commonly called Buster – was an earnest little boy with a powerful forehead above shrewd brown eyes. His elder brother, Cooke Phelps, had had marginal employment in a few films of the late Twenties, and Buster was apprenticed to the trade at five months in gurgling roles. He spent two early years as a very small member of the 'Mickey McGuire' troupe.

Buster's career went strongly till he was eleven or so, then tailed off. Among his last featured roles were ones in *And the Angels Sing* (44), *Tomorrow Is Forever* (46) and *Mother Is a Freshman* (49).

28-30 'Mickey McGuire' comedies
30 Feet First
31 Indiscreet
Leftover Ladies
One Way Passage
32 Frisco Jenny
Handle With Care
Little Orphan Annie
Scandal for Sale

Buster Phelps with James Dunn

Three on a Match
33 Broken Dreams
Laughing at Life
One Man's Journey
Sailor's Luck
The World Gone Mad
34 Now and Forever
Servants' Entrance
Strange Wives
35 The Affair of Susan
Little Men
36 Anna Karenina
Libeled Lady
Small Town Girl
Too Many Parents
37 Girl Loves Boy
38 Little Tough Guy
39 Hero for a Day
40 The Blue Bird
The Howards of Virginia
41 The Wagons Roll at Night

Akihiko Katayama

JAPAN

b: 11 Nov 26 (Kyoto)

Akihiko, son of the actor and director Koji Shima, was a beautiful child with a cropped, gleaming head and large expressive eyes. He was greatly admired in *Shinjitsu ichiro*, and is magnificent

in Tomotaka Tasaka's *Robo no ishi* – a kind of Japanese 'Childhood of Gorki', with several other child players of strong personality.

Katayama continued to act for the next three decades, with film roles in *Kakute kamikaze wa fuku* (44), *Maihime* (51), *Ketto kagiya no tsuji* (51), *Okasan* (52), *Gero no kubi* (55) and *Bakumatsu* (70).

In 1972 ill health obliged him to leave the profession; but he recovered, and turned to directing documentaries.

37 Kagirinaki zenshin (Forever forward)
Shinjitsu ichiro (The way to truth)
38 Robo no ishi (Pebble by the wayside)
39 Bakuon (Airplane drone)
40 Kaze no Matasaburo
(Whirlwind Matasaburo)

Terry Kilburn

BRITAIN/USA

b: 25 Nov 26 (London)

Terence Kilbourne was the son of a London bus-driver, and as a child appeared in seaside concert parties, giving his impersonations of famous movie stars from Charles Laughton to Freddie Bartholomew °. (With his huge blue eyes

Terry Kilburn and Robert Donat in Goodbye, Mr Chips

and sad smile he would have made a very good Bing Crosby.)

In spite of his obvious talent, no quick breakthrough into London show business was made, so his parents scraped all their money together and (with the aid of a Los Angeles lawyer they had met in London) took him to Hollywood. Still, for nearly a

Kilburn in They Shall Have Music

year, nothing happened. Then, just as hope was fading, he got a nice offer of a spot on Eddie Cantor's radio show, and gave a heart-rending recitation about a boy and his dog. MGM took note, and eventually he was given a part in *Lord Jeff*, opposite the very Bartholomew he had not so long ago been mimicking.

Little Kilburn was a tremendous heart-render when he put his mind (and eyes) to it. He did so most energetically as Tiny Tim in *A Christmas Carol*, and as the endlessly reborn new boy in that apotheosis of the maudlin, *Goodbye, Mr Chips*. Less emotionally, he was with Mickey Rooney ◇ in one of his 'Andy Hardy' films, and with Rooney again (and Bartholomew) in *A Yank at Eton*.

Away from MGM after 1939, Kilburn got plenty of work, but the leads dwindled to supporting roles and then cameos. He was in *National Velvet* and *Keys of the Kingdom* (44), *Black Beauty* (46), two *Bulldog Drummond* movies (47), *The Fortunes of Captain Blood* (50) and a few other films of the Forties and Fifties. His final screen credit seems to have been in *Lolita* (62).

By this time, though, he had largely turned to the live theatre, as an actor – he played Marchbanks in Shaw's 'Candida' opposite Olivia de Havilland, and took over the lead from Eli Wallach in 'The Teahouse of the August Moon' – then as director, notably of London productions of such American plays as 'Inherit the Wind', 'Look Homeward, Angel' and 'The Dark at the Top of the Stairs'. He won considerable critical applause for these, and in the Seventies became artistic director of a fine professional theatre in Rochester, Michigan.

Raino Hämäläinen

FINLAND

b: circa 1926

Like another Finnish boy epic of twenty years earlier, *Ollin oppivuodet*, Orvo Saarikivi's *Tottisalmen perilinnen* was based on a children's story by Anni Swan, and again dealt with the changing fortunes of a boy of gentle birth. The emphasis this time, though, is on role-reversals.

The rich child, Klaus (Kalevi Koski) is freckly and obstreperous – so much so that for the good of his soul he is packed off to live in the chastening atmosphere of the local vicarage. There he meets an orphan called Yrjö (Hämäläinen), employed as a general odd-job, who is injured saving Klaus from harm in a typical exploit with a wild horse. Klaus's father expresses his gratitude to Yrjö by taking him on at the manor-house, but the boy is framed up for a theft of valuables by a wicked servant, and gets thrown out

Raino Hämäläinen (right) in Tottisalmen perilinnen

again. He is then kidnapped and drugged by a mysterious man in a fez . . . and so on and so forth.

The final upshot is that Yrjö turns out to be Klaus's elder brother and the rightful heir to Tottisalmi: but he declines the inheritance and leaves to rejoin his mother in Greece, where his disowned father had died, and the now much improved Klaus inherits after all.

Hämäläinen, a slender, curly-haired, very un-Finnish-looking boy of the sensitive, Philippe DeLacy ◇ type, is a striking performer who deserved better than a rags-to-riches story.

40 Tottisalmen perilinnen
(The heir of Tottisalmi)

Li Keng

CHINA

b: circa 1926 (Guangdong Province)
d: 1965

Keng was the son of the famous actress Lin Chuchu, and was in several films with her. His finest performance was in *Shennü*, as the child of a prostitute (played by the glamorous star Ruan Lingyu).

He continued to act in films as an adult: *Lianai zhi dao* (48), *Minzhu qingnian jinxingqu* (52), and was assistant director on two films of the early 1960s. But he died prematurely.

34 Renshen (Life)
   Shennü (Goddess)
35 Tian lun (Family relations)
37 Tsimu qu (Song of a loving mother)

Li Keng and Ruan Lingyu in Shennü

Dickie Jones

USA

b: 25 Feb 27 (Snyder, Texas)

In a horse-mad community, even the son of the local newspaper editor was obliged to conform, and young Dick did so with such alacrity that by the age of five this neat little Texan was appearing in public in exhibitions of ridin' and ropin'. It was in such a rodeo, in Dallas, that he was spotted by the cowboy film hero Hoot Gibson, who engaged Dick to ride with his travelling circus and took him and his mother to Hollywood.

The boy, gifted with humorous dark eyes and a saucy manner, soon got work in movies (his first was *Wonder Bar*), though not with Hoot himself. He guested with 'Our Gang', and his list of other credits is vast. In one of his most famous performances he was unseen, providing the voice of the puppet hero in Disney's *Pinocchio*.

Dick Jones was in a famous 1942 film, *This Gun For Hire*, but unfortunately his part was left on the cutting-room floor. It had been a nice compliment to him, though, that in *Mr Smith Goes to Washington* he had played James Stewart's faithful Senate page-boy 'Dick Jones', a role repeated in a sort of junior spin-off the following year: *Adventure in Washington*. (This had been originally called *Senate Page Boys*.) From 1942 Dick was heard coast-to-coast in the title role of the 'Henry Aldrich' radio series.

Films continued: *Heaven Can Wait* (43), *The Adventures of Mark Twain* (44), *The Strawberry Roan* (48), *Sands of Iwo Jima* (49), and a further ten or so in the Fifties and Sixties. On TV, he used his ridin' and stuntin' skills in the series 'The Range Rider' (from 1951) and 'Buffalo Bill, Jr.' (from 1954), starring in the latter.

But he was sick of being typecast in a dying genre, and sick also of horses: 'stupid and untrustworthy animals', he told Richard Lamparski. From then on Dick devoted himself to real estate.

Dickie Jones (as Dick Jones) with James Stewart in Mr Smith Goes to Washington

34 Fifteen Wives
   Little Men
   Strange Wives
   Washee Ironee ('OG')
   Wonder Bar
35 Call of the Savage (serial)
   The Crusades
   The Hawk
   Moonlight on the Prairie
   Our Gang Follies of 1936
   Reckless
   Westward Ho
36 The Black Legion
   Daniel Boone
   The First Baby
   Gasoloons
   The Pinch Singer ('OG')
   Smoke Tree Range
   Sutter's Gold
37 Blake of Scotland Yard (serial)
   Border Wolves
   Hollywood Round-Up
   The Kid Comes Back
   Love Is on the Air
   Our Gang Follies of 1938
   Pigskin Palooka ('OG')
   Ready, Willing and Able
   Renfrew of the Royal Mounted
   Stella Dallas
38 The Devil's Party
   Flying Fists
   The Great Adventures
     of Wild Bill Hickok

Land of Fighting Men
A Man to Remember
Woman Doctor
39 Beware Spooks!
   Destry Rides Again
   The Frontiersman
   The Man Who Dared
   Mr Smith Goes to Washington
   Nancy Drew – Reporter
   Sergeant Madden
   Sky Patrol
   Young Mr Lincoln
40 Brigham Young – Frontiersman
   Hi-Yo Silver!
   The Howards of Virginia
   Knute Rockne – All American
   Maryland
   Pinocchio
   Virginia City
41 Adventure in Washington
   The Vanishing Virginian
42 The Major and the Minor
   Mountain Rhythm

Tommy Baker

USA

b: 5 Mar 27

Tommy Baker was a busy trouper with petulant eyebrows.

39 Danger Flight
   Joe and Ethel Turp Call on the President
   Mr Smith Goes to Washington
   Saga of Death Valley
   Scouts of the Air
40 The Blue Bird
   Knute Rockne – All American
   My Love Came Back
41 Brother Orchid
   Coffins on Wheels
   A Dispatch from Reuters

Jean Claudio

FRANCE

b: 28 Mar 27 (Neuilly-sur-Seine)

This dark, pale-skinned, aristocratic-looking boy – he played the Tsarevich in *La tragédie impériale* – was born Claude Martin, but was billed at the start of his acting career as 'Claudio'. Then, as if this was a surname, he prefixed it with a 'Jean'. His biggest roles were in *Les disparus de Saint Agil* and *L'enfer des anges*.

From his mid-teens there was a ten-year gap in Claudio's career, but in his mid-twenties he returned to the screen and was busy for the next two decades. Among his films were *Le déjeuner sur l'herbe* (60), *Le cocu magnifique* (64) and some British-based productions: *The Beauty Jungle* (64), *Darling* (65) and *Triple Cross* (66).

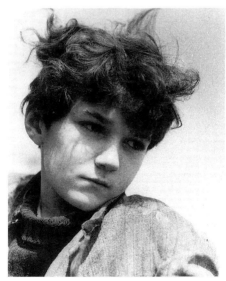

Jean Claudio in L'enfer des anges

38 Carrefour (Crossroads)
   Les disparus de Saint Agil
      (The lost boys of Saint-Agil)
   La tragédie impériale
      (The imperial tragedy)
39 La charrette fantôme (The phantom cart)
   L'enfer des anges (Angels' hell)
40 Untel père et fils
      (So-and-So senior and junior)
41 Andorra
42 Les cadets de l'Océan
      (Cadets of the Ocean)

Norbert Rohringer in Jakko

Norbert Rohringer

AUSTRIA/GERMANY

b: 9 Apr 27 (Vienna)

Yet another non-German who became
an Aryan pin-up. The wavy blond hair
and dazzling blue eyes of the Austrian
Rohringer were seen exclusively in German films from 1939. (He had already
adorned the Viennese stage.)

His leading role in *Jakko* showed him as
a successor to the 'sensitive' Claus Detlef
Sierck ◇: a circus child (artistic, wilful)
whom fate throws at the world's mercy,
saved – lucky chap! – by falling in with
sea cadets of the Hitler Youth. Rohringer
had a lot of charm and deserved better
than such rubbish.

Just too young to be caught up in the
fighting, Rohringer was in three more
films: *Das war mein Leben* (44), *Ein Mann
wie Maximilian* (44) and the unfinished
Wir beide liebten Katharina (45). After the
war he returned to Vienna and made his
living as a press reporter and as a pianist.

36 Mädchenpensionat (Girls' school – AT)
39 Anton der Letzte (Anton the Last)
   Mutterliebe (A mother's love)
40 Der Sündenbock (The scapegoat)
41 Heimaterde (Native earth)
   Jakko
   Mein Leben für Irland (My life for Ireland)
42 Der Fall Rainer (The Rainer case)
   Symphonie eines Lebens
      (Symphony of a life)
43 Freunde (Friends)
   Die Hochstaplerin (The crooked lady)
   Die Jungfern vom Bishofsberg
      (The maids of Bishop's Hill)
   Kollege kommt gleich
      (My colleague's just coming)
   Liebesgeschichten (Love stories)
   Die Wirtin zum Weissen Rössl
      (The landlady of the White Horse)

David Holt

USA

b: 14 Aug 27 (Jacksonville, Florida)

David was a brilliant dancer as a child,
and proved a competent though not an
exciting actor in films of the Thirties. His
parents twice took him to be interviewed
by Hollywood studios, and eventually he
got started with a part in *Mary Stevens,
M.D.*. After his performance in *Now and
Forever*, Paramount signed him up on a
long contract.

He was more fun in unsympathetic roles.
Like his great predecessor Jackie Searl ◇,
he played sneaky brother Sid in *Tom
Sawyer*.

By his mid-teens Holt was growing tall
and rather languid. He was in another ten
or so films over the next ten years, including *The Human Comedy* (43), *The Cheaters*
(45), *Courage of Lassie* (46), *Battleground*
(49) and *Combat Squad* (53).

33 Mary Stevens, M.D.
34 Black Moon

*David Holt with Madge Evans (a child star of 20
years earlier) in* Men Without Names

   The Cat's Paw
   The Defense Rests
   Now and Forever
   Shock
   You Belong to Me
35 The Age of Indiscretion
   Big Broadcast of 1936
   The Last Days of Pompeii
   Men Without Names
36 Big Broadcast of 1937
   It's a Great Life
   Straight from the Shoulder
   Trouble for Two
37 The Adventures of Tom Sawyer
38 Kentucky
   Sons of the Legion
39 Beau Geste
   Hero for a Day
40 Military Academy
41 Remember the Day
42 The Pride of the Yankees

David's considerably younger brother
Ricky appeared as a baby in *Gone With the
Wind* (39), and once or twice more.

Bennie Bartlett

USA

b: 16 Aug 27 (Independence, Kansas)

Not many Hollywood kids came from
Kansas, but red-haired Bennie Bartlett
did. His parents (Floyd and Nina) were
vaudeville people, and he was born on

Bennie Bartlett with Mr Towser, 1936

tour, making his debut at 10 days, though it's not known what he sang. At the age of three he learnt the trumpet, and at four was running his own dance band, with himself as vocal and trumpet soloist. It must have been terrible.

Bennie (or Benny) now learnt piano and drums, and began writing his own songs. Soon he was singing them, and trumpeting, on the local radio station. At this point, whether by request of the Kansans or in search of higher things, the Bartlett family upped stakes and moved to California, where father Floyd got work as a dance music arranger. The boy became a public figure, in a small but noisy way, and by the time he was nine had had 15 of his songs published. He had also landed a Paramount contract.

Music apart, there was clearly some intention to set up the rowdy redhead as a new Rooney ◇. He had that sort of pudgy truculence. But it didn't quite happen. Behind the brass there was an anxious streak that showed, an earnestness that was actually rather redeeming. He made a nice foil for Dickie Moore ◇, Virginia Weidler or Shirley Temple.

Bennie was in six 1943 films, including *He Hired the Boss*, *Next of Kin* and *Thank Your Lucky Stars*, and in many more over the next two decades, such as *Cheaper by the Dozen* (50), *Rear Window* (54), *High Society* (55) and *The Scapegoat* (59).

Larry Nunn

USA

b: 23 Aug 27 (Marshfield, Oregon)

If he'd been born a few years earlier, Nunn, a fair, skinny-eyed boy with a hard-bitten expression, would have been a natural Dead End Kid. But street-wisdom tangled effectively with pathos in *Men of Boys Town*.

He appeared on stage in Seattle at the age of four, after which he performed in theatres, clubs and churches. He was a member of a well-known children's orchestra, and became a regular on a local radio show. Busby Berkeley heard him, and gave him a leading role in *Strike Up the Band*.

Nunn was in *The Navy Way* (44), and had a good part in *Desperate* (47). After that his screen career faded.

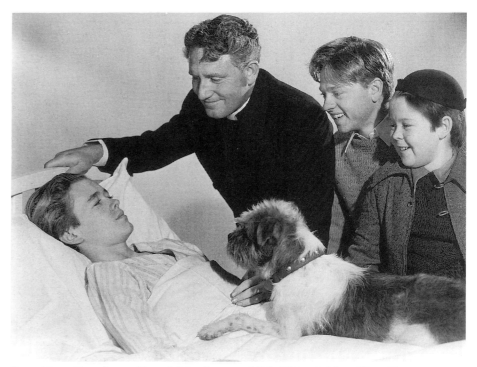

(l. to r.:) Larry Nunn, Spencer Tracy, Mickey Rooney and Bobs Watson in Men of Boys Town

Bengt Dalunde

SWEDEN

b: 9 Sep 27 (Bräcke)

39 Emilie Högqvist
40 Lillebror och jag (Me and my kid brother)
   Snurriga familjen (The crazy family)
41 I natt eller aldrig (Tonight or never)
   Landstormens lilla argbigga
      (The reservist's nagging wife)
42 Flickan i fönstret mittemot
      (The girl in the window opposite)
   Ungdom i bojor (Youth in chains)

Tommy Bond

USA

b: 16 Sep 27 (Dallas, Texas)

It was strange that such a chubby, good-natured creature should have first won fame as a menacing heavy: but so it was with Tommy Bond, the bully 'Butch' in 'Our Gang' comedies between 1932 and 1940. In fact, after a two-year lay-off, he didn't become 'Butch' until *Glove Taps* (February 1937), in which he's a tough kid who moves into the Gang's neighbourhood, accompanied by a baleful-looking henchman called 'The Woim' (Sidney Kibrick ◇). For the next three years he remained an oppressor, extortionist and general pain.

Outside the Gang, Tommy — first featured as a warbling tot on radio — was much in demand in the comedy shorts of Laurel and Hardy, Charlie Chase, Andy Clyde and Thelma Todd. He could scowl and rage like the best of brats, but he could also be the jolly, companionable friend-and-buddy. In 1939-40 he was one of the 'Five Little Peppers' in the film series.

After 1941 Tommy Bond acted for a further decade, in films like *This Land Is Mine* (43), *The Man from Frisco* (44) and *The Beautiful Cheat* (45). With 'Alfalfa' Switzer ◇ he was in the *Gas House Kids* movies (47), and he played Jimmy Olsen in the second *Superman* serial (48) and in the next one, *Atom Man versus Superman* (50). In 1951 he ended with *Bedtime for Bonzo* and *Call Me Mister*.

That year he graduated in theater arts at Los Angeles State College, and went to work as property master at KTTV, and later as stage manager at Channel 30 in Fresno.

Tommy Bond with Gloria Jean in A Little Bit of Heaven

32 'Our Gang' (one short)
33 Beauty and the Bus
   'Our Gang' (5)
34 The Cracked Iceman
   I'll Take Vanilla
   Kid Millions
   'Our Gang' (6)
   You Said a Hatful
35 Alimony Aches
36 Libeled Lady
37 Hideaway
   Knee Action
   Married Before Breakfast
   'Our Gang' (4)
   Rosalie
38 Block-Heads
   City Streets
   'Our Gang' (5)
39 Career
   Five Little Peppers and How They Grew
   Now It Can Be Sold
   'Our Gang' (5)
40 Five Little Peppers at Home
   Five Little Peppers in Trouble
   A Little Bit of Heaven
   'Our Gang' (1)
   Out West with the Peppers
41 Adventure in Washington
   New York Town

Bobby Breen

USA

b: 4 Nov 27 (Montreal, Canada)

Bobby's precocious singing talent, carefully nurtured, led to a 1931 debut in the Silver Slipper Night Club in Toronto. Soon afterwards, with the club's band, he sang on the radio. Then came a stream of vaudeville and restaurant engagements.

After he had performed in Illinois and New York, he went to study at the Professional Children's School in Hollywood. There he was seen by Eddie Cantor, who in 1936 gave him (like Terry Kilburn ◇) a regular spot on his radio show. Bobby, a dab hand with languages, could also sing in French, Italian and Spanish, and won wide popularity. RKO signed him up, and he starred and sang till the golden voice left him — a cheerful trouper without any particular charm or individuality.

His last acting assignment in the cinema was in *Johnny Doughboy* (42), along with

Bobby Breen (right) with Tommy Bupp in Fisherman's Wharf

other kid actors of the past like Spanky McFarland◇ and Robert Coogan◇. But he continued as a singer in nightclubs and stage musicals, and in occasional films such as *London Entertains* (51) and *Curse of the Voodoo* (65).

36 Let's Sing Again
   Rainbow on the River
37 Make a Wish
38 Breaking the Ice
   Hawaii Calls
39 Escape to Paradise
   Fisherman's Wharf
   Way Down South

Martin Spellman

USA

b: 1927

Young Spellman got on chatting terms with the stars while working as a newsboy at the MGM studios. He also shone their shoes.

   As a Christmas present, Clark Gable arranged for the 12-year-old to have two days' work as an extra in *Test Pilot*. Soon afterwards, Martin had his picture taken selling a paper to Myrna Loy – obviously with real commitment, for studio executives who saw it 'commented on the sincerity in his eyes'. Norman Taurog signed him up on the spot for *Boys Town*.

   Spellman's best parts came in *Streets of New York* and *Son of the Navy*.

38 Boys Town
   I Am a Criminal
   Santa Fe Stampede
   Sharpshooters
   Test Pilot
39 Beau Geste
   Let Us Live
   Streets of New York
40 Hold That Woman
   Son of the Navy
41 Law of the Wild
   Meet the Chump

Ram Apte

INDIA

b: circa 1927

33 Krishna Sudama
34 Gunsundari
   Sitamgar (The cruel beloved)
   Toofan Mail
35 Barrister's Wife
   Dev dasi (Temple dancer)

   Noor-e-watan (Light of the nation)
   Raat ki Rani (Queen of the night)
36 Laheri lala
   Matlabi duniya (The selfish world)
   Prabhu ka pyara (Favourite of the God)
37 Dil farosh (The heart-seller)
   Sarafi loot
   Toofani toli (The stormy group)
   Zamin ka chand (Moon on the earth)
38 Ban ki chidiya (Forest bird)
   Billi (The cat)
   Gorakh aya (Here comes Gorakh)
   Prithvi putra (Son of the earth)
39 Pukar (The call)
   Sant Tulsidas (St Tulsidas)
40 Bharosa (Faith)

Gabriel Farguette

FRANCE

b: circa 1927

In *La guerre des gosses* Gaby Farguette played 'Tigibus', the role played in the 1962 *Guerre des boutons* by Martin Lartigue◇. (A male scamp provided contrast to Gaby's appearance as 'la petite Muriel' in *L'île des veuves*.) He also had leading roles in *Ceux de demain* and *Un gosse en or*.

35 Jérôme Perreau
36 Bach détective (Bach the detective)
   Le coeur dispose (The heart disposes)
   La guerre des gosses (The kids' war)
   L'île des veuves (Widows' island)
   La peur (Fear)
   La rose effeuillée (The rose without petals)
37 Liberté
38 Ceux de demain (Tomorrow's people)
   Les disparus de Saint-Agil
    (The lost boys of Saint-Agil)
   Un gosse en or (A darling kid)
40 Retour au bonheur (Return to happiness)

Pat Fitzpatrick

BRITAIN

b: circa 1927

A pert but rather icy little boy, best remembered as Nova Pilbeam's youngest brother in Hitchcock's *Young and Innocent* – the one who produces a dead rat at the lunch table. He was also the child Mozart in *Whom the Gods Love*.

33 The Bermondsey Kid
   Call Me Mame
   Sleeping Car
34 Falling in Love
   Give Her a Ring
   My Old Dutch
   Red Wagon
35 Brewster's Millions
   The Tunnel
36 Calling the Tune
   Gaolbreak
   Royal Eagle
   Whom the Gods Love
37 Young and Innocent
38 You Live and Learn
39 The Good Old Days

Anant Marathe

INDIA

b: circa 1927

35 Dharma ki devi (Goddess of religion)
36 Chhaya (Shadow)
37 Mere lal (My son)
   Usne kya socha (What he thought)
38 Mr X
   Nand Kumar
39 Flying Ranee
   Hukum ka ekka (Ace of Spades)
40 Anuradha
   Geeta
44 Ramshastri

Anant's brother, RAM MARATHE, was also in *Mere lal*, and played child parts in other films of the late Thirties: *Shan chorr* (36), *Jagirdar / The landlord* (37), *Sagar ka sher / Lion of Sagar* (37) and *Gopal Krishna* (38).

Pepito del Rio

MEXICO

b: circa 1927

Raphael del Rio – who was billed as such in *Corazón de niño* – was famous as 'Pepito' for most of his childhood career. After 1940 he acted as 'Pepe del Rio', in films like *La pequeña madrecita* (44), *Amor prohibido* (45) and many more till the end of the decade.

37 No basta ser madre
   (It's not enough to be a mother)

¡Ora Ponciano! (Now, Ponciano!)
38 Allá en el Rancho Chico
   (Over at Boys' Ranch)
39 La canción del huerfano
   (Song of the orphan)
   La casa del ogro (The ogre's house)
   Corazón de niño (Heart of a child)
40 La canción del milagro
   (Song of the miracle)
   Odio (Hatred)

Livi Shchipachev

USSR

b: circa 1927

Livi, the son of the poet Stepan Shchipachev, played the lead in the two *Timur* films, which retained their popularity with Soviet youth for many years. They are something like a rural and more improving version of *Nous les gosses* (see Jean-Pierre Geffroy ◇): a band of boys have fun and do good, helpful, patriotic things.

40 Timur i yevo komanda
   (Timur and his gang)
42 Klyatva Timura (Timur's oath)

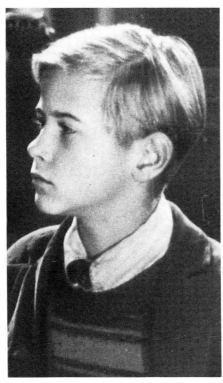

Livi Shchipachev in Timur i yevo komanda

Vova Tumalaryants

USSR

b: circa 1927

Though most of his films are forgotten nowadays, the blond Tumalaryants was arguably the star Soviet child actor of his period. He had three outright leads in *Poyezd idyot, Vozvrashcheniye* and *Volshebnoye zerno*, plus an important secondary role in *Visokaya nagrada* – no Russian boy since the silent era had been so honoured, and not even the extraordinary Kolya Burlyayev ◇ would be in the 1960s.

In *Vesoliye artisti*, however, Vova was merely one of several 'child entertainers'.

37 Vozdushnoye priklyucheniye
   (Aerial adventure)
38 Poyezd idyot v Moskvu
   (The train leaving for Moscow)
   Vesoliye artisti (Merry artistes)
39 Visokaya nagrada (High award)
40 Vozvrashcheniye (The return)
41 Volshebnoye zerno (The magic seed)

Bobby Winkler

USA

b: 1927
d: 28 Dec 89 (Woodland Hills, Cal.)

Bobby Winkler (*né* Winckler, as which he appeared till 1939) had flat fair hair and an obstinate, enthusiastic expression. You could tell he was trouble, as he proved in his most celebrated role as the joy-riding kid in *Sullivan's Travels*. But before that he had done masses of screen work, including a few appearances with 'Our Gang' and a leading role in the 1939 serial *Daredevils of the Red Circle*.

After 1943, Bobby hurtled on through a few more films: in the following year *The Adventures of Mark Twain, Gambler's Choice* and *Incendiary Blonde*, in 1947 *Prairie Express* and in 1948 *Criss Cross*. On the last occasion he was billed as 'Robert Winkler', and with this expression of adulthood it seems to have ended. He's not the father of Henry, 'the Fonz'.

155

Bobby Winkler in Daredevils of the Red Circle

Sonny Bupp

USA

b: 10 Jan 28 (New York)

Moyer (or Sonny) Bupp was the kid brother of Tommy Bupp ◇, and they appeared together in *Star for a Night*, as in many films afterwards. Like (it often seems) about half the kid population of Hollywood, he had a one-film stand with Our Gang but failed to be re-engaged. His round baby face hadn't the engaging malice of Tommy's.

Sonny is best remembered now for his role in *Citizen Kane*: not as Kane in the childhood flashback (that was Buddy Swan ◇) but as Kane's son near the end. He was in short comedies with – among others – Robert Benchley, Edgar Kennedy, Our Gang and the Three Stooges.

35 Dante's Inferno
Dinky
It Happened in New York
36 Star for a Night
We Who Are About to Die
37 Cash and Carry
Hollywood Hotel
Love Is on the Air
Love on Toast
My Dear Miss Aldrich
Woman Wise
38 Angels with Dirty Faces
Hunted Men
Men in Fright ('OG')
Penrod's Double Trouble
Swing Your Lady
Valley of the Giants
The Young in Heart
39 Boy Trouble
The Day of Rest
Emergency Squad
Feathered Pests
Fixer Dugan
No Place to Go
On Borrowed Time
Renegade Trail
She Couldn't Say No
Sudden Money
When Tomorrow Comes
40 Abe Lincoln in Illinois
Comin' Round the Mountain
Half a Sinner
I Take This Woman
Knute Rockne – All American

36 Pay As You Exit ('OG')
37 Dangerous Holiday
The Man in Blue
'Our Gang' *(4)*
38 Weather Wizards
Football Romeo ('OG')
39 Blue Montana Skies
Daredevils of the Red Circle *(serial)*
While America Sleeps
40 Cherokee Strip
Keeping Company
Knute Rockne – All American
Overture to Glory
Riders of Pasco Basin
Waterloo Bridge
41 Bad Men of Missouri
Father's Son

Last of the Duanes
Lucky Devils
Men of Boys Town
Pass of the Pecos
The Wagons Roll at Night
West Point Widow
The Wildcat of Tucson
42 Eyes in the Night
Life Begins for Andy Hardy
My Favorite Blonde
The Pride of the Yankees
Sullivan's Travels
This Gun for Hire
Wings for the Eagle
43 The Good Fellows
I Dood It
True to Life

Sonny Bupp with Fred Stone in No Place to Go

Little Orvie
Parole Fixer
Queen of the Mob
Slightly Tempted
Three Faces West
The Villain Still Pursued Her
41 All That Money Can Buy
Citizen Kane
Doctors Don't Tell
Father's Son
Four Mothers
International Squadron
42 Eyes of the Underworld
The Loves of Edgar Allan Poe
Syncopation
Wings for the Eagle

Jun Yokoyama

JAPAN

b: Jan 1928 (Niigata Prefecture)

Jun entered the Shochiku studio in 1933 and, presumably because of his shattering energy, acquired the nickname 'Bakudan-Kozo' ('Bomb Boy'). He played mainly in the films of Shimizu and Saito – and in fact could be quite a sensitive child.

33 Shima no musume (Island woman)
35 Kare to kanojo to shonentachi
    (He, she and the boys)
36 Daigaku yoitoko (Up with school!)
    Kuruma ni tsunda takaramono
    (Treasure in the cart)
    Yurei ga shindara (If the ghost died)
37 Haha no shori (Mother's victory)
    Kaze no naka no kodomo
    (Children in the wind)
    Koi mo wasurete (Forget love too)
38 Anma to onna
    (The masseurs and a woman)
39 Kodomo no shiki (Four seasons of children)
40 Tomodachi (Friends)
41 Mikaeri no tou
    (The tower of introspection)

Kaj Hjelm

SWEDEN

b: 24 Jun 28 (Stockholm)
d: September 1983

*Jun Yokoyama (right) and Masao Hayama (left)
in* Kaze no nakano kodomo

Kaj Hjelm wags a cheerful finger in Frun
tillhanda

The cheeky, chirpy Hjelm was a great asset to Swedish cinema as a boy in the early 1940s, and continued acting for a further twenty years or so.

39 Frun tillhanda (Lady in waiting)
   Vi på Solgläntan (We from Solgläntan)
40 Hanna i societen (Hanna in society)
   Swing it, magistern! (Swing it, Sir!)
41 Livet går vidare (Life goes on)
   Magistrarna på sommarlov
      (Sirs on summer vacation)
   Så tuktas en äkta man
      (How to tame a real man)
42 I gult och blått (Yellow and blue)
   Vårat Gäng (Our Gang)
   Vi hemslavinnor (We domestic slaves)
43 I mörkaste Småland (In darkest Småland)
   Kajan går till sjöss (The Kaja goes to sea)
   Katrina
   Lille Napoleon (Little Napoleon)
   En melodi om våren (A melody of Spring)

Gunnar Möller

SWEDEN/GERMANY

b: 1 Jly 28 (Berlin)

Gunnar Thor Karl Möller was Swedish-born, but his father (an optician) settled in Germany and they received German citizenship in 1937, the year before his father's death. Gunnar – a naïvely good-natured-looking boy – made his film debut in 1939, and in 1942 was given a two-year contract to portray the typical

Gunnar Möller in Kopf hoch, Johannes!

'Pimpf' (or junior member of the Hitler Youth) in a series of short propaganda films. He was also chosen to be in a film (*Die sieben Stäbe*) about the Savings Bank. A non-German had made good again.

Gunnar Möller continued to act in films up to the end of the War and after it – mainly in East Germany up to 1950 – and became of one of his country's leading young actors. He starred in *Hans im Glück* (49), *Die Jungen vom Kranichsee* (50) and *Ich denke oft an Piroschka* (55).

In September 1979, living in London, Möller murdered his wife, the actress Brigitte Rau, in a fit of drunken rage. (She had been married to him for 25 years, and they had three children.) At his trial in 1980 evidence of Brigitta's malicious taunting was accepted in mitigation. Möller was given a five-year jail sentence. He was, however, freed in November 1981, since when his acting career has resumed, quietly.

40 Unser Fräulein Doktor (Our Miss Doctor)
41 Das andere ich (The other I)
   Immer nur du (Nothing but you)
   Kopf hoch, Johannes! (Chin up, Johannes!)
   Sein Sohn (His son)
   Die sieben Stäbe (The seven staves)
42 Meine Freundin Josefine
      (My friend Josephine)
   Der Strom (The river)
   Zwischen Himmel und Erde
      (Between heaven and earth)
43 Das Bad auf der Tenne
      (The bath on the threshing-floor)
   Floh im Ohr (Flea in the ear)
   Fritze Bollmann wollte angeln
      (Fritze Bollmann goes fishing)
   Zirkus Renz (The Renz Circus)

Sidney Kibrick

USA

b: 2 Jly 28 (Minneapolis)

Sidney and his elder brother Leonard both had a cloud of coppery curls overhanging a cloud of coppery freckles. The effect appealed to their father, a scrap-metal dealer. (Opinions were divided as to the classic beauty of their faces.) With a third Kibrick, they went on the vaudeville stage

as 'the Casey brothers', and must have gleamed delightfully, whatever the other merits of their act.

In 1935 Sidney followed Leonard into 'Our Gang', and became even more a fixture after Leonard dropped out, when he took on the character of 'the Woim', sinister henchman of the bully 'Butch' (Tommy Bond ◇).

When their Gang days were over, and their education completed, both Sidney and Leonard Kibrick joined their father in the scrap-metal business. Then they switched to contracting and did very, very well out of it.

35 'Our Gang' (*5 shorts*)
36 'Our Gang' (*5*)
37 'Our Gang' (*6*)
   Dead End
38 'Our Gang' (*4*)
   Annabel Takes a Tour
   Boys Town
   Just Around the Corner
39 'Our Gang' (*5*)
   Everybody's Baby
   Gone with the Wind
   Jesse James
   A Trip to Paris
40 'Our Gang' (*1*)
42 Flight Lieutenant

Roddy McDowall

BRITAIN/USA

b: 17 Sep 28 (London)

If any ex-child-star has lost almost nothing of his youthfulness after half a century in the movies, it must be Roderick Andrew Anthony Jude McDowall, the most puckish 60-something in the business. He still has, when required, the earnestness of a boy, but even more the mischievous-ness. Sometimes he goes completely ape.

His Scottish father was in the Merchant Navy (and seldom home), and his mother was Irish – a good pedigree for pucks. From the age of four he did commercial modelling, for breakfast cereal advertise-ments and the like. A film producer signed him up for *Murder in the Family* after

Roddy McDowall firewatches in Confirm or Deny

seeing him in a Shakespearean production at a London drama school.

In 1940, after he had been in sixteen British films, he went on a visit to the USA with his mother and sister. They made the round of the Hollywood studios, where people were already looking for a boy for *The Yearling*: filming actually started on two other versions which were aborted before MGM and Clarence Brown got it in the can. But Master McDowall was felt to be too British for the part.

No one, in fact, showed much interest until he came to Fox. There they were auditioning for *How Green Was My Valley*, and everything fell into place, including his Britishness. He made his name as young Huw, and confirmed it with his gallant office-boy in *Confirm or Deny* and his mercurial cabin-boy in *Man Hunt*. After that, gradually switching to American backgrounds, he had less

interesting partnerships with dogs and horses.

After three films in 1945, (including a 'Son of Flicka') and in 1946 *Holiday in Mexico*, Roddy had the lead in a remake of Stevenson's *Kidnapped* and played Malcolm in the Orson Welles *Macbeth* (both 1948). He was in *The Steel Fist* (52), but the rest of the Fifties was spent in theatre work, from Shakespeare and Shaw to modern plays, mainly on Broadway. He also became a distinguished portrait photographer.

Roddy was in 45 more movies during the Sixties and Seventies (including the 'Planet of the Apes' quartet, in which he starred behind an impressive mask), not counting TV work. He hasn't slowed down a lot in the last decade, and remains in amazingly good shape, with the slightly waspish charm that has become his trademark.

McDowall takes to the saddle in My Friend Flicka

159

Spanky McFarland in Our Gang, 1932

George 'Spanky' McFarland

USA

b: 2 Oct 28 (Fort Worth, Texas)
d: 30 Jun 93 (Grapevine, Texas)

To the cereal-besotted image-makers of 'Our Gang' – 'Farina' Hoskins ◇ already installed, 'Buckwheat' Thomas ◇ to come – any chubby child on a bread advertisement must have seemed an offer not to be refused. An 18-month-old baby called George Robert Phillips McFarland had been such a hit on a Dallas bakery's posters in 1929 that they proceeded to star him in a cinema commercial. That's how he was spotted by an 'Our Gang' scout, and it didn't take long for the Roach studio to acquire a slice of the action.

Spanky (the name taken from his mother's recurrent threat to the roaming toddler) was rotund, self-contained and intelligent. The Gang director Robert McGowan said of him: 'He's the first genius I've directed since Jackie Cooper ◇'. Certainly he had wonderful comic timing, and was as drily laid-back as Stymie Beard ◇. His 'okey-dokey' was the essence

of good-humoured equanimity.

From *Free Eats* in 1932 to *Unexpected Riches* in 1942, Spanky was a top favourite in the Gang's shorts. He was in 94 altogether, plus his own star vehicle, the full-length feature *General Spanky*, in which he leads a Southern kids' militia against a Union army. The transplantation of the Gang into a historical setting with awkward overtones of real bloodshed didn't work, although Spanky, aided by Alfalfa Switzer ◇, Buckwheat Thomas ◇ and other Gang stalwarts, is still a formidable little pudding.

He was sometimes featured with the studio's adult comics like Charlie Chase, or loaned out to other studios. (In *O'Shaughnessy's Boy* he played Jackie Cooper as a small child.) I've been unable to discover if a putative 1936 short called *Alone, Alas* really existed, but the title is too good to lose.

After 1944, no more acting work came his way. When he was old enough Spanky joined the Air Force for a while, then worked at a soft drink factory, briefly hosted a TV show that showed old Gang movies, sold hamburgers and wine (not together), promoted oil, and finally, after one or two other projects, rose to a solid position in the sales department of Philco-Ford TV. However, he made at least one modest comeback, in *Moonrunners* (75).

McFarland with Alfalfa Switzer (left) in General Spanky

Maltin and Bann, interviewing Spanky in 1977, liked him enormously: 'a guy without any pretense . . . a man's man . . . plucky, talented, pleasantly grumpy.'

Masaru Kodaka

JAPAN

b: 3 Nov 28 (Tokyo)

At the age of eight Masaru began training at the Shinko Oizumi Studio, and in 1938 was signed up by Toho.

He had a teenage role in *Santaro ganbaru* (44), but nothing more till *Itto madame to santo danna* ten years later.

Benny Fagerlund

DENMARK

b: 6 Dec 28 (Søborg, nr. Copenhagen)

Benny Fagerlund (right) with Ilselil Larsen (left) and Lasse Steen-Hansen in Vi kunne ha' det så rart

Benny and his younger brother Ib (born 13 June 1937, and also in *Familien Gelinde*) were members of the Danish Radio Boys' Choir when spotted by a film scout. The fair-haired Benny, praised by critics for his beautiful voice, intelligence and soulful eyes — well used in his 'singing scenes' which moved audiences deeply — became for a few years the biggest Nordic child star since Martin Herzberg ◇.

The singing was a particular asset in *Jeg har elsket og levet*, an operettish biopic, in the *Lilac Time* manner, about the Danish romantic composer Christoph Ernst Friedrich Weyse. Benny also had great success in the family comedies *Vi kunne ha' det så rart* and *Familien Gelinde* — the former cosily bourgeois, the latter scattily bohemian.

Benny became a consultant anaesthetist in Copenhagen, and Ib a business executive living in England.

Phillip Hurlic

USA

b: 20 Dec 28 (Los Angeles)

'Lucky' Hurlic, a handsome child with a sweet personality, appeared in Educational comedies, in a Paramount short with an all-black cast, with Moran and Mack, and a few times with 'Our Gang'. He was extremely elegant.

Phillip Hurlic (right) with Billy Mauch in Penrod's Double Trouble

36 The Green Pastures
37 The Adventures of Tom Sawyer
   Hearts Divided
   Our Gang Follies of 1938
   Penrod and Sam
   Wings Over Honolulu
38 The Awful Tooth ('OG')
   Feed 'Em and Weep ('OG')
   Jezebel
   Penrod and His Twin Brother
   Penrod's Double Trouble
39 Cousin Wilbur ('OG')
   Mr Smith Goes to Washington
   Son of Frankenstein
   The Sun Never Sets
   Zenobia
40 Young Tom Edison
41 Father's Son
   Golden Hoofs
42 Scattergood Rides High

Ronnie Cosbey

USA

b: 22 Dec 27 (Alhambra, Cal.)

Well-favoured little Ronald – the child of non-theatrical parents – was a standard-issue blond moppet of the early talkies, a plump, handsome Cupid. (His elder brother Jackie also acted for a time. They can be seen together in *Carolina*.)

By the age of ten Ronnie was becoming somewhat jowly, and he wisely packed it in when the teens arrived.

31 East Lynne
   Hush Money
   Wicked
32 The Big Broadcast
   If I Had a Million
   The Man from Yesterday
33 Broadway Bad
   Dance Hall Hostess
   Ever in My Heart
   Heroes for Sale
   The Iron Master
   King of the Jungle
34 Carolina
   The Circus Clown
   Housewife
   Now and Forever
   Now I'll Tell
   Registered Nurse
35 I Live My Life
   Little Men
   Moonlight on the Prairie
   Oil for the Lamps of China
   Personal Maid's Secret
   Public Opinion
   Straight From the Heart
   West Point of the Air
36 Boulder Dam
   The Man I Marry
   Next Time We Love
   Sutter's Gold
37 Madame X
   Wells Fargo
38 The Marines Are Here
   The Telephone Operator
41 The Birth of the Blues

Ronnie Cosbey with June Travis in The Marines Are Here

Billy Dawson

USA

b: circa 1928

The solid, dimply Dawson had leads in two Warner films with more than a similarity of title. *Father Is a Prince* was provisionally called 'Father's Son', but *Father's Son* (with scenario by Booth Tarkington) had quite a different story. To confuse matters further, John Litel, as well as Billy, played a leading part in both.

Stardom wasn't to go much further for the busy Dawson. He was one of many senate page boys in *Adventure in Washington*, and never again rose above the second or third rank.

40 A Dispatch from Reuters
   Father Is a Prince
   Knute Rockne – All American
   Ladies Must Live
41 Adventure in Washington
   Father's Son
   Here Comes Mr Jordan
   Nine Lives Are Not Enough
   Nothing But the Truth
   Remember the Day
   Steel Against the Sky
42 The Major and the Minor
43 Nobody's Darling
44 Lady in the Dark
   Sweet and Lowdown

Polito Ortin

MEXICO

b: circa 1928

Polito was a son of the actor Leopoldo Ortin; his leading roles were in *La canción del huerfano* and *Los dos pilletes*.

Later, as Polo Ortin, he was in *Dos tenorios de barrio* (49) and *Vive come sea* (51).

36 Malditas sean las mujeres
   (A curse on all women)
38 Allá en el Rancho Chico
   (Over at Boys' Ranch)
39 La canción del huerfano
   (Song of the orphan)
   Luces de barriada (Lights of the quarter)
42 Los dos pilletes (The two rascals)
   Regalo de reyes (Gift of kings)

Saul Zamora

MEXICO

b: circa 1928
d: circa 1939

This singing boy, not enjoyed by the film historian Emilio García Riera, was known as 'el Gordito' (Little Fatty). He had a leading role in *Los desheredados*.

Sad to say, little Fatty died of a 'fulminant pneumonia' during the filming of *Diablillos*. He had been one of its stars.

34 La mujer del puerto (Woman of the port)
35 Los desheredados (The disinherited)
   Madre querida (Darling mother)
36 El calvario de una esposa
   (A wife's torment)
37 A la orilla de un palmar
   (At the edge of the palm-grove)
38 Allá en el Rancho Chico
   (Over at Boys' Ranch)
39 Diablillos de arrabal
   (Little devils of the suburbs)

Tao Ferrari

ITALY

b: 2 Feb 29 (Brussels)

Paolo Ferrari – known as Tao in childhood – was in two early films. Then, after nearly fifteen years of silence, Ferrari sprang on to the screen again in the mid-Fifties: *Totò cerca pace* (54), *Ridere, ridere, ridere* (55), *Susanna tutta panna* (57), *Camping* (58) and so on for the next quarter of a century, combining film work with theatre and TV.

38 Ettore Fieramosca
40 Kean

Bobby Samarzich

USA

b: 17 Feb 29

This was a boy whose professional name was changed with almost shirt-like regularity.

He began as 'Bobby Smarzich', but in 1938 appeared as 'Bobby Samrich'. In 1943, for *The Human Comedy* and for his one leading role in *The Boy from Stalingrad* – a flower of the brief 'glorious Russian allies' era – he changed to 'Samarzich', which does seem to be his own name. (At least, it's the one he lives under as an adult.)

He made a highly likeable little

Bobby Samarzich (centre) and Scotty Beckett (right) in The Boy from Stalingrad

Russian hero, given stardom over the head of Scotty Beckett ◇ on this occasion. Nevertheless, the following year, he was back as 'Samrich'. He was even billed sometimes as plain 'Bobby Rich', and had a brother who acted as 'Vido Rich'.

34 Black Fury
   Million Dollar Baby
   The Scarlet Letter
35 Tomorrow's Youth
36 Under Your Spell
38 Gateway
39 The Great Commandment
   Woman Doctor
43 The Boy from Stalingrad
   The Human Comedy
44 Tall in the Saddle

Freddie Mercer

USA

b: 6 Mar 29 (Detroit)

Freddie first sprang to fame as a boy soprano. At nine he sang with the Detroit Symphony Orchestra, and (more frequently) in church and on the radio.

Apart from an odd casting as the young Edgar Allan Poe, this cheeky-looking boy with big ears, wide mouth and small chin – a handsomer version of Mad magazine's Alfred E. Neumann – was best known in the popular 'Gildersleeve' series.

Freddie Mercer in The Loves of Edgar Allan Poe

40 Five Little Peppers in Trouble
41 On the Sunny Side
42 The Great Gildersleeve
   The Loves of Edgar Allan Poe
43 Gildersleeve on Broadway
   Gildersleeve's Bad Day
   Shadows on the Sage
44 Gildersleeve's Ghost
   My Gal Loves Music

Tyler with Ann Todd in the 1941 Danny Boy

Grant Tyler

BRITAIN

b: 12 Apr 29 (London)

Fair-haired Grant Tyler was a natural smiler. His biggest part was the lead in *Danny Boy*, a remarkably quick remake of the story last filmed in 1934 with Ronnie Hepworth ◇.

Soon after it, Grant shot up by a foot, which put a premature end to his career as a child actor. In 1948 he was in *Daughter of Darkness* and *Eureka Stockade*, but was mainly seen henceforth in the theatre, often in musicals like 'The Dancing Years', or revues like 'Sigh No More'.

40 They Came by Night
41 The Common Touch
   Danny Boy
   The Prime Minister
42 The Young Mr Pitt

Michel François

FRANCE

b: 22 Jly 29 (Nice)

This slender, sensitive, dark-eyed creature – who always looked younger than his age – made his debut at five years old, and at twelve was acting with the Comédie Française. He played Edwige Feuillère's son in Ophüls' *Sans lendemain*, and Madeleine Renaud's in *Le ciel est à vous*. In *La cage aux rossignols* he was a conscience-wracked orphan. *Air pur* was never completed.

Michel continued to appear in films for another decade or so. He was Gérard Philipe's fellow-student in *Le diable au corps* (46), and had the male lead in *Les dernières vacances* (47) and again in *Clara de Montargis* (50). He was also the unseen narrator in Truffaut's early film about early teens, *Les mistons* (57).

Gradually, in fact, his interest shifted to the aural side of film. Michel François became one of France's leading special effects technicians, with his own much-in-demand sound studio, and later a producer.

35 Rose
36 Sous les yeux de l'Occident
   (Under western eyes)
37 L'affaire du courrier de Lyon
   (The Lyons Mail case)
38 J'étais une aventurière
   (I was an adventuress)
39 Air pur (Clean air)
   La charrette fantôme (The phantom cart)
   Circonstances atténuantes
   (Extenuating circumstances)
   Jeunes filles en détresse
   (Young girls in distress)
   Menaces (Threats)
   Sans lendemain (No tomorrow)
41 L'assassinat du Père Noël
   (The murder of Father Christmas)
   Péchés de jeunesse (Sins of youth)
42 L'amant de Bornéo
   (The lover from Borneo)
   Patricia
   Le voile bleu (The blue veil)
43 Le ciel est à vous (Heaven is yours)
44 La cage aux rossignols
   (The cage of nightingales)

Michel François with Noël-Noël in La Cage aux rossignols

Douglas Croft with Elsa Janssen in The Pride of the Yankees

Douglas Croft

USA

b: 12 Aug 29 (Seattle)

His real name was Douglas Malcolm Wheatcroft. The star-struck boy was spotted hanging around the film studios by an agent who signed him up and eventually got him a small part. (His first big one was in *Not a Ladies' Man*.) The agent decided his name was too long, so shortened it (for *King's Row*) to 'Douglas Wheat'. Meeting sales resistance, he then dropped the Wheat and kept the Croft. It spelt home run for the serious, curly-haired Douglas, who went on to play the baseball hero Lou Gehrig (as a boy, before turning into Gary Cooper) in *Pride of the Yankees*.

There was no doubt which role won him greatest fame: he was Robin in the screen's first *Batman*, the 15-part serial of 1943 with Lewis Wilson as the Caped Crusader.

This proved a hard act to follow. Douglas was in *River Gang* (45) and *Killer McCoy* (47) – and the cinema didn't see him again except in flashback, in 1965, in a 4½-hour potted version of the old serial, called *An Evening with Batman and Robin!*

41 King's Row
   Remember the Day
42 Flight Lieutenant
   George Washington Slept Here
   Not a Ladies' Man
   The Pride of the Yankees
   Yankee Doodle Dandy
43 Batman *(serial)*
   Harrigan's Kid
   Presenting Lily Mars

Billy Lee

USA

b: 12 Sep 29 (Nelson, Indiana)
d: 17 Nov 89 (Beaumont, Cal.)

When Billy Lee Schlenaker was only two his family moved to Los Angeles. The bright kid was enrolled at the Meglin School, and soon showed singing, dancing

Billy Lee in Thunder Trail

and acting talent. He began appearing semi-publicly in L.A. before he was four. Hal Roach saw him, and cast him in the 'Our Gang' comedy *Mike Fright* – not as a Gang member, but as a little smartypants tap-dancer. Almost at once Paramount signed him up for *Wagon Wheels* and a healthy contract.

Billy Lee's shining morning face and cheerful professionalism kept him busily employed till the onset of the teens and the realities of life. During *Cocoanut Grove* he learned to play the drums, and later formed the Billy Lee Band. He also toured in vaudeville as a dancer.

Scotty Beckett

USA

b: 4 Oct 29 (Oakland, Cal.)
d: 8 May 68 (Hollywood)

Scott Hastings Beckett's life started and ended, as many lives do, in hospital. But the first impulse to his career came there too, when a Hollywood casting director spotted him entertaining his sick father with a medley of pop songs. The rest, for a decade or so, was stardust. Ashes came later.

He was a girlishly pretty child, with fine dark eyes somewhat in the Jackie Coogan◊ mould. The expression, though, lacked Coogan's steel – it was sweet, but slightly weary and petulant. It was the resemblance to the great Jackie, un-doubtedly, which led Hal Roach, when he signed him up with Our Gang in 1934, to dress Scotty in a big cap (baseball, sideways on) and super-sloppy sweater. He was teamed with Spanky McFarland◊ in a shrimp duo, rather as another cherub, Dickie Moore◊, had been teamed with Stymie Beard◊ a couple of years earlier.

Beckett moved on even sooner than Moore. After less than two years he yielded to Alfalfa Switzer◊ as Spanky's partner in mischief, and ceased to be a

Scotty Beckett in The Boy from Stalingrad

regular ganger. But he made one notable return in the title role of *Cousin Wilbur*, as Alfalfa's relative, a bespectacled dandy who turns out to be a business wizard and a prize fighter.

He was in constant demand elsewhere, looking particularly well in patrician garb and settings, for instance as the Dauphin in *Marie Antoinette*. He was in innumerable front-line productions, starring Errol Flynn, Greta Garbo, Fredric March, Norma Shearer, Spencer Tracy and the like, usually as offspring or younger-self. Till his late teens, Scotty was doing fine. He had also won fine notices on the Broadway stage in 'Slightly Married' in 1943.

But now, in Scotty's teens, the screen parts were beginning to thin out, and his big eyes were losing their confidence and lustre. In 1945 he was seen in *Circumstantial Evidence* and *Junior Miss*, in 1946 as young Al Jolson in *The Jolson Story*, and in 1947 in *Cynthia* and *Dangerous Years*. 1948 gave him, too old, the lead in a remake of the preposterous *Michael O'Halloran*, but not in *A Date with Judy*. He had a rewarding lead on radio in the popular series 'The Life of Riley'.

There followed *Battleground* (49), submission to Dean Stockwell in *The Happy Years*, plus *Louisa* and *Nancy Goes to Rio* (50) and another very B-rated lead in *Corky of Gasoline Alley* (51). He was given

opportunities for comedy in the TV serial *Rocky Jones, Space Ranger* (54) but largely ignored in his last film, the courtroom drama *Three for Jamie Dawn* (56).

His youthful appeal had almost gone. Far from being pretty, he was beginning to look, on his rougher days, like Ernest Borgnine. His private life was in a mess and he hadn't quite the brains or stability to cope. His first drunken driving charge had come in 1948, and two years later he was divorced from his first wife, whose life he had allegedly threatened. In 1954 he was twice arrested, for carrying a concealed weapon and for passing a dud cheque. A drugs charge came in 1957, with a second divorce the following year and what looked like a suicide attempt.

Show business no longer an option, he tried real estate and car dealing, neither with much success. In 1964 he was given a 180-day suspended jail sentence for hitting his stepdaughter, child of his third wife, over the head with a crutch. At the beginning of May 1968, unemployed and hopeless, he got badly beaten up in a brawl, and was admitted to a Hollywood rest home. After two days he was found dead in bed, apparently of an overdose. Poor Scotty had been beamed up at last.

33 Gallant Lady
34 Babes in Toyland
    George White's Scandals
    I Am Suzanne
    'Our Gang' (8)
    Romance in the Rain
    Sailor Made Widow
    Stand Up and Cheer
    Whom the Gods Destroy
35 Dante's Inferno
    I Dream Too Much
    'Our Gang' (7)
    Pursuit
36 Anthony Adverse
    The Case Against Mrs Ames
    The Charge of the Light Brigade
    Little Boy Blue
    Old Hutch
37 Bad Man of Brimstone
    Conquest
    A Doctor's Diary
    It Happened in Hollywood
    King Without a Crown
    Life Begins With Love

'Our Gang' Follies of 1938
Wells Fargo
When You're in Love
38 The Devil's Party
    Four's a Crowd
    Listen, Darling
    Marie Antoinette
    No Time to Marry
    Smashing the Rackets
    You're Only Young Once
39 Blind Alley
    Cousin Wilbur ('OG')
    Days of Jesse James
    Dog Daze ('OG')
    The Escape
    The Flying Irishman
    Love Affair
    Mickey the Kid
    Our Neighbors – the Carters
    The Royal Rodeo
40 The Blue Bird
    Cinderella's Feller
    Flag of Humanity
    Gold Rush Maisie
    My Favorite Wife
    My Son, My Son!
    Street of Memories
41 Aloma of the South Seas
    Father's Son
    King's Row
    The Vanishing Virginian
42 Between Us Girls
    It Happened in Flatbush
43 Ali Baba and the Forty Thieves
    The Boy from Stalingrad
    Good Luck Mr Yates
    Heaven Can Wait
    My Reputation
    The Youngest Profession
44 The Climax

Master Suresh

INDIA

b: 13 Oct 29

His real name was Nasir Ahmed Khan, and he acted mainly in Hindi films. In his late teens he re-emerged in leading juvenile roles, in films like *Sona chandi* (46), *Rang mahal* (48), *Dulari* (49), *Dastan* (50) and *Jadoo* (51).

37 Saqi
38 Bazigar
39 Adhuri kahani
    Mirza sahiban

40 Bandhan
41 Anjan
    Naya sansar
42 Basant

Olsson in Göranssons pojke

Tom Olsson

SWEDEN

b: 6 Nov 29 (Stockholm)

Tom, a jolly blond somewhat like a handsomer Tommy Bond ◇, had been a busy professional for many years when he got his biggest chance in the title role of *Göranssons pojke*. He returned briefly to films in the early Sixties, and had a small part in Ingmar Bergman's *Djävulens öga* (The devil's eye).

35 Ebberöds Bank (Ebberöd's Bank)
36 Äventyret (The adventure)
37 Familjer Andersson (The Anderssons)
   Vardag i varuhuset
      (Every day at the big store)
   Vi gå landsvägen (We take the high road)
39 Folket på Högbogården
      (The folks at Högbo's farm)
   Gläd dig i din ungdom
      (Rejoice in your youth)
40 Hjältar i gult och blått
      (Heroes in yellow and blue)
   Juninatten (June nights)
   Mjölkens mirakler (Miracles of milk)
   Som en tjuv om natten
      (Like a thief in the night)
   Swing it, magistern! (Swing it, Sir!)
41 Göranssons pojke (Göransson's boy)
43 Prästen, som slog knockout
      (The K.O. priest)

Michael Gainsborough

BRITAIN

b: circa 1929

Michael's principal role was as sidekick to a dog, the eponymous hero of *Scruffy*. This mutt was briefly famous enough in Britain to have a ghosted book of his movie memoirs published.

37 Sensation
38 John Halifax, Gentleman
   Scruffy
39 All Living Things
41 Quiet Wedding
43 The Shipbuilders
44 Mr Emmanuel

Cordell Hickman

USA

b: circa 1929

Cordell was a serious, likeable black boy seen in many films of the early 1940s. He was teamed with Billy Lee in *The Biscuit Eater* and with Bobby Blake in *Mokey*.

40 The Biscuit Eater
41 The Little Foxes
   Tarzan's Secret Treasure
   West of Cimarron
   You're the One
42 Arabian Nights
   Deep in the Heart of Texas
   Mokey
   Tales of Manhattan
44 Buffalo Bill
   Tale of a Dog ('OG')
45 The Big Bonanza

Martin Schmidhofer

GERMANY

b: circa 1929

After his boyhood appearances, Martin made one or two more films in the early Fifties: *So sind die Frauen* (50), *Der Klosterjäger* (53).

38 Der Edelweisskönig (The edelweiss king)
   Frau Sixta
39 Heimatland (Home country)

Waldrausch (Forest murmur)
40 Beates Flitterwochen (Beate's honeymoon)
   Links der Isar – rechts der Spree
      (Isar on the left, Spree on the right)
41 Der laufende Berg (The moving mountain)

Kenneth Anger

USA

b: 3 Feb 30 (Santa Monica, Cal.)

The occultist and *avant-garde enfant terrible* was brought up in Hollywood and is said to have appeared in several films as a child, as well as beginning – aged nine – his own controversial career as a filmmaker with the short *Who Has Been Rocking My Dream Boat?* – though a version of *Ferdinand the Bull* apparently preceded this.

Anger's real-life capers would often have made fine cinema. He once crept out of a darkened house, naked but for a tastefully draped sheet, to achieve midnight congress with an unsuspecting shrub – only to limp back shortly afterwards, unfulfilled and punctured, having trodden on a hedgehog.

His most glamorous film role was undoubtedly in Max Reinhardt's spectacular *Midsummer Night's Dream*, dressed in white silk tunic and turban and riding a white unicorn, as the 'little changeling boy' over whose custody Oberon and Titania wrangle. This was the film in which Mickey Rooney ◇ played Puck, and Billy Barty ◇ was the fairy Mustardseed.

35 A Midsummer Night's Dream

Serge Emrich

FRANCE

b: 6 Apr 30 (Paris)
d: June 1979

Serge had four years of stage experience, from 1941, with the Théâtre du Petit Monde. On radio he played leads in 'David Copperfield', 'Peter Pan' and 'The Prince and the Pauper'. All the first three film roles were distinguished: for instance he was the Dauphin in *Paméla,* and Louis XVI in *Le Capitan.*

In his late teens Serge made two more films: *La vie en rose* (47) and *D'homme à hommes* (48). But ill health was already dogging him, and he had to abandon the profession.

44 Paméla
45 Le Capitan (The Captain)
   Les malheurs de Sophie
      (The misfortunes of Sophie)

Tommy Cook

USA

b: 5 Jly 30 (Duluth, Minnesota)

After a good deal of radio experience, the dark, curly-haired Tommy won visible acclaim in two serials, and went on to be a familiar face of the Forties.

He had five films in 1946, including *Humoresque, Song of Arizona* and *Tarzan and the Leopard Woman* (in which he was a fairly dangerous savage), and he continued to appear regularly until the Sixties; after that only in *The Thing with Two Heads* (72).

Away from the studios, he became a noted professional tennis player – foreshadowing Vincent Van Patten ◇ – and won over 100 trophies.

40 Adventures of Red Ryder (serial)
   Mutiny in the County
41 Mr District Attorney
   Jungle Girl (serial)
42 The Greenie
   The Tuttles of Tahiti
43 Good Luck Mr Yates
   Hi, Buddy!
44 Mr Winkle Goes to War
45 The Gay Senorita
   Strange Holiday
   The Suspect
   Wanderer of the Wasteland

Tommy Cook spotted in Tarzan and the Leopard Woman

Billy Mahan

USA

b: 9 Jly 30 (Port Townsend, Washington)

Billy's sister was a well-known radio performer, and he made his own radio debut at the age of two. He became the smallest boy (with George Ernest ◇ as his senior) in the 'Jones Family' movies of 1936-1940.

After a sizeable gap, William Mahan made sporadic returns to the screen; *Take Care of My Little Girl* (52), *Strange Lovers* (63), *What a Way to Go!* (64).

36 Back to Nature
   Educating Father
   Every Saturday Night
37 Big Business
   Off to the Races
38 Borrowing Trouble
   Down on the Farm
   Hot Water
   Love on a Budget
   A Trip to Paris
39 Everybody's Baby
   The Jones Family in Hollywood
   Safety in Numbers
40 On Their Own
   Quick Millions
   Too Busy to Work
   Young As You Feel

Darryl Hickman

USA

b: 25 Jly 30 (Los Angeles)

One of Hollywood's most appealing boy actors – no relation to Cordell Hickman ◇, who was somewhat darker – was named by his screen-struck mother after Darryl F. Zanuck. The views of his father, an insurance salesman, aren't known, but it was when he was talking insurance with a lady called Ethel Meglin – who happened to run a famous drama school for children – that the boy's die was finally cast. He had been showing off almost as soon as he could walk ('I was the biggest hambone that ever lived', he said later) and it was now a matter of developing and polishing the talent.

Darryl Hickman

In his early years Darryl had the air of a soulful duckling – irresistible when he was also trying to look tough and independent. One eye he caught was that of Bing Crosby, visiting the Meglins to pick some song-and-dance kids for *The Star Maker*. Bing's brother Everett, an agent, was sufficiently impressed to take Darryl on, and soon afterwards landed him a five-year contract with MGM.

Archer Winston of the New York Post described his performance in *Men of Boys Town* as 'equal parts Al Capone and Tiny Tim'.

Darryl's younger brother DWAYNE HICKMAN (b: 18 May 1934) appeared with him in *Captain Eddie*, and went on to play more parts in the late Forties, largely in the *Rusty* (dog and boys) series. He returned to the screen a decade later and played several adult leads in the Sixties, besides achieving TV fame as Dobie Gillis.

Darryl himself has continued more or less unabatedly in show business, apart from an unexpected moment in 1951 when he entered a seminary to study for the priesthood. (A month later he was out again.) He was a regular screen teenager for some time, in films like *Fighting Father Dunne* (48) and *The Happy Years* (50, playing opposite a new boy star, Dean Stockwell $^\diamond$).

His twenty or so films in the Fifties and Sixties included *Destination Gobi* (53), *Tea and Sympathy* (56), *The Iron Sheriff* (57), *The Tingler* (59) and *Johnny Shiloh* (62). He had also been doing some stage work of a song-and-dance nature, and in 1963 took over from Robert Morse on Broadway in 'How to Succeed in Business Without Really Trying'. He wrote for TV, and in the 1970's was a TV programmer for CBS, then executive producer on the soap opera 'Love of Life'. At the same time he and Dwayne had taken over the running of their father's insurance business.

Darryl still played occasional screen roles, as in *Network* (76) and *Sharky's Machine* (81).

36 Three Cheers for Love
38 If I Were King
39 Emergency Squad
   The Star Maker
40 The Farmer's Daughter
   The Grapes of Wrath
   Mystery Sea Raider
   Untamed
   The Way of All Flesh
   Young People
41 Coffins on Wheels

Glamour Boy
Men of Boys Town
Mob Town
Sign of the Wolf
42 Going to Press ('OG')
   Heart Burn
   Jackass Mail
   Joe Smith, American
   Keeper of the Flame
   Northwest Rangers
   Young America
43 Assignment in Brittany
   The Human Comedy
   Song of Russia
44 And Now Tomorrow
   Henry Aldrich – Boy Scout
   Meet Me in St Louis
   Salty O'Rourke
   Two Years Before the Mast
      (*not released till 1946*)
45 Boogie Woogie
   Captain Eddie
   Kiss and Tell
   Leave Her to Heaven
   Rhapsody in Blue
46 Boys' Ranch
   The Strange Love of Martha Ivers

In-joke in Glamour Boy: *Darryl Hickman impersonates the young Jackie Cooper, in the presence of Cooper himself (centre) and William Demarest (right)*

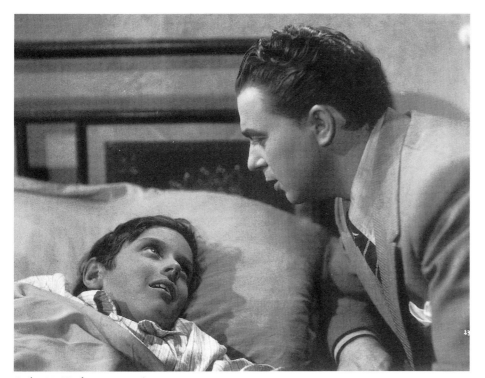

Barbetti in Voglio vivere così

Cesarino Barbetti

ITALY

b: 29 Sep 30 (Palermo)

After his childhood career, Cesare Barbetti continued in films like *La leggenda di Faust* (49), *Messalina* (51), *La grande rinuncia* (51) and *Guerra e pace* (56) – and so to the present day, often in prestige costume pieces like *Agostino d'Ippona* (72).

34 Il cappello a tre punte
   (The three-cornered hat)
35 Darò un milione (I'll give a million)
40 Melodie eterne (Immortal melodies)
   Giorni di festa (Holidays)
41 I promessi sposi (The betrothed)
   Voglio vivere così (That's the way to live)
42 L'angelo bianco (The white angel)
   La contessa Castiglione
   (Countess Castiglione)
43 Dagli Appennini alle Ande
   (From the Apennines to the Andes)
   La freccia nel fianco (Arrow in the side)

Arthur Fritz Eugens

GERMANY

b: 31 Oct 30

His authentic name was Arthur Fritz Schumacher, and he and Peter Bosse ◇ pretty well cornered the maternal instincts of late 1930s Germany.

36 Kinderarzt Dr Engel
   (Dr Engel, paediatrician)
   Maria, die Magd (Maria the maid)
37 Patrioten (Patriots)
   Vor Liebe wird gewarnt
   (A warning of love)
38 Du und ich (You and I)
   Familie auf Bestellung (Family to order)
   Heimat (Homeland)
   Mordsache Holm (The Holm murder case)
   Skandal um den Hahn
   (Scandal over a cockerel)
   Ziel in den Wolken
   (Target in the clouds)
39 Irrtum des Herzens (Error of the heart)
   Männer müssen so sein
   (That's how men have to be)
   Roman eines Arztes (A doctor's story)
40 Bismarck
   Feinde (Enemies)
41 Sonntagskinder (Sunday children)
42 Geliebte Welt (Beloved world)
   Ein Zug fährt zu (A train rolls on)
43 Gefährlicher Frühling
   (Dangerous spring)
   Der kleine Grenzverkehr
   (Frontier traffic)

Lutz Moik

GERMANY

b: 10 Nov 30 (Berlin)

Wavy-haired, good-natured Lutz-Jürgen Moik was in three films in the aftermath of World War Two. *Frühlingsmelodie* was never completed. In the other two Lutz was partnered by a younger boy, Hans Neie.

Moik remained busy in films, in East Germany till 1950 (with the leading role in *Das kalte Herz*), but thereafter mainly in the West.

45 Frühlingsmelodie (Melody of spring)
   Meine Herren Söhne (My worthy sons)
   Eine reizende Familie (A delightful family)

Lutz Moik in Vor dem neuen Tag

Bobs Watson

USA

b: 16 Nov 30 (Los Angeles)

Bobs was not to be confused with the character actor Bobby Watson (1888-1965) who five times impersonated Hitler on the screen. He was born on the 18th birthday of his eldest brother, Coy ◇, and was the last of nine Watson siblings (six of them boys), all of whom appeared in

Bobs Watson and hound in Men of Boys Town

movies. Their father, Coy Watson, Senior, had been a prop-man and assistant director in the Mack Sennett studio.

The pudgy Bobs was valued for his sassiness and pathos, most famously as 'Pee Wee' in *Boys Town* and as 'Pud' in *On Borrowed Time*. His style hasn't, in fact, worn too well. He's hard-working, delivers a good line like a trouper (no Watson would have done less) and sobs with facility; but he's rather shrill, and seldom delivers anything unpredictable.

Having squeaked and sobbed himself to a standstill, Bobs Watson went very quiet for the next decade or so, but resurfaced in the Fifties for a few more films: *The Bold and the Brave* (56), *Saintly Sinners* (62), *Whatever Happened to Baby Jane?* (62), *First to Fight* (67).

He then become a Methodist minister, and appeared in Ron Howard's ◇ directorial debut, *Grand Theft Auto* (77), as 'Rev. Bobs Watson'.

33 The Fisherman
35 Life Begins at Forty
36 Love on the Run
   Mary of Scotland
   Pay As You Exit ('OG')
   Show Boat
37 Our Gang Follies of 1938
   She's Dangerous
38 Boys Town
   Go Chase Yourself
   In Old Chicago
   Kentucky
   Young Dr Kildare
39 Blackmail
   Calling Dr Kildare
   Dodge City
   Everything's On Ice
   On Borrowed Time
   The Story of Alexander Graham Bell
40 Dr. Kildare's Crisis
   Dreaming Out Loud
   Wyoming
41 Hit the Road
   Men of Boys Town
   Scattergood Pulls the Strings
43 Hi, Buddy!

Bill 'Butch' Lenhart and Kenneth 'Buddy' Brown

USA

b: 14 Dec 30 (Edmond, Oklahoma)
   and 20 Jan 32 (Baltimore)

On this occasion it's necessary to break with chronology and let Kenneth Brown in ahead of his time, since 'Butch and Buddy' formed an inseparable duo (and were billed as such) for virtually the whole of their screen careers. They seem seldom to have appeared separately: Lenhart in *Melody of the Plains* and *Two-Gun Troubadour*, before the partnership was established, and Brown in *Bomber's Moon*, when it was nearly over.

Bill Lenhart – the relatively phlegmatic 'Butch' – is said to have played the bass fiddle (presumably rather a small one) from the age of three. (In *Two-Gun Troubadour* Butch was rather confusingly credited as Buddy *(sic)* 'Bull Fiddle Bill' Lenhart.) Certainly it was a sizeable 'cello he supported in his movies.

Kenneth Brown – the smaller, sprightlier 'Buddy' – was wowing Baltimore on the accordion from four: indeed he is advertised in 1937, rashly, as 'the world's smallest accordionist' (there was bound to be a smaller one somewhere) and that year won himself a music scholarship with the instrument.

The two boys met at an audition, and while awaiting their turn improvised a little duet. The fun they had decided them to join forces, and they became the screen's one famous non-sibling kid partnership, appearing in films with W. C. Fields and Abbott and Costello among others. The following titles involved both of them except where otherwise noted.

37 Melody of the Plains *(Butch only)*
39 Two-Gun Troubadour *(Butch only)*
   The Under-Pup
40 A Little Bit of Heaven
   Sandy Is a Lady
   Spring Parade
41 In the Navy
   Man from Montana
   Melody Lane
   Never Give a Sucker an Even Break
42 Johnny Doughboy
43 Bomber's Moon *(Buddy only)*
   Cinderella Swings It
   A Lady Takes a Chance
   Spotlight Scandals
44 Army Wives

Horácio Silva

PORTUGAL

b: 1930

It would be impossible for a Portuguese boy to make a big career in the cinema, since the domestic market is so tiny and the Brazilians, for instance, use their own

Butch Lenhart (left) and Buddy Brown, 1940

Precarious romance: Horacio Silva and Fernanda Matos in Aniki-Bóbó

actors. But Horácio Silva had the luck to play the lead in one of the most charming and atmospheric of all children's films: *Aniki-Bóbó*, which Manoel de Oliveira directed in the precipitous old waterfront city of Oporto, while the Second World War rumbled to the north and east of the Peninsula.

It's a story of chivalry and rivalry among the local kids, with the gentle, high-minded Carlitos (Silva) so romantically obsessed with Terezinha (Fernanda Matos) – to the fury of the thuggish Eduardo (António Santos, a splendid Mussolini-in-short-pants) – that he steals a doll from the 'Shop of Temptations' to present her with.

What distinguishes *Aniki-Bóbó*, aside from the humour and excitement of its plot, is the grubby beauty of the setting, and the strain of dreamy poetry that surrounds the characters. It would have been worthy of Pagnol, and the kids are terrific.

42 Aniki-Bóbó

Buddy Swan

USA

b: circa 1930

He seems to have had musical ambitions, since the Academy Casting Directory for December 1940 prints a photo of him conducting an orchestra, with the caption 'Maestro Buddy Swan'. He is best known as the Hero as Child, with Toboggan, in *Citizen Kane*.

In his late teens Buddy was in at least seven more films: in 1949 *Roaring Westward*, in 1950 *Destination Murder*, *Military Academy* and *Sentence Suspended*. Later ones included *Frigid Wife* (60) and *A Modern Marriage* (62).

40 The Haunted House
41 Citizen Kane
44 The Sullivans
    Sweet and Low-Down
45 Scared Stiff
46 Centennial Summer
    Gallant Journey

Dear little boy: Peter Bosse, 1936

Peter Bosse

GERMANY

b: 15 Jan 31

Germany's *'Lieblingskind'* of the late Thirties was the cuddlesome Peter Bosse, whose mother was the actress Hilde Maroff. His *Moppethaftigkeit* was indescribable. But though he was hardly of military age by 1939, that's where his childhood career stopped.

He appeared on the screen again in East Germany after the war, in his late twenties, in *Kapitäne bleiben an Bord* (58), *Der Prozess wird vertagt* (58) and one or two more. He also worked as an adaptor and director for East German radio.

35 Alles weg'n dem Hund
   (All because of the dog)
   Besuch im Zoo (Visit to the Zoo)
   Vergiss mein nicht (Forget me not)
36 Das Gässchen zum Paradies
   (Little road to paradise)
   Reisebekanntschaft (Travel acquaintance)
   Schloss Vogelöd (Vogelöd Castle)
   Schlussakkord (Final chord)
37 Frauenliebe, Frauenleid
   (Woman's love and grief)
   Heinz hustet (Harry has a cough)
   Mutterlied (Song of a mother)
38 Es leuchten die Sterne
   (The stars are shining)
   Die Frau am Scheidewege
   (Woman at the crossroads)
39 Robert und Bertram

Conrad Binyon

USA

b: 30 Jan 31

Conrad was a delightfully unglamorous boy who radiated humour and common sense. Hugh (Dewey) Binyon – a few outings with 'Our Gang' – was probably his elder brother, and the director and writer Claude Binyon his father. One of his best parts came as a Russian boy fighter in *The Boy from Stalingrad*.

Having been in *Blue Sierra, Courage of Lassie* and *The Gallant Journey* in 1946, Binyon returned in 1950 with *My Blue Heaven, Sentence Suspended* and the snappily titled *Military Academy with That 10th Avenue Gang*. This was enough to finish anyone's screen career, and it seems to have finished Conrad's.

40 The Howards of Virginia
41 On the Sunny Side
   This Woman Is Mine
42 The Glass Key
   Young America
43 The Boy from Stalingrad
   First Comes Courage
   Good Luck Mr Yates
   The Human Comedy
   The Meanest Man in the World
   The Underdog
44 And Now Tomorrow
   The Keys of the Kingdom
   Since You Went Away
45 Love Letters
46 Blue Sierra
   Courage of Lassie
   The Gallant Journey

Conrad Binyon in The Boy from Stalingrad

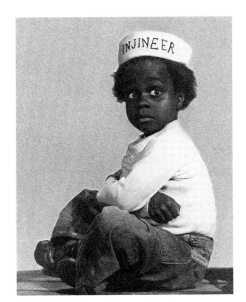

Buckwheat Thomas, circa 1936

William 'Buckwheat' Thomas

USA

b: 12 Mar 31 (Los Angeles)
d: 10 Oct 89 (Los Angeles)

After the departure of Stymie Beard◇ it seemed time in 'Our Gang' for a return to those old cereal values represented by 'Farina' Hoskins◇: so when a tiny black applicant turned up with a huge smile and irresistible eyes, 'Buckwheat' was what he became. Like Farina, he was for some time curiously unisex – the character had originally been planned as a little girl, and was once or twice played by girls, so that 'Buckwheat' had to mutate, as near imperceptibly as possible, into virility. He had a whole decade to do it in.

Billy Thomas made all those Gang shorts, and loved every minute of it in his quiet way. But he didn't make much effort to continue acting after 'Our Gang' was dissolved in 1944. He served in the Korean war, then worked for MGM (his former employers) as a lab technician. Although his marriage broke up, he seems to have been a good father and a contented man, with many friends, till his sudden death in 1980.

34-44 'Our Gang' *(91)*
42 Mokey
45 Colorado Pioneers

Johnny Sheffield

USA

b: 11 Apr 31 (Los Angeles)

Almost incredibly, the child who was to become Tarzan's muscular 'Boy' in the 1940s, and the beefy 'Bomba' of the early 1950s, was so delicate at birth that he had to spend his early weeks in an incubator. The treatment must indeed have been brilliant.

Johnny was the son of the actor Reginald Sheffield, once a leading child actor in England (see Eric Desmond◇). He made his own debut on stage, at the age of seven, as 'Pud' in a touring production of 'On Borrowed Time'. When it came to his home town a studio scout was on hand. Sheffield junior was whisked off for a test (Tarzan already in mind), and in no time was fitted out with a leather fig-leaf and dispatched to the MGM

Johnny Sheffield in Little Orvie

jungle. Though the jungle's proprietors changed over the years, Johnny became a fixture – but it's worth noting that until he was 15, less than half his roles had been in *Tarzan* films.

While he wasn't the lithest of Tarzan's junior partners – that was surely Steve Bond◇ of *Tarzan and the Jungle Boy* – Sheffield was a great little swimmer and

New Boy, old ape: Johnny Sheffield and Cheetah

swinger (crocodiles and lianas permitting), and the kind of Darned Good Sort any childless hero would be happy to have around the place. He held the role, on and off, for eight years, and made it completely his own while Johnny Weissmuller was boss of the jungle.

After *Tarzan and the Huntress* (47) Johnny Sheffield, now an unusually hunky teenager, left the Tarzan series. (Weissmuller himself was to leave it two years later, handing over the role to Lex Barker and becoming 'Jungle Jim' at Columbia.) In 1949 Sheffield acquired his own series as *Bomba the Jungle Boy*, which was the title of the first of these twelve cut-price productions. The last, in 1955, was *Lord of the Jungle*. He was also seen in *The Sun Comes Up* (49), *That Forsyte Woman* (49), *Scaramouche* (52), *Young Bess* (53) and a few more.

He had meanwhile put in some time at UCLA, studying business administration with a view to a life outside the cinema. His old career petered out with minor roles in *The Swan* (56) and *Midnight Lace* (60).

39 Babes in Arms
    Tarzan Finds a Son!
40 Knute Rockne – All American
    Little Orvie
    Lucky Cisco Kid
41 Million Dollar Baby
    Tarzan's Secret Treasure
42 Tarzan's New York Adventure
43 Tarzan's Desert Mystery
    Tarzan Triumphs
44 The Great Moment
    The Man in Half Moon Street
    Our Hearts Were Young and Gay
    Wilson
45 Roughly Speaking
    Tarzan and the Amazons
    Tarzan and the Leopard Woman

Johnny's younger brother Bill appeared in many films of the Forties, from *Knute Rockne* to *The Boy with Green Hair*.

Gianni Glori

ITALY

b: 3 Aug 31 (Milan)

Buzzy Henry (centre) in the 1946 Danny Boy

Gianni was the son of Enrico Glori, who acted in early French talkies and was for many years the favourite villain of Italian films. The lad (sometimes billed as Gianni Musy-Glori) looked as if he might have been handy in the villainy line himself, but his main child part, in the boxing drama *Harlem,* was a sympathetic one.

After a brief educational pause, Gianni's career resumed in 1947 with *L'onorevole Angelina.* Two or three years later he really got going, in films like *Il vespro Siciliano* (50), *Quo vadis?* (51), *Totò e il re di Roma* (52), and one or two films every year thereafter. Now he had every chance to play crooks, in his father's footsteps.

41 Oro nero (Black gold)
43 Harlem

Robert 'Buzzy' Henry

USA

b: 4 Sep 31 (Colorado)
d: 30 Sep 71 (Los Angeles)

Robert – who soon adopted the nickname of 'Buzzy', in the tradition of ridin' boys like Buzz Barton ◊ – won a medal for trick riding at the age of two in a Colorado rodeo. A mere month or two later he was

filming in a Western with Buck Jones, and had made more than a dozen such pictures by the time he was five.

Buzzy or not, he was a very untypical ridin' boy: sensitive-looking (with soulful brown eyes), slender, almost delicate. Starting earlier than Barton, he had ten years as Boy Rider of the Silver Screen.

In his late teens, he continued with hardly a let-up. There were four films in 1947: *King of the Wild Horses, Last of the Redmen, Law of the Canyon* and *Rolling Home.* In 1948 he was in the *Tex Granger* serial, and in one or two films a year during the Fifties, including *The Indian Fighter* (55), *Jubal* (56) and *Cowboy* (58). Between times he toured the rodeo circuits.

Buzz Henry was seen in some popular films of the Sixties, like *Spencer's Mountain* (63), *Shenandoah* and *Von Ryan's Express* (65) and *Tony Rome* (67). But he was also in demand as a technical adviser, stunt coordinator and sequence director, and was frequently the second unit director, for instance on *The Cowboys* (72). His untimely death came at the age of 40.

35 Western Frontier
36 The Unknown Ranger
37 Ranger Courage
    Rio Grande Ranger

Narciso Busquets

MEXICO

b: 9 Sep 31 (Mexico City)
d: 14 Sep 88

This romantic-looking boy, with a wide, dreamily sensual face, was the leading Spanish-speaking child actor of his period, presumably son of the actor Joaquin Busquets (1875-1942).

The Mexican film historian Emilio García Riera registers with profound boredom his 'unremittingly tearful face' in one sentimental drama after another. Summarising *El intruso*, 'the intruder,' writes García, 'was Narciso Busquets, snivelling even more than usual, and crippled and illegitimate into the bargain . . . a sort of Cinderella on crutches.'

The uncritical Mexican public liked Narciso, clearly. His other leads included *Una luz en mi camino*, *Los dos pilletes*, *Dulce madre mia* and *La pequeña madrecita*.

Busquets continued to act in films of the Forties and Fifties, and was still acting in the late Seventies. He also did much dubbing work.

37 Allá en el Rancho Chico
      (Over at Boys' Ranch)
   La gran cruz (The great cross)
38 Los bandidos de Rio Frio
      (The bandits of Cold River)
   Estrellita (Little star)
   Hombres de mar (Men of the sea)
   Una luz en mi camino (A light on my way)
   Por mis pistolas (Because of my pistols)
   Refugiados en Madrid
      (Refugees in Madrid)
39 El cobarde (The coward)
   Corazon de niño (A boy's heart)
40 Ahí está el detalle (That's the whole point)
   Hombre o demonio (Man or demon)
41 ¡Ay, Jalisco, no te rajes!
      (Don't weaken, Jalisco!)
   La gallina clueca (The broody hen)
   El gendarme desconocido
      (The unknown policeman)
42 Los dos pilletes (The two rascals)
   Dulce madre mia (My sweet mother)
   Historia de un gran amor
      (Story of a great love)
   El padre Morelos (Father Morelos)
   Regalo de reyes (Gift of kings)
43 Cuando habla el corazon
      (When the heart speaks)
   Distinto amanacer (Definite daybreak)
   El espectro de la novia (The maid's ghost)
   La pequeña madrecita (The little mother)
44 Alma de bronce (Soul of bronze)
   La barraca (The farmhouse)
   El intruso (The intruder)

Roger Krebs

FRANCE

b: circa 1931

One of the most popular and often-revived French films of the Forties was Jean Dréville's *La cage aux rossignols*, a sentimental comedy set in a school, with Noël-Noël as a teacher trying simultaneously to win the hand of Micheline Francey and to subdue a rebellious class of 12-to-14-year-olds. Since there were to be opportunities for song, the pupils were almost all recruited from France's favourite boys' choir of the period, the Petits Chanteurs à la Croix de Bois.

Narciso Busquets with Andrea Palma in Dulce madre mia

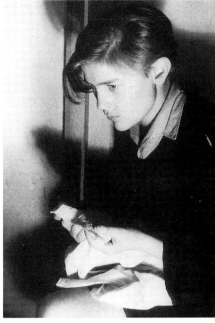

Roger Krebs (Laugier) in Le visiteur

There were two important featured roles among the boys: a sensitive one, played by Michel François ◇, and a smoulderingly uncooperative one called Laugier, played by 'le petit Krebs' (as he was billed). The blond Laugier surprisingly proved to be the school's star singer, and redeemed himself by singing the solo in a highly romantic arrangement of a chorus by Rameau.

Three years later, Dréville made another film with a school setting, *Le visiteur*. This was an effective sentimental drama in which Pierre Fresnay starred as a criminal on the run, who holes up in his old school and is offered hospitality as a distinguished Old Boy.

Fresnay is hero-worshipped (and in due course protected) by an introverted 14-year-old called Clarens, and Clarens is played by a smouldering blond called Roger Laugier who is, sure enough, the not-quite-so-petit Krebs. Like Mickey Kuhn ◇, the boy had jettisoned his real surname, no doubt uncomfortably German-sounding at the time, to replace it with his fictional one from *La cage aux rossignols*.

Krebs/Laugier, proudly throwing back a lock of hair which falls over his right eye, is a striking performer in both films:

Mickey Kuhn with Virginia Weidler in Bad Little Angel

obstinate, vulnerable and disturbingly real.

In the 1948 remake of *La maternelle*, one of the boys is played by 'Laugier' (presumably the same ex-Krebs), and the name recurs in the cast of *Tête blonde* (49). But never again: and Roger Krebs, alias Laugier, is thought to have emigrated to Canada.

43 La cage aux rossignois
        (The cage of nightingales)
46 Le visiteur (The visitor)

Mickey Kuhn

USA

b: circa 1931

Slim Mickey had an interesting, edgy screen personality which earned him a good deal of work – sometimes as a sensitive, sometimes a meanie.

In 1941, in a wave of patriotism, he too dumped his Germanic surname and adopted the hugely Anglo-Saxon 'Mickey

McCune' for screen purposes. By the end of 1944, though, he was back as Kuhn, still with a characteristic expression of scornful distaste.

In 1947 Mickey was in *High Conquest, Magic Town* and *Rusty Leads the Way*, plus an important role in Howard Hawks's *Red River*. Then he was seen, more sporadically, in such films as *The Broken Arrow* (50), *On the Loose, A Streetcar Named Desire* and *That's My Boy* (51), and *The Last Frontier* (55).

Nearly thirty years later Mickey Kuhn made a long-delayed comeback in *The House on Sorority Row* (83), but by now he had moved into a different field, as Flight Administrator at Logan International Airport.

35 Unwelcome Stranger
36 Gorgeous Hussy
        Libeled Lady
37 A Doctor's Diary
        The Prisoner of Zenda
38 Change of Heart
        Young in Heart
39 Bad Little Angel
        Gone with the Wind

Juarez
        King of the Underworld
        SOS – Tidal Wave
        When Tomorrow Comes
40 I Want a Divorce
41 One Foot in Heaven
        Rags to Riches
43 Presenting Lily Mars
45 Dick Tracy
        Roughly Speaking
        This Love of Ours
        A Tree Grows in Brooklyn
46 The Return of Rusty
        Roaring Rangers
        The Searching Wind
        The Strange Love of Martha Ivers

Leon Tyler

USA

b: circa 1931

Leon, blond and sleek, played amusing wimplets in films of the early 1940s, though his appearances with Our Gang never got beyond three. He could afford to snap his elegant fingers at them.

He also outlived most of them as a performer, continuing in *It Happened in Brooklyn* (47), *Magic Town* (47), *Mickey* (48), *Mr Soft Touch* (49), *Military Academy with That 10th Avenue Gang* (50), *Carrie* (51) and so on to Disney fims of the 1950s: *The Absent-Minded Professor* (61), *Son of Flubber* (63) and *The Monkey's Uncle* (65).

40 On Their Own
        Spots Before Your Eyes
41 Come Back, Miss Pipps ('OG')
        Helping Hands ('OG')
        Melody for Three
        They Met Again
        Whistling in the Dark
42 The Loves of Edgar Allan Poe
        On the Sunny Side
        Surprised Parties ('OG')
43 Bomber's Moon
        I Dood It
44 The Great Mike
        The Hitler Gang
        The Seventh Cross
45 Circumstantial Evidence
        The Great Stagecoach Robbery
        Son of Lassie
        This Love of Ours

Hans Lindgren in Barnen från Frostmofjället

Hans Lindgren

SWEDEN

b: 6 Jan 32 (Österåkers)

Hans was a capable blond, active as a boy in Swedish films of the mid-Forties. Most of his roles were marginal – working boys in stables or smithies – but he had the leading character of 'Ante' in the energetic children's adventure *Barnen från Frostmofjället*.

He resumed his film career in 1950, and averaged one a year thereafter.

43 Kajan går till sjöss (The Kaja goes to sea)
    När ungdomen vaknar
      (When youth awakes)
44 Den heliga lögnen (The holy lie)
    Rännstensungar (Guttersnipes)
    Vår Herre luggar Johansson
      (The Almighty rebukes Johanson)
45 Barnen från Frostmofjället
      (The kids from Frostmo Mountain)
    Trav, hopp och kärlek
      (Faith, hope and chariots)
46 Barbacka (Bareback)

Kenneth 'Buddy' Brown

USA

b: 20 Jan 32

(See BILL 'BUTCH' LENHART, page 172.)

Göran Bernhard

SWEDEN

b: 20 Jan 32 (Stockholm)

This plumply handsome little brunet played the heir-to-a-fortune whom governess Ingrid Bergman was supposed to knock off in *En kvinnas ansikte* – an almost instant Swedish remake of MGM's *A Woman's Face*, in which Joan Crawford was supposed to do likewise to Richard Nichols ◇. (This idea had crossed the minds of many filmgoers of the period.)

Miss Bergman's heart, of course, rapidly softened. Göran (whose actual surname was Streijflert) was Sweden's Dear Little Gentleman of the period – the equivalent of Peter Bosse ◇ in Germany, Johnny Russell ◇ or Scotty Beckett ◇ in the USA.

Oddly, Göran seldom worked twice for the same director.

36 Äventyret (The adventure)
    Familjens hemlighet (The family secret)
37 Häxnatten (Night of the witch)
38 Två år i varje klass
    (Two years in every class)
    En kvinnas ansikte (A woman's face)
39 Herr husassistenten (Mister Housemaid)
40 Västkustens hjältar
    (Heroes of the West Coast)
    Den blomstertid (Flowering time)
41 Soliga Solberg (Sunny Mr Solberg)
    Stackars Ferdinand (Poor old Ferdinand)
43 Jag dräpte (I killed)
44 Jag är eld och luft (I am fire and air)

Baby LeRoy

USA

b: 12 May 32 (Altadena, Cal.)

Since babies generally gurgle rather than act, they have to be rather special ones to get into this book. Ronald LeRoy Winebrenner was definitely special, the best-known baby of the talkies.

He won a 'photogenic baby' contest, which led to his being chosen to appear in *A Bedtime Story* with Maurice Chevalier. He filmed four times with the great child-hater W.C.Fields, who is said to have

Pliant and affable: Baby Leroy

spiked the tot's orange juice with gin and then, when LeRoy grew woozy, remarked: 'The kid's not a trouper – can't hold his liquor.'

In the words of Marc Best, Baby LeRoy was 'an even-tempered and jolly infant with a pliant and affable disposition towards strangers.' He also had the knack of mimicking the expressions of people talking to him – Fields included.

In 1936 Paramount declined its option to renew LeRoy's contract, but he didn't become an embittered four-year-old. At 18 he was discovered working in his step-father's delicatessen on Sunset Boulevard, and from 1951 to 1965 he was a lifeguard on San Pedro beach. Fields's gin didn't appear to have stunted his growth.

33 Alice in Wonderland
    A Bedtime Story
    Tillie and Gus
    The Torch Singer
34 It's a Gift
    The Lemon Drop Kid
    Miss Fane's Baby Is Stolen
    The Old-Fashioned Way
35 It's a Great Life!

Yukihiko Sugi

JAPAN

b: 12 Jne 32 (Fukuoka Prefecture)

He worked briefly for the Toho studio, around his tenth year.

A decade or so later, after graduating from Meiji University, Sugi returned to acting, in *Tsuyiko no kasa* (55), *Zakkyo kazoku* (56), *Arashi o yobu yujo* (59).

From 1972 he has been a producer of educational programmes for TV.

41 Jiro monogatari (Tales of Jiro)
42 Tsubasa no gaika (Song of victory)

Anthony Wager

BRITAIN

b: 24 Jne 32 (Willesden, London)

Anthony Alexander Wager's father was a plumber and decorator in North-West London, and Anthony was chosen from more than 700 candidates for the part of Young Pip in David Lean's *Great Expectations*.

In 1949 Wager appeared in secondary parts in *Fame Is the Spur* and *No Place for Jennifer*, and in 1951 in *Scrooge*. He was in *Above Us the Waves* (55), *The Captain's Table* (58), *Night of the Prowler* (62), *Shadow of Fear* (63), *Be My Guest* (65), and many other films of the period – too often, he complained, as soldiers or sailors.

Moving to Australia, he could be seen – as a grander kind of soldier – in an early scene of the TV film *Bodyline* (AU 85).

Raiding the larder: Anthony Wager in the 1946 Great Expectations

46 Great Expectations
47 Cagliostro (US)
   Hungry Hill
   The Secret Tunnel
48 The Guinea Pig

Billy 'Froggy' Laughlin

USA

b: 5 Jly 32 (San Gabriel, Cal.)
d: 10 Aug 48 (Hacienda Heights, Cal.)

At the age of 3½, as Richard Lamparski relates, William Robert Laughlin, a meat-cutter's son, was overheard by his mother talking to what she assumed was a gravelly-voiced man. When she went out to see, she found he was talking to himself. The 'Froggy' voice had been born. Training with a Popeye dummy, he began to entertain the local kids and then perform at church socials. At Christmas 1939, through the agency of an entrepreneur called Bud Murray, he did a solo turn (as a top-hatted politician) in a children's show at a Los Angeles theatre.

Its success led to a contract with 'Our Gang', and he was with them non-stop, as 'Froggy', in 29 shorts, from 1940 till the Gang's dissolution in 1944. He was a highly distinctive figure with his square, sandy-thatched head, slightly crossed eyes behind wire-framed specs, and suspender-hitched trousers. His weird voice delighted kids but got on the nerves of most adults, who found it too ponderous for real comedy.

He was in one non-Gang film, *Johnny Doesn't Live Here* (44), immediately after the series ended, but told his parents he wasn't interested in making any more. In his mid-teens he got a newspaper round, and a motor-bike to do it with. One day, forgetting his promise not to let other kids go on it, he allowed a friend to drive the bike while he slung his newspapers out from the back. They collided with a truck. The friend survived; poor Froggy didn't.

Brian Weske

BRITAIN

b: 23 Dec 32 (London)

This fair, waifish boy, a favourite urchin of British films of the late Forties, was the son of the actor J. Victor Weske. His first featured role was as 'Limpy' in *Medal for the General*, but he was better known later as 'Henry' in the *William* films.

He had minor parts in films for another twenty years or so, for instance in *The High Bright Sun* (65) and *A Hole Lot of Trouble* (69).

44 Medal for the General
45 Perfect Strangers
46 Hospital Services
   Quiet Weekend
47 Fame Is the Spur
   Fortune Lane
   Just William's Luck
48 Pen Picture from Rhodesia
   William Comes to Town

Brian Smith

BRITAIN

b: 24 Dec 32 (Nottingham)

Although a mid-teenager when he was in *The Browning Version* and *No Place for Jennifer*, Brian Smith was amazingly small and young-looking for his age, and these were unmistakably 'boy roles'.

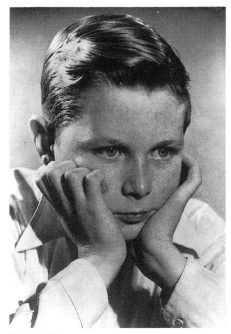

Brian Smith, 1949

A year or two earlier he had read stories on BBC Radio, and played in 'A Month in the Country' for Hugh Hunt at the Bristol Old Vic. At the end of 1948 he played Jim in a London production of 'Treasure Island', and in 1949 was 'Moth' in Hunt's magical production of 'Love's Labours Lost', starring Michael Redgrave.

He was then in the Redgrave 'Hamlet', and the Redgrave-Smith partnership at last came before the cameras in the crucial scene of *The Browning Version*, played with memorable delicacy and feeling.

Brian Smith, who has grown into a mature and subtle actor (still uncannily youthful), had the delicious satisfaction in 1982 of appearing in 'The Browning Version' at York Repertory Theatre — not as Taplow, but as Crocker-Harris.

49 No Place for Jennifer
50 The Browning Version

William Graham

BRITAIN

b: 1932 (Darlington)

The most important if not the most picturesque impersonator of 'William',

grubby hero of Richmal Crompton's popular series of children's books and England's answer to America's *Penrod*, was the curly-haired son of a blacksmith.

47 Just William's Luck
48 William Comes to Town

Bobby Larson

USA

b: 1932

This slight, tow-haired boy, with a lordly oval face, had been performing on radio from the age of six. His first notable screen role was as the 'Gettysburg address' kid who inspires James Stewart in *Mr Smith Goes to Washington*. He played 'Davie' in the *Little Peppers* series, and had two leading parts in 1943, in *The Underdog* and *You Can't Beat the Law*. He also appeared in some middle-period 'Blondie' films, and was excellent in sly, needling roles..

As 'Bob Larson' he was later seen in *Redwood Forest Trail* (50), and continued for at least another fifteen years.

39 Mr Smith Goes to Washington
40 The Bank Dick
   The Courageous Dr Christian
   The Doctor Takes a Wife
   Earthbound
   Five Little Peppers at Home
   Five Little Peppers in Trouble
   The Howards of Virginia
   Out West with the Peppers
41 Bachelor Daddy
   Design for Scandal
   Half Shot at Sunrise
   Here Comes Mr Jordan
   Her First Beau
   The Lady from Cheyenne
   Lydia
   The Stork Pays Off
   Woman of the Year
42 The Affairs of Jimmy Valentine
   Jackass Mail
   Leather Burners
   Quiet, Please, Murder
   Riders of the Northland
   Ship Ahoy
43 The Adventures of Mark Twain
   Good Luck Mr Yates
   The Iron Major
   Smart Guy
   The Underdog
   You Can't Beat the Law

Bobby Larson with Charles Starrett (left) and Shirley Patterson in Riders of the Northland

44 An American Romance
    Mr Winkle Goes to War
    My Pal Wolf
    The Sullivans
    The Unwritten Code
45 The Adventures of Rusty
    Sagebrush Heroes
    You Came Along
46 Blondie's Lucky Day
    Cross My Heart
    Life with Blondie
    Personality Kid
    The Unknown
47 Blondie's Holiday

Billy Cummings

USA

b: circa 1932

Cummings was a tough, dark, dogged, rather Italian-looking boy, much in demand in the mid-1940s.

44 The Sullivans
    Sunday Dinner for a Soldier
    Three Men in White
45 Circumstantial Evidence
    Colorado Pioneers
47 Oregon Trail Scouts
48 Fighting Father Dunne

Ducky Louie

USA

b: circa 1932

This endearing Chinese-American boy – possibly related to Roland Lui, 'the

Ducky Louie in China Sky

Merrill Rodin (right) with Charlie Bates in The Strange Death of Adolph Hitler

younger son' in *The Good Earth* of 1937 – played leading roles in South-East Asia war films of the late 1940s. He was seen again in *Smuggler's Island* (51).

In *China's Little Devils* he was a heroic resistance fighter, but had a richer part in *China Sky*, as 'Little Goat', loyal and humorous houseboy to doctor Randolph Scott.

45 Back to Bataan
    China Sky
    China's Little Devils
47 Black Gold

Merrill Rodin

USA

b: circa 1932

Merrill Guy Rodin was a neat, freckled boy with a serious face and sandy hair – the last not too apparent in his first notable role, as a Dutch refugee child in

The Pied Piper, for which he had been shaved virtually bald. He's probably better remembered, with his normal thatch, as the younger of the heroine's brothers in *The Song of Bernadette*.

42 The Pied Piper
43 American Empire
    Chetniks!
    Hail the Conquering Hero
    Sagebrush Law
    Seventh Column
    The Song of Bernadette
    The Strange Death of Adolph Hitler
44 And Now Tomorrow
    Buffalo Bill
    In the Meantime, Darling
    The Master Race
    The Sullivans
    Sweet and Lowdown
45 Anchors Aweigh
    The House I Live In
46 Abilene Town
    Gay Blades
    The Virginian
47 I Wonder Who's Kissing Her Now

182

Dimplomatic: Johnny Russell with Shirley Temple in the 1946 Blue Bird

Johnny Russell

USA

b: 25 Jan 33 (Brooklyn, New York)

John Russell Countryman had fair curls
and a pretty-pudgy face. (Unlike the
granite-faced adult John Russell, born
1921, whose screen career started at
almost the same moment.) On an L.A.
holiday with his mother, the child was
auditioned and given a part in *The Duke
Comes Back*. His playing was praised but
seemed to lead nowhere; then he landed a
role in *Always Goodbye*, and ten more films
smoothly followed.

   In his last, *The Blue Bird*, he co-starred
with Shirley Temple – and in adult life,
by an odd coincidence, John Countryman,
like Miss Temple, entered the diplomatic
service. He must have dimpled charmingly
as the American consul in, for instance,
Bahrain.

37 The Duke Comes Back
38 Always Goodbye
   Five of a Kind
   Headline News
   Prison Break
39 Jesse James
   The Man Who Dared

Mr Smith Goes to Washington
   Sabotage
40 The Blue Bird
   Lady with Red Hair
   The Man I Married

Rinaldo Smordoni

ITALY

b: 5 Feb 33 (Rome)

Rinaldo, a carpenter's son, was chosen
to play the younger of the two 'innocent
delinquents' in De Sica's harrowing
Sciuscia. (The 16-year-old FRANCO
INTERLENGHI – born 29 October 1930 –
who played his older companion, went on
to marry the actress Antonella Lualdi and
become a leading man in Italian films of
the Fifties and Sixties.) Young Smordoni
knew the background well enough: he had
for some time been shining Roman shoes
on his own account. In *Sciuscia* he
graduates to black-marketeering, and so
to prison, escape and sudden death.

   He played one more important role, a
classic one for French boy actors: that of
Gavroche in an Italian version of 'Les
misérables', directed by Riccardo Freda.

   When last heard of, he was still living in
Rome, working as a bus-driver.

46 Sciuscia (Shoe-shine)
49 I miserabili (The poor and wretched)

Rinaldo Smordoni (left) with Franco Interlenghi in Sciuscia

Nyström in Barnen från Frostmofjället

Anders Nyström

SWEDEN

b: 8 Feb 33 (Stockholm)

The wry Master Nyström was in no less than twenty films between the ages of eight and fourteen.

At the end of his teens he made one more appearance in *Trots* (52). Then, nearly twenty years later, in 1971-72, he was in three TV films.

41 Landstormens lille argbigga
  (The home guard's nagging wife)
42 Himlaspelet (Mystery play)
  Kan doktorn komma?
  (Can the doctor come?)
43 Brödernas kvinna (The brothers' woman)
  Herre med portfolj
  (Gentleman with portfolio)
  Katrina
  När ungdom vaknar (When youth awakes)
44 Hets (Frenzy)
  Kejsaren av Portugallien
  (The Emperor of Portugal)
  Och alla dessa kvinnor
  (And all these women)
  Vändkorset (Crossroads)
  Vi på Vallberga (We from Vallberga)
45 Barnen från Frostmofjället
  (The kids from Frostmo Mountain)
  I som här inträden (Ye who enter here)
  Maria på Kvarngården
  (Maria at Kvarngård)
46 Hundra dragspel och en flicka
  (100 accordions and a girl)
  Ödermarksprästen (The country priest)
47 Det kom en gäst (A guest is coming)
  Maria
  Pappa sökes (Daddy wanted)

Ebbe Langberg

DENMARK

b: 1 Aug 33 (Copenhagen)
d: February 1989 (Copenhagen)

Langberg, celebrated for his dominant role in *De pokkers unger*, provided a Danish voice for Disney's *Peter Pan* (52), and from the late 1950s was one of Denmark's most popular juvenile leads on both stage and screen.

He directed his first film in 1963, and from 1968 managed the Aalborg Theatre.

46 Ditte menneskebarn (Ditte, child of man)
47 De pokkers unger (Those bloody kids)
48 Kristinus Bergman

Brian Roper

BRITAIN

b: 9 Aug 33 (Doncaster)

This amiable, freckled redhead – 'Ginger' in the *William* films – had the sort of cosmopolitan career denied to most Doncaster boys. After acting in local dramatic shows, he toured Britain with a company organised by the National Association of Boys' Clubs, and at 14, in London, played the title role (created, oddly enough, by Elisabeth Bergner) in Barrie's biblical play 'The Boy David'.

Roper as Dickon in The Secret Garden

In *The Naked Heart* he acted with Michèle Morgan, in *The Secret Garden* – somewhat woodenly, inhibited by a 'compromise' Yorkshire accent – with Hollywood's leading child actors, Margaret O'Brien and Dean Stockwell ◊, and in *The Miniver Story* with Greer Garson and Walter Pidgeon.

The puppyish Roper – 15 or 16 when this last film was being shot – was still reasonably convincing in short trousers. He subsequently appeared in *Time Gentlemen Please!* (52), *The Girl on the Pier* (53), *The Rainbow Jacket* (54) and *The Blue Peter* (55). He then went to work in the USA, and was seen in *Hong Kong Confidential* (US 58) before moving into the agency business.

47 Just William's Luck
48 William Comes to Town
49 The Naked Heart
  The Secret Garden (US)
50 The Miniver Story (US)

Ted Donaldson

USA

b: 20 Aug 33 (New York)

It somehow restored one's faith in Hollywood's integrity that the boy who probably had more leading parts than any other in the Forties was so magnificently unglamorous and un-All-American. 'Pudge' Donaldson, in his earlier films at least, was not just pudgy but downright flabby. You couldn't help warming to the lad – especially as he turned out to have a nice crisp way with lines and a tough-guy accent to deliver them in.

His parents, Will Donaldson and Muriel Pollock, wrote and arranged light music for the radio, the medium on which their ginger-haired four-year-old launched his career and became known for his command of dialects and foreign accents and his powers of mimicry. He began training as an actor, and played in such stage hits of the early Forties as 'Life with Father' and 'Sons and Soldiers'.

Ted Donaldson in Once upon a Time

Bobby Blake

USA

b: 18 Sep 33 (Nutley, New Jersey)

That tough little nut Robert Blake – as he
now is – was born Michael James Vijencio
Gubitosi, and until 1942 acted as Mickey
Gubitosi. His parents were a song-and-
dance duo known as The Hillbillies, and
when he was only two he and his sister
replaced their mother and made it a trio.
Three years later Michael joined 'Our
Gang', almost by an act of will: like the
Switzers, he simply turned up and started
performing, and they took him on.

  He got landed with a rather whiney
character (which can't have delighted him,
although it was called 'Mickey') and
remained with the increasingly charmless
Gang till its demise in 1944. He later said
that his whole childhood was lousy, and
the acting not the least lousy part of it.
With two alcoholic parents to support,
he felt less like a child star than a child
labourer.

  Young Gubitosi had always had a few
film jobs outside 'Our Gang', and at the
age of eight he got a starring one in a film
called *Mokey*: difficult child redeemed by
dog, etcetera. For the occasion he (or his
agent) decided to ditch his Italian name.
He re-christened himself Bobby Blake;
and from mid-1942 it was Bobby Blake,
too, not Mickey Gubitosi, who played
'Mickey' in 'Our Gang'.

  When the Gang broke up, he found a
niche almost at once in the 'Red Ryder'
Western series, in which he played a Red
Indian boy called 'Little Beaver', junior
sidekick at first to 'Wild Bill' Elliott (in
films like *Tucson Raiders* and *Wagon Wheels
Westward*) and then, during 1946-47, to
Allan Lane (*Conquest of Cheyenne* and so
on).

Then he was chosen to co-star with
Cary Grant in a whimsical film comedy,
Once Upon a Time, about a little boy called
Pinky who keeps a dancing caterpillar in a
match-box. While it dances, it sings 'Yes
sir, that's my baby', to the delight of
Grant, who sees in it a means of restor-
ing his fortunes. He behaves with ruth-
less cynicism, till shamed into decency by
Master Donaldson.

  While Ted's looks improved as he
entered his teens, he became identified
(like Mark Dennis ◇, Teddy Infuhr ◇ and
others) with an interminable series centred
on a dog called Rusty, though he also had
leads in *Personality Kid*, *The Red Stallion*

and *The Decision of Christopher Blake*.

  Ted Donaldson had two films in 1952,
Phone Call from a Stranger and *Raging
Waters*, but the roles were secondary and
the screen career got no further. In the
late 1970s he was working in a movie
bookstore in Hollywood.

With his Mexican kid in Huston's 1948 classic *The Treasure of Sierra Madre*, Blake was back to ethnic roles, and for a time such small parts (with the emphasis on 'small') were his lot, in films like *The Black Rose* (50), *The Black Hand* (50), *Apache War Smoke* (52) and *The Veils of Bagdad* (53). When he finally got a leading role, in *The Purple Gang* (60), it was as a pint-sized, power-crazed delinquent. It looked as if Robert Blake, a notably embittered character who made no bones about his past unhappiness, was to have a depressing adult career playing nasty little men, a trend confirmed, though more sympathetically, by his young murderer in *In Cold Blood* (67).

The turning-point came with his role in *Tell Them Willie Boy Is Here* (69), as the formidably noble Indian of the title, ruefully pursued by Robert Redford; and Blake's screen rehabilitation was completed in 1973 by his brilliant – and lovable – performance as John Wintergreen, the traffic cop with detective aspirations, in *Electra Glide in Blue*. When he played a real cop, though, in the lead of the TV series 'Baretta', Blake (who knew all about real cops, from his own chequered history) made a pretty bleak figure.

Having got this out of his system, he then produced and starred in three TV movies as the more benign, off-beat investigator Joe Dancer.

39 'Our Gang' *(4 shorts)*
   Bridal Suite
40 'Our Gang' *(9)*
   I Love You Again
   Spots Before Your Eyes
41 'Our Gang' *(8)*
42 Andy Hardy's Double Life
   China Girl
   Kid Glove Killer
   Mokey
   'Our Gang' *(8)*
43 'Our Gang' *(7)*
   Lost Angel
   Salute to the Marines
   Slightly Dangerous
44 'Our Gang' *(3)*
   The Big Noise
   Cheyenne Wildcat
   Marshal of Reno
   Meet the People
   The San Antonio Kid
   The Seventh Cross
   The Sheriff of Las Vegas
   Tucson Raiders
   Vigilantes of Dodge City
   The Woman in the Window
45 Colorado Pioneers
   Dakota
   The Great Stagecoach Robbery

   A Guy Could Change
   The Horn Blows at Midnight
   Lone Texas Ranger
   Marshal of Laredo
   Phantom of the Plains
   Pillow to Post
   Wagon Wheels Westward
46 California Gold Rush
   Conquest of Cheyenne
   Home on the Range
   Humoresque
   In Old Sacramento
   Out California Way
   Santa Fe Uprising
   Sheriff of Redwood Valley
   Stagecoach to Denver
   Sun Valley Cyclone
47 Homesteaders of Paradise Valley
   The Last Round-Up
   Marshal of Cripple Creek
   Oregon Trail Scouts
   The Return of Rin Tin Tin
   Rustlers of Devil's Canyon
   Vigilantes of Boomtown
48 The Treasure of the Sierra Madre

Donn Gift

USA

b: 14 Dec 33 (Danville, Illinois)

The haggard, sad-eyed Gift – genuinely frail, after a childhood illness – is mainly remembered now as Claude Jarman's °° ailing friend in *The Yearling*; but he had his own starring role in *The Enchanted Valley*.

Donn was a great reader and naturalist, and a dedicated member of the Audubon Society.

46 The Yearling
48 The Enchanted Valley
   Fighting Father Dunne
50 The Happy Years

Lanny Rees

USA

b: 14 Dec 33 (Veradale, Washington)

Lanny was a busy and personable boy actor without any marked screen personality. He had the human lead in *My Dog Shep*, which is fairly self-explanatory.

Bobby Blake and redeeming dog in Mokey

Lanny Rees with Barbara Hale, 1948

46 Home in Oklahoma
   Little Iodine
   My Dog Shep
47 Banjo
   Law Comes to Gunsight
   A Likely Story
48 California Firebrand
   Overland Trails
   The Time of Your Life
49 The Life of Riley

Tommy Tucker

USA

b: 1933

38 Test Pilot
39 Boy Trouble
   Call a Messenger
   Vigil in the Night
40 The Blue Bird
   Junior G-Men *(series)*
41 On the Sunny Side
   Shadow of the Thin Man
42 The Falcon's Brother
   Little Tokyo, U.S.A.
   Mrs Miniver
43 Election Daze ('OG')
46 California

Bobby Anderson

USA

b: circa 1933

Bobby Anderson, 1948

The whole Bobby Anderson situation could hardly be more confusing – since there was *another* boy actor called Robert Anderson, a year or two older than this one, who *also* called himself 'Bobby' until about 1943.

The older Anderson was the busier performer, but the younger one – who looked like a fairer-haired junior version of Montgomery Clift – had the better roles, such as the hero-as-boy in *It's a Wonderful Life*. The two Robert Andersons actually appeared *together* in this film, and in *Magic Town*. One of them – or both? – appeared once or twice with 'Our Gang'.

47 The Bishop's Wife
   It's a Wonderful Life
   Magic Town
48 Kidnapped
   Ruthless
49 Samson and Delilah

Mark Dennis

USA

b: circa 1933

This erect, dignified boy, with rather old-fashioned good looks, was unlucky to get embedded in the mediocre *Rusty* series; but he had worthwhile parts elsewhere, notably in the horse-racing story *Sport of Kings*.

Mark Dennis, circa 1948

In adult life Mark Dennis had the occasional acting assignment, such as *Targets* (68) and *Nickelodeon* (76); but he was credited as a still photographer on *Pagan Island* (61).

46 The Return of Rusty
47 The Millerson Case
   Riders of the Lone Star
   Sport of Kings
   The Thirteenth Hour
48 The Secret Beyond the Door
49 Rusty's Birthday

Ernest Severn

USA

b: 3 May 33 (Johannesburg, S.A.)
d: 27 Nov 87 (Thousand Oaks, Cal.)

There were no less than eight little Severns, all of whom acted in Hollywood. They were the sons and daughters of Dr Clifford Severn, an English dietician and physical culture specialist who moved first to South Africa and then, in the mid-1930s, to Los Angeles.

The first two children (Venetia and Clifford junior) were born in London in the Twenties, the next three (Yvonne, Raymond and Ernest) in Johannesburg in the early Thirties, and the last three (Christopher, William ◊ and Winston) in Los Angeles between 1936 and 1943. The girls did less film work than the boys, but

Ernest Severn, circa 1946

Danny Mummert

USA

b: 20 Feb 34 (Dallas, Texas)

By virtue of being born some seven months earlier, Alvin Fuddle of the *Blondie* series – Baby Dumpling's next-door buddy – gets into this book ahead of Dumpling himself. In fact the three-year-old Danny Mummert auditioned for the role of Alexander (alias Baby Dumpling till 1942), but Larry Simms ◇ landed it. The two of them were identified with the series over a period of twelve years, growing from toddlers to mid-teenagers. Only seven of Mummert's films were 'non-Blondies'.

Whereas Dumpling/Alexander represents the mischievous but four-square American boy, Alvin has intellectual and artistic pretensions and regards Alexander as a handy audience. He will burst into song to entertain the Bumsteads; or he will dazzle them with some pearl of erudition. 'Sometimes I frighten myself', he comments modestly. The slender, whimsical Mummert plays him with great charm.

He showed his own mental prowess when, as a two-year-old, he dumbfounded visitors to the Texas Centennial Fair by reeling off the names of all the Presidents of the United States, plus the states themselves and their capitals. If, when the time came, he failed to win Columbia's vote as Dumpling, he could console himself by reflecting that he had far the more amusing part.

Danny was in all the 'Blondie' films listed for Larry Simms (page 190) except, it seems, *Life with Blondie* and *Blondie's Lucky Day* in 1946. In his absence Bobby Larson ◇ made the first two of his three appearances in the series.

Danny Mummert continued to act as a late-teenager in such films as *The Member of the Wedding* (52), *The Sniper* (52) and *Bitter Creek* (54). A 'Don Mummert' was credited as recently as 1980, in *Bronco Billy*.

The films Danny was in as a boy *without* Simms were:—

the siblings claimed to have notched up more than 200 movie credits between them by the end of the Forties.

Ernest was an uncharacteristic member of the generally dark-and-wavy Severn clan: Nordic-looking, with straight fair hair and piercing blue eyes in the manner of David Bowie. He is powerful in the flashback scenes of *Pursued*, struggling with frightening memories and with the scowling Charley Bates ◇.

Ernest Severn, like Christopher, later became an elder in the Mormon Church.

CLIFFORD SEVERN (born 1927) could also be seen in *Forever and a Day*, RAYMOND in *A Guy Named Joe*, *The Man from Down Under* and *The Hour Before the Dawn*, and CHRISTOPHER in the first two of these.

Clifford had other supporting roles in films from *Jalna* (35) to *Journey for Margaret* (42) and beyond; and Raymond was particularly prominent in *We Are Not Alone* (39). WINSTON (born 1943) was in *Her Sister's Secret*, *If Winter Comes* and *Lost Honeymoon* (all 47) and *A Man Called Peter* (55). And so on. But Bill ◇ was to become probably the most lauded of the Severns.

Danny Mummert (left) enlightens Larry Simms

Donny Dunagan

USA

b: 16 Aug 34 (San Antonio, Texas)

The dread word 'moppet' might have been coined for this chrysanthemum-headed reincarnation of Richard Headrick °. The son of a professional golfer, he began to walk at six months and could roller-skate before he was two.

Claude Jarman, Jr.

USA

b: 27 Sep 34 (Nashville, Tennessee)

With the drooping fair hair, soulful blue eyes and oval face of a boy saint in a 19th-century painting, the ten-year-old 5th-grader Jarman must have presented a touching sight in a Nashville classroom, one winter's day, to a man posing as a school inspector. The man, happily, was the film director Clarence Brown, travelling incognito in search of a leading boy for *The Yearling*. (This was Hollywood's third attempt since 1940 to get the Marjorie Kinnan Rawlings boy-and-fawn story filmed.)

Brown later called on Mr and Mrs Jarman to express his interest – only to find that Claude, though alerted to the visit, had forgotten to tell his parents about it and had gone out to a Cub Scout meeting. He was never that keen on acting anyway.

But Brown talked with Jarman senior (a railroad accountant) and persuaded him to bring his bashful son across country to Hollywood for a screen test. Young Claude impressed everyone, MGM gave him a five-year contract, and he was showered with awards for his performance as Jody.

To tell the truth, Jarman was no great shakes as an actor and had no illusions about it. But his simple feeling is hard to resist, and the relationship with kind, stern father Gregory Peck is admirably painful, though the folksy sanctimony of their dialogue grows no less toe-curling with the passing years.

Claude never repeated his initial success, and MGM didn't really make the best of him. (In *High Barbaree*, where he played

Claude Jarman and fawn in The Yearling

Van Johnson in flashbacks, they curled his hair and he looked awful.) His young-adult films were *Inside Straight* (51), *Hangman's Knot* (52), *Fair Wind to Java* (53) and finally, for Disney, *The Great Locomotive Chase* (56). Apart from a guest appearance in the TV series 'Wagon Train', that was the end of his acting.

In the 1960s he worked in public relations, then in the Seventies moved into film production, and also had a stint as executive director of the San Francisco Film Festival.

Larry Simms

USA

b: 1 Oct 34 (Santa Monica, Cal.)

This blond three-year-old with the huge, rather cold blue eyes and centre parting was the screen offspring of that beloved cartoon duo Dagwood Bumstead and his wife Blondie (Arthur Lake and Penny Singleton). While the parents, thanks to impeccable studio make-up, scarcely changed through the unprecedented 12-year run of the *Blondie* series, their little Alexander (Simms) – known for the first few years as 'Baby Dumpling' – and his friend Alvin from next door (Danny Mummert ◇) grew before one's very eyes.

Larry's mother was the nightclub singer Margaret Lawrence, and his own first break came in 1938 when his portrait appeared on the cover of the Saturday Evening Post. Honour enough for a tot; but that wasn't the end of it. After his debut as Dumpling, he was awarded an honorary mayorship of Venice: Venice, California, that is.

Simms was a glamorous baby and a neat performer, though usually outscored when Mummert's Alvin was on hand. Like Mummert, he had a few assignments

outside the series – notably as James Stewart's elder son in *It's a Wonderful Life*, and as Justin in *Madame Bovary* – but he was wholly identified with the 28 *Blondie* films. His younger brother Michael also appeared in one: *Blondie Goes to College*.

Interestingly enough, Arthur Lake, *né* Silverlake – perpetrator of Dagwood, the dithering, simpering superwimp with the intellect of a retarded cockroach – had himself once been a child actor, and at the age of twelve had played in a movie version of *Jack and the Beanstalk*.

Larry Simms was happy to quit acting when the series ended. He went off and studied aeronautical engineering, to such effect that from 1956 till his retirement in 1974 he worked for the Jet Propulsion Laboratory at Pasadena. Dumpling for Victory – or Beware of Dumpling?

(In the following Simms filmography, the two 1943 films marked 'B' are 'Blondies' in spite of the neutral title.)

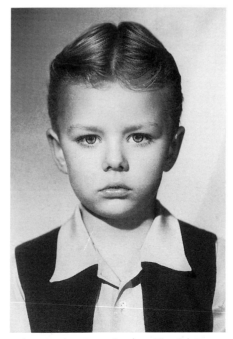

Baby Dumpling: Larry Simms in Blondie Goes Latin

Richard Lyon

BRITAIN/USA

b: 8 Oct 34 (London)

As a four-year-old London orphan, Richard was adopted by the American stars Ben Lyon and Bebe Daniels, who had made their home in Britain. (Ben, famous flyer of *Hell's Angels* in 1930, served with the Royal Air Force during World War Two, and was later awarded the Order of the British Empire.) As soon as Richard was old enough, the Lyons began to involve him and his sister Barbara in their screen and radio work, and when he was sent to the USA during the war, the fine-boned boy got offers on his own merit.

His biggest role was in *The Tender Years*, but his best-known one was as Irene Dunne's son in *Anna and the King of Siam*. He was the homeless boy from the poster who gave moral courage to Dean Stockwell ◇ in *The Boy With Green Hair*, and the odious patrol-leader of Bob Hope's Boy Foresters in *The Great Lover*.

Richard Lyon with Irene Dunne in Anna and the King of Siam

Returning to London with the family around 1950, Richard and Barbara became household voices in the popular comedy series 'Life with the Lyons' on BBC radio. He became visible again in the spin-off films *Life with the Lyons* (GB 53) and *The Lyons in Paris* (GB 54), and later in *The Headless Ghost* (GB 59). Afterwards he worked as a photographer in London.

40 The Howards of Virginia
44 Secret Command
   The Unseen
46 Anna and the King of Siam
   The Green Years
47 The Tender Years
48 The Boy with Green Hair
   Smart Woman
49 The Great Lover

Gino Leurini

ITALY

b: 11 Nov 34 (Rome)

The handsome Leurini had only two screen years in which he could be considered a child, but was notable in *Cuore* and *Molti sogni per le strade*, and had a lead as a romantic schoolboy in the faintly absurd sex-education drama *Domani e troppo tardi*.

He continued smoothly from his mid-teens to his early twenties in *Vento d'Africa*

(51), *Guardi e ladri* (51), *La vendetta di una pazza* (51), *Il caimano del Piave* (51), *Wanda la peccatrice* (52), *La regina di Saba* (52), *I vitelloni* (IT/FR 53), *Ricordami* (55) and many more. Leurini has now retired.

47 Cuore (Heart)
   Fabiola
   Legge di sangue (Law of blood)
48 Molti sogne per le strade
   (The street has many dreams)
49 Domani è troppo tardi
   (Tomorrow is too late)

Alfonso Mejía

MEXICO

b: 16 Nov 34 (Mexico City)

Los olvidados, Buñuel's frightening study of poverty and delinquency, was shot during February and March of 1950, when Mejía was a very young-looking 15. He came in fact from a middle-class family and a quite different background from the film's, but his absorption in its horrors is intense and unsentimental.

For several years Alfonso Mejía was one of the most highly-regarded of young Mexican actors, with important roles in *El martir del Calvario* (52), *Padre nuestro* (53), *El tunel seis* (55), *El boxeador* (57), *Quinceañera* (58), *La edad de la tentación* (58) and so on throughout the next decade. He was twice nominated for the 'Best Young Actor of the Year' award before finally winning it for his performance in *Quinceañera*.

Self-defence: Alfonso Mejía in Los olvidados

Mejía studied political sciences and dramatic art in tandem, and showed himself a powerful actor in the theatre as well as in films.

50 Los olvidados (The forgotten ones)
51 La bien amada (The well-beloved)
   Mi esposa y la otra
      (My wife and the other woman)

Charlesworth as East in the 1950 Tom Brown's Schooldays

John Charlesworth

BRITAIN

b: 21 Nov 34 (Leicester)
d: 2 Apr 60 (Birmingham)

John William Charlesworth, like Alfonso Mejía,[◇] came late to acting, but the slight, boyish appearance persisted throughout his teens. He had reddish hair, a light creamy voice and a level blue gaze of disturbing intensity. Besides work in radio, he gave several brilliant performances on the London stage, ranging from the anguished child of divorcing parents in 'Background', and a stalwart Jim Hawkins opposite Donald Wolfit's Long John Silver, to the licentious school prefect in 'Quaint Honour'.

His best screen role was as the hero's friend East in *Tom Brown's Schooldays*, where he ran the gamut from cocky exuberance through staunch loyalty to manly grief. (He would in fact have been a superb Tom, but the role was predestined for the younger and more tremulous John Howard Davies ◇, who had already starred in *Oliver Twist* and *The Rocking Horse Winner*.)

Charlesworth showed his power in emotional scenes in *Scrooge* and *The Magic Box*, and had an adventurous lead in the Children's Film Foundation's *John of the Fair*. He appears only in the opening minutes of *The Oracle*, as a worried office-boy.

He continued to be seen in the cinema, in *Yield to the Night* (56), *A Question of Adultery* (56), *Yangtse Incident* (57), *Battle Hell* (57), *The Adventures of HAL 5* (58) and seven or eight more films. Tragically, having recently married, and while playing leading roles at Birmingham Repertory Theatre, John Charlesworth gassed himself in April 1960.

50 Last Holiday
   Tom Brown's Schooldays
51 The Magic Box
   Scrooge
52 John of the Fair
   The Oracle

Rusty Tamblyn

USA

b: 30 Dec 34 (Los Angeles)

Being red-haired, there was no way Russell Irving Tamblyn could avoid being called Rusty, though he later preferred Russ. He attracted local notice in childhood as a gymnast, and did a bit of stage acting; but he didn't reach the screen until a bit part in 1948.

Russ Tamblyn had two films in 1951: *Father's Little Dividend* (a 'Father' sequel) and *As Young As You Feel*, with two more the following year: *Retreat, Hell!* and *The Winning Team*. After *Take the High Ground* (53) came *Seven Brides for Seven Brothers* (54) – the very first, he swears, of only five times he actually *danced* on screen. Another of these, *Hit the Deck*, came in 1955, the sensational *Tom Thumb* in 1958

and *West Side Story* in 1961. In all of them his happy athleticism was a joy.

He got an Oscar nomination for his performance in *Peyton Place* (57), and his many later films included *How the West Was Won* (62), *The Haunting* (63), *The Long Ships* (64), *The Last Movie* (71) and *Black Heat* (76).

In his spare time, though, Tamblyn had revealed definite talent as a painter and collagist, and in 1962 he made his bow as a choreographer in *Human Highway*. He co-produced this film with an old friend and contemporary – Dean Stockwell, ◇ one-time star of *The Boy With Green Hair*, which had seen his own modest screen debut over 30 years earlier.

A more recent role was as the 'wacko shrink' Lawrence Jacoby in David Lynch's TV serial *Twin Peaks*, which also saw a starring comeback by Russ's *West Side Story* co-star, Richard Beymer.

48 The Boy with Green Hair

49 Captain Carey, U.S.A.
   Gun Crazy
   The Kid from Cleveland
   Reign of Terror
   Samson and Delilah
50 Father of the Bride
   The Vicious Years

Jan Prokeš

CZECHOSLOVAKIA

b: 1934

Prokeš gives a remarkable performance in *Svedomí*, as the son of a hit-and-run driver who has killed a child while combining business with adultery on a night away from home. As he realises what his father has done, and sees him pathetically lying in the attempt to cover his tracks, the pain and growing contempt in the boy's eyes are unforgettable.

48 Svedomí (Conscience)
51 Vitězna kridla (Wings of victory)

Jan Prokeš with his guilty father (Miloš Nedbal) in Svedomí

Charley Bates

USA

b: circa 1934

The dark, usually disruptive Bates was in many famous films of the Forties. He was Teresa Wright's kid brother, for instance, in *Shadow of a Doubt*, Gregory Peck's guilty buried self in *Spellbound* and Ernest Severn's ◇ antagonist in *Pursued*.

Later, Charley was in *Shockproof* (49) and *The Snows of Kilimanjaro* (53) before fading from the scene.

41 Blossoms in the Dust
   The Mexican Spitfire's Baby
   Tall, Dark and Handsome
   The Vanishing Virginian
42 I Married a Witch
   Shadow of a Doubt
43 The North Star
   The Song of Bernadette
   Son of Dracula
   The Strange Death of Adolph Hitler
44 An American Romance
   The Curse of the Cat People
   Destiny
   Lady in the Dark
   Once Upon a Time
   San Diego, I Love You
45 A Miner Affair
   Spellbound
46 Danny Boy
   The Green Years
   The Hoodlum Saint
   Night in Paradise
   Three Wise Fools
47 Golden Earrings
   Her Husband's Affairs
   Pursued

Freddy Fernández

MEXICO

b: circa 1934

Freddy was famous around 1950 in the Hispanic film-going world for his repeated screen appearances as the street-boy 'el Pichi', first seen in *Callejera*.

He was in several films in 1950, and remained in a high state of exposure throughout the Fifties, still often as 'Pichi'.

43 Cristóbal Colón (Christopher Columbus)
44 El medico de las locas
   (Mad women's doctor)
   Tribunal de justicia (Police court)
45 Arsenio Lupin (Arsène Lupin)
   Bartolo toca la flauta
   (Bartolo plays the flute)
48 Ustedes los ricos (You are the rich ones)
49 Amor de la calle (Street love)
   Callejera (Streetwalker)

Antonín Mikulič

CZECHOSLOVAKIA

b: circa 1934

This darkish, square-faced, sharp-chinned boy was much in demand in Czech films of the late 1940s and early 1950s.

46 Pravě začiname (We're just beginning)
47 Nezbedny bakalar (The mischievous tutor)
   Předtucha (Presentiment)
48 Na dobré stopě (On the right track)
   Zelena knižka (The green book)
49 Dva ohně (Two fires)

Yura Yankin

USSR

b: circa 1934

The pudgily serious Yura had been discovered in a war orphans' home by the director of *Sin polka*, Vasili Pronin. Though based on a different original, its story – about a determined waif attaching himself to a fighting group and making himself indispensable through his skills as a spy – is remarkably like that of Tarkovski's more celebrated *Ivan's Childhood* of 1962. Unlike *Ivan*, it has a happy ending.

46 Sin polka (Son of the regiment)

Charles Knetschke

GERMANY

b: 3 Jly 35 (Berlin)

Cheeky little Charly Knetschke was the most memorable of the roaming boys in

Charly Knetschke (later Charles Brauer) in Irgendwo in Berlin

Lamprecht's 1946 drama set in the ruins of Berlin, like a nightmare distortion of his great 1931 *Emil and the Detectives* where the kids had better games to play. (Even Fritz Rasp, *Emil*'s 'Man in the Bowler Hat', lingers on, comic no more, as a seedy thief.)

Of a typical Berlin school class of 41 twelve-to-fourteen-year-old boys, a journalist recorded at the time, nine had lost both parents and were fending for themselves, half had no fathers and a quarter no mothers, only four had their own bed to sleep in, and only nine had not yet been caught stealing. . . .

Charly continued to act in his later teens, henceforth as Charles Brauer, and mainly in West Germany. He had a good part in 1952 in *Der Kampf der Tertia*, a remake of a popular school story – directed this time by a former child actor, Erik Ode, later to be a beloved veteran on German TV. Charly's became a familiar teenage face in films like *Mit 17 beginnt das Leben* (53), *Christina* (53) and *Reifende Jugend* (55). A quarter of a century later he was still acting, in *Neonstadt* (81).

46 Irgendwo in Berlin (Somewhere in Berlin)
48 Und wieder 48! ('48 again!)

Netscher in A Journey for Jeremy

Robin Netscher

BRITAIN

b: 16 Sep 35 (Bombay, India)

Robin's father, who had worked in the British colonial service in India, returned to Britain in 1945. The intelligent little boy, with a blunt, endearingly doggy face, appeared many times on the London stage over the next few years, in shows as various as 'High Button Shoes', 'Life With Father', 'All My Sons' and 'Six Characters in Search of an Author'. He also broadcast frequently on BBC Radio, and played leading roles (such as 'The Winslow Boy') in the provinces.

His screen debut found him acting with Jean Simmons, but his best part, admirably taken, was in *Journey for Jeremy*, about a boy whose railway dreams came true.

In his later teens Robin switched his allegiance from acting to light music. Doing military service with the Royal Artillery, he became a member of the regimental band, and tried his hand as an arranger and conductor. Afterwards he won a scholarship to the Guildhall School of Music (where he also studied

composition), and around 1960 formed a group called the Beltones, with whom he played trumpet. Working in South Africa in the early Seventies, he conducted the Johannesburg Pops Orchestra and won some SARI awards.

Robin Netscher then worked in Hollywood – Hollywood, Florida, to be precise – as shoreside Entertainment Director for Royal Caribbean Cruise Lines in Miami. He still has a hand in film music and commercial jingles.

47 Uncle Silas
48 No Room at the Inn
49 Journey for Jeremy
50 The Dragon of Pendragon Castle
    Waterfront

Veli-Matti Kaitala

FINLAND

b: 24 Oct 35 (Tampere)

'Veli-Matti' – he usually performed without a surname – was the only Finnish boy actor who got to play two star parts in the cinema: Finland's films are not too thick on the ground. This likeable, sensitive boy, more bony than bonny, was directed by Edvin Laine first as 'Little Matty' and then,

Veli-Matti in Pikku-Matti maailmalla

the following year, as 'Lucky Peter'. He became a considerable national favourite in these two roles.

Pikku-Matti contrasts the sober virtue of rural life with the drunkenness and vice of the city, whither Matty travels after the death of his grandmother. Little does he know that his lost mother lives there, a fallen woman and (dear God) an artist's model. Our boy experiences the life of hoboes and bohemians but remains unsullied, to be reunited at last with his redeemed mater – in the countryside, of course.

With *Onnen-Pekka* we are back with a story of an orphan and an inheritance, in which rural ghostbusting frustrates a dastardly plot. A classic Finnish romance rewards deserving poverty with money from beyond the grave.

In both these films the serious Veli-Matti warbles like a Baltic Bobby Breen ◇, and finds an ally in a little girl called Ritva-Leena, who had also been with him in *Nokea ja kultaa*.

Veli-Matti made only one more screen appearance, when he was nearly 20, but it was in the most famous of all Finnish films: *Tuntematon sotilas* (55, The unknown soldier). He married an artist, then became an economist and primary school teacher.

45 Nokea ja kultaa (Soot and gold)
46 Kirkastuva sävel (Brightening note)
47 Pikku-Matti maailmalla
    (Little Matty out in the world)
48 Laitakaupungin laulu (Song of the suburbs)
    Onnen-Pekka (Lucky Peter)
49 Aaltoska orkaniseeraa
    (Mrs Aaltonen gets organised)

Tomihiro Aoki

JAPAN

b: circa 1935

Tomihiro – known as Fatso, and also as Aoki the Farter, from a particular talent of his – was half-brother to the great 'Tokkan-Kozo', Tomio Aoki ◇. (Tomio's mother had now married the actor Shigeru Ogura.) Ozu couldn't resist the idea of directing a new Aoki.

Johnny Calkins

USA

b: circa 1935

Calkins had a mild, sweet face and curly reddish hair. He returned to acting in adult life, for instance in *Once upon a Texas Train* (88).

Richard Nichols

USA

b: circa 1935

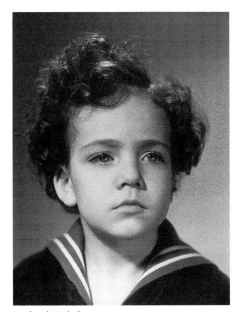

Richard Nichols, 1941

Jaime Jiménez Pons (right) in Rio Escondido

This limpid, curly child had been preceded on to the screen by four elder brothers: Paul, Ray, Buster and Eddie. (All but Paul are on display in *Vigil in the Night*, and Paul and Ray were in *Boys Town*.)

It's not Richard's fault that because he looked angelic he was made to play, by and large, a series of lacrimose little creeps.

Jaime Jiménez Pons

MEXICO

b: 6 Jan 36

Hispanic names formally honour both father and mother, in that order: so Jaime's father was a Jiménez and his mother a Pons. It's permissible to call him simply Jaime Jiménez, but not Jaime Pons. As Jiménez is roughly as common, in Hispanic terms, as Jackson, it's not a bad idea to use both parts of his name – particularly as there were several subsequent Mexican kid actors called Jiménez Pons, who we can thus reasonably assume may have been related. (Though Pons too is anything but uncommon. The hell with it.)

This little Jiménez, at any rate, won the Mexican Film Academy's 'Best Child Performance of the Year' award for his work in *Rio escondido*.

Lasse Sarri

SWEDEN

b: 3 Feb 36 (Stockholm)

Sarri's later films included *Trots* (52), *Ogift fader sökes* (53), *Danssalongen* (55), *Swing it, fröken!* (56) and *Vägen genom Skå* (57).

45 Sextetten Karlsson (The Karlsson Sextet)
46 Iris och löjtnantshjärtan
   (Iris and the lieutenant's heart)
47 Får jag lov, magistern! (Please, Sir!)
   Konsten att älska (The art of loving)
   Kvinna utan ansikte
   (Woman without a face)
48 Eva
   Kvarterets olycksfågel (The local Jonah)
49 Fängelse (Prison)
50 Kastrullresan (Voyage in a saucepan)
   Kvartetten som sprängdes
   (The quartet that split up)
51 Bärande hav (Seaborne)

Dean Stockwell

USA

b: 5 Mar 36 (North Hollywood)

His father, Harry Stockwell, was an actor, and his mother a dancer. When Dean was seven, he and his younger brother Guy played leading parts in a Theater Guild production of 'The Innocent Voyage'. The critics raved, Hollywood swooped, and

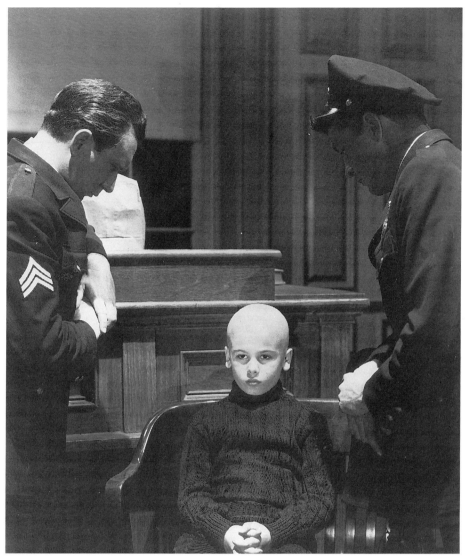

Stockwell (hairless) in The Boy with Green Hair

Dean Stockwell, 1946

MGM signed him up. He had a whale of a time with Gene Kelly and Frank Sinatra in *Anchors Aweigh*.

Stockwell, a plump, pouting, curly-headed cherub with knowing brown eyes, often seemed something of a prima donna in his early years, yet he could express spontaneous gaiety or genuine pain, and was deservedly the most sought-after boy actor of the Forties. Sometimes, as with Freddie Bartholomew ◊, his arrogance was exploited in a 'humbling' drama, for instance in *The Secret Garden* and *The Happy Years* – the latter showing him at his best.

After an educational pause in his career, a leaner and nervier Dean Stockwell returned in *Gun for a Coward* (56) and *The Careless Years* (57). (He must have been sick of Years by now.) Then came three important 'classic' parts: as the young nietzschean co-murderer in *Compulsion* (59), as the D.H. Lawrence figure in *Sons and Lovers* (GB 60) and as the Eugene O'Neill figure (the consumptive younger son) in *A Long Day's Journey into Night* (62). He was an intelligent and personable young actor doing a good professional job. Predictions of his becoming a major star proved ill-founded, and during the Sixties he was seldom on the screen.

The next decade began better, with leads in *The Dunwich Horror* (70) and *The Werewolf of Washington* (73), and in two

1971 TV movies: *Paper Man* and *The Failing of Raymond*. Films now came thick and fast as Stockwell's hair thinned and a wary, hard-bitten middle-aged actor emerged – more interesting, actually, than the younger one. He has lent strength to such varied films as *Human Highway* (82), *The Man with the Deadly Lens* (82), *Alsino y el condor* (NI/MX/CU/CR 82), *Paris, Texas* (84), *Blue Velvet* (86) and *Catchfire* (89). His portrayal of Howard Hughes in *Tucker* (88) is a small *tour de force*.

45 Abbott and Costello in Hollywood
   Anchors Aweigh
   The Valley of Decision
46 The Green Years
   Home Sweet Homicide
   The Mighty McGurk
47 The Arnelo Affair
   Gentleman's Agreement
   A Really Important Person
   The Romance of Rosy Ridge
   Song of the Thin Man
48 The Boy with Green Hair
   Deep Waters
49 Down to the Sea in Ships
   The Secret Garden
   Stars in My Crown
50 The Happy Years
   Kim
51 Cattle Drive

Allan Martin, Jr.

USA

b: 10 Mar 36

Allan, a pudgier American version of Roddy McDowall, was signed up for the lead in *Johnny Holiday*, and given a contract with United Artists, after touring in a play with the Lunts.

Johnny Holiday was a traditional moral tale. Landing in a reformatory of the open-air, agricultural type, our hero was pulled one way by the vicious delinquent Stanley Clements, the other by the rough-hewn but saintly over-seer William Bendix. An uneven contest, of course.

49 Johnny Holiday
51 Her First Romance

Michel Rob

FRANCE

b: 13 Apr 36 (Paris)

A fair boy with a square, narrow-eyed boxer's face, Michel nevertheless graced the boards of the Comédie Française. His important character in *Sous le ciel de Paris* is fittingly named 'Pirate'.

46 Vertiges (Vertigo)
47 Danger de mort (Mortal danger)
   La révoltée (Woman in revolt)
50 Sous le ciel de Paris (Under the Paris sky)
   Souvenirs perdus (Lost memories)
51 Monsieur Leguignon, lampiste
   (M. Leguignon, lamp-man)
52 Rires de Paris (Paris laughter)

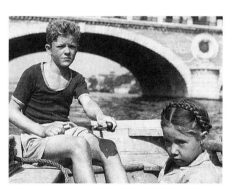

Michel Rob with Marie-France in Sous le ciel de Paris

Tommy Ivo

USA

b: 18 Apr 36 (Denver, Colorado)

Ivo was a toothy, tow-haired boy with the air of an emaciated chipmunk. This brought him a mass of work, often of a Western nature, which he handled good-humouredly but without blazing talent. His stab at a Devon accent in *Plymouth Adventure* is highly engaging.

Though looking nothing like his age, Ivo dropped out after 1952 for a change of voice, and returned two or three years later (often as 'Tom' rather than 'Tommy') to play teenage roles until the early Sixties. These included *You're Never Too Young* (55), *In Times Like These* (55), *Dragstrip Girl* (57), *The Beast of Budapest* (57), *The*

Ghost of Dragstrip Hollow (59) and *The Cat Burglar* (61).

45 Earl Carroll Vanities
46 Song of Arizona
47 Carnival in Costa Rica
   Stepchild
48 Fighting Back
   I Remember Mama
   Moonrise
   Secret Service Investigator
   Smoky Mountain Melody
   Song of Idaho
   Trail to Laredo
49 Feudin' Rhythm
   Horsemen of the Sierras
   Laramie
   Outcasts of the Trail
   Prejudice
   Take One False Step
50 Father Is a Bachelor
   The Killer That Stalked New York
   Kill the Umpire
   The Lost Volcano
   Operation Haylift
   Sunset Blvd.
   Trail of the Rustlers
51 The Lemon Drop Kid
   Snake River Desperadoes
   The Treasure of Lost Canyon
   Whirlwind
52 Belles on Their Toes
   Plymouth Adventure
   The Rough Tough West

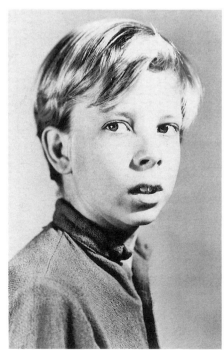

Tommy Ivo in Treasure of the Lost Canyon

Chapin with William Gargan in Night Editor

Michael Chapin

USA

b: 25 Jly 36 (Hollywood)

Debonair Michael was the elder brother of Billy Chapin ◇ of *Night of the Hunter* fame. Their maternal grandfather was William Graham, owner and publisher of Harper's and Graham's magazines. None of Michael's films was as distinguished as *Hunter*, but he made a tidy living in open-air parts, some of them leading ones – for instance in *Buckaroo Sheriff of Texas*, *Arizona Manhunt* and *The Dakota Kid*. He was as near as we got around 1950 to a Buzz Barton ◇ or Buzzy Henry ◇. (Only Kelly Reno ◇ has emulated him of late, in a strictly non-fancy way.)

Roy Rogers taught Michael various shooting and riding tricks, including hanging by one stirrup from a galloping horse with his face only inches from the ground. He survived it.

Michael Chapin pressed on into his teens, with another starring role in *Wild Horse Ambush* (52). Then came *Wagons West* (52), *Springfield Rifle* (52), *Pride of the Blue Grass* (54) and a small part in his kid brother's star outing, *Night of the Hunter* (55).

44 The Sullivans
45 The Corn is Green
46 Backlash
     The Farmer's Daughter
     It's a Wonderful Life
     Night Editor
     Song of Arizona
     Swamp Fire
47 Call Northside 777
     Heaven Only Knows
48 Night Wind
     Under California Stars
49 El Paso
     Strange Bargain
50 Buckaroo Sheriff of Texas
     Summer Stock
51 Arizona Manhunt
     The Dakota Kid
     Wells Fargo Gunmaster

Pascal Tabary

FRANCE

b: 24 Aug 36 (Savigny-sur-Orge, Essonne)

Tabary was an enchanting elf, son of a violinist, who started as he meant to go on, acting with Pierre Fresnay, Jean-Louis Barrault and Danielle Darrieux in his three films.

He made an immediate hit as the irrepressible 'Bouton' in Dréville's generally sombre *Le visiteur* (see Roger Krebs ◇) – after which Fresnay chose him to play a scurvy boy scout in the Marcel Achard comedy 'Savez-vous planter les choux?' at the Michodière, with Pierre Larquey.

But Pascal Tabary pursued his acting career no further, and eventually went into publishing. He became director of the Swiss subsidiary of Editions Dargaud, who publish the Astérix books.

46 Le visiteur (The visitor)
48 D'homme à hommes (Man to man)
49 Occupe-toi d'Amélie (Look after Amelia)

Teddy Infuhr

USA

b: 9 Nov 36 (St Louis)

His family moved to Hollywood when he was three, and two years later he made his film debut in *The Tuttles of Tahiti*, playing not a Tuttle but a Tahitian, a role he more or less repeated for Abbott and Costello in *Pardon My Sarong*. He was a strange little boy, unlike any other in the movies, with spiky fairish hair and a beaky face with coldly defiant blue eyes. It would have been fascinating to see him in a major role – but he was invaluable in secondary ones, as even an incomplete list of his credits (from *Tuttles* to *Kettles*) testifies.

Teddy bewildered Nigel Bruce's Dr Watson in a memorable performance as Gale Sondergaard's fly-snapping brat in *The Spider Woman*. ('Extraordinary child, Holmes.') He later got embroiled in the *Rusty* series – nobody's perfect – but redeemed himself with a splendid junior Jonathan in *David and Jonathan*.

Ted Infuhr appeared in one or two more films as a teenager – in 1952 *Ma and Pa Kettle at the Fair* and *Scaramouche*, in 1953 *Mister Scoutmaster* and *The Juggler*, in 1954 *Men of the Fighting Lady* – before devoting himself to more serious matters. He is now a successful dental surgeon.

42 The Ghost of Frankenstein
     Pardon My Sarong
     The Tuttles of Tahiti

Teddy Infuhr (right) with supercilious Bobby Larson in The Unwritten Code

Gary Gray

USA

b: 18 Dec 36 (Los Angeles)

Anagrammatic Gary Gray's father, a businessman, let him do a little acting as a tot. He got picked as an extra for a Joan Crawford weepie, but everyone liked him so much he was given a few lines. He hardly stopped working in movies for the next dozen years, besides playing in several 'little theater' stage productions.

Gary was fair and blue-eyed, with an earnest, doggy expression. (In his early teens he frequently co-starred with dogs – Pal, Shep, Lassie, etc. – when not playing a junior member of Raymond

Gary Gray with William Holden in Father Is a Bachelor

Gary Gray and Lassie No. 5 in The Painted Hills

Walburn's family in the 'Henry' and 'Father' comedies. But he managed to avoid most of the 'Rusty' series.) Though occasionally stroppy or mischievous, as in *Rachel and the Stranger*, he was almost invariably the Good Guy – brave, honest and loyal to the end.

Father Is a Bachelor, by the way – which also features the unrelated but equally admirable Billy Gray ◊ – was *not* part of the 'Father' series, in which the tough little George Nokes ◊ played Gary's kid brother.

Gary made a few more films after 1952: *Emergency Hospital* (56), *Teenage Rebel* (56), *The Party Crashers* (58), *Wild Heritage* (58) and *Terror at Black Falls* (62).

Dale Belding

USA

b: circa 1936

This goofy, dithering blond – like a younger Billy Benedict – was first seen, under a liberal sprinkling of studio freckles, in two pieces of belated Our Gangery produced for Hal Roach. Then, growing leggier by the day, he became a member of the Kettle brood, which also embraced Teddy Infuhr ◊, George Arglen, George and Donald MacDonald and Richard Eyer ◊ among others.

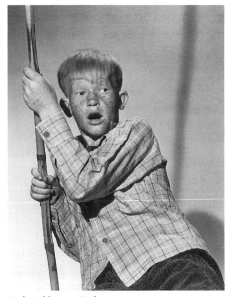

Dale Belding in Curley

After one last outing with *Ma and Pa Kettle at the Fair* (52), the perpetually startled Dale Belding left our screens.

Billy Kimbley

USA

b: circa 1936

It was said that William Kimberley (as he was billed in early years) had made over 600 appearances on the Broadway stage, as actor, dancer and singer, before he was twelve. Since he was also a healthy-looking curly blond, with a determined bull-froggish look that recalled the pre-war German Wolfgang Kieling ◊, it's not clear why his only lead was as the hero of a gloriously silly boy-and-dog adventure called *Shep Comes Home*.

In this he evades consignment to an orphanage, and while on the run with Shep contrives to outwit and capture a brace of bank-robbers. It's an epic — directed by the reliable Ford Beebe — that richly deserves revival on TV.

Billy Kimbley doesn't seem to have made any film appearances after 1951.

Meschke in Germania, Anno Zero

Edmund Meschke

GERMANY

b: circa 1936

Edmund, the pathetic little anti-hero of De Sica's chilling melodrama *Germania, Anno Zero*, set in the ruins of 1945 Berlin, is one of the screen's most expressionless children, and not without reason. What must once have been an angelic face has aged before its time, its main function now to conceal such flickers of emotion as may threaten to surface.

His bedridden elderly father is slowly dying, sustained only by expensive medicines which reduce the family to poverty and theft. An older brother, having deserted from the army, is holed up in a stupor of self-pity, contributing nothing. The only person Edmund trusts, a shifty schoolmaster, remarks casually that the old man would be better off dead, for everyone's sake. The boy gets hold of some poison and slips it into his father's soup.

Rejected by the appalled teacher, who

Billy Kimbley in Shep Comes Home

had not expected this development, Edmund wanders blankly through the city, and at last lets himself fall (the action is too wearily offhand to be called suicide) from the top of a ruined building.

It's a desolate story, with a performance of utter desolation from little Meschke. (Whose name has occasionally been given as Moeschke.)

47 Germania, Anno Zero
(Germany, Year Zero – IT/FR/DE)

Jandl in The Search

Ivan Jandl

CZECHOSLOVAKIA

b: 24 Jan 37
d: circa 1990

Little Jandl won an Academy Award for his performance in *The Search* – where, as a terrified and almost mute survivor of a concentration camp, he is befriended and taught to speak again by Montgomery Clift.

He was also in at least two films in his native Czechoslovakia. In *Zelená knížka* he is one of a group of children who expose a dishonest shopkeeper, and in *Svedomí* a boy who witnesses a hit-and-run accident. His stoical face did most of his speaking for him.

He needed stoicism, for his international success brought him little happiness at home. According to Fred Zinneman's autobiography, the communist authorities in Czechoslovakia not only refused Ivan permission to travel, but effectively aborted his acting career.

48 Zelená knížka (The green book)
The Search (US/CH)
Svedomí (Conscience)

Bobby Driscoll

USA

b: 3 Mar 37 (Cedar Rapids, Iowa)
d: circa Jan 68 (New York)

Bobby Driscoll, finally one of the most tragic of screen children, seemed to have everything going for him. He was pleasant-looking, alert, plucky, intelligent, with a sense of humour and great acting talent. He had all the chances a kid actor could have wished, and took them beautifully. And his was a face the camera loved, alive with fleeting shadows and nuances.

His mother, born Isabella Kretz, was a schoolteacher. His father, Cletus Driscoll, was a roofing contractor whose sinus trouble caused him to move from Iowa to California in search of warmth and sunshine. A friend in Pasadena, where they came to live in 1942, arranged for Bobby to attend a studio audition, and he was given a tiny part in *Lost Angel*. Even this was enough for people to notice something fresh and special about him, and he was signed up by 20th-Century Fox. His early films included *Identity Unknown*, a title that was to prove ominous.

He went on to win Critics' Awards for his performances in *Song of the South* (a semi-animated Disney, based on the 'Uncle Remus' stories), *So Dear to My Heart* (boy and black lamb) and *The Window* (cry-wolf tale of a child who witnesses a murder but is not believed) – all these made before he was twelve. He was equally endearing in grubby denims or in velvet and lace.

He went on to play Jim Hawkins to the

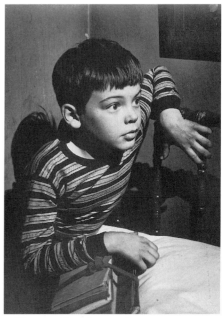

Bobby Driscoll in The Window

legendary, eye-rolling Long John Silver of Robert Newton, though this was one of his less interesting efforts, perhaps cowed by the magnificent ham of his companion. And, at 15, he was the voice of Disney's *Peter Pan*.

In his mid teens, Driscoll was still a handsome fellow, but the ground was crumbling under his feet. Suddenly Walt Disney had no further plans for him, nor did anyone else. For the next five years the only job he got was in a Colonial-period piece called *The Scarlet Coat* (55). In 1956 he got married – and was arrested on a narcotics charge, which was to be the first of many. In 1958 came his last movie, a teenage gang melodrama called *The Party Crashers*. His lead in this mediocre affair wasn't among his happiest.

The year after, Bobby was jailed as a heroin addict. Then came a curious incident with a handgun, a robbery charge, and a six-month jail sentence for drugs and forgery. In his statement to the court he said he had been experimenting with drugs since he was 17, and at the time had the money to pay for it. Now he was hooked and broke.

The last five years of Bobby Driscoll's life are a sad blur of addiction, mostly spent in hippie circles of New York's

Lower East Side. His family and friends lost sight of him for ever. In March 1968 a young man's body was found by some children playing in an empty tenement. There was no identification, but there were needle marks and there were 'certain substances' in what was left of the bloodstream. The body went into a pauper's grave.

When, a year or so later, Bobby's mother renewed her appeals to the FBI to find her missing son, the unidentified man's fingerprints were among those compared with Bobby's. They were a perfect match, and so the mystery was solved – just after his father's death.

Walsh in Hans Christian Andersen

Joey Walsh

USA

b: 11 Jne 37 (New York)

The young Joey, whose father owned and drove a sightseeing bus in New York, had a pleasingly unusual face, with a snipey nose, a tiny chin and a general expression of puzzlement. From 1949 he was getting work, and some good parts, on TV.

Hollywood now beckoned. Joey is well remembered as Danny Kaye's jealously devoted apprentice Peter in *Hans Christian Andersen*, but rather forgotten as another apprentice, to Kirk Douglas's *Juggler*.

He returned to New York and TV work for a year or two, playing innumerable tough kids. But California lured him back, though he now supported himself there less by acting – *Captain Newman, M.D.* (63), *Invitation to a Gunfighter* (64), *Drive, He Said* (70) – than by gambling, an art he passed on to Elliott Gould.

This in turn bore fruit when he wrote and co-produced *California Split* (74), in which he also played a small part. It starred Gould and carried Walsh's message that gamblers, like drunks, were not a total disaster but could also have fun and be fun. (Altman's kaleidoscope of a film, Jonathan Rosenbaum helpfully wrote, changed form 'from a noun into a verb'.)

Joseph Walsh appeared again in *The*

Driscoll as Jim Hawkins in the 1950 Treasure Island

Driver (75) and continued to act on TV and on the New York stage, but from now on was principally a screenwriter, and a fine one.

52 Hans Christian Andersen
53 The Juggler

Jeremy Spenser

BRITAIN

b: 16 Jly 37 (London)

Jeremy's father was Sri Lankan and his mother, a musician and teacher, Italian. His elder brother David (born 12 March 34) was a fine boy actor, largely on radio, but also in the film *Mr Perrin and Mr Traill* (48). After a sporadic adult career in theatre and cinema, David became one of Britain's best radio drama directors, winning two Pye Awards.

It was David who suggested Jeremy for two child parts he was too old for, in *Anna Karenina* and *Kind Hearts and Coronets*. But Jeremy shot to overnight fame as a boy conductor in *Prelude to Fame*. This was a straight crib of a French film of 1949, *Prélude à la gloire*, which had starred a real-life prodigy called Roberto Benzi. (Another, Pierino Gamba, had already done virtually the same in Italy: there was a general European craze for boy conductors at the time.)

Jeremy Spenser was no musical prodigy, but he was a keen mimic. The highpoint of *Prelude to Fame* is his conducting of a symphony orchestra in Weber's entire 'Oberon' overture – laughable as musicianship, but irresistible as a portrait of a temperamental little boy having a ball. With his brooding dark looks, Jeremy was like a twelve-year-old Orson Welles, every inch the mini-maestro.

He remained Britain's leading boy actor for the next two or three years, and was sinisterly memorable on the London stage in 1952, his hair dyed blond, as Miles in 'The Innocents' a version of Henry James's 'The Turn of the Screw'. (Later filmed, with Martin Stephens ◇ in the part.)

Jeremy Spenser in Prelude to Fame

In his late teens Jeremy Spenser continued in *The Devil on Horseback* (54), *Summer Madness* (55), *Escapade* (55), *Wonderful Things* (57) and *The Prince and the Showgirl* (57), in which he repeated his stage role (with Laurence Olivier) as the young King Nicholas of Carpathia.

Then, after *Ferry to Hong Kong* (59), he was an Italian teenager dogging Vivien Leigh in *The Roman Spring of Mrs Stone* (61), a temperamental young painter in *Vengeance* (GB/DE 62), a soldier in Losey's *King and Country* (64), and after *He Who Rides a Tiger* (65) an emblematic personage in Truffaut's *Fahrenheit 451* (68).

An actor good enough to work with Losey and Truffaut should have faced the future with confidence – but Jeremy Spenser abandoned his acting career at this point, in favour of drama teaching and directing, and later antique dealing.

47 Anna Karenina
49 The Dancing Years
   Kind Hearts and Coronets
   The Spider and the Fly
50 Portrait of Clare
   Prelude to Fame
51 Appointment With Venus
52 The Planter's Wife
53 Background

Christian Simon as the 1951 'Poil de Carotte'

Christian Simon

FRANCE

b: 22 Jly 37 (Paris)

Cricri, as he was called in his smaller days, began as a touching Parisian mite. By the time he came (too late) to play 'Poil de Carotte', in the story's third film incarnation, he was a complicated-looking fourteen-year-old.

46 L'arche de Noé (Noah's ark)
   Le bataillon du ciel (The sky battalion)
   Berlin Express
   Les portes de la nuit (The gates of night)
   Voyage-surprise (Mystery trip)
47 Aubervilliers
48 Le bal des pompiers (The firemen's ball)
   Buffalo-Bill et la bergère
      (Buffalo Bill and the shepherdess)
49 Amédée (Amadeus)
   Plus de vacances pour le Bon Dieu
      (No let-up for Almighty God)
50 Les anciens de Saint-Loup
      (Old Saint-Loup boys)
   Souvenirs perdus (Lost memories)
51 Passion
   Poil de Carotte (Carrots)

Jackie 'Butch' Jenkins

USA

b: 19 Aug 37 (Los Angeles)

His mother was the Broadway actress Doris Dudley, and the sandy little five-year-old was spotted by the ever-alert Clarence Brown, who as usual swept all objections aside and engaged him for his film of the Saroyan novel *The Human Comedy*. Butch played the benjamin of the nuclear family, Ulysses.

There was something so disarmingly real about this sleepy, blear-eyed dormouse of a child that he became a national favourite, and also got Critics' Awards for his performances in *National Velvet, Our Vines Have Tender Grapes*, and *The Bride Goes Wild*.

Butch's attitude to acting was quite straightforward. 'I hate it,' he told a startled Rouben Mamoulian, who had just signed him up for *Summer Holiday*, his version of O'Neill's 'Ah, Wilderness'. During 1947 the boy developed a serious stammer. As his mother was already worried about the strain filming was imposing on Jackie and his education,

Butch Jenkins in Summer Holiday

she called a halt to his career – without, we can be sure, too many tears from the dormouse.

Butch Jenkins, having turned his back on Hollywood, grew up to be an emperor of many car washes and supervisor of the East Texas Water System.

Jackie 'Butch' Jenkins and Margaret O'Brien in Our Vines Have Tender Grapes

43 The Human Comedy
44 An American Romance
   National Velvet
45 Abbott and Costello in Hollywood
   Our Vines Have Tender Grapes
46 Boys' Ranch
   Little Mister Jim
   My Brother Talks to Horses
47 Stork Bites Man
   Summer Holiday
48 Big City
   The Bride Goes Wild

Cerusico in Altri tempi

Enzo Cerusico

ITALY

b: 22 Oct 37 (Rome)

Cerusico, always a good actor, came to
the screen when he was twelve. He took
the classic 'Cuore' role of the Sardinian
drummer boy – earlier played on screen
by Luigi Petrungaro ◇ – in an episode of
Blasetti's compendium film *Altri tempi*.

    After a busy three years he paused
to finish his education, then resumed a
career he obviously enjoyed. He was in
Il mattatore (59), *La dolce vita* (60), *Una
storia di notte* (64), *Faustina* (68), *L'invasione*
(69)....etcetera, more or less to the present
day.

50 Camicie rosse (Red shirts)
   Lebbra bianca (White leprosy)
   Piume al vento (Feather in the wind)
51 Altri tempi (Times gone by)
   I due derelitti (The two down-and-outs)

52 Gli angeli del quartiere (Local angels)
   Una croce senza nome (A nameless cross)
   La figlia del diavolo (The devil's daughter)
   Viva il cinema! (Long live cinema)

Adi Lödel

EAST GERMANY

b: 1937
d: 2 Jne 55 (Hamburg)

Lödel, the obsessed young sharpshooter
in *Kinder, Mutter und ein General*, hanged
himself shortly afterwards.

51 Decision Before Dawn (US)
   Hilfe, ich bin unsichtbar
     (Help! I'm invisible)
   Lockende Gefahr (Danger beckons)
   Die verschleierte Maja (The hidden Maja)
52 Ich hab' mein Herz in Heidelberg verloren
     (I lost my heart in Heidelberg)
53 Liebeskrieg nach Noten
     (A musical war of love)
55 Kinder, Mütter und ein General
     (Children, mothers and a general)

'Alfio'

ITALY

b: circa 1937

All the actors in *La terra trema*, Visconti's
semi-documentary drama of Sicilian fisher-
folk, were anonymous non-professionals,
inhabitants of the village of Aci-Trezza.

    The splendid portrayer of the boy 'Alfio'
may have been Turiddu Vicari – his is the
last male name in Visconti's own non-

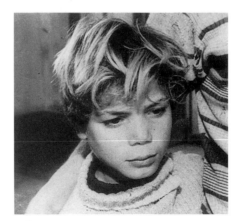

'Alfio' in La terra trema

alphabetical listing of the real-life players
of his Aci-Trezza 'family'.

47 La terra trema (The earth shakes)

George Nokes

USA

b: circa 1937

George, a tough, rather mean-looking
little blond, had only one leading role – in
Shaggy, a dog story – but seemed to be in
almost all family films for a few years. He
was a torment to Bing Crosby and Bobby
Driscoll ◇, and finally to Raymond Walburn in the *Father* films.

42 The Hard Way
43 Happy Land
   The Iron Major
   The North Star
44 Going My Way
   The Keys of the Kingdom
   The Purple Heart
   The Story of Dr Wassell
45 The Bells of St Mary's
   Incendiary Blonde
46 Angel on My Shoulder
   The Best Years of Our Lives
   It's a Wonderful Life
   Night and Day
   Song of the South
47 Curley
   For the Love of Rusty
48 Shaggy
   Slippy McGee
   State of the Union
49 You're My Everything
50 Father Makes Good
   Father's Wild Game
51 Father Takes the Air

Billy Gray

USA

b: 13 Jan 38 (Los Angeles)

His mother, Beatrice, was an actress whose
career was effectively halted by Billy's arrival: she withdrew from a publicity tour
for her last film, and was shown the door
by the ever-compassionate RKO.

    From his movie debut at seven, Billy
proved to have one of the strongest personalities of all Hollywood's children, and

Billy Gray in The Guy Who Came Back

to be equally adept at comedy or drama. With a formidable scowl, he had an impatient honesty that marked him out from the normal run of ingratiating studio kids.

He was bolshy and argumentative, a natural for the Penrod-based character he played in the Doris Day musicals *On Moonlight Bay* and *By the Light of the Silvery Moon*. (His name, as Doris's kid brother, was 'Wesley' – surely in homage to the first Penrod, Wesley Barry ◇.) Choked by dust or food in these well-loved films, he would come up with a graveyard cough of which he was justly proud.

His most often-seen performance, nowadays, is in *The Day the Earth Stood Still*, one of the most moral and seminal of flying-saucer movies. His hero-worship fighting with deep suspicion of Michael Rennie (Klaatu, alias Mr Carpenter) gives the formula story one of its most human elements, and few could have delineated the basic expressions of scepticism, alarm and wonder as Billy did – all this while incarnating the normal American kid worried about his homework.

In the mid-1950s Billy Gray became involved in the TV series 'Father Knows Best', with Jane Wyman and Robert

Young as his parents, plus a brace of sisters. His all too gosh-and-golly role of 'Bud' was an embarrassment to this down-to-earth boy, not accustomed to deal in such old-hat currency. The steady income was hard to spurn, though, so he held his nose and got on with it – for the next six years or so.

The occasional feature film cropped up: *The Seven Little Foys* (55), *The Explosive Generation* (61), *Two for the Seesaw* (62), *The Navy vs. the Night Monsters* (66), *Dusty and Sweets McGee* (71), *Werewolves on Wheels* (71).

Billy Gray (later Bill) shouldn't, incidentally, be confused with Bill Gray (sometimes Billy), a squashy-faced character actor who died in 1978.

In 1962 he got a three-year sentence for driving under the influence of drink and/or drugs (hotly denied by Gray, though he didn't deny that marijuana and alcohol had passed his lips in the past). He was an expert driver, particularly of motorcycles in his early days. But above all he was an excellent and salty actor, who has been sadly neglected in his adult prime.

45 The Strange Affair of Uncle Harry
46 Cluny Brown
    Our Old Car
    To Each His Own
47 Curley
    The Gangster
48 Fighting Father Dunne
49 Abandoned Woman
    Bad Men of Tombstone
50 Father Is a Bachelor
    Gene Autry and the Mounties
    The Good Humor Man
    In a Lonely Place
    Singing Guns
    Three Little Words
51 The Day the Earth Stood Still
    The Guy Who Came Back
    Jim Thorpe – All American
    On Moonlight Bay
    Sierra Passage
52 The Girl Next Door
    The Return of Gilbert and Sullivan
    Talk About a Stranger
53 All I Desire
    By the Light of the Silvery Moon
    Hurricane at Pilgrim Hill
    The Outlaw Stallion

Shashi Kapoor

INDIA

b: 18 Mar 38 (Calcutta)

Shashi was a member of the mighty Kapoor dynasty of the Indian cinema: son of Prithviraj, and younger brother of Raj °.

He went on to become a popular Indian leading actor, and has also been seen abroad in films like *Sammy and Rosie Get Laid* (GB 87), where he plays the haunted torturer Rafi.

44 Meena
45 Bachpan (Childhood)
    Tadbir (The endeavour)
47 Bhakt Dhruva
    Renuka
48 Bhakt Bilwamangal
    Bhakt Gopalbhaiya
    Aag (Fire)
    Shaheed (The martyr)
50 Ram darshan
    Samadhi (The shrine)
    Veer Babruwahan
51 Awara (The tramp)
52 Mordhwaj
    Sansar

Peter Miles (Gerald Perreau)

USA

b: 1 Apr 38 (Tokyo, Japan)

The sensitive, innocent-looking French-bred Gerald Richard Perreau-Saussine had fled France in 1940 with his French father and American mother: after crossing the Atlantic on a tramp steamer, they went to join his mother's parents in Los Angeles. His pretty younger sister Gigi Perreau (Ghislaine, born 1941) entered movies before Gerald, and became a well-known child actor, as to a lesser extent did another sister, Janine.

The boy acted as Gerald Perreau until 1948, when – with the big time looming – he was persuaded to adopt the homelier screen name of Peter Miles. He and Gigi appeared together in *Enchantment, Family Honeymoon* and *Roseanna McCoy*. His own best-remembered lead was in *The Red Pony*, Lewis Milestone's effective version of a John Steinbeck story.

In the 1950s Peter abandoned acting, and rather than going into his father's banking business devoted himself to writing. In both 1966 and 1967 he won the Samuel Goldwyn Creative Writing Award for his novels 'Angel Loves Nobody' (originally called 'Crooked Children') and 'The Moonbathers'. In 1969 Robert Altman filmed an earlier novel of his, *That Cold Day in the Park*. In a last switch of name, Gerald/Peter now decided to publish as Richard Miles.

Peter Saussine remains in reserve.

43 Passage to Marseille
44 Dark Waters
    San Diego, I Love You
45 This Love of Ours
47 Curley
    Heaven Only Knows
    Possessed
48 Enchantment
    Family Honeymoon
    Who Killed Doc Robbin?
49 The Red Pony
    Roseanna McCoy
    Song of Surrender
50 California Passage
    The Good Humor Man
    Trigger, Jr.
51 Quo Vadis
52 At Sword's Point

Peter Miles with Louis Calhern in The Red Pony

Wolfgang Jansen

WEST GERMANY

b: 3 Apr 38 (Danzig)
d: 9 Jan 88 (Hamburg)

Wolfgang's father, Bernhard, was a sculptor, and his mother, Elli, a singer. He was a dark, plumpish, good-natured creature, seen in his debut film as an enterprising schoolkid smuggling coffee and coal across the German-Dutch border in the aftermath of World War Two.

Wolfgang's biggest role was as one of the ringleaders of *Der Kampf der Tertia*. He had three films in 1954: *Mädchen mit Zukunft*, *Der Raub der Sabinerinnen* and *Schlagerparade*. Then, two years later, a part in the Austrian film *Die Deutschmeister*, but he had to wait a whole decade more for his next film, *Die Heiden von Kummerow und ihre lustigen Streiche*.

By the 1970s poor Wolfgang Jansen was presenter of a pre-school TV show with puppets and plastic gnomes.

51 Sündige Grenze (Frontier of sin)
52 Der keusche Lebemann (The chaste libertine)
53 Hollandmädel (Dutch girl)
   Der Kampf der Tertia
      (The battle of Form 4)
   Postlagernd Turteltaube
      (Poste Restante Turtle-Dove)
   Der Vetter aus Dingsda
      (The cousin from Thingummy)

Maurizio Di Nardo

ITALY

b: 4 May 38 (Rome)

Maurizio, son of an engineer, was chosen from school auditions for his debut role in *Cuore*. He had the traditional over-ripe looks of an Italian tenor – which may have helped him land the part of Caruso as a boy in the 1951 biopic.

He was prominent in *La fiamma che non si spegne* and *Altri tempi* and, resisting the temptation to let his films of 1952 extend into a series about handicapped women,

Maurizio di Nardo in Enrico Caruso

took the title role in the Swiss film *Il piccolo bandito*.

Maurizio di Nardo went no further in show business, and followed his father into engineering.

47 Cuore (Heart)
48 Fabiola
49 La fiamma che non si spegne
      (The undying flame)
51 Altri tempi (Times gone by)
   Enrico Caruso, leggenda di una voce
      (Caruso: legend of a voice)
52 La cieca di Sorrento
      (The blind woman of Sorrento)
   La muta dei Portici
      (The dumb woman of Portici)
   Melodie immortale (Deathless melodies)
   Il piccolo bandito (The little bandit – CH)
53 Il sacco di Roma (The sack of Rome)

Peter Blitz

SWEDEN

b: 15 Aug 38 (Solna)

The eleven-year-old Peter was picked to play Kalle, one of the classic heroes of Swedish children's literature. The book had twice been filmed before, and would be again in the Seventies.

Blitz returned as a teenager to play in *Swing it, fröken!* (56).

50 Anderssonskans Kalle
      (The Anderssons' Kalle)
   Den vita katten (The white cat)
51 Valley of Eagles (GB)

Tommy Kearins

BRITAIN

b: 31 Aug 38 (Govan, Glasgow)

Alexander Mackendrick's *The Maggie* – known in the U.S. as *High and Dry* – is one of the best of the Ealing comedies. It tells how an American tycoon (Paul Douglas), chartering a boat to carry a valuable load of central heating equipment and other basic necessities of life to a remote Scottish island where he has bought a house, falls into the clutches of a devious old mariner who owns a 'puffer' or tiny Clyde steamboat. The crew of three includes a 'wee boy' (Kearins) who is the general dogsbody, but a valued one.

At a moment of total despair – when it seems his cargo is doomed never to reach haven – Douglas threatens to buy the boat over their heads and get a new crew. The Wee Boy, appalled at the possibility, decides to eliminate it by stunning the American with a carefully dropped trap-door. After a sickening thud, he goes ashore to break the news to his mates. 'You'd better go aboard,' he says bleakly. 'I think I've killed him.'

The scenes between Douglas and Kearins, before and after the trapdoor incident, dramatise the irreconcilable: cost-effective capitalism versus noble, unpractical humanity. The Wee Boy, passionate and implacably moral, wins the debate hands down, and Douglas accepts the inevitable with something like grace.

Tommy Kearins, the son of a Clydeside riveter, was fully worthy of this delectable film. He had never acted, but was spotted by a studio scout working behind the

Tommy Kearins initiates Hubert Gregg into the joys of poaching in The Maggie

scenes at an amateur show in Glasgow. After *The Maggie*, Ealing paid for Tommy to go to a London stage school, but he couldn't get on with it and soon dropped out. He returned to Glasgow and became an apprentice engineer at Harland and Wolff's shipyard, till it closed down.

He then joined the Merchant Navy and saw the world, but in the process became an alcoholic. With typical determination he pulled himself together, joined Alcoholics Anonymous and kicked the habit, which he is rightly proud of. Tommy was made a partner in a company to make independent TV productions – including a well-earned one on Scottish Humour.

54 The Maggie

Bill Severn

USA

b: 16 Oct 38 (Hollywood)
d: after 1978

William Churchill Roosevelt Severn – the penultimate Severn boy, clear-eyed and curly – was probably the most winsome

of the brood, even when competing with Lassie.

Bill Severn, following the family trend, became a Doctor of Theology. Sadly, he died in his forties.

42 Eagle Squadron
   Journey for Margaret
44 The Story of Dr Wassell
45 The Enchanted Forest
   Son of Lassie
48 The Bride Goes Wild

Billy Severn, 1943

Brenner and Greif in Junges Herz voll Liebe

Hansl Brenner

WEST GERMANY

b: 25 Nov 38 (Innsbruck)

Brenner acted on the stage in Innsbruck as a boy, and later became a popular actor in West Germany, Switzerland and Austria, with strong left-wing sympathies. After working for many years in Berlin, he and a few friends established an 'actors' commune' in Munich, which ran for seven years, putting on shows and pooling all receipts. He has been in more than fifty TV films.

53 Junges Herz voll Liebe
   (Young heart full of love)

Raul de Anda, Jr.

MEXICO

b: circa 1938

His father (of the same name) was a film director. After his childhood Raul de Anda, Jr., was only in one film: *Señoritas* (58). But from 1956 he began to act as executive producer to his father and others. From 1965, with *Tierra de violencia*, he became a director in his own right.

49 El Charro Negro en el Norte
   (Charro Negro in the north)
   La fe en Dios (Faith in God)
51 Con todo el corazón (With all one's heart)
53 Frontera norte (Northern frontier)

Jimmy Boyd

USA

b: 9 Jan 39 (McComb, Mississippi)

The boy-and-horse story *Racing Blood* was directed and part-written by Wesley Barry ◇, the great boy star of the early 1920s. Young Boyd was better known for his pop records, like 'Tell Me a Story' with Frankie Laine. 'Boy platter artist Jimmy Boyd warbles capably enough,' reported Variety, 'but as an actor he's on the yelling side.'

Yelling or not, Boyd made several more screen appearances. He was in *King of the Rodeo* (55), *The Second Greatest Sex* (55), *Platinum High School* (60), *Inherit the Wind* (60), *High Time* (60), *The Two Little Bears* (61), *Norwood* (70) and *That's the Way of the World* (75).

54 Racing Blood

John Howard Davies

BRITAIN

b: 9 Mar 39 (London)

John's mother was an actress, and his father the screenwriter Jack Davies; acting went back four generations in the family. He was suitably delicate, at nine, for the job of playing Oliver Twist: not as heart-rendingly pretty as the 1960 Oliver, Mark Lester ◇, but a better actor.

His range, it's true, was limited to expressions of wide-eyed wonder or fear, plus rather exaggerated enthusiasm and politeness, but this was the manner of the time and not his fault. Drenched and filthy in *Oliver Twist*, he looked the most pitiful (yet distinguished) of drowned rats; and if he was a disappointingly bland Tom Brown, he was at his best in *The Rocking Horse Winner*, with the horse-haunted mania bursting satisfyingly through impeccable English charm.

Davies now abandoned acting. After public school and university education, he went into TV production with EMI and the BBC, where he became Head of Light

Bug-eyed punter: Davies in The Rocking Horse Winner

Entertainment. There he produced or directed such classic series as 'Steptoe and Son', 'Monty Python's Flying Circus' and 'Fawlty Towers', and so earned the gratitude of the whole English-speaking world.

48 Oliver Twist
49 The Rocking Horse Winner
50 Tom Brown's Schooldays
51 The Magic Box

John Howard Davies in the 1950 Tom Brown's Schooldays

Mario Girotti

ITALY

b: 29 Mar 39 (Venice, Italy)

The fair-haired Girotti, of partly German ancestry, was a graceful and confident child performer – but not yet a household name.

Mario Girotti continued to appear in films from his late teens: *Mamma sconosciuta* (56), *La grande strada azzurra* (57), *Quaglione* (57), *Lazzarella* (57), *Anna di Brooklyn* (58), *Il padrone delle ferriere* (58), *La spada e il croce* (58), *Cartagine in fiamme* (59) and so on. During the following five years he had supporting roles in movies like *Giuseppe venduto dai fratelli* (61), *The Roman Spring of Mrs Stone* (GB/US 61) and *Il gattopardo* (IT/FR 62).

In 1967, graduating to leading roles in innumerable spaghetti Westerns, he changed his professional name to Terence Hill, and became an internationally famous blue-eyed gunman.

51 Vacanze col gangster
    (Holiday with a gangster)
52 La voce del silenzio (The voice of silence)
53 Villa Borghese
55 La vena d'oro (The vein of gold)

Lecointe in Les anciens de Saint-Loup

Serge Lecointe

FRANCE

b: 26 Apr 39 (Paris)

Serge made his debut on radio at three, on the stage (with Charles Dullin) at five, and in the cinema at eight. He was a plain, serious, sensitive kid.

He was also in a TV version of Pagnol's *Merlusse*, and appeared in one or two more movies in his teens: *Chiens perdus sans collier* (55), *Mitsou* (56).

47 Si jeunesse savait (If youth but knew)
    La vie en rose (Rose-coloured life)
48 Le coeur sur la main (Heart on hand)
49 Plus de vacances pour le Bon Dieu
    (No holidays for Almighty God)
50 Les anciens de Saint-Loup
    (Old Saint-Loup boys)
    Chabichou
    Dieu a besoin des hommes
    (God needs mankind)
51 Un grand patron (The Chief)
    La porte ouverte (The open door)
    Seuls au monde (Alone in the world)
52 Le dernier Robin des Bois
    (The last Robin Hood)
    Le rideau rouge (The red curtain)

Chet Allen

USA

b: 6 May 39 (Chickasha, Oklahoma)
d: 17 Jne 84 (Columbus, Ohio)

The wandering orphan given an extend-ed lift by medicine man Dan Dailey in

Travelling hopefully: Chet Allen in Meet Me at the Fair

Douglas Sirk's musical *Meet Me at the Fair* was an admired soloist of the Columbus Boychoir. On TV he created the name part in Menotti's popular Christmas opera 'Amahl and the Night Visitors', and he sang in Honegger's oratorio 'King David' at the 1952 Los Angeles Music Festival. (The name 'Chet Allen' is sometimes given in inverted commas, implying that it may not have been his true name.)

In his only film he sang some rather awful songs very prettily, and acted with good will and a helpful smile more or less throughout. But poor Chet didn't strike one as likely to make a successful adult career, and, unhappily, this proved the case.

After 1952 most of his singing was in churches, though he had the role of an opera singer's son in the 1953 TV series 'Bonino'. He was credited as art director on Altman's *The Delinquents* in 1956; but later he worked as a stockboy in stores, and as a volunteer helper at a drop-in center. Finally, in 1984, depressed beyond endurance, he took his own life.

52 Meet Me at the Fair
53 Bonino (TVS)

William Fox

BRITAIN

b: 19 May 39 (London)

William (later James) was the younger brother of Edward Fox, but the first of the

two by several years to take up acting. He was the nicest kind of upper-middle-class English schoolboy: polite but spirited, larky but easily embarrassed.

In the peacetime sequel to *Mrs Miniver* he played Greer Garson's schoolboy son, back from evacuation in the USA with a baseball bat and some frightful slang. Then he had the lead in *The Magnet*, a modest and charming comedy in which he believes he has caused the death (through a broken heart) of a smaller boy whom he has tricked out of his dearest possession, a giant magnet. (He has in fact misunder-stood an overheard conversation about a deceased budgerigar.)

A decade later, when young Fox reap-peared as an adult actor, he had changed his first name to James because there was already a British actor called William Fox. He began to play a long series of usually decent, though sometimes weak, English ex-public-schoolboys: in *The Loneliness of the Long-Distance Runner* (62), *The Servant* (63), *Tamahine* (63), *Those Magnificent Men in Their Flying Machines* (65), *King Rat* (US 65), *The Chase* (US 65), *Thoroughly Modern Millie* (US 67), *Arabella* (IT 67), *Isadora* (68), *Duffy* (US/GB 68) and *Performance* (70).

His most remarkable roles among these were in *The Servant*, as the foolish rich youth ruthlessly victimised by Dirk Bogarde as his theoretical valet, in *King Rat* as George Segal's prison-camp catspaw, and – far more complex and interesting – in *Performance*, as the London crook whose personality dissolves, under the drugs proffered by Mick Jagger's retired pop star, into a weird simulacrum of his host's. This was far from normal James Fox territory.

At this point, however, Fox abruptly gave up show business to devote himself to evangelical religion, and for the next decade his only film appearance was in a Billy Graham production, *No Longer Alone* (US 78).

Then, in the early Eighties, he returned to the secular cinema as a lean, worn but impressively gentle middle-aged man, in films like *Runners* (83), *A Passage to India*

William (later James) Fox with Greer Garson in The Miniver Story

a memorable and much-publicised film debut in the title role of *The Mudlark*, with Irene Dunne as Queen Victoria and Alec Guinness as Disraeli: the innocent waif finally succeeded in making the reclusive monarch smile again. Perched on the royal throne, muddy Andrew was irresistible.

Two years later, a skinny 12-year-old, he had another lead in *The Yellow Balloon*, where he is frightened into becoming a criminal's accomplice – a conventional melodrama, but well done. He had three more good secondary roles over the next three years.

Now Ray started to shoot up, but he remained useful in teenage parts in *Woman in a Dressing Gown* (57), *Gideon's Day* (58) and *Serious Charge* (59) – a rare unsympathetic part in this last, as a malignant Teddy Boy who accuses his sporting vicar of indecent advances. Nearly always, he was cast as a nervous, gentle creature.

After some mainly uninteresting films in the Sixties – *Twice Round the Daffodils* (62), *The System* (64), *Coplan sauve sa peau* (FR/IT 68) – he appeared on the West End stage as the shy, stammering King George VI in 'Crown Matrimonial', a play based on the romance of the Windsors. He did it so well that he was cast as King George again in 1978 in 'Edward and Mrs

(85) and *Comrades* (86). In 1991 he was memorable as Anthony Blunt in a TV version of Alan Bennett's 'A Question of Attribution'.

49 No Place for Jennifer
50 The Lavender Hill Mob
   The Magnet
   The Miniver Story (US)
   One Wild Oat

Brand Inglis

BRITAIN

b: 31 May 39

In Pat Jackson's hospital drama *White Corridors* he played – quite beautifully – the cheerful little boy who proves to have a

fatal blood infection. His entry into British cinema was as brief as his life in the film. We could have done with a lot more of Brand Inglis.

He came to no great harm, though: he became a Bond Street art dealer.

51 White Corridors

Andrew Ray

BRITAIN

b: 31 May 39 (Southgate, London)

He was the younger of two actor sons of the comedian Ted Ray. (His elder brother Robin abandoned the stage in his 20s and became a TV personality.) Andrew made

Andrew Ray in The Mudlark

Before the fall: Enzo Staiola in Ladri di biciclette

Simpson', a TV dramatisation of the same story. In a sense, of course, it was a part he had long been prepared for: even as a mudlark he had sat on the throne of England.

Though he has done a fair amount of TV work since then, his only notable screen parts have been in the remake of *Great Expectations* (75 – as Herbert Pocket) and in the Burt Reynolds jewel caper *Rough Cut* (US 80).

Enzo Staiola

ITALY

b: 15 Jne 39 (Rome)

The father-and-son relationship in De Sica's *Ladri di biciclette* was so intense and desperate – tramping round Rome in search of the stolen bicycle without which the poor father's long-awaited job as bill-poster would also disappear – that Enzo Staiola's remains an unforgotten face for anyone who ever saw the film. A whole tragic, hopeless, footsore day was mirrored in the eyes of the increasingly exhausted little boy who had so joyfully

polished the machine for its first shift the day before.

De Sica knew he need look no further for his 'Bruno' once he saw this roly-poly but wonderfully soulful urchin, one of the most endearing in all cinema. Blundering into a church service and bolting after the sketchiest of genuflections, untimely ripped from a much-needed pee against a wall, sulking with wounded dignity after a slap from his father, Staiola has the air of a small bear in grave need of honey, never quite giving up hope but becoming sceptical.

At the end, Bruno experiences the misery of seeing his old man as a despised criminal – a common bicycle-thief like the wretched youth they had spent so long tracking and had even, uselessly, found. Both Bruno and his father (marvellously played by Lamberto Maggiorani, who died in 1983) are heartbreaking figures.

Such a debut and such instant fame couldn't fail to be followed up in a series of films, both at home and abroad. Enzo worked for directors like Blasetti, Dieterle, Duvivier, Mankiewicz and Zampa, and with foreign stars like Bogart, Raft and Ava Gardner, but though he was always a welcome sight, lovable and often touching, he never knew another film like his first.

Staiola's only adult film appearance was in 1961, in *Spade senza bandiera*. He became a clerk in the Ministry of Finance.

48 Ladri di biciclette (Bicycle thieves)
49 Marechiaro Vulcano (Volcano)
   Cuori senza frontiere
      (Hearts without frontiers)
   Marakatumba, ma non e una rumba
      (Marakatumba, never a rumba)
50 Strano appuntamento
      (Strange rendezvous)
51 Altri tempi (Times gone by)
   Buon viaggio pover' uomo
      (Bon voyage, poor fellow)
   I'll Get You for This (GB)
   A Tale of Five Cities (GB)
52 Penne nere (Black plumes)
   Le retour de Don Camillo
      (Il ritorno di Don Camillo
      Don Camillo's return – FR/IT)
   L'ingiusta condanna (The wronged woman)
54 The Barefoot Contessa
      (La contessa scalza – US/IT)

Bobby Henrey

BRITAIN

b: 26 Jne 39 (Villers-sur-Mer, Calvados, France)

Bobby, son of the novelist Mrs Robert Henrey, was spotted by an acute studio scout in a photo on the dust-jacket of one of his mother's books. They were looking for a posh but innocent child to play the French diplomat's son in Graham Greene's story *The Fallen Idol*, and this lordly ham-

ster of a boy proved, on interview, to be ideal.

With a bleary but obstinate air, civil manners and a trace of French accent, little Henrey was great in Carol Reed's near-perfect comedy thriller – whether communing with his grass snake McGregor or (after the latter's regrettable demise) ganging up against its executioner, Mrs Baines. He forms a rewarding alliance with her forgivably adulterous husband (Ralph Richardson, wonderfully and uncharacteristically subdued), and his increasingly frantic, counter-productive attempts to shield Baines, suspected by the police of killing his wife, are magnificent.

The pompous little voice calling 'Baines! Baines!' in the marbled caverns of the embassy is one of the cinema's most memorable child sounds. And no one could have delivered with more exquisite boredom the line (on seeing Michèle Morgan, as Richardson's girl friend): 'Oh look, there's your niece again.'

That it was, however, a one-off performance was cruelly demonstrated two or three years later when Bobby was cast as a musical prodigy in Mittel-Europa. Plumper than before, burdened with Tyrolean-style dress, an atrocious

hair-do, and script and direction as far beneath Greene and Reed as could be imagined, the poor little chap looked terrible and acted likewise.

48 The Fallen Idol
51 The Wonder Kid

ABOVE: *Translated: Henrey in* The Wonder Kid

BELOW: *Bobby Henrey and McGregor in* The Fallen Idol

Foreshadowing: Orley Lindgren with John Garfield in Under My Skin

Orley Lindgren

USA

b: 18 Jly 39 (Long Beach, Cal.)

'A child with an unforgettable face,' 20th-Century Fox called him in the pre-publicity for *Under My Skin*.

It was indeed the face, rather than vast temperament, that was his fortune. It was wide and thoughtful, with a short Scandinavian nose (he had Swedish parents) and some rather chipped teeth; he had a passion for football. The expressiveness of the level grey eyes was striking; his voice was soft, gentle and low, a rare blessing in boy actors; and he moved with the grace of a wild pony.

He often appeared in the first reel of a film as the hero-as-a-boy. He was Bix Beiderbecke (alias Rick Martin) as a kid, discovering music; he was young John Ridd, scaling the great cliff to the high kingdom of the Doones; he was transmuted, variously, into Kirk Douglas, Richard Greene, Charlton Heston and Ben Johnson – the last being the only

remotely suitable match. Because he was an 'outdoor' boy with a certain air of stoicism, and good with horses, he fitted naturally into a Western context.

Under My Skin was a sentimentalised but not worthless version of Ernest Hemingway's bitter little narrative 'My Old Man'. Orley played the son of a famous but corrupt jockey (John Garfield) who is banned from racing in the U.S. and in much of Europe, but remains a hero to the boy. Joe Butler sees his father vilified – like Bruno in *Bicycle Thieves* – as well as

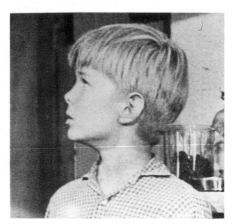

Lindgren in Saddle Tramp

killed. The anguished face on the screen was indeed unforgettable.

Orley's only other starring role was with Guy Madison and Andy Devine in *Behind Southern Lines*, directed and produced (respectively) by former child stars Thomas Carr ◇ and Wesley Barry ◇ for the United Artists TV series 'The Adventures of Wild Bill Hickok'.

After 1953 Lindgren, now a leggy teenager, did no more professional acting, though he developed technical skills and kept some links with the film world. (Many years later, in 1970 – misspelt – he was one of the team of sound recordists on *Gimme Shelter*.) His parents, former teachers who had evolved into realtors, felt he should complete his education. He did so to such effect that he got a PhD at Berkeley and became a business consultant at Davis University.

43 Hitler's Children
45 Anchors Aweigh
47 On Our Merry Way
48 Sorrowful Jones
50 Saddle Tramp
 Under My Skin
 Young Man with a Horn
51 Lorna Doone
52 Behind Southern Lines
 Japanese War Bride
 Red Planet Mars
 The Savage
 Wild Stallion
53 Mister Scoutmaster

Jimmy Hunt

USA

b: 4 Dec 39 (Los Angeles)

Jimmy was the quintessential 'kid next door' – small, freckled and rather strident, with sandy curls, definitely a menace. He was small enough for his age to play one of Orley Lindgren's ◇ younger brothers in *Saddle Tramp*.

But besides nuisance value he could convey the bewilderment of an ordinary boy at encountering *Invaders from Mars* or the like.

46 My Brother Talks to Horses
47 High Barbaree

Jimmy Hunt in Pitfall

48 Family Honeymoon
   The Fuller Brush Man
   The Mating of Millie
   Pitfall
   The Sainted Sisters
   Sorry, Wrong Number
   So This Is New York
49 Rusty's Birthday
   Rusty Saves a Life
   Shadow on the Wall
   Special Agent
   Top o' the Morning
50 The Capture
   Cheaper by the Dozen
   Louisa
   The Mating Season
   Rock Island Trail
   Saddle Tramp
51 Her First Romance
   Katie Did It
   Weekend with Father
52 Belles on Their Toes
53 All American
   Invaders from Mars
   Lone Hand
54 She Couldn't Say No

Enrico Olivieri

ITALY

b: 14 Dec 39 (Torino)

Enrico Olivieri was an outrageously handsome boy with brown hair and an aristocratic bearing. Later, in 1960, he was in *La maschera del demonio.*

48 Fuga in Francia (Escape into France)
   Guglielmo Tell (William Tell)
51 I figli di nessuno (Nobody's sons)
   Ragazzo (Boy)
52 Bufere (Gales)
   Chi e senza peccato (He that is without sin)
   Menzogna (Untruth)
54 La donna del fiume
      (The woman by the river)
55 War and Peace (Guerra e pace – US/IT)

Glyn Dearman

BRITAIN

b: 30 Dec 39

Dearman, the charming Tiny Tim in *Scrooge* and the pathetic Arthur in *Tom Brown's Schooldays,* later became an accomplished BBC radio drama producer.

48 The Small Voice
50 Tom Brown's Schooldays
51 Scrooge
53 Four Sided Triangle

Larry Joe Olsen in Who Killed Doc Robbin?

Larry Joe Olsen

USA

b: 1939 (Marshalltown, Iowa)

Larry Joe – rather like a wavy-haired, over-ripe Larry Simms◊ – was apparently

Enrico Olivieri with Serge Reggiani in Bufere

unrelated to the slightly younger Chris Olsen ◇. His father was an inspector for Northrop Aviation.

43 The Chance of a Lifetime
   Happy Land
44 Address Unknown
   Casanova Brown
   My Pal Wolf
   The Seventh Cross
45 Divorce
   Lone Texas Ranger
   Sergeant Mike
47 Curley
48 Isn't It Romantic?
   Sitting Pretty
   Who Killed 'Doc' Robbin?
50 Kill the Umpire
   Winchester '73
51 Room for One More
52 The Story of Three Loves
53 Her Twelve Men

Jaime Calpe, Jr.

MEXICO

b: circa 1939

Jaime won the Mexican Film Academy's award for the best child performance of 1948-49 for his work in *El dolor de los hijos*, and was runner-up two years later in *El papelerito*.

46 Los que volvieron (Those who will return)
48 El dolor de los hijos (The grief of the sons)
49 La dama del alba (Lady of the dawn)
   Lluvia roja (Red rain)
50 Madre querida (Darling mother)
   El papelerito (The paper boy)
   Tambien de dolor se canta
    (There are sad songs too)
   Vagabunda (The lady tramp)
51 Una mujer sin amor
    (A woman without love)

52 El martir del Calvario
    (The martyr of Calvary)
53 Angeles de la calle
    (Angels of the street – CU/MX)
   Los que no deben nacer
    (Those who should not be born)
55 El tesoro de la Isla de Pinos
    (Treasure on the Isle of Pines)

Bobby Hyatt

USA

b: circa 1939

Bobby made his screen debut, modestly, at ten months. When he was seven, he contracted polio, and the forecast for his future was grim. However, he made a total recovery and resumed work without the slightest ill effects.

His lively eyes and soft, good-natured profile made him a welcome ingredient of many movies of his time. He was particularly engaging in the 'Four Eyes' episode of *It's a Big Country*, and was spunky enough to play Gavroche in the 1952 version of *Les Misérables*.

In his later teens he made one more appearance, in *The Careless Years* (57).

46 Stagecoach to Denver
47 High Wall
   Miracle on 34th Street
48 The Babe Ruth Story
   Caught
   Mr Peabody and the Mermaid
   No Minor Vices
49 The Dark Past
   The Reckless Moment
   Undertow
50 Everybody's Dancin'
   It's a Big Country
51 The Basketball Fix
   He Ran All the Way
   Tomorrow Is Another Day
   When I Grow Up
52 Carbine Williams
   Les Misérables
   Small Town Girl
   Toughest Man in Arizona
53 The Farmer Takes a Wife
   Gypsy Colt
   The Trail Blazers

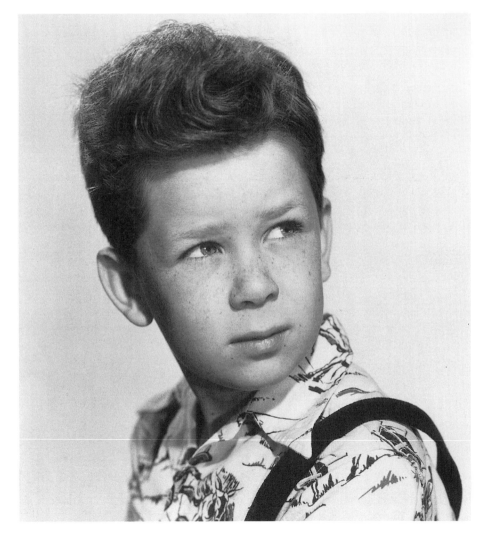

Bobby Hyatt in The Dark Past

Tough stuff: Peter Edward Price with Jean Peters in Love That Brute

Angelo Maggio

ITALY

b: circa 1939

Angelo, a fair-haired negro, was the abandoned child of an Italian girl and an American G.I. He was adopted by the Neapolitan actor Dante Maggio, and began his screen career with two leading roles.

49 Il mulatto
50 Angelo tra la folla (Angel in the crowd)
51 Il capitano di Venezia
    (The captain of Venice)
52 Amo un assassino (I love a murderer)
    Don Lorenzo
53 Il grande addio (The big farewell)

Peter E. Price

USA

b: circa 1939

The initials of Peter Edward Price were probably chosen with care: this was a forceful personality. He was fearsomely bratty in *Please Believe Me*, and of his performance in *Love That Brute*, the New York Times critic wrote: 'The kid is a pip. ... The way he swaggers around and

tosses out tough stuff is just remarkable.'
    More languishingly, however, Price mustered his reserves of soul to play the boy Caruso. Maurizio di Nardo ◇ had done the same in Italy.

49 Please Believe Me
50 Annie Get Your Gun
    Love That Brute
51 The Great Caruso
    New Mexico
    On the Sunny Side of the Street
54 The Phantom Stallion

Joaquin Roche, Jr.

MEXICO

b: circa 1939

43 Divorciadas (Divorcees)
44 La barraca (The farmhouse)
    Diario de una mujer (A woman's diary)
    Imprudencia (Imprudence)
    Tribunal de justicia (Police court)
45 Las abandonadas (Abandoned women)
    La mujer que engañamos
    (The woman we deceive)
46 Contra la ley de Dios (Against divine law)
    Cuando lloran los valientes
    (When brave men weep)
    El hijo de nadie (Nobody's son)
    Yo fui una usurpadora (I was a usurpatress)
47 Algo flota sobre el agua
    (Something floats on the water)

Barrio de pasiones (Passionate quarter)
48 Cara sucia (Dirty face)
    Ojos de juventud (Eyes of youth)

Masahiko Kato

JAPAN

b: 2 Jan 40 (Kyoto)

Masahiko came from a famous theatrical family in Japan, and was to become a leading actor himself.
    After his childhood film appearances, he continued in *Kurutta kajitsu* (56), *Juunana sai no teiko* (57), *Kokoni otoko ari* (59), *Taiyo no hakaba* (60) and many more. Latterly he acted under the name of Masahiko Tsugawa. His recent films include *Marusa no onna* (87) and *Kyoshu* (88).

45 Kitsune no kureta akanbo
    (Gift of the Gods)
53 Yoake mae (Before dawn)
54 Sansho dayu (Sansho the bailiff)

Bert Brandt

WEST GERMANY

b: 3 Jan 40

Bert, an actor's son, was a cheeky boy with a brush of fair hair. He was outstanding in Kurt Hoffmann's film of the Erich Kästner story *Das fliegende Klassenzimmer* – the film that also launched the future German pop idol PETER KRAUS (Peter Siegfried Krausenecker, born 18 March 1939).

54 Das fliegende Klassenzimmer
    (The flying classroom)
55 Marianne de ma jeunesse
    (Marianne of my youth – FR/DE)

Heiki Eis

AUSTRIA

b: 19 Jan 40

Heinrich Kilian Gereon Fanta – Heiki for short – was a son of the famous Austrian actress Maria Theresia Eis (1896-1954) by her third husband, Professor Robert Fanta.

Angelic: Heiki Eis with Attila Hörbiger in Gottes Engel sind überall

He had one celebrated screen hit, in *Gottes Engel sind überall*, as a lost child during World War Two. Around the same time Heiki was playing leads on the Viennese stage. At the Burgtheater he was in 'Henne und Küchlein', and starred as Cedric Fauntleroy in 'Der kleine Lord'; at the Volkstheater he was Pud in 'The Vinegar Tree'.

Ten years later he appeared in *Panoptikum 59*, and went on to do film and video work for the Staatsoper ballet school.

49 Gottes Engel sind überall
   (God's angels are everywhere)

Georges Poujouly

FRANCE

b: 20 Jan 40 (Garches, Seine-et-Oise)

The memorable creator of 'Michel', farmboy protector and slave of the little war-orphaned Parisienne Brigitte Fossey in *Jeux interdits*, was discovered by the film's director, René Clément, at a children's holiday camp in the Yonne. Soon after his first film his unmarried mother left her factory job and spent all his earnings.

In *Jeux interdits*, Michel's first service to Paulette is to help her bury her dead puppy, which has been machine-gunned from the air, together with her parents, among the fugitives on the crowded highroad from Paris. Burials of further creatures (birds, mice, even an earthworm) take place in a mounting ecstasy of sub-limated mourning: a barn is transformed into a grotto of funereal splendour, aided largely by crosses pilfered from the village churchyard. The outcome is inevitable and, in its authentically childish way, tragic.

Poujouly's muddy Michel is a touch-ing, sometimes grumpy cavalier to Fossey's capricious Paulette. Two high-

points of his performance, though, are solos: his recital of the Lord's Prayer in a furious temper, and his final heartbroken destruction of the fantastic cemetery in the mill.

His defiant little face was seen power-fully again the following year in *Nous sommes tous des assassins* and several other films. (In his more genial moments he reminded one faintly of a small snub-nosed Jean-Pierre Aumont.) On disc he partnered Gérard Philipe in *Le petit prince*. Later, in his teens, he had leading parts in Italian films.

In the mid-Fifties Poujouly was the original choice to play the boy in *The Old Man and the Sea*, but by the time it was ready to shoot he was too old, and the Mexican FELIPE PAZOS (born 22 Nov 1944) took his place.

Poujouly didn't lack work, though: in *Et Dieu créa la femme* (56, with Brigitte Bar-dot), *Les oeufs de l'autruche* (57), a lead in *Ascenseur pour l'échafaud* (57, Louis Malle's first feature), *Guingette* (58), *Pêcheur d'Is-lande* (59), *Une fille pour l'été* (59, FR/IT), *Vacances en enfer* (60), *Une grosse tête* (61, another lead) and *Le vice et le vertu* (62).

Then the parts thinned out, and apart from *Paris brûle-t-il?* (66), *Helle* (71) and

Rough: Georges Poujouly in Nous sommes tous des assassins

Smooth: studio portrait, circa 1952

Biribi (71) not much more was seen of this admirable lad in the cinema. He became a floor manager for Fox, and also did dubbing work – providing, for instance, the voice of Dustin Hoffman in *Marathon Man*.

51 Jeux interdits (Forbidden games)
52 Chevaliers de France (Knights of France)
   Hold-up en musique (Musical hold-up)
   La jeune folle (The mad girl)
   Nous sommes tous des assassins
      (We are all murderers)
   Quitte ou double (Double or quits)
   Son dernier Noël (His last Christmas)
53 Gangsters en jupons (Petticoat crooks)
54 Les diaboliques (The fiends)
   Dix-huit heures d'escale
      (Eighteen-hour stop-over)
   Il tesoro del Bengala
      (The treasure of Bengal – IT)
55 Les assassins du dimanche (Sunday killers)
   Il cortile (The yard – IT)
   Il piccolo vetraio (The glazier's boy – IT)
   Si tous les gars du monde
      (If all the world's boys)

Matija Barl

YUGOSLAVIA

b: 17 Feb 40 (Ljubljana)

The popular story of the intrepid shepherd boy Kekec was filmed three times, and directed each time by Jože Gale. In *Srečno, Kekec!* (63, Hang on, Kekec!) the hero was played by VELIMIR GJURIN, and in *Kekčeve ukane* (69, Sharp-witted Kekec) by ZLATKO KRASNIC. Each had his points, but Barl in Gale's first *Kekec* had the most personality. The film won the prize for best full-length children's feature at the 1952 Venice Film Festival.

A children's course on railways, which Matija Barl attended at the age of eight, led indirectly to an acting course, and this was where the producer of *Kekec* found him three years later. Out of more than 1000 little Slovenians auditioned, he got the part.

Acting on Radio Ljubljana followed, and at 14 he was also working as an announcer and presenter. In later teens he moved on to studies at the Ljubljana Dramatic Academy, and had a small part in a 1959 film called *Dobri stari pianino*.

When he was 22 Barl moved to West Germany, eventually becoming a free-lance producer in Munich, via TV work as production manager, assistant director and occasional actor. Privately, his passion was for flying: he holds a pilot's licence.

51 Kekec

Sean Barrett

BRITAIN

b: 4 May 40 (London)

His father was a film stunt man, and Sean made his professional debut in 1952 in a BBC TV play called 'The Twelfth Brother'. In the years that followed he played John in 'Peter Pan' on the London stage, and Puck in 'A Midsummer Night's Dream' on radio.

He had to play a dim-witted boy in *Bang! You're Dead* – but made up for this with his ardent Petya in King Vidor's *War and Peace*.

With his honest, innocent manner, the curly-haired Barrett remained in demand for teenage roles: *Dunkirk* (58), *A Cry from the Streets* (59), *Sons and Lovers* (60). Later films were *Attack on the Iron Coast* (67), *Great Catherine* (67), *Hell Boats* (73), *The Zoo Robbery* (73) and *Robin Hood Junior* (75) – these last two for the Children's Film Foundation.

Meanwhile he was acting widely in the theatre, and was with Noël Coward in the London premiere of his 'Suite in Three Keys'. In 1969 he began a spell with the

The first Kekec: Matija Barl

BBC Drama Repertory on radio, and since then his fine, incisive voice has often been heard, both as actor and poetry reader. It is heard too in the later films *Return to Oz* (US 85) and *Lorca and the Outlaws* (85).

53 Bang! You're Dead
   Four Sided Triangle
55 Escapade
56 War and Peace (US/IT)

Ricky Nelson

USA

b: 8 May 40 (Teaneck, N.J.)
d: 31 Dec 85 (DeKalb, Texas)

Eric Nelson, like his elder brother David (born 24 Oct 36), was a son of the band-leader and actor Ozzie Nelson and his wife Harriet, who had a long-running family show on radio and TV. The boys became part of it, and first took to the large screen in a Nelson family vehicle. David was in no further feature films till 1957, but Ricky was in the 'Mademoiselle' episode of *The Story of Three Loves*.

From his early teens Rick Nelson began to make a name as a rock singer, and has been called 'the first teen rock idol'. He appeared in a few more films from his late teens: *Rio Bravo* (58), *The Pigeon That Took Rome* (62) and *Love and Kisses* (65 – a singing lead).

Over the following decade or so both aspects of his career faded, but in the Eighties he began to regain his status as a master of rock. It was on his way from Dallas to a concert in Guntersville, Alabama, that his private plane crashed on the last day of 1985.

51 Here Come the Nelsons
52 The Story of Three Loves

Wang Longji

CHINA

b: 13 Jne 40 (Sichuan Province)

Western filmgoers are used to films based on comic-strips (the Gumps, the Newlyweds, Blondie and so on), and a more socially-conscious eastern equivalent led to *San-Mao liulang ji*, the most memorable of Longji's films.

Zhang Leping's original appeared in a left-wing Shanghai newspaper in the late 1940s, and became a popular favourite. It celebrates the resilience of an enterprising street urchin who is almost bald – it's often known as *The Winter of Three-Hairs* – and has, by Chinese standards, rather a long nose.

In the film, a sort of satirical comedy, San-Mao is taken up (to his amused disgust, tempered with gastronomic pleasure) by a rich family, but finally escapes back to the streets. At least, that was how it ended in the spring of 1949, when government censors forbade its release. After the liberation of Shanghai, it took the screen in triumph, plus an added finale in which San-Mao cheers the P.L.A.'s victory parade.

Wang Longji, who perfectly incarnates the bizarre little hero, was the elder son of Wang Yunjie, a famous composer of music for Chinese films. He was a familiar figure in the Kunlun Film Studios where his father worked, and was chosen for the role because of his big head and thin neck – the image of the cartoon character – and his general air of under-nourishment.

Longji, in fact, could empathise well with San-Mao's struggle for existence, having himself learnt the taste of hunger in earlier childhood at a time when his father was unemployed. He also liked Three-Hairs' honest, good-natured character, 'typical,' he said, 'of thousands of poor children in the old society'.

He had made his film debut the year before, playing an orphan in *Yan yang tian*, written and directed by the playwright Tsao Yu. After several more starring roles in childhood he quit acting, but graduated in 1963 from the Film Literature department of the Shanghai Film School. He is now the director of a factory in Shanghai.

48 Yan yang tian (Bright sunny skies)
   Wan jia denghuo (Myriads of lights)
49 San-Mao liulang ji
   (The story of San-Mao's wanderings)
51 Liang jia chun (Two families)
53 Wei haizimen zhufu (Bless the children)

Ozzie's boys: David (left) and Ricky Nelson

Three-Hairs: Wang Longji in San-Mao liulang ji

Fella Edmunds

BRITAIN

b: 25 Oct 40 (Chiswick)

Edwin Terua Edmonds, a boy with Australian connections, had the starring role of a boy jockey in *The Rainbow Jacket*. His two subsequent leads were in films produced by the Children's Film Foundation.

52 To the Rescue
54 The Rainbow Jacket
55 The Stolen Airliner
56 Supersonic Saucer

Tim Considine

USA

b: 31 Dec 40 (Los Angeles)

Timothy Daniel Considine was born into the Hollywood purple: his father had produced films as diverse as *The Sheik* and *Boys Town*, and his maternal grandsire was the theatrical magnate Alexander Pantages.

Tim played the comedian's doleful son in *The Clown*, a maudlin Red Skelton vehicle which tried to do for vaudeville what *The Champ* had done for boxing. Thereafter, as a child, he was generally cast in mean, neurotic roles – which was a pity because, as he showed in the teenage comedy series 'Spin and Marty', opposite the slightly younger David Stollery ◇, he had a nice sense of humour.

'Spin and Marty' ran on TV for 88 episodes between 1955 and 1958, and two years later Considine started a long stint as one of the senior-junior members of 'My Three Sons', with Fred Mac-Murray as the eternal father.

The series ran from 1960 to 1972, but Considine continued to appear in films: *The Shaggy Dog* (59), *Sunrise at Campobello* (60), *Patton: Lust for Glory* (69), *Tarzan's Deadly Silence* (70), *The Daring Dobermans*

Tim Considine in The Clown

(73). He has also served as scriptwriter, and is acting still.

52 The Clown
53 Executive Suite
   Her Twelve Men
54 Unchained
55 The Private War of Major Benson

Nicky Yardley in Bush Christmas

Nicky Yardley

AUSTRALIA/BRITAIN

b: 1940

With his elder brother Michael, the aboriginal Neza Saunders and the bespectacled Morris Unicomb, Nicky was the junior member of a notable quartet in *Bush Christmas*, one of the first Australian-based films to achieve world-wide popularity. Ralph Smart was to direct him again three years later in *Bitter Springs*, but perhaps his best part came in Harry Watt's *Eureka Stockade*.

Nick Yardley made a comeback in *Pudding Thieves* (AU 67).

47 Bush Christmas (GB)
49 Eureka Stockade (GB)
50 Bitter Springs (GB)

Alain Emery

FRANCE

b: circa 1940

The intense, horse-loving hero of Albert Lamorisse's *Crin Blanc* had leads in two further horse-shorts directed by Denys Colomb de Daunant.

He returned once more in *Comment les séduire* (67): not about horses.

53 Crin Blanc, cheval sauvage
   (White Mane, the wild horse)
55 Braco
57 Glamador

Alain Emery with the small Pascal Lamorisse in Crin Blanc

Ismael Perez

MEXICO

b: circa 1940

The plain but characterful Ismael Perez was a fixture for nearly ten years of Mexican cinema: a Hispanic Tommy Bupp ◇ or David Hannaford ◇.

He never got a real star part – the 'Papelerito' of 1950 was the boy singer Joselito Jiménez ◇ – but had a good early supporting role as little Felipe in *Pueblerina*, one of many films in which he was directed by Emilio Fernandez.

Ismael became known as 'Poncianito' (Little Lemon) from the character he played in *Víctimas del pecado*, for which he also won a nomination for the 'best child actor of the year' award. But after 1956, now a larger and less cute lemon, he packed in the acting. He may have been unsettled, two years earlier, by a film called *Your life in my hands*, originally entitled *My life in your hands*.

48 Bamba
   Maclovia
   Medianoche (Midnight)
   Prisión de sueños (Prison of dreams)
   Pueblerina (Town girl)
49 Duelo en las montañas
   (Duel in the mountains)
   El rey del barrio
   (King of the neighbourhood)
   Yo soy charro de levita
   (Rough but respectable)
50 The Bullfighter and the Lady (US)
   Inmaculada (Spotless)
   El papelerito (The paper-boy)
   Siempre tuya (Forever yours)
   Víctimas del pecado (Victims of sin)
51 El ruiseñor del barrio
   (The local nightingale)
52 La bestia magnífica (The gorgeous beast)
53 Angeles de la calle (Angels of the street)
   Orquídeas para mi esposa
   (Orchids for my wife)
54 Dos mundos y un amor
   (Two worlds, one love)
   La rebelion de los colgados
   (The failures' revolt)
   Tu vida entre mis manos
   (Your life in my hands)
55 El tesoro de la Isla de Piños (MX/CU)
   (Treasure on the Isle of Pines)
56 El camino de la vida (The road of life)

Lucky Lemon: Ismael Perez rides with Columba Dominguez in Pueblerina

Van Dyke Parks

USA

b: 3 Jan 41 (Hattiesburg, Mississippi)

As a boy, sleek and brown-eyed, Parks was a lively, witty Dickie Jones ◇ type. He was a young Ruritanian prince in *The Swan*, and – less convincingly – goat-boy Peter in *A Gift for Heidi*. He also studied classical piano and composition.

(The down-to-earth role of the goat-boy had been played by Delmar Watson ◇ in the 1937 *Heidi* opposite Shirley Temple, and by Thomas Klameth in two Swiss films of 1952-54 with Elsbeth Sigmund. In the popular Austrian TV version of 1979, with Katia Polletin as Heidi, a delectably solemn lad called Stefan Arpagäus proved the best of all the Peters.)

As it turned out, music rather than acting was to form Van Dyke Parks' life. In his early twenties he was groomed by MGM to write soundtrack music for them, but turned to song-writing on his own account and had a considerable hit with a folk-rock number, 'High Coin'. He wrote lyrics for the Beach Boys, arranged and produced for many leading groups and soloists, and put out three solo LPs of his own which earned him the accolade of 'the first art rocker'. He made a brief appearance in Altman's *Popeye* (80), on which he was music director.

56 The Swan
58 A Gift for Heidi

David Stollery

USA

b: 18 Jan 41 (Los Angeles)

David John Stollery III was a dark-eyed blond, and a fine actor in a quiet, rather aristocratic way. In 1955-58 he was the junior partner, with Tim Considine, in the long-running TV Disney comedy series 'Spin and Marty'. He landed the Disney contract after his performance in the title role of a TV play called 'The Prodigy', with Ray Milland.

Apart from the 1960 film *Ten Who Dared*, he didn't do much more acting, but majored in art and mathematics.

48 A Connecticut Yankee
   in King Arthur's Court
50 Peggy
   Where Danger Lives

David Stollery, circa 1950

51 Darling, How Could You!
   Jack and the Beanstalk
   Tales of Robin Hood
53 Her Twelve Men
55 Storm Fear
56 Westward Ho the Wagons
57 Drango

Wolfgang Condrus

WEST GERMANY

b: 11 Feb 41 (Berlin)

This large, rather pouting blond was the son of the film actor Siegfried Breuer. He was a popular screen child of the Fifties, and played 'Gustav with the hooter' in Stemmle's 1954 remake of *Emil and the Detectives*.

Condrus continued to perform busily on film, stage and radio.

52 Postlagernd Turteltaube
   (Poste restante: Turtle-Dove)
53 Briefträger Müller (Postman Müller)
   Hab' Sonne im Herzen
   (Sunshine in my heart)
   Der Raub der Sabinerinnen
   (Rape of the Sabines)
54 Emil und die Detektive
   (Emil and the detectives)
   Hänsel und Gretel (Hansel and Gretel)
   So ein Affentheater! (What a farce!)

55 Ein Herz bleibt allein (A heart on its own)
   Liebe, Tanz und 1000 Schlager
   (Love, dance and 1000 hits)
   Mein Leopold (My Leopold)
   Die schöne Müllerin
   (The miller's pretty daughter)
56 Charleys Tante (Charley's Aunt)
57 Kalle wird Bürgermeister
   (Kalle becomes mayor)
   Robinson soll nicht sterben
   (Robinson shall not die)

Peter Feldt

AUSTRIA

b: 1 Apr 41 (Klagenfurt)

This serious boy with an interesting, often worried expression, played a rich little girl's humble but admirable friend in *Pünktchen und Anton*, the first filming of Erich Kästner's book.

The 'Little Dot' was Sabine Eggerth, and Feldt partnered her again in the follow-up vehicle, *Maxie*. But his promising film career seems to have been taken no further.

53 Pünktchen und Anton
   (Little Dot and Anton)
   Maxie

Fritz von Friedl

AUSTRIA

b: 17 Apr 41 (Berlin)

It's strange that one of the few other well-known boys in Austrian films should have been born only 16 days after Peter Feldt ◇, and born in Germany. His father, Fritz senior, had worked in German and Austrian films since 1926, latterly with UFA. But he returned to Austria after the war, and his saucy little blond son soon began to get work on stage and screen.

The boy's first two movies, open-air adventures in lush scenery, were filmed in Austria for the Children's Film Foundation in Britain. Four years later, he would be with Feldt in *Pünktchen und Anton*.

After the usual pause for education, Fritz von Friedl returned to the screen in *Der Page vom Palast-Hotel* (58), *Im Prater blüh'n*

Home helping: Fritz von Friedl in Der Sonnblick ruft

Damian Damiecki (left) in Tajemnica starego szybu

---

wieder die Bäume (58) and *Lulu* (62). Later films have included *Das gelbe Haus am Pinnasberg* (69), *Permission to Kill* (US/AT 75), *Alles Leben ist Chemie* (78) and *Rote Hitze* (DE/US 85).

The greater part of Friedl's work has been on the stage, frequently at the Wiener Burgtheater, and with leads, for instance, in Shakespeare, Shaw and Brecht.

49 The Lone Climber (GB)
   The Mysterious Poacher (GB)
51 Der fidele Bauer (The merry peasant)
   Schwindel in Dreivierteltakt
     (Swindle in three-four time)
52 Der Bauernrebell (The peasant rebel)
   Frühlingsstimmen (Voices of spring)
   Ideale Frau gesucht
     (Wanted: the ideal woman)
   Der Sonnblick ruft (Call of the Sonnblick)
   Der Verschwender (The spendthrift)
53 Du bist die Welt für mich
     (You are the world to me)
   Pünktchen und Anton
     (Little Dot and Anton)

54 Kaisermanöver (Imperial manoeuvres)
   Ein Haus voll Liebe (A house full of love)
   Der rote Prinz (The red prince)
   Verliebte Leute (People in love)

Damian Damięcki

POLAND

b: 16 Jly 41 (Podszkodzie, nr Ostrowiec
            Świętokrzyski)

Damian – or Dudek – and his younger brother MACIEJ (b: 11 Jan 44) were both remarkable actors. So were both their parents – Dobiesław Damięcki and Irena Górska – who became heroes of the anti-Fascist resistance. They were suspected of having murdered the collaborator Igo Sym, a former actor who had become the Warsaw propaganda chief.

Whether they had or not, they spent the rest of the war in hiding, and young Damian first saw the light of day in somewhat Christ-like style, laid in a box of straw. (Whereupon Damian senior got wildly drunk and ran out into the streets shouting: 'You're all looking for me, you bastards, and now I've got a son!' By incredible luck, he didn't run into a policeman.)

Damian junior was only in two films as a boy, but they were both leading roles. In *Tajemnica starego szybu* he was joined by Maciej, who threw himself so deeply into his neurotic part that according to the director, Wadim Berestowski, he underwent a marked change of personality and took some time to 'recover'.

Maciej was later in *Spotkania w mroku / Begegnung im Zwielicht* (PL/DD 60), and then back home in *Ludzie z pociągu* (61), *Pingwin* (64), *Banda* (65 – a leading part), *Bokser* (66), *Sąsiedzi* (68), *Droga* (74), etcetera.

Damian continued to act, in supporting roles, but many years later had another lead in *Zasieki* (77). His childhood films had been:

54 Opowieść atlantycka (Atlantic story)
55 Tajemnica starego szybu
     (Secret of the old pit)

Michael Caridia

BRITAIN

b: 2 Aug 41 (nr Swaffham, Norfolk)

There was something splendidly snide and haughty about Michael Caridia even at twelve, in his early appearances on TV. He was the son of wealthy parents (his father something important in the car trade) and clearly knew his worth.

He excelled in spiteful parts, and in *The Gamma People* was an enthusiastic member of a totalitarian youth movement, almost a mini-Hitler. In *Up in the World*, with Norman Wisdom, he plays the sadistic little Sir Reginald, given to playing cruel practical jokes on the staff. (Happily, he gets slightly duffed up himself.)

Caridia went on acting into his late teens, with some fine performances on TV and the London stage.

Boy scout Hitler: Michael Caridia in The Gamma People

55 The Gamma People
   The Reluctant Bride
56 Odongo
   Up in the World

Vittorio Manunta

ITALY/BRITAIN

b: 25 Aug 41 (Rome)

Vittorio, when he was five, was one of three Italian war-orphans adopted by an aristocratic American lady – Molly, last Countess of Berkeley – following an agonising vision she experienced in England at the Cenacle of Our Lady at Grayshott, Hampshire.

A scion of the poetic Lowells of Boston, she had married an English earl, had become a Roman Catholic convert in London during World War Two, and was now rich, childless and scattily emotional. After purchasing and transforming a 'half-ruined confraternity' on a magnificent hilltop in Assisi – evicting a few nuns in the process – Lady Molly acquired the orphans from an Italian charity (rather as if ordering a brace of partridges from Harrods), installed them at the villa and spoiled them outrageously.

When the British film producer Anthony Havelock-Allan came to Assisi looking for locations for his adaptation of Paul Gallico's popular story 'The Little Miracle', he met Lady Molly and her brood, and persuaded her to allow Vittorio (now nine) to test for the leading role of the little peasant boy who takes his sick donkey Violetta to meet the Pope in Rome. He proved a natural, and in spite of frequently behaving like a demon – biting photographers and terrorising press agents, locking himself in the bathroom and refusing to perform – created a highly winning character.

After *Stranger on the Prowl,* in which he co-starred with Paul Muni, Vittorio was featured in a TV play called 'His Boy'. He then went off to school in England and Switzerland, going through a some-what gangsterish phase in adolescence but emerging into maturity and full-scale adoption as Vittorio Manunta Lowell.

51 Never Take No for an Answer (GB)
52 Imbarco a mezzanotte
   (Midnight departure – IT/US – Stranger on the Prowl)

Vittorio Manunta in Never Take No for an Answer

Gordon Gebert, prehensile

Gordon Gebert

USA

b: 7 Oct 41 (Des Moines, Iowa)

Gordon Alan Gebert III, a sly moppet with an almost prehensile pout, is most often seen nowadays riding pillion to a medieval Burt Lancaster in *The Flame and the Arrow.* He is undeniably charming.

Gebert returned in 1958 for a teenage role in *Summer Love.*

49 Come to the Stable
   Holiday Affair
50 The Flame and the Arrow
   Saddle Tramp
51 Chicago Calling
   Flying Leathernecks
   The House on Telegraph Hill
   Night Into Morning
   Operation Pacific
   Something to Live For
52 The Narrow Margin
55 To Hell and back

Jacky Gencel

FRANCE

b: 14 Oct 41 (Paris)

Jacky, with his worn, wary little bruiser's face, had a show-business pedigree: a

Wary: Jacky Gencel and ally in Plus de vacances pour le bon Dieu

mother who had been a singer, a father who had been a theatrical hatter. He made his debut on the Paris stage in 1944 in 'Le grand Poucet' at the Théâtre Montparnasse, the first of many appearances in Paris and elsewhere.

His film career started two years later, but it was certainly his performance in *Plus de vacances pour le bon Dieu* which caught the eye of Hollywood and led to his role in the Capra comedy *Here Comes the Groom*, as a French war orphan destined for adoption by Bing Crosby.

In 1954, after five years' absence from the stage, Jacky settled in for a 3-year run at the Châtelet, as the page-boy in Maurice Lehmann's revival of 'White Horse Inn'. In 1959 came his last screen role, in *La verte moisson* – after which the much-loved Jacky Gencel retired from the acting profession to take over his father's hattery.

46 Un flic (A cop)
47 Une mort sans importance
    (An unimportant death)
48 Mademoiselle s'amuse
    (The young lady has fun)
   La maternelle (The nursery school)
   Retour à la vie (Return to life)
49 Le jugement de Dieu (Divine judgment)
   Plus de vacances pour le bon Dieu
    (No let-up for Almighty God)

50 Les anciens de Saint-Loup
    (Old Saint-Loup boys)
   Le marinier (The seaman)
   Passion
   La peau d'un homme (A man's skin)
   Le roi des camelots (King of the hawkers)
51 La composition de calcul (The maths test)
   La demoiselle et son revenant
    (The young lady and her ghost)
   Here Comes the Groom (US)
   Monsieur Leguignon lampiste
    (Monsieur Leguignon, lamp-man)
52 Le dernier Robin des Bois
    (The last Robin Hood)
53 Gamins de Paris (Paris kids)
   L'oeil en coulisse (The sidelong look)

David Hemmings

BRITAIN

b: 18 Nov 41 (Guildford)

Hemmings, a pupil of the Arts Educational School in London, was only 14-15 when his 1957 films were shot. He was first heard of as a remarkable boy singer, creating the part of Miles in the first production of Britten's opera 'The Turn of the Screw' in 1954. (He is on the original LP recording.) His film debut was in the Children's Film Foundation serial *Five Clues to Fortune*.

Treble chance: David Hemmings in Five Clues to Fortune

He was in four films in 1959: *The Challenge, In the Wake of a Stranger, Men of Tomorrow* and *No Trees in the Street*. Then followed *Some People* (62), *The System* (63) and *Live It Up* (63) – in which the former opera singer stars as the leader of a beat group called the Smart Alecs.

In due course he was to go on to better things as an international actor, as well as directing and producing. In 1967 he formed Hemdale Enterprises, which among other things handled the affairs of Mark Lester ◇ and Jack Wild. ◇ (He directed Wild in the lead of his 1973 film *The 14.*)

Hemmings's son Nolan appeared in a 1986 TV serialisation of 'David Copperfield'.

57 Five Clues to Fortune (serial)
   The Heart Within
   Saint Joan (GB/US)

Beau Bridges

USA

b: 9 Dec 41 (Los Angeles)

Lloyd Vernet Bridges III, alias Beau, appeared from the age of five in the 'Sea Hunt' TV series of his father, Lloyd Bridges. (Beau's younger brother Jeff – born 4 Dec 49 – was also carried on as a baby in 'Sea Hunt', and in the 1950 film *The Company She Keeps*.)

It was ten years or so later that pudgy Beau Bridges returned to the screen in films like *The Explosive Generation* (61), *Village of the Giants* (65), *The Incident* (67) and *For Love of Ivy* (68), before his first important lead in *The Landlord* (70). He has seldom stopped working since. Nor, come to that, has Jeff.

48 Force of Evil
   No Minor Vices
49 The Red Pony
   Zamba

The coloured actor Todd Bridges (born 1965), familiar from TV series like 'Diff'rent Strokes', is an adopted son of Beau.

Tommy Kirk

USA

b: 10 Dec 41 (Louisville, Kentucky)

When he was only one, Tommy's family moved to Los Angeles. After stage work at the Pasadena Playhouse he was noticed by TV scouts and got increasingly good parts in various series as his dramatic skill became evident. Besides being a 'regular boy', he had considerable emotional power.

In 1956 he landed an important lead in the TV series 'The Hardy Boys', was featured in Walt Disney's 'Mickey Mouse Club', and for the next eight years was very much identified with Disney productions (as Kevin Corcoran ◇ and Kurt Russell ◇, for instance, were later to be) in a series of leading roles. These began with a testing one in *Old Yeller*, where he has to shoot the beloved dog to deliver it from hydrophobia.

He also dubbed the voice of Kay for the US release of a Russian cartoon version (*Snezhnaya koroleva*, 57) of Hans Andersen's 'Snow Queen'.

For seven whole years Tommy Kirk was *the* Disney boy actor. He starred for them in *The Shaggy Dog* (59), *The Absent-Minded Professor* (61), *Babes in Toyland* (61), *The Horsemasters* (GB 61), *Moon Pilot* (61), *Bon Voyage!* (62), *Son of Flubber* (62), *Savage Sam* (63) and *The Misadventures of Merlin Jones* (63).

It was hereabouts, though, that Kirk's own misfortunes began. He had not only come out and told the world he was gay — which was brave, but rash for a boy with a 'regular' image — he was also absorbing large quantities of drugs and drink and behaving in a tiresomely unprofessional manner. Disney dropped him, and so did the producers of *The Sons of Katie Elder*, which he was to have been in.

He starred in *Pajama Party* (64), and all he could get from now on were parts in cheapo movies, too painful to name. After about 1970 even these began to dry up.

Between odd non-acting jobs he did some theatre work, but mainly concen-

Exercised: Tommy Rettig in The 5,000 Fingers of Dr. T

trated on kicking the addictions and getting his act together again.

57 Back from the Dead
   Old Yeller

Tommy Rettig

USA

b: 10 Dec 41 (Jackson Heights, N.Y.)
d: 15 Feb 96 (Marina del Rey, Cal.)

Like so many child actors, Thomas Noel Rettig reminded one of a small Disney-ish animal. Chipmunk? Gopher? Gerbil? Something at least with bright brown eyes, healthy incisors and a tendency to sit up looking startled.

When he was five, Tommy got the part of Little Jake in a touring production of 'Annie Get Your Gun', with Mary Martin, which was on the road for nearly two

years, playing in 42 cities. Catching many eyes, he was offered roles in two stage plays ('Member of the Wedding' and 'Peter Pan') and two films (*Panic in the Streets* and *Two Weeks with Love*). He opted for the films.

In 1954 he won the main two-legged part in CBS's 'Lassie' series on TV — the sequence called 'Jeff's Collie' — a lucrative assignment which occupied him for nearly four years before he got free. A new and younger boy hero, 'Timmy' (played by Jon Provost ◇), was installed in his place.

Tom Rettig's work after 1956 was sporadic. Though clearly a teenager, he was small and not easy to cast. In the mid-Sixties things looked brighter: a romantic lead at the Los Angeles Players' Ring, and a regular role in the TV series 'See Here, Private Hargrove'. But it led to nothing more, and he drifted from job to job outside the profession.

In the Seventies, almost inevitably in his milieu and situation, came trouble with drugs, and periods of probation though not imprisonment. The intelligent and articulate Rettig has since said, with some firmness: 'I never had trouble with drugs. I had trouble with the *law* over drugs.' And for all its apparent checkeredness, he says of his life: 'From my perspective, it's been absolutely terrific.' He subsequently worked as a computer programmer.

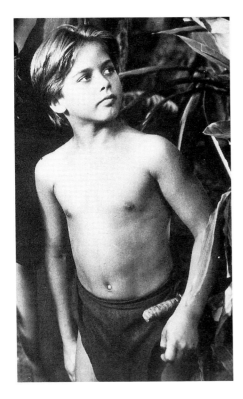

Tommy Carlton

USA

b: circa 1941

The glamorous and muscular 'Joey' of *Tarzan's Savage Fury*, initially used as live bait by crocodile-hunters, became for this one film the surrogate son our hero (now Lex Barker) had lacked since the departure of Weissmuller's 'Boy', Johnny Sheffield ◇.

Carlton acted prettily, but was only to be the first of a series of short-lived surrogates – Ricky Sorensen ◇, 'Jai', Ricky Der, Manuel Padilla ◇, Steve Bond ◇.

Jimmy Hawkins

USA

b: circa 1941 (12 Nov)

This Jim Hawkins never played the lead in *Treasure Island*, on screen at least, but did become well known between 1953 and 1958 as Annie's kid brother Tagg in the 'Annie Oakley' TV series for ABC.

He stayed in show business for some years afterwards, and was seen for instance in *Zotz!* (62), *Girl Happy* (65) and *Spinout* (66). A brother, Timmy, had been nearly as busy but didn't persist as long.

Jimmy's many film appearances of 1945-55 included:

Muscular: Tommy Carlton in Tarzan's Savage Fury

Láci Horváth in Valahol Európában

László Horváth

HUNGARY

b: circa 1941

László (or Láci) was the wiry little 'Kuksi' of Geza Radvanyi's *Somewhere in Europe* – a story of homeless orphans living wild and lawless in the aftermath of war. They hole up in a ruined castle, only to find it already tenanted by an elderly and once-famous musician. In return for having his life spared (he's almost lynched on the spot) the old aesthete tames these savage breasts with a crash course in classical music, until tragedy intervenes.

An unlikely and soppy story, but the kids are highly impressive, particularly ENDRE HARKANYI – born 26 Mar 34 – as one of the wildest. (Apart from the unfinished *Uttörök*, this was Harkányi's only film as a child, but he went on to become a well-known adult actor in Hungary.)

With little Horváth it was the reverse: a whole string of further appearances as a kid, but nothing much afterwards.

The name of László Horváth reappears in later Hungarian films, but it's more or less the Hungarian equivalent of Tommy Jones and is not thought to be the former Kuksi.

The good shepherd: Tsai Yuanyuan in Jimao xin

Tsai (Cai) Yuanyuan

CHINA

b: 1 Mar 42 (Beijing)

His father, Tsai Songling, was a famous stage actor in modern Chinese plays, and the director of *Jimao xin* was the film actor Shi Hui.

Yuanyuan threw himself with boyish impetuousness into the role of little Haiwa, carrying a vital military message through enemy lines and proving what obscure parts of a sheep you can hide things in. His scampering energy was hugely likeable, and he deservedly became an idol of his child contemporaries in China.

For some time he pursued an acting career, graduating from the Performing Department of the Beijing Film Academy in 1965. He is now an independent producer.

53 Jimao xin
   (The letter with the feathers)

Brandon DeWilde

USA

b: 9 Apr 42 (Brooklyn, N.Y.C.)
d: 6 Jly 72 (nr Denver, Colorado)

Both Brandon's parents were former actors, and it was his dad's presence as stage manager with the 'Member of the Wedding' company that led to Brandon being auditioned for the role of the quaint John Henry when Tommy Rettig ◊ proved unavailable. Having got it, he played it triumphantly for 492 performances in New York (from 1950) and 56 more on the road. He was the first child to win a Donaldson award for an outstanding performance in the theatre.

It provided his screen debut too, when the play was filmed in 1952. But *Shane*, the following year, made him famous with a wider audience (and won him an Oscar nomination) as the little boy who hero-worships Alan Ladd's eponymous outsider. Then he was given vehicles of his own, including – of course – a boy-and-dog story, *Goodbye, My Lady*, whose main distinction was that the dog was, for a change, a basenji. In that respect it was a silent movie.

In 1953-54 Brandon starred in the TV series 'Jamie'.

Having graduated to teenage roles, his boyish looks – with a slight, endearing squint, gradually corrected – enabled him to keep on playing them for the rest of his short life. He was in *Blue Denim* (59), *All Fall Down* (62), *Hud* (63), *In Harm's Way* (65), *Those Calloways* (65), *The Trip* (67), *La spina dorsale del diavolo* (IT/YU/US 70 – *The Deserter*), *Wild in the Sky* (71) and *Black Jack* (72), before dying in a car crash on his way to Denver, where he was to appear on the stage.

52 The Member of the Wedding
   Shane
55 Good-Bye, My Lady
57 The Missouri Traveler
   Night Passage

Christian Fourcade

FRANCE

b: 22 Apr 42 (Vincennes, Seine)

This sad-eyed child was already popular in France before becoming the second French boy in three years to be flown across the Atlantic to the bosom of Bing Crosby – who this time, in *Little Boy Lost*, was searching for his own son rather than a potential adoptee. Prophetically, Christian had been in *Voyage en Amérique* the year before. He enjoyed Hollywood, but admitted to an occasional longing for a dish of snails.

In *Brelan d'as*, a portmanteau film, he was in the episode 'A choirboy's evidence'. Later he was to play some of the classic French boy-roles, such as Le Souris in *Crainquebille*, Gavroche in *Les misérables* and Rémi in *Sans famille*.

After 1957, Fourcade's acting career continued for another decade or so. He was in *Par-dessus le mur* (59), *Le capitan* (60) and many more. But their importance dwindled, to him at least. By the early Seventies he was running a stud-farm at Rambouillet.

Sad eyes: Christian Fourcade in Un grand patron

48 Dernier amour (Last love)
   L'inconnue no.13
      (Unknown woman No.13)
   La maternelle (The nursery school)
49 La Marie du port (Mary of the port)
50 Caroline chérie (Darling Caroline)
   Trois télégrammes (Three telegrams)
51 Un grand patron (The Chief)
   Le voyage en Amérique
      (Journey to America)
52 Brelan d'as (Three aces)
   La jeune folle (The mad girl)
   Little Boy Lost (US)
   Suivez cet homme (Follow that man)
53 Les compagnes de la nuit (Night partners)
   Crainquebille
   Gamins de Paris (Paris kids)
   Le petit Jacques (Little Jacques)
   Le rafle est pour ce soir
      (The raid is tonight)
55 Le dossier noir (The black file)
56 Bonjour jeunesse (Hello youth – FR/CH)
   Fric-frac en dentelles (Burglars in lace)
57 Echec au porteur (Pay out bearer)
   Les misérables (The poor and wretched)
   Sans famille (No relations)

Peter Finkbeiner

WEST GERMANY

b: 15 Jly 42

Germany's second 'Emil', a generation later than Lamprecht's Rolf Wenkhaus◇ of 1931, was the son of a Berlin gynae-cologist. Peter Finkbeiner, a thoughtful brown-eyed boy, hadn't acted before but

Brandon DeWilde with Ernest Truex in the TV series Jamie

Thoughtful: Peter Finkbeiner in the 1954 Emil und die Detektive

got good notices and went on to make further films.

54 Emil und die Detektive
    (Emil and the detectives)
55 Der fröhliche Wanderer
    (The happy wanderer)
56 Du darfst nicht länger schweigen
    (Now you can speak out)
    Wo die alten Wälder rauschen
    (Where the old forests rustle)
58 Stephanie

Ratan Kumar (Master Ratan)

INDIA

b: 21 Aug 42 (Ajmer)

'Master Ratan' – whose real name was Syed Nazir Ali – studied in Bombay and had leading roles in many films, most notably *Do bigha zamin* (Two acres of land) and *Boot polish*.

The latter begins as a traditionally roguish Indian proletarian musical, then plunges into sentimental drama and reaches an almost operatic climax of pathos as the children are separated and a surprisingly plump Ratan 'starves' in the streets while his little sister (Baby Naaz) is pampered by rich adopters.

A similar suspension of disbelief is required when watching Pavarotti taking the role of a starving poet.

'Master Ratan' credits are asterisked.

47 *Dekhoji (Look, dear)
48 Dil ki awaz (The heart speaks)

Ratan Kumar in Do bigha zamin

*Gowlan
*Phool aur kante
  (The flower and the thorns)
*Shyama
49 Balam (Darling)
   Hamari manzil (Our goal)
   *Maa ka pyar (Mother's love)
   Roomal (The handkerchief)
50 *Alakh Niranjan
   *Apni chhaya (One's own shadow)
   *Hamari beti (Our daughter)
   Sargam (Seven-note scale)
   Sartaj
51 Afsana (The story)
   *Humlog (We people)
   *Malhar
   Saudagar (The trader)

52 Baghdad
   Baiju bawra (Crazy Baiju)
   *Betaab (The restless one)
   Diwana (The crazy one)
   *Indrasan
   Laila Majnu
   Moti Mahal
   Rajarani Damayanti
53 Bhagyawan (The lucky one)
   Dard-e-dil (Anguish of the heart)
   Do bigha zamin (Two acres of land)
   Naya ghar (The new house)
54 Angarey (Embers)
   Boot polish
   Jagriti (Awakening)
55 Ekadashi (The eleventh day)
   Jalwa

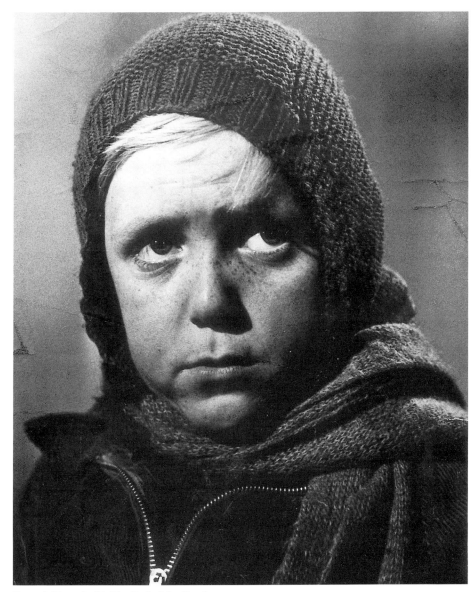
Dogged: Hannaford in The End of the Road

David Hannaford

BRITAIN

b: 1 Oct 42 (Leyton, E.London)

This fair-haired Cockney urchin, a cheer-fully recurring presence in British films of the Fifties, crashed into show business at the age of 3½, at the wheel of a runaway bus.

A friend of the Hannafords worked at the Leyton Bus Garage, where the little boy was more or less adopted as a mascot. Seated one day, as often before, unsupervised at the wheel of a slumbering London Transport bus, David casually disengaged the hand brake, unaware that this particular one wasn't standing on the level. Slowly gathering speed, the bus rumbled down the slope, ploughed straight across a main road and came to a shuddering halt in someone's garden on the other side. A rather shaken David Hannaford stepped out.

The incident naturally got his picture in the local papers, and a film studio scout, spotting the dogged little face, did the rest. Over the next ten years this tough, comical child, with the lugubrious eyes of a St Bernard who has lost his brandy, was in something like 50 films, plus occasional West End shows like 'Summer Song' or 'The Desperate Hours' and a fair amount of TV.

One of his most important roles was in *The Second Mate*, where a little boy dreams of a naval career carrying him to the highest ranks. (The aircraft-carrier 'Theseus' was engaged to play the ship he ended up commanding, but unfortunately it had to leave at short notice for Korea, and was replaced by the battleship 'Vanguard'.)

David's finest 'mature' part was in *The End of the Road*, as the grandson of an old craftsman who has been superannuated by his firm. (Played by the Scottish actor Finlay Currie, so memorable as Magwitch in the 1947 *Great Expectations*.) The scenes between the old man and the little boy are enormously touching and funny.

The 1957 *Carry On Admiral*, incidentally, is not one of the 'Carry On' series, which started in 1958.

David Hannaford's last important role was in 'The Littlest Sergeant', an episode in the 'O.S.S.' TV series. He then toyed with ideas of becoming a professional boxer (he was a very good amateur one), but this didn't materialise. He settled for less glamorous work with more secure prospects, and later ran his own delivery firm in Basildon, Essex.

A nice thing happened to him a few years ago. A new soundtrack had to be dubbed for *The Dragon of Pendragon Castle*, a Children's Film Foundation piece which had given him one of his first leading parts. This time, he was engaged to dub one of the adult roles, and his son Mark dubbed his own old one.

48 The Last Load
    No Room at the Inn
    William comes to Town
49 Journey for Jeremy
    Now Barabbas Was a Robber
    Three Bags Full *(serial)*
50 The Dragon of Pendragon Castle
    The Second Mate
    Trio
51 I Believe in You
    The Magic Marble
    Scrooge

Stefan Danailov

BULGARIA

b: 9 Dec 42 (Sofia)

Danailov and the slightly older GEORGI NAUMOV (born 11 Sep 41) had leading roles in Petr Vasilev's improving but lively *Sledite ostavat*, about children tracking down a spy.

Both of them went on to be popular young leading actors in Bulgaria – Danailov in *Inspectorat i noshta* (63), *S dah na bademi* (67), *Parviat kurier* (68), *Ivan Kondarev* (73), etcetera.

Stefan Danailov in Sledite ostavat

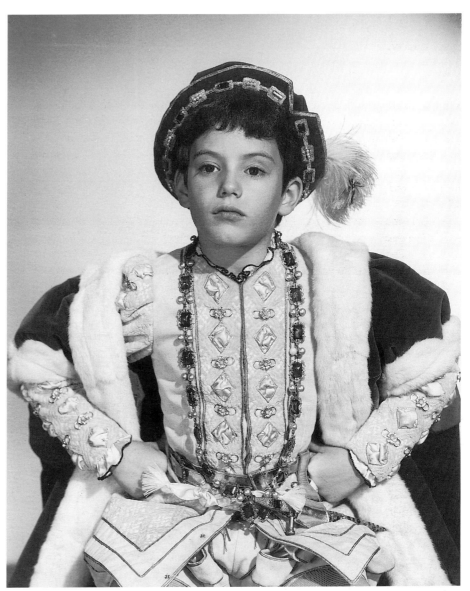

The well-named Rex Thompson as King Edward VI in Young Bess

Rex Thompson

USA

b: 14 Dec 42 (New York)

Rex, son of actor-turned-businessman John Thompson, made his stage debut in a 1949 Broadway revue called 'Alive and Kicking'. He went on to play in 'The King and I', 'Escapade' and 'King of Hearts' over the next four years. He then became more active in television, in adaptations of 'David Copperfield', 'Great Expectations' and Saki's 'Sredni Vashtar' – perfect casting for this last.

He was an intense-looking brunet with a wide, slightly ruthless mouth. He started by playing a boy king in *Young Bess* (and would be royal again, in 1957, when he played the double lead in a TV version of 'The Prince and the Pauper'). He went on to specialise in rich, spoilt, or even English children, though he had a huskier part in *All Mine to Give*, as the son of a pioneer family in Wisconsin.

Vladimír Pucholt

CZECHOSLOVAKIA

b: 1942

A few years after his child roles, Pucholt became one of the most popular of young Czech actors, known all over the world through his superb faux-naïf performances in the films of Milos Forman, notably as the bewildered young hero of *A Blonde in Love*.

He was in about ten more films before leaving the cinema in 1967 to study medicine in England. In 1970, however, he was in the West German film *Malatesta*.

55 Návštěva z oblak (Visit from the clouds)
   Punta a čtyřlistek (Doggy and the three)
56 Vzorný kinematograf Haška Jaroslava
   (Jaroslav Hašek's model cinema)
57 Brankář bydlí v naší ulici
   (The goalkeeper lives in our street)

Kit Taylor

AUSTRALIA

b: 1942

He was the son of the actor Grant Taylor. When Robert Newton, four years after his eye-rolling triumph as Long John Silver in the 1955 *Treasure Island*, was persuaded to revive the role in an Australian Cinema-scope sequel, fair-haired Kit was cast as Jim Hawkins.

Newton and Taylor went on to star in a 'Long John Silver' series on Australian TV (1955-56). *Under the Black Flag* and *South Sea Pirates* were cobbled together from episodes in this series, so Kit was in fact only 13-14 at the time of filming.

Kit Taylor later went to work abroad, appearing for instance in *Assault* (GB 70). But in 1974 he returned to Australia, and has since then acted in numerous cinema

Jim down under: Kit Taylor in Long John Silver

and TV movies: *Harness Fever* (75), *Don's Party* (76), *Born to Run* (76), *Weekend of Shadows* (77), *Newsfront* (78), etcetera. Two of these – *Born to Run* and *Harness Fever* – featured the boy actor Robert Bettles◇.

54 Long John Silver
   Under the Black Flag
56 The Crisis
   Ship o' the Dead
   Tale of a Tooth
57 South Sea Pirates

Barry Curtis

USA

b: circa 1942

Fair-haired Barry is remembered as Ricky North, the naïvely good-natured hero of the CBS TV Western series 'The Adventures of Champion'. (It was better known as 'Champion the Wonder Horse'.) But he escaped occasionally into cinema films.

52 The Marrying Kind
54 One Desire
55-56 'The Adventures of Champion' (TVS)
57 The Missouri Traveler
   3:10 to Yuma

Bewildered: Vladimír Pucholt (r.) with Vladimír Bejval (l.) in Vzorný kinematograf Haška Jaroslava

Kálmán Koletár

HUNGARY

b: circa 1942
d: circa 1966

Kálmán was, on a modester scale, a Hungarian Mickey Rooney ◇. He had brown eyes, ludicrously floppy fair hair and the slack mouth of a clown. He radiated vulnerability and fecklessness.

Viktor Gertler cast him opposite Gyula Gózon as the junior co-star of *Me and Grandpa*. Grandpa was a boozer who drifted from job to job; little Berci, who lived with him, was a brilliant cyclist and footballer but hardly a model pupil. Great affection united this disorganised couple, and with the aid of Berci's schoolmates their lives got sorted out, more or less.

Kálmán never had another lead, but his sweetly silly face popped up in eight more films over the next two years.

From his late teens to his mid-twenties Koletár was in frequent demand as a character actor in films, working for directors like Fábri, Makk and Máriássy. His credits included *Dúvad* (59), *A megfelelö ember* (60), *Mindennap élünk* (63), *Tücsök* (63), *Egy ember aki nincs* (64), *Karambol* (64) and *Vizivárosi nyár* (65).

He was well-liked – and imprudent. Around 1966, attempting to cross to the West, perhaps in hopes of furthering his career, Kálmán Koletár was shot dead by a border guard.

54 Én és a nagyapám (Me and Grandpa)
55 Egy pikoló világos (One glass of beer)
   Budapesti tavasz (Springtime in Budapest)
   Mindenki iskolája (Everyone's school)
56 A kabát (The overcoat)
   Dollárpapa (Dollar daddy)
   Több, mint jatek (More than a game)
   Jól megjárta (They've had it)
   A legokosabb ember (The cleverest man)
57 Éjfélkor (At midnight)
   Fapados szerelem (Simple love)
   Két vallomás (Two confessions)
   Külvárosi legenda (Legend of the suburbs)

Thomas Schmidt

EAST GERMANY

b: circa 1942

Thomas was seen in the title role of Wolfgang Staudte's *Geschichte vom kleinen Muck*, based on a fairytale by E.T.A. Hoffmann, about a little hunchbacked boy who finds fortune through a magic stick and a pair of magic slippers. When these are stolen from him, he recovers them through native cunning.

Little Muck was shown widely in Eastern and Central Europe.

53 Die Geschichte vom kleinen Muck
   (The tale of Little Muck)

Andrea Scirè

ITALY

b: circa 1942

Franco Rossi's *Amici per la pelle* – known to the English-speaking public as *Friends for Life* – is a remarkable, deeply-felt study of a schoolboy friendship: emotionally intense, but completely without sensuality.

The extrovert Mario, son of a ceramic artist, befriends a new boy who arrives at his school: Franco, the shy, serious son of a diplomat. Theirs is a relationship of opposites, with Franco hopelessly vulnerable to Mario's bouncy insensitivity. What finally shatters it is an act of spite by Mario, betraying a secret about Franco's dead mother after his intellectual friend has, somewhat improbably, beaten him in a long-distance race.

GERONIMO MEYNIER (born 5 July 41) is brilliant as the attractive, affectionate but shallow Mario. Meynier went on to become a leading young actor in Italy in the Sixties. He was in *Amore e chiacchiere* (57), *Il cocco di mamma* (57), *Ragazzi della marina* (58), *Vacanze d'inverno* (59), *Il magistrato* (59), *La grande guerra* (IT/FR 59) and many more, including Renzo Rossellini's Italian episode of *Love at Twenty* (FR/IT/JP/DE/PL 62) and *Giulietta e Romeo* (IT/ES 64, as Romeo). He has now retired.

But Andrea Scirè's sweet-natured Franco carries the real charge of *Amici per la pelle*. It's a sad study in disillusionment, and his is a face that registers pride, diffidence and pain with perfect truthfulness.

Solidarity: Kálmán Koletár with Gyula Gózon in Én és a nagyapám

Vulnerability: Andrea Scirè (right) with Geronimo Meynier

Scirè – rumoured to be a distant scion of the Buonaparte dynasty – never made another film.

55 Amici per la pelle (Bosom friends)

Anthony Sydes

USA

b: circa 1942

The stocky, blond Anthony Sydes was a frequent sight in Hollywood films at the end of the 1940s. He continued at least until *Gunsmoke in Tucson* (58).
   Among his credits were:

46 Claudia and David
   Johnny Comes Flying Home
47 Driftwood
   It Happened on Fifth Avenue
   It's a Joke, Son
   Miracle on 34th Street
   Song of Love
48 Canon City
   Chicken Every Sunday
   Sitting Pretty
49 The Life of Riley
   Reign of Terror

50 Cheaper by the Dozen
   Shadow on the Wall
52 Belles on Their Toes
   The Lady Says No
53 The Glenn Miller Story
56 Lust for Life

Lars Henning-Jensen

DENMARK

b: 22 Feb 43 (Copenhagen)

Lars was the son of the directors Bjarne and Astrid Henning-Jensen, one or both of whom directed his first three films. He provided voice only to *Hvor bergene sejler*. Later, he studied music.

46 Ditte menneskebarn
   (Ditte, child of man)
47 De pokkers unger
   (Those bloody kids)
49 Palle alene i verden
   (Palle alone in the world)
50 Vesterhavsdrenge (North sea boys)
52 Ukendt mand (Unknown man)
54 Balletens børn (Children of the ballet)
55 Hvor bjergene sejler
   (Where mountains float)

Peter Czeike

AUSTRIA

b: 2 Apr 43 (Prague)

Peter, son of the actress Isolde Kaspar, was born in the capital of the German 'protectorate' of Bohemia-Moravia. After the war they moved to Austria, first living in Linz (where he made his stage debut at the age of three and then, from 1948, in Vienna. He began to appear in films.
   Peter acted on the Vienna stage, for instance in 'Wilhelm Tell' at the Burg-theater, and was in one later film: *Die vergessenen Jahre* (62).

48 Die Schatztruhe (The treasure-chest)
49 Die Sonnhofbäuerin
   (The Sonnhof farmer's wife)
51 K -- das Haus des Schweigens
   (K -- the house of silence)
   Das letzte Rezept (The last prescription)
   Stadtpark (City park)
   Wien tanzt (Vienna dances)
55 Der Kongress tanzt (Congress dances)
57 Die liebe Familie (The dear family)
58 Meine schöne Mama (My beautiful Mama)

Roland Kaiser

WEST GERMANY

b: 9 Apr 43 (Damsdorf, nr Berlin)

Roland Ernst Wolf Kaiser, with his pale, sharp face, cornered the screen's market in worldly-wise street kids in 1950s West Germany. Having started modestly as little 'Tuesday' in *Emil*, he ended up as the confident elder statesman of scruff. He was also in demand in the theatre.
   His parents had brought him and seven siblings over from the Eastern Zone. His father died soon afterwards, and Roland became the family's breadwinner.
   He kept on acting after 1959, but devoted himself more to pop singing.

54 Emil und die Detektive
   (Emil and the detectives)
   Keine Angst vor Schwiegermüttern
   (Mothers-in-law are OK)
   Der treue Husar (The faithful hussar)
55 Meine Kinder und ich (My children and I)

Roland Kaiser, circa 1957

56 Drei Männer im Schnee
  (Three men in the snow)
57 Casino de Paris
  Ferien auf Immenhof
  (Holidays at Immenhof)
  Heute blau und morgen blau
  (Blue today, blue tomorrow)
  Liebe, Jazz und Übermut
  (Love, jazz and high spirits)
  Münchhausen in Afrika
  (Münchhausen in Africa)
  Robinson soll nicht sterben
  (Robinson shall not die)
  Vater, unser bestes Stück
  (Father, the family treasure)
  Zürcher Verlobung (Zürich engagement)
58 Ihr 106. Geburtstag (Her 106th birthday)
  Kleine Leute -- mal ganz gross
  (Little big people)
  Der Mann im Strom (Man in the river)
  Ohne Mutter geht es nicht
  (You can't do without mother)
  Was eine Frau in Frühling träumt
  (A woman's dreams in spring)
59 Rosen für den Staatsanwalt
  (Roses for the Public Prosecutor)

Celal Ersöz

TURKEY

b: 20 Apr 43 (Giresun)

Celal Ersöz acted on stage as a boy as well as on screen. As a young man he became an assistant director, and later moved to England.

55 Günahkâr baba (Guilty father)
56 Fakir kizin kismeti (A poor girl's luck)

Patrick Adiarte

USA

b: 2 Aug 43 (Philippines)

Patrick's father, a Filipino captain in the US Army, was killed in action just before the boy was born. Patrick – with his mother, Purie – spent nearly four years on Broadway in 'The King and I', working his way up through the ranks of the royal children and finally succeeding Sal Mineo as the Crown Prince.

After repeating the role in the film, he was in *High Time* (60) with Bing Crosby, and then -- again repeating a Broadway role -- in *Flower Drum Song* (61). He was seen later in *John Goldfarb, Please Come Home!* (65), and as Hawkeye's Korean houseboy Ho-John in the great TV series 'M*A*S*H'.

56 The King and I

John Hall

BRITAIN

b: 22 Aug 43 (Haywards Heath, Sussex)

Hall, a sly, intelligent child with reserves of feeling, played parts as diverse as Jim Hawkins, Auntie Mame's nephew and Little Eyolf on the London stage, but got his finest reviews as John Henry in the British premiere of 'The Member of the Wedding'. (To a wider public he was familiar as the insolent 'Taplow' in the Jimmy Edwards TV series 'Whacko!')

He played Michael Redgrave's son in *The Dam Busters*, and was a smartass sea-scout – a Taplow derivative – tormenting the hapless David Tomlinson in *Further Up the Creek*.

While doing a little more stage acting, John Hall studied composition under Alan Bush and in 1966 won a scholarship at the Royal Academy of Music, where he subsequently became a Professor. His Organ Concerto won the Royal Philharmonic Prize in 1969, one of innumerable composition prizes he was to win. Several of his works have been broadcast by the BBC.

55 The Dam Busters
58 Further Up the Creek

Bobby Diamond

USA

b: 23 Aug 43 (Los Angeles)

For many years from 1955, Diamond became nationally known as 'Joey' in NBC's long-running TV Western series 'Fury'. To begin with, he was no great shakes in the saddle, and was doubled in long-shot by a girl rider known as 'the Whiz of San Fernando Valley': nor was she wholly silent about the fact. Bobby, nettled, brushed up his horsemanship, and the Whiz got the push.

After later appearances in *Airborne* (62) and *Billie* (65) Robert Diamond retired from acting, studied law, and became an attorney.

48 The Mating of Millie
51 Young Man with Ideas
52 The Greatest Show on Earth
  The Lady Wants Mink
53 The Silver Whip
55 Untamed

Nettled: Bobby Diamond in the TV series 'Fury'

Václav Postránecký

CZECHOSLOVAKIA

b: 8 Sep 43

After his leading screen roles as a boy, Václav continued acting. He had a few more movies: *Chlap jak hora* (60), *Posledni etapa* (62), *Bylo nas deset* (63).

55 Punta a čtyřlistek (Doggy and the Four)
56 Vzorný kinematograf Haška Jaroslava
    (Jaroslav Hašek's model cinema)
57 Malí medvědáři (Young bear-keepers)

Lee Aaker

USA

b: 25 Sep 43 (Inglewood, California)

This stocky, defiant little blond -- surname deriving from the Danish Aakjaer -- was a kind of pocket Poujouly [◇], or American Hannaford [◇], and just as likeable. His mother ran a dancing school in his home town, and he got spots on stage and TV.

Lee's first good chance came with the crippled title role of the short *Benjy*, and

he won two Critics' Awards for his work in *The Atomic City* and *Hondo*. (He also auditioned hereabouts for the kid in *Shane*, and was even told he'd got it, only to learn the following week that it had gone instead to Brandon DeWilde [◇].)

A characteristic Lee Aaker part was as the insufferable kidnappee in the 'Ransom of Red Chief' story in *O. Henry's Full House*, but he was also fine at keeping a stiff upper lip, as in *Desperate Search*. He did a lot of TV, most inescapably as Rusty, the dog's best friend, in ABC's 'Adventures of Rin Tin Tin' series (164 episodes between 1954 and 1958).

Lee made a momentary comeback in the musical *Bye Bye Birdie* (63), then worked as a TV production assistant. Finally he settled down contentedly as a professional carpenter.

47 The Governor of Louisiana
51 Los Alamos
   Something to Live For
52 The Atomic City
   Benjy
   Desperate Search
   The Greatest Show on Earth
   High Noon
   Monkey Business

My Son John
No Room for the Groom
O.Henry's Full House
53 Arena
   Hondo
   Jeopardy
   Take Me to Town
54 Destry
   The Raid
   Ricochet Romance

Lee's elder brother DEE AAKER appeared in some movies, such as *Mister Scoutmaster* (53), *Her Twelve Men* (54) and *Bigger Than Life* (56).

Stray dancer: Jimmy Urbain in Chiens perdus sans collier

Jimmy Urbain

FRANCE

b: 6 Dec 43 (Paris)

Many child actors have had some initial dance training. James Maurice Urbain is a rare example of a successful child actor who then went on to win even greater fame as a ballet dancer.

His father worked in the cinema, both as scriptwriter and production manager, and Jimmy came before the cameras when he was five. He stayed so for the next ten years, combining the cinema with some stage work — with Pierre Fresnay, for instance, in 'Bille en tête'.

Defiant: Lee Aaker in No Room for the Groom

His best screen roles came in Delannoy's *Chiens perdus sans collier* and in *Les misérables* (where he was the Gavroche).

Urbain danced in Roland Petit's 'Cyrano de Bergerac' in 1959. He was then in the Marquis de Cuevas' company 1960-62, with Golovine 1962-63, in the Grand Ballet Classique de France from 1965 and the Ballet Théâtre Contemporain from 1968. He won the Prix Nijinsky in Paris in 1966, and Gold Medals in Paris, Milan and Venice. He danced many of the star roles in the classic repertory, and created new ones both in France and Italy.

He later ran his own dance school at Angers.

49 On n'aime qu'une fois (You only love once)
  Le trésor de Cantenac
    (The treasure of Cantenac)
51 La poison (Poison)
52 Lettre ouverte à un mari
    (Open letter to a husband)
  La loterie du bonheur
    (The lottery of happiness)
53 Gamins de Paris (Paris kids)
  Tourments (Torment)
54 Leguignon guérisseur
    (Leguignon the healer)
55 Ces sacrées vacances
    (These bloody holidays)
  Chiens perdus sans collier
    (Lost dogs without collars -- FR/IT)
  Culottes courtes (Short pants)
  Les diaboliques (The fiends)
  Un jeudi à Paris (Thursday in Paris)
56 Les carottes sont cuites
    (The goose is cooked)
  Fric-frac en dentelles (Burglars in lace)
  The Happy Road (US)
  Miss Catastrophe
57 Les misérables
    (The poor and wretched -- FR/PL)
58 Les jeux dangereux (Dangerous games)

Billy Chapin

USA

b: 28 Dec 43 (Los Angeles)

Not many boy actors began their film careers by playing Gary Cooper's baby daughter, but this honour went in 1944 to the 22-day-old Billy Chapin in *Casanova Brown*. Drunk with self-importance, he

Down the river: Billy Chapin in The Night of the Hunter

then played Lana Turner's baby in *Marriage Is a Private Affair*.

Handsome Billy rested on his laurels for most of the next decade. In 1952 he at last got a plum part in a stage musical called 'Three Wishes for Jamie', which won him the New York Critics' Award as the year's most promising young actor. Then he did some TV work, and at nine returned to the cinema, with a good role as Dan Dailey's baseball-crazy son in *The Kid from Left Field*.

He had an attractively dreamy expression, and sometimes needed galvanising into action. This happened to him forcefully enough when Charles Laughton directed him in *The Night of the Hunter*. Laughton praised him afterwards as an 'acting technician', but the effect is

sometimes as if Billy were acting by numbers, responding to instructions from the director: strange, abrupt, startled-fawn reactions which are undoubtedly beautiful yet not quite real.

It hardly matters, though, in the nightmarish atmosphere of his escape and flight (with his bizarre, rag-doll-like little sister) from the richly evil Robert Mitchum. At the end, his three mounting cries of 'Don't!' when he sees the hated Mitchum struck down by the police, just like his father at the beginning of the story, are almost operatic in effect, and curiously shaking.

44 Casanova Brown
  Marriage Is a Private Affair
46 The Cockeyed Miracle
48 No Minor Vices

242

Vladimír Bejval

CZECHOSLOVAKIA

b: circa 1943

Vladimír was a droll little blond who provided comic relief -- and now and then solemnity -- in Czech films of the early Fifties.

Haunted: Vladimír Bejval in Konec strašidel

Brad Mora hoisted by Betty Hutton in Annie Get Your Gun, *with Keenan Wynn (left)*

Brad Mora

USA

b: circa 1943

Bradley Mora, the flaxen imp in the Davy Crockett hat in *Annie Get Your Gun*, later lengthened his Mora to Morrow. (His younger brother Scott acted under the name of Scotty Morrow.) Brad reappeared briefly in *Son of Flubber* (63).

Anthony Richmond

BRITAIN

b: circa 1943

Oddly enough this was not the famous British cameraman (born 1942) but a square-jawed little chap who played the lead in *Bang! You're Dead* and appeared in a few subsequent films of the Fifties. His last two, leading roles again, were for the Children's Film Foundation.

Aleš Kosnar

CZECHOSLOVAKIA

b: 2 Jan 44

Kosnar's dark, intense look was an asset to several Czech films. After his lead on home territory in *Doggy* he went Arabian

Illegal dogging: Aleš Košnar gives himself up in Punta a Čtyřlistek

for *Labakan*, based on one of Hauff's exotic fairy-tales.

55 Punta a čtyřlistek (Doggy and the Three)
56 Labakan
   Obušku z pytle ven! (Stick, start beating!)
57 Legenda o lasce (Legend of love)
   Škola otců (School for fathers)

Hiroshi Yamate

JAPAN

b: 17 Feb 44 (Yokohama Prefecture)

Yamate acted only as a child, mainly in period subjects filmed by the Toei company. In adult life he became an architect.

54 Beni kujaku (Red pickle)
   Mikazuki doji (Child of the crescent moon)
   Tsuigeki sanjuki (Attack by thirty soldiers)
56 Fuun Kuroshio maru
      (The Kuroshio in a storm)
57 Fuji ni tatsukage (In the shadow of Fuji)

58 Kotengu Kiritaro (Kiritaro the devil's son)
   Sonen tantei dan – tomei kaijin
      (Detective stories for boys)

Jacques Moullières

FRANCE

b: 15 Apr 44 (Villeneuve-le-Roi)

Jacques Moulière (as he was born) was a dark, fierce, sensitive boy who contributed memorably to French films of the Fifties. In streetwise or gypsyish parts he was matchless.

  After 1959 he appeared in at least one more feature film, *Un clair de lune à Maubeuge* (62). But Jacky Moulière – he reverted to his authentic name – now turned himself into a pop singer, making records as well as performing in live concerts and broadcasting.

53 La dot de Sylvie (Sylvie's dowry)
   Les fruits sauvages (Wild fruits)
54 Les amants du Tage
      (The lovers of the Tagus)
   Obsession
   Le sixième art (The sixth art)
55 L'affaire des poisons
      (The affair of the poisons)
   Les assassins du dimanche (Sunday killers)
   Chiens perdus sans collier
      (Lost dogs without collars)
   Coup dur chez les mous
      (Hard strike on a soft target)
   Le dossier noir (The black file)
   La meilleure part (The better part)
56 The Happy Road (US)
57 Les amants de demain (Tomorrow's lovers)
   Reproduction interdite
      (Copyright reserved)
   Sans famille (No relations)
58 Les jeux dangereux (Dangerous games)
59 Les loups dans la bergerie
      (Wolves in the sheepfold)

Yves-Marie Maurin

FRANCE

b: 19 Apr 44 (Toulouse)

Six Maurin siblings took to the stage and screen in the Forties and Fifties; but their mother – the singer Mado Maurin – married three times, and they came in three lots. By Mado's first husband, the sailor and writer Bourdeaux-Maurin de Kerguelen, there were Yves-Marie and his elder brother Jean-Pierre; by her second

Jacques Moullières in Chiens perdus sans collier

there was Patrick; and by her third there were three: Dominique, Jean-François and Marie-Véronique. Of the later Maurins, Dominique◊ and Jean-François◊ made the most impact on film.

The witty and whimsical little Yves-Marie made his Paris stage debut when he was five, in Mauriac's 'Le feu sur la terre', and soon afterwards was in his first movie, *Le traqué*, or *Gunman in the Streets*. Hereabouts also he began doing TV, and reciting poems in cafés and bars. Further plays included 'The Merry Wives of Windsor', 'Anna Karenina' and 'The Innocents', and he appeared at the Cirque d'Hiver in 'Davy Crockett et Jimmy Boy'.

He has continued to act tirelessly, on the stage in Sophocles, Molière, Racine, Giraudoux, Lorca, Sartre and Stoppard among others, as well as in his own production of Cocteau's 'La machine infernale'. His films as an adult include *La française et l'amour* (60), *Goodbye Again* (Aimez-vous Brahms? – US/FR 61), *Paris brûle-t-il?* (66), *Salut l'artiste* (FR/IT 73), *Les onze mille verges* (FR/IT) and *Collections privées* (79). And he has been in countless plays on TV.

He has also written poetry (praised by Montherlant), plays and novels, and latterly has been known simply as 'Yves-Marie'. This is a Renaissance Maurin.

50 Le traqué (The hunted man – FR/US)
   Trois télégrammes (3 telegrams)
51 Monsieur Fabre
   Le plus joli péché du monde
      (The loveliest sin in the world)
52 La jeune folle (The mad girl)
   Suivez cet homme (Follow that man)
53 Dortoir des grandes (Big girls' dormitory)
   La même route (The same way)
   Sidi-bel-Abès
54 Les diaboliques (The fiends)
55 Ces sacrées vacances
      (These bloody holidays)
56 En effeuillant la marguerite
      (He loves me, he loves me not)
   The Happy Road (US)
   Je reviendrai à Kandara
      (I shall return to Kandara)
57 Clara et les méchants
      (Clara and the naughty boys)
   Isabelle a peur des hommes
      (Isabelle's afraid of men)
59 Monsieur Suzuki

Yves-Marie's half-brother PATRICK MAURIN – born 26 Jan 47 – was in *Les espions* (57), besides much stage and TV work. For Dominique and Jean-François, see their separate entries.

Jean-Pierre Léaud

FRANCE

b: 5 May 44 (Paris)

His father, Pierre Léaud, was a film writer and a former actor and journalist, and his mother the actress Jacqueline Pierreux. Jean-Pierre's Antoine Doinel in Truffaut's *Les quatre cents coups* is rightly regarded as one of the greatest child performances of the screen. Its humour, insolence, anger and tragic emotion were fused into something extraordinary through the genius of Truffaut, for whom the story was thinly disguised autobiography.

Jean Cocteau, who admired *Les quatre cents coups* enormously, gave Jean-Pierre a small part in his farewell caprice *Le testament d'Orphée*.

Léaud continued to work for Truffaut – mentor and second father – and became the subject of a fascinating experiment in film-making: because Antoine Doinel didn't vanish for good, but reappeared in a series of films between 1962 and 1978, showing him growing older as Jean-Pierre Léaud was.

The first Doinel resurrection was in the 'Antoine and Colette' story of the omnibus film *L'amour à vingt ans* (62), in which he was reunited with his faithful buddy René (Patrick Auffay) from *Les quatre cents coups*, to compare notes about Life at 20. We later followed Antoine's progress from first love and first sex to marriage, fatherhood and infidelity in *Baisers volés* (68), *Domicile conjugal* (71) and *L'Amour en fuite* (78). They add up to a subtle, funny and touching story of half a life.

In between, Léaud acted for Jean-Luc Godard in *Pierrot le fou* (65), *Masculin féminin* (FR/SE 66), *Le gai savoir* (FR/DE 67), *La chinoise* (67) and *Week-end* (FR/IT 67) before resuming the mantle of Doinel, and playing leads for Truffaut also in *Les deux anglaises et le continent* (71) and *La nuit américaine* (73). In this last film, playing a *jeune premier*, Léaud gave a perfect demonstration of the peevish, twitchy but somehow endearing persona he had made his own on the screen.

Yves-Marie Maurin (right) with Georges Poujouly in Les diaboliques

Jean-Pierre Léaud (left) with Patrick Auffay in Les quatre cents coups

Professional: Léaud, circa 1959

He worked too, during the Sixties and Seventies, for Pasolini, Skolimowski, Glauber Rocha and other important directors.

Truffaut's untimely death in October 1984 had a devastating effect on Léaud, who became for a long time a recluse, unable to work. In a tragi-comic incident which Truffaut would have appreciated, he was convicted in May 1987 (but let off with a suspended sentence) for attacking an 80-year-old neighbour with a pot of

geraniums because she was driving him mad with her noise.

Purely coincidentally, one hopes, a recent film of Léaud's is called *I Hired a Contract Killer* (FI/SE 90).

58 Les quatre cents coups (The 400 blows)
59 Le testament d'Orphée
   (The testament of Orpheus)
60 Boulevard

Childhood – boyhood in particular – continued to evoke passionate identification from Truffaut, and scarcely one of his films is without a telling appearance from a boy, however fleeting. Before *Les quatre cents coups* came the two-wheeled prowlers of *Les mistons* (58), and after it. . .

Tirez sur le pianiste (60, Shoot the pianist): RICHARD KANAYAN ◇ as the kidnapped Fido.

Fahrenheit 451 (66): MARK LESTER ◇, making an early appearance as a mouselike schoolboy, and DENIS GILMORE ◇ as the reader of 'the Martian Chronicles'.

La mariée était en noir (68, The bride wore black): CHRISTOPHE BRUNOT as 'Cookie', child of one of Jeanne Moreau's revenge-victims.

Baisers volés (68, Stolen kisses): JEROME ZUCCA, to appear later in *Une belle fille comme moi*, and as the victimised hero of

Edouard Niermans' film *Anthracite* (72).

L'enfant sauvage (70, The wild child): JEAN-PIERRE CARGOL ◇.

Une belle fille comme moi (72, A lovely girl like me): JEROME ZUCCA as the schoolboy film-maker with a scoop on his hands.

La nuit américaine (73, Day for night): CHRISTOPHE VESQUE as the small Truffaut-surrogate stealing *Citizen Kane* stills from a cinema foyer.

L'histoire d'Adèle H. (75, The story of Adèle H.): DAVID FOOTE as the little boy under the shop counter.

L'argent de poche (76, Small change): GEORY DESMOUCEAUX as the moonstruck lover of LAURENT DEVLAEMINCK's mum, then later of Pascale Bruchon, a bit more his own age; PHILIPPE GOLDMANN as abused truant Julien, battered by his drunken mother; RICHARD GOLFIER who gets a disastrous haircut from CLAUDIO and FRANCK DELUCA; SEBASTIEN MARC as determinedly mute Oscar, and many others, right down to the toddler GRÉGORY, who falls to certain death from a ninth-floor window, but merely bounces.

L'homme qui aimait les femmes (77, The man who loved women): MICHEL MARTI playing the hero as a boy.

La chambre verte (78, The green room): PATRICK MALÉON as Truffaut's deaf-mute nephew.

L'amour en fuite (79, Love on the run): JULIEN DUBOIS as Jean-Pierre Léaud's son.

Le dernier métro (80, The last tube train): FRANCK PASQUIER as the caretaker's boy Jacquot, who becomes a child actor.

La femme d'à côté (81, The woman next door) – OLIVIER BECQUAERT as Gérard Depardieu's small son.

Richard O'Sullivan

BRITAIN

b: 7 May 44 (Chiswick, London)

His father was a mechanic, and Richard started elocution and dancing lessons when he was four. Three years later he made his film debut, playing Trevor Howard's son in *The Stranger's Hand*, and two years after that, in *Dangerous Exile*, he was royalty: a somewhat fictional version of poor Louis XVIII, happily escaped to Wales.

O'Sullivan, by now sporting his characteristic twisted smile, pressed on into a mixture of teenage rave-ups and grown-up weepies: *The Nun's Story* (60), *A Story of David* (60), *And Women Shall Weep* (60), *Spare the Rod* (61), *The Young Ones* (62), then *Cleopatra* (63, as Ptolemy), *Wonderful Life* (64), *A Dandy in Aspic* (68), *The Haunted House of Horror* (69) and so on into the Seventies.

Hereafter, though, his career lay largely in television. In comedy series like 'Doctor at Large', 'Doctor in Charge', 'Father, Dear Father', 'Man about the House', 'Robin's Nest', 'Me and My Girl' and 'Trouble in Mind', O'Sullivan became one of Britain's most popular light comedians of the wry, homely kind. As a change of scene, he also played the title role in a 'Dick Turpin' series.

Eavesdropping: Peter Asher in Isn't Life Wonderful!

Richard O'Sullivan takes a call in The Stranger's Hand

53 La mano dello straniero
  (The Stranger's Hand – IT/GB)
54 Dance, Little Lady
  The Dark Avenger
  Forever Is a Long Time
  The Green Scarf
  Make Me an Offer
55 The Secret
56 Dangerous Exile
  It's Great to be Young
  Jacqueline
  Raiders of the River *(serial)*
57 No Time for Tears
59 Carry On Teacher
  Witness in the Dark

Peter Asher

BRITAIN

b: 22 Jne 44 (London)

Peter, elder brother of the beautiful Jane Asher, went into films (though not the same ones) at about the same time she did. He was a dogged-looking little boy with curly red hair, and his biggest part was in *Isn't Life Wonderful!*

In 1961 he joined up with Gordon Waller to form the pop duo 'Peter and

Gordon' which enjoyed great success for a few years, and split up in 1968. Then, after working briefly as a scout for Apple Records (Jane was Paul McCartney's girl-friend at the time), Peter moved to Los Angeles, where he worked as producer for James Taylor, Linda Ronstadt and Bonnie Raitt among others.

52 Isn't Life Wonderful!
    The Planter's Wife
55 Escapade

Tinted: Ray in The Brave One

Michel Ray

BRITAIN/USA

b: 21 Jly 44 (Gerrards Cross)

Michel Ray Popper was his full name. His father was a London company director, and his mother had studied singing and drama in Vienna. Michel spoke French and German as well as English, and went to the Lycée Française in London. His languages, plus some skill in skiing, won him a central role in *The Divided Heart*, as a war orphan with German foster-parents. This in turn led to his being spotted by RKO scouts for the lead in *The Brave One*, as a little Mexican with a little bull, and the remainder of his leads were in the States.

With his dark curly hair and wide-set blue eyes, Michel was a picturesque child in his natural state. This was not enough for his Hollywood masters, who sometimes gilded the lily till he looked like a male Elizabeth Taylor.

After a four-year lay-off, Ray returned to British films for one more 'tinted' role, in *Lawrence of Arabia* (62).

54 The Divided Heart (GB)
56 The Brave One (US)
57 The Tin Star (US)
    Flood Tide (US)
58 The Space Children (US)

Frazer Hines

BRITAIN

b: 22 Sep 44 (Horsforth, Yorkshire)

He trained at the Corona Stage School in London, and was in show business from the age of eight.

After his teens, Hines continued in further films: *Go Kart Go!* (64), *The Last Valley* (70) and *Zeppelin* (71).

In the late Seventies he was cast as Joe in Yorkshire TV's new series 'Emmerdale Farm', little knowing that it would still be running, with him in it, more than 15 years later. He has latterly done little else.

55 On the Twelfth Day
    Stock Car
    Windfall
56 The Dodo
    The Long Arm
    Peril for the Guy
    The Weapon
    X – the Unknown
58 The Salvage Gang
59 Witness in the Dark
    The Young Jacobites (serial)

Michael Ande

WEST GERMANY

b: 5 Oct 44 (Bad Wiessee, Bavaria)

It was Julien Duvivier who discovered the curly-haired Michael Ande and put him in his Franco-German co-production *Marianne*.

Ande and Oliver Grimm◇ (his junior by 3½ years, but earlier on the scene) were the two golden children of German cinema in the Fifties. They were together in *Griff nach den Sternen*, and again (with

Michael Ande with Josef Egger in Der schönste Tag meines Lebens

Neapolitan: Ande in Don Vesuvio und das Haus der Strolche

Günther Hoffmann °) in R.A. Stemmle's *Majestät*, a trio-adventure in which Ande plays the young King Maximilian III of Slovaria, Grimm a child film-star and Hoffmann a hotel lift-boy. All three came well out of the romp.

In *Das Hirtenlied* Michael was a little goatherd, in the *Trapp* films (sadly lacking the verve of *The Sound of Music*) was the elder Trapp boy, and in *Der schönste Tag meines Lebens* ended up as a Wiener Sängerknabe. In *Skandal in Ischl* he was an Archduchess's ailing grandson, but in *Don Vesuvio* died a noble death as a Neapolitan urchin.

The sheer Peter-Pannishness of Michael Ande was well illustrated when at the age of 21 he played quite a convincing Jim Hawkins in a TV version of 'Treasure Island': *Die Schatzinsel* (DE/FR 66). His few cinema films in this period included *Verdammt zur Sünde* (64).

From 1976, after more TV work, he partnered Siegfried Löwitz in the long-running cop-series 'Der Alte'.

54 Marianne de ma jeunesse
   (Marianne of my youth – FR/DE)
55 Griff nach den Sternen
   (Reaching for the stars)
   Ich weiss, wofür ich lebe
   (I know what I'm living for)
56 Das Hirtenlied vom Kaiserthal

(Shepherd's song from the
   Kaiserthal – AT)
Die Stimme der Sehnsucht
   (The voice of longing)
Die Trapp-Familie (The Trapp Family)
Zärtliches Geheimnis (Tender secret)
57 El Hakim
Die Prinzessin von St Wolfgang
   (The Princess of St Wolfgang)
Der schönste Tag meines Lebens
   (The most beautiful day of
      my life – AT)
Skandal in Ischl (Scandal in Ischl – AT)
58 Der Arzt von Stalingrad
   (The doctor of Stalingrad)
Don Vesuvio und das Haus der Strolche
   (Don Vesuvio and the house
      of waifs – DE/IT)
Majestät auf Abwegen
   (His Majesty goes astray)
Die Trapp-Familie in Amerika
   (The Trapp Family in America)
59 Wenn die Glocken hell erklingen
   (When the bells ring brightly – AT)

Johnny Washbrook

USA

b: 16 Oct 44 (Toronto, Canada)

Washbrook, a ridin' boy, was mainly identified with the TV series 'My Friend Flicka', which ran on NBC during 1957-58. But he had been acting from the age of **six**, and by the time he was ten had notched up more than 200 live TV shows.

However, he made a few films, and later continued to act on stage and TV.

56 Laura
   These Wilder Years
57-8 'My Friend Flicka' (TVS)
58 Lonelyhearts
   The Space Children

Claudy Chapeland

FRANCE

b: 27 Nov 44 (Levallois-Perret, Seine)

50 Trois télégrammes (Three telegrams)
53 Le retour de don Camillo
   (The return of Don Camillo – FR/IT)
   Tourments (Torment)
54 Napoléon

55 Impasse des Vertus
   (Cul-de-sac of the Virtues)
   Mademoiselle de Paris
   Quatre veuves (Four widows)
56 Je reviendrai à Kandara
   (I shall return to Kandara)

Malcolm Brodrick

USA

b: 3 Dec 44 (New York)

Malcolm – who would have made a good brother for Peggy Ann Garner – was of English origins: his parents (father an engineer) came from Blackpool, and an uncle became Lord Mayor of Burnley. Having done modelling from the age of three, he was discovered by Jan Peerce, who required him to sing 'What Is a Boy?' on his radio show.

Young Brodrick made a strong mark on the New York stage, notably (in 1953) in 'The Desperate Hours'. He did a lot of stage and television work in the years that followed, and it's a great pity that he only had one sizeable screen role.

In *Man on Fire*, as a cool, humorous boy who is gradually being torn apart by the manoeuvres of his parents' divorce, Brodrick is painfully real and touching.

Torn apart: Malcolm Brodrick in Man on Fire

Rural reproach: Nuţă Chirlea and Nicolae Tomazoglu in Ciulinii Bărăganului

Bing Crosby, to his credit, shirks none of the ugliness and indignity of the father's well-written part.

57 Man on Fire
   That Night

Nuţă Chirlea

ROMANIA

b: circa 1944

Chirlea was a fine, reproachful presence in this harrowing drama of rural poverty, directed in Romania by the French socialist Louis Daquin. At first sight it's about as far from his *Nous les gosses* of 1941 as could be imagined – but the themes of endurance and solidarity underlie both.

It was Nuţă Chirlea's only film. After graduating from high school, he worked as a driver at the National Film Production Centre. More recently, he returned to his native village in the Teleorman district.

57 Ciulinii Bărăganului
   (The thistles of Baragan)

Pinaki Sen Gupta

INDIA

b: circa 1944

Young Gupta played Apu in the central film of Satyajit Ray's great trilogy. (The watchful little Apu of the opening film, *Pather panchali* – 1955, Song of the Road – WAS SUBIR BANERJI.)

During the unhappy sojourn in Benares,

Gupta's Apu roams the city while his ailing father works as a prayer-caller on the banks of the Ganges and his timid, ailing mother stays at home washing, cooking and scrubbing. He is happiest feeding monkeys in a temple.

56 Aparajito (The unvanquished)
58 Jalsaghar (The music room)

Stefan Haar

WEST GERMANY

b: circa 1944

55 Suchkind 312 (Missing child no.312)
56 Das Donkosakenlied
   (The Don Cossack song)
   Tierarzt Dr Vlimmen
   (Dr Vlimmen, veterinary surgeon)
57 Das einfache Mädchen (The simple girl)

Günter Hoffmann

WEST GERMANY

b: circa 1944

This curly-haired blond, whose mother worked as a presser in Berlin, made a fine foil for the smaller Oliver Grimm ◇ in *Mein Vater, der Schauspieler* and *Majestät auf Abwegen*; but the fun ended in *Die Brücke*, where he was one of Hitler's boy soldiers defending a doomed bridge.

He appeared again in an Austrian film of 1963, *Die lustigen Vagabunden*.

Leif Nilsson

SWEDEN

b: circa 1944

Vova Siluyanov

USSR

b: circa 1944

The beefy Volodya Siluyanov had his biggest roles in *V 6 ráno na letišti* – known in Russia as *Udivitelnoye voskresene* – and in *Lyuboi tsenoi*.

John Pike

BRITAIN

b: 7 Jan 45

John Pike, a doggedly handsome Scot, played in many British films of the 1950s, frequently for the Children's Film Foundation.

He continued in *And Women Shall Weep* (60), the serials *The Young Jacobites* (60) and *Four Winds Island* (61), *Live It Up* (63) and *Reach for Glory* (63).

John's younger brother PETER PIKE – born 17 Jly 51 – was in *The Challenge* (59), *Hand in Hand* (60), *The Pirates of Blood River* (61), *The Heroes of Telemark* (65) and *Drop Dead, Darling* (66).

Jeremy Bulloch

BRITAIN

b: 16 Feb 45 (Market Harborough)

The amiable sandy-haired Bulloch was the son of a Scottish electrician, and attended the Corona Stage School in London from the age of twelve. He first won fame on

On your marks: Jeremy Bulloch (left) and John Pike in The Cat Gang

TV as Philip Copper in the serial 'The Newcomers'. When he was 15 he played Bob Cherry in the 'Billy Bunter' series.

Jeremy Bulloch remained highly employable: never a star, but a good, reliable supporting actor. Over the next few years he was in *Spare the Rod* (61), *Play It Cool* (62), *The Devil's Agent* (62), *Summer Holiday* (62), *All in Good Time* (64), *The Idol* (66) and *Money-Go-Round* (66).

Since then his films have included *Las Leandras* (ES 69), *The Virgin and the Gypsy* (69), *Mary, Queen of Scots* (71), *O Lucky Man!* (73), *The Spy Who Loved Me* (77), *The Empire Strikes Back* (US 80), *Return of the Jedi* (US 83) and *Octopussy* (83). On TV, widening his usual scope, he has played a gay doctor in the series 'Agony' (81) and a slippery villain in the series 'Chocky' (84).

59 The Cat Gang
   Crow's Nest
   The Dawn Killer *(serial)*
   The Young Jacobites *(serial)*
60 Caught in the Net
   A French Mistress

Bulloch's chubby son CHRISTIAN – born 22 Nov 65 – also became a useful performer, with a lead in the children's film *The Boy Who Never Was* (79).

Jon Whiteley

BRITAIN

b: 19 Feb 45 (Monymusk, Aberdeenshire)

In 1951 the six-year-old Jon, son of a village schoolmaster, won a prize for verse-speaking at the Aberdeen Music Festival. A BBC van visited his school, and Jon repeated his recitation for the benefit of Scottish radio listeners. It was overheard by a talent scout, who reported back to studios in the south – and so Britain discovered one of its most unusual and likeable child actors.

Charming as his appearance was – a serious, square little face with watchful features beneath a tangle of blond hair – Jon's most precious attribute was his beautifully old-world Aberdeenshire

Whiteley in The Kidnappers

voice: melodious, quaintly measured, almost pedantic. No child's voice quite like it had been heard in the cinema before, and it added a special quality to the parts he had to play, which were in general of the John Howard Davies ◇ type (delicate child thrown into tough or harrowing situations).

The Whiteley manner was perfectly suited to *The Kidnappers*, conversing with an even smaller Scot, Vincent Winter ◇, over the ownership of an unidentified but hearty baby they had stumbled on. 'Is it our babby now, Harry?'

asks Winter. 'It's mine,' says Whiteley with sweet solemnity, 'but you can have a loan of it while I've other business. You can feel it. Go on, feel it, if you crave to.' (There is later a wonderful argument about a name for the baby. Winter favours 'Rover'.)

An attractive TV remake of *The Kidnappers* – now called *The Little Kidnappers*, which had been the original film's US release title anyway – was shown in 1990, with two very similar-looking children (Leo Wheatley and Charles Miller) as the two boys.

Old-world: Whiteley in Moonfleet

In Jon Whiteley's other roles (a frightened runaway in *Hunted*, a puzzled orphan in *Moonfleet*, a supposed murderer in *The Weapon*, and the affection-starved son of a diplomat in *The Spanish Gardener*) his sober charm was used with varying success. But he was always a pleasure to watch and listen to.

Whiteley got a degree at Oxford, wrote books on Ingres and the Pre-Raphaelites, and became curator of an Oxford college art collection.

52 Hunted
53 The Kidnappers
55 Moonfleet (US)
56 The Weapon
   The Spanish Gardener

Richard Eyer

USA

b: 6 May 45 (Santa Monica, Cal.)

The small, snub-nosed Richard – son of an experimental mechanic at North American Aircraft – was the elder of two acting brothers, and a late recruit to the *Kettles* series. He was a pugnacious little number, a sort of brunet answer to Lee Aaker ◇. After good featured parts in films like *The Desperate Hours* and *Friendly Persuasion*, he had leads in *The Invisible Boy* and *Johnny Rocco*, and played the Genie in *The Seventh Voyage of Sinbad*.

Later, in his mid-20s, Richard Eyer had a supporting part in the 1971 'Lassie' TV series.

53 It Happens Every Thursday
54 Ma and Pa Kettle at Home
55 Come Next Spring
   The Desperate Hours
   The Kettles in the Ozarks
   Sincerely Yours
56 Canyon River
   Friendly Persuasion
   Overnight Haul
   Slander
57 Bail Out at 43,000
   The Invisible Boy
58 Fort Dobbs
   Johnny Rocco
   The Seventh Voyage of Sinbad
60 Hell to Eternity

Richard's more solemn-looking younger brother ROBERT EYER – born 6 May 48 – was featured in *The Dark at the Top of the Stairs* (60) and *Back Street* (61).

Tim Hovey

USA

b: 19 Jne 45 (Los Angeles)
d: 9 Sep 89 (Watsonville, Cal.)

Tiny Tim, a child seemingly endowed with double-jointed dimples, not only talked but read at an alarmingly early age. His father owned a sports shop in the San Fernando Valley, and took little interest in offers to get Tim into the movies. But

Quaker oat: Richard Eyer in Friendly Persuasion

Double-jointed dimples: Tim Hovey and eponym in Toy Tiger

Rocket and module: Jock Mahoney and Hovey in
Slim Carter

eventually the boy went to a studio audition and landed a small part in the 'Lassie' series. At a subsequent audition he went one better and was cast in the plum role of a military academy's smallest cadet in *The Private War of Major Benson.*

This set the tone of cuteness which was to dog all his major parts, though not that of a troubled child of Joan Crawford in *Queen Bee.* In *Slim Carter* he was teamed with ex-stuntman hero Jock Mahoney.

Both Tim and his parents were very relaxed about his career, which came about with almost no effort. When he was 15 he simply decided to stop acting, although he'd enjoyed it well enough and had just been offered a part on Broadway in 'Critic's Choice'.

After Jesuit high school and study at the University of Colorado he applied to

join the Air Force, but was rejected as being too small. For the next few years he travelled widely in Europe, Asia and Africa, then in the Seventies became sound engineer with The Grateful Dead and Kingfish.

Well-invested earnings from his four years of stardom saved him from the need to work too intensively, and Hovey was said to be a notably unbitter and untwisted man. He nevertheless died of a drug overdose.

55 The Private War of Major Benson
   Queen Bee
56 Everything But the Truth
   Toy Tiger
57 Man Afraid
   Slim Carter
58 Money, Women and Guns

Kim Charney

USA

b: 2 Aug 45

54 The Bounty Hunter
   The Long, Long Trailer
   Overland Pacific
   Pushover
   Ricochet Romance
   Run For Cover
   Suddenly
55 Bobby Ware Is Missing
   Foxfire
56 The Bottom of the Bottle
   The Guns of Fort Petticoat
   The Mole People
   The Werewolf
57 Drango
   Girl in the Woods
   New Day at Sundown

58 Crash Landing
   Man from God's Country
   Quantrill's Raiders
59 Hey Boy! Hey Girl!
62 How the West Was Won

Master Mohan

INDIA

b: 4 Sep 45 (Madras)

52 Dharma devata (God of religion)
   Pelli chesi choodu
53 Pempudu koduku
54 Koondu killi
   Manohara (Winner of hearts)

Bibhu Bhattacharjee

INDIA

b: September 1945 (Jharia)

Master Bibhu, as he was known in the cinema, was brought up in Calcutta.

51 Bhakta Raghunath
   Prahlad
   Pratiyabartan (The return)
52 Andhi
   Bindur chheley
   Nil darpan
53 Dhruba
54 Agni pariksha (Tested by fire)
   Bakul
   Ladies seat
55 Prashna
56 Mahakavi Girish Chandra

Harry Kratz

AUSTRIA

b: 5 Nov 45

Some years after his prime as an Austrian child star, Kratz became a successful Viennese doctor.

55 Seine Tochter ist der Peter
   (Peter is his daughter)
   Die Sennerin von St Kathrein
   (The dairymaid of St Kathrein)
56 Försterliesl (Liesl the forester's daughter)
   Ihr Korporal (Her corporal – AT/DE)
57 Der Wilderer vom Silberwald
   (The poacher of Silver Forest – DE)

   Wie schön, dass es Dich gibt
   (Thank God for you)
58 So ein Millionär hat's schwer
   (Tough on a millionaire like that)
   Der veruntreute Himmel
   (Heaven embezzled)

Kevin Coughlin

USA

b: 13 Dec 45 (New York)
d: 19 Jan 76 (North Hollywood)

Kevin was a fair, delicate-looking boy, good at conveying anguish. He had modelled from the age of three, and from his seventh birthday began a four-year stint on the CBS soap 'I Remember Mama'. Thereafter he did much stage and TV work.

He had melodrama in *Storm Center* and crude comedy in *Happy Anniversary*, but in between was the little boy who shot Tony Curtis in *The Defiant Ones*.

He returned to films in his twenties in *Duel at Diablo* (65), *Mary Jane* (68), *Wild in the Streets* (68), *The Young Runaways* (68) and *The Gay Deceivers* (69). In this deplorable last film he starred as a young draft-dodger posing as a homosexual.

Kevin Coughlin in Storm Center

Poor Coughlin wasn't to have many more chances. In January 1976, having got out of his car to clean the windscreen, he was knocked over and killed by a hit-and-run driver.

56 Storm Center
58 The Defiant Ones
59 Happy Anniversary

Dalenius in Luffaren och Rasmus

Eskil Dalenius

SWEDEN

b: 28 Dec 45 (Stockholm)

The frail, thoughtful little Dalenius made a most endearing 'Rasmus' in three children's comedies of the Fifties, based on radio plays by Astrid Lindgren.

53 Mästerdetektiven och Rasmus
   (The master-detective and Rasmus)
55 Luffaren och Rasmus
   (The tramp and Rasmus)
56 Rasmus, Pontus och Toker

Pierre Devis

FRANCE

b: circa 1945

The dark, elegant hero of Franju's short romance *La première nuit*, set in the Paris Métro, certainly deserves his place here, though his role consists of nothing more than looking lovesick.

Following a mysterious little fair-haired girl into the Underground and into a series of trains, then getting shut in for the night, Devis is the moonstruck image of first love, dignified but dazed. It's a most endearing and poetic little film, and from Franju's point of view a hymn of love to the Métro.

Twenty-two years later, in *Le dernier métro*, Truffaut borrowed a clip of a few seconds from *La première nuit* as a linking shot: at a junction of two Métro passages, you can just see Master Devis emerging from the crowd and beginning to walk towards the camera.

58 La première nuit (The first night)

Romi Kapoor

INDIA

b: circa 1945

Master Romi had leads in *Munna* and in Sadajiv Rao's *Hum panchi ek dal ke*. In *Munna* – directed by Khwaja Ahmad Abbas, Indian pioneer of social realism – he was touchingly intense as a kind of casteless Oliver Twist who falls in with an Indian Fagin.

53 Dil-e-nadan (The narve heart)
    Shole (Sparks)
54 Mastana (The carefree one)
    Munna (The lost child)
    Toote khilone (Broken toys)
57 Ab Dilli door nahin (Not far to Delhi)
    Dushman (The enemy)
    Hum panchi ek dal ke
       (We birds of one branch)
58 Do phool (Two flowers)
60 Maa baap (Parents)

Richard Palmer

BRITAIN

b: circa 1945

The distinguished-looking Richard was, briefly, Britain's best boy actor at the end of the 1950s – playing leads like Jim Hawkins and Ronnie Winslow on TV – but apart from the lead in *Treasure at the*

Rope-trick: Romi Kapoor in Munna

Mill (for the Children's Film Foundation) he didn't get enough opportunity in the cinema.

He abandoned his acting career, and many years later was working for IBM.

57 Five on a Treasure Island *(serial)*
    Saint Joan (GB/US)
    Treasure at the Mill
59 Whirlpool
60 A French Mistress
    Linda

György Weiser

HUNGARY

b: circa 1945

György, a strong but haunted-looking boy, was striking in the title role of *Dani*, an unhappy and rather unusual story of an abandoned child whom, ten years later, neither his natural mother nor his foster-mother really want. Threatened with boarding school, Dani runs away and collides with a train, which knocks sense into all of them.

55 A szánkó (The sledge)
56 Szakadak (Precipice)
    Több, mint jatek (More than a game)
57 Dani
58 Aranybalta (The golden axe)
    Langok (Flames)
    A sóbálvány (Pillar of salt)

In nearly all these films (though not in *Dani*) György's brother ANTAL WEISER is also in the cast. In 1958 Antal has a big role of his own in *Bogáncs*, a story about a black sheepdog called Thistle. Neither Weiser seems to have acted after that.

Colin Petersen

AUSTRALIA/BRITAIN

b: 24 Mar 46 (Kingaroy)

Sandy, freckly and brown-eyed, the nine-year-old Queenslander was a happy choice for Anthony Kimmins' *Smiley*, an adventure set in the Australian bush. (By the time Kimmins made his follow-up film, *Smiley Gets a Gun*, in Australia two years

György Weiser (right) in Dani

Healthy waif: Colin Petersen in A Cry from the Streets

later, Petersen wasn't available and was replaced by the less individual KEITH CALVERT.)

Colin moved to Britain for his films directed by Wolf Rilla and Lewis Gilbert, and in these his Australian-ness was toned down, though he remained an engaging and touching child.

In the Sixties he joined the Beegees pop group as their drummer. Later he returned to Australia, and was seen in a bit part in *Barney* (AU 76).

56 Smiley (GB)
57 The Scamp (GB)
58 A Cry from the Streets (GB)

George Winslow

USA

b: 3 May 46 (Los Angeles)

Art Linkletter's 'People Are Funny' show was a TV favourite. A viewer called Karl Wentzlaff wrote to him asking if he'd like to interview a little boy with a deep, deep voice. Art replied that he would, and the tiny George Wentzlaff appeared on the show dressed in overalls and dubbing himself Casey Jones. With his droll, solemn manner he was the hit of the season.

Cary Grant happened to be watching the show, and rang Norman Taurog suggesting George for *Room for One More*. George joined the cast. His surname was anglicised, and he became known to the public as George 'Foghorn' Winslow. His wasn't an assumed voice like Froggy Laughlin's ◇; it was simply the way he talked, with dignity and a laid-back sense of humour. George, Marc Best wrote, was 'an individualist who never thought of himself as a child.' He was a boy of few but pithy words.

He made countless returns to Art Linkletter's shows on TV and radio, and also appeared with the Nelsons. In the mid-Fifties he starred in the series 'Dear Phoebe'.

In the cinema he became a valuable star for two or three years, acting opposite

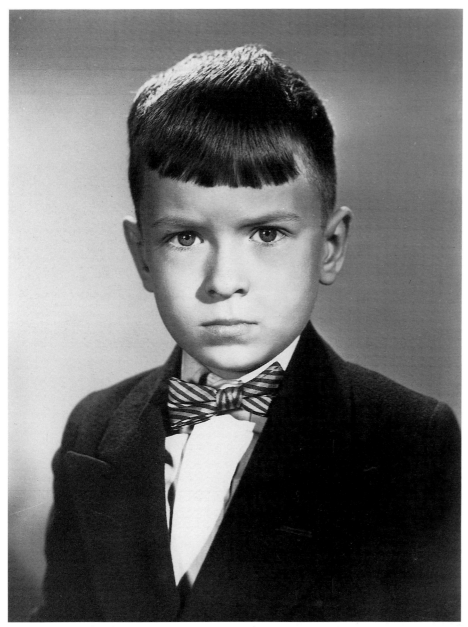

Pithy: George Winslow

Johnny Crawford

USA

b: 26 May 46 (Los Angeles)

John Ernest Crawford – not to be confused with the adult actor John Crawford, whose career overlaps with his – came of powerful showbiz stock. His grandfather was a Broadway producer and music publisher, his father a film editor and his elder brother an actor. (They were all called Robert. A younger brother was called Corydon, which doesn't happen to everyone.) John also had musical grandparents on his mother's side.

He began appearing on TV at the age of four, and was one of Walt Disney's early 'Mouseketeers': as was PAUL PETERSON of *Houseboat* (58) and 'The Donna Reed Show' – later cashiered for, in his own words, 'conduct unbecoming a mouse'.

Johnny Crawford became a household face as Chuck Connors' son Mark in ABC's Western series 'The Rifleman' (1957-59). He was a slim, brown-eyed, shy-looking ridin' boy somewhat in the Buzzy Henry ◇ mould, but more cheerful than soulful.

Around 1960 Crawford emerged as a singer, with teenage hits like 'Cindy's Birthday', 'Your Nose Is Gonna Grow' and 'Rumors' between 1961 and 1964. He continued to act in films, though: *Indian Paint* (64), *The Restless Ones* (66), *Village of*

Cary Grant, Richard Widmark and Clifton Webb, and paying court to Marilyn Monroe in *Gentlemen Prefer Blondes*. He was in fact a striking little boy, with fine, rather severe eyes, capable of exerting considerable moral authority. He was unique, and because he was straight-faced and never ingratiating, his comedy has worn very well.

By the late 1950s George was approaching his teens, and self-consciousness ambushed his poise. He later spent four years in the Navy, then took up photography. His voice, Richard Lamparski reports, is now quite unremarkable.

51 Room for One More
52 Monkey Business
My Pal Gus
53 Gentlemen Prefer Blondes
Mister Scoutmaster
54 The Rocket Man
55 Artists and Models
56 Rock, Pretty Baby
57 An Affair to Remember
58 Summer Love
Wild Heritage

Johnny Crawford in Courage of Black Beauty

the Giants (66), *El Dorado* (67). In 1969 he starred in a short called *The Resurrection of Broncho Billy*, and had leading roles in *The Naked Ape* (73) and *Dynamite Woman* (76).

50 Lonely Hearts Bandits
53 Conquest of Cochise
   Serpent of the Nile
   Slaves of Babylon
54 Captain Kidd and the Slave Girl
57 Courage of Black Beauty
   'The Rifleman' *(TVS, till 1959)*
58 The Space Children
60 Exodus
   I Aim at the Stars (US/DE)

Koji Shitara

JAPAN

b: 4 Jne 46 (Yamagata Prefecture)

He was a sensitive child, memorable as the jealous little hero of Gosho's *Yellow Crow* who feels dispossessed by a repatriated father and a new baby. He was also the elder brother (of Masahiro Shimazu ◊) in *Ohayo*, Ozu's brilliant re-think of his more painful *I Was Born, But . . .* of 1932. (The casus belli is now TV-watching, with the earlier boys' hunger-strike replaced by a silence-strike, but the critique of adults' ingratiating silliness is no less to the point.)

Silent protest: Koji Shitara (left) and Masahiko Shimazu in Ohayo

After a couple of late films – *Onna girai* (64) and *Ohanahan* (66) – Shitara turned from acting to music. He graduated from music school in 1969, and studied in Los Angeles from 1971-75.

52 Ochazuke no aji (Green tea with rice)
   Sono yo no tsuma (That night's wife)
   Yume to shiriseba
      (If I knew it was a dream)
53 Aijo ni tsuite (About love)
57 Kiiroi karasu (Yellow crow)
59 Ohayo (Good morning)
60 Akibiyori (Late autumn)
62 The Big Wave (US/JP)

Takao Zushi

JAPAN

b: 25 Jne 46 (Osaka Prefecture)

After his childhood Zushi continued in the profession, as a supporting actor in Toho films, and with much TV work. His later films included *Sara no mon* (64), *Ousho* (73), *Okita soushi* (74) and *Akuma no temariuta* (77).

56 Kurama tengu – goyo toihen
      (The curious robbery)
58 Kusabue no oka (The grass flute on the hill)
   Noren (The Japanese curtain)
   Tsuzuri kata kyodai
      (Brother and sister like writing)

Brooding: Burlyayev in Ivanovo detstvo

Kolya Burlyayev

USSR

b: 3 Aug 46

Nikolai Burlyayev was one of the screen's most remarkable child actors. His best part, unquestionably, was as the hero of Andrei Tarkovski's early film *Ivan's Childhood* – a twelve-year-old orphan who sees his mother and sister gunned down by Germans, and finds a meaning in life by infiltrating enemy lines as a spy during World War Two.

The frail Ivan is no shrinking violet: returning from an assignment, he demands to be put in immediate touch with headquarters, and throws an impressive tantrum when lower ranks try to head him off. Only when his friend the captain arrives to confirm Ivan's star status does the boy relax at all. Burlyayev, skinny, brooding and old before his time, is wonderful in these scenes, allowing the child in him to peep only occasionally through the grim mask of revenge. He's less well suited to the pseudo-idyllic flashback scenes of sun, sand and rolling apples.

Visionary: Burlyayev in Ivanovo detstvo

Tugomir Štiglic

YUGOSLAVIA

b: 8 Nov 46 (Ljubljana)

Though he looks considerably older, the leggy hero of *Dolina miru* – and son of its director, France Štiglic – was only nine when it was filmed. Tugo played a Slovenian boy, in the closing phase of World War Two, who befriends a little girl of German parentage (Evelyne Wohlfeiler) and, later, a shot-down American pilot (John Kitzmiller). This mini-League of Nations tries its best to survive, and two of the three do.

Tugo Štiglic – who got the part on merit, surviving auditions in competition with others, despite being the director's son – was an athletic boy with a finely intent brown-eyed face, and it's sad that no more parts came his way. However, he went on to graduate in the History of Fine Arts at Ljubljana University; then, returning to films, worked as assistant to several Slovenian directors.

Tarkovski used him again in *Andrei Rubloff* (66), as the youth who casts the bell – Nikolai's personality was just as intransigent – and Tarkovski reported that though brilliant, he was also wilful and exhausting to handle. Then he was in *Ot nechego delat* (70), and had leads in *Stihove* (BG 70), *Legenda* (PL 71) and *Proverka na dorogakh* (71) before playing Dostoyevski's gambler in *Igrok* (72). He played in and directed one episode of *Poshekhon* (75), graduating in the same year from the state faculty of film direction.

After some time out of films he re-appeared as the hero of *Voyenno-polevoi roman* (84), and two years later directed himself in the title role of *Lermontov*.

61 Sud sumashchedshikh
    (Judgment of the mad)
    Malchik i golub (The boy and the dove)
62 Ivanovo detstvo (Ivan's childhood)
    Bez strakha i upryoka
    (Without fear or reproach)
    Vstupleniye (Beginning)
63 Strogaya igra (Hard play)

Tugo Štiglic as the hero of Dolina miru

In the mid-Seventies he began directing short films of his own, and also directed for TV. His first feature was a children's film called *Leto u školjci* (Summer in a seashell), made in 1985. Its success made a sequel possible.

56 Dolina miru (Valley of peace)

Bobby Clark, 1956

Bobby Clark

USA

b: 1946 (Seattle, Washington)

Bobby is the little dark boy at the start of *Invasion of the Body Snatchers*, terrified of his mother whom he no longer recognises. (He calms down, of course, when he himself is 'podded'.)

There had been an earlier juvenile Bobby Clark in Hollywood – a ridin' boy of twelve or so who had been active in 1939: in *Trigger Smith*, in the serial *Overland with Kit Carson*, and in the *Sagebrush Family* series. The unrelated Bobby II was born about 20 years later, and was acting by the time he was seven.

Gene Kelly chose him as co-star in his French-based vehicle *The Happy Road*, and paired him with Brigitte Fossey, five years after *Jeux interdits*. The other French children in the film are led by Jimmy Urbain ◇, Jacques Moullières ◇ and Yves-Marie Maurin ◇.

Bobby Clark also starred as the hero's son in the TV series 'Casey Jones'.

54 There's No Business Like Show Business
55 Bring Your Smile Along
   Invasion of the Body Snatchers
   Ransom!
56 The Happy Road
   Rebel in Town
57 'Casey Jones' (TVS)
   Destination 60,000
   Gun Duel in Durango

Joselito Jiménez

SPAIN

b: 1946 (Jaén)

This famous boy warbler of the 1950s – Spain's answer to Italy's Robertino Loreti ◇ – came from an Andalusian peasant family, and had his first performing success in a Valencian fiesta. He made his national debut on radio, then appeared in public concerts with Luis Mariano, who helped him to get recording contracts in France, with further radio and TV spots.

Since he was a confident, good-looking child, and by now widely popular, his introduction to the large screen was inevitable. The vehicle, *The Little Nightingale*, was directed by Antonio del Amo, who would direct him eight more times over the next seven years. (The Mexican venture *El caballo blanco* was Joselito's only non-Amo film before 1964.) A drowsy numbness would pain almost anyone's sense at the stream of full, throaty Ds that followed.

The Spanish and Mexican industries and publics are so closely linked that a get-together seemed desirable between him and his junior, the Mexican child idol, Cesareo 'Pulgarcito' Quezadas. ◇ This was effected in 1959 with *Joselito's Adventures in America*, a reunion following in 1966 with *El falso heredero*.

Joselito's co-vagabond in *Los dos golfillos* was another successful Spanish child actor, PABLO ALONSO, who was also seen in *Dos años de vacaciones* (62), *Héros sans retour* (62 – BE/IT/ES/DE) and *Vacaciones para Ivette* (64).

José Jiménez, now too big to be diminutive, continued in Spanish films till his

mid-20s: *El secreto de Tomy* (63, ES/FR), *Loca juventud* (64, ES/FR/IT), *La vida nueva de Pedrito de Andia* (65), *El falso heredero* (66, ES/MX) and *Prisionero en la ciudad* (68).

56 El pequeño ruiseñor (The little nightingale)
57 Saeta del ruiseñor (Song of the nightingale)
58 El ruiseñor de las cumbres
   (Nightingale of the peaks)
   Escucha mi canción (Listen to my song)
59 El pequeño coronel (The little colonel)
   Aventuras de Joselito en America
   (Joselito's adventures in America
   – ES/MX)
60 Los dos golfillos (Two little vagabonds)
61 Bello recuerdo (Sweet memory)
   El caballo blanco
   (The white horse – ES/MX)

Richard Williams in Heart of a Child

Richard Williams

BRITAIN

b: 1946

The pretty but somewhat expressionless Master Williams had two or three leading parts, most notably in the Tyrolean setting of *Heart of a Child*, where with the aid of a photogenic St Bernard he triumphs over the brutality of his father (Donald Pleasence).

57 Action of the Tiger
58 Heart of a Child
59 The Child and the Killer
61 The Greengage Summer

Lyonya Babich

USSR

b: circa 1946

All Babich's roles were leading ones.

58 Flagi na bashnyakh
  (Flags on the towers)
  Sashko
59 Malchiki (Boys)
61 Morskaya chaika (The seagull)

Steen Flensmark

DENMARK

b: circa 1946

Nearly 30 years before his international triumph with *Babette's Feast*, the young Gabriel Axel was chosen to direct the first filming of Denmark's most popular early-teen novel, *Flemming og Kvik*. Its author, Gunnar Jørgensen, was the much-loved headmaster of one of Copenhagen's leading boys' schools.

A former pupil of his, 13-year-old Steen Flensmark, was chosen by Axel to incarnate the honest and intelligent but rebellious Flemming, who takes strong exception to the methods of two of his teachers. He made a fine job of it, and repeated his characterisation in the sequel, *Flemming på kostskole*. In both films his lively friend Kvik was played by PER GECKLER.

Rebellious: Steen Flensmark in Flemming og Kvik

Vova Guskoff and Anya Kamenkova in Devochka ishet otsa

A foreign interloper in *Flemming på kostskole* was the then famous Italian boy soprano ROBERTINO (Roberto Loreti, b: 22 Oct 46), for whom a situation was engineered to deliver his popular rendering of the 'Ave Maria'. Robertino, a nightingale with all the soulfulness of a pocket battleship, had much earlier piped his way into *Le petit monde de Don Camillo* (FR/IT 51), and was to be in the 1961 Austrian film *Im Schwarzen Rössl* (Black Horse Inn). He was on the whole better heard than seen.

60 Flemming og Kvik
  (Flemming and Quick)
61 Flemming på kostskole
  (Flemming at boarding school)
62 Prinsesse for en dag (Princess for a day)

Vova Guskoff

USSR

b: circa 1946

The stocky, fair-haired Volodya Guskoff had no less than six leading roles in his eight films, a degree of stardom unheard of since the earliest days of the Soviet cinema. (Though he doesn't have the title role in *The Star Child* – based, surprisingly, on an Oscar Wilde story.)

A characteristic Guskoff performance was in *Mikolka the Locomotive*, as a little boy living by a railway station in Byelorussia around the time of the October Revolution – protesting against the station-master's ill-treatment of his grandfather, setting free imprisoned workers, fighting with the partisans.

54 Dva druga (Two friends)
56 Mikolka, paravoz
  (Mikolka the locomotive)
  Seri razboinik (The grey bandit)
57 Zvyozdni malchik (The Star Child)
59 Devochka ishet otsa
  (A little girl looks for her father)
  Golubiye Pestsi Peti Sinyavina
  (Petya Sinyavin's Blue Foxes)
60 Prostaya istoriya (A simple story)
61 Zelyoni patrul (The green patrol)

Richard Kanayan

FRANCE

b: circa 1946

This dark, scruffy little cove had a long moment of glory in the first classroom scene of *Les 400 coups*, making a total write-off of his exercise book, spattering it with ink-blots and tearing out page after page. Truffaut, sensing a kindred spirit, cast him in *Shoot the Pianist* (in a Franco-Armenian duo) as Charles Aznavour's kidnapped kid brother Fido. Kanayan is as splendid as ever.

He next tried unsuccessfully to make a career as a music-hall singer. Finally he became a tailor.

58 Les quatre cents coups (The 400 blows)
60 Tirez sur le pianiste (Shoot the pianist)

Oscar Orlegui

ARGENTINA

b: circa 1946

He and the younger CARLOS LOPEZ MONET were two of the children chosen by the Argentine Leopoldo Torre-Nilsson for his films *La caida* and *El secuestrador*. They were performers of considerable sophistication – Orlegui romantic and slightly sinister, Monet curly and cheeky. Orlegui had one more film in the same year.

58 La caida (The fall)

He nacido en Buenos Aires
(Born in Buenos Aires)
El secuestrador (The kidnapper)

Alain Dekock

FRANCE

b: 10 Jan 47 (Paris)

Alain – his surname sometimes spelt 'Dekok', 'Decock', etc. – played on the professional stage, once as the divine emissary in 'Waiting for Godot'.

His big screen chance came in *Le petit garçon de l'ascenseur*, as a 14-year-old lift-boy at a posh Monte Carlo hotel. With adult help, he wins a newspaper competition whose prize is a weekend in the same hotel's Royal Suite. He then makes rather an exhibition of himself.

Alain was fine, but it led to nothing much. His career continued for a time in such films as *Dis-moi qui tuer* (65) and *L'armée des ombres* (69).

59 Les dragueurs (Girl crazy)
   Les petits chats (The little cats)
62 Cartouche (FR/IT)
   Les mystères de Paris (Secrets of Paris)
   Le petit garçon de l'ascenseur
   (The little lift-boy)

Just thinking of you: Ladd in Misty

David Ladd

USA

b: 5 Feb 47 (Los Angeles)

David was the son of Alan Ladd and his second wife, Sue Carol. As a child he won several awards for dancing. His part in *The Big Land* was only marginal, but he had leads in his other four early films. He was an outstandingly gentle little boy, quite without his father's cold-eyed cockiness. (Alan starred in his first two films.)

In *The Proud Rebel* – which earned him a Critics' Award – David plays a mute boy; in *A Dog of Flanders*, a sensitive child who learns to paint; in *The Sad Horse*, a little cripple. Pathos was his strong suit, but he kept sickliness at bay. When his father wasn't in the film, he often shared the honours with a dog and/or horse.

In his 20s David returned to movies, with supporting roles in *R.P.M.* (70), *Catlow* (GB 71), *Death Line* (GB 72), *Jonathan Livingston Seagull* (73), *The Klansman* (74), *The Day of the Locust* (75), *Evil in the Deep* (76), *The Wild Geese* (GB 77), *Captive* (80) and *Beyond the Universe* (81).

Fallen sophisticates: Carlos Lopez Monet (left) and Oscar Orlegui in El secuestrador

Flemish master: David Ladd in the 1959 Dog of Flanders

57 The Big Land
58 The Proud Rebel
59 A Dog of Flanders
   The Sad Horse
60 Raymie
61 Misty

Eddie Hodges

USA

b: 5 Mar 47 (Hattiesburg, Miss.)

Redhead Eddie's family moved to New York in 1953. He appeared on TV in 'The Jackie Gleason Show', and then on 'Name That Tune' where he won himself a $25,000 prize. Soon afterwards he was playing on Broadway in 'The Music Man', before being cast as Frank Sinatra's son in *A Hole in the Head* and joining him in the joyous duet 'High Hopes'.

He was too young and too well-washed, though, to be up to playing Huck Finn opposite Archie Moore (who himself packed too light a punch on this occasion). They both did their best.

Later, like Johnny Crawford[◇], Eddie became better known as a singer than an actor. His first hit was 'I'm Gonna Knock On Your Door', and (perhaps in an effort to up-Huck himself) he recorded the original version of 'Ain't Gonna Wash for a Week'. His last appearance in the charts was in 1965.

On screen, he was in *C'mon, Let's Live a Little* (67), *The Happiest Millionaire* (67) and *Live a Little, Love a Little* (68).

59 A Hole in the Head
60 The Adventures of Huckleberry Finn
62 Advise and Consent
   Johnny Shiloh
   Summer Magic

Pablito Calvo

SPAIN

b: 16 Mar 47 (Madrid)

Little Pablo Calvo Hidalgo (to give him his final matronymic as well) had two or three years as quite a big international star, in successive films directed by Ladislao Vajda. As the darling of a Franciscan monastery in *Marcelino*, he brings bread to the image of a crucified Christ, and is rewarded with a vision; as Pepote, he helps his drunken old uncle Jacinto to fulfil a humble role in the bull-ring; and so on.

Saucer-eyed, modulating effortlessly from despair to joy, this Spanish Jackie Coogan[◇] was really too good to be true. But thanks to his naturalness, and to Vajda's considerable tact and skill, the vehicles remained roadworthy and didn't

Hodges in The Adventures of Huckleberry Finn

Well drilled: Eddie Hodges and Frank Sinatra in A Hole in the Head

Seeing things: Pablito Calvo in Marcelino pan y vino

bog down in syrup. With lesser directors, and cuteness draining away, Pablito couldn't command the same success, though he carried on till he was 14.

There had been some theatrical precedents in the family: both his grandfathers had worked behind the scenes, with prompter's and other duties. Pablo himself, when he withdrew from the cinema, became in due course an industrial engineer.

55 Marcelino pan y vino
    (Bread-and-wine Marcelino)
56 Mi tio Jacinto (My uncle Jacinto – ES/IT)
57 Un angel paso por Brooklyn
    (An angel comes to Brooklyn – ES/IT)
58 Totò e Marcelino
    (Toto and Marcelino – IT/FR)
60 Juanito (ES/DE)
61 Alerta en el ciel (Alert in the sky)
62 Barcos de papel (Paper boats – ES/AR)
   Dos años de vacaciones
    (The two-year holidays – ES/MX)

Danny Chang

USA

b: 25 Mar 47 (China)

His father was an importer of jade and oriental goods. When his parents returned to the USA, Danny was 6 months old.

51 Hong Kong
52 Battle Circus
53 South Sea Woman
55 Soldier of Fortune
58 China Doll

Luke Halpin

USA

b: 4 Apr 47 (New York)

Luke had appeared on TV from the age of five, but was 15 before striking up his slippery partnership with the screen's favourite dolphin. The *Flipper* films came out during the 'Flipper' series on TV, which ran from 1963-66.

There was a quick follow-up with *Flipper's New Adventure* in 1964. Then Halpin was in *Island of the Lost* (67), *If It's Tuesday,*

Luke Halpin dries off in Flipper's New Adventure

Eddie Axberg in Briggen 'Tre Liljor'

This Must Be Belgium (69), *Shock Waves* (70), *Hot Stuff* (79), *Eyes of a Stranger* (80) and *The Ordeal of Dr Mudd* (80).

57 Street of Sinners
63 Flipper

Péter Benkö

HUNGARY

b: 1 Jne 47 (Budapest)

Péter was the son of the actor Endre Benkö, with whom he appeared in his first film, playing one of two Jewish children given shelter by a circus clown.

When he was 18, Peter return to acting. His films included *Játék amúzeumban* (66),

A koppányi aga testamentuma (67), *Egri csillagok* (68), *Az utolsó kör* (68) — all good parts, leading up to joint stardom in the musical *Csínom palkó* (73). He appears frequently in the theatre and on television.

54 Fel a fejjel (Chin up!)
56 Több, mint játék (More than a game)

Eddie Axberg

SWEDEN

b: 9 Jly 47 (Stockholm)

Like his elder brother Conny and younger brother Rick, Eddie Axberg began performing on radio and TV around 1960. He was in two films in his mid-teens, and

thereafter in many more, as actor or sound director, or sometimes both.

61 Briggen 'Tre Liljor'
   (The good ship 'Three Lilies')
63 Nattvardsgästerna (The communicants)

RICK AXBERG — born 24 Nov 50 — was seen in *Vaxdocken* (62, Wax doll) and *Här har du ditt liv* (66, This is your life).

Borya Tokaryoff

USSR

b: 20 Aug 47

After sharing the lead in *Vstupleniye* with Kolya Burlyayev $^\lozenge$, a year his senior, Tokaryoff was in *Sinyaya tetrad* (63).

He completed the actors' course at VGIK in 1969, and in 1977 the directors' course. Meanwhile he appeared in *Goryachi sneg* (73), *Visokoye zvaniye* (74), *Eto mi ne prokhodili* (76), *Dva kapitana* (77) and the lead in *Aleksandr malenki* (82). In 1983 he directed his first feature, *Nas venchali ne v tserkvi*.

Boris Tokaryoff is now — or was — an Honoured Artist of the RSFSR.

59 Spasyonnoye pokoleniye
   (The saved generation)
62 Gde ti teper, Maksim?
   (Where are you now, Maxim?)
   Vstupleniye (Beginning)

James Aubrey

BRITAIN

b: 28 Aug 47 (Klagenfurt, Austria)

James Aubrey Tregidgo was born in Austria because his father, a British Army officer, was stationed there at the time. When he was 13 he was chosen by Peter Brook to play the tragic hero, Ralph, in the film of William Golding's *Lord of the Flies* – shot in 1961, though it wasn't released till 1963.

James's Ralph was perfect: the decent, conventional upper-middle-class British schoolboy to the life. As the unwilling leader defeated and hunted down by darker forces, he is a profoundly touching figure: baffled, disappointed, honourable to the last. His reluctant dependance on the self-appointed aide Piggy (the wonderful HUGH EDWARDS) is delicately drawn.

Directly after the shooting of *Lord of the Flies*, James Aubrey was in a Broadway play called, by a happy chance, 'Isle of Children'.

Several years later, back home in Britain, he reappeared in a film called *The Sex Thief*

(73). Then, in 1978, he had a leading role in *Terror* and the lead – as a songwriter disastrously entangled with an under-age girl – in *Home before Midnight*. He was also one of the principals, around this time, in the controversial TV serial *A Bouquet of Barbed Wire*. More recent films were *The Final Frame* (89), *La grieta* (ES 89) and *Buddy's Song* (90).

61 Lord of the Flies

A new version of *Lord of the Flies* was filmed in America (or rather in Jamaica) in 1989, by Harry Hook, talented director of *The Kitchen Toto*. In many ways it works better than Peter Brook's oddly tentative first filming. There's much more of the feel of the island and the terrors of settling into it. But the American principals, intelligent as they are – Paul Balthazar Getty as Ralph, Daniel Pipoly as Piggy, Badge Dale as Simon and Chris Furrh as Jack – haven't the individuality of their English prep school forerunners, and there seems nothing very surprising or shocking about the boys of a military school sliding into barbarism. Soldiers are designed to kill.

Racial victim: Jimmy Sterman in Paw

Jimmy Sterman

HOLLAND DENMARK

b: 30 Aug 47 (Amsterdam)

The hero of Astrid Henning-Jensen's short film *Paw* – about racial prejudice among children – had a Dutch mother and a West Indian father. He was so obviously sweet-natured and unassuming that it came as a shock to see him, on the screen, persecuted by a group of healthy little Danes.

Paw comes to live in a coastal village in Zealand, and his life is made such hell by the local kids – a blond brute called Marius, played by Freddy Pedersen, is particularly hateful – that he escapes into a nearby forest where he is befriended, briefly, by a poacher, before being sent to a reformatory, escaping again, and living on an island with only a fox cub for companion.

Paw won a Grand Prix at the 1960 Cannes Film Festival, plus a Gold Medal from the Council of Europe and a Hollywood nomination for best foreign film of the year. It has been sadly ignored of late.

59 Paw (DK)

Hero and aide: James Aubrey (right) with Hugh Edwards in the 1961 Lord of the Flies

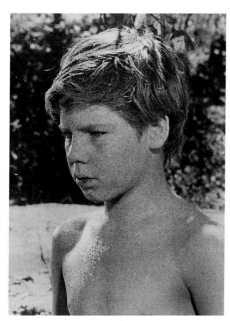

Sandy: Rangno in The Little Savage

Terry Rangno

USA

b: 25 Sep 47 (Los Angeles)

Rangno played Paul Newman as a boy in *Somebody Up There Likes Me*, and wasn't at all a bad likeness, with a defiant nobility of bearing.

56 Somebody Up There Likes Me
58 The Long, Hot Summer
59 The Little Savage
    The Remarkable Mr Pennypacker

Ole Neumann

DENMARK

b: 16 Oct 47

Ole was known almost entirely, as a child, as 'Lille Per' (little Peter) in the popular *Father to Four* series that spanned nearly a decade. But he was in one or two other films, and also recorded the Danish narration for Lamorisse's *Voyage en ballon*.

When the *Far til fire* series was over, Ole appeared in two or three more linked films: *Kampen om Næsbygård* (64), *Næsbygårds arving* (65), *Krybskytterne på Næsbygård* (66). He became a pop guitarist and led his own group, 'His Newmen'.

53 Far til fire (Father to four)
    Fløjtespilleren (The flautist)
54 Far til fire i sneen (FTF in the snow)
55 Far til fire pæ landet (FTF in the country)
56 Far til fire i byen (FTF in town)
57 Far til fire og Onkel Sofus
    (FTF and Uncle Sophus)
58 Far til fire og ulveungerne
    (FTF and the Wolf Cubs)
59 Far til fire på Bornholm (FTF on Bornholm)
60 Det skete på Møllegården
    (It happened at Møllegård)
61 Far til fire med fuld musik
    (FTF goes musical)

Lille Per's elder brother Ole in the *Far til fire* films was played by OTTO MØLLER JENSEN (b: 31 July 40), who was also in *Fløjtespilleren* (53) and *Arvingen* (The heir, 54). Later, after studying in Paris, Otto became a fashion designer.

Master Babua

INDIA

b: 19 Nov 47 (Calcutta, Bengal)

Babua's actual name was Prosanta Kumar Roy.

53 Bhagwan Sri Krishna Chaitanya
    Bhore hoye elo
    Hari Laxmi
    Jog bijog (Meeting and parting)
    Nishkriti (The exit)
    Sarala
54 Chheley kar
    Moner mayur (The restless heart)
55 Atma darshan (Self-encounter)
    Dristi (The vision)
    Kankabatir ghat (The banks of Kankabati)
    Pratishodh (Vengeance)
56 Asabarna
    Chhaya sangini
57 Baksiddha
    Gharer math (The home temple)

Hiroyuki Ota

JAPAN

b: 25 Nov 47 (Shizuoka Prefecture)

When he was nine, Hiroyuki joined the Wakakusa troupe's training school. His introduction to films came with the help of the director Daisuke Ito, a distant relative. One of his leading roles was in a remake of Tasaka's 1938 film *A Pebble by the Wayside*.

Ota continued to act for a further fifteen years or so, but he also became a professional singer in the late Sixties. His films included *Aitsu tono boken* (65), *Nogiku no gotoki kimi nariki* (66), *Kagiri aru hi o ai ni ikite* (67), *Bakumatsu* (70) and *Sri Lanka no ai to wakare* (76). He then took to management.

56 Niizuma kagami (The new wife's mirror)
59 Oja no ken (The king's sword)
    Chiyoda jo enjo (Chiyoda castle is
    burning)
60 Robo no ishi (Pebble by the wayside)
61 Kaachan umiga shitteruyo
    (The little fisherman)
62 The Big Wave (US/JP)
63 Wakai Tokyo no yane no shita
    (Under the roof of young Japan)

Vincent Winter

BRITAIN

b: 29 Dec 47 (Aberdeen, Scotland)

One of the screen's most treasurable children was the younger of *The Kidnappers*, two small Scots in Nova Scotia who chance on a lost baby in a wood and decide to appropriate it. 'We could call it Rover,' suggests five-year-old Winter, not wholly lucid about the man-beast demarcation. This is borne out later when the boys' austere grandfather (Duncan Macrae) discovers what's going on, takes the baby from them and strides off towards the house with the bundle in his arms. 'Grandaddy!' yells the tiny Winter, racing after him with a wild surmise, 'Don't eat it, Grandaddy, it ain't fittin'!'

After some less inspired parts in British films, chubby Vincent was taken up by Walt Disney for his last few films as an actor, and was unfailingly likeable, with or without his native accent. He sang (dubbed) with the Vienna Boys' Choir, agonised over a bereaved Skye terrier, showed understanding of a sea-monster

Plotting: Vincent Winter (left) and Jon Whiteley in The Kidnappers

Ludwik Halicz

POLAND

b: 1947 (Warsaw)

In *Krol Macius I*, this curly redhead played not the spoilt little King (Juliusz Wyrzykowski) but his exasperated adjutant. In Wadim Berestowski's *Bitwa o Kozi Dwor*, an exhilarating story of juvenile gangs based on a novel by Jozef Hen, he was the intrepid leader of the 'good gang'.

Halicz later emigrated to Israel.

57 Krol Macius I (King Macius I)
60 Spotkania w mroku
  (Twilight encounter – PL/DD)
  Szatan z siódmej klasy
  (Seventh grade Satan)
61 Bitwa o Kozi Dwor
  (The battle of Goat Yard)

that devastates London, foiled train-robbers, and so on. But he never again got a script like *The Kidnappers*.

Though his acting days were now over, Vincent Winter's connection with the cinema wasn't. He trained in the technical side of the business, and re-emerged as an assistant director in British films of the Seventies. He has worked, for instance, on *The Sailor's Return* (78), as production manager on *Superman II* (80) and as Second Unit assistant on *The Dark Crystal* (82).

53 The Kidnappers
55 The Dark Avenger
56 The Door in the Wall
57 Day of Grace
  Time Lock
59 Beyond This Place
  The Bridal Path
61 Gorgo
  Greyfriars Bobby
62 Almost Angels (US)
63 The Horse Without a Head
  The Three Lives of Thomasina (GB/US)

Furtive Winter in The Kidnappers

Aspiring: Chris Olsen in The Fastest Gun Alive

Christopher Olsen

USA

b: 1947 (Los Angeles)

Chris (or Christy, or Christopher Robin) was in movies from the age of fourteen months, and grew to be totally convincing as the average, amiable White American Boy: blond but unglamorous, vulnerable but plucky. In this capacity he was much used, for instance as James Stewart's son in the remake of *The Man Who Knew Too Much* and James Mason's in *Bigger Than Life*. His reactions to fun or fear were natural and unaffected.

Scully in Hunted in Holland

Sean Scully

BRITAIN/AUSTRALIA

b: 1947

During much of his childhood, this highly intelligent young Australian lived with his mother in London, where he trained as an actor and was seen on the stage, notably in 'Treasure Island' at the Mermaid, playing a spunky Jim Hawkins to the Long John Silver of Bernard Miles. ('A bright-eyed squirrel of a boy who spits delight-

fully,' said the New Statesman.) Then he was spotted and signed up by the Disney organisation.

In *Almost Angels*, a kind of *All About Eve* rethought in terms of the Vienna Boys' Choir, Sean played the Bette Davis part of the supplanted prima donna, and Vincent Winter ◇ an innocent version of the Anne Baxter. It's a hilarious exercise, saved from total fatuity by Winter's all-conquering niceness and by Scully's angry grief when his voice breaks at the school concert.

Luckily Scully's super-treble has a second string to his bow: he is also a gifted composer and conductor. (Just a kid like any other.) Handing out manuscript parts to his Sängerknabe colleagues for an at-sight try-out on a convenient hillside, he has only to wave his arms for the lads to break into impeccable polyphony. And further triumphs are to follow. This feast of genius and Gemütlichkeit adds up to a film not to be missed.

Scully was in fact an unusually clever fellow. A year or two before *Almost Angels*, he had stood up on the spur of the moment and addressed bystanders at Speakers' Corner in Hyde Park, London. 'An hour later,' reported the 'Evening Standard,' 'twelve-year-old Sean from Sydney, Australia, was still talking. The audience had swelled to more than 100, and jostled around Sean to hear his views on religion, politics, racial prejudice – the lot. Then he calmly thanked them for their attention, and went home two hours late for tea.' This was clearly someone who would have few problems with a mere symphony orchestra.

In his stint for Disney, Scully starred in a British remake of *The Prince and the Pauper*, playing both parts without the aid of a twin, and doing so with enormous spirit. He had the lordliness, malice and humour – reminiscent of the young Katharine Hepburn – to make the dual role convincing and interesting, and the film should be revived more often. His last performance for Disney, and his last as a boy, was a rather thankless one in *Dr Syn* as sidekick to the clerical smuggler.

Sean Scully – no connection, incidentally, with an artist of the same name – returned to his native Australia, where he became a valuable member of the acting community. His antipodean films have included *A City's Child* (71), *Sunday Too Far Away* (74), *The Rollicking Adventures of Eliza Fraser* (76), *Cactus* (86), and many others

Ricky Sorensen

USA

b: 1947

Ricky, a muscular little boy who had been in one or two films, plus a TV series based on the 1951 film *Room for One More*, was chosen as the new 'Boy' for some TV Tarzan movies starring Gordon Scott. He was to be the 'adopted son' of Scott and the new Jane, Eve Brent. (Ricky wasn't in fact

Ricky Sorensen in The Hard Man

called 'Boy' in the films but 'Tartu' – apparently a compression of 'Tarzan Two', though the name must have puzzled many Estonians.)

Tarzan and the Trappers, not screened until May 1966, was a conflation of three TV pilot films that preceded *Tarzan's Fight for Life*. But it made Ricky Sorensen the only boy since Johnny Sheffield ◇ to make more than a one-off appearance in Tarzan movies. He didn't do much more after 1958, but supplied the voice of 'Wart' (King Arthur as a child) in Disney's cartoon version of *The Sword in the Stone*.

Fifteen years later, Disney gave Rick a small part in *The Cat from Outer Space* (78).

57 The Hard Man
    Man of a Thousand Faces
58 Tarzan and the Trappers
    Tarzan's Fight for Life
60 Underworld USA
63 The Sword in the Stone *(voice only)*

Danny Bravo

USA

b: circa 1947

Danny, whose real name appears to have been Danny Zaldivar, had the lead in *For the Love of Mike*. Almost inevitably, he returned to the screen a few years later in *For Pete's Sake!* (66)

60 For the Love of Mike
    The Magnificent Seven

Wolfgang Glaser

EAST GERMANY

b: circa 1947

In *Der Moorhund* the sad-faced Glaser plays a boy on a summer holiday visit to his father, a lieutenant in the border guard. He solves the mystery of a shaggy dog, repeatedly sighted by locals, which turns out to be a tool of imperialist agents. This may be the first four-footed tool in European films.

60 Der Moorhund (Dog of the moorland)

Ivan Kauzlarič

CZECHOSLOVAKIA

b: circa 1947

The severe-looking Kauzlarič makes a powerful impression in an episode of the omnibus film *Třinactileti*, as a boy who becomes tragically obsessed with a bicycle called The Silver Favourite. He has an equally tormented time in the title role of *Jerguš Lapin*, as a dead outlaw's son who leaves the mountains to work in a factory – but finds only unhappiness there, and returns to the mountains.

60 Třinactileti (Thirteen-year-olds)
61 Jerguš Lapin

Nerius Narkis

USSR – Lithuania

b: circa 1947

In *Zhiviye gyeroyi*, a four-story celebration of children in recent Lithuanian history, the blond Narkis is the hero of the first part, 'No need'. He plays a peasant boy who is sold to a kulak as a shepherd.

In the second episode, 'The nightingale', VITAUTAS BUYZIS plays a boy who can imitate birds on his pipe, and so lures a Nazi detachment into a guerrilla ambush; in the third, 'The last shot', ZHIVILLE JAKELAITITE is a little girl killed by a German soldier; and in the last, LEONIDAS MALASHAZHKAS is a boy of today, learning about his country's history.

59 Zhiviye gyeroyi (Living heroes)

Dhimitër Pecani

ALBANIA

b: circa 1947

DEBATIK was Albania's second home-directed feature. Its title is an acronym, standing for 'Djemt e bashkuar antifashistë të ideve komuniste' – the League of Anti-Fascist Boys of Communist Ideas.

It tells a story of schoolboy heroism under Italian occupation. Agim (Dhimitër Pecani) and Coli (Shpëtim Zani), helping the patriotic guerrillas, are caught and tortured by the Italians, but refuse to give information and finally escape and give a vital warning to their comrades. Coli, unusually on the screen, earns his living by selling tortoises.

Zani seems to have made no more films, but Pecani was in supporting roles in *Vitet e para* (65), *Oshëtimë në bregdet* (66), *Njësiti gueril* (69), *Përse bie kjo daulle* (69) and *I treti* (78). Finally, in 1979, he had another lead in *Ne vinim nga lufta*, a story of the fight against post-war bourgeois subversion.

61 DEBATIK
    (Communist boys against fascism)

Phillips in Hot Shots

Phil Phillips

USA

b: circa 1947

The robust Phil – who won a children's talent contest in Boston in 1952 – could hardly have had less similar roles than in his first two films: one a Bowery Boys knockabout, and the other a bloodstained frontier melodrama with Joel McCrea.

271

He handled both so well that it's a puzzle he didn't do more on screen.

56 Hot Shots
57 The Tall Stranger
60 Tall Story

Pepito Romay

MEXICO

b: circa 1947

Both Pepito and his elder sister Titina became popular child stars in Mexico in the mid-Fifties. They (and a younger sister, Lichita) were the children of Joselito Rodriguez, who directed most of their films.

The handsome, jolly Pepito got a nomination for 'Best Child Performance of the Year' after *Pintame angelitos blancos* (its working title was 'My colour condemns me'); and he won the award for *Despues de la tormenta*. All his remaining roles were leads, sometimes co-starring with Titina.

54 Pintame angelitos blancos
    (Imagine white angels)
55 Despues de la tormenta (After the storm)
    La pequeña enemiga (The little devil)
    Dos diablillos en apuros
    (Two little devils in a fix)
56 Pepito as del volante (Pepito, ace driver)
57 Pepito y el monstruo
    (Pepito and the monster)
    Pepito y los robachicos
    (Pepito and the kidnappers)

Yoshiro Ichikawa

JAPAN

b: 10 Jan 48 (Tokyo)

Yoshiro was a member of the children's theatre company Gekidan Himawari, and scored a considerable success with his first film. Thereafter he did a lot of TV, and took part in a song contest.

Latterly Ishikawa returned to acting, and was in the 1977 film *Yakuza senso, nihon no don*.

62 Kyupora no aru machi (Cupola)
63 Kemuri no osama (King of smoke)

Fancier: Yoshiro Ichikawa in Kyupora no aru machi

Martin Stephens

BRITAIN

b: 30 Jan 48 (London)

Martin Angel Keller — with a middle name like that, it's ironic that he became famous for playing evil children — initially appeared before the camera as a commercial model, before acting (as Martin Keller) in the refugee drama *The Divided Heart*. He was the younger version of Michel Ray's ◇ 'Toni'. After this, and a lapse of some years, he became Stephens.

Martin had an alert, intelligent little face which was capable of being funny or mischievous. He was demure and touching in films like *The Witness*, where he was threatened by crooks and exploited by police, and amused everyone as crafty Sigismond, the child of Deborah Kerr and

Reign of terror: Martin Stephens in Count Your Blessings

aristocratic Rossano Brazzi in *Count Your Blessings*.

It was only as the leader of the mysteriously-spawned alien children of *The Village of the Damned* – sporting a loathsome bleached coiffure and luminescent eyes – that he joined the ranks of hell, consolidating his status with his chilling Miles in Henry James's 'Turn of the Screw', filmed as *The Innocents*. By this time the icy look was second nature.

He was saved from further creepies by taking over from Keith Hamshere in the title role of Lionel Bart's 'Oliver!', on the London stage in 1961.

He reappeared in his mid-teens in two more films: *The Battle of the Villa Fiorita* (US/GB 65) and *Le streghe* (IT/FR 66). But finally he quit show business and became a lawyer.

54 The Divided Heart
58 Another Time, Another Place
   Harry Black
   Law and Disorder
   Passionate Summer
59 Count Your Blessings (US)
   Please Turn Over
   A Touch of Larceny
   The Witness
60 The Hellfire Club
   No Kidding
   The Village of the Damned
61 The Innocents

Mike McGreevey

USA

b: 7 Feb 48 (Phoenix, Arizona)

This cheerful, freckled redhead was the son of a screen and TV writer. There is no way a film called *Chartroose Caboose* is going to get left out of this book, and there was no way young Michael, the epitome of boy-next-door as well as a useful actor, would be spurned by the Disney studio. He claimed to have made more than 100 TV appearances by the time he was twelve.

McGreevey went on to be in *Treasure in the Haunted House* (64), *The Way West* (67), *The Impossible Years* (68), *Death of a*

Pillow talk: Mike McGreevey and Molly Bee in Chartroose Caboose

Gunfighter (69), *The Computer Wore Tennis Shoes* (70), and so forth.

57 The Girl Most Likely
59 Day of the Outlaw
   The Man in the Net
60 Chartroose Caboose
61 The Clown and the Kid
62 Sammy – the Way Out Seal

Edoardo Nevola

ITALY

b: 23 Feb 48 (Rome)

Edoardo was a sweet but slightly unmemorable Italian favourite of the latter Fifties.

55 Il ferroviere (The railwayman)
56 Guardia, guardiascelta, brigadiere
   e maresciallo
   (Guard, leading guard, brigadier
   and marshal)
57 Il cocco di mamma (Mummy's darling)
   Il maestro (The schoolmaster – IT/ES)
   L'uomo di paglia (Man of straw)
58 Sogno a Venezia (Dream in Venice)
   Tal vez mañana (Perhaps tomorrow – ES)
   L'uomo dai calzoni corti
   (The man in short pants)
59 La cento chilometri (The 100 kilometres)
   Il mondo nella mia tasca
   (The world in my pocket)
61 Il gladiatore invincibile
   (The invincible gladiator – IT/ES)
63 La noia (Boredom – IT/ES)

Edoardo Nevola in Il ferroviere

Pugnacious: Dennis Waterman, circa 1960

Dennis Waterman

BRITAIN

b: 24 Feb 48 (London)

Sandy-haired Dennis, who attended the Corona School from the age of eleven, was the younger brother of the European welterweight boxing champion Peter Waterman, and shared some of his pugnaciousness.

Around 1960 he had the lead on an 'alternative' LP of Bart's 'Oliver!', played in Shakespeare at Stratford-on-Avon and in 'The Music Man' on the London stage, and became TV's first incarnator of Richmal Crompton's 'William'. In 1962 he landed a five-year contract with Desilu for a TV series called 'Fair Exchange', about a cockney family in New York. His biggest film role was for the Children's Film Foundation in *Go Kart Go!*

Dennis did little filming in his mid-teens. Then he returned with a vengeance. Subsequent films included *Up the Junction* (67), *The Smashing Bird I Used to Know* (69), *My Lover, My Son* (69), *Wedding Night* (69), *The Scars of Dracula* (70), *Man in the Wilderness* (US 71), *Fright* (71), *The Belstone Fox* (73), *Sweeney!* (76) and *Sweeney 2* (78).

These last two were derived from the long-running TV cop series 'The Sweeney', in which he had an important part; a lead in another similar series, 'Minder', followed and lasted even longer. Since then Waterman has developed into a popular leading man, mainly on stage and television, but without any particular charm or lightness of touch.

59 Night Train for Inverness
60 Ali and the Camel *(voice only)*
   Snowball
61 The Pirates of Blood River
62 Crooks Anonymous (US)
63 Go Kart Go

Oliver Grimm

WEST GERMANY

b: 3 Apr 48 (Munich)

Oliver's mother was the former UFA actress Hansi Wendler; his father, Hans Grimm, was a director, and in fact directed

Oliver Grimm

many of the boy's films. But his first lead, as 'Niki', was in a film by Rudolf Jugert.

Oliver, with his happy yet vulnerable teddy-bear face – rather like a pocket Fischer-Dieskau – rapidly became a favourite of the German public, equally delighted to see him being mischievous or pathetic, bringing adults together in the manner of a male Shirley Temple, or humbling himself to the problems of life at street-level as a boy King in *Majestät auf Abwegen*. O.W.Fischer as a Shakespearean actor and Heinz Rühmann as a circus clown were among his many adoring screen fathers.

In spite of being everyone's dear little boy for nearly a decade, Oliver adroitly skirted the swamp of sickliness and never became over-cute. There was certainly nothing cute about his last child role, in the British film *Reach for Glory*, as a Jewish refugee from Vienna, dumped among schoolboy chauvinists in East Anglia. At the end of this first screen version of John Rae's novel 'The Custard Boys' he lies

Grimm with Harald Juhnke in Schick' deine Frau nicht nach Italien

dead in a coalyard, victim of a 'mock execution' which went wrong.

So ended Oliver Grimm's career as a child star. But, after an educational pause, he returned to acting, and was seen in popular TV series like 'Derrick' (75) and 'Dalli-Dalli' (76).

52 Ich heisse Niki (My name is Nicky)
    Vater braucht eine Frau
        (Father needs a wife)
53 Moselfahrt aus Liebeskummer
        (Lovelorn trip down the Moselle)
54 Morgengrauen (Dawn of day)
    Frühlingslied (Spring song)
55 Griff nach den Sternen
        (Reaching for the stars)
    Wenn der Vater mit dem Sohne
        (Fathers and sons)
56 Mein Vater, der Schauspieler
        (My father the actor)
57 Kleiner Mann – ganz gross (Little big man)
58 Der schwarze Blitz (Black lightning)
    Majestät auf Abwegen
        (His Majesty goes astray)
59 Das schöne Abenteuer
        (The beautiful adventure)
60 Frau Irene Besser
    The Magnificent Rebel (US/WG)
    Schick' deine Frau nicht nach Italien
        (Don't send your wife to Italy)
61 Isola Bella
63 Reach for Glory (GB)

Gregory Phillips

BRITAIN

b: 18 May 48 (Hitchin, Herts.)

Gregory's success as Judy Garland's son in *I Could Go On Singing* brought him a leading part in ABC Television's children's serial *Emerald Soup* (63). His later films included *Who Killed the Cat?* (66), *I Start Counting* (69) and *The Virgin Soldiers* (69).

63 I Could Go On Singing
64 The Pumpkin Eater

Jerry Mathers

USA

b: 2 Jne 48 (Sioux City, Iowa)

His father was a teacher who became a high school principal. The family having moved to Los Angeles before he was two, Jerry began modelling and TV work (initially on the Ed Wynn Show) before appearing – together with his sister Susie – in *This Is My Love*.

The rest of Jerry's child career was occupied by his role as Theodore Cleaver, known as 'Beaver', in the TV series 'Leave It to Beaver', which opened on CBS in October 1957. (It later moved to NBC and then ABC.) The pudgy, accident-prone boy became so well-liked by the nation over the next six years that he was actually made an honorary citizen of the Beaver State, Oregon, for services to beaverhood.

His elder brother Wally in the show was played by Tony Dow (born 13 Apr 45), and the sneaky boy-next-door, Eddie, by Ken Osmond. Years later, in 1979-80, Mathers and Dow teamed up again to tour in a play called 'So Long, Stanley'. It was Wally's childhood inability to pronounce 'Theodore', incidentally, that led to the name 'Beaver'.

Apart from the odd guest appearance on TV, though, Mathers didn't make any great effort to prolong his teenage career. He had the unnerving experience of being reported killed in action in Korea; but his Air Force experience didn't include death. He returned to acting in 1981 in a TV movie called *The Girl, the Gold Watch and the Dynamite*.

54 This Is My Love
    The Seven Little Foys
56 Bigger Than Life
    The Shadow on the Window
    That Certain Feeling
    The Trouble With Harry
58 The Deep Six

Alford in To Kill a Mockingbird

Philip Alford

USA

b: 11 Sep 48 (Gadsden, Alabama)

The serious young Alford does well in *To Kill a Mockingbird*, a story of racial bigotry set in the 1930s in his own home state of Alabama. (The novel is by Harper Lee.)

As the son of noble liberal lawyer Atticus Finch (Gregory Peck), preparing to defend a negro on a rape charge, he has a hard job competing with his enterprising kid sister 'Scout' (the superb Mary Badham), but just about holds his own.

Philip Alford appeared again in *Shenandoah* (65), in *The Intruders* (67) and in the Disney adventure *Bristleface*.

62 To Kill a Mockingbird

Hennie Scott

BRITAIN

b: 25 Sep 48

Hennie — born Hendrik Momberg, of a South African father — was a handsome boy with an air of sardonic self-confidence. He had leads in two CFF films, *The Missing Note* and *Wings of Mystery*, and a supporting role in Disney's Vienna Boys' Choir drama, *Almost Angels*.

Oddly, he abandoned acting in favour of a career with the Metropolitan Water Board.

59 Bottoms Up
60 Circle of Deception
61 The Missing Note
62 Almost Angels (US)
63 Wings of Mystery

Barry Gordon

USA

b: 21 Dec 48 (Brookline, Mass.)

Barry, the son of a radio announcer, won a singing competition at three, and from four to six was a regular in the children's TV show 'Startime'. Then, with Art Mooney's band, he made a hit on disc with a song called 'Nuttin' for Christmas', which sold a cool two million copies. He followed this up in *The Girl Can't Help It* by singing 'Blue Suede Shoes', and in *Pressure Point* grew up to be Bobby Darin: but this was no song-and-dance since Darin was cast as a young Nazi.

In the early Sixties, Barry Gordon spent over a year acting with Jason Robards, Jr. – on Broadway, and then on tour – in Herb Gardner's play 'A Thousand Clowns'. Their brilliant characterisations were enshrined in the 1965 film.

Gordon continued in *The Spirit Is Willing* (66), *Double-Stop* (68), and *Out of It* (69). In 1977 he became a celebrity again when he played a child-psychiatrist in the TV series 'Fish', and he had a small part in the delightful Dracula comedy *Love at First Bite* (79). He starred, though, as the bigot Archie Bunker – the US equivalent of Britain's Alf Garnett – in the TV series

Radio off: Barry Gordon in A Thousand Clowns

'All in the Family' and its sequel, 'Archie Bunker's Place'.

56 The Girl Can't Help It
60 Cinderfella
   Hands of a Stranger
62 Pressure Point
65 A Thousand Clowns

Charles Herbert

USA

b: 23 Dec 48 (Culver City, Cal.)

Charles Herbert Saperstein was a square-faced little boy with some droll expressions and tones of voice, good value in films of the late Fifties. He made his bow in 1953 on TV's 'Half-Pint Panel', and was later active on the stage, where he earned an Emmy nomination for his performance as a blind child in a play called 'The Miracle Hour'.

After 1960 Charles Herbert made one or two more appearances in TV series like 'The Twilight Zone' and 'The Outer Limits', but not much more.

54 The Long, Long Trailer
55 The Night Holds Terror
   The View from Pompey's Head
56 Gunfight at the O.K. Corral
   These Wilder Years
57 No Down Payment
   The Tattered Dress
58 The Colossus of New York
   The Fly
   Houseboat

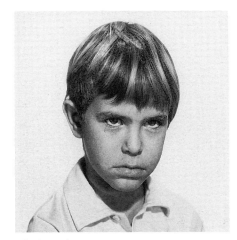

Charles Herbert, circa 1959

59 The Five Pennies
   The Man in the Net
60 The Boy and the Pirates
   Please Don't Eat the Daisies
   Thirteen Ghosts

Georgia on his mind: Daneliya in Mamlyuk

Dato Daneliya

USSR — Georgia

b: 1948 (Tbilisi)

This young Georgian had three leading roles as a child: in *Mamlyuk, Dedushka Gigiya* and *Raskaz nishchevo*. In the last two of them – the first was a story of Turkish slavery in 18th-century Georgia – he played 'Dato' and 'Datiko'. It looked as if cult of personality was setting in.

His later films included *Matzi Khvitya* (67), *Tariel Golua* (68), *Abesalom i Eteri* and *Gimilis Bichebi* (69). Eventually, however, he chucked in the glory of the screen. He became a handball trainer, and in due course an international referee.

55 Magdanas lurdzha (Magdana's donkey)
58 Mamlyuk (The Mameluke)
   Ori odzhaki (Two families)
   Skhvisi shvilebi
      (Another woman's children)
59 Den posledni, den pervi
      (Last day, first day)
   Ganacheni (The judgment)
   Sluchai na plotine (Incident on the dam)
60 Dedushka Gigiya (Grandpa Gigiya)
61 Raskaz nishchevo (The pauper's tale)

Sheepwatcher: Peppeddu Cuccu in Banditi a Orgosolo

Peppeddu Cuccù

ITALY

b: circa 1948

Peppeddu is the hero's younger brother in this tragedy of Sardinian shepherding, which ends with an oddly *Bicycle-Thieves*-like twist as the endlessly wronged and luckless Michele turns bandit himself and steals the flock of an almost equally miserable shepherd. Peppeddu can only watch.

61 Banditi a Orgosolo
      (Bandits of Orgosolo)

Gilles Payant

USA

b: circa 1948

This relaxed French-Canadian was chosen by Disney to co-star with an even hand-somer Red Setter. The film's hopeless, but Payant's almost comically expressive face and quaint accent would win anyone's heart. (He's at his best when giving Red a lesson in 'pointing'.)

He is the very embodiment of eager helpfulness, but not above a good 14-year-old sulk when his good nature is abused beyond normal bounds. Why didn't Disney give such an endearing fellow another film?

62 Big Red

Fantasist: Vitya Perevalov in Starozhil

Vitya Perevalov

USSR

b: circa 1948

Viktor, or Vitya, was a funny moon-faced blond who had leads in most of his films.

In the folk-tale *Marya* he joins up with a soldier, returning from the war, who helps him rescue his gifted mother from a particularly nasty Water Goblin. (Russian courage and cunning finally reduce this threat to a dirty puddle.) In the school story *Starozhil* he plays a seemingly in-curable fantasist whose good friend Boris undertakes his reformation.

Vitya's later films included *Dolgaya shchastlivaya zhizn* (66), *Respublika Shkid* (66), and a lead in the teenage comedy-romance *Ya vas lyubil* (68).

57 Tambu-Lambu
58 Gorod zazhigayet ogni
    (The town lights up)
59 Marya, iskusnitsa
    (Maria the nimble weaver)
    Sombrero
61 Baltiskoye nebo (Baltic sky)
    Starozhil (The old-timer)

Javier Tejeda

MEXICO

b: circa 1948

The touching hero of Emilio Gomez Muriel's *Simitrio*, Javier won the Mexican Film Academy's award for best child actor of the year, as a mischievous boy who takes advantage of his village school-master's near-blindness by impersonating an absent boy, but ends up feeling sorry for him.

60 Simitrio

Láci Tóth

HUNGARY

b: circa 1948

For the new film version of Zsigmund Moricz's novel *Légy jó mindhalálig*, little László Tóth, from the spa town of Hajdu-böszörmeny, was chosen out of 27,000 possible schoolboys in his province – the story takes place in Debrecen, and they wanted a hero with a Hajdu accent. He proved capable of intense tragic feeling.

At the San Francisco Film Festival of 1960 Láci won the prize for the year's best child performance. He went on to more ordinary leading roles in settings of 1920 revolutionary Hungary and 1956 post-monarchist Egypt.

60 Légy jó mindhalálig (Always be good)
61 Puskák és galambok (Guns and doves)
63 Egyiptomi törtenet (Egyptian story)

Tomáš Sedláček

CZECHOSLOVAKIA

b: 15 Jan 49

The stolid-looking but expressive little Sedláček was referred to by some Czech sources, in his first film (about a boys' hockey team), as Tomáš Sláma. He partnered the even more stolid Russian boy Vova Siluyanov ◇ in *V 6 ráno*, in which Tomáš stows away on a TU-104 to Moscow to take part in an International Youth Festival.

He returned to films in his mid-teens in *Misto v houfu* (64) and *Každy mlady muž* (65).

Sticking together: Láci Tóth in Légy jó mindhalálig

Tomáš Sedláček in V 6 ráno na letišti

Jon Provost

USA

b: 12 Mar 49 (Pomona, Cal.)

Jonathan Provost, son of an aeronautical engineer, was too peaches-and-cream as a child to be very interesting on the screen. He was blond, blue-eyed, cuddly, and not overburdened with artistic temperament.

After some early bits, his charming looks landed him a leading role in *Escapade in Japan,* as a diplomat's child who is deposited in the sea by the ill-fated airliner bringing him to join his parents, and then picked up by a Japanese fishing boat. The fisherman's small son (Roger Nakagawa) rashly undertakes the job of getting him to Tokyo, and they undergo none-too-thrilling adventures.

On the strength of this, little Jon was installed in 1957 in the main child role of the CBS 'Lassie' series on TV. His 'Timmy' replaced the 'Jeff Miller' of Tommy Rettig◊, who had been a regular for the three previous years, and the new sequence ('Timmy and Lassie') ran till 1964.

Even at 13, there was still a certain meringue-like quality about Provost's looks and playing. By 1966, though, when he appeared in the framing scenes of *This Property Is Condemned,* the puppy-fat had fallen away to reveal a personable teenager. He appeared again in *The Computer Wore Tennis Shoes* (69) and *The Secret of the Sacred Forest* (70).

After this Jon retired, went to college, and in due course became an estate agent. But, in a wave of nostalgia, he played an important adult role in a 'New Lassie' TV series in 1989, with Will Nipper as the bitch's new boy friend.

Crabbed youth: Jon Provost on location for Escapade in Japan

Dominique Maurin

FRANCE

b: 1 Apr 49

Dominique was one of six gifted children of the singer Mado Maurin – see under Yves-Marie Maurin ◇ (p.244) for a detailed tally of the siblings. He was less aristocratic in feature and manner than his older brothers and sisters, and put this to good use in some cheeky characterisations on stage and screen.

Among Dominique's subsequent films were *Erotissimo* (68), *Les grandes vacances*

Dominique Maurin, circa 1951

(68), *Les anarchistes* (69), *On est toujours trop bon avec les femmes* (70), the serial *La maison des bois* (71) and *Les princes* (82).

Giancarlo Damiani

ITALY

b: 1 Apr 49 (Setteromano)

The director Luigi Comencini cast the son of a skilled worker as the sad little boy in his *Finestra sul Luna Park* when he met him playing in the street.

Giancarlo grew up to be a civil servant.

Toshitaka Ito

JAPAN

b: 27 May 49 (Tokyo)

Toshitaka Ito entered the Toei training school for child actors when he was ten. His performance in *Hadakakko* was a powerful one.

Ito continued to appear in films like *Ah, yokaren* (68), *Aoba shigereru* (74) and *Hakkodasan* (77), and became a valuable supporting actor.

Kevin Corcoran

USA

b: 10 Jne 49 (Santa Monica)

The father of the eight Corcoran children (Bill, Noreen, Brian, Hugh, Donna, Kerry, Kevin and Kelly) was head of MGM's maintenance department, and brought them along for a crowd scene in *Show Boat*. All the little Corcorans subsequently

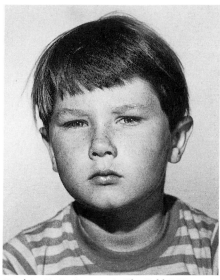

Resolute: Kevin Corcoran in The Rabbit Trap

appeared in films or on TV, but most notably Noreen and Donna – and Kevin, who went on to be a stalwart of Disney films.

He had been a 'Mouseketeer' on the 'Mickey Mouse Club' since 1956, and from *Old Yeller* the following year played a whole string of Disney leads, usually as Tommy Kirk's ◇ footloose kid brother.

His chunky, resolute little figure, with ice-blue eyes and obstinate mouth set in a round face, became a reassuring Hollywood presence as he grappled with an assortment of dogs (yellow, shaggy or savage), plus a chimpanzee and a tiger – in or out of the circus. From a part he played in a Disney TV serial, *Adventures in Dairyland*, Kevin became generally known as 'Moochie', which suited him fine.

After one late-teens film, *Blue* (68), Kevin Corcoran gave up acting. But he stayed with Disney as an assistant producer, or in the case of *Treasure of Matecumbe* (76) assistant director.

60 Moochie of Pop Warner Football
   Pollyanna
   Swiss Family Robinson
   Toby Tyler
61 Babes in Toyland
62 Bon Voyage!
   Johnny Shiloh
   The Mooncussers
63 Savage Sam
64 A Tiger Walks

Don't forget the Fruit Gums: Gilmore, 1960

Denis Gilmore

BRITAIN

b: 14 Aug 49 (Hillingdon)

Denis was the English Menace – a well-known freckled model-child of the 1950s, associated in the national psyche with the slogan 'Don't forget the Fruit Gums, Mum!' (Though the voice was in fact supplied by the boy-impersonating radio actress Denise Bryer.)

Towards the age of ten the red-haired teddy-bear got into acting, appearing in several popular TV series and, with Vincent Winter ◇, in a trio of films for Disney. In 1964 he starred in his own series, 'Mike', for ITV, and the following year had a lead in *Cup Fever* for the Children's Film Foundation.

In 1966 Denis Gilmore was in the last scene of Truffaut's *Fahrenheit 451* – as the memoriser of 'Martian Chronicles' – and after that in *Gates to Paradise* (GB/YU 67), *H2S* (IT 68), *Satan's Skin* (70) and *Psychomania* (US 72).

58 The Horse's Mouth
   Them Nice Americans
60 Hand in Hand
   The Unstoppable Man
62 Almost Angels (US)
63 The Horse Without a Head
   The Three Lives of Thomasina (GB/US)
64 The Golden Head (US/HU)
   The Tomb of Ligeia
65 Cup Fever

In the 1980s, Denis's little son Denis was advertising ('a chip off the old block') in British casting directories.

Razvan Petrescu

ROMANIA

b: 8 Sep 49 (Bucharest)

The internationally successful co-production *Codine*, directed by Henri Colpi, was not about a pain-killer but a pain-causer in the form of a large Balkan bandit, to whom a young boy becomes nervously attached. Loyalties are divided in the manner of a far less joky 'Treasure Island'.

Razvan Petrescu, a warm-hearted performer, didn't pursue an acting career. After graduating at the Faculty of Philology, he taught English at a Bucharest high school.

63 Codine (FR/RO)

Giannis Kalatzopoulos

GREECE

b: 1949 (Athens)

Giannis, who also spoke English and French, made his stage debut in 1954 at the Children's Theatre in Athens in a play called 'The Two Urchins'. Soon afterwards, Grigoris Lambrinis cast him in his film *To koritsi me ta paramithia*.

Kalatzopoulos had an important film role in *I thissia mias ginekas* (69), but his career henceforth lay mainly in the theatre, where he has played such leading parts as Brecht's Galileo.

56 Kinigontas ton erota (Hunting for love)
   To koritsi me ta paramithia
     (The girl with the stories)
57 Thelo na zissis manula
     (I want you to live, Mummy)
   Tis nichtas ta kamomata
     (What happened in the night)
61 Choris mitera (Without a mother)
   To paidi tou dromou (Child of the street)
62 Den gnorissa mitera
     (I never knew a mother)
   I katatregmeni (The persecuted)
   Psila ta cheria Hitler (Hands up, Hitler)

Marco Paoletti

ITALY

b: 1949 (Siena)

Like Edoardo Nevola ◇, the elegant, humorous Marco made his debut in *Il ferroviere*. He went on to make fewer films but with more glamorous roles, notably as the adventurous heroes of the oft-filmed *Dagli Appennini alle Ande* and *Lazarillo de Tormes*.

Paoletti made at least one further appearance, in *Saul e David* (IT/ES 65).

55 Il ferroviere (The railwayman)
57 Il maestro (The schoolmaster – IT/ES)
58 Dagli Appennini alle Ande
     (From Apennines to Andes – IT/AR)
   Pia de' Tolomei
59 El lazarillo de Tormes
     (The little guide from Tormes – ES)

Traveller: Marco Paoletti in the 1958 version of Dagli Appennini alle Ande

Tadzio Wiśniewski

POLAND

b: 1949

Tadzio's enchantingly flustered face – he would have made an ideal silent comic – is memorable in the films of the best Polish directors of children, Janusz Nasfeter and Wadim Berestowski. He has supporting roles in all of these, but deservedly a lead to himself in *Moj stary*.

58 Male dramaty (Little dramas)
60 Kolorowe ponczochy (Coloured stockings)
   Przejażdżka (The excursion)
61 Bitwa o Kozi dwor (The battle of Goat Yard)
   Moj stary (My old man)

Mustapha Brick

MOROCCO

b: circa 1949

In Casablanca, the 12-year-old bootblack Abdou works to keep his mother and kid brother, but becomes the tool of criminals. He saves up to buy his mother a sewing machine. Having bought it, he drops it.

61 Les enfants du soleil (Children of the sun)

Francisco Javier Cebrian

SPAIN

b: circa 1949

The exuberant Francisco had leads in both his films, and in *Pascualin* was billed simply as 'Francisco Javier'.

63 Se necesita chico (Boy wanted)
65 Pascualin

Vasso Gabriel

LEBANON

b: circa 1949

The Lebanese film *Le petit étranger* is about 13-year-old Dori, who has always wanted to be an airman, and builds himself a

Flustered: Tadzio Wisniewski in Moj stary

wooden plane. When his elder brother is jailed for a *crime passionnel*, Dori rides away on a white horse, leaving family and friends behind. Seeking adventure, he finds brutality and prejudice.

A white plane would have been better.

62 Le petit étranger (The little stranger)

Miguelito Gil

SPAIN

b: circa 1949

Miguelito's most starry (not to say tacky) part was in *Un traje blanco*, as a six-year-old who dreams of making his first communion in a white suit. To deter him from continually stealing suitable suits, a dying woman gives him some money, but his soldier brother gambles it away.

Whiter than white: Miguelito Gil in Un traje blanco

Little Marcos then loses an arm while working in a foundry. . . . Whereupon, when the story reaches the public prints, rich gifts are showered on the maimed child from all over the world, and he is thus able to take a whiter-than-white communion.

55 Recluta con niño (Recruit with child)
56 Un traje blanco (A white suit)
58 Cafe de Puerto
59 El hombre de la isla
      (The man on the island)

Juan José

SPAIN

b: circa 1949

Boy singers were now top box-office in Latin countries. Juan José had the lead in *Demonio con angel*.

62 Las travesuras de Morucha (Morucha's
      pranks)
63 Un demonio con angel (Demon and angel)

Prickles of conscience: Lutz Manke in
Igelfreundschaft

Stepson: Tuukka Tanner in Pikku Pietarin piha

Lutz Manke

EAST GERMANY

b: circa 1949

To quote the Czech catalogue of children's films, on Hermann Zschoche's heart-warming *Igelfreundschaft*:

'Heiner lives near the Czechoslovak frontier. Using a wooden pipe which he has carved himself, he lures a little hedgehog to him. The animal has a ring on its foot which means that it belongs to somebody. Yet Heiner doesn't want to give it back and hides it.

'One day he is invited to visit a village on the other side of the frontier. There he meets a girl called Jana, and discovers that she has lost a pet hedgehog. He says nothing. But when the Czech children send their favourite rabbit as a gift to the German Pioneers, Heiner has a twinge of conscience. In an adventurous way, he returns the hedgehog to Jana.'

For all lovers of adventure, hedge-hogs and the prickles of conscience, *Igelfreundschaft* is a must.

61 Igelfreundschaft
      (Hedgehog friendship – DD/CS)

Tuukka Tanner

FINLAND

b: circa 1949

Pikku Pietarin piha was based on a recent children's book by Aapeli. It was a rather subtle little saga of childhood, seen through the eyes of an unusual child.

Pietari, its hero, is the son of a market vendor in a small provincial town, and the story falls into three sections: Before, During and After Karoliina – this being the name of a step-mother whom the father marries and who both arrives and leaves dramatically but without explanation. Karoliina is a powerful woman, well-disposed towards Pietari, for whom she makes new trousers. Her mysteriousness is in convincing proportion to a child's understanding of adult goings-on.

Pietari, vividly depicted by the sturdy Tuukka Tanner, is a real character, talking things over man-to-man with a very per-sonal God and caught up in all the serious concerns of courtyard life: singing hymns, burying rats and teaching local toddlers to pee standing up.

Jack Witikka's film, shot in Porvoo in the late summer of 1961, has a directness and realism that doesn't preclude poetry, and is one of the finest products of the Finnish cinema. The story was filmed again in 1977 as *Aika hyvä ihmiseksi*, with OSSI ARONEN as Peter.

61 Pikku Pietarin piha (Little Peter's yard)

Karel Smyczek

CZECHOSLOVAKIA

b: 31 Mar 50 (Mělník)

The round-faced, intelligent Smyczek, usually bespectacled, was one of the best Czech boy actors of the early 1960s. He went on acting for a time, and appeared in some 25 films before turning to work as an assistant director.

After five years of training at the Prague Film Faculty, he began writing and directing for TV, and in 1979 directed *Housata*, his first feature film for the cinema. In further films, such as *Jen si tak trochu písknout* (Just a little whistle) he has showed great insight in directing children.

59 Bila holubice (The white dove)
   Zpivajici pudřenka
     (The musical powder-compact)
60 Pochodne (Torches)
   Zle pondělí (Black Monday)
61 Pohadka o stare tramvaji
     (Tale of an old tram)
64 Láska nebeska (Heavenly love)
   Tato, sežeň štěně (Buy me a puppy, Dad)
65 Volejte Martina (Send for Martin)

Nicholas Hammond

BRITAIN/USA

b: 15 May 50 (Washington, D.C.)

His mother was the English actress Eileen Bennett, and when he was eleven Nicholas appeared on the Broadway stage in 'The Complaisant Lover', playing Michael Redgrave's son. He was only one of the anonymous schoolboys in *Lord of the Flies*, but played the elder Trapp son in *The Sound of Music*.

Karel Smyczek in Zle pondělí

After appearing in *Skyjacked* (71), *Superdad* (74) and *Law of the Land* (76), Nicholas Hammond — now a graduate of Princeton — landed a star part no one could have anticipated, becoming *Spider-Man* (77) both in the cinema and in the TV series 'The Amazing Spider-Man' (78).

Since tangling with a spider proved to have more useful side-effects than mixing it with a fly, this particular young scientist, Peter Parker, continued to scale walls in vertical chase of crime in *Spider-Man Strikes Back* (78) and *Spider-Man: the Dragon's Challenge* (79) before arachnoid heroes lost their charm.

Hammond now branched out into a second career as a photo-journalist, but hit the screen again in *The Challenge* (86).

61 Lord of the Flies
65 The Sound of Music

Matthieu Carrière

WEST GERMANY

b: 2 Aug 50 (Hannover)

Handsome Matthieu, the son of a psychiatrist, acted on stage from the age of ten before being cast as hero-as-boy in the screen version of Thomas Mann's *Tonio Kröger*. By the time he landed the conscience-racked lead in another literary adaptation for the cinema, *Der junge Törless* — this time from Musil — he had played Kästner's 'Emil' and 'Anton' on stage.

Completing his education in France, Carrière, with his Franco-German parentage and trilingual abilities, now embarked on perhaps the most co-productional career in screen history. He was in *Gates to Paradise* (GB/DE 67), *La maison des Bories* (FR 69), *Le petit matin* (FR 69), *Rendez-vous à Bray* (FR/BE/DE 71), *Malpertuis* (FR/BE/DE 71), *Etat de siège* (FR/IT/DE 72), *L'homme au cerveau greffé* (FR/IT/DE 72), and has continued to play leads not only for directors in France and Germany, but also in Italy, Belgium, Switzerland, Holland and Canada.

64 Tonio Kröger (FR/DE)
66 Der junge Törless
 (Young Törless – DE/FR)

Christopher Witty

BRITAIN

b: 26 Aug 50

The amiable curly-haired Witty was seldom a star, outside of children's films, but had a central role as a kidnapped Arab crown prince in *Masquerade*.

He was seen later in *Baby Love* (68) and *The Railway Children* (70).

56 The Passionate Stranger
57 No Time for Tears
58 Life in Emergency Ward 10
59 The Adventures of Rex (serial)
 Life in Danger
 Sapphire
60 No Kidding
 Rockets in the Dunes
61 The Damned
63 Go Kart Go
64 Masquerade

Fergus McClelland

BRITAIN

b: 10 Sep 50 (Hampstead, London)

Like Christian Bale ◇ in *Empire of the Sun*, young Fergus – son of the Irish actor Allan McClelland – was required in *Sammy Going South* to represent a middle-class British schoolboy brought face to face with war and the grim realities of life. Since Sammy's ordeal involves finding his way the length of Africa, from Port Said to Durban, it is less claustrophobic than imprisoned Jim's.

Though a rather confected Odyssey, and no more Alexander Mackendrick's finest film than *Empire* is Spielberg's, this softened version of W.H. Canaway's novel offered Fergus McClelland the chance to see spectacular landscapes and to meet an assortment of exotic animals, including Edward G. Robinson as a grizzled hunter with a Hemingway beard and a sideline in smuggled diamonds. As the pompously manly little Brit, Fergus was superb, rightly suspicious of the motives of most of his 'helpers', and singing defiantly to himself when alone.

On the strength of his performance he got work with the Royal Shakespeare company, and played Jim Hawkins in the Mermaid Theatre's 'Treasure Island' of Christmas 1963. He did a good deal of TV work, including several weeks in the hospital soap opera 'Emergency Ward 10'.

After marginal roles in *Press for Time* (66) and the musical *Goodbye Mr Chips* (69) Fergus abandoned the acting profession. He now supports himself, and his interest in music and ancient religions, by work in electronics, and has been writing a novel on an Old Testament subject.

63 Sammy Going South
64 The Pumpkin Eater

Dennis Holmes

USA

b: 10 Oct 50

Dennis – who made his film debut at the age of six weeks – should not be confused with the adult British actor Denis Holmes, who was active at the same time. (Since British Denis usually wore a heavy moustache, you would not confuse them if you saw them.)

Although determined little blond Dennis made a solid fistful of cinema films, he was best known for his resident role as Mike in the TV series 'Laramie' (1959-63) though he also appeared in 'Wagon Train' and 'Tales of Wells Fargo'.

51 Operation Pacific
59 Hound Dog Man
 Woman Obsessed
60 Key Witness
61 The Fiercest Heart
63 The Miracle of Santa's White Reindeer

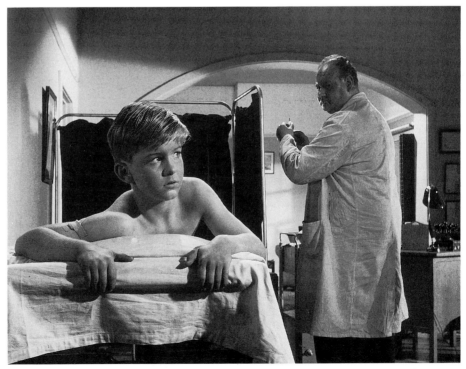

This won't hurt: Fergus McClelland faces inoculation from Guy Deghy in Sammy Going South

Kondrat quits the cloister in Historia żółtek cizemki

Marek Kondrat

POLAND

b: 18 Oct 50 (Cracow)

Marek, son of the actor Tadeusz Kondrat, had a leading role in *Historja żółtek cizemki* as a 15th-century village boy who aspires to be a wood-carver. After a marathon footslog to Cracow, he is accepted as an apprentice and helps to work on a great altar-piece – but at the moment of unveiling is accused of theft.

Marek later followed in his father's footsteps. He had starring roles in *Dvoji svet v Hotelu Pacifik* (75) and *Smuga cienia* (76). He was, more modestly, in *Dreszcze* (81), in Wajda's *Danton* (FR/PL 82) and in *Rok spokojnego słonca* (84), among many other films.

61 Historja żółtek cizemki
     (Story of a yellow slipper)
62 Miedzy brzegami (Between the coasts)

Hanuš Bor

CZECHOSLOVAKIA

b: 26 Dec 50

60 Černa sobota (Black Saturday)
     Valčik pro milion (Waltz for a million)
61 Každa koruna dobra (Each good crown)
62 Klaun Ferdinand a raketa
     (Ferdinand the clown and a rocket)
63 Einstein kontra Babinsky
     (Einstein versus Babinsky)
66 Ukradena vzducholod (The stolen airship)

Joël Flateau

FRANCE

b: 28 Dec 50 (Paris)

Joël sprang from the union of two great French theatrical families. His maternal great-great-grandfather, for instance, Jules Barbier, wrote the libretti for Gounod's 'Faust' and 'Roméo et Juliette'; one of his great-grandfathers, Jean d'Yd, was a famous actor, and another, Léon Flateau,

Classic hero: Jöel Flateau in the 1957 Sans famille

directed a Paris theatre, La Cigale. His own parents were the actors Serge Flateau and Pierrette Castan. It was almost inevitable that he would be the leading boy actor of his generation in France.

When he was five he auditioned as a pianist at the Paris Conservatoire (he would later play the child Mozart on TV), and at six made his screen debut as a sick child in *Echec au porteur*. At seven he had the classic role of Rémi in André Michel's remake of *Sans famille*, and the leads now came thick and fast. On TV he was Little Lord Fauntleroy, l'Aiglon, Pip in 'Great Expectations', the Lazarillo and the Bon Petit Diable.

In the cinema, he played Césariot in Joshua Logan's remake of *Fanny*, and in Carl Foreman's *The Victors* – bravely – a boy prostitute offering himself to exhausted GIs. He was fluent in English and Spanish.

After playing a lead in Bernard Romy's *L'acte* (CH 68) much of his activity transferred to Switzerland, where he formed his own pop groups 'Phoetus' (contributing keyboard and vocals) and later 'Magic Power'. For the time being, at least, he has turned his elegant back on acting.

57 Echec au porteur
    (Pay out bearer)
    Sans famille (No relations – FR/IT)
58 Drôles de phénomènes
    (Curious happenings)
    Les jeux dangereux
    (Dangerous games – FR/IT)
59 Si le ciel s'en mêle (If heaven takes a hand)
60 Fanny (US)
63 The Victors (GB)
64 En France comme si vous y étiez
    (Imagine you're in France)

Pascal Lamorisse

FRANCE

b: 1950

Pascal appeared only in the open-air films of his father Albert Lamorisse – and only briefly, as a toddler, in *Crin Blanc*.

Then, in Lamorisse's famous *Ballon*

Adjustments: Pascal Lamorisse in Voyage en ballon

rouge, the little boy makes friends with a toy balloon which follows him everywhere before it is stoned by hostile boys, dies, and rises again, escorted to heaven by all the balloons of Paris.

In *Voyage en ballon*, four years later, Pascal is himself up in the sky in a hot-air balloon, travelling with his scientific grandfather from Paris down to Provence and then, alone, to the Alps, the Camargue and the Atlantic coast.

In both films the balloon, having survived a disaster, escapes. The disasters in real life, though, were all too real. When the balloon in *Voyage* burst alarmingly

into flames, this was not in the script: it was a potentially lethal accident which Lamorisse in his hovering helicopter had caught on film and decided to incorporate into the story.

In 1970, while he was shooting *Le vent des amoureux* in Iran, Albert Lamorisse's helicopter crashed and he was killed. Pascal helped to complete the film, which later won an Oscar nomination.

53 Crin Blanc, cheval sauvage
    (White Mane, the wild horse)
56 Le ballon rouge (The red balloon)
60 Voyage en ballon (Journey by balloon)

Marietto, circa 1961

Marietto Angeletti

ITALY

b: circa 1950

The frail but engaging Marietto – simply billed by his first name until about 1964 – made himself an international starlet by his command of languages. He acted with Clark Gable, Gregory Peck and Charlton Heston, as well as guesting in France and Germany.

He has a central role in Zinnemann's *Behold a Pale Horse*, a rather stiff post-Spanish-civil-war drama of treachery and revenge, playing opposite Peck's exiled veteran guerrilla.

57 La ballerina e il Padreterno
  (The ballerina and the Everlasting Father)
58 Kleine Leute – mal ganz gross
  (Little big people – DE)
60 It Started in Naples (US)
  Giuseppe venduto dai fratelli
  (Joseph sold by his brothers)
61 Blond muss man sein auf Capri
  (Better be blond on Capri – DE)
62 Giganta di Metropolis
  (The giant of Metropolis)
  Jusqu'au bout du monde
  (To the world's end – FR/IT)
  The Pigeon That Took Rome (US)
64 Behold a Pale Horse (US)

Angel Gomez

SPAIN

b: circa 1950

This singing cherub won considerable celebrity as 'Pachin' in two lightweight vehicles. But as 'Angelito' in *Los desheredados* (the Spanish release title was 'An angel on trial') a bid for larger wings was discernible.

He played a Spanish boy who travels with his father to Porto Rico, and is orphaned in a car smash soon after as they land. His ancient uncle, once a famous guitarist, is alcoholic and reduced to playing in the streets of San Juan. Angelito sings along with him, to the delight of passers-by.

Uncle is then denounced as an exploiter of minors, and the boy is sent to a home, where he is miserable until his voice is heard by a visiting TV star. Angelito now hits the heights. But the school bully frames him for a theft and he has to stand trial. . . . Will evil rout good?

61 Pachin
  Pachin almirante (Admiral Pachin)
64 Los desheredados (The disinherited –
  MX/ES/PR)

Apartness: Roger Mobley in A Dog's Best Friend

Roger Mobley

USA

b: circa 1950

In any Jacqueline Onassis prize for wide-apart eyes in the boy-actor class, Roger Mobley would have to start co-favourite with the later Sean Kelly °.

Following the fleet: Angel Gomez and friend in Pachin almirante

The inseparable air of dogged integrity stood him in good stead, with the Disney studio among others.

He played several leads, though not in *Emil*, where Bryan Russell ◊ had the title role and Roger, in a hideous hat, was the all-fixing Gustav. The remaining films of 1964-65 were TV specials in the NBC series 'Walt Disney's Wonderful World of Color'.

Many years afterwards Mobley made a screen comeback for the old firm in *The Apple Dumpling Gang Rides Again* (79).

60 A Dog's Best Friend
61 The Boy Who Caught a Crook
   The Comancheros
   Jack the Giant Killer
   The Silent Call
63 Dime With a Halo
64 Emil and the Detectives
   A Taste of Melon
   Treasure in the Haunted House
65 Gallegher
   The Further Adventures of Gallegher

Vangelis Joannides

GREECE

b: circa 1950

In classical times, an apparently all-female fishing village is stumbled on by a group of shepherds down from the mountains. The youngest shepherd boy, Skymnos, is fascinated by a teenage girl called Chloe. At the end, seeing her seduced by another, he drowns himself.

Nikos Koundouros's *Little Aphrodites* won many festival awards, and with its evocation of the pastoral world of Longus and Theocritus was seen as unassailably poetic. To some, with its interminable mooching over rocks, its symbolic dead pelican and gloomy bouts of heavy breathing, it seemed a load of classical rubbish.

Young Joannides' luminous study in puppy-love, however – 'Skymnos' more or less means 'puppy' – is hard to forget.

62 Mikres Afrodites (Little Aphrodites)

Slightly foxed: Vangelis Joannides in Mikres Afrodites

Michal Koblic

CZECHOSLOVAKIA

b: circa 1950

The fair-haired, dark-eyed Koblic made a memorable debut in *Práče* as the frail but heroic 'Slinger' (historically the name for Hussite boy soldiers). In the closing days of World War Two little František is liberated from a Nazi concentration camp, and fights his way back to Czech soil.

He had another outstanding lead in *Králíci*, a satire on human hypocrisy seen through a child's eyes.

Road to ruin: Michal Koblic takes a sip in Králíci ve vysoké trávě

60 Práče (The slinger)
   Lidé jako ty (People like you)
   Osevni (Sowing)
61 Králíci ve vysoké trávě
   (Rabbits in the tall grass)
62 Neklidna hladina (Troubled surface)
   Oranžový měsíc (Orange moon)
   Střevicky (The shoes)

Cesareo Quezadas

MEXICO

b: circa 1950

The cheeky little Quezadas was for some time identified with his debut role as 'Tom Thumb', and continued to be referred to as 'Pulgarcito'. But he soon graduated from mischief to pathos, and *El sordo* was a marvellously grotesque wallow, with the comedian Antonio Espino playing soppy Chaplin to his Coogan and praying to the Virgin to restore his hearing – lost while defending a girl from rape – so he can hear what the desperate child is shouting. (Which is, as it happens: 'I've been bitten by a poisonous spider!')

In *Joselito vagabundo* he was teamed for the second time, after an interval of six years, with the Spanish boy singer 'Joselito' (José Jimenez ◇). Though Joselito was the elder by four years or so, his career was to continue longer.

57 Pulgarcito (Tom Thumb)
58 Angelitos del trapecio
   (Little angels of the trapeze)
   Mi niño, mi caballo y yo
   (My boy, my horse and me)
   El sordo (The deaf man)
59 Aventuras de Joselito en America
   (Joselito's adventures in America –
   ES/MX)
   El dolor de pagar la renta
   (The pain of paying the rent)
   Santa Claus
60 Caperucita y Pulgarcito contra los
   monstruos (Red Riding Hood and Tom
   Thumb versus the monsters – MX)
   El globero (The balloon-seller)
61 La banda de los ocho
   (The gang of eight – ES/MX)
   Ha llegado un angel (An angel has arrived)
62 ¿Chico o chica? (Boy or girl? – ES)
65 Duelo de pistoleros (Duel of gunmen)
   Joselito vagabundo
   (Joselito the wanderer)

Tom Thumb meets the Nightingale: Cesareo Quezadas (left) and Joselito Jiménez (right) in Aventuras de Joselito in America

Hwang Hag Yun

NORTH KOREA

b: 21 Feb 51 (Pyongyang)

Hwang Hag Yun, born in the Songyo district of the North Korean capital, began his acting career when he was a pupil in the first grade of middle school. He continued in his later teens with roles in *The unfinished struggle* (67), *The flourishing village* (69) and *The flower girl* (71), and in 1976 joined the Korean Feature Film Studio.

Hwang has appeared in more than twenty of the Studio's films – notably *I'll beat the drum* (77) and *Hasty marriage* (87) – winning great popularity as a comedian. In 1988 he was awarded the title of Meritorious Actor.

64 People's Teacher
   Boy Company Member
65 Stormy Days

Jan Priskorn Schmidt

DENMARK

b: 22 Feb 51 (Copenhagen)

Jan (sometimes Priiskorn) Schmidt made his film debut at the age of nine, and was Denmark's leading boy actor throughout the Sixties. He also dubbed one of the leading roles in *Amici per la pelle*, and in one or two Disney films.

Venus fra Vestø, incidentally, was a remake of Britain's *Appointment with Venus*, with Jan playing the Jeremy Spenser ◇ part, and the eponymous cow on a Danish island.

Jan continued for a while, in *Min søsters børn* (66) and its sequel, *Min søsters børn på bryllupsrejse* (67), then in *Threesome* (US/DK 69), otherwise known as *Ursula*.

60 Flemming og Kvik (Flemming and Quick)
61 Flemming på kostskole
   (Flemming at boarding school)
   Mine tossede drenge (My crazy boys)
   Soldaterkammerater på efterårsmanøvre
   (Comrades-in-arms on autumn
   manoeuvres)
   Sorte Shara (Black Shara)

Cow-catcher: Jan Priskorn Schmidt in Venus fra Vestø

Kurt Russell

USA

b: 17 Mar 51 (Springfield, Mass.)

The father, Bing Russell, was a baseball pro who became an actor. His baby was bound to be beefy, but Kurt has always offered an interesting combination of the square-jawed and the feline.

A passion for motor-racing reared its head when he was only eight, but four more years passed before his first movie appearance: hacking Elvis Presley's shins in *It Happened at the World's Fair*. In 1963 he landed the title role, as the son of an itinerant doctor, in a TV Western series called 'The Travels of Jaimie McPheeters',

and more or less simultaneously played Jaimie in a film, *Guns of Diablo*, drawn from the same book. He also made guest appearances in other series like 'The Fugitive' and 'Gilligan's Island'.

Soon afterwards he was signed up by the Walt Disney studios, and had his first outing in *Follow Me, Boys!* as a recalcitrant orphan (named, oddly, Whitey White) who is adopted, and turned into a God-fearing Boy Scout, by Fred McMurray. It was a film that left nearly everyone feeling recalcitrant.

In *Willie and the Yank*, he more or less reprised Kevin Corcoran's ◇ Disney role in *Johnny Shiloh*, as a boy soldier in the Civil War.

For a further eight years Russell was

Feline: Kurt Russell in The Travels of Jamie McPheeters

Jörgen Lindström

SWEDEN

b: 19 May 51

Jörgen, best known for his performances in the 1960's for Ingmar Bergman and Mai Zetterling, made an early bow in a TV dramatisation of *Åke and His World*. Bertil Malmberg's semi-autobiographical novel of 1924 told of childhood in a Swedish village, with its joys, ordeals and terrors. (Another admirable Lindström, Martin, was to play Åke for Allan Edwall 25 years later.)

Bergman, fascinated by Jörgen's huge, troubled blue eyes and innocently sensual tadpole mouth, made powerful use of them in two of his weirdest films. In *The Silence* the boy played the ten-year-old son of a spiteful nymphomaniac (Gunnel Lindblom), observing in a cavernous hotel her sexual couplings and her cruelty to her sister, his aunt (Ingrid Thulin).

Four years later, in *Persona* – which could equally well have been called *The Silence* – he is the emblematic child, at the opening and close of the film, reaching out towards the image of a woman's face.

In Zetterling's *Night Games* – this time as Ingrid Thulin's son – Jörgen is present at an alarming party of decadents, at the climax of which his pregnant mother gives birth to a dead baby. (What a great party this is.) Although he retreats from the orgy, he is undergoing his own crisis of identity, given to painting his face and drawn incestuously towards his mother.

Few of Jörgen's films would have appealed to Disney, but his strangely receptive face became a part of cinema history.

almost exclusively the clean-limbed Disney teenager, usually directed by Robert Butler or Vincent McEveety, with leads in *The One and Only Genuine Original Family Band* (68), *The Horse in the Grey Flannel Suit* (68), *Guns in the Heather* (68), *The Computer Wore Tennis Shoes* (69), *The Barefoot Executive* (70), *Now You See Him, Now You Don't* (72), *Charley and the Angel* (73), *Superdad* (74), *The Deadly Tower* (75) and *The Strongest Man in the World* (75).

Meanwhile, however, on furlough from Disney, he played the younger of James Stewart's ex-convict companions in *Fools' Parade* (71), and, after a lead in the TV series 'The Quest' (76), landed his break-through role in 1978 as – of all people – *Elvis*, the very man whose ankles he had assaulted fifteen years earlier. His fair hair dyed dark, he had a sporting stab at impersonating someone he was quite unlike.

Since then, increasingly beefy and often mean, Kurt Russell has starred in two of John Carpenter's films, *Escape from New York* (81) and *The Thing* (82), as well as in *Used Cars* (80), *Silkwood* (83), *Swing Shift* (84), *The Mean Season* (85), *Overboard* (87), *Tequila Sunrise* (88), *Tango and Cash* (89), *Backdraft* (91) and many more

He gives good value, and one welcome feature of the break from Disney is that his film titles have got shorter.

His early performances brought him to international attention, and three of his four next films had Spanish or Italian connections.

Further ones included *Top Crack* (IT 66), *Hello-Goodbye* (US 70), *Promise at Dawn* (US/FR 70), *Time for Loving* (GB 71) and *Hellé* (72). He has since worked for such directors as Carné (*Les assassins de l'ordre*, 72), Tavernier (*Le juge et l'assassin*, 75), Visconti (*L'innocente*, FR/IT 76) and Goretta (*Les chemins de l'exil*, 78).

Haudepin has also made a film of his own: *Paco l'infaillible*, starring Patrick Dewaere, which won a prize at the 1979 Cannes Festival. Writing and directing are his main aims now.

Troubled: Jörgen Lindström in Tystnaden

Didier Haudepin

FRANCE

b: 15 Aug 51 (Paris)

His parents were schoolteachers. His younger sister, Sabine, worked for Truffaut in films as far apart as *Jules et Jim* and *Le dernier Métro*.

Didier was blessed (or cursed) with one of the most beautiful faces any child has brought to the screen: sensitive without being drippy, thoughtful but not dopy, vulnerable yet with a certain sharpness. He was touching as Jeanne Moreau's little son in *Moderato cantabile*, and even more so as the hapless object of a schoolboy passion in the film of Peyrefitte's 'Les amitiés particulières'.

Between these, in the theatre, he had played the Barry Gordon ◇ role in 'A Thousand Clowns', opposite Yves Montand, and for three years he was in another famous story of school-bound passion, Montherlant's 'La ville dont le prince est un enfant'.

Love-object: Didier Haudepin (right) with Francis Lacombrade in Les amitiés particulières

Cor van der Linden

HOLLAND

b: 2 Oct 51

He was the son of H.J. van der Linden, who between 1952 and 1978 directed some thirty comedies and adventure stories for children. Cor and his sister Jos (born 10 March 1953) appeared in many of them, though whereas he was eight before he began, she started at two.

The 'Sjors en Sjimmie' films are drawn from a popular comic strip featuring a white and a black boy. ('Sjimmie', the black one, was sometimes played by a girl – twice by Jos.) In the 1962 film, Cor played 'Sjors', but not in the later ones.

Between 1969 and 1978 Cor van der Linden had parts in eight more of his father's films, including the very last, but not in leading roles.

60 Avonturen van een zigeunerjongen
   (A gypsy boy's adventures)
62 Het verraad van de Zwarte Ridder
   (The Black Knight's treason)
   Robin Hood en zijn schelmen
   (Robin Hood and his merry men)
   Sjors en Sjimmie op Pirateneiland
   (George and Jimmie on Pirates'
   Island)
64 De avonturen van Pietje Bell
   (The adventures of Pete Bell)
   De jongen uit het Wilde Westen
   (The boy from the Wild West)
65 Vrijbuiters van het woud
   (Robbers of the forest)
66 Sjors en Sjimmie en de gorilla
   (George and Jimmie and the gorilla)
   De man met het zwarte masker
   (The man in the black mask)

The title role in *De avonturen van Pietje Bell* was played by JEU CONSTEN (born 1951), whose father, the actor Hub Consten, appeared in many of H.J. van der Linden's films. In 1966 Jeu played Sjors to the Sjimmie of Jos van der Linden, the director's daughter, and was in eight more Van der Linden films, the last in 1975.

Stephan Schwartz

WEST GERMANY

b: 18 Oct 51 (Berlin)

56 Der Glockengiesser von Tirol
   (The bell-founder of Tyrol)
58 Solang' die Sterne glühn
   (As long as the stars shine)
59 Der Haustyrann (The domestic tyrant)

Pereira Neto

PORTUGAL

b: circa 1951

One doesn't associate Portugal with doggy dramas, but Pereira Neto had the lead in two.

63 Nove rapaces e um cão
   (Nine boys and a dog)
65 Um cão e dois destinos
   (A dog and two destinies)

Roberto Chevalier

ITALY

b: 14 Mar 52

57 Giovani mariti (Young husbands)
58 The Naked Maja (US)
59 Il nemico di mia moglia (My wife's enemy)
   Gli scontenti (The discontented)
   Quartiere ovest (West district)
   Pulcinella cetrulo d'Acerra
   (Pulcinella, the Acerra cucumber)
   Centomila leghe nello spazio
   (100,000 leagues into space)
61 La vendetta di Ursus
   (The vengeance of Ursus)

Pat Cardi

USA

b: 2 May 52

Pat, son of a construction engineer, was a natural and touching actor. His two starring roles were interestingly contrasted. In *And Now Miguel* he was a devout Mexican boy with aspirations to prove himself as a shepherd, and in *Let's Kill*

Gone astray: Pat Cardi and lost lamb in And Now Miguel

Uncle a wealthy orphan with a murderous English guardian who plans to hijack his fortune by eliminating him.

Cardi returned to films in his early twenties, with roles in *Battle for the Planet of the Apes* (73) and *Horror High* (74).

58 The Naked and the Dead
63 Youngblood Hawke
65 Brainstorm
66 ... And Now Miguel
   Let's Kill Uncle

Kevin Brodie

USA

b: 31 May 52 (Burbank, Cal.)

Kevin, son of the actor Steve Brodie, made his debut at the age of seven in the 'Wyatt Earp' series on TV.

In 1972 he was in the Lassie film *Joyous Sound* for TV, and three years later in *The Great Spider Invasion*, on which he was also an assistant director.

Toshio Egi

JAPAN

b: 4 Jne 52 (Tokyo)

Toshio started acting at the age of four. When he was 21 he returned to the screen, and was seen in *Isoge wakamono* (74), *Tarao Bannai* (78) and *Kindaichi Kosuke no daiboken* (79)

Jay North

USA

b: 3 Aug 52 (North Hollywood)

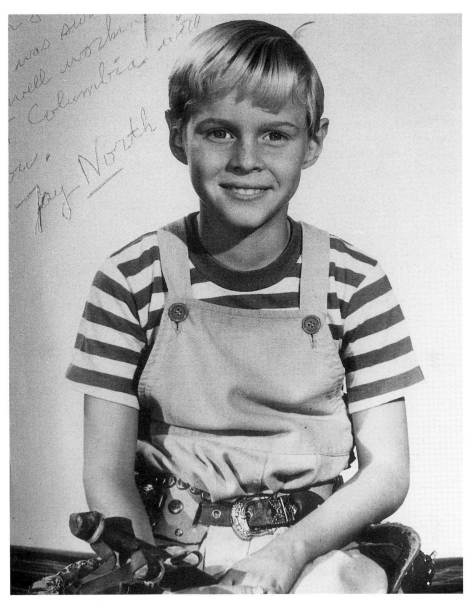

Unmelting: Jay North as Dennis

At the age of six a platinum blond child with unbelievably innocent blue eyes (it was unwise to believe them) became a national figure on CBS Television when he incarnated 'Dennis the Menace', the beloved brat of Hank Ketcham's strip cartoon – chosen by Ketcham himself out of 500 auditionees. Jay North's insolently charming smile and air of butter-wouldn't-melt made him, almost overnight, the kid every American parent wanted to spank. The series ran from 1959 to 1963.

   He had already appeared on TV in shows like 'Queen for a Day' or '77 Sunset Strip' before landing Dennis. Between 1959 and 1963 the role was to take him through four series and 146 episodes, and earn him nearly $90,000 not counting residuals, a tidy little fortune which, shrewdly invested in real estate, has saved him from further worries about cash. (It was as Dennis, incidentally, that he made a brief guest appearance in the Cantinflas vehicle *Pepe*.)

   The end of 'Dennis', though, wasn't the end of Jay. In the grotesque *Zebra in the Kitchen* he had the star part as a born-free animals'-libber, causing high-principled havoc when given a holiday job at a zoo –

and releasing the animals. He was by now a handsome and earnest, not to say priggish 12-year-old, and a year later, in *Maya*, he shared an Indian adventure with a boy called SAJID KHAN. (This duly got developed into a TV series.)

   Hereafter, for all his fame and glamour, Jay North's career spluttered. He toured in stage plays, and made one or two ill-starred returns to filming: in *Joyous Sound* (72) he was acted off the TV screen by Lassie, in *The Teacher* (74, AKA *The Seductress*) was seduced and strangled, and in *Scout's Honor* (80) had little to do. In the meantime he had served briefly in the

Navy before becoming a prison guard and then a 'nutritional consultant'.

   Reacting against what was clearly a traumatic childhood, North developed into a personable but under-employed and disgruntled young man of right-wing views: pro decent dress and capital punishment, anti long hair and rock 'n' roll.

Michael Newport, 1965

Michael Newport

BRITAIN

b: 23 Sep 52

This delightfully unaffected, freckly, often bespectacled boy got his big break as Frank Sinatra's kidnapped son in *The Naked Runner*, but had had rather more fun, a year or two before, as a stalwart little Cornishman in *The Devil-Ship Pirates*.

He also appeared with the Royal Shakespeare Company at Stratford-upon-Avon, for instance in the Paul Scofield 'Macbeth'.

In 1968 he was a bold Jim Hawkins in a BBC-TV serialisation of *Treasure Island*, and in 1969 made one last cinema appearance in *Mischief*. Thereafter he quit acting, and much of his work was connected with photography.

Around 1980 he invented a form of illuminated chess, called 'Spectrum Satellite'.

63 The Devil-Ship Pirates
65 Life at the Top
66 The Naked Runner
68 Decline and Fall . . . of a Bird-Watcher!
   If . . .

Jack Wild

BRITAIN

b: 30 Sep 52 (Royton, Lancs.)

Though frankly delinquent, the Artful Dodger is as near as English literature got to a Gavroche-character: and, advanced into the vale of teens as he was — fifteen at the time of filming — Jack Wild was so tinily terrific in the film of Bart's musical *Oliver!* that he really cannot be overlooked as a 'child actor'. (He had in fact appeared marginally in the original London stage production of 'Oliver!', but was then considered too small to play the Dodger.)

His only previous film appearance of note had been in a Children's Film Foundation production called *Danny the Dragon*, but this gave little hint of the swagger and patronising geniality his Dodger was to display. As a singing-and-dancing Cockney sparrow, a Phiz

Still dodging: Jack Wild in S.W.A.L.K.

caricature brought to exuberant life, all hat and boots and flapping, dandyish rags, he could not have been surpassed. The angelic Oliver of Mark Lester ◇ was never going to get much of a look-in.

When the popular American TV series 'H.R.Pufnstuf' was filmed as *Pufnstuf* (US 70), Wild made a brilliant hero, holding his own with witches, puppets and an animated flute. He then returned to Britain and was reunited with Mark Lester in the unsatisfying *S.W.A.L.K.* (71) – this mysterious title a schoolgirl acronym for Sealed With A Loving Kiss. Childhood romance, buddyhood and crude satire rode uneasily together in Alan Parker's script.

In the same year he was also reunited with Ron Moody (his ex-Fagin) in *Flight of the Doves*, he and a kid sister (Helen Raye) eluding both wicked uncle and wicked stepfather in a whimsical Irish adventure. He loyally supported Donovan in Jacques Demy's version of *The Pied Piper* (71), and in David Hemmings' *The 14* (73) showed leadership quality as the eldest of a rabble of orphaned siblings.

But this was his last worthwhile screen role. Since *Keep It Up Downstairs* (76) he has contented himself with being an 'all-round entertainer', and making the occasional guest appearance on TV.

66 Danny the Dragon
68 Oliver!

Masahiko Shimazu

JAPAN

b: 1 Oct 52 (Kagoshima Prefecture)

The young Masahiko trained for three years with the Wakakusa Troupe, and studied Japanese traditional dance with Fujima-ryu. He was in several of Ozu's later films, for instance as the younger brother in *Ohayo* (the remake of *I Was Born, But . . .*). He proved a hilarious pug-faced purveyor of dumb insolence, continually distracted by natural needs.

After one more film, *Mangan ryoko* (70), Shimazu abandoned acting.

Bryan Russell

USA

b: 1952 (Los Angeles)

In spite of his square jaw, Bryan was unrelated to Kurt Russell ◇, the Disney stable's other chief boy of the mid-1960s. He was a darker, more placidly handsome fellow, whose mother had been a concert pianist and whose sister Jeanie also acted.

He played the title role in the rather unatmospheric *Emil* of 1964, and in *Bullwhip Griffin* was paired with his great predecessor, Roddy McDowall ◇.

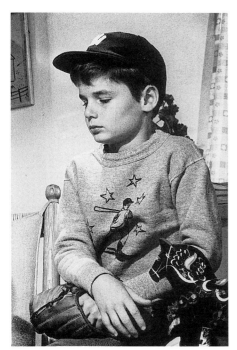

Placid: Bryan Russell in A Ticklish Affair

Pain in the shoulder: Martin Lartigue cadges a lift in Bébert et l'omnibus

Martin Lartigue

FRANCE

b: circa 1952

The irrepressible 'Tigibus' of *La guerre des boutons* — the most popular French children's film of the last 40 years — was the son of a painter, and grandson of the great photographer Jacques-Henri Lartigue, who died as recently as 1986.

Louis Pergaud's 'gallic, epic and rabelaisian' story of the few-holds-barred warfare between the boys of the villages of Longeverne and Velrans had been a minor classic since its appearance in 1912. Its name was taken from the Velrans' tactic of disabling captured Longevernes by cutting the buttons off their trousers — a tactic the Longevernes eventually trumped by going into battle stark naked and with nothing to lose.

It was filmed in 1936 – debuttoned – as *La guerre des gosses*, with Serge Grave ◇ playing Lebrac, the tough and charismatic Longeverne leader. When the actor Yves Robert decided to make a new version a quarter of a century later he restored the proper title and made a jolly romp of it, though in some respects making it too squeaky-clean for such an earthy affair.

He found a fine, Burt Lancasterish Lebrac in ANDRE TRETON, and an admirably dour Aztec (the Velrans' Rommel) in MICHEL ISELLA, and these two forged the epic link.

Martin Lartigue had the comic role of the baby of the party, Petit Gibus or Tigibus — younger brother of Grangibus — and made it his field-day, showing a total lack of soldierly qualities, getting drunk on patrol, and grumbling incessantly and ungrammatically. He was perhaps over-cute, but hammed it up to good effect.

An attempt to repeat the triumph a year later, starring Martin as a child who repeatedly gets mislaid 'with hilarious results', proved a mistake. The spectacle of a child of ten or more behaving like a rather moronic five-year-old was merely embarrassing.

After playing the lead in a TV serialisation of *Huckleberry Finn*, Martin held his peace for a few years, and then – still holding it – began to study mime. He did theatre work with Robert Dhéry, and made a cartoon film with Xavier Gélin, then decided to give up performing. He had been a great fluffer of lines and, surprisingly, a martyr to stage fright.

In his mid-twenties he left Paris for the Auvergne and began to paint in a naïf style, following in his father's footsteps. He has had several exhibitions.

In 1994 a very spirited Irish version of *Boutons* was directed by John Roberts. The rival commanders (Gregg Fitzgerald and John Coffey) were fine, but Little Con – the Tigibus figure, engagingly played by Anthony Cunningham – was much reduced in importance.

Bibi Morat

FRANCE

b: circa 1952

This comic *joli-laid* moppet, a hit in his first film, proved exportable, and was taken up by Hollywood and Spain.

60 La française et l'amour
 (The Frenchwoman and love)
 Tête folle (Crazy head)
62 Come Fly With Me (US)
 Le couteau dans la plaie
 (Knife in the wound)
64 Vacaciones para Ivette
 (Holiday for Ivette – ES)
65 Up from the Beach (US)

Bruce Ritchey

USA

b: circa 1952

With a face like a locked door, Ritchey was fiercely impressive in *A Child Is Waiting*, as the retarded child for whose mind and soul an unusually subdued Judy Garland struggles.

Owing to a conflict of intentions between the producer (Stanley Kramer) and the director (John Cassavetes) its release was delayed for four years; but the result, however compromised, has a troubling power.

62 A Child Is Waiting

Steve Bond

USA

b: 22 Apr 53 (Haifa, Israel)

When the hulking ex-football star Mike Henry made his last appearance as Tarzan he was not in peak condition. He was exhausted from the pressures of the two previous films, and this extra one, *Tarzan and the Jungle Boy*, had been set up at short notice to make the most of some Brazilian sets and locations.

In addition he was suffering from

Bibi Morat wishes the kindly German commandant (Marius Goring) good luck in Up from the Beach. *Between them, Françoise Rosay and Raymond Bussières.*

dysentery, and had only recently recovered from 'monkey fever' – this deriving from a facial injury inflicted on him, at equally short notice, by an enraged elderly chimpanzee called Dinky. During the shooting of the film itself, infections of the liver and ear were added to his burden. It's a miracle that the poor man could walk, let alone yell and swing from trees.

The Jungle Boy of the title, round whom the story revolved, was a blond child called Erik Brunik who had accompanied his geologist father, many years earlier, on an exhibition into the jungle. Their canoe had overturned, and the father had been drowned. Stranded in the jungle, Erik (now about 12) had learned Tarzanesque skills and acquired the company of a leopard, when discovered by the Apeman on behalf of some visiting journalists.

The story develops along the corniest of Tarzanian lines – but this time the great man's 'boy' really is something of a find. The young Steve Bond, an earnest and decent deliverer of silly speeches, has a cat-like grace that matches the pard's. His

barefoot running through trees and rocks has genuine exhilaration.

If the jungle boy's accent also seemed exotic, this was neither intentional nor surprising. Steve's real name was Shlomo Goldberg, and he had been born in Israel. After divorce from his father, a ship's steward, little Shlomo's mother had emigrated and taken him to Los Angeles, where she had friends. He had already done some stage work in Israel, and was resuming his career in America when the Tarzan assignment came up, and the dark boy was dyed blond.

A mix-up in the role allocations, presumably from some erroneous handout, has been repeatedly copied over the years, though it has no relation to what appears on the film. Just to put the record straight, Eric really *is* played by Steve Bond – and not by Ronald Gans, who (not Ed Johnson) plays the photographer-journalist. The good and bad jungle princes are played, respectively, by Ed and his Olympic brother Rafer Johnson. Bond says he appeared in two more

298

Tarzan films shot in Brazil at the same time as *Tarzan and the Jungle Boy*, but for some reason these were never released. Apart from playing Kirk Douglas as a boy in *The Arrangement*, he had no more screen roles before growing up. He worked by turns as waiter, bouncer, truck-driver and model. (In this last *métier* he achieved some fame as a nude centrefold in 'Playgirl' in 1973.)

Finally he broke back into acting, with leads in *Cat Murkil and the Silks* (76), *Massacre at Central High* (76), *Gas Pump Girls* (79) and *The Prey* (84). He also became a glamorous regular in the TV soap opera 'General Hospital'.

67 Don't Just Stand There!
   Tarzan and the Jungle Boy (US/CH)
69 The Arrangement

Yanush Alurkov

BULGARIA

b: 30 May 53

Yanush, son of the director Georgi Alurkov – who in fact only directed him once, in *Konnikut* – was a strong, passionate brunet who graduated from appealing cameos to emotional leading roles.

In the last of these, *Mezhdu dvamata* (he has no part to mention in *The Pied Piper*) he is, as the title suggests, happy with neither of his parents. To attempt a rapprochement with his uncaring father, he stows away and confronts him on a river-barge.

Dimiter Petrov, who gets a superb performance from young Alurkov, had earlier directed him in another boat-film, *Kapitanat*. This was one of the most popular Bulgarian movies of its decade, with the deeply-felt conflicts of friendship and peer pressure one associates with good old-fashioned boy's fiction. (In France it would have been illustrated by Pierre Joubert.)

Yanush Alurkov played the benjamin of the 'good' gang. Its leader, the 'Captain' of the title, was played by Raiko Bodurov, a mature teenager; but a formidable meanie – heading a breakaway group competing for ownership of the prized boat – was created by EDUARD SHAKHPAZYAN (b: 23 Dec 49), a swarthy boy interestingly dyed blond. He was memorable.

60 Vyaternata melnica (The windmill)
63 Kapitanat (The Captain)
64 Konnikut (The horseman)
   Trenadeset dni (Thirteen days)
66 Mezhdu dvamata (Between his parents)
   Svirachat (The Pied Piper – US/BG)

John Moulder-Brown

BRITAIN

b: 3 Jne 53 (London)

In his early years John was the schoolboy equivalent of an English Rose: huge, pale blue eyes blinked demurely through a fringe of fair hair, and he couldn't, you'd think, have said boo to a goose. But he was more than just a pretty face, and when he graduated from modelling to acting, and gained in experience and confidence, a touch of scornful pride crept in which made him less sweet and more complicated.

Most often, though, he was cast in sincere, sympathetic roles which didn't call for huge displays of temperament – and got abundant work as a child, including several leads with the Children's Film Foundation.

In the 1969 co-production of *The Boys of Paul Street* – a remake of the classic Molnar story, filmed in 1934 as *No Greater Glory* – Moulder-Brown was too mature for the leading role, which was taken this time by Anthony Kemp ◊.

However, instead of faltering and fading like the careers of so many well-favoured children, Moulder-Brown's now blossomed. Jerzy Skolimowski gave him two starring roles: as the young swimming-pool attendant in *Deep End* (DD/US 70), fatally obsessed with Jane Asher, and as the enterprising nephew of David Niven and

Yanush Alurkov in Konnikut

John Moulder-Brown in First Love

John Moulder-Brown had further leading roles in *The Grass Is Singing* (ZM/SE 81), *Ellis Island* (84) and *Killing Heat* (US 84).

57 Death Over My Shoulder
58 A Cry from the Streets
   The Man Inside
   Room at the Top
59 Night Train for Inverness
60 Doctor in Love
61 The Missing Note
   Two Living, One Dead (GB/SE)
62 55 Days at Peking (US)
   Night Without Pity
63 Becket
   Go Kart Go
64 Beware of the Dog
   The Uncle
65 The Heroes of Telemark
   Runaway Railway
66 Operation Third Form
67 Calamity the Cow
   Half a Sixpence (GB/US)
68 Heidi (US/DE)
69 The Boys of Paul Street (US/HU)
   La Residencia (The big house – ES)

Gina Lollobrigida in *Herzbube* (DE/US 72 – *Sex, Love and Murder*), a delightful adaptation of Nabokov's 'King, Queen, Knave'.
   He played another love-sick adolescent in *Erste Liebe* (DD/CH/HU 71), based on a Turgenev story. Robert Young's *Vampire Circus* (71) proved less nourishing than the smaller part of Prince Otto, unhappy younger brother of the Wagner-crazy King of Bavaria, in Visconti's *Ludwig* (IT/FR/DE 72). He looked suitably sheepish in the appalling *Confessions from the David Galaxy Affair* (78), but had another prestige lead as Thomas Mann's charming twister in the TV film *Bekenntnisse des Hochstaplers Felix Krull* (DE 81).
   Felix in boyhood, incidentally, was played with amazing suavity by OLIVER WEHE, to be seen again in a leading role in Ruy Guerra's *Erendira* (US 83).

Armand Oprescu
ROMANIA

b: 11 Sep 53 (Bucharest)

Romania's answer to the Jean-Pierre Léaud ◇ of *Les quatre cents coups* has in fact more the broken-nosed look of a Jean-Paul Belmondo. Young Oprescu is tremendous in Gheorghe Naghi's *Who'll Open the Door?*, a story of a boy returning home from two years in reformatory – and almost instantly being framed up for a crime he hasn't committed.
   Oprescu has the relaxed presence of a true actor – brooding, drily humorous, always in control but never predictable. He can surprise one, for instance, with an effortless evocation, sketched in two or three scornful gestures, of the boring, slippers-by-the-fire adult life he doesn't want for himself. It's a great performance in a film that should be seen.

Brooding: Armand Oprescu in Cine va deschide uşa?

Armand Oprescu was never in another, which is our loss. The happy end from his point of view was that he became a professional acrobat in the State Circus in Bucharest.

67 Cine va deschide uşa?
   (Who'll open the door?)

David Bradley

BRITAIN

b: 27 Sep 53 (Barnsley, Yorkshire)

The unforgettable Billy Casper of Ken Loach's tragic film *Kes* had one of the bleakest faces in the cinema's history. Its real-life owner was David Bradley, son of a coalminer and a seamstress, and 14½ at the time of shooting. The film was made in and around Barnsley, David's own home town and that of Barry Hines, on whose novel 'Kestrel for a Knave' it was based.

As a boy at odds with family, school and job-orientated society – not speaking the same language, though sharing a dialect – David was superb, and as often funny as sad. His blank interview with the careers master and his uncoordinated attempts at goal-keeping take place in the same stupor of alienation. He can only come alive, beyond reach of satanic mills, in the countryside where wild things live – and so meets the little predator that teaches him, for a time, about freedom and beauty. (At the expense of mice, with whom Billy might even better have identified.)

David Bradley was now fired with ambition to act, and his immense hit in *Kes* led immediately to offers, though it was two or three years before he made another film. He got a lead in Yorkshire Television's serial *The Flaxton Boys* (70), and worked on stage at the Leeds Playhouse.

Then in 1971 – henceforth known as Dai Bradley to avoid confusion with an older actor called David – he joined the National Theatre company, and was to stay with them for five years, during which time he played in Shakespeare,

Knave and kestrel: David Bradley in Kes

Wedekind and O'Casey among others, and in 1974 took over the lead in Peter Schaffer's 'Equus', a role which won him awards when the production toured South Africa and the USA.

Television appearances had continued, and in the cinema he had a lead with the Children's Film Foundation in *The Seaweed Children* (73), and a small part in *Zulu Dawn* (US/NL 78), before getting another big one in Anthony Page's *Absolution* (78) – unfortunately a fairly ludicrous thriller set in a Catholic school. (In which, I regret to say, Bradley murders Dominic Guard ◊, star of *The Go-Between*.) He was also in a remake of *All Quiet on the Western Front* (79) and *The Glory Glory Days* (83).

More recently, he has been acting on stage in South Africa, including the leads in 'Billy Liar' (a role he had already played at Nottingham), 'For King and Country' and 'The Wound' (which he co-directed).

69 Kes

Frazer McIntosh

BRITAIN

b: 17 Nov 53 (Adelaide, Australia)

Frazer – generally known as 'Fizz' – was the son of the broadcaster and TV newsreader Alex McIntosh. His film career was short, unusual and distinguished.

Both his roles were leading ones, in Yugoslav co-productions, and both were

Guerrilla bootblack: Frazer McIntosh in Vojnik

directed by George Breakston◊, who had been an American child actor of the 1930s. In *Vojnik* Frazer played a Yugoslav boy who runs messages, discreetly spies and finally fights and dies for the partisans during World War Two; and in *The Boy Cried Murder* – more or less a remake of *The Window*, in which Bobby Driscoll◊ starred in 1949 – he is the witness of a murder, hunted by the murderer. In both films he showed a strong and appealing personality.

Yugoslav cinemas, with their ruthlessly logical phoneticisation of foreign names – 'Dzejms Mejsn in *Dzuljus Sizr*', and the like – always billed Fizz as 'Frejzer Mekintoš'.

He nearly made it a trio of leads, with the most glamorous to come last. For some time Orson Welles had been toying with the idea of a new *Treasure Island*, with himself as Long John Silver. Money was advanced, and Welles went to Alicante in Spain for a 'test shoot' – building a full-scale model of the Hispaniola for the occasion, and engaging Frazer as his Jim Hawkins.

The great man and the boy were there for nearly a month, filming scenes. . . . But, mysteriously, nothing more happened, and Welles decided instead to start the film he had always wanted to make: *Chimes at Midnight*. It was quite widely believed that Falstaff had made off with Long John Silver's gold.

(Six years later, Welles finally did play Silver in a *Treasure Island* directed by John Hough. But by now Frazer was pushing 20, and Jim was played by Kim Burfield◊ – erring, in fact, on the small side.)

It wasn't only Welles who had shown interest at this time: the Disney studio wanted to sign Frazer up for two or three films, but his mother vetoed the idea and said he should now concentrate on his education.

After some inattentive years at a minor public school, Frazer studied electronics. He worked as a gas tester, then in music publishing with EMI, then in a company formed with two friends. He worked in video films, in rebuilding cars, in house conversions and (as pianist) in music groups. Not a very coherent career to date, but he has enjoyed it.

65 Vojnik (The Soldier – YU/US)
66 The Boy Cried Murder (GB/DE/YU)

Jan Koester

AUSTRIA

b: 29 Dec 53

The beefy Jan, who worked largely in Austrian productions or co-productions, was in fact a Bavarian. He first came to notice as a ten-year-old in the Austrian TV series 'Unsere grosse Schwester', then played Peter in Werner Jacobs' 1965 *Heidi* and was in two other popular films. The rich local diet eventually made him rather a podge.

The location of Jan's 1964 film got shifted from the north of Austria to the south. Originally it was to have been *Happy End am Attersee*!

64 Happy-End am Wörthersee
   (Happy end by Lake Wörth – DE/AT)
65 An der Donau, wenn der Wein blüht
   (By the Danube when the vines are
   flowering – DE/AT)
   Heidi
66 Der Spielplatz (The playground)

Jan Koester as Peter, with Eva-Maria as the heroine in the 1965 Heidi

Vassilis Kailas

GREECE

b: 1953

After his debut in Cacoyannis' *Telefteo psema*, young Kailas is said to have clocked up more than a hundred film appearances. Among his teenage ones were *Brosta stin aghoni* (68), *Oikogenia Khorafa* (68), *Oniro apatilo* (68) and *Ston daskalo mas me agapi* (69).

58 To teleftteo psema (The last lie)
62 Dio manes ston stavro tou ponou
      (Two mothers on the cross of pain)
    O lustrakos (The little bootblack)
    I nifi toskasse (The bride escaped)
63 Gia ligi storgi (For a little affection)
    Kardies stin kategida (Hearts in the storm)
    To megalo amartima (The great sin)
    I pseftra (The girl who lied)
    Enas vlakas me patenda (A patent fool)
64 Ime mia distikhismeni
      (I'm an unhappy woman)
    Katatregmeni tis miras (Persecuted by fate)
    Kathe limani ke kaimos
      (A grief in every port)
    To koritsi tou ponou (A girl of sorrow)
65 Angeli khoris ftera (Angels without wings)
    O megalos orkos (The great oath)
    O nikitis (The winner)
    Tha zisso gia sena (I'll live for you)
    Thiela se pediki kardia
      (Storm in a child's heart)
66 Isaya khoreve (Isaya dance)
67 O emborakos (The little merchant)

Zdeněk Lstibůrek

CZECHOSLOVAKIA

b: circa 1953

The little Lstibůrek is a furious presence in Karel Kachyňa's *Aťžije Republika!*, a tragicomic view of the last days of the war in rural Moravia: a hyperactive first-person narrator of chaos, hypocrisy and disillusionment.

   He sees brutal men strutting as patriots, gentle men stoned as collaborators, and his friendship with a much-put-upon horse is more meaningful than with any adults. Reckless of self-interest, he taunts and exasperates parents, authorities and

Baleful: Zdeněk Lstibůrek in Aťžije Republika!

schoolmates alike, with a kind of mad-eyed, gadfly intensity, a balefulness akin to David Bennent's ◊ as Oskar in *The Tin Drum*.

   One feels for him an admiration tinged with fear: he has the indestructibility of a force of nature.

   Kachyňa, incidentally, one of Czecho-slovakia's finest directors since the 1950s, has brought remarkable performances out of many other Czech boy actors, such as Vladimír Dlouhý ◊, Michal Koblic ◊, Martin Mikuláš ◊ and Michal Vavruša ◊.

65 Ať žije Republika!
      (Long live the Republic!)

Billy Mumy

USA

b: 1 Feb 54

As Jackie Coogan ◊ should have been kid brother to Louise Brooks, the sandy-haired Billy Mumy should have been to Sissy Spacek. Shy, freckled, pale-eyed and plucky, with a most charming smile, the young Bill was praised by James Stewart, his father in *Dear Brigitte*, as 'the only kid actor I knew who was worth a damn'.

He was barely seven when he appeared in two little TV dramas (*The Door without a Key* and *Bang! You're Dead*) in the 'Alfred Hitchcock Presents' slot. After a minuscule part in *A Child Is Waiting*, Billy made his first film for the Disney studio, partnering the redder-headed Michael McGreevey ◊ as the saviours of *Sammy – the Way Out Seal*.

   His last boyhood lead, in *Rascal*, was again for Disney, but in the meantime he had had his best role as the mathematical prodigy Erasmus, surprising child of a bewildered poet and academic (Stewart), flabbergasting computer operators and racing tipsters alike before achieving his heart's desire in a meeting with Brigitte Bardot. His swooning adoration of the great lady – archly playing herself – is a joy.

   Hereabouts, too, he became a national figure on TV as Will Robinson in the barely effable series 'Lost in Space' (65-68), and between this and the claims of education had little time for major filming.

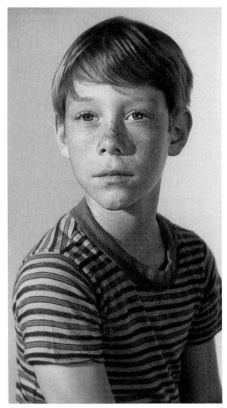

Prodigy: Billy Mumy as Erasmus in Dear Brigitte

303

Matchmaker: Ronny Howard with Glenn Ford in The Courtship of Eddie's Father

In 1971, following the boy-and-raccoon romance *Rascal*, the now gangling and long-haired Bill Mumy had a lead in the animal-rights drama *Bless the Beasts and Children*. Subsequent films have included *Sunshine* (73), *Papillon* (73), *Twilight Zone the Movie* (83) and *Captain America* (89).

61 Tammy Tell Me True
62 A Child Is Waiting
   Sammy – the Way Out Seal
63 Palm Springs Weekend
   A Ticklish Affair
64 A Taste of Melon
   Treasure in the Haunted House
65 Dear Brigitte
   'Lost in Space'
69 Rascal

Ronny Howard

USA

b: 1 Mar 54 (Duncan, Oklahoma)

From the age of three this red-haired child, sharply honest and cheerful, began entertaining cinemagoers and TV-viewers. (He had already made his stage debut with his actor parents, Rance and Jean Howard.) For eight years he was in 'The Andy Griffith Show' as Andy's son Opie, and he was the little boy who sang 'Gary, Indiana' in the film of *The Music Man*.

His best part, though, was as Glenn Ford's son in *The Courtship of Eddie's Father* – a role later played on TV by Brandon Cruz – gamely overcoming grief at the loss of his mother by taking a rational interest in the selection of her eventual successor. Vincente Minnelli's sentimental comedy worked admirably, and Ronnie had delightful solidity as a boy who isn't going to be fobbed off with just any old mother.

In *The Wild Country* (69) Ron and his younger brother CLINT HOWARD – born 10 Apr 59 – played the two sons of a Pittsburgh family of the 1880s facing raw life in Wyoming. (The blond, stocky, broad-browed Clint, famous himself in the mid-Sixties as a black bear's buddy in the TV series 'Gentle Ben', was often to be in Ron's films over the next twenty years or more.)

After *Smoke* (70) and *The Hunting Party* (71), Ron had a lead in one of the decade's most influential films, George Lucas's *American Graffiti* (73). For TV he was in *The Migrants* (73) and had the title role in *Huckleberry Finn* (74) – far too old, of course, past 20, but no older than Jack Pickford◇ when he played Tom Sawyer in 1917. There followed leads in *The Spikes Gang* (74), *The Shootist* (76), *Eat My Dust* (76) and *I'm a Fool* (77).

On TV he was winning wider recognition in 'Happy Days', the series that sealed the fame of Henry Winkler; and he also turned to directing, making his debut with *Grand Theft Auto* (77). He directed Bette Davis in the TV film *Skyward*, and Henry Winkler in *Night Shift* (82), before achieving his first definite hit, the mermaid comedy *Splash* (84). *Cocoon* (84) was poor but popular, and *Gung Ho* (86) and *Willow* (88) established Ron Howard as one of America's most prominent young directors.

56 Frontier Woman
58 The Journey
61 Come September
   The Music Man
62 The Courtship of Eddie's Father
   Five Minutes to Live
65 Village of the Giants
66 Door-to-Door Maniac
67 A Boy Called Nuthin'

Sean Bury

BRITAIN

b: 15 Aug 54 (Brighton)

Sean was trained for the stage at the Corona School in London, and was a member of the Westminster Cathedral Choir. A few years after co-starring with a Great Dane in a Children's Film Foundation serial, he was priceless as the diffident new boy, Jute, in Lindsay Anderson's *If. . . .*

After a small part in the musical *Goodbye, Mr Chips,* Sean Bury touchingly shared the lead with Anicée Alvina in a teenage romance, *Friends* (US 71), written and directed by Lewis Gilbert for Paramount. He was in *The Abominable Dr Phibes* (71), *The Story of a Love Story* (73),

New bug: Sean Bury in If . . .

and starred again in *Paul et Michelle* (FR/GB 74, more or less a sequel to *Friends*) before being reduced to the naval ranks in *The Spy Who Loved Me* (77).

64 Beware of the Dog *(serial)*
68 If. . . .
69 Goodbye, Mr Chips

Sascha Hehn

WEST GERMANY

b: 11 Oct 54 (Munich)

Alexander, or Sascha, was the son of the former UFA actor Albert Hehn, who persuaded Willy Fritsch to give the boy his first chance in films. He was a lively and adventurous child, given to leaping over bonfires and similar displays of panache. A few years later the parents separated, and Sascha, left in his mother's custody, became her chief breadwinner.

At 17 he made his first 'shocker': *Schüler-Report* (72), closely followed by *Die liebestollen Apothekerstöchter* (72), *Babysitter gesucht* (72), *Alexander und die Töchter* (73), *Blau blüht der Enzian* (73) and *Verbrechen nach Schulschluss* (75). He was, for a time, the idol of the German sex film.

But in the late Seventies, having had (in his own words) 'enough of this shit', Hehn

Panache: Sascha Hehn in Drei weisse Birken

quit the movie and TV scene and departed for the Caribbean, where he worked as a shipboard waiter, diving instructor and tourist guide. This led to him being taken up by the international jet set; but eventually, disillusioned with life among the Beautiful People (and by losing all his savings in a dubious real-estate venture), he returned to acting.

Apart from appearing on stage as Orlando in 'As You Like It' at the 1981 Salzburg Festival, and a film lead in the motor-racing drama *Burning Rubber* (81), he has – after a long and undignified dispute about his military service – regained his star ranking mainly in TV serials like 'Das Traumschiff' (as a glamorous Chief Steward) and 'Die Schwarzwaldklinik' (as a glamorous doctor).

59 Hubertusjagd (Saint Hubert's hunt)
  Ein Student ging vorbei
    (A student passed by)
60 Ein Sommer, den man nie vergisst
    (An unforgettable summer)
  . . . Und keiner schämte sich
    (No-one was ashamed)
61 Drei weisse Birken (Three silver birches)
62 Alarm in den Bergen
    (Mountain alert – TVS)
65 Das Mädel aus dem Böhmerwald
    (The girl from the Bohemian Forest)

Anthony Kemp

BRITAIN

b: 3 Nov 54

Anthony, a whimsical snub-nosed child with a wide mouth and expressive eyes, somewhat resembled a pocket version of Ian McKellen. After making a great impression as a lonely little boy in the TV play *Toggle*, he won a lead as the wolf-crying hero of a Children's Film Foundation Production. (His participation in *Oliver!* was negligible.)

Anthony's biggest and best role, manfully taken, was as the gallant little Nemecsek – the character played, in former years, by Gyuri Faragó and George Breakston◇ – in a new, dual-

Anthony Kemp as Nemecsek in The Boys of Paul Street

language version of Molnar's story *The Boys of Paul Street*. In *Cromwell* he played the future Protector's son Henry.

At this point, like David Bradley◇ before him, Anthony had to change his professional name because it duplicated that of an existing actor, and became instead 'Jason Kemp'. He was in one of

BBC-TV's 'Wessex Tales', *Barbara of the House of Grebe* (73), and then in *The Swordsman* (74).

67 Toggle
68 Cry Wolf
  Oliver!
69 The Boys of Paul Street
    (A Pal utcai fiuk – US/HU)
  Twinky
70 Cromwell

His younger brother EDWARD KEMP – born 3 April 60 – also appeared in *Cromwell*, and went on to be in *Fragment of Fear*, *Fiddler on the Roof*, *The Spy's Wife* and *Blinker's Spy-Spotter* in 1971, and *A Touch of Class*, *Swot* and *Crossplot* in 1972.

Pedro Mari Sanchez

SPAIN

b: 1954

Perhaps the most attractive child actor in Spanish films of the 1960s, Pedro Mari (he was often billed thus, without surname) offered a satisfying blend of youthful

Trainer and brother: Pedro Mari Sanchez with Marisol (right) in Cabriola

ardour and calm good nature. In *Cabriola* – produced and directed by Mel Ferrer, and released in the USA as *Every Day Is a Holiday* – he was the helpful kid brother of a girl toreador (the pop singer Marisol).

La primera aventura was released in Mexico as *El niño y el ladron*, 'The child and the robber'.

64 La primera aventura
   (First adventure – ES/MX)
   Juego de hombres (A man's game)
   Los siete bravisimos (Seven brave boys)
65 Cabriola
   La familia y...uno mas
   (The family . . . plus one)
   El misterio de las naranjas azules
   (The mystery of the blue oranges)
66 Huyendo del halcon (Flight from the hawk)
67 El dedo del destino (The finger of Fate)

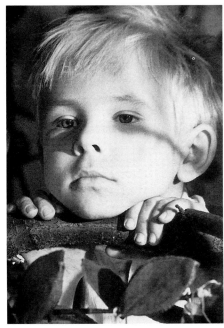

Barkhatov in the title role of Seryozha

Borya Barkhatov

USSR

b: circa 1954

The tiny blond Barkhatov had a hit first time out, as the eponymous hero of *Seryozha*, subtitled 'a few stories from the life of a very small boy'. (It won a Grand Prix at the Karlovy Vary Festival, and was often shown in the West as *A Summer to Remember*.)

Seryozha had lost his father in the war, and now – in a sex-reversal of *The Courtship of Eddie's Father* – contemplates his mother's choice of a new one. It is a very lovable piece.

Borya had a further leading role in *Bratya Komarovi*.

60 Seryozha
61 Bratya Komarovi (The Komarov brothers)
62 Greshni angel (Sinful angel)

Juliancito Bravo

MEXICO

b: circa 1954

Little Julian was born in Spain but moved to Mexico at quite a tender age. After a prominent part in *La batalla de los pasteles* he had leads in *Seguiré tus pasos* and (of course) in *Los aventuras de Juliancito*. To play yourself is to have arrived.

64 Alias el Rata (Alias the Rat)
   La gran aventura (The great adventure)
   Los hijos que yo soñé
   (The sons I dream of)
   Primera comunion (First communion)
   Su precio unos dolares
   (His price a few dollars)
65 La tierna infancia (Tender childhood)
66 La batalla de los pasteles
   (The battle of the pies)
   Seguiré tus pasos
   (I'll follow in your footsteps)
   Los tres mosqueteros de Dios
   (God's three musketeers)
68 Los aventuras de Juliancito
   (The adventures of Juliancito)
70 El tunco Maclovio
   (That swine Maclovio)

Darko Cesar

YUGOSLAVIA

b: circa 1954

The blond Darko – a sterner John Howard Davies ◊ – had the lead in Bato Čengić's *Mali vojnici*, an impressive film set in a home for waifs at the end of World War Two.

He had a complex role as a German

orphan mortally threatened by his vengeful fellow-inmates. The children, led by the grim teenager 'Bomber' (Sead Cakal), are excellent.

67 Mali vojnici (Little soldiers)

Marinko Ćosić

YUGOSLAVIA

b: circa 1954

Marinko, reckoned the finest Yugoslav child performer of his day, was superb in Mate Relja's *Opasan put*.

63 Ljubav (Love)
   Opasan put (Dangerous road)

Lutz Bosselmann

EAST GERMANY

b: circa 1954

The chunky little Bosselmann had leads in both his films. As Lütt Matten, a fisherman's son, he attempts to improve his striking-rate by finding a legendary shell which lures fish into the nets. The appeal to magic proves disastrous, and he is saved by purely human means.

61 Das Märchenschloss (Fairy tale castle)
63 Lütt Matten und die weisse Muschel
   (Lütt Matten and the white shell)

Lutz Bosselmann in Lütt Matten und die weisse Muschel

Luis de la Cuesta

ARGENTINA

b: circa 1954

Ricardo Güiraldes' 1926 novel 'Don Segundo Sombra' has been described as a sort of Argentine 'Huckleberry Finn'. A boy learns the secrets of life under the tutelage of the wise, eponymous gaucho guru, 'a man of action who eschews violence'.

Young Luis de la Cuesta is superb in Manuel Antín's serenely powerful film.

68 Don Segundo Sombra
   El santo de la espada
   (The saint with the sword)

Tomáš Hádl

CZECHOSLOVAKIA

b: circa 1954

Hadl, an interesting, subtle boy of russet complexion, didn't play little Bobeš: this was Jiří Lukeš◇, whom he also partnered in Kouzelný den. In his 1964 film, a study of courage and cowardice under the occupation, he is memorable as the child of devious middle-class parents.

60 Kouzelný den (Magical day)
61 Malý Bobeš (Little Bobeš)
62 Deštivý den (Rainy day)
   Malý Bobeš ve městě
   (Little Bobeš goes to town)
63 Tři zlate vlasy děda Vševěda
   (Grandpa Knowall's three golden hairs)
64 ...A pátý jezdec je Strach
   (And the fifth horseman was Fear)

Jiří Lukeš

CZECHOSLOVAKIA

b: circa 1954

This serious little blond, with some droll expressions, was the favourite child of Czech cinema in the early 1960s. In Kouzelný den he led a cast of small children rehearsing a 'musical fairy-tale' to perform at a gymnastic festival.

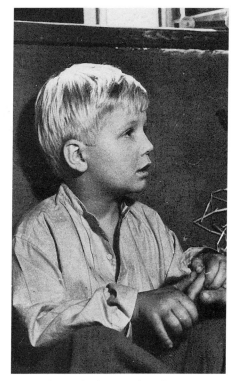

Country boy: Jiří Lukeš in Malý Bobeš

In the two Bobeš films, drawn from a book by Josef Václav Pleva, he is a pre-1914 child living first in the country, then in the town.

Lukeš' later appearances were for TV.

60 Kouzelný den (Magical day)
61 Malý Bobeš (Little Bobeš)
62 Malý Bobeš v městě
   (Little Bobes goes to town)
63 Barnabášek
   (Little Barnaby)
   Modrý autobus
   (The blue bus)

Björn Andresen

SWEDEN

b: 26 Jan 55 (Stockholm)

There was deep insecurity behind the apparently classic beauty of the boy Visconti chose to incarnate Tadzio in Death in Venice. Björn Andresen's father was unknown (but rumoured to be intellectual), and his adoptive father divorced his mother when the child was four. Six years later she disappeared and was in due course found to have killed herself. Thereafter Björn lived mainly with grandparents.

He turned out to have musical gifts, and trained as a pianist at a Swedish music school, until his grandmother rashly sent a photograph of him to a film studio. It led to his taking a secondary part in a Swedish teen-film, and then the emblematic one in the Visconti spectacular – which brought him worldwide fame but little happiness.

Androgynously styled in the fashion of the early Seventies rather than the period of Thomas Mann's story, Björn was of course too old to suggest Aschenbach's 'little Phaeax' or to provide the moral disorientation that Mann intended. But as Visconti's atmospheric wallow descends into terminal farce, with poor Bogarde expiring more of cosmetics than cholera – such a vulgar, incompetent hotel barber would have been lucky to keep his job two days – Andresen has his finest hour, languidly pointing towards the horizon of death.

The resulting adulation, plus general mismanagement of his professional career, unsettled him hopelessly for most of the next ten years. He married and became a father, but found himself unable to sustain the responsibilities that this entailed. At last, aided by intelligence and sensitivity, he began to get his act together.

In 1985, after earning his living as a music arranger and teacher, and appearing in one or two films such as Bluff Stop! (77) and Den enfaldige mördaren (82, The simple murderer), he began to train seriously as an actor, and eventually won a major role in Camus' 'Caligula' on the Stockholm stage. (Another stage role, ironically in view of his early musical ambitions and own brief pop-idol status, was as John Lennon.)

'I can't wait to age,' he told John James in an interview. 'I'm looking forward to the peace and quiet. I was born with a face I didn't ask for.'

70 En kärlekshistoria (A love story)
71 Morte a Venezia
   (Mort à Venise/Death in Venice – IT/FR)

Fatal: Björn Andresen

Mann's real-life Tadzio, Władysław Moes

The real-life 'Tadzio', the Polish boy whose beauty fascinated Thomas Mann on a visit to Venice in the summer of 1911, is now revealed to have been Władysław Moes (1900-86), known as 'Adzio' and later a Baron. At the age of six he had similarly enchanted the Polish writer Henryk Sienkiewicz, author of 'Quo vadis?' – but spoilt it all by leaking on the great man's trousers .

William Dix

BRITAIN

b: 29 Jan 55

Grey-flanneled English prep-school angel turned devil, the machiavellian Master Dix was a fair match in *The Nanny* for his deranged keeper, Bette Davis – whether confronting her with jowly truculence or a fake suicide.

Machiavellian: William Dix in The Nanny

Transformed into jolly, helpful Tommy Stubbins in the messy whimsy of the *Doctor Dolittle* musical, he was inevitably less riveting, and after this, like Tom Brown before him, young William went off to Rugby.

65 The Nanny
67 Doctor Dolittle (US)

Stefano Colagrande

ITALY

b: 2 May 55 (Rome)

Luigi Comencini's screen version of 'Misunderstood', the admirable Victorian novel by Florence Montgomery, is much superior to Jerry Schatzberg's 1983 remake, which is only made bearable by the peerless honesty of Henry Thomas ◇.

The more conventionally good-looking Colagrande (son of a businessman, and discovered by Comencini in Florence) is not quite in Thomas's league, but gives an immensely touching and dignified performance as the wronged boy who can't do right in his father's eyes. SIMONE GIANNOZZI plays the charming but irresponsible younger brother.

66 Incompreso (Misunderstood)

Teddy Eccles

USA

b: 9 Jne 55

The pleasant, sandy-haired Eccles had his only starring part – as a 13-year-old botanist on a self-imposed survival course – in *My Side of the Mountain*. Though Jean George's novel hardly lent itself to drama, Teddy Eccles made a resolute figure of this junior Thoreau.

He had in fact already had several years in films (his first commercial was at two months), and caught the eye as the bottle-collecting boy of *In Cold Blood*. He was often to be seen on TV.

After twenty years in films and TV, Ted Eccles left the acting business. (A 'dying' role in 'General Hospital' seemed a fitting exit.) Instead he turned to the craft of special effects, then trailers and music videos. After working in turn for Paramount and Disney, he went into a partnership in 1986 to make promotional videos for new films.

60 Cimarron
   The Crowded Sky
62 My Six Loves
65 The Family Jewels
67 In Cold Blood
68 My Side of the Mountain (CA)
70 The Phynx
   San Francisco International Airport
71 The Honkers

'Heintje'

HOLLAND/WEST GERMANY

b: 12 Aug 55 (Bleijerheide, Holland)

Hein Nicolaas Theodoor Simons, son of a Dutch coalminer and a restaurateuse, was an appealing child with a pealing voice. After success in a local talent contest, he cut his first record and in no time was topping the West German charts, wowing the housewives with his 'Mama', 'Heidschi Bumbeidschi', and other numbing numbers invoking stars and tears.

It wasn't possible for Heintje to build a career at home because of stringent Dutch laws on 'child labour', but this hardly inconvenienced him. Before long he was a Deutschmark-millionaire, and the silver screen beckoned.

Many of his films, such as *Zum Teufel mit der Penne* and *Morgen fällt die Schule aus*, belonged to a deplorable school series with the generic title of 'Die Lümmel von der ersten Bank' (The Front Row Louts), in which hearty knockabout alternated with sadistic pranks at the expense of the ancientry. Heintje naturally didn't get involved with the worst of these, and occasionally burst into song, but it was a bad idea to be even on the fringe.

More characteristic vehicles for the warbler, with the slenderest of soppy plots but at least no loutish sadism, were

Warbler: Heintje Simons in Heintje – ein Herz geht auf Reisen

Heintje – ein Herz geht auf Reisen and *Heintje, mein bester Freund*: titles that his dimmest fans couldn't miss.

In 1972 it was announced that Heintje would be co-starring with Danny Kaye, Maria Schell and Peter Ustinov in an international co-production to be made in Yugoslavia and based on 'The Shoes of

the Fisherman', but nothing came of it. The golden voice cracked, and he retired to rest on his laurels, acquiring a wife and some riding stables.

68 Zum Teufel mit der Penne
   (Damn the dosshouse)
69 Einmal wird die Sonne wieder scheinen
   (The sun will shine again one day)
   Heintje – ein Herz geht auf Reisen
   (Heintje – a travelling heart)
   Heintje, mein bester Freund
   (My best friend Heintje)
   Hurra, die Schule brennt
   (Hurrah, the school's on fire)
71 Morgen fällt die Schule aus
   (End of term tomorrow)

Kim Chol

NORTH KOREA

b: 28 Aug 55 (Pyongyang)

Young Chol, who began acting when he was 13, was born in the Central district of Pyongyang. After *Story on the Potong river* (73) he withdrew from the career for a time, but followed a one-year course at the Actors' Training Centre.

Kim Chol takes charge in The Engine-Driver's Son

In 1981 Kim graduated from Pyong-yang College of Cinematography, then resumed acting. He has appeared in more than 24 films with the Korean Feature Film Studio, developing into a fine dramatic actor with a flair for passion – a quality he had shown even as a child. He was in *Mother's Wish*, a medal-winner at the first Pyongyang Film Festival for Non-Aligned and Developing Countries, and had good parts in *Kwangju calls* (85), *Run, Korea* (85) and *Rim Kog* (88).

In 1988 he, like Hwang Hag Yun ◇, was named an Actor of Merit.

68 A Boy in Keumdol
69 Sea of Blood
71 The Engine-Driver's Son

Benoît Ferreux

FRANCE

b: 29 Sep 55

In the notorious and wholly charming *Souffle au coeur*, released in English-speaking countries under the feeble title of *Dearest Love*, a 15-year-old boy longs to lose his virginity.

After gentle homosexual attraction to a younger schoolmate (Eric Walter), a cruelly aborted first visit to a brothel, and some hapless passes at teenage girls at the clinic where he is sent for his heart murmur, young Laurent is finally initiated by his erring mother – though the incest is slight, accidental and 'never to be mentioned again'. In its afterglow, the boy almost immediately makes his first conquest.

Louis Malle's film is so good-hearted, funny and affectionate that only a true sex-hater could find offence in it.

The likeable Benoît Ferreux, nephew of Jean-Louis Trintignant, continued to act, with small parts in *La messe dorée* (73), *Violette Nozière* (77), *Escape to Victory* (US 81) and *Five Days One Summer* (US 82) among others. But in between times he has been barman, photographer, demolition worker and assistant director to Roger Vadim.

Stockinged feet: Benoît Ferreux makes a quiet exit in Le souffle au coeur

70 Le souffle au coeur
   (Heart murmur /Dearest Love –
   FR/IT/DE)

Oleg Kovachev

BULGARIA

b: 19 Oct 55

This sensitive boy, son of the cameraman Hristo Kovachev, had a memorable lead in his first film, *Knight without armour*, as a

Moral litmus: Oleg Kovachev in Ritsar bez bronya

child hurt and baffled by the unpleasant illogicalities of adult behaviour.

In due course Oleg grew up and became a film director. His son Boyan played an important role in *Ti, koito si na nebeto* (89, Thou which art in heaven).

65 Ritsar bez bronya (Knight without armour)
66 The Pied Piper (US/BG)
69 Nai dulgata nosht (The longest night)

Roman in Wyrok

Grzegorz Roman

POLAND

b: 30 Oct 55

The delightful Grzegorz was first seen in *Wyrok*, at the centre of a harrowing drama of family break-up, and had a smaller part in Nasfeter's *Moj stary*. Six years later, as 'Freckled Mark', he starred in his own TV series.

61 Wyrok (The sentence)
   Moj stary (My old man)
66 Kochankowie z Marony
   (The lovers of Marona)
67 Dziadek do orzechow (The Nutcracker)
   Niewiarygodne przygody Marka Piegusa
   (The amazing adventures of
   Freckled Mark)

Multi-exotic: Domasin in Island of the Blue Dolphins

Larry Domasin

USA

b: circa 1955 (Los Angeles)

The multi-exotic Larry – boasting a Hawaiian-Portuguese mother and a Filipino father – made his professional debut when he was six in the TV series 'Follow the Sun', then was in 'Adventures in Paradise' and 'Seven against the Sea'.

His biggest screen hit was in *Island of the Blue Dolphins*, as a boy marooned with his sister (Celia Kaye) on a lonely Pacific isle.

63 Dime with a Halo
   Fun in Acapulco
64 Island of the Blue Dolphins
65 The Rare Breed
   Ride Beyond Vengeance
66 Valley of Mystery

Nasret Dubashev

USSR – Kirghizia

b: circa 1955

Dogged little Nasreddin Dubashev represented the spirit of Kirghizia in *Nebo nashego detstva*, a visually glorious film by Tolomush Okeyev.

In a harsh world of mountains and sheep, the sorely-tried boy tries to pursue his own education while mediating between a brutal chauvinist father and a resigned, put-upon mother. Nasret's face is ageless.

66 Nebo nashego detstva
   (The sky of our childhood)
69 Dzhamilya

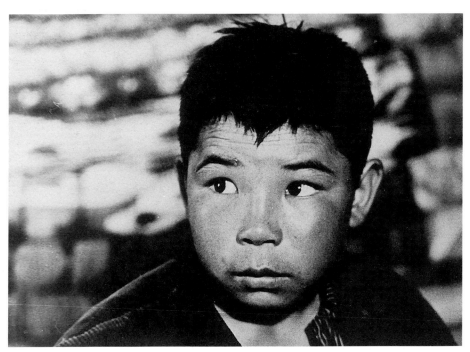

Sorely tried: Nasret Dubashev in Nebo nashevo detstva

Mitch Vogel

USA

b: 17 Jan 56 (Alhambra, Cal.)

The good-natured, red-headed Mitchell Vogel hit the heights in feisty duo with Steve McQueen in *The Reivers*, a road movie set in tough, turn-of-the-century Mississippi and based (minus a dimension or two) on a William Faulkner novel. Vogel's Lucius, glorying in the bright yellow Winston Flyer they travel in, and rising to the challenge of his first brothel with enthusiasm and gallantry, is a cheering creation.

As a late-teenager, Mitch was in *Born Innocent* (74) on TV, but also in series like 'Bonanza' (where he had a leading role), 'Petrocelli' and 'The Little House on the Prairie'.

68 Yours, Mine and Ours
69 The Reivers
71 The Boy from Dead Man's Bayou
72 Menace on the Mountain

Josef Filip in Tony, tobě přeskočilo

Josef Filip

CZECHOSLOVAKIA

b: circa 1955

Burly, oval-faced Filip delighted Czech moviegoers with two performances in 1963 and made a welcome comeback five years later. In his mid-teens he was featured in the popular 'Pan Tau' TV films.

Máte doma lva? is a musical dream of childhood wish-fulfilments: being a traffic-cop on crossroad duty, roller-skating through a museum, attending a congress of ghosts – and, of course, owning a lion.

In *Na Žižkově válečném voze* he and Jan Kraus are two boys fighting with the Hussites, and in *Tony* he is one of four siblings who escape from a children's home to take refuge with a benevolent hermit.

63 Máte doma lva?
(Do you have a lion at home?)
Povídky o dětech (Stories about children)
68 Na Žižkově válečném voze
(On Žižka's fortified wagon)
Tony, tobě přeskočilo (Tony, you're crazy)

Flowers and freckles: Mitch Vogel in The Reivers

'Mehdi' (Mehdi el Glaoui)

FRANCE

b: 26 May 56 (Choisy-le-Roi)

Mehdi, although he acted almost exclusively for TV, was such a popular child
actor that he can't be omitted. He was also
the grandson of a Pasha of Marrakesh.
In 1954 the petite starlet Cécile Aubry
had secretly married Prince Si Brahim, and
Mehdi was born at the Prince's country
house, the Blue Mill, some 25 miles from
Paris.

By the age of four the engaging child
and his eager, earnest expressions – he
was slightly like a male Elisabeth Bergner
– caught the eye of some of his mother's
show-business acquaintances, and the rest
was French TV history. Mehdi was best
known in the three 'Sébastien' series,

which opened with an adventure in which
the tiny boy was partnered by a huge
dog, and ended with a maritime mystery.
Most of his work was to be directed by
Cécile Aubry herself.

In his mid-teens Mehdi returned to
the TV screen as *Le jeune Fabre* (72), in
a celebration of the great zoologist. He
was then in *Un amour de pluie* (73), the TV
serial *Jérôme et Isabelle* (74), *Catherine et Cie.*
(FR/IT 75), and another TV serial, *Kick.*
He also worked for Claude Goretta on the
technical side of *Les chemins de l'exil* (78).

61 La merveilleuse histoire de Poly
   (The amazing story of Poly)
65 Belle et Sébastien
   (Belle and Sebastian)
67 Sébastien parmi les hommes
   (Sebastian out in the world)
69 Sébastien et la Mary-Morgane
   (Sebastian and the 'Mary Morgan')

Princely: Mehdi el Glaoui

Dominic Guard

BRITAIN

b: 18 Jne 56 (Hammersmith,London)

Dominic's parents were the actors Philip
Guard and Charlotte Mitchell; his brother
Christopher also became an actor, though
not in childhood.

Dominic's performance in *The Go-
Between* was a miracle of modesty and
feeling. As Leo, the shabby-genteel boy
hero of L.P.Hartley's novel, unexpectedly
invited to spend part of his summer
holidays at a rather grand country house
in Norfolk, he never put a foot wrong.

Inappropriately dressed for a swelter-
ing July, he glows; and his temperature
is further raised by his employment as
'Mercury', or letter carrier, between the
daughter of the house and her two
lovers: Lord Trimingham, for whom she
is destined, and Ted Burgess, a young
yeoman farmer, whom she meets secretly.
Leo longs to know what on earth is going
on behind these messages. When Burgess
promises to tell him what is meant by
'spooning' (in other words, the secrets of
sex), the boy not only blushes but seems
to break out in a sweat of guilty curiosity.

Dominic, a devout vegetarian, was one
of the screen's most endearing children,
and it was regrettable that only two more
screen parts came his way before his late
teens. But his painful scene with Lady
Nelson in *Bequest to the Nation* – the
cast-off wife superbly played by Margaret
Leighton, Dominic's hostess in *The Go-
Between*) – found him at his best, emotion
struggling with embarrassment, awkward
words literally bursting from his flushed
face.

He continued as an increasingly striking
actor, darkly sensitive and romantic-
looking but still with that residual air of
baffled decency which had made his Leo
so touching. He was particularly inter-
est- ing in 'complicated' parts, such as the
obsessed, rather shifty young Englishman
in Peter Weir's *Picnic at Hanging Rock*
(AU 75).

Green party: Dominic Guard in The Go-Between

in *Le cri du coeur*, as a boy who after losing a leg in an accident becomes a prey to sexual obsession. But by now he had other irons in the fire: he and his father set up a transport firm, and with some mates he launched a pop group called V.O.

67 Jacquou le Croquant (Jacko the clodhopper)
68 Le temps de vivre (A time to live)
71 Le drapeau noir flotte sur la marmite
   (The black flag flies on the stewpot)

Sean Kelly

USA

b: 19 Nov 56 (Burbank, Cal.)

The tawny-haired, splay-eyed Sean – who should not be confused with a British Sean Kelly of the Fifties and Sixties, though his own grandmother had farmed in Ireland – played Stuttering Bob in *The Cowboys*, cured of his affliction by the invitation to swear his bitter heart out at John Wayne.

He was a most likeable performer, with an expressive face and some depth of feeling. Even this couldn't bring alive the tedious Lassie film *Well of Love*.

Sean was also in a TV version of Arthur Miller's 'Incident at Vichy', which Stacy Keach directed.

71 The Cowboys
   Well of Love

His later credits include *The Count of Monte Cristo* (74), *How Green Was My Valley* (76, TV serial), *Able's Will* (77), *Lord of the Rings* (78, voice only), *One Fine Day* (78), *Absolution* (78), *An Unsuitable Job for a Woman* (81), *Cousin Phyllis* (82, TVS).

71 The Go-Between
72 The Hands of Cormac Joyce
73 Bequest to the Nation

Eric Damain

FRANCE

b: 18 Sep 56 (Boulogne-Billancourt)

Eric was just ten when his father – a worker at the Renault plant – saw that

Stellio Lorenzi was looking for a young boy to play the lead in the TV serial *Jacquou le Croquant*. After several competitive auditions young Damain got the part, which involved five months' filming in Périgord. He was subsequently offered a role in *Le temps de vivre*, and four years later teamed up with Jean Gabin in *Le drapeau flotte*.

In the wake of his success as Jacquou, Eric – a very gifted singer – recorded an LP, and in 1971 was also on a commercial recording of Saint-Exupéry's 'Le Petit Prince', with Jean-Louis Trintignant as the narrator. (Just as Georges Poujouly ◇, a generation earlier, had done with Gérard Philipe.)

In 1974 Damain returned to the screen

Eric Damain, circa 1968

315

Padilla in Tarzan and the Valley of Gold

Manuel Padilla

USA

b: 1956

This highly photogenic little Mexican had proved his worth in several films before he became involved with Tarzan.

Unlike Johnny Sheffield◇ and Ricky Sorensen◇, he had a different fictional name for each outing with Tarzan. In *The Valley of Gold* he was a kidnapped child called Ramel, in *The Great River* a cabin boy called Pepe, and in NBC's spin-off TV series (1966-68, with Ron Ely succeeding Mike Henry as the Apeman) Manuel became Jai — even more confusing, since this name had already belonged, five years earlier, to the little elephant boy of *Tarzan Goes to India*.

Later films included *American Graffiti* (73), *More American Graffiti* (79) and *Scarface* (83).

63 Dime with a Halo
   The Young and the Brave
64 Black Spurs
   Robin and the 7 Hoods
   Sylvia
   Taffy and the Jungle Hunter
65 Tarzan and the Valley of Gold (US/CH)
67 Tarzan and the Great River (US/CH)
   Tarzan's Deadly Silence
   Tarzan's Jungle Rebellion
69 Cutter's Trail
70 The Great White Hope
   A Man Called Horse

Estonian Jim: Aare Laanemets in Ostrov Sokrovishch

Aare Laanemets

USSR — Estonia

b: circa 1956

It probably never occurred to Robert Louis Stevenson that his Jim Hawkins might one day be impersonated by an Estonian. The tall, distinguished-looking Laanemets is really too old for Jim, but makes a graceful, oddly romantic hero.

He had earlier, in *Vesna*, been a schoolboy in pre-revolutionary Estonia.

70 Vesna (Spring)
71 Ostrov sokrovishch (Treasure Island)

Soldiering on: Vitya Zhukov in Eto bilo v razvedke

Vitya Zhukov

USSR

b: circa 1956

Vitya was a bright, sensitive-looking boy, and a fine performer. In *Eto bilo*, a story of World War Two, he is rather like the hero of *Ivan's Childhood*, serving with the Soviet army and performing deeds of enormous daring.

In *Malchishki*, a two-part film, he has the lead in the second story, as a scholarly, non-athletic boy who is persuaded to train as a boxer, and does so to some effect.

69 Eto bilo v razvedke
   (It happened on reconnaissance)
   Malchishki (Kids)

Stephen Hudis

BRITAIN/USA

b: 17 May 57 (London)

Stephen, son of the screenwriter Norman Hudis, moved to Los Angeles in 1965 with his British parents. His large, enthusiastic eyes and pleasingly irregular features made him a useful addition to Hollywood's stable of boy actors.

In *The Cowboys* he is the gallant Jewish boy Charlie Schwartz who is trampled to death by cattle while attempting to retrieve Nicolas Beauvy's ◊ spectacles.

He had leads in his other two films listed here, both made for TV. *Sam Hill* is an entertaining Western romp starring Ernest Borgnine, while the Lassie film is a hymn to the warm, deep humanity of US Air Forces Strategic Command. (The ineffable bitch does her bit by moving birds' nests off a rocket range.) Stephen was later seen on British TV in the serial *Ski Boy* (GB 74).

70 Sam Hill: Who Killed Mr Foster?
71 The Cowboys
72 Lassie: Peace Is My Profession

Tord Tjädersten

SWEDEN

b: 17 May 57

The Swedish children's classic was first filmed in 1922, with Gösta Alexandersson ◊ as Kalle. Tjädersten, with his straw-like hair, made a worthy successor.

72 Anderssonskans Kalle
     (The Anderssons' Kalle)
73 Anderssonskans Kalle i busform
     (The Anderssons' Kalle in top form)

Staffan Hallerstam

SWEDEN

b: 21 May 57

1970 must have been an interesting year for young Hallerstam, moving between the worlds of Pippi Longstocking and

Ingmar Bergman. In *Beröringen*, carrying the fatal Bergman surname of Vergerus, he was the hapless son of Bibi Andersson and Max von Sydow.

67 Kullamannen (The man from Kulla)
69 Kråkguldet (False gold)
70 Beröringen (The Touch – SE/US)
     Pippi Långstrump på de sju haven
        (Pippi Longstocking on the Seven Seas)

Jean-Pierre Cargol

FRANCE

b: 24 May 57 (Montpellier)

The real name of Truffaut's *Enfant sauvage*, the 'wild boy of Aveyron', was Reyes Baliardo. He was one of fourteen gypsy siblings. His uncle was the guitarist Manitas de Plata, in whose band his father, Hippolyte Baliardo, also played. Reyes himself was later to do the same.

In his performance as wild Victor he empathised astoundingly with the bewildered creature of the forest: the sheer difficulty of grappling with basic, unfamiliar concepts was wonderfully conveyed. No one who saw it will forget the sight of him alone, outdoors, at night, swaying on his haunches in the moonlight – or his fury of grief when Dr Itard (played by Truffaut) tests his moral sense by inflicting a brutal injustice on him.

Truffaut's actual kindness to Jean-Pierre was shown by putting his mother and one of his brothers on the payroll, so that he shouldn't feel too homesick.

Wild eye: Jean-Pierre Cargol in L'enfant sauvage

Cargol with his teacher: François Truffaut as Dr Itard

Reyes Baliardo still plays flamenco guitar, either alone or with his uncle – and loves to be called 'the Wild Child'.

70 L'enfant sauvage
    (The wild child)
74 Caravan to Vaccares
    (Caravane à Vaccarès – GB/FR)

Raimondas Banionis

USSR – Lithuania

b: 13 May 57 (Panevėžys)

The Lithuanian boy in Tarkovski's con-voluted space epic had the best possible pedigree for the job: his father, Donatas Banionis, was playing his father, the investigative astronaut.

Though Donatas was a star, Raimondas was not too keen on acting. He neverthe-less appeared in three more films in 1972.

At the age of 14 he wrote, directed and shot a film of his own at school, and before graduating from Moscow's film academy had directed another, called *Speed is my God*. Two short films followed, and his next feature was *My little wife* (84).

70 Pyaterka otvazhnikh (The fearless five)
72 Solaris
    Prisvoit zvaniye geroya
    (To him the name of hero)

Jean-François Maurin

FRANCE

b: 21 Jun 57

The last important cinematic son of Mado Maurin was Jean-François, a full brother of Dominique ◇ and Marie-Véronique Maurin. He had sandy-reddish hair, a lot of freckles, and rather fine pale-blue eyes.

After comic outings with Bourvil (in *Trois enfants*) and Fernandel (*L'homme à la Buick*) he tackled the emotional role of a withdrawn orphan in *La promesse*, practising strange rituals in a tree-house and intoxicating himself with the perfume of a young woman (Jacqueline Bisset).

66 Trois enfants dans le désordre
    (Three chaotic kids)
67 L'homme à la Buick
    (The man with the Buick)
69 La promesse (The promise)
70 La maison des Bories
    (The house of the Bories)

Intoxicated: Jean-François Maurin with Jacqueline Bisset in La promesse

Dreamer: Nino del Arco (right) in Grandes amigos

Fredrik Becklén

SWEDEN

b: circa 1958

Kjell Grede's beautiful *Hugo och Josefin* is about a little girl living in the Swedish countryside and needing a playmate. When she goes to the village school she falls in with the oddball of her class, a strange loner called Hugo, prone to vanish on private quests and safaris. He has his own sorrow, since his father is in prison (as a conscientious objector), but he also has a kindly uncle who looks after him.

Josefin is played by the enchanting Marie Öhman – a child of utter happiness who often subsides in helpless giggles – and Hugo by one of the most endearing and individual of all the screen's children.

Nino del Arco

SPAIN

b: circa 1958

In *El niño y el muro* he played a half-German boy – whose German postman father, to add to the ethnic confusion, is played by Daniel Gélin. The Wall is the Berlin one, and the tenuous plot involves a ball, a white mouse, border guards and supramural romance.

In *La primera aventura* (released in Mexico as *The boy and the thief*) a poor peasant is arrested for theft of a church collection, three village children try to prove him innocent and some avenging dogs hound the true culprit to a confession.

Nino, an ornament to both these moral tales, continued to act, with for instance the second lead in *Kaltman, el hombre increíble* (75).

64 El niño y el muro
    (The child and the wall – MX/ES)
   La primera aventura
    (The first adventure – ES/MX)
66 Grandes amigos
    (Great friends – ES)

Troll: Fredrik Becklén in Hugo och Josefin

Fredrik Becklén is a wise little troll, with an unpretentious dignity and the most winning of grins. Solemnly explaining his long absence from school as a research project on water-spiders, or bowling along the country lanes on an old penny-farthing bicycle (while the soundtrack, with justified effrontery, bursts into 'For Unto Us a Child Is Born'), he is a magical creation.

An attempt to team Fredrik up, two years later, with another director and another little girl – and the sort of cute, interminable title popular at the time – was unhappily less inspired.

67 Hugo och Josefin
(Hugo and Josephine)
69 Hur Marie träffade Fredrik, åsnan Rebus, Kangarun Ploj och ...
(How Mary met Frederick, Rebus the donkey, Ploughman the kangaroo and...)

Jacques Gagnon

CANADA

b: circa 1958

Claude Jutra's sympathetic study of the general-storekeeper Antoine, one snowbound Christmas in Quebec Province, is made through the eyes of young nephew Benoît. Antoine's 'general' services include – reluctantly – those of undertaker, and much of the film is

Jacques Gagnon in Mon oncle Antoine

Fastidious: Filip Łobodzinski (left) with Henryk Gołebiewski in Stawiam na Tolka Banana

devoted to a long and increasingly drunken journey to pick up a corpse. Benoît, who goes along for the ride, learns a good deal about life, death and human weakness, and Jacques Gagnon's face soaks it all in.

71 Mon oncle Antoine
(Uncle Antoine)

Stephen Lindholm

SWEDEN

b: circa 1958

Stephen played 'Pelle' in a popular series of comedies, adapted from radio plays by Astrid Lindgren. He retained the part when it moved on into the TV series *Saltkråkar* (69).

64 Vi på Saltkråkar
(We from Salty Crow Island)
Tjorven, Båtsman och Moses
(Tjorven, Boatman and Moses)
65 Tjorven och Skrållan
(Tjorven and Little Yeller)
66 Tjorven och Mysak
67 Skrållan, Ruskprick och Knorrhane

Filip Łobodzinski

POLAND

b: circa 1958

Łobodzinski, too schematically set up as a victimised wimp in Nasfeter's school drama *Abel twoj brat*, showed enormous charm in his two TV serials of 1972 for Stanisław Jędryka. In these, fastidious Filip was satisfyingly partnered by one of his tormentors from *Abel*, the streetwise yob of HENRYK GOŁEBIOWSKI.

70 Abel twoj brat (Your brother Abel)
72 Podroz za jeden usmiech
(Journey for a smile)
Stawiam na Tolka Banana
(I'm betting on Tolek Banana)

Loris Loddi

ITALY/USA

b: circa 1958

Bilingual Loris, after adorning several spaghetti epics, deserved better than to see his (fictional) mother raped and murdered in the awful Harold Robbins-based *Adventurers*. This sort of thing has an embittering effect on a lad.

He was later seen in *Ladyhawke* (US 85).

63 Cleopatra (US/GB)
64 Ercole sfida Sansone
   (Hercules challenges Samson)
   La rivolta dei sette (Revolt of the Seven)
   Maciste nelle miniere di Re Salomone
   (Maciste in King Solomon's Mines)
66 Un fiume di dollari (A river of dollars)
70 The Adventurers (US)

Kiril Petrov

BULGARIA

b: circa 1958

Kushti bez ogradi was Kircho Petrov's biggest role in his many films of the early Seventies.

71 S deca na more
   (With children at the seaside)
   Taralezhite se razhdat bez bodli
   (Hedgehogs aren't born prickly)
72 Tatul (Thornapple)
73 Kato pesen (Like a song)
   Kushti bez ogradi (Houses without fences)
   Siromashko lyato (Indian summer)
74 Bashta mi boyadzhiyata
   (My father the housepainter)

Rauf Pojani

ALBANIA

b: circa 1958

The burly Pojani had a leading role in *Mëngjeze lufte*, as one of four schoolboy

Rauf Pojani in Mëngjeze lufte

Sardonic: Cristian Sofron in Atunci i-am condamnat pe toti la moarte

members of the Albanian resistance under Nazi occupation.

71 Mëngjeze lufte (Mornings of war)
72 Kapedani (The Captain)

Cristian Sofron

ROMANIA

b: 9 May 59 (Bucharest)

Cristian was very impressive in Sergiu Nicolaescu's 1972 drama of World War Two, originally to have been given the less cumbersome title of *Moarte lui Ipu* (Ipu's death). It's a searching story of hostages and scapegoats, involving a fiercely independent boy in a Transylvanian village, and an innocent simpleton called Ipu who makes a heroic gesture against the occupying Germans.

As the boy, somewhat reminiscent of Tarkovski's Ivan, Cristian Sofron veers excitingly between the emotional and the sardonic, like a darker Kolya Burlyayev ◇ with a dash of Jack Wild ◇.

In the two 1975 co-productions, both based on Jules Verne adventures, Sofron

partnered the French boy MARC DI NAPOLI. After graduating as an actor from the Bucharest Institute for Theatre and Cinema Arts, he went on to appear in *Doi ani de vacanța, Toate pînzele sus, Pentre patrie* and several more films.

72 Atunci i-am condamnat pe toți la moarte
   (I'd condemned them all to death)
75 Insula comorulor
   (Cormorant Island – RO/FR)
   Piratii din Pacific
   (Pirates of the Pacific – RO/FR)

Claude Amazan

FRANCE

b: 18 Jne 59 (Paris)

Claude, son of a doctor and a midwife, was a striking black child actor.

In the title role of *Le petit Bougnat* he had a disagreement with a little girl about the desirability of a summer camp holiday. He then played the page Zamore in a TV serialisation of a novel by Dumas père.

70 Le petit Bougnat (Little Charcoal)
72 Balzamo

Innocent eye: Bogdan Untaru in Năică și barza

Bogdan Untaru
ROMANIA

b: 13 Jly 59 (Bucharest)

After earlier studies of urban children in *Mingea* (58, The ball) and *Pustiul* (61, The kid), Elisabeta Bostan's series of short films about the little village boy Năică finally established her reputation as one of the world's finest directors of films about children. She saw the world with a child's innocent eye, but captured it with a skill and delicacy that also delighted adults.

Young Bogdan Untaru, who became enormously popular as Năică, had the perfect blend of wonder, curiosity and mischief. He never meant to be an actor, and after graduation from High School became something rarer and just as valuable: a wood-carver.

However, in 1987 Elisabeta Bostan persuaded him to make a brief comeback in the framing scenes of a Năică compilation called *Unde eşt copilarie?* (Where are you, childhood?), together with his former little-girl partner from the Năică films, Sanda Foamete (born 15 Oct 60).

63 Năică
66 Năică și barza
   (Naica and the stork)
67 Năică și veverița
   (Naica and the squirrel)
   Năică pleacă la București
   (Naica goes to Bucharest)

A slightly longer Bostan film about rustic childhood, from the same period, was *Amintirie din copilărie* (Childhood memories), released in 1965. It starred the wholly delightful ION BOCANCEA (born 7 Feb 51) as 'Nică', a slightly older version of Năică. Like Untaru, Bocancea became a father but not an actor. He is now an economist.

Ömer Dönmez
TURKEY

b: 13 Aug 59 (Adapazar)

In 1965 Ömer won second prize in a child actor contest promoted by the Turkish film magazine Ses, and made his film debut in the same year. By 1970 had appeared in more than 50 films, often billed simply as 'Ömercik' (Little Ömer).

65 Sevgim ve gururum (My love and pride)
68 Artik sevmeyeceğim (I'll never love again)
   Funda
   Yuvana dön baba (Come home, Daddy)
69 Ayşecikle Ömercik
   (Little Ayşe and little Ömer)
   Tatli günler (Sweet days)
   Ana kalbi (Mother's heart)
72 Aci sevda (Bitter love)
   Elveda meyhaneci (Farewell, mine host)
73 Anneler günü (Mother's day)

Lance Kerwin
USA

b: 6 Nov 59 (Newport Beach, Cal.)

Lance was probably America's leading boy actor of the late Seventies, in constant demand for TV movies, series and serials. With his huge eyes and mouth, he was a

Lance Kerwin, circa 1975

funny child who matured into a handsome teenager – though always looking much younger than he was – and developed considerable sensitivity as an actor.

He sometimes needed courage too, as when cast in the lead of an agonising drama about bed-wetting (*The Loneliest Runner*). But, wet or dry, Lance's integrity shone through.

Kerwin's generally anguished appeal continued undiminished in *The Death of Richie* (77), *'James at 15'* (77, TVS), *Young Joe, the Forgotten Kennedy* (77), *Salem's Lot* (79), *Side Show* (79), *The Boy Who Drank Too Much* (79, with Scott Baio ◇ in the title role), *Children of Divorce* (80), *The Mysterious Stranger* (82), *The Shooting* (82), *A Killer in the Family* (83) and *Enemy Mine* (85).

74 The Bridge of Adam Rush
   The Cloning of Richard Swimmer
   Escape to Witch Mountain
   The Greatest Gift
   The Healers
   Reflections of Murder
   To Hear a Rainbow Sing
75 'The Family Holvak' (TVS)
76 The Amazing Cosmic Awareness of Duffy
   Moon
   Amelia Earhart
   The Loneliest Runner

Johnny Whitaker

USA

b: 13 Dec 59 (Van Nuys, Calif.)

Red-mopped Johnny, son of Mormon parents, was no oil painting but a considerable performer. With the homely appeal of Jimmy Hunt ◇ a generation earlier, he had bigger opportunities than Hunt and took them with both freckled hands.

From the age of three he sang solos in the local Mormon church, and at four made his first commercial (for Chevrolet). In his acting debut, on the live TV show 'A Day in Court', he wept impressive buckets as his father was jailed.

He first impinged on the public conscience at the age of five, when he landed

Gun-toting Mormon: Johnny Whitaker in the TV series 'Family Affair'

the role of Jody in what was to be a long-running TV sitcom, 'A Family Affair' (1966-71). He was signed up by the Disney studio, with whom he made the majority of his films, for the cinema or for TV.

This was his cosy, kid-next-door side, which reached its apotheosis in the musical *Tom Sawyer* of 1973. On the way he had partnered George Spell ◇ in a remake of *The Biscuit Eater* (boys and dog) and Jodie Foster in *Napoleon and Samantha* (boy, girl and aged lion).

However, he had also shown his teeth as a boy possessed by Dark Powers in *Something Evil*, one of Steven Spielberg's early essays for TV: writhing and snarling on the floor, he has some of the horror of Mikael Rundquist, the boy-demon who savages Max von Sydow in Ingmar Bergman's *Hour of the Wolf*.

Tom Sawyer was pretty well the end of Whitaker's child career; but he later took a degree in film directing at Brigham Young University, and appeared in a film called *Magic Pony* (79).

65 The Russians Are Coming, the Russians
   Are Coming
71 The Biscuit Eater
   The Littlest Angel
   Something Evil
72 Napoleon and Samantha
   Snowball Express
73 Tom Sawyer

Vladimír Dlouhý

CZECHOSLOVAKIA

b: 1959

Vladimír is best remembered for his role as the polio-stricken boy who learns to ride horses, in a Czech version of 'I Can Jump Puddles' by the Australian Alan Marshall. Although much of the film is dangerously sentimental, the boy's courage is touchingly rendered.

Vladimír Dlouhý continued to win leading roles, in films like *Ostrov stříbrných volavek* (76), *Šestapadesát neomluvených hodin* (77) and *Hop...a je tu lidoop!* (77).

70 Už zase skáču přes kaluže
   (I'm jumping over puddles again)
72 Počkam, až zabiješ (I'll wait, you kill him)
73 Kvočny a Král (Hens and a King)
   Osud jmenem Kamila (Fate, alias Camilla)
74 Robinsonka (Girl Crusoe)
76 Plaveni hřibat (Foals in the river)

Vladimír Dlouhy in Už zase skáču přes kaluže

Brook Fuller

USA/FRANCE

b: 1959

Brook's part in *Il gattopardo* is a tiny one; in *L'arbre de Noël* it is large and extremely maudlin, an early entry in the Dying Boy genre later to be dominated by Renato Cestiè◇.

The unfortunate Pascal expires (of radioactive contamination) serenely and in the utmost comfort, in a château bought by his millionaire father, and in the company of two tame wolves. The American release title, *When Wolves Cry*, might have been amended to *When Critics Howl*.

63 Il Gattopardo
   (Le Guépard /The Leopard – IT/FR)
69 L'arbre de Noël
   (The Christmas tree – FR/IT)

Doomed: Fuller in L'arbre de Noël

Szergej Elisztratov

HUNGARY

b: circa 1959

Elisztratov's big role was in *Vállald ön-magadat*, based on the novel 'Children Are Born Twice' by Sándor Somogyi Tóth. He gives an unusual and intriguing portrait of an adolescent unable to relate either to his peer-group or to girl friends.

71 Holt vidék (Dead landscape)
74 Száznegyvenegy perc a Befejezetlen
    mondatból
    (Unfinished sentence of 141 minutes)
    Vállald önmagadat (Be yourself!)

Malicious: Philip Frame in The Little Ark

Philip Frame

USA

b: circa 1959

This agreeably malicious boy made a convincing henchchild to the vampire Count Yorga, and a somewhat acid war orphan in *The Little Ark*. He is notably ungallant to his fellow-refugee Alinda (Genevieve Ambas) in this adventure set amid the Dutch floods of 1953, but witty and watchable.

71 The Little Ark
   The Return of Count Yorga

Aleko Kochev

BULGARIA

b: circa 1959

The son of scientist parents, Aleko was discovered by Ivanka Grubcheva, who gave him a small part in *Deca igrayat ven* and then the lead in *Pri nikogo*, an admirably unsentimental drama of divorce. Its title, 'With no one', is the boy's answer in court when asked which of his parents he wants to go and live with.

Having finished his military service, Aleko – who once described himself to Grubcheva as 'your lazy boy' – hoped to return to acting.

73 Deca igrayat ven
   (Children playing out of doors)
74 Pri nikogo (With no one)

Roman Mosior

POLAND

b: circa 1959 (Wrocław)

Roman – small, dark, slightly dangerous – had an animal intensity that was irresistible to directors like Janusz Nasfeter. He cast him as the 'nasty cruel boy' who torments a nervous schoolmate (Piotr Szczerkowski), and then, in *Motyle*, as a rough kid experiencing the agonies of first love for an alluring girl of his own age (the devastating Bożena Fedorczyk, for whose sole benefit *Lolita* ought to have been remade).

In his late teens Mosior reappeared in *Zanim nadejdzie dzień* (76).

70 Abel – twoj brat (Your brother Abel)
   Dzięcioł (Woodpecker)
   Wakacje z duchami
   (Haunted holidays)
71 Pan Samochodzik i Templariusze
   (Mr Motor and the Templars)
   Rurka z kremem (Cream puff)
72 Ten okrutny nikczemny chłopiec
   (That cruel, disgusting boy)
   Motyle (Butterflies)

Dangerous: Roman Mosior in Ten okrutny nikczemny chłopiec

Tomislav Žganec

YUGOSLAVIA

b: circa 1959

68 Imam dvije Mame i dva Tate
(I've got two Mums and two Dads)
70 Družba Pere Kvržice
(Peter Kvržic's gang)
71 Tko pjeva zlo ne misli
(You can't go wrong with a song)

Eric Shea

USA

b: 14 Feb 60

Eric was a floridly freckled little chap who, given a bristling moustache and some pince-nez, would have had a certain Teddy Roosevelt quality. His screen image was plucky and argumentative, not to say uppity.

He showed true American grit as the SS 'Poseidon' capsized around him, and (well cast) as Mitch Vogel's ◇ kid brother in the Civil War adventure *Menace on the Mountain*; he was resourceful in *Castaway Cowboy*, a sort of Hawaiian Western, and peddled nude snapshots of aspiring beauty queens in *Smile*.

Many of his cinema and TV films were for Disney, and when Yul Brynner made a comeback as the King of Siam in a TV serialisation of *Anna and the King*, Eric played astonished son to Samantha Eggar's Anna.

One of his later performances, a break from his normal role of dear little pest, was as a bullying lout in *When Every Day Was the Fourth of July* (78).

68 Yours, Mine and Ours
69 Gaily, Gaily
70 The Cockeyed Cowboys of Calico County
72 Menace on the Mountain
The Poseidon Adventure
73 Ace Eli and Rodger of the Skies
74 Bobby Parker and Company
The Castaway Cowboy
Houston, We've Got a Problem
Smile
The Whiz Kid and the Mystery at Riverton
The Secret of the Pond

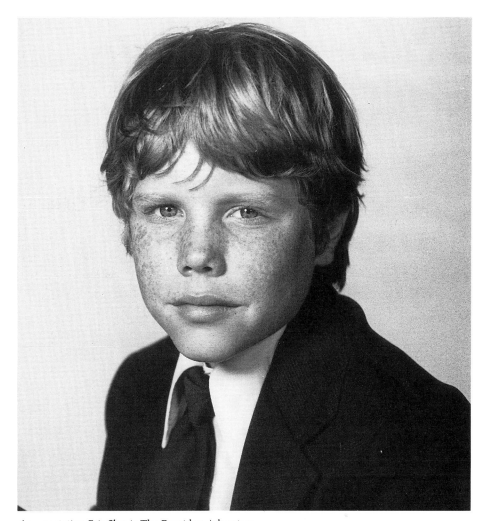

Argumentative: Eric Shea in The Poseidon Adventure

Eric had two elder brothers, Michael and Chris, both of whom were useful actors around the same time. MICHAEL SHEA was featured in *Namu, the Killer Whale* (66), *Welcome to Hard Times* (66) and *Ride a Northbound Horse* (69). CHRIS SHEA was in the TV series 'Shane' (66), then in *Firecreek* (68), *Yours, Mine and Ours* (68), *Smith!* (69), another TVS, 'My World and Welcome to It' (70), and *A Little Game* (71).

Svetislav Goncić

YUGOSLAVIA

b: 5 May 60 (Kladovo, Serbia)

As a hopeful boy Svetislav joined Radio Belgrade's junior drama studio, as a result of which he got many radio and TV roles, for instance in the TV series 'Kamiondžije' (Truck drivers). On stage he was in 'Nagrada' (The prize), the last production of the great director Bojan Stupica.

In *The boy and the violin* Goncić didn't play the young fiddler: that was STEVAN MARKOVIC, a real-life violin prodigy in the Heimo Haitto ◇ mould. In *Winter in Jakobsfeld* he acted with Slavko Štimac ◇.

After his two film roles in 1975 he studied acting at the Belgrade Faculty of Dramatic Arts, and from 1982 was a member of the important theatre group 'Atelier 212'. He became one of Serbia's leading actors, winning many awards for his work, and had the lead in *Oktoberfest* (87).

c.73 Kamiondžije (Truck-drivers – TVS)
75 Dečak i violina (The boy and the violin)
Zimovanje u Jakobsfeldu
(Winter in Jakobsfeld)

Indonesian Romeo: Karno in Romi dan Juli

Štimac in Vuk samotnjak

Rano Karno

INDONESIA

b: 8 Oct 60 (Jakarta)

Rano Karno, son of the well-known actor Sukarno M. Noor (1931-86), scored a big hit in *Si Doel anak Betawi*, and was seen in many films over the next two or three years. He had a heavily impressive face and a strong dramatic sense.

In 1974 he won two 'Best Child Actor' awards, at the Indonesian Film Festival in Surabaya and then at the Asian Film Festival in Taiwan.

After *Wajah tiga perempuan* (Faces of three women, 76) Rano graduated to adult roles, and has become a leading Indonesian actor, winning further awards in films like *Ranjau-ranjau cinta* (84), *Arini* (86), *Macan kamus* (87) and *Arini II* (88).

71 Lewat tengah malam (After midnight)
72 Si Doel anak Betawi
   (Si Doel, son of Batavia)
73 Rio anakku (Rio, my child)
74 Romi dan Juli (Romi and Juli)
   Si Rano (Rano)
75 Sebelum usia 17 (Under 17)

Slavko Štimac

YUGOSLAVIA

b: 15 Oct 60 (Perušić, Croatia)

Slavko was born in a remote village in the Croatian hills, and as a little boy had to walk several miles to and from school every day. While attending secondary school at Gospić, he was discovered by the film director Obrad Gluščević, hunting the region for a leading child for *Vuk samotnjak*.

His brave, cheerful countenance became a great favourite in Yugoslavia, where he took several leading parts. He was also spotted by Sam Peckinpah, who cast him in the important role of the captured Russian boy soldier taken under James Coburn's wing in *Cross of Iron*. Even with his dark hair dyed a dubious blond, Slavko (actually billed as 'Mikael Slavko Stimac') made a striking and touching figure. He was fine again as the hapless delinquent of *Special education*, a pitiful teenage teddy-bear in a school of hard knocks.

Štimac continued to act with steady success in his later teens: for instance *Aller retour* (78), *Tigar* (78), *Dvoboj za jukna prugu* (78), *Ko to tamo peva* (80). His first 'adult' lead came in Emin Kusturica's *Sjecas li se Dolly Bell* (81, Do You Remember Dolly Bell?).

72 Vuk samotnjak (The lone wolf)
75 Zimovanje u Jakobsfeldu
   (Winter in Jakobsfeld)
76 Vlak i snijegu (The snowbound train)
   Salaš u Malom Ritu (Farm in Mali Rit)
77 Cross of Iron
   (Steiner: das eiserne Kreuz – GB/DE)
   Specijalno vaspitanje (Special education)

Al Coster

MEXICO

b: 1960

Al Coster was the screen name of René Cardona III, son of the director René Cardona II, who had himself been a child actor twenty years or so earlier.

70 El pequeño Robin Hood
71 Un pirata de doce años
   (A twelve-year-old pirate)
72 La mula de Cullen Baker
72 Zindy, el niño de los pantanos
   (Zindy, child of the swamps)

Shane Simms

NEW ZEALAND

b: 1960
d: 1978

One of the world's most engaging children's films was made by the pupils and staff of Lincoln High School, near Christchurch in New Zealand. It was a spoof Western, directed and scripted by Tony Brittenden, a teacher at the school, and shot in the suitably rocky local landscape.

Lincoln County Incident told of the adventures of the bookish but resourceful Samson Peabody Jones, an innocent traveller stranded among hard-drinking, quick-shooting thieves and rustlers. He discovers a gold mine with a resident ghost who hands him a parcel 'only to be opened in an emergency'. (When the final

Shane Simms in Lincoln County Incident

crisis arrives and Samson opens the parcel, it proves to contain a telephone and the number of a Dial-a-Cowboy service.)

Shane Simms' Samson – quaintly attired in bowler-hat, gold-rimmed spectacles and a sober suit of bottle-green velvet – is a dandyish scholar one can't fail to warm to: not only brighter but far cooler than his brutish adversaries, whom he outwits with dreamlike precision. It's a triumph of intelligence.

Brittenden's film took five years to complete, with the help of parents, well-wishers and a clever brother. By the time it was released (in 1980) poor Shane Simms was dead – killed in a car crash. His dry, first-person narration in *Lincoln County Incident* is spoken well by an American, Stephen Trail. But Shane's Samson will live on as the most charming of memorials.

75 Lincoln County Incident

Kim Burfield

BRITAIN

b: circa 1960

After an inauspicious start as the hero-worshipper of a clapped-out soccer star (Richard Harris, who also directed with maudlin abandon) young Kim's career was resurrected when Orson Welles chose him as Jim Hawkins to his oft-postponed

Orson's Jim: Kim Burfield in the 1971 Treasure Island

Long John Silver. The introduction was presumably made by Wolf Mankowitz, who scripted both films, but Kim was too young and cute to be a convincing Jim, though he performed with spirit.

His final lead – as a boy called David Hawkins, oddly enough – was in a rather plodding time-travel fantasy from the Children's Film Foundation.

69 Bloomfield (GB/IL)
71 Treasure Island (GB/FR/DE/ES)
74 The Flying Sorcerer

César Chauveau

FRANCE

b: circa 1960

After *Le clan des Siciliens*, César played the lead in two films directed by Gérard Blain. In *Le pélican* he was obsessively hunted by his father, severed from him by divorce, and in *Un enfant dans la foule* he was the child of unloving, often brutal parents.

He also appeared in Blain's 1978 film *Un second souffle* (FR/DE).

68 Le clan des Siciliens (The Sicilian clan)
73 Le pélican (The pelican)
75 Un enfant dans la foule
    (A child in the crowd)

César Chauveau in Le clan des Siciliens

Mischievous: Eser as 'Gaylord'

Archibald Eser

WEST GERMANY

b: circa 1960

Archibald's performance as the sweetly mischievous 'Gaylord' in both these films (with Werner Hinz as his doting grandad) made him the nation's moppet-of-the-moment.

68 Morgens um sieben ist die Welt noch in Ordnung (7 a.m. and all's well)
69 Wenn süss das Mondlicht auf den Hügeln schläft (When the sweet moonlight sleeps upon the hills)

Hauntingly sad: Sutherland in Montreal Main

blonds, are fine in their secret games — all, it turns out, fermenting in the warped mind of Niles. Robert Mulligan, directing with bravura, plays his own game of double-bluff on the audience. By never showing the twins incontrovertibly together in full shot until the closing moments of the film, he encourages our belief that the 'double act' is the usual fake: the final shock, when one sees that the twins really *are* separate boys, is worth waiting for.

72 The Other

Wynand Uys

SOUTH AFRICA

b: circa 1960

In *Dirkie*, a relatively static epic of survival — a sort of *Sammy Going Nowhere*, whose foreign release title was *Lost in the Desert* — an ailing little boy is dumped in the Kalahari desert, sole human survivor of a plane crash, with only his dog for company. It's actually rather well done. The poor child has to cope with attacks by snake, scorpion and hyaena, and his attempt to cook ostrich eggs provides perfect culinary farce.

Not only the title was transformed for foreign consumption. Both the boy and his father and director, the actor Jamie

Johnny Sutherland

CANADA

b: circa 1960

Montreal Main was a brave, sympathetic but ultimately slightly wet story of love between a man and a boy. (The relationship is left shadowy, and the man caves in too easily under social attack.)

Johnny Sutherland makes a hauntingly sad figure of the boy, a child of the flower-power era who proves stronger in both emotion and character than the man who loved him.

74 Montreal Main

Chris and Martin Udvarnoky

USA

b: circa 1960

In *The Other*, a curious, effective horror-melodrama scripted by Tom Tryon from his own novel, the Udvarnoky twins play twins Niles and Holland — the complication being that Holland is really dead, and only kept alive in Niles' fantasy as a playmate and convenient scapegoat for his own wickeder and more vindictive acts, which don't stop short of murder.

The Udvarnokies, a pair of pudgy

Overheated: Wynand Uys in Dirkie

Double bluff: Martin and Chris Udvarnoky in The Other

Uys, altered their surnames to Hayes, with Wynand adding a pseudo-autobiographical touch by becoming 'Dirkie Hayes'.

70 Dirkie

Clay O'Brien

USA

b: 6 May 61 (Ray, Arizona)

With his honest, puzzled, meat-and-potatoes face – a bit like a cub version of Joel McCrea – Clay O'Brien was a particularly endearing screen kid of the early Seventies (even when he was masquerading, without notable conviction, as a semi-white Red Indian). His father Gene had long been a horse-handler for movies, and also a stuntman (e.g. for Alan Ladd in *Branded*).

In *Cahill* he was daunted by the fatherly example of John Wayne (the youngest of whose *Cowboys* he had been two years earlier) and terrorised by the snarling George Kennedy: here Clay enacted straightforward fear as touchingly as he elsewhere embodied dogged courage.

He was the eldest of three comically off-loaded orphans in *The Apple Dumpling Gang*, and was a spunky T.J. to the Mackintosh of Roy Rogers in the old cowboy's return to the screen after an absence of 23 years. Later he was in *The Town That Dreaded Sundown* (77).

71 The Cowboys
72 Climb an Angry Mountain
73 Cahill United States Marshal
   One Little Indian
74 The Apple Dumpling Gang
   The Whiz Kid and the Mystery at Riverton
75 Mackintosh and T.J.

Jackie Haley

USA

b: 14 Jly 61 (Northridge, Calif.)

Jackie Earle Haley – as he was known from *The Bad News Bears* onwards – is the son of the actor Bud Haley. He was appearing on TV from the age of six, his earliest important job being to supply the voice of the protagonist in the animated TV version of 'Dennis the Menace'. He created his first big impression, though, as the maliciously epicene child actor in *The Day of the Locust*. (See Bubbles Noisom °.)

Epicene: Jackie Haley in The Day of the Locust

He was fine as the abrasive Kelly Leak, odd star out of *The Bad News Bears*, and soldiered on through this glorious film's two increasingly awful sequels: *The Bad News Bears in Breaking Training* (77) and *The Bad News Bears Go to Japan* (78). He was a post-holocaust orphan in *Damnation Alley* (77), but had better luck in *Breaking Away* (79) and *Losin' It* (83).

Wary little Haley may not have been the most charming of child actors, but he has never lacked for personality.

72 Un homme est mort
       (The Outside Man – FR/IT)
74 The Day of the Locust
76 The Bad News Bears

Scott Baio

USA

b: 22 Sep 61 (Brooklyn, New York)

The actual, original Bugsy Malone grew from pint-size to robust six-footer in three or four years, with surprisingly little change to the oval face which had entranced Blousey Brown. His large, gentle, rather anxious eyes – no longer obliged to affect world-weary coolness under a soft hat – learned to express increasing warmth and humour, till he deservedly became a pillar of the more admirable TV sitcoms.

In a whole series of series, like 'Happy Days' (as cousin to 'the Fonz'), 'Muggsy', 'Joanie Loves Chachi' and 'Charles in Charge', Scott was a delight to watch and listen to: relaxed, intelligent and almost, dare one say, wise. In the cinema, *Foxes* (79) hardly extended him, but in the title role of the TV movie *The Boy Who Drank Too Much* (80) he rose to a quite new challenge. He also starred in *Zapped!* (82).

76 Bugsy Malone (GB)
       Luke Was There
78 Legs
79 Skatetown USA

His younger brother JIMMY BAIO (born 15 Mar 62) was often seen in sitcoms of the last decade or two: for instance in 'Joe and

World-weary: Scott Baio in Bugsy Malone

Sons' (75) and in the perennial 'Soap'. His cinema films have included *Lepke* (74), *The Bad News Bears in Breaking Training* (77) and *Playing for Keeps* (84).

Lee Montgomery

USA

b: 3 Nov 61 (Winnipeg, Canada)

Elliot and Olivia, the Irish-Canadian parents of Lee Harcourt Montgomery, were both actors, and their pudgy little lad made a predictably early start in show

business, aged about four. The family moved to California in 1969, and two years later Lee was working for Walt Disney and co-starring with a golden-egg-laying duck. In *Ben* (sequel to *Willard*) he co-starred with a rat, and in *Burnt Offerings* with Oliver Reed.

Lee, a pleasant kid-next-door type, was good at conveying mounting panic, and was often required to. He had particular trouble with screen fathers, at least two of whom (in *Cry in the Wilderness* and *Burnt Offerings*) tried to kill him.

His later films included *True Grit, a Further Adventure* (78), *Split Image* (82),

Death with father: Lee Montgomery in
Burnt Offerings

Mutant (83), *Staying Together* (84, a lead),
Night Shadows (84) and *Girls Just Wanna
Have Fun* (85).

71 The Harness
   Million Dollar Duck
72 Ben
   Bobby
   Pete 'n' Tillie
73 A Cry in the Wilderness
   Female Artillery
   Runaway!
74 Doctor Dan
   The Savage Is Loose
75 Man on the Outside
76 Baker's Hawk
   Burnt Offerings

Dschingis Bowakow
b: 23 Jan 62 (Dachau, near Munich)

and Uwe Enkelmann
b: 7 Nov 61 (Hamburg-Wilhelmsburg)

WEST GERMANY

Dschingis' parents were Kalmuks, from a
Mongolian race which lives between the
Caspian and Black seas. By an accident of
history, the boy was born in a place with
an accursed name.

His elder sister, Natalia, married the
young German film director Hark Bohm,
who later starred the ten-year-old brother-
in-law, opposite his own actor brother
Marquard Bohm, as the roaming Indian
boy Chetan. In this story, set in Montana
around 1880, a shepherd saves Chetan
from a rancher's vengeance and gradually
befriends him.

Galloping on horseback, with long
flying hair, dressed only in a few strips
of leather, Dschingis presents an image
straight out of Fenimore Cooper. His
impassive, sculptured face contrasts
fascinatingly with the lithe speed of his
movements. (He grew up to be a devotee
of Kung Fu and Kobudo.)

72 Tschetan, der Indianerjunge
   (Chetan, Indian boy)
75 Nordsee ist Mordsee
   (North Sea is Death Sea)

In *Nordsee ist Mordsee* Dschingis co-starred
with UWE ENKELMANN, a tawny, freckled
boy more or less adopted by Hark Bohm
– he had already had the lead in Bohm's
1973 film *Ich kann auch 'ne Arche Bauen*
(I can build an ark too).

Uwe plays a tough local boy who revels
in persecuting the 'slit-eyed outsider'; his
gang smashes up a huge raft which
Dschingis had been patiently building in
the hope of sailing away on it one day.
After routing the gang and defeating Uwe
in fair fight, Dschingis forces his enemy to
help him rebuild the raft. Gradually they
become friends and allies, and in the end
sail off together into the perils of the
North Sea. (This idealistic story is much
less starry-eyed than it sounds.)

73 Ich kann auch 'ne Arche bauen
   (I can build an ark too)

Dschingis Bowakow in Tschetan, der Indianerjunge

In Hark Bohm's 1977 film *Moritz, lieber Moritz* (Dear Moritz), a new early-teenager, MICHAEL KEBSCHULL — with a memorable face of doleful beauty — took the title role in a boy-and-girl romance which had some charm, but alienated at least its British public in a scene where Moritz summarily executes a cat. (The cat had killed his pet rat, so his action followed perfectly accepted traditions of buddy-avenging.) Uwe and the saxophone-playing Moritz overcome class differences to become friends and fellow pop-musicians, and Dschingis again uses his martial arts to scatter a crowd of hostile yobs.

Dschingis had the tiny role of a Russian soldier at the end of Volker Schlöndorff's *Die Blechtrommel* (DE/FR 78, The tin drum), and Uwe again played a pop-drummer in Peter F. Bringmann's *Die Heartbreakers* (82). But meanwhile the two had co-starred once more in *Im Herzen des Hurrican* (79).

Leif Garrett

USA

b: 8 Nov 61 (Hollywood)

Leif Garrett is his stage name; his mother is the actress Carolyn Stellar. He was a glamorous child with the eyes of a knowing doe, and began acting professionally as a five-year-old.

Although he was in continuous demand and acquired a considerable teeny-bopper following, his star roles, as in *Skateboard* and the lurid *Kid Vengeance*, didn't come till he was 15. (He was unlucky to be only eight or nine when Visconti was casting *Death in Venice*, though this would have actually been nearer the age of the real-life Tadzio — Władysław Moes — at the moment Thomas Mann saw and was entranced by him in Venice in the summer of 1911. See Björn Andresen°, p.308.)

Leif Garrett now began making rock LP's; but his acting career continued strongly, with roles in *Sergeant Pepper's Lonely Hearts Club Band* (78), *The Outsiders* (83), *Thunder Alley* (84), and a near-lead —

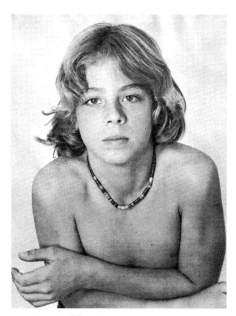

Knowing: Leif Garrett

as a motor mechanic — in Bruce Morrison's *Shaker Run* (NZ 85).

69 Bob and Carol and Ted and Alice
73 Macon County Line
   Walking Tall
74 Devil Times Five
   Strange Homecoming
75 The Last Survivors
   Part 2 Walking Tall
   Three for the Road
76 Flood
77 God's Gun
   Kid Vengeance
   Peter Lundy and the Medicine Hat Stallion
   Skateboard
   Walking Tall the Final Chapter

Simon Burke

AUSTRALIA

b: 1961

Simon, who also developed talents as a singer and dancer, had only one child part in the cinema, but a meaty one. As the confused Tom Allen of *The Devil's Playground*, a pupil in an Australian Catholic seminary in the 1950, he moves bashfully through the steamy atmosphere of an adolescence riddled with religion-induced shame and guilt: masturbation, sado-masochistic hanky-panky and (in Tom's case) torrential bed-wetting.

The nice thing is that, against all the odds, innocence and humour continually win out, in cascades of schoolboy giggles. There are hilarious scenes of mutual confession among the pupils, and would-be sexy fights. ('You've won. What are you going to do to me?')

Simon Burke — wholly delightful and sympathetic in this weird film — later had leading roles in *The Irishman* (78) and *The Clinic* (82), and supporting ones in *Slippery Slide* (80), *May I Have a Normal Life* (81), *Red* (81), and *Slate, Wyn and Me* (87). He also had leads in the 1983 TV series 'Scales of Justice' and 'Kings'.

76 The Devil's Playground

Master Alankar

INDIA

b: circa 1961

Forceful little Alankar had genuine passion, a refreshing change from the glazed soulfulness and formal snivelling of the Indian child-actor tradition. One is inclined to cheer when, as a proud shoe-shiner, he rejects a client's coin tossed on the ground, and demands (successfully) that it be picked up and handed to him.

71 Andaz (Style)
   Jai Bangla Desh
      (Long live Bangladesh)
72 Aage badho (Forward march)
   Bharat ke shaheed (Martyrs of India)
   Dharkan (Heartbeat)
   Gomti ke kinare
      (On the banks of Gomti)
   Haar jeet (Defeat and victory)
   Jaanwar aur insaan (Man and beast)
   Seeta aur Geeta (Seeta and Geeta)
73 Anolkhi (Unknown)
   Barkha bahar (Love's bloom)
   Jugnu (Glow-worm)
   Naag mere saathi
      (Snake, my companion)
74 Balak aur janwar (The boy and the animal)
   Balak Dhruv (The child Dhruv)
   Chatis Ghante (36 Ghante)
   Khote sikkay (Counterfeit coins)
   Majboor (Helpless)
   Naga kanni (Snake girl)

Ilir Çelia

ALBANIA

b: circa 1961

'Two brothers, Qetsor the Dictator and Erlet the Foolish, have become the terror of their toys and the most quarrelsome children of the building. Because of their bad behaviour, their friends shun them. The two begin to have frightful dreams. To Erlet it seems that his toys are chasing him through a dark forest, whereas Qetsor sees himself in the dock with damaged toys as his judges. The brothers wake and realize their mistakes.'

Ilir Çelia played Qetsor in this classic moral tale, and Kristaq Burdhima was Erlet. Çelia later had a lead in *Me hapin e shokëve* (79) and a supporting part in *Partizani i vogël Velo* (80).

72 Kryengritje ne pallat (Palace revolution)
75 Lumë drite (Flood of light)

András Márkus

HUNGARY

b: circa 1961

In *A locsolókocsi*, the arrival of a Bardot-like girl (Erika Maretics) in his class arouses the passion of the conceited Omasics (Markus). However, she prefers his unpretentious friend Totyi (Péter Lengyel), and this drives Omasics to deplorable acts of treachery, for which he duly has to atone.

74 A locsolókocsi (The water-truck)

Marek Sikora

POLAND

b: circa 1961

Things really pile up against poor Jurek, the fourteen-year-old hero of Stanisław Jędryka's *Koniec wakacji*. He stands help-lessly by as teenage thugs blackmail a schoolmate; he is told that his mother has gone off to a sanatorium, and later learns

that she has gone off with a lover; and to cap it all, his own newly-acquired girl-friend lets him down.

After the TV series 'Szaleństwo Majki Skowron', the excellent Marek Sikora had a supporting role in Nasfeter's *Królowa pszczół* (77).

75 Koniec wakacji (End of the holidays)
   Szaleństwo Majki Skowron (Majek Skowron's madness)

Peter Malmsjö

SWEDEN

b: 1 Mar 62 (Saltsjö-Boo)

Peter played Niklas in the 1971 film, to the 'Figur' – oddball, weirdo, goon – of STEFAN GRYBE (b: 19 Nov 62). It's all about a hunt for a lost dog.

70 Grisjakten (The pig-hunt)
71 Niklas och Figuren
   (Nicholas and the Goon)
72 Ture Sventon, privatdetektiv
   (Ture Sventon, private detective –
   NO/SE)

Johnny Doran

USA

b: 25 May 62

The strawberry-blond John Allen Doran had, in childhood, a button of a nose and a round sucking mouth. Angry green eyes, however, proclaimed that he was nobody's pushover. He began acting when he was three, made dozens of commercials, and experienced two New York stage flops – one of them a musical based on 'A Member of the Wedding'.

No pushover: Johnny Doran in From the Mixed-Up Files. . .

339

(He also played John Henry in the straight stage version.)

In his 1973 film with the interminable title (*The Hideaways*, its re-release name, was a great improvement) he made a fine fist of surviving overnight incarceration in the Metropolitan Museum of Art, and was quite unintimidated by Ingrid Bergman in a white wig.

Three years later, for Disney, he and a delightful black buddy of his own age (Billy Attmore) allied themselves with a Southern belle and a quack doctor (Joan Hackett and Peter Ustinov) in the search for his late father's treasure. He had a good part in the TV series 'Salty'.

Most of his later work was for TV. He took the Rooney part in a remake of *Captains Courageous* – opposite the exquisitely hateful Jonathan Kahn – and played Jackie Cooper ◇ in a Judy Garland biopic called *Rainbow*. He also appeared in the series 'The Fantastic Journey' and 'Mulligan's Stew', and later films included *Superstition* (82).

73 From the Mixed-Up Files of Mrs Basil E. Frankweiler
76 Treasure of Matecumbe
77 Captains Courageous

Jan Ohlsson

SWEDEN

b: 3 Jne 62 (Uppsala)

His was not Erich Kästner's Emil, but a mischievous rustic one created by the inevitable Astrid Lindgren; the equally inevitable (and equally excellent) Olle Hellbom directed the three films.

Jan played the lead in *Dante*, a story of boy detectives tracking down jewel thieves.

71 Emil i Lönneberga (Emil at Lönneberga)
72 Nya hyss av Emil i Lönneberga
   (New pranks of Emil at Lönneberga)
73 Emil och grisaknoen (Emil and the piglet)
77 Dante, akta're för Hajen!
   (Mind the Shark, Dante!)

Swedish Emil: Jan Ohlsson in Emil i Lönneberga

Ike Eisenmann

USA

b: 21 Jly 62 (Houston, Texas)

Ike, a round-faced little boy of exceptional intelligence – and usually cast as such, by the Disney studio in particular – was the son of the actor Al Abel. His brother, Al Eisenmann, also acted.

From 1970 Ike was seen episodically in several TV series such as 'Gunsmoke' and 'Kung Fu', and had a leading role in 'The Fantastic Journey' when the film spawned a series.

Ike's later credits included *Return from Witch Mountain* (78, lead), *The Bastard* (78), *Black Beauty* (78), *Devil Dog: the Hound of Hell* (78), two leads in 1979, *The Healer* and *Shadow of Fear*, then *The Formula* (80), *Star Trek the Wrath of Khan* (82) – this was when film titles abandoned even punctuation – *So Young, So Deadly* (82), *Cross Creek* (83) and *Gobots: Battle of the Rocklords* (86, voice only).

The talented Ike, who had acquired a taste for magic after his 'Witch Mountain' films – in which he casually levitated – also painted and played the viola.

74 Escape to Witch Mountain
   The Secret of the Pond
75 The Sky's the Limit
76 The Amazing Cosmic Awareness
   of Duffy Moon
   Banjo Hackett
   Kit Carson and the Mountain Men
   Roamin' Free
   Terror Out of the Sky

Ivan Arshinkov

BULGARIA

b: 1 Oct 62

The finest movies of the frail, sensitive little Arshinkov were written by those princes of Bulgarian scenarists, the 'brothers Mormarev' – not brothers at all, in fact, but old friends and collaborators (Marko Stoychev and Moritz Yomtov) whose delectable but different senses of humour have combined to produce some

Keyboard trouble: Ivan Arshinkov in Spomen

of the world's subtlest and funniest film scripts for children. Their tales (*Hedgehogs, Children at the Seaside*) are moral in the best sense, with lessons learnt through laughter, not preaching.

In *The Wind of Travel* Ivan played a little peasant boy who one day bids farewell to the buffalo he tends, and sets out alone to discover the world and what it means to be a man. *Memory* pitted him against a piano and a piano-teacher.

68 Nebeto na Veleka (The sky of Veleka)
69 Priznanie (Confession)
70 Staretsat (The old man)
   Taralezhite se razhdat bez bodli
      (Hedgehogs aren't born prickly)
71 S deca na more
      (With children at the seaside)
72 Vyaturut na puteshestviyata
      (The wind of travel)
73 Mazhe bez rabota (Men without work)
   Siromashko lyato (Indian summer)
   Spomen (Memory)

Eric Olson

USA

b: 17 Nov 62 (Santa Monica, Cal.)

Eric was a gentle, likeable boy whose best parts came in 1976. In the Ibsenite disaster-movie *Flood* he nearly drowns as the son of the mayor (Richard Basehart) who puts the local economy above the public safety, and in *Viva Knievel* gives moral support as the son of the stuntman's mechanic (Gene Kelly).

74 Mixed Company
   Sarah T.
75 Conspiracy of Terror
   The Swiss Family Robinson (TVS)
76 Flood
   Viva Knievel!
   Widow
78 King

Robert Bettles

AUSTRALIA

b: 1962

Bettles, a tough, square-faced boy with riding skills, was thundering across our screens four years before Kelly Reno◊ of *Black Stallion*. If not such a dazzling rider as Reno, he was at least as good an actor, and could be very touching in the understated Australian manner. The Disney studio took him up, and his honest chips of eyes and pleasingly unreconstructed teeth shone through six leading roles.

75 The Fourth Wish
   Harness Fever
   Ride a Wild Pony (US)
76 Let the Balloon Go
77 Born to Run (US)
   Shimmering Light (AU/US)

Alfred J. Lutter

USA

b: 1962

Freckled, myopic and a sharp-witted ad-libber, Alfred Lutter III made an instant hit

341

in *Alice Doesn't Live Here Any More* as the bored little son Ellen Burstyn drags from Socorro via Phoenix to Tucson in her forlorn quest for singing stardom. He then made a perfect sketch of Woody Allen, as a child, confronting the sheeted figure in *Love and Death*. ('We shall meet again!' 'Don't bother.')

The nearest Alfred came to conventional Boy's Adventure was in *The Cay*, as a stranded and blinded child buffeted by sea and sandstorm. After that the spectacles came on again for his role as Ogilvie, the intellectual and sporting statistician of *The Bad News Bears*.

74 Alice Doesn't Live Here Any More
75 Love and Death
   The Cay
76 The Bad News Bears
   It Must Be Love 'Cos I Feel So Dumb
77 The Bad News Bears in Breaking Training

Unsmiling: Stephen Archibald in My Ain Folk

Stephen Archibald

BRITAIN

b: circa 1962

The autobiographical trilogy of the Scot Bill Douglas – completed in 1978 with *My Way Home* – was one of the landmarks of British cinema in the Seventies. Bleak and laconic, it compares fascinatingly with Russia's Gorki trilogy of some 35 years earlier, whose terrors were balanced by human warmth and moments of great emotional release.

Douglas's childhood was in every way more deprived – his surrogate never smiles after the departure of his only childhood friend, a German POW – and a desolating coldness hangs over the recreation of life with his bitter old grandmother (the absolute antithesis of

Gorki's), and in and out of orphanages after her death.

Stephen Archibald, who continued to play the hero in his early teens and at National Service age in *My Way Home*, was the ideal interpreter of the boy Douglas – hungry for affection but wary of rebuff, and only occasionally giving vent to the rage within him.

72 My Childhood
73 My Ain Folk

Master Ramu

INDIA

b: circa 1962

Ramu had leads in *Paapam pasivadu* and *Pasi hridalayu*.

72 Paapam pasivadu (Alas, boy)
   Vasantha Maaligai
73 Deivakkuzhandaigal (God's children)
   Dhanama? Daivama? (Money or God?)
   Geetha
   Manitharil manickam (Jewel among men)
   Pasi hridalayu (Tender hearts)
   Pillai selvam (Son is wealth)
74 Devudu chesina pelli
      (Marriage made in heaven)
   Doctoramma (Lady doctor)
   Maha bhakta tukaram
   Peddalu marali (Reform the grown-ups)
   Ramayya thandri (Father Ramayya)

Master Satyajit

INDIA

b: circa 1962

Satyajit played a leading role in *Jai Radhe Krishna*.

71 Hare Rama hare Krishna
72 Anuraag (Blind love)
   Bijli (Lightning)
   Jawani diwani (Crazy youth)
   Mere bhaiya (My brother)
   Samadhi (The shrine)
   Shadi ke baad (After marriage)
   Shor (The noise)
   Theerthayathra (Pilgrimage)
73 Hum sub chor hain (The criminals)
   Joshila (Flaming youth)
   Jugnu (Glow-worm)

Pyar ka rishta (Love's relation)
Sabak (Lesson)
74 Balak Dhruv (The child Dhruv)
Bidaai (Farewell)
Jai Radhe Krishna (Glory to Radha Krishna)
75 Dharam karam (Ritual acts)
Maya Machchindra
Tyag (The sacrifice)

Akihiro and Masahiro Tomikawa

JAPAN

b: circa 1962

The brothers Tomikawa – Akihiro in the first film and Masahiro in the second – were the small observers and narrators in these two blood-spattered stories of wandering samurai life, which were amalgamated and reissued in a dubbed American version under the title *Shogun Assassin* (80).

The impassive infant Daigoro watches his father, 'Lone Wolf', formerly the Shogun's executioner, in heroic, pitiless and ceaseless action. The audience's incomprehension faithfully echoes the infant's.

71 Kozure ohkami – ko wo kashi ude
 kashi tsukamatsuru
 (Lightning swords of death)
72 Kozure ohkami – sanzu no kawa
 no ubaguruma
 (A pram at the Styx)

Michal Vavruša

CZECHOSLOVAKIA

b: circa 1962

Michal Vavruša, a proud, sensitive, distinguished-looking boy with huge dark eyes, was unusual in Czech films in playing four leading roles: on two occasions with absent or unsympathetic fathers, and once with a dog.

In *Ostrov stříbrných volavek*, set towards the close of World War One, Michal is the son of an army officer who has been killed in action. He lives unhappily with

Liberal anguish: Michal Vavruša in Ostrov stříbrných volavek

his grandfather (Erwin Geschonneck), a cold, haughty officer of the old school, and finally defies him by allying himself with working-class boys to protect two deserters from discovery.

70 Kapitan Korda (Captain Korda)
72 Vlak do stanice Nebe
 (The train to Heaven station)
75 Sirius
76 Ostrov stříbrných volavek
 (The isle of silver herons)

Renato Cestiè

ITALY

b: 11 Jan 63 (Rome)

This charming sandy-haired boy, the picture of health with his bright eyes and freckled button of a nose, became Italy's unlikely flag-bearer in the 'Beautiful Death' genre launched by Terence Young's *L'arbre de Noël* and Arthur Hiller's *Love Story*.

In *L'ultima neve di primavera*, a big international box-office hit, Renato played the emotionally neglected son of a successful lawyer (Bekim Fehmiu). When his father shows belated affection and takes him off on a skiing holiday – luxurious surroundings pointing the familiar moral that money cannot buy love – Luca succumbs to leukaemia, and after a long illness bravely borne dies late at night, in his father's arms, in a deserted funfair.

Clearly believing that one could not have too much of a bad thing, the same marshmallow-peddler who had conceived this lamentable tale, Mario Gariazzo, rewrote it with a few differences as *Il venditore di palloncini* and directed the

Death's bright angel: Renato Cestiè in L'ultima neve di primavera

result himself. This time Renato, as the neglected son of a drunken comedian (James Whitmore), wears himself to the point of terminal exhaustion and malnutrition in trying to earn, provide and housekeep for his father.

His death scenes are now even more prolonged and beautiful – with no disfiguring tubes up the nose – and doctors, nurses, parents and friends gather at the bedside to proclaim the radiant boy a saint and martyr. Following its predecessor to the ultimate gasp, the film allows him to expire at a circus, guided heavenwards by the gnomic balloon-seller of the title.

This wallow in glycerine tears, released in America and Britain (dubbed) as *Last Moments*, should survive as a monument to the corrupted sentiments of our age.

Renato Cestiè, now the darling of Italy, had played nine further leads by his mid-teens, and by public demand was frequently allowed to survive till the final credits. He continued his career in more modest roles, and was seen for instance as the mute youth in the framing scenes of Zeffirelli's excellent film version of *La traviata* (NL 83). He must have felt a pang of jealousy at the heroine's musical death.

Cestiè in Ritorno di Zanna Bianca

69 Leonardo da Vinci
72 Così sia (So be it)
73 L'ultima neve di primavera
    (The last snow of spring)
   Si può fare...amigo
    (Make himself a friend – IT/FR/ES)
74 L'albero dalle foglie rosa
    (The pink-leaved tree)
   Il ritorno di Zanna Bianca
    (The return of White Fang)
   Cuore (Heart)
   Il venditore di palloncini
    (The balloon-seller, AKA Last Moments)
75 Giubbe rosse (Red jackets)
   Bianchi cavalli di agosto
    (White horses of August)
   Noi non siame angeli (We're no angels)
76 Come ti rapisco il pupo
    (How I kidnap the baby)
77 Nero veneziano (Venetian black)
78 Enfantasme (Spooks)

Menderes Utku

TURKEY

b: 5 Apr 63 (Istanbul)

Menderes – the roguish 'Afacan' of his late films – is the son of the Turkish producer-director Ümit Utku (who in fact only directed his films of 1968-69). His sister Nilgün also acted as a child.

65 Suçlu çocuklar (Guilty children)
68 Yara (The wound)
69 Ana mezari (Mother's grave)
   Sabirtaşi (The patience stone)
   Iffet (Honour)
71 Afacan küçük serseri
    (Afacan the little rascal)
72 Afacan harika coçuk
    (Afacan the wonder-boy)

Panchito Gomez

USA

b: circa 1963

Panchito's best parts were in *Paco* and *Walk Proud*. During 1977 he was also in an episode of the TV series 'The Winners'. He was seen again in *Max Dugan Returns* (83), *Tuff Turf* (84) and *Cold Dog Soup* (89).

74 Doctor Max
75 Paco
78 Run for the Roses

Panchito Gomez with Phillip R. Allen in the ABC Afterschool Special Gaucho

79 Walk Proud
80 Borderline
   Gaucho

Tudor Petruţ

ROMANIA

b: 1 Dec 63 (Bucharest)

'Adrian', co-hero of Geta Doina Tarnavschi's enjoyable adventure, was played by the curly-haired son of the leading Romanian actor Emanoil Petruţ. (His pal 'Onoriu' was CRISTIAN ORASCU.) Aptly, in the former Roman province of Dacia, the plot involves Roman relics, and fantasies of Roman days.

Tudor went on to study drama and direction, but after leaving university returned to film acting in *Femeia din Ursa Mare* (The woman from Ursa Major) and *Liceenii* (Teenagers).

76 Misterul lui Herodot
    (The Herodotus mystery)

Peter Welz

EAST GERMANY

b: 1963

In Heiner Carow's *Ikarus*, the great dream of young Mathias is to go up in an aeroplane. His journalist father promises

Peter Welz in Ikarus

him, for his birthday treat, a flight over Berlin – then goes out on an assignment and forgets all about it. In mounting desperation, Mathias scours the city for him. Peter Welz gives a fine, passionate performance.

A different kind of desperation awaited him in *Ich zwing dich zu leben*. As a boy of the Hitler Youth, in the closing days of World War Two, he is determined to die for his country – with a father equally determined that he shan't.

Welz was seen again in *Pugowitza* (80) and – very marginally – in *Der Name der Rose* (The Name of the Rose, DE/IT/FR 86). Meanwhile, though, he was training as a director at the DDR's film academy, and having graduated began working as an assistant director.

75 Ikarus (Icarus)
77 Ich zwing dich zu leben
     (I'll force you to live)

Dainius Bratkauskas

USSR – Lithuania

b: circa 1963

The most gifted and poetic director of Lithuanian children's films is Arunas Žebriunas (born 1930), much of whose best work came in the 1970s. In 1959 he had directed 'The Last Shot', an episode in a four-story film about his country's

children, mainly during World War Two. (See Nerius Narkis °.) His section was singled out for a special State Prize.

After 1½ full-length films (he shared direction of the first) Žebriunas returned to subjects featuring children in *The Last Day of the Holidays* (64), *The Little Prince* (66, based on Saint-Exupéry's fable), and *Death and the Cherry-Tree* (68, from an H.E.Bates story). *The Beauty* (69) featured a little girl called Inga Mickyte, who won a special prize at the next Minsk Film Festival.

Then came *Night-Bird* (73), *The Adventures of Detective Kalle* (76, from an Astrid Lindgren story filmed in Sweden some 30 years earlier as *Mästerdetektiven Blomkvist*) and *Nut-Bread* (78). Among his work for adults, Žebriunas in 1974 directed Lithuania's first screen musical, *The Devil's Bride*.

After melancholy early themes, he decisively rejected the Soviet tradition of 'apple-cheeked pioneers and sweet simple babbling', and treated children as equals. His work became increasingly frisky and fantastical, even grotesque. *Night-Bird* is a captivating piece about a junior Walter Mitty who dreams of performing some heroic deed and being congratulated by a venerable general – which of course is exactly what happens.

Dainius Bratkauskas, a sophisticated little lad, holds the screen with his own brand of eccentric charm.

73 Polunochnik (Night-Bird)

The most engaging of Lithuania's other boy actors in the cinema have been EDVINAS MENCIKOVAS in *Andrius* (80) and GIEDRIUS CAIKAUSKAS in *I Am* (89).

Julio Cesar Cruz

BRAZIL

b: circa 1963

The first and third of Julio Cesar's roles were leading ones.

70 O meu pé de laranja lima
     (My beloved orange tree)
71 Rua Descalça (Barefoot Street)
72 Som, amor e curtição (Music, love and fun)

Dainius Bratkauskas in Night-Bird

Zoltán Csoma

HUNGARY

b: circa 1963

Glamorous Zoltán played the boy genius in *Álmodó ifyúság*, a dramatisation of the childhood of the Hungarian writer and movie-maker Béla Balázs (1884-1949) – who, among other things, directed the 1921 film *A megfagyott gyermek* (starring Ferko Szécsi ◇) and 25 years later scripted *Valahol Europaban* (which starred Lászlo Horváth ◇).

   The hero's dangerous friend Ödön was played by Csaba Damenija.

74 Álmodó ifyúság
    (Dreaming youth)

Geory Desmouceaux and Philippe Goldmann

FRANCE

b: circa 1963

L'argent de poche was Truffaut's most soft-centred film. In fact it's so whimsically anecdotal as hardly to have a centre at all: there are tiny episodes about a tot who survives a several-storey fall from a window-ledge, a little girl at another window appealing for food from kindly neighbours, some boys involved in un-qualified haircuts, and so on.

   The only developed characters are a romantically inclined boy (Desmouceaux, sandy and gentle) who finally finds true love with a girl of suitable age, and an incipient delinquent (the smouldering Goldmann) who is regularly knocked around at his wretched home. This last is the film's only serious strand, but it's marred by a too directly moralising summing-up.

76 L'argent de poche
    (Pocket-money/Small Change)

Victim: Hiroyuki Kawase with his crazed father (Noboru Mitsutani) in Dodes'ka-den

Hiroyuki Kawase

JAPAN

b: circa 1963

In Kurosawa's *Dodes'ka-den*, a luridly stylised 'Lower Depths' set in a shanty-town outside modern Tokyo, Hiroyuki plays the loyal child of an idiotic beggar who lives in the shell of an old car. After wearing himself out begging for food for the two of them, the little boy eventually falls ill and dies, his father scarcely noticing what is happening.

   Hiroyuki, funny and indomitable as the tiny victim, reappeared the following year in the latest exploit of the deathray-dealing monster Godzilla, now firmly on the side of humanity. This time, some-what more privileged as the brilliant son of a brilliant scientist, he invokes God-zilla's aid to combat an evil, living mass of industrial waste from the sea (really a Sludge Monster rather than the one sug-gested in the English release title, *Godzilla vs. the Smog Monster*). Godzilla wins.

70 Dodes'ka-den (Trundle-ting)
71 Gojira tai Hedora
    (Godzilla versus Hedora)

Riton Liebman

FRANCE

b: circa 1963

In Bertrand Blier's hilariously bad-taste tale of the redemption of a female wimp, Riton (billed without surname in his debut) plays an apparently floppy and victimised boy who ends up like a more successful Cherubino – Mozart is a constant presence – not merely bedding but impregnating the heroine. He is priceless.

   Later (as Riton Liebman) he was in *Vénus* (83), *L'addition* (84) and *On ne meurt que deux fois* (85).

77 Préparez vos mouchoirs
    (Get out your handkerchiefs)

346

Roberto Maccanti and Paolo Pavesi

ITALY

b: circa 1963

Bertolucci's epic melodrama of Italian society from 1900 to 1945 pivots on the stormy friendship of two boys born on the same day on the same rural estate: Alfredo, grandson of the old laird, and Olmo, son of the workers' overseer. The arrival of Fascism drives them further apart. While the socialist Olmo fights bravely against it, Alfredo is feebly acquiescent.

There are magnificent passages in this vast two-part film, but also patches of crude sensationalism and naïve flag-waving. The childhood scenes are among the finest. Plump Alfredo, smug little inheritor of riches, is admirably played by Paolo Pavesi, but the honours are easily taken by Roberto Maccanti's Olmo — lean, leggy catcher of frogs and breeder of silkworms. His straw hat fringed with impaled, kicking frogs is a grave trial for animal-lovers, though undeniably picturesque. Maccanti conveys the angry pride of an oppressed class, and does it with humour and elegance.

There are two fearsome uncredited boy-roles in Part Two of *1900*. A vengeful young proletarian called Leonidà arrests the middle-aged Olmo at gunpoint as the Fascists forces flee at the end of World War Two; and in a horrifying scene from the 1930s, the twelve-year-old Patrizio Avanzini, son of a rich bourgeois, is raped and murdered by the drunken Attila (Donald Sutherland), a half-crazy Fascist lout who has become the estate manager. Patrizio appears to be played by more than one boy.

76 Novecento (1900 – IT/FR/DE)

Junior Mehmood

INDIA

b: circa 1963

Junior Mehmood, an engagingly cocky and unpretty performer, was hugely popular in India for many years. He had the lead in *Do bachchey dus haath* — released abroad as *Young James Bond*.

68 Anjana (Stranger)
   Brahmachari (The celibate)
   Farishta (The angel)
   Vaasna (Passion)
69 Balak (The lad)
   Chanda aur Bijli ('Moon' and 'Lightning')
   Do raaste (Two ways)
   Nateeja (The result)
   Pyar hi pyar (Love, only love)
   Simla Road
   Vishwas (The faith)
70 Aan milo sajna (Join me, darling)
   Bachpan (Childhood)
   Ghar ghar ki kahani
     (Every household's story)
   Harishchandra Taramati
   Kati patang (Kite without string)
   Yaadgaar (Remembrance)
71 Behroopiya (The clown)
   Caravan
   Choti bahu (Younger daughter-in-law)
   Hare Rame hare Krishna
   Haathi mere saathi
     (Elephants, my companions)
   Hungama (Chaos)
   Johar Mehmood in Hong Kong
   Khoj (The search)
   Ladki pasand hai (The girl's O.K.)
72 Bansi birju (Love-birds)
   Bharat ke shaheed (Martyrs of India)
   Bijli (Lightning)
   Bombay to Goa
   Do bachchey dus haath
     (Two kids, ten hands)
   Munimji (The manager)
   Rivaaj (The custom)
   Sazaa (Crime and punishment)
   Shararat (A naughty game)
   Tangewala (Horse-cart driver)
   Tanhai (Solitude)
73 Dhamkee (The threat)
   Ek nari do roop (Two-faced woman)
   Jheel ke us paar (Across the lake)
   Kora aanchal (Untouched virgin)
   Maa da ladla (Mother's darling)
74 Aap ki kasam (By oath)
   Amir garib (Rich and poor)
   Nirdosh (The innocent)
   Thokar (Kick)
   Ujala hi ujala (Light, more light)
75 Geet gata chal (Walk singing)
76 Aap beati (My own story)
   Deewangee (Madness)
   Koi jeeta koi hara (One wins, one loses)
79 Bagula bhagat (Hypocrite)

Different ain't worse: Chris Petersen (right) with Guillermo San Juan in Joey and Redhawk

Chris Petersen

USA

b: circa 1963

Chris, elder brother of the dynamic Patrick Petersen◊, had a lazily handsome face with a useful sidelong look of scorn. He tended to be given roles in which arrogance gave way to underlying decency. In *When Every Day Was the Fourth of July*, a weak echo of *To Kill a Mocking-Bird*, his father defended a gentle, brain-damaged war-veteran on a charge of anarchist murder; and in *Joey and Redhawk* his best friend (Guillermo San Juan) was a part-Indian boy, teaching him that 'different ain't worse'.

Chris had a lead in the TV series 'The Baxters', but in the worthy TV movie *The House at 12 Rose Street*, on the other hand, he embodied an out-and-out racist teenager, ripe for the KKK.

76 The Little Dragons
78 Joey and Redhawk
   The Swarm
   When Every Day Was the Fourth of July
80 Brave New World
   The House at 12 Rose Street

Néstor Yujira

BOLIVIA

b: circa 1963

Néstor, an Aymara Indian, played the lead
in the first episode of Antonio Eguino's
three-part film, as a country boy who
goes to work first in the local market
town and then in the capital, La Paz.
He had a memorable stolid dignity.

77 Chuquiago

Chris Makepeace

CANADA/USA

b: 22 Apr 64 (Toronto)

Curly Chris did his best as a holiday-camp
misfit in the gruesomely hearty and un-
funny *Meatballs*. As another gentle victim,
he had a more rewarding role in *My
Bodyguard*, where he recruits a brooding
giant of a boy (Adam Baldwin) as
protector against the school bully (Matt
Dillon). For all its traditional elements,
Tony Bill's directorial debut is very
likeable.

   Chris Makepeace's later films included
The Last Chase (81), *Going Great* (82),
Mazes and Monsters (82), *The Mysterious
Stranger* (82), *The Terry Fox Story* (83), *The
Oasis* (84), *The Falcon and the Snowman*
(85), *The Undergrads* (85) and *Vamp* (86).

79 Meatballs (CA)
80 My Bodyguard (US)

Eric Clerckx

BELGIUM

b: 30 May 1964 (Lummen)

For *De Witte*, tough, dark-haired Eric
was dyed blond to play 'Whitey' in
Robbe de Herdt's remake of Ernst Claes'
classic novel, previously filmed in 1934
with Jefke Bruyninckx ◊ in the role. He
was a rawer, more realistic rogue and
peasant than the graceful Bruyninckx had
been.

Randy Rossino: Domenico Tittone in Dimenticare Venezia

His 1981 film showed him enthusiasti-
cally leaping into sex with mature girls.

79 De Witte van Sichem
   (Whitey from Sichem)
81 Twee vorstinnen en en vorst
   (Two princesses and a prince)

Whitey of 1979: Eric Clerckx in De Witte van
Sichem

Domenico Tittone

ITALY

b: 4 Aug 64 (Rome)

This book is devoted to boys who have
played leading roles in the cinema, and
many hundreds who have done so have
had to be left out for reasons of space. But
there are occasions where quality must
transcend lack of quantity, and where the
effect of a minor role is so vivid that it
would be wrong not to celebrate it.

   Franco Brusati's *Dimenticare Venezia* is
an extremely beautiful film about the need
to free yourself from memories and obses-
sions, and allow yourself to grow old. Its
central character, the homosexual Nicky,
strives to remain a youthful buddy to a
lover half his age. He is in thrall to
memories of his childhood, enlivened by
torrid friendship for a fellow-chorister
called Rossino.

At an open-air restaurant in a forest, he catches sight of a young boy who reminds him uncannily of that playmate of so long ago. It turns out to be the son of Rossino, now a bald middle-aged paterfamilias (to whom the prim middle-aged Nicky is unpardonably churlish).

With two different shades of hair and a complete transformation of personality, Domenico Tittone plays both the young Rossino (in flashbacks) and Rossino's son: the latter a shy creature, puzzled and alarmed by the wild-eyed stranger who appears to be stalking him, the former a flame-haired, scarlet-cassocked epitome of randy pubescence. (His reaction to the sudden sight of a group of young women bathing in the nude is magnificently over-the-top.)

This is probably the most amazing dual-role performance any boy has given in the cinema, yet the film's credits don't even say who gives it – which may have been why the remarkable Tittone wasn't at once given major roles to play.

The young Nicky is portrayed by ALESSANDRO DORIA, with a face of utter vulnerability.

79 Dimenticare Venezia (Forget Venice)
    La chambre aux dames
       (The ladies' room – FR)

Drier, circa 1976

Alessandro Doria as the young Nicky

Moosie Drier

USA

b: 6 Aug 64 (Chicago)

There was no first name on Master Drier's original birth certificate: his parents wanted time to think about it. Pressed by the registrar a month or two later, all they could come up with was 'Moosie', a name he had acquired in the family from his wearing of Moose pyjamas. The following year – still blushing – they left Chicago for Los Angeles.

Moosie Drier is little known in Britain because none of his main roles have been in the cinema, but familiar in the USA from his many leads in TV films. With his wide mouth and large eyes struggling between happiness and worry, he was one of the small screen's most entirely lovable children.

He made his debut at five, in a TV commercial with his sister Peggy, memorably delivering one line. At seven he was perfect in the James Thurber-inspired *War between Men and Women*, as the youngest of the brood to whom Jack

Lemmon becomes unwelcome stepfather. Little David is 'scared of everything', deeply concerned about pollution (even about polluted waffles), and in the habit of sleeping on the floor outside people's bedroom doors like a human draught-excluder, desperate for moral support.

He owed his early fame, though, largely to his appearances in 'Rowan and Martin's Laugh-In', where he gave 'Kid News' from the branches of a tree. His enchanting mixture of insecurity and insouciance won him vast affection. He also turned up in 'Doc' and 'Executive Suite'.

Around the same time Moosie played the lead in a TV film based on Albert Lamorisse's *Voyage en ballon*, after which he became a regular on 'The Bob Newhart Show', as the neighbour's son Howie. Some years later, in *Rainbow*, a Judy Garland biopic, he took the role of Mickey Rooney ◇. (Johnny Doran ◇ played Jackie Cooper ◇.)

The Moose's later films included *Homeward Bound* (80), *The House at 12 Rose Street* (80) and *Charlie and the Great Balloon Race* (81), as well as guesting in many TV series.

Griffin O'Neal

USA

b: 28 Oct 64 (Los Angeles)

After a fleeting appearance in the frightful *Nickelodeon*, the younger brother of *Paper*

Cool: Griffin O'Neal

Moon's Tatum O'Neal got his own big chance – and took it with both hands. The opportunity came in Caleb Deschanel's flawed but fascinating film *The Escape Artist* (not released till 1982).

Griffin's earlier life with his actor parents Ryan O'Neal and Joanne Moore – variously plagued by drink and drugs – had been given exhaustive coverage in the press: repeatedly being thrown out of school for fighting, for instance, and getting his front teeth knocked out by Ryan in a domestic brawl, after he had followed Tatum's lead by moving in with his father and Farrah Fawcett.

Having been a serious contender (finally ruled out on grounds of age) for Ricky Schroder's ◇ part in the 1979 Zeffirelli remake of *The Champ*, Griffin revealed himself in *The Escape Artist* as an amazingly self-contained player. He was the embodiment of cool, with a face every bit as watchable as his sister's – blunt and freckled, illuminated by large, light, alert eyes. 'A great-looking gamin daredevil,' Pauline Kael called him in the New Yorker.

Griffin – an under-sized 15 at the time of shooting – plays Danny Masters, a boy illusionist and escapologist following the craft of his father, who had died while

Prestidigitators: O'Neal with Jackie Coogan in The Escape Artist

Griffin's real life, however, had taken the kind of ugly turn that many had predicted. In August 1983 his father, Ryan O'Neal, committed him to a strict drug clinic to fight his addiction to cocaine; and when he was released nearly three years later, he began drinking heavily. This may have led to the tragedy of 26 May 1987.

He and Gian Carlo, son of Francis Ford Coppola – who at the time was directing Griffin in *Gardens of Stone* – had hired a speedboat on a river near Annapolis. The boat ran under a tow-line stretched between two other craft, and in the whiplash of the snapping rope Gian Carlo was killed. Griffin, though at first he denied it, had been at the wheel, and was indicted for Gio Coppola's manslaughter. He was eventually cleared of this, and found guilty simply of 'recklessly operating a boat'.

76 Nickelodeon (US/GB)
79 The Escape Artist (*released 1982*)

Greg Rowe

AUSTRALIA

b: 1964

The international success of Henri Safran's sentimental boy-and-pelican drama *Storm Boy* made Greg Rowe's gentle face familiar all round the world – more familiar than those of Moosie Drier ◇, Griffin

attempting to break out of jail. Danny falls in with Stu, the near-psychopathic son of a crooked mayor, and challenges the local jail that if they lock him manacled in a cell he can escape within the hour. Succeeding in this, he breaks into the mayor's office and removes some incriminating ledgers which he hands over to the FBI, thus incurring Stu's homicidal displeasure.

The film's jumpy story-line, tinkered with by a multitude of hands, bewildered critics and public alike when it was finally released in 1982. But it has enormous virtues, with sunny wit in some scenes, and a dark poetry in others.

The dangerous Tom-and-Jerry relationship with Stu (Raul Julia, memorable) culminates with Danny holed up in a street mail box, while Stu drums on it with a carving knife. Afterwards, Griffin O'Neal walks off into the night with magic flowers springing from his heels, having given one of the screen's greatest boy performances.

In 1984, still looking only about 14, he had another taxing lead as the wrestler hero of *Hadley's Rebellion*. Again he acted admirably, as well as showing superb wrestling skill. Two years later he was a short-lived hot-rod driver in *The Wraith*.

Buffeted: Greg Rowe in Storm Boy

351

O'Neal ◇ and Domenico Tittone ◇ put together. (1964 was a rich birth-year for boy film actors.)

Greg didn't have the talent of any of those three young men, but it probably didn't worry him or his audiences. He had a small role in the opening scenes of Peter Weir's ambitious film, *The Last Wave*, and then another lead – of the proving-his-manhood type – opposite Hardy Kruger (once himself a boy film actor) in the tuna-fishing adventure *Blue Fin*.

In his later teens Greg appeared in an episode of the TV serial *Young Ramsey* (80), in *Dead Man's Float* (80) and in *Freedom* (82).

76 Storm Boy
77 The Last Wave
79 Blue Fin

Kazuhito Ando

JAPAN

b: circa 1964

This enchanting child, son of a Japanese civil servant, had been acting in movies (and making TV commercials for Hitachi) for four or five years before he was cast opposite the ageing David Niven in *Paper Tiger*.

In this popular film Niven, in a comic reprise of his *Separate Tables* characterisation, plays the distinguished-looking but hollow Walter Bradbury, an inveterate coward given to boasting of his war exploits. Bradbury, engaged as English tutor to a diplomat's 11-year-old son, is hero-worshipped by little Koichi when by pure accident he foils an attempted assassination. Tutor and charge are then kidnapped, and the dithering Bradbury finally rouses himself to a genuine act of courage.

It's a corny and unconvincing tale, largely redeemed by the charm of the two principals. Little Kazuhito – simply billed as 'Ando' – won many hearts with his demure courtesy and his wholly misplaced reverence for 'Mister Bladbelly'.

74 Paper Tiger (GB)

Freedom fighter: Cherstvoff in Podranki

Alyosha Cherstvoff

USSR

b: circa 1964

The central narrative of Nikolai Gubenko's fine *Podranki* – generally known as *Orphans* in Britain and the USA – is a flashback into the narrator's past life, as a war orphan at a children's home after World War Two: a tough establishment with an honestly portrayed mixture of good and bad teachers.

As the young hero fighting injustice, Alyosha Cherstvoff is superb, the suspicion born of experience masking a sensitive and passionate nature. The smaller but no less impressive role of the vengeful Valya Gandin, who blows himself up while attempting to lob a home-made grenade into an enclosure of German prisoners – a performance of painful intensity – is in fact taken by a girl, the remarkable Natalya Gundareva.

77 Podranki (Wounded birds, AKA Orphans)
78 A u nas bila tishina (It was quiet over here)

Norman Knox

SOUTH AFRICA

b: circa 1964

e'Lollipop was a slightly worrying film directed by Ashley Lazarus and set in the 'black homeland' of Lesotho (formerly Basutoland), west of Durban. It was released in the US under the deeply

Togetherheid: Norman Knox (left) and Muntu Ben Louis N'debele in e'Lollipop

boring title of *Forever Young, Forever Free*.

A white orphan, Jannie (Norman Knox), is brought up in a black mission run by an Italian priest, Father Alberto (José Ferrer). Jannie forms a devoted friendship with a boy of his own age called Tsepo (Muntu Ben Louis N'Debele), who at the climax of the film sacrifices his life to save his white friend's.

Basically this is a sentimental essay in together-heid, designed to make middle-of-the-road South African whites feel warmer about their black brothers. No harm in that. But some patronising attitudes unwittingly emerge, and Tsepo's noble act is uncomfortably reminiscent of the faithful black servant of colonial novels having the privilege of dying for his white master. Perhaps Jannie might have been allowed to die for Tsepo, just this once?

The delightful Muntu seems to have had no further screen roles, but Norman had two minor ones the following year.

75 e'Lollipop
76 Terrorist
   Tigers Don't Cry

Ivan Kojundžić

YUGOSLAVIA

b: circa 1964

The terrible sufferings of Eastern Europe during Hitler's War had more than an economic bearing on its countries' subsequent artistic development. In the cinema at least they were doomed to fight their patriotic battles over and over again, raking through the embers of hatred for 20, even 30 years after the war's end.

Each country had its schoolboy hero, fighting with the army or the partisans, and Boško Buha was Yugoslavia's. Branko Bauer's film tells his moving story, embroidering it with interludes of fun or first love. Ivan Kojundzic, a more dogged version of Slavko Štimac ◇, plays him nobly.

78 Boško Buha

Magic jacket: Gabor Szücs in Kincskeresö kisködmön

Jeremy Levy

USA

b: circa 1964

Jeremy, after making a striking impression as Aaron, the heroic Gavroche of the Jewish ghetto in *Holocaust*, was mainly concerned in *Rich Kids* with the problems of well-heeled adolescence and the love lives of his elders. He showed intelligence and droll humour.

78 Holocaust
79 Rich Kids

Brett Maxworthy

AUSTRALIA

b: circa 1964

To quote Colin Pahlow's review in the Monthly Bulletin of the British Film Institute, 'an obnoxious male child, a marshmallow-hearted pickpocket and a grunting wombat trek across familiar Australian Tourist Board terrain in search of the boy's even more unpleasant father.' Other critics liked the film better, but not much. (It was released in Britain as *Lost in the Wild*.)

Brett Maxworthy, far from obnoxious in himself, had already sung and acted on TV, and got landed with some pretty embarrassing ditties in *Barney*. A former child actor, Colin 'Smiley' Petersen ◇, surfaced briefly in a marginal role.

76 Barney

Gabor Szücs

HUNGARY

b: circa 1964

In *Kincskeresö kisködmön* a poor cobbler makes his little son Ferkó a magic jacket. Ferkó is too busy in daydreams to concentrate at school, but the jacket does his work for him, and finally helps him to save

353

as well as holding 8th-dan in Japanese Karate and 6th in Judo. He seemed a natural to cash in on the bionic craze.

Yap's two films were directed by Bobby A. Suarez and Leody M. Diaz respectively. *Dynamite Johnson* was originally slated as *The Twelve Million Dollar Boy*, which may have been an overstatement.

76 Bionic Boy
78 Dynamite Johnson (GB)

Enea Zhegu (left) with Herion Mustafaraj (right) in Tomka dhe shokët e tij

Enea Zhegu

ALBANIA

b: circa 1964

Enea was not unlike an Albanian Barret Oliver ◇. Good to see the classical name 'Aeneas' adorning a boy star.

76 Lulëkuqet mbi mure (Poppies on the walls)
77 Njeriu me top
Tomka dhe shokët e tij
(Tommy and his friends)

the life and win the friendship of a crippled boy he has previously wronged.

Gabor Szücs is delectable as Ferkó, and István Gruber very touching as the clever little cripple.

Three years later Gabor had another leading role in *Tüzgömbök*.

72 Kincskeresö kisködmön (The magic jacket)
74 A locsolókocsi (The watering-truck)
75 Tüzgömbök (Balls of fire)

Johnson Yap

SINGAPORE

b: circa 1964 (Singapore)

Johnson Yap, 'Asia's youngest Master of Martial Arts', began to learn the Korean art of Taekwondo at the age of five. In 1978 he was said to be the youngest 9th-dan Black Belt holder in Chinese Kung Fu,

Richard Constantini

FRANCE

b: 24 Jan 65

As well as being a capable performer in routine family vehicles, Constantini more than once showed himself capable of power and feeling.

In *Les passagers*, on a three-day drive

from Rome to Paris with his new step-father (Jean-Louis Trintignant) he was pursued by a vehicle of a different kind, in the murderous tradition of Spielberg's *Duel*: though in this case the hostile van-driver, a deranged ex-lover of his mother, was visible enough.

In *Un sac de billes* he was the capable elder in a subtle story of two Jewish children who leave Paris during World War Two and succeed in crossing into the Zone Libre, there to cope with patriots and quislings while concealing their race. His younger brother was played by the engaging PAUL-ERIC SCHULMANN, who was also in Raul Ruiz's film *La vocation suspendue* (77).

76 Les passagers (The passengers — FR/IT)
77 Un sac de billes (A bag of marbles)
78 Vas-y, maman (Go on, Mum)
    Attention! Les enfants regardent
    (Look out, the children are watching)

Todd Lookinland

USA

b: 1 Mar 65 (Torrance, California)

Todd, younger brother of tough Mike Lookinland (of 'The Brady Bunch' and *The Towering Inferno*), had made many TV appearances, for instance in the 'Petrocelli' series, before being cast as Tyltyl in the ill-fated remake of Maeterlinck's *Blue Bird*, which was filmed in the Soviet Union with Elizabeth Taylor doubling (rather well) as Mother and Witch.

Most of the other players betray an embarrassing lack of conviction, and the magnificently expressive faces of Todd (and of Patsy Kensit as his kid sister Mityl) are wasted on this charmless magic.

In his later teens Todd appeared in *Beulah Land* (80), *Every Stray Dog and Kid* (81) and *The Karate Kid* (84), as well as the TV serial *The New Land*.

73 Guess Who's Been Sleeping In My Bed
76 The Blue Bird (US/SU)
77 How the West Was Won
    A Sensitive, Passionate Man
78 Big Wednesday
79 The Suicide's Wife

Tommy Ohrner

WEST GERMANY

b: 3 Jne 65 (Munich)

The handsome, long-haired and extro-vert Tommy — whose elder sister Carolin also acted, in more modest roles — was Germany's favourite TV boy of the skateboard era, rather like Leif Garrett ◇ in the USA. Most of his early films were noisy family comedies, but when he was ten he played (on TV) the dramatic role of the son in *Brennendes Geheimnis*, as Peter Eysoldt ◇ had in 1923 and Hans Joachim Schaufuss ◇ in 1933, and the brilliant David Eberts would in 1988.

Tommy had the lead in the popular TV serial *TimmThaler* — known in English-speaking countries as *Tim Tyler* — about a boy with a wonderful laugh, so wonderful that it got him kidnapped by a villain who couldn't laugh at all.

When his career resumed in his late teens, he was in *Im Dschungel ist der Teufel los* (82), *Ein dicker Hund* (82), *Manni, der*

Tyltyl visits Russia: Todd Lookinland in the 1976 Blue Bird

Tommy Ohrner in Das Haus der Krokodile

Libero (82, TVS), *Plem, plem, die Schule brennt* (83) and *Die ungläublichen Abenteuer des Guru Jakob* (83).

68 Helga und Michael
70 Hurra, unsere Eltern sind nicht da
  (Hurrah, our parents are out)
  Nachbarn sind zum Ärgern da
  (Neighbours are a nuisance)
71 Hilfe, die Verwandten kommen
  (Help, here come the relatives)
75 Brennendes Geheimnis
  (Burning secret)
  Das Haus der Krokodile
  (The house of crocodiles – TVS)
  Timm Thaler (Tim Tyler – TVS)

Michael Sharrett

USA

b: 18 Jly 65 (Ventura, California)

As a child, Michael Sharrett had a round, sweet face which appealed to the Disney studio. He didn't have a lot of personality, but what there was was pleasant, and he did his best with some formula stories.

Adult life brought sterner things, including being nearly killed by a robotised girl in Wes Craven's *Deadly Friend* (86).

78 Hanging by a Thread
  Hot Lead and Cold Feet
  The Magic of Lassie
79 Joe's World (TVS)
  Night Rider
  A Shining Season
80 Strange Companions

Filip Renč

CZECHOSLOVAKIA

b: 17 Aug 65 (Prague)

Filip, an attractive brunet with a wide humorous mouth, played the hero as a boy in *Julek* – a biopic about the composer Julius Fučik.

He went on to become a very popular juvenile lead on Czech TV and cinema screens, in films like *Bili jeleni, Život je tvrdolin, Motiv pro vraždu* and *Leve křidlo*.

73 Družina Černého Pera
  (The Black Feather playschool)
76 Jakub
79 Nechci nic slyšet (Leave me alone)
80 Julek

Private person: Filip Renč in Nechci nic slyšet

Bernd Riedel

WEST GERMANY

b: August 1965 (Berlin)

Die Kinder aus Nr.67, a proud re-creation of working-class Berlin in the Thirties, carries the defiant subtitle 'Heil Hitler, ich hätt gern 'n Paar Pferdeappel' (Heil Hitler, and two bits of horse-shit, please). The inhabitants of the building at No.67 are almost solidly socialist: the few Nazi supporters are bigots or proto-yuppies.

The wiry little Erwin (Riedel) and his plump friend Paul (René Schaaf) harass the local Hitlerjugend flock tirelessly, surviving all pressures to conform with 'patriotic' society outside until finally, to Erwin's disgust, Paul turns coat and joins the HJ.

The film's directors, Usch Barthelmess-Weller and Werner Meyer, spent four months searching for their central group of fifteen kids, only two of them middle-class. These then spent a week living together in a youth hostel, wearing their film clothes and getting to know each other. Besides learning some of the technical side of filming, they watched movies of the Thirties and talked to people who had been children at the time.

The preparation paid off. The kids are entirely convincing, and Bernd Riedel makes a brave, dry socialist hero.

80 Die Kinder aus Nr.67 (The kids at No.67)

Ilker Inanoğlu

TURKEY

b: 20 Aug 65

Ilker's pa (who directed his first three films) was the producer-director Türker Inanoglu, his ma the actress Filiz Akin.

Ilker spoke English, French and German, and went to school in Switzerland. All his parts were leading ones.

69 Yumurcak (The kid)
70 Yumurcak köprüalti çocuğu
  (The kid from under the bridge)
  Tatli rüyalar (Sweet dreams)

Integrity: Bernd Riedel (left) with his turncoat friend (René Schaaf) in Die Kinder aus Nr.67

71 Küçük kovboy (The little cowboy)
72 Küçük Sahit (The little witness)
73 Veda (Farewell)
74 Belâli tatil (Troubled holiday)

Tomasz Hudziec

POLAND

b: 3 Dec 65 (Wrocław)

All these four roles were leading ones, except in *Z biegiem lat*, a turn-of-the- century family saga directed for TV by Andrzej Wajda.

In *Zmory*, based on a novel by Emil Zegadłowicz, Tomasz played a sensitive boy living in a mysterious old house in the provinces with his ex-schoolmaster father. When obliged to emerge from his private imaginative world and go off to secondary school, he is distressed by the stupidity and dishonesty he finds, but powerless to fight it. (In the hero's later teens he is played by Piotr Łysak, a sort of Polish John Moulder-Brown ◇.)

Zmory was set in pre-Communist Poland. But three years later its director, Wojciech Marczewski, cast Tomasz

Hudziec again as the out-of-step hero in an intriguingly different context nearer to the present day: that of the mindless conformism and bigotry of some young communists. Hudziec has a powerful screen personality, adept in fastidious distress.

His later films have included *Zygfryd* (86) and *Zero życia* (87).

Haunted: Tomasz Hudziec in Zmory

78 Zmory (Nightmares)
   Nauka latania (Learning to fly)
79 Ucieczka (Escape)
80 Z biegiem lat, z biegiem dni
   (As days and years pass)
81 Dreszcze (The creeps)

Brad Savage

USA

b: 9 Dec 65 (Livonia, nr Detroit)

Brad Savage, a beefy child, was a bit like a dark, curly-haired Kurt Russell ◇, with sharp blue eyes in a pudgy face. He started his stage career playing Auntie Mame's nephew in a touring production.

On screen Brad usually played uncomplicated, cheerful kid brothers, but when for a change he played an elder brother (to Ronnie Scribner ◇) in *Salem's Lot* he found himself being an involuntary blood donor to his junior, who by an unfortunate accident had become a boy vampire. Once bitten, Brad of course became one too.

After *Mayday! Mayday!* (81), he was one of the high school guerrillas in John Milius' egregious *Red Dawn* (84).

72 Second Chance
73 The Bait
74 Another April
   The Apple Dumpling Gang
75 All Together Now
   Echoes of a Summer (US/CA)
   Grandpa Max
   My Father's House
   The Other Side of the Mountain
76 No Deposit, No Return
   Islands in the Stream
   Two-Minute Warning
78 Return from Witch Mountain
79 Salem's Lot
   Second Time Around

Krisztián Kovács

HUNGARY

b: 1965 (Budapest)

Krisztián, a jolly teddy-bear of a boy, became popular on both large and small

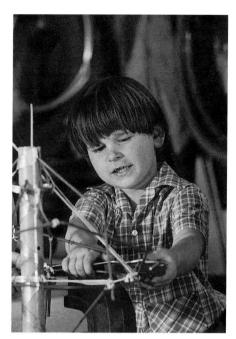

Nautical dreams: Krisztián Kovács in
Hahó, a tenger!

screens in Hungary after his 1971 appearance as the eponymous Öcsi, who performs miracles in the bathroom, and sails off to find Time. (The next year's sequel, in which he sulks after not being consulted about a new baby, also ends with a vision of the sea.)

Kemenykalap es krumpliorr was a condensation of a popular TV series of 1974, which won an award as 'Best Children's TV series' in the 1975 Hollywood Festival of World Television.

69 A varászló (The magician)
70 Szerelmi álmok (Dreams of love)
71 Hahó, Öcsi! (Hi, Öcsi!)
   Reménykedok (A charming family)
72 Hahó, a tenger! (Sea ahoy!)
78 Kemenykalap es krumpliorr
   (Bowler hat and potato nose)

Chris Barnes

USA

b: circa 1965

Chris was the most daffily blond of the Bad News Bears, and one of the least mannerly. Much of his subsequent work was done for TV. The two 1978 roles

were in pilots for CBS sitcom series with Austin Pendleton, and he was in yet another pilot – *Two Plus Two* – in 1982, also for CBS (which could as well stand for Chris Barnes Station).

Big Henry won a mass of awards, including an Emmy as Outstanding Children's Special. *Through the Magic Pyramid* was directed – well before 1981, in fact – by former child actor Ron Howard ◇.

76 The Bad News Bears
77 The Bad News Bears in Breaking Training
78 You're Gonna Love It Here
   Big City Boys
79 Big Henry and the Polka Dot Kid
81 Through the Magic Pyramid

Peter Bjerg and Anders Agensø

DENMARK

b: circa 1965

The hero of *You Are Not Alone*, Kim (Peter Bjerg), discovers first love with a slightly older schoolmate, Bo (Agensø). Their schoolmates behave with predictable

savagery, but love surprisingly wins through. It's frank, funny, tender – terribly Danish – and the boys are excellent.

78 Du er ikke alene (You are not alone)

Dexter Fletcher

BRITAIN

b: 31 Jan 66

Dexter – one of the few remarkable child actors who are clearly going to be remarkable adult actors – followed two talented elder brothers into the profession: Steve (born 27 Mar 62) and Graham (born 3 Nov 63, now Graham Fletcher-Cook).

His 1972 film debut was in a short Road Safety film, and his role in the 'Steptoe' spinoff was marginal to say the least. He had a genuine lead in the first *Chimpmates* series for the Children's Film Foundation, but sprang to worldwide notice in the small part of 'Babyface' in *Bugsy Malone*, giving a sublime bit of method acting before yelling 'Geronimo!' and hurtling off to rout the forces of evil with a baseball bat.

Chris Barnes and blind Wolfie in Big Henry and the Polka Dot Kid

him added stage experience. None of this was to be wasted.

At 17, still looking a mere kid, he played a sort of modern-dress Puck in a whimsical documentary on Covent Garden, and had a good secondary role in the crew of *The Bounty* (84). Then he played Al Pacino's long-suffering son Ned in his older phase in the churlishly undervalued *Revolution* (85) – the earlier Ned being taken by the impressively dour SID OWEN (born 12 Jan 72).

Dexter next played, with sly humour, the decorative hero-as-youth in Derek Jarman's *Caravaggio* (86). Then, after small parts in two bizarre films, Ken Russell's *Gothic* (86) and Bob Spiers' *Didn't You Kill*

ABOVE: Dexter Fletcher and Alice in the Children's Film Foundation's first series of Chimpmates.

RIGHT: Artist as a young man: Fletcher in Caravaggio

After *Bugsy*, Dexter was retained on option for two films that failed to materialise, one for Alan Parker and one for David Puttnam. The latter was to have been a Charlie Chaplin biopic, with Dexter playing the great man as a child; but Chaplin himself vetoed the project.

During 1977 Dexter played Puck in the Royal Shakespeare Company production of 'A Midsummer Night's Dream', and a year later repeated the role (non-singing) in Benjamin Britten's operatic version at Glyndebourne. Also in 1978 he played – quite magnificently – the classic role of Gavroche in an Anglo-French TV film of *Les misérables*, confirming not only his intelligence and passion but an enviable command of physical acting: his death-fall when struck by a bullet in mid-stride, the instantly lifeless body flopping into the gutter like a rag doll, was amazing.

With searching, sometimes baleful eyes and an upper lip so long and curling that it made Gordon Gebert ◇ look positively under-developed, Dexter's face was always watchable, but his talent came across almost as strongly on radio. A further spell with the RSC in 1982 gave

My Brother? (87), he had a romantic lead in Bob Hoskins' *Raggedy Rawney* (88) as a young gypsy deserter from a middle-European army.

After a small part in the disappointing *When the Whales Came* (89) came another lead in a misconceived version of *The Rachel Papers* (89) – some way after the novel by Martin Amis (born 25 Aug 49), who had once himself acted as a near-child in *A High Wind in Jamaica* (65).

72 Mind Where You're Going
73 Steptoe and Son Ride Again
75 Chimpmates *(first series)*
76 Bugsy Malone
78 Les misérables (FR/GB)
79 The Long Good Friday
80 The Elephant Man
81 4D Special Agents
    Memoirs of a Survivor

Jan Potměšil

CZECHOSLOVAKIA

b: 31 Mar 66

The elegant Potměšil, fair-haired and in turn-of-the-century dress, played a serious, passionate boy hero in the Jules-Verne-based *Secret of Steel City*. Two years later, dark-haired, in T-shirt and jeans, he was a co-hero with horse trouble in *Don't look round*.

In between, he had been in films called *Bachelors*, *The secret of the Devil's pocket* and *The woman behind the counter*, and some time afterwards was in one called *Proč?* (Why?).

78 Tajemstvi ocelového mesta
    (The secret of Steel City)
80 Neohližej se, jde za námi kuň
    (Don't look round, there's a horse
    following us)

Doug McKeon

USA

b: 10 Jne 66 (New Jersey)

Doug, whose father was a stockbroker and mother a teacher, began earning money from modelling when he was five. He had four siblings, at least one of whom

Doug McKeon happy for once with Burt Young and Talia Shire in Daddy I Don't Like It Like This

– his younger brother Keith – also acted. (PHILIP McKEON of the TV series 'Alice', born 20 Nov 64, was oddly enough unrelated.)

Doug got stage work off-Broadway when he was eight, and made his TV bow soon afterwards in *The Silent Eye*. He was in the series 'Colorado Saga' and 'Big Shamus, Little Shamus'.

Europe was hardly aware of him before *On Golden Pond*, when he was pushing 15 and playing a surly teenager. But in 'Big Shamus', for instance, with the bear-like Brian Dennehy as his private-eye father, Doug was a most sophisticated performer, managing the off-hand wrynesses of filial affection with rare delicacy and feeling.

Later, he was in *Night Crossing* (82, with brother Keith), *An Innocent Love* (82), *Desperate Lives* (82), *Heart and Soul* (85) and *Breaking Home Ties* (87).

77 Daddy I Don't Like It Like This
    Tell Me My Name
78 Centennial
    Uncle Joe Shannon
80 The Comeback Kid
81 On Golden Pond

Ronnie Scribner

USA

b: 23 Jly 66

Ronnie – once said to have 'the saddest eyes and most beautiful mouth in the business' – was the first recruit to James

Ronnie Scribner, circa 1982

Mason's boy vampire club in *Salem's Lot*, and made a powerful impression in 'Dallas' around the same time when embraced as a surrogate son by Bobby Ewing.

Other series he was seen in were 'Me and Maxx', 'The Little House on the Prairie' and 'Archie Bunker's Place', and he was Kenny Rogers' son in the pilot for 'The Gambler' – though by the time the series spawned a further episode Scribner was too old, and was replaced by the radically different though no less estimable Charlie Fields ◊.

Pat Petersen

USA

b: 9 Aug 66 (Los Angeles)

Patrick J. Petersen, younger brother of Chris ◊, had none of Chris's watchful calm, but the eye-flashing, teeth-gnashing hyperactivity of a born barnstormer. He was a Terror.

After an early debut with his brother in the feeble *Little Dragons*, Pat found an ideal vehicle in the title role of O. Henry's famous tale *The Ransom of Red Chief*, shown as an ABC Weekend Special in September 1977.

Two bumbling kidnappers (here, ideally, Strother Martin and Jack Elam) have such a wretched time with the rich man's brat they have grabbed that they end up paying the father to take him back. With hot stones in boots, punctured coffee-mugs and all-too-believable threats of scalping, little Petersen exhausts and terrorises his captors. Probably no future Red Chief will take his Chiefdom in such deadly earnest.

Confirming his ability in the TV series 'The Kallikaks' – about a poor Appala-

Hyperactive: Pat Petersen in ABC's 1977 Ransom of Red Chief

chian family in California – Patrick was given star billing in *The Contest Kid* and its sequel. (A sequel was also concocted to *The Ransom of Red Chief.*) He played a beastly boy in *The Man in the Santa Claus Suit*, but redeemed himself by offering, briefly, to take on the computerised monster of *Alligator*.

Among his later films were *Best Kept Secrets* (84) and *Little Miss Perfect* (87).

Master Rajoo (Fahim)

INDIA

b: 15 Aug 66 (Bombay)

This prolific little performer won the Best
Child Actor award in 1976 for his role in
Chitchor. In his late teens he cropped up
again in *Woh 7 din* (83) and *Farishta* (84).

72 Bawarchi (The cook)
   Parichay (Introduction)
   Samadhi (The shrine)
73 Daag (Stigma)
   Gaddaar (Traitor)
   Hindustan ki kasam (Soldier's pledge)
   Nafrat (Hatred)
74 Benaam (Nameless)
   Dost (Friend)
   Duniya ka mela
      (The world's a merry-go-round)
75 Faraar (The absconder)
   Himalaya se ooncha
      (Higher than the Himalayas)
   Kushboo (Fragrance)
   Uljhan (Confusion)
76 Chitchor (Stealer of hearts)
77 Inkaar (The refusal)
   Khatta meetha (Sour and sweet)
   Kitaab (The book)
   Mamta (Maternal love)
   Palkhon ki chhaon main
      (Under the eyelashes)
   Shirdi ke Sai Baba (The Sai Baba of Shirdi)
78 Ankhiyon ke jharonkon se
      (Through the eyes' windows)
   Badaltey rishtey (Changing relations)
   Bandi (The prisoner)
   Trishna (Insatiable desire)
   Trishul (The trident)
   Tumbhri kasam (Swear by you)
79 Aatish (Fire)
80 Bin maa ke bachchey (Motherless children)
81 Chameli Memsaab
   Kanhaiyya

David Bennent

WEST GERMANY

b: 9 Sep 66 (Lausanne)

David, whose mother is a dancer, and
father the actor Heinz Bennent – seen
for example as the hidden Jewish theatre-
director of Truffaut's *Dernier Métro*, and as
the ill-fated scoutmaster in *The Tin Drum*

All-seeing: David Bennent in Die Blechtrommel

– was born with a condition called the
Nonan syndrome, which means that full
growth is limited to 5 feet or so. He was
twelve when he played, unforgettably, the
tiny hero of Günter Grass's weird story in
Volker Schlöndorff's film.

Oskar is first glimpsed blissfully reclining in his mother's womb, which he later
wishes he had never left. However, the
gift of the promised tin drum when he is
three, with the discovery that his special
scream can shatter glass, gives a satisfying
purpose to his life. He decides to stop
growing, and achieves this by a fall down
the cellar steps. The rest of the film shows
him infuriating the local Nazis, achieving
sex (and possibly fatherhood) with a girl
twice his size, finding friendship and love
with midgets, settling some old scores –
and drumming, drumming.

The whole film is narrated by David
Bennent himself, from Oskar's point
of view, in the dry, factual voice of a
pedantic child. But his old-young face
with its hypnotic, coldly all-observing
eyes and terrible capacity for rage,
dominates the whole of this visually
marvellous film. (Grass himself had
insisted that Oskar must be played by a
child, but he could never have expected
such sublime luck in the casting.)

David, like his father, speaks fluent
French, and dubbed his own role for the
French version of *Blechtrommel*. His later
films have included *Canicule* (FR 83) and
Ridley Scott's *Legend* (US 85, as top elf
Honethorn Gump). In 1988 he won fine
reviews as the Fool in a Berlin Schaubühne
production of 'King Lear', and in 1990 for
his 'furious urchin' of a Caliban in Peter
Brook's French 'Tempest'.

His elder sister Anni (born 1963) also
acts: in 1976, for instance, she played Hed-
wig in Ibsen's 'Wild Duck', and in 1979
the title role in Borowczyk's film of *Lulu*.

79 Die Blechtrommel (The tin drum – DE/FR)

Tomas Fryk

SWEDEN

b: 18 Sep 66

In *Barnens Ö* the divorced mother of
eleven-year-old Reine Larssen goes off
on a trip with her new lover, despatch-
ing Reine (as she believes) to a summer
camp known as Children's Island. Reine,
however, who has no intention of wasting
his time in organised games, climbs back
into his empty home and his own private
world. His main preoccupations are the

Stranded: Tomas Fryk in Barnens Ö

existence of God and his own genital development, together with hatred of his mother's boy-friend and the possibility of holding his breath for a record three minutes.

In excursions into the outside world he has interesting, sometimes exciting but finally unsatisfying meetings with girls and women: he is repeatedly brushed aside as superfluous, and furious to find himself crying for his mother. But not a single man he knows offers an adequate role-model, only 'mythical' figures like Chaplin or Björn Borg. Children, he sees, really are stranded on an island of their own.

Kay Pollak's film is a truthful study of early adolescence, and the proud, sceptical, gaze of Tomas Fryk probes his dilemma deeply, with interludes of wild resentment or lust.

In his late teens he made a comeback on TV in *Femte generationen* (86).

79 Barnens Ö (Children's Island)

Matthew Laborteaux

USA

b: 8 Dec 66 (Los Angeles)

This dark, handsome, intelligent boy played dark, handsome, intelligent boys: more remarkable than it might seem, since he had been adopted by the Laborteaux couple as a nine-month-old baby with grave physical and mental handicaps which included autism and a hole in the heart. All these, through love and devotion, he triumphantly overcame.

In the mid-1970s Matthew was for some time a regular in the popular TV series 'The Little House on the Prairie', and had the first lead in the serial *The Red Hand Gang*.

In his later teens, he was the whizzest of the 'Whiz Kids' (83, TVS), and his technological genius led him into deep waters in *Deadly Friend* (86) when he fitted an electronic brain into a brain-dead girl, who then turned nasty.

74 A Woman Under the Influence
76 Bravo Two
   A Circle of Children
   Papa and Me
77 Tarantulas: the Deadly Cargo
78 Killing Stone
   King of the Gypsies
80 The Aliens Are Coming

Matthew's 'elder brother' PATRICK LABOR-TEAUX (also adopted at nine months, and also overcoming appalling handicaps) proved a busy and gifted actor too.

Charley Boorman

BRITAIN

b: 1966 (Wimbledon)

John Boorman's blond son Charley was first seen, briefly, as Jon Voight's son at the end of *Deliverance*, and most of his parts have been brief ones in his father's films – though often very striking, such as his mordant young Mordred in *Excalibur*.

He was later a red-haired delinquent in *Dream One* (GB/FR 84, originally entitled *Nemo*), and had his only lead, as the white child destined to be 'rescued' from a tribe of South American Indians who have raised him for ten years as one of their

own, in *The Emerald Forest* (85). John Boorman's diary of the film's setting-up and shooting is a riveting read.

Charley had the part of the young German pilot who comes to earth in *Hope and Glory* (87), in which the central Boorman-as-a-child figure is taken by the delightful SEBASTIAN RICE EDWARDS. He was then in *Mister Frost* (FR/GB 85).

72 Deliverance (US)
74 Zardoz (IE)
78 The First Great Train Robbery
81 Excalibur (US)

Alexander and Andreas Bauer

AUSTRIA

b: circa 1966

In *What price victory?*, a thoughtful Austrian soccer version of *The Bad News Bears*, the bad news is not incompetence but success and its corruptions, and the price – it clearly says – can be too high.

An ambitious sports master at a Viennese grammar school starts a football team and trains it furiously for participation in the Austrian school championship. All goes well – too well. What started as fun becomes an increasingly ugly striving for success at all costs: easy-going boys turn into arrogant prima-donnas, team spirit takes second place to selfish goal-hunting, professional fouls are practised, and education gets shoved into the background.

A pair of Viennese brothers give fine performances in the poles-apart leads: Alexander plays the team captain, a brilliant goal-scorer who becomes such a monster of egoism that his own team-mates vote to drop him, while Andreas is the calm, good-natured goalkeeper who uses diplomacy to keep the side together.

Walter Bannert's admirable film should be seen by sports-mad schoolboys everywhere.

81 Was kostet der Sieg?
   (What price victory?)

Vladimir Buljan

YUGOSLAVIA

b: circa 1966

Vladimir Buljan was a true-life ace horse-boy in the Kelly Reno ◇ class, and did all his own riding in *The last race*.

Its story, simple but sympathetic, tells of a former champion racehorse called Zimzelen – beloved of the local school-children – which is condemned to the slaughterhouse by the hard-nosed management of the horse farm he lives on.

Some of the children steal Zimzelen and run away with him. The adults search their hearts and readjust their priorities. The children return with the reprieved horse, and Buljan rides Zimzelen to victory in a veterans' race.

He later studied oil engineering with a view to following his father's career.

79 Poslednja trka (The last race)

Alexander Buss
and Barnaby Holm

BRITAIN

b: circa 1966

The screenwriter Andrew Birkin (elder brother of Jane), who had also been an assistant director on Kubrick's *2001*, worked on a TV musical adaptation of *Peter Pan* in 1975, and became fascinated by the strange personality of its author, J.M.Barrie. Three years later BBC Television broadcast his three-part dramatic biography of Barrie, *The Lost Boys*, and in 1979 Birkin published a remarkable study, 'J.M.Barrie and the Lost Boys'.

The whimsical, melancholy little Scot was himself an example of the Peter Pan syndrome. In so far as he grew up at all – he married twice, though hardly for sexual reasons – psychologically he remained in many ways a child. He was haunted by the innocence and sadness of his own childhood (with an elder brother who was killed at 13 in a skating accident and

Barrie's Michael: Alexander Buss in The Lost Boys *of 1978*

whom he could never replace in his mother's affections) and captivated by the innocence and happiness of ordinary little boys. 'Nothing that happens after we are twelve,' he wrote, 'matters very much.'

After divorcing his first wife in 1909, Barrie attached himself to Sylvia Llewelyn Davies, mother of three beautiful boys he had met in Kensington Gardens. Later, after her husband's death of cancer, he became surrogate father to the boys (now numbering five), whom he loved obsessively though quite unsexually. But tragedy stalked them. Sylvia herself died of cancer in 1910; the eldest boy, George, was killed in action in 1915 at the age of 21, and Michael (Barrie's special favourite) was drowned in 1921, aged 20.

At this point Birkin's book ends: but his five-hour TV drama takes Barrie's life right to its lonely end in 1937. It is one of British television's undisputed master-pieces – desperately sad, but with such wit and psychological acuity as to be com-pletely absorbing – and the performance of Ian Holm as Barrie is simply a miracle, a maddening, fascinating, tragic little figure

masking his vulnerability with gruffness.

Holm's own son BARNABY – who had been in *Juggernaut* (74), and later had a featured role in the Birkin-scripted *Omen* sequel *The Final Conflict* (US 81) – played the young George at the time of his first meeting with Barrie, and in the subtlest emotional scenes (particularly one over a game of draughts in a Swiss hotel) the remarkable ALEXANDER BUSS is Michael at the age of nine or so.

78 The Lost Boys

Jeffrey Frank

USA

b: circa 1966

Jeffrey Frank is Michael Caine's schoolboy son in *The Island*, an enjoyably ludicrous story of a colony of inbred pirates on an island off Florida, who capture the pair of them and brainwash the boy into (nearly) shooting his father once the latter has per-formed a necessary act of fertilisation on the colony's only viable woman.

Jeffrey, having smouldered balefully in his 'changed' state, was subsequently engaged for a leading role as a member of the Hitler Youth in a West German TV serial called *Blut und Ehre – Jugend unter Hitler* (DE 82).

80 The Island

Lars Herrmann

EAST GERMANY

b: circa 1966

Lars is excellent in Hans Kratzert's *Ottokar*, a film full of shifting emphases. It's about a small boy sworn to fight injustice in all its forms. This leads him to appear sometimes a prig, sometimes a hero, sometimes a hypocrite.

Finally a good use is found for the well-meaning meddler.

76 Ottokar, der Weltverbesserer
   (Ottokar the world-reformer)

Jan Johansen

DENMARK

b: circa 1966

In *Kundskabens træ*, probably the most truthful film ever made about adolescence, Nils Malmros took advantage of the physical and psychological changes of puberty by filming his two-year story over a full two-year period, so that we actually watch the changes happening. The children's bodies elongate, their expressions become more cagey and pensive, most get interested in the opposite sex. Some get nicer, others don't.

One boy revenges himself on a shy, attractive girl who has rebuffed him, by launching a campaign of slander, ridicule and ostracism which reduces her to a tragic wreck. Loyalties slither, conformism makes cowards of previously decent boys. We wait to see who, if anyone, will go to Elin's aid, and at last someone does; but it is too little, and too late.

In the quaintly formal early-teen society of classless Denmark around 1960, this film never strikes a false note. It is unpredictable, often wonderfully funny, and sometimes appallingly painful.

As the weak, good-natured Niels-Ole, the central male character, Jan Johansen is perfect. Brian Theibel (a crewcut oddball) and Bo von der Lippe (a puckish anatomist) are outstanding among the other boys.

81 Kundskabens træ (The tree of knowledge)

Herion Mustafaraj
(Herion Spiro)

ALBANIA

b: circa 1966

Herion Spiro – his surname later changed to Mustafaraj in accordance with the Albanisation law – made a great popular hit in his first film, *Beni ecën vetë*.

Wide-open: Jan Johansen (right) with Andres Ørgård in Kundskabens træ

Urban wimplet: Herion Spiro (later Mustafaraj) with Selma Sotiriadhi in Beni ecën vetë

Beni, pampered son of over-protective urban parents, is taken off by a country uncle to spend part of his summer on a farm. Away from the stifling home, confronted by strange animals and befriended by village children, the little wimp becomes a man.

It sounds awful. Actually, in the hands of Xhanfise Keko, doyen of Albanian directors, it's very charming.

75 Beni ecën vetë (Benny walks by himself)
77 Tomka dhe shokët e tij
    (Tommy and his friends)
78 Pas gjurmëve (After the tracks)
81 Shoku ynë Tili (Our friend Til)

Petro Papakosta

ALBANIA

b: circa 1966

The Albanian cinema, still fighting the National Liberation War in 1980, produced yet another drama of a young pioneer who longs to get a rifle and kill foreign soldiers. The partisan commanders keep turning him down on grounds of age, but eventually, by an act of cunning, Velo gets a gun from an enemy outpost, and he and his faithful dog climb up the mountain to join the patriots.

However heroic, such childish determination to kill is not a pretty sight, but Petro Papakosta, a vehement teddy-bear of a boy, takes some of the curse off it.

80 Partizani i vogël Velo
    (Little partisan Velo)

Heroics: Eric Rosen in Rové huliet

Eric Rosen

ISRAEL

b: circa 1966

Rové huliet, written and directed by Ilan Moshenson, is set in the austere early days of the Israeli state and paints a bravely unflattering picture of chauvinist teachers and parents living in the past, their hang-ups echoed in the depressingly 'heroic' war-games of the children, which end – inevitably – in tears.

Eric Rosen, as a boy in whom gut patriotism struggles with common sense and conscience, is extremely fine.

79 Rové huliet (The wooden gun)

Jan Schwarzbauer

WEST GERMANY

b: circa 1966

Robert Muller's superb novel, on which *The World That Summer* is closely based, was published in 1959 in Britain, where he has lived since leaving Germany, as a part-Jewish schoolboy, in the 1930s.

The story, set in Hamburg at the time of the 1936 Olympics and largely auto-biographical, tells of a boy with a much-loved Jewish grandmother whose racial origins he and his family hush up. Hannes visits her regularly and goes to the opera with her; but at the same time he belongs to the Hitler Youth and is keenly interested in making the grade and winning his HJ knife.

He keeps cravenly quiet as his playmates smash the windows of Jewish shopkeepers, and when his granny is moved in on by a Nazi lout (her former milkman) whose price for silence is bed, board and the bulk of her earnings, Hannes is jealous and contemptuous rather than sympathetic, and simply disowns her. At last, when his family has been pretty well destroyed by fear and caution, shame catches up with him.

Moral courage, let alone heroism, is a large thing to ask, particularly of such a naturally conformist creature as a boy. Nils Malmros' film *Kundskabens træ* (see Jan Johansen ◊) offers a corresponding picture of young male cowardice in democratic Denmark. Few can be sure they would have behaved better in

Hannes' circumstances, so ingrained is the instinct for self-preservation.

Jews understood that as well as any. A telling scene shows Hannes, in a brief mood of racial solidarity, pausing outside a Torah school and asking one of the pupils if it would be possible for him to enrol. 'I wouldn't, if you don't have to,' says the Jewish boy with dignity.

Die Welt in jenem Sommer (finely directed by Ilse Hoffmann for Westdeutscher Rundfunk) is an agonising story. It is also extremely funny – richly informative, for instance, about German schoolboy smut of the period and the devout absurdities of the Hitler Youth. The characterisation of the grisly gang Hannes hangs around with is spot-on, most memorably the sly little bourgeois Rolfi (Jörg Doleh) with his smart bike and his snigger.

As Hannes, Jan-Claudius Schwarzbauer is tremendous: on the surface just an ordinary, sport-loving boy, but with nervous calculation seething behind his cool exterior. We watch his self-respect eroded a little more with each act of betrayal until he reaches an abject state of moral numbness.

80 Die Welt in jenem Sommer
   (The world that summer)

Unheroic: Jan Schwarzbauer in Die Welt in jenem Sommer

Söderdahl in Bröderna Lejonhjärta

Lars Söderdahl

SWEDEN

b: circa 1966

Olle Hellbom, the regular director of Astrid Lindgren stories, had an untypical one in *The Brothers Lionheart*, a straight-faced adventure set in the middle ages (though it is in fact the dream of a dying present-day child).

Jonathan, the teenage brother of little 'Crispy' – as the English version has it – gets involved in the rescue of a resistance fighter imprisoned by a cruel tyrant. He refuses to let Crispy accompany him into the perils of Wild Rose Valley, but after Jonathan is captured Crispy goes on his own rescue mission.

The story, standard saga-stuff with none of Lindgren's usual whimsicality, is not a major bundle of fun, but Lars Söderdahl's Crispy is completely captivating: scared but brave, serious and determined. He looks wonderful, but the poignant little voice supplied by Nicholas Barnes ◊ on the British dubbing makes a vital contribution to the film's undoubted magic.

77 Bröderna Lejonhjärta
   (The brothers Lionheart)

Nikolaus Vogel

AUSTRIA

b: circa 1966

Both his grandfather and father – Rudolf Vogel (1900-1967) and Peter Vogel (1937-1978) – were famous German actors, and his mother, Gertraud Jesserer, was an Austrian actress. Since Peter Vogel's suicide, Nikolaus had lived in Vienna with his mother and elder brother, and was spotted by the director Walter Bannert on a trawl through Viennese schools for young actors for his soccer morality film.

In *Was kostet der Sieg?* Nikolaus had only the third or fourth role, but Bannert was so impressed that he gave him a lead in *Die Erben*.

81 Was kostet der Sieg? (What price victory)
82 Die Erben (The inheritors)

Ganev in Izpiti po nikoye vreme

Dimiter Ganev

BULGARIA

b: 10 Apr 67

This whimsical mouse, a lawyer's son, rapidly became a Bulgarian favourite in his early films. Two of them – *Children playing* and *Exams* – were directed by Ivanka Grubcheva: delightful episodic affairs in which Dimiter's droll expressions and attitudes were prominent.

In *Houses without fences* he is an orphan cared for, with varying success, by a succession of friends and neighbours before being entrusted to a children's home. His innocent frankness at once disconcerts and disarms. He also had a lead in *The hedgehogs' war*, a TV serial of the mid-1970s which was released several years later in condensed cinema form.

73 Deca igrayet ven
    (Children playing outdoors)
    Kashti bez ogradi (Houses without fences)
74 Izpiti po nikoye vreme
    (Exams any old time)
80 Usadeni dushi (The hedgehogs' war)

Adrian Vîlcu

ROMANIA

b: 13 Jly 67

Adrian Vîlcu was nearly fourteen before his big chance came, in Elisabeta Bostan's two circus films (condensed from a long TV serial). He played Geo, son of the clown Cezar Marcelloni. Geo's sister Fanny is a trapeze artist, and he is destined to succeed his father as a clown, though his real ambition is to be a polar explorer. After triumphs and tragedies in turn-of-the-century Romania and Russia, the Marcellonis add a baby polar bear to their troupe; and in the end it is the bear, Fram, who is instrumental in getting Geo to the North Pole.

After some rather exhausting musicals and fairytales in the 1970s, Bostan, earlier known as the miniaturist of the *Năică* films, got back to top form in her handsomely mounted circus chronicle. As the romantic Geo, Vîlcu was a revelation: a gentle, sensitive, humorous boy capable of great vivacity as well as frequent sadness. This was clearly a born actor, as he showed in his subsequent work.

73 Veronica
78 Revanşa (Revenge)

Adrian Vîlcu as the aspirant clown in Saltimbancii

81 Saltimbancii (The clowns)
   Un saltimbanc la Polul Nord
      (A clown at the North Pole)
82 Prea cald pentru lună mai
      (Too hot for May)
   Prea tineri pentru riduri
      (Too young for wrinkles)
   Racheta alba (The white rocket)

Lionel Melet

FRANCE

b: 14 Oct 67 (Paris)

Lionel had the male lead in *Trocadéro*, a skateboarding romance for teenies. He employs every device of infant blackmail to persuade his mother to let him see his Juliet (the beautiful and resoundingly named Bérangère de Lagatinerie) at the skateboarders' mecca at the Trocadéro. It's a story of some wit and charm.

77 L'Hôtel de la Plage (Beach Hotel)
78 Trocadéro bleu citron
      (Trocadero blue and yellow)
80 Blue jeans

Fernando Ramos da Silva

BRAZIL

b: 29 Nov 67 (São Paulo)
d: 25 Aug 87 (São Paulo)

Pixote, Hector Babenco's tragedy of juvenile delinquency, was more drily documentary than Buñuel's *Los olvidados* of thirty years earlier, but no less nightmarish in its way. Its picture of a boys' reformatory supervised by cynically helpless adults, where the inmates sniff glue and the stronger ones beat up, rape and even kill the weaker almost at will, is depressing enough; but when the tough little Pixote and three companions succeed in breaking out, things don't improve much, since their efforts to survive begin with pocket-picking and mugging and graduate through drug-selling to murder.

With his steam-rollered face and sad, splayed eyes which spoke volumes of bitter experience, the grim urchin Fernando Ramos da Silva looked many times his age, which made his rare moments of childish glee the more poignant. At the end, having just accidentally shot one of his friends while attempting his own second murder, Pixote curls into a foetal position on the bed of a middle-aged prostitute, who suckles him briefly before throwing him out to fend for himself in a world he ought not to grow up in.

Fernando Ramos, in brutal fact, was never to grow far. His princely payment for *Pixote* – about $1000 – didn't last him long. (Hector Babenco, the director who had plucked him from obscurity, went on to fame and fortune with *Kiss of the Spiderwoman*.) Fernando was given a part in a Brazilian TV soap opera, but proved too unreliable and was written out of it.

Incorrigible: Fernando Ramos da Silva in Pixote

When a film was derived from the series – *Gabriela* (83) – he got his part back; but it led to nothing more, and he drifted into a life of petty crime. In 1984 he was arrested while trying to steal a TV set from a shop: witnesses helpfully identified him as the star of *Pixote*.

He was incorrigible; the police grew sick of picking him up. Three years later they caught him and an accomplice engaged in further robbery. The friend surrendered; Fernando, in true Cagney style, elected to shoot it out with the cops, and so died. It is probably the end he would have chosen, had he ever had a real choice.

79 Pixote a lei do mais fraco (Pixote, the law of the weakest)

Nicholas Barnes

BRITAIN

b: 4 Dec 67

The art of dubbing shouldn't be ignored in any consideration of foreign films shown on English-speaking screens. Crude dubbing can destroy a film, while a careful and sensitive job can, just occasionally, make you forget you aren't listening to the original actors. It demands a sympathy, intelligence and quickness of response which is simply beyond most child actors – but not beyond the remarkable Nicholas Barnes.

He was an outstanding solo performer on BBC Radio, in readings which ranged from the tragic concentration-camp journal of the Polish child David Rabinowicz to the hilarious diary of the pubescent Adrian Mole. He also took the lead in John Challen's radio play 'Out of the Mouths' in 1980.

Nicholas supplied – perfectly – the English voices for Lars Söderdahl◇ in *The Brothers Lionheart* and Stefan Arpagäus◇ in the 1979 *Heidi* serial, as well as one of the leads in the US cartoon version of *The Lion, the Witch and the Wardrobe*.

He can actually be *seen* in one or two films like *The Brute* (76) and *Outland* (81, as Sean Connery's son).

76 The Brute
78 The Lion, the Witch and the Wardrobe
   (US, *voice only*)
81 Outland

Paul Medford

BRITAIN

b: 1967

In Anthony Simmons' *Black Joy* – a Dickensian comedy set in Brixton's black community – Paul Medford, the son of a London Transport bus inspector, made a joyous debut as a West Indian Artful Dodger. In due course he got two substantial roles for the Children's Film Foundation.

He was later to have a leading part in the TV soap opera 'East Enders' and appeared in many films.

77 Black Joy
79 A Horse Called Jester
   Yesterday's Hero
81 4D Special Agents

Francesco Bonelli

ITALY

b: circa 1967

Luigi Comencini, for more than 30 years a master of children's psychology and problems, turned in *Voltati Eugenio* to the crumbling institution of the modern family, or 'non-family': not accusing, he said, but merely stating facts.

The parents of twelve-year-old Eugenio are separated and self-absorbed, concentrating on their careers and love-affairs. They have vague affection for their son, but on the whole he is an inconvenience, to be fed and educated, shuttled from house to house, and bought off with pocket money.

Above all, he has long since ceased to be cute. A telling final scene shows the family out on a farm, cooing over a newborn calf: 'Dear little thing! Isn't he sweet!' Eugenio, no longer little or sweet, walks away and leaves them to it.

Francesco Bonelli's disillusioned face, longing for affection – or even consideration – but not expecting it, tells the whole story. He briefly finds a friend in a little shop-boy called Guerrino (the engaging Alessandro Bruzzese) who plies him with greens for his rabbit.

81 Voltati Eugenio (Turn round, Eugenio)

Arben Latifi

ALBANIA

b: circa 1967

Arben Latifi makes a jaunty protagonist in *Our friend Til*, the story of an 'impossible' boy: generally absent from school, inattentive and insufferable when present. Albania's school system comes under critical scrutiny, and so do parents who think none of the responsibility is theirs.

Four years later, as an older teenager, Arben returned to the screen in *Lundrimi i parë*, a breathless drama about the adaptation of fishermen to modern methods.

81 Shoku ynë Tili (Our friend Til)

Harun Yeşilyurt

TURKEY

b: circa 1967

This sandy, worried-looking young Turk played the heroine's husband in *Hazal* – a ten-year-old husband in an arranged marriage in a remote mountain village – and had reason to look worried since he was about to become the screen's first ten-year-old cuckold. Harun accepted his fate with dignity and magnanimity.

He had further tribulations in *At* (one of the world's briefer titles) as a country boy coming to the big city with his father. Their aim is to earn enough to buy him an education: but when their horse is stolen, their hope goes with it – a situation reminiscent of *Bicycle Thieves*. Father, son and horse have a wretched time of it in Ali Ozgentürk's harrowing story of life at survival level.

Unhorsed: Harun Yeşilyurt in At

Undiscouraged, however, Harun continued to act throughout his teens.

80 Hazal
82 At (The horse – TR/DE)
83 Gülibik (TR/DE)

Christos Zannides

CYPRUS

b: circa 1967

The Turkish military take-over of Cyprus in July 1974 is seen in *Avrianos polemistis*

through the eyes of a Greek-Cypriot boy.

His grandparents refuse to budge as the Turkish forces approach (one subsequently dies, the other is deported), but Orestes leaves with his parents, only to end up, after a serious of close shaves, in the numbing tedium of a refugee camp. At last, deciding that death is preferable to dishonour, he sets off across the minefields in the direction of his home village.

In this strictly black-and-white propaganda film (in ravishing colour) Christos Zannides makes a splendidly passionate junior hero. Dimitri Andreas, incidentally, who plays his father, appeared as a child in *Ill Met by Moonlight* (GB 58).

81 Avrianos polemistis (Tomorrow's warrior)

Patrick Bach

WEST GERMANY

b: 3 Mar 68 (Hamburg)

Patrick, a lordly child who had appeared in commercials since he was nine, won international fame in two popular TV serials.

In *Silas*, a rambling 19th century saga based on books by Cecil Bødker, he was

Lordly waif: Patrick Bach in the TV serial Silas

a footloose waif with a magic flute. Silas runs away from a travelling circus, not wishing to train as a sword-swallower; wins a black horse in a bet with a horse-dealer, only to have it stolen from him; falls in with a lame boy called Godik (Lucky Molocher) who proves a faithful friend, but also with an evil old female smuggler called The Shrew. And so on: almost every adult a dangerous brute, endless escapes through windows, across mud-flats and through reed-beds.

The tiny Bach is certainly a picturesque mini-hero in his patched jacket, leather breeches and 19th-century leg-warmers, and acts with enormous eyes, teeth and vehemence, but the story (dimly dubbed for Anglo-Saxon consumption) is neither subtle nor gripping.

Jack Holborn (brilliantly dubbed by the same firm that bungled *Silas*) was altogether more fun, and with a livelier source in a pirate adventure by the peer-less Leon Garfield. Jack, a supposed orphan – he eventually finds his mother – goes to sea as a cabin-boy, but becomes embroiled in a mutiny, and much confused by a pair of twin aristocrats, one of whom is a judge and the other a buccaneer.

Though we lose Garfield's quirky narrative prose, much of his crisp dialogue is retained, and Patrick Bach is if anything better than in *Silas*: the eyes even huger and more self-righteous, the lips thrust out by even more tombstone-like incisors. For those who like their boy heroes proud and stroppy, little Bach had no equal. He was in addition a splendid athlete and rider.

There were to be no more serials, but in 1984 he had a lead in Siggi Götz's comedy *Drei und eine halbe Portion*. No prizes for guessing who was the half-pint.

81 Silas (TVS)
82 Jack Holborn (DE/NZ, TVS)
84 Drei und eine halbe Portion
    (Three and a half portion)

OPPOSITE: *Lordly waif: Patrick Bach in the TV series* Silas

Billy Jacoby
USA

b: 10 Apr 68 (Queens, NYC)

Billy was the half brother of the excellent Scott Jacoby ◇ (born 1955), and elder of Bobby (born 1973). He was seen later in *Reckless* (84).

79 North Dallas Forty
80 Bloody Birthday
81 Back Roads
    X-Ray
82 The Beastmaster
    Cujo
    Hospital Massacre
    Man, Woman and Child
    Nightmares
    Superstition

Lee Whitlock
BRITAIN

b: 17 Apr 68

Lee made his name as Stanley Moon in the admirable 1982 serial *Shine On, Harvey Moon*, a rich evocation of wartime Britain. His subsequent material varied widely, in-cluding the abysmal schoolboy series 'Be-hind the Bike Sheds' (84), *Comrade Dad* (84), 'Hold the Back Page' (TVS 85), *The Best Years of Your Life* (86), *Wish You Were Here* (87) and *The Two of Us* (88).

He showed much sensitivity as a dying teenager in *The Best Years of Your Life* and a gay one in *The Two of Us*.

82 Shine On, Harvey Moon (TVS)
83 The Merry Wives of Windsor

Filip Yankovski
USSR

b: 10 Nov 68

Filip, the son of actor Oleg Yankovski, plays the artist (Alexei) aged five in Tarkovski's autobiographical kaleido-scope, *Mirror*: a little shaven-headed creature with dark, non-committal eyes, walking through the forest with his

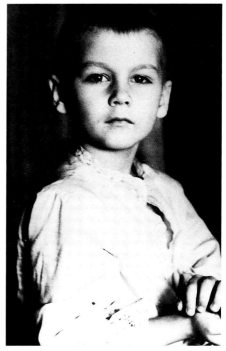

Non-committal: Filip Yankovski in Zerkalo

grandmother or watching a neighbour's barn burn spectacularly down. In this magically evocative, sometimes confusing film he is the neutral observer, simply absorbing what he sees but saying nothing. His real-life father, of course, is playing the Tarkovski figure.

Alexei at 12, and in the 'later' scenes Alexei's son Ignat at the same age, are played by the shaggier IGNAT DANILTSEV: equally watchful, with the grudging eyes of one being pulled unwillingly through other people's lives. Daniltsev, impressive as he was, chose not to become an actor but instead studied art at the Surikov School of Painting in Moscow.

The brief but vivid role of Asafiev – a bitter, rebellious orphan at a military school, who electrifies his fellow-pupils by rolling an apparently live grenade on to their firing range – is taken by Yuri Sventikov. And there is a seraphic baby.

Filip Yankovski went on to become a student at the Moscow Arts Theatre School Studio, and in his late teens returned to filming in *Sentimentalnoye puteshestviye na kartoshki* (86).

74 Zerkalo (Mirror)
75 Pod kamennim nebom (Under a stone sky)

Anthony Michael Hall

USA

b: circa 1968 (Boston)

Hall, a frail, snaggle-tooth version of Boris Becker, was a good actor, with leading roles in several films. In the TV serial *Rascals and Robbers* he played Huck Finn to the Tom Sawyer of Patrick Creadon.

He later had leads in *Out of Bounds* (86) and *Johnny Be Good*, and would have had one in *Full Metal Jacket* had he not fallen foul of Stanley Kubrick through some unprofessional conduct.

82 Rascals and Robbers
    Six Pack
83 National Lampoon's Vacation
    Running Out
84 Sixteen Candles
85 Breakfast Club
    Weird Science

Hershewe in Casey's Shadow

Michael Hershewe

USA

b: circa 1968

Hershewe was a lively boy with a wide mouth and dark eyes, seen to advantage as Walter Matthau's horse-loving youngest son in *Casey's Shadow*.

77 Casey's Shadow
78 The Big Fix
    Bloodbrothers
80 American Dream

Kelly Reno

USA

b: circa 1968

The Black Stallion was the first product of Francis Ford Coppola's Omni Zoetrope studio, and the first feature film of the director, Carroll Ballard. (Its brilliant photographer, Caleb Deschanel, was to make a fascinating directorial debut in 1982 with *The Escape Artist*.)

This is a delightfully traditional story of a shipwreck and its only survivors, a boy and a desperate Arab stallion, who meet on a desert island. The boy, Alec Ramsey, patiently tames the horse before they are rescued. On their return to America, Alec meets a retired trainer (played by Mickey Rooney ◊), and after secret preparations rides 'The Black' to victory over two of the world's fastest thoroughbreds.

Kelly – son of Bud Reno, a Colorado cattle-breeder and one of the 'wranglers' on the two *Black Stallion* films – was brought up on an 8000-acre ranch near Pueblo. He was a genuinely brilliant rider from an early age, and did most of his own stunts in the film, though he gave way to a professional jockey for the climactic race.

He makes an unglamorous but endearing hero, whose rather flat face, bleared with freckles, occasionally offers a radiant,

Rode to Morocco: Kelly Reno in The Black Stallion Returns

bruised smile. After his screen debut, his next appearance was on a TV show called 'Big Blue Marble'.

Alec Ramsey and the Arab stallion (Cass-Olé) returned four years later in a further adventure in which the horse's original Arab owners forcibly reclaim him. The scene shifts to North Africa, whither Alec also flies and where he becomes embroiled in dangerous tribal rivalries involving a vital horse-race. Kelly Reno, now well into his teens, is as appealing as ever, but the treatment is less fresh.

He had further riding leads in *The Long Ride* (AKA *Brady's Escape*, a US-Hungarian co-production directed by Pál Gábor of *Angi Vera* fame) and, in 1985, in one of NBC's 'Amazing Stories'.

79 The Black Stallion
83 The Black Stallion Returns
   The Long Ride (Hosszú vágta – US/HU)

Sven Valsecchi

ITALY

b: circa 1968

Little half-Swedish Sven had the sort of gap-toothed beauty that pierces maternal bosoms. He appeared only in the opening scenes of the ineffable *Venditore* (see Renato Cestiè ◇), but had the lead in the other two tearjerkers: in *Nene*, and in *Questo si che e' amore* (distributed abroad as *The Last Night of Christmas* or *The Day*

Sven Valsecchi in Nene

Santa Claus Cried) as a poor little rich boy with an absentee daddy.

His films, and their titles, were not Sven's fault.

74 Il venditore di palloncini
   (The balloon-seller)
77 Nene
   Questo si che e' amore
   (This thing called love, AKA The Last Night of Christmas)

Bateman, 1981

Jason Bateman

USA

b: 14 Jan 69 (Westchester, N.Y.)

Handsome Jason, son of a film producer, made a modest start at the age of ten in an educational film. His shrewdest move, though, was to become Ricky Schroder's ◇ tormentor, Derek, in the TV sitcom 'Silver Spoons' – a schoolboy master of sneak and smarm.

He then got his own series, co-starring with David Garrison in 'It's Your Move', and was the elder brother of Jeremy Licht ◇ and Danny Ponce in the more entertaining 'Valerie', transmogrified after the departure of its star, Valerie Harper, to 'The Hogan Family', with Sandy Duncan as the new matriarch.

Leads followed in *Can You Feel Me Dancing?* (86), *Teen Wolf Too* (88) and *Crossing the Mob* (88).

Jason was a keen sportsman: when he was twelve, for instance, he went to Australia as a member of the American Youth Soccer Organisation team. His sister Justine became a successful actress, in 'Family Ties' and other TV series.

79 The Veldt
81 Legends of the West
83 Just a Little More Love
   'Silver Spoons' (TVS)
84 The Fantastic World of D.C. Collins
   'It's Your Move' (TVS)

Meeno Peluce

USA

b: 26 Feb 69 (Holland)

Meeno, a popular TV kid with a shock of dark curly hair, was in fact Dutch by birth, but moved to the US when he was four. His mother became a Hollywood studio caterer, and so in due course he was spotted. His younger sister, the comprehensively named Soleil Moon Frye, also acted.

Meeno's style was laid-back and charming. He was perfect in the Wild West sitcom 'Best of the West' (as the son of the liberal sheriff from the city, fastidiously learning to hold his own in rough new surroundings) and in the time-warp fantasy stories of 'Voyagers'. He was also seen in other series, such as 'The Incredible Hulk', 'The Bad News Bears' and 'Diff'rent Strokes', as well as some pilots.

78 Ghost of Flight 401
   Night Cries
   The Pirate
79 The Amityville Horror
   Fast Friends
80 The Jazz Singer
   Scout's Honor
   'Best of the West' (TVS)
81 Don't Go Near the Park
82 Million Dollar Infield
   'Voyagers' (TVS)
   World War III

Ross Harris

USA

b: 13 Mar 69

Ross Harris, the youngest of seven children, was an extrovert-looking boy generally associated with comedy, though *Testament* was to show that he could do a good deal more. His first job, at six, was a public service plea on the perils of drunken driving.

He was already a familiar face from his role as Dylan in the TV series 'Married' when he got his small but delectable role in the spoof disaster movie *Airplane!* – as the boy who is vouchsafed a look at the cockpit, and a rather dubious interview with pilot Peter Graves. In a beautiful sight gag, the extremely rowdy nun who is to play a damaging part in the action is seen to be reading 'Boy's Life' magazine; across the gangway, Rossie is immersed in 'Nun's Life'.

Lynne Littman's *Testament* was one of a spate of nuclear-war films, more moving than the others because of its low-key, unsensational approach. We don't even know precisely where or why the missiles have struck, but watch the inhabitants of a small California town gradually dying of radiation sickness, in particular one family of which, after his father's disappearance, Ross is the oldest male. Serious and practical, and himself visibly weakening, he sees his sister (Roxana Zal) and his younger brother (Lukas Haas ◊) succumb before the desolate end.

73 The Crazies
77 A Christmas Coal Mine Miracle
   Un autre homme, une autre chance
      (FR – Another man, another chance)
80 Airplane!
83 My Brother's Wedding
   Testament

Mark Luxford

BRITAIN

b: 27 Jne 69

Since 1951, the main source of films for children in Britain – where there is no specialist producer like Disney in America – has been the CHILDREN'S FILM FOUNDATION. With the aid of a levy or grant from the film industry the CFF has been invaluable, making mainly comedy or adventure stories for showing at Saturday morning cinema shows, or more recently (as the CFTF) for TV. It also buys in, dubs and distributes foreign children's films, often from Eastern Europe.

Besides its own 'specialist' regulars, it has attracted guest directors as various as Jacques Brunius, Alberto Cavalcanti, Charles Frend, Lewis Gilbert, Pat Jackson and Michael Powell. Actors like Francesca Annis, Michael Crawford, Judy Geeson, Susan George, David Hemmings ◊ and Richard O'Sullivan ◊ have been among the CFF's child stars.

The plots, usually contemporary and open-air, seldom centre on a particular child. A duo or trio of protagonists is preferred, or sometimes a small gang. There have been decadent periods where the treatment has fallen into predictable formulas: child gangs carefully balanced for race, sex and 'types', comic crooks

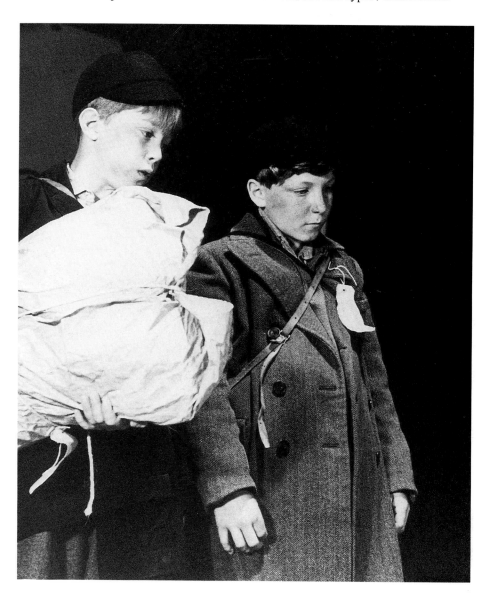

John Holmes (left) and Mark Luxford in Friend or Foe

(usually a crafty middle-aged one with a younger, near-moronic sidekick), pompous policemen, ineffectual teachers, and lots of busy, jolly music of a currently popular kind, to make you feel you're having a good time.

But at their best — and recent years have been good ones — the low-budget CFF films have been refreshing entertainments, which raise moral issues in an unheavy way and make the young audience reflect as well as keeping it amused and excited.

A fine example was John Krish's *Friend or Foe*, about two evacuees from wartime London billeted on a Welsh farm: the calm, thoughtful Tucky (Mark Luxford) and the troubled David (John Holmes), whose sailor father was machine-gunned in the water after his ship was sunk. A German plane is shot down nearby, and the boys find two survivors hiding in the woods — find them because one of the Germans saves David from drowning in the river. They let the boys go on condition that they say nothing.

Tucky thinks they should honour their promise, bring these 'good Germans' food and let them go; the vengeful David, in spite of owing his life to them, wants to turn them in at once. Tucky's view narrowly prevails, but their dilemma is solved when the unwounded pilot escapes and is captured (he keeps quiet about the boys) and his wounded comrade allows them to hand him over and be regarded, in an ironic finale, as heroes.

Tucky, the one who rightly concludes that war is stupid, is most sympathetically played by Mark Luxford, with eyes like searchlights and a meditative face of enormous character. Mark had also acted on stage with the Royal Shakespeare Company, and done much TV.

81 Friend or Foe

Lyubomir Tsvetkov

BULGARIA

b: 14 Aug 69 (Sofia)

After his parents divorced, Lyubomir's father moved to Poland, and it was there that he was chosen as the boy hero of two co-productions directed by Pawel Komorowski. (His roles in the Bulgarian films had only been minor ones.)

The 'Eye of the Prophet' is a precious stone sought by zealots and crooks alike. Lyubomir, a rangy blond with interesting, angular features, moves through exotic adventures in a series of exotic costumes.

78 Talisman
82 Oko proroka (Eye of the Prophet – PL/BG)
83 Za edna troika
   (Getting a third)
84 Przeklete oko proroka
   (Accursed Eye of the Prophet – PL/BG)

Sanz in La leyenda del tambor

Jorge Sanz

SPAIN

b: 26 Aug 69 (Madrid)

A tougher nut than 'Pitusin' ◇ or Pablito Calvo ◇, Jorge Sanz is the finest Spanish kid actor of recent years, with a lot of humour and personality. For his vivid

Dangerous quest: Lyubomir Tsvetkov in Przeklete oko proroka

performance as the sturdy little Romeo of Antonio J. Betanco's early-teen romance *Valentina* (she was played by Paloma Gomez) Jorge won a citation at the 1983 Manila Film Festival. He had been 'young Conan' in the American film.

He continued busily into his teens, with *Dos mejor que uno* (84), *Mambru se fue a la guerra* (85), *El año de las luces* (86), *El luta mañana sere libre* (87), *Monte Bajo* (88) and *Si te dicen que cai* (88). There were also many TV appearances, such as in *Goya* (84), *Pepe Carvallo* (84), *Segunda enseñenza* (85) and *Gallego* (87).

He had the lead in *El año de las luces*, which won the Silver Bear award at the Berlin Film Festival, and another in *Amantes* (91). Sanz had become a star.

79 La miel (Honey)
80 El canto de la cigarra (Song of the cicada)
   Dos pillos y pico (Two rascals and a bit)
   Dos y dos son cinco
     (Two and two are five)
   Los locos vecinos del segundo
     (The deputy's crazy neighbours)
81 Conan the Barbarian (US)
   La leyenda del tambor
     (Legend of the drummer)
   Mar brava (Angry sea)
   La rebelion de los pajaros
     (Revolt of the birds)
82 Valentina
83 Vivir mañana (Live tomorrow)

Mark Kounnas

AUSTRALIA

b: 1969

It was especially piquant that a boy with a Greek father should have incarnated the child Don Bradman in the national epic *Bodyline*. The tough, confident Mark was also in a TV serial called *Catch Us If You Can*.

82 Ginger Meggs
   Run Rebecca Run
83 The Winds of Jarrah
84 Bodyline
85 Mad Max Beyond Thunderdome

Seryozha Bobrovski in Detski sad

Seryozha Bobrovski

USSR

b: circa 1969

In his two films of 1984 – as a boy dancer in *Detski sad* and a boy poet in *Vera, Nadezhda* – Bobrovski showed himself the finest kind of young Russian actor, with an athlete's body and a strong, sensitive face full of humour and panache.

81 Vasili i Vasilisa (Vasili and Vasilissa)
84 Detski sad (Kindergarten)
   Vera, Nadezhda, Lyuboff
     (Faith, Hope, Charity)

Alan Esquivel

NICARAGUA

b: circa 1969

In a Nicaragua torn by civil war, a boy dreams of flying like a condor, and in trying to turn fantasy into reality falls from a tree and is crippled. Even this

Alan Esquivel in Alsino y el condor

fails to quell his imagination; but his first experience of flying, by an ironical twist, is in the helicopter of an American pilot fighting with the Contras. (Played, in a further twist, by the former child star Dean Stockwell◇.)

82 Alsino y el condor (Alsino and the condor – NC/MX/CU/CR)

Holý in Za trnkovym keřem *with Gustáv Valach*

Tomáš Holý

CZECHOSLOVAKIA

b: circa 1969

Tomáš, a pudgy little comedian, became a national favourite in Václav Gajer's three films of country life during 1979-80, and also in a TV serial called 'On the Way to Atlantis'.

78 Setkáni v červenci (July meeting)
79 Na pytlácke stezce (On the poacher's path)
Pod jezevči skálou (Under Badger's Rock)
Postaveni mimo hru (Off-side)
Upir ve věžáku
   (Vampire in the tower block)
80 Prázdniny pro psa (Holiday for a dog)
Za trnkovym keřem (Behind the sloe-bush)
81 Utěky domů (Escaping home)

Martin Mikuláš

CZECHOSLOVAKIA

b: circa 1969

The hero of *The Golden Eels* is Prdelka, a little boy of eight or so who goes with his family on a fishing holiday in the autumn of 1939. His Jewish father develops an obsession with the famous eels of the local river, but catches few.

After war breaks out, the Germans remove Prdelka's father and elder brothers to a concentration camp. The child and his mother remain in the 'golden eels' district, moving into a cottage that had been his grandmother's, and he takes over his father's passion for fishing, braving all sorts of dangers from river bailiffs and German soldiers to practise his art. At last, one day, he gets a miraculous haul of eels – but at his moment of triumph decides they are too beautiful to die, and lets them go again. (They represent, clearly, the souls of the imprisoned.)

Karel Kachyňa's lyrical direction, abetted by the stirring music score of Luboš Fišer, makes *The Golden Eels* an unforgettable film, but Martin Mikuláš' contribution as Prdelka is vital: a slender, frisky little boy with a clownishly thoughtful face, easily dashed and easily cheered again.

Kachyňa gave him a marginal role a couple of years later in his TV movie *Counting Sheep.*

79 Zláti úhoří (The golden eels)
81 Počitani oveček (Counting sheep)

Oussama Nadir

EGYPT

b: circa 1969

In the final 'judgment scene' of Youssef Chahine's film, Oussama appears, his hair silver-lacquered and unicorn-quiffed, as 'the spirit of puerile irresponsibility'.

82 Hadduta misriya (Egyptian Story)

Mads M. Nielsen

DENMARK

b: circa 1969

Mads, who played the lead in Ebbe Nyvold's film, is the son of actors Ole Møllegaard and Lane Lind. In this bicyclistic road movie he flees Denmark's hard-pressed police force, shearing his

Liberator: Martin Mikuláš in Zláti úhoří

377

ample locks and falling in with a girl of his own age. The two of them precipitate a fair amount of human misery.

83 Drengen der forsvandt
   (The boy who disappeared)

Eloquent: Yanogo in Wěnd Kûuni

Serge Yanogo

BURKINA FASO

b: circa 1969

The remarkable *Wěnd kûuni*, directed by Gaston J.M. Kaborè, set out beautifully the tough life of a mute boy employed as shepherd in the wilds of Burkina Faso (formerly the Upper Volta) in a folk-tale which revealed, Kaborè said, 'the psychology, the ghosts, the contradictions and the ethics of a society whose everyday tranquillity is sometimes host to sudden, tragic upheavals.'

The strongest social theme is the cruel tribal law of the arranged marriage (as in the Chinese film *Yellow Earth*), which is indirectly responsible both for the boy's loss of speech and its recovery.

82 Wênd kûuni (Gift of God)

Cocky: de Munk

Danny de Munk

HOLLAND

b: 19 Feb 70 (Amsterdam)

This irresistible urchin – somewhat in the Darryl Hickman ◇ mould – made a powerful debut in Guido Peters' remake of the *Ciske* story (from a novel by Piet Bakker) first filmed by Wolfgang Staudte in 1955, with DICK VAN DER VELDE in the title role.

Danny was far cockier than Van der Velde, presenting an almost suicidally uncompromising character. Ciske empties a pot of ink over his schoolmistress, kicks a local crook up the backside, and in due course (after great provocation, it must be said) sticks a carving-knife into his appalling mother. He moves inexorably from reformatory to reformatory, alienating nearly everyone on his way. But his long calvary from cheeky chappie to matricide is made absorbing by Danny's unmistakable star quality – the anger, the amazing grin.

Peters' film is marred, however, by two-dimensional acting from the adults and by the music score, ill-suited to a

story set in the slums of 1934 Amsterdam. There is even a 'theme song', a sort of mournful rock ballad, belted out by Danny himself. (He had a powerful voice and in due course became a pop star.)

After making many records and many TV appearances, Danny was recalled by Guido Peters in 1986 to play a further lead, as a young fisherman, in *Op hoop van zegen*, based on a turn-of-the-century stage play. It didn't do as well as *Ciske*.

84 Ciske de Rat (Ciske the rat)
86 Op hoop van zegen (In hope of blessing)

Borislav Tsankov

BULGARIA

b: 24 Mar 70 (Sofia)

Borislav's father was an engineer and chemist, his mother an economist, so the child was likely to be formidably intelligent. Just as important, from the point of view of his first director and screenwriter, Ranghel Vulchanov, he had a marvellously open and expressive face.

Reformer: Borislav Tsankov in Lachenite obouvki na neznainiya voin

As the observing eye of *Lachenite obouvki* – representing, really, Vulchanov himself as a child in the 1930s – Borislav watches the pomp and revelry of a village wedding, then dreams of imposing village justice on the decadent city.

Ricky Schroder

USA

b: 13 Apr 70 (Staten Island)

Both Richard Schroder, Jr., and his elder sister Dawn modelled and did TV commercial work from early childhood. Their father was Brooklyn district manager of the New York Telephone Company.

When Franco Zeffirelli chose Ricky to play the Jackie Cooper ◇ role in his updated Florida remake of *The Champ*, everyone's advance reaction was: 'Far too pretty, far too cute.' But Zeffirelli worked hard to remove the professional cuteness, and having done so regarded Schroder as more spontaneous than Cooper. 'I treated him like an adult,' he said.

As the small son of Jon Voight's divorced and gone-to-seed boxer, the cherubic Ricky conquered all doubts

Well suited: Ricky Schroder goes visiting in the 1978 Champ

False hopes: Schroder with Jon Voight in The Champ

with one of the most emotional child performances ever seen. His face would at one moment be radiant with joy, but a minute later redden and crumple into a flood of tears: he was, by general consent, the champion weeper of our times, and it was genuinely painful to watch the tiny creature racked and heaving with grief.

If Ricky hadn't the delightful grubbiness of Jackie Cooper, he could equal him for sheer feeling. For instance, the reunion in an empty stadium with his father, newly released from prison, left audiences in a sodden heap. As a film, though – Schroder for Cooper, Voight for Beery, Zeffirelli for Vidor – it was indeed too pretty by far.

After this triumph, a follow-on vehicle was the next problem, and a cinematic toughening-up of Ricky was decided on. In *The Last Flight of Noah's Ark*, Disney teamed him with Elliott Gould, Genevieve Bujold and a cargo of farmyard animals in

a desert island adventure. In *The Earthling*, abruptly orphaned when his parents' camper topples into a grand Australian canyon, he was taught lifecraft by a haggard old William Holden, who had gone up into the mountains to die.

Thus masculated, he was castable in the sissy role of all time. In Jack Gold's *Little Lord Fauntleroy* – opposite an Alec Guinness almost as crusty as William Holden had been – Ricky was wholly enchanting and produced an almost definitive Ceddie: as pure and plucky an angel of *noblesse oblige* as could have hovered in Mrs Burnett's wildest dreams, though we were denied the shoulder-length curls, and the lace collars were rather skimpy.

In 1984 he started a long run in the TV sitcom 'Silver Spoons'. In this – as the pampered but unspoilt son of a quaint young millionaire (Joel Higgins) whose chief pastime is playing with toy trains –

he had an amusing script and a chance to sharpen up his comic timing. Needless to say, he proved as professional in this genre as in his previous ones. Though he was allowed some poignant moments, not a tear was shed.

In *Something So Right* he was less convincing as an incipient delinquent, but *A Reason to Live* had him at full strength in the attempt to stop his father (Peter Fonda) from committing suicide. It was a grotesque weepie, but Ricky handled his role with grace as well as desperation.

At this point he took something of a break from filming, but returned in *Too Young the Hero* (84) and *Apt Pupil* (84). Another lead was in *Terror on Highway 91* (88). In between, he proved his toughness by undertaking a trapeze act in TV's 'Circus of the Stars'.

78 The Champ
80 The Earthling (AU/US)
   The Last Flight of Noah's Ark
   Little Lord Fauntleroy (GB)
82 Hansel and Gretel
   'Silver Spoons' (TVS)
   Something So Right
83 Two Kinds of Love
84 A Reason to Live

Corey Feldman

USA

b: 16 Jly 70 (Reseda, Cal.)

Corey, a kind of Jackie Searl◊ for our times, specialised in nerds and meanies and made a good living from it. He was notable in *The Goonies* and *Stand By Me*.

His later films included *The Lost Boys* (87), *License to Drive* (88), *The 'Burbs* (88), *Dream a Little Dream* (88), *Goonies II* (89), *Friday the 13th IV* (89), *V* (89), etcetera. *License to Drive* was his first real starring role, and in *Dream a Little Dream* he not only danced but sang one of his own original songs. He supplied the voice of 'Donatello' in *Teenage Mutant Ninja Turtles* (90).

78 Born Again
79 Americathon 1998

Strong and silent: River Phoenix in Stand By Me

   Time After Time
   Willa
80 Father Figure
81 The Fox and the Hound
82 The Kid with the Broken Halo
83 Still the Beaver
84 Friday the 13th – the Final Chapter
   Gremlins
85 Friday the 13th – a New Beginning
   The Goonies
86 Stand By Me

River Phoenix

USA

b: 23 Aug 70 (Madras, Oregon)
d: 31 Oct 93 (Hollywood)

River Jude Phoenix, the son of high-principled vegetarian ex-missionaries – his father had at one stage been 'Arch-bishop of Venezuela and the Caribbean' for a cult called The Children of God – was a child of the flower-power era, as were his siblings Rain, Leaf, Liberty and Summer. (Though these wondrous names, and the surname Phoenix itself, were post-cult adoptions.)

River's first major part was as the computer-freak Wolfgang of *Explorers*, building his own spacecraft out of junk and harnessing it to an invisible motor force. Though cast as the Type B nerd (learned, bespectacled, liable to be beaten up by louts) he stayed cool even on a TV-crazed alien planet.

River Phoenix – Rio to his friends – had two important roles in 1986, which clinched his position as the strong, silent boy of contemporary US cinema, and a deep, untricksy actor. In Peter Weir's *The Mosquito Coast*, he was the worried elder son of a manic inventor (Harrison Ford) who plans to bring self-sufficiency to a Central American wilderness through a vast ice-machine. River's struggle between loyalty to his father and exasperation at his excesses was genuinely felt.

In Rob Reiner's *Stand by Me* he is the troubled but courageous Chris Chambers (in adult life his courage would be the death of him) who sustains three school-boy companions – admirably played by Wil Wheaton ◇, Corey Feldman ◇, and Jerry O'Connell – on a gruesome, manhood-proving quest for a dead body. This leads them through encounters with a guard-dog, a train on a high bridge and a pondful of leeches, but also through conflicts with each other which are often comic but sometimes upsetting. Each of the four boys experiences a dark night of the soul along the way, but River's is most memorable for his raw honesty and the nakedness of his expression. He was the least meretricious of boy actors.

In 1988 he starred in *A Night in the Life of Jimmy Reardon*, *Little Nikita* and *Running on Empty* before a brief hero-as-boy appearance in *Indiana Jones and the Last Crusade* (89). After offbeat roles in *I Love You to Death* (90) and *Dogfight* (91), he had an even odder lead in *My Private Idaho* (91) as a narcoleptic prostitute, and almost redeemed this profoundly infuriating film. The comedy-thriller *Sneakers* followed in 1992.

Then, appallingly, at the end of October 1993, with a leading role in *Interview with the Vampire* awaiting him, River Phoenix collapsed and died of drugs after leaving a night club. Hardly any actor of his age could have been worse spared. The gods really pick them.

82 'Seven Brides for Seven Brothers' *(TVS)*
84 Celebrity
85 Explorers
   Robert Kennedy and His Times
   Surviving
86 Circle of Violence
   The Mosquito Coast
   Stand By Me

River's younger brother LEAF PHOENIX (born 28 Oct 74), who had also been acting for some years, had leads in *Space Camp* (86), *Russkies* (87), *Secret Witness* (87) and *Parenthood* (89).

Alan Cox

BRITAIN

b: 6 Aug 70

Alan, son of the actor Brian Cox, has his father's talent but in a less bullish form. As a boy at least, he was a dreamer and a doubter, with a baffled British decency which made him a delightful Young Doctor Watson in *Young Sherlock Holmes*.

He was capable of considerable feeling, as he showed when playing the much-parodied role of the doomed William in *East Lynne*. It was impossible to laugh when, pallid and sweat-soaked, he took leave of his little brother: 'Goodbye, Archie dear. I'm going to heaven – that bright blue sky, you know.' The spectre of 19th-century child mortality, when such farewells must have been all too common, was chillingly present, and Cox was tremendous.

As the author-as-a-boy figure in John Mortimer's *Voyage Round My Father* he had little acting to do, but had a ball in the title role of the TV play *Man of Letters*, as a schoolboy in love with a waitress at the local tea-shop, plaguing her with ill-directed declarations of passion.

82 East Lynne
   A Voyage Round My Father
84 Man of Letters
85 Young Sherlock Holmes and the
   Pyramid of Fear

Bertil Guve

SWEDEN

b: 9 Sep 70

Fanny and Alexander, Ingmar Bergman's 'farewell to the cinema', is a glorious plumcake of nostalgia, melodrama, semi-autobiography and magic, showing the master so much at the height of his powers that it seems inconceivable he won't make another major film. Mixed in with the fun there is grief and horror enough, but none of the gloomy self-torment of his middle period.

The 'ladies first' title is a misnomer, since poor Fanny (the sweetly stolid Pernilla Allwin) is not only the younger and alpha-betically the second, but hardly says a word or lifts a finger in the film. It's

Floppy fighter: Bertil Guve in Fanny och Alexander

her ten-year-old brother Alexander (Bertil Guve), intellectual and dreamer, who is at the centre of the action throughout. When his father, a provincial actor-manager, collapses while rehearsing as the Ghost in 'Hamlet' and dies, his mother – before those shoes are old, etcetera – marries the handsome Bishop who conducts the funeral. Then, Alexander's father returns as a ghost. The Bishop hasn't poisoned the father, it's true, but there can be little doubt what role Alexander is playing. Even his mother comments on it.

Bishop Vergerus removes his wife and children from their comfortable home and relatives and imprisons them in his own icy house. Alexander rebels, and is brutally punished. But he and Fanny are mysteriously rescued by his grand-mother's old lover, a Jewish antiquarian, and by further magic – or accident – Alexander, at one or two supernatural removes, kills his hated stepfather, and the family is reunited. (Though the Bishop's ghost now replaces the father's, and threatens to be a less benign presence.)

Bertil Guve, a pale, dark, brooding bean-pole, has a deceptive softness of appear-ance as we see him playing with his toy theatre or feasting and dancing in the family's Christmas celebrations. When the bad business starts, he reveals courage, bitter humour and a smouldering fury: his exchanges with the cunning Bishop are memorable. The floppy boy has become a resistance fighter.

Bergman used him again, but only mar-ginally, in *After the rehearsal*, a chip from the artist's workbench.

81 Fanny och Alexander
    (Fanny and Alexander)
83 Efter repetitionen (After the rehearsal)

Indars Lācis

USSR – Latvia

b: 1970 (Riga)

Aivars Freimanis' *Puika* (The Boy) was based on a popular autobiographical novel. In the setting of a Latvian farm-

Little Latvia: Indars Lācis in Puika

house at the end of the 19th century, the child Jancis develops the eye of a poet as he watches the beauties and difficulties of the world around him. *Puika* won the 'Big Christopher' prize as the best Latvian film of its year, and little Indars Lācis was superb.

77 Puika (The boy)

Eight years later, *Sprīdītis* (Tom Thumb) was a kind of fairy tale in which a brave but undersized Latvian boy travels the world in search of the Happy Land of his imagination, only to discover in the end that Happy Land is the very home he had left behind. Gunars Piesis' fine film won international prizes at the Gidron and Buenos Aires festivals, greatly helped by the irresistible eagerness of RONALDS NEILANDS (born in Riga in 1975).

Vitali Sedletski

USSR

b: 1970

The Black Hen is a 19th-century children's classic by Antoni Pogorelski, who wrote it for his little nephew, Alexei Tolstoi. It's about a boy called Alyosha Lanskoi, whose kind parents send him away – for his own good, of course – to a posh

Bewildered: Vitali Sedletski in Chernaya kuritsa

boarding school where he is bewildered by the rough-and-tumble. To bolster his somewhat tottering morale he dabbles in a childish kind of magic, and suffers pangs of conscience.

Viktor Gres, who directed this film, remembered the book as one which had touched him deeply when he was a child, but which he now saw as too didactic. He played this element down, and chose an angelic little boy from Murmansk, Vitali Sedletski — who was eight when the film was shot, and a newcomer to acting — as its hero.

80 Chernaya kuritsa, ili podzemniye zhiteli
(The black hen, or the dwellers underground)

Tobias Asphaug

NORWAY

b: circa 1970

In the unusual and sympathetic *Sølvmunn* — a near-comedy about a child coping with parental separation and realignment of loyalties — Tobias Asphaug is memorable, a passionate pudding with a mouthful of orthodontic silverware.

81 Sølvmunn (Silver-mouth)

Gary Cadenat

MARTINIQUE/FRANCE

b: circa 1970

Euzhan Palcy's moving *Rue Cases Nègres* — also known as *Sugar Cane Alley* — is a sort of black *Childhood of Gorki* set in 1930 Martinique.

José, an orphan, lives with his tough old grandmother in a shanty-area for cane plantation-workers. He is exceptionally bright, and her dream is to see him get a proper education. José wins a modest scholarship, but his school essays are so remarkable that he is accused of plagiary. He wins through in the end, but his grandmother dies, worn out by her work for him.

Ardent: Gary Cadenat in Rue Cases Nègres

As the old lady, a worthy successor to Gorki's grandma, Darling Legitimus is sublime; but Gary Cadenat's ardent José makes one feel that her sacrifice was not wasted.

83 Rue Cases Nègres
(FR – Black Shack Alley)

A variant on the educational theme came from Mali in 1986 in Cheick Oumar Sissoko's magnificent *Nyamanton*, AKA *Lessons from the Garbage*. This is a tragi-comedy of wrong priorities, which proved a huge hit in its own country. The schools were so underfunded that children had to provide their own seats: no seat, no education.

Since the poor parents of Kalifa (Macire Kanté) can't spare one, he has to collect rubbish to earn enough to buy a seat for himself, then to pay the school fees, which keep going up. It's a desperate film, but often hilarious and exhilarating too, and the children are splendid.

Mads Ole Erhardsen

DENMARK

b: circa 1970

Nils Malmros, director of the remarkable *Tree of Knowledge* (see Jan Johansen ◇), had four years earlier made a study of male character-forming in *Drenge*.

In its first episode, little Mads Ole learns the mysteries of sex — ignorance of which had not been among his major worries — from an appallingly worldly-wise cousin, not much older than himself, who comes to stay. It is a beautiful comedy of innocence and pretended sophistication. (The other stories are more soulful but less entertaining.)

Mads Ole, not surprisingly, had several subsequent calls from TV.

77 Drenge (Boys)

Fabrizio Forte

ITALY

b: circa 1970

A shepherd's life, however peaceful in theory, isn't always a happy one, particularly if you work, as in *Padre Padrone*, for a violent and neurotic father in the mountains of Sardinia. Gavino Ledda's only slightly fictionalised autobiography gave the Taviani brothers the canvas for a beautiful but disturbing film whose childhood scenes are among its most unforgettable.

The little Gavino is brusquely removed from school by his father and assigned to a life of almost total isolation. When he tries to run away, he is caught and beaten. When he meets and talks to another shepherd boy, he is beaten. The only release for the boys is sex with chickens or a resigned donkey. After ten years of lonely boredom, Gavino becomes almost an animal himself, even losing the power of speech. But eventually he escapes, wins himself an education, and becomes a writer.

The crop-headed Fabrizio Forte conveys marvellously the gradual chilling of natural warmth and the loss of hope, in surroundings which at first are frightening and then merely miserable. To those not condemned to work there, of course, they look idyllic.

77 Padre padrone
(Father and master)

Tabaek Jiradith

THAILAND

b: circa 1970

Kampoon Boonthavee's prize-winning book, which inspired Vichit Kounavudhi's *Luk Isan*, told of his bleak childhood in a notoriously drought-stricken area in north-east Thailand, and the endless migrations in search of water which his people were obliged to make in spite of their attachment to their homeland.

Tabaek Jiradith plays the boy with sinuous stoicism.

82 Luk Isan (Man from Isan)

Lee Yu-Tin and Chan Sun

HONG KONG

b: circa 1970

Fuzi qing, written and directed by Allen Fong (Fong Yuk-Ping) is, again, auto-biographical, but tells of a poor urban childhood relieved by fantasy and, in due course, the cinema. After a first experience of magic-lantern shows, Ka-Hing and his friend Siu-Chung rig up one of their own at home, which unfortunately burns most of the house down.

Lee Yu-Tin as the wide-eyed Ka-Hing and Chan Sun as the extrovert friend are a finely contrasted pair.

81 Fuzi qing (Father and son)

Thomas Lücking

SWITZERLAND

b: circa 1970

Thomas Koerfer's *Glut*, set in the Switzerland of 1944, offers metaphors of his country as the still centre of a hurricane, and as a snow-capped lid on a volcano.

Andres, twelve-year-old son of a rich arms manufacturer and art-collector who is earnestly supplying the needs of the German army, finds himself being moulded to his father's image of manhood

and success. It is not enough for him to put aside childish things: Andres has to burn his toy soldiers and watch his teddy-bear ritually drowned by his father.

Thomas Lücking presents Andres with iron control, masking his pain behind near-inscrutability.

83 Glut (CH/DE – Heat)

Yang Tong in Fei lai de xianhe

Yang Tong

CHINA

b: circa 1970 (Qingdao, Shandong)

Yang Tong had leads from 1981 onwards.

80 Di shi ge dankong (The tenth bullet scar)
81 Si ge xiao huoban (Four buddies)
82 Fei lai de xianhe (The crane flies back)
   Mama, nizai nali
      (Where are you now, Mum?)
84 Shenmi de jianta
      (The mysterious sword tower)

Rafał Węgrzyniak

POLAND

b: circa 1970

Young Węgrzyniak, a Warsaw schoolboy, gives a terrific performance in *Kochankowie mojej mamy* as a fatherless boy with an out-of-control mother – played by the unique Krystyna Janda, a sort of blonde Anna Magnani – who finds that the best way to pay the household bills is to look

Desperate: Rafał Węgrzyniak in Kochankowie mojej mamy

for 'protectors', dulling her distaste with drink and pills.

Her young son finds himself doing the shopping and cooking and, between times, having to restrain his mother from drug-dependency and even suicide attempts. There is a terrible scene where he has to tie her up as if she were a mad-woman, which by this time she practically is.

Radosław Piwowarski's film is not all grim by any means, nor is the mother a monster – merely a weak, lost, some-times violent charmer. There is abundant humour and understanding, but a growing sense of hopelessness and a desperate concern about the boy. Rafał Węgrzyniak reveals himself as one of the finest child actors of the European cinema.

85 Kochankowie mojej mamy
(My mum's lovers)
86 Pociag do Hollywood
(Train to Hollywood)
Złota mahmudia (The gold coin)

Another fine Pole was WOJCIECH KLATA in the first of Krzysztof Kieslowski's remarkable *Ten Commandments* series, *Dekalog* (88). He was also the cheekiest of the doomed children in *Korczak* (90).

Jeremy Licht

USA

b: 4 Jan 71 (Los Angeles)

This charming, handsome, intelligent boy – who probably beat his wife, if we only knew – was at his best as the mysterious Anthony in the episode of *Twilight Zone the Movie* where he lures people into a weird house. There they become his doting slaves while he conjures up cartoon monsters from the TV.

He also guested in the soap opera 'St Elsewhere' among others, and had a front-line role as one of the heroine's younger sons in the long-running sitcom 'Valerie': the smooth, successful one, paired with the clumsy, touchingly unsuccessful Willie of Danny Ponce. Jason Bateman◊ was their elder brother, David.

Jeremy Licht, circa 1984

79 And Your Name Is Jonah
The Seekers
80 The Comeback Kid
A Cry for Love
Father Figure
Once upon a Family
81 The Ordeal of Bill Carney
82 Lois Gibbs and the Love Canal
Skeezer
83 Twilight Zone the Movie
84 All the Kids Do It

Victor Chuchkov

BULGARIA

b: 20 Feb 71

Yo-Ho-Ho brought together two doyens of the Bulgarian cinema: the poet and scenarist Valeri Petrov and the director Zacco Heskiya. It chronicles a strange friendship in hospital between a child with a broken arm and a bitter young actor with an agonising injury he despairs of conquering.

The boy, Leonid, senses an affinity with him and asks him to invent a story. The young man embarks on a romantic tale: doubly satisfying to an actor, since he is not only the narrator but (in his imagination) the star as well – the Black Pirate. Leonid, though bored by the repeated intrusions of a glamorous

Damsel in Distress, enjoys the adventure and is bitterly resentful when the actor, in too much pain, tells him to go away.

Finally the actor tricks the boy into stealing some drugs from the dispensary which he can use to kill himself. But in the 'final instalment' of the Black Pirate story – in which Leonid joins him as swordsman and ally – he finds the courage to fight on.

The stormy relationship between these two temperamental creatures is movingly developed by Kiril Variski (the actor) and Victor Chuchkov (Leonid). Chuchkov has a remarkable face, proud and vulnerable, and great delicacy of feeling.

81 Yo-Ho-Ho

Victor Chuchkov in Yo-ho-ho

Sean Astin

USA

b: 25 Feb 71 (Los Angeles)

Sean and his younger brother Mackenzie (born 12 May 73) were the sons of suc-cessful actors: John Astin and the former child actress Patty Duke.

Sean, brace-toothed and endearingly earnest, brought stability to the frenetic *Goonies*, and had the right breathless elan to deliver speeches beginning 'But what if, you guys, just *what if* this map...' He has continued to act, for instance in *The War of the Roses* (89), *Staying Together* (89) and *Memphis Belle* (GB 90), with a lead in *Encino Man* (92).

Peter Billingsley in Death Valley

82 The Rules of Marriage
85 The Goonies
   White Water Summer
86 The BRAT Patrol
87 Like Father, Like Son

Mackenzie, seen mainly on TV, was in *Lois Gibbs and the Love Canal* (81), *I Dream of Jeannie: 15 Years Later* (85) and *The Garbage Pail Kids* (87), as well as the popular sitcom 'The Facts of Life'.

Peter Billingsley

USA

b: 16 Apr 71 (New York)

Peter, as a child, was a kind of bespectacled, de luxe version of Britain's David Hannaford ◇ of the 1950s. With platinum blond hair and china-blue eyes, somewhat too good to be true, he had little of Hannaford's grubby charm – but could act when required.

Having made a modest name for himself as 'Messy Marvin' in Hershey Syrup commercials (he wasn't *always* clean), Peter brought a touch of class to the deplorable Burt Reynolds comedy *Paternity*, and dodged a homicidal maniac in *Death Valley*. In *Massarati* he was the Brain, a tiresomely two-dimensional child genius.

Late in 1981 he joined the TV chat show 'Real People' as one of the hosts and interviewers.

Far his best part came as Ralphie, the demurely manly little hero of *A Christmas Story*, determined come what may to get a Red Ryder air rifle in honour of Our Saviour's birth. His school teacher disapproves, as does Santa Claus himself, in the local department store. But Ralphie finally gets his gun – and breaks his glasses.

The muffled childhood of snowbound Indiana is lovingly depicted in Bob Clark's nostalgic comedy, but there is no joking about the temperature – a boy challenged to lick a metal pole finds his tongue frozen to it. Billingsley is splendid.

He was later seen in *The Last Frontier* (86), *Beverly Hills Brats* (88) and *Russkies* (88).

78 If Ever I See You Again
81 Death Valley
   Honky Tonk Freeway
   Paternity
82 Memories Never Die
83 A Christmas Story
   Massarati and the Brain

Justin Henry

USA

b: 25 May 71 (New York)

In the most famously emotion-manipulative movie of its time, cuddly Justin was the *casus belli* between the Kramers. He's irresistible, though it's doubtful if he can be said to act.

Manipulator: Justin Henry in Kramer vs. Kramer

Three or four years later he decided to have a stab at acting professionally.

79 Kramer vs. Kramer
80 A Christmas Story *(TV special)*
83 Tiger Town
84 Martin's Day *(CA)*
   Sixteen Candles

Graham McGrath

BRITAIN

b: 29 Jly 71

Graham, a middle-class Brit with real temperament, first emerged as Young Pip in a BBC TV serialisation of *Great Expectations*. He didn't have much to do except look brave and loyal in the magical mystery adventure *Krull*, and played Albert Speer as a boy in *Third Reich*.

His first proper lead came in Derek Banham's short TV movie *Last Day of Summer*, based on a short story by Ian McEwan about a friendship between a conventional schoolboy – orphaned and living in a hippy commune – and a fat girl hired as their housekeeper. Annette Badland stole the show, but Graham played with crispness and feeling.

His best role, though – orphaned again, as so often – was in a TV production of Michael Wilcox's wise and delectably characterised play *Lent*, set in an English prep school during the Easter holidays. Graham plays the son of the deceased headmaster, now succeeded by the bone-headed senior member of staff, whom the boy despises and rebels against, being obliged to live under the same roof even out of term. Graham's pride and anger are exhilarating: he defies the wretched Mr Edwards with a panache worthy of the Bishop-defying hero of *Fanny and Alexander*.

It's a great pity that the intelligent and personable McGrath was seen so little in the cinema. He played the young Czar in the historical TV extravaganza *Peter the Great*, but his subsequent parts were less rewarding.

81 Great Expectations
82 Krull
   Third Reich
83 Last Day of Summer
84 Lent
   Peter the Great (US)
86 Paradise Postponed
   The Children of Dynmouth

Graham McGrath in Last Day of Summer

Ke Huy Quan

USA

b: 20 Aug 71 (Saigon, Vietnam)

Ke, the first Boat Person to break into Hollywood, arrived in the USA via Hong Kong, with his family, in 1979. (His Chinese father had owned a plastics company in Saigon.) They settled in Los Angeles the following year, and Ke became the quicksilver 'Short Round' in Spielberg's *Indiana Jones* prequel – a side-kick with a real kick, since he's an expert in martial arts. He's equally adept in escapes through passages and catacombs, by underground railway or collapsing bridge.

In *The Goonies* he is no longer the junior partner but a respected equal, indeed generally superior to his disorganised companions, with a hilarious array of life-preserving inventions. Ke is the new-style Oriental performer – all-action and far from inscrutable.

He has also been seen in the CBS series 'Together We Stand' and 'Nothing Is Easy'.

84 Indiana Jones and the Temple of Doom
85 The Goonies

Henry Thomas

USA

b: 9 Sep 71 (San Antonio, Texas)

The boy hero of *E.T.* was unusual among child actors in being quite without charm, at least of the ingratiating kind. He seldom smiled; his square, thoughtful face was generally worried and, as he got older, rather forbidding. Far from making Henry Thomas unsympathetic, this made one warm to a serious kid facing serious problems.

The problems in *E.T.*, of course, were themselves unusual: the discovery and concealment of a superior alien like a withered, unshelled turtle with haunting eyes. In *Misunderstood* (a lame remake of Luigi Comencini's fine *Incompreso* of 1966) Thomas is a boy thought by his father

No ingratiation: Henry Thomas in E.T.

to be irresponsible and unfeeling: a strong 19th-century story with a tragic ending.

The issues in *Cloak and Dagger* were more traditional: fantasising child witnesses murder and becomes embroiled in Hitchcockian spy-plot. *Frog Dreaming*, the best of the post-*E.T.* vehicles – AKA *The Quest* – transported Henry to Australia, where he stalked a Loch-Ness-type monster in a haunted lake.

Since then, Thomas's biggest screen role has been as Danceny in Milos Forman's *Valmont* (89), a relatively romantic version of *Les liaisons dangereuses*.

81 Raggedy Man
   The Steeler and the Pittsburgh Kid
82 E.T.
83 Misunderstood
84 Cloak and Dagger
85 Frog Dreaming (AU)

Obstinate: Hicks in A Swarm in May

Thomas with Gene Hackman in Misunderstood

Oliver Hicks

BRITAIN

b: 10 Sep 71

The Children's Film Foundation (see pp. 374-5) was founded in Britain in 1951. Thirty years later there came into being a completely separate and much modester organisation called the CHILDREN'S FILM UNIT

This sprang from the work of the playwright and former teacher Colin Finbow, who in the Seventies had started a film unit at Forest Hill Comprehensive School in South-East London. He supplied his own equipment, and a group of film-mad pupils got together at weekends to shoot short documentaries or features – at first a few minutes long, then half an hour, then feature-length. It would hire a van and go off on location during the school holidays, often to Wales or the south coast.

The unit was wholly amateur: the few adult parts taken by parents, teachers and friends, the rest by the kids, who also undertook the camerawork, sound recording, costumes, props and lighting. Only the direction and coordination came from Finbow.

In 1978 the 'Forest Hill Film Unit' made (for £400) its first full-length film, based on Ray Bradbury's *Something Wicked This Way Comes* and arguably, for all its roughness, more atmospheric than Jack Clayton's Hollywood shot of four years later. This was followed in 1979 by an impressive new version of John Rae's anti-jingoist novel *The Custard Boys* (filmed by Philip Leacock in 1961 as *Reach for Glory*). There were some fine performances, and ravishing camerawork by the teenager Amos Richardson. Production costs soared to £1,000. . . .

Two years later, having given up his teaching job, Colin Finbow and some supporters launched the Children's Film Unit as an educational charity, largely funded by grants from industry or local authorities, opening up participation to any kids who were free and eager to make films in their school holidays. Since then, latterly supported and screened by TV's Channel Four, the CFU has produced at least one full-length feature a year. Adult roles henceforth were played by well-known professionals (including Peter Bayliss, Glenda Jackson, Martin Jarvis, Freddie Jones, Charles Kay, Jack May, Ron Moody and Susannah York).

The stories tend to be more sophisticated than the CFTF's, and a particularly exotic one was the 1982 version of William Mayne's novel *A Swarm in May*, about a cathedral chorister who is saved from opting out of a difficult solo by involvement with bee-keeping and ghosts. Eleven-year-old Oliver Hicks was remarkable in the role – shy, troubled, obstinate and enormously winning. He was also in *Captain Stirrick* (81) and *Dark Enemy* (83).

The best of the CFU's other boy 'stars' have been CHRIS CHESCOE in *The Custard Boys*, RORY McFARQUHAR in *Dark Enemy*, ORLANDO WELLS in *Mister Skeeter* (84), JEREMY COSTER in *School for Vandals* (86) and *Doombeach* (90), MAX RENNIE in *Hard Road* (89), BEN BRAZIER in *How's Business* (91), and LEE TURNBULL in *Willie's War* (94).

Outside the CFU, Wells (son of Miss York) has been in films like *The Ploughman's Lunch* and *Maurice*, Rennie has had a lead in *When the Whales Came*, and Brazier plays Peter the goat-boy in Disney's excellent new *Heidi* (94).

Charlie Fields

USA

b: 16 Sep 71 (Brooklyn, NYC)

Charles Fields – as he later billed himself – had the same sharp, pinched face as the hero of *Kes*, David Bradley ◇. He had the air of one used to fending for himself, quick, resourceful and rightly suspicious of the world.

He was marvellous as Kevin Dobson's motherless son in the TV series 'Shannon' – boarded out with grandparents while his detective father earned their bread. Charlie's rare, frosty little smiles were worth waiting for. He was terrifying, though, as a possessed child in *The Demon Murder Case*.

77 The Betsy
79 Orphan Train

81 Fish Hawk (CA)
82 The Electric Grandmother
83 The Demon Murder Case
   The Gambler – the Adventure Continues
   'Shannon' (TVS)
85 The Beniker Gang

Noah Hathaway

USA

b: 13 Nov 71 (Orange, New Jersey)

Noah, who as the boy-warrior Atreyu rode the benign flying dragon (a sort of dog-cum-otter) in Wolfgang Petersen's *Never-Ending Story*, was a graceful and good-looking but not particularly interesting actor. Although his father Robert (an actor too) is half Mohican Indian, Noah seemed too bland to be any kind of warrior.

The 1978 cinema release of *Battlestar Galactica* was a two-hour boil-down of the insipid TV space series.

77 Best Friends
78 Battlestar Galactica
79 High Midnight
   The Last Convertible
80 It's My Turn
81 Separate Ways

Charlie Fields with Will Sampson in Fish Hawk

Corey Haim

USA

b: 23 Dec 71 (Toronto, Canada)

Corey Haim was a strong, serious, sensitive boy with a face the camera loved. His career began in Canada, in a TV series called 'The Edison Twins'.

He then moved down to the USA, and had particularly rewarding leads in *Silver Bullet* and *Lucas*.

Corey's later films included *The Lost Boys* (87), *License to Drive* (88) and *Prayer of the Rollerboys* (90). He was also in the TV series 'Roomies'.

E.T. junior: Cary Guffey in Lo sceriffo e l'extraterrestre

Cary Guffey

USA

b: 10 May 72 (Douglasville, Georgia)

The innocent face of Cary Guffey, holding his arms out in welcome to the UFO visitors to Indiana, became one of the key images of Outer Space mysticism. Extra-terrestrials, Steven Spielberg's story said (and he would say the same in *E.T.*) are not frightening but friendly and morally superior. Hollywood has been saying this – sometimes tremulously – at least since the early 1950s, in films like *The Next Voice You Hear*, *The Day the Earth Stood Still* and *Red Planet Mars*, but Spielberg's spectacular evocation of hopes and fears goes far beyond these in sheer emotional sweep, to a conclusion which is virtually religious.

After this, Stanley Kubrick wanted Cary to be the 'eerie little kid' in *The Shining* – but his parents said no, and Danny Lloyd got the part. Instead, Cary went off to Italy and co-starred with the vast Bud Spencer in a Michele Lupo film. This time *he* was the visitor from outer space (through a slight electronic fault in his space-ship), creating havoc in the local police force and electricity supply, and casually talking to animals.

Wil Wheaton

USA

b: 29 Jly 72 (Burbank, Cal.)

Richard William Wheaton III was a supernaturally skinny kid: at 5'9" he weighed only 113 pounds, or a shade over 8 stone. With enormous brown eyes, he looked as fragile as a new-born fawn, and was inevitably likened to Bambi. (Though in fact it was the voice of a mouse he supplied in *The Secret of NIMH*, a cartoon by defecting Disney animators.)

Wil's big opportunity, to which he rose perfectly, was as Gordie Lachance, the narrator-as-boy in Rob Reiner's *Stand By Me*. Gordie was the future writer, the sensitive member of the corpse-hunting quartet, reassured by his friendship with the staunch Chris Chambers (River Phoenix ◇).

Fawnlike: Wil Wheaton in Stand By Me

His varied encounters with nature – watching a deer cross the railway line, or fainting after plucking a leech from his private parts – are vital, but his robust line in schoolboy fantasy is shown, too, in the campfire story of Lardass Hogan, who wins a pie-eating contest and then spews copiously over the applauding crowd.

81 A Long Way Home
82 The Secret of NIMH *(voice only)*
   The Shooting
84 The Buddy System
   The Last Starfighter
85 The Defiant Ones
86 Stand By Me
   Young Harry Houdini

Draško Roganović

YUGOSLAVIA

b: 24 Aug 72 (Belgrade)

Draško, son of a production manager, made many appearances on TV, with a leading role in the serial *Čitanka*. He was very fine in *Mahovina na asfaltu*, as a mountain village boy who has to go to school in town, an element he finds unutterably alien. Like Gordie Lachance in *Stand By Me*, he will grow up to be a writer.

83 Mahovina na asfaltu (Moss on the asphalt)
84 Citanka (Reading book)
85 Neka druga zena (Some other woman)

Basal el-Abyad

SYRIA

b: circa 1972

Muhammad Salas' *Ahlam al-medina* is virtual autobiography, taking as its hero a country boy called Dib who moves to Damascus with his parents in 1954, in the dying days of the military regime. His grandfather takes them in, and they live precariously and with some uneasiness, never fully accepted but ideally placed to see the tragicomic fermentations of nationalism in their family and in the streets.

Portraits of deposed leaders are regularly removed from the walls and replaced by the next man in. Some way off, the Suez canal is nationalised. Tubthumping patriots prove to be rogues and cowards, and political hysteria reigns.

All the same, there is a lot of human warmth in the film, even nostalgia. 'The past was full of repression,' Salas wrote, 'but there was also a kind of honesty and purity that is absent now....Now there is just prudence and calculation.' Basal el-Abyad's Dib watches it all with a kind of nervous eagerness.

84 Ahlam al-medina (City dreams)

Liu Qiang

CHINA

b: circa 1972

In 1939, a military folk-song collector travels to the mountains of a remote northern province of China. He is shocked to find that the twelve-year-old daughter of the family he's billeted on is likely soon to become the bride of an arranged marriage. (Women in this society are hardly more than chattels and objects of barter.) Her younger brother is withdrawn almost to the point of muteness.

Liu Qiang's face, as Hanhan in *Huang tudi*, is a picture – or rather a blank canvas, revealing nothing. He watches, he listens: and then one day, quite suddenly, up on the mountainside, he bursts into song. His

Blank canvas: Liu Qiang with Wang Xueqi in Huang tudi

ballad, a gift for the serious collector, tells of the joys of bed-wetting, even in wedlock. The surprise is so complete and delightful that the collector laughs helplessly: he teaches Hanhan a communist song, and thereafter the boy is almost chatty.

Qiang, with an interesting proto-punk hairstyle consisting of a frontal brush of hair on an otherwise shaven head, demonstrates that if silence is golden, its breaking can be priceless.

84 Huang tudi (Yellow earth)

Majid Nirumand

IRAN

b: circa 1972

Amir Naderi's exhausting, exhilarating *Dawandeh* celebrates a boy's life on the waterfront of a Persian Gulf port. Survival money is earned by water-selling, shoe-shining, carrying blocks of ice, or retrieving bottles from the sea.

In stifling heat, the kids' favourite pastime is running, manically, after vehicles (even trains), or against each other, or simply solo. At least it expresses their desperation. One young boy, Amiro, finds relief in yelling at ships out at sea.

Finally he decides that he can only get out of his rut through education, and throws himself into it with characteristic fury, bellowing out the alphabet against the crashing waves of the sea-shore. And still, amid extraordinary images of ice and fire, Majid Nirumand runs.

He kept on running in Naderi's *Aab, baad, khak*, a drama of drought set in the parched land of the Iranian-Afghan border. But the Iranian authorities, who had already castigated *Dawandeh* as a slur on their country, and had failed to get Naderi to apologise for it, now banned the showing of both films. Naderi was granted political asylum in the USA, and Majid and his elder brother Mansur Nirumand fled into Pakistan.

84 Dawandeh (The runner)
85 Aab, baad, khak (Water, wind and sand)

Ice and fire: Majid Nirumand in Dawandeh

Another outstanding Iranian film of recent years was Bahram Beyzaie's *Bashu* (86), the story of an orphan boy (ADNAN AFRAVIAN) who flees to the peaceful north of the country from the war-torn south. The urban dialect of this dark-skinned stranger renders him unintelligible to the rural community he lands up in, and his far from silent relationship with the peasant woman who adopts him (in her husband's absence) is extremely moving. Cries and gestures seize the screen with elemental power.

Charlie Condou

BRITAIN

b: 8 Jan 73

This gentle, round-faced boy played Cliff Robertson's son in *The Key to Rebecca*, facing tamish villainy from David Soul as a Nazi. He then played, for the CFTF, the middle-class intruder on rural strife in a new version of Thomas Hardy's 'Our Exploits at West Poley'. On TV in 1987 Charlie gave a moving performance, in *Every Breath You Take*, as a schoolboy coping simultaneously with solos in the cathedral choir, his mother's chaotic love life and his recently diagnosed diabetes.

85 The Key to Rebecca
86 Exploits at West Poley
87 Every Breath You Take

André Gower

USA

b: 27 Apr 73 (Los Angeles)

The handsome André, a pathetic tot in *The Man in the Santa Claus Suit*, waited eight more years for the lead in *The Monster Squad*, but had meanwhile been featured in a mass of TV series and one-offs.

André Gower, circa 1987

Robby Kiger, circa 1985

Robby Kiger

USA

b: 11 Jne 73 (Encino, Cal.)

After 1984 the impish Kiger, touching as epileptic Frank in *Who Will Love My Children?* and plucky in the horror film *Children of the Corn*, was largely occupied as Jack Warden's grandson in the TV series 'Crazy Like a Fox'.

Barret Oliver

USA

b: 24 Aug 73 (Los Angeles)

In *The Never-Ending Story*, Wolfgang Petersen's spectacular movie tribute to reading, Barret was Bastian, the boy with the book, sitting alone in an attic and discovering that the imagination could be more exciting than TV. (If not more exciting than spectacular movies. But presumably Bastian will progress to George Eliot and Tolstoi in due course.)

He had, incidentally, already encountered his storybook champion, Noah Hathaway ◇, in an episode of the TV series 'Battlestar Galactica', in which Hathaway had a featured role.

The brown-eyed Barret Oliver brought such passion and intensity to his gradual involvement in this confused moral fairy-tale – centred on a notably unappetising Ivory Tower – that he became a hot property from now on.

In *Cocoon*, a fantasy about geriatric rejuvenation, he had a somewhat fatuous role as Wilford Brimley's grandson, but had more to chew on in *D.A.R.Y.L.* (stands for Data Analysing Robot Youth Lifeform), as a super-intelligent bionic boy who is also a knockout at baseball and ends up escaping from his military pursuers in a supersonic jet. Barret's sensitive face made Daryl the most human robot of our time.

He continued in films such as *Scenes from the Class Struggle in Beverly Hills* (89).

Uncommon reader: Barret Oliver in The Never-Ending Story

82 The Circle Family
Jekyll and Hyde...Together Again
Kiss Me Goodbye
83 Uncommon Valor
White Dog
84 Frankenweenie
Invitation to Hell
Die unendliche Geschichte
(The Never-Ending Story – DE)
85 Cocoon
D.A.R.Y.L. (GB)
86 Gramma
The Legend of Sleepy Hollow
Spot Marks the X
87 The Secret Garden (TVM)

In *The Neverending Story II: The Next Chapter* (GE 89), Barret was succeeded as Bastian by JONATHAN BRANDIS, a beautiful and intelligent hero with an amazingly plastic face capable of expressing any extreme emotion but few subtle ones.

Emil Minty

AUSTRALIA

b: circa 1973

Minty was not winsome, but full of character. His wildest role was as the Feral Kid in *Mad Max 2*, a terrifying child with a lethally sharp metal boomerang.

81 Mad Max 2
82 Fluteman
Moments
Rubbish
83 The Winds of Jarrah

Christian Bale

BRITAIN

b: 30 Jan 74

Christian, the English boy chosen by Steven Spielberg to play the star role of Jim, survivor of Japanese prison-camps in J.G.Ballard's semi-autobiographical novel 'Empire of the Sun', wasn't exactly a household face at the time.

He had appeared – as a Thatcherite child with strong views about the Idle Workers – in a TV serialisation of Fay Weldon's novel 'The Heart of the Country'. About the same time he was filming, in the role of the doomed young Tsarevich, in the TV block-buster *Anastasia*. There was an extraordinary distinction about both these characterisations, and an underlying vulnerability.

He was seen by Spielberg – and also by the Russian Vladimir Grammatikov, preparing an Astrid Lindgren film in co-production with Sweden. Christian Bale was engaged in *Mio, min Mio*, not in the title role – the excellent NICHOLAS PICKARD starred – but as Mio's loyal friend Jum-Jum. (A very un-Bale name.) It's a fairy-tale set in a modern framework, in the tradition of *The Brothers Lionheart*, and his first wholly sympathetic role.

Jim in *Empire of the Sun* was his first lead, and just about as testing as it could have been. But Christian handled the transformation from pampered middle-class schoolboy to weathered fixer of the camps, with astonishing skill and sureness: the bright eyes dimmed, but they could still glint at the sniff of a deal.

Christian Bale's intelligence and poise, plus his look of pained hauteur, were slightly wasted in his next assignments, playing Jim Hawkins opposite the Long John Silver of Charlton Heston, and the Boy in Kenneth Branagh's star-studded *Henry V*.

87 Anastasia (US/GB)
Empire of the Sun (US)
Heart of the Country (TV series)
Mio min Mio
(Mio, my Mio – SE)
89 Henry V

Bogdan Carp

ROMANIA

b: 23 Nov 74 (Bucharest)

The splendidly unglamorous Carp was a popular, droll Romanian kid-next-door.

80 Muşchetarii în vacanţa
(Musketeers on holiday)
Buna seara Irina (Good evening, Irina)
81 Alo, aterizeaza Strabunica
(Hello, great-grandma has landed)

Spoilt junior: Huckleberry Fox in Misunderstood

Huckleberry Fox

USA

b: circa 1974

Huckleberry, an interesting child with a lopsided smile, was mere George when he started into commercials at the age of six months. His father and mother – a doctor and a nurse – nicknamed three of his siblings Tigger, Bear and Spanky, so he could have done worse.

He was wonderful (as was Polly Holliday) in *Konrad*, a TV version of Christine Nostlinger's fantasy: a lonely lady receives through the post a factory-made child, whom she can't remember ordering. And in *Misunderstood*, as the trouble-stirring younger brother, he was perfect.

83 Konrad
Misunderstood
84 American Dreamer
Terms of Endearment
85 Blue Yonder
Time Flyer
87 The Incredible Ida Early

Michael Nezer in Kidnapning

Michael Nezer

DENMARK

b: circa 1974

Michael's parents were the pianist Ole Nezer and the actress Beatrice Palner.

In two popular family comedies directed by Sven Methling he played the mischievous little Bertram, youngest of three boys. (His elder brothers were played by Tobias Fog and Jesper Lund.)

82 Kidnapning (The kidnap)
   Tre engle og fem løver
      (Three angels, five lions)

Dávid Vermes

HUNGARY

b: circa 1974

In *Hol volt* Dávid (or Arpad — the film and publicity credits differ) plays a boy called Andris who is on the run, searching for his father — with difficulty, since his mother is dead and his birth certificate carries not his own name but the registrar's. What's more, the registrar has

had a nervous breakdown, destroyed all his files and gone missing too. The two of them, plus a disillusioned nurse, meet up and form an anti-bureaucratic cadre. Eventually, cornered, they escape on the creaking wings of a vast iron eagle.

Gyula Gazdag's film is a delightfully subversive story in the spirit of Jean Vigo. Its hero, Andris, a runner almost to equal Majid Nirumand ◇, is splendidly taken by Master Vermes, a burly, resolute boy with the jaw and eyebrows of (unmistakably) Marlon Brando.

87 Hol volt, hol nem volt...
      (It was and it wasn't)
88 Piroska és Farkas
      (Red Riding Hood and the Wolf)

Jamshid Habib

PAKISTAN

b: 7 Oct 75 (Mustafabad Lulaini)

The spirited Jamshid, born in a small town in the district of Kasur, south of Lahore, has been employed in cinema and TV films almost non-stop since 1987.

87 Badal
   Choroon ki barat
   Dulari
   Janbaz
88 Aik jan hain hum
   Allah dad
   Allah ditta
   Bardhast
   Commando action

Jamshid Habib, circa 1987

Anton Glanzelius

SWEDEN

b: 1975 (Copenhagen)

The hero of *My Life as a Dog* is Ingemar
Johansson – not *the* Ingemar Johansson,
though the latter, a national hero in 1959
Sweden, is about to knock out Floyd
Patterson in the USA. Little Ingemar's
mother is dying of TB, and his boyish
high spirits are too much for her, so she
sends him away to a jolly uncle in the
country.

Ingemar, given to barking at moments of
stress, has two dogs on his mind: his own
Sickan, in kennels pending his return, and
the Russian dog Laika, which had died
two years earlier – first martyr of the
space-race. Now his mother dies, and
Sickan, he eventually learns, has been
put down. Feeling anguished and

Nicer than it looks: Anton Glanzelius and Susanna Wetterholm in Mitt liv som hund

betrayed, Ingemar locks himself in his
uncle's summer-house and communicates
only in barks. Thanks to his uncle's
sympathy, however, and big Ingemar's
victory, he pulls through.

Lasse Hallström's treasurable film, bursting with rich and eccentric detail, has a
great hero in the accident-prone Ingemar
of Anton Glanzelius, with his cowlicked
head and features at once blunt and
angular – half beaver, half hedgehog.
(A girl friend, stroking his head, says:
'How nice it feels! I thought it would be
prickly.') Hall Hinson in the Washington
Post described him as 'a pint-size Jack
Nicholson, with devilish eyebrows'.

Anton's father, Ingmar Glanzelius, is a
journalist, and his mother, Margita Åhlin,
an actress. She was playing the title role
in a production of 'Antigone' when her
eight-year-old son had his first walk-on.

Hallström had originally intended to
cast an older boy as Ingemar, but having
once met Anton found him so special
that the part was tailored to fit him. He
identified strongly with it, in spite of sensing that it was really 'a bit grown-up' for
him. By the time it was over he himself

had matured rapidly and found it hard to
snap back into relationships with school
friends. 'A lot of people say a lot of shit to
me,' he complained. 'I don't say anything.
I can hold it in for three months, then I
cry for a whole day. I still live with the
film. . . .'

He was later featured, less successfully,
in a TV film called *Who Can Be Safer Than
a Child?*

85 Mitt liv som hund (My life as a dog)

Pelle Hvenegaard

DENMARK

b: 1975 (Copenhagen)

The novelist Martin Andersen Nexø was
a Danish counterpart of Maxim Gorki, but
the autobiographical childhood volume of
his great proletarian tetralogy 'Pelle the
Conqueror' appeared in 1906, seven years
before the equivalent book of Gorki's
memoirs. In a manner owing more to
Zola, it tells of a Swedish widower and his
young son who emigrate to find work on
a Danish farm. There they undergo every

Christened for the role: Pelle Hvenegaard as the hero of Pelle erobreren

Veselin Prahov

BULGARIA

b: 27 Jan 76

Brown-eyed, innocently knowing Veselin Prahov really could be called the Bulgarian Jackie Coogan ◇, if time hadn't made it a rather meaningless comparison. There's a definite similarity, if Prahov hasn't quite Coogan's cheeky hauteur. He scored a hit in *Dog in a Drawer*, and has starred regularly since then.

82 Kuche v chekmedje (Dog in a drawer)
83 Gore na chereshata (Up in the cherry tree)
84 Tursi su suprug za mama
    (Finding Mummy a husband)
85 Amigo Ernesto (My friend Ernesto)
88 Byagashti kucheta (Running dogs)

Bulgarian Coogan: Veselin Prahov in Kuche v chekmedje

kind of indignity and oppression, until the boy Pelle finally sets off to earn his living in the city (where he will become a trades union activist).

Bille August, director in 1983 of a fascinating schoolboy film called *Zappa*, himself wrote the scenario of his 1987 film of Pelle's childhood, and engaged the magnificent Max von Sydow to play the father. The boy he found for Pelle might have been born for the role, and was in fact christened for it, through his mother's lifelong passion for Nexø's book. With proud, indignant brown eyes, young Hvenegaard has one of the screen's most transparently honest and vulnerable faces, as memorable as Alyosha Lyarski's ◇ as the boy Gorki.

86 Pelle erobreren
    (Pelle the conqueror)

A shorter and sketchier film version of Nexø's childhood story had been directed in 1986 for East German TV by Christian Steinke. His Pelle, a touching little blond called STEPHAN SCHRADER, was more a Mark Lester ◇ than a Lyarski.

Lukas Haas

USA

b: 6 Apr 76

When Lukas was four, his kindergarten class took part in the annual Los Angeles Festival of Masks. He was so committed to his characterisation as a spider that he insisted on *crawling* the entire mile-long parade route – such was the artistic seriousness and iron will of this deceptively meek-looking, jug-eared little boy.

He is best known as the Amish child perilously guarded by Harrison Ford in *Witness*, but was admirable too in *Testament*, though he could do little to redeem the feebleness of *Lady in White*.

83 Testament
84 The Doctor
   Love Thy Neighbor
85 Witness
   Amazing Stories
88 Lady in White
   See You in the Morning
   The Wizard of Loneliness
89 Music Box
91 Alan and Naomi
   A Perfect Tribute

Fang Chao

CHINA

b: circa 1976 (Guizhou Province)

Little Chao has been a star from the age of two-and-a-half, when he played the part of Yuansheng, an orphan brought up in a nursery school, in Xie Jin's film *A, yaolan*.

79 A, yaolan (O cradle)
81 Ku guo (Bitter fruit)
82 Mu ma ren (The herdsman)
   Quanshui dingdong (Bubbling spring)
83 Da qiao xiamian (Under the bridge)
84 Dianti shang (In the elevator)
85 Tuofeng shang de ai (Camel love)
87 Wo zhi liu san tsi lei
      (Lonely cried three times)

Harley Cross

USA

b: 1978 (New York)

84 Mrs Soffel
85 Where are the Children?
86 Once Again
87 The Believers
   Someone to Watch over Me
89 The Fly II
   Hobo's Christmas
   Stanley and Iris

Macaulay Culkin

USA

b: 26 Aug 80 (New York)

While this volume has been going laboriously to press, a new boy star has risen and fallen in the west: a delicate, porcelain-skinned, slightly effete child of huge confidence and little subtlety. After three amusing cameos came the lead in *Home Alone*, which to general amazement (for it was nothing to write home about) was a smash hit, breaking all box-office records short of *E.T.*'s.

The response caught Fox on the hop, but after secondary roles in *Jacob's Ladder* and *My Girl* ('his first screen kiss') came *Home Alone 2*, a fairly shameless rematch, with the same silly burglars being sadistically worsted all over again. *The Good Son* tried Culkin (more convincingly) in a mean role opposite the virtuous Elijah Wood: audiences cheered as Mac fell to his death. By 1994 the porcelain bubble seemed to have burst.

88 Rocket Gibraltar
   See You in the Morning
89 Uncle Buck
90 Home Alone
   Jacob's Ladder
91 My Girl
   Only the Lonely
92 Home Alone 2: Lost in New York
93 The Good Son
   The Nutcracker
94 Getting Even with Dad
   The Pagemaster
   Richie Rich

Elijah Wood

USA

b: 28 Jan 81 (Cedar Rapids, Iowa)

A genuine actor, intelligent and emotional, though no Huck. (Leonardo DiCaprio of *This Boy's Life* would have been near-perfect.)

89 Back to the Future 2
90 Avalon
   Internal Affairs
91 Paradise
   Radio Flyer
92 Forever Young
   Day-O
93 The Good Son
   The Adventures of Huck Finn
94 North

REASONS OF SPACE have prevented our featuring many later famous actors or directors who made brief or obscure screen appearances as children. These include such people as Charles Aznavour, Noah Beery, Jr., Eddie Bracken, Cyril Cusack, George Formby, Lewis Gilbert, Anthony Harvey, Tim Holt, David Janssen, Brian Keith, Hardy Krüger, Arthur Lake, Sidney Lumet, Lon McCallister, Chester Morris, Marius Müller-Westernhagen, Erik Ode (Odemar), Richard Quine, Gene Raymond (Raymond Gion).

Also many who really emerged in their teens, such as Michael Anderson, Jr., Richard Beymer, Frankie Burke, Stanley Clements, Jeff East, Douglas Fairbanks, Jr., Skip Homeier, Franco Interlenghi, James Lydon, Sidney Miller, Graham Moffatt, Anthony Newley, Charles Peck.

Some of their names and early films will nevertheless be found in the indexes.

Boy Film Actors
(Alphabetical Listing)

Those in **bold** type have 'featured entries' in the book, and the page of their entry follows. (If they are 'one-film boys', or remembered for particular films, these may be mentioned – often in the form best known in the English-speaking world.)

The remaining actors – ordinary print – are followed by the titles of films they were in, plus page numbers if they are referred to in others' featured entries. Translations of foreign titles will be found in the *Titles Index*. Notes on Russian transliteration are on pp viii-ix. For the *Nationality Code*, see p 8.

* = Born; † = Died.

Aaker, Dee (US): 241 *Hans Christian Andersen (52)*, *The Kid from Left Field (53)*, *Mister Scoutmaster (53)*, *Bigger Than Life (56)*
Aaker, Lee (US, 25 Sep 43): 241
Abe, Tetsue (JP): *Shonen (69)*
Abélard, Anatole (FR) – *see* **Mary, Anatole 'Bébé'**, 25
Aber, Nestor (US): *Halfway to Heaven (29)*, *Penrod and Sam (31)*, *Chandu the Magician (32)*
Ackles, David (US, *20 Feb 37): *The Adventures of Rusty (45)*, *Son of Rusty (47)*, *My Dog Rusty (48)*
Adames, John (US): *Gloria (80)*
Adams, Brandon (US): *The People under the Stairs (91)*
Adel, Léo (BE): *Un gamin de Bruxelles (25)*
Adeyev, Viktor (SU): *Pod stuk kolyos (58)*
Adiarte, Patrick (US, *2 Aug 43): 240
Adrien, le petit (FR): *Le roman d'un mousse (13)*, *The Curse of Greed (14)*, *Roses of Life (15)*
Afravian, Adnan (IR): *Bashu, gharibeh kuchak (89)*
Agdamov, Ravshan (SU): *Desyat tisyakh malchikov (61)*
Agensø, Anders (DK): 358 *You are not alone (78)*
Ageyev, Volodya (SU): *Slepaya ptitsa (63)*
Ahromi, Hassan Haydari (IR): *Entezar (74)*
'Ahui' (MX): *Robinson Crusoe and the Tiger (69)*, *Johnny Raton (69)*
Aidinyan, A. (SU): *Serdtse poyot (56)*
Airey, Paul (NZ): *Children of Fire Mountain (80)*
Åkerblom, Johan (SE): *Jim och piraterna Blom (87)*
Akimovich, Lenya (SU): *Priklyucheniye Petrushki (36)*
Akopyan, M. (SU): *Karo (37)*
Alankar, Master (IN): 338
Albee, Josh (US): *Jeremiah Johnson (72)*, *Slaughterhouse-Five (72)*, *Tom Sawyer (73)*

Albert, Edward, Jr. (US, *20 Feb 51): *The Fool Killer (64)*
Albright, Wally (US, *3 Sep 25): 138
Alejandro, Miguel (US, *24 Oct 57): 320
Aleksandrov, Borya (SU): *Priklyucheniya Artyomki (56)*, *Na perelome (57)*
Aleksanian, M. (SU): *The colour of pomegranates (74)*
Alekseyev, Igor (SU): *Rikki-Tikki-Tavi (76)*
Alexander, Ben (US, *26 May 11; †c.1 Jly 69): 49
Alexander, Louis (US): *Prince of Players (54)*
Alexander, Tad (US, *29 Dec 22): 113
Alexandersson, Gösta (SE, *16 Oct 09; †17 Mar 88): 40
'Alfalfa' (US) – *see* **Switzer, Carl**, 145
Alfaro, Angel Diaz (ES): *El camino (64)*
'Alfio' (IT): 206 *La terra trema (47)*
Alford, Philip (US, *11 Sep 48): 276
Aliyev, Ibrahim (SU): *Ya budu tantsevat! (62)*
Allen, Ali (GB) – *see* **Alleney, Ali**
Allen, Chad (US, *5 Jne 74): *The Bad Seed (85)*, *Help Wanted: Kids (86)*, *TerrorVision (86)*
Allen, Chet (US, *6 May 39; †17 Jne 84): 212 *Meet Me at the Fair (52)*
Allen, Willi (GE): 42
Alleney, Ali (GB): *Peril for the Guy (56)*, *The Salvage Gang (58)*
Alleney, Tamba (GB): *The Beggar's Opera (53)*, *Moby Dick (56)*
Almgren, Sven (SE): *Luffaren och Rasmus (55)*, *Nattbarn (56)*, *Rasmus, Pontus och Toker (56)*, *Swing it, fröken! (56)*, *Mamma tar semester (57)*, *Mästerdetektiven lever farligt (57)*, *Vägen genom Skå (57)*
Alonso, José Luis (ES): *Los parajos de Badenbaden (74)*, *Paisaje con figuras (75)*, *Camada negra (77)*
Alonso, Pablo (ES): *Los dos golfillos (61)*, *Dos años de vacaciones (62)*, *Marcia o crepa (62)*, *Vacaciones para Ivette (64)*
Alonso, Tito (AR): *Eramos seis (45)*, *A sangre fria (47)*, *Apenas un delincuente (49)*
Alurkov, Yanush (BG, *30 May 53): 299
Alvarez, Pedro (CL): *Valparaiso mi amor (70)*
Amazan, Claude (FR, *18 Jne 59): 327
Ammon, Bernard (CH): *Marie-Louise (43)*
Ancona, Ricardo (MX): *Yanco (61)*
Anda, Raoul de, Jr. (MX): 210
Ande, Michael (DE, *5 Oct 44): 248
Anderiesen, Hansje (NL, *8 Nov 29): *De big van het regiment (35)*
Andersen, Mads Bugge (DK): *Busters verden (84)*
Andersen, Poul (DK): *Barnehjertets heltemod (13)*
Anderson, Bobby (US): 187

Baukov, Vasya (SU): *Detstvo marshala (38)*

Baulch, Alan (GB, *15 Jne 50): *Strictly for the Birds (63), First Men in the Moon (64), The Amorous Adventures of Moll Flanders (65)*

Baxter, Clive (GB, †22 Aug 78): 113

Beard, Matthew 'Stymie' (US, *1 Jan 25; †8 Jan 81): 132

Beaumont, Martin (GB): *Cry Wolf (68), If.... (68), The Boys of Paul Street (69), Blinker's Spy-Spotter (71)*

Beaumont, Richard (GB, *5 Jne 61): *Scrooge (70), Whoever Slew Auntie Roo? (71), Digby the Biggest Dog in the World (73), Great Expectations (75)*

Beauvy, Nicolas (US, *9 Jly 58): 322

Beban, George, Jr. (US, *16 Jne 14; †28 Sep 77): *Lost in Transit (17), Hearts of Men (18), One Man in a Million (20)*

Bebè (IT) – *see* **Notari, Eduardo**, 20

Bébé (FR) – *see* **Mary, Anatole**, 25

Beck, Cornish (US): *The Lone Wolf (17), Broadway Bill (18), Just a Woman (18), White and Unmarried (21)*

Beck, Pierre-Michel (FR, *1938): *Le garçon sauvage (51), Le blé en herbe (52), L'età dell' amore (53)*

Becker, Tony (US): *'The Texas Wheelers' (74), Cody (77), The Onion Field (79)*

Beckett, Scotty (US, *4 Oct 29; †10 May 68): 166

Becklén, Fredrik (SE): 325 *Hugo och Josephin (67)*

Bécourt, Alain (FR, *18 May 46): *Mon oncle (58)*

Becquaert, Olivier (FR): 246 *La femme d'à côté (81)*

Bédarieux, Gérard de (FR): 94 *Zéro de conduite (32)*

Beeny, Christopher (GB, *7 Jly 41): *The Long Memory (52), The Kidnappers (53), Child's Play (54), It's a Great Day (55), Man of the Moment (55)*

Bejan, Gheorghe (RO): *Pustiul (61)*

Bejval, Vladimír (CS): 243

Belding, Dale (US): 200

Belmon, Jean-Pierre (FR): *Les enfants du paradis (43), La fiancée des ténèbres (44)*

Benham, Leland (US, *20 Sep 05; †26 Sep 76): 26

Benkö, Peter (HU, *1 Jne 47): 266

Bennent, David (DE, *9 Sep 66): 362 *The tin drum (79)*

Bennett, Andrew (GB): *Black Jack (79)*

Bennett, Kevin (GB): *I've Gotta Horse (65), Runaway Railway (65), Operation Third Form (66)*

Bennett, Mickey (US, *1914; †6 Sep 50): 69

Ben Youb, sami (FR): *La vie devant soi (77)*

Benzi, Roberto (IT/FR, *12 Dec 38): *Prélude à la gloire (49), L'appel du destin (52)*

Bergman, Johan (SE): *Fimpen (74)*

Berlinger, Milton (US, *12 Jly 08): 36

Bernard, Butch (US): *The Seven Year Itch (55), Toy Tiger (56), All Mine to Give (57), Man Afraid (57)*

Berneis, Peter (GE) – *see* **Eysoldt, Peter**, 43

Bernhard, Göran (SE, *20 Jan 32): 179

Bettles, Robert (AU, *1962): 341

Beymer, Richard (US, *21 Feb 39): *Stazione Termini (52), So Big (53)*

Bhattacharjee, Bibhu (IN, *Sep 45): 388

Bhattacharya, Niren (IN): *Babla (51)*

Bhattarak, Param (IN): *Bari theke paliye (59)*

Bibhu, Master (IN) – *see* **Bhattacharjee, Bibhu**, 255

Bichkoff, Yura (SU): *Patriot (39)*

'Big Boy' (US) – *see* **Sabiston, Malcolm**, 119

Billings, Elmo (US, *24 Jne 12; †6 Feb 64): 54

Billings, George (US, *1925): 142

Billingsley, Peter (US, *16 Apr 71): 386

Binyon, Conrad (US, *30 Jan 31): 174

Biru, Banyu (ID): *Langitku rumahku (90)*

Biryukoff, Gena (SU): *Dressirovshchiki (61), Trudniye deti (63)*

Bishop, Piers (GB): *Tomorrow at Ten (62), Ballad in Blue (64)*

Bjerg, Peter (DK): 358 *You are not alone (78)*

Bjørnsson, Fredbjørn (DK, *10 Sep 26): *Balletten dansar (38), Vagabonden (40)*

Black, Buck (US, †): 84

Blackton, Charles Stuart (GB/US): *The Little Strategist (17), The Common Cause (18), A House Divided (18), The Littlest Scout (18), The Moonshine Trail (19), Passers-By (20), A Gipsy Cavalier (22), On the Banks of the Wabash (23)*

Blake, Bobby (US, *18 Sep 33): 185

Blanch, Jaime (ES): *Jeromin (53)*

Blankenship, Harold (US): *Medium Cool (69)*

Blawut, Jacek (PL): *Echo (63)*

Bleger, Lucas (DE): *Die Linden von Lautenbach (85)*

Blitz, Peter (SE, *15 Aug 38): 209

Blomfield, Derek (GB, *31 Aug 20; †1964): 100

Blusch, Walter (GE): *Das Hermannchen (36)*

Boal, Raymond (GB, *11 Feb 62): *Where's Johnny? (74)*

Boardman, True, Jr. (US, *28 Oct 09): 40

Bobikin, Tolya (SU): *Maksimka (52)*

Bobrovski, Seryozha (SU): 376

Bocancea, Ionel (RO, *7 Feb 51): 328 *Amintiri din copilarie (65)*

Bock, Raoul de (NL, *16 Jly 26): *Mysterie van de Mondschein-Sonate (35)*

Boda, Benjamin (FR): *Judex (63)*

Bodianu, Ion (RO): *Mingea (58), Valurile Dunarii (60)*

'Bodo' (ZA/IT): *Piedone l'Africano (78), Piedone d'Egitto (80)*

Bohigas, Fernandito (MX): *Ya tengo a mi hijo (46)*

Böhme, Matthias and Wolfgang (DD): *Die Jagd nach dem Stiefel (62)*

Bois, Curt (GE, *5 Apr 01; †25 Dec 91): 18

Boitot, Pascal and Patrick (FR): *Six chevaux bleus (67)*

Bolme, Thomas (SE, *21 Apr 45): *Mälarpiraten (59), Pojken i trädet (61)*

Bond, James III (US): *The Sky Is Grey (80)*

Bond, Steve (US, *22 Apr 53): 298 *Tarzan and the Jungle Boy (67)*

Bond, Tommy (US, *16 Sep 27): 153

Bonelli, Francesco (IT): 369 *Eugenio (81)*

Bonnefous, Jean-Pierre (FR, *25 Apr 43): *Les fruits sauvages (53), Les diaboliques (54), Culottes courtes (55)*

Bonsall, Brian (US, 3 Dec 82): *Angel of Death (90), False Arrest (91), Father Hood (93), Blank Check, Lily in Winter, Father and Scout (94)*

Boorman, Charley (GB, *1966): 363

Bor, Hanuš (CS, *26 Dec 50): 286

Borisevich, Ye. (SU): *Konduit (35)*

Boriskin, Pavlik (SU): *Annushka (59), Sudba cheloveka (59), Zare navstrechu (59), Pervoye svidaniye (60), Kiyevskaya sonata (62)*

Borsi, József (HU): *Jutalomutazás (74)*

Borzunoff, Alyosha (SU): *Neobiknovennoye puteshestviye Mishki Strekachova (59), Drug moi, Kolka (61)*

Boss, Yale (US, *18 Oct 1899; †16 Nov 77): 14

Bosse, Peter (GE, *15 Jan 31): 174

Bosselmann, Lutz (DD): 307

Botha, Louwtjie (ZA): *Met liefde van Adele (77)*

Boudreaux, Joseph (US): *Louisiana Story (48)*

Boudwin, Jimsy (US, *29 Apr 17): *The Shining Adventure (25), The Ancient Mariner (25), My Lady's Lips (25), The Scrappin' Kid (25), The Johnstown Flood (26), North Star (26), The Unknown Cavalier (26), One Woman to Another (27)*

Boughedir, Selim (TN): *Halfaouine – l'enfant des terrasses (90)*

'Bout de Zan' (FR) – see **Poyen, René,** 36

Bowakow, Dschingis (DE, *7 Nov 61): 337

Bowyer, Ivor (GB): *Riders of the New Forest (46), The Secret Tunnel (47), The Last Load (48)*

Boyd, Jimmy (US, *9 Jan 39): 211

Brackmann, Günther (GE, *1 Apr 20; †28 Mar 49): *Die blonde Carmen (35), Hilde Petersen postlagernd (35), Die Taler der Tante Sidonie (35), Die törichte Jungfrau (35)*

Braden, Christopher (CA/GB): *The Kid from Canada (56)*

Bradford, Jesse (US): *King of the Hill (93)*

Bradley, David (GB, *27 Sep 53): 301 *Kes (69)*

Brambilla, Franco (IT): *1860 (33), Aldebaran (35), Vecchia guardia (35), Tredici uomini e un cannone (36)*

Branald, Adolf (CS, *4 Oct 10): 45

Brandis, Jonathan (US, *13 Apr 76): *The Secret Garden (87), Poor Little Rich Girl (87), Wrong Guys (88), The Neverending Story II (89), Stepfather II (89), It (90)*

Brandt, Bert (DE, *3 Jan 40): 219

Brantford, Mickey (GB, *26 Mar 11): 48

Brassard, Georgie (GB): *'Rainbow Comedies' (22)*

Brassett, Stephen (GB, *24 Nov 58): *Junket (70), The Trouble with 2B (72)*

Bratkauskas, Dainius (SU): 345 *Polunochnik (73)*

Brauer, Charles (DD) – see **Knetschke, Charly,** 193

Bravo, Danny (US): 271

Bravo, Juliancito (MX): 307

Bray, Richard (US): *Pie in the Sky (65)*

Brazier, Ben (GB, *17 Sep 80): *The Krays (90), How's Business (91), Let Him Have It (91)*

Breakston, George (US, *22 Jan 20; †21 May 73): 95

Brécourt, Jacques (FR): *Champions de France (38), Les trois tambours (40)*

Breen, Bobby (US, *4 Nov 27): 153

Brenner, Hansl (AT/DE, *25 Nov 38): 210

Brick, Mustapha (MA): 282 *Les enfants du soleil (61)*

Bridges, Beau (US, *9 Dec 41): 229

Bridges, Jeff (US, *4 Dec 49): 229

Brignoli, Omar (IT): *L'albero degli zoccoli (78)*

Bristol, Igor (SU): *Zolotiye yabloki (54), Taina dvukh okeanov (55-56), Zare navstrechu (59)*

Brockwell, Leonard (GB, *21 May 55): *Heavens Above! (63), Darling (65), I've Gotta Horse (65), The Heroes of Telemark (65), Headline Hunters (68), S.W.A.L.K. (70)*

Brodie, Kevin (US, *31 May 52): 294

Brodrick, Malcolm (US, *3 Dec 44): 249 *Man on Fire (57)*

Brooke, Michael, jr. (GB): *The Magnet (50), The Mudlark (51), The Long Arm (56), X the Unknown (56), The Secret Place (57)*

Brouwers, Daan (NL): *Wierook en tranen (77)*

Brown, Kenneth 'Buddy' (US, *20 Jan 32): 172

Brown, Tom (US, *13 Jan 13; †3 Jne 90): 58

Brunius, Palle (SE, *5 Nov 09): 41

Brunot, Christophe (FR): 246 *La mariée était en noir (68)*

Bruyninckx, Jefke (BE, *13 Aug 19): 92 *De Witte (34)*

Buckton, Ben (GB, *1964): *The Battle of Billy's Pond (76), The Glitterball (77)*

'Buckwheat' (US) – see **Thomas, William,** 175

'Buddy' (US) – see **Brown, Kenneth,** 172

Budin, Gilles (FR): *Blue jeans (80)*

Buljan, Vladimir (YU): 364 *Poslednja trka (79)*

Bulloch, Christian (GB, *22 Nov 65): 252 *The Boy Who Never Was (79), The Strange Affair of Adelaide Harris (79)*

Bulloch, Jeremy (GB, *16 Feb 45): 251

Bunty, Master (IN): *Nanha shikari (73), Amir garib (74)*

Bupp, Sonny (US, *10 Jan 28; †): 156

Bupp, Tommy (US, *2 Feb 25; †25 Dec 83): 133

Buquet, Jean (FR, *18 Apr 26): 144

Burfield, Kim (GB): 333

Bürger, Peter (GE): *Die Zeit mit Dir (48), Begegnung mit Werther (49), Kein Engel ist so rein (50), Die Tat des Anderen (50), Der Theodor im Fussballtor (50), Hanna Amon (51), Das seltsame Leben des Herrn Bruggs (51), Kinder, Mütter und ein General (55)*

Burke, Simon (AU, *1961): 338

Burlyayev, Borya (SU): *Dva druga (54), Sudba barabanshchika (55), Urok istori (56), Semya Ulyanovikh (57)*

Burlyayev, Kolya (SU, *3 Aug 46): 259 *Ivan's Childhood (62)*

Burns, Bobby (GE): 103

Burns, Michael (US, *30 Dec 47): *The Wizard of Baghdad (60), Mr Hobbs Takes a Vacation (62)*

Burrud, Billy (US, *12 Jan 25; †11 Jly 90): 133

Bury, Sean (GB, *15 Aug 54): 305

Busck, Ole (DK): *Der var engang en krig (66)*

Busquets, Narciso (MX, *9 Sep 31; †14 Sep 88): 177

Buss, Alexander (GB): 364 *The Lost Boys (78)*

Bustamante, Michel (PL): *Opowiesc atlantycka (54), Tajemnica starego szybu (55)*

But, Igor (SU): 122 *Beleyet parus odinoki (36)*

'Butch' (US) – see **Lenhart, Bill,** 172

'Butch and Buddy' (US, Kenneth Brown and Bill Lenhart): 172

Butler, Jimmy (US, *24 Sep 21; †18 Feb 45): 107

Butterworth, Ernest (US, *1906): 27

Butterworth, Frank (US, *12 Dec 03; †6 Aug 75): 27 *The Honorable Algernon (13), When You and I Were Young (13), The Children of the Mission (15), The Circus (15), When Hearts Were Trumps (15), The Bold, Bad Burglar (16), It Can't Be True (16), Storming the Trenches (16), When the Minstrels Came to Town (16), The Young Sleuths (16)*

Butterworth, Joe (US): 52

Butts, Billy (US, *8 Sep 19): 92

Buyl, Nand (BE, *12 Feb 23): 115

Buyzis, Vitautas (SU): 271 *Zhiviye geroyi (59)*

Byrne, Josh (CA): *The Wild Stallion (83)*

Cada, Roman (CS): *Muj brácha ma prima brachu (75)*

Cadenat, Gary (MT): 383 *Rue Cases Nègres (83)*

Caikauskas, Giedrius (SU): 345 *I am (89)*

Caldwell, Peter (US): *Manpower (41), One Foot in Heaven (41), To Be or Not to Be (42), My Heart Belongs to Daddy (43)*

Calenda, Carlo (IT): *Cuore (84)*

Calkins, Johnny (US): 195

Call, Brandon (US, *17 Nov 76): *Jagged Edge* (85), *The Adventures of Ford Fairlane* (90), *Blind Fury* (90)

Callis, Clifford (US): *Kiddus, Kidds and Kiddo* (16), *Charity Castle* (17)

Calloway, Kirk (US, *22 Sep 60): *Summertree* (71), *Cinderella Liberty* (73)

Calpe, Jaime, Jr. (MX): 218

Calvert, Billy (US): *Mr Up's Trip Tripped Up* (12)

Calvert, Keith (AU, *1947): 257 *Smiley Gets a Gun* (58)

Calvo, Pablito (ES, *16 Mar 47): 264

Canstell, Billy (AU): *Those Terrible Twins* (25)

Capelli, Franco (IT): 37

Capra, Francis (US): *A Bronx Tale* (93), *Free Willy 2* (95)

Cardi, Pat (US, *2 May 52): 294

Cardiff, Jack (GB, *18 Sep 14): *Tiptoes* (27)

Cardona, René II (MX, *c.1936): 332

Cardona, René III (MX) – *see* **Coster, Al,** 332

Cardwell, Barry (US): *The Sand Castle* (60)

Carey, Denis (GB): *The Greedy Boy's Dream* (49), *Children of Chance* (49), *Oh...Rosalinda!!* (55)

Cargol, Jean-Pierre (FR, *24 May 57): 317 *The Wild Boy* (70)

Caridia, Michael (GB, *2 Aug 41): 227

Carlsson, Sven-Axel (SE, *1932; †1971): *Sextetten Karlsson* (45), *Maj på Malö* (47), *Nyckeln och ringen* (47), *Mästerdetektiven Blomkvist* (47)

Carlton, Tommy (US): 231 *Tarzan's Savage Fury* (52)

Carnahan, Junior (US, *1904): 24

Carney, Anthony (GB): *Time Trouble* (85), *Fighting Back* (86)

Carp, Bogdan (RO, *23 Nov 74): 394

Carpenter, Francis (US, *9 Jly 11): 51

Carr, Johnny (US, †27 Nov 56): 30

Carr, Stephen (US, †20 May 86): 30

Carr, Thomas (US, *4 Jly 07): 30

Carrière, Matthieu (DE, *2 Aug 50): 284

Carrington, William (GB): *Two Little Vagabonds, or The Pugilistic Parson* (03), *Dotheboys Hall* (03), *The Apple Woman* (04)

Carson, Hunter (US, *26 Dec 75): *Paris, Texas* (84), *Invaders from Mars* (86)

Carson, Shawn (US): *The Funhouse* (80), *Cry for the Strangers* (82), *Something Wicked This Way Comes* (82)

Casarotti, Ettore (IT, *22 Oct 11): 51

Cascio, Salvatore (IT): *Nuovo Cinema Paradiso* (88), *Stanno tutti bene* (90), *The Pope Must Die* (GB 91)

Casey, Kenneth (US, *10 Jan 1899; †10 Aug 65): 12

Cavell, Marc (US, *26 Jne 39): *Thunder in the East* (52), *The Man from the Alamo* (53), *Diane* (55)

Çelia, Ilir (AL): 338

Çelik, Engin (TR): *Yol* (82)

Černohorský, Ilja (CS): *Dobrodružství na Zlaté Zátoce* (55)

Černý, Vladimír (CS): *Janošik* (63)

Cerusico, Enzo (IT, *22 Nov 37): 206

Červenka, Mirek (CS): *Honzíkova cesta* (56)

Cesar, Darko (YU): 307

Cestiè, Renato (IT, *11 Jan 63): 343 *The Last Snows of Spring* (73)

Chakravarty, Kushal (IN): *Sonar kella* (74)

Chambot, Jean-Georges (FR, *27 Apr 36): *Le sorcier du ciel* (48), *Singoalla* (49), *Les anciens de Saint-Loup* (50)

Chan Sun (HK): 384

Chaney, Chubby (US, *18 Jan 18; †29 May 36): 85

Chang, Danny (US, *25 Mar 47): 265

Chant, Cyril (GB): *The Lone Scout* (29), *When Scouting Won* (30)

Chaouch, Mahdi (TN): 320 *Viva la Muerte* (71)

Chapeland, Claudy (FR, *27 Nov 44): 249

Chapin, Billy (US, *28 Dec 43): 242 *Night of the Hunter* (55)

Chapin, Michael (US, *25 Jly 36): 198

Chapin, Tom (GB): *Lord of the Flies* (61)

Chaplin, Michael (US): *Limelight* (51), *A King in New York* (57)

Charles, Richard (GB, *17 Jne 71): *Oliver Twist* (82)

Charlesworth, John (GB, *21 Nov 34; †2 Apr 60): 191 *Tom Brown's Schooldays* (50)

Charney, Kim (US, *2 Aug 45): 254

Chassay, Clancy (GB): *Wittgenstein* (93)

Chatterji, Siddhartha (IN): *Sonar kella* (74)

Chauveau, César (FR): 333

Chelidze, Rodam (SU): *Mayakovski nachinalsa tak* (58)

Chernishoff, Yura (SU): 70

Chernoff, Misha (SU): *Pedagogicheskaya poema* (55), *Kogda poyut solovyi* (56)

Cherstvoff, Alyosha (SU): 352 *Orphans* (77)

Chescoe, Chris (GB, *19 Jly 66): 389 *The Custard Boys* (79), *Captain Stirrick* (81)

Chevalier, Roberto (IT, *14 Mar 52): 294

Chilikin, Andrei (SU): *Chuk i Gek* (53)

Chinn, B. Cave (GB): *Where the Rainbow Ends* (21)

Chirlea, Nuţă (RO): 250 *Ciulinii Baraganului* (57)

Chitaya, Otar (SU): *Kolibel poeta* (47)

Choloyev, S. (SU): *Zub akuli* (59)

Chorbadjiev, Kliment (BG): *Ivan i Aleksandra* (88)

Christiansen, Albert (SE): *Mälarpirater* (23)

Chuchkov, Victor (BG, *20 Feb 71): 385 *Yo-Ho-Ho* (81)

Chugunoff, Yura (SU): *Chuk i Gek* (53), *Poema o more* (58)

Chursin, Kolya (SU): *Dva Fyodora* (58), *Malchiki* (59)

Chusseau, Gilles (FR): *Paris vu par...* (64)

Chylek, Eugeniusz (PL/GB): *Johnny on the Run* (54)

Ciamaca, Julien (FR): *La gloire de mon père* (90), *Le château de ma mère* (90)

'Cinessino' (IT) – *see* **Giunchi, Eraldo,** 28

Claessen, Abel (NL): *De nachttocht* (83)

Clark, Andy (US, *Mar 03; †16 Nov 60): 21

Clark, Bobby I (US, *c.1926): *Trigger Smith* (39), *Overland with Kit Carson* (39), *The Sagebrush Family* (39)

Clark, Bobby II (US, *1946): 261 *'Casey Jones'* (57)

Clark, Peter (GB): *Bloody Kids* (79)

Clark, Roy (US): 21

Claudio, Jean (FR, *28 Mar 27): 150

Clay, Noland (US, *24 May 57): *The Stalking Moon* (68)

Clerckx, Eric (BE, *30 May 64): 348

Clifford, Tommy (GB/US, *19 Sep 18): *Song o' My Heart* (30), *Part Time Wife* (30)

'Clo-Clo' (FR) – *see* **Machin, Claude,** 109

Cobb, Joe (US, *7 Nov 17): 82

Coffey, Cameron (US): *Little Brownie's Bravery* (16), *The Heart of Youth* (19), *The Woman Michael Married* (19), *Polly of the Storm Country* (20), *The Little Clown* (21), *Passing Thru* (21)

Coffey, John (IE): *War of the Buttons* (93)

Coghlan, Junior (US, *15 Mar 16): 71

East, Jeff (US, *27 Oct 57): *Tom Sawyer (73)*
Eastwood, Kyle (US): *Honkytonk Man (82)*
Eberts, David (US): 355 *Burning Secret (88)*
Eccles, Teddy (US, *9 Jne 55): 309
Edmonds, Fella (GB, *25 Oct 40): 223
Edwards, Hugh (GB): 267 *Lord of the Flies (61)*
Edwards, Sebastian Rice (GB): 363 *Hope and Glory (87)*
Egi, Toshio (JP, *4 Jne 52): 295
Einarsson, Einar Örn (IS, *23 Sep 76): *Nonni i Manni (87)*
'Eiros' (ZA): *The Gods Must Be Crazy II (88)*
Eis, Heiki (AT, *19 Jan 40): 219
Eisenmann, Ike (US, *21 Jly 62): 340
El-Abyad, Basal (SY): 391 *Ahlam al-medina (84)*
Elikomov, Oleg (SU): *Vzlomshchik (87)*
Eliztratov, Szergej (HU): 330
Ellis, Christopher (GB): *The Flood (63), The Pumpkin Eater (64), The Sandwich Man (66), The Nightcomers (71)*
Ellis, Ian (GB): *The Day the Earth Caught Fire (61), The War Game (62), The Flood (63), The Sky Bike (67), The Magnificent 6½ (68)*
Emery, Alain (FR): 224 *The Wild Stallion (53)*
Emrich, Serge (FR, *6 Aug 30; †June 79): 160
Enchev, Ivan (BG): *Nezavursheni igri (63)*
Enkelmann, Uwe (DE, *23 Jan 62): 337
Epstein, Sasha (SU): *Yevreiskoye shchaste (25), Kirilcho (26)*
Erdélyi, Dáni (HU): *Apa (66)*
Erhardsen, Mads Ole (DK): 383 *Drenge (77)*
Erimitchoi, Ivan (FR, *11 Feb 58; †5 May 75): 321 *Pic et pic et colégram (71)*
Ernest, George (US, *20 Nov 21): 108
Ershov, Alyosha (SU): *Dodumalsya, pozdravlayu! (77)*
Ersöz, Celal (TR, *20 Apr 43): 240
Erven, Peter (NL): *Dik Trom en zijn dorpsgenoten (73), Dik Trom knapt 't op (74)*
Eser, Archibald (DE): 333
Esquivel, Alan (NC): 376 *Alsino and the condor (82)*
Ess, Misha (SU): *Polyot k tisyacham solnts (63)*
Eugens, Arthur Fritz (GE, *31 Oct 30): 171
Evans, Angelo (US): *Angelo My Love (83), Saving Grace (85)*
Evans, Lucas (CA): *Tommy Tricker and the Stamp Traveller (88)*
Eyer, Richard (US, *6 May 45): 253
Eyer, Robert (US, *6 May 48): 253 *The Dark at the Top of the Stairs (60), Back Street (61)*
Eysoldt, Peter (GE, *1 Apr 10; †4 Nov 85): 43

Fagerlund, Benny (DK, *6 Dec 28): 161
Fairbanks, Douglas, jr. (US, *9 Dec 09): *Stephen Steps Out (23), Air Mail (24)*
Faith, Dale (US): *The Accusing Toe (18)*
Falk, Lauritz (SE, *16 Nov 09; †1966): 41
Fang Chao (CN): 398
Faragó, Gyuri (HU): 61 *A Pál utcai fiuk (24)*
Farguette, Gabriel (FR): 154
'Farina' (US) – *see* **Hoskins, Allen**, 99
Fehér, Gábor (HU): *Jób lázadása (83)*
Fehér, Hans (AT, *14 Sep 22; †1 Apr 58): 112
Fejtö, Raphael (FR): *Au revoir les enfants (87)*
Feldman, Corey (US, *16 Jly 70): 380

Feldt, Peter (AT, *1 Apr 41): 226
Fenton, Simon (US): *The Power of One (91), Matinee (93)*
Ferendeles, Massimiliano (IT): *Cuore di mamma (69)*
Fernandez, Freddy (MX): 193
Ferrari, Tao (IT, *2 Feb 29): 163
Ferrario, Adrian (AR): *Tiro al aire (80)*
Ferreira, Nuno (PT): *O sangue (89)*
Ferrell, Ray (US, *24 Aug 49): *Zero Hour (57), Hell's Five Hours (58), The Remarkable Mr Pennypacker (59), Plunderers (60), Strangers When We Meet (60)*
Ferreux, Benoît (FR, *29 Sep 55): 311 *Souffle au coeur (70)*
Fesechko, Lenya (SU): 123
Fields, Charlie (US, *16 Sep 71): 389
Figueroa, Ruben (US, *5 Dec 58): 320 *Popi (69)*
Fijewski, Tadzio (PL, *14 Aug 11; †1977): 87
Filatov, Andrei (SU): *Priklyucheniya Tolya Klyukvina (64)*
Filip, Josef (CS): 313
Filip, Mihai (RO): *Prea mic pentru un razboi atit de mare (69), Padurea perduta (71)*
Finkbeiner, Peter (DE, *15 Jly 42): 233 *Emil and the Detectives (54)*
Finzi, Christopher and Nigel (GB): *The Starfish (52)*
Fioravanti, Giusva (IT, *28 Mar 58): 322
Fischer, Xander (NL): *Monsieur Hawarden (68)*
Fisenko, Yura (SU): *Taina Vip (59), Devchonka, s kotoroi ya druzhil (61), Rodnaya krov (63)*
Fisher, Jasen (US): *Parenthood (89), Hook (91)*
Fitzgerald, Ciarán (IE): *Into the West (92), All Things Bright and Beautiful (94)*
Fitzgerald, Gregg (IE): *War of the Buttons (93)*
Fitzpatrick, Christian (US): *Santa Claus (85)*
Fitzpatrick, Pat (GB): 154
Fiuzat, Allen (US): *Benji (74), For the Love of Benji (77)*
Flateau, Joël (FR, *28 Dec 50): 286
Flensmark, Steen (DK): 262
Fletcher, Dexter (GB, *31 Jan 66): 358
Flohr, Norbert (DD): *Schritt für Schritt (60), Kuttel (61)*
Fomchenko, Igor (SU): *Katok i skripka (61)*
Fønss, Mogens (DK, *5 Dec 18): *Den store dag (30)*
Forest, Jean (FR, *27 Sep 12; †27 Mar 80): 54
Forlong, James (GB, *14 Jne 59): *Lionheart (68), Raising the Roof (71), Rangi's Catch (72), Hijack! (75)*
Formato, Domenico (IT): *Le quattro giornate di Napoli (62)*
Formby, George (GB, *26 May 04; †6 May 61): *By the Shortest of Heads (15)*
Forte, Fabrizio (IT): 383 *Padre padrone (77)*
Fortunato, Pasquale (IT): *Il conformista (69)*
Foster, Richard R. (GB/US): *The River (51), Damn Citizen (57)*
Fourcade, Christian (FR, *22 Apr 42): 233
Fox, Huckleberry (US): 394
Fox, Johnny, Jr. (US): 42
Fox, William (GB, *19 May 39): 212
Frame, Philip (US): 330
Frana, H. (CS): *Pětikoruna (60)*
Franchina, Sandro (IT, *25 Sep 39): *Europa 51 (52)*
Francis, Jon (US): *Will Penny (67)*
François, Michel (FR, *22 Jly 29): 164

Frank, Jeffrey (US): 364 *The Island (80)*

Frątczak, Jozef (PL): *Pieklo i niebo (66)*

Frayne, Stephen (GB): *Froggy's Little Brother (22)*

Freddy-Karl, Serge (FR): *Napoléon (26), La route est belle (29)*

Frederick, Freddie Burke (US, *13 Jan 22; †31 Jan 86): 109

Freitas, Ruben and Marco de (PT): *Les destins de Manoel (85)*

Frerichs, Christian (DE): *Rosa und Lin (72)*

Frezza, Giovanni (IT): *Quella villa accanto il cimitero (82), I nuovi barbari (83)*

Friedl, Fritz von (AT, *17 Apr 41): 226

Friedrikh, Vitya (SU): *Senka s 'Mimozi' (33)*

'Froggy' (US) – see **Laughlin, Billy**, 180

Frost, Philip (GB): *The Last Journey (35), Scrooge (35), Wings of the Morning (37), Kipps (40)*

'Frugolino' (IT) – see **Roveri, Ermanno**, 21

Fryk, Tomas (SE, *18 Sep 66): 362 *Barnens Ø (79)*

Fuehrer, Bobby (US): *'Universal Ike' series (14), Bobby's Bandit (15), Bobby's Medal (15), The Choir Boys (15), A Dark House (15), The Little Soldier Man (15), Safety (15)*

Fuller, Brook (US, *1959): 330 *The Christmas Tree (69)*

Fuller, Jean (FR): *Feu de paille (39)*

Furlong, Edward (US, *2 Aug 77): *American Heart (91), Terminator 2 (91), Pet Sematary 2 (92), A Home of Our Own (93), Brainscan (94)*

Furlong, Kirby (US): *Mame (74)*

Gabriel, Vasso (LB): 282 *Le petit étranger (62)*

Gabriëlse, Bart (NL): *Martijn en de magier (79), De bende van hiernaast (80)*

Gabrovski, Slavyan (BG): *Chicho krustnik (87), Plemennikut chuzhdenets (89), Muzhe bez mustatsi (90)*

Gaete, Emilio (CL): *Largo viaje (67)*

Gagnon, Jacques (CA): 326 *My Uncle Antoine (71)*

Gaillard, Jimmy (FR, *11 Nov 16; †17 Apr 85): 74

Gainsborough, Michael (GB): 168

Galle, Gianluca (IT): *Cuore (84)*

Galo, Igor (YU): *Imam dvije mame i dva tate (68)*

Gaman, Tom (GB): *Lord of the Flies (61)*

Gamble, Mason (US): *Dennis (93)*

Ganev, Dimiter (BG, *10 Apr 67): 367

Ganguly, Rajiv (IN): *Phatikchand (83)*

Ganichev, Tolya (SU): *Malchik s okraini (47), Selskaya uchitelnitsa (47), Krasni galstuk (48)*

Garber, Matthew (GB, *25 Mar 56; †13 Jne 77): *The Three Lives of Thomasina (63), Mary Poppins (64), The Gnome-Mobile (66)*

Garcha, Kiran (GB, *12 Jne 65; †Aug 1984): *Sredni Vashtar (76), Stalemate (77)*

Garcia, Lolo (ES): *La guerra de Papa (77)*

Garlick, Stephen (GB, *7 Jly 59): *Carry On Doctor (68), Headline Hunters (68), The Oxbone Buccaneers (68), Crossplot (69), The Oxbone Buccaneers (69), Scrooge (70)*

Garrett, Leif (US, *8 Nov 61): 338

Garvolt, Jaromír (CS): *Varuj...! (47)*

Gašević, Boško (YU): *Izgubljena olovka (60)*

Gauster, Harald (AT): *Waldheimat (83)*

Gavrilov, Tolya (SU): *Novi attraktsion (57)*

Ge Zuozhi (CN, *c.1924): 130

Gebert, Gordon (US, *7 Oct 41): 228

Geckler, Per (DK): 262 *Flemming og Kvik (60), Flemming på kostskole (61)*

Géczy, István (HU): *Gyermekbetegségek (65)*

Geffroy, Jean-Pierre (FR, *22 Sep 25): 140 *Nous les gosses (41)*

Gemini, Marco (IT): *8½ (63)*

Gencel, Jacky (FR, *14 Oct 41): 228

Genevois, Emile (FR, *1 Jan 18): 84

'Gennariello' (IT) – see **Notari, Eduardo**, 20

Georgadze, Dato (SU): *Malenkiye ritsari (63)*

Gervais, Gérard (FR): *Fantômas (46), Torrents (46), Les dernières vacances (47), Ombre et lumière (50), Trois télégrammes (50)*

Getty, Balthazar (US, *22 Jan 75): 267 *Lord of the Flies (89), Young Guns II (90)*

Geula, Jack (DE): *Regentropfen (81)*

Gévai, G. Simon (HU): *Csók, Anyu (87)*

Gharbi, Ahmed (MA): *Brahim (58)*

Giai, Henri (FR): *L'Ibis Bleu (18)*

Gibson, Colin (GB): *Tim Driscoll's Donkey (54), John and Julie (55)*

Gift, Donn (US, *14 Dec 33): 186

Gil, Miguelito (ES): 282

Gilmore, Denis (GB, *14 Aug 49): 281

Gilpin, Jay (US): *The Southerner (45), Angel on My Shoulder (46), Arch of Triumph (48)*

Gilpin, Marc (US, *26 Sep 66): *Jaws 2 (78), Where's Willie? (78), Earthbound (81), The Legend of the Lone Ranger (81)*

Gion, Raymond (US, *13 Aug 08): *The Kid Comes Through (21)*

Gipps-Kent, Simon (GB, *25 Oct 58): *Lost Hearts (73), The Fire Fighters (74), Great Expectations (75)*

Giraudi, Nicolas (FR): *Le lieu du crime (86)*

Girotti, Mario (IT, *29 Mar 39): 211

Giunchi, Eraldo (IT): 28

Gjurin, Velimir (YU): 221 *Potraga za zmajem (61), Romanca o solzi (61), Ti lovis (61), Srečno, Kekec! (63)*

Glanzelius, Anton (SE, *1975): 396 *My Life as a Dog (85)*

Glaoui, Mehdi el (FR, *26 May 56): 314

Glaser, Darel (US): *Bless the Beasts and Children (71)*

Glaser, Wolfgang (DD): 271 *Der Moorhund (60)*

Gledhill, Nicholas (AU, *1975): *Careful, He Might Hear You (83), Bodyline (84)*

Glori, Gianni (IT, *3 Aug 31): 176

Godet, Thomas (FR): *Toto le héros (91)*

Godorikov, Andrik (SU): *Rvaniye bashmaki (33)*

Golden, Sidney (US): *Little Buster (13)*

Goldmann, Philippe (FR): 346 *L'argent de poche (76)*

Goldsteinkehler, Constantin (FR) – see Golstein, Coco, 94

Gołębiewski, Henryk (PL): 326 *Abel – twoj brat (70), Wakacje z duchami (70), Podroz za jeden usmiech (72)*

Golfier, Richard (FR): 246 *L'argent de poche (76)*

Goloborodko, Yegor (SU): *Kazhdi okhotnik zhelayet znat (86)*

Golstein, Coco (FR): 94 *Zéro de conduite (32)*

Gomba, Peter (HU): *Az igazi égszinkék (57)*

Gomez, Angel (ES): 288

Gomez, Jaime (FR): *Pourquoi? (77)*

Gomez, Panchito (US, *2 Nov 63): 344

Gonçalves, Sidonio (PT): *O miudo de bica (63)*

Goncic, Svetislav (YU, *5 May 60): 331

Goodwin, Harold (US, *1 Dec 02; †12 Jly 87): 20

Gordon, Barry (US, *21 Dec 48): 293
Gordon, Bobby (US, *21 Aug 13): 58
Gorst, Eldon (GB, *14 Aug 22; †2 Mar 50): 111
Goryunoff, Lyosha (SU): *Ai-Gul (36)*, *Rodina zovyot (36)*
Gosselin, François (CA): *The Christmas Martian (71)*
Gottlieb, Cyril (US): *Bread Cast upon the Waters (12)*, *The Drummer of the Eighth (12)*, *Orphan of the War (13)*, *The Social Ghost (14)*
Gower, André (US, *27 Apr 73): 392
Goxhi, Sokol (AL): *Tingujt e luftës (76)*
Graham, William (GB, *1932): 181
Granberg, Lars (SE, *20 Jan 27): *Vi som går koksvägen (32)*, *Synnove Solbakken (34)*, *Våran pojke (36)*
Granberg, Olof (SE, *6 Oct 28): *Vi som går koksvägen (32)*, *Bränningar (35)*, *Våran pojke (36)*
Grant, Eldon (GB) – see Gorst, Eldon, 111
Grauer, Ben (US, *2 Jne 08; †31 May 77): 35
Grave, Serge (FR, *21 Sep 19): 93
Gravey, Fernand (BE) – see Mertens, Fernand, 23
Gray, Billy (US, *13 Jan 38): 206
Gray, Gary (US, *18 Dec 35): 199
Gréco, Fabrice (FR): *Le jouet (77)*
Green, Hughie (GB, *2 Feb 20): 96
Green, Seth (US): *The Hotel New Hampshire (84)*, *Radio Days (87)*
Grendon, Stephen (GB): *Swallows and Amazons (74)*
Grey, Eric (GB): *Where the Rainbow Ends (21)*
Griffen, Ray (AU): *Those Terrible Twins (25)*
Griffin, Russell Francis (US): 89
Griffith, Gordon (US, *4 Jly 07; †12 Dec 58): 30
Grimm, Oliver (DE, *3 Apr 48): 274
Grönros, Roland (SE): *Villervalle i Söderhavet (63)*, *Modiga mindra män (67)*
Gruden, Matjaž (YU): *Sreca na vrvici (77)*
Gruner, Mark (US): *A Little Game (71)*
Grybe, Stefan (SE, *19 Nov 62): *Niklas och Figuren (71)*
Guard, Dominic (GB, *18 Jne 56): 314 *The Go-Between (71)*
Gubitosi, Michael (US) – see Blake, Bobby, 185
Guerin, Bruce (US, *18 Jan 19): 90
Guffey, Cary (US, *10 May 72): 390
Guichard, Roby (FR, *9 Apr 14): 63
Güler, Murat (TR): *Gülibik (84)*
Gupta, Pinaki Sen (IN): *Aparajito (56)*, *Jalsaghar (58)*
Gurev, Seryozha (SU): *Neokonchennaya pesa dlya mekhanicheskovo pianino (77)*
Gusak, Sergei (SU): *Detski sad (84)*
Gusev, Andrei (SU): *Dve ulbki (71)*
Gusev, Valeri (SU): *Taina Vip (59)*
Guskoff, Vova (SU): 262
Guve, Bertil (SE, *9 Sep 70): 381 *Fanny and Alexander (81)*

Haar, Stefan (DE): 250
Haas, Hansi (AT): *Singende Jugend (36)*
Haas, Lukas (US, *6 Apr 76): 398
Habib, Jamshid (PK) – see Jamshid Habib, 395
Haccard, Olivier (FR): *Ce que savait Morgan (73)*
Hack, Hans Peter (DE): *Ina, Peter und die Rasselbande (55)*, *Struwwelpeter (55)*, *Die Gansemagd (57)*
Hackett, Albert (US, *16 Feb 00; †16 Mar 95): 16

Hackett, Raymond (US, *15 Jly 02; †7 Jly 58): 16
Hadl, Tomáš (CS): 308
Haig, Douglas (US, *9 Mar 20): 97
Haim, Corey (US, *23 Dec 71): 390
Haines, Donald (US, *1918): 89
Haitto, Heimo (FI, *27 May 25): 137
Haley, Jackie Earle (US, *14 Jly 61): 335
Halicz, Ludwik (PL, *1947): 269
Hall, Anthony Michael (US, *14 Apr 68): 372
Hall, John (GB, *22 Aug 43): 240
Hall, Newton (US): 61
Hallberg, Nils (SE, *18 Sep 21): 107
Hallerstam, Staffan (SE, *21 May 57): 317
Halm, Florian (DE, *1964): *Ein Jahr ohne Sonntag (70)*, *Wie sag ich's meinem Kinde (70)*, *Hoopers letzte Jagd (71)*, *Wickie (75)*
Halpin, Luke (US, *4 Apr 47): 265
Hämäläinen, Raino (FI): 148
Hammond, Brian (GB): *Innocent Sinners (58)*, *Tiger Bay (59)*, *Make Mine Mink (60)*, *The Loneliness of the Long Distance Runner (62)*
Hammond, Nicholas (GB/US, *15 May 50): 284
Hamrick, Burwell (US, *1906; †21 Sep 70): 27
Hamshere, Keith (GB, *1946): *In Search of the Castaways (62)*, *Play It Cool (62)*
Handzlik, Jan (US, *21 Sep 45): *Auntie Mame (58)*
Hanke, Jochen and Jürgen (DE): *Alle Tage ist kein Sonntag (59)*
Hanley, Thomas (US): *On the Waterfront (54)*
Hannaford, David (GB, *1 Oct 42): 235
Hann-Byrd, Adam (US): *Little Man Tate (91)*
Harkányi, Endre (HU, *26 Mar 34): 231 *Valahol Európában (48)*, *Úttörök (49)*
Harper, Tommy (US): *Bill's Boy (14)*, *The Chimney Sweep (16)*, *The Pacifist (16)*
Harris, Buddy (US, *c.1906): *Daddy's Soldier Boy (13)*, *The Little Bugler (14)*, *The Little Sheriff (14)*, *Tommy's Tramp (14)*, *The Way to Heaven (14)*, *The Man He Might Have Been (14)*
Harris, Neil Patrick (US, *15 Jne 73): *Too Good to Be True (88)*, *Clara's Heart (88)*, *Home Fires Burning (88)*, *'Doogie Howser, MD' (89)*
Harris, Ross (US, *13 Mar 69): 374
Harrison, Andrew (GB): *The Secret Garden (75)*, *Escape from the Dark (76)*
Harrison, Simon (GB): *The Wind and the Lion (75)*, *Sky Riders (76)*
Harron, Bobby (US, *24 Apr 1893; †1 Sep 20): 10
Hartleben, Dale (US): *Inside Straight (51)*, *Her Twelve Men (53)*, *Artists and Models (55)*
Hartleben, Jerry (US): *King of the Wild Stallions (58)*
Harvey, Anthony (GB, *3 Jne 31): *Caesar and Cleopatra (45)*
Hašler, Karel (CS): *Jurašek (56)*, *Žalobníci (60)*
Hathaway, Noah (US, *13 Nov 71): 389
Hauck, Roy (US): 17
Haudepin, Didier (FR, *15 Aug 51): 293 *Special Friendships (64)*
Hawke, Ethan (US, *6 Nov 71): *Explorers (85)*
Hawkes, Ian (GB, *27 Oct 77): *Queen of Hearts (89)*, *Cello (90)*, *The Children (90)*, *Truly, Madly, Deeply (90)*
Hawkins, Jimmy (US): 231
Hawley, Andrew (GB): *The Innocent (84)*
Hayama, Masao (JP, *1 Aug 25): 137
Hayes, Dirkie (ZA) – see Uys, Wynand, 334

Haziza, Fabien (FR, *1906): 28
Headrick, Richard (US, *29 Apr 17): 77
Hebert, Chris (US): *Fuzzbucket (84)*, *The New Man (84)*
Hegedüs, Tommy (HU): *Macko ur kalandjai (20)*
Hehn, Sascha (DE, *11 Oct 54): 305
Heimann, Kai (DK): 47
'Heintje' (Hein Simons, NL/DE, *12 Aug 55): 310
Hemmings, David (GB, *18 Nov 41): 229
Henderson, Dick, Jr. (GB, *30 Oct 22; †22 Sep 85): *The Man from Blankley's (30)*, *Cavalcade (33)*, *Things Are Looking Up (35)*
Henderson, Simon (GB, *18 Mar 65): *Henry VIII and His Six Wives (72)*, *It's a 2'6' above the Ground World (72)*, *Rosie Dixon Night Nurse (78)*, *Danger on Dartmoor (80)*
Hénin, Georges (FR, *22 Nov 13): 40 *Napoléon (26)*, *La passion de Jeanne d'Arc (27)*
Hennig, Mike (DE): *Reifezeit (76)*
Henning-Jensen, Lars (DK, *22 Feb 43): 239
Henrey, Bobby (GB, *26 Jne 39): 215 *The Fallen Idol (48)*
Henry, Justin (US, *25 May 71): 386 *Kramer vs. Kramer (79)*
Henry, Robert 'Buzzy' (US, *4 Sep 31): 176
Henties, Torsten (DE): *Stunde Null (77)*, *David (78)*
Hepworth, Henry (GB): 103
Hepworth, John (GB): 103
Hepworth, Ronnie (GB, *1920): 103
Herbert, Charles (US, *23 Dec 48): 277
Herbert-Bond, John (US): *Tower of London (39)*, *Raffles (40)*
Herranz, Miguel Angel (ES): *¿Que he hecho YO para merecer esto!! (84)*
Herrmann, Lars (DD): 365
Hershewe, Michael (US): 372
Herzberg, Martin (GE/DK, *15 Jan 11): 47
Heuzé, André (FR): 62 *Poil de Carotte (25)*
Hickman, Cordell (US): 168
Hickman, Darryl (US, *25 Jly 30): 169
Hickman, Dwayne (US, *18 May 34): 170 *Captain Eddie (45)*, *Hoodlum Saint (46)*, *The Return of Rusty (46)*, *The Secret Heart (46)*, *For the Love of Rusty (47)*, *The Boy with Green Hair (48)*, *My Dog Rusty (48)*, *Rusty Leads the Way (48)*
Hicks, Oliver (GB, *10 Sep 71): 388 *Captain Stirrick (81)*, *A Swarm in May (82)*, *Dark Enemy (83)*
Hidalgo, Luis Maria (ES): *Miguelin (64)*
Higgins, Jamie (NZ): *The God Boy (75)*
Hill, Trevor (GB, *1936): *Bobby Rings the Bell (51)*, *Skid Kids (52)*, *The Secret Cave (53)*, *Unser Dorf (53)*
Hillien, Hervé (FR): *Il était une fois un flic (72)*
Hines, Frazer (GB, *22 Sep 44): 248
Hintsch, Gyuri (HU): *Egigerö fü (79)*
Hirabayishi, Kiyoshi (JP): *Kaachan shiguno iyada (61)*
Hirst, Stephen (GB): *Black Jack (79)*
Hjelm, Kaj (SE, *24 Jne 28; †Sep 83): 157
Hodges, Eddie (US, *5 Mar 47): 264
Hodges, Greg (US): *The Double McGuffin (79)*
Hodges, Hal (US): *Frogs (72)*
Hoff, Morten (DK): *Zappa (83)*
Hoffmann, Günter (DE): 251
Hogdon, John Philip (US): *Visit to a Chief's Son (74)*
Holden, Peter (US, *28 Sep 30): *The Great Man Votes (89)*

Holm, Barnaby (GB): 364 *Juggernaut (74)*, *The Lost Boys (78)*, *The Final Conflict (80)*
Holmberg, Dagfinn (DK): *Ta' Pelle med (52)*, *Altid ballade (55)*, *Hvad skal jeg være? (55)*
Holmes, Dennis (US, *10 Oct 50): 285 *'Laramie' (59-63)*
Holmes, Leon (US, *26 Nov 13): 60
Holt, David (US, *14 Aug 27): 151
Holt, Tim (US, *5 Feb 18; †15 Feb 73): *Born to the West (26)*, *The Vanishing Pioneer (28)*
Holý, Tomáš (CS): 377
Homeier, Skippy (US, *5 Oct 30): *Tomorrow, the World (44)*
Hooks, Eric (US): 324 *Sounder (72)*, *Just an Old Sweet Song (76)*
Hooks, Kevin (US, *19 Sep 58): 324
Hopson, Nicholas (US/GB): *Missing the Tide (18)*, *In the Gloaming (19)*, *Her Son (20)*
Horneff, Wil (US): *Ghost in the Machine (93)*, *The Sandlot Kids (93)*
Horváth László (HU): 231
Hoskins, Allen 'Farina' (US, *9 Aug 20; †26 Jly 80): 99
Hould, Ra (NZ/US) – *see* Sinclair, Ronald, 125
House, Chandler (US): *The Father (15)*, *Intolerance (16)*, *Pillars of Society (16)*, *The Little Orphan (17)*
House, Newton (US, *10 Jan 11): 47
Hovey, Tim (US, *19 Jne 45; †9 Sep 89): 253
Howard, Clint (US, *10 Apr 59): 304 *The Courtship of Eddie's Father (63)*, *An Eye for an Eye (66)*, *Gentle Giant (67)*, *The Jungle Book (67)*, *Winnie the Pooh and the Blustery Day (68)*, *The Wild Country (69)*, *The Red Pony (73)*, *Salty (73)*, *Huckleberry Finn (74)*
Howard, Ronny (US, *1 Mar 54): 304
Hrušecký, A. (CS): *Daniel (60)*, *OK 12 startuje (61)*, *Chlapec a srna (62)*
Hryniewicz, Henryk (PL): *Świadectwo urodzenia (61)*
Hubbard, Allan (US): *Tender Mercies (82)*, *Daddy's Dyin' Who's Got the Will? (89)*
Hudis, Stephen (US, *17 May 57): 317
Hudziec, Tomasz (PL, *3 Dec 65): 357
Hunaerts, Geert (BE): *Crazy love (87)*
Hundscheidt, Francisco (NL): *Sjors en Sjimmie en de Rebellen (72)*
Hunt, Jimmy (US, *4 Dec 39): 216
Hunter, Jerry (US): *Happy Land (43)*, *A Boy, a Girl and a Dog (46)*, *Heaven Only Knows (47)*, *The Great Lover (49)*, *Sorrowful Jones (49)*, *It's a Big Country (50)*
Hupp, George (US): 29
Hurlic, Phillip (US, *20 Dec 28): 162
Hurtado, Alfredo 'Pitusin' (ES, *6 Dec 17; †1965): 82
Hutchins, Bobby 'Wheezer' (US, *29 Mar 25): 134
Hvenegaard, Pelle (DK, *1975): 396 *Pelle the Conqueror (87)*
Hwang Hag Yun (KN, *21 Feb 51): 290
Hyatt, Bobby (US): 218

Ichikawa, Yoshiro (JP, *10 Jan 48): 272
Idström, Alfred (FI): 35
Ilagan, Jay (PH): *Maruja (67)*
Ilnitski, Kostya (SU): *Zvyozdochka (62)*
Inagaki, Hiroshi (JP, *30 Dec 05; †21 May 80): *films pre-1920*
Inanoglu, Ilker (TR, *20 Aug 65): 356
Inayoshi, Tiharu (JP): *Malenki beglets (67)*
Infuhr, Teddy (US, *9 Nov 36): 198
Inglis, Brand (US, *31 May 39): 213 *White Corridors (51)*

Losby, Donald (US, *24 Sep 47): *Raintree County* (57), *The Mating Game* (58), *The Remarkable Mr Pennypacker* (58), *Critic's Choice* (62), *Tower of London* (62)

Louie, Ducky (US): 182

Lstibůrek, Zdeněk (CS): 303 *At zije Republika!* (65)

Lubej, Bogdan (YU): *Ne joči, Peter* (64)

Lubinsky, Tibi (AT): 38

Lucieer, Leonard (NL): *De Noordelingen/The Northerners* (92)

Lücking, Thomas (CH): 384 *Glut* (83)

Lukeš, Jiří (CS): 308

Lukyanov, L. (SU): *Pashka* (30)

Lundberg, Sven (SE): *Nils Holgerssons underbara resa* (62)

Lupino, Dicky (GB, *1929): *Just – William* (39)

Lutter, Alfred J. (US, *1962): 341

Lutz, Hermin (GE): *Kindertragödie* (27)

Luxford, Mark (GB, *27 Jne 69): 374 *Friend or Foe* (81)

Lyarski, Alyosha (SU): 143 *The Childhood of Gorki* (38)

Lydon, Jimmy (US, *30 May 23): *Back Door to Heaven* (39)

Lykke-Seest, Esben (NO, *10 Jly 05; †8 Feb 88): 27 *Æresgjesten* (19), *Historien om en gut* (19)

Lynas, Jeffrey (CA): *Lies My Father Told Me* (75), *Breaking Point* (76), *Killer on Board* (77), *Something for Joey* (77)

Lynen, Robert (FR, *24 May 21; †1 Apr 44): 104

Lyon, Richard (GB/US, *8 Oct 34): 190

Lyudvinski, Vasya (SU): 70

McBan, Mickey (US, *27 Feb 19): 91

Maccanti, Roberto (IT): 347 *1900* (76)

McClelland, Fergus (GB, *10 Sep 50): 285 *Sammy Going South* (63)

McCloskey, Brooks (US): *'Buster' films* (12), *The Doctor's Romance* (14), *The Urchin* (15)

McComas, Kendall (US): *Daddy Long Legs* (31), *The Spider* (31), *'Our Gang'* (32), *Man's Castle* (33)

McCormack, Leigh (GB): *The Long Day Closes* (92)

McDermott, Russell (US): 24

McDonald, Donald (US): *Her Twelve Men* (53), *Ma and Pa Kettle at Home* (54), *Great Day in the Morning* (55), *The Kentuckian* (55), *The Brass Legend* (56)

MacDougall, Robin (US): *The Blue Bird* (18)

McDowall, Roddy (GB/US, *17 Sep 28): 158

McFarland, Spanky (US, *2 Oct 28): 160

McFarlane, Craig (GB): *Fern, the Red Deer* (76)

McFarlane, Hamish (GB): *The Navigator* (88)

McFarquhar, Rory (GB, *9 Jly 71): 389 *A Swarm in* May (82), *Dark Enemy* (83)

McGrath, Graham (GB, *29 Jly 71): 387

McGreevey, Michael (US, *7 Feb 48): 273

Machin, Claude (FR, *1921): 109

McIntosh, Frazer (GB, *17 Nov 53): 301

Mackay, Mathew (CA): *The Peanut Butter Solution* (86)

McKeag, Michael (GB): *Here We Come Gathering* (45), *White Cradle Inn* (47)

McKeen, Lawrence 'Snookums' (US, *1924; †2 Apr 33): 124

Mackenzie, Alistair (GB): *David Copperfield* (70), *The Man Who Haunted Himself* (70)

McKeon, Doug (US, *10 Jne 66): 360

McKeon, Philip (US, *20 Nov 64): *Up the Sandbox* (72)

McKim, Harry (US, *1930): 130 *Cowboys from Texas* (39), *I Love You Again* (40), *Men of Boys Town* (41), *The Great Gildersleeve* (42), *Johnny Doughboy* (42), *Dixie* (43), *Hitler's Children* (43), *Henry Aldrich, Boy Scout* (44), *Mr Winkle Goes to War* (44), *The Mojave Firebrand* (44), *Nevada* (44), *Sweet and Low-Down* (44)

McKim, Sammy (US, *20 Dec 24): 130

MacLaine, Ian (GB): *The Boy and the Bridge* (59)

Mac Liammóir, Michael (IE) – *see* **Willmore, Alfred**, 15

McNicholl, Jack (GB, *17 Nov 72): *Terry on the Fence* (85)

Madden, Jerry (US, *29 Jne 23): 117

Madore, Douglas (US): *Bad Little Angel* (39), *She Couldn't Say No* (39), *Soak the Old* (40), *Babes on Broadway* (41), *Blossoms in the Dust* (41), *Here Comes Mr Jordan* (41), *One Foot in Heaven* (41), *On the Sunny Side* (41), *Sun Valley Serenade* (41), *You're the One* (41), *The Great Gildersleeve* (42), *A Yank at Eton* (42), *The Human Comedy* (43), *The Very Thought of You* (44), *The Adventures of Rusty* (45), *The Horn Blows at Midnight* (45)

Madyanov, Roma (SU): *Sovsem propashchi* (74)

Maggio, Angelo (IT): 219

Magimel, Benoît (FR): *La vie est une longue fleuve tranquille* (88)

Magnusson, Toni (SE): *Paradistorg* (76)

Mahan, Billy (US, *9 Jly 30): 168

Mahinda, Edwin (GB): *The Kitchen Toto* (87), *White Mischief* (87)

Maiya, Marik (SU): *Fedkina pravda* (25)

Makepeace, Chris (CA/US, *22 Apr 64): 348

Makhonin, Viktor (SU): *Ivan Makarovich* (68)

Makutonin, Syova (SU): 114

Malašažkas, Leonidas (SU): *Zhiviye geroyi* (59)

Malaska, Jan (CS): *Pohadka o stare tramvaji* (61), *Anička jde do školy* (62)

Maléon, Patrick (FR): 246 *La chambre verte* (78)

Malinger, Ross (US): *Late for Dinner* (91), *Sleepless in Seattle* (93)

Malmsjö, Peter (SE, *1 Mar 62): 339

Malone, Cavan (GB, *25 Nov 39; †1982): *Captain Boycott* (47), *The Root of All Evil* (47), *When the Bough Breaks* (47), *It's Hard to Be Good* (48), *Mr Perrin and Mr Traill* (48), *Kind Hearts and Coronets* (49)

Maltsev, Petya (SU): *Anna na sheye* (54), *Za vlast Sovetov* (56), *Golubiye Pestsi Peti Sinyavina* (59), *Verniye serdtsa* (59)

Mambetov, Murat (SU): *Suda priletayut lebedi* (75)

Mandzhiyev, E. (SU): *Gaichi* (38)

Manesse, Gaspard (FR): *Au revoir les enfants* (87)

Manke, Lutz (DD): 283 *Hedgehog Friendship* (61)

Mannu, Finn (DK): 123 *The Boy Millionaire* (36)

Manu, Ion (RO, *1901; †1968): *Joffre la Mizil* (15)

Manunta, Vittorio (IT, *25 Aug 41): 228

Marathe, Anant (IN): 155

Marathe, Ram (IN): 155

Marchenko, Valya (SU): *Malchiki* (59), *Morskaya chaika* (61)

'Marietto' (IT) – *see* **Angeletti, Marietto**, 288

Marion, Don (US, *9 Oct 17): 81

Marion, Francis (US, *22 Jly 07): 32

Mark, Flip (US, *22 Dec 48): *The Journey* (59), *Please Don't Eat the Daisies* (60), *Safe at Home!* (62), *Marriage on the Rocks* (65)

Markarian, S. (SU): *Rozhdyonniye zhit* (60)

Markersen, Kristjan (DK): *Otto er et næsehorn* (83)

Markin, Arkadi (SU): *Nove priklucheniya Kapitana Vrungelya* (79)

Marković, Stevan (YU): 331 *Dečak i violina* (75)

Markus, Andras (HU): 339

Marriot, Robert (US): *Roogie's Bump (54)*

Marshall, Sean (US, *19 Jne 65): *The Deadly Trackers (73), Pete's Dragon (77)*

Marsuni, Dani (ID): *Serangan fajar (82)*

Martaguet, Christian (FR, *28 May 36): *La vie en rose (47), Le coeur sur la main (48), Au revoir Monsieur Grock (49), L'homme aux mains d'argile (49), Dieu a besoin des hommes (50), Nez de cuir (51)*

Martaguet, Michel (FR): *Trique, gamin de Paris (60)*

Martin, Allen, Jr. (US, *10 Mar 36): 197

Martin, Eugene (US): *Tower of London (62)*

Martin, Jeffery (CA): *The Boy Who Stopped Niagara (47)*

Martin, Raul (PE): *La muralla verde (69)*

Martinez, Flavio (MX): *Mustang (73)*

Martinov, Lenya (SU): *Poyezd idyot v Moskvu (38)*

Martins, Danny (US): *The Hostage (66)*

Marx, Brett (US): *The Bad News Bears (76), The Bad News Bears in Breaking Training (77), The Bad News Bears Go to Japan (78), The Lucky Star (80)*

Mary, Anatole 'Bébé' (FR, *18 Jly 05; †6 Oct 74): 25

Masner, Martin (CS): *Žirafa v okně (68)*

Mason, Morgan (GB/US): *Hero's Island (61), The Sandpiper (65)*

Master Ratan (IN) – *see* **Kumar, Rattan,** 234

Mastryukoff, Volodya (SU): *Moneta (62)*

Matałowski, Jerzy (PL): *Sąsiedzi (68)*

Mathers, Jerry (US, *2 Jne 48): 275

Mathieu, Maurice (FR): 28

Mauch, Billy (US, *6 Jly 24): 128

Mauch, Bobby (US, *6 Jly 24): 128

Maurin, Dominique (FR, *1 Apr 49): 280

Maurin, Jean-François (FR, *21 Jne 57): 318

Maurin, Patrick (FR, *26 Jan 47): 245 *Les espions (57)*

Maurin, Yves-Marie (FR, *19 Apr 44): 244

Maxian, František (CS): *Zpivajici pudřenka (59), Zle pondělí (60), Pohadka o stare tramvaji (61)*

Maxworthy, Brett (AU): *Barney (76)*

May, Gavin (GB, *12 Dec 73): *Infantile Disorders (87)*

Mazayev, Volodya (SU): *Zare navstrechu (59)*

Mazurkiewicz, Maciej (PL): *Dolina Issy (82)*

Mazzello, Joseph (US): *Jersey Girl (92), Jurassic Park (93), Shadowlands (93), The River Wild (94), The Cure (95)*

Mazzola, Eugene (US): *Wait till the Sun Shines, Nellie (52), Cry of the Hunted (53), The Prodigal (55), The Ten Commandments (56), Walk the Proud Land (56)*

Medford, Paul (GB, *1967): 369

'Mehdi' (FR) – *see* **Glaoui, Mehdi el,** 314

Mehmood Junior (IN): 347

Meier, Ludwig (GE): *Peterle (43), Ein Herz schlägt für dich (45)*

Meinshausen, Hans Jürgen (DD): *Der neue Fimmel (60)*

Mejía, Alfonso (MX, *16 Nov 34): 191 *Los olvidados (50)*

Mejias, José Antonio (ES): *El camino (64)*

Melet, Lionel (FR, *14 Oct 67): 368

Melford, Judson (US): 17

Mencikovas, Edvinas (SU): 345 *Andrius (80)*

Mende, Ulrich (DD): *Die Suche nach dem wunderbunte Vögelchen (63)*

Mendenhall, David (US, *13 Jne 71): *Space Raiders (83), Over the Top (86), My African Adventure (87)*

Mercanton, Jean (FR, *17 May 20; †4 Nov 47): 97

Mercer, Freddie (US, *6 Mar 29): 164

Merkulov, Misha (SU): *Volnitsa (55), Polyushko-pole (56), Oni vstretilis v puti (57)*

Mertens, Fernand (BE, *25 Dec 04; †2 Nov 70): 23

Meschke, Edmund (DE): 201 *Germany Year Zero (47)*

Meskhi, Mishko (SU): *Sazhentsi (73)*

Mesnier, Christian (FR): *Bruno, l'enfant du dimanche (68)*

Messinger, Buddy (US, *26 Oct 07; †25 Oct 65): 34

Meynier, Geronimo (IT, *5 Jly 41): 238 *Amici per la pelle (55)*

Mezzanotte, Aldo (IT) – *see* 'Patatà', 38

Michenaud, Gerald (US): *The Naked Kiss (64), A Big Hand for the Little Lady (66), In Enemy Country (67), Buckskin (68), Welcome Home, Johnny Bristol (71)*

Michl, Janko (CS): *Cesar a detektivi (68)*

Micinski, Ryszard (PL): *Karuzela zycia (30)*

Mickelsen, Jerry (US): *Journey for Margaret (42), Edge of Darkness (43), The North Star (43), Circumstantial Evidence (45), My Pal Wolf (45), Duel in the Sun (46), Backlash (47), Emergency Wedding (50), The Happy Years (50), Lorna Doone (51)*

Mietek, Kucyk (PL, *c.1919; †1945): *Jeden z trzydziestu sresciu (25), Iwonka (25)*

Mikaliunas, Evaldas (SU): *Malenki prints (67)*

Mikuláš, Martin (CS): 377 *The Golden Eels (79)*

Mikulič, Antonín (CS): 193

Miles, Chris Cleary (GB): *Second Best (94)*

Miles, Peter (US, *1 Apr 38): 208

Miller, Frank (GB): *Oh That Doctor's Boy! (06), The Terror and the Terrier (10)*

Miller, Sergius (PL): *Na dworze króla Tuszynka (77), Ballada o niepokonanym Jasiu (78)*

Miller, Winston (US, *22 Jne 10): 44

Millington, Norris (US): *'Buster Brown' series (14)*

Milrad, Josh (US): *The Beastmaster (82)*

Mimica, Srdan (YU, *1957): *Ponedeljak ili utorak (66), Dogadjaj (69)*

'Mimmo' (IT) – *see* **Palermi, Mimmo,** 83

Minayev, Lora (SU): *Lichnoye delo (39)*

Mincer, Edward (PL): *Świadectwo urodzenia (61)*

Minty, Emil (AU, *1973): 394

'Mircha' (?AT/FR): 114

Mirski, Lyova (SU): *Lichnoye delo (39), Brat geroya (40)*

Mirzoyev, Dzheik (SU): *Machekha (58), Nastoyashchi drug (59), Kompaneros (62)*

Mitayev, Yura (SU): *Semiklassniki (38)*

Mitchell, John (GB, *9 Jne 46): *Bottoms Up (59)*

Mitchell-Smith, Ilan M. (US, *29 Jne 69): *Daniel (83)*

Mkrtchiyan, Robert (SU): *Taina gornovo ozera (54), Plenniki Barsova Ushchelya (56)*

Mobley, Roger (US): 288

Mock, Gérard (FR): *Le tournoi dans la cité (28), La Venenosa (28)*

Modak, Shahu (IN): 114

Mohan, Master (IN, *4 Sep 45): 255

Moik, Lutz (DD, *10 Nov 30): 171

Mokatsian, Tolik (SU): *Dochka (42)*

Molen, Michael Walma van de (NL): *Knokken voor twee (83)*

Molina, Vicente (MX): *Corazon de niño (39)*

Möller, Gunnar (GE, *1 Jly 28): 158

Monahan, Joseph 'Chip' (US, *16 May 07): 29

Monda, Dick (US, *10 Aug 40): *The Eddie Cantor Story (53)*, *The Glass Wall (53)*

Monet, Carlos Lopez (AR) – see Lopez Monet, Carlos, 263

Montgomery, Lee (US, *3 Nov 61): 336

Moore, Dickie (US, *12 Sep 25): 139

Moore, Micky (US, *14 Oct 16): 73

Moore, Pat (US, *20 Oct 12): 64

Mora, Bradley (US): 243

Moran, Jackie (US, *26 Jan 23; †20 Sep 90): 114

Morat, Bibi (FR): 298

Morell, Arnaud (GB): *Daemon (85)*

Moreno, José Luis (MX): *Medianoche (48)*, *Amor de la calle (49)*, *Coqueta (49)*, *Madre querida (50)*, *Pata de palo (50)*, *El pecado de ser pobre (50)*, *Nunca debieron amarse (51)*

Morgan, Jackie (US, *7 Jly 16; †25 Jly 81): 73

Morihara, Yukio (JP): *Te o tsunagu kora (62)*

Morrell, Joshua (US, *19 Nov 74): *Joey (85)*

Morrison, Ernie (US, *20 Dec 12; †24 Jly 89): 56

Morrow, Brad (US) – see **Mora, Bradley**, 243

Mosho, Genci (AL): *Qyteti më i ri në botë (74)*, *Tomka dhe shokët e tij (77)*, *Pas gjurmëve (78)*, *Partizani i vogël Velo (80)*

Mosior, Roman (PL): 330

Moss, Jimmy (US): *Inside Job (46)*, *They Live by Night (48)*, *Stars in My Crown (49)*, *The Damned Don't Cry (50)*, *Jim Thorpe - All American (51)*, *Les Misérables (52)*, *Mister Scoutmaster (53)*

Moss, Paul (GB): *The Black Windmill (74)*

Moulder-Brown, John (GB, *3 Jne 53): 299

Moulière, Jacky (FR) – see **Moullières, Jacques**, 244

Moullières, Jacques (FR, *15 Apr 44): 244

Mouloudji, Marcel (FR, *16 Sep 22; †14 Jne 94): 112

Mukotinin, Syova (SU) – see **Makutonin, Syova**, 114

Müller, Dirk (DD): *Moritz in der Litfasssäule (83)*

Müller, Waldemar (GE): *Ein Kind, ein Hund, ein Vagabund (34)*

Mullins, Peter (GB): *Mr Emmanuel (44)*, *Caravan (46)*

Mummert, Danny (US, *20 Feb 34): 188

Mumy, Billy (US, *1 Feb 54): 303 *'Lost in Space' (65-68)*

Munier, Jean (FR): *L'enfant-roi (23)*

Munk, Danny de (NL, *19 Feb 70): 378 *Ciske de Rat (84)*

Munteanu, Ion (RO): *Nufarul roşu (55)*

Murphy, Jack (US, *1912): 59 *Peter Pan (24)*, *The Lost World (25)*, *Stella Dallas (25)*, *Tumbleweeds (25)*, *The Texas Streak (26)*

Murphy, Maurice (US, *3 Oct 13; †23 Nov 78): 59

Musin, Rifat (SU): *I togda ya skazal: Net (73)*, *Vkus khalvi (75)*

Mustafaraj, Herion (AL): 365 *Beni ecën vetë (75)*

Nacu, Gabriel (RO): *Aventurile lui Babuşcă (73)*

Nadir, Oussama (EG): 377

Nagy, Geza (HU): *Negyen az arban (61)*

Nagy, Zoltán (HU): *Elysium (86)*

Nakagawa, Hideo (JP): *Kaze no naka no mendori (48)*

Nakov, Plamuk (BG): *Hot Noon (64)*

Narkis, Nerius (SU): 271 *Living Heroes (59)*

Nash, Damien (GB, *11 Nov 67): *Charlie Was a Rich Man (81)*, *Twilight Time (82)*

Nash, Simon (GB, *7 Sep 72): *Xtro (82)*, *Breakout (84)*, *Brazil (85)*

Nataraj, G.S. (IN): *Kaadu (73)*

Natulu, Bala (IN): *Baala bharathamu (72)*

Naumenko, Volodya (SU): *Pozovi menya v dal svetluyu (77)*

Naumov, Georgi (BG, *11 Sep 41): 236 *Sledite ostavat (55)*

Nazarov, Pavel (SU): *Zamri umi voskresni (89)*

Nazarov, Seryozha (SU): *Ten (61)*

N'Debele, Muntu Ben Louis (ZA): 352 *e'Lollipop (75)*

N'Diaye, Mame (SN): *N'diangane (74)*

Needs, Philip (GB, *5 Nov 51): *Hand in Hand (60)*

Negron, Miguel Angel (MX): *Raices (55)*

Neie, Hans (DE): *Meine Herren Söhne (45)*, *Eine reizende Familie (45)*, *Wie sagen wir es unseren Kindern? (45)*, *Kein Platz für Liebe (47)*, *Und finden dereinst wir uns wieder... (47)*, *Eins - zwei - drei Corona (48)*

Neilands, Ronalds (SU, *1975): 382 *Spriditis (85)*

Nelson, Bobby (US, *1923): 122

Nelson, Ricky (US, *8 May 40; †31 Dec 85): 222

Neto, Pereira (PT): *Nove rapaces e um cão (63)*, *Um cão e dois destinos (65)*

Netscher, Robin (GB, *16 Sep 35): 194

Neumann, Ole (DK, *16 Oct 47): 268

Nevola, Edoardo (IT, *23 Feb 48): 273

Newport, Michael (GB, *23 Sep 52): 296

Ney, Geraldo del (BR): *Menino de engenho (66)*

Nezer, Michael (DK): 395 *Kidnapning (82)*

Nicholas, Thomas Ian (US): *Rookie of the Year (93)*

Nichols, Richard (US): 195

Nielsen, Mads M. (DK): 377 *Drengen der forsvandt (83)*

Nievelstein, Jef (NL): *Nieuwe avonturen van Dik Trom (58)*

Nilsson, Leif (SE): 251

Nipper, Will (US): 279

Nirumand, Majid (IR): 392 *The Runner (84)*

Noël, Yves (FR): *L'amour est en jeu (57)*, *Drôles de phénomènes (58)*, *Le premier mai (58)*

Noisom, George 'Bubbles' (US): 75

Nokes, George (US): 206

Nolman, Volodya (SU): *Vanka i mstitel (28)*

Norborg, Anders (SE): *Det store aventyret (55)*

Norden, Tommy (US, *25 Sep 52): *Le couteau dans la plaie (62)*

Norman, B.G. (US): *The Clock (45)*, *The Valley of Decision (45)*, *Night and Day (46)*, *Miracle on 34th Street (47)*, *The Big Clock (48)*, *Reckless Moment (49)*, *The Gunfighter (50)*

North, Jay (US, *3 Aug 52): 295

North, Neil (GB, *18 Oct 32): *The Winslow Boy (48)*

Notari, Eduardo (IT, *1 Jan 03; †1986): 20

Novikov, Tolya (SU): *Na grafskikh razvalinakh (57)*

Nowak, Leopold (PL): *Pierwszy start (52)*

Nucci, Danny (US, *15 Sep 68): *American Drive-In (82)*

Nueci, Rodolfo di (AR): *Tacuara y Chamorro (68)*

Nunn, Larry (US, *23 Aug 27): 152

Nyberg, Ernst (SE): *Vinden från väster (42)*

Nyström, Anders (SE, *8 Feb 33): 184

O'Brien, Austin (US): *The Lawnmower Man (92)*, *Last Action Hero (93)*, *Prehysteria (93)*, *My Girl 2 (94)*, *Lawnmower Man 2 (95)*

O'Brien, Clay (US, *6 May 61): 335

O'Brien, Kieran (GB, *1973): *Bellman and True (87)*

Očenášek, Ladislav (CS): *Máte doma lva? (63)*, *Kdyby tisíc klarinetů (64)*

O'Connor, Donald (US, *30 Aug 25): 137

O'Conor, Hugh (GB): *Lamb (86)*, *My Left Foot (89)*

Odemar, Erik (GE, *6 Nov 10; †19 Jly 83): *I.N.R.I.* (23)

O'Donnell, Walter 'Spec' (US, *9 Apr 11; †14 Oct 86): 49

Ohlsen, Jürgen (GE): 95 *Hitlerjunge Quex* (33)

Ohlsson, Jan (SE, *3 Jne 62): 340

Ohrner, Tommy (DE, *3 Jne 65): 355

Ohsawa, Yukihiro (JP): *Jiro monogatari* (55)

Oizumi, Akira (JP, *1 Jan 25): 132

Okimura, Takeshi (JP): *Nianchan* (59), *Chiku-no kodomotachi* (60)

Okumoyama, George (JP): *Kiku to Isamu* (59)

Oliszewski, Olek (PL): *Chciałbym się zgbuić* (79)

Oliver, Barret (US, *24 Aug 73): 393

Oliver, Michael (US): *Problem Child* (90), *Problem Child 2* (91)

Olivieri, Enrico (IT, *14 Dec 39): 217

Olsen, Chris (US, *1947): 269

Olsen, Larry Joe (US, *1939): 217

Olson, Eric (US, *17 Nov 62): 341

Olsson, Tom (SE, *6 Nov 29): 168

O'Neal, Griffin (US, *28 Oct 64): 350 *The Escape Artist* (79)

Opatrny, Miloš (CS): *Kluci na řece* (44)

Oprescu, Armand (RO, *11 Sep 53): 300 *Cine va deschide uşa?* (67)

Orascu, Cristian (RO): *Misterul lui Herodot* (76)

Ordell, Robin (AU, *19 Jan 18; †13 Aug 42): 85 *The Kid Stakes* (27)

Orlegui, Oscar (AR): 263

Orloff, Oleg (SU): *Tak nachinalas legenda* (76)

Ortin, Polito (MX): 163

Osawa, Kenzaburo (JP): *Aki tachinu* (61)

Osherov, Shuy (IL): *Shlosha yamin ve yeled* (66)

Osorno Barona, Luis, Jr. (MX)

Ostrum, Peter (US, *1 Nov 57): 320 *Willy Wonka and the Chocolate Factory* (71)

O'Sullivan, Richard (GB, *7 May 44): 246

Ota, Hiroyuki (JP, *25 Nov 47): 268

Otterman, Gabi (IL): *Ani ohev otach Rosa* (71)

Ouedraogo, Noufou (BF): *Yaaba* (88), *Tilaï* (90)

'Our Gang' (US) – *see* Albright, Bailey Sd., Beard, Beckett, Blake, Bond T., Chaney, Cobb, Condon, Cooper Ja., Daniels M., Downs, Hoskins, Hutchins, Kaye, Kibrick L. and S., Laughlin, Lee P., McComas, McFarland, Moore D., Morrison E., Spear, Switzer, Thomas W. and many more.

Overgaard, Jeppe (DK): *Altid ballade* (55)

Owen, Sid (GB. *12 Jan 72): *Revolution* (85)

Owen, Tony (AU): *Norman Loves Rose* (82)

Oxenbould, Ben (AU): *Fatty Finn* (80)

'Pachin' (ES) – *see* **Gomez, Angel**, 288

Padilla, Manuel (US, *1956): 316 'Tarzan' (66-68)

Palermi, Mimmo (IT, *1917; †Aug 1925): 83

Palmer, Richard (GB): 256

Pankhurst, Garry (AU, *1952): *The Intruders* (69)

Pankratov, A. (SU): *Vreditel* (29)

Paoletti, Marco (IT, *1949): 281

Papakosta, Petro (AL): 366

Pâqui, Jean (FR, *15 Apr 21, RN Jean-Francois de Thunel, Chevalier d'Orgeix): *L'assommoir* (33), *Ame de clown* (34), *La maison du mystère* (35)

Parks, Van Dyke (US, *3 Jan 41): 225

Parrish, Robert (US, *4 Jan 16): 71

Parry, George S. (US): *A Christmas to Remember* (78), *Special Olympics* (78)

Pasarić, Tomica (YU): *Sedmi kontinent* (60)

Pasca, Alfonsino (IT): *Paisa'* (46), *Au revoir Monsieur Grock* (49)

Pasquier, Franck (FR): 246 *Le dernier métro* (80)

Passendorfer, Thomas (PL): *Zabijcie czarna owcę* (71)

Pässler, Franz (GE): *Das Ferienkind* (43)

Pastor, Daniel (MX): *Virgen que forjo una patria* (42), *Las aventuras de Cucuruchito y Pinocho* (43), *Cristobal Colon* (43), *La barraca* (45), *La culpable* (45), *La hora de la verdad* (45), *Marina* (45), *El ahijado de la muerte* (46), *Ave de paso* (46), *La otra* (46), *Por un amor* (46), *Tabaré* (46)

'Patatà' (IT, *c.1908; †Oct 1926): 38

Patrick, Butch (US, *2 Aug 53): *Hand of Death* (61), *The Two Little Bears* (61), *Pressure Point* (62), *One Man's Way* (64), *Munster Go Home!* (66), *Way Down Cellar* (67)

Paul, Ellis (US): *Our Boys* (17), *The Saint's Adventure* (17), *Seventy and Seven* (17), 'Do Children Count?' series (17)

Paul, Jack (US): *The Little Straw Wife* (15), *Joyce's Strategy* (16), 'Do Children Count?' series (17)

Pavesi, Paolo (IT): 347 *1900* (76)

Pavitt, Eric (GB, *7 Jly 22): 110

Payant, Gilles (CA/US): 277 *Big Red* (62)

Pazos, Felipe (MX, *22 Nov 44): 220 *The Old Man and the Sea* (58)

Pecani, Dhmitër (AL): 271 *DEBATIK* (61)

Peck, Charles (US): *Dead End* (37), *Mad About Music* (38)

Peluce, Meeno (US, *26 Feb 69): 373

Pender, Tommy (GB, *31 Dec 63): *Mind Where You're Going* (72), *Steptoe and Son Ride Again* (73), *The Water Babies* (77)

Pendharkar, Dnyanesh (IN): *Aai mi kuthe javoo* (72)

Penrose, Peter (GB): *Almost a Divorce* (31), *Sorrell and Son* (33), *Lorna Doone* (34), *The Man Who Changed His Name* (34), *The Old Curiosity Shop* (35)

Pera, Radames (US, *14 Sep 60): *A Dream of Kings* (69), *Incident in San Francisco* (71), *Gidget Gets Married* (72)

Perels, Martin (NL, *16 Nov 60): *Q & Q* (78)

Perevalov, Vitya (SU): 278

Perez, Ismael (MX): 225

Perl, Lloyd (US): *Let Katy Do It* (15), *Little Dick's First Case* (15), *The Defenders* (16), *A Sister of Six* (16), *Aladdin and the Wonderful Lamp* (17), *Treasure Island* (17), *Ace High* (18), *The Girl with the Champagne Eyes* (18)

Perreau, Gerald (US) – *see* **Miles, Peter**, 208

Perry, Steven (US): *The Man in the Net* (59), *The Sound and the Fury* (59), *A Raisin in the Sun* (61)

Peterhans, Hans Peter (GE, *19 May 14): 63

Petersen, Casper (DK): *Fugleskræmslet* (10), *Lattermaskinen* (10), *Medbejlerens hævn* (10)

Petersen, Chris (US): 347

Petersen, Colin (AU, *26 Mar 46): 256

Petersen, Patrick (US, *9 Aug 66): 361

Peterson, Paul (US, *23 Sep 45): *Houseboat* (58)

Peterson, Vidal (US): *Something Wicked This Way Comes* (82)

Petrescu, Razvan (RO, *8 Sep 49): 281 *Codine* (63)

Petrov, Kiril (BG): 327

Petrungaro, Luigi (IT, *10 Feb 04): 22

Shirley, Thomas (US): *Jimmy* (13), *Tapped Wires* (13), *What George Did* (13)

Shitara, Koji (JP, *4 Jne 46): 259

Short, Antrim (US, *11 Jly 00; †24 Nov 72): 16

Shuford, Andy (US, *1917): 83

Siani, Ryp (US): *Robby* (68)

Sieniawski, Wojciech (PL): *Dziewczyna i chłopak* (80)

Sierck, Claus Detlev (GE, *30 Mar 25; †6 Mar 44): 135

Sikora, Marek (PL): 339

Siluyanov, Vova (SU): 251

Silva, Fernando Ramos da – see **Ramos da Silva, Fernando**, 368

Silva, Horacio (PT): 172 *Aniki-Bóbó* (42)

Silvester, Julian (GB): *Captain Stirrick* (81)

Simanovich, Kolya (SU): *Konnitsa skachet* (29), *Chelovek s portfelem* (29), *Fritz Bauer* (30), *Lyagavi* (30)

Simmons, Gary (GB, *23 Feb 71): *Haunters of the Deep* (84)

Simms, Larry (US, *1 Oct 34): 190

Simms, Shane (NZ, *1960; †1978): 332

Simon, Christian (FR, *22 Jly 37): 205

Simons, Hein (NL/DE) – see **'Heintje'**, 310

Simons, William (GB): *No Place for Jennifer* (49), *The Happiest Days of Your Life* (50), *Prelude to Fame* (50), *Where No Vultures Fly* (51), *West of Zanzibar* (53)

Sinclair, Ronald (NZ/US, *21 Jan 24; †1992): 125

Singer, Johnny (GB, *4 Dec 23; †7 Jly 87): 119

Singh, Leikhendra (IN): *Imagi ningthem* (81)

Sinutko, Shane (US, *16 Apr 65): *The Shaggy D.A.* (76), *Pine Canyon Is Burning* (77), *The Immigrants* (78), *Lassie: the New Beginning* (78), *Samurai* (79), *Resurrection* (80)

Sinyakin, Vanya (SU): *Kostyor v lesu* (41)

Sira, Puneet (GB, *3 Dec 67): *Arabian Adventure* (79)

Şişko, Şaban (TR/FR): *Le mur* (83)

Skamene, Roman (CS): *Útěk* (67)

Skarsgård, Stellan (SE, *13 Jne 51): *Bombi Bitt och jag* (68)

Skinner, Keith (GB, *17 Aug 49): *Mademoiselle* (66)

Skol, Jerry (PL/GB): *Success Is the Best Revenge* (84)

Skolimowski, George (PL/GB) – see Skol, Jerry

Slade, Max Elliott (US): *3 Ninja Kids* (92), *3 Ninjas Kick Back* (93)

Slawe, Heinz (GE): *Ein Kind – ein Hund* (23)

Šlosar, Josef (CS): *Malý partyzán* (51)

Smarzich, Bobby (US) – see **Samarzich, Bobby**, 163

Smestad, Stian (NO): *Håkon Håkonsen / Shipwrecked* (90)

Smirnoff, Igor (SU): *Detstvo Gorkovo* (38), *Timur i yevo komanda* (40), *Yakov Sverdlof* (40)

Smith, Brian (GB, *24 Dec 32): 180

Smith, Erle, Ronald and Graham (GB): *Terrors* (30)

Smith, Jack (US, *18 Aug 1896; †3 Jan 33): 10

Smith, Paul (AU, *1968): *Fighting Back* (82), *Waterloo Station* (82)

Smorchkoff, Kolya (SU): *Gavroche* (37), *Druzya iz tabora* (38)

Smordoni, Rinaldo (IT, *5 Feb 33): 183 *Shoeshine* (46)

Smyczek, Karel (CS, *31 Mar 50): 284

Snelling, Leonard (GB, *1921): *The Three Maxims* (36), *The Gang Show* (37), *London Melody* (37)

'Snookums' (US) – see **McKeen, Lawrence**, 124

Snyders, Sammy (US): *Huckleberry Finn and His Friends* (79)

Sobolev, Yura (SU): *Pastushonok* (35)

Söderblom, Jan (SE): *Da capo* (85)

Söderdahl, Lars (SE): 367

Sofron, Cristian (RO, *9 May 59): 327

Sokoloff, Sasha (SU): *Malchik s okraini* (47)

Sokoloff, Shura (SU): *Krasni galstuk* (48)

Sorensen, Ricky (US, *1947): 270

Spain, Mark (AU): *My Brilliant Career* (79), *Harlequin* (80), *Bush Christmas* (83)

Spallone, Daniele (IT): *La steppa* (62)

'Spanky' (US) – see **McFarland, George**, 160

Spear, Harry (US, *16 Dec 21; †10 Feb 69): *The Flying Horseman* (26), *The Midnight Kiss* (26), *Gigolo* (26), *'Our Gang'* (26-29)

Spell, George (US, *1960): 322

Spell, Winston (US): 322 *Hickey and Boggs* (72)

Spellman, Martin (US, *1927): 154

Spenser, David (GB, *12 Mar 34): 204 *Mr Perrin and Mr Traill* (48)

Spenser, Jeremy (GB, *16 Jly 37): 204

Spindola, Robert (US): *Ramona* (36), *The Firefly* (37)

Spiro, Herion (AL) – see **Mustafaraj, Herion**, 365

Spree, Titus (DE): *Zwischen Mond und Sonne* (81)

Spurrier, Paul (GB, *23 May 67): *The Wild Geese* (77), *Anna Karenina* (77), *The Lost Boys* (78), *Vice Versa* (81)

Stahl, Nick (US): *The Man without a Face* (93), *Tall Tale* (94)

Staiola, Enzo (IT, *15 Jne 39): 214 *Bicycle Thieves* (48)

Stallone, Sage (US, *5 May 76): *Rocky V* (90)

Stalmaster, Hal (US, *29 Mar 40): *Leap to Heaven* (56), *Johnny Tremain* (57)

Stanfield, Devin (GB, *20 Feb 71): *Crime Story* (83), *Chocky* (84), *The Box of Delights* (84)

Stark-Gstettenbaur, Gustl (GE, *1 Mar 14): 62

Starý, Petr (CS): *Dobrodruzství s Blasem* (74), *Páni kluci* (75)

Steele, Bob (US, *23 Jan 06; †22 Dec 88): *The Adventures of Bill and Bob* (22)

Steele, Jadrien (US, *22 Nov 74): *Mosquito Coast* (86)

Steele, Richard (US): *With Six You Get Eggroll* (68)

Steen-Hansen, Lasse (DK): *Vi kunne ha' det så rart* (42), *Møllen* (43)

Steinbeck, Jan (DE, *20 May 76): *Hatschipuh* (87)

Stellman, Michael (US/IT): *Il relitto* (60)

Stensgård, Per (DK): 46

Stephens, Harvey (GB, *12 Nov 70): *The Omen* (76), *Gauguin the Savage* (79)

Stephens, Martin (GB, *30 Jan 48): 272

Sterman, Jimmy (NL/DK, *30 Aug 47): 267 *Paw* (59)

Steuart, Maury (US, *1909): 42

Štiglic, Tugomir (YU, *8 Nov 46): 260

Štimac, Slavko (YU, *15 Oct 60): 332

Stockwell, Dean (US, *5 Mar 36): 196

Stollery, David (US, *18 Jan 41): 225

Stone, Georgie (US, *1911): 51

Stoyanov, Marin (BG, *3 Mar 69): *Pokhishteniyé v zhulto* (80), *Kuche vuv chekmedzhe* (81)

Straburzynski, Igor (PL): *Legenda* (70)

Strachan, Gordon R. (GB): *Venus Peter* (88)

Stremovski, Zhora (SU): *Orlyonok* (57)

Strohbach, Rolf (DD): *Die Reise nach Sundevit* (66)

Stukov, Fedya (SU): *Neskolko dnei iz zhizni I.I. Oblomova* (79), *Priklyucheniya Tomi Soyera* (81), *Rodnya* (82)

Umnig, Andreas (AT): *Schöne Tage* (81)

Untaru, Bogdan (RO, *13 Jly 59): 328 *'Naica' films* (63-67)

Urbain, Jimmy (FR, *6 Dec 43): 241

Urchs, Sascha (DE): *Der kleine Vampir* (68)

Utku, Menderes (TR, *5 Apr 63): 344

Uys, Wynand (ZA): 334

Valiyev, Kambar (SU): *Lyuti* (73)

Valsecchi, Sven (IT): 373

Van — for Dutch and Belgian names, see under following word

Van Atta, Lee (US, *22 Jly 24): 129

Van de, Van der, Van 't — as Van, see next word of name

Van Horn, Jimmy (US, *24 Sep 17; †20 Apr 66): *The Cherokee Kid* (27)

Van Patten, Dick (US, *9 Dec 28): *Reg'lar Fellers* (41)

Van Patten, Vincent (US, *17 Oct 57): 319

Vargas, — de (UY): *El pequeño heroe del Arroyo* (29)

Vasilev, Borya (SU): *Alyosha Ptitsin virabativayet kharakter* (53), *Odna noch* (56), *Andreika* (58), *Ezop* (60)

Vasilev, V. (SU): *Kontsert Betkhovena* (36)

Vasilev, Vladimir (BG): *Tigurcheto* (72), *Migove v kibritena kutiika* (79)

Vasilev, Volodya (SU): *Chudotvornaya* (60)

Vasiliu, Sorin (RO): *Alarma in Delta* (75)

Vavruša, Michal (CS): 343

Velasquez, Andres (US): *One Big Affair* (52), *The Littlest Outlaw* (54)

Velasquez, Ernesto (MX): 143

Velde, Dick van der (NL, *20 Mar 42): *Ciske de Rat* (55)

Veldt, Govert (NL): *Pan* (61)

'Veli-Matti' — *see* **Kaitala, Veli-Matti,** 194

Velkov, Ivan (BG, *7 Nov 70): *Da obichash na inat* (85)

Verdi, Freddie (US, *1909): *The Prima Donna's Husband* (16), *The Foolish Virgin* (17), *The Little Chevalier* (17), *The Light Within* (18), *Love's Conquest* (18), *Satan on Earth* (19), *Cousin Kate* (21), *The Glimpses of the Moon* (23)

Vermes, David (HU): 395 *Hol volt, hol nem volt* (87)

Vesque, Christophe (FR): 246 *La nuit américaine* (73)

Vidal, Jorge (MX): *Allá en el Rancho Chico* (38), *Corazon de niño* (39), *Diablillos de arrabal* (39)

Vidan, Tonči (YU): *Kapetan Mikula Mali* (74)

Vîlcu, Adrian (RO, *13 Jly 67): 368

Vincent, Alex (US): *Child's Play* (88), *Wait until Spring, Bandini* (89), *Child's Play 2* (90)

Visca, Renato (IT, *1905): 27

Vishnev, Oleg (SU): *Vasek Trubachov i yevo tovarishchi* (55), *Otryad Trubachova srazhayetsa* (57)

Vitushin, Sasha (SU): *Pervi myach* (62)

Vogel, Mitch (US, *17 Jan 59): 313 *The Reivers* (69)

Vogel, Nikolaus (AT): 367

Voigt, Cai (DK, *c.1897): 12

Voinovski, Andrei (SU): *Chudak iz 5B* (72)

Voinyagovski, Nasko (BG): *Smurtta na zaeka* (81)

Von (prefix) — see under name following

Voříšek, Petr (CS): *Pani kluci* (75), *Ostrov střibrnych volavek* (76)

Voronov, Stefan (BG, *10 Apr 75): *Lyubovna terapiya* (87)

Voronovski, —. (SU): *Kak Petyunka yezdil k Ilyichi* (24)

Vries, Martijntje de (NL, *18 Sep 13; †30 Apr 43): 59

Vulkov, Valentin (BG): *Nespokoen dom* (65)

Vychopeň, Daniel (CS): *Lukáš* (82)

Wager, Anthony (GB, *24 Jne 32): 180

Wagner, Claude (LU): *Schacko Klak* (80)

Wain, Kit (GB/US, *1919): *The King of Kings* (27), *Four Devils* (28), *Tom Brown of Culver* (31)

Waintrop, Thomas (FR): *Folle à tuer* (75)

Wallbridge, David (GB): *Thunder Rock* (42), *For Those in Peril* (44), *Pink String and Sealing Wax* (45), *The Rake's Progress* (45), *The Captive Heart* (46), *Take My Life* (47)

Walsh, Joey (US, *11 Jly 37): 203 *Hans Christian Andersen* (52)

Walter, Eric (FR): *Souffle au coeur* (70)

Wang Jiayi (CN): *Liangjia funü* (85)

Wang Longji (CN, *13 Jne 40): 222 *San-Mao liulang ji* (49)

Wang Qiguang (CN): *Dongdong de Jiaqi* (84)

Ward, Jay Walter (US): *Reducing* (31), *Emma* (32), *Goodbye Again* (33), *Pilgrimage* (33), *To the Last Man* (33), *Big Hearted Herbert* (34), *In Spite of Danger* (35), *Captains Courageous* (37)

Wargin, Karol (PL): *Żolnierz zwyciestwa* (53)

Warner, Steven (GB, *1966): *The Little Prince* (74), *The Blue Bird* (76)

Warnock, Craig (GB, *22 Feb 70): *Time Bandits* (81), *To the Lighthouse* (83)

Warnock, Grant Ashley (GB, *7 Dec 71): *Blood Money* (81), *St George and the Dragon* (81), *Stig of the Dump* (81)

Warren, Gary (GB, *5 Jly 54): *Up in the Air* (69), *The Railway Children* (70)

Washbrook, Johnny (US, *16 Oct 44): 249

Waterman, Dennis (GB, *24 Feb 48): 274

Watson, Billy (US, *25 Dec 23): 121

Watson, Bobs (US, *16 Nov 30): 171

Watson, Coy, Jr. (US, *16 Nov 12): 56

Watson, Delmar (US, *1 Jly 26): 144

Watson, Garry (US, *1928): 144

Watson, Harry (US, *31 Aug 21): 105

Wawrzyszczyk, Janusz (PL): *Gromada* (51)

Webster, Rupert (GB): *If....* (68)

Węgrzyniak, Rafał (PL): 384 *Kochankowie mojej mamy* (85)

Wehe, Oliver (DE): *Bekenntnisse des Hochstaplers Felix Krull* (80), *Erendira* (83)

Weinert, Michael (DE): *Der Fussgänger* (73)

Weiser, Antal (HU): 256

Weiser, György (HU): 256

Wells, Orlando (GB, *9 Jne 73): 389 *The Ploughman's Lunch* (83), *A Christmas Carol* (84), *Mister Skeeter* (84), *Maurice* (87)

Welz, Peter (DD, *1963): 344 *Ikarus* (76)

Wenkhaus, Rolf (GE, *9 Sep 17; †31 Jan 42): 80 *Emil and the Detectives* (31)

Weske, Brian (GB, *23 Dec 32): 180

West, James (US): *The Way of All Flesh* (40), *On the Sunny Side* (41), *Happy Land* (43)

West, Simon (GB): *Swallows and Amazons* (74)

Whalley, Tat (GB, *12 Jan 75): *Queen of Hearts* (89), *The Gift* (90)

Wheaton, Wil (US, *29 Jly 72): 390

'Wheezer' (US) — *see* **Hutchins, Bobby,** 134

Whitaker, Johnny (US, *13 Dec 59): 329 *'Family Affair'* (66-71)

'White, Bob' (US) — *see* Beban, George, Jr.

White, Richard (US): *The Grandmother* (70)

Whiteley, Jon (GB, *19 Feb 45): 252

Whitlock, Lee (GB, *17 Apr 68): 371

Titles Index

The names following each title are those of boy actors involved in the film: see ALPHABETICAL LISTING p 399. (For NATIONALITY CODES, see p 8.)

Srl = serial, Srs = series, TVS = TV series. Translations of foreign-language titles won't be repeated for remakes.

The alphabetical listing follows the 'straight-through' system now adopted by most libraries, which regards the **whole title** as if it were one word. Thus, we don't list all those beginning with the word 'cat' before proceeding to 'cataclysm' and so on. A film called *Herringbones* (or indeed *Herring Bones*) would come **between** *Her Right Hand* and *Her Ring Finger*.

'Our Gang' implies multiple participation. In their films, only names of boys who weren't regular Gangers will be added.

Actors' names will in general be listed alphabetically after each film, except where one or more had obviously star roles.

Aab, baad, khak /*Water, wind and sand* (IR 85): Nirumand
Aag /*Fire* (IN 48): Kapoor S.
Aage badho /*Forward march* (IN 72): Alankar
Aai mi kuthe javoo /*Where shall I go, Mother?* (IN 72): Pendharkar
Aakhri khat /*The last letter* (IN 66): Bunty
Aaltoska orkaniseera /*Mrs Aaltonen gets organised* (FI 49): Kaitala
Aan milo sajna /*Join me, darling* (IN 70): Mehmood
Aap beati /*My own story* (IN 76): Mehmood
Aap ki kasam /*By oath* (IN 74): Mehmood
Aatish /*Fire* (IN 79): Rajoo
Abandonadas, Las /*Abandoned women* (MX 45): Roche
Abandoned Woman (US 49): Gray B.
Abbé Constantin, L' /*Father Constantine* (FR 25): Guichard
Abbott and Costello in Hollywood (US 45): Jenkins, Stockwell
Ab Dilli door nahin /*Not far to Delhi* (IN 57): Kapoor R.
Abe Lincoln in Illinois (US 40): Bupp S.
Abel – twoj brat /*Your brother Abel* (PL 70): Łobodzinski, Izdebski, Mosior
Abenteuer eines jungen Herrn in Polen /*A young gentleman's adventure in Poland* (GE 34): Richter
Abenteuer im Südexpress /*Adventure on the Southern Express* (GE 34): Richter

Abenteuer in Bamsdorf /*Adventure at Bamsdorf* (DD 57): Kuss, Schmidt P.
Abie's Irish Rose (US 28): Janney
Abilene Town (US 46): Rodin M.
Above All Things (57 US) – *see* Flood Tide
Above and Beyond (US 52): Olsen C.
Abraham Lincoln (US 24): Hall N., Lee Ra., Moore M.
Abysmal Brute, The (US 23): Messinger
Accusing Toe, The (US 18): Faith
Ace Eli and Rodger of the Skies (US 73): Shea E.
Ace High (US 18): Sargent
Ace Lucky (49 US) – *see* Feudin' Rhythm
Achatmurmel, Die /*The agate marble* (DD 60): Schimkus
Aci sevda /*Bitter love* (TR 72): Dönmez
Across the Alley (US 13): Jacobs P.
Action of the Tiger (GB 57): Williams R.
Actor's Children, The (US 10): Boss
Addams Family Values (US 93): Workman
Address Unknown (US 44): Gray G., Olsen L.
Adhuri kahani /*Unfinished story* (IN 39): Suresh
Admirable Crichton, The (19 US) – *see* Male and Female
Admirable Crichton, The (GB 57): Hannaford
A dónde van nuestros hijos /*Where are our sons going?* (MX 56): Jiménez Pons R.
Adres Lenina /*Lenin's address* (SU 29): Litkin, Zavyaloff
Advent (CS 56): Rosenberg V.
Adventure in Diamonds (US 40): Downing R.
Adventure in Washington (US 41): Jones D., Bond T., Dawson
Adventurers, The (US 70): Loddi
Adventures and Emotions of Edgar Pomeroy, The (US 20-21): Jones J.
Adventures at Rugby (50 GB) – *see* Tom Brown's Schooldays
Adventures in Dairyland (US 59): Corcoran
Adventures of Andy, The (US 14): Clark A.
Adventures of Bill and Bob, The (US 22): Steele B.
Adventures of Bullwhip Griffin, The (US 65): Russell B.
'Adventures of Champion, The' (US 55-56, TVS): Curtis
Adventures of Ford Fairlane, The (US 90): Call
Adventures of Huck Finn, The (US 93): Wood E.
Adventures of Huckleberry Finn, The (US 38): Watson Bl.
Adventures of Huckleberry Finn, The (US 60): Hodges E.
Adventures of Mark Twain, The (US 43): Larson
Adventures of Prince Courageous (US 21): Trimble
Adventures of Red Ryder, The (US 40): Cook T.

Adventures of Rex, The (GB 59): Pike J., Witty

'Adventures of Rin-Tin-Tin, The' (US 54-58, TVS): Aaker L.

Adventures of Rusty, The (US 45): Donaldson T., Gray G., Larson, Madore

Adventures of Sherlock Holmes, The (US 39): Kilburn

Adventures of Tom Sawyer, The (US 37): Kelly T., Moran, Holt D., Billings G., Hurlic, Rentschler

Adventures of Tom Sawyer and His Friends, The (79 US) – see Huckleberry Finn and His Friends

Advise and Consent (US 62): Hodges E.

Æresgjesten / The guest of honour (NO 19): Lykke-Seest

Afacan harika coçuk / Afacan the wonder-boy (TR 72): Utku

Afacan küçük serseri / Afacan the little rascal (TR 71): Utku

Affaire des poisons, L' / The affair of the poisons (FR 55): Moullières

Affaire du courrier de Lyon, L' / The Lyons Mail case (FR 37): François

Affair of Susan, The (US 35): Phelps

Affairs of Annabel, The (US 38): Van Atta

Affairs of Jimmy Valentine, The (US 42): Larson

Affair to Remember, An (US 57): Winslow G.

Affair with a Stranger (US 53): Chapin B.

Afraid of Love (GB 25): Brantford

Afraid of the Dark (GB 91): Keyworth

African Interlude, An (21 US) – see Adventures and Emotions of Edgar Pomeroy

Afsana / Story (IN 51): Kumar

After Divorce (32 US) – see Divorce in the Family

After Midnight (49 US) – see Captain Carey, USA

After the Thin Man (US 36): Hoskins

Age of Desire, The (US 23): Guerin, Lee F.

Age of Indiscretion, The (US 35): Holt D.

Aggressor, The (US 11): Pickford

Agni pariksha / Tested by fire (IN 54): Bhattacharjee

Agonie des aigles, L' / The eagles' agony (FR 20): Rauzéna

Agostino (IT 62): Colombo

Agustina de Aragon / Augustina of Aragon (ES 28): Hurtado

Ahí está el detalle / That's the whole point (MX 40): Busquets

Ahijado de la muerte, El / Death's godchild (MX 46): Pastor

Ahlam al-medina / City dreams (SY 84): El-Abyad

Ah, Wilderness! (US 35): Rooney, Bupp T., Kibrick L.

Ah, Wilderness! (47 US) – see Summer Holiday

Ai-Gul (SU 36): Kim, Goryunoff, Makutonin

Aijo ni tsuite / About love (JP 53): Shitara

Aika hyvä ihmiseksi / Not bad for a human (FI 77): Aronen

Aik jan hain hum (PK 88): Jamshid

Ai no ikko / A family of love (JP 41): Oizumi

Air Mail (US 25): Fairbanks

Airplane! (US 80): Harris R.

Air pur / Clean air (FR 39): François

Ajab tuzhe sarkar / Well done! (IN 71): Sachin

Åke och hans värld / Åke and his world (SE 59): Lindström J.

Åke och hans värld (SE 84): Lindström M.

Akibiyori / Late autumn (JP 60): Shimazu, Shitara

Aki tachinu / Approach of autumn (JP 61): Osawa

Akvalangi na dne / Aqualungs on the sea-bed (SU 65): Barsov

Aladdin and the Wonderful Lamp (US 17): Carpenter, Messinger, Sargent, Lee Ra., Perl

Aladdin's Lantern (US 38): 'Our Gang'

Alakh Niranjan (IN 50): Kumar

Alan and Naomi (US 91): Haas L.

A la orilla de un palmar / At the edge of a palm-grove (MX 38): Zamora

Alarma in Delta / Danger in the Delta (RO 75): Popescu, Vasiliu

Alarm auf Station III / Alert at Station 3 (GE 39): Dann

Alarm in den Bergen / Mountain alert (DE 62, srl): Hehn

Albero dalle foglie rosa, L' / The pink-leaved tree (IT 74): Cestiè

Albero degli zoccoli, L' / The tree of clogs (IT 78): Brignoli

Aldebaran (IT 35): Brambilla

Alerta en el ciel / Alert in the sky (ES 61): Calvo

Alex (90 PT) – see Idade maior

Alfalfa's Aunt (US 39): 'Our Gang'

Alfalfa's Double (US 40): 'Our Gang'

Alfons Zitterbacke / Alphonse Aguecheek (DD 65): Rossmann

Algo flota sobre el agua / Something floats on the water (MX 47): Roche

Algy's Tormentor (GB 13): Royston R.

Ali and the Camel (GB 60): Rifai, Waterman

Alias El Rata / Alias the Rat (MX 64): Bravo J.

Alias Jimmy Valentine (US 29): Butts

Alias the Bandit (US 30): Nelson B.

Alias the Deacon (US 28): Murphy M.

Alias the Deacon (34 US) – see Half a Sinner

Alias the Deacon (US 40): Bartlett

Ali Baba and the Forty Thieves (US 18): Messinger, Sargent, Stone, Lee Ra.

Ali Baba and the Forty Thieves (US 43): Beckett

Alice Doesn't Live Here Any More (US 74): Lutter

Alice in Wonderland (US 33): Barty, Leroy, Searl

Aliens Are Coming, The (US 80): Laborteaux M.

Alimony Aches (US 35): Bond T.

All About Hash (US 40): 'Our Gang'

Allá en el Rancho Chico / Over at Boys' Ranch (MX 37): Busquets, Ortin, Rio, Velasquez E., Zamora

Allah dad (PK 88): Jamshid

Allah ditta (PK 88): Jamshid

All American (US 53): Hunt

Allan Field's Warning (GB 13): Barker

Alleen voor U / Just for you (BE 35): Buyl

Alles für Geld / Anything for money (GE 23): Herzberg

Alles weg'n dem Hund / All because of the dog (GE 35): Bosse

Alle Tage ist kein Sonntag / It's not Sunday every day (DE 59): Hanke

Alley Cowboy (46 US) – see Boys' Ranch

Allez France! (FR 64): Lester

All I Desire (US 53): Gray B.

Alligator (US 80): Petersen P.

All in a Day (US 20): Morrison E.

All in a Day's Work (GB 14): Desmond

All I Want for Christmas (US 91): Randall

All Lit Up (US 20): Morrison E.

All Mine to Give (US 57): Thompson R., Bernard, Provost

All on Account of a Portrait (US 13): Boss

All on Account of the Milk (US 10): Pickford

All Quiet on the Western Front (US 30): Parrish

All Souls' Eve (US 21): Moore M.

All That Money Can Buy (US 41): Bupp S.
All the Kids Do It (US 84): Licht
All Things Bright and Beautiful (GB/IE 94): Fitzgerald C.
All This, and Heaven Too (US 40): Nichols
All Together Now (US 75): Drier, Savage B.
All Woman (US 18): Sargent
Alma de bronce /Soul of bronze (MX 44): Busquets
Álmodó ifyúsag /Dreaming youth (HU 74): Csoma
Almost a Divorce (GB 31): Penrose
Almost Angels (US 62): Scully, Winter, Gilmore, Scott H.
Alo, aterizeaza strabunica /Hello, great-grandmama has landed
   (RO 81): Carp
Aloha (US 31): Moore D.
Alois vyhrál los /Alois wins the lottery (CS 18): Branald
Aloma of the South Seas (US 41): Beckett, Roy
Alone in Moscow (62 SU) – see Ya kupil papu
Alone in the Streets (54 IT) – see Soli per le strade
Alone in the World (US 16): Short
Along Came Baby (47 US) – see On Our Merry Way
Along Came Youth (US 31): Ernest
Alsino y el condor /Alsino and the condor (NC/MX/CU/CR 82):
   Esquivel
Altid ballade /Always trouble (DK 55): Holmberg, Klahn, Overgaard
Altri tempi /Times gone by (IT 51): Cerusico, Di Nardo, Staiola
Alupusu taisho /Alpine master (JP 34): Ito K.
Always Goodbye (US 38): Russell J.
Alyosha Ptitsin virabativayet kharakter /Alyosha Ptitsin's character-
   training (SU 53): Kargopoltsev, Podmasterev, Vasilev B.
Amant, L' / The lover (FR/US 92): Poupaud
Amant de Bornéo, L' /The lover from Borneo (FR 42): François
Amants de demain, Les /Tomorrow's lovers (FR 57): Moullières
Amants du Tage, Les /The lovers of the Tagus (FR 54): Moullières
Amapola (ES 25): Hurtado
Amarilly of Clothes-Line Alley (US 18): Barry W., Butterworth F.
Amateur Daddy (US 32): Darro
Amateur Gentleman, The (GB 36): Singer
Amatörfilmen /The amateur film (SE 22): Alexandersson
Amazing Cosmic Awareness of Duffy Moon, The (US 76):
   Eisenmann, Kerwin
Amazing Mrs Holliday, The (US 43): Infuhr
Amazing Stories (US 85): Haas L.
Ambassador Bill (US 31): Alexander T.
Ambrose's Cup of Woe (US 16): Jacobs
Ambush (US 39): Lee B.
Ame de clown/ A clown's soul (FR 34): Pâqui
Amédée /Amadeus (FR 49): Simon
Ame des moulins, L' (12 NL/FR) – see Molens die juichen en weenen
Amelia Earhart (US 76): Kerwin
America (44 US) – see American Romance
American, The (US 27): Murphy M.
American Dream (US 80): Hershewe
American Dreamer (US 84): Fox H.
American Drive-In (US 82): Nucci
American Empire (US 43): Rodin M.
American Heart (US 91): Furlong E.
American Hot Wax (US 77): Drier
American Romance, An (US 44): Bates, Jenkins, Larson

Americathon (US 79): Feldman
Ames d'enfants /Children's souls (FR 27): Guichard
A mi-chemin du ciel /Halfway to heaven (FR 30): Mercanton
Amici per la pelle /Bosom friends (IT 55): Meynier, Scirè
Amigo Ernesto /My friend Ernesto (BG 85): Prahov
Amintiri din copilarie /Childhood memories (RO 64): Bocancea
Amir garib /Rich and poor (IN 74): Bunty, Mehmood
Amitiés particulières, Les /Special friendships (FR 64):
   Haudepin, Maurin D.
Amityville Horror, The (US 79): Peluce
Among the Living (US 41): Watson D.
Amor de la calle /Street love (MX 50): Fernandez, Jiménez Pons J.,
   Moreno
Amore /Love (IT 35): Sannangelo
Amore più bello, L' (58 IT/ES) – see Uomo dai calzoni corti
Amor, estranjo amor /Strange love (BR 81): Ribeiro
Amori di una calda estate (65 ES/FR/IT) – see Pianos mecanicos
Amorous Adventures of Moll Flanders, The (GB 65): Baulch
Amo un assassino /I love a murderer (IT 52): Maggio
Amour est en jeu, L'/Love at stake (FR 57): Noël
Amour en fuite, L' /Love on the run (FR 79): Dubois
Amsterdam (NL 28): Klein H.
Amy (US 81): Scribner
Ana kalbi /Mother's heart (TR 69): Dönmez
Anak dalita /Child of sorrow (PH 56): Bacani
Ana mezari /Mother's grave (TR 69): Utku
Anastasia (GB 87): Bale
Anchors Aweigh (US 45): Stockwell, Lindgren O., Rodin M.
Anciens de Saint-Loup, Les /Old Saint-Loup boys (FR 50): Gencel,
   Lecointe, Simon, Chambot
Ancient Mariner, The (US 25): Boudwin, Jones B.
And a Little Child Shall Lead Them (US 09): Tansey J.
Andaz /Style (IN 71): Alankar
An der Donau, wenn der Wein blüht /By the Danube when
   the vines are flowering (DE/AT 65): Koester
Andere Ich, Das /The other I (GE 41): Möller
Anderson Tapes, The (US 71): Jacoby S.
Anderssonskans Kalle /The Anderssons' Kalle (SE 22): Alexandersson
Anderssonskans Kalle (SE 34): Hallberg
Anderssonskans Kalle (SE 50): Blitz
Anderssonskans Kalle (SE 72): Tjädersten
Anderssonskans Kalle i busform /The Anderssons' Kalle in top form
   (SE 73): Tjädersten
Anderssonskans Kalle på nya upptag /New adventures of the
   Anderssons' Kalle (SE 23): Alexandersson
Andhi /Thunderstorm (IN 52): Bhattacharjee
...And Now Miguel (US 66): Cardi, Robbins
And Now Tomorrow (US 44): Binyon, Rodin M.
Andorra (FR 41): Claudio
André Cornélis (FR 27): Roudenko
Andreika (SU 58): Vasilev Vo.
Andrius (SU 80): Mikaliunas
And So They Were Married (US 36): Moran, Scott D.
And So They Were Married (44 US) – see Johnny Doesn't Live Here
And Sudden Death (US 36): Lee B.
And Women Shall Weep (GB 60): O'Sullivan
'Andy' series (US 13-14): Clark A.

Andy Goes on the Stage (US 14): Clark A., Boss

Andy Hardy Gets Spring Fever (US 39): Kilburn

Andy Hardy's Double Life (US 42): Blake

And Your Name Is Jonah (US 79): Licht

Ane de Buridan, L' /Buridan's ass (FR 32): Bara

Anekdoten um den alten Fritz /Stories about Old Fritz (GE 35): Teetzmann

Angarey /Embers (IN 54): Kumar

Angeles de la calle /Angels of the street (CU/MX 53): Calpe, Perez

Angel Eyes (US 28): Sabiston

Angeli del quartiere, Gli /Local angels (IT 52): Cerusico

Angeli khoris ftera /Angels without wings (GR 65): Kailas

Angelito (61 ES) – see Pachin almirante

Angelitos del trapecio /Little angels of the trapeze (MX 58): Quezadas

Angelo bianco, L' /The white angel (IT 42): Barbetti

Angelo è sceso a Brooklyn, Un (57 ES/IT) – see Angel pasó por Brooklyn

Angel of Death (US 90): Bonsall

Angelo My Love (US 83): Evans A.

Angel on My Shoulder (US 46): Gilpin J., Nokes

Angelo tra la folla /Angel in the crowd (IT 50): Maggio

Angel pasó por Brooklyn, Un /An angel comes to Brooklyn (ES/IT 57): Calvo

Angel's Face, An (70 PL) – see Twarz aniola

Angels with Dirty Faces (US 38): Jordan, Bailey Sd., Bupp S.

Anička jde do školy /Little Annie goes to school (CS 62): Malaska

Aniki /Elder brother (JP 33): Sugawara

Aniki-Bóbó (PT 42): Silva

Ani ohev otach Rosa /I love you, Rosa (IL 71): Otterman

Anjan (IN 41): Suresh

Anjana /The stranger (IN 68): Mehmood

Ankhiyon ke jharonkon se /Through the eyes' windows (IN 78): Rajoo

Än leva de gamla gudar /The old gods live still (SE 37): Winther

Anma to onna /The masseurs and a woman (JP 38): Yokoyama

'Anna and the King' (US c.72, TVS): Shea E.

Anna and the King of Siam (US 46): Lyon

Annabel Lee (US 21): Grauer

Annabelle's Affairs (US 31): Parrish

Annabel Takes a Tour (US 38): Kibrick S., Severn Cl.

Anna Karenina (DK 22): Herzberg

Anna Karenina (27 US) – see Love

Anna Karenina (US 35): Bartholomew, Phelps

Anna Karenina (GB 47): Spenser J.

Anna Karenina (GB 77, srl): Spurrier

Anna na sheye /Anna round your neck (SU 54): Maltsev

Année de l'éveil, L' /Year of awakening (FR 91): Colin

Anneler günü /Mother's day (TR 73): Dönmez

Anne-Liese von Dessau, Die /Anne-Liese of Dessau (GE 25): Pottier

Anne of Windy Poplars (US 40): Moran

Annette im Paradies /Annette in paradise (GE 34): Schaufuss

Annie Get Your Gun (US 50): Mora, Price

Annie Laurie (US 27): Janney

Annie Oakley (US 35): Watson D.

Annie Rowley's Fortune (US 13): Hackett A. and R.

Anniversary Trouble (US 35): 'Our Gang'

Anolkhi /Unknown (IN 73): Alankar

Another April (US 74): Savage B.

Another Man, Another Woman (77 FR) – see Autre homme, une autre chance

Another Time, Another Place (GB 58): Stephens M.

Ansigtet /The face (DK 14): Schønberg

Anthony Adverse (US 36): Mauch Bl., Beckett

Anthracite (FR 79): Zucca

Anton der Letzte /Anton the Last (GE 39): Rohringer

Anty (US 89): Rushton

Anuraag /Blind love (IN 72): Satyajit

Anuradha (IN 40): Marathe A.

Anything Goes (US 36): Bartlett, Tucker J.

Aozora ni naku /Crying to the blue sky (JP 32): 'Tokkan-Kozo', Sugawara

Apa /Father (HU 66): Erdélyi

Aparajito /The unvanquished (IN 56): Gupta

...A pátý jezdec je Strach /And the fifth horseman was Fear (CS 64): Hádl

Apenas un delincuente /Hardly a delinquent (AR 49): Alonso T.

Apni chhaya /One's own shadow (IN 50): Kumar

Appel du destin, L' /The call of destiny (FR 52): Benzi

Appel du silence, L' /The call of silence (FR 36): Buquet

Apple Dumpling Gang, The (US 74): O'Brien C., Savage B.

Apple-Tree Girl, The (US 17): Clark A.

Appointment with Venus (GB 51): Spenser J.

Après l'amour /After love (FR 31): Bara

April Fool (US 11): Boss

April Fool (US 26): Holmes L., Moore P.

Arabian Adventure (GB 79): Sira

Aranybalta /The golden axe (HU 58): Weiser A. and G.

Ara! Sono shunkan yo! /That's just when! (JP 30): 'Tokkan-Kozo'

Ara! Tairyo dane! /What a catch! (JP 30): 'Tokkan-Kozo'

Arbor Day (US 36): 'Our Gang'

Arbre de Noël, L' /The christmas tree (FR/IT 69): Fuller B.

Arche de Noé, L' /Noah's ark (FR 46): Simon

Archie and the Bell-Boy (US 13): Boss, Clark A.

Arch of Triumph (US 48): Gilpin, J.

Are Husbands Necessary? (39 US) – see Honeymoon in Bali

Arena (US 53): Aaker L.

Are These Our Children? (US 31): Butts

Are We All Murderers? (52 FR) – see Nous sommes tous des assassins

Argent, L' /Money (FR 28): Gaillard

Argent de poche, L' /Pocket money (FR 76): Desmouceaux, Goldman

Arizona Ames (37 US) – see Thunder Trail

Arizona Badmen (US 35): Bupp T.

Arizona Bound (US 27): Butterworth J.

Arizona Mahoney (US 36): Lee B.

Arizona Manhunt (US 51): Chapin M.

Arizona Streak, The (US 26): Darro

Arizona Sweepstakes, The (US 26): Morgan, Schaeffer

Arizona Wildcat, The (US 38): Downing R.

Arkansas Traveler (US 38): Cook B., Moore D.

Arlésienne, L' /The girl from Arles (FR 30): Mercanton

Arme Sünderin, Die /The poor sinner (GE 23): Pottier

Armored Attack (43 US) – see North Star

Army Brat (46 US) – see Little Mister Jim

Army Wives (US 44): Brown K., Lenhart

Babes in Toyland (US 34): Beckett, Bupp T.
Babes in Toyland (US 61): Corcoran, Russell B.
Babes on Broadway (US 41): Madore
Babies à la Mode (US 30): Scott D.
Babla (IN 51): Bhattacharya
Baby, The (US 15): Carpenter
Baby Blues (US 41): 'Our Gang'
Baby Brother (US 27): 'Our Gang'
Baby Clothes (US 26): 'Our Gang'
Baby Follies (US 30): Scott D.
Baby Marie's Round-Up (US 19): Morrison E.
Baby's Diplomacy (US 17): Morrison E.
Baby Talks (US 29): McKeen
Bach détective /Bach the detective (FR 36): Farguette
Bachelor Daddy, The (US 22): Guerin
Bachelor Daddy (US 41): Larson
Bachelor Husband, A (GB 20): Craig
Bachelor's Christmas, A (US 15): Roubert
Bachelor's Waterloo, A (US 12): Johnson R.
Bachpan /Childhood (IN 45): Kapoor S.
Bachpan (IN 70): Mehmood
Back Door to Heaven (US 39): Lydon
Backfield (34 US) – see Band Plays On
Back from Eternity (US 56): Provost
Back from the Dead (US 19): Eason
Back from the Dead (US 57): Kirk
Background (GB 53): Spenser J.
Backlash (US 46): Chapin M., Gray G., Mickelsen
Back Porch (34 US) – see It's a Gift
Back Roads (US 81) Jacoby B.
Back Stage (US 23): 'Our Gang'
Back Street (US 61): Eyer Ro.
Back to Bataan (US 45): Louie
Back to Nature (US 36): Ernest, Mahan
Back to the Future 2 (US 89): Wood E.
Back to the Kitchen (US 19): Marion D.
Backward - the Riddle of Dyslexia (US 83): Phoenix R.
Backyard Theater, A (US 14): Griffith, Jacobs
Badal (PK 87): Jamshid
Badaltey rishtey /Changing relations (IN 78): Rajoo
Bad and the Beautiful, The (US 52): Olsen C.
Bad auf der Tenne, Das /The bath on the threshing-floor (GE 43): Möller
Badge 373 (US 73): Alejandro
Bad Guy (US 37): Billings G.
Bad Lands, The (US 25): Black B.
Bad Little Angel (US 39): Reynolds, Kuhn, Madore
Bad Man from Red Butte, The (US 40): Billings G.
Bad Man of Brimstone (US 37): Beckett
Bad Man of Wyoming (40 US) – see Wyoming
Bad Men of Missouri (US 41): Winkler
Bad Men of Tombstone (US 49): Gray B.
Bad News Bears, The (US 76): Barnes C., Haley, Lutter, Marx
Bad News Bears Go to Japan, The (US 78): Haley, Marx
Bad News Bears in Breaking Training, The (US 77): Barnes C., Haley, Lutter, Marx
Bad Ronald (US 74): Jacoby S.
Bad Seed, The (US 85): Allen Chd.

Bad Sister, The (US 31): Durand, Butler
Baghdad (IN 52): Kumar
Bagula bhagat /Hypocrite (IN 79): Mehmood
Baiju bawra /Crazy Baiju (IN 52): Kumar R.
Bail Out at 43,000 (US 57): Eyer
Baisers volés /Stolen kisses (FR 68): Zucca
Bait, The (US 73): Savage B.
Bajaderens hævn /The bayadere's revenge (DK 16): Schønberg
Baker's Hawk (US 76): Montgomery
Baksiddha (IN 57): Babua
Bakul (IN 54): Bhattacharjee
Bakuon /Airplane drone (JP 39): Katayama
Balak /The kid (IN 69): Mehmood Jr.
Balak aur janwar /The boy and the animal (IN 74): Alankar
Balak Dhruv /The child Dhruv (IN 74): Alankar, Satyajit
Balam /Darling (IN 49): Kumar R.
Bal des pompiers, Le /The firemen's ball (FR 48): Simon
Ballada o niepokonanym Jasiu /Ballad of John the Invisible (PL 78): Miller S.
Ballad in Blue (GB 64): Bishop
Ballad of Josie, The (US 67): Quinn T.
Ballerina e il Padreterno, La /The ballerina and the Everlasting Father (IT 57): Angeletti M.
Balletten dansar /The ballet dances (DK 38): Bjørnsson
Ballettens börn /Children of the ballet (DK 54): Henning-Jensen
Ball of Fire (US 41): Ryan T.
Ballonrejsen /Trip in a balloon (DK 60): Neumann
Ballon rouge, Le /The red balloon (FR 56): Lamorisse
Baltiskoye nebo /Baltic sky (SU 61): Perevalov
Bamba (MX 48): Perez
Bambi (US 42): Dunagan
Bambini ci guardano, I /The children are watching (IT 42): De Ambrosis
Banda de los ochos, La /The Gang of Eight (ES/MX 61): Quezadas
Bandhan (IN 40): Suresh
Bandi /The prisoner (IN 78): Rajoo
Bandidos de Rio Frio, Los /The bandits of Cold River (MX 38): Busquets
Banditi a Orgosolo /Bandits of Orgosolo (IT 61): Cuccù
Bandit of Sherwood Forest, The (US 46): Tauzin
Bandit's Baby, The (US 25): Jones B., Noisom
Bandit Tamer, The (US 25): Black B.
Band Plays On, The (US 34): Durand, Haines
Bang! You're Dead (GB 53): Richmond, Barrett
Bang! You're Dead (US 61): Mumy
Banjo (US 47): Rees
Banjo Hackett (US 76): Eisenmann
Bank Detective, The (40 US) – see Bank Dick
Bank Dick, The (US 40): Larson
Ban ki chidiya /Forest bird (IN 38): Apte
Banshun /Late spring (JP 49): Aoki (Tomihiro)
Bansi birju (IN 72): Mehmood
Bantam Cowboy, The (US 28): Barton
Bärande hav /Seaborne (SE 51): Sarri
Barbacca /Bareback (SE 46): Lindgren H.
Barber Shop, The (US 33): Watson H.
Barbier von Filmersdorf, Der /The barber of Filmville (GE 15): Zilzer
Barcos de papel /Paper boats (ES/AR 62): Calvo
Bar-C Mystery, The (US 26): Fox J.

Bardhast (PK 88): Jamshid
Barefoot Boy, The (US 23): Lee F.
Barefoot Boy (US 38): Moran
Barefoot Contessa, The (US/IT 54): Staiola
Bargain Day (US 31): 'Our Gang'
Bari Didi /Elder sister (IN 39): Kapoor Ra.
Bari thekey paliye /The runaway (IN 59): Bhattarak
Barkhar bahar /Love's bloom (IN 73): Alankar
Barnabašek /Little Barney (CS 63): Lukeš
Barnehjertets heltemod /A child's heroism (DK 15): Andersen P.
Barnen från Frostmofjället /The kids from Frosty Hill (SE 45): Lindgren H., Nyström
Barnens Ö /Children's Island (SE 79): Fryk
Barney (AU 76): Maxworthy
Barnum & Ringling, Inc. (US 28): 'Our Gang'
Barnyard Follies (US 40): Kaye, Switzer
Barraca, La /The farmhouse (MX 45): Roche
Barrier, The (US 17): Carr J., S., T., Jones J.
Barrio de pasiones /District of passion (MX 47): Roche
Barrister's Wife (IN 35): Apte
Bartolo toca la flauta /Bartolo plays the flute (MX 45): Fernandez
Basant (IN 42): Suresh
Bashta mi boyadzhiyata /My pa the housepainter (BG 74): Petrov
Bashu, gharibeh kuchak/Bashu the little stranger (IR 89): Afravian
Basketball Fix, The (US 51): Hyatt
Bastard, The (US 78): Eisenmann, Doran
Bataillon du ciel, Le /The sky battalion (FR 46): Simon
Batalla de los pastelas, La /The battle of the pies (MX 66): Bravo J.
Batman, The (US 43): Croft
Battaglia, La /The battle (IT 42): Artese
Battle, The (US 14): Jacobs
Battle at Bloody Beach (US 61): Brodie
Battle Circus (US 52): Chang
Battle of Billy's Pond, The (GB 76): Buckton, Ashby A.
Battle of Greed (US 37): Butler
Battle of Youth (US 19): Alexander B.
Battlestar Galactica (US 78): Hathaway
Battling Brewster (US 24): Holmes L.
Battling Buckaroo, The (US 28): Darro
Battling Kid, The (US 30): Nelson B.
Bauernrebell, Der /The peasant rebel (AT 52): Friedl
Bawarchi /The cook (IN 72): Rajoo
Bayou Boy (71 US) — see Boy from Dead Man's Bayou
'Baywatch' (US 89–, TVS): Call
Baxter Millions, The (35 US) — see Three Kids and a Queen
Bazar-e-Hasan (PK 89): Jamshid
Bazigar (IN 38): Suresh
Beach Romance, A (US 14): Jacobs
Bear, The (US 84): Guffey
Bear Facts, The (US 14, 'Sonny Jim'): Connelly
Bear Facts, The (US 38): 'Our Gang'
Bear Shooters, The (US 30): 'Our Gang', Janney
Beastmaster, The (US 82): Jacoby Bl., Milrad
Beast of the City, The (US 32): Rooney
Beates Flitterwochen /Beata's honeymoon (GE 40): Schmidhofer
Beau Geste (US 26): DeLacy, McBan, Murphy M.
Beau Geste (US 39): Cook B., O'Connor, Holt D., Spellman

Beautiful but Broke (US 44): Gray G., Mummert
Beautiful but Dangerous (54 US) — see She Couldn't Say No
Beauty and the Bus (US 33): Bond T.
'Bébé' series (FR 10-14): Mary
Bébé adopte un petit frère /Baby adopts a little brother (FR 12): Mary, Poyen
Bébé, Bout de Zan et le voleur /Baby, Nipper and the burglar (FR 12): Mary, Poyen
Bébert et l'omnibus /Bébert and the bus (FR 63): Lartigue, Isella
Becket (GB 64): Moulder-Brown
Bedstermoders vuggevise /Grandma's lullaby (DK 12): Crone
Bedtime Story, A (US 33): Leroy
Bedtime Worries (US 33): 'Our Gang'
Begegnung im Zwielicht (60 PL/DD) — see Spotkania w mroku
Begegnung mit Werther /Meeting with Werther (DE 49): Bürger
Beggar in Purple, A (US 20): Butterworth E.
Beggar's Opera, The (GB 53): Alleney T.
Beginner's Luck (US 35): 'Our Gang'
Behind Southern Lines (US 52): Lindgren O.
Behold a Pale Horse (US 64): Angeletti M.
Behold Thy Son (57 JP) — see Kiiroi karasu
Behroopiya /The clown (IN 71): Mehmood
Bei, baraban /Beat, drum (SU 62): Krivchenkov
Bekenntnisse des Hochstaplers Felix Krull /Confessions of Felix Krull, confidence man (DE 80): Wehe
Belâli tatil /Troubled holiday (TR 74): Inanoğlu
Beleyet parus odinoki /A white sail gleams (SU 38): But, Runge
Believe it or not (62 SU) — see Ya kupil papu
Believers, The (US 87): Cross
Bellamy Trial (US 28): Lee D.
Belle aventure, La /The glorious adventure (FR 42): Geffroy
Belle équipe, La /The great team (FR 36): Lynen
Belle et Sébastien /Belle and Sebastian (FR 61, srl): 'Mehdi'
Belle fille comme moi, Une /A lovely girl like me (FR 72): Zucca
Belles on Their Toes (US 52): Hunt, Ivo, Sydes
Bellman & True (GB 87): O'Brien K.
Bello recuerdo /Sweet memory (ES 61): Jiménez
Bells of St Mary's, The (GB 28): Pavitt
Bells of St Mary's, The (US 45): Nokes, Tyler D.
Beloved (US 34): Butler, Ernest, Rooney
Beloved Brat (US 38): Beard
Beloved Enemy (US 36): Sinclair
Beloved Rogue, The (US 27): Moore D.
Beloved Vagabond, The (36 FR) — see Vagabond bien-aimé
Beloved Vagabond, The (GB 36): Tester
Ben (US 72): Montgomery
Benaam /Nameless (IN 74): Rajoo
Ben Blair (US 16): Griffith
Bende van hiernaast, De /The next door gang (NL 80): Gabriëlse
Benefits Forgot (38 US) — see Of Human Hearts
Benefiz-Vorstellung der Vier Teufel, Die /The Four Devils' benefit performance (GE 20): Herzberg
Beni ecën vetë /Benny walks alone (AL 75): Mustafaraj (Spiro)
Beniker Gang, The (US 85): Fields, Pintauro
Beni kujaku /Red pickle (JP 54): Yamate
Benjamin Blake (41 US) — see Son of Fury
Benjamin Franklin, Jr. (US 43) 'Our Gang'

Benji (US 74): Fiuzat
Benjy (US 52): Aaker L.
Bennie Bartlett's Band (US 38): Bartlett
Benny Goodman Story, The (US 55): Kasday
Be Prepared! (53 US) – *see* Mr Scoutmaster
Bequest to the Nation (GB 73): Guard
Berlin Express (FR 46): Simon
Berlin Story (52 GB) – *see* Man Between
Bermondsey Kid, The (GB 33): Fitzpatrick P., Singer
Beröringen / *The touch* (SE/US 70): Hallerstam
Berth Quakes (US 37): Bartlett
Besprizorniye / *Little vagabonds* (SU 28): Chernishoff, Lyudvinski
Bessmertni garnizon / *The immortal garrison* (SU 56): Saifulin
Best Friends (US 77): Hathaway
Bestia magnifica, La / *The gorgeous beast* (MX 52): Perez
Best of the West (US 80): Peluce
Best Man Wins (US 48): Gray G., Sheffield B.
Best Years of Our Lives, The (US 46): Infuhr, Nokes
Besuch im Zoo / *Visit to the Zoo* (GE 35): Bosse
Be Sure Your Sins (GB 15): Desmond
Betaab / *Restless* (IN 52): Kumar
Betrayal (US 29): Haig
Betsy, The (US 77): Fields
Better Movies (US 25): 'Our Gang'
Better Wife, The (US 19): Alexander B.
Between Heaven and Hell (US 56): Mora
Between Us Girls (US 42): Beckett
Beware, My Lovely (US 52): Mora, Pollock
Beware of Blondes (26 US) – *see* Poker Faces
Beware of Blondie (US 50): Simms L., Mummert
Beware of Children (60 GB) – *see* No Kidding
Beware of the Dog (GB 64, srl): Moulder-Brown, Bury
Beware Spooks! (US 39): Jones D., Bupp T.
Beyond the Law (37 US) – *see* Californian, The
Beyond the Rainbow (US 22): Griffin
Beyond the Rockies (US 26): Nelson B.
Beyond This Place (GB 59): Winter
Bezhin lug / *Bezhin meadow* (SU 37): Kartashoff
Bez strakha i uproka / *Without fear or reproach* (SU 62): Burlyayev K.
Bhagwan Sri Krishna chaitanya (IN 53): Babua
Bhagyawan / *The lucky one* (IN 53): Kumar
Bhakta Raghunath (IN 51): Bhattacharjee
Bhakt Bilwamangal (IN 48): Kapoor S.
Bhakt dhruva (IN 47): Kapoor S.
Bhakt Gopalbhaiya (IN 48): Kapoor S.
Bharat ke shaheed / *Martyrs of India* (IN 72): Mehmood, Alankar
Bharat mata (57 IN) – *see* Mother India
Bharosa / *Faith* (IN 40): Apte
Bhore hoye elo (IN 53): Babua
Bianchi cavalli di agosto / *White horses of August* (IT 75): Cestiè
Bicz Bózy / *The scourge of God* (PL 66): Zarzycki
Bidaai / *Farewell* (IN 74): Satyajit
Bien amada, La / *The well-beloved* (MX 51): Mejía
Big (US 88): Rushton
Big and the Bad, The (73 IT/FR/ES) – *see* Si può fare....amigo
Big Ben Calling (GB 35): Green H.
Big Bonanza, The (US 44): Driscoll, Hickman C.

'Big Boy' Juvenile Comedies (US 27-29): Sabiston
Big Broadcast, The (US 32): Cosbey
Big Broadcast of 1936, The (US 35): Holt D.
Big Broadcast of 1937, The (US 36): Holt D., Lee B.
Big Brother (US 23): Bennett M.
Big Brother Bill (US 15): Benham
Big Business (US 24): 'Our Gang'
Big Business (US 37): Mahan
Big Cage, The (US 33): Rooney
Big Chance, The (US 33): Rooney
Big Chief Little Pimple (GB 14): Collet
Big City (US 48): Jenkins
Big City Boys (US 78): Barnes C.
Big Clock, The (US 48): Norman
Big Dan (US 23): Black B.
Big Decision, The (51 US) – *see* Basketball Fix
Big Ears (US 31): 'Our Gang'
Big Fall, The (50 US) – *see* Under My Skin
Big Fella, The (GB 37): Gorst
Big Fish, The (55 CS) – *see* Dobrodružstvi na Zlate Zatoce
Big Fix, The (US 78): Hershewe
Bigger Than Life (US 56): Olsen C., Mathers
Big Hand for the Little Lady, A (US 66): Michenaud
Big Heart, The (47 US) – *see* Miracle on 34th Street
Big Hearted Herbert (US 34): Ward
Big Henry and the Polka Dot Kid (US 79): Barnes C.
Big Land, The (US 57): Ladd
Big Noise, The (US 44): Blake
Big Operator, The (US 59): North J.
Big Pal (US 25): Bennett M., Black B.
Big Premiere, The (US 40): 'Our Gang'
Big Race, The (30 US) – *see* Texan, The
Big Red (US 62): Payant
'Big Shamus, Little Shamus' (US 79, TVS): McKeon D.
Big Show, The (US 23): 'Our Gang'
Big Sister, The (US 16): Roubert
Big Stampede, The (US 33): Bailey Sd.
Big Thrill, The (33 US) – *see* Return of Casey Jones
Big Town, The (US 25): 'Our Gang'
Big Trail, The (US 30): Shuford, Parrish
Big Tremaine (US 16): Alexander B.
Big van het Regiment, De / *The regimental piglet* (NL 35): Anderiesen
Big Wave, The (US/JP 62): Ota, Shitara
Big Wednesday (US 78): Lookinland T.
Bijli / *Lightning* (IN 72): Mehmood, Satyajit
Bila holubice / *The white dove* (CS 59): Smyczek
'Bill and Andy' series (US 31-32): Shuford
Billet de mille, Le / *The thousand-franc note* (FR 34): Genevois
Billi / *The cat* (IN 38): Apte
Billie (US 12): Porter W.
Bill's Boy (US 14): Harper
Bill's Wife (16 US) – *see* Grouches and Smiles
'Billy' films (US 13-14): Jacobs
Billy l'enfant terrible / *Beastly little Billy* (FR c.29): Barty
Billy's Burglar (US 12): Kelly P.
Billy Turf, het dikste studentje ter wereld / *Billy Turf, the world's fattest schoolboy* (NL 78): Janssen T.

Bimbo (20 US) – see Just Pals
Bindur chheley (IN 52): Bhattacharjee
Bin maa ke bachchey / Motherless children (IN 80): Rajoo
Bionic Boy, The (US 76): Van Patten V.
Bionic Boy, The (SG 76): Yap
Birbal (IN 72): Sachin
Birds and the Bees, The (US 55): Corcoran
Biribì, il piccolo poliziotto di Parigi / Biribi, the little Paris policeman
   (IT 21): Capelli
Birth Certificate (61 PL) – see Swiadectwo urodzenia
Birthday Blues (US 32): 'Our Gang', McComas
Birth of the Blues, The (US 41): Cosbey
Birthright (US 20): Berlinger
Biscuit Eater, The (US 40): Lee B., Hickman C
Biscuit Eater, The (US 71): Spell G., Whitaker
Bishop's Wife, The (US 47): Anderson B., Infuhr
Biskoppen / The bishop (DK 44): Fagerlund
Bismarck (GE 40): Eugens
Bit o' Heaven, A (US 17): Clark R.
Bits of Life (US 21): Barry W.
Bitter Springs (GB 50): Yardley N.
Bitwa o Kozi Dwor / Battle of Goat Yard (PL 61): Halicz, Wiśniewski
Black Ace, The (US 28): Butts
Black and white (FR 29): Machin, 'Colibri'
Black Bandit, The (US 38): Downing R.
Black Beauty (US 20): Hamrick
Black Beauty (GB/DE/ES 71): Lester
Black Book, The (49 US) – see Reign of Terror
Black Cauldron, The (US 85): Call
Black Fear (US 15): Hackett A., Tansey J.
Black Fury (US 34): Albright, Nelson B., Rentschler, Samarzich
Black Gold (US 47): Louie
Blackguard, The (GB 25): Herzberg
Black Hand Gang, The (GB 30): Pavitt, Singer
Black Hen, The (80 SU) – see Chernaya kuritsa
Black Island (GB 78): Murphy M.
Black Jack (GB 79): Hirst, Bennett A.
Black Joy (GB 77): Medford
Black Legion (US 36): Jones D.
Black Lightning (US 24): Butterworth J.
Blackmail (GB 29): Ashby J.
Blackmail (US 39): Watson Bs.
Black Moon (US 34): Holt D.
Black Noon (US 71): Garrett
Black Panther's Cub, The (US 21): Jackson C.
Black Pawl (20 US) – see Godless Men
Black Rider, The (GB 54): Pike J.
Black Rose, The (US/GB 50): Blake
Black Sheep, The (46 US) – see Boys' Ranch
Black Spurs (US 64): Padilla
Black Stallion, The (US 79): Reno
Black Stallion Returns, The (US 83): Reno
Black Wall, The (US 12): Casey
Blå drenge, De / Those boys in blue (DK 33): Larsen
Blake Murder Mystery, The (40 US) – see Haunted House
Blake of Scotland Yard (US 37, srl): Jones D.
Blank Check (US 94): Bonsall

Blank Wall, The (49 US) – see Reckless Moment
Blau blüht der Enzian / Gentian blue (DE 73): Doff
Blaue vom Himmel, Das / Sky blue (DE 32): Richter
Blå undulater, De / The surge of the sea (DK 65): Schmidt J.P.
Blaze o' Glory (US 29): Darro
Blazing Barriers (23 US) – see Jacqueline
Blechtrommel, Die / The tin drum (DE/FR 79): Bennent
Blé en herbe, Le / Green corn (FR 52): Beck P.-M.
Blessing, The (59 US) – see Count Your Blessings
Blick zurück, Ein / A look back (GE 44): Möller
Blind Alibi (US 38): Bupp T.
Blind Alley (US 39): Beckett
Blind Date (US 34): Rooney
Blinde Passagier, Der / The stowaway (GE 22): Allen W.
Blind Fury (US 90): Call
Blind Man's Buff (US 16): Roubert, Clark A.
Blinker's Spy-Spotter (GB 71): Beaumont M.
Block-Heads (US 38): Bond T.
Block Signal, The (US 26): Holmes L.
Blodets bånd / The ribbon of blood (DK 11): Stensgård
Blomstertid, Den / Blossom time (SE 40): Bernhard
Blonde Carmen, Die / The blonde Carmen (GE 35): Brackmann
Blonde Reporter, The (31 US) – see Sob Sister
Blonde Venus (US 32): Moore D., Tucker J.
Blondie (US 38): Simms L., Mummert
Blondie Brings Up Baby (US 39): Simms L., Mummert
Blondie Buys a Horse (43 US) – see It's a Great Life
Blondie for Victory (US 42): Simms L., Mummert
Blondie Goes Latin (US 41): Simms L., Mummert
Blondie Goes to College (US 42): Simms L., Mummert
Blondie Has Servant Trouble (US 40): Simms L., Mummert
Blondie Hits the Jackpot (US 49): Simms L., Mummert
Blondie in Society (US 41): Simms L., Mummert
Blondie in the Dough (US 47): Simms L., Mummert
Blondie Knows Best (US 46): Simms L., Mummert
Blondie Meets the Boss (US 39): Simms L., Mummert
Blondie on a Budget (US 40): Simms L., Mummert
Blondie Plays Cupid (US 40): Simms L., Mummert
Blondie's Anniversary (US 47): Simms L., Mummert
Blondie's Big Deal (US 49): Simms L., Mummert
Blondie's Big Moment (US 47): Simms L., Mummert
Blondie's Blessed Event (US 42): Simms L., Mummert
Blondie's Hero (US 50): Simms L., Mummert, Infuhr
Blondie's Holiday (US 47): Simms L., Mummert, Larson
Blondie's Lucky Day (US 46): Simms L., Larson
Blondie's Reward (US 48): Simms L., Mummert
Blondie's Secret (US 48): Simms L., Mummert
Blondie Steps Out (39 US) – see Blondie Meets the Boss
Blondie Takes a Vacation (US 39): Simms L., Mummert
Blond muss man sein auf Capri / Better be blond on Capri (DE 61):
   Angeletti M.
Blood Brother, The (32 US) – see Texas Pioneers
Bloodbrothers (US 78): Hershewe
Bloodhound, The (US 25): Black B.
Blood Money (GB 81, TVS): Warnock G.
Blood Seedling, The (US 15): Clark R.
Bloody Birthday (US 80): Jacoby Bl.

Bloody Kids (GB 79): Thomas R.2, Clark P.

Bloomfield (GB 69): Burfield

Blossoms in the Dust (US 41): Nichols, Bates C., Madore

Blow Your Own Horn (US 23): Fox J.

Blue Bird, The (US 18): MacDougall

Blue Bird, The (US 40): Russell J., Baker, Beckett, Cook B., Moore D., Phelps, Tucker T.

Blue Bird, The (US/SU 76): Lookinland T., Warner

Blue Boy, The (US 26): DeLacy

Blue Eagle, The (US 26): Madden

Blue Fin (AU 79): Rowe

Blue Grass of Kentucky (US 50): Henry R.

Blue jeans (FR 80): Budin, Melet

Blue Kite, The (HK/CN 92) − see Lan fengzheng

Blue Montana Skies (US 39): Winkler

Blue Skies (US 29): Frederick, Moore D., Scott D., Watson D. and H.

Blue Squadron, The (GB 34): Singer

Blue Streak McCoy (US 20): Eason

Blue Veil, The (US 51): Pollock

Blumenmädchen vom Grand-Hotel, Das / The flower-girl at the Grand Hotel (DE 34): Richter

Blut und Ehre - Jugend unter Hitler / Blood and Honour: youth under Hitler (DE 82): Frank

B-Men (US 89): Arnott

Bob and Carol and Ted and Alice (US 69): Garrett

Bob and Rowdy (US 11): Boss

Bobbed Hair (US 22): Coghlan

'Bobby' comedies (US 17): Connelly

Bobby (US 72): Montgomery

Bobby and the Roses (US 16): Hamrick

Bobby auf der Fährte / Bobby on the ferry (GE or AT 21): Lubinsky

Bobby, der Benzinjunge / Bobby the petrol boy (GE 29): Burns B.

Bobby Parker and Company (US 74): Shea E.

Bobby Rings the Bell (GB 51): Hill

Bobby's Baby (US 13): Short

Bobby's Bandit (US 15): Fuehrer

Bobby's Dream (US 12): Boss

Bobby's Kodak (US 08): Harron

Bobbys krig / Bobby's war (NO 74): Andersson

Bobby's Long Trousers (US 12): Boss, Clark A.

Bobby's Medal (US 15): Fuehrer

Bobby's Plot (US 14): Hauck

Bobby Ware Is Missing (US 55): Charney

Bob Hampton of Placer (US 21): Barry W.

Bodyline (AU 84): Gledhill, Kounnas

Bofuu no bara / Rose in the storm (JP 31): 'Tokkan-Kozo'

Bogáncs / Thistle (HU 58): Weiser A.

Boiling Point, The (US 32): Nelson B.

Bold, Bad Burglar, The (US 16): Butterworth F.

Bold Bad Pirate, A (US 20): Roubert

Bolshiye i malenkiye / Big and small (SU 63): Klimov

Bomans pojke / Boman's boy (SE 33): Winther

'Bomba' series (US 49-56): Sheffield J.

Bombay to Goa (IN 72): Mehmood

Bomber's Moon (US 43): Brown K., Tyler L.

Bombi Bitt och jag / Bombi Bitt and I (SE 68): Skarsgård

Bonds of Love (US 19): Lee F.

Bondwomen (US 15): Steuart

Bonjour jeunesse / Hello youth (FR/CH 56): Fourcade

Bon petit diable, Un / A good little devil (FR 23): Rauzéna

Bon petit diable, Un (FR 83): Courtois

Bon Voyage! (US 62): Corcoran

Boogie Woogie (US 45): Hickman Dl.

Boothill Brigade (US 37): Nelson B.

Boot Polish (IN 54): Kumar

Boots and Saddles (US 37): Sinclair

Borderland (US 22): Lee F.

Borderline (US 80): Gomez P.

Border Whirlwind, The (US 26): Nelson B.

Border Wolves (US 37): Jones D.

Bored of Education (US 36): 'Our Gang'

Bore of a Boy, A (GB 13): Royston R.

Born Again (US 78): Feldman

Born of the Cyclone (24 US) − see Untamed Youth

Born to Battle (US 26): Black B., Darro

Born to Dance (US 36): Watson Bl.

Born to Run (US 77): Bettles

Born to Sing (US 42): Nunn

Born to Sing (62 US) − see Almost Angels

Born to the West (US 26): Holt T., Butterworth J.

Borrowing Trouble (US 37): Ernest, Mahan

Bors Istvan / Istvan Bors (HU 39): Dévényi

Boshi-zo / Mother and son (JP 55): Yamate

Boško Buha (YU 78): Kojundžić

Boss of the Lazy Y (US 18): Lee F.

Boss Said No, The (42 US) − see Blondie Goes to College

Bottom of the Bottle, The (US 56): Charney

Bottom of the Well, The (US 17): Connelly

Bottoms Up (GB 59): Mitchell, Scott H., Robinson D.

Boulder Dam (US 36): Breakston, Cosbey

Boule de gomme / Jujube (FR 31): Bara

Boulevard (FR 60): Léaud

Bouncing Babies (US 29): 'Our Gang'

Bounty Hunter, The (US 54): Charney

Bouquetière des innocents, La / The flower-girl of the innocent (FR 22): Guichard

Bout de Chou / Little pet (FR 35): Buquet, 'Mircha'

'Bout de Zan' series (FR 13-15): Poyen

Bowery, The (US 33): Cooper Ja., Alexander T., Kibrick L.

Bowery Boys (US 14): Griffith, Jacobs

Bow Wow (US 22): Marion D.

Boxeador, El / The boxer (MX 57): Jiménez Pons R.

Boxing Gloves (US 29): 'Our Gang'

Box of Delights, The (GB 84): Stanfield

Boy (US 14): Jackson C.

Boy, The (19 US) − see Heart of Youth

Boy, The (69 JP) − see Shonen

Boya banzai / Three cheers for Boya (JP 35): 'Tokkan-Kozo'

'Boy Adventure' series (US 27): Janney

Boy, a Girl and a Dog, A (US 46): Hunter

Boy and a Bad Man, A (US 29): Nelson B.

Boy and His Dog, A (US 47): Sheffield B.

Boy and the Bridge, The (GB 59): MacLaine

Boy and the Girl, The (US 12): Boss
Boy and the Pirates, The (US 60): Herbert
Boy at the Throttle, A (US 15): Boardman
Boy Called Nuthin', A (US 67): Howard R.
Boy Company Member (KN 64): Hwang
Boy Cried Murder, The (GB/DE/YU 66): McIntosh
Boy Detective, The (US 08): Harron
Boy from Barnardo's, The (38 US) – see Lord Jeff
Boy from Dead Man's Bayou, The (US 71): Lookinland M., Vogel
Boy from Stalingrad, The (US 43): Samarzich, Beckett, Binyon
Boyhood He Forgot, The (US 17): Short
Boyhood of Dr Noguchi, The (56 JP) – see Noguchi hideyo no shonen-jidai
Boy in Keumdol, A (KN 68): Kim C.
Boy Named Charlie Brown, A (US 69): Robbins
Boy of Flanders, A (US 24): Coogan J.
Boy of Mine (US 23): Alexander B.
Boy of the Revolution, A (US 11): Pickford
Boy of the Streets, A (US 27): Bennett M
Boy of the Streets (US 37): Cooper Ja.
Boy of Two Worlds (59 DK) – see Paw
Boy Rider, The (US 27): Barton
Boy Scouts to the Rescue (US 18): Carr J. and S.
Boys from Brazil, The (US 78): Black J.
Boy Slaves (US 39): Daniel
Boys of Paul Street, The (24 HU) – see Pál utcai fiuk
Boys of Paul Street, The (US/HU 69): Kemp, Moulder-Brown, Beaumont M., Younger
Boys' Prison (49 US) – see Johnny Holiday
Boys' Ranch (US 46): Hickman Dl., Homeier, Jenkins
Boys' School (38 FR) – see Disparus de Saint-Agil
Boys to Board (US 23): 'Our Gang'
Boys Town (US 38): Rooney, Watson Bb., Butler, Kibrick L. and S., Rentschler, Reynolds, Spellman, Thomas F.
Boys Will Be Joys (US 25): 'Our Gang'
Boy Ten Feet Tall, A (63 GB) – see Sammy Going South
Boy Trouble (US 39): O'Connor, Lee B., Albright, Billings G., Bupp S., Tucker T.
Boy Wanted (US 13): Boss
Boy Who Caught a Crook, The (US 61): Mobley
Boy Who Cried Bitch, The (US 90): Cross, Bradford
Boy Who Never Was, The (GB 79): Bulloch C.
Boy Who Stole a Million, The (GB 60): Reyna
Boy Who Stole an Elephant, The (US 69): Lester
Boy Who Stopped Niagara, The (CA 47): Martin J.
Boy Who Talked with Animals, The (GB 80): Spurrier
Boy Who Turned Yellow, The (GB 72): Dightam
Boy With Green Hair, The (US 48): Stockwell, Lyon, Calkins, Hickman Dw., Infuhr, Sheffield B., Tamblyn
Bracelet de la Marquise, Le / The marchioness's bracelet (FR 11): Mary
Braco (FR 55): Emery
Brady's Escape (83 US/HU) – see Long Ride
Brahim (MA 58): Gharbi
Brahmachari / The celibate (IN 68): Mehmood, Sachin
Brainscan (US 94): Furlong E.
Brainstorm (US 65): Cardi
Brancolando nel buio / Groping in the dark (IT 13): Petrungaro

Brand of Hate, The (US 34): Rentschler
Brankář bydlí v naší ulici / The goalie lives in our street (CS 57): Sedláček, Pucholt
Bränningar / Breakers (SE 35): Granberg O.
Brass (US 23): Guerin
Brass Legend, The (US 55): MacDonald D.
Brat geroya / The hero's brother (SU 40): Mirski
BRAT Patrol, The (US 86): Astin S.
Bratya Komarovi / The Komarov brothers (SU 61): Barkhatov
Brave New World (US 80): Petersen Chr.
Brave One, The (US 56): Ray M.
Bravest of the Brave (US 38): Downing R.
Bravos, The (US 72): Van Patten V.
Bravo Two (US 76): Laborteaux M.
Brazil (GB 85): Nash S.
Bread (US 24): Sabiston, Lee Ra.
Bread Cast upon the Waters (US 12): Gottlieb
Breakfast Club (US 85): Hall A.M.
Breaking Point (CA 76): Lynas
Breaking the Ice (US 38): Breen
Breakout (GB 84): Nash S.
Break the News to Mother (US 19): Grauer
Breed of the Treshams, The (GB 20): Craig
Brelan d'as / Three aces (FR 52): Fourcade
Brennende Geheimnis, Das (23 GE) – see Mutter, dein Kind ruft
Brennendes Geheimnis / Burning secret (GE 33): Schaufuss, Richter
Brennendes Geheimnis (DE 75): Ohrner
Brewster's Millions (GB 35): Fitzpatrick P.
Brick Top (US 16): Clark R.
Bridal Path, The (GB 59): Winter
Bridal Suite (US 39): Blake
Bride Goes Wild, The (US 48): Jenkins, Severn B.
Bride of Frankenstein (US 35): Barty
Bride-To-Be, The (US 22): Condon
Bride Wore Red, The (US 37): Moore D.
Bridge Destroyer, The (GB 14): Desmond
Bridge of Adam Rush, The (US 74): Kerwin
Bridges Burned (US 17): Steuart
Brieftträger Müller / Postman Müller (DE 53): Condrus
Briggen 'Tre Liljor' / The good ship 'Three Lilies' (SE 61): Axberg E.
Brigham Young – Frontiersman (US 40): Jones D.
Bring Home the Turkey (US 27): 'Our Gang'
Bring Your Smile Along (US 55): Clark B.2
Bristleface (US c.66): Alford
Britton of the Seventh (US 16): Connelly
Broadcasting Night Life in Hollywood (US 22): Jones J.
Broadway Bad (US 33): Cosbey
Broadway Bill (US 18): Beck C.
Broadway to Hollywood (US 33): Cooper Ja., Rooney, Alexander T.
Bröderna Lejonhjärta / The brothers Lionheart (SE 77): Söderdahl
Brödernas kvinna / The brothers' woman (SE 43): Nyström
Broken Chains (US 16): Tansey J.
Broken Doll, The (US 14): Jacobs
Broken Dreams (US 33): Phelps
Broken Laws (US 24): Moore P.
Broken Mask, The (US 28): DeLacy
Broken Rosary, The (GB 34): Hepworth H.

Broken Silence, The (US 22): Depew
Broken Strings (US 40): Beard
Broke to the Wide (26 US) – *see* Cowboy Cop
Brokiga blad /*Miscellany* (SE 31): Winther
Bronx Tale, A (US 93): Capra
Bronze Bride, The (US 17): Lee F.
Brother For Sale (US 30): McKeen
Brother Orchid (US 40): Baker
Brother Rat and a Baby (US 40): Bupp T.
Brothers Lionheart, The (77 SE) – *see* Bröderna Lejonhjärta
Broth of a Boy, A (US 15): Clark A.
Brownies, The (US 17): Carpenter, Messinger
Browning Version, The (GB 50): Smith B.
'Brown Kiddies' series (US 27): Janney
Brücke, Die /*The bridge* (DE 59): Hoffmann
Bruno, l'enfant du dimanche /*Bruno, Sunday's child* (FR 68): Mesnier
Bruscolo /*Titch* (IT 19): Roveri
Brute, The (GB 76): Barnes N.
Brute Breaker, The (US 19): Hamrick
Bubbling Troubles (US 40): 'Our Gang'
Bübchen (68 DE) – *see* Kleine Vampir
'Bubi' series (10-14 FR) – *see* 'Bébé'
Buccaneers, The (US 24): 'Our Gang'
Buckaroo Kid, The (US 26): House N.
Buckaroo Sheriff of Texas (US 50): Chapin M.
Buck Privates (US 28): Searl, Shuford
Buck Rogers serial (US 39): Moran
Buckskin (US 68): Michenaud
Buckskin Days (US 28): House N.
Budapesti tavasz /*Springtime in Budapest* (HU 55): Koletár
Bud Blossom (US 15): Benham
Buddy's Downfall (US 14): Kelly P.
Buddy's First Call (US 14): Kelly P.
Buddy System, The (US 84): Wheaton
Buenaventura de Pitusin, La /*Pitusin's good luck* (ES 23): Hurtado
Bufere /*Gales* (IT 52): Olivieri
Buffalo Bill (US 44): Hickman C., Rodin M.
Buffalo-Bill et la bergère /*Buffalo Bill and the shepherdess* (FR 48): Simon
Bugle Call, The (US 16): Collier
Bugle Call, The (US 27): Coogan J.
Bugsy Malone (GB 76): Baio S., Fletcher
Bukhta smerti /*Bay of death* (SU 26): Lyudvinski
Bulbule Punjab /*Nightingale of Punjab* (IN 33): Modak
Bulldog Drummond's Revenge (US 37): Bartlett
Bulldog Pluck (US 27): Nelson B.
Bullet for a Badman (US 64): Tate
Bullets or Ballots (US 36): Madden, Watson H.
Bullfighter and the Lady (US 50): Perez
Bumps (US 12): Casey
Buna seara Irina /*Good evening, Irina* (RO 80): Carp
Bunny's Mistake (US 13): Connelly
Bunt na kuklite /*The doll's revolt* (YU 57): Ruben
Bunty Pulls the Strings (US 20): Lee F.
Buon natale! /*Merry Christmas!* (IT 14): Roveri
Buon sangue non mente /*Good blood doesn't lie* (IT 17): Petrungaro
Buon viaggio pover' uomo /*Bon voyage, poor fellow* (IT 51): Staiola
Bureau of Missing Persons (US 33): Alexander T.

Burglar's Mistake, A (US 09): Harron
Burgomaster of Stilemonde, The (GB 28): Brantford
Buried Treasure (US 26): 'Our Gang'
Burning Daylight (US 20): Hall N.
Burning Secret (33 GE and 75 DE) – *see* Brennendes Geheimnis
Burning Secret (GB/US 88): Eberts
Burnt Offerings (US 76): Montgomery
Bush Christmas (GB 47): Yardley M. and N.
Bush Christmas (AU 83): Spain
Bush Leaguer, The (US 27): Shuford
Business of Love, The (US 25): Hall N.
'Buster' films (US 12): Johnson R., McCloskey
Buster Brown (DK 11): Rosenberg M.
'Buster Brown' series (US 14): Millington
'Buster Brown' comedies (US 25-29): Hutchins, Trimble
Buster's Dream (US 12): Johnson R., Carr S.
Busters verden /*Buster's world* (DK 84): Andersen M. B.
Buti nga sa iyo /*You are really good* (PH 84): Ummar
Butterfly (US 24): Wilkinson
Buttons (GB 15): Royston G.
Buttons (US 27): Coogan J., Watson C.
Buzzy and the Phantom Pinto (US 41): Henry R.
Byagashti kucheta /*Running dogs* (BG 88): Prahov
Bye Bye Birdie (US 63): Russell B.
Bye-Bye Red Riding Hood (CA/HU 88): Vermes
By Hook or by Crook (43 US) – *see* I Dood It
By Speshul Delivery (US 17): Lee F.
By the Light of the Silvery Moon (US 53): Gray B.

Caballo blanco, El /*The white horse* (MX/ES 62): Jiménez
Cabriola (ES 65): Sanchez
Cactus Nell (US 17): Jacobs
Cadets de l'Océan, Les /*Cadets of the 'Ocean'* (FR 42): Claudio
Caesar and Cleopatra (GB 45): Harvey
Café de Puerto (ES 58): Gil
Cage aux rossignols, La /*Cage of nightingales* (FR 44): François, Krebs
Cagliostro (US 47): Wager
Cahill United States Marshal (US 73): O'Brien C.
Caida, La /*The fall* (AR 58): Orlegui, Lopez Monet
Caillaux Case, The (US 18): Grauer
Cairo (US 42): Nunn
Cajus Giulius Caesar (IT 12): Visca
Calamity the Cow (GB 67): Moulder-Brown,
California (US 46): Tucker T.
California Firebrand (US 48): Rees
California Gold Rush (US 46): Blake
Californian, The (US 37): Reynolds
California or Bust (US 27): Fox J.
California Passage (US 50): Miles P.
Call a Messenger (US 39): Tucker T.
Callejera /*Streetwalker* (MX 49): Fernandez, Jiménez Pons J.
Call for Mr Caveman, A (US 19): Morrison E.
Call from the Past, A (GB 15): Desmond
Call from the Wild (US 21): Lee F.
Calling All Kids (US 43): 'Our Gang'
Calling Dr Kildare (US 39): Watson Bs.
Calling the Tune (GB 36): Fitzpatrick P.

Call Me Mame (GB 33): Fitzpatrick P.
Call Northside 777 (US 47): Chapin M.
Call of the Cumberlands, The (US 16): Griffith
Call of the Heart, The (US 27): Murphy M.
Call of the Ring, The (37 US) — see Duke Comes Back
Call of the Savage (US 35, srl): Jones D.
Call the Mesquiteers (US 38): McKim S.
Call to Glory (US 85): Hathaway
Calvaire du mousse, Le (12 NL/FR) — see Lijden van de scheepsjongen
Calvario de una esposa, El /A wife's torment (MX 36): Zamora
Camada negra /Black brood (ES 77): Alonso J.L.
Camelot (US 67): Beauvy
Camera Fiend, The (GB 13): Desmond
Came the Brawn (US 38): 'Our Gang'
Camicia nera /Blackshirt (IT 33): Locchi
Camicie rosse /Redshirts (IT/FR 50): Cerusico, Leurini
Camino, El /The road (ES 64): Alfaro, Mejias
Camino de la vida, El /The road of life (MX 56): Jiménez Pons H. and R., Perez
Campo di maggio /May Field (IT 35): Locchi
Campus Honeymoon (US 48): Infuhr
Canadian, The (US 26): Butts
Canale degli angeli, Il /Angels' canal (IT 34): Locchi
Canary Murder Case, The (US 29): Scott D.
Cancion del huerfano, La /Orphan's song (MX 39): Ortin, Rio, Velasquez E.
Cancion del milagro, La /Song of the miracle (MX 40): Rio
Cancre, Le (70 FR) — see Cinéma de Papa
Canicule /Dog-days (FR 83): Bennent
Canker of Jealousy, The (15 GB) — see Be Sure Your Sins
Canned Fishing (US 38): 'Our Gang'
Canon City (US 48): Sydes
Canta y no llores /Sing, don't cry (MX 49): Jiménez Pons J.
Canto de la cigarra, El /Song of the cicada (ES 80): Sanz
Cantoniera N.13, La /Signal-girl 13 (IT 19): Casarotti
Canyon Hawks (US 30): Barton
Canyon River (US 56): Eyer Ri.
Can You Hear Me, Mother? (GB 35): Pavitt, Singer
Cão e dois destinos, Um /A dog and two destinies (PT 65): Neto
Caperucita y Pulgarcito contra los monstruos /Red Riding Hood and Tom Thumb versus the Monsters (MX 60): Quezadas
Capitan, Le /The Captain (FR 45): Emrich
Capitano di Venezia, Il /The Captain of Venice (IT 51): Maggio
Cappello a tre punte, Il /The three-cornered hat (IT 34): Barbetti
Capricciosa (DK 08): Voigt
Captain Barnacle's Waif (US 12): Kelly P.
Captain Blood (US 24): Noisom
Captain Blood (US 35): Beard
Captain Boycott (GB 47): Malone
Captain Carey, USA (US 49): Tamblyn
Captain Eddie (US 45): Hickman Dl. and Dw.
Captain Grant's Children (36 SU) — see Deti Kapitana Granta
Captain Grant's Children (62 GB) — see In Search of the Castaways
Captain January (US 36): Tucker J.
Captain Kidd and the Slave Girl (US 54): Crawford J.
Captain Kiddo (US 17): Clark R.

Captains Courageous (US 37): Bartholomew, Rooney, Bupp T., Burrud, Reynolds, Thomas F., Van Atta, Ward
Captains Courageous (US 77): Kahn, Doran
Captains of the Clouds (US 42): Roy
Captain Spanky's Show Boat (US 39): 'Our Gang'
Captain Stirrick (GB 81): Silvester, Hicks
Captive Heart, The (GB 46): Wallbridge
Capture, The (US 50): Hunt
Captured in Chinatown (US 36): Nelson B.
Cara sucia /Dirty face (MX 48): Roche
Caravan (GB 46): Mullins
Caravan (IN 71): Mehmood
Caravane à Vaccarès (74 GB/FR) — see...
Caravan to Vaccares (GB/FR 74): Cargol
Carbine Williams (US 52): Hyatt
Career (US 39): Billings G., Bond T.
Careful, He Might Hear You (AU 83): Gledhill
Carlos und Elisabeth (GE 24): Herzberg
Carman's Romance (US 14): Jacobs
Carmen (US 28): Madden
Carnet de bal /Dance card (FR 37): Lynen
Carnevalesca /Carnival (IT 17): Visca
Carnival Girl, The (US 26): Darro
Carnival in Costa Rica (US 47): Ivo
Carolina (US 34): Cosbey
Caroline chérie /Darling Caroline (FR 50): Fourcade
Carottes sont cuites, Les /The goose is cooked (FR 56): Urbain
Carpenter, The (US 13): Connelly
Carrefour /Crossroads (FR 38): Claudio
Carrefour des enfants perdus, Le /The crossroads of missing children (FR 43): Demorget
Carringford School Mystery, The (GB 58, srl): Richmond
Carry On Admiral (GB 57): Hannaford
Carry On Doctor (GB 72): Garlick
Carry On Teacher (GB 59): O'Sullivan
Cartas marcadas /Marked cards (MX 48): Cardona II
Cartoons in a Seminary (US 15): Boss
Cartoons in the Kitchen (US 15): Clark A.
Cartouche (FR/IT 62): Dekock
Casa del ogro, La /The ogre's house (MX 39): Rio
Casa de vecindad /House nearby (MX 50): Roche
Casanova Brown (US 44): Chapin B., Olsen L.J.
Case against Mrs Ames, The (US 36): Beckett
Casebusters (US 86): Hathaway
Case of Eugenics, A (US 15): Connelly
Case of Lena Smith, The (US 29): Albright
Case of the Silk King, The (US 90): Allen Chd.
'Casey Jones' (US 57, TVS): Clark B.2
Casey's Shadow (US 77): Hershewe
Cash and Carry (US 37): Bupp S.
Casino de Paris (DE/IT/FR 57): Kaiser
Castaway Cowboy, The (US 74): Shea E.
Castle in the Air (GB 52): Hannaford
Cat, The (US 66): Redlin
Catch Me a Dream (75 ZA) — see Vang vir my 'n droom
Catch My Smoke (US 22): Griffith
Catch Us If You Can (AU 83): Kounnas

Edward Albert

José Luis Alonso

Two Penrods: Ben Alexander (l.) defers to Wesley Barry

Ricardo Ancona

Ilir Çelia

Cat, Dog & Co. (US 29): 'Our Gang'
Cat Gang, The (GB 59): Bulloch J., Pike J.
Cat's-Paw, The (US 34): Holt D.
Cattle Drive (US 51): Stockwell
Caught (US 48): Hawkins, Hyatt
Caught in a Cabaret (US 14): Griffith
Caught in the Net (GB 60): Bulloch J.
Caught Short (US 30): Conlon, Haig
Cause for Alarm! (US 50): Mora
Cause for Divorce (US 23): Coghlan
Cause for Thanksgiving (US 14, 'Sonny Jim'): Connelly
Cavalcade (US 33): Henderson D., Scott D.
Cavalcade of the West (US 36): Tucker J.
Cave Dwellers, The (US 14, 'Sonny Jim'): Connelly
Caves du Majestic, Les / The Majestic's cellars (FR 44): Demorget
Cay, The (US 75): Lutter
Cecilia of the Pink Roses (US 18): Jackson C.
Celebrity (US 84): Phoenix R.
Cello (GB 90): Hawkes
Cenere / Ashes (IT 16): Casarotti
Centennial (US 78): McKeon D.
Centennial Summer (US 46): Swan
Cento chilometri, La / The 100 kilometres (IT 59): Nevola
Centomila leghe nello spazio/ 100,000 leagues into space (IT 59): Chevalier
Ce que savait Morgan / What Morgan knew (FR 73): Haccard
Cerf-volant du bout du monde / Kite from the world's end (FR/CN 58): Baradine
Černa sobota / Black Saturday (CS 60): Bor
Certain Rich Man, A (US 21): Lee F.
Cesar a detektivi / Caesar and the detectives (CS 68): Michl
Ces chers petits (58 FR) − see Drôles de phénomènes
Československý Jekišek / A Czech Jekyll (CS 18): Branald
Ces sacrées vacances / These bloody holidays (FR 55): Urbain, Maurin Y.-M.
Cesta do hlubin studakový duše / Journey to the depths of a student's soul (CS 39): Salač
Cesta do pravěkou / Journey into prehistory (CS 55): Bejval
Cestou křizovou / The way of the cross (CS 38): Jedlička V.
C'est pour les orphelins / It's for the orphans (FR 16): Poyen
Ceux de demain / Tomorrow's people (FR 38): Bara, Buquet, Farguette
Chabichou (FR 50): Lecointe
Chained (US 34): Rooney, Bupp T.
Challenge, The (GB 59): Pike P.
Chambre des dames, La / The ladies' room (FR 79): Tittone
Chambre verte, La / The green room (FR 78): Maléon
Chameli Memsaab (IN 81): Rajoo
Champ, The (US 31): Cooper Ja., Shuford
Champ, The (US 78): Schroder
Champeen, The (US 23): 'Our Gang'
Champions de France / Champions of France (FR 38): Brécourt
'Champion the Wonder Horse' (55-56 US) − see Adventures of Champion
Champi-Tortu / Runty (FR 20): Duc
Chance of a Lifetime, The (US 43): Olsen L.J.
Chanda aur Bijli / 'Moon' and 'Lightning' (IN 69): Mehmood, Sachin
Change of Heart (US 38): Kuhn, Watson D.

Channel Crossing (GB 33): Hepworth J., H., R.
Chant de l'amour, Le / Love song (FR 35): Rodon, Tarride
Chardons du Baragan, Les (57 RO) − see Ciulinii Baraganului
Charge of the Light Brigade, The (US 36): Beckett
Charity Castle (US 17): Callis
Charleys Tante / Charley's aunt (DE 56): Condrus
Charlie Chan's Chance (US 31): Conlon
Charlie, the Lonesome Cougar (US 67): Russell B.
Charrette fantôme, La / The phantom cart (FR 39): Buquet, Claudio, François,
Charro Negro en el norte, El / Charro Negro in the North (MX 49): Anda
Chartroose Caboose (US 60): McGreevey
Chasing Trouble (US 31): Coghlan
Château de ma mère, Le / My mother's mansion (FR 90): Ciamaca
Chatis Ghante / 36 Ghante (IN 74): Alankar
Chavala, La / The lass (ES 25): Hurtado
Chciałbym się zgbuić / I want to get lost (PL 79): Jankowski A., Oliszewski, Wiśniewski W.
Cheaper by the Dozen (US 50): Hunt, Sydes
Cheating the Public (US 18): Lee F.
Checkers (US 24): Black B.
Cheerful Givers (US 17): Stone
Cheer Leader, The (US 27): Nelson B.
Chelovek idyot za solntsem / A man follows the sun (SU 61): Krimnus
Chelovek rasseyanni / An absent-minded man (SU 38): Seleznyov
Chelovek s portfelem / Man with a briefcase (SU 29): Simanovich
Cherevichki / The slippers (SU 27): Lyudvinski
Chéri-Bibi (31 US) − see Phantom of Paris
Chernaya kuritsa / The black hen (SU 80): Sedletski
Cherokee Kid, The (US 27): Van Horn
Cherokee Strip, The (US 37): Bupp T.
Cherokee Strip (US 40): Winkler
Chess Players, The (77 IN) − see Shatranj ke khilari
Chetniks! (US 43): Rodin M.
Chevaliers de France / Knights of France (FR 52): Poujouly
Chew Chew Land (US 10): Casey
Cheyenne Cyclone (US 32): Darro
Cheyenne Wildcat (US 44): Blake
Chhaya / Shadow (IN 36): Marathe A.
Chhaya sangini (IN 56): Babua
Chheley kar (IN 54): Babua
Chicago Ben (38 GB) − see Hey! Hey! USA!
Chicago Calling (US 51): Gebert
Chicago, Chicago (69 US) − see Gaily, Gaily
Chicago Sal (US 23): Headrick
Chichi / Father (JP 30): Sugawara
Chicho krustnik / Uncle Godfather (BG 87): Gabrovski
Chicken Chaser (US 14): Griffith
Chicken Every Sunday (US 48): Sydes
Chicken Feed (US 27): 'Our Gang'
Chicken-Wagon Family (US 39): Billings G.
¿Chico o chica? / Boy or girl? (ES 62): Quezadas
Chief, The (US 33): Rooney
Chiefly Concerning Males (US 14, 'Sonny Jim'): Connelly
Chiefs (US 83): Guffey

Chiens perdus sans collier / *Lost dogs without collars* (FR/IT 55):
Urbain, Moullières, Lecointe, Maurin Y.-M.

Chi è senza peccato / *He that is without sin* (IT 52): Olivieri

Chiisakobe / *Little kid* (JP 62): Ito T.

Chiku-no kodomotachi / *Children of the mining town* (JP 60): Okimura

Child and the Killer, The (GB 59): Williams R.

Child for Sale, A (US 20): Connelly

Child in Judgment, A (US 15): Steuart

Child Is Waiting, A (US 62): Ritchey, Mumy

Children, The (GB/DE 90): Hawkes

Children in the House, The (US 16): Carpenter, Stone

Children in the Wind (37 JP) − *see* Kaze no naka no kodomo

Children of Chance (GB 49): Carey

Children of Divorce (US 27): Marion D.

Children of Dreams (US 31): Janney

Children of Dust (US 23): Hall N., Lee F., O'Donnell

Children of Dynmouth, The (GB 86): McGrath

Children of Fire Mountain (NZ 80, TVS): Airey

Children of the Feud (US 16): Stone

Children of the Fog (GB 35): Pavitt, Rietti

Children of the Forest (GB 12): Royston R.

Children of the Mission, The (US 15): Butterworth F.

Children's Conspiracy, The (US 13): Benham

Child's Devotion, A (US 12): Hackett R.

Child's Influence, A (US 13): Butterworth E.

Child's Remorse, A (US 12): Steuart

Child's Stratagem, A (US 10): Pickford

Child Thou Gavest Me, The (US 21): Headrick

Chili-Chala the Magician (69 HU) − *see* Varázsló

Chilly Days (US 28): Sabiston

Chimney Sweep, The (US 16): Harper

Chimp Mates (GB 75): Fletcher

China Doll (US 58): Chang

China Girl (US 42): Blake

China Hilaria, La / *The girl Hilaria* (MX 38): Velasquez E.

China Sky (US 45): Louie

China's Little Devils (US 45): Louie

Ching (US 19): Lee F.

Chino (73 IT/ES/FR) − *see* Valdez, il mezzosangue

'Chip' series (US 15-16): Monahan

Chip Off the Old Block, A (US 15): Monahan

Chipollino (SU 73): Yelistratov

Chi sei tu? / *Who are you?* (IT 38): Locchi

Chissà perchè...capitano tutto a me / *A captain all to myself: Why?*
(IT 80): Guffey

Chitchor / *Stealer of hearts* (IN 76): Rajoo

Chitty Chitty Bang Bang (GB 68): Hall A.

Chlapec a srna / *The boy and the deer* (CS 62): Hrušecky

Chocolate Girl (32 JP) − *see* Chokoreto garu

Choir Boys, The (US 15): Fuehrer

Chokoreto garu / *Chocolate girl* (JP 32): 'Tokkan-Kozo'

Chota baap / *Little father* (IN 77): Alankar

Choti bahu / *The younger daughter-in-law* (IN 71): Mehmood

Chris and the Wonderful Lamp (US 17): Carnahan

Christian, The (US 23): Wood E. H.

Christmas (US 22): DeLacy

Christmas Carol, A (16 US) − *see* Right to Be Happy

Christmas Carol, A (US 38): Kilburn, Sinclair, Severn Cl.

Christmas Carol, A (51 GB) − *see* Scrooge

Christmas Coal Mine Miracle, A (US 77): Harris R.

Christmas Story, A (US 83): Billingsley

Christmas Strike, The (GB 13): Desmond

Christmas to Remember, A (US 78): Parry

Christmas Tree (69 FR/IT) − *see* Arbre de Noël

Christoph Columbus (GE 22): Szécsi

Christus (IT 16): Roveri, Visca

Chronicles of Bloom Center, The (US 15): Barry W.

Chudesni korabl / *The marvellous ship* (SU 36): Tulubev

Chudo s samogonom / *The illicit vodka miracle* (SU 25):
Konstantinov

Chuk i Gek / *Chuk and Gek* (SU 53): Chilikin, Chugunoff

Chuquiago (BO 77): Yujira

Cieca di Sorrento, La / *The blind woman of Sorrento* (IT 52):
Di Nardo

Ciel est à vous, Le / *The sky is yours* (FR 43): François

Cigalon / *Hopper* (FR 36): Dubrou

Cimarron (US 30): Jackson E., Scott D.

Cimarron (US 60): Eccles

Cinderella Liberty (US 73): Calloway

Cinderella's Feller (US 40): Beckett

Cinderella Swings It (US 43): Brown K., Lenhart

Cinderfella (US 60): Gordon Ba.

Cinéma de Papa, Le / *Dad's cinema* (FR 70): Cohen

Cinema Paradiso (88 IT/FR) − *see* Nuovo Cinema Paradiso

'Cinessino' series (IT 10-13): Giunchi

Cine va deschide uşa? / *Who'll open the door?* (RO 67): Oprescu

Cinquième empreinte, La (FR 34): Genevois

Circle, The (US 25): McBan

Circle Family (US 82): Oliver B.

Circle of Children, A (US 76): Laborteaux M. and P.

Circle of Deception (GB 60): Scott H.

Circle of Fear (US 51): Kimbley

Circle of Violence (US 86): Phoenix R.

Circonstances attenuantes / *Extenuating circumstances* (FR 39):
François

Circumstantial Evidence (US 45): Beckett, Cummings, McKim H.,
Mickelsen, Tyler L.

Circus, The (US 15): Butterworth F.

Circus, The (US 28): Jones B.

Circus and the Boy, The (US 14, 'Sonny Jim'): Connelly

Circus Boy (GB 47): Scott P.

Circus Clown, The (US 34): Cosbey

Circus Day (US 20): Roubert

Circus Days (US 23): Coogan J.

Circus Fever (US): 'Our Gang'

Circus Jim (NL/GB 22): Doxat-Pratt

Circus Kid, The (25 FR) − *see* Coeur des gueux

Circus Kid, The (US 28): Darro

Cisco Kid, The (US 31): Haig

Ciske de Rat / *Ciske the rat* (NL 55): van der Velde

Ciske de Rat (NL 84): de Munk

Ciske -- ein Kind braucht Liebe / *Ciske: a child needs love*
(DE/NL 55): van der Velde

Čitanka / *Reading book* (YU 84): Roganović

Citizen Kane (US 41): Swan, Bupp S.
City Lights (US 31): Jewell, Parrish
City of Beautiful Nonsense, The (GB 34): Hepworth H.
City Sparrow, The (US 20): Fox J.
City Streets (US 38): Bond T.
Ciudad de los Niños, La /Boys' town (MX 56): Jiménez Pons R.
Ciulinii Baraganului /The thistles of Baragan (RO 57): Chirlea
Cjamango (IT 67): Fioravanti
Clan des Siciliens, Le /The Sicilian clan (FR 68): Chauveau
Clan of the Cave Bear (US 85): Cramer
Clara et les méchants /Clara and the bad boys (FR 57):
    Maurin Y.-M.
Clara's Heart (US 88): Harris N. P.
Clash of Steel, The (US 17): Marion F.
Claude Duval (GB 24): Brantford
Claudia and David (US 46): Sydes
Claudine à l'école /Claudine at school (FR 37): Mouloudji
Clay Dollars (US 21): Depew, Devine
Clean Heart, The (US 24): Butts
Clearing the Trail (US 27): House N.
Cleopatra (US 63): Loddi, O'Sullivan
Client, The (US 94): Renfro
Climax (US 44): Beckett
Climb an Angry Mountain (US 72): O'Brien C.
Clipped Wings (US 38): Watson D.
Cloak and Dagger (US 84): Thomas H.
Clock, The (US 45): Gray G., Norman
Clockwork Mice (GB 94): Conroy
Clodhopper, The (US 25): McBan
Cloister's Touch, The (US 10): Pickford
Cloning of Richard Swimmer, The (US 74): Kerwin
Close Encounters of the Third Kind (US 77): Guffey
Clothes Line Quarrel, The (US 13): Benham
Clown, The (US 16): Jacobs
Clown, The (US 52): Considine
Clown and the Kid, The (US 61): McGreevey
Clown Princes (US 39): 'Our Gang'
Clown's Best Performance, The (US 11): Casey
Cluny Brown (US 46): Gray B.
Coals of Fire (US 14): Benham
Cobarde, El /The coward (MX 39): Busquets
Cobbler, The (US 23): 'Our Gang'
Cobweb, The (US 55): Rettig
Cocco di mamma, Il /Mummy's darling (IT 57): Nevola
Cockeyed Cowboys of Calico County, The (US 70): Shea E.
Cockeyed Miracle, The (US 46): Chapin B.
Cock o' the North (GB 35): Hepworth R.
Cocoanut Grove (US 38): Lee B.
Cocoon (US 85): Oliver B.
Code of the Outlaw (US 42): Bartlett
Code of the West (US 25): Lee F.
Codine /Codin (FR/RO 63): Petrescu
Cody (US 77): Becker
Coeur de Paris, Le /The heart of Paris (FR 31): Gaillard
Coeur des gueux, Le /The beggars' heart (FR 25): Machin
Coeur dispose, Le /The heart disposes (FR 36): Farguette
Coeurs héroïques, Les /Heroes' hearts (FR 27): Forest

Coeur sur la main, Le /Heart on hand (FR 48): Lecointe
Coffins on Wheels (US 41): Baker, Hickman Dl., Nunn
Cognasse (FR 32): Mercanton
Cohens and Kellys, The (US 26): Gordon Bo., Bennett M.
Cold River (US 81): Petersen P.
Colonel Redl (84 HU/DE/AT) — see Redl ezredes
Colorado Pioneers (US 45): Blake, Cummings, Thomas W.
Colossus of New York, The (US 58): Herbert
Colour of Pomegranates, The (74 SU) — see Nran gouyne
Colton, U.S.N. (US 15): Kelly P.
Comancheros, The (US 61): Mobley
Comeback Kid, The (US 80): Licht, McKeon D.
Come Back, Miss Pipps (US 41): 'Our Gang'
Come Fly with Me (US 62): Morat
Come Next Spring (US 55): Eyer Ri.
Come Out of the Kitchen (US 19): Morrison E.
Come September (US 61): Howard R.
Come ti rapisco il pupo /How I kidnap the baby (IT 76): Cestiè
Come to Papa (US 28): Sabiston
Come to the Stable (US 49): Gebert
Coming Generation, The (US 12): Roubert
Coming of Age (91 FR) — see Année de l'éveil
Coming of the Law, The (US 18): Sargent
Comin' Round the Mountain (US 40): Bupp S.
Comisario en turno /Policeman on duty (MX 49): Jiménez Pons J.
Commanding Officer, The (US 15): Carpenter
Commando Action (PK 88): Jamshid
Commencement Day (US 24): 'Our Gang'
Common Cause, The (US 18): Blackton
Common Touch, The (GB 41): Tyler G.
Communale, La (FR 65): Haudepin
Compagnes de la Nuit, Les /Night partners (FR 53): Fourcade
Composition de calcul, La /The math test (FR 51): Gencel
Compromised (US 31): Watson D.
Comrades (US 28): Janney
Comte Kostia, Le /Count Kostya (FR 24): Guichard
Conan the Barbarian (US 81): Sanz
Confessions (GB 25): Shaw L.
Confessions of a Co-Ed (US 31): Moore D.
Confessions of a Nazi Spy (US 39): Billings G., Bupp T.
Confessions of a Queen (US 25): Darro
Confirm or Deny (US 41): McDowall
Conflict (US 36): Bupp T.
Conformista, Il (IT/FR/DE 69): Fortunato
Connecticut Yankee in King Arthur's Court, A (US 48):
    Hawkins, Nokes, Stollery
Conquered Hearts (US 18): Tansey S.
Conquerors, The (US 32): Albright
Conquest (US 37): Beckett
Conquest of Cheyenne (US 46): Blake
Conquest of Cochise (US 53): Crawford J.
Conquest of the Air (GB 36): Hepworth R.
Conscripts of Misfortune (GB 23): Brantford
Consequences (GB 18): Craig
Conspiracy of Terror (US 75): Olson
Conspirators, The (US 44): Roy
Consuming Love (US 11): Casey

Contessa Castiglione, La / *Countess Castiglione* (IT 42): Barbetti
Contessa scalza, La (54 US/IT) — *see* Barefoot Contessa
Contest Kid, The (US 79): Petersen P.
Contest Kid Strikes Again, The (US 79): Petersen P.
Con todo el corazon / *With all one's heart* (MX 51): Anda
Contraband (US 25): Fox J.
Contra la ley de Dios / *Against divine law* (MX 46): Roche
Convicted: a Mother's Story (US 87): Savage F.
Convict 99 (GB 38): McDowall
Convict's Heart, The (US 11): Pickford
Cop, The (37 US) -- *see* Man in Blue
Cop on the Beat, The (US 14): Clark R.
Cops and Watches (14 US) — *see* Twenty Minutes of Love
'Copter Kids, The (GB 76): Scott-Taylor
Coqueta / *Flirt* (MX 49): Moreno
Corazon / *Heart* (AR 47): Barbieri
Corazon de niño / *A child's heart* (MX 39): Molina, Busquets, Rio
Corazones sin rumbo / *Aimless hearts* (ES 28): Hurtado
Corn is Green, The (US 45): Chapin M., Roy
Corporal Billy's Comeback (US 16): Short
Cortile, Il / *The yard* (IT 55): Poujouly
Così sia / *So be it* (IT 72): Cestiè
Cotolay (ES 65): Haudepin
Could a Man Do More? (US 15): Willis
Counselor Bobby (US 13): Kelly P.
Countdown (US 67): Riha
Counterfeit Constable, The (64 FR) — *see* Allez France!
Count of Monte Cristo, The (US 34): Albright
Country Doctor, The (US 27): Coghlan
Country Doctor, The (US 36): Watson D.
Country Gentlemen (US 36): McKim S.
Country Girl, The (US 54): Provost
Country Kid, The (US 12): Connelly
Country Kid, The (US 23): Barry W., Gordon Bo., Guerin, O'Donnell
Count Three and Pray (US 55): Hawkins
County Chairman, The (US 35): Rooney
County Fair, The (US 20): Barry W.
County Fair, The (US 37): Butler
Count Your Blessings (US 59): Stephens M.
Coupable, Le / *The guilty man* (FR 36): Rodon
Coup dur chez les mous / *Hard strike on a soft target* (FR 55): Moullières
Courage (US 30): Janney, Marion D.
Courage of Black Beauty (US 57): Crawford J.
Courage of Silence, The (US 17): Johnson W.
Courageous Dr Christian, The (US 40): Larson
Courtship of Eddie's Father, The (US 62): Howard R. and C.
Cousin Kate (US 21): Verdi
Cousin Pons, Le / *Cousin Pons* (FR 23): Guichard
Cousin Wilbur (US 39): 'Our Gang', Hurlic
Couteau dans la plaie, Le / *Knife in the wound* (FR/IT/US 62): Morat, Norden
Covent Garden (GB 83): Fletcher
Covered Wagon, The (US 23): Fox J.
Cover Girl (US 44): Wissler
Cowboy and the Bandit, The (US 35): Nelson B.
Cowboy and the Kid, The (US 19): Eason
Cowboy and the Kid, The (US 36): Burrud

Cowboy and the Lady, The (US 38): Henry R.
Cowboy Cop, The (US 26): Darro
Cowboy Counsellor, The (US 32): Nelson B.
Cowboy Kid, The (US 12): Reulos
Cowboy Musketeer, The (US 25): Darro
Cowboys, The (US 71): Beauvy, Hudis, Kelly S., O'Brien C.
Cowboys from Texas (US 39): McKim H.
Cowboy Star, The (US 36): Albright
Crab, The (US 17): Butterworth E.
Cracked Iceman, The (US 34): Beard, Bond T., McFarland
Cracked Wedding Bells (US 20): Morrison E.
Cradle Robbers (US 24): 'Our Gang'
Cradle Song (US 33): Durand, Moore D.
Crainquebille (FR 22): Forest
Crainquebille (FR 33): Genevois
Crainquebille (FR 53): Fourcade
Crash Landing (US 58): Charney
Crashout (US 55): Olsen C.
Crazies, The (US 73): Harris R.
Crazy House (US 28): 'Our Gang'
Crazy Love (BE 87): Hunaerts
Cricket, The (US 17): Hupp
Crime at Blossoms, The (GB 33): Singer
Crime School (US 38): Jordan
Crime Story (GB 83): Stanfield
Crimson Trail, The (US 35): Nelson B.
Crin Blanc / *White mane* (FR 53): Emery, Lamorisse
Crisis, The (AU 56): Taylor K.
Crisscross (US 91): Arnott
Cristobal Colon / *Christopher Colombus* (MX 43): Fernandez
Cristo del oceano, El / *Christ of the sea* (ES 71): del Arco
Critic's Choice (US 62): Kelman, Losby
Croce senza nome, Una / *A nameless cross* (IT 52): Cerusico
Cromwell (GB 70): Kemp A. and E.
Cronica de un niño solo / *A boy on his own* (AR 64): Puente
Crooked Alley (US 23): Fox J.
Crooks Anonymous (US 62): Waterman
Croquette (FR 27): Mercanton
Cross Creek (US 83): Guffey
Crossed Trails (US 24): Black B.
Cross My Heart (US 46): Larson
Cross My Heart (90 CA) — *see* Fracture du myocarde
Cross of Iron (GB/DE 77): Štimac
Cross of Lorraine, The (US 43): Roy
Crossplot (GB 69): Garlick
Cross Your Heart (US 12): Benham
Crowd, The (US 28): Downs, Frederick
Crowded Sky, The (US 60): Eccles
Crowd Roars, The (US 38): Rentschler, Reynolds
Cruising Casanovas (52 US) — *see* Gobs and Gals
Crusades, The (US 35): Jones D.
Crutch, The (US 14): Connelly
Cry for Love, A (US 80): Licht
Cry for the Strangers (US 82): Carson S.
Cry from the Mountain (US 87): Kidd C.
Cry from the Streets, A (GB 58): Petersen Col., Moulder-Brown
Cry in the Wilderness, A (US 73): Montgomery

Cry of the Children, The (US 12): Benham
Cry of the City (US 48): Cook T.
Cry of the First-Born, The (US 15): Short
Cry of the Hunted (US 53): Mazzola
Cry Wolf (GB 68): Kemp A., Beaumont M.
Csodagyerek, A /The child prodigy (HU 20): Lubinsky
Csók, Anyu /Love, Mother (HU 87): Gévai
Cuando habla el corazon /When the heart speaks (MX 43): Busquets
Cuando lloran los valientes /When brave men weep (MX 46): Roche
'Cub' Reporter, The (US 12): Boss
Cuckoo Patrol (GB 65): Lester
Cujo (US 82): Pintauro, Jacoby Bl.
Culottes courtes/Short pants (FR 55): Bonnefous, Urbain
Culpable, La /Guilty woman (MX 45): Pastor
Cumberland Romance, A (US 20): Fox J.
'Cuore' series (IT 14-16): Petrungaro, Roveri
Cuore (39 MX) — see Corazon de niño
Cuore /Heart (IT 47): Leurini, Di Nardo
Cuore (IT 74): Cestiè
Cuore (IT 84): Calenda, Galle
Cuore di mamma /Mummy's darling (IT 69): Ferendeles
Cuori senza frontiere /Hearts without frontiers (IT 49): Staiola
Cup Fever (GB 65): Gilmore, Rolls
Cupid by Proxy (US 18): Morrison E.
Cupid Forecloses (US 19): Griffith
Cure, The (US 95): Mazzello, Renfro
Cure for Crime, A (US 11): Boss
Curing the Office Boy (US 12): Boss
Curley (US 47): Olsen L.J., Belding, Gray B., Miles P. (Perreau), Nokes
Curley and His Gang in the Haunted Mansion (48 US) — see Who Killed 'Doc' Robbin?
Curly (44 US) — see Once Upon a Time
Curse of the Cat People, The (US 44): Bates
Curtain Call (US 40): Kelly T.
Custard Boys, The (61 GB) — see Reach for Glory
Custard Boys, The (GB 79): Chescoe, Milliet
Custard Cup, The (US 23): Devine
Custer's Last Stand (21 US) — see Bob Hampton of Placer
Cutey Tries Reporting (US 13): Kelly P.
Cutter's Trail (US 69): Padilla
Cut the Cards (US 20): Morrison E.
Cyclone of the Range (US 27): Darro
Cyclone of the Saddle (US 35): Nelson B.
Cytherea (US 24): Moore M.
Czardaskönig, Der /The czardas king (DE 58): Haar

Daag /Stigma (IN 73): Rajoo
Da capo (FI/SE 85): Söderblom
Daddy (GB 17): Barker E.
Daddy (US 23): Coogan J.
Daddy I Don't Like It Like This (US 77): McKeon D.
Daddy Long Legs (US 19): Barry W., Lee F., Boardman, Condon
Daddy Long Legs (US 31): Barty, McComas
Daddy's Boy and Mammy (US 11): Casey
Daddy's Darlings (GB 13): Royston R.
'Daddy's Didums' series (GB 10-13): 'Didums'
Daddy's Dyin' Who's Got the Will? (US 89): Hubbard

Daddy's Girl (US 18): Morrison E.
Daddy's Soldier Boy (US 13): Harris B.
Dad for a Day (US 39): 'Our Gang'
Dad's Outlaws (US 16): Goodwin
Daemon (GB 85): Morell
Daens (BE 92): Baetens
Dagli Appennini alle Ande /From Apennines to Andes (IT 16): Roveri
Dagli Appennini alle Ande (42 MX) — see Dulce madre mia
Dagli Appennini alle Ande (IT 43): Barbetti
Dagli Appennini alle Ande (IT/AR 58): Paoletti
Daigaku yoitoko /Up with school! (JP 36): Yokoyama
Daisogen no wataridori /Rider with a guitar (JP 60): Egi
Dak ghar /Post office (IN 66): Sachin
Dakota (US 45): Blake
Dakota Kid, The (US 51): Chapin M.
Dama del alba, La /Lady of the dawn (MX 49): Calpe
Damaged Hearts (US 24): Devine
Dam Busters, The (GB 55): Hall J.
Damen i svart /The lady in black (SE 58): Nilsson
Dames Ahoy (US 34): Watson H.
Damien - Omen II (US 78): Scott-Taylor
Damn Citizen (US 57): Foster
Damned, The (GB 61): Witty
Damned Don't Cry, The (US 50): Moss J.
Dämon der Frauen (32 GE) — see Rasputin
Damsel in Distress, A (US 37): Watson H.
Danapani /Basic foodstuff (IN 53): Kapoor S.
Dance Hall Hostess (US 33): Cosbey
Dance Little Lady (GB 54): O'Sullivan
Dance Madness (US 26): Billings E.
Dancing Romeo (US 44): 'Our Gang'
Dancing Years, The (GB 49): Spenser J.
Dandy Dick (GB 35): Singer
Danger Claim (US 30): Nelson B.
Danger de mort /Mortal danger (FR 47): Rob
Danger Flight (US 39): Baker
Danger - Love at Work (US 37): Bartlett
Danger on Dartmoor (GB 80): Henderson S.
Danger on the Air (US 38): Kaye
Dangerous Crossroads (US 33): Searl
Dangerous Days (US 29): Nelson B.
Dangerous Exile (GB 56): O'Sullivan
Dangerous Fingers (GB 37): Pavitt
Dangerous Holiday (US 37): Sinclair, Winkler
Dangerous Intrigue (US 36): Billings G.
Dangerous Paradise (US 20): Steuart
Dangerous Partners (US 45): Infuhr
Danger Trail, The (US 28): House N.
Dani (HU 57): Weiser G.
Daniel (CS 60): Hrůsecký
Daniel (US 83): Mitchell-Smith
Daniel Boone (US 36): Jones D.
Daniel Boone's Bravery (US 11): Melford
Daniel und der Weltmeister /Daniel and the World Champion (DD 63): Schmidt R.
Danjo oshikurabe /Strong men, strong women (JP 31): 'Tokkan-Kozo'

Dann schon lieber Lebertran /*I'd rather have cod-liver oil* (GE 31): Klein G.

Danny Boy (GB 34): Hepworth R.

Danny Boy (GB 41): Tyler G.

Danny Boy (US 46): Henry R., Bates

Danny the Champion of the World (GB 89): Irons

Danny the Dragon (GB 66): Wild

Dante, akta're för Hajen! /*Mind the Shark, Dante!* (SE 77): Ohlsson

Dante's Inferno (US 35): Beckett, Bupp S.

Da obichash na inat /*We love each other, though* (BG 85): Velkov

Da qiao xiamian /*Under the bridge* (CN 83): Fang

Dard-e-dil /*Heart's anguish* (IN 53): Kumar, Surendra

Daredevils of the Red Circle (US 39, srl): Winkler

Daring Danger (US 32): Nelson B.

Daring Years, The (US 23): Depew

Daring Young Man, The (US 42): Mummert

Dark Angel, The (US 25): Jones B., Noisom

Dark Angel, The (US 35): Breakston, Butler

Dark at the Top of the Stairs, The (US 60): Eyer Ro.

Dark Avenger, The (GB 55): O'Sullivan, Winter

Dark Enemy (GB 83): MacFarquhar, Hicks

Dark House, A (US 15): Fuehrer

Dark Past, The (US 49): Hyatt

Dark Waters (US 44): Miles P. (Perreau)

Darling (GB 65): Brockwell, Younger

Darling, How Could You! (US 51): Stollery

Darling of New York, The (US 23): Coghlan, O'Donnell

Darò un milione /*I'll give a million* (IT 35): Barbetti

Darts Are Trumps (GB 38): Singer

D.A.R.Y.L. (GB 85): Oliver B.

Dary Magow /*The gifts of the magi* (PL 72): Samosionek

Dastan /*Faith* (IN 50): Surendra

Dastan /*Faith* (IN 72): Sachin

Das war mein Leben /*That was my life* (GE 44): Rohringer

Daughter of France, A (GB 14): Cricks

Daughter of the West, A (US 18): Morrison E.

Daughters of Desire (US 29): Searl

David (DE 78): Henties

David and Bathsheba (US 51): Infuhr

David and Goliath (20 US) – *see* 'Edgar' series

David and Jonathan (GB 20): Wood S.

David Copperfield (GB 13): Desmond

David Copperfield (DK 22): Herzberg

David Copperfield (US 35): Bartholomew

David Copperfield (GB 70): Mackenzie

David Copperfield (GB 75): Kahn

David, Goliat i petel /*David, Goliath and the cock* (YU 61): Ćortošev

Dawandeh /*The runner* (IR 84): Nirumand

Dawn (GB 28): Ashby J.

Dawn, The (82 ID) – *see* Serangan fajar

Dawn Killer, The (GB 59): Bulloch J.

Dawn of a Tomorrow, The (US 24): McBan

Dawn of Truth, The (GB 20): Wood S.

Daybreak (US 31): Searl

Day in the Country, A (GB 12): Royston R.

Day-O (US 92): Wood E.

Day of Grace (GB 57): Winter

Day of Reckoning (US 33): McFarland

Day of Rest, The (US 39): Bupp S.

Day of the Locust, The (US 74): Haley

Day of the Outlaw (US 59): McGreevey

Day on Rollers, A (GB 13): Royston R.

Day Santa Claus Cried, The (77 IT) – *see* Questo si che è amore

Day's Diet, A (21 US) – *see* 'Edgar' series

Days of Jesse James (US 39): Beckett

Day's Pleasure, A (US 19): Coogan J., Lee Ra.

Day the Earth Caught Fire, The (GB 61): Ellis I.

Day the Earth Stood Still, The (US 51): Gray B.

Day They Gave Babies Away, The (57 US) – *see* All Mine to Give

Daytime Wives (US 23): McBan

Dead End (US 37): Peck, Jordan, Kibrick S.

Deadline (US 31): Ernest

Deadly Cargo, The (77 US) – *see* Tarantulas: the Deadly Cargo

Deadly Trackers, The (US 73): Marshall

Dead Man's Shoes (GB 39): McDowall

Dead Men Tell No Tales (US 71): Lookinland M.

Dear Boys Home for the Holidays, The (GB 03): Williamson S. and T.

Dear Brigitte (US 65): Mumy

Dear Departed, The (US 20): Morrison E.

Dearest Love (70 FR/IT/DE) – *see* Souffle au coeur

Death in Venice (71 IT/FR) – *see* Morte a Venezia

Death of a Champion (US 39): O'Connor

Death on the Diamond (US 34): Rooney

Death Over My Shoulder (GB 57): Moulder-Brown

Death Valley (US 81): Billingsley

DEBATIK (AL 61): Pecani, Zani

Debout, là-dedans! /*Stand up in there!* (FR 35): Buquet, Grave

Deca igrayet ven /*Children playing outdoors* (BG 73): Ganev, Kochev

Dečak i violina /*The boy and the violin* (YU 75): Marković, Gončić

Dečak je isao za suncem /*The boy who followed the sun* (YU 82): Jablan

Dečak je vikao ubistvo (66 GB/DE/YU) – *see* Boy Cried Murder

Deception (US 32): Moore D.

Decision Before Dawn (US 51): Lödel

Decision of Christopher Blake, The (US 48): Donaldson T.

Decline and Fall...of a Birdwatcher! (GB 68): Newport

Dedo del destino, El /*The finger of fate* (ES 67): Sanchez

Dedushka Gigiya /*Grandpa Gigiya* (SU 60): Daneliya

Deedar (IN 51): Surendra

Deep in the Heart of Texas (US 42): Hickman C.

Deep Six, The (US 58): Mathers

Deep Waters (US 48): Stockwell

Deewangee /*Madness* (IN 76): Mehmood

Defenders, The (US 16): Carpenter, Perl, Stone

Defense Rests, The (US 34): Holt D.

Defiant Ones, The (US 58): Coughlin

Defiant Ones, The (US 85): Wheaton

Deivakkuzhandaigal /*God's children* (IN 73): Ramu

Dekabristi /*The Decembrists* (SU 26): Konstantinov

Dekalog /*The ten commandments* (PL 88): Klata

Dekhoji /*Look, dear* (IN 47): Kumar

Dekigokoro /*Passing pancy* (JP 33): 'Tokkan-Kozo'

De la jungle à l'écran /*From jungle to screen* (FR 28): Machin

Delikatessen (GE 30): Stark-Gstettenbaur

Deliverance (US 19): Boardman

Deliverance (US 72): Boorman
Delo Rumyantseva / *The Rumyantsev case* (SU 55): Koval
Deloviye lyudi / *Businessmen* (SU 62): Tikhonov
Del rosa al amarillo / *From pink to yellow* (ES 63): del Corral
De Mayerling à Sarajevo / *From Mayerling to Sarajevo* (FR 40): Buquet
Demoiselle et son revenant, La / *The young lady and her ghost* (FR 51): Gencel
Demonio con angel, Un / *Demon and angel* (ES 63): Juan José
Demonios en el jardin / *Demons in the garden* (ES 82): Sanchez-Prieto
Demon Murder Case, The (US 83): Fields
Den gnorissa mitera / *I never knew a mother* (GR 62): Kalatzopoulos
Dennis (US 93): Gamble
'Dennis the Menace' (US 59-63, TVS): North J.
Den posledni, den pervi / *Last day, first day* (SU 59): Daneliya
De pokkers unger / *Those bloody kids* (DK 47): Henning-Jensen, Langberg
Derby Day (US 23): 'Our Gang'
Derelict Reporter, The (US 11): Casey
Dernier amour / *Last love* (FR 48): Fourcade
Dernières vacances, Les / *Last holidays* (FR 47): François, Gervais
Dernier métro, Le / *The last tube train* (FR 80): Pasquier
Dernier Robin des Bois, Le / *The last Robin Hood* (FR 52): Gencel, Lecointe
Der var engang en krig / *Once there was a war* (DK 66): Busck
Deserted at the Altar (US 22): Lee F.
Desert Pirate, The (US 27): Darro
Desert Rider (US 23): Wilkinson
Desert Tribesman, The (US 14): Benham
Desheredados, Los / *The disinherited* (MX 35): Zamora
Desheredados, Los (ES/MX 64): Gomez A.
Design for Scandal (US 41): Larson
Desperate (US 47): Infuhr
Desperate Hours, The (US 55): Eyer Ri.
Desperate Motives (US 92): Bonsall
Desperate Search (US 52): Aaker L.
Desperate Trails (US 21): Stone
Des Pfarrers Töchterlein / *The parson's little daughter* (GE 12): Bois
Despues de la tormenta / *After the storm* (MX 55): Romay
Destination 60,000 (US 57): Clark B.2
Destins de Manoel, Les / *Manoel's destinies* (FR/PT 85): de Freitas M. and R.
Destiny (US 44): Bates
Deštivý den / *Rainy day* (CS 62): Hádl
Destry (US 54): Aaker L.
Destry Rides Again (US 32): Ernest
Destry Rides Again (US 39): Jones D.
10,000 malchikov / *10,000 boys* (SU 61): Agdamov
Det ender med bryllup / *It ends in marriage* (DK 43); Kaas
Deti Kapitana Granta / *Captain Grant's children* (SU 36): Segel
Deti partizana / *A partisan's children* (SU 54): Komissarov
Det kom en gäst / *A guest is coming* (SE 47): Nyström
Det skete på Møllegården / *It happened at Møllegård* (DK 60): Neumann
Detski sad / *Kindergarten* (SU 84): Gusak, Bobrovski
Detstvo Gorkovo / *Gorki's childhood* (SU 38): Lyarski, Smirnoff
Detstvo marshala / *A marshal's childhood* (SU 38): Baukov
Deutsche Helden in schwerer Zeit / *German heroes in hard times* (GE 24): Peterhans
Deux gamines, Les / *Two saucy girls* (FR 20): Poyen
Deux gamines, Les (FR 36): Grave
Deux gosses, Les / *Two boys* (FR 24): Forest, Shaw L., Mercanton
Deux gosses, Les (FR 36): Grave, Tavoli
Devchata / *Girls* (SU 61): Krivchenkov
Devchonka, s kotoroi ya druzhil / *The little girl I knew* (SU 61): Fisenko
Dev dasi / *Temple dancer* (IN 35): Apte
Devil and Daniel Webster, The (41 US) − see All That Money Can Buy
Devil and Max Devlin, The (US 81): Rich
Devil Girl from Mars (GB 54): Richmond
Devil Horse, The (US 32, srl): Darro
Devil is a Sissy, The (US 36): Bartholomew, Cooper Ja., Rooney, Bailey Sd.
Devil is Driving, The (US 32): Moore D.
Devil's Cargo, The (US 25): O'Donnell
Devil-Ship Pirates, The (GB 63): Newport
Devil's Own, The (66 IT/FR) − see Streghe
Devil's Party, The (US 38): Beckett, Bupp T., Jones D., Rentschler
Devil's Playground, The (AU 76): Burke
Devil's Squadron (US 36): Burrud
Devil-Stone, The (US 17): Hamrick
Devil Takes the Count, The (36 US) − see Devil is a Sissy
Devil Times Five (US 74): Garrett
Devochka ishet otsa / *A little girl looks for her father* (SU 59): Guskoff
Devochka na shariye / *Girl on a ball* (SU 67): Tsirghiladze
Devotion (US 31): Scott D.
Devudu chesina pelli / *Marriage made in heaven* (IN 74): Ramu
Dhamkee / *The threat* (IN 73): Mehmood
Dhanama? Daivama? / *Money or God?* (IN 73): Ramu
Dharam karam / *Ritual acts* (IN 75): Satyajit
Dharkan / *Heartbeat* (IN 72): Alankar
Dharma devata / *God of religion* (IN 52): Mohan
Dharma ki devi / *Goddess of religion* (IN 35): Marathe A.
D'homme à hommes / *Man to man* (FR 48): Tabary
Dhruba (IN 53): Bhattacharjee
Diable au coeur, Le / *Devil in the heart* (FR 26): Heuzé
Diablillos de arrabal / *Little devils of the outskirts* (MX 39): Vidal, Zamora
Diaboliques, Les / *The fiends* (FR 54): Poujouly, Maurin Y.-M., Urbain, Bonnefous
Dial Hot Line (US 70): Van Patten V.
Diamant noir / *Black diamond* (FR 40): Rétaux
Diamond from the Pie, A (US 16): Monahan
Diane (US 55): Cavell
Dianti shang / *In the elevator* (CN 84): Fang
Diario de una mujer / *A woman's diary* (MX 44): Roche
Dicen que soy comunista / *They say I'm a communist* (MX 51): Roche
Dick's Fairy (GB 21): Craig
Dick Tracy (US 37, srl): Van Atta
Dick Tracy (US 45): Kuhn
Dick Tracy (US 90): Korsmo
Dick Tracy Returns (US 38, srl): Tucker J.
Dick Turpin (GB 33): Hepworth H., J. and R.
Dieu a besoin des hommes / *God needs mankind* (FR 50): Lecointe, Martaguet C.
Digby the Biggest Dog in the World (GB 73): Beaumont R.
Digger (US 93): Hann-Byrd

Dik Trom en zijn dorpsgenoten / *Dik Trom and his village friends* (NL 47): Koridon

Dik Trom en zijn dorpsgenoten (NL 73): Erven

Dik Trom knapt 't op / *Dik Trom eats his fill* (NL 74): Erven

Dik Trom weet raad / *Dik Trom knows best* (NL 76): Janssen T.

Dil-e-nadan / *The naïve heart* (IN 53): Kapoor Ro.

Dil farosh / *The seller of hearts* (IN 37): Apte

Dil ki awaz / *The heart speaks* (IN 48): Kumar

Dimenticare Venezia / *Forget Venice* (IT 79): Tittone, Doria

Dime with a Halo (US 63): Domasin, Mobley, Padilla

Dimka (62 SU) − see Ya kupil papu

Dimples (US 36): Kibrick L.

Dim v lesu / *Smoke in the woods* (SU 55): Saifulin

Dink Stover (50 US) − see Happy Years

Dinky (US 35): Cooper Ja., Bupp S., Butler, Ernest

Dinner Hour (US 20): Morrison E.

Dinosaurus! (US 60): Roberts A.

Dinty (US 20): Barry W., Hall N.

Dio manes ston stavro tou ponou / *Two mothers on the cross of pain* (GR 62): Kailas

Dirkie (ZA 70): Uys

Dirty Face Dan (US 15): Carpenter, Stone

Discounters of Money, The (US 17): Connelly

Di shi ge dankong / *The tenth bullet scar* (CN 80): Yang

Dis-moi qui tuer / *Tell me who to kill* (FR 65): Dekock

Disorderly Conduct (US 32): Moore D.

Disparus de St. Agil, Les / *Missing boys of St. Agil* (FR 38): Claudio, Grave, Mouloudji, Buquet, Farguette, Rétaux

Dispatch from Reuters, A (US 40): Baker, Dawson, Moore D., Nichols

Disputed Passage (US 39): Cook B.

Distant Cry from Spring, A (80 JP) − see Harukanaru yama no yobigoe

Distinto amanacer / *Signs of daybreak* (MX 43): Busquets

Díszmagyar / *The dress suit* (HU 49): Horváth

Ditte menneskebarn / *Ditte, child of man* (DK 46): Henning-Jensen, Langberg

Ditya gostsirka / *A child of the State Circus* (SU 25): Konstantinov

Divided Heart, The (GB 54): Ray M., Stephens M.

Divine Lady, The (US 28): Parrish

Divorce (US 23): DeLacy

Divorce (US 45): Calkins, Olsen L.J.

Divorce Coupons (US 22): Berlinger

Divorcee, The (US 30): Shuford

Divorce in the Family (US 32): Cooper Ja.

Divorciadas / *Divorcees* (MX 43): Roche

Divot Diggers (US 36): 'Our Gang'

Diwana / *the crazy one* (IN 52): Kumar

Dix-huit heures d'escale / *Eighteen-hour stop-over* (FR 54): Poujouly

Dixiana (US 30): Jackson E.

Dixie (US 43): McKim H. and S.

Do bachchey dus haath / *Two kids, ten hands* (IN 72): Mehmood

Do bigha zamin / *Two acres of land* (IN 53): Kumar

Dobrodružství na Zlate Zatoce / *Adventure on Golden Bay* (CS 55): Černohorský

Dobrodružství s Blasiem / *Adventure with Blasius* (CS 74): Starý

Dobrodružství s nahým klukem / *Adventure with a naked boy* (CS 64): Tomšů

Dobro pozhalovat / *Welcome!* (SU 64): Kosikh

Doch Gilyana / *Gilyan's daughter* (SU 28): Safarov

'Do Children Count?' series (US 17): Paul E. and J.

Dochka / *Little daughter* (SU 42): Mokatsian

Doctor, The (US 84): Haas L.

Doctoramma / *Lady doctor* (IN 74): Ramu

Doctor Dan (US 74): Montgomery

Doctor Dolittle (US 67): Dix

Doctor in Love (GB 60): Moulder-Brown

Doctor Jack (US 22): Daniels M.

Dr Jekyll and Mr Hyde (US 31): Tucker J.

Dr Kildare's Crisis (US 40): Watson Bs.

Doctor Max (US 74): Gomez P.

Doctor Rameau (US 15): Carnahan

Doctor's Diary, A (US 37): Beckett, Kuhn, Sinclair

Doctors Don't Tell (US 41): Bupp S.

Doctor Sinkum (US 07): Harron

Dr Socrates (US 35): Madden

Doctor's Romance, The (US 14): McCloskey

Dr Syn - Alias the Scarecrow (GB 63): Scully

Doctor Takes a Wife, The (US 40): Larson

Døden kommer til middag / *Death comes to dinner* (DK 64): Schmidt J.P.

Dodes'ka-den / *Trundle-ting* (JP 70): Kawase

Dodge City (US 39): Watson Bs.

Dodumalsya, pozdravlayu! / *Bravo - you got it!* (SU 77): Yershoff A.

Does It Pay? (US 23): Grauer

Dogadjaj / *The event* (YU 69): Mimica

Dogalog, The (US 31): Nelson B.

Dog Days (US 25): 'Our Gang'

Dog Daze (US 39): 'Our Gang'

Dog Doctor, The (US 31): Barty

Dog Heaven (US 27): 'Our Gang'

Dog of Flanders, A (US 35): Thomas F.

Dog of Flanders, A (US 59): Ladd

Dog of the Wild (US 49): Gray G.

Dog's Best Friend, A (US 59): Mobley

Dog's Good Deed, A (US 14): Benham

Dogs Is Dogs (US 31): 'Our Gang'

Dogs of War (US 23): 'Our Gang'

Dog's Pal, A (US 27): Madden

Dog's Tale, A (US 11): Pickford

Doing Time (US 20): Morrison E.

Doin' Their Bit (US 42): 'Our Gang'

Do It Now (US 24): Fox J.

Doktor Aibolit / *Dr Ouch-It-Hurts* (SU 38): Seleznyoff

Dolina Issy / *The Issa valley* (PL 82): Mazurkiewicz

Dolina miru / *Valley of peace* (YU 56): Štiglic

Dollar Mark, The (US 24): Marion D.

Dollárpapa / *Dollar daddy* (HU 56): Koletár

Doll House Mystery, The (US 15): Stone

Doll's House, A (US 22): DeLacy

Doll's Revenge, The (GB 07): Potter

Dolly Does Her Bit (US 18): Morrison E.

Dolly macht Karriere / *Dolly the career girl* (GE 30): Stark-Gstettenbaur

Dolly of the Dailies (US 14, srl): Boss

Dolly's Vacation (US 18): Morrison E.

Dolor de los hijos, El / *Grief of the sons* (MX 48): Calpe

Dolor de pagar la renta, El / *The pain of paying the rent* (MX 59): Quezadas

Domani è troppo tardi / *Tomorrow's too late* (IT 49): Leurini

Domingo feliz, Un / *A happy Sunday* (VE 88): Sauce

Don Carlos (24 GE) — *see* Carlos und Elisabeth

Donde nacen los pobres / *Where the poor are born* (MX 50): Jiménez Pons J.

Dondi (US 61): Kory

Dongdong de Jiaqi / *Summer at Grandpa's* (TW 84): Wang Q.

Don Juan (US 26): DeLacy

Donkosakenlied, Das / *The Don Cossack song* (DE 56): Haar

Don Lorenzo (IT 52): Maggio

Donna del fiume, La / *The woman by the river* (IT 54): Olivieri

Don Segundo Sombra (AR 68): de la Cuesta

Don't (US 25): Fox J.

Don't Ever Marry (US 20): Barry W.

Don't Get Me Wrong (GB 37): Singer

Don't Go Near the Park (US 81): Peluce

Don't Just Stand There! (US 67): Bond S.

Don't Lie (US 42): 'Our Gang'

Don't Turn 'Em Loose (US 36): Nichols

Don't Weaken (US 20): Morrison E.

Don Vesuvio und das Haus der Strolche / *Don Vesuvio and the house of waifs* (DE/IT 58): Ande

'Doogie Howser, MD' (US 89–, TVS): Harris N. P.

Doombeach (GB 89): Coster J.

Door in the Wall, The (GB 56): Winter

Door That Has No Key, The (GB 21): Craig

Door-to-Door Maniac (US 66): Howard R.

Doorway to Hell, The (US 30): Janney

Door without a Key (US 61): Mumy

Do phool / *Two flowers* (IN 58): Kapoor R.

Do raaste / *Two ways* (IN 69): Mehmood

Doroga v mir / *Road to the world* (SU 29): Zavyaloff

Dorogoi malchik / *Dear boy* (SU 73): Yelistratov

Doro no kawa / *Muddy river* (JP 81): Asahara, Sakurai

Dorothy Vernon of Haddon Hall (US 24): Watson C.

Dortoir des grandes / *Big girls' dormitory* (FR 53): Maurin Y.-M.

Dos años de vacaciones / *Two years' holiday* (ES/MX 62): Calvo, Alonso P.

Dos diablillos en apuros / *Two little devils in a fix* (MX 55): Romay

Dos golfillos, Los / *Two little rascals* (ES 61): Jiménez, Alonso P.

Dos mundos y un amor / *Two worlds, one love* (MX 54): Perez

Dos pilletes, Los / *Two vagabonds* (MX 42): Busquets, Ortin

Dos pillos y pico / *Two-and-a-bit rascals* (ES 80): Sanz

Dossier noir, Le / *The black file* (FR/IT 55): Fourcade, Moullières

Dost / *Friend* (IN 74): Rajoo

Dos y dos son cinco / *Two and two are five* (ES 80): Sanz

Dot de Sylvie, La / *Sylvia's dowry* (FR 53): Moullières

Dotheboys Hall (GB 03): Carrington

Doublecross (GB 56): Pike J.

Double Event, The (GB 21): Wood S.

Double Life of Mr Alfred Burton, The (GB 19): Craig

Double Lives (29 US) — *see* Trail of the Horse Thieves

Double McGuffin, The (US 79): Hodges G.

Doubling for Romeo (US 22): Rogers J.

Do Unto Others (US 15): Benham

Do Unto Others (GB 15): Barker K.

Dovitljivi Kekec (69 YU) — *see* Kekčeve ukane

Down on the Farm (US 20): Marion D.

Down on the Farm (NZ 35): Sinclair

Down on the Farm (US 38): Ernest, Mahan

Down the Stretch (US 36): Rooney

Down to the Sea in Ships (US 49): Stockwell, Hawkins

Drag (US 29): Watson Bl., G., H.

Drághfy Éva / *Eva Draghfy* (HU 20): Lubinsky

Dragon of Pendragon Castle, The (GB 50): Netscher, Hannaford

Dragonwyck (US 46): Henry R.

Dragueurs, Les / *Girl crazy* (FR 59): Dekock

Drama of Heyville, The (US 14): Clark A.

Drango (US 57): Charney, Howard R., Stollery

Drapeau noir flotte sur la marmite, Le / *The black flag flies on the stewpot* (FR 71): Damain

Dream, A (US 11): Pickford

Dream Fairy, The (US 13): Boss

Dream for Christmas, A (US 73): Spell G.

Dreaming Out Loud (US 40): Watson Bs.

Dream of Eugene Aram, The (US 16): Clark R.

Dream of Kings, A (US 69): Pera

Dreamscape (US 83): Yothers

Dreamspeaker (CA 76): Tracey

Dream Street (US 21): Depew

Dream Time (GB 73): Lester

Drei blaue Jungs -- ein blondes Mädel / *Three blue boys, one blonde girl* (GE 33): Richter

Drei Männer im Schnee / *Three men in the snow* (GE 56): Kaiser

Drei Tanten, Die / *The three aunts* (GE 21): Allen W.

Drei und eine halbe Portion / *Three and a half portions* (DE 84): Bach

Drei weisse Birken / *Three silver birches* (DE 61): Hehn

Drenge / *Boys* (DK 77): Erhardsen

Drengen der forsvandt / *The boy who disappeared* (DK 83): Nielsen

Dressirovshchiki / *Animal-trainers* (SU 61): Biryukoff

Dressmaker from Paris, The (US 25): O'Donnell

Dreszcze / *The creeps* (PL 81): Hudziec

Drie flinke kerels / *Three rough types* (BE 38): Buyl

Drifting (US 23): Guerin

Driftwood (US 16): Roubert

Driftwood (US 24): Billings E.

Driftwood (US 47): Infuhr, Sydes

Drink Hearty (US 20): Morrison E.

Dristi / *The vision* (IN 55): Babua

Driver of the Deadwood Coach, The (US 12): Melford

Drôles de phénomènes / *Weird happenings* (FR 58): Noël, Flateau

Droomkoninkje / *Little dream king* (NL 26): Klein H.

Droom van een H.F.C.-ertje, De / *An H.F.C. fan's dream* (NL 23): Dalmeijer

Drop Dead, Darling (GB 66): Lester, Pike P.

Drops wird Flieger / *Drops becomes a pilot* (GE 38): 'Drops'

Drudge, The (US 14): Connelly

Druha směna / *The second shift* (CS 40): Salač

Drum, The (GB 38): Sabu, Tester

Drummer of the Eighth, The (US 12): Gottlieb

Drunkard, The (US 36): Nelson B.

Družba Pere Kvržice /*Peter Kvržic's gang* (YU 70): Žganec

Druzhok /*Little friend* (SU 57): Koval, Ptichkin

Družina Cerného Péra /*The Black Feather playschool* (CS 73): Renč

Druzya iz tabora /*Gypsy friends* (SU 38): Smorchkoff

Druzya - tovarishch /*Friends and comrades* (SU 59):
    Rakitin, Semyonov S.

Dry Rot (GB 56): Pike J.

Du bist die Welt für mich /*You're the world to me* (AT 53): Friedl

Du darfst nicht länger schweigen /*Now you must speak out* (DE 55):
    Finkbeiner

Due derelitti, I /*The two down-and-outs* (IT 51): Cerusico

Duel, Le /*The duel* (FR 39): Buquet

Duel in the Sun (US 46): Mickelsen

Duelo de pistoleros /*Duel of gunmen* (MX 65): Quezadas

Duelo en las montañas /*Duel in the mountains* (MX 49): Perez

Duel Personalities (US 39): 'Our Gang'

Due macchinisti, I /*The two mechanics* (IT c.10): Visca

Du er ikke alene /*You're not alone* (DK 78): Bjerg, Agensø

Dugan of the Bad Lands (US 31): Shuford

Duke Comes Back, The (US 37): Russell J.

Dulari (PK 87): Jamshid

Dulce madre mia /*Darling mother* (MX 42): Busquets

Duma pro kazaka Golotu /*Saga of the cossack Golota* (SU 37):
    Shekhtman, Tirtov

Dummy, The (US 29): Bennett M., Holmes L.

Duniya ka mela /*The world's a merry-go-round* (IN 74): Rajoo

Durand of the Bad Lands (US 25): Black B., Lee F.

Du rififi chez les hommes /*Free fight* (FR/IT 54): Maurin D.

Dushman /*The enemy* (IN 57): Kapoor R.

Dutch (US 91): Randall

Du und ich /*You and I* (GE 38): Eugens

Dva druga /*Two friends* (SU 54): Burlyayev B., Guskoff

Dva Fyodora /*The two Fyodors* (SU 58): Chursin

Dva ohně /*Two fires* (CS 49): Mikulič

Dva shaluna /*The two pranksters* (SU 27): Ratiani

Dvě matky /*Two mothers* (CS 20): Pražský

Dve ulbki /*Two smiles* (SU 71): Gusev A.

Dvoye iz odnovo kvartala /*Two from the same district* (SU 57):
    Semyonov R.

Dynamite (US 29): Scott D.

Dynamite Johnson (GB 78): Yap

Dynamite's Daughter (US 25): Haig

Dzhamilya (SU 69): Dubashev

Dziadek do orzechow /*The Nutcracker* (PL 67): Roman, Pomaski

Dzięcioł /*Woodpecker* (PL 70): Mosior

Dziesieciu z Pawiaka /*Ten from Pawiak* (PL 31): Rogulski

Dziewczyna i chłopak /*Girl and boy* (PL 80): Sieniawski

Each Pearl a Tear (US 16): Alexander B.

Eagle and the Hawk, The (US 33): Scott D.

Eagle Rock (GB 64): Rolls

Eagle Squadron (US 42): Severn B., Sheffield B.

Eagle's Talons, The (US 28): Darro

Earl Carroll Vanities (US 45): Ivo

Earl of Chicago, The (US 40): Sinclair

Earthbound (US 40): Larson

Earthbound (US 81): Dungan, Gilpin M., Porter T.

Earthling, The (AU/US 80): Schroder

Earth Women, The (US 26): Butterworth J.

Easiest Way, The (US 31): Shuford

Easter Lily, An (US 14, 'Sonny Jim'): Connelly

East Is East (52 US) — *see* Japanese War Bride

East Lynne (GB 13): Barker K.

East Lynne (US 25): Headrick

East Lynne (US 31): Albright, Cosbey

East Lynne (GB 82): Cox A.

East of Fifth Avenue (US 33): Moore D.

Easy Does It (49 US) — *see* Great Lover

Easy Living (US 37): Bartlett

Easy Money (US 15): Connelly

Easy Street (US 16): Berlinger

Easy to Take (US 36): Lee B., Scott D., Switzer

Eavesdroppers, The (US 12): Casey

Ebberöds Bank /*Ebberöd's Bank* (SE 35): Olsson

Echec au porteur /*Pay out bearer* (FR 57): Flateau, Fourcade

Echelle blanche, L' (69 FR) — *see* Promesse, La

Echo (PL 63): Blawut

Echoes of a Summer (US/CA 75): Savage B.

Eddie Cantor Story, The (US 53): Monda

Eddie's Exploit (US 12): Porter W.

Eddy Duchin Story, The (US 56): Thompson R.

Edelweisskönig, Der /*The edelweiss king* (GE 38): Schmidhofer

'Edgar' series (US 20-21): Jones J., Messinger, Trebaol E.

Edge of Darkness (US 43): Mickelsen

Edison, Marconi & Co. (US 28): 'Our Gang'

Edle Blut, Das /*Noble blood* (GE 27): Pottier

Edna's Imprisonment (US 11): Boss

Educating Father (US 36): Ernest, Mahan

Education du Prince, L' /*The prince's education* (FR 38): Lynen

Efter repetitionen /*After the rehearsal* (SE 83): Guve

Egg and I, The (US 47): Infuhr

Égigérö fü /*Rising gas* (HU 79): Hintsch

Egyhuszasos leany, Az /*A girl for two farthings* (HU 23):
    Lubinsky

Egyiptomi történet /*Egyptian story* (HU 62): Tóth L., Kiss

Egy pikoló világos /*One glass of beer* (HU 55): Koletár

Egyptian, The (US 54): Rettig

Ehrenschuld, Die /*Debt of honour* (GE 21): Pottier

Eight o'Clock Walk (GB 53): Hannaford

8 on the Lam (US 66): Brodie

80 Steps to Jonah (US 69): Quinn T.

Einfache Mädchen, Das /*The simple girl* (DE 57): Haar

Einmal wird die Sonne wieder scheinen /*The sun will shine again one day*
    (DE 69): 'Heintje'

Einstein kontra Babinsky /*Einstein versus Babinsky* (CS 63): Bor

Eins - zwei - drei Korona /*One, two, three Coronas* (DE 48): Neie

Eiserne Faust, Die /*The iron fist* (GE 21): 'Patatà'

Ejfélkor /*At midnight* (HU 56): Koletár

Ek (22 US) — *see* One Glorious Day

Ekadashi /*The eleventh day* (IN 55): Kumar

Ek nari do roop /*Two-faced woman* (IN 73): Mehmood

Ekspeditricen /*The shopgirl* (DK 11): Crone

Elder Sister (81 IN) — *see* Oppol

Election Day (US 29): 'Our Gang'

Election Daze (US 43): 'Our Gang', Tucker T.
Electric Grandmother, The (US 82): Fields
Elegy, The (US 27): DeLacy
Elephant Boy (GB 37): 'Sabu'
Elephant Man, The (GB 80): Fletcher
Elephants Never Forget (39 US) – see Zenobia
El Hakim (DE 57): Ande
Elnémult harangok / The bells stop ringing (HU 21): Szécsi, Lázár
e'Lollipop (ZA 75): Knox, N'Debele
Elopement (US 51): Rettig
El Paso (US 49): Chapin M.
Elveda meyhaneci / Farewell, mine host (TR 72): Dönmez
Elvis Elvis (SE 76): Dorazio
Elysium (HU 86): Nagy Z.
Emborakos, O / The little merchant (GR 67): Kailas
Emerald of the East (GB 28): Rive
Emergency Squad (US 39): Bupp T. & S., Hickman Dl.
Emergency Wedding (US 50): Mickelsen
Emil and the Detectives (31 GE) – see Emil und die Detektive
Emil and the Detectives (GB 35): Williams J., Blomfield, Rietti, Singer, Tester
Emil and the Detectives (US 64): Russell B., Mobley
Emila nedarbi / Emil's pranks (SU 86): Zonnenbergs-Zombergs
Emilie Högqvist (SE 39): Dalunde
Emil i Lönneberga / Emil at Lönneberga (SE 71): Ohlsson
Emil och grisaknoen / Emil and the piglet (SE 73): Ohlsson
Emil und die Detektive / Emil and the detectives (GE 31): Wenkhaus, Schaufuss, Richter
Emil und die Detektive (DE 54): Finkbeiner, Condrus, Kaiser
Emma (US 32): Ward
Empire of the Sun (US 87): Bale
Empty Canvas, The (63 IT/FR) – see Noia
Empty Cradle, The (US 23): Bennett M.
Empty Hearts (US 24): Black B.
Enchanted Barn, The (US 19): Butterworth F.
Enchanted Forest, The (US 45): Severn B.
Enchanted Valley, The (US 48): Gift
Enchantment (US 48): Miles P.
End of Summer, The (61 JP) – see Kohayagawa-ke no aki
End of the Road, The (GB 54): Hannaford
End of the Trail, The (US 33): Albright
En effeuillant la marguerite / He loves me, he loves me not (FR 56): Maurin Y.-M.
Enemy, The (US 27): Schaeffer
Enemy to Society, An (US 15): Carnahan
Én és a nagyapám / Me and Grandpa (HU 54): Koletár, Horváth
Enfance nue, L' / Naked childhood (FR 68): Tarrazon
Enfantasme / Spooks (IT 78): Cestiè
Enfant dans la foule, Un / Child in the crowd (FR 75): Chauveau
Enfant de l'amour, L' / Child of love (FR 30): Mercanton
Enfant de la roulotte, L' / The caravan kid (FR 14): Poyen
Enfant du dimanche, L' (68 FR) – see Bruno, l'enfant du dimanche
Enfant-roi, L' / The boy king (FR 23, srl): Munier
Enfant sauvage, L' / The wild boy (FR 69): Cargol
Enfants du paradis, Les / Children of paradise (FR 43): Belmon
Enfants du placard, Les / Closet children (FR 77): Balvet
Enfants du soleil, Les / Children of the sun (FR/MA 61): Brick

Enfer des anges, L' / Angels' hell (FR 39): Buquet, Claudio
En France comme si vous y étiez / Imagine you're in France (FR 64): Flateau
Engine-Driver's Son, The (KN 71): Kim C.
Englische Heirat, Die / The English wedding (GE 34): Richter
Englishman's Home, An (GB 38): Tester
Enigme du Mont Agel, L' / The mystery of Mont Agel (FR 23): Machin
Enken / The widow (DK 13): Stensgård
En la tierra del sol / In the land of the sun (ES 27): Hurtado
Enoch and Ezra's First Smoke (US 13): Boss, Clark A.
Enoch Arden (GB 14): Willmore
Enoken no Kondo Isamu / Enoken's Isamu Kondo (JP 35): Ito K.
Enredos de una gallega, Los / Spanish intrigue (MX 51): Roche
Enrico Caruso, leggenda di una voce / Caruso, the legendary voice (IT 51): Di Nardo
Entente cordiale (FR 39): Buquet
Entertaining Uncle (GB 14): Desmond
Entezar / Waiting (IR 74): Ahromi
Entotsu otoko / Man on a chimney (JP 31): 'Tokkan-Kozo'
Entraîneuse, L' / The lady trainer (FR 38): Mouloudji
Environment (US 22): Headrick
Episode de Waterloo, Un / Waterloo episode (BE 13): Mertens
Equipage, L' / The crew (FR 28): Guichard
Eraku nare / Get wise (JP 32): 'Tokkan-Kozo'
Eramos seis / We were six (AR 45): Alonso T., Barbieri
Erben, Die / The inheritors (AT 82): Vogel N.
Erborgtes Glück / Borrowed happiness (GE 18): Pottier
Ercole / Hercules (IT 18): Roveri
Ercole sfida Sansone / Hercules challenges Samson (IT 64): Loddi
Erdekházasság / Marriage of convenience (HU 18): Lubinsky
Erendira (DE 83): Wehe
Erkel (HU 52): Horváth
Erlkönig, Der (30 FR) – see Roi des Aulnes
Errant Errand Boy, The (GB 02): Williamson T.
Erste Recht des Kindes, Das / A child's first right (GE 32): Klicks
Escapade (GB 55): Spenser J., Asher, Barrett, Ray A.
Escapade in Japan (US 57): Provost
Escape, The (US 39): Beckett, Downing R.
Escape Artist, The (US 79): O'Neal
Escape by Night (GB 53): Ray A.
Escape from the Dark (GB 76): Harrison A.
Escape to Paradise (US 39): Breen
Escape to Witch Mountain (US 74): Eisenmann, Kerwin
Escucha mi canción / Hear my song (ES 59): Jiménez
Es leuchten die Sterne / The stars are shining (GE 38): Bosse
Espectro de la novia, El / The maid's ghost (MX 43): Busquets
Espions, Les / The spies (FR 57): Maurin P.
Estrellita / Little star (MX 38): Busquets
E.T. (US 82): Thomas H.
Età dell' amore, L' / Summer of love (IT 53): Beck P.-M.
Eto bilo v razvedke / It happened on reconnaissance (SU 69): Zhukov
Ettefaghe sadeh, Yek / A simple incident (IR 73): Zamani
Ettore Fieramosca (IT 38): Ferrari
Eugenio (81 IT) – see Voltati Eugenio
Eureka Stockade (GB 49): Yardley N.
Europa '51 (IT 52): Franchina

Noland Clay

Zoltán Csoma

Gardar Thór Cortes

Jeremy Cooper runs from horror in The Reflecting Skin

Sanzhar Dzhaksilikov

David Eberts

449

Eva (SE 48): Sarri
Even Break, An (US 18): Stone
Ever in My Heart (US 33): Cosbey
Ever-Living Isles, The (US 15): Goodwin
Ever-Open Door, The (GB 20): Wood S.
Everybody's Baby (US 39): Ernest, Kibrick S., Mahan
Everybody's Dancin' (US 50): Hyatt
Everybody's Hobby (US 39): Moran
Every Breath You Take (GB 87): Condou
Every Day Is a Holiday (65 ES) − see Cabriola
Every Man for Himself (US 24): 'Our Gang'
Every Saturday Night (US 36): Ernest, Mahan
Every Stray Dog and Kid (US 81): Petersen P.
Everything But the Truth (US 56): Hovey
Everything's On Ice (US 39): Watson Bs.
Évforduló /Anniversary (HU 36): Dévényi
Evidence (US 15): Steuart
Evidence (US 29): Frederick
Examination Day at School (US 10): Pickford
Excalibur (US 81): Boorman
Exclusive (US 37): Bartlett, Lee B.
Executive Suite (US 53): Considine
Exit the Vamp (US 21): Moore M.
Exodus (US 60): Crawford J.
Expensive Shine, An (US 12): Kelly P.
Expert, The (US 32): Moore D.
Exploits at West Poley (GB 86): Condou
Explorers (US 85): Hawke, Phoenix R., Presson, Jaffe
Exposed (US 32): Hutchins
Exquisite Sinner, The (US 26): Janney
Extra Day, The (GB 56): Hannaford
Extra Man, The (US 23): Fox J.
Eyes in the Night (US 42): Winkler
Eyes of the Night (US 26): Black B.
Eyes of the Underworld (US 42): Bupp S., Lee B.
Eyewitness (GB 70): Lester
Ezop /Aesop (SU 60): Vasilev B.

Fabiola (IT 18): Visca
Fabiola (IT 47): Leurini
Fable of the Back-Trackers from the Hot Sidewalks, The
    (US 17): McDermott
Fable of the Toilsome Ascent and the Shining Table Land, The
    (US 17): McDermott
Face at the Telephone, The (GB 15): Royston G.
Face Between, The (US 22): Hamrick
Facing the Music (GB 33): Singer
Fahrenheit 451 (GB 66): Gilmore, Lester, Younger
Fahrt ins Grüne, Die /Country excursion (GE 33): Richter
Fahrt nach Bamsdorf, Die /Trip to Bamsdorf (DD 56): Kuss, Schmidt P.
Fair and Muddy (US 28): 'Our Gang'
Fairies and Witches (US 15): Benham
Fair Warning (US 37): Burrud
Faisons du cinéma /Let's make a movie (FR 38): Rodon
Faithful (GB 36): Pavitt
Faith of Sonny Jim, The (US 15): Connelly
Fakir kizin kismeti /A poor girl's luck (TR 56): Ersöz

Falcon's Brother, The (US 42): Tucker T.
Fall, The (58 AR) − see Caida
Fallen Idol, The (GB 48): Henrey
Falling in Love (GB 34): Fitzpatrick P.
Falling in Love (US 84): Bradford
Fall of a Nation, The (US 16): Willis
Fall Rainer, Der /The Rainer case (GE 42): Rohringer
False Arrest (US 91): Bonsall
False Hero (46 US) − see Roaring Rangers
Falso heredero, El (66 MX/ES) − see Joselito vagabundo
Falstaff in Wien /Falstaff in Vienna (GE 40): Kieling
Fame is the Spur (GB 47): Wager, Weske
Fame Street (US 31): Janney
Famiglia Benvenuti, La /The Benvenutis (IT 67): Fioravanti
Familia y...uno mas, La /The family, plus one (ES 65): Sanchez
Familie auf Bestellung /Family to order (GE 38): Eugens
Familien Gelinde /The Gelindes (DK 44): Fagerlund
Familie Schimek /The Schimeks (GE 35): Teetzmann
Familjen Andersson /The Anderssons (SE 37): Olsson
Familjens hemlighet /The family secret (SE 36): Bernhard
'Family Affair, A' (US 66-71, TVS): Whitaker
Family Group, The (US 28): Haig
'Family Holvak, The' (US 75, TVS): Kerwin
Family Honeymoon (US 48): Hunt, Miles P.
Family Honor, The (US 20): Alexander B.
Family Jewels, The (US 65): Eccles
Family Next Door, The (US 39): Bartlett, Billings G.
Family Picnic, A (US 15): Kelly P.
Family Troubles (US 43): 'Our Gang'
'Famous Poems of George R. Sims' series (GB 22): Brantford
Fan Fan (US 18): Carpenter, Messinger, Sargent
Fängelse /Prison (SE 49): Sarri
Fangs of Justice (US 26): Frederick
Fanny (US 60): Flateau
Fanny och Alexander /Fanny and Alexander (SE 81): Guve
Fans (21 US) − see 'Edgar' series
Fantastic World of D.C. Collins, The (US 84): Bateman
Fantômas (FR 46): Gervais
Fapados szerelem /Simple love (HU 57): Koletár
Faraar /The absconder (IN 75): Rajoo
Farfalla della morte, La /Butterfly of death (IT 20): Casarotti
Farishta /The angel (IN 68): Mehmood
Får jag lov, magistern! /Please, Sir! (SE 47): Sarri
Farmer's Daughter, The (US 28): Watson D.
Farmer's Daughter, The (US 40): Hickman Dl.
Farmer's Daughter, The (US 46): Chapin M.
Farmer Takes a Wife, The (US 53): Hyatt, Mora
Farm Hands (US 43): 'Our Gang'
'Far til fire' series /Father to four (DK 53-61): Jensen O.M., Neumann
Fascination (GB 31): Bartholomew
Fast Companions (US 32): Rooney
Fast Company (US 24): 'Our Gang'
Fastest Gun Alive, The (US 56): Olsen C.
Fast Freight (US 26): Frederick
Fast Freight (US 29): 'Our Gang'
Fast Friends (US 79): Peluce
Fatal Card, The (26 US) − see Arizona Streak

Fate's Awful Jest (US 12): Casey
Fate's Plaything (20 NL/GB) – *see* Wat eeuwig blijft
Father, The (US 15): House C.
Father and Scout (US 94): Bonsall
Father and Son (US 29): McBan
Father and Son (81 HK) – *see* Fuzi qing
Father Dunne's Newsboys (48 US) – *see* Fighting Father Dunne
Father Figure (US 80): Licht
Father Hood (US 93): Bonsall
Father is a Bachelor (US 50): Gray B. and G., Ivo
Father is a Prince (US 40): Dawson
Father Makes Good (US 50): Gray G., Nokes
Father of the Bride (US 50): Tamblyn .
Father of the Bride (US 91): Culkin K.
Fathers of Men (US 16): Connelly
Father's Son (US 30): Janney, Bennett M.
Father's Son (US 41): Dawson, Beckett, Bupp S., Hurlic,
    McKim S., Winkler
Father's Wild Game (US 50): Gray G., Nokes
Father Takes the Air (US 51): Gray G., Nokes
Fatty Finn (AU 80): Oxenbould
Fearless Lover (US 25): Darro
Feathered Pests (US 39): Bupp S.
Federal Manhunt (US 38): Tucker J.
Fedka (SU 36): Kat-Oglu
Fedkina pravda /*Fedka's truth* (SU 25): Zimin, Maiya
Feed 'Em and Weep (US 38): 'Our Gang', Hurlic
Fe en Dios, La /*Faith in God* (MX 49): Anda
Feet First (US 30): Phelps
Fei lai de xianhe /*The crane flies back* (CN 82): Yang
Feinde /*Enemies* (GE 40): Eugens
Fekete gyémántok /*Black diamonds* (HU 38): Dévényi
Fel a fejjel! /*Chin up!* (HU 54): Benkö, Horváth
Felicità, La /*Happiness* (IT 17): Roveri
Felix Krull (80 DE) – *see* Bekenntnisse des Hochstaplers
    Felix Krull
Fellow Citizens (US 20): Morrison E.
Female Artillery (US 73): Montgomery
Femme d'à côté, La /*The woman next door* (FR 81): Becquaert
Femme infidèle, La /*The faithless woman* (FR/IT 68): Di Napoli S.
Femme poisson, La /*The woman-fish* (FR 32): Mercanton
Femme sans importance, Une /*A woman of no importance* (FR 37):
    Buquet
Ferien auf Immenhof /*Holidays at Immenhof* (DE 57): Kaiser
Ferien in Tirol (56 DE) – *see* Zärtliches Geheimnis
Ferienkind, Das /*The holiday child* (GE 43): Pässler, Reck
Ferme du pendu, La /*Hanged man's farm* (FR 45): Demorget
Fern, the Red Deer (GB 76): McFarlane C.
Ferroviere, Il /*The railwayman* (IT 55): Nevola, Paoletti
Festa di maggio (58 FR/IT) – *see* Premier mai
Festival of Nations (US 26): Janney
Feu de paille /*Flash in the pan* (FR 39): Fuller J.
Feudin' Rhythm (US 49): Ivo
Feudists, The (US 13): Kelly P.
Fiacre n.13 /*Cab no. 13* (IT 17): Casarotti
Fiamma che non si spegne, La /*The flame that never dies* (IT 49):
    Di Nardo

Fiancée des ténèbres, La /*Shadow fiancée* (FR 44): Belmon
Fiat voluntas Dei /*God's will be done* (IT 35): Locchi
Fickle Finger of Fate, The (67 ES) – *see* Dedo del destino
Fidele Bauer, Der /*The merry peasant* (GE 08): Bois
Fidele Bauer, Der (AT 51): Friedl
Field of Honor, The (US 17): Lee F.
Fiercest Heart, The (US 61): Holmes D.
Fiete im Netz /*Fiete in the net* (DD 57): Schimanski
Fietsen naar de Maan /*Cycling to the moon* (NL 62): Kerbosch
Fifteen Wives (US 34): Jones D.
Fifth Avenue (US 26): Noisom
Fifth Form at St Dominic's, The (GB 21): Thompson M.
Fifth Horseman, The (US 24): Depew
55 Days at Peking (US 62): Moulder-Brown
Fightin' Fools (US 41): 'Our Gang'
Fighting Back (US 48): Gray G., Ivo
Fighting Back (AU 82): Smith P.
Fighting Boob, The (US 26): Nelson B.
Fighting Cressy (US 20): Stone
Fighting Father Dunne (US 48): Cummings, Gift, Gray B., Roberts E.
Fighting Fools (US 49): Infuhr
Fighting for Fame (US 27, srl): Alexander B.
Fighting Guardsman, The (US 45): Tauzin
Fighting Job (US 20): Alexander B.
Fighting Joe (US 16): Messinger
Fighting Kid, The (US 28): House N.
Fighting Sons (40 US) – *see* Gallant Sons
Fighting Sullivans, The (44 US) – *see* Sullivans
Fighting the Flames (US 25): Darro
Fightin' Redhead, The (US 28): Barton
Fig Leaves (US 26): Watson C.
Figlia del diavolo, La /*The devil's daughter* (IT 52): Cerusico
Figli di nessuno, I /*Nobody's sons* (IT 51): Olivieri
Filasse (34 BE) – *see* Witte, De
Fille bien gardée, La /*The guarded girl* (FR 23): Poyen
Fille de Delft, La (14 NL/BE/FR) – *see* Meisje uit de bloemenvelden
Fille du juge d'instruction, La /*The magistrate's daughter* (FR 11): Mary
Film du poilu, Le /*The French soldier's film* (FR 28): Guichard
Filmens datter /*Daughter of the cinema* (DK 15): Reinwald
Film von der Königin Luise, Der /*The Queen Louisa film* (GE 13):
    Reinwald
Fils d'un autre, Le /*Another man's son* (FR c.14): Touzé
Fimpen /*Stubby* (SE 74): Bergman
Final Chapter, The (US 27): Holmes L.
Final Conflict, The (US 80): Holm
Final Extra, The (US 27): Holmes L., Jones B.
Find the Girl (US 20): Morrison E.
Find the Lady (GB 36): Pavitt
Finestra illuminata, La /*The lighted window* (IT c.13): Visca
Finestra sul Luna Park, La /*Window on Luna Park* (IT 56): Damiani
Finn and Hattie (US 31): Searl
Finsternis ist ihr Eigentum, Die /*Darkness is hers* (GE 22): Pottier
Firecreek (US 67): Tate
Fire Fighters (US 22): 'Our Gang'
Fire Fighters, The (GB 74): Gipps-Kent
Firefly, The (US 37): Spindola
Fire in the Stone (AU 83): Smith P.

Fireman, Save My Child (US 27): Haig
Fireman, Save My Child (US 32): Moore D., Ernest
Fireside Brewer, A (US 20): Marion D.
Fires of Fate (US 19): Moore P.
First Aid (US 18): Hamrick
First Baby, The (US 36): Jones D.
Firstborn (US 84): Haim
First Comes Courage (US 43): Binyon
First Great Train Robbery, The (GB 78): Boorman
First Men in the Moon (GB 64): Baulch
First Round-Up, The (US 34): 'Our Gang'
First Seven Years, The (US 30): 'Our Gang'
Fisher Maid, The (US 11): Pickford
Fisherman, The (US 33): Watson Bs.
Fisherman's Wharf (US 39): Breen, Bupp T., Kibrick L.
Fish Hawk (CA 81): Fields
Fish Hooky (US 33): 'Our Gang'
Fishy Tales (US 37): 'Our Gang'
Fiul munților / Son of the mountains (RO 80): Baltațescu
Fiume di dollari, Un / A river of dollars (IT 66): Loddi
Five Clues to Fortune (GB 57, srl): Hemmings
Five Little Peppers and How They Grew (US 39): Peck, Sinclair, Bond T.
Five Little Peppers at Home (US 40): Peck, Sinclair, Bond T., Larson
Five Little Peppers at School (40 US) – see Five Little Peppers in Trouble
Five Little Peppers in Trouble (US 40): Peck, Sinclair, Bond T., Larson, Mercer
Five Miles to Midnight (62 FR/IT/US) – see Couteau dans la plaie
Five Minutes to Live (US 62): Howard R.
Five of a Kind (US 38): Russell J.
Five on a Treasure Island (GB 57, srl): Palmer
Five Pennies, The (US 59): Herbert
Five Senses, The (US 15): Roubert
5,000 Fingers of Dr T., The (US 52): Rettig
Fixer (US 29): Sabiston
Fixer Dugan (US 39): Bupp S., Dunagan
Flådens friske fyre / Lively lads of the fleet (DK 65): Schmidt J.P.
Flagi na bashnyakh / Flags on the towers (SU 58): Babich
Flag of Humanity (US 40): Beckett
Flame, The (GB 20): Wood S.
Flame and the Arrow, The (US 50): Gebert
Flame of Life, The (US 23): Lee F.
Flames of Desire (US 24): Billings E.
Flaming Hearts (US 22): Lee F.
Flaming Love (US 25): Alexander B.
Flaming Waters (US 26): Darro
Flamme, La / The flame (FR 25): Guichard
Flapper, The (US 20): Connelly, Steuart
Flash the Sheepdog (GB 67): Younger
Flat Broke (US 20): Morrison E.
Flemming og Kvik / Flemming and Kvik (DK 60): Flensmark, Geckler, Schmidt J.P.
Flemming på kostskole / Flemming at boarding school (DK 61): Flensmark, Geckler, Schmidt J.P., Loreti
Flesh and Fantasy (US 43): Infuhr
Flesh and the Devil (US 26): Darro, De Lacy, Murphy M., Noisom

Flic, Un / A cop (FR 46): Gencel
Flicka kommer till stan, En / A girl comes to town (SE 37): Winther
Flickan i fönstret mittemot / The girl in the window opposite (SE 42): Dalunde
Flickornas Alfred / Their darling Alfred (SE 35): Hallberg
Fliegende Klassenzimmer, Das / The flying classroom (DE 54): Kraus, Brandt, Hoffmann
Flight Lieutenant (US 42): Croft, Kibrick S.
Flight of the Navigator (US 86): Cramer
Flipper (US 63): Halpin
'Flipper' (US 63-66, TVS): Halpin, Norden
Flipper's New Adventure (US 64): Halpin
Flirt, The (US 16): Short
Flirt, The (US 22): Messinger, Boardman
Floh im Ohr / Flea in the ear (GE 43): Möller
Fløjtespilleren / The flautist (DK 53): Jensen O.M., Neumann
Flood, The (GB 63): Ellis I. and C.
Flood (US 76): Olson, Garrett
Flood Tide (US 57): Ray M.
Floor Below, The (US 19): Morrison E.
Florodora Girl, The (US 30): Albright
Flower Drum Song (US 61): Adiarte
Fluch der Schönheit / Curse of beauty (GE 15): Reinwald
Fluchtversuch / Escape attempt (DE 76): Savic
Fluke (US 94): Pomeranc
Fluteman (AU 82): Minty
Fly, The (US 58): Herbert
Flying Blind (US 41): Kaye
Flying Carpet, The (56 SU) – see Starik Khottabich
Flying Eye, The (GB 55): Hannaford
Flying Fists (US 38): Jones D.
Flying G-Men (US 39): McKim S.
Flying Horseman, The (US 26): Butts, Holmes L., Spear, Watson C.
Flying Irishman, The (US 39): Beckett, Reynolds
Flying Leathernecks (US 51): Gebert
Flying Ranee, The (IN 39): Marathe A.
Flying Sorcerer, The (GB 74): Burfield
Flying U Ranch (US 27): Darro
Flying with Music (US 42): Roy
Flying Without Wings (76 NL) – see Peter en de vliegende autobus
Fly My Kite (US 31): 'Our Gang', Ernest
Fly II, The (US 89): Cross
Folket på Högbogården / The folks at Högbo's farm (SE 39): Olsson
Folkets ven / The people's friend (DK 18): Jensen S.C.
Folle à tuer / Crazy to kill (FR 75): Waintrop
Following the Scent (US 15): Connelly
Follow Me, Boys! (US 66): Russell K.
Follow That Blonde (US 46): Infuhr
Follow the Swallow (US 30): Barty
Follow Your Heart (US 36): Rentschler
Follow Your Leader (GB 14): Desmond
Foolish Matrons, The (US 21): Lee F., Marion D.
Foolish Virgin, The (US 17): Tansey S., Verdi
Foolish Virgin, The (US 24): O'Donnell
Fool Killer, The (US 64): Albert
Fools for Luck (US 28): Haig

Football Crazy (60 DD) – *see* Neue Fimmel
Football Romeo (US 38): 'Our Gang', Winkler
Footlight Glamour (US 43): Simms L., Mummert
Footlight Parade (US 33): Barty
Footlights and Fools (US 29): Bennett M.
For Better, for Worse (US 19): Barry W., Moore M.
Forbidden Adventure (31 US) – *see* Newly Rich
Forbidden Company (US 32): Durand
Forbidden Fire (US 19): Moore P.
Forbidden Music (36 GB) – *see* Land Without Music
Forbidden Room, The (US 19): Carpenter
Forbidden Thing, The (US 20): Hall N., Wilkinson
Force of Evil (US 48): Bridges B.
Foreign Correspondent (US 40): Kilburn
Forest Pony (46 GB) – *see* Riders of the New Forest
Forever and a Day (US 43): Severn E.
Forever Young (US 92): Wood E.
Forever Young, Forever Free (75 ZA) – *see* e'Lollipop
Forget Venice (79 IT) – *see* Dimenticare Venezia
Forgotten Babies (US 33): 'Our Gang'
Forgotten Woman, The (US 39): Dunagan
For Heaven's Sake (US 50): Rettig
For Her Brother's Sake (US 11): Pickford
For His Sake (US 22): Jackson C.
For Love of Mary Ellen (US 15): Stone
For Pete's Sake (US 34): 'Our Gang'
For Pete's Sake (US 67): Jensen J.
Forsaken, The (GB 13): Desmond
For Sale, a Daddy (US 16): Monahan
Försterliesl / *The forester's daughter* (AT 56): Kratz
For Such Is the Kingdom of Heaven (13 GB) – *see*
   Christmas Strike
Fort Dobbs (US 58): Eyer Ri.
For the Love of Benji (US 77): Fiuzat
For the Love of Mike (US 60): Bravo D.
For the Love of Rusty (US 47): Donaldson T., Hickman Dw., Infuhr,
   Nokes
For the Queen (US 11): Boss, Tansey R.
For Those in Peril (GB 44): Wallbridge
Fort na obozowej (61 PL) – *see* Bitwa o Kozi Dwor
Fortunate Life, A (AU 85, srl): Richards
Fortune Hunter, The (US 27): Gordon Bo.
Fortune Lane (GB 47): Barr, Weske
For You My Boy (US 23): Roubert
Fotygraft Gallery (US 19): Carr J. & S.
Foundling, The (US 15): Barry W.
Four Devils (US 28): DeLacy, Wain
4D Special Agents (GB 81): Fletcher, Medford
Four Feathers, The (US 29): DeLacy
Four Feathers, The (GB 39): Baxter
Four Feathers, The (GB 78): Scott-Taylor
Four Hundred Blows, The (58 FR) – *see* Quatre cents coups
Four Mothers (US 41): Bupp S.
Four Parts (US 34): Beard
Four's a Crowd (US 38): Beckett
Four Seasons (US 17): Benham
Four Seasons of Children (39 JP) – *see* Kodomo no shiki

Four Sided Triangle (GB 53): Barrett, Dearman
Four Sons (US 28): Parrish
Fourth Alarm, The (US 26): 'Our Gang'
Fourth Commandment, The (US 26): Shuford
Fourth Horseman, The (US 32): Watson D.
Fourth Musketeer, The (US 23): Stone, Coghlan
Fourth Wish, The (AU 75): Bettles
Fox, The (US 21): Eason
Fox and the Hound, The (US 81): Feldman
Foxfire (US 55): Charney
Fox Movietone Follies of 1929 (US 29): Cooper Ja.
'Fox Rascals' series (US 28): Holmes L.
Fracture du myocarde, La / *Heart rupture* (CA 90): Copans
Fraid Cat (US 14, 'Sonny Jim'): Connelly
Framing Youth (US 37): 'Our Gang'
Française et l'amour, La / *The Frenchwoman and love* (FR 60): Morat
Frankenstein (US 73): Garrett
Frankenweenie (US 84): Oliver B.
Frau am Scheidewege, Die / *Woman at the crossroads* (GE/HU 38): Bosse
Fraudeur, Le / *The swindler* (FR 37): Lynen
Frauen, die nicht lieben dürfen / *Women forbidden to love* (GE 24): Lázár
Frauen für Golden Hill / *Women for Golden Hill* (GE 38): Kieling
Frauenliebe, Frauenleid / *Women's love and grief* (GE 37): Bosse
Frau im Mond / *Woman in the moon* (GE 29): Stark-Gstettenbaur
Frau Irene Besser (DE 60): Grimm
Frau Sixta (GE 38): Schmidhofer
Freccia nel cuore, La / *Arrow in the heart* (IT 24): Palermi
Freccia nel fianco, La / *Arrow in the side* (IT 43): Barbetti
Freckled Rascal, The (US 29): Barton
Freckles (US 28): Fox J., Holmes L.
Freddie's Dumb Playmates (GB 13): Royston R.
Free and Easy (US 30): Coogan J.
Freedom Is Paradise (89 SU) – *see* SER
Free Eats (US 32): 'Our Gang', McComas
Free Soul, A (US 28): Albright
Free Wheeling (US 32): 'Our Gang', McComas
Free Willy (US 93): Richter
Free Willy 2 (US 94): Richter, Capra
French Mistress, A (GB 60): Bulloch J., Palmer
Freshman, The (US 25): McBan
Fresh Paint (US 20): Morrison E.
Freunde / *Friends* (GE 43): Rohringer
Friaren från landsvägen / *Proposal on the highway* (SE 23):
   Alexandersson
Fric-frac en dentelles / *Burglars in lace* (FR 56): Fourcade, Urbain
Friday the 13th – a New Beginning (US 85): Feldman
Friday the 13th – the Final Chapter (US 84): Feldman
Friendly Enemies (US 25): Fox J.
Friendly Persuasion (US 56): Eyer Ri.
Friend or Foe (GB 81): Luxford
Friends for Life (55 IT) – *see* Amici per la pelle
Friends for Life (55 IT) – *see* Amici per la pelle
Frisco Jenny (US 32): Phelps
Frisco Sally Levy (US 27): Holmes L.
Fritz Bauer (SU 30): Simanovich
Fritze Bollmann wollte angeln / *Fritze Bollmann went fishing*
   (GE 43): Möller
Frivolous Sal (US 24): Alexander B.

Frog Dreaming (AU 85): Thomas H.
Froggy's Little Brother (GB 21): Thompson M., Frayne
Frogs (US 72): Hodges H.
Fröhliche Wanderer, Der / The happy wanderer (DE 55): Finkbeiner
Fröken blir piga / From miss to maid (SE 36): Hallberg
From Out of the Past (US 16): Connelly
From the Mixed-Up Files of Mrs Basil E. Frankweiler (US 73): Doran
From This Day Forward (US 46): Driscoll
Frontera norte / Northern border (MX 53): Anda
Frontiersman, The (US 39): Jones D.
Frontier Woman (US 56): Howard R.
Front Page Story, A (US 22): Messinger
Frozen River (US 29): Lee D.
Früchtchen / Fruitlet (AT 34): Richter
'Frugolino' series (IT 14): Roveri
Frühlingslied / Spring song (DE 54): Grimm
Frühlingsmelodie / Melody of spring (DE 45): Moik
Frühlingsstimmen / Voices of spring (AT 52): Friedl
Fruitful Vine, The (GB 21): Dear
Fruits sauvages, Les / Wild fruits (FR 53): Moullières, Bonnefous
Frun tillhanda / Lady in waiting (SE 39): Hjelm
Fuga in Francia / Flight into France (IT 48): Olivieri
Fugleskræmslet / The scarecrow (DK 10): Petersen Cas.
Fuji ni tatsukage / In Fuji's shadow (JP 57): Yamate
Fukeiki jidai / Age of depression (JP 30): 'Tokkan-Kozo'
Fuller Brush Man, The (US 48): Hunt
Full House (52 US) – see O.Henry's Full House
Funda (TR 68): Dönmez
Funhouse, The (US 80): Carson S.
Fun in Acapulco (US 63): Domasin
Fuochi d'artificio / Fireworks (IT 38): Locchi
Further up the Creek (GB 58): Hall J.
Fury (US 36): Van Atta
'Fury' (US 55-66, TVS): Diamond B.
Fussgänger, Der / The pedestrian (DE/CH 73): Weinert
Futen rojin nikki (JP 62): Shimazu
Fuun Kuroshio maru / The 'Kuroshio' in a storm (JP 56): Yamate
Fuzi qing / Father and son (HK 81): Lee Y.-T., Chan

Gabriel over the White House (US 33): Moore D.
Gaddaar / Traitor (IN 73): Rajoo
Gaichi (SU 38): Mandzhiyev
Gaietés de l'Exposition, Les / Exhibition Follies (FR 39): Mouloudji
Gaily, Gaily (US 69): Shea E.
Gallant Defender (US 35): Billings G.
Gallant Journey (US 46): Binyon, Cook T., Swan
Gallant Lady (US 33): Moore D., Beckett
Gallant Sons (US 40): Kelly T.
Gallegher (US 17): Clark A.
Gallegher (US 65): Mobley
Gallina clueca, La / The broody hen (MX 41): Busquets
Gamble in Hearts, A (26 US) – see Wild to Go
Gambler, The (US 80): Scribner
Gambler of the West, The (US 15): Short
Gambler: the Adventure Continues, The (US 83): Fields
Gamble with Hearts, A (GB 23): Brantford
Gambling Terror, The (US 37): Nelson B.

Game of Life, The (GB 22): Brantford
Game of Three, The (US 15): Stone
Game That Kills, The (US 37): McKim S.
Gamin de Bruxelles, Un / A Brussels urchin (BE 25): Adel
Gamin de Paris, Le / The Parisian urchin (FR 23): Poyen
Gamins de Paris / Paris kids (FR 53): Fourcade, Gencel, Urbain
Gamma People, The (GB 55): Caridia
Ganacheni / The judgment (SU 59): Daneliya
Gang Bullets (US 37): Bartlett
Gang Show, The (GB 37): Snelling
Gangster, The (US 47): Gray B.
Gangsters en jupons / Petticoat crooks (FR 53): Poujouly
Gansemagd, Die / The goose-girl (DE 57): Hack
Gaolbreak (GB 36): Fitzpatrick P.
Garbage Pail Kids, The (US 87): Astin M.
Garçon sauvage, Le / The wild boy (FR 51): Beck P.-M.
Garden of Allah, The (US 16): Jacobs
Gariftar (PK 88): Jamshid
Garrison's Finish (US 23): Coghlan
Garri zanimayetsa politikoi / Harry goes into politics (SU 33): Shelontsev
Gaslight (US 44): Gray G.
Gas Logic (US 18): Connelly
Gasoloons (US 36): Jones D.
Gässchen zum Paradies, Das / Little road to paradise (GE 36): Bosse
Gate, The (CA 86): Dorff
Gateway (US 38): Samarzich
Gattopardo, Il / The leopard (IT/FR 62): Fuller B.
Gaucho (US 80): Gomez P.
Gauguin the Savage (US 79): Stephens H.
Gavroche (SU 37): Smorchkoff
Gay Blades (US 46): Rodin M.
Gay Old Dog (GB 35): Singer
Gay Retreat, The (US 27): Madden
Gay Senorita, The (US 45): Cook T.
Gay Sisters, The (US 42): Simms L.
Gay Tuttles, The (42 US) – see Tuttles of Tahiti
GB VII (US 74): Wixted
Gde ti teper, Maksim? / Where are you now, Maxim? (SU 62): Tokaryoff
Geared to Go (US 24): Butterworth J.
Geeta (IN 40): Marathe A.
Geet gata chal / Walk singing (IN 75): Mehmood
Geetha (IN 73): Ramu
Gefährliche Frühling / Dangerous spring (GE 43): Eugens
Gefährlicher Urlaub (52 GB) – see Man Between
Geheimnis des Abbe X, Das / The Abbé X's secret (GE 27): Rive
Geheimnisse von London, Die / London mysteries (GE/AT 20): Lubinsky
Geheimnisse von New York, Die / New York mysteries (GE 20): Allen W.
Geheimnisvolle Wrack, Das / The mysterious wreck (DD 54): Rettschlag
Geheimnis von Schloss Holloway, Das / The mystery of Holloway Castle (GE 19): Herzberg
Gehetzte Menschen (32 CS/AT/GE) – see Štvaní lidé
Geliebte Welt / Beloved world (GE 42): Eugens
Gendarme desconocido, El / The unknown policeman (MX 41): Busquets
Gene Autry and the Mounties (US 50): Gray B., Infuhr
General Crack (US 29): DeLacy
General Spanky (US 36): McFarland, Switzer, Downing R., Tucker J., 'Our Gang'

Generals Without Buttons (36 FR) — *see* Guerre des gosses
Genkanban to ojosan / *The porter and the lady* (JP 34): 'Tokkan-Kozo'
Gentle Julia (US 36): Searl
Gentleman for a Day (US 14): Hauck
Gentleman Jim (US 42): Calkins
Gentleman of Paris, A (GB 31): Lawford
Gentleman's Agreement (US 47): Stockwell
Gentlemen Prefer Blondes (US 53): Winslow G.
George Washington, Jr. (US 23): Barry W.
George Washington Slept Here (US 42): Croft
George White's Scandals (US 34): Beckett
Gerald Cranston's Lady (US 24): Headrick
Germania Anno Zero / *Germany, Year Zero* (IT/FR/DE 47): Meschke
Geschenk des Inders, Das / *The Indian's gift* (GE 13): Bois
Geschichte der stillen Mühle, Die / *Story of the silent mill* (GE 14): Reinwald
Geschichte vom kleinen Mück, Die / *Story of little Muck* (DD 53): Schmidt T.
Getaway, The (36 US) — *see* Tough Guy
Get Off My Foot (GB 35): Pavitt
Get Out and Get Under (US 20): Morrison E.
Get Rich Quick (US 34): Ernest
Get-Rich-Quick Edgar (US 20): Jones J., Messinger
Getting Andy's Goat (US 14): Clark A.
Getting 'Em Right (US 25): Holmes L.
Getting Even with Dad (US 94): Culkin M.
Getting His Goat (US 20): Morrison E.
Get Your Man (US 27): Durand
Gharer math / *The home temple* (IN 57): Babua
Ghar ghar ki kahani / *Every household's story* (IN 70): Mehmood
Ghariboon ka badshah (PK 88): Jamshid
Ghost City (US 32): Shuford
Ghost in the Machine (US 93): Horneff
Ghost of Flight 401 (US 78): Peluce
Ghost of Frankenstein, The (US 52): Infuhr
Ghost of Mother Eve, The (US 14): Boss
Ghost of St Michael's, The (GB 40): Baxter
Ghost Rider, The (US 36): Nelson B.
Ghost Talks, The (US 28): Bennett M.
Gia ligi storgi / *For a little affection* (GR 63): Kailas
Gian Burrasca (IT 43): Battaglia
Giants vs. Yanks (US 23): 'Our Gang'
Gibigianna, La / *The popinjay* (IT 19): Casarotti
Gidget Gets Married (US 72): Beauvy, Pera
Gift, The (GB 89): Whalley
Gift for Heidi, A (US 58): Parks
Giftgas / *Poison gas* (GE 29): Burns B.
Gift of Gab, The (US 34): Barty
Gift of God (82 BF) — *see* Wênd Kûuni
Giganta di Metropolis / *Giant of the metropolis* (IT 60): Angeletti M.
Gigolette (FR 21): Haziza
Gigolo (US 26): Spear
Gij zult niet dooden / *Thou shalt not kill* (NL/GB 21): Doxat-Pratt
Gikor (SU 34): Pogosian
Gildersleeve on Broadway (US 43): Mercer, Infuhr
Gildersleeve's Bad Day (US 43): Mercer

Gildersleeve's Ghost (US 44): Mercer
Ginger (US 35): Searl, Bupp T.
Ginger (US 46): Calkins, Collins
Ginger Meggs (AU 82): Kounnas
Ginger Snaps (US 29): Sabiston
Gingham Girl, The (US 27): Haig
Giorni di festa / *Holidays* (IT 40): Barbetti
Giovani mariti / *Young husbands* (IT/FR 57): Chevalier
Giovanni Episcopo (IT 16): Visca
Gipsy Cavalier, A (GB 22): Blackton
Girl, The (27 US) — *see* What Every Girl Should Know
Girl Can't Help It, The (US 56): Gordon Ba.
Girl Crazy (US 32): Lee D.
Girl Expert, The (US 24): Butts
Girl from Jones Beach, The (US 49): Gray G.
Girl in the Woods (US 57): Charney
Girl in White, The (US 52): Mora (Morrow)
Girl Loves Boy (US 37): Bailey Sd., Phelps
Girl Most Likely, The (US 57): McGreevey
Girl Next Door, The (GB 13): Royston R.
Girl Next Door, The (US 52): Gray B.
Girl of Good Family, A (85 CN) — *see* Liangjia funü
Girl of the Limberlost, A (US 24): Black B., Hall N.
Girl of the Limberlost, A (US 34): Bupp T.
Girl Overboard (US 37): Burrud
Girl Said No, The (US 30): Coghlan
Girl Shy (US 24): Daniels M.
Girl Was Young, The (37 GB) — *see* Young and Innocent
Girl Who Dared, The (US 15): Boardman
Girl Who Wrecked His Home, The (GB 16): Bennett C.
Girl with the Champagne Eyes, The (US 18): Carpenter, Perl
Giro del mondo di un birichino, Il / *A scamp goes round the world* (IT 21): Capelli
Girovaghi, I / *The strollers* (IT 56): Autiero
Giubbe rosse / *Red jackets* (IT 75): Cestiè
Giugno / *June* (IT 56): Damiani
Giuseppe venduto dai fratelli / *Joseph sold by his brothers* (IT 60): Angeletti M.
Give Her a Ring (GB 34): Fitzpatrick P.
'Gjenerali' kapet rob, Një / *A general is captured* (AL 80): Lohja
Gläd dig i din ungdom / *Rejoice in your youth* (SE 39): Olsson
Gladiador invencible, El (61 IT/ES) — *see* Gladiatore invincibile
Gladiator, The (US 38): Moore D.
Gladiatore invincibile, Il / *The unbeatable gladiator* (IT/ES 61): Nevola
Glamador (FR 57): Emery
Glamour Boy (US 41): Hickman Dl.
Glass Cage, The (GB 55): Richmond
Glass Key, The (US 35): Ernest
Glass Key, The (US 42): Binyon
Glass Wall, The (US 53): Monda
Glenn Miller Story, The (US 53): Sydes
Glimpses of the Moon, The (US 23): Verdi
Glitterball, The (GB 77): Buckton
Globero, El / *The balloon-seller* (MX 60): Quezadas
Glockengiesser von Tirol, Der / *The bell-caster of Tyrol* (DE 56): Schwartz S.
Gloire de mon père, La / *My father's glory* (FR 90): Ciamaca

Gloom Chaser, The (US 28): Sabiston, Watson D.

Gloria (US 80): Adames

Gloriana (US 16): Griffith, Messinger

Gloria's Romance (US 16): Hauck, Steuart

Glorious Adventure, The (US/GB 22): Brantford, Craig

Glorious Fourth, The (US 27): 'Our Gang'

Głos serca / Voice of the heart (PL 30): Rogulski

Glove Taps (US 37): 'Our Gang', Tucker J., Winkler

Glut / Heat (CH/DE 83): Lücking

Gnome-Mobile, The (US 66): Garber

Go and Get It (US 20): Barry W.

Go-Between, The (GB 71): Guard

Gobs and Gals (US 52): Rettig

Go Chase Yourself (US 38): Watson Bs.

God Boy, The (NZ 75): Higgins

Godless Girl, The (US 28): Marion D.

Godless Men (US 20): Lee F.

God's Crucible (US 16): Lee F.

Gods Must Be Crazy II, The (ZA 88): 'Eiros'

Godzilla versus the Smog Monster (71 JP) — see Gojira tai Hedora

Gogi - otvazhni lyotchik / Gogi the fearless pilot (SU 28): Ratiani

Gogi Ratiani (SU 27): Ratiani, Dadeshkeliani

Goin' Fishin' (US 40): 'Our Gang'

Going Ga-Ga (US 28): Albright, Watson D.

Going My Way (US 44): Nokes

Going of the White Swan, The (US 14): Clark R.

Going Straight (US 16): Carpenter, Collier, Stone

Going to Press (US 42): 'Our Gang', Hickman Dl.

Gojira tai Hedora / Godzilla versus Hedora (JP 71): Kawase

Go Kart Go! (GB 63): Moulder-Brown, Waterman, Witty

Gold and the Woman (US 16): Eason

Gold Diggers of 1933 (US 33): Barty

Golden Bed, The (US 25): Billings E., Marion D.

Golden Earrings (US 47): Bates, Simms L.

Golden Eels, The (79 CS) — see Zlátí úhoří

Golden Fortress, The (74 IN) — see Sonar kella

Golden Head, The (US/HU 64): Gilmore

Golden Hoofs (US 41): Hurlic

Golden Princess, The (US 25): Marion D.

Golden Strain, The (US 25): Lee F., Watson C.

Gold Heels (US 24): Black B.

Goldie (US 31): Barty

Gold Is Not All (US 10): Pickford

Gold Rush Maisie (US 40): Beckett

Golos Tarasa / The voice of Taras (SU 40): Tsigankov

Golubiye Pestsi Peti Sinyavina / Petya Sinyavin's Blue Foxes (SU 59): Guskoff, Maltsev

Goluboi portret / The blue portrait (SU 77): Savishchev

Gomti ke kinare / On the banks of the Gomti (IN 72): Alankar

Gone with the Wind (US 39): Cook B., Kaye, Kelly T., Kibrick S., Kuhn, Moran

Good as Gold (US 27): Moore M.

Good Bad Boy, The (US 24): Butterworth J., Gordon Bb.

Good Bad Boys (US 40): 'Our Gang'

Goodbye Again (US 33): Ward

Goodbye, Mr Chips (GB 39): Kilburn

Goodbye, Mr Chips (GB 69): Bury

Good-Bye, My Lady (US 55): DeWilde

Goodbye Summer (US 14): Connelly

Good Cheer (US 26): 'Our Gang'

Good Fellows, The (US 43): Winkler

Good Guys and the Bad Guys, The (US 69): Riha

Good Humor Man, The (US 50): Miles P., Gray B.

Good Little Devil, A (US 08): Kelly P.

Good Luck, Mr Yates (US 43): Beckett, Binyon, Cook T., Larson, Roy, Wissler

Good Morning (59 JP) — see Ohayo

Goodness Gracious (US 13): Connelly

Good Old Days, The (GB 39): 'Our Gang'

Good Son, The (US 93): Wood E., Culkin M.

Good Times (US 67): Robbins

Goonies, The (US 85): Astin S., Feldman, Quan

Gopal Krishna (IN 29): Batto

Gopal Krishna (IN 38): Marathe R.

Gorakh aya / Here comes Gorakh (IN 38): Apte

Göranssons pojke / Göransson's boy (SE 41): Olsson

Gorechto pladre / Hot noon (BG 64): Nakov

Gore na chereshata / Up in the cherry-tree (BG 83): Prahov

Gorgeous Hussy (US 36): Kuhn

Gorgo (GB 61): Winter

Gorod zazhigayet ogni / The town lights up (SU 58): Perevalov

Gosse en or, Un / A darling kid (FR 38): Farguette

Gosseline, La / That little girl (FR 23): Poyen

Gottes Engel sind überall / God's angels are everywhere (AT 49): Eis

Governor of Louisiana, The (US 47): Aaker L.

Gowlan (IN 48): Kumar

Grabbarna i 57: an / The kids at No.57 (SE 35): Hallberg

Grabbing Grabbers (US 26): Bennett M.

Grabenplatz 17 / No.17, Grabenplatz (DE 58): Haar

Grab the Ghost (US 20): Morrison E.

Grail, The (US 23): Headrick

Graine au vent / Seed in the wind (FR 28): Heuzé

Gramma (US 86): Oliver B.

Gran aventura, La / The great adventure (MX 64): Bravo J.

Gran cruz, La / The great cross (MX 37): Busquets

Grandaddy's Boy (US 13): Clark R.

Grande addìo, Il / The big farewell (IT 53): Maggio

Grande épreuve, La / The big test (FR 27): Heuzé

Grand élan, Le / Snow speed (FR 39): Mouloudji

Grandes amigos / Great friends (ES 66): Arco

Grand Escapade, The (GB 46): Artemus

Grandmother, The (US 70): White R.

Grandpa Max (US 75): Savage B.

Grand Parade (US 26): O'Donnell

Grand patron, Un / The Chief (FR 51): Fourcade, Lecointe

Grand-père / Grandad (FR 38): Rodon

Grand Prix (GB 34): Hepworth R.

Grands, Les / The big boys (FR 36): Grave

Granitsa na zamke / Closed frontier (SU 37): Tirtov

Granujas, Los / The urchins (ES 24): Hurtado

Grapes of Wrath, The (US 40): Hickman Dl., Albright

Grass Orphan, The (GB 22): Dear

Grate Impeeryul Sirkus, The (US 14): Clark R.

Grausige Nächte /*Nights of horror* (GE 21): Pottier
Great Adventure, The (53 SE) — *see* Stora äventyret
Great Adventures of Wild Bill Hickok, The (US 38): Jones D., McKim S.
Great Bradley Mystery, The (US 17): Clark A.
Great Caruso, The (US 51): Price
Great Commandment, The (US 39): Samarzich
Great Companions (52 US) — *see* Meet Me at the Fair
Great Day, The (56 ES) — *see* Traje blanco
Great Day in the Morning (US 55): MacDonald
Great Divide, The (US 15): Carr J. and S.
Greater Love, The (US 17): Thaw
Greatest Gift, The (US 74): Kerwin
Greatest of These Is Charity, The (US 12): Benham
Greatest Show on Earth, The (US 52): Diamond, Hawkins
Great Expectations (22 DK) — *see* Store forventninger
Great Expectations (US 34): Breakston, Searl
Great Expectations (GB 46): Wager
Great Expectations (GB 75): Gipps-Kent, Beaumont R.
Great Expectations (GB 81, srl): McGrath
Great Gildersleeve, The (US 42): Mercer, McKim H., Madore
Great Guns (US 41): Nichols
Great Impostor, The (GB 18): Wood S.
Great Jasper, The (US 33): Durand, Line
Great Love, The (US 25): Coghlan
Great Lover, The (US 49): Lyon, Gray G., Hunter, Lindgren O.
Great Man Votes, The (US 39): Holden, Bartlett
Great Meadow, The (US 31): Shuford
Great Mike, The (US 44): Henry R., Tyler L.
Great Mr Nobody, The (US 41): Moore D.
Great Moment, The (US 44): Sheffield B. and J.
Great O'Malley, The (US 36): Watson D.
Great Stagecoach Robbery, The (US 45): Blake, Tyler L.
Great White Hope, The (US 70): Padilla
Great White Way, The (US 24): Watson H.
Greed (US 23): Jewell
Greedy Boy's Dream, The (GB 49): Carey
Greedy George (US 13): Clark A.
Greek Street (GB 30): Pavitt
Greengage Summer, The (GB 61): Williams R.
Greenie, The (US 42): Cook T.
Green Pastures, The (US 36): Hurlic
Green Promise, The (US 49): Donaldson T.
Green Scarf, The (GB 54): O'Sullivan
Green Years, The (US 46): Stockwell, Lyon, Bates
Gregorio (PE 84): Torre
Gremlins (US 84): Feldman
Greshni angel /*Sinful angel* (SU 62): Barkhatov
Gretchen the Greenhorn (US 16): Carpenter, Stone
Gretel zieht das grosse Los /*Gretel wins the lottery* (GE 33): Schaufuss
Greyfriars Bobby (GB 61): Winter
Greystoke (GB 84): Potts
Gribiche (FR 25): Forest
Griff nach dem Sternen /*Reaching for the stars* (DE 55): Ande, Grimm
Grisjakten /*The pig-hunt* (SE 69): Malmsjö

Grit (US 24): Depew
Gromada /*Community* (PL 51): Wawrzyszczyk
Grosse König, Der /*The great king* (GE 42): Sierck
Grouches and Smiles (US 16): Lee F.
Grouchy (US 16): Johnson R.
Growing Pains (US 28): 'Our Gang'
'Gruby' /*Fatty* (PL 73, TVS): Dudek
Guardia, guardiascelta, brigadiere e maresciallo /*Guard, senior guard, brigadier and marshal* (IT 56): Nevola
Guépard, Le (62 IT/FR) — *see* Gattopardo
Guer jiu zu ji /*An orphan saves his grandfather* (CN 22): Zheng
Guerra de Papa, La /*Daddy's war* (ES 77): Garcia
Guerra e il sogno di Momo, La /*The war and Momo's dream* (IT 16): Petrungaro
Guerra italo-libica tra scugnizzi napoletani, La /*The war between Italy and Libya as fought by Neapolitan urchins* (IT 12): Notari
Guerre des boutons, La (36 FR) — *see* Guerre des gosses
Guerre des boutons, La /*War of the buttons* (FR 62): Treton, Lartigue, Isella
Guerre des boutons, La /*War of the buttons* (GB/FR 93): Fitzgerald G., Coffey J., Cunningham
Guerre des gosses, La /*War of the kids* (FR 36): Grave, Farguette, Mouloudji, Buquet, Tavoli
Guess Who's Been Sleeping in My Bed (US 73): Lookinland T.
Guglielmo Tell /*William Tell* (IT 48): Olivieri
Guilty or Not Guilty (US 14): Benham, Hauck
Guinea Pig, The (GB 48): Wager
Guldhørnene /*Golden horns* (DK 14): Heimann
Gülibik (TR/DE 83): Güler, Yeşilyurt
Gummi-Tarzan /*Rubber Tarzan* (DK 81): Svanbjerg
'Gumps' series (US 23-27): Morgan, Butts
Günahkâr baba /*Guilty father* (TR 55): Ersöz
Gun Crazy (US 49): Tamblyn
Gun Duel in Durango (US 57): Clark B.2
Gunfight at the OK Corral (US 56): Herbert
Gun Fighter, The (US 16): Stone
Gunfighter, The (US 50): Norman
Gun Gospel (US 27): Madden
Gun Law (US 29): Darro
Gun Lords of Stirrup Basin (US 37): Nelson B.
Gunman in the Streets (50 FR/US) — *see* Traqué
Gun Point (US 55): Rettig
Gunsmoke Ranch (US 37): McKim S.
Gun Smugglers (US 48): Gray G.
Guns of Diablo (US 64): Russell K.
Guns of Fort Petticoat, The (US 56): Charney
Gunsundari (IN 34): Apte
Gus Edwards' International Colortone Revue (US 29): Scott D.
Guten Abend, Gute Nacht /*Good evening, good night* (GE 36): Kieling
Gute Reise, Herr Meyer /*Bon voyage, Herr Meyer* (GE 38): Kieling
Guttaperchevi malchik /*The rubber boy* (SU 57): Popoff
Guximtarët /*The brave one* (AL 70): Sento
Guy, a Gal and a Pal, A (US 45): Donaldson T.
Guy Could Change, A (US 45): Blake
Guy Fawkes (GB 23): Dear
Guy Named Joe, A (US 43): Severn Chr. and E.
Guy Who Came Back, The (US 51): Gray B.

Gyanu, A /Suspicion (HU 17): Szécsi
Gyermekbetegségek /Childhood ailments (HU 65): Géczy
Gyermekszív /A child's heart (HU 20): Szécsi, Lázár
Gypsy Colt (US 53): Hyatt
Gypsy Trail, The (US 18): Stone

Haar jeet /Defeat and victory (IN 72): Alankar
Haathi mere saathi /Elephants, my companions (IN 71): Mehmood
Habanera, La (GE 37): Schulz-Dornburg
Hab' Sonne im Herzen /Sunshine in my heart (DE 53): Condrus
Hadakakko /The naked child (JP 61): Ito T.
Hadduta misriya /Egyptian story (EG 82): Nadir
Hævnen er sød /Revenge is sweet (DK 11): Voigt, Crone
Haflinger Sepp, Der (53 DE) – see Junges Herz voll Liebe
Haha no shori /Mother's victory (JP 37): Hayama, Yokoyama
Haho, a tenger! /Sea ahoy! (HU 72): Kovács
Haho, Öcsi! /Hi, Öcsi! (HU 71): Kovács, Laluja
Hail the Conquering Hero (US 43): Rodin M.
Hair Trigger Baxter (US 26): Nelson B.
Hakoiri musume /An innocent maid (JP 35): 'Tokkan-Kozo'
Hakumat (PK 88): Jamshid
Half-a-Dollar Bill (US 24): Darro
Half a Sinner (US 34): Rooney
Half a Sinner (US 40): Bupp S.
Half a Sixpence (GB/US 67): Moulder-Brown
Halfaouine, l'enfant des terrasses /Halfawin, child of the terraces (TN/FR 90): Boughedir
Half Shot at Sunrise (US 41): Larson
Half-Way to Heaven (US 29): Aber
Half-Way to Hollywood (US 38): Billings G.
Ha llegado un angel /An angel has arrived (ES 61): Quezadas
Hallelujah! (US 29): Beard
'Hallroom Boys' comedies (US 21): Condon
Hal Roach Comedy Carnival (47 US) – see Curley
Halunkengeiger, Der /The crooked fiddler (GE 22): Herzberg
Ha maaza marg ekla (IN c.60): Sachin
'Ham and Bud' series (US 14-16): Barry W., Griffith
Hamari beti /Our daughter (IN 50): Kumar
Hamari manzil /Our goal (IN 49): Kumar
Hammerhead (GB 68): Younger
Hanagata senshu /Star athlete (JP 37): 'Tokkan-Kozo'
Hanamuko no negoto /The bridegroom talks in his sleep (JP 35): 'Tokkan-Kozo'
Hände aus dem Dunkel /Hands from the darkness (GE 33): Richter
Hand in Hand (GB 60): Needs, Gilmore, Pike P.
Handle With Care (US 32): Ernest, Phelps
Hand of Death (US 61): Patrick
Hand of God, The (US 15): Connelly
Hands of a Stranger (US 60): Gordon Ba.
Hands of Cormac Joyce, The (GB 72): Guard
Hands of Hope (US 24): Quinn B.
Hands Up! (US 26): Billings G.
Hanging by a Thread (US 78): Sharrett
Hangman, The (43 US) – see Hitler's Madman
Hangmen Also Die (US 43): Roy
Hanna Amon (DE 51): Bürger
Hanna i societen /Hannah in society (SE 40): Hjelm

Hans Christian Andersen (US 52): Walsh
Hansel and Gretel (US 82): Schroder
Hänsel und Gretel /Hansel and Gretel (DE 54): Condrus
Hantise, La /Obsession (FR 12): Mathieu
Hao gege /Good brother (CN 25): Zheng
Happiest Days of Your Life, The (GB 50): Simons W.
Happy (GB 34): Rietti
Happy Anniversary (US 59): Coughlin
Happy-End am Attersee (64 AT) – see....
Happy-End am Wörthersee /Happy end by the Wörthersee (AT 64): Koester
Happy Jack, a Hero (US 10): Pickford
Happy Land (US 43): Hunter, Nokes, Olsen L.J., West J.
Happy Road, The (US 56): Clark B.2, Urbain, Moullières, Maurin Y.-M.
Happy Time, The (US 52): Driscoll
Happy Warrior, The (US 25): Gordon Bo., Holmes L.
Happy Years, The (US 50): Stockwell, Gift, Mickelsen, Mummert
Hard Boiled (US 26): O'Donnell
Hard-Boiled Canary, The (US 41): Haitto
Hard Man, The (US 57): Sorensen
Hard Road (GB 89): Rennie
Hard Way, The (US 42): Nokes
Hare Rama hare Krishna (IN 71): Mehmood, Satyajit
Här har du ditt liv /This is your life (SE 66): Axberg R.
Hari Laxmi (IN 53): Babua
Harishchandra Taramati (IN 70): Mehmood
Här kommer Pippi Långstrump /Here comes Pippi Longstocking (SE 72): Sundberg
Harlem (IT 43): Glori
Harlequin (AU 80): Spain
Harmony Row (AU 33): Kerr
Harness, The (US 71): Montgomery
Harness Fever (AU 75): Bettles
Három árva, A /The three orphans (HU 23): Szécsi
Három hét /Three weeks (HU 17): Szécsi
Harp in Hock, A (US 27): Coghlan, Jewell, Jones B.
Harrigan's Kid (US 43): Croft
Harry Black (GB 58): Stephens M.
Harukanaru yama no yobigoe /A distant cry from Spring (JP 80): Yoshioka
Haškovy povidky /Stories by Hašek (CS 52): Bejval
Hasty Marriage, The (US 31): Billings G.
Hat, Coat and Glove (US 34): Durand
Hatschipuh (DE 87): Steinbeck
Hatsukoi mondou /First love questionnaire (JP 50): 'Tokkan-Kozo'
Haunted House, The (US 40): Swan
Haunted Ship, The (US 27): Madden
Haunted Spooks (US 22): Morrison E.
Haus der Krokodile, Das (DE 75, srl): Ohrner
Haustyrann, Der /The domestic tyrant (DE 59): Schwartz S.
Haus voll Liebe, Ein /A house full of love (AT/DE 54): Friedl
Haut les mains /Hands up! (FR 12): Mary
Havenmusiek /Music of the port (BE 37): Bruyninckx, Buyl
Having Wonderful Time (US 38): Bailey Sd.
Hawaii Calls (US 38): Breen
Hawk, The (US 35): Jones D.

Häxnatten /Night of the witch (SE 37): Bernhard
Hazal (TR 80): Yeşilyurt
Hazel Kirke (US 12): Tansey R.
Headin' for Trouble (US 31): Shuford
Headless Horseman, The (US 22): Devine
Headline Hunters, The (GB 68): Brockwell, Garlick
Headline News (US 38): Russell J.
Headlines (US 25): O'Donnell
Headmaster, The (GB 21): Craig
Head of the Family, The (US 28): Bennett M.
Heads We Go (GB 33): Rietti
Healer, The (US 35): Rooney
Healers, The (US 74): Kerwin
Hear My Song (GB 91): Conroy
Heart Breaker, The (US 25): Madden
Heart Burn (US 42): Hickman Dl.
Heart Line, The (US 21): Alexander B.
Heart of a Child, The (US 13): Benham
Heart of a Child (39 MX) – see Corazon de niño
Heart of a Child (GB 58): Williams R.
Heart of a Fool (US 16): Moore P.
Heart of a Hero, The (US 16): Jackson C.
Heart of Maggie Malone, The (US 14): Clark R.
Heart of Nora Flynn, The (US 16): Jacobs
Heart of Rachel, The (US 18): Alexander B.
Heart of the Country (GB 87): Bale
Heart of the Rockies (US 37): McKim S.
Heart of Youth, The (US 19): Sargent, Coffey C.
Heart o' the Hills (US 10): Goodwin
Hearts Aflame (US 23): Headrick
Hearts and Flowers (US 15): Carpenter
Hearts and Hoofs (US 28): Darro
Hearts and Spangles (US 26): Darro
Hearts Are Thumps (US 37): 'Our Gang', Winkler
Hearts Divided (US 37): Hurlic
Heartsease (US 13): Casey, Kelly P.
Heart's Haven (US 22): Lee F.
Hearts in Dixie (US 29): Beard, Jackson E.
Hearts of Humanity (US 32): Searl
Hearts of Men (US 18): Beban
Hearts of the World (US/GB 18): Alexander B., Marion F.
Heart Within, The (GB 57): Hemmings
Heaven Can Wait (US 43): Beckett, Gray G., Larson
Heavenly Days (US 44): Infuhr
Heaven On Earth (US 27): Janney
Heaven Only Knows (US 47): Chapin M., Gray G., Hunter, Miles P. (Perreau)
Heavens Above! (GB 63): Brockwell
Hedgehog Friendship (61 DD/CS) – see Igelfreundschaft
Heebee Jeebees (US 27): 'Our Gang'
Heideschulmeister Uwe Karsten /Village teacher Uwe Karsten (GE 33): Lohmeyer
Heidi (US 37): Watson D.
Heidi (CH 52): Klameth
Heidi (AT 65): Koester
Heidi (US/DE 68): Moulder-Brown
'Heidi' (AT c.79, srl): Arpagäus

Heidi und Peter (CH 54): Klameth
Heilige Hass, Der /Holy hate (GE 21): Allen W.
Heimat /Homeland (GE 38): Eugens
Heimaterde /Native earth (GE 41): Rohringer
Heimatland /Home country (GE 39): Schmidhofer
Heimkehr ins Glück /Happy homecoming (GE 33): Klicks
Heimweh /Homesickness (GE 37): Kieling
Heintje - ein Herz geht auf Reisen /Heintje: a travelling heart (DE 69): 'Heintje'
Heintje, mein bester Freund /My best friend, Heintje (DE 69): 'Heintje'
Heinz hustet /Harry's cough (GE 37): Bosse
Heixin fu /Evil-hearted (CN 34): Ge
Helen and Warren (US 26, srl): McBan
Helen Intervenes (US 15): Benham
Helga und Michael (DE 68): Ohrner
Heliga lögnen, Den /The holy lie (SE 44): Lindgren H.
Helldorado (US 34): Hurlic
Hellfire Club, The (GB 60): Stephens M.
Hello, Everybody! (US 33): Tucker J.
Hell's Five Hours (US 58): Ferrell
Hellship Bronson (US 28): Watson D. and H.
Hell to Eternity (US 60): Eyer Ri.
He Loved Her So (14 US) – see Twenty Minutes of Love
Helping Grandma (US 31): 'Our Gang'
Helping Hand, The (US 08): Harron
Helping Hands (US 41): 'Our Gang', Tyler L.
Helter Skelter (US 29): Sabiston
Hemmelighedsfulde X, Det /The mysterious X (DK 13): Reinwald
He nacido en Buenos Aires /Born in Buenos Aires (AR 58): Orlegui
Hen in the wind (48 JP) – see Kaze no naka no mendori
Henry Aldrich, Boy Scout (US 44): Hickman Dl., Holt D., McKim H.
Henry and Dizzy (US 42): Switzer
Henry V (GB 89): Bale
Henry VIII (GB 11): Willmore
Henry VIII and His Six Wives (GB 72): Henderson S.
Henry, the Rainmaker (US 49): Gray G., Nokes
He Ran All the Way (US 51): Hyatt
Her Bad Quarter of an Hour (US 16): Connelly
Her Benny (GB 20): Wood S.
Her Big Brother (US 14): Hauck
Hercules, Samson and Ulysses (64 IT) – see Ercole sfida Sansone
Here Comes Mr Jordan (US 41): Dawson, Larson, Madore
Here Comes the Band (US 35): McFarland
Here Comes the Groom (US 51): Gencel, Hawkins
Here Comes the Sun (GB 45): Artemus
Here Come the Nelsons (US 51): Nelson R.
Here's Boomer (US 79): Drier
Here We Come Gathering (GB 45): McKeag
Her Father Said No (US 27): Darro
Her Filmland Hero (US 15): Griffith, Jacobs
Her First Beau (US 41): Larson
Her First Romance (US 40): Daniel
Her First Romance (US 51): Martin A., Hunt
Her Fling (US 18): Lee F.
Her Greatest Story (US 16): Lee F.
Her Husband's Affairs (US 47): Bates, Infuhr
Her Husband's Faith (US 16): Lee F.

Her Husband's Honor (US 16): Lee F.
Her Husband's Secret (US 25): Darro
Heritage, The (US 18): Hamrick
Heritage (US 20): Roubert
Héritiers de l'oncle James, Les /Uncle James's heirs (FR 23): Machin
Her Kingdom of Dreams (US 19): Barry W.
Her Mad Bargain (US 21): Butterworth E.
Herman (NO 90): Lie
Hermannchen, Das /Little Hermann (GE 36): Blusch
Her Man o' War (US 26): Coghlan
Her Marriage Vow (US 24): Wilkinson
Her Mistake (US 18): Thaw
Her New Yob (US 15): Roubert
Her Night of Nights (US 22): Daniels M.
Hero, The (US 22): Lee F.
Hero, The (69 GB) – see Bloomfield
Heroes for Sale (US 33): Cosbey
Heroes of Telemark, The (GB 65): Brockwell, Moulder-Brown, Pike P.
Heroes of the Saddle (US 40): Kaye
Heroes of the Street (US 22): Barry W., Butterworth J.
Hero for a Day (US 39): Bupp T., Holt D., Phelps
Hero's Island (US 61): Mason
Héros sans retour (62 IT/DE/ES/BE) – see Marcia o crepa
Herre med portfolj /Gentleman with portfolio (SE 43): Nyström
Herren der Meere /Lords of the sea (AT 22): Lubinsky
Herr husassistenten /Mr Housemaid (SE 39): Bernhard
Her Right to Live (US 17): Connelly
Herrin und ihr Knecht, Die /The lady and her squire (GE 29): Stark-Gstettenbaur
Her Salvation (US 17): Clark R.
Her Sister's Secret (US 47): Severn Wn.
Her Son (GB 20): Hopson
Hers to Hold (US 43): Infuhr
Her Twelve Men (US 53): Considine, Hartleben D., Olsen L.J., Stollery, Thompson R.
Herz bleibt allein, Ein /A heart on its own (DE 55): Condrus
Herzen ohne Ziel (28 ES) – see Corazones sin rumbo
Herz geht auf Reisen, Ein (69 DE) – see Heintje – ein Herz geht auf Reisen
Herz geht vor Anker /Heart at anchor (GE 40): Kieling
Herz schlägt für Dich, Ein /A heart beats for you (GE 45): Meier
He Swore Off Smoking (US 13): Boss
Hets /Frenzy (SE 44): Nyström
Heure du destin, L' /The hour of destiny (FR 28): Gaillard
Heute blau und morgen blau /Blue today, blue tomorrow (DE 57): Kaiser
Hewitt's Just Different (US 79): Drier
Hey Boy! Hey Girl! (US 59): Charney
Hey! Hey! U.S.A.! (GB 38): Bupp T., McDowall
Hi, Buddy! (US 43): Cook T., Watson Bs.
Hickey and Boggs (US 72): Spell W.
Hidden Power (US 39): Moore D.
Hidden Truth, The (US 19): Grauer
Hidden Woman, The (US 22): Thaw
Hide and Shriek (US 38): 'Our Gang'
Hideaway (US 37): Bond T.
Hideaways, The (73 US) – see From the Mixed-Up Files of Mrs Basil E. Frankweiler

Hide-Out (US 34): Rooney
Hiding Place, The (77 DD) – see Ich zwing dich zu leben
Hier irrt Schiller /Schiller is wrong (GE 36): Kieling
Hige no chikara /Moustache power (JP 31): 'Tokkan-Kozo'
High and Low (63 JP) – see Tengoku to jigoku
High Barbaree (US 47): Jarman, Hunt
Highbinders, The (US 26): Alexander B.
High Conquest (US 47): Kimbley, Kuhn
Higher Mercy, The (US 12): Casey
High Gear (33 US) – see Return of Casey Jones
High Jinx, A (US 25): McBan
Highly Dangerous (GB 50): Secretan
High Midnight (US 79): Hathaway
High Noon (US 52): Aaker L.
High Society (US 24): 'Our Gang'
High Speed (US 32): Rooney
High Time (US 60): Adiarte
High Treason (GB 29): Singer
High Wall (US 47): Hyatt
High, Wide and Handsome (US 37): Bupp T.
Hijack! (GB 75): Forlong
Hija de la otra, La /Someone's daughter (MX 51): Jiménez Pons J.
Hijo de la calle /Son of the street (AR 49): Poggio
Hijo de nadie, El /Nobody's son (MX 46): Roche
Hijos de la oscuridad /Sons of darkness (MX 51): Jiménez Pons J.
Hijos que yo soñe, Los /The sons I dream of (MX 64): Bravo J.
Hilde Petersen postlagernd /Hilda Petersen, poste restante (GE 35): Brackmann, Teetzmann
Hilfe, die Verwandten kommen /Help! Here comes the family (DE 71): Ohrner
Hilfe, ich bin unsichtbar /Help! I'm invisible (DE 51): Lödel
Hills of Kentucky (US 27): Schaeffer
Hills of Peril (US 27): Black B.
Himalaya se ooncha /Higher than the Himalayas (IN 75): Rajoo
Himlaspelet /Mystery play (SE 42): Nyström
Hindustan ki kasam /Soldier's oath (IN 73): Rajoo
Hi'-Neighbor! (US 34): 'Our Gang', Bupp T.
Hipolito el de Santa (MX 50): Jiménez Pons J.
Hirtenlied vom Kaiserthal, Das /Shepherd's song from the Kaiserthal (AT 56): Ande
His Brother's Keeper (GB 39): McDowall
His Dearest Possession (GB 19): Barker E.
His Divorced Wife (US 19): Moore P.
His First Commission (US 09): Boss
His First Experience (US 13): Johnson R.
His First Sweetheart (GB 14): Collet
His Hour (US 24): Noisom
His Lying Heart (US 16): Jacobs
His Mother's Hope (US 12): Porter W.
His Mother's People (US 21): Lee F.
His Night Out (US 35): Burrud
His Own Law (US 23): Barry W.
His People (US 25): Gordon Bo.
His Private Secretary (US 33): Rentschler
His Reward (US 14): Benham
His Secretary (US 25): Billings E.
His Sister (US 13): Clark R.

Mads Ole Erhardsen

Henryk Fogiel

Jeffrey Frank

Darby Hinton

Tom Gaman

Allan Hubbard

Scott Jacoby

Albin Johnson

461

His Sister's Kids (US 13): Griffith, Jacobs
Histoire de cirque, Une (27 FR) — *see* Croquette
Historia de un gran amor /*Story of a great love* (MX 42): Busquets
Historia żółtek cizemki /*Story of a yellow slipper* (PL 61): Kondrat
Historien om en Gut /*A boy's story* (NO 19): Lykke-Seest
Hitler Gang, The (US 44): Tyler L.
Hitlerjunge Quex /*Hitler Youth Quex* (GE 33): Ohlsen, Richter, Wenkhaus
Hitler's Children (US 43): Lindgren O., McKim H.
Hitler's Madman (US 43): Nichols
Hitori musuko /*The only son* (JP 36): 'Tokkan-Kozo', Hayama
Hit the Road (US 41): Watson Bs.
Hit the Saddle (US 37): McKim S.
Hitting the High Spots (US 18): Griffith
Hittin' the Trail (US 37): Bupp T.
Hi-Yo Silver! (US 40): Jones D., McKim S.
Hjältar i gult och blått /*Heroes in yellow and blue* (SE 40): Olsson
Hjulskøjterne (08 DK) — *see* Rulleskøjterne
H'mida (EG/TU 66): Aouini, Lefebvre F.
H.M.S. Defiant (GB 62): Robinson D.
H.M.S. Pinafore (17 US) — *see* Pinafore
Hoà-Bình /*Peace* (FR 70): Phi Lân
Hochstaplerin, Die /*The crooked lady* (GE 43): Rohringer
Hogan's Alley (US 12): Boss, Tannura
Hogan's Alley (US 25): Holmes L., Noisom
Hog Wild (US 72): Beauvy, O'Brien C.
Hogy állunk fiatelember? /*Well, young man?* (HU 63): Kosztolányi
Hold Back the Dawn (US 41): Lee B.
Hold-up en musique /*Musical hold-up* (FR 52): Poujouly
Hole in the Head, A (US 59): Hodges E.
Holiday Affair (US 49): Gebert
Holiday in Britain (74 HU) — *see* Jutalomutazás
Hollandmädel /*Dutch girl* (DE 53): Jansen
Hollands jeugd /*Dutch youth* (NL 34): Klein H.
Holloway's Treasure (GB 24): Brantford
Hollywood (US 23): Fox J., Reisner
Hollywood Hotel (US 37): Bupp S.
Hollywood Round-Up (US 37): Daniel, Jones D.
Holnap kezdődik az élet /*Life begins tomorrow* (HU 24): Lázár
Holocaust (US 78): Levy
Holt vidék /*Dead landscape* (HU 71): Elisztratov
Hol volt, hol nem volt /*It was and it wasn't* (HU 87): Vermes
Holy Terror, The (US 29): 'Our Gang'
Holy Terror, The (63 FR) — *see* Bébert et l'omnibus
Hombre (US 67): Lazer
Hombre de la isla, El /*The man on the island* (ES 59): Gil
Hombre o demonio /*Man or demon* (MX 40): Busquets
Hombres do mar /*Men of the sea* (MX 38): Busquets
Home Alone (US 90): Culkin M.
Home Alone 2: Lost in New York (US 92): Culkin M. and K.
Home Fires Burning (US 88): Harris N. P.
Home for the Holidays (13 GB) — *see* Three Little Vagabonds
Home in Oklahoma (US 46): Rees
Home Maker, The (US 25): Murphy M., Schaeffer
Home of Our Own, A (US 93): Furlong E.
Home on the Range (US 46): Blake
Home Run for Love (US 79): Scribner

Homesick (US 28): Watson H.
Homesteaders of Paradise Valley (US 47): Blake
Homestretch (US 47): Cook T.
Home Sweet Home (US 24): Headrick
Home Sweet Homicide (US 46): Stockwell
Homeward Bound (US 80): Drier
Home Work (US 35): Watson D.
Homme à la Buick, L' /*The man with the Buick* (FR 67): Maurin J.-F.
Homme aux mains d'argile, L' /*Clay-handed man* (FR 49): Martaguet C.
Homme du jour, L' /*Man of the day* (FR 36): Lynen
Homme est mort, Un /*A man is dead* (FR/IT 72): Haley
Hommes d'airain, Les (41 FR) — *see* Andorra
Hondo (US 53): Aaker L.
Honest Hutch (US 20): Trebaol E., F. and Y.
Honesty - the Best Policy (US 26): Bennett M.
Honeychile (US 51): Mora
Honey, I Shrunk the Kids (US 89): Rushton
Honeymoon in Bali (US 39): Bartlett
Honey Siege, The (GB 87, srl): Davies L.
Hong Kong (US 51): Chang
Honhar /*One who promises* (IN 36): Modak
Honkers, The (US 71): Eccles
Honky Donkey (US 34): 'Our Gang'
Honky Tonk Freeway (US 81): Billingsley
Honkytonk Man (US 82): Eastwood
Honorable Algernon, The (US 13): Butterworth F.
Honor Among Men (US 24): Wilkinson
Honzíkova cesta /*Johnny's journey* (CS 56): Červenka
Hoodlum, The (US 19): Messinger, Condon
Hoodlum Saint, The (US 46): Bates, Hickman Dw.
Hook and Ladder (US 32): 'Our Gang', McComas
Hoopers letzte Jagd /*Hooper's last chase* (DE 71): Halm
Hoosier Romance, A (US 18): Jacobs
Hoosier Schoolmaster, The (US 24): Brown T.
Hoosier Schoolmaster, The (US 35): Bupp T.
Hope and Glory (GB 87): Edwards S.R.
Hop Harrigan (US 46, srl): Henry R.
Hora de la verdad, La /*The moment of truth* (MX 45): Pastor
Hordubalove /*Hordubal's people* (CS 37): Davidik
Horn Blows at Midnight, The (US 45): Blake, Madore
Horouci srdce /*Burning heart* (CS 62): Polak
Horse, The (82 TR) — *see* At
Horse Called Jester, A (GB 79): Medford
Horsemen of the Sierras (US 49): Ivo
Horse's Mouth, The (GB 58): Gilmore
Horse Thief, The (US 13): Jacobs
Horse without a Head, The (GB 63): Winter, Gilmore
Hospital Massacre (US 82): Jacoby Bl.
Hospital Services (GB 46): Weske
Hosszú az út hazáig /*It's a long way home* (HU 60): Sebók
Hosszú vagta (83 US/HU) — *see* Long Ride
Hostage, The (US 66): Martins
Hostinec u kamenneho štolu /*The inn with the stone gallery* (CS 49): Mikulič
Hotel Berlin (US 45): Tyler D.
Hôtel de la Plage /*Beach Hotel* (FR 77): Melet

Hôtel du Libre-Echange / *Free Trade Hotel* (FR 34): Grave

Hotelgeheimnisse / *Hotel secrets* (GE 28): Burns B.

Hotel New Hampshire, The (US 84): Green S.

Hot Lead and Cold Feet (US 78): Sharrett

Hot Luck (US 28): Sabiston

Hot Noon, A (64 BG) – *see* Gorechto pladre

Hot Off the Press (US 35): Rentschler

Hot Shots (US 56): Phillips P.

Hot Water (US 24): McBan

Hot Water (US 38): Ernest, Mahan

Hound Dog Man (US 59): Holmes D.

Hound of Silver Creek, The (US 27): Jones B.

Hour Before the Dawn, The (US 44): Severn E.

Hour of the Wolf (68 SE) – *see* Vargtimmen

House at 12 Rose Street (US 80): Drier, Petersen Chr.

Houseboat (US 58): Herbert, Peterson P.

House Divided, A (US 18): Blackton

House I Live In, The (US 45): Infuhr, Rodin M.

Housemaster (GB 38): Hepworth H.

House of Fear, The (US 15): Boss, Carr J. and S.

House of Our Own, A (US 75): San Juan

House on Telegraph Hill, The (US 51): Gebert

House Party, The (US 15): Hackett A.

House That Jack Built, The (US 11): Pickford

House That Screamed, The (69 ES) – *see* Residencia, La

House II: the Second Story (US 87): Arnott

Housewife (US 34): Cosbey

House with the Golden Windows, The (US 16): Jacobs

Houston, We've Got a Problem (US 74): Shea E.

How a Horseshoe Upset a Happy Family (US 13): Boss

Howards of Virginia, The (US 40): Binyon, Jones D., Larson,
      Lyon, Phelps

How Billy Kept His Word (GB 14): Desmond

How Bobby Called Her Bluff (US 14): Boss

How Bobby Joined the Circus (US 12): Boss

How Cissy Made Good (US 15): Connelly

How Could You Jean? (US 18): Barry W., Hamrick

How Green Was My Valley (US 41): McDowall

How Millie Became an Actress (US 12): Kelly P.

How's Business (GB 91): Brazier

How the Boys Fought the Indians (US 12): Boss, Clark A.

How the West Was Won (US 62): Charney, Russell B.

How the West Was Won (US 77): Lookinland T., Petersen P.

How to Handle Women (US 28): Billings E.

How Tommy Saved His Father (US 12): Casey

Hrabĕnka z Podskali / *The Countess of Podskal* (CS 25): Branald

Hsiao taofan / *Teenage fugitive* (TW 84): Wang C.

Huang tudi / *Yellow earth* (CN 84): Liu

Hubertusjagd / *St Hubert's hunt* (DE 59): Hehn

Huckleberry Finn (US 19): Sargent, Griffith

Huckleberry Finn (US 31): Durkin, Coogan J., Searl

Huckleberry Finn (60 US) – *see* Adventures of Huckleberry Finn

Huckleberry Finn (US 74): East

Huckleberry Finn (US 74): Howard R. and C.

Huckleberry Finn (74 SU) – *see* Sovsem propashchi

Huckleberry Finn and His Friends (US 79): Snyders, Tracey

Hue and Cry (GB 46): Barr

Hugo och Josefin / *Hugo and Josephine* (SE 67): Becklén

Hukum ka ekka / *Ace of spades* (IN 39): Marathe A.

Hullabaloo (US 40): Nunn

Human Comedy, The (US 43): Binyon, Hickman Dl., Holt D.,
      Jenkins J., Kaye, Samarzich

Humanité (25 FR) – *see* Coeur des gueux

Human Jungle, The (GB 66): Lester

Human Side, The (US 34): Ernest, Moore D.

Human Sparrows (26 US) – *see* Sparrows

Humlog / *We people* (IN 51): Kumar

Humoreska / *Humoresque* (CS 39): Salač

Humoresque (US 20): Connelly, Berlinger

Humoresque (US 46): Blake, Cook T.

Hum panchhi ek dai ke / *We birds of one branch* (IN 56):
      Kapoor Ro.

Hum sub chor hain / *The criminals* (IN 73): Satyajit

Hunchback, The (GB 14): Desmond

Hund, der Herr Bozzi hiess, Der (57 ES/IT) – *see* Angel paso por
      Brooklyn

Hundra dragspel och en flicka / *100 accordions and a girl* (SE 46):
      Nyström

Hungama / *Chaos* (IN 71): Mehmood

Hungarian Fairy Tale, A (87 HU) – *see* Hol volt, hol nem volt

Hungry Arms (US 26): Holmes L.

Hungry Hill (GB 47): Wager

Hunted (GB 52): Whiteley

Hunted in Holland (GB 61): Scully

Hunted Men (32 CS/AT/GE) – *see* Štvaní lidé

Hunted Men (US 38): Bupp T. and S., McKim S., Watson D.

Hunters of the Reef (US 78): Drier

Hur Marie träffade Fredrik, âsnan Rebus, kangarun Ploj och... / *How
      Mary met Frederick, Rebus the donkey, Ploughman the kangaroo, and....*
      (SE 69): Becklén

Hurra, die Schule brennt / *Hurrah, the school's on fire* (DE 69):
      'Heintje'

Hurra, unsere Eltern sind nicht da / *Hurrah, our parents aren't there*
      (DE 70): Ohrner

Hurricane at Pilgrim Hill (US 53): Gray B.

Husarenfieber / *Hussar fever* (GE 25): Pottier

Husarenliebe / *Hussar love* (GE 32): Rive

Husband's Holiday (US 31): Moore D.

Hushed Hour, The (US 19): Alexander B.

Hush Money (US 21): Devine

Hush Money (US 31): Cosbey

Huyendo del halcon / *Flight from the hawk* (ES 66): Sanchez

Hvad skal jeg være? / *What shall I be?* (DK 55): Holmberg

Hvide hingst, Den / *The white stallion* (DK 61): Wilner

Hvor bjergene sejler / *Where mountains float* (DK 55): Henning-Jensen

I Aim at the Stars (US/DE 60): Crawford J.

I Am (SU 89): Caikauskas

I Am a Criminal (US 38): Spellman

I Am an American (US 44): Gray G.

I Am Guilty (US 21): Moore M.

I Am Suzanne (US 34): Beckett

I Believe in You (GB 51): Hannaford

Ibis Bleu, L' / *The Blue Ibis* (FR 18): Giai

Icebound (US 24): Depew

Ice Flood, The (US 26): Schaeffer

Ice Follies of 1939 (US 39): Switzer

Ich - bin - Du /I am you (GE 20): Pottier

Ich hab' mein Herz in Heidelberg verloren /I lost my heart in Heidelberg (DE 52): Lödel

Ich hatt' einen Kameraden /Once I had a comrade (GE 24): Eysoldt

Ich heisse Niki /My name is Nicky (DE 52): Grimm

Ich kann auch 'ne Arche bauen /I can build an ark too (DE 73): Enkelmann

Ich liess mein Herz am Wörthersee (59 DE) — see Sommer, den man nie vergisst

Ich weiss, wofür ich lebe /I know what I'm living for (DE 56): Ande

Ich zwing dich zu leben /I'll force you to live (DD 77): Welz

Iconoclast, The (US 10): Pickford

I Could Go On Singing (GB 63): Phillips G.

Idade maior, A /Coming of age (PT 90): Colares

Idaho Red (US 29): Darro

Ideale Frau gesucht /Wanted: the ideal woman (AT 52): Friedl

Idée de génie, Une /A brilliant idea (FR 31): Mercanton

Idée fumante, Une /A smoking idea (FR, c.33): Tarride

Identity Unknown (US 45): Driscoll

I Did It, Mama (US 09): Boss

Idler, The (US 14): Connelly

Idle Tongues (US 24): Black B.

I Do (US 21): Morgan

Idol Dancer, The (US 20): Carr T., Grauer

Idol of the Crowds (US 37): Burrud

I Dood It (US 43): Tyler L., Winkler

I Dream Too Much (US 35): Beckett

I Escaped from the Gestapo (US 43): McFarland

If.... (GB 68): Webster, Bury, Newport

If Ever I See You Again (US 78): Billingsley

Iffet /Honour (TR 69): Utku

If I Had a Million (US 32): Cosbey

If I'm Lost, How Come I Found You? (US 78): Drier

If I Were Boss (GB 37): Singer

If I Were King (US 38): Hickman Dl.

Ifjú szívvel /Young at heart (HU 53): Horváth

If My Country Should Call (US 16): Griffith

If Only the Rain (81 DE) — see Regentropfen

I Found a Dog (US 49): Gray G.

If Winter Comes (US 47): Severn Wn.

If You Knew Susie (US 48): Driscoll

Igazi égszinkék, Az /The true azure (HU 57): Gomba

Igelfreundschaft, Die /Hedgehog friendship (DD/CS 61): Manke

I Give My Love (US 34): Alexander T.

I guld och blått /Yellow and blue (SE 42): Hjelm

Ihre Hoheit befiehlt /Her Highness commands (GE 31): Rive

Ihr 106. Geburtstag /Her 106th birthday (DE 58): Kaiser

Ihr Junge (30 GE/CS/AT) — see Když struny lkají

Ihr Korporal /Her corporal (AT/DE 56): Kratz

Ijdijk (NL 63): Bakker

Ikarus /Icarus (DD 76): Welz

Ikh ulitsa /Their street (SU 30): Chernishoff

Il a été perdu une mariée /Wife goes missing (FR 32): Bara

Ile au trésor, L' /Treasure Island (FR/US 86-89): Poupaud

Ile des veuves, L' /Widows' Island (FR 36): Farguette

Ile enchantée, L' /The magic island (FR 26): Guichard

Ile sans nom, L' /The nameless island (FR 22): Rauzéna

Il est charmant /He's charming (FR 31): Mercanton

Il était une fois /Once upon a time (FR 33): Bara

Il était une fois un flic /Once there was a cop (FR 72): Hillien

I Like It That Way (US 34): Rooney

I Live My Life (US 35): Cosbey

I'll Be Seeing You (US 44): Gray G.

I'll Cry Tomorrow (US 55): Kasday

I'll Fix It (US 34): Butler

I'll Get You For This (GB 50): Staiola

I'll See You in My Dreams (US 51): Olsen C.

I'll Take Vanilla (US 34): Bond T.

I Love You Again (US 40): Blake, McKim H., Switzer

I Love You, Rosa (71 IL) — see Ani ohev otach Rosa

Imagi ningtham /Precious son (IN 81): Singh

Imam dvije mame i dva tate /I've got two mums and two dads (YU 68): Galo

I-Man (US 86): Cramer

I Married a Witch (US 42): Bates

Imbarco a mezzanotte /Midnight departure (IT/US 52): Manunta

Ime mia distikhismeni /I'm an unhappy woman (GR 64): Kailas

I'm from Missouri (US 39): Cook B.

I'm Jumping Over Puddles Again (70 CS) — see Už zase skáču přes kaluže

Immer nur du /Nothing but you (GE 41): Möller

Immigrants, The (US 78): Sinutko

I mörkaste Småland /In darkest Småland (SE 43): Hjelm

Impasse des Vertus, L' /Cul-de-sac of the Virtues (FR 55): Chapeland

Impossible Mrs Bellew, The (US 22): Moore P. and M., Wilkinson

Imprudencia /Imprudence (MX 44): Roche

Im Schützengraben /In the trench (GE 14): Reinwald

In a Garden (US 12): Benham

In a Lonely Place (US 50): Gray B.

Ina, Peter und die Rasselbande /Ina, Peter and the Rattlers (DE 55): Hack

I natt eller aldrig /Tonight or never (SE 41): Dalunde

Incendiary Blonde (US 45): Nokes

Incident in a Small Town (US 94): Stahl

Incident in San Francisco (US 71): Pera

In Cold Blood (US 67): Eccles

Incompreso /Misunderstood (IT 66): Colagrande

Inconnue no.13, L' /Unknown woman No. 13 (FR 48): Fourcade

Indiana Jones and the Temple of Doom (US 84): Quan

Indianapolis Speedway (US 39): Bupp T.

Indian Trapper's Vindication, The (US 15): Willis

Indiscreet (US 31): Phelps

Indiscretion of an American Wife (52 IT/US) — see Stazione Termini

Indrasan (IN 52): Kumar

In Enemy Country (US 67): Michenaud

Infamous Miss Revell, The (US 21): Carpenter

Infantile Disorders (GB 87): May

Infermiere di Tata, L' /Daddy's male-nurse (IT 15): Roveri

Ingenuity (US 12): Casey

Ingiusta condanna, L' /The wronged woman (IT 52): Staiola

Ingratitude of Liz Taylor, The (US 15): Clark R.

Inkaar / *The refusal* (IN 77): Rajoo
In Love with Life (US 34): Moore D.
Inmaculada / *Spotless* (MX 50): Perez
Inner Sanctum (US 48): Belding
Innocent, The (GB 84): Hawley
Innocent Moves (93 US) – see Searching for Bobby Fischer
Innocents, The (GB 61): Stephens M.
Innocent Sinners (GB 58): Hammond
Innocents of Paris (US 29): Durand
Innocent Theft, An (US 12): Casey
In Old Chicago (US 37): Reynolds, Watson Bl., Bs. and D.
In Old Madrid (US 11): Pickford
In Old Monterey (US 39): Lee B.
In Old Sacramento (US 46): Blake
In Peril's Path (US 14): Benham
Inqilab / *Revolution* (IN 35): Kapoor Ra.
I.N.R.I. (GE 23): Odemar
In Search of Eden (79 US) – see Gauguin the Savage
In Search of the Castaways (GB 62): Hamshere
Inside Job (US 46): Moss J.
Inside Straight (US 51): Hartleben D.
In Slumberland (US 17): Stone
In Spite of Danger (US 35): Ward
Insula Comorulor / *Cormorant Island* (RO/FR 75): Sofron
Insulting the Sultan (US 20): Morrison E.
Intègre, L' / *The upright man* (FR 14): Poyen
Intermezzo (US 39): Scott D.
Internal Affairs (US 90): Wood E.
International Squadron (US 41): Bupp S.
In the Dog House (US 34): Watson D.
In the Gloaming (GB 19): Hopson
In the Meantime, Darling (US 44): Rodin M.
In the Name of the Law (US 22): Alexander B.
In the Navy (US 41): Brown K., Lenhart
In the Shadow (US 13): Carnahan, Casey
In the Sultan's Garden (US 11): Pickford
In Times Like These (56 US) – see These Wilder Years
Intolerance (US 16): Carpenter, House C., Lee Ra.
Into the West (IE 92): Conroy, Fitzgerald C.
Intrigue (US 17): Connelly
Intruder in the Dust (US 49): Jarman
Intruders, The (US 67): Alford
Intruders, The (AU 69): Pankhurst
Intruso, El / *The intruder* (MX 44): Busquets
Invaders from Mars (US 53): Hunt
Invaders from Mars (US 86): Carson H.
Invasion of the Body Snatchers (US 55): Clark B.2
Inventor's Sketch, The (US 13): Boss
Invisible Boy, The (US 57): Eyer Ri.
Invitation to Happiness (US 39): Cook B.
Invitation to Hell (US 84): Oliver B., Presson
Invitation to the Dance (US 54): Kasday
Io mi chiamo Frugolino / *My name is Scamp* (IT 13): Roveri
I Remember Mama (US 48): Ivo
Irene (US 40): Kelly T.
Irgendwo in Berlin / *Somewhere in Berlin* (DD 46): Knetschke
Iris och löjtnantshjärtan / *Iris and the lieutenant's heart* (SE 46): Sarri

Irma in Wonderland (US 16): Hupp
Iroke dango suduki / *Story of a wild passion* (JP 30): 'Tokkan-Kozo'
Iron Curtain, The (US 48): Olsen C.
Iron Horse, The (US 24): Miller W.
Iron Major, The (US 43): Larson, Nokes, Roy
Iron Mask, The (US 29): Parrish
Iron Master, The (US 33): Cosbey, Frederick
Irrtum des Herzens / *Error of the heart* (GE 39): Eugens
Isabella a peur des hommes / *Isabella's afraid of men* (FR 57): Maurin Y.-M.
Isaya khoreve / *Isaya dance* (GR 66): Kailas
I See Ice! (GB 38): McDowall
Ishikawa Goemon no hoji / *Goemon's memorial service* (JP 30): 'Tokkan-Kozo'
Island, The (US 80): Frank
Island Comedy, An (US 11): Boss
Island of Regeneration, The (US 15): Connelly
Island of the Blue Dolphins (US 64): Domasin
Islands in the Stream (US 76): Savage B., Wixted
Isle of Lost Ships, The (US 29): Watson G.
Is Matrimony a Failure? (US 22): DeLacy
Isn't It Romantic? (US 48): Olsen L.J.
Isn't Life Wonderful! (GB 52): Asher
Isola Bella (DE 61): Grimm
I som här inträden.... / *Ye who enter here* (SE 45): Nyström
Is Zat So? (US 27): DeLacy
Is Zat So? (35 US) – see Two-Fisted
It (US 27): Billings E., Shuford
It (US 90): Brandis
I Take This Woman (US 40): Billings G., Bupp S.
Itazura kozo / *Naughty young priest* (JP 35): Ito K.
It Can't Be True (US 16): Griffith, Butterworth E. and F.
It Grows on Trees (US 52): Pollock
It Had to Happen (US 36): Bupp T.
It Happened at Lake Wood Manor (US 76): Drier
It Happened at the World's Fair (US 63): Russell K.
It Happened in Brooklyn (US 46): Kimbley
It Happened in Flatbush (US 42): Beckett
It Happened in Hollywood (US 37): Beckett, Burrud
It Happened in New York (US 35): Bupp S.
It Happened in Springfield (US 45): Gray G.
It Happened One Night (US 34): Breakston
It Happened on Fifth Avenue (US 47): Sydes
It Happens Every Spring (US 49): Calkins
It Happens Every Thursday (US 53): Eyer Ri.
It Must Be Love 'Cos I Feel So Dumb (US 76): Lutter
I togda ya skazal: Net / *Then I said No* (SU 73): Musin
It Pays to Advertise (US 31): Coghlan
It's a Bear (US 24): 'Our Gang'
It's a Big Country (US 50): Hyatt, Hunter
It's About Time (66 US) – see Let's Kill Uncle
It's a Boy (US 14): Jacobs
It's a Boy (US 20): Marion D.
It's a Date (US 40): Kelly T.
It's a Gift (US 34): Bupp T., Leroy
It's a Great Day (GB 55): Beeny
It's a Great Life! (US 35): Holt D., Leroy

It's a Great Life (US 43): Simms L., Mummert, Gray G.

It's a Joke, Son (US 47): Sydes

It's a Pleasure (US 45): Janssen D.

It's a 2'6 above the Ground World (GB 72): Henderson S.

It's a Wonderful Life (US 46): Anderson B., Chapin M., Hawkins, Nokes, Rettig, Simms L.

It's a Wonderful World (US 39): Kibrick L.

It's Great to Be Young (GB 56): O'Sullivan

It's Hard to Be Good (GB 48): Malone

It's in the Bag (US 45): Tyler D.

It's My Turn (US 80): Hathaway

It's Never Too Late to Mend (GB 37): Singer

It Started in Naples (US 60): Angeletti M.

It's the Old Army Game (US 26): Bennett M.

It's Your Move (US 84, TVS): Bateman

It Wasn't Poison After All (US 13): Clark A.

Ivan Grozni /Ivan the Terrible (SU 44): Pirev

Ivanhoe (GB 52): Pike J.

Ivan i Aleksandra /Ivan and Alexandra (BG 88): Chorbadjiev

Ivan Makarovich (SU 68): Makhonin

Ivanovo detstvo /Ivan's childhood (SU 62): Burlyayev K.

Ivan's Childhood (62 SU) — see Ivanovo detstvo

I've Gotta Horse (GB 65): Bennett K., Brockwell

I've Lived Before (US 56): Mora (Morrow)

Ivory Snuff Box, The (US 15): Boss

I Wanna Hold Your Hand (US 78): Juttner

I Want a Divorce (US 40): Kuhn

I Want to Forget (US 18): Thaw

I Was an Adventuress (US 40): Cook B.

I Was a Spy (GB 33): Singer

I Was Born, But... (32 JP) — see Umarete wa mita keredo

I Wonder Who's Kissing Her Now (US 47): Rodin M.

Iwonka (PL 25): Mietek

Izgubljena olovka /The missing pencil (YU 60): Gašević

Izpiti po nikoe vreme /Exams any old time (BG 74): Ganev

Jaanwar aur insaan /Man and beast (IN 72): Alankar

Jack (FR 25): Forest

Jack and the Bean Stalk (US 13): Benham

Jack and the Beanstalk (US 17): Carpenter, Lake, Lee Ra., Messinger

Jack and the Beanstalk (US 51): Stollery

Jack and the Beanstalk (US 67): Riha

Jackass Mail (US 42): Hickman Dl., Larson

Jack Chanty (US 15): Short

Jack Holborn (DE/NZ 82, srl): Bach

Jackie (US 21): Stone

Jackie Cooper's Christmas Party (US 31): Cooper Ja.

Jack o' Clubs (US 24): Fox J.

Jackpot, The (US 50): Rettig

Jack's the Boy (GB 32): Singer

Jack the Giant Killer (US 61): Mobley

Jacob's Ladder (US 90): Culkin M.

Jacqueline (GB 56): O'Sullivan

Jacqueline, or Blazing Barriers (US 23): Depew, Griffin

Jacques et Jacotte (FR 36): Rodon

Jacquou le Croquant /Jacko the Clodhopper (FR 69, srl): Damain

Jade Love (84 TW) — see Yu qing sao

Jadria (PL 36): Kudla

Jag är eld och luft /I am air and fire (SE 44): Bernhard

Jagd nach dem Stiefel, Die /Hunt the boot (DD 62): Böhme M. and W.

Jag dräpte /I killed (SE 43): Bernhard

Jagged Edge (US 85): Call

Jagirdar /The landlord (IN 37): Marathe R.

Jagriti /Awakening (IN 54): Kumar

Jaguëy de las ruinas, El /Jaguar in the ruins (MX 44): Jiménez Pons J.

Jahr ohne Sonntag, Ein /A year without Sundays (DE 70, TVS): Halm

Jai Bangla Desh /Long live Bangladesh (IN 71): Alankar

Jailbreak (US 36): Rentschler

J'aime toutes les femmes /I love all women (FR 35): Grave

Jai Radhe Krishna /Glory to Radha Krishna (IN 74): Satyajit

Jakko (GE 41): Rohringer

Jakub (CS 76): Renč

Jaldeep /The lighthouse (IN 56): 'Ashok', Dube

Jalna (US 35): Severn Cl.

Jalsaghar /The music room (IN 58): Gupta

Jalwa (IN 55): Kumar

Jam Closet, The (US 12): Porter W.

Janbaz (PK 87): Jamshid

Jang (PK 88): Jamshid

Janitor's Flirtation, The (US 14): Boss

Janitor's Quiet Life, The (US 13): Boss

Janko muzykant /Janko the musician (PL 30): Rogulski

Janošik (CS 35): Davidik

Janošik (CS 63): Černy

Jan Pieter en zijn zusje /Jan Peter and his little sister (NL 34): van Putten

Japanese War Bride (US 52): Lindgren O.

Jardinier et le petit espiègle, Le (1895 FR) — see Arroseur arrosé

'Jarr Family' series (US 15): Kelly P.

Java Head (US 23): Depew

Jawani diwani /Crazy youth (IN 72): Satyajit

Jaws 2 (US 78): Gilpin M.

Jazz Cinderella (US 30): Durand, Frederick

Jazz Singer, The (US 27): Gordon Bo., Holmes L.

Jazz Singer, The (US 80): Peluce

Jazz Waiter, The (14 US) — see Caught in a Cabaret

Jealous Husbands (US 23): Alexander B., Marion D.

Jean Goes Fishing (US 11): Casey

Jeden z trzydziestu sresciu /One from the 30th (PL 25): Mietek

Jeepers Creepers (US 39): Lee B.

'Jeff's Collie' (54-57 US, TVS) — see 'Lassie'

Jeg har elsket og levet /I've loved and lived (DK 40): Fagerlund

Jekyll and Hyde...Together Again (US 82): Oliver B.

Jennie Gerhardt (US 33): Durand

Jenny (FR 36): Mouloudji

Jeopardy (US 52): Aaker L.

Je reviendrai à Kandara /I'll come back to Kandara (FR 56): Chapeland, Maurin Y.-M.

Jergus Lapin (CS 61): Kauzlarič

Jernbanens datter /Daughter of the railway (DK 11): Crone

Jérôme Perreau (FR 35): Bara, Buquet, Farguette, Grave

Jeromin (ES 53): Blanch

Jerry the Giant (US 26): Madden

Jersey Girl (US 92): Mazzello

Jes' Call Me Jim (US 20): Rogers J.
Jesse James (US 27): Downs
Jesse James (US 39): Kibrick L. and S., Russell J.
Jess of the Mountain Country (US 14): Short
J'étais une aventurière / I was an adventuress (FR 38): François
Jeudi à Paris, Un / Thursday in Paris (FR 55): Urbain
Jeune fille d'une nuit, La / The one-night girl (FR 34): Genevois
Jeune folle, La / The mad girl (FR 52): Fourcade, Maurin Y.-M., Poujouly
Jeunes filles en détresse / Young girls in distress (FR 39): François
Jeux dangereux, Les / Dangerous games (FR/IT 58): Flateau, Moullières, Urbain
Jeux interdits / Forbidden games (FR 51): Poujouly
Jewish Prudence (US 27): Fox J.
Jezebel (US 38): Beard, Hurlic
Jheel ke us paar / Across the lake (IN 73): Mehmood
Jikatsu suru onna / Independent woman (JP 35): Sugawara
Jimao xin / Letter with the feathers (CN 53): Tsai
Jim Bludso (US 16): Stone
'Jimmie' series (10-14 FR) – see 'Bébé'
Jimmie's Job (US 11): Kelly P.
Jimmie Straightened Out (US 16): Hamrick
Jimmy (US 13): Shirley
Jimmy (FR 30): Gaillard
Jimmy bruiteur / Jimmy's sound-effects (FR 28): Gaillard
Jim och piraterna Blom / Jim and the pirates Blom (SE 87): Åkerblom
Jim Thorpe - All American (US 51): Gray B., Hawkins, Moss J.
Jinsei no onimotsu / The burden of life (JP 35): Hayama
Jiro monogatari / Tales of Jiro (JP 55): Ohsawa
Jób lázadása / Job's revolt (HU 83): Fehér G.
Jocaste / Jocasta (FR 24): Forest
Jochukko / The maid's kid (JP 55): Tanabe
Joe and Ethel Turp Call on the President (US 39): Baker, Bupp T.
'Joe and Sons' (US 75, TVS): Baio J.
Joe Smith, American (US 42): Hickman Dl.
'Joe's World' (US 79, TVS): Sharrett
Joey (US 85): Morrell
Joey and Redhawk (US 78): Petersen Chr., San Juan
Joffre la Mizil (RO 15): Manu
Jog bijog / Meeting and parting (IN 53): Babua
Johanna Enlists (US 18): Barry W.
Johannes' hemmelighed / Johannes' secret (DK 85): Katz
Johar Mehmood in Hong Kong (IN 71): Mehmood
John and Julie (GB 55): Gibson
John Barleycorn (US 14): Roubert, Short
John Ermine of the Yellowstone (US 17): Hamrick
John Halifax, Gentleman (GB 38): Gainsborough, McDowall
'John Henry' comedies (US 19-22): Marion D.
Johnny Apollo (US 40): Albright
Johnny Comes Flying Home (US 46): Sydes
Johnny Doesn't Live Here (US 44): Laughlin
Johnny Doughboy (US 42): Brown K., Lenhart, McFarland, McKim H., Switzer
Johnny Get Your Hair Cut (US 27): Coogan J.
Johnny Holiday (US 49): Martin A.
Johnny on the Run (GB 54): Chylek
Johnny Rocco (US 58): Eyer Ri.
Johnny Shiloh (US 62): Corcoran, Hodges E.

Johnny's Travels (56 CS) – see Honzíkova cesta
Johnny Tremain (US 57): Stalmaster
John of the Fair (GB 52): Charlesworth
Johnstown Flood, The (US 26): Billings E., Boudwin
Joi i Druzhok / Joy and Buddy (SU 28): Litkin, Zavyaloff
Jól megjarta / They've had it (HU 56): Koletár
Jones Family in Hollywood, The (US 39): Mahan
Jones Family in Hot Water, The (38 US) – see Hot Water
Jongen uit het Wilde Westen, De / Boy from the Wild West (NL 64): van der Linden C.
Jonny Roova (SE 85): Dytlow-Kozlowski
Joselito vagabundo / Joselito the wanderer (MX/ES 66): Quezadas
Josh and Cindy's Wedding Trip (US 11): Boss
Joshila / Flaming youth (IN 73): Satyajit
Josselyn's Wife (US 19): Alexander B.
Jouet, Le / The toy (FR 77): Gréco
Jour de vacances / Holiday (FR 31): Bara
Journey, The (US 58): Howard R., Mark
Journey for Jeremy (GB 49): Netscher, Hannaford
Journey for Margaret (US 42): Mickelsen, Severn B. and Cl.
Joy (20 NL/GB) – see Zonnetje
Joyce's Strategy (US 16): Paul J.
Joyland (US 29): Bailey Sd.
Joy Scouts (US 39): 'Our Gang'
Joy Tonic (US 29): Sabiston
J.T. (US 69): Hooks K.
Juanito (ES/DE 60): Calvo
Juarez (US 39): Kuhn
Jubilo, Jr. (US 24): 'Our Gang'
Judex (FR 16, srl): Poyen, Haziza
Judex (FR/IT 63): Boda
Judgment of the Hills (US 27): Darro, Winslow D.
Judgment of the Storm (US 23): Darro
Judy of Rogues' Harbor (US 20): Lee F.
Juego de hombres / A man's game (ES 64): Sanchez
Jugement de Dieu, Le / Divine judgment (FR 49): Gencel
Jugendliebe / Youthful love (GE 18): Herzberg
Juggernaut (GB 74): Holm
Juggler, The (US 53): Walsh, Infuhr
Jugnu / Glow-worm (IN 73): Alankar, Satyajit
Juicio contra un angel / An angel on trial (ES 64): Gomez A.
Julek (CS 80): Renč
Julesburg (US 56): Chapin B.
July Days (US 23): 'Our Gang'
Jumping for Joy (GB 55): Hannaford
Junge Adler / Young eagles (GE 44): Krüger
Junge schrie Mord, Ein (66 GB/DE/YU) – see Boy Cried Murder
Junges Herz voll Liebe / Young heart full of love (DE 53): Brenner
Junge Törless, Der / Young Törless (DE/FR 66): Carrière
Jungfern vom Bischofsberg, Die / The maids of Bishop's Hill (GE 43): Rohringer
Jungfrukällan / Virgin's Spring (SE 59): Porath
Jungle Girl (US 41, srl): Cook T.
Jungle Trail, The (US 19): Stone
Jungle Trail of the Son of Tarzan (23 US) – see Son of Tarzan (US 20)
Juninatten / June night (SE 40): Olsson

'Junior G-Men' series (US 40): Tucker T.
Junior Miss (US 45): Beckett
Junker Hinrichs verbotene Liebe (25 GE) – see Zur Chronik
    von Grieshuus
Junket (GB 70): Brassett
Jurašek (CS 56): Hašler
Jurassic Park (US 93): Mazzello
Jus' Passin' Through (US 23): Condon
Jusqu'au bout du monde / To the world's end (FR/IT 62):
    Angeletti M.
Just a Little More Love (US 83): Bateman
Just an Old Sweet Song (US 76): Hooks E. and K.
Just Another Dame (42 US) – see Not a Ladies' Man
Just Around the Corner (US 38): Bartlett, Kibrick L. and S.
Just a Woman (US 18): Beck C.
Just 'Kids' (US 15): Benham
Just Pals (US 20): Stone
Just Pals (36 US) – see Cowboy and the Kid
Just Pretending (US 12): Hackett A.
Just What Bobby Wanted (US 17): Connelly
Just - William (GB 39): Lupino, McDowall
Just William's Luck (GB 47): Graham, Roper, Weske
Jutalomutazás / The prize holiday (HU 74): Borsi
'Juvenile Comedies' series (US 24): Alexander B.
Juvenile Court (US 38): Billings G.
Juvenile Love Affair, A (US 12): Casey, Kelly P.

Kaachan shiguno iyada / Don't die, Mummy! (JP 61): Hirabayishi
Kaachan umiga shitteruyo / The little fisherman (JP 61): Ota
Kaadu / The forest (IN 73): Nataraj
Kabat, A / The overcoat (HU 56): Koletár
Kadetten / Cadets (GE 39): Sierck
Kådisbellan / The slingshot (SE 93): Salén
Kagirinaki zenshin / Forever forward (JP 37): Katayama
Kaisermanöver / Imperial manoeuvres (AT 54): Friedl
Kaiser, the Beast of Berlin, The (US 18): Hupp
Kaishain kubiyoke senjutsu / The company-man strategy (JP 30):
    'Tokkan-Kozo'
Kaishain seikatsu / An office-worker's life (JP 29): 'Tokkan-Kozo'
Kajan går till sjöss / The 'Kaja' goes to sea (SE 43): Hjelm, Lindgren H.
Kakadu und Kiebitz (GE 20): Allen W.
Kak Petyunka yezdil k Ilyichi / How little Peter visited Lenin
    (SU 24): Voronovski
Kak ya bil samostoyatel nim / I take charge of the house (SU 63):
    Semyonov Vo., Yershoff
Kalle wird Bürgermeister / Kalle becomes mayor (DE 57): Condrus
Kampf der Tertia, Der / The battle of the Third Form (GE 28):
    Stark-Gstettenbaur
Kampf der Tertia, Der (DE 53): Jansen
Kan doktorn komma? / Can the doctor come? (SE 42): Nyström
Kanhaiyya (IN 81): Rajoo
Kanikuli / The holiday (SU 62): Kokochashvili
Kankabatir ghat / The banks of the Kankabati (IN 55): Babua
Kann kvinder fejler? / Can women do wrong (DK 24): Herzberg
Kapedani / The captain (AL 72): Pojani
Kapetan Mikula Mali / Little Captain Mike (YU 74): Vidan
Kapitanat / The captain (BG 62): Alurkov, Shakhpazyan

Kapitani Goluboi Laguni / Captains of the Blue Lagoon (SU 62):
    Baranov, Kokin
Kapitan Korda / Captain Korda (CS 70): Vavruša
Kapronoviye seti / The Kapronov nets (SU 62): Kharonski
Kardies stin kategida / Hearts in the storm (GR 63): Kailas
Kare to kanojo to shonentachi / He, she and the boys (JP 35):
    'Tokkan-Kozo', Yokoyama
Karl Brunner (SU 36): Fesechko
Kärlekshistoria, En / A love story (SE 70): Andresen
Karl Valentin, der Sonderling / The strange Karl Valentin (GE 29):
    Stark-Gstettenbaur
Karo (SU 37): Akopyan M.
Karusellen / The roundabout (SE 23): Pottier
Karuzela życia / Life's roundabout (PL 30): Micinski
Kashtanka / Little Chestnut (SU 26): Zimin
Kastrullresan / Voyage in a saucepan (SE 50): Sarri
Katastrofen i Kattegat / Disaster in the Kattegat (DK 15): Reinwald
Katatregmeni, I / The persecuted (GR 62): Kalatzopoulos
Katatregmeni tis miras / Persecuted by fate (GR 64): Kailas
Kathe limani ke kaimos / A grief in every port (GR 64): Kailas
Katie Did It (US 50): Hunt
Kati patang (IN 70): Mehmood
Katok i skripka / Steam-roller and violin (SU 60): Fomchenko
Kato pesen / Like a song (BG 73): Petrov
Katrina (SE 43): Hjelm, Nyström
Kaufmann von Venedig, Der / The merchant of Venice (GE 23): Allen W.
Kawaii gokesan / The pretty widow (JP 32): 'Tokkan-Kozo'
Každa koruna dobra / Every good crown (CS 61): Bor
Kaze no Matsaburo / Whirlwind Matsaburo (JP 40): Katayama, Oizumi
Kaze no naka no kodomo / Children in the wind (JP 37): 'Tokkan-Kozo',
    Hayama, Yokoyama
Kaze no naka no mendori / A hen in the wind (JP 48): Aoki (Tomihiro),
    Nakagawa
Kazhdi okhotnik zhelayet znat / What every hunter wants to know
    (SU 86): Goloborodko
K - das Haus des Schweigens / K: house of silence (DE 51): Czeike
Kdyby tisic klarinetů / If a thousand clarinets (CS 64): Očenašek
Když má svátek Dominika / Dominica's name-day (CS 67): Pospišil
Když struny lkají / When strings weep (CS/AT/GE 30): Fehér H.
Kean (IT 40): Ferrari
Keby som mal pušku / If I had a gun (CS 71): Dernat
Keeper of the Flame (US 42): Hickman Dl.
Keeping Company (US 40): Winkler
Kees, de zoon van de stroper / Kees, the poacher's son (NL 50): van Driel
Keine Angst vor Liebe / No worry about love (GE 33): Richter
Keine Angst vor Schwiegermüttern / Mothers-in-law are OK
    (DE 54): Kaiser
Kein Engel ist so rein / No angel so pure (DE 50): Bürger
Kein Platz für Liebe / No room for love (DE 47): Neie
Kejsaren av Portugallien / The Emperor of Portugal (SE 44): Nyström
Kekčeve ukane / Sharp-witted Kekec (YU 69): Krasnić
Kekec (YU 51): Barl
Kelly the Second (US 36): Switzer
Kéménykalap es krumpliorr / Bowler-hat and Potato-nose (HU 78):
    Kovács
Kemuri no osama / King of smoke (JP 63): Ichikawa
Kentuckian, The (US 55): MacDonald

Kentucky (US 38): Holt D., Watson Bs. and D.
Kentucky Colonel, The (US 20): Griffith
Kentucky Foes (US 13): Tansey R.
'Kentucky Jones' (US 64-65, TVS): Der
Kentucky Kernels (US 34): McFarland
Kentucky Pride (US 25): Miller W.
Kes (GB 69): Bradley
Kessen no ozora e / To the air of battle (JP 43): Kodaka
Kétlelkü asszony, A / Woman with two souls (HU 17): Szécsi
Kettles in the Ozarks, The (US 55): Eyer Ri.
Kettles on Old MacDonald's Farm, The (US 57): Arglen
Két vallomás / Two confessions (HU 57): Csógör, Koletár
Keusche Lebemann, Der / The chaste libertine (DE 52): Jansen
Keys of the Kingdom, The (US 44): Binyon, McDowall, Nokes
Key to Power, The (US 20): Carr S.
Key to Rebecca, The (GB 85): Condou
Key Witness (US 60): Holmes D.
Khatta meetha / Sour and sweet (IN 77): Rajoo
Khoj / The search (IN 71): Mehmood
Khoris mitera / Motherless (GR 61): Kalatzopoulos
Khote sikkay / Counterfeit coins (IN 74): Alankar
Kibo ni tatsu / Ever hopeful (JP 38): Hayama
Kick Out (US 22): Morgan
Kid, The (US 10): Pickford
Kid, The (US 21): Coogan J., Lee Ra.
Kid Auto Races at Venice (US 14): Griffith, Jacobs
Kidco (US 84): Schwartz S.
Kid Colossus, The (54 US) – see Roogie's Bump
Kid Comes Back, The (US 37): Jones D.
Kid Comes Through, The (US 21): Gion (Gene Raymond)
Kid Comes Through, The (US 29): Nelson B.
Kiddie Cure (US 40): 'Our Gang'
Kiddies' Christmas, The (US 12): Johnson R.
Kiddus, Kidds and Kiddo (US 16): Callis
Kid for Two Farthings, A (GB 54): Ashmore
Kid from Borneo, The (US 33): 'Our Gang'
Kid from Canada, The (GB 56): Braden
Kid from Cleveland, The (US 49): Tamblyn
Kid from Left Field, The (US 53): Chapin B.
Kid from Left Field, The (US 80): Coleman G.
Kid from Nowhere, The (US 82): Petersen P.
Kid Glove Killer (US 42): Blake
Kid Hayseed (US 28): Sabiston, Watson D.
Kid Magicians, The (US 15): Stone
Kid Millions (US 34): Albright, Beard, Bond T., Bupp T., Jordan, Kibrick L., Rentschler
Kidnapning / Kidnap (DK 82): Nezer
Kidnapped (US 38): Bartholomew, Watson Bl.
Kidnapped (US 48): Anderson B.
Kidnapped (GB 59): Pike J.
Kidnapped Child, The (GB 04): Barker K.
Kidnappers, The (GB 53): Whiteley, Winter, Beeny
Kids (US 14): Jacobs
Kid Stakes, The (AU 27): Ordell
Kid Stakes, The (AU 80): Oxenbould
Kid Vengeance (US 77): Garrett
Kid with the Broken Halo (US 82): Feldman

Kiiroi karasu / The yellow crow (JP 57): Shitara
Kiken shingo / Danger signal (JP 31): 'Tokkan-Kozo'
Kiki (US 26): Darro
Kiku to Isamu / Kiku and Isamu (JP 59): Okumoyama
Killer! (69 FR/IT) – see Que la bête meure
Killer, The (US 21): Lee F.
Killer McCoy (US 47): Roberts E.
Killer on Board (US 77): Lynas
Killer That Stalked New York, The (US 50): Ivo
Killing Stone (US 78): Laborteaux M.
Kill the Umpire (US 50): Ivo, Olsen L.J.
Kilmeny (US 15): Griffith
Kim (US 50): Stockwell
Kincskeresö kisködmön / The magic jacket (HU 72): Szücs
Kind - ein Hund, Ein / A child and a dog (GE 23): Slawe
Kind, ein Hund, ein Vagabund, Ein / Child, dog and tramp (GE 34): Müller W.
Kinderarzt Dr. Engel / Dr Engel, paediatrician (GE 36): Eugens
Kinder aus Nr.67, Die / The kids at No.67 (DE 80): Riedl
Kinder, Mütter und ein General / Children, mothers and a general (DE 55): Bürger, Lödel
Kinderseele / Children's soul (DE 81): Schäfer
Kindertragödie / Children's tragedy (GE 27): Lutz
Kind Hearts and Coronets (GB 49): Malone, Spenser J.
Kindred of the Dust (US 22): Guerin
King (US 78): Olson
King and I, The (US 56): Thompson R., Adiarte
Kingdom of Nosyland (US 15): Butterworth E.
Kingdom Within, The (US 22): Marion F.
King for a Night (US 33): Billings G.
King in New York, A (GB 57): Chaplin M.
King of Kings, The (US 27): Moore M., Holmes L., Jewell, Wain
King of the Arena (US 33): Nelson B.
King of the Castle (GB 36): Singer
King of the Gypsies (US 78): Laborteaux M.
King of the Hill (US 93): Bradford
King of the Jungle (US 33): Cosbey
King of the Ritz (GB 33): Singer
King of the Sierras (US 36): Albright
King of the Turf (US 39): Daniel
King of the Wild Horses (US 47): Sheffield B.
King of the Wild Stallions (US 58): Hartleben J.
King of the Underworld (US 39): Bailey Sd., Kuhn
King René's Daughter (US 13): Benham
King's Row (US 41): Beckett, Croft, Scott D.
King Without a Crown (US 37): Beckett
Kinigontas ton erota / Hunting for love (GR 56): Kalatzopoulos
Kino (CS 61): Pospišil
Kipps (GB 40): Frost
Kira-Kiralina (SU 27): Krestinski
Kirilcho / Little Cyril (SU 25): Epstein
Kirkastuva sävel / Brighter note (FI 46): Kaitala
Kish i Dva Portfelya / Kish and 'Double-Satchel' (SU 74): Kondratev
Kis Lord, A / The little Lord (HU 18): Lubinsky
Kis Lord, A (HU 22): Szécsi
Kiss and Tell (US 45): Hickman Dl.
Kiss Me Goodbye (US 82): Oliver B.

Kitaab / *The book* (IN 78): Rajoo

Kit Carson and the Mountain Men (US 76): Eisenmann

Kitchen Cynic, The (US 44): Infuhr

Kitchen Toto, The (GB 87): Mahinda

Kitsune no kureta akanbo / *Gift of the gods* (JP 45): Kato

Kitty Foyle (US 40): Nichols

Klaun Ferdinand a raketa / *Ferdinand the clown and a rocket* (CS 62): Bor

Klebolin klebt alles / *Sticko sticks everything* (GE 09): Bois

Kleine Detektiv, Der / *The little detective* (GE 09): Bois

Kleine Grenzverkehr, Der / *Frontier traffic* (GE 43): Eugens

Kleine Herzog, Der / *The little Duke* (GE 24): Peterhans

Kleine Kavalier, Der / *The little cavalier* (AT/HU 36): 'Mircha'

Kleine Leute - mal ganz gross / *Little people, not so little* (DE 58): Kaiser, Angeletti M.

Kleine Muck, Der / *Little Muck* (GE 21): Allen W.

Kleiner Mann, ganz gross / *Little big man* (GE 38): Dann

Kleiner Mann, ganz gross (DE 57): Grimm

Kleiner Mann was tun / *What's to be done, little man?* (DE 82): Aykol

Kleine Vampir, Der / *The little vampire* (DE 68): Urchs

Klein Svend und seine Mutter / *Little Svend and his mother* (GE 13): Kaulbach

Klich (SU 35): Assadullayev

Klimbusch macht Wochenende / *Klimbusch's weekend* (GE 38): Kieling

Kluci na řeče / *Boys in the river* (CS 44): Opatrny

Klyatva Timura / *Timur's oath* (SU 42): Shchipachev, Pupko

Knee Action (US 37): Bond T.

Knight before Christmas, The (US 14, 'Sonny Jim'): Connelly

Knight in London, A (GB 29): Rive

Knights of the Square Table (US 17): Clark A.

Knocknagow (GB 18): Cusack

Knock-out (FR 23): Allen W.

Knock-Out, The (GB 23): Brantford

Knokken voor twee / *Thumps for two* (NL 83): van de Molen

K novomu beregu / *To a new shore* (SU 55): Koval

Knute Rockne - All American (US 40): Baker, Billings G., Bupp S., Dawson, Jones D., Sheffield B. and J., Winkler

Kochankowie mojej Mamy / *My mum's lovers* (PL 85): Węgrzyniak

Kochankowie z Marony / *The lovers of Marona* (PL 66): Roman

Kodomo no koro senso na atta / *There was a war when I was a kid* (JP 80): Saito

Kodomo no shiki / *Four seasons of children* (JP 39): Hayama, Yokoyama

Kogda poyut solovyi / *When nightingales sing* (SU 86): Chernoff

Kohayagawa-ke no aki / *The Kohayagawas' autumn* (JP 61): Shimazu

Kohlhiesels Töchter / *Kohlhiesel's daughters* (GE 30): Stark-Gstettenbaur

Koi jeeta koi hara / *One wins, one loses* (IN 76): Mehmood

Koi mo wasurete / *Forget love too* (JP 37): Yokoyama

Koi no shakkin gurui no senjutsu / *Money for love* (JP 30): 'Tokkan-Kozo'

Kojo no tsuki / *Moon over the ruins* (JP 37): Hayama

Koldusgróf, A / *The beggar Count* (HU 17): Szécsi

Kolibel poeta / *A poet's cradle* (SU 47): Chitaya

Kollege kommt gleich / *My colleague's just coming* (GE 43): Rohringer

Kolorowe pończochy / *Coloured stockings* (PL 60): Rzegocki, Wiśniewski

Komanda s nashei ulitsi / *The team from our street* (SU 53): Yevgeniyev

Komödianten des Lebens / *Life's mummers* (GE 23): Herzberg

Kompaneros / *Buddies* (SU 62): Krimnus, Mirzoyev

Komptoiristka / *The shop-girl* (CS 22): Branald

Konduit / *Conduct* (SU 35): Borisevich

Konec strašidel / *An end to ghosts* (CS 53): Bejval

Konets Staroi Berezovski / *The end of old Berezovska* (SU 60): Likhin

Kongress tanzt, Der / *Congress dances* (AT 55): Czeike

Koniec wakacji / *End of the holidays* (PL 75): Sikora

König der Manege, Der / *King of the sawdust ring* (GE 21): 'Patatà'

Königsgrenadiere, Die / *The King's grenadiers* (GE 25): Lázár

König und die kleinen Mädchen, Der / *The King and the little girls* (GE 25): Allen W.

Koningin Elisabeth's dochter / *Queen Elisabeth's daughter* (NL 15): de Vries

Konnikut / *The horseman* (BG 64): Alurkov

Konnitsa skachet / *The cavalry gallops* (SU 29): Simanovich

Konoko sutezaraba / *If I don't get rid of the child* (JP 35): 'Tokkan-Kozo'

Konrad (US 73): Fox H.

Konsten att älska / *The art of loving* (SE 47): Montin, Sarri

Kontsert Betkhovena / *The Beethoven concerto* (SU 36): Taimanov, Vasilev V.

Konzert za fleita i momiche / *Concerto for flute and girl* (BG 79): Ivanov D.

Koondu killi (IN 54): Mohan

Kopf hoch, Johannes! / *Chin up, Johnny!* (GE 41): Sierck, Möller

Kora aanchal / *Untouched virgin* (IN 73): Mehmood

Korczak (PL/GE/FR/GB 90): Klata

Koritsi me ta paramithia / *The girl with the stories* (GR 56): Kalatzopoulos

Koritsi tou ponou, To / *A girl of sorrow* (GR 64): Kailas

Koshi no nuketa onna / *A woman out of joint* (JP 34): 'Tokkan-Kozo'

Kosmonavt No. .... / *Cosmonaut No. ....* (SU 61): Diyev

Kostyor v lesu / *Camp-fire in the forest* (SU 41): Sinyakin

Kotengu Kiritaro / *Kiritaro the devil's son* (JP 58): Yamate

Kouzelný den / *Magical day* (CS 60): Lukeš, Hádl

Kozure ohkami - ko wo kashi ude kashi tsukamatsuru (JP 71): Tomikawa

Kozure ohkami - sanzu no kawa no ubaguruma (JP 72): Tomikawa

Krajczár története, Egy / *The story of a kreutzer* (HU 17): Szécsi

Kråkguldet / *False gold* (SE 69): Hallerstam

Králíci ve vysoké travě / *Rabbits in tall grass* (CS 61): Koblic

Kramer vs. Kramer (US 79): Henry J.

Krasni galstuk / *Red kerchief* (SU 48): Sokoloff Sh., Kotoff S.

Krayat na edna vakantsiya / *End of the holidays* (BG 64): Karamiltsev

Krays, The (GB 90): Brazier

Kreutzersonate, Die / *The Kreutzer Sonata* (GE 37): Kieling

Krishna Sudama (IN 33): Apte

Kristinus Bergman (DK 48): Langberg

Król Macius I / *King Macius I* (PL 57): Wyrzykowski, Halicz

Królowa pszczól / *Queen bee* (PL 77): Karwatka, Sikora

Krull (GB 82): McGrath

Kryengritje ne pallet / *Palace revolution* (AL 72): Çelia

Kuche v chekmedje / *Dog in a drawer* (BG 82): Prahov, Stoyanov

Küçük kovboy / *The little cowboy* (TR 71): Inanoğlu

Küçük sahit / *The little witness* (TR 72): Inanoğlu

Ku guo / *Bitter fruit* (CN 81): Fang C.

Kuksi (47 HU) – *see* Valahol Európában

Kullamannen / *The man from Kulla* (SE 67): Hallerstam

Külvárosi legenda / *Legend of the suburbs* (HU 57): Koletár

Kundskabens træ / *The tree of knowledge* (DK 81): Johansen

Kurama tengu - goyo toihen / *The curious robbery* (JP 56): Zushi
Kuruma ni tsunda takaramono / *Treasure in the cart* (JP 36): Yokoyama
Kusabue no oka / *The grass flute on the hill* (JP 58): Zushi
Kushboo / *Fragrance* (IN 75): Rajoo
Kushti bez ogradi / *Houses without fences* (BG 73): Ganev, Petrov
Küsschen und der General / *Küsschen and the General* (DD 61): Kersten
Kuttel (DD 61): Flohr
Kvarterets olycksfågel / *The local Jonah* (SE 48): Sarri
Kvartetten som sprängdes / *The quartet that split up* (SE 36): Winther
Kvartetten som sprängdes (SE 50): Sarri
Kvinnas ansikte, En / *A woman's face* (SE 38): Bernhard
Kvinna utan ansikte / *Faceless woman* (SE 47): Montin, Sarri
Kvočny a král / *Hens and a King* (CS 73): Dlouhy
Kyupora no aru machi / *Cupola* (JP 62): Ichikawa

Labakan (CS 56): Košnar
Lachenite obouvki na neznainiya voin / *The unknown soldier's patent leather shoes* (BG 79): Tsankov
Lacrime del popolo / *A people's tears* (IT 20): Casarotti
Lad an' a Lamp, A (US 32): 'Our Gang'
Ladder of Life, The (US 12): Benham
Laddie (US 26): Fox J.
Laddie (US 35): Butler
Laddie (US 40): McKim S.
Ladies Love Brutes (US 30): Durand, Frederick
Ladies' Man, A (US 22): Reisner
Ladies Must Live (US 40): Dawson
Ladies Seat (IN 54): Bhattacharjee
Ladki pasand hai / *The girl's O.K.* (IN 71): Mehmood
Ladri di biciclette / *Bicycle thieves* (IT 48): Staiola
Lady, The (US 25): Darro, Fox J.
Lady and Gent (US 32): Butts
Ladybugs (US 92): Brandis
Lady from Cheyenne, The (US 41): Larson
Lady from Hell, The (US 26): Moore M.
Lady in the Dark (US 44): Dawson, Bates
Lady in White (US 88): Haas L.
Lady Lies, The (US 29): Brown T.
Lady of the Dugout, The (US 18): Alexander B.
Lady of the Lighthouse, The (US 15): Desmond
Lady Says No, The (US 52): Sydes
Lady's Profession, A (US 33): Searl
Lady Takes a Chance, A (US 43): Brown K., Lenhart
Lady Wants Mink, The (US 52): Diamond, Rettig
Lady with Red Hair (US 40): Russell J.
La Habanera (37 GE) – *see* Habanera, La
Laheri lala (IN 36): Apte
Laila Majnu (IN 52): Kumar
Laitakaupungin laulu / *Song of the suburbs* (FI 48): Kaitala
Lake of Dreams, The (US 12): Clark R.
Lamb (GB 86): O'Conor
Land Beyond the Law, The (US 27): Butts
Land of Fighting Men (US 38): Jones D.
Land of Wanted Men (US 32): Shuford
Landstormens lille argbigga / *The reservist's nagging wife* (SE 41): Dalunde, Nyström
Land Without Music (GB 36): Hepworth J.

Lan fengzheng / *The blue kite* (HK/CN 92): Zhang
Langitku rumahku / *My sky, my home* (ID 90): Biru, Sunaryo
Lángok / *Flames* (HU 58): Weiser A. and G., Ragó
Laramie (US 49): Ivo
'Laramie' (US 59-63, TVS): Holmes D.
Largo viaje / *Long journey* (CL 67): Gaete
Lariat Kid, The (US 28): Barton
Láska je utrpením / *Love is suffering* (CS 19): Pražský
Láska nebeska / *Heavenly love* (CS 64): Smyczek
Lasse Mansson fra Skaane / *Lasse Mansson from Skaane* (DK 21): Herzberg
'Lassie' (US 54-64, TVS): Rettig, Provost
Lassie Come Home (US 43): McDowall
Lassie: Peace Is My Profession (72 US) – *see* Peace Is My Profession
Lassie's Great Adventure (US 63): Provost
Lassie: The New Beginning (US 78): Sinutko
Lassie: Well of Love (71 US) – *see* Well of Love
Last Action Hero (US 93): O'Brien A.
Last Convertible, The (US 79): Hathaway
Last Day of Summer (GB 83): McGrath
Last Days of Pompeii, The (US 35): Holt D.
Last Flight of Noah's Ark, The (US 80): Schroder
Last Frontier, The (US 26): Coghlan
Last Gangster, The (US 37): Scott D.
Last Holiday (GB 50): Charlesworth
Last Journey, The (GB 35): Frost
Last Lesson, The (US 42): Roy
Last Load, The (GB 48): Barr, Bowyer, Hannaford
Last Man on Earth, The (US 24): Black B., Murphy M.
Last Moment, The (US 23): Bennett M.
Last Moments (74 IT) – *see* Venditore di palloncini
Last Night of Christmas, The (77 IT) – *see* Questo si che è amore
Last of the Duanes (US 41): Winkler
Last Outlaw, The (US 27): Butts
Last Round-Up, The (US 47): Blake
Last Snows of Spring, The (73 IT) – *see* Ultima neve di primavera
Last Stand, The (US 30): Nelson B.
Last Starfighter, The (US 84): Wheaton
Last Survivors, The (US 75): Garrett
Last Trail, The (US 27): Madden
Last Train from Gun Hill (US 55): Kelman
Last Valley, The (GB 70): Alejandro
Last Wagon, The (US 56): Rettig
Last Wave, The (AU 77): Rowe
Late for Dinner (US 91): Malinger
Late Lodgers (US 21): Morrison E.
Late Mr Jones, The (US 13): Carnahan
Latest From Paris, The (US 28): Frederick, Holmes L.
Lattermaskinen / *The laughter-machine* (DK 10): Petersen Cas.
Laufende Berg, Der / *The moving mountain* (GE 41): Schmidhofer
Laughing at Life (US 33): Phelps
Laughter in Hell (US 32): Condon
Laura (US 56): Washbrook
Lavender Hill Mob, The (GB 50): Fox W.
Law and Disorder (GB 58): Stephens M.
Law and the Lady, The (US 24): Depew

Law Comes to Gunsight (US 47): Rees
Law Decides, The (US 16): Connelly
Lawful Larceny (US 23): Griffin
Lawnmower Man, The (US 92): O'Brien A.
Lawnmower Man 2 (US 95): O'Brien A.
Law of Man, The (US 19): Lee F.
Law of the North (US 32): Shuford
Law of the Sea, The (US 32): Albright
Law of the Wild (US 41): Spellman
Law Unto Herself, A (US 18): Hamrick
Lazarillo de Tormes, El / *The little guide from Tormes* (ES 25): Hurtado
Lazarillo de Tormes, El (ES 59): Paoletti
Lazy Days (US 29): 'Our Gang'
Lazy Lightning (US 26): Gordon Bo.
Léanybecsület / *A maiden's honour* (HU 23): Szécsi
Leap to Heaven (US 56): Stalmaster
Leather Burners (US 42): Larson
Leave Her to Heaven (US 45): Hickman Dl.
'Leave It to Beaver' (US 57-63, TVS): Mathers
Leave It to Blondie (US 45): Simms L., Mummert
Leave It to Henry (US 49): Gray G.
Lebbra bianca / *White leprosy* (IT 50): Cerusico
Leftover Ladies (US 31): Phelps
Leg and the Legacy, The (US 12): Roubert
Legenda / *Legend* (PL 70): Straburzynski
Legenda o lásce / *Legend of love* (CS 57): Košnar
Legend of the Boy and the Eagle, The (US 67): Lomakema
Legend of the Lawman (75 US) – *see* Part 2 Walking Tall
Legend of the Lone Ranger, The (US 81): Gilpin M.
Legends of the West (US 81): Bateman
Legge di sangue / *Law of blood* (IT 47): Leurini
Legion of Death, The (US 18): Marion F.
Legion of the Lawless (US 40): Watson D.
Legion ulicy / *Legion of the streets* (PL 32): Rogulski
Legokosabb ember, A / *The cleverest man* (HU 56): Kolétar
Legs (US 78): Baio S.
Leguignon guérisseur / *Leguignon the healer* (FR 54): Urbain
Légy jó mindhalálig / *Always be good* (HU 36): Dévényi
Légy jó mindhalálig (HU 60): Tóth L., Kiss
Leidensweg der Inge Krafft, Der / *Inge Krafft's path of sorrow* (GE 21): Pottier
Lélek órása, A / *Watchmaker of souls* (HU 23): Lázár
Lemon Drop Kid, The (US 34): Leroy
Lemon Drop Kid, The (US 51): Ivo
Lena Rivers (US 25): Berlinger
Lengyelvér / *Polish blood* (HU 20): Szécsi
Lent (GB 84): McGrath
Léolo (CA 92): Collin
Leonardo da Vinci (IT 69): Cestiè
Leopard, The (62 IT/FR) – *see* Gattopardo
Lepke (US 74): Baio J.
Les misérables (FR) – *see* Misérables, Les
Les Miserables (US 18): Phillips A.
Les Miserables (US 52): Hyatt, Moss J.
Lesnoi chelovek / *Man from the forest* (SU 27): Chernishoff
Lessons from the Garbage (86 ML) – *see* Nyamanton
Letat zhuravli / *The cranes are flying* (SU 57): Popoff

Letayushchi korabl / *The flying ship* (SU 60): Yershoff I.
Let 'Er Go (US 20): Marion D.
Let 'Er Go Gallagher (US 27): Coghlan
Let Him Have It (GB 91): Brazier
Let Katy Do It (US 15): Carpenter, Perl, Stone
Let's Go Gallagher (US 25): Darro
Let's Go Naked (32 GB) – *see* Strip, Strip, Hooray!
Let's Kill Uncle (US 66): Cardi
Let's Make Music (US 41): Bartlett
Let's Sing Again (US 36): Breen
Letter with the Feathers, The (53 CN) – *see* Jimao xin
Let the Balloon Go (AU 76): Bettles
Let Them Live! (US 37): Bartlett
Lettre, La / *The letter* (FR 30): Mercanton
Lettre au petit Jésus, La / *Letter to baby Jesus* (FR 10): Mary
Lettre ouverte à un mari / *Open letter to a husband* (FR 52): Urbain
Let Us Be Gay (US 30): Frederick, Moore D.
Let Us Live (US 39): Lee B., Spellman
Letzte Rezept, Das / *The last prescription* (DE 51): Czeike
Leugen van Pierrot, De / *Pierrot's lie* (NL 22): de Vries
Lewat tengah malam / *After midnight* (ID 71): Karno
Leyenda del tambor, La / *Legend of the drummer* (ES 81): Sanz
Liangjia chun / *Two families* (CN 51): Wang L.
Liangjia funü / *A girl of good family* (CN 85): Wang J.
Libeled Lady (US 36): Bond T., Kuhn, Phelps, Reynolds
Liberté / *Freedom* (FR 37): Farguette
Lichnoye delo / *A private matter* (SU 39): Minayev, Runge, Mirski
Lide jako ty / *People like you* (CS 60): Koblic
Liebe dumme Mama / *Dear silly Mama* (GE 34): Richter
Liebe Familie, Die / *The dear family* (AT 57): Czeike
Liebe, Jazz und Übermut / *Love, jazz and jollity* (DE 57): Kaiser
Liebesgeschichten / *Love stories* (GE 43): Rohringer
Liebeskrieg nach Noten / *Musical war of love* (DE 53): Lödel
Liebeslegende (38 GE) – *see* Preussische Liebesgeschichte
Liebe, Tanz und 1000 Schlager / *Love, dance and 1000 hits* (DE 55): Condrus
Lies My Father Told Me (CA 75): Lynas
Lieu du crime, Le / *The scene of the crime* (FR 86): Giraudi
Lieutenant Pie's Love Story (GB 13): Desmond
Life at the Top (GB 65): Newport
Life Begins at Forty (US 35): Watson Bl., Bs., D., G.
Life Begins for Andy Hardy (US 41): Winkler
Life Begins with Love (US 37): Beckett
Life Hesitates at Forty (US 36): Switzer
Life in Danger (GB 59): Witty
Life in Emergency Ward 10 (GB 58): Witty
Life of an Actress, The (US 27): Nelson B.
Life of Emile Zola, The (US 37): Moore D.
Life of Jimmy Dolan, The (US 33): Rooney, Durand, Hoskins
Life of Riley, The (US 49): Rees, Sydes
Life Returns (US 35): Breakston, Bupp T.
Life with Blondie (US 46): Simms L., Larson
Life with Father (US 47): Calkins
Lightning Lariats (US 27): Darro
Lightning Swords of Death (71 JP) – *see* Kozure ohkami
Lightning Warrior, The (US 31, srl): Darro
Lights of Old Broadway (US 25): Black B.

Maciré and Alikaou Kanté in Nyamanton

Sasha Karamiltsev

Michael Kebschull

Dicky Lupino

Angelo Maggio

Hardy Krüger in Junge Adler

Lights o' London (GB 22): Brantford
Light That Failed, The (US 23): Miller W.
Light That Failed, The (US 39): Sinclair
Light Within, The (US 18): Verdi
Lijden van de scheepsjongen, Het / *The cabin-boy's torment*
    (NL/FR 12): Mathieu
Like Babes in the Wood (US 17): Griffith
Like Father, Like Son (US 87): Astin S.
Likely Story, A (US 47): Rees
Lillebror och jag / *Me and my kid brother* (SE 40): Dalunde
Lille Napoleon / *Little Napoleon* (SE 43): Hjelm
Lille Teddy / *Little Teddy* (DK 14): Schønberg
Lille virtuos, Den / *The little virtuoso* (DK 17): Jensen S.C.
Lillian's Dilemma (US 14): Kelly P.
'Lilliput' series (IT 19-21): 'Arnold' and 'Patatà'
Lily Christine (US 32): Bartholomew
Lily in Winter (US 94): Bonsall
Limelight (US 51): Chaplin
Limpy (32 US) – *see* When a Feller Needs a Friend
'Lincoln' cycle (US 17): Monahan, Jackson C.
Lincoln County Incident (NZ 80): Simms S.
Lincoln in the White House (US 39): Moore D.
Linda (GB 60): Palmer
Linden von Lautenbach, Die / *The lime-trees of Lautenbach*
    (DE 85): Bleger
Line of Destiny, The (56 LK) – *see* Rekava
Links der Isar - rechts der Spree / *Iser on the left, Spree on the right*
    (GE 40): Schmidhofer
Lin McLean (18 US) – *see* Woman's Fool
Lionheart (GB 68): Forlong
Lion, the Witch and the Wardrobe, The (GB 78): Barnes N.
Listen, Darling (US 38): Bartholomew, Beckett
Liszt (70 HU/SU) – *see* Szerelmi álmok
Little Adventurer, The (GB 72): Lester
Little American, The (US 17): Alexander B.
Little Annie Rooney (US 25): Butterworth J., O'Donnell,
    House N., Jackson E., Rudolph
Little Ark, The (US 71): Frame
Little Artist of the Market, The (US 12): Boss, Tansey R.
Little Belgian, The (17 US) – *see* Little Orphan
Little Billy's City Cousin (US 14): Griffith, Jacobs
Little Billy's School Days (US 16): Jacobs
Little Billy's Strategy (US 14): Griffith, Jacobs
Little Billy's Triumph (US 14): Griffith, Jacobs
Little Bit of Heaven, A (US 40): Bond T., Brown K., Lenhart
Little Boy Blue (US 12): Hackett R., Johnson R.
Little Boy Blue (US 36): Beckett
Little Boy Bountiful (GB 14): Desmond
Little Boy Lost (US 52): Fourcade
Little Breeches (US 14): Carr T.
Little Bride of Heaven, The (US 12): Tannura
Little Brother (US 16): Berlinger
Little Brownie's Bravery (US 16): Coffey C.
Little Buckaroo, The (US 28): Barton
Little Bugler, The (US 14): Harris B.
Little Buster (US 13): Golden
Little Captain, The (US 14): Connelly

Little Captain of the Scouts, The (US 15): Benham
Little Captive, The (US 14, 'Sonny Jim'): Connelly
Little Chevalier, The (US 17): Verdi
Little Church Around the Corner (US 23): Miller W.
Little Clown, The (US 21): Coffey C.
Little Cripple, The (US 11): Butterworth E.
Little Cupids, The (US 15): Stone
Little Daddy (US 31): 'Our Gang'
Little Darling, The (US 09): Harron
Little Delicatessen Store, The (US 12): Boss
Little Dick's First Case (US 15): Perl, Stone
Little Diplomat, The (US 19): Morrison E.
Little Dragons (US 78): Petersen Chr. and P.
Little Dramas (58 PL) – *see* Male dramaty
Little Duchess, The (US 17): Tansey S.
Little Foxes, The (US 41): Hickman C.
Little Friend (GB 34): Green H.
Little Fugitive, The (US 53): Andrusco
Little Game, A (US 71): Gruner, Shea C.
Little Girl Next Door, The (US 11): Boss
Little Girl Shall Lead Them, A (GB 13): Barker K.
Little Guide from Tormes, The (59 ES) – *see* Lazarillo de Tormes
Little Hero, A (US 13): Clark R.
Little Indian Martyr, The (US 12): Clark R.
Little Iodine (US 46): Rees
Little Johnny Jones (US 23): O'Donnell
Little Jungle Boy (US/AU 70): Rahmin
Little Kaintuck (US 13): Willis
Little Kidnappers, The (53 GB) – *see* Kidnappers
Little Kidnappers, The (US 90): Miller C., Wheatley
Little Lad in Dixie, A (US 11): Casey
Little League Moochie (US c.58): Corcoran
Little Life Guard, The (US 15): Stone
Little Lord Fauntleroy (GB 14): Royston G.
Little Lord Fauntleroy (18 & 22 HU) – *see* Kis Lord
Little Lord Fauntleroy (US 21): Condon, Marion F.
Little Lord Fauntleroy (US 36): Bartholomew, Rooney, Searl
Little Lord Fauntleroy (GB 80): Schroder
Little Lumberjack, The (US 15): Willis
Little Man Tate (US 91): Hann-Byrd
Little Man, What Now? (US 34): Haines
Little Mariana's Triumph (US 17): Lee F.
Little Matchmakers, The (US 15): Willis
Little Men (US 34): Alexander T., Bupp T., Cosbey, Durand,
    Ernest, Jones D., Moore D., Phelps
Little Men (US 40): McKim S., Nichols
Little Mickey Grogan (US 27): Darro
Little Minister, The (GB 15): Willmore
Little Minister, The (US 21): Daniels M.
Little Minister, The (US 34): Watson Bl.
Little Miss Big (US 46): Infuhr
Little Miss No-Account (US 18): Carr S.
Little Miss Nobody (US 36): Watson D.
Little Miss Pinkerton (US 43): 'Our Gang'
Little Mister Jim (US 46): Jenkins
Little Monsters (US 88): Savage F.
Little Mother (US 29): 'Our Gang'

Little Nell's Tobacco (US 11): Pickford
Little Old New York (US 23): Watson H.
Little Orphan, The (US 17): House C., Hupp
Little Orphan Annie (US 32): Moore D., Phelps
Little Orphan Annie (US 38): Bupp T.
Little Orphans, The (US 15): Goodwin
Little Orphant Annie (US 18): Alexander B., Jacobs B.
Little Orvie (US 40): Sheffield B., Bupp S.
Little Pal (29 US) – see Say It With Songs
Little Papa (US 35): 'Our Gang'
Little Patriot, The (US 17): Morrison E.
Little Pirate, The (US 17): Hamrick
Little Prince, The (67 SU) – see Malenki prints
Little Prince, The (US 74): Warner S.
Little Ranger, The (US 38): 'Our Gang'
Little Red Schoolhouse, The (US 36): Moore D.
Little Robinson Crusoe (US 24): Coogan J., Butterworth J.
Little Roughneck (18 US) – see Nine Tenths of the Law
Little Savage, The (US 29): Barton
Little Savage, The (US 59): Rangno
Little School Ma'am, The (US 16): Carpenter, Stone
Little Sheriff, The (US 14): Harris B.
Little Shoes (US 17): Paul J.
Little Shots (US 83): Kiger
Little Sinner (US 35): 'Our Gang'
Little Soldier Man, The (US 15): Fuehrer, Willis
Little Spy, The (US 11): Casey
Littlest Angel, The (US 71): Whitaker
Little Stephen (GB 21): Dear
Littlest Outlaw, The (US 54): Velasquez A.
Little Strategist, The (US 17): Blackton
Little Straw Wife, The (US 15): Paul J.
Littlest Scout, The (US 18): Blackton, Carr S.
Littlest Sergeant, The (GB c.57): Hannaford
Little Sunset (US 15): Griffith
Little Tokyo, USA (US 42): Tucker T.
Little Tough Guy (US 38): Billings G., Phelps
Little Tough Guys in Society (US 38): Thomas F.
Little Willie's Adventures with a Tramp (GB 10): Sanders
Little Willie's Apprenticeships (GB 13): Royston R.
Live and Learn (US 20): Morrison E.
Live and Learn (US 30): Durand
Livet går vidare /Life goes on (SE 41): Hjelm
Livets storme /Life's storms (DK 10): Crone
Live Wire, The (GB 37): Singer
Living Heroes (59 SU) – see Zhiviye geroyi
Lizzie's Watery Grave (US 15): Jacobs
Ljubav /Love (YU 63): Cosić
Lloyds of London (US 36): Bartholomew, Scott D.
Lluvia roja /Red rain (MX 49): Calpe
Locked Doors (US 24): Billings E.
Lockende Gefahr /Danger beckons (DE 51): Lödel
Locos vecinos del segundo, Los /The deputy's crazy neighbours
   (ES 80): Sanz
Locsolókocsi, A /The water-truck (HU 74): Márkus, Lengyel, Szücs
Lodge Night (US 23): 'Our Gang'
Loin du foyer /Far from home (FR 20): Haziza

Lois Gibbs and the Love Canal (US 82): Astin M., Licht
Lola Casanova (MX 49): Jiménez Pons J.
London Bobby, A (US 20): Morrison E.
London Melody (GB 37): Snelling
Lone Climber, The (GB 49): Friedl
Lone Cowboy (US 33): Cooper Ja.
Lone Hand (US 53): Hunt
Lone Hand Saunders (US 26): Butts
Loneliest Runner, The (US 76): Kerwin
Loneliness of the Long Distance Runner, The (GB 62): Hammond
Lonely Heart Bandits (US 50): Crawford J.
Lonelyhearts (US 58): Washbrook
Lonely Road, The (GB 36): Pavitt
Lone Ranger, The (US 38, srl): McKim S.
Lone Scout, The (GB 29): Chant
Lonesome Trailer, The (US 36): Albright
Lone Star Ranger, The (US 23): Carpenter
Lone Star Ranger, The (US 29): Butts, Watson D.
Lone Texas Ranger (US 45): Blake, Olsen L.J.
Lone White Sail, The (38 SU) – see Beleyet parus odinoki
Lone Wolf, The (US 17): Beck C.
Long Arm, The (GB 56): Brooke, Hines
Long Day Closes, The (GB 92): McCormack
Long Days of Summer, The (US 80): Scribner
Longest Night, The (US 36): Bupp T.
Long Good Friday, The (GB 79): Fletcher
Long, Hot Summer, The (US 58): Rangno
Longing for a Mother (US 13): Hackett R.
Long John Silver (AU 54): Taylor
Long Live the King (US 23): Coogan J., Lee Ra.
Long, Long Trailer, The (US 54): Charney, Herbert, Olsen C.
Long Memory, The (GB 52): Beeny
Long Odds (GB 22): Thompson M.
Long Pants (US 27): Darro, Noisom
Long Ride, The (US/HU 83): Reno
Long Time Gone (US 84): Wheaton
Long Way Home, A (US 81): Wheaton
Looking for Trouble (US 19): Morrison E.
Looking on the Bright Side (GB 32): Singer
Loosened Plank, The (GB 14): Royston R.
Lord Babs (GB 32): Singer
Lord Jeff (US 38): Bartholomew, Daniel, Kilburn, Lawford
Lord Loves the Irish, The (US 20): Butterworth E.
Lord of the Flies (GB 61): Aubrey, Edwards H., Gaman,
   Chapin T., Hammond N.
Lord of the Flies (US 89): Getty
Lorna Doone (GB 34): Penrose
Lorna Doone (US 51): Lindgren O., Mickelsen
Los Alamos (US 51): Aaker L.
Los que no deben nacer /Those who should not be born (MX 53): Calpe
Los que volvieron /Those who will return (MX 46): Calpe
Lost (US 33): Cooper Ja.
Lost, a C(r)ook (US 17): Jacobs
Lost Angel (US 43): Blake, Driscoll
Lost at Sea (US 26): Schaeffer
Lost Boys, The (GB 78): Buss, Holm, Spurrier
Lost Boys, The (US 87): Haim

Lost Flight (US 70): Wixted
Lost Hearts (GB 73): Gipps-Kent
Lost Honeymoon (US 47): Severn Wn.
'Lost in Space' (US 65-68, TVS): Mumy
Lost in the Desert (70 ZA) – see Dirkie
Lost in the Studio (US 14): Jacobs
Lost in the Wild (76 AU) – see Barney
Lost in Transit (US 17): Beban
Lost Jungle, The (US 33): Rooney
Lost Lambs (36 CN) – see Mitu de gaoyang
Lost Necklace, The (US 11): Pickford
Lost Romance, The (US 21): Moore M.
Lost Volcano, The (US 50): Ivo
Lost World, The (US 25): Murphy J.
Loterie du bonheur, La / The lottery of happiness (FR 52): Urbain
Lotus Eater, The (US 21): Barry W.
Loud Speaker, The (US 35): Bailey Sd.
Louisa (US 50): Hunt
Louisiana Story (US 48): Boudreaux
Loupiote, La / The wee girl (FR 36): Grave
Loups dans la bergerie, Les / Wolves in the sheepfold (FR 59): Moullières
Love (US 27): DeLacy
Love Affair (US 39): Beckett, Nichols
Love among the Geysers (US 12): Rothermel
Love and Death (US 75): Lutter
Love and Lions (US 25): Janney
Love and the Frenchwoman (60 FR) – see Française et l'amour
Love at Second Sight (GB 34): Singer
Love Before Ten (US 13): Clark R.
Love Birds (US 34): Rooney
Love Boat (US 79) : Scribner
Love Bug, The (US 25): 'Our Gang'
Love Business (US 31): 'Our Gang'
Love Finds Andy Hardy (US 38): Reynolds
Love-Friend (14 US) – see Twenty Minutes of Love
Love, Honor and Behave (US 38): Moore D., Bupp T.
Love in a Bungalow (US 37): Tucker J.
Love in the Dark (US 22): Guerin
Love Is a Racket (US 32): Ernest
Love Is News (US 37): Kibrick L., Watson H.
Love Is On the Air (US 37): Billings G., Bupp S. and T., Jones D., Tucker J.
Love Letters (US 45): Binyon
Love Light, The (US 21): Condon
Love, Live and Laugh (US 29): Watson Bl., C., G. and H., Winslow D.
Love Makes 'Em Wild (US 27): Watson C.
Love My Dog (US 27): 'Our Gang'
Love Net, The (US 18): Jackson C.
Love on a Budget (US 38): Mahan
Love on the Run (US 36): Downing R., Watson Bs.
Love on the Spot (GB 32): Singer
Love on Toast (US 37): Bupp S.
Love on Wheels (GB 32): Blomfield
Love Piker, The (US 23): Miller W.
Lover of Camille, The (US 24): Moore P.
Lovers Courageous (US 32): Searl
Lover's Lane (US 24): Guerin

Love's Conquest (US 18): Verdi
Loves of Edgar Allan Poe, The (US 42): Mercer, Bupp S., Tyler L.
Love Special, The (US 21): Butterworth E.
Love's Sunset (US 13): Connelly
Love That Brute (US 50): Price, Hawkins
Love Thy Neighbor (US 84): Haas L.
Loyal Lives (US 23): Bennett M.
Lucas (US 86): Haim
Luce del mondo, Il / Light of the world (IT 35): Locchi
Luces de barriada / Lights of the quarter (MX 39): Ortin
Luck in Pawn (US 19): Moore P.
Luck of Geraldine Laird, The (US 20): Alexander B.
Luck of the Irish, The (US 19): Butterworth E., Messinger
Lucky (46 US) – see Boy, a Girl and a Dog
Lucky Cisco Kid (US 40): Sheffield J.
Lucky Corner, The (US 36): 'Our Gang'
Lucky Devils (US 41): Winkler
Lucky Dog (US 12): Boss
Lucky Gold Piece, A (US 16): Tansey S.
Lucky Nick Cain (50 GB) – see I'll Get You For This
Lucky Star, The (CA 80): Marx
Ludwig from Germany (US 12): Tansey R.
Luffaren och Rasmus / The tramp and Rasmus (SE 55): Dalenius
Lügen auf Rügen / Lies on Rügen (GE 31): Rive
Lugina e pushkatarëve / Valley of rifleman (AL 70): Prela
Luitenant, De / The lieutenant (BE 64): Tant
Lukáš / Luke (CS 82): Vychopeň
Luke Was There (US 76): Baio S.
Luk Isan / Man from Isan (TH 82): Jiradith
Lukrezia Borgia (GE 22): Lubinsky
Lulëkuqet mbi mure / Poppies on the walls (AL 76): Arifi, Zhegu
Lumë drite / Flood of light (AL 75): Çelia
Lumikuningatar / The Snow Queen (FI 86): Kaatrasalo
'Lümmel von der ersten Bank' series (DE 67-71): 'Heintje'
Lummox (US 30): Moore D.
Luna, La / The moon (IT 79): Barry M.
Lure of Luxury, The (US 18): Hupp
Lure of the Jungle, The (59 DK) – see Paw
Lure of the Wild, The (US 25): Jones B.
Lust for Life (US 56): Sydes
Lustigen Vier von der Tankstelle, Die / The jolly foursome from the gas station (DE 72): Doff
Lustrakos, O / The little boot-black (GR 62): Kailas
Luther (GE 27): Stark-Gstettenbaur
Lütt Matten und die weisse Muschel / Lütt Matten and the white shell (DD 63): Bosselmann
Luz en mi camino, Una / A light on my way (MX 38): Busquets
Lyagavi / The sneak (SU 30): Litkin, Simanovich
Lyatif (SU 30): Safarov
Lyckliga Vestköping / Lucky Vestköping (SE 37): Hallberg
Lydia (US 41): Larson, Roy
Lykken / Fortune (DK 16): Schønberg
Lyuboi tsenoi / Money no object (SU 59): Siluyanov
Lyubovna terapiya / Love therapy (BG 87): Voronov
Lyuti / The fierce one (SU 73): Valiyev

Maa baap / The parents (IN 60): Kapoor Ro.

476

Maa da ladla / *Mother's darling* (IN 73): Mehmood
Maa ka pyar / *Mother's love* (IN 49): Kumar
Ma and Pa Kettle (US 49): Arglen, Belding, Infuhr
Ma and Pa Kettle at Home (US 54): Arglen, Eyer Ri., McDonald
Ma and Pa Kettle at the Fair (US 51): Arglen, Belding, Infuhr
Ma and Pa Kettle Back on the Farm (US 51): Belding, Infuhr
Ma and Pa Kettle Go to Town (US 49): Arglen, Belding, Infuhr
Macbeth (US 16): Alexander B., Carpenter, Marion F.
Macbeth (GB 71): Dightam
McCluskey Strikes a Blow (54 US) ′ – *see* Rocket Man
Machekha / *The stepmother* (SU 58): Mirzoyev
Machi no hanauri musume / *The flower girl* (JP 39): Sugawara
Machi no rumpen / *Tramp in the street* (JP 31): 'Tokkan-Kozo'
Maciste contro la morte / *Maciste versus death* (IT 20): Allen W.
Maciste nelle miniere di Re Salomone / *Maciste in King Solomon's mines* (IT 64): Loddi
Mackintosh and T.J. (US 75): O'Brien C.
Macko ur kalandjai / *Adventures of Mr Teddy* (HU 20): Hegedüs
Maclovia (MX 48): Perez
Macon County Line (US 73): Garrett
Mad About Music (US 38): Moran, Peck
Madam Bavri (PK 89): Jamshid
Madame Bovary (US 49): Simms L., Infuhr
Madame Curie (US 43): Infuhr
Madame Rosa (77 FR) – *see* Vie devant soi
Madame X (US 20): Moore P.
Madame X (US 29): Cosbey, Moore D., Scott D.
Madame X (US 37): Moore D., Reynolds
Madame X (US 65): Quinn T.
Mädchen mit Zukunft / *Girl with a future* (DE 54): Jansen
Mädchenpensionat / *Girls' boarding school* (AT 36): Rohringer
Mädel aus dem Böhmerwald / *The girl from the Bohemian forest* (DE 65): Hehn
Madeleine (GB 49): Barr
Mädels von heute / *Young girls today* (GE 33): Klicks
Mademoiselle (52 US) – *see* Story of Three Loves
Mademoiselle (GB/FR 66): Skinner
Mademoiselle de Paris (FR 55): Chapeland
Mademoiselle Parley-Voo (GB 28): Ashby J.
Mademoiselle s'amuse / *The young lady has fun* (FR 48): Gencel
Mad Genius, The (US 31): Darro
Madla zpívá Evropě / *The young lady sings for Europe* (CS 40): Jedlička A. and V.
Mad Max Beyond Thunderdome (AU 85): Kounnas
Mad Max 2 (AU 81): Minty
Madre querida / *Darling mother* (MX 35): Zamora
Madre querida (MX 50): Calpe, Moreno
Mad Woman, The (US 19): Grauer
Maestro, Il / *The schoolmaster* (IT/ES 57): Nevola, Paoletti
Magdanas lurdzha / *Magdana's donkey* (SU 55): Daneliya
Maggie, The (GB 53): Kearins
Magic Box, The (GB 51): Charlesworth, Davies J.H.
Magic Extinguisher, The (GB 01): Williamson C.
Magic Garden, The (US 27): DeLacy, Wilkinson
Magic Glass, The (GB 14): Desmond
Magic Lamp, The (US 57): Kasday
Magic Marble, The (GB 51): Hannaford

Magic of Lassie, The (US 78): Sharrett
Magic Town (US 47): Anderson B., Kuhn, Mummert
Magistrarna på sommarlov / *Masters on summer vacation* (SE 41): Hjelm
Magnas Miska / *Mickey the magnate* (HU 48): Horváth
Magnet, The (GB 50): Fox W., Brooke, Secretan
Magnificent Ambersons, The (25 US) – *see* Pampered Youth
Magnificent Brute, The (US 36): Burrud
Magnificent Rebel, The (US/DE 60): Grimm
Magnificent Seven, The (US 60): Bravo D.
Magnificent 6½, The (GB 68): Ellis I.
Magnificent 6½, The: second series (GB 69): Ellis I.
Magyarenfürstin, Die / *The Magyar princess* (GE 23): Herzberg
Maha bhakta tukaram (IN 74): Ramu
Mahakavi girish chandra (IN 56): Bhattacharjee
Mahapuja (IN 54): Kapoor S.
Maharajahens yndlingshustru / *The maharajah's favourite wife* (DK 17): Heimann
Mahovina na asfaltu / *Moss on the asphalt* (YU 83): Roganović
Maid of Salem (US 37): Bartlett
Maid's Night Out (US 38): Tucker J.
Mail and Female (US 37): 'Our Gang', Winkler
Main Street (US 23): Griffith, O'Donnell
Maison de mystère, La / *The house of mystery* (FR 22): Haziza
Maison des bois, La / *The house in the woods* (FR/IT 71): Tarrazon
Maison des Bories, La / *The house of the Bories* (FR 69): Maurin J.-F.
Maison du mystère, La / *House of mystery* (FR 35): Pâqui
Maja zwischen zwei Ehen / *Maja between two marriages* (GE 38): Dann
Majboor / *Helpless* (IN 74): Alankar
Majestät auf Abwegen / *His Majesty goes astray* (DE 58): Grimm, Ande, Hoffmann
Majhli didi / *Middle sister* (IN 67): Sachin
Major and the Minor, The (US 42): Cook B., Dawson, Jones D., Nunn, Roy
Maj på Malö / *May on Malö* (SE 47): Carlsson
Make a Wish (US 37): Breen, Bupp T., Lee B.
Make Me an Offer! (GB 54): O'Sullivan
Make Mine Mink (GB 60): Hammond
Make Way for Tomorrow (US 37): Bupp T.
Making a Convert (US 14): Clark A.
Making of an American, The (US 12): Benham
Makin' Movies (US 22): Jones J.
Maksimka / *Young Maxim* (SU 52): Bobikin
Malachi's Cove (GB 73): Bradley
Mälarpiraten / *The pirate of Lake Mälar* (SE 59): Bolme
Mälarpirater / *Pirates of Lake Mälar* (SE 23): Christiansen
Malchiki / *Boys* (SU 59): Babich, Chursin, Marchenko
Malchik i golub / *The boy and the dove* (SU 62): Burlyayev K.
Malchik iz tabora / *Boy from the gypsy camp* (SU 29): Lyudvinski
Malchik s konkami / *Boy with the skates* (SU 62): Selyuzhenok
Malchik s okraini / *Boy from the outskirts* (SU 47): Ganichev, Sokoloff Sa.
Malchishki / *Kids* (SU 69): Zhukov
Malditas sean las mujeres / *A curse on all women* (MX 36): Ortin
Male and Female (US 19): Barry W.
Male dramaty / *Little dramas* (PL 58): Rzegocki, Wiśniewski
Malenki beglets / *The little runaway* (SU/JP 67): Inayoshi

Malenki prints / *The little prince* (SU 67): Mikaliunas

Malenki serzhant / *The little sergeant* (SU 76): Klimenkov

Malenkiye ritsari / *Little knights* (SU 63): Georgadze

Malhar (IN 51): Kumar

Malheurs de Sophie, Les / *The misfortunes of Sophie* (FR 45): Demorget, Emrich

Mali čovek / *Little man* (YU 57): Ruben

Malí medvědáři / *Little bear-keepers* (CS 57): Rosenberg V., Kříž, Postránecký, Bejval

Mali vojnici / *Little soldiers* (YU 67): Cesar

Malvado Carabel, El / *The wicked Carabel* (ES 34): Ripoll

Malvaloca (ES 26): Hurtado

Malý Bobeš / *Little Bobby* (CS 61): Lukeš, Hádl

Malý Bobeš ve městě / *Little Bobby goes to town* (CS 62): Lukeš, Hádl

Malý partyzán / *The little partisan* (CS 50): Šlosar, Bejval

Mama, nizai nali / *Where are you now, Mother?* (CN 82): Yang

Mama Runs Wild (US 37): McKim S.

Mama's Little Pirate (US 34): 'Our Gang'

Mamba (US 29): Beard, Frederick

Mame (US 74): Furlong K.

Mamlyuk / *The mameluke* (SU 58): Daneliya

Mammy's Chile (US 13): Roubert

Mamta / *Maternal love* (IN 77): Rajoo

Man Afraid (US 57): Hovey, Bernard

Man and Boy (US 71): Spell G.

Man and Maid (US 25): Miller W.

Man Behind the Curtain, The (US 16): Connelly

Man Between, The (GB 52): Krause

Man Called Horse, A (US 70): Padilla

Man Called Peter, A (US 55): Chapin B., Cook C., Kelman, Pike J., Severn Wn.

Manchara (IN 54): Mohan

Mandolinata a mare / *Mandolin concert at sea* (IT 17): Notari

Mandrake the Magician (US 39): Downing R.

Manewry miłosne / *Amorous manoeuvres* (PL 34): Kudla

Man from Blankley's, The (GB 30): Henderson D.

Man from Down Under, The (US 43): Severn Chr. and E.

Man from Fleet Street, The (40 US) — *see* Dispatch from Reuters

Man from God's Country (US 58): Charney

Man from Hell, The (US 34): Bupp T.

Man from Montana, The (US 41): Brown K., Lenhart

Man from Red Gulch, The (US 25): Moore M.

Man from the Alamo, The (US 53): Cavell

Man from Yesterday, The (US 32): Cosbey

Mang günü / *The blind orphan girl* (CN 25): Zheng

Manhattan Melodrama (US 34): Butler, Rooney, Haines

Manhattan Parade (US 32): Moore D.

Man He Might Have Been, The (US 16): Harris B.

Man Hunt (US 36): Ernest

Man Hunt (US 41): McDowall

Man I Love, The (US 29): Scott D.

Man I Married, The (US 40): Russell J.

Man I Marry, The (US 36): Cosbey

Man in Blue, The (US 25): Morgan

Man in Blue, The (US 37): Burrud, Watson D, Winkler

Man in Half Moon Street, The (US 44): Sheffield J.

Man Inside, The (GB 58): Moulder-Brown

Man in the Net, The (US 59): Herbert, McGreevey, Perry

Man in the Santa Claus Suit, The (US 79): Petersen P., Gower

Manitharil manickam / *Jewel among men* (IN 73): Ramu

Manly Man, A (US 11): Pickford

Man met het zwarte masker, De / *The man in the black mask* (NL 66): Consten

Männer müssen so sein / *That's how men have to be* (GE 39): Eugens

Mann im Strom, Der / *Man in the river* (DE 58): Kaiser

Mano dello straniero, La / *The stranger's hand* (IT/GB 53): O'Sullivan

Manoel na ilha das maravilhas (85 FR/PT) — *see* Destins de Manoel

Man of Aran (GB 34): Dillane

Man of a Thousand Faces (US 57): Sorensen

Man of Iron (55 IT) — *see* Ferroviere

Man of Letters (GB 84): Cox A.

Man of Nerve, A (US 25): Holmes L.

Man of the Moment (GB 55): Beeny

Manohara / *Winner of hearts* (IN 54): Mohan

Man on Fire (US 57): Brodrick

Man on the Outside (US 75): Montgomery

Man on the Rock, The (US 38): Downing R.

Man on the Train, The (51 US) — *see* Tall Target

Man or Mouse (US 42): Switzer

Manpower (US 41): Caldwell

Man's Awakening, A (US 13): Roubert

Man's Best Friend (US 35): Haig

Man's Castle (US 33): Moore D., McComas, Watson H.

Manslaughter (US 22): Moore M.

Man sollte es nicht für möglich halten / *You wouldn't believe it possible* (GE 22): Allen W.

Man That Might Have Been, The (US 14): Kelly P.

Man That Never Smiled, The (US 25): Black B.

Man the Army Made, The (GB 17): Brantford

Man to Beat Jack Johnson, The (GB 10): Sanders

Man to Man Talk (58 FR/IT) — *see* Premier mai

Man to Remember, A (US 38): Jones D.

Man Under the Bed, The (US 12): Casey

Man Who Came Back, The (US 24): Wilkinson

Man Who Changed His Name, The (GB 34): Penrose

Man Who Dared, The (US 39): Jones D., Russell J.

Man Who Fell to Earth, The (US 86): Wheaton

Man Who Found Himself, The (US 25): Griffin

Man Who Haunted Himself, The (GB 70): Mackenzie

Man Who Knew Too Much, The (US 55): Olsen C.

Man Who Played God, The (US 22): Bennett M.

Man Who Smiled, The (US 24): Guerin

Man Who Vanished, The (US 15): Boss

Man Who Wagged His Tail, The (57 ES/IT) — *see* Angel paso por Brooklyn

Man Who Won, The (US 23): McBan

Man Without a Conscience, The (US 25): Rudolph, Schaeffer

Man Without a Face, The (US 93): Stahl

Man, Woman and Child (US 82): Dungan, Jacoby Bl.

Ma petite marquise / *My little marchioness* (FR 37): Buquet, Rodon

Marakatumba, ma non e una rumba / *Marakatumba, never a rumba* (IT 49): Staiola

Marauders, The (US 55): Kasday

Mar brava / *Angry sea* (ES 81): Sanz

Marcelino, pan y vino / *Bread-and-wine Marcelino* (ES 55): Calvo

Märchenschloss, Das / *The fairy-tale castle* (DD 61): Bosselmann

Marching On (US 29): Madden

Marcia o crepa / *March or die* (IT/DE/ES/BE 62): Alonso P.

Marechiaro (IT 49): Staiola

Mare Nostrum (US 26): Brantford

Margi (83 BG) — *see* Za edna troika

Margie (US 40): Collins

Maria (SE 47): Olsson

Maria Chapdelaine (FR 34): Genevois

Maria, die Magd / *Maria the maid* (GE 36): Eugens, Kieling

Marianne (US 29): Scott D., Winslow D.

Marianne (54 FR/DE) — *see* Marianne de ma jeunesse

Marianne de ma jeunesse / *Marianne of my youth* (FR/DE 54): Ande, Brandt

Maria på Kvarngården / *Maria at Kvarngård* (SE 45): Nyström

Maria Walewska (37 US) — *see* Conquest

Marie Antoinette (US 38): Beckett

Marie du port, La / *Mary of the port* (FR 49): Fourcade

Marie-Louise (CH 43): Ammon

Marina (MX 45): Pastor

Marines Are Here, The (US 38): Cosbey

Marinier, Le / *The seaman* (FR 50): Gencel

Marions-nous / *Let's get married* (FR 31): Mercanton

Marito in condominio, Un / *Husband as joint owner* (IT 63): Nevola

Marked Money (US 28): Coghlan

Mark of Zorro, The (US 20): Berlinger

Marquise von Pompadour, Die / *The Marquise of Pompadour* (GE 30): Stark-Gstettenbaur

Marriage Is a Private Affair (US 44): Chapin B.

'Marriage License?' (US 26): Brantford

Marriage Morals (US 23): Bennett M., Griffin

Marriage Playground, The (US 29): DeLacy

Married Before Breakfast (US 37): Bond T.

Married Life (US 20): Marion D.

Marrying Kind, The (US 52): Curtis, Olsen C.

Marry the Girl (US 28): Frederick

Marry the Girl (GB 35): Singer

Marschall Vorwärts / *Marshal Forwards* (GE 32): Klicks

Marshal of Cripple Creek (US 47): Blake

Marshal of Laredo (US 45): Blake

Marshal of Reno (US 44): Blake

Martha's Vindication (US 16): Carpenter, Stone

Martijn en de magier / *Martin and the magician* (NL 79): Gabriëlse

Martin's Day (CA 84): Henry J.

Martir del Calvario, El / *The martyr of Calvary* (MX 52): Mejía, Calpe

Maruja (PH 67): Ilagan

Marya - iskussnitsa / *Mary the nimble weaver* (SU 59): Perevalov

Mary from America (US 17): Marion F.

Maryland (US 40): Anderson B., Jones D.

Mary Lou (GE 28): Burns B.

Mary of Scotland (US 36): Watson Bs.

Mary Poppins (US 64): Garber

Mary, Queen of Tots (US 25): 'Our Gang'

Marys grosses Geheimnis / *Mary's big secret* (GE/IT/FR 28): Machin

Mary Stevens, M.D. (US 33): Holt D.

Marzy nel vasto mondo / *Marzy in the great wide world* (IT 17): Casarotti

Mas alla de Rio Mino / *Beyond the River Mino* (ES 69): del Arco

Mashiroki Fuji no ne / *The white peak of Fuji* (JP 35): Hayama

Mask, The (US 21): Moore M.

Masked Raiders (US 49): Gray G.

Mason of the Mounted (US 32): Shuford

Masoom gawah (PK 88): Jamshid

Masquerade (GB 64): Witty

Masquerade Bandit, The (US 26): Darro

Massacre Hill (49 GB) — *see* Eureka Stockade

Massarati and the Brain (US 83): Billingsley

Mastana / *The carefree one* (IN 54): Kapoor Ro.

Mästerdetektiven Blomkvist / *Master-detective Blomkvist* (SE 47): Carlsson

Mästerdetektiven lever farligt / *The master-detective lives dangerously* (SE 57): Nilsson

Mästerdetektiven och Rasmus / *The master-detective and Rasmus* (SE 53): Dalenius, Dam

Master Race, The (US 44): Rodin M.

Máte doma lva? / *Do you have a lion at home?* (CS 63): Filip J., Očenášek

Mateo Falcone (FR 28): Roudenko

Mater amatisima / *Beloved mother* (ES 80): de la Cruz

Maternelle, La / *The nursery school* (FR 48): Fourcade, Gencel

Maternité / *Motherhood* (FR 29): Gaillard

Matinee (US 93): Fenton

Mating, The (US 18): Carr S.

Mating Game, The (US 58): Losby

Mating of Marcus, The (GB 24): Brantford

Mating of Millie, The (US 48): Diamond, Hunt

Matlabi duniya / *The selfish world* (IN 36): Apte

Matrimonial Bed, The (US 30): Moore D.

Matter of Life and Death (US 81): Kiger

Maurice (GB 87): Wells

Mausi / *Mousie* (GE 34): Teetzmann

Max and Maurice (US 12): Boss

Maxie (AT 53): Feldt

Maya (US 65): North J., Khan

Mayakovski nachinalsa tak / *This is how Mayakovsky started* (SU 58): Chelidze

Maya machchindra (IN 32): Batto

Maya machchindra (IN 75): Satyajit

Maybe Moonshine (16 US) — *see* 'Ham and Bud' series

Mayor, The (US 19): Redden

Mayor of Filbert, The (US 19): Alexander B.

Mayor of Hell, The (US 33): Hoskins

Maytime (US 37): Watson D.

Mazhe bez rabota / *Men without work* (BG 73): Arshinkov

Me (68 FR) — *see* Enfance nue

Me and Bill (US 12): Clark R.

Meanest Man in the World, The (US 42): Binyon, Gray G.

Measure of a Man, The (US 24): Gordon Bo.

Meatballs (CA 79): Makepeace

Medal for the General, A (GB 44): Weske

Medalla del torero, La / *The bull-fighter's medal* (ES 24): Hurtado

Medbejlerens hævn / *The outcast's revenge* (DK 10): Petersen Cas.

Medianoche / *Midnight* (MX 48): Moreno, Perez

Medicine Man, The (US 30): Butts
Medico de las locas, El / The mad women's doctor (MX 44): Fernandez
Medico delle pazze, Il / The mad women's doctor (IT 19): Casarotti
Medium Cool (US 69): Blankenship
Meena (IN 44): Kapoor S.
Meet Doctor Christian (US 39): Moran
Meeting, Le / The meeting (FR 31): Bara, Mercanton
Meet John Doe (US 41): Bartlett
Meet Me at the Fair (US 52): Allen (Chet), Arglen
Meet Me in St Louis (US 44): Hickman Dl.
Meet the Chump (US 41): Spellman
Meet the Nelsons (51 US) — see Here Come the Nelsons
Meet the People (US 44): Blake
Meet the Prince (US 26): Holmes L.
Meet the Stewarts (US 42): Mummert
Megalo amartima, To / The great sin (GR 63): Kailas
Megalos orkos, O / The great oath (GR 65): Kailas
Megfagyott gyermek, A / The frozen child (HU 21): Szécsi
Meilleure part, La / The better part (FR/IT 55): Moullières
Meine Freundin Josefine / My friend Josephine (GE 42): Möller
Meine Herren Söhne / My worthy sons (DE 45): Moik, Neie
Meine Kinder und ich / My children and I (DE 55): Kaiser
Meine schöne Mama / My beautiful Mama (DE/AT 58): Czeike
Meine Tante - deine Tante / My aunt and yours (GE 27): Allen W.
Mein Herz ist eine Jazzband / My heart's a jazz band (GE 28): Burns B.
Mein Leben für Irland / My life for Ireland (GE 41): Rohringer
Mein Leopold / My Leopold (DE 55): Condrus
Mein Vater, der Schauspieler / My father the actor (DE 56): Grimm, Hoffmann
Meisje uit de bloemenvelden, Het / The girl from the tulip-fields (NL/BE/FR 14): Mertens
Mela / The fair (IN 71): Sachin
Mélo / Melodrama (FR 32): Bara
Melodie eterne / Timeless melodies (IT 40): Barbetti
Melodie immortale / Immortal melodies (IT 52): Di Nardo
Melodies Old and New (US 42): 'Our Gang'
Melodi om våren, En / A melody of spring (SE 43): Hjelm
Melody (70 GB) — see S.W.A.L.K.
Melody for Three (US 41): Tyler L.
Melody for Two (US 37): O'Connor
Melody Lane (US 41): Brown K., Lenhart
Melody of the Plains (US 37): Lenhart
Melody Time (US 48): Driscoll
Méltóságos kisasszony, A / The honorable young lady (HU 36): Dévényi
Member of the Wedding, The (US 52): DeWilde
Même route, La / The same way (FR 53): Maurin Y.-M.
Memoirs of a Survivor (GB 81): Fletcher
Memories Never Die (US 82): Billingsley
Memory (GB 14): Desmond
Memory Lane (US 26): Darro
Menace on the Mountain (US 72): Shea E., Vogel
Menaces / Threats (FR 39): François
Men Don't Leave (US 90): Korsmo
Mëngjeze lufte / Mornings of war (AL 71): Pojani
Ménilmontant (FR 36): Mouloudji, Rodon
Men in Fright (US 38): 'Our Gang', Bupp S.

Men in Her Diary (US 45): Gray G.
Menino de engenho / Skilled lad (BR 66): del Ney
Men of Boys Town (US 41): Hickman Dl., McKim H., Nunn, Watson Bs., Winkler
Men of Yesterday (GB 36): Hepworth H. and J.
Men on Call (US 30): Ernest
Menschen / Humans (GE 19): Pottier
Mensonges / Lies (FR 45): Demorget
Men Without Names (US 35): Holt D.
Men Without Women (US 29): Parrish
Men With Wings (US 38): Cook B., O'Connor, Reynolds
Menya zovut Kozha / My name is Kozha (SU 63): Segizbayev
Menzogna / Untruth (IT 52): Olivieri
Mercy Island (US 41): Kilburn
Mere bhaiya / My brother (IN 72): Satyajit
Mere lal / My son (IN 37): Marathe A. and R.
Meri awaz (PK 88): Jamshid
Merijntje Gijzen's jeugd / The youth of Merijntje Gijzen (NL 36): Krols
Merlusse / Codfish (FR 35): Dubrou
Merry Widow, The (US 25): Rudolph
Merry Wives of Windsor, The (GB 82): Whitlock
Merveilleuse histoire de Poly, La / The amazing story of Poly (FR 61): 'Mehdi'
Mes, Het / The knife (NL 61): van der Linden R.
Meseország / Fairyland (HU 22): Szécsi, Lázár
Mes petites amoureuses / My little loves (FR 75): Loeb
Message in the Bottle, The (US 11): Pickford
Messenger Boy, The (US 31): Billings G.
Metin (DE 79): Yüksel
Met liefde van Adele / Love from Adèle (ZA 77): Botha
Metropolitan (US 35): Watson D.
Meu pé de laranja lima, O / My beloved orange-tree (BR 70): Cruz J.C.
Mexicali Rose (US 39): Albright
Mexican Spitfire's Baby, The (US 41): Bates
Mezhdu dvamata / Between his parents (BG 66): Alurkov
Miami Story, The (US 54): Kasday
Miarka, la fille à l'ourse / Miarka and the she-bear (FR 20): Mercanton
Micha (IE/RS 92): Korkhin
Michael O'Halloran (US 23): Boardman
Michael O'Halloran (US 37): Moran, Downing R.
Michael O'Halloran (US 48): Beckett, Cook T.
Michigan Kid, The (US 28): Murphy M.
'Mickey McGuire' series (US 27-32): Rooney, Barty
Mickey the Kid (US 39): Beckett, Ryan
Micki + Maude (US 84): Kiger
Midnight Flyer, The (US 25): Darro, Billings E.
Midnight Kiss, The (US 26): Spear
Midnight Message, The (US 26): Fox J.
Midshipman Easy (GB 35): Green H., Tester
Midsummer Night's Dream, A (US 35): Rooney, Anger, Barty
Mi, dvoye muzhchin / We two men (SU 62): Korol
Między brzegami / Between the coasts (PL 62): Kondrat
Miel, Le / Honey (ES 79): Sanz
Mi esposa y la otra / My wife and the other woman (MX 51): Mejía
Mighty Lak a Goat (US 42): 'Our Gang'
Mighty McGurk, The (US 46): Stockwell

Mighty Moose and the Quarterback Kid (US 76): Cruz B.

Mignon è partita /Mignon has left (IT/FR 88): Ruta

Migove v kibritena kutiika /Moments in a matchbox (BG 78): Vasilev Vl.

Miguelin (ES 64): Hidalgo

Mikado, The (US 17): Carpenter, Messinger

Mikaeri no tou /The tower of introspection (JP 41): Yokoyama

Mikazuki doji /Child of the crescent moon (JP 54): Yamate

Mike (US 26): Coghlan, Darro

'Mike' (GB 64, TVS): Gilmore

Mike Fright (US 34): 'Our Gang', Lee B.

Mike's Elopement (US 15): Goodwin

Mikolka, paravoz /Mikolka the locomotive (SU 56): Guskoff

Mikres Afrodites /Little Aphrodites (GR 62): Joannides

Milady o' the Beanstalk (US 18): Morrison E.

Milestones of Life (US 15): Benham

Military Academy (US 40): Holt D., Kelly T.

Millerson Case, The (US 47): Dennis

Millionærdrengen /The boy millionaire (DK 36): Mannu

Million dans un main d'enfant, Un /A million in a child's hand
  (FR 20): Touzé

Million Dollar Baby (US 34): Samarzich

Million Dollar Baby (US 41): Sheffield J.

Million Dollar Duck (US 71): Montgomery

Million Dollar Infield (US 82): Peluce

Million Dollar Legs (US 32): Moore D.

Million Dollar Legs (US 39): O'Connor

Million Dollar Mystery, The (US 14): Hauck

Millions in the Air (US 35): Bartlett

Mill on the Floss, The (GB 37): Gorst

Mindenki iskolaja /Everyone's school (HU 55): Koletár

Mind Where You're Going (GB 72): Fletcher, Pender

Miner Affair, A (US 45): Bates

Mine to Keep (US 23): Moore P. and M.

Mine tossede drenge /My crazy boys (DK 61): Schmidt J.P.

Mingea /The ball (RO 58): Bodianu

Mi niño, mi caballo y yo /My boy, my horse and me (MX 58):
  Quezadas

Miniver Story, The (US 50): Fox W., Roper

Min søsters børn /My sister's children (DK 66): Schmidt J.P.

Min søsters børn på bryllupsrejse /My sister's children
  on honeymoon (DK 67): Schmidt J.P.

Mio min Mio /Mio, my Mio (SE 87): Pickard, Bale

Miracle, The (US, c.70): Wixted

Miracle des loups, Le /Miracle of the wolves (FR 30): Gaillard

Miracle from Mars (52 US) −see Red Planet Mars

Miracle Makers, The (US 23): Headrick

Miracle Man, The (US 19): Lee F.

Miracle Man, The (US 32): Coogan R., Searl, Tucker J.

Miracle of Santa's White Reindeer, The (US 63): Holmes D.

Miracle of the Hills, The (US 59): North J.

Miracle on 34th Street (US 47): Hyatt, Norman, Sydes

Mirages (FR 37): Mouloudji

Miriam Rozella (GB 23): Craig

Mirko i Slavko /Mirko and Slavko (YU 74): Radenković, Radonjić

Mirror, The (74 SU) − see Zerkalo

Mirza sahiban (IN 39): Suresh

Miserabili, I (IT 47): Smordoni

Misérables, Les (18 US) − see Les Miserables

Misérables, Les /The poor and wretched (FR 25): Badiole

Misérables, Les (FR 33): Genevois

Misérables, Les (47 IT) − see Miserabili

Misérables, Les (52 US) − see Les Miserables

Misérables, Les (FR/IT 58): Fourcade

Misérables, Les (FR/PL 58): Urbain

Misérables, Les (FR/GB 78): Fletcher

Misérables, Les (FR 83): Curtil

Mishka protiv Yudenicha /Mishka versus Yudenich (SU 25): Zavalyoff

Mishka, Seryoga i ya /Mishka, Seryozha and me (SU 61): Semyonov Vi.

Mishka Zvonov (SU 25): Konstantinov

Miss Adventure (US 19): Sargent

Miss Catastrophe (FR 56): Urbain

Misses Finch and Their Nephew Billy, The (US 11): Casey

Miss Fane's Baby Is Stolen (US 34): Leroy, McFarland

Miss Gingersnap (US 19): Morrison E.

Missing Link, The (US 27): Janney, Jones B., Shuford

Missing Note, The (GB 61): Moulder-Brown, Scott H.

Missing the Tide (GB 18): Hopson

Missouri Traveler, The (US 57): DeWilde, Curtis

Miss Susie Slagle's (US 45): Driscoll

Mistake in Judgment, A (US 13): Boss

Mr Celebrity (US 41): Henry R.

Mr District Attorney (US 41): Cook T.

Mr Emmanuel (GB 44): Gainsborough, Mullins

Mr Hobbs Takes a Vacation (US 62): Burns M.

Misterio de las naranjas azules, El /Mystery of the blue oranges
  (ES 65): Sanchez

'Mr Jarr' series (US 15): Kelly P.

Mr Newcombe's Necktie (US 13): Boss, Clark A.

Mr Peabody and the Mermaid (US 48): Hyatt

Mr Perrin and Mr Traill (GB 48): Malone, Spenser D.

Mr Pickwick's Predicament (US 12): Boss

Mr President (US 87): Gower

Mister Scoutmaster (US 53): Winslow G., Hawkins, Infuhr,
  Lindgren O., Pollock

Mr Skeeter (GB 84): Wells

Mr Skitch (US 33): Albright

Mr Smith Carries On (GB 37): Singer

Mr Smith Goes to Washington (US 39): Jones D., Baker, Bupp T.,
  Hurlic, Infuhr, Larson, Russell J., Simms L., Watson Bl., D., G., H.

Misterul lui Herodot /The Herodotus mystery (RO 76): Orascu, Petruţ

Mr Up's Trip Tripped Up (US 12): Calvert B.

Mr Winkle Goes to War (US 44): Cook T., Donaldson T., Larson,
  McKim H.

Mr X (IN 38): Marathe A.

Mrs Miniver (US 42): Tucker T.

Mistress of His House (US 14): Clark R.

Mrs Soffel (US 84): Cross

Mrs Wiggs of the Cabbage Patch (US 34): Breakston, Butler

Mrs Wiggs of the Cabbage Patch (US 42): Lee B., Switzer

Misty (US 61): Ladd

Misunderstood (66 IT) − see Incompreso

Misunderstood (US 83): Thomas H., Fox H.

Mi tio Jacinto /My Uncle Jacinto (ES/IT 56): Calvo

Mitka Lelyuk (SU 38): Fesechko

Mitt hem är Copacabana /*My home is Copacabana* (SE 65): de Lima, dos Santos

Mitt liv som hund /*My life as a dog* (SE 85): Glanzelius

Mitu de gaoyang /*Stray kids* (CN 36): Ge

Miudo de bica, O /*The street kid* (PT 63): Gonçalves

Mi vas lyubim /*We love you* (SU 62): Barsov

Mixed Company (US 74): Olson

Mjølkens mirakler /*Miracles of milk* (SE 40): Olsson

Młody las /*Young wood* (PL 36): Kudla

Mniejsky szuka dużego /*Small seeks tall* (PL 76): Schmidt R.

Moan & Groan, Inc. (US 29): 'Our Gang'

Moarte lui Ipu (72 RO) − *see* Atunci i-am condamnat pe toti la moarte

Mob, The (28 US) − *see* Crowd, The

Mob Rule (US 36): Watson D.

Mob Town (US 41): Hickman Dl.

Moby Dick (US 30): Shuford

Moby Dick (US/GB 56): Alleney T.

Model, The (US 15): Casey

Moderato cantabile (FR/IT 60): Haudepin

Moderne landevejsridder, En /*An up-to-date tramp* (DK 17): Heimann

Modern Hero, A (US 34): Rentschler

Modern Prodigal, The (US 10): Pickford

Modiga mindra män /*Brave little men* (SE 67): Grönros

Modry autobus /*The blue bus* (CS 63): Lukeš

Mohammedan Conspiracy, A (US 14): Benham

Moi dom na zelyonikh kholmakh/*My home in the green hills* (SU 86): Dzhaksilikov

Mojave Firebrand, The (US 44): McKim H.

Moj stary /*My old man* (PL 61): Wiśniewski, Roman, Rzegocki

Moj tata na odredjeno vreme /*My part-time Daddy* (YU 82): Kojo

Mokey (US 42): Blake, Hickman C., Thomas W.

Molens die juichen en weenen, De /*The mills rejoice and weep* (NL/FR 12): Mathieu

Mole People, The (US 56): Charney

Møllen /*The mill* (DK 43): Steen-Hansen

Molly the Drummer Boy (US 14): Boss

Molodiye kapitani /*Young captains* (SU 39): Serchevski

Molti sogni per le strade /*Many dreams on the street* (IT 48): Leurini

Moments (AU 82): Minty

Moment to Moment (US 66): Robbins

Mondo nella mia tasca, Il /*The world in my pocket* (IT 59): Nevola

Moner mayur /*The restless heart* (IN 54): Babua

Moneta /*The coin* (SU 62): Mastrukoff

Money Grabbers, The (25 US) − *see* Wyoming Wildcat

Money Moon, The (GB 20): Craig

Money to Burn (US 20): Morrison E.

Money, Women and Guns (US 58): Hovey

Mon gosse (58 IT/FR) − *see* Totó e Marcelino

Monkey Business (US 26): 'Our Gang'

Monkey Business (US 31): Barty

Monkey Business (US 52): Aaker L., Mora, Winslow G.

Mon oncle /*My uncle* (FR/IT 58): Bécourt

Mon oncle Antoine /*My Uncle Antoine* (CA 71): Gagnon

Mon oncle Benjamin /*My Uncle Benjamin* (FR 23): Guichard

Mon père avait raison /*My father was right* (FR 36): Grave

Mon p'tit /*My kid* (FR 22): Guichard

Monsieur Albert (FR 32): Mercanton

Monsieur Beulemeester, garde civique /*M. Beulemeester, civil guard* (BE 13): Mertens

Monsieur Fabre (FR 51): Maurin Y.-M.

Monsieur Hawarden (BE/NL 68): Fischer

M. Leguignon lampiste /*Monsieur Leguignon the lamp-man* (FR 51): Gencel, Rob

Monsieur Papa /*Mr Daddy* (FR 77): Reboul

Monsieur Pipelet (FR 55): Maurin D.

Monsieur Suzuki (FR 59): Maurin Y.-M.

Monster, The (US 25): Billings E.

Monster Squad, The (US 87): Gower, Kiger

Montalvo et l'enfant /*Montalvo and the child* (FR 88): Ducret

Montana Kid (US 31): Shuford

Montana Mike (47 US) − *see* Heaven Only Knows

Montreal Main (CA 74): Sutherland

Moochie of Pop Warner Football (US 60): Corcoran

Moochie of the Little League (US 59): Corcoran

Mooncussers, The (US 62): Corcoran

Moonfleet (US 55): Whiteley

Moonlight on the Prairie (US 35): Cosbey, Jones D.

Moon Madness (US 20): Lee F.

Moonraker, The (GB 57): Anderson M.

Moonrise (US 48): Calkins, Ivo

Moonshine Trail, The (US 19): Blackton

Moorhund, Der /*Dog of the moorland* (DD 60): Glaser W.

Mordet i Bakerstreet /*Murder in Baker Street* (DK 10): Crone

Mord for åbent tæppe /*Murder with open curtains* (DK 64): Schmidt J.P.

Mordhwaj (IN 52): Kapoor S.

Mordsache Holm /*The Holm murder case* (GE 38): Eugens

More to Be Pitied Than Scorned (US 22): Griffith

Morgengrauen /*Dawn of day* (DE 54): Grimm

Morgen fällt die Schule aus /*End of term tomorrow* (DE 71): 'Heintje'

Morgens um sieben ist die Welt noch in Ordnung /*7 a.m. and all's well* (DE 68): Eser

Moritz in der Litfasssäule /*Maurice in the advertising pillar* (DD 83): Müller D.

Moritz, lieber Moritz /*Maurice, dear Maurice* (DE 78): Kebschull, Enkelmann, Bowakow

Morskaya chaika /*The seagull* (SU 61): Marchenko

Mors lilla vän /*Mother's little friend* (SE 55): Dam

Morte a Venezia /*Death in Venice* (IT/FR 71): Andresen

Mort sans importance, Une /*An unimportant death* (FR 47): Gencel

Mosby's Marauders (66 US) − *see* Willie and the Yank

Moselfahrt aus Liebeskummer /*Lovelorn trip down the Mosel* (DE 53): Grimm

Mosquito Coast, The (US 86): Phoenix R.

Moth and the Flame, The (US 15): Steuart

Mother Carey's Chickens (US 38): Moran, Dunagan

Mother Goose in a Sixteenth Century Theater (US 12): Boss, Clark A., Porter W.

Mother India (IN 57): Sajjid

Mother-in-Law's Day (US 32): Billings G.

Mother Machree (US 27): DeLacy, Parrish

Mother Riley Meets the Vampire (GB 52): Hannaford

Mothers Cry (US 30): Frederick

Mothers of Men (GB 38): Singer

Moti Mahal (IN 52): Kumar
Motyle /*Butterflies* (PL 72): Mosior, Izdebski, Szczerkowski
Moulders of Men (US 27): Darro
Mountain of Fear (64 YU) – *see* Srečno, Kekec!
Mountain Rhythm (US 42): Jones D.
Mountains of Manhattan (US 27): Gordon Bo.
Mouse and the Lion, The (US 13): Kelly P.
Movie Struck (26 US) – *see* Tom and His Pals
Movin' Pitchers (US 13): Clark R.
Mózg elektronowy /*The electronic brain* (PL 68): Samosionek
Muddy Bride, A (US 21): Morgan
Muddy River (81 JP) – *see* Doro no kawa
Mudlark, The (GB 50): Ray A., Brooke
Muj brácha ma prima bráchu /*My brother's got a super brother*
   (CS 75): Cada
Mujer del puerto, La /*Woman of the port* (MX 34): Zamora
Mujer que engañamos, La /*The woman we deceive* (MX 45): Roche
Mujer sin amor, Una /*A loveless woman* (MX 51): Calpe
Mula de Cullen Baker, La /*Cullen Baker's mule* (MX 70): Coster A.
Mulatto, Il /*The halfbreed* (IT 49): Maggio
Mu ma ren /*The herdsman* (CN 82): Fang
Munango Story, The (US 54): Pollock
Münchhausen in Afrika /*Münchhausen in Africa* (DE 57): Kaiser
Munimji /*The manager* (IN 73): Mehmood
Munna /*The lost child* (IN 54): Kapoor Ro.
Munster Go Home! (US 66): Patrick
Muqaddar ka sikundar /*Conqueror of fate* (IN 78): Mayur
Muqin /*The mother* (CN 49): Wang L.
Mur, Le /*The wall* (FR 83): Şişko
Muralla verde, La /*The green wall* (PE 69): Martin R.
Murder Case (US 29): Scott D.
Murder in the Family (GB 38): McDowall
Murder on the Blackboard (US 34): Searl
Murder Will Out (GB 39): McDowall
Murphy's Romance (US 85): Haim
Muşchetarii în vacanţa /*Musketeers on holiday* (RO 80): Carp
Mush Again (US 29): McKeen
Mush and Milk (US 33): 'Our Gang'
Musical Romance (34 US) – *see* Beloved
Music Box (US 89): Haas L.
Music Man, The (US 61): Howard R.
Music Room, The (58 IN) – *see* Jalsaghar
Music School (39 US) – *see* They Shall Have Music
Musique portuaire (37 BE) – *see* Havenmusiek
Musketeers of Pig Alley, The (US 10): Pickford
Mustang (PL 69): Samosionek
Mustang (MX 73): Martinez
Muta di Portici, La /*The dumb woman of Portici* (IT 52): Di Nardo
Mutant (US 83): Guffey
Mutiny in the County (US 40): Cook T.
Mutter, dein Kind ruft /*Mother, your child is calling* (GE 23): Eysoldt
Mutterliebe /*Mother's love* (GE 39): Rohringer
Mutterliebe: Bauernhof und Grafenschloss /*Mother's love in farm
   and castle* (GE 09): Bois
Mutterlied /*Song of a mother* (GE/IT 37): Bosse
Muzhe bez mustatsi /*Men without moustaches* (BG 90): Gabrovski
Muž přes palubu /*Man overboard* (CS 81): Kral

My Ain Folk (GB 73): Archibald
My Best Girl (US 29): Beard
My Bill (US 38): Moore D., Jordan
My Bodyguard (US 80): Makepeace
My Boy (US 21): Coogan J., Winslow D.
My Brilliant Career (AU 79): Spain
My Brother's Wedding (US 83): Harris R.
My Brother Talks to Horses (US 46): Jenkins, Gray G., Hunt
My Childhood (GB 72): Archibald
My Dear Kuttichetan (IN 86): Aravind
My Dear Miss Aldrich (US 37): Bupp S.
My Dog Rusty (US 48): Donaldson T., Ackles, Hickman Dw., Infuhr
My Dog Shep (US 46): Rees
My Father's House (US 75): Savage B.
My Favorite Blonde (US 42): Switzer, Winkler
My Favorite Redhead (49 US) – *see* Great Lover
My Favorite Wife (US 40): Beckett
My Friend Flicka (US 43): McDowall
'My Friend Flicka' (US 57-58, TVS): Washbrook
My Friend, the Devil (US 22): Grauer
My Friend the King (GB 31): Pavitt
My Gal Loves Music (US 44): Mercer
My Girl (US 91): Culkin M.
My Girl 2 (US 94): O'Brien A.
My Heart Belongs to Daddy (US 43): Caldwell
My Heart is Calling (GB 34): Singer
My Kid (US 26): Sabiston
My Left Foot (GB 89): O'Conor
My Life as a Dog (85 SE) – *see* Mitt liv som hund
My Little Chickadee (US 40): Billings G., Watson D.
My Love Came Back (US 40): Baker
My Lucky Star (US 38): Kibrick L.
My Mamie Rose (US 24): Butts
My Mother's Lovers (85 PL) – *see* Kochankowie mojej mamy
My Name Is Ivan (62 SU) – *see* Ivanovo detstvo
My Old Dutch (US 26): Hall N., Noisom
My Old Dutch (GB 34): Fitzpatrick P., Pavitt, Singer
My Pal Gus (US 52): Winslow G., Olsen C.
My Pal the King (US 32): Rooney
My Pal Wolf (US 44): Larson, Mickelsen, Olsen L.J.
My Reputation (US 43): Beckett, Kaye
My Side of the Mountain (CA 68): Eccles
My Sister Eileen (US 42): Mummert
My Six Loves (US 62): Eccles, Livingston B.
My Son Alone (43 US) – *see* American Empire
My Song Goes Round the World (GB 34): Rietti
My Son John (US 52): Aaker L.
My Son, My Precious (81 IN) – *see* Imagi ningtham
My Son, My Son! (US 40): Beckett
Mystère de la Tour Eiffel, Le /*The Eiffel Tower mystery* (FR 27): Gaillard
Mystère de la Villa Rose, Le /*Mystery of the Villa Rose* (FR 29):
   Mercanton
Mystères de Paris, Les /*Secrets of Paris* (FR 22): Guichard
Mystères de Paris, Les (FR 62): Decock
Mysteriet på Duncan Slot /*Mystery at Castle Duncan* (DK 16): Kaulbach
Mysterie van de Mondschein-Sonate, Het /*The Moonlight Sonata
   mystery* (NL 35): de Bock

Mysterious Mission, The (22 US) — see You Never Know
Mysterious Mystery, The (US 24): 'Our Gang'
Mysterious Poacher, The (GB 49): Leidinger, Friedl
Mysterious Rider, The (US 27): Butts
Mysterious Rider, The (US 33): Bailey Sd.
Mystery in Mexico (US 48): Jiménez Pons J.
Mystery of Dracula's Castle, The (US c.73): Kolden, Whitaker
Mystery of Edwin Drood, The (US 35): Ernest
Mystery Plane (US 39): Bupp T.
Mystery Sea Raider (US 40): Hickman Dl.
Mystery Valley (US 28): Darro
Mystiske Z-Stråler, De / The mysterious Z-rays (DK 15): Kaulbach
My Summer Story (US 93): Culkin K.
'My Three Sons' (US 60-72, TVS): Livingston B. and S.
My tři a pes z Pětipes / We three and the dog from Five-Dogs
    (CS 71): Kúkol
My Way Home (GB 78): Archibald
My Wild Irish Rose (US 22): Daniels M.
'My World and Welcome to It' (US 70, TVS): Shea C.

Naag mere saathi / Snake, my companion (IN 73): Alankar
Nachbarn sind zum Ärgern da / Neighbours are a nuisance (DE 70):
    Ohrner
Nachey nagun (PK 88): Jamshid
Nachtgestalten / Shapes of the night (GE 20): Allen W.
Nacht in London, Eine (29 GB) — see (sic) Knight in London
Nachtkolonne / Night column (GE 31): Lohmeyer
Nachttocht, De / The night wind (NL 83): Claessen
Na dobré stopě / On the right track (CS 48): Mikulič
Na dworze krola Tuszynka / At the court of King Tuszynko (PL 77):
    Miller S.
Nafrat / Hatred (IN 73): Rajoo
Naga kanni / Snake girl (IN 74): Alankar
Nagaya shinshi roku / Record of a tenement gentleman (JP 47):
    Aoki (Tomihiro)
Na grafskikh razvalinakh / On the ruined estate (SU 56): Novikov
Nagyur, A / The big gentleman (HU 17): Szécsi
'Naica' films (RO 63-67): Untaru
Nai dulgata nosht / The longest night (BG 67): Kovachev
Naked Alibi (US 54): Chapin B.
Naked and the Dead, The (US 58): Cardi
Naked Heart, The (GB 49): Roper
Naked Hearts (US 16): Griffith, Hupp
Naked Hills, The (US 55): Olsen C.
Naked Kiss, The (US 64): Michenaud, Spell G.
Naked Maja, The (US 58): Chevalier
Naked Runner, The (GB 66): Newport
Nakhalyonok / Little cheeky (SU 61): Semyonov Vo.
Na lunu s peresadkoi / To the moon, with one change (SU 34):
    Kuzdryavtsev
Namerareta aitsu / A disrespectful fellow (JP 34): 'Tokkan-Kozo'
Namida no aikyomono / Tears of happiness (JP 31): 'Tokkan-Kozo'
Namonaku mazushiku utsukushiku / We're so happy by ourselves (JP 61):
    Shimazu
Namu, the Killer Whale (US 66): Shea M.
Nancy Drew - Detective (US 38): Bupp T.
Nancy Drew - Reporter (US 39, srs): Jones D.

Nancy's Birthright (US 16): Short
Nand ke Lala (IN 34): Modak
Nand kishore (IN 51): Surendra
Nand Kumar (IN 38): Marathe A.
Nanha shikari / The young hunter (IN 73): Bunty
Nanny, The (GB 65): Dix, Younger
Nanon (GE 23): Allen W.
Na perelome / At the turning-point (SU 57): Aleksandrov
Napoléon (FR 26): Roudenko, Freddy-Karl, Hénin
Napoléon (FR 54): Chapeland
Napoleon and Samantha (US 72): Whitaker
Napoleon, Jr. (US 26): Madden
Napoleon's Barber (US 28): DeLacy
Na pytlácke stezce / On the poacher's path (CS 79): Holý
Når man kun er ung / As long as you're young (DK 43): Kaas
Narrow Margin, The (US 52): Gebert
Narrow Street, The (US 24): Butterworth J.
När ungdomen vaknar / When youth awakes (SE 43): Lindgren H.,
    Nyström
Na sluneční straně / On the sunny side (CS 33): Schulhoff
Nastoyashchi drug / A real friend (SU 59): Mirzoyev
Nastoyashchi tovarishch / A real comrade (SU 36): Denisov
Natale di bebè, Il / Baby's birthday (IT 32): Locchi
Nateeja / The result (IN 69): Mehmood
National Lampoon's Vacation (US 83): Hall A.M.
National Velvet (US 44): Jenkins
Natsukashi no kao / A nostalgic face (JP 41): Kodaka
Nattbarn / Night child (SE 56): Almgren
Nattlek / Night games (SE 66): Lindström J.
Nattvardsgästerna / The night communicants (SE 62): Axberg E.
Naufragio / Shipwreck (IT 16): Roveri
Nauka latania / Learning to fly (PL 78): Hudziec
Navajo (US 51): Teller
Naval Academy (US 41): Cook B., Scott D.
Navigator: a Medieval Odyssey, The (NZ/AU 88):
    McFarlane H.
Návštěva z oblak / Visit from the clouds (CS 55): Pucholt
Navy Beans (US 28): Sabiston
Naya ghar / The new house (IN 53): Kumar
Naya sansar (IN 41): Suresh
Nayezdnik iz Kabardi / Rider from Kabarda (SU 39): Lakotkin
Na zazoryavane / At dawn (BG 72): Zahariev
Na Žižkově válečném voze / On Zizka's fortified wagon (CS 68): Filip J.
N'diangane (SN 74): N'Diaye
Nebeto na Veleka / The sky of Veleka (BG 68): Arshinkov
Ne bolit golova u dyatla / The woodpecker never has a headache
    (SU 75): Zhezlayev
Nebo nashego detstva / The sky of our childhood (SU 66): Dubashev
Nechci nic slyšet / Leave me alone (CS 79): Renč
Negyen az arban / Four in the flood (HU 61): Nagy G.
Neighbors (US 18): Grauer
Ne joči, Peter / Don't cry, Peter (YU 64): Lubej
Neka druga zena / Some other woman (YU 85): Roganović
Neklidna hladina / Troubled surface (CS 62): Koblic
Nelson (GB 18): Barker E.
Nemico di mia moglie, Il / My wife's enemy (IT 59): Chevalier
Nene (IT 77): Valsecchi

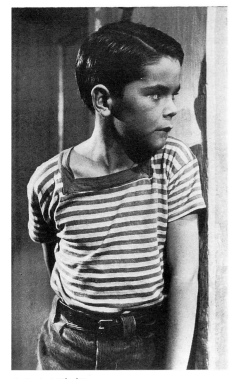

Antonín Mikulič

Sid Owen in Revolution

Ronalds Neilands

Radames Pera

Snowbound: Hans Fehér in The Robber Symphony

Neobiknovennoye delo / *An unusual case* (SU 56): Koval

Neobiknovennoye puteshestviye Mishki Strekachova / *Mishka Strekachov's unusual journey* (SU 59): Devkin, Borzunoff

Neohližej se, jde za námi kuň / *Don't look round, there's a horse following us* (CS 80): Potměšil

Neokonchennaya pesa dlya mekhanicheskovo pianino / *Unfinished piece for player-piano* (SU 77): Gurev

Ne plači, Petre (64 YU) — *see* Ne joči, Peter

Ne pleure pas / *Don't cry* (FR 78): Labouze

Nero - Hass war sein Gebet, Il (67 DE/IT) — *see* Odio è il mio Dio

Nero veneziano / *Venetian black* (IT 77): Cestiè

Në shtëpinë tonë / *In our family* (AL 79): Lohja

Neskolko dnei iz zhizni I.I.Oblomova / *A few days in the life of I.I.Oblomov* (SU 79): Stukov

Nespokoen dom / *A restless home* (BG 65): Vulkov

Neue Fimmel, Der / *The latest craze* (DD 60): Meinshausen

Neue Schiffsjunge, Der / *The new cabin-boy* (GE 36): Teetzmann

Nevada (US 44): McKim H.

Nevada City (US 41): Lee B.

Neverending Story, The (84 DE) — *see* Unendliche Geschichte

Neverending Story II: The Last Chapter, The (GE 89): Brandis, Morrison K.

Never Give a Sucker an Even Break (US 41): Brown K., Lenhart

Never Take No for an Answer (GB 51): Manunta

Never Too Young (48 US) — *see* Sorrowful Jones

Nevlovime mstiteli / *The elusive avengers* (SU 66): Kosikh

Névtelen vár / *Castle without a name* (HU 20): Szécsi

New Folks in Town (US 19): Carr J. and S.

New Frontier, The (US 39): McKim S.

Newly Rich (US 31): Searl, Line, Butts, Haines, Tucker J.

'Newlyweds and Their Baby, The' (US 26-28, srs): McKeen

New Mexico (US 51): Price

New Partner, The (US 14): Clark A.

New Pupil, The (US 40): 'Our Gang'

Newsboy's Dream, A (GB 13): Cricks

New School Teacher, The (US 24): Bennett M., Griffin

New Teacher, The (US 22): Moore P.

New Year's Eve (US 29): Frederick

New York Town (US 41): Bond T.

Next Door Neighbor (52 US) — *see* Talk about a Stranger

Next Time We Love (US 36): Cosbey

Next Voice You Hear, The (US 50): Gray G.

Nezavursheni igri / *Unfinished games* (BG 63): Enchev

Nezbedny bakalar / *The mischievous tutor* (CS 47): Mikulič

Nez de cuir / *Leather nose* (FR 51): Martaguet C.

Nga mesi i errësirës / *From deepest darkness* (AL 78): Arifi

Nianchan / *Second brother* (JP 59): Okimura

Nichemu plokhomu ne uchili / *We didn't do anything wrong* (SU 58): Ivanov S.

Nicholas Nickleby (03 GB) — *see* Dotheboys Hall

Nickelodeon (US/GB 76): O'Neal

Nieuwe avonturen van Dik Trom / *Dik Trom's new adventures* (NL 58): Nievelstein

Niewiarygodne przygody Marka Piegusa / *Amazing adventures of Freckled Mark* (PL 67): Roman

Nifi toskasse, I / *The bride escaped* (GR 62): Kailas

Night and Day (US 46): Nokes, Norman

Night-Bird (73 SU) — *see* Polunochnik

Night Club Queen (GB 34): Tester

Nightcomers, The (GB 71): Ellis C.

Night Cries (US 78): Peluce

Night Editor, The (US 46): Calkins, Chapin M.

Night Games (66 SE) — *see* Nattlek

Night Hair Child (GB 71): Lester

Night Hawk, The (US 38): Burrud

Night Holds Terror, The (US 55): Herbert

Night in Paradise (US 46): Bates

Night into Morning (US 51): Gebert

Nightmares (US 82): Jacoby Bl.

Night 'n' Gales (US 37): 'Our Gang'

Night of June 13, The (US 32): Butts

Night of the Grizzly (US 66): Brodie

Night of the Hunter, The (US 55): Chapin B.

Night Passage (US 57): DeWilde

Night Rider (US 79): Sharrett

Night Riders, The (US 39): McKim S.

Night Shadows (US 84): Guffey

Night Train for Inverness (GB 59): Waterman, Moulder-Brown

Night Wind (US 48): Chapin M., Gray G.

Night Without Pity (GB 62): Moulder-Brown

Night Work (US 30): Billings G., Scott D.

Night Work (US 39): Lee B., O'Connor

Niizuma kagami / *The new wife's mirror* (JP 56): Ota

Nikitis, O / *The winner* (GR 65): Kailas

Niklas och Figuren / *Nicholas and the Goon* (SE 71): Grybe, Malmsjö

Nil darpan (IN 52): Bhattacharjee

Nils Holgerssons underbara resa / *Nils Holgersson's wonderful journey* (SE 62): Lundberg

Nine Lives Are Not Enough (US 41): Dawson

Nine Miles to Noon (US 64): Lazer

1900 (76 IT/FR/DE) — *see* Novecento

Nine Tenths of the Law (US 18): Eason

Niño y el ladron, El (64 ES/MX) — *see* Primera aventura

Niño y el lobo, El (65 ES) — *see* Cotolay

Niño y el muro, El / *The child and the wall* (ES/MX 64): del Arco

Nirdosh / *The innocent* (IN 74): Mehmood

Nischt geht über die Gemütlichkeit / *Good nature is essential* (GE 34): Schaufuss

Nishi Ginza eki mae / *West Ginza station* (JP 58): Shimazu

Nishkriti / *Exit* (IN 53): Babua

Ni slova o futballe / *Not a word about soccer* (SU 74): Kharitonov

Njeriu me top (AL 77): Zhegu

Noah's Ark (US 28): Moore D.

No basta ser madre / *It's not enough to be a mother* (MX 37): Rio

Nobody's Boy (25 FR) — *see* Sans famille

Nobody's Children (29 US) — *see* Blue Skies

Nobody's Children (US 40): Lee B.

Nobody's Darling (US 43): Dawson

No Boy Wanted (US 29): McKeen

No Deposit, No Return (US 76): Savage B.

No Down Payment (US 57): Herbert

Noël du père Lathuille, Le / *Father Lathuille's Christmas* (FR 22): Guichard

No Escape (43 US) — *see* I Escaped from the Gestapo

No Fare (US 28): Sabiston
No Greater Glory (US 34): Breakston, Searl, Alexander T., Butler, Haines, Line
No Greater Love (US 32): Moore D.
Noguchi hideyo no shonen-jidai / *The boyhood of Dr Noguchi* (JP 56): Daigenji
Noia, La / *Tedium* (IT/FR 63): Nevola
Noi non siame angeli / *We're no angels* (IT 75): Cestiè
Noisy Noises (US 29): 'Our Gang', Black B.
Noisy Six, The (US 13): Clark R.
Nokea ja kultaa / *Soot and gold* (FI 45): Kaitala
No Kidding (GB 60): Stephens M., Witty
No Man of Her Own (US 32): Conlon
No Man's Gold (US 26): Moore M.
No Minor Vices (US 48): Bridges B., Chapin B., Hyatt
None But the Brave (US 28): Butts
None But the Brave (60 US) – *see* For the Love of Mike
Non far piangere la bambina / *Don't make the baby cry* (IT 13): Giunchi
Nonni i Manni / *Nonni and Manni* (IS/DE 87, srl): Cortes, Einarsson
No Noise (US 23): 'Our Gang'
Non-Stop New York (GB 37): Tester
Noon Hour, The (US 15): Goodwin
Noordelingen, De / *The Northerners* (NL 92): Lucieer
Noor-e-watan / *Light of the nation* (IN 35): Apte
No Parking (GB 38): Singer
No Place for Jennifer (GB 49): Smith B., Fox W., Simons W.
No Place to Go (US 39): Bupp S. and T.
Nordsee ist Mordsee / *North Sea, death sea* (DE 75): Bowakow, Enkelmann
No Relations (25 FR) – *see* Sans famille
Noren / *The Japanese curtain* (JP 58): Zushi
Norman Loves Rose (AU 82): Owen T.
No Room at the Inn (GB 48): Netscher, Hannaford
No Room for the Groom (US 52): Aaker L.
Norrtullsligan / *The Norrtull Gang* (SE 23): Falk
North (US 94): Wood E.
'North and South' (US 86, TVS): Guffey
North Dallas Forty (US 79): Jacoby Bl.
North of Fifty-Three (US 17): Lee F.
North of Nevada (US 24): Butterworth J.
North Star, The (US 43): Bates, Infuhr, Mickelsen, Nokes, Roberts E.
Northwest Rangers (US 42): Hickman Dl.
Nose in a Book, A (US 20): Eason
Not a Drum Was Heard (US 24): McBan
Not a Ladies' Man (US 42): Croft
Not For Sale (GB 24): Brantford
Nothing But the Truth (US 41): Dawson
Nothing Sacred (US 37): Barty
Nothing Venture (GB 47): Artemus
No Time for Tears (GB 57): O'Sullivan, Witty
No Time to Marry (US 37): Beckett
Not Mine to Love (66 IL) – *see* Shlosha yamin ve yeled
Not One to Spare (US 24): Black B., House N., Winslow D.
Notorious Mrs Sands, The (US 20): Alexander B.
Notre-Dame de la Mouise / *Our Lady of Poverty* (FR 40): Rodon
Not So Dusty (GB 36): Singer
Not To Be Trusted (US 26): Rooney

Nous les gosses (36 FR) – *see* Guerre des gosses
Nous les gosses / *Us kids* (FR 41): Geffroy, Buquet
Nous sommes tous des assassins / *We are all murderers* (FR 52): Poujouly
Nouvelle mission de Judex, La / *Judex's new mission* (FR 17, srl): Poyen
1900 (IT/FR/DE 76): Maccanti, Pavesi
Nove priklucheniya Kapitana Vrungelya / *New adventures of Captain Wrangel* (SU 79): Markin
Nove rapazes e um cão / *Nine boys and a dog* (PT 63): Neto
Novi attraktsion / *The latest attraction* (SU 57): Gavrilov
Now and Forever (US 34): Cosbey, Holt D., Phelps
Now Barabbas Was a Robber (GB 49): Hannaford
Nowhere to Hide (US 94): Pomeranc
Nowhere to Run (US 92): Culkin K.
Now I'll Tell (US 34): Cosbey
Now It Can Be Sold (US 39): Bond T.
No Woman Knows (US 21): Fox J., Lee Ra.
Nran gouyne / *The colour of pomegranates* (SU 74): Aleksanian
Nufarul roşu / *The pink water-lily* (RO 55): Munteanu
Nuit de mai / *May night* (FR 34): Bara
Number, Please (US 22): Morrison E.
Nunca debieron amarse / *They never should have been in love* (MX 51): Moreno
Nun's Story, The (GB 60): O'Sullivan
Nuovi barbari, I / *The new barbarians* (IT 83): Frezza
Nuovo Cinema Paradiso / *The new Paradise Cinema* (IT/FR 88): Cascio
Nurse, The (US 12): Porter W.
Nurse Brown (21 NL/GB) – *see* Zuster Brown
Nurse Edith Cavell (US 39): Downing R.
Nurse Marjorie (US 20): Lee F.
Nutcase (NZ 80): Donaldson A.
Nutcracker, The (US 93): Culkin M.
Nya hyss av Emil i Lönneberga / *New adventures of Emil at Lönneberga* (SE 72): Ohlsson
Nyamanton / *Lessons from the garbage* (ML 86): Kante A. and M., Thiocary
Nyckeln och ringen / *The key and the ring* (SE 47): Carlsson
Nye huslærer, Den / *The new tutor* (DK 10): Crone, Voigt

Obey the Law (US 33): Moore D.
Object - Alimony (US 28): Moore D.
Objev na Střapaté hůrce / *The discovery on Shaggy Hill* (CS 61): Polák, Zoula
Oblomov (79 SU) – *see* Neskolko dnei iz zhizni I.I.Oblomova
Obsessão, Em / *Obsession* (PT 88): Lavos
Obsessed with a Married Woman (US 85): Gower
Obsession (FR 33): Bara
Obsession (FR/IT 54): Moullières
Obušku z pytle ven! / *Stick, start beating!* (CS 56): Košnar
Occupe-toi d'Amélie / *Look after Amelia* (FR 49): Tabary
Och alla dessa kvinnor / *And all these women* (SE 44): Nyström
Ochazuke no aji / *Green tea with rice* (JP 52): Shitara
Oddballs (CA 84): Wodchis
Odds on Gallegher (25 US) – *see* Let's Go Gallegher
Ödermarksprästen / *The country priest* (SE 46): Nyström
Odio / *Hatred* (MX 40): Rio
Odio è il mio Dio, L' / *Hatred is my God* (IT/DE 67): Fioravanti
Odna noch / *One night* (SU 56): Vasilev B.

Odongo (GB 56): Caridia
Odwiedziny Prezydenta / *Visit from the President* (PL 61): Pomaski
O dwoch takich co ukradli księżyc / *The two who stole the moon*
   (PL 62): Kaczynski J. and L.
Oeil en coulisse, L' / *The sidelong look* (FR 53): Gencel
Office Boy's Birthday, The (US 13): Boss
Officer Cupid (US 21): Marion D.
Officer 174 (US 12): Moore J.
Officer Thirteen (US 32): Searl
Official Officers (US 25): 'Our Gang'
Off the Record (US 39): Bupp T.
Off to the Races (US 37): Mahan
Of Human Hearts (US 38): Reynolds
Ofumi no hyoban / *Popular Ofumi* (JP 36): Hayama
Ogni na reke / *Lights on the river* (SU 53): Kopelev
Ogotte chodaiyo! / *Give me a treat!* (JP 30): 'Tokkan-Kozo'
Ohayo / *Good morning* (JP 59): Shitara, Shimazu
O.Henry's Full House (US 52): Aaker L.
Ohé! Ohé! / *Hi! Hi!* (FR 31): Mercanton
Oh, God! (US 77): Drier
Ohne Fleiss kein Preis / *No work, no prizes* (GE 37): Teetzmann
Ohne Mutter geht es nicht / *You can't do without mother* (DE 58): Kaiser
Oh... Rosalinda!! (GB 55): Carey
Oh That Doctor's Boy! (GB 06): Miller F.
Oh! What a Surprise! (GB 04): Williamson T. and S.
Oil for the Lamps of China (US 35): Cosbey
Oja no ken / *The King's sword* (JP 59): Ota
Ojos de juventud / *Eyes of youth* (MX 48): Roche
OK 12 startuje / *OK 12 takes off* (CS 61): Hrušecky
Oklahoma Jim (US 31): Shuford
Oko proroka / *The prophet's eye* (PL/BG 82): Tsvetkov
Okoto na proroka (82 PL/BG) — see Oko proroka
Okrągły tydzień / *Week without end* (PL 77): Jakubik
Okusama no moryoku / *Violent wives* (JP 33): 'Tokkan-Kozo'
Old Barn Dance, The (US 38): McKim S.
Old Clothes (US 25): Coogan J.
Old Curiosity Shop, The (GB 35): Penrose
Old Dutch (US 28): Janney
Old English (US 30): Janney
Old Fashioned Boy, An (US 20): Lee F.
Old Fashioned Way, The (US 34): Leroy
Old Good-For-Nothin' (US 15): Connelly
Old Gray Hoss (US 28): 'Our Gang'
Old Heidelberg (US 15): Carpenter, Goodwin
Old Hutch (US 36): Beckett, Watson D. and H.
Old Ironsides (US 26): O'Donnell
Old Louisiana (US 37): Albright
Old Maid's Baby, The (US 19): Morrison E.
Old Man and the Sea, The (US 58): Pazos
Old Nest, The (US 21): Jones J., Messinger
Old Oaken Bucket, The (US 21): Connelly
Old Silver Watch, The (US 12): Casey
Old Soldiers (GB 38): Singer
Old Sweetheart of Mine, An (US 23): Moore P.
Old Swimmin' Hole, The (US 21): Messinger
Old Wallop, The (US 27): 'Our Gang'
Old West, The (US 52): Pollock

Old Wives' Tale, The (GB 21): Dear
Old Yeller (US 57): Kirk, Corcoran
Oliver! (GB 68): Lester, Wild, Kemp A.
Oliver Oliver (FR 92): Colin
Oliver Twist (19 HU) — see Twist Oliver
Oliver Twist (20 GE/AT) — see Geheimnisse von London
Oliver Twist (US 22): Coogan J., Trebaol E.
Oliver Twist (US 33): Moore D., Nelson B., Searl
Oliver Twist (US 40): Kidd R.
Oliver Twist (GB 48): Davies J.H.
Oliver Twist (GB 82): Charles R.
Olive's Love Affair (US 15): Jacobs
Olive's Pet (US 15): Jacobs
Ollin oppivuodet / *Olli's apprenticeship* (FI 20): Idström
Olvidados, Los / *The forgotten ones* (MX 50): Mejía
Olympic Games (US 27): 'Our Gang'
O'Malley of the Mounted (US 20): Headrick
Omar the Tent-Maker (US 22): DeLacy
Ombre et lumière / *Shade and light* (FR 50): Gervais
Ombytta roller / *Changing roles* (SE 20): Brunius
Omen, The (GB 76): Stephens H.
On Borrowed Time (US 39): Watson Bs., Bupp S.
Once Again (US 86): Cross
Once a Hero (US 37): Burrud
Once upon a Family (US 80): Licht
Once upon a Murder (83 US) — see Chiefs
Once upon a Time (US 44): Donaldson T., Bates, Gray G.
One and Only, Genuine, Original Family Band, The (US 68):
   Russell K., Riha
One Big Affair (US 52): Velasquez A.
One Desire (US 54): Curtis
One Foot in Heaven (US 41): Caldwell, Kuhn, Madore
One Glorious Day (US 22): Fox J.
One Hour to Zero (GB 76): Ashby A.
One Jump Ahead (GB 55): Hannaford
One Little Indian (US 73): O'Brien C.
One Live Ghost (US 36): Watson D.
One Man in a Million (US 20): Beban
One Man's Journey (US 33): Ernest, Phelps
One Man's Way (US 64): Patrick
One Plus One Equals One (US 15, 'Sonny Jim'): Connelly
One Romantic Night (US 30): DeLacy
One Terrible Day (US 22): 'Our Gang'
One Touch of Nature (US 14): Clark A.
One Touch of Sin (US 17): Lee F.
1 - 2 - 3 Go! (US 41): 'Our Gang'
One Way Passage (US 31): Phelps
One Wild Oat (GB 50): Fox W.
One Wild Ride (US 25): 'Our Gang'
One Wish Too Many (GB 56): Pike J., Richmond
One Woman, The (US 18): Alexander B.
One Woman to Another (US 27): Boudwin
One Year Later (US 33): Searl
On Golden Pond (US 81): McKeon D.
Onion Field, The (US 79): Becker
Oni vstretilis v puti / *They met on the way* (SU 57): Merkulov
Only the Lonely (US 91): Culkin

Only Yesterday (US 33): Butler
On Moonlight Bay (US 51): Gray B.
On n'aime qu'une fois / You only love once (FR 49): Urbain
Onna wa nete mate / Going to sleep without a woman (JP 32):
    'Tokkan-Kozo'
Onna wa tsuyokute hitorimono / Woman is strong and independent
    (JP 31): 'Tokkan-Kozo'
Onna wa tsuyokute yowai mono / Woman is both strong and weak
    (JP 31): 'Tokkan-Kozo'
Onnen-Pekka / Lucky Peter (FI 48): Kaitala
On Our Merry Way (US 47): Lindgren O.
On Our Selection (AU 20): Wilson
On Probation (US 12): Benham
On purge Bébé / Baby's purge (FR 31): Tarride
On the Banks of the Wabash (US 23): Blackton
On the Breast of the Tide (US 14): Clark R.
On Their Own (US 40): Kaye, Mahan, Tyler L.
On the Right Track (US 81): Coleman G.
On the Sunny Side (US 41): Binyon, McDowall, Madore, Mercer,
    Tucker T., Tyler L., West J.
On the Sunny Side of the Street (US 51): Price
On the Twelfth Day (GB 55): Hines
On the War Path (US 11): Melford
On the Waterfront (US 54): Hanley
On to Reno (US 28): Daniels M.
On Your Guard (US 33): Nelson B.
On Your Toes (US 27): Janney
On Your Toes (US 39): Bupp T., O'Connor
Opasan put / Dangerous road (YU 63): Cosić
Open Range (US 27): Shuford
Open Road, The (19 US) − see Sleeping Lion
Operation Haylift (US 50): Ivo
Operation Pacific (US 51): Gebert, Holmes D.
Operation Third Form (GB 66): Moulder-Brown, Bennett K.
Op hoop van zegen / In hope of blessing (NL 86): de Munk
Op med lille Martha / Cheers for little Martha (DK 46): Uglebjerg
Opowieść Atlantycka / Atlantic story (PL 54): Bustamante, Damiecki D.
Oppol / Elder sister (IN 81): Aravind
Oracle, The (GB 52): Charlesworth
Orage / Storm (FR 37): Buquet
Orange Peel (GB 07): Williamson T.
Oranžový měsíc / Orange moon (CS 62): Koblic
¡Ora Ponciano! / Now, Ponciano! (MX 37): Rio
Orchids and Ermine (US 27): Rooney
Ordeal of Bill Carney, The (US 81): Licht
Oregon Trail Scouts (US 47): Blake, Cummings
Orfana del ghetto, L' / Orphan girl of the ghetto (IT 17): Casarotti
Organization, The (US 71): Spell G.
Orias, Az / The giant (HU 60): Rago
Ori odzhaki / Two families (SU 58): Daneliya
Orlyonok / The eaglet (SU 57): Stremovski
Oro nero / Black gold (IT 41): Glori
Orphan of the Sage (US 28): Barton
Orphan of the Wagon Trails (US 29): Nelson B.
Orphan of the War (US 13): Gottlieb
Orphan of the Wilderness (AU 36): Ryan D.
Orphans (77 SU) − see Podranki

Orphans of the Street (US 37): Ryan
Orphan Train (US 79): Fields
Orquideas para mi esposa / Orchids for my wife (MX 53): Perez
Örszem, Az / The sentry (HU 24): Szécsi
Osevni / Sowing (CS 60): Koblic
O'Shaughnessy's Boy (US 35): Cooper Ja., Albright, McFarland
O.S.S. (US 46): Driscoll
Ostrov Sokrovishch / Treasure Island (SU 71): Laanemets
Ostrov stříbrných volavek / The Isle of Silver Herons (CS 76):
    Vavruša, Vořišek
Osud jmenem Kamila / Fate, alias Camilla (CS 73): Dlouhý
Otac na službenom putu / When Father was away on business
    (YU 85): De Bartolli
Otec / Father (CS 81): Angst
Other, The (US 72): Udvarnoky C. and M.
Other Half, The (US 19): Redden
Other Men's Shoes (US 20): Connelly
Other Side of the Mountain, The (US 75): Savage B.
Other Woman, The (US 16): Griffith
Other Woman, The (US 21): Lee F.
Otoko narya koso / I am a man, therefore... (JP 37): Kodaka
Otoko yamome no Gansan / Gansan the widower (JP 33):
    'Tokkan-Kozo'
Otome gokoro sannin shimai / Three pure-hearted sisters (JP 35): Ito K.
Otra, La / The other woman (MX 46): Pastor
Otryad Trubachova srazhayetsa / Trubachov's detachment in action
    (SU 57): Devkin, Vishnev
1860 (IT 33): Brambilla
8½ (IT/FR 63): Gemini
Otto er et næsehorn / Otto is a rhino (DK 83): Markersen
Ottokar der Weltverbesserer / Ottokar the world-reformer (DD 77):
    Herrmann
Otto yo naze nakuka / Why does the husband weep? (JP 31):
    'Tokkan-Kozo'
Our Boys (US 17): Paul E.
Our Children (US 13): Griffith, Jacobs
Our Gang (US 22): 'Our Gang'
Our Gang Follies of 1936 (US 35): 'Our Gang', Downing R., Hurlic,
    Jones D., Watson D.
Our Gang Follies of 1938 (US 37): 'Our Gang', Beckett, Hurlic,
    Jones D., Watson Bs., Winkler
Our Hearts Were Young and Gay (US 44): Sheffield J.
Our Mother's House (GB/US 67): Lester
Our Neighbors, the Carters (US 39): Bartlett, Beckett
Our New Errand Boy (GB 05): Williamson A. and T.
Our Old Car (US 46): Gray B.
Our Vines Have Tender Grapes (US 45): Jenkins
Out All Night (US 27): Holmes L.
Out All Night (US 33): Barty
Out California Way (US 46): Blake
Outcast (US 37): Moran
Outcasts of the Trail (US 49): Ivo
Outland (GB 81): Barnes N.
Outlaws of Red River (US 27): Downs
Outlaw Stallion, The (US 53): Gray B.
Out of a Clear Sky (US 18): Connelly
Out of the Dust (US 19): Moore M.

Out of the Sky (US 20): Eason
Out of the Storm (US 26): Holmes L.
Out of the West (US 26): Darro
Outriders, The (US 49): Jarman, Belding
Outside Man, The (72 FR/IT) – see Homme est mort
Outsider, The (GB 39): McDowall
Outside the Law (US 30): Watson D.
Outside These Walls (US 39): Bupp T.
Out West with the Peppers (US 40): Sinclair, Bond T., Larson
O velkou cenu / For the Grand Prix (CS 22): Pražský
Overboard (US 87): Rushton
Overland Pacific (US 54): Charney
Overland Trails (US 48): Rees
Overland with Kit Carson (US 39, srl): Clark B.1
Overnight Haul (US 56): Eyer Ri.
Over Silent Paths (US 10): Pickford
Over the Hill (US 17): Carr J., Benham
Over the Hill (US 31): Conlon, Barty
Over the Hill to the Poorhouse (US 20): Carr S. and T., Tansey S., Devine
Over the Top (US 86): Mendenhall
Over the Wall (US 37): Bupp T.
Overture to Glory (US 40): Winkler
Oxbone Buccaneers, The (GB 68): Garlick, Turner, Younger

Paapam pasivadu / Alas, boy (IN 72): Ramu
Pablo and the Dancing Chihuahua (US 72): Islas
Pachin (ES 61): Gomez A.
Pachin almirante / Admiral Pachin (ES 61): Gomez A.
Pacifist, The (US 16): Harper
Paciorki jednego rózanca / The beads of one rosary (PL 79): Rzepka
Pacjent / The patient (PL 69): Samosionek
Paco (US 75): Gomez P.
Paco el elegante / Paco the dandy (MX 52): Jiménez Pons J.
Paddy O'Day (US 35): Bailey Sd., Bupp T., Watson H.
Padre Morelos, El / Father Morelos (MX 42): Busquets
Padre padrone / Father and master (IT 77): Forte
Padurea perduta / The lost forest (RO 71): Filip M.
Paganini (GE 23): Herzberg
Pagemaster, The (US 94): Culkin M.
Page vom Dalmasse-Hotel, Der / The page from the Hotel Dalmasse (GE 33): Richter
Paidi tou dromou, To / Child of the street (GR 61): Kalatzopoulos
Painted Hills, The (US 51): Gray G.
Painted Stallion, The (US 37, srl): McKim S.
Painted Veil, The (US 34): Watson D.
Paisa' / Countryman (IT 46): Pasca
Paisaje con figuras / Landscape with figures (ES 75): Alonso J.L.
Paisan (46 IT) – see Paisa'
Pajaros de Baden Baden, Los / Birds of Baden-Baden (ES 74): Alonso J.L.
Pal, Canine Detective (US 49): Gray G.
Pal, Fugitive Dog (US 50): Gray G.
Palkhon ki chhaon main / Under the eyelashes (IN 77): Rajoo
Palle alene i verden / Palle alone in the world (DK 49): Henning-Jensen
Palm Springs Weekend (US 63): Mumy
Paloma, La (GE 34): Teetzmann
Pals (25 US) – see Big Pal

Pal's Adventure (US 50): Gray G.
Pal's Gallant Journey (US 50): Gray G.
Pals of the Prairie (US 29): Barton
Pál utcai fiúk, A / The boys of Paul Street (HU 24): Faragó, Szecsi
Pál utcai fiúk, A (69 US/HU) – see Boys of Paul Street
Paméla (FR 44): Emrich
Pampered Youth (US 25): Alexander B.
Pan (NL 61): Veldt
Panic in the Streets (US 50): Rettig
Pani kluci / Young gentlemen (CS 75): Dymek M., Starý, Voříšek
Pan Samochodzik i Templariusze / Mr Motor and the Templars (PL 71, srl): Mosior, Samosionek
Pants (US 17): McDermott
Papa and Me (US 76): Laborteaux M.
Papa by Proxy (US 16): Benham
Papa's Sweetheart (US 11): Boss
Papa's Vacation (US 28): Bennett M.
Papelerito, El / The paper-boy (MX 51): Calpe, Jiménez Pons J., Perez
Paper Tiger (GB 74): Ando
Pappa sökes / Daddy wanted (SE 47): Nyström
Paprikajancsi / Harlequin (HU 58): Rago
Paquito (ES 84): Rincon
Paradise (US 91): Wood E.
Paradise Garden (US 17): Hupp
Paradise Postponed (GB 86, srl): McGrath
Paradiso / Paradise (IT 23): Palermi
Paradistorg / Paradise Place (SE 76): Magnusson
Paragon gola! / Shoot, Paragon! (PL 70): Tchórznicki
Paraíso escondido / Hidden paradise (MX 58): Osorno
Parasite, The (US 25): Guerin
Pardes (IN 50): Surendra
Pardon My Gun (US 30): Watson H.
Pardon My Sarong (US 42): Infuhr
Pards (US 21): Barry W.
Parentage (US 17): Roubert
Parenthood (US 89): Fisher, Phoenix L.
Parenthood (US 90, TVS): DiCaprio
Parents terribles, Les / Awful parents / (FR 35): Grave
Parias de l'amour, Les / Love's pariahs (FR 21): Haziza
Parichay / Introduction (IN 72): Rajoo
Paris Bound (US 29): Scott D.
Parishodh (IN 55): Babua
Paris Incident (50 FR) – see Trois télégrammes
Paris Plane (GB 34): Pavitt
Paris, Texas (US 84): Carson H.
Paris vu par... / Paris as seen by... (FR 64): Chusseau
Park Row (US 52): Pollock
Park Your Car (US 20): Morrison E.
Parole Fixer (US 40): Bupp S., Lee B.
Parted Curtains (US 20): Moore M.
Partizani i vogël Velo / Little partisan Velo (AL 80): Papakosta
Partners (28 US) – see Avenging Rider
Partners (US 32): Nelson B.
Part Time Wife (US 30): Clifford
Part 2 Walking Tall (US 75): Garrett
Party Fever (US 38): 'Our Gang'
Partyzánská stezka / In the steps of the partisans (CS 59): Kohák

Parusa moyego detstva /*Sails of my childhood* (SU 82): Prokopchuk

På rymmen med Pippi Långstrump /*On the run with Pippi Longstocking* (SE/DE 70): Sundberg

Pasand apni apni /*Each to his choice* (IN 72): Dean

Pascualin (ES 65): Cebrian

Pas de coup dur pour Johnny /*No tough luck for Johnny* (FR 55): Seidel

Pas gjurmëve /*After the tracks* (AL 78): Mosho, Mustafaraj

Pashka (SU 30): Lukyanov

Pasi hridalayu /*Tender hearts* (IN 73): Ramu

Passager, Le /*The passenger* (FR 27): Mercanton

Passagers, Les /*The passengers* (FR/IT 76): Constantini

Passage to Marseille (US 43): Miles P. (Perreau), Roy

Passer passer piger /*Come on, girls* (DK 65): Schmidt J.P.

Passers-By (US 20): Blackton

Passing of J.B.Randall & Company, The (US 12): Tansey R.

Passing of Wolf MacLean, The (US 24): Fox J.

Passing Thru (US 21): Coffey C.

Passion (FR 50): Simon, Gencel

Passionate Friends (GB 22): Dear

Passionate Stranger, The (GB 56): Witty

Passionate Summer (GB 58): Stephens M.

Passion de Jeanne d'Arc, La /*The passion of Joan of Arc* (FR 27): Hénin

Passion Flower (US 30): Moore D.

Passionnément /*Passionately* (FR 33): Mercanton

Pass of the Pecos (US 41): Winkler

Pasteur (FR 22): Rauzéna

Pasteur (FR 35): Rodon

Pastushonok /*The little shepherd boy* (SU 35): Sobolev

Pata de palo /*Wooden leg* (MX 50): Moreno

Patches (US 16): Eason

Paternity (US 81): Billingsley

Pather panchali /*Song of the road* (IN 55): Banerjee

Path of Happiness, The (US 16): Benham

Patricia (FR 42): François

Patricia Neal Story, The (US 81): Kiger

Patriot, The (US 15): Connelly

Patriot, The (US 16): Carpenter, Stone

Patriot (SU 39): Bichkoff

Patrioten /*Patriots* (GE 37): Eugens

Patsani /*Tough kids* (SU 83): Zikov

Paula (US 52): Rettig

Pavilion on the Links, The (20 US) — *see* White Circle

Pavlukha /*Little Paul* (SU 62): Semyonov Vo.

Paw (DK 59): Sterman

Pay As You Exit (US 36): 'Our Gang', Watson Bs., Winkler

Peace Is My Profession (US 72): Hudis

Peacemaker, The (GB 22): Thompson M.

Peacock Feathers (US 25): Noisom

Peanut Butter Solution, The (CA 86): Mackay

Pearl of Love, The (US 25): Griffin

Peau de Pêche /*Peach-Skin* (FR 28): Gaillard

Peau d'un homme, Le /*A man's skin* (FR 50): Gencel

Pecado de ser pobre, El /*The sin of poverty* (MX 50): Moreno

Péchés de jeunesse /*Sins of youth* (FR 41): Buquet, François

Peck's Bad Boy (US 21): Coogan J., Griffith, Reisner

Peck's Bad Boy (US 34): Cooper Ja., Searl

Peck's Bad Boy with the Circus (US 38): Kelly T., McFarland, Rentschler, Kibrick L.

Pedagogicheskaya poema /*Pedagogical poem* (SU 55): Chernoff, Poplavets, Yevgeniyev

Peddalu marali /*Reform the grown-ups* (IN 74): Ramu

Pedra no bolso, Uma /*A stone in the pocket* (PT 90): Leite

Peggy (US 50): Stollery

Peggy Does Her Darndest (US 18): Morrison E.

Peinture et les cochons, La /*Painting and pigs* (NL/FR 12): Mathieu

Pélican, Le /*The pelican* (FR 73): Chauveau

Pelle der Eroberer /*Pelle the conqueror* (DD 86): Schrader

Pelle erobreren /*Pelle the conqueror* (DK 87): Hvenegaard

Pelle the Conqueror (86 DD, 87 DK) — *see above*

Pelli chesi choodu (IN 52): Mohan

Pelota de trapo /*Rag ball* (AR 48): Poggio

Pempudu koduku (IN 53): Mohan

Penalty, The (US 20): Trebaol E.

Pengenes magt /*The power of money* (DK 15): Reinwald

Penne nere /*Black plumes* (IT 52): Staiola

Penny of Top Hill Trail (US 21): Stone

Pen Picture from Rhodesia (GB 48): Weske

Penrod (US 20): Barry W., Griffith, Condon, Hall N., Morrison E.

Penrod and His Twin Brother (US 38): Mauch B. and B., Bartlett, Hurlic, Tucker J.

Penrod and Sam (US 23): Alexander B., Butterworth J., Messinger, Hall N., Gordon Bo., Jackson E.

Penrod and Sam (US 31): Janney, Coghlan, Aber, Parrish

Penrod and Sam (US 37): Mauch Bl., Watson H., Billings G., Hurlic, Madden, Tucker J.

Penrod's Double Trouble (US 38): Mauch B. and B., Hurlic, Bupp S., Tucker J.

People in Love (51 US) — *see* Night into Morning

People under the Stairs, The (US 91): Adams

People vs. Nancy Preston, The (US 25): Darro

Pepánek Nezdara /*No-hope Joey* (CS 23): Pražský

Pepe (US/MX 60): North J.

Pepito as del volante /*Ace driver Pepito* (MX 56): Romay

Pepito y el monstruo /*Pepito and the monster* (MX 57): Romay

Pepito y los robachicos /*Pepito and the kidnappers* (MX 57): Romay

Pepote (56 ES/IT) — *see* Mi tio Jacinto

Peppeniello (IT 14): Capelli

Pepper (US 36): Bupp T.

'Peppino' (IT 83, TVS): Pulvirenti

Peppino e Violetta (51 GB) — *see* Never Take No for an Answer

Pequeña enemiga, La /*The little enemy* (MX 55): Romay

Pequeña madrecita, La /*The little mother* (MX 43): Busquets

Pequeño coronel, El /*The little colonel* (ES 60): Jiménez

Pequeño heroe del Arroyo, El /*The little hero of the Arroyo* (UY 29): de Vargas

Pequeño Robin Hood, El /*The little Robin Hood* (MX c.70): Coster A.

Pequeño ruiseñor, El /*The little nightingale* (ES 56): Jiménez

Percy (US 25): Marion D.

Peregrine Hunters, The (GB 78): Dundavan

Perfect Strangers (GB 45): Weske

Perfect Tribute, A (US 91): Haas L.

Peril for the Guy (GB 56): Alleney A., Hines
Perils of Pauline, The (US 14, srl): Berlinger
Perplexing Pickle Puzzle, A (US 15): Benham
Persona (SE 66): Lindström J.
Personal Affair, A (US 11): Boss
Personality (US 30): Black B.
Personality Kid (US 46): Donaldson T., Larson
Personal Maid's Secret (US 35): Cosbey
Pervi ekzamen /The first exam (SU 58): Kurban-Annakurbanov
Pervi myach /The first ball (SU 62): Vitushin
Pervoye svidaniye /First meeting (SU 60): Boriskin
Pescatore del Rhone, Il /The fisherman of the Rhône (IT 17):
    Casarotti
Pessi ja Illusia /Pessi and Illusia (FI 84): Kangas
Pete 'n' Tillie (US 72): Montgomery
Peter en de vliegende autobus /Peter and the flying bus (NL 76):
    Van Kruysen
Peter Ibbetson (US 18): Monahan
Peter Ibbetson (US 35): Moore D.
Peterle /Little Peter (GE 43): Meier
Peter Lundy and the Medicine Hat Stallion (US 77): Garrett
Peter Pan (US 24): Murphy J. and M., DeLacy, McBan
Peter Pan (US 52): Driscoll
Peter, Paul und Nanette (GE 34): Richter
Peters landlov /Peter's shore leave (DK 63): Schmidt J.P.
Peter the Great (US 84, srl): McGrath
Peter und das Einmaleins mit der Sieben /Peter and the seven-times table
    (DD 62): Dutz
Pete's Dragon (US 77): Marshall
Pětikoruna /The five-kroner piece (CS 60): Frana
Petimata ot Moby Dik /The five from the Moby Dick (BG 69):
    Djambazov
Petit Bougnat, Le /Little Charcoal (FR 70): Amazan
Petit criminel, Le /The little criminal (FR 90): Thomassin
Petite bonne du Palace, La /The maid at the Palace (FR 26): Mercanton
Petit étranger, Le /The little stranger (LB 62): Gabriel
Petit garçon de l'ascenseur, Le /The little lift-boy (FR 62): Dekock
Petit Jacques, Le /Little Jack (FR 53): Fourcade
Petit monde de Don Camillo, Le /The little world of Don Camillo
    (FR/IT 51): Loreti
Petit Poucet, Le /Tom Thumb (FR 12): Mary
Petit prince, Le — see Malenki prints (SU 67), Little Prince (US 74)
Petit roi, Le /The little King (FR 33): Lynen
Petit roi de Rome, Le /The little King of Rome (FR 10): Mary
Petits chats, Les /The little cats (FR 59): Dekock
Pettersson i Annorlunda /Pettersson at Annorlunda (SE 56): Nilsson
Petukhi /Fighting cocks (SU 25): Konstantinov
Peur, La /Fear (FR 36): Farguette
Phantom, The (US 31): Sabiston
Phantom Express (US 25): Darro
Phantom Flyer, The (US 28): Jones B.
Phantom Light, The (GB 35): Singer
Phantom of Paris, The (US 31): Scott D.
Phantom of the Plains (US 45): Blake
Phantom of the Range (US 28): Darro
Phantom Stallion, The (US 54): Price
Phantom Valley (US 48): Infuhr

Phatikchand /Phatik and the juggler (IN 83): Ganguly
Phool aur kante /The flower and the thorns (IN 48): Kumar
Phynx, The (US 70): Eccles
Physician, The (GB 29): Ashby J.
Pianos mecanicos, Los /The player-pianos (ES/FR/IT 65): Haudepin
Piccola vedetta lombarda, La /The little Lombard lookout (IT 15):
    Petrungaro, Roveri
Piccoli naufraghi /Little castaways (IT 39): Artese
Piccolo alpino /Boy of the Alps (IT 40): Artese, Sannangelo
Piccolo bandito, Il /The little bandit (CH 52): Di Nardo
Piccolo cerinaio, Il /The little match-seller (IT 14): Roveri
Piccolo mondo di Don Camillo, Il (51 FR/IT) — see Petit monde de Don
    Camillo
Piccolo patriota padovano, Il /The little Paduan patriot (IT 15): Roveri
Piccolo scrivano fiorentino, Il /The little Florentine scrivener (IT 15):
    Roveri
Piccolo vetraio, Il /The glazier's boy (IT 55): Poujouly
Piccolo vom Goldenen Löwen, Der /The page-boy at the Golden Lion
    (GE 28): Stark-Gstettenbaur
Pic et pic et colégram /Eeny meeny mina mo (FR 71): Erimitchoi
Pickaninny, The (US 21): Morrison E.
Pick a Star (US 37): McFarland, Switzer
Pickles (GB 72): Daniels P.
Pickwick Papers, The (GB 52): Hannaford
Picture Mommy Dead (US 66): Corcoran
Pie (US 16): Hupp
Piedone d'Egitto /Bigfoot in Egypt (IT/DD 80): 'Bodo'
Piedone l'Africano /Bigfoot the African (IT/DD 78): 'Bodo'
Pied Piper, The (US 42): McDowall, Rodin M., Tauzin
Pied Piper (US/BG 66): Alurkov, Kovachev
Pie in the Sky (US 65): Bray
Piekło i niebo /Heaven and hell (PL 66): Frątczak
Pierre Fabien et Cie. /Pierre Fabien and Co. (BE 79): Debecq
Pierwszy start /First start (PL 52): Nowak
Pieseň o sivom holubovi /Song of the grey dove (CS 60): Poláček,
    Krajčovič
Pigen og millionæren /The girl and the millionaire (DK 65): Schmidt J.P.
Pigen og pressefotografen /The girl and the press photographer
    (DK 63): Schmidt J.P.
Pige og 39 sømænd, En /A girl and 39 sailors (DK 65):
    Schmidt J.P.
Pigeon That Took Rome, The (US 62): Angeletti
Pigeon That Worked a Miracle, The (US 58): Payne
Pige uden lige /A singular girl (DK 43): Kaas
Pigskin Palooka (US 37): 'Our Gang', Jones D., Watson D.
Pikku-Matti maailmalla /Little Matt out in the world (FI 47): Kaitala
Pikku pelimanni /The little fiddler (FI 39): Haitto
Pikku Pietarin piha /Little Peter's yard (FI 61): Tanner
Pikro psomi, To /Bitter bread (GR 51): Kouris
Pilgrim, The (US 23): Reisner, Lee Ra.
Pilgrimage (US 33): Ward
Pilipko (62 SU) — see Zvyozdochka
Pillai selvam /Son is wealth (IN 73): Ramu
Pillars of Society (US 16): House C.
Pillow to Post (US 45): Blake
Pilluelo de Madrid, El /The scamp of Madrid (ES 26): Hurtado

Pilsudski kupil Petluri (26 SU) — *see* P.K.P.

Pim, de schrik van de familie / *Pim, the family terror* (NL c.18): 'Pim'

Pinafore (US 17): Carpenter, Messinger

Pinch Singer, The (US 36): 'Our Gang', Jones D., Watson D.

Pine Canyon Is Burning (US 77): Sinutko

Pink Gods (US 22): Trimble

Pink String and Sealing Wax (GB 45): Wallbridge

Pink Tights (US 20): Eason

Pinocchio (US 40): Jones D.

Pinocchio (IT 71, srl): Balestri

Pinocchio in Outer Space (US 65): Lazer

Pintame angelitos blancos / *Imagine white angels* (MX 54): Romay

Pinto Kid, The (US 28): Barton

'Pioneer Kid' series (US 29-30): Nelson B.

Pi-Pa-Po (GE 22): Lázár

Pippi ausser Rand und Band (70 SE/DE) — *see* På rymmen med Pippi Långstrump

Pippi i Taka-Tuka Land / *Pippi in Taka-Tuka-Land* (SE 70): Sundberg

Pippi Långstrump / *Pippi Longstocking* (SE/DE 69): Sundberg

Pippi Långstrump på de sju haven / *Pippi Longstocking on the Seven Seas* (SE/DE 70): Sundberg, Hallerstam

Pippin up to His Pranks (GB 12): Barker K.

Pirata de doce años, Un / *A 12-year-old pirate* (MX 71): Coster A.

Pirate, The (US 78): Peluce

Pirates of Blood River, The (GB 61): Pike P., Waterman

Piratii din Pacific / *Pirates of the Pacific* (RO/FR 75): Sofron

Piroshka és Farkas (88 CA/HU) — *see* Bye-Bye Red Riding Hood

Piso pisello / *Big pea, little pea* (IT 81): Porro

Pitfall (US 48): Hunt

Piume al vento / *Feather in the wind* (IT 50): Cerusico

Pixote (BR 80): Ramos da Silva

P.K.P. (SU 26): Lyudvinski

Place in the Sun, A (US 51): Anderson B.

Plainsman, The (US 36): Bailey Sd., Ernest

Planter's Wife, The (GB 52): Spenser J., Asher

'Plattfuss' films (78-80 IT/DD) — *see* 'Piedone'

Plavecky marias / *Swimmer's card-game* (CS 52): Bejval

Plaveni hřibat / *Foals in the river* (CS 76): Dlouhý

Playing With Souls (US 25): Marion D.

Playin' Hookey (US 28): 'Our Gang'

Play It Cool (GB 62): Hamshere

Playthings of Destiny (US 21): Headrick

Pleasant Journey, A (US 23): 'Our Gang'

Please Believe Me (US 49): Price

Please Don't Eat the Daisies (US 60): Herbert, Mark, Livingston S.

Please Turn Over (GB 59): Stephens M.

Plemennikut chuzhdenets / *The foreign nephew* (BG 89): Gabrovski

Plotina prorvana / *The dam has burst* (SU 28): Krestinski

Plot Thickens, The (US 36): Kaye

Plough and the Stars, The (US 36): McKim S.

Ploughman's Lunch, The (GB 83): Wells

Plow Woman, The (US 17): Hupp

Plunderers (US 60): Ferrell

Plus de vacances pour le bon Dieu / *No let-up for Almighty God* (FR 49): Gencel, Lecointe, Simon

Plus joli péché du monde, Le / *The loveliest sin in the world* (FR 51):

Maurin Y.-M.

Plymouth Adventure (US 52): Ivo

Pocharde, La / *The inebriate woman* (FR 21): Haziza

Pochodne / *Tortures* (CS 60): Smyczek

Pociag do Hollywood / *Train to Hollywood* (PL 86): Węgrzyniak

Počitani oveček / *Counting sheep* (CS 81): Mikuláš

Počkam, až zabiješ / *I'll wait, you kill him* (CS 72): Dlouhý

Pod jezevči skálou / *Under Badger's Rock* (CS 79): Holý

Pod kamennim nebom / *Under a stone sky* (SU 75): Yankovski

Podranki / *Wounded birds* (SU 77): Cherstvoff

Podróz za jeden uśmiech / *Journey for a smile* (PL 72): Gołębiewski, Łobodzinski

Pod stuk kolyos / *Rattle of the wheels* (SU 58): Adeyev

Poema o more / *Sea poem* (SU 58): Chugunov

Pogrzeb świerszcza / *Burial of a cricket* (PL 78): Tomczak

Pohádka o stare tramvaji / *Tale of an old tram* (CS 61): Malaska, Maxian, Smyczek

Poil de Carotte / *Carrots* (FR 25): Heuzé

Poil de Carotte (FR 32): Lynen

Poil de Carotte (FR 51): Simon

Poil de Carotte (FR 73): Cohn

Point, The (US 70): Lookinland M.

Pointing Finger, The (US 19): Redden

Poison, Le / *Poison* (FR 51): Urbain

Poisoned Paradise (US 24): Lee F.

Poison Pen (GB 39): McDowall

Pojken i trädet / *The boy in the tree* (SE 61): Bolme

Poker Faces (US 26): Holmes L.

Pokhishteniyé v zhulto / *Kidnap in yellow* (BG 80): Bakavliev, Stoyanov

Pokkers unger, De (47 DK) — *see* De pokkers unger

Police Court (US 32): Janney

Pollyanna (US 19): Condon

Pollyanna (US 60): Corcoran

Polly of the Circus (US 17): Carr J. and S.

Polly of the Storm Country (US 20): Coffey C., Moore M.

Polly Put the Kettle On (US 16): Hamrick

Polly the Girl Scout and Grandma's Medals (GB 13): Barker K.

Polonez Oginskogo / *Oginsky's polonaise* (SU 71): Tsukker

Polunochnik / *Night-Bird* (SU 73): Bratkauskas

Poly (61 FR) — *see* Merveilleuse histoire de Poly

Polyot k tisyacham solnts / *Flight to thousands of suns* (SU 63): Ess

Polyushko-pole / *Little field* (SU 56): Merkulov

Ponedeljak ili utorak / *Monday or Tuesday* (YU 66): Mimica

Pony Express, The (US 25): Fox J.

Pony Express Kid, The (US 30): Nelson B.

Pony Who Paid the Rent, The (GB 12): Royston R.

Pooch, The (US 32): 'Our Gang', McComas

Poor Folks' Boy, The (US 14): Willis

Poor Little Rich Girl (US 87): Brandis

Poor Men's Wives (US 23): McBan

Poor Old Bill (GB 31): Lawford

Poor Relation, A (US 15): Steuart

Popaul et Virginie (FR 19): Touzé

Popi (US 69): Alejandro, Figueroa

Poppy Girl's Husband, The (US 19): Stone

Por mis pistoles / *For my pistols* (MX 38): Busquets

Portafoglio rosso, Il / *The red notebook* (IT 14): Roveri, Visca

Porte ouverte, La / *The open door* (FR 51): Lecointe

Portes de la nuit, Les / *The gates of night* (FR 46): Simon

Portrait, The (US 14): Connelly

Portrait of Clare (GB 50): Spenser J.

Portrait of Innocence (41 FR) — *see* Nous les gosses

Por un amor / *For one love* (MX 46): Pastor

Poseidon Adventure, The (US 72): Shea E.

Po sledam geroya / *In a hero's footsteps* (SU 35): But

Poslednja trka / *The last race* (YU 79): Buljan

Possessed (US 47): Miles P. (Perreau)

Postal Inspector (US 36): Burrud

Postaveni mimo hru / *Off-side* (CS 79): Holý

Postlagernd Turteltaube / *Poste-Restante Turtle-Dove* (DE 52): Condrus, Jansen

Post of Honor, The (US 30): Nelson B.

Potash and Perlmutter (US 23): Devine

Poteryannaya fotografiya / *The lost photograph* (SU/CS 59): Sedláček, Kekish

Potraga za zmajem / *Quest for the dragon* (YU 61): Gjurin

Poucette, ou le plus petit détective du monde / *Thumbscrew, the world's smallest detective* (FR 19): Touzé, Duc

Pouponnière, La / *The day nursery* (FR 32): Bara

Pourquoi? / *Why?* (FR 77): Gomez J.

Poverty of Riches, The (US 21): Lee F., Coghlan

Povidky o dětech / *Stories about children* (CS 63): Filip J.

Power and the Glory, The (US 18): Tansey S., Jackson C.

Power Dive (US 41): Lee B.

Power of a Hymn, The (US 12): Melford

Power of a Lie, The (US 22): Miller W.

Power of One, The (US 91): Fenton, Witcher

Power of Right, The (GB 19): Wood S.

Poyezd idyot v Moskvu / *The train leaving for Moscow* (SU 38): Martinov, Tumalaryants

Poznanskie słowiki / *Nightingales of Poznan* (PL 65): Jankowski P.

Pozovi menya v dal svetluyu / *Call me to the bright distance* (SU 77): Naumenko

Prabhu ka pyara / *Favourite of the God* (IN 36): Apte

Práče / *The slinger* (CS 60): Koblic

Practical Jokers (US 38): 'Our Gang'

Prahlad (IN 51): Bhattacharjee

Prairie Gold (US 19): Moore P.

Prairie Moon (US 38): Ryan

Pram at the Styx, A (72 JP) — *see* Kozure ohkami - sanzu no kawa no ubaguruma

Pranks (US 09): Harron

Prashna (IN 55): Bhattacharjee

Prästen, som slog knockout / *The K.O. priest* (SE 43): Olsson

Přátelé na moři / *Comrades at sea* (CS 59): Sedláček

Pratiyabartan / *The return* (IN 51): Bhattacharjee

Pravě začiname / *We're just beginning* (CS 46): Mikulič

Prázdniny pro psa / *Holiday for a dog* (CS 80): Holý

Pražské švadlenky / *Dressmakers of Prague* (CS 29): Pražský

Prea cald pentru luna mai / *Too hot for May* (RO 82): Vîlcu

Prea mic pentru un razboi atit de mare / *Too small for such a big war* (RO 69): Filip M.

Prea tineri pentru riduri / *Too young for wrinkles* (RO 82): Vîlcu

Předtucha / *Presentiment* (CS 47): Mikulič

Prehysteria (US 93): O'Brien A.

Prejudice (US 49): Ivo

Prélude à la gloire / *Prelude to fame* (FR 49): Benzi

Prelude to Fame (GB 50): Spenser J., Simons W.

Premier mai, le / *May Day* (FR/IT 58): Noël

Première nuit, La / *The first night* (FR 58): Devis

Premières armes, Les / *The first campaign* (FR 49): Cordier

Prem pujari / *Worshipper of love* (IN 70): Sachin

Préparez vos mouchoirs / *Handkerchiefs ready!* (FR/BE 77): Liebman

Presenting Lily Mars (US 43): Croft, Kuhn

Pressure Point (US 62): Gordon Ba., Patrick

Preussische Liebesgeschichte / *Prussian love story* (GE 38): Sierck

Price of a Ruby, The (US 14): Hackett R.

Price of a Song, The (GB 35): Singer

Price of Divorce, The (GB 28): Ashby J.

Price of Redemption, The (US 20): Moore M.

Price of Silence, The (US 17): Griffith

Price of Success, The (US 25): O'Donnell

Price on His Head, A (GB 14): Desmond

Pride of Pawnee, The (US 29): Darro

Pride of the Force, The (GB 33): Singer

Pride of the Marines (US 36): Burrud

Pride of the Yankees, The (US 42): Croft, Collins, Roy, Winkler

Přijdu hned / *I'll come in a moment* (CS 42): Jedlička A.

Příklady táhnou / *The power of example* (CS 39): Salač

Priklyucheniya Artyomki / *Artyomka's adventures* (SU 56): Aleksandrov

Priklyucheniya Petrushki / *Petrushka's adventures* (SU 36): Akimovich

Priklyucheniya Toli Klyukvina / *Tolya Klyukvin's adventures* (SU 64): Filatov

Priklyucheniya Tomi Soyera / *Tom Sawyer's adventures* (SU 81): Stukov, Suhakov

Prima Donna's Husband, The (US 16): Verdi

Primal Law, The (US 21): Lee F.

Prime Minister, The (GB 41): Tyler G.

Primera aventura, La / *The first adventure* (ES/MX 64): Arco, Sanchez

Primera comunion / *First communion* (MX 64): Bravo J.

Primite telegrammu v dolg / *Send telegram on charge* (SU 79): Tikhonchik

Primrose Path, The (US 25): Moore P.

Primrose Ring, The (US 17): Jacobs

Prince and the Pauper, The (20 AT) — *see* Prinz und Bettelknabe

Prince and the Pauper, The (IN 32): Modak

Prince and the Pauper, The (US 37): Mauch Bl. and Bb.

Prince and the Pauper, The (US 57): Thompson R.

Prince and the Pauper, The (GB 62): Scully

Prince and the Pauper, The (PA 77): Lester

Prince Chap, The (US 16): Barry W.

Prince in a Pawnshop, A (US 16): Connelly

Prince in Disguise, The (US 15): Connelly

Prince of a King, A (US 23): Reisner

Prince of Players (US 54): Alexander L., Cook C.

Princes in the Tower, The (GB 13): Desmond

Princess Bride, The (US 87): Savage F.

Princess Comes Across, The (US 36): Bartlett

Princesse, à vos ordres / *At your service, Princess* (FR 31): Mercanton

Pri nikogo / *With no-one* (BG 74): Kochev

Prinsesse för en dag / *Princess for a day* (DK 62): Flensmark

Printer's Devil, The (US 23): Barry W.

Prinzessin und der Geiger, Die / *The princess and the fiddler*
(GE 25): Herzberg
Prinzessin von St Wolfgang, Die / *The Princess of St Wolfgang*
(DE 57): Ande
Prinz Louis Ferdinand (GE 27): Rive
Prinz und Bettelknabe / *The prince and the pauper* (AT 20): Lubinsky
Prision de sueños / *Prison of dreams* (MX 48): Perez
Prison Break (US 38): Russell J.
Prisoner for Life, A (US 19): Moore P.
Prisoner of Zenda, The (US 37): Kuhn
Prisvoit zvanie geroya / *To him the name of hero* (SU 72): Banionis
Prithvi putra / *Son of the earth* (IN 38): Apte
Private Hell 36 (US 54): Hawkins
Private Izzy Murphy (US 26): O'Donnell
Private Life of Don Juan, The (GB 34): Rietti
Private War of Major Benson, The (US 55): Hovey, Considine
Prize of Gold, A (GB 55): Ray A.
Priznanie / *Confession* (BG 69): Arshinkov
Prizvanie / *Vocation* (SU 56): Demyanov
Probation (US 32): Durand
Probationer, The (US 13): Clark R.
Problem Child (US 90): Oliver M.
Prodigal, The (US 55): Mazzola
Professional Soldier (US 35): Bartholomew
Professor's Antigravitational Fluid, The (GB 08): Potter
Professor's Romance, The (US 15): Connelly
Proie, La / *The prey* (FR 20): Poyen
Proklyatieto (84 PL/BG) – *see* Przeklete oko proroka
Proletardrengen / *The working-class boy* (DK 15): Reinwald
Promesse, La / *The promise* (FR 69): Maurin J.-F.
Promesse de l'aube, La (70 US/FR) – *see* Promise at Dawn
Promessi sposi, I / *The betrothed* (IT 41): Barbetti
Promise at Dawn (US/FR 70): Raffoul
Pro obezyanku / *About a little monkey* (SU 35): Makutonin
Prosím, pane Profesore! / *Please, Sir!* (CS 41): Jedlička A.
Prosperity (US 32): Tucker J.
Prostaya istoriya / *A simple story* (SU 60): Guskoff
Proud Rebel, The (US 58): Ladd
Pro Vityu, pro Mashu i Morskuyu Pekhotu / *Vitya, Masha and the Marines* (SU 74): Svetlichni
Prvak / *The first-former* (CS 59): Krajčovič
Przejażdżka / *The excursion* (PL 60): Wiśniewski
Przeklete oko proroka / *Accursed Eye of the Prophet* (PL/BG 84): Tsvetkov
Pseftra, I / *The girl who lied* (GR 63): Kailas
Psila ta kheria Hitler / *Hands up, Hitler!* (GR 62): Kalatzopoulos
Psyllos, O / *The Flea* (GR 90): Trivizas
Public Enemy, The (US 31): Coghlan, Darro
Public Opinion (US 35): Cosbey
Pueblerina / *Town girl* (MX 48): Perez
Puika / *The boy* (SU 77): Lacis
Pukar / *The call* (IN 39): Apte
Pulcinella, cetrulo d'Acerra / *Punch, the Acerra cucumber* (IT 59): Chevalier
Pulgarcito / *Tom Thumb* (MX 58): Quezadas
Pullman Nightmare, A (US 13): Benham
Pumpkin Eater, The (GB 64): Phillips G., McClelland, Ellis C.

Pünktchen und Anton / *Little Dot and Anton* (AT 53): Feldt, Friedl
Punktur punktur komma strik / *Dot dot comma dash* (IS 81): Jónsson
Punťa a čtyřlistek / *Doggy and the Three* (CS 55): Košnar, Postránecký, Pucholt
Puppe vom Lunapark, Die / *The Luna Park doll* (GE 24): Eysoldt
Pups Is Pups (US 30): 'Our Gang'
Pure in Mind (39 US) – *see* Boy Slaves
Purple Heart, The (US 44): Nokes
Pursued (US 47): Severn E., Bates
Pursuing Vengeance, The (US 16): Hamrick
Pursuit (US 35): Beckett
Pursuit of Happiness, The (US 34): Billings G.
Pushover (US 54): Charney
Puskák és galambok / *Guns and doves* (HU 61): Tóth L., Kiss
Pustiul / *The kid* (RO 61): Bejan
Puteshestviye / *The journey* (BG 80): Tsankov
Putyovka v zhizn / *The road to life* (SU 31): Dzhagofarov
Pyar hi pyar / *Love, only love* (IN 69): Mehmood
Pyar ka rishta / *Love's relation* (IN 73): Satyajit
Pyaterka otvazhnikh / *The fearless five* (SU 70): Banionis
Pyšna princezna / *The proud princess* (CS 52): Bejval

Qatloon kay qatil (PK 88): Jamshid
Q & Q (NL 78): Perels
Quack Doctor, The (US 20): Marion D.
Quality Street (US 27): Jewell, McBan, Watson C.
Quality Street (US 37): Bailey Sd., Kaye
Quanshui dingdong / *Bubbling spring* (CN 82): Fang
Quantrill's Raiders (US 58): Charney
Quarantined (US 14): Clark A.
Quartiere ovest / *West district* (IT 59): Chevalier
Quatre cents coups, Les / *The 400 blows* (FR 58): Léaud, Auffay, Kanayan
Quatre veuves / *Four widows* (FR 55): Chapeland
Quattro giornate di Napoli, Le / *The four days of Naples* (IT/US 62): Formato
Queen Bee (US 55): Hovey
Queen of Hearts (GB 36): Pavitt
Queen of Hearts (GB 89): Hawkes, Whalley
Queen of Sheba, The (US 21): Moore P.
Queen of the Mob (US 40): Bupp S.
¡¡Que he hecho YO para merecer esto!! / *What have I done to deserve this?* (ES 84): Herranz
Que la bête meure / *The beast must die* (FR/IT 69): Di Napoli M. and S.
Quella villa accanto il cimitero / *The house by the cemetery* (IT 82): Frezza
Quest, The (US 15): Clark R.
Quest, The (85 AU) – *see* Frog Dreaming
Question Mark, The (US 11): Boss
Questo si che è amore / *This thing called love* (IT 77): Valsecchi
Quick Millions (US 39): Mahan
Quick Money (US 37): Bailey Sd.
Quicksand (US 18): Lee F.
Quiet Fourth, A (US 35): Watson D.
Quiet One, The (US 48): Thompson D.
Quiet, Please, Murder (US 42): Larson
Quiet Street, A (US 22): 'Our Gang'
Quiet Wedding (GB 41): Gainsborough

Quiet Weekend (GB 46): Weske
Quitte ou double /Double or quits (FR 52): Poujouly
Quo Vadis (US 51): Miles P.
Qyteti më i ri në botë /The youngest city in the world (AL 74): Mosho

Raaste aur manzil /Way and destination (IN 69): Sachin
Raat ki Rani /Queen of the night (IN 35): Apte
Rabbit Trap, The (US 58): Corcoran
Race for Life, A (US 14): Jacobs
Race for Life, A (US 28): Gordon Bo.
Rachel (47 US) − see Rachel and the Stranger
Rachel and the Stranger (US 47): Gray G.
Racheta alba /The white rocket (RO 82): Vîlcu
Racketeer, The (US 29): Parrish
Racing Blood (US 54): Boyd
Racing for Life (US 24): Darro
Racing Luck (US 35): Ernest
Racing Strain, The (US 32): Moore D.
Radio Bugs (US 44): 'Our Gang'
Radio Days (US 87): Green S.
Radio Flyer (US 91): Wood E., Mazzello
Radio Hound, The (US 22): Fox J., Morgan
Radio Lover (GB 36): Pavitt
Radio Parade (GB 33): Pavitt
Radio Patrol (US 37, srl): Rentschler
Radio Star, The (35 US) − see Loud Speaker
Rad na odredjeno vreme /Part-time work (YU 80): Kojo
Raffles (US 40): Herbert-Bond
Rafle est pour ce soir, Le /The raid is tonight (FR 53): Fourcade
Ragazzi (46 IT) − see Sciuscia
Ragazzo /Boy (IT 51): Olivieri
Ragazzo di Calabria /Boy of Calabria (IT/FR 87): Polimeno
Rage (US 72): Beauvy
Raggedy Man (US 81): Thomas H.
Rag Man, The (US 25): Coogan J.
Rags to Riches (US 22): Barry W.
Rags to Riches (US 41): Kuhn
Raices /Roots (MX 55): Negron
Raid, The (US 54): Aaker L., Rettig
Raiders of the River (GB 56, srl): O'Sullivan
Raiders of Tomahawk Creek (US 50): Kimbley
Railroadin' (US 29): 'Our Gang'
Railway Children, The (GB 70): Warren, Witty
'Rainbow' Comedies (GB 22): Brassard
Rainbow (US 78): Doran, Drier
Rainbow Jacket, The (GB 54): Edmonds
Rainbow Man, The (US 29): Darro
Rainbow on the River (US 36): Breen, Beard, Watson Bl.
Raintree Country (US 57): Losby
Rainy Day, A (US 19): Carr J.
Rainy Days (US 28): 'Our Gang'
Raising the Roof (GB 71): Forlong
Raisin in the Sun, A (US 61): Perry
Raja Harishchandra (IN 12): Phalke
Rajarani Damayanti (IN 52): Kumar
Rake's Progress, The (GB 45): Wallbridge
Rakudai wa shita keredo /I flunked, but... (JP 30): 'Tokkan-Kozo'

Rally 'Round the Flag, Boys! (US 58): Livingston S.
Ramayya thandri /Father Ramayya (IN 74): Ramu
Rambling Rose (US 91): Haas L.
Ram darshan (IN 50): Kapoor S.
Ramona (US 36): Spindola
Ramshastri (IN 44): Marathe A.
Random Harvest (US 42): Kilburn
Range Buzzards (US 25): Jones B.
Range Courage (US 27): Winslow D.
Ranger Courage (US 37): Henry R.
Rangi's Catch (GB 72, srl): Forlong
Rango (US 31): Scott D.
Rani Saheba /Her Majesty the Queen (IN 30): Batto
Rännstensungar /Guttersnipes (SE 44): Lindgren H.
Ransom! (US 55): Clark B.2
Ransomed (US 10): Casey
Ransom of Red Chief, The (US 11): Boss
Ransom of Red Chief, The (52 US) − see O.Henry's Full House
Ransom of Red Chief, The (US 77): Petersen P.
Rare Breed, The (US 65): Domasin
Rascal (US 69): Mumy
Rascals and Robbers (US 82): Hall A.M.
Rasmus, Pontus och Toker /Rasmus, Pontus and Nutter (SE 56): Dalenius, Almgren
Rasputin (GE 32): Rive
Rasputin and the Empress (US 32): Alexander T.
Rasskaz nishchevo /The pauper's tale (SU 61): Gachechiladze, Daneliya
Rätselhafter Blick, Ein /An enigmatic look (GE 18): Lindau-Schulz
Ratten der Grossstadt /Rats of the metropolis (GE 20): Allen W.
Raub der Sabinerinnen, Der /The rape of the Sabines (DE 54): Jansen
Räuberbande, Die /The robber band (GE 28): Stark-Gstettenbaur
Raymie (US 60): Ladd
Reach for Glory (GB 61): Tomlinson, Grimm
Readin' and Writin' (US 32): 'Our Gang', McComas
Ready, Willing and Able (US 37): Jones D.
Really Important Person, A (US 47): Stockwell
Reason to Live, A (US 84): Schroder
Rebecca of Sunnybrook Farm (US 17): Barry W.
Rebecca of Sunnybrook Farm (US 32): Conlon, Albright
Rebel in Town (US 56): Clark B.2
Rebelion de los colgados, La /Revolt of the failures (MX 54): Perez
Rebelion de los pajaros /Revolt of the birds (ES 81): Sanz
Recht auf Liebe, Das /The right to love (GE 39): Sierck
Reckless (US 35): Rooney, Hoskins, Jones D.
Reckless Living (US 38): Billings G., Tucker J.
Reckless Moment, The (US 49): Hyatt, Norman
Reckless Youth (29 US) − see Daughters of Desire
Reckoning, The (US 32): Scott D.
Reclaimed: the Struggle for a Soul Between Love and Hate (US 19): Connelly
Recluta con niño /Recruit with child (ES 55): Gil
Reconciled in Blood (US 14): Clark R.
Redeeming Sin, The (US 25): Noisom
Redeeming Sin, The (US 29): DeLacy
Redemption (US 17): Thaw
Redemption (US 30): Frederick
Red Hand Gang, The (US c.78, srl): Laborteaux M.

Mechanical laughter: Casper Petersen (r.) and family in Lattermaskinen

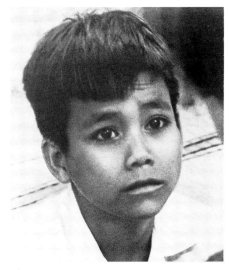

Phi Lân

Jiří Polák

Jungle chic: Bobby Nelson borne by Frank Merrill in Tarzan the Mighty

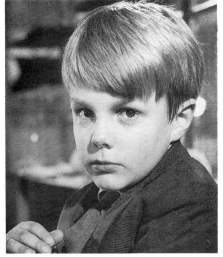

Clive Powell

Redheads Preferred (US 26): Holmes L.
Red Hot Hoofs (US 26): Darro
Red Hot Hottentots (US 20): Morrison E.
Redl ezredes /*Colonel Redl* (HU/DE/AT 84): Svidrony
Redman and the Child, The (US 08): Tansey J.
Red Mill, The (US 27): Janney
Redneck (72 IT/GB) — *see* Senza ragione
Red Planet Mars (US 52): Lindgren O.
Red Pony, The (US 49): Miles P., Bridges B.
Red Pony, The (US 73): Howard C.
Red River (US 47): Kuhn
Red River Range (US 38): McKim S.
Red Rope, The (US 37): Nelson B.
'Red Ryder' series (US 44-47): Blake, McKim H.
Red Stallion, The (US 47): Donaldson T.
Red Sundown (US 55): Kasday
Red Sword, The (US 29): Darro
Reducing (US 31): Ward
Red Wagon (GB 34): Fitzpatrick P.
Red Warning, The (US 27): House N.
Reflecting Skin, The (GB 90): Cooper Jy.
Reflections of Murder (US 74): Kerwin
Reformation of the Gang, The (US 14): Kelly P.
Reformatory (US 38): Bailey Sd., Bupp T., Daniel, Jordan,
   McKim S.
Refugee, The (US 15): Benham
Refugiados en Madrid /*Refugees in Madrid* (MX 38): Busquets
Regalo de reyes /*Gift of kings* (MX 42): Busquets, Ortin
Regentropfen /*Raindrops* (DE 81): Geula
Registered Nurse (US 34): Cosbey
Reg'lar Fellers (US 41): Switzer, Lee B., Van Patten D.
Regular Scout, A (US 26): Black B.
Reifezeit /*Maturity* (DE 76): Hennig
Reign of Terror (US 49): Tamblyn, Sydes
Reisebekanntschaft /*Travel acquaintance* (GE 36): Bosse
Reise nach Sundevit, Die /*The journey to Sundevit* (DD 66): Strohbach
Reise nach Tilsit, Die /*The journey to Tilsit* (GE 39): Kieling
Reivers, The (US 69): Vogel
Reizende Familie, Eine /*A charming family* (GE 45): Moik, Neie
Rekava /*Line of destiny* (LK 56): Dharmapriya
Relitto, Il /*The wastrel* (IT 60): Stellman
Reluctant Bride, The (GB 55): Caridia
Reluctant Dragon, The (US 41): Lee B.
Remarkable Mr Pennypacker, The (US 58): Ferrell, Losby, Rangno
Remember the Day (US 41): Croft, Dawson, Holt D., Kaye
Remember When (GB 37): Singer
Remembrance (US 22): Trimble
Reménykedok /*A charming family* (HU 71): Kovács
Remontons les Champs-Elysées /*Let's go up the Champs-Elysées* (FR 38):
   Buquet
Remorseless Love (US 21): Devine
Rendezvous (51 US) — *see* Darling, How Could You!
Rendezvous 24 (US 46): Gray G.
Renegade Trail (US 39): Bupp S.
Renfrew of the Royal Mounted (US 37): Jones D.
Reno (US 30): Scott D.
Renoir, My Father (GB 78): Spurrier

Renshen /*Life* (CN 34): Li
Rented Man, The (US 17): Marion F.
Renuka (IN 47): Kapoor S.
Repaying the Debt (GB 12): Royston R.
Reported Missing (US 22): Bennett M.
Reproduction interdite /*Copyright reserved* (FR 57): Moullières
Rescue from the Desert (US 11): Melford
Residencia, La /*The big house* (ES 69): Moulder-Brown
Responding brother (CN 82): Ji
Rest Cure, The (GB 23): Brantford
Restless Sex, The (US 20): Carr S.
Resurrection (US 80): Sinutko
Retour, Le (28 GE/IT/FR) — *see* Marys grosses Geheimnis
Retour à la vie /*Return to life* (FR 48): Gencel, Lecointe
Retour au bonheur /*Return to happiness* (FR 40): Farguette
Retour de Don Camillo, Le /*The return of Don Camillo* (FR/IT 53):
   Staiola, Chapeland
Return from Witch Mountain (US 78): Eisenmann, Juttner, Savage B.
Return of Casey Jones, The (US 33): Searl, Haig
Return of Count Yorga, The (US 71): Frame
Return of Frank James, The (US 40): Beard
Return of Gilbert and Sullivan, The (US 52): Gray B.
Return of Monte Cristo (US 46): Infuhr
Return of Peter Grimm, The (US 26): Janney, McBan
Return of Peter Grimm, The (US 35): Breakston
Return of Rin Tin Tin, The (US 47): Blake
Return of Rusty, The (US 46): Donaldson T., Collins, Dennis,
   Hickman Dw., Infuhr, Kuhn
Return of the Bad Men (US 48): Gray G.
Return of the Big Cat (US 74): Juttner
Return of the Texan (US 52): Mora
Return to Warbow (US 58): Olsen C.
Reunion (GB 32): Pavitt
Reunion (US 36): Ernest
Reunion in Rhythm (US 37): 'Our Gang'
Revanche /*A debt repaid* (AT 22): Lubinsky
Revanşa /*Revenge* (RO 78): Vîlcu
Revelation (US 24): Guerin
Revenge Is Sweet (US 12): Boss
Revenge of Red Chief (US 79): Petersen P.
Révolté, Le /*The rebel* (FR 38): Buquet
Révoltée, La /*Woman in revolt* (FR 47): Rob
Revoltosa, La /*The wild girl* (ES 25): Hurtado
Revolution (GB 85): Owen S.
Rey del barrio, El /*King of the neighbourhood* (MX 49): Perez
Rhapsody in Blue (US 45): Hickman Dl.
Rich But Honest (US 27): Watson C.
Richest Man in the World, The (US 30): DeLacy
Richie Rich (US 94): Culkin M.
Rich Kids (US 79): Levy
Rich Man's Folly (US 31): Durand
Rich Men's Wives (US 22): Headrick
Ricochet Romance (US 54): Aaker L., Charney
Riddle: Woman, The (US 21): DeLacy
Ride a Northbound Horse (US 69): Shea M.
Rideau rouge, Le /*The red curtain* (FR 52): Lecointe
Ride a Wild Pony (US 75): Bettles

Ride Beyond Vengeance (US 65): Domasin
Ride for Help, The (US 28): House N.
Rider of the Plains, A (US 31): Shuford
Riders of Pasco Basin (US 40): Winkler
Riders of the Lone Star (US 47): Dennis
Riders of the New Forest (GB 46, srl): Bowyer
Riders of the Northland (US 42): Larson
Ridin' Down the Canyon (US 42): Henry R.
Riding Gold (US 27): House N.
Riding to Fame (US 27): Watson D.
Ridin' Kid from Powder River, The (US 24): House N.
Ridin' Whirlwind, The (US 27): House N.
Rififi (54 FR/IT) − see Du rififi chez les hommes
Riffraff (US 35): Rooney
Right in Your Lap (US 37): Switzer
Right Off the Bat (US 15): Hauck
Right of the Strongest, The (US 23): Watson C.
Right to Be Happy, The (US 16): Lee F.
Right to Live, The (US 15): Stone
Right to Love, The (US 30): Parrish
Right to Romance, The (US 33): Watson D.
Rike enke, Den / The rich widow (DK 62): Schmidt J.P.
Rikki-Tikki-Tavi (SU 76): Alekseyev
Riley the Cop (US 28): Parrish
Ringtailed Rhinoceros, The (US 15): Hackett R.
Ring Up the Curtain (33 US) − see Broadway to Hollywood
Rio anakku / Rio, my child (ID 73): Karno
Rio escondido / Hidden river (MX 47): Jiménez Pons J.
Rio Grande (US 20): Stone
Rio Grande (US 50): Jarman
Rio Grande Ranger (US 37): Henry R.
Rip and Stitch Tailors (US 19): Marion D.
Rip Van Winkle (US 14): Steuart
Rip Van Winkle (US 21): Carpenter
Rires de Paris / Paris laughter (FR 52): Rob
Ritorno di Don Camillo, Il (53 FR/IT) − see Retour de Don Camillo
Ritorno di Zanna Bianca, Il / The return of White Fang) (IT 74): Cestiè
Ritsar bez bronya / Knight without armour (BG 65): Kovachev
Rivaaj / The custom (IN 72): Mehmood
Rivals, The (US 15): Stone
Rivaux de la piste, Les / Rivals of the track (FR 32): Mercanton
River, The (US 50): Foster
River, The (US 84): Bailey Sn.
River of No Return (US 54): Rettig
River Pirate, The (US 28): Lee D.
River's End, The (US 19): Barry W.
River's End (US 30): Coghlan, Janney
River Wild, The (US 94): Mazzello
Rivolta dei sette, La / Revolt of the Seven (IT 64): Loddi
Rizhik / Ginger (SU 60): Zolotaryoff
Road to Divorce, The (US 20): Redden
Road to Eldorado, The (US 28): Darro
Road to Happiness, The (US 42): Lee B.
Road to Heaven, The (GB 22): Brantford
Road to Life, The (31 SU) − see Putyovka v zhizn
Road to Yesterday, The (US 25): Coghlan, Jones B.
Road Warrior, The (81 AU) − see Mad Max 2

Roamin' Holiday (US 37): 'Our Gang'
Roaring Oaks (US 20): Carr S.
Roaring Rails (US 24): Darro
Roaring Ranch (US 30): Nelson B.
Roaring Rangers (US 46): Kuhn
Roarin' Guns (US 36): Bupp T.
Roarin' Lead (US 37): Bupp T.
Robber Symphony, The (GB/FR 36): Fehér
Robby (US 68): Raum, Siani
Robert (DE 66): Rosengarten
Robert Kennedy and His Times (US 85): Phoenix R.
Roberto (49 FR) − see Prélude à la gloire
Robin and the 7 Hoods (US 64): Padilla
Robin Hood en zijn schelmen / Robin Hood and his merry men (NL 62): van der Linden C.
Robin Hood, Jr. (US 23): Lee F.
Robinson Crusoe (MX 69): 'Ahui'
Robinson Crusoe and Son (US 32): Durand
Robinson Junior (29 FR) − see Black and White
Robinsonka / Girl Crusoe (CS 74): Dlouhý
Robinson soll nicht sterben / Robinson shall not die (DE 57): Condrus, Kaiser
Robo-no ishi / Pebble by the wayside (JP 38): Katayama
Robo-no ishi (JP 60): Ota
Robot Wrecks (US 41): 'Our Gang'
Rock-a-Bye Baby (US 20): Morrison E.
Rocket Boy (54 US) − see Rocket Man
Rocket Gibraltar (US 88): Culkin M.
Rocket Man, The (US 54): Winslow G.
Rockets in the Dunes (GB 60): Witty
Rocking Horse Winner, The (GB 49): Davies J.H.
Rock Island Trail (US 50): Hunt
Rock, Pretty Baby (US 56): Winslow G.
Rocky V (US 90): Stallone
Rocky Mountain Rangers (US 40): McKim S.
Rodeo (US 52): Gray G.
Rodina zovyot / Call of the motherland (SU 36): Goryunoff
Rodnaya krov / Blood kinship (SU 63): Fisenko, Selyuzhenok
Rodnya / Kinsfolk (SU 82): Stukov
Roger-la-Honte (FR 45): Demorget
Rogues' Gallery, The (US 13): Jacobs
Rogue's Romance, A (US 19): Moore P.
Rohanj velem! / Run with me! (HU 82): Jambor
Roi des Aulnes, Le / The Erl King (FR 30): Lapon
Roi des camelots, Le / King of the Hawkers (FR 50): Gencel
Rois mages, Les / The Magi (FR 31): Mercanton
Roll Along Cowboy (US 37): Albright
Roll, Freddy, Roll! (US 74): Drier
Roma città aperta / Rome, open city (IT 45): Annichiarico
Romain Kalbris (FR 22): Haziza
Romanca o solzi / Romance of the tear (YU 61): Gjurin
Romance in Manhattan (US 34): Butler
Romance in the Rain (US 34): Beckett
Romance of Billy Goat Hill, The (US 16): Hamrick, Lee F.
Romance of Rosy Ridge, The (US 47): Stockwell
Romance of Tarzan, The (US 18): Griffith
Romance of the Redwoods, A (US 17): Alexander B.

'Romances of Youth' series (US 20): Roubert
Roman de Werther, Le / *The story of Werther* (FR 38): Buquet
Roman d'un mousse, Le / *A cabin-boy's story* (FR 13): Adrien
Roman d'un tricheur, Le / *The story of a cheat* (FR 36): Grave
Roman eines Arztes / *A doctor's story* (GE 39): Eugens
Roman Scandals (US 33): Barty
Romanza di un cane povero, Il / *The story of a poor dog* (IT 16): Visca
Romi dan Juli / *Romi and Juli* (ID 74): Karno
Roogie's Bump (US 54): Marriot
Rookie, The (US 16): Connelly
Rookie of the Year (US 93): Nicholas
Roomal / *The handkerchief* (IN 49): Kumar
Room at the Top (GB 58): Moulder-Brown
Room for One More (US 51): Olsen L.J., Winslow G.
Roomies (US 87): Haim
Root of All Evil, The (GB 47): Malone
Ropin' Romance (US 28): House N.
Roppa no dadakko touchan / *Roppa's naughty daughter* (JP 40): Kodaka
Roquevillard, Les (FR 22): Rauzéna
Rosa de Xochimilco / *Rose of Xochimilco* (MX 38): Velasquez E.
Rosalie (US 37): Bond T.
Rosarote Brille, Die / *Rose-coloured spectacles* (GE 34): Teetzmann
Rosary, The (US 15): Clark R.
Rosa und Lin / *Rosa and Lin* (DE 72): Frerichs
Rose (FR 35): Buquet, François
Roseanna McCoy (US 49): Miles P.
Rose Bowl (US 36): Lee B.
Rose effeuillée, La / *Rose without petals* (FR 36): Farguette
Rosen für den Staatsanwalt / *Roses for the Public Prosecutor* (DE 59): Kaiser
Rose of Washington Square (US 39): Kibrick L.
Roses de la vie, Les / *The roses of life* (FR 15): Adrien
Roses in the Dust (GB 21): Craig
Rosie Dixon Night Nurse (GB 78): Henderson S.
Rosita (US 23): DeLacy
Rossignol et les cloches, Le / *The nightingale and the bells* (CA 44): Barbeau
Rote Prinz, Der / *The red prince* (AT 54): Friedl
Roti (PK 89): Jamshid
Rough and Ready (US 24): Butts
Rough Going (US 25): Black B.
Roughly Speaking (US 45): Calkins, Kuhn, Sheffield J.
Rough Riding Rangers (US 35): Nelson B.
Rough Riding Romance (US 19): Lee F.
Rough Ridin' Justice (US 45): Infuhr
Rough Ridin' Red (US 28): Barton
Roughshod (US 49): Jarman
Rough Tough West, The (US 52): Ivo
Route est belle, La / *The glorious way* (FR 29): Freddy-Karl
Route heureuse, La / *The happy road* (FR 35): Sannangelo
Rové huliet / *The wooden gun* (IL/US 78): Rosen
Rover's Big Chance (US 42): 'Our Gang'
Rovin' Tumbleweeds (US 39): McKim S.
Rowdy and His New Pal (US 11): Tannura, Boss
Royal Cavalcade (GB 35): Singer
Royal Eagle (GB 36): Fitzpatrick P.
Royal Oak, The (GB 23): Dear

Royal Rider, The (US 29): DeLacy
Royal Rodeo, The (US 39): Beckett
Royce (US 76): Drier
Rozhdyonniye burei / *Born of the storm* (SU 57): Siluyanov
Rozhdyonniye zhit / *Born to live* (SU 60): Markarian
Rua Descalça / *Barefoot Street* (BR 71): Cruz J.C.
Rubber Tires (US 27): Coghlan
Ruchome piaski / *Shifting Sands* (PL 68): Zuchowicz
Rue Cases Nègres / *Black Shack Alley* (FR 83): Cadenat
Ruiseñor de las cumbres, El / *Nightingale of the peaks* (ES 58): Jimenez
Ruiseñor del barrio, El / *The local nightingale* (MX 51): Perez
Rules of Marriage, The (US 82): Astin S.
Ruling Voice, The (US 31): Scott D.
Rulleskøjterne / *Roller-skates* (DK 08): Voigt
Runaway, The (US 17): Tansey S.
Runaway (US 73): Montgomery
Runaway (US 84): Cramer
Runaway Boy, The (IN 59) — *see* Bari thekey paliye
Runaway Girls (US 28): Watson D.
Runaway Railway (GB 65): Moulder-Brown, Bennett K., Brockwell
Runaways, The (US 12): Melford
Runaways, The (US 15): Stone
Runaways, The (GB 59): Stephens
Runaway Train, The (73 US) — *see* Runaway
Run Boy Run (87 IT/FR) — *see* Ragazzo di Calabria
Run for Cover (US 54): Charney
Run for the Roses (US 78): Gomez P.
Runner, The (84 IR) — *see* Dawandeh
Running Out (US 83): Hall A.M.
Run on Percy, The (US 15): Clark R.
Run Rebecca Run (AU 82): Kounnas
Run Wild, Run Free (GB 69): Lester
Ruota del falco, La / *The falcon's wheel* (IT 20): Casarotti
Rüpel (DD 62): Dieckmann
Rurka z kremem / *Cream puff* (PL 71): Mosior, Samosionek
Rushin' Ballet (US 37): 'Our Gang'
Russ Farrell, Aviator (US 28, srs): Black B.
Russians Are Coming, the Russians Are Coming, The (US 65): Whitaker
Russkies (US 87): Phoenix L., Billingsley
Rustlers of Devil's Canyon (US 47): Blake
Rusty and the Falcon (US 66): Lee Ru.
Rusty Leads the Way (US 48): Donaldson T., Hickman Dw., Infuhr, Kuhn
Rusty Saves a Life (US 49): Donaldson T., Hickman Dw., Hunt, Infuhr
Rusty's Birthday (US 49): Donaldson T., Dennis, Hickman Dw., Hunt, Infuhr
Ruthless (US 48): Anderson B.
Ruth's Millions (US c.18): Trebaol E.
Ruth's Remarkable Reception (US 16): Steuart
Rvaniye bashmaki / *Shabby boots* (SU 33): Godorikov
Ryan White Story, The (US 89): Haas L.

Saat geht auf, Die / *The seed springs up* (GE 35): Sierck
Sabak / *The lesson* (IN 73): Satyajit
Sabirtaşi / *The patience stone* (TR 69): Utku
Sables mouvants, Les / *Shifting sands* (FR 29): Heuzé

Sabotage (GB 36): Tester
Sabotage (US 39): Russell J.
Sacco di Roma, Il / The sack of Rome (IT 53): Di Nardo
Sac de billes, Un / A bag of marbles (FR 75): Constantini, Schulmann
Saddle Tramp (US 50): Lindgren O., Hunt, Gebert
Sad Horse, The (US 59): Ladd
Sadie Goes to Heaven (US 17): McDermott
Saeta del ruiseñor / Song of the nightingale (ES 57): Jiménez
Safar / The journey (IN 70): Sachin
Safe at Home! (US 62): Russell B., Mark
Safe Passage (US 94): Stahl
Safety in Numbers (US 39): Mahan
Safety Last (US 23): Daniels M.
Saga of Death Valley (US 39): Baker, Bupp T.
Sagar ka sher / Lion of Sagar (IN 37): Marathe R.
Sagebrush Family, The (US 39, srl): Clark B.l
Sagebrush Heroes (US 45): Larson
Sagebrush Law (US 43): Rodin M.
Sage Hen, The (US 21): Headrick
Sahara (US 19): Moore P.
Saida a enlevé Manneken Pis / Saida kidnaps Manneken Pis
 (BE 13): Mertens
Sailor Beware (GB 56): Pike J.
Sailor Made Widow (US 34): Beckett
Sailor's Luck (US 33): Phelps
Sailor Who Fell from Grace with the Sea, The (GB 76): Kahn
Sainted Sisters, The (US 48): Hunt
St George and the Dragon (GB 81): Warnock G.
Saint Joan (GB/US 57): Hemmings, Palmer
St Martin's Lane (GB 38): Singer
Saint's Adventure, The (US 17): Paul E.
Salaam Bombay! (IN 88): Syed
Salaš u Malom Ritu / The farm in Mali Rit (YU 76): Štimac
Salem's Lot (US 79): Kerwin, Savage B., Scribner
Sal Grogan's Face (GB 22): Brantford
Sally (US 25): Rudolph
Salomy Jane (US 19): Jones J.
Salomy Jane (32 US) — see Wild Girl
Saloon Bar (GB 40): McDowall
Saltimbancii / The clowns (RO 81): Vîlcu
Saltimbanc la Polul Nord, Un / A clown at the North Pole (RO 81): Vîlcu
Saltkrakan (SE 69, srl): Lindholm
Salty O'Rourke (US 44): Hickman Dl.
Salute to the Marines (US 43): Blake
Salvage Gang, The (GB 58): Alleney A., Hines
Salvation Hunters, The (US 25): Guerin
Salvation Joan (US 16): Connelly
Salvation Nell (US 31): Albright
Salvation of Nance O'Shaughnessy, The (US 14): Clark R.
Samadhi / The shrine (IN 50): Kapoor S.
Samadhi (IN 72): Rajoo, Satyajit
S.A.Mann Brand / Brownshirt Brand (GE 33): Wenkhaus
Sam Hill: Who Killed Mr Foster? (US 70): Hudis
Sami gryazni / The dirtiest boy (SU 34): Makutonin
Sammy Going South (GB 63): McClelland
Sammy - the Way Out Seal (US 62): McGreevey, Mumy
Sam's Boy (GB 22): Rudd

Samson and Delilah (US 49): Tamblyn, Anderson B.
Samurai (US 79): Sinutko
San Antonio Kid, The (US 44): Blake
Sand Castle, The (US 60): Cardwell
San Diego, I Love You (US 44): Miles P. (Perreau), Bates, Infuhr, Wissler
Sandlot Kids, The (US 93): Horneff
Sandpiper, The (US 65): Mason
Sandwich Man, The (GB 66): Ellis C.
Sandy is a Lady (US 40): Brown K., Lenhart
Sane Fourth of July, A (US 11): Boss
San Francisco (US 36): Bupp T.
San Francisco International Airport (US 70): Eccles
Sangue, O / Blood (PT 89): Ferreira
Sangue romagnolo / Blood of Romagna (IT 16): Roveri, Petrungaro
San-Mao liulang ji / The story of San-Mao's wanderings (CN 49): Wang L.
Sansar / World (IN 52): Kapoor S.
Sans famille / No relations (BE 12): Mertens
Sans famille (FR 25): Shaw L., Guichard
Sans famille (FR 34): Lynen, Grave
Sans famille (44 IT) — see Senza famiglia
Sans famille (FR/IT 57): Flateau, Fourcade, Moullières
Sansho dayu / Sansho the bailiff (JP 54): Kato
Sans lendemain / No tomorrow (FR 39): François
Santa and the Three Bears (US 70): Riha
Santa Claus (US 85): Fitzpatrick C.
Santa Claus and the Clubman (US 11): Boss
Santa Fe Stampede (US 38): Spellman
Santa Fe Trail (US 30): Durkin
Santa Fe Uprising (US 46): Blake
Santiago's Ark (US 73): Figueroa
Santo de la Espada / The saint with the sword (AR 68): Cuesta
Sant Tulsidas / St Tulsidas (IN 39): Apte
Sap, The (US 26): Janney, Jones B.
Sapho / Sappho (FR 34): Bara
Sapphire (GB 59): Witty
Saqi (IN 37): Suresh
Sarafi loot (IN 37): Apte
Sarah and Son (US 30): DeLacy, Winslow D.
Sarah Siddons (GB 39): McDowall
Sarah T. (US 74): Olson
Sarajevo (HU 40): Dévényi
Sarala (IN 53): Babua
Sarfrosh (PK 89): Jamshid
Sargam / Seven-note scale (IN 50): Kumar
Sartaj (IN 50): Kumar
Sashko (SU 58): Babich
Sąsiedzi / Neighbours (PL 68): Matałowski
Satan on Earth (US 19): Verdi
Så tuktas en äkta man / Taming a real man (SE 41): Hjelm
Saturday Morning (US 22): 'Our Gang'
Saturday Night (US 22): Marion D.
Saturday's Lesson (US 29): 'Our Gang'
Saudagar / The trader (IN 51): Kumar
Savage, The (US 52): Lindgren O.
Savage Frontier (US 53): Hawkins
Savage Is Loose, The (US 74): Montgomery
Savage Sam (US 63): Corcoran

Saving Grace (US 85): Evans A.
Sawdust Doll, The (US 18): Morrison E.
Sawdust Ring, The (US 17): Goodwin
Sayat Nova (74 SU) − see Nran gouyne
Say It in French (US 38): Lee B.
Say It with Songs (US 29): Lee D.
Sazaa (IN 72): Mehmood
Sazhentsi /Saplings (SU 73): Meskhi
Scalawag (US/YU/IT 73): Lester
Scamp, The (GB 57): Petersen Col.
Scandal (US 29): Albright
Scandale, Le /Scandal (FR 34): 'Mircha'
Scandal for Sale (US 32): Phelps
Scandal Sheet (US 31): Searl
Scandal Street (US 38): Switzer
Scaramouche (US 52): Infuhr
Scaramouches, The (GB 10): Potter
Scarecrow of Romney Marsh, The (63 GB) − see Dr Syn - Alias the
    Scarecrow
Scared Stiff (US 45): Swan
Scarlatine, La /Scarlet fever (FR 83): Jaulmes
Scarlet Letter, The (US 26): Haig, Jewell
Scarlet Letter, The (US 34): Rentschler, Samarzich
Scarlet Mark, The (US 15): Roubert
Scarlet Pimpernel, The (GB 35): Rietti
Scarlet River (US 33): Butts
Scarlet Weekend, A (US 32): Nelson B.
Scattergood Pulls the Strings (US 41): Watson Bs.
Scattergood Rides High (US 42): Hurlic
Sceriffo e l'extraterrestre, Lo /The sheriff and the extraterrestrial
    (IT 79): Guffey
Schacko Klak (LU 90): Wagner
Schatten über St Pauli /Shadow over St Pauli (GE 38): Kieling, Sierck
Schatztruhe, Die /The treasure-chest (AT 48): Czeike
Schermerhorn (NL 66): Tromp
Schick' deine Frau nicht nach Italien /Don't send your wife to Italy
    (DE 60): Grimm
Schlagerparade /Hit parade (DE 63): Jansen
Schloss Vogelöd /Vogelöd Castle (GE 36): Bosse
Schlussakkord /Final chord (GE 36): Bosse
Schmuggler von Bernina, Die /The smugglers of Bernina (GE 24): Eysoldt
Schöne Abenteuer, Das /The beautiful adventure (DE 59): Grimm
Schöne Müllerin, Die /The miller's pretty daughter (DE 55): Condrus
Schöne Tage /Fine days (AT 81): Umnig
Schönste Tag meines Lebens, Der /The most beautiful day of my life
    (AT 57): Ande
School Begins (US 28): 'Our Gang'
Schoolboy Love (US 21): Watson C.
Schoolboys' Revolt, The (GB 08): Potter
School Days (16 US) − see 'Sonny Boy' series
School Days (US 21): Barry W.
School for Husbands (GB 37): Baxter
School for Vandals (GB 86): Coster J.
School Principal, The (US 13): Hackett A.
School's Out (US 30): 'Our Gang'
Schritt für Schritt /Step for step (DD 60): Flohr
Schuhe einer schönen Frau, Die /A lovely woman's shoes (GE 22): Allen W.

Schwarze Blitz, Der /Black lightning (DE 58): Grimm
Schwarze Walfisch, Der /The black whale (GE 34): Richter
Schwindel in Dreivierteltakt /Swindle in three-four time (AT 51): Friedl
Scipione l'Africano /Scipio Africanus (IT 37): Angeletti R.
Sciuscia /Shoeshine (IT 46): Interlenghi, Smordoni
Scoffer, The (US 20): Stone
Scogliera della morte, La /The reef of death (IT 20): Capelli
Scoiattolo del mare, Lo /The sea squirrel (IT 20): Capelli
Scontenti, Gli /The malcontents (IT 59): Chevalier
Scoperta, La /The discovery (IT 69): Fioravanti
Scotty of the Scouts (US 26, srl): Alexander B.
Scout Camp (IN 58): 'Ashok', Dube
Scout's Honor (US 80): Peluce
Scouts of the Air (US 39): Baker
Scrapper, The (US 22): Lee F.
Scrooge (GB 35): Frost
Scrooge (GB 51): Dearman, Charlesworth, Hannaford
Scrooge (GB 70): Beaumont R., Garlick
Scruffy (GB 38): Gainsborough, McDowall
S deca na more /Children at the seaside (BG 71): Arshinkov, Djambazov,
    Petrov
Sea Children, The (73 GB) − see Oxbone Buccaneers (GB 68)
Sea Hawk, The (US 24): Wilkinson
Seal of Silence, The (US 18, srl): Connelly, Moore P.
Sea of Blood (KN 69): Kim C.
Search, The (US/CH 48): Jandl
Searching for Bobby Fischer (US 93): Pomeranc
Searching Wind, The (US 46): Kuhn
Sébastien et la Mary-Morgane /Sebastian and the 'Mary Morgan'
    (FR 69, srl): 'Mehdi'
Sébastien parmi les hommes /Sebastian out in the world (FR 67, srl):
    'Mehdi'
Sebelum usia 17 /Under 17 (ID 75): Karno
Second Best (US 93): Miles C. C.
Second Chance (US 72): Savage B.
Second Childhood (US 36): 'Our Gang'
Second Mate, The (GB 50): Hannaford
Second Time Around (US 79): Savage B.
Second to None (GB 26): Brantford
Second Wife (US 30): Frederick
Second Wife (US 36): Breakston, Downing R., Van Atta
Second Youth (US 24): Bennett M.
Secret, The (GB 55): O'Sullivan
Secret Admirer (US 84): Haim
Secret Beyond the Door, The (US 48): Dennis
Secret Cave, The (GB 53): Hill
Secret Command (US 44): Lyon
Secret Garden, The (US 49): Stockwell, Roper
Secret Garden, The (GB 75, srl): Harrison A.
Secret Garden, The (US 87): Brandis, Steele J.
Secret Garden, The (US 93): Knott, Prowse
Secret Heart, The (US 46): Hickman Dw.
Secret of NIMH, The (US 82): Wheaton
Secret of the Pond, The (US 74): Shea E., Eisenmann
Secret Place, The (GB 57): Brooke
Secrets (US 24): Miller W.
Secret Service (US 31): Jackson E.

Secret Service Investigator (US 48): Ivo
Secret Tunnel, The (GB 47): Bowyer, Wager
Secret Witness (US 88): Phoenix L.
Secret World (69 FR) — see Promesse, La
Secuestrador, El /The kidnapper (AR 58): Orlegui, Lopez Monet
Sedmi kontinent /The seventh continent (YU/CS 60): Pasarić
Seed (US 31): Moore D.
Seeds of Vengeance (US 20): Hamrick, Stone
Seeing the World (US 27): 'Our Gang'
Seein' Things (US 24): 'Our Gang'
Seekers, The (US 79): Licht
Seeta aur Geeta /Seeta and Geeta (IN 72): Alankar
See You in the Morning (US 88): Culkin M., Haas L.
Seger i mörker /Victory in the darkness (SE 54): Montin, Nilsson
Segreto nel chiostro, Un /A secret in the cloister (IT 19): Roveri
Seguiré tus pasos /I'll follow in your footsteps (MX 66): Bravo J.
Sehnsucht nach Afrika /Longing for Africa (GE 39): Sierck
Seine erste Liebe /His first love (GE 33): Richter
Seine Tochter ist der Peter /His daughter Peter (AT 55): Kratz
Sein letzter Trick /His last trick (GE 20): Allen W.
Sein Sohn /His son (GE 41): Möller
Seitensprünge /Something on the side (GE 40): Kieling
Selfish Yates (US 18): Butterworth E.
Self-Made Failure, A (US 24): Alexander B.
Self-Made Wife, The (US 23): Murphy M.
Selskaya uchitelnitsa /The village schoolmistress (SU 47): Ganichev
Seltsame Leben des Herrn Bruggs, Das /The strange life of Herr Bruggs (DE 51): Bürger
Semiklassniki /Seventh-graders (SU 38): Mitayev
Semya Ulyanovikh /The Ulyanovs (SU 57): Burlyayev B.
Senate Page Boys (41 US) — see Adventure in Washington
Se necesita chico /Boy wanted (ES 63): Cebrian
Senka s 'Mimozi' /Senka from 'Mimosa' (SU 33): Friedrikh
Sennerin von St Kathrein, Die /The dairymaid of St Kathrein (AT 55): Kratz
Senor Daredevil (US 26): Black B.
Senorita from the West (US 45): Mummert
Sensation (GB 37): Gainsborough
Sensitive, Passionate Man, A (US 77): Lookinland T.
Sentimentalnoye puteshestviye na kartoshki /Sentimental journey for potatoes (SU 86): Yankovski
Senza famiglia /No relations (IT 44): De Ambrosis
Senza ragione /Mindless (IT/GB 72): Lester
Separate Ways (US 81): Hathaway
SER /Freedom is paradise (SU 89): Kozirev
Serangan fajar /Daybreak (ID 82): Marsuni
Serdtse poyot /The heart sings (SU 56): Aidinyan
Serenade (GE 37): Sierck
Sergeant Jim (56 YU) — see Dolina miru
Sergeant Madden (US 39): Jones D.
Sergeant Mike (US 45): Olsen L.J.
Sergeant Pepper's Lonely Hearts Club Band (US 78): Garrett
Sergeant York (US 41): McKim S.
Seri razboinik /The grey bandit (SU 56): Guskoff, Kopelev
Serpent of the Nile (US 53): Crawford J.
Servants' Entrance (US 34): Phelps
Seryozha (SU 60): Barkhatov

Setkáni v červenci /July meeting (CS 78): Holý
Sette giorni cento lire /Seven days, 100 lire (IT 32): Locchi
Seuls au monde /Alone in the world (FR 51): Lecointe
Seva Sadan (IN 34): Modak
'Seven Brides for Seven Brothers' (US 82, TVS): Phoenix R.
7 Faces of Dr Lao (US 63): Tate
Seven Little Foys, The (US 54): Mathers
Seventh Column (US 43): Rodin M.
Seventh Cross, The (US 44): Blake, Olsen L.J., Tyler L.
Seventh Voyage of Sinbad, The (US 58): Eyer Ri.
Seventy and Seven (US 17): Paul E.
Seven Year Itch, The (US 55): Bernard
Severnaya lyuboff /Northern love (SU 27): Litkin
Sevgim ve gururum /My love and pride (TR 65): Dönmez
Sex Lure, The (US 16): Carnahan
Sextetten Karlsson /The Karlsson Sextet (SE 45): Carlsson, Sarri
Shabbies, The (US 15): Kelly P.
Shadi ke baad /After marriage (IN 72): Satyajit
Shadowed (US 46): Roberts E.
Shadowlands (US 93): Mazzello
Shadow of a Doubt (US 42): Bates
Shadow of the Thin Man (US 41): Tucker T.
Shadow of Tragedy, The (US 14): Hackett R.
Shadow on the Wall (US 49): Hunt, Sydes
Shadow on the Window, The (US 56): Mathers
Shadows (US 22): Messinger
Shadows on the Sage (US 43): Mercer
Shaggy (US 47): Nokes
Shaggy D.A., The (US 76): Sinutko
Shaggy Dog, The (US 59): Corcoran
Shaheed /The martyr (IN 48): Kapoor S.
Shall We Dance? (US 37): Bailey Sd.
Shame (US 21): Lee F., Moore M.
Shamrock Alley (US 27): Sabiston
Shamrock and the Rose, The (US 27): Watson C., Holmes L.
Shan chor (IN 36): Marathe R.
Shane (US 52): DeWilde
'Shannon' (US 83, TVS): Fields
Shararat /A naughty game (IN 72): Mehmood
Shark (US/MX 69): Spell G.
Sharpshooters (US 38): Spellman
Shatranj ke khilari /The chess players (IN 77): Narain
Shattered (76 FR/IT) — see Passagers, Les
Shattered Idols (US 21): Lee F.
Shattered Lives (US 25): House N.
Shazdeh Ehtejab /Prince Ehtejab (IR 74): Khansarri
Shchastlivovo plavaniya /Safe journey (SU 49): Klimenkov
Sheba (GB 19): Barker E.
She Couldn't Say No (US 39): Bupp S., Madore
She Couldn't Say No (US 54): Hunt
Sheehy and the Supreme Machine (US 77): Drier
Shehnshah (PK 88): Jamshid
Shenandoah (US 65): Alford
Shenmi de jianta /The mysterious sword-tower (CN 84): Yang
Shennü /Goddess (CN 34): Li
Shep Comes Home (US 48): Kimbley
Shepherd of the Hills, The (US 19): Jones J.

Shepherd of the Hills, The (US 27): Murphy M.
Sheriff, The (US 18): Morrison E.
Sheriff of Las Vegas, The (US 44): Blake
Sheriff of Redwood Valley (US 46): Blake
Sheriff's Son, The (US 18): Lee F.
Sherlock Holmes (US 22): Devine
Sherlock Holmes and the Spider Woman (44 US) − see Spider Woman
Sher Shah (PK 89): Jamshid
She's a Boy (US 27): Sabiston
She's a He (US 30): McKeen
She's a Vamp (US 20): Roubert
She's Dangerous (US 37): Watson Bs.
She's for Me (US 43): Infuhr
She Wanted a Millionaire (US 32): Conlon
She Was a Lady (US 34): Searl
Shiinomi gakuen / The Shiinomi school (JP 55): Kawarazaki
Shima no musume / Island woman (JP 33): Yokoyama
Shimmering Light (AU/US 77): Bettles
'Shine On, Harvey Moon' (GB 82, TVS): Whitlock
Shining, The (US 80): Lloyd
Shining Adventure, The (US 25): Alexander B., Billings E., Boudwin
Shining Season, A (US 79): Sharrett
Shinjitsu ichiru / The way to truth (JP 37): Katayama
Ship Ahoy (US 42): Larson
Shipbuilders, The (GB 43): Gainsborough
Shipmates o' Mine (GB 36): Blomfield
Ship o' the Dead (AU 56): Taylor
Ships With Wings (GB 41): Baxter
Ship Was Loaded, The (57 GB) − see Carry On Admiral
Shirdi ke Sai Baba / The Sai Baba of Shirdi (IN 77): Rajoo
Shirobanba / Children of Izu (JP 62): Shimamura
Shivering Shakespeare (US 30): 'Our Gang'
Shivering Spooks (US 26): 'Our Gang'
Shiver My Timbers (US 31): 'Our Gang', Ernest, Tucker J.
Shlosha yamin ve yeled / Three days and a child (IL 66): Osherov
Shock (US 34): Holt D.
Shockproof (US 49): Bates
Shoeshine (46 IT) − see Sciuscia
Shogun Assassin (US 80): Tomikawa A. and M.
Shojo to fusen / The little girl and the balloon (JP 58): Shimazu
Shoku ynë Tili / Our friend Til (AL 81): Latifi, Mustafaraj
Shole / Sparks (IN 53): Kapoor Ro.
Shonen / The boy (JP 69): Abe
Shooting, The (US 82): Wheaton
Shooting of Dan McGrew, The (US 24): DeLacy
Shootin' Indians (US 25): 'Our Gang'
Shoot on Sight (US 20): Morrison E.
Shoot Out (US 71): Beauvy
Shoot the Pianist (60 FR) − see Tirez sur le pianiste
Shopworn Angel (US 38): Butler
Shor / The noise (IN 72): Satyajit
Shore Acres (US 20): Hamrick, Headrick
Shorty (US 14): Boss
Should a Woman Tell? (US 19): Headrick
Shoulder Arms (US 18): Boardman
Should Ladies Behave (US 33): Janney
Show Boat (US 29): Beard

Show Boat (US 36): Watson Bs. and D.
Show Boat (US 51): Corcoran
Showdown (US 63): Brodie
Show Kids (US 34): Alexander T.
Show People (US 28): Watson C.
Shri Krishna Leela (IN 70): Sachin
Shrimps for a Day (US 34): 'Our Gang', Watson D.
Shriveled Soul, The (US 16): Lee F.
Shukujo wa nani o wasuretaka / What did the lady forget? (JP 37): 'Tokkan-Kozo', Hayama
Shuttle, The (US 18): Jones J.
Shyama (IN 48): Kumar
Shyam Sunder / Lord Krishna (IN 32): Modak
Sibiryaki / The boys from Siberia (SU 40): Pupko
Sic 'Em, Brownie (US 22): Morgan
Sidekicks (US 93): Brandis
Side Street (US 49): Hickman Dw.
Sidi Bel-Abès (FR 53): Maurin Y.-M.
Si doel anak Betawi / Son of Batavia (ID 72): Karno
Sidste dans, Den / The last dance (DK 22): Herzberg
Sieben Sommersprossen / Seven freckles (DD 77): Rathmann
Sieben Stäbe, Die / The seven staves (GE 41): Möller
Siedma pevnina (60 YU/CS) − see Sedmi kontinent
Siempre tuya / Forever yours (MX 50): Perez
Sie nannten ihn Amigo / They called him Amigo (DD 58): Schwill
Sierra Passage (US 51): Gray B.
Siete bravisimos, Los / Seven brave boys (ES 64): Sanchez
Si ge xiao huoban / Four buddies (CN 81): Yang
Signal Tower, The (US 24): Darro
Sign of the Cactus, The (US 24): Gordon Bo.
Sign of the Cross, The (US 32): Conlon
Sign of the Dagger (48 US) − see Trail to Laredo
Sign of the Wolf (US 41): Hickman Dl.
Signore desidera, Il / The gentleman wishes (IT 33): Locchi
Si jeunesse savait / If youth but knew (FR 47): Lecointe
Silas (DE 81, srl): Bach
Si le ciel s'en mêle / If heaven takes a hand (FR 59): Flateau
Silence, The (63 SE) − see Tystnaden
Silence of Dean Maitland, The (AU 34): Kerr
Silent Avenger, The (US 27): Black B.
Silent Call, The (US 61): Mobley
Silent Man, The (US 17): Goodwin
Silent Stranger, The (US 24): Headrick
Silent Witness, A (GB 13): Desmond
Silken Shackles (US 26): Janney
Silk Hat Kid, The (US 35): Lee B.
Silly Billies (US 36): Watson D.
Silver Bullet (US 85): Haim
Silver City Bonanza (US 51): Kimbley
Silver Dollar (US 32): Durand
Silver Lining, The (US 31): Albright
'Silver Spoons' (US 83, TVS): Schroder, Bateman
Silver Whip, The (US 53): Diamond
Silver Wings (US 21): Monahan
Simitrio (MX 60): Tejeda
Simla Road (IN 69): Mehmood
Simple Sis (US 27): Schaeffer

Simplicio (VE 78): Rodriguez S.A.
Sinbad the Sailor (54 US) — see Invitation to the Dance
Sincerely Yours (US 55): Eyer Ri.
Since You Went Away (US 44): Binyon, Laughlin
Sinews of Steel (US 27): Gordon Bo.
Sing As We Go (GB 34): Pavitt
Singende Jugend /Singing youth (AT 36): Lojda, Haas H.
Singing Detective, The (GB 86, TVS): Davies L.
Singing Fool, The (US 28): Lee D.
Singing Guns (US 50): Gray B.
Single Standard, The (US 29): Albright
Singoalla (FR/SE 49): Chambot
Sing, You Sinners (US 38): O'Connor
Sinister House (48 US) — see Who Killed 'Doc' Robbin?
Sin of Madelon Claudet, The (US 31): Darro
Sin of Martha Queed, The (US 20): Lee F., Stone
Sin polka /Son of the regiment (SU 46): Yankin
Sins of Her Parent (US 16): Lee F.
Sins of Man (US 36): Reynolds, Rentschler
Sins of the Fathers (US 28): Haig, Scott D.
Sin's Pay Day (US 32): Rooney
Sinut na Maria /Mary's son (BG 82): Delchev
Si può fare...amigo /Make himself a friend (IT/FR/ES 73): Cestiè
Si Rano /Rano (ID 74): Karno
Siren of Corsica, A (US 15): Hackett R.
Sirius (CS 75): Vavruša
Siromashko lyato /Indian summer (BG 73): Arshinkov, Petrov
Sissybelle (US 13): Clark R.
Sister of Six, A (US 16): Carpenter, Perl, Stone
Sisters (US 11): Pickford
Sitamgar /The cruel beloved (IN 34): Apte
Si tous les gars du monde /If all the world's boys (FR 55): Poujouly
Sitting Pretty (US 38): Tucker J.
Sitting Pretty (US 48): Olsen L.J., Sydes
Six chevaux bleus /Six blue horses (FR 67): Boitot
Six-Gun Justice (US 30): Nelson B.
Sixième art, Le /The sixth art (FR 54): Moullières
Six Pack (US 82): Hall A.M.
Six Shooter Andy (US 18): Sargent, Messinger, Stone, Lee Ra.
Sixteen Candles (US 84): Hall A.M., Henry J.
Sjors en Sjimmie en de Rebellen /George and Jimmy and the rebels (NL 72): Hundscheidt
Sjors en Sjimmie en der gorilla /George and Jimmy and the gorilla (NL 66): Consten, van der Linden C.
Sjors en Sjimmie en het zwaard van Krijn /George and Jimmy and the sword of Krijn (NL 77): Daemen, Janssen T.
Sjors en Sjimmie in het land der reuzen /George and Jimmy in the land of giants (NL 67): Ayal
Sjors en Sjimmie op Pirateneiland /George and Jimmy on Pirates' Island (NL 62): van der Linden C.
Skandal in Ischl /Scandal at Ischl (AT 57): Ande
Skandal um den Hahn /Scandal over a rooster (GE 38): Eugens
Skateboard (US 77): Garrett
Skating Master, The (US 14): Benham
Skeezer (US 82): Licht
Skeleton, The (US 12): Roubert
Skeppargatan 40 /40 Skipper Street (SE 25): Alexandersson

Skepp kommer lastat, Ett /A ship and its cargo (SE 32): Winther
Skhvisi shvilebi /Another woman's children (SU 58): Daneliya
Skid Kids (GB 52): Hill
Skin Deep (US 29): Lee D.
Skin Game, The (GB 20): Doxat-Pratt
'Skinnay' series (US 19): Carr J. and S.
Skinner's Baby (US 17): Coogan J.
Skipper & Co. (DK 74): Jacobsen
Skipper's Wooing, The (GB 22): Rudd
Skippy (US 31): Cooper Ja., Searl, Coogan R., Haig, Haines
'Skippy' (AU 65-68, TVS): Pankhurst
Škola otců /School for fathers (CS 57): Košnar
Škola, základ života /School prepares you for life (CS 38): Salač
Skråköpings Rundradio inviges /Radio Skråköping takes the air (SE 32): Winther
Skrållan, Ruskprick och Knorrhane (SE 67): Lindholm
Sky Bike, The (GB 67): Ellis I.
Sky Bride (US 32): Coogan R.
Sky High Saunders (US 27): Jones B.
Sky Is Grey, The (US 80): Bond J.
Sky Parade, The (US 36): Bartlett, Lee B.
Sky Patrol (US 39): Jones D.
Sky Pilot, The (US 21): Alexander B.
Sky Riders (US 76): Harrison S.
Skyrocket, The (US 26): Coghlan
Sky's the Limit, The (US 75): Eisenmann
Sladký čas Kalimagdory /Happy days with Kalimagdora (DE/CS 68): Gogal
Sla først, Frede! /Strike first, Freddy! (DK 65): Schmidt J.P.
Slander (US 56): Eyer Ri.
Slanderers, The (US 24): Morgan
Slaughterhouse-Five (US 72): Albee
Slave Ship (US 37): Beard, Scott D.
Slaves of Babylon (US 53): Crawford J.
Slaves of Beauty (US 27): Bennett M.
Sledite ostavat /Traces remain (BG 55): Danailov, Naumov
Sleeping Car (GB 33): Fitzpatrick P.
Sleeping Fires (US 17): Steuart
Sleeping Lion, The (US 19): Moore P.
Sleepless in Seattle (US 93): Malinger
Slepaya ptitsa /The blind bird (SU 63): Ageyev
Slickers (US 87): Call
Slide, Kelly, Slide (US 27): Coghlan
Slight Case of Murder, A (US 37): Bupp T., Jordan
Slightly Dangerous (US 43): Blake
Slightly Tempted (US 40): Bupp S.
Slim Carter (US 57): Hovey
Slingshot, The (93 SE) — see Kådisbellan
Slingshot Kid, The (US 27): Barton
Slippy McGee (US 48): Nokes
Slow as Lightning (US 23): Jones B.
Slow Down (US 26): Shuford
Sluchai na plotine /Incident at the dam (SU 59): Fazilov, Daneliya
Sluchai v pustine /Desert incident (SU 57): Suponev
Small Change (76 FR) — see Argent de poche
Small Talk (US 29): 'Our Gang'
Small Town Girl (US 36): Breakston, Phelps, Watson Bl.

505

Small Town Girl (US 52): Hyatt
Small Voice, The (GB 48): Dearman
Smart Guy (US 43): Larson
Smart Set, The (US 28): Watson C.
Smart Woman (US 48): Lyon
Smash and Grab (GB 37): Singer
Smashing the Rackets (US 38): Beckett
Smashing Through (32 US) − see Cheyenne Cyclone
Smile (US 74): Shea E.
Smile, Brother, Smile (US 27): DeLacy
Smile Wins, The (US 28): 'Our Gang'
Smiley (GB 56): Petersen Col.
Smiley Gets a Gun (AU 58): Calvert
Smiling All the Way (US 20): Redden
Smith! (US 69): Shea C.
'Smitty' comedies (US c.28): Haines, Searl, Ernest, Jackson E.
Smoke Tree Range (US 36): Jones D.
Smoky (US 33): Albright
Smoky Joe's Revenge (GB 74): Cox N.
Smoky Mountain Melody (US 48): Ivo
Smoldering Embers (US 20): Hamrick
Smorfie di Pulcinella /Punch's grimaces (IT 19): Casarotti
Smurtta na zaeka /Death of the hare (BG 81): Voinyagovski
Smutjes Schwester /Smutje's sister (GE 36): Teetzmann
Snake River Desperadoes (US 51): Ivo
Snap Shots (US 15): Clark A.
Sněženky /Snowdrops (CS 20): Pražský
Snezhnaya skazka /Snow story (SU 59): Yershoff I.
'Snookums' comedies (US 26-27): McKeen
Snowball (GB 60): Waterman
Snowball Express (US 72): Whitaker
Snowdrift (US 23): Black B.
Snows of Kilimanjaro, The (US 52): Bates
Snow Treasure (US 68): Austad
Snow White (US 13): Roubert
Snug Harbor (US 18): Jackson C.
Snurriga familjen /The crazy family (SE 40): Dalunde
Soak the Old (US 40): Madore
Soapbox Derby (GB 58): Crawford M.
Sóbálvány, A /The pillar of salt (HU 58): Weiser G.
So Big (US 24): Darro
So Big (US 32): Moore D.
So Big (US 53): Beymer, Provost, Rettig
Sobirayushchi oblaka /The cloud-collector (SU 63): Kokorev
Sob Sister (US 31): Albright, Moore D.
Social Ghost, The (US 14): Gottlieb
Society Architect, The (US 27): Shuford
So Dear to My Heart (US 48): Driscoll
So ein Affentheater! /What a farce! (DE 54): Condrus
So ein Millionär hat's schwer /A hard-done-by millionaire (AT 58): Kratz
Soeurs d'armes /Sisters in arms (FR 37): Buquet
Sogno a Venezia /Dreams in Venice (IT 58): Nevola
Sogno patriotico di Cinessino, Il /Cinessino's patriotic dream (IT 15): Giunchi
So Goes My Love (US 46): Driscoll
Solang' die Sterne glühn /As long as the stars shine (DE 58): Schwartz S.

Solaris (SU 72): Banionis
Soldaterkammerater på efterårsmanøvre /Comrades-in-arms on autumn manoeuvres (DK 61): Schmidt J.P.
Soldatski sin /A soldier's son (SU 32): Kuzdryavtsev
Soldier, The (65 YU/US) − see Vojnik
Soldier of Fortune (US 55): Chang
Soliga Solberg /Sunny Solberg (SE 41): Bernhard
Solitary Sin, The (US 19): Griffith, Redden
Soll man heiraten? /Should one marry? (GE 25): Szécsi
Solo per te (37 GE/IT) − see Mutterlied
Sol sale todos los dias, El /The sun shines every day (ES 56): Rodriguez M.A.
Solskinbørnene /The sunshine children (DK 17): Heimann
Sølvmunn /Silver-mouth (NO 81): Asphaug
Som, amor e curtição /Music, love and fun (BR 72): Cruz J.C.
Sombras de circo /Shadows of the circus (ES 31): Hurtado
Sombrero (SU 59): Kulakoff, Perevalov
Somebody's Mother (US 26): McBan
Somebody Up There Likes Me (US 56): Rangno
Som en tjuv om natten /Like a thief in the night (SE 40): Olsson
Someone to Watch Over Me (US 87): Cross
Something Always Happens (GB 34): Singer
Something Evil (US 71): Whitaker
Something for Joey (US 77): Lynas
Something Money Can't Buy (GB 52): Hannaford
Something So Right (US 82): Schroder
Something to Live For (US 51): Aaker L., Gebert
Something to Think About (US 20): Moore M.
Something Wicked This Way Comes (US 82): Carson S., Peterson V.
Sommer, den man nie vergisst, Ein /An unforgettable summer (DE 59): Hehn
Sommer i Tyrol /Summer in the Tyrol (DK 64): Schmidt J.P.
Sommernachtstraum in unserer Zeit, Ein /A modern midsummer night's dream (GE 13): Reinwald
Sonar kella /The golden fortress (IN 74): Chatterjee, Chakravarty
Sonatas (ES/MX 59): Jiménez Pons R.
Son autre amour /His other love (FR 33): Lynen
Son dernier Noël /His last Christmas (FR 52): Poujouly
Sonen tantei dan - tomei kaijin /Detective stories for boys (JP 58): Yamate
Son frère de lait /His foster-brother (FR 35): Bara
Song of Arizona (US 46): Calkins, Chapin M., Cook T., Ivo
Song of Bernadette, The (US 43): Rodin M., Bates
Song of Idaho (US 48): Ivo
Song of Life, The (US 21): Headrick
Song of Love, The (US 29): Durand
Song of Love (US 47): Sydes
Song of My Heart (US 47): Kimbley
Song of Russia (US 43): Hickman Dl.
Song of Surrender (US 49): Miles P.
Song of the Road (55 IN) − see Pather panchali
Song of the Saddle (US 36): Ernest
Song of the Soul, The (US 18): Carr S.
Song of the South (US 46): Driscoll, Nokes
Song of the Thin Man (US 47): Stockwell
Song o' My Heart (US 30): Clifford, Albright
Song to Remember, A (US 44): Tauzin
Sonnblick ruft, Der /Call of the Sonnblick (AT 52): Friedl

Sönndagsbarn / *Sunday's child* (SE 92): Linnros
Sonnhofbäuerin, Die / *The Sonnhof farmer's wife* (AT 49): Czeike
Sonntagskinder / *Sunday children* (GE 41): Eugens
'Sonny Boy' films (US 16): Johnson W.
Sonny Boy (US 29): Lee D., Ernest
'Sonny Jim' series (US 14-15): Connelly
Sonny Jim and the Great American Game (US 15): Connelly
Sonny Jim's First Love Affair (US 15): Connelly
Son of Courage (US 30): Nelson B.
Son of Democracy, A (US 17): Jackson C.
Son of Dracula (US 43): Bates
Son of France, A (GB 14): Royston G.
Son of Frankenstein (US 39): Dunagan, Hurlic
Son of Fury (US 41): McDowall, Severn Cl.
Son of India (IN 62): Sajjid
Son of Lassie (US 45): Severn B., Tyler L.
Son of Neptune, A (US 16): Griffith
Son of Rusty (US 47): Donaldson T., Ackles, Hickman Dw., Infuhr
Son of Tarzan (US 20, srl): Griffith
Son of the Border (US 33): Durand
Son of the Frontier, A (US 28): House N.
Son of the Gods (US 30): Moore D.
Son of the Guardsman (US 46, srl): Henry R.
Son of the Navy (US 40): Spellman
Sono yo no tsuma / *That night's wife* (JP 52): Shitara
Sons of the Legion (US 26): Brown T.
Sons of the Legion (US 38): Albright, Bartlett, Billings G.,
    Cook B., Holt D., Lee B., O'Connor
Sooky (US 31): Cooper Ja., Searl, Coogan R., Tucker J.
Sorcier du ciel, Le / *Wizard of the sky* (FR 48): Chambot
Sordo, El / *The deaf man* (MX 58): Quezadas
So Red the Rose (US 35): Moore D.
Sorrell and Son (US 27): McBan
Sorrell and Son (GB 33): Penrose
Sorrell and Son (GB 84, srl): Critchley
Sorrowful Jones (US 48): Hunter, Lindgren O.
Sorry, Can't Stop! (GB 09): Williamson S.
Sorry, Wrong Number (US 48): Hunt
Sorte familie, Den / *The black family* (DK 13): Stensgård
Sorte Shara / *Black Shara* (DK 61): Schmidt J.P.
SOS Kindtand / *Molar emergency* (DK 43): Kaas
SOS - Tidal Wave (US 39): Kuhn
So This Is New York (US 48): Hunt
Sotlugg och Linlugg / *Blackie and Whitey* (SE 48): Thorsell, Järnmark
Souffle au coeur / *Heart murmur* (FR/IT/DE 70): Ferreux, Walter
Soul of Satan, The (US 17): Lee F.
Soul's Awakening, A (GB 22): Thompson M.
Sound and the Fury, The (US 59): Perry
Sounder (US 72): Hooks K. and E.
Sound of Music, The (US 65): Hammond
Sound Your A (US 29): Madden
Sous le ciel de Paris / *Under the Paris sky* (FR 50): Rob
Sous les yeux de l'Occident / *Under western eyes* (FR 36): François
South Central (US 92): Coleman C.
Southerner, The (US 31): Albright
Southerner, The (US 45): Gilpin J.
Southern Exposure (US 35): Switzer

South of Algiers (GB 52): Messaoud
South Sea Pirates (AU 57): Taylor K.
South Seas Adventure (AU 58): Scully
South Sea Woman (US 53): Chang
Souvenirs perdus / *Lost memories* (FR 50): Rob, Simon
Sovsem propashchi / *Hopelessly lost* (SU 74): Madyanov
Sowing of Alderson Cree, The (20 US) − *see* Seeds of Vengeance
Space Camp (US 86): Phoenix L.
Space Children, The (US 58): Ray M., Crawford J., Washbrook
Space Flight IC-1 (GB 65): Lester
Space Raiders (US 83): Mendenhall
Spanish Dancer, The (US 23): Black B.
Spanish Gardener, The (GB 56): Whiteley
Spanking Age, The (US 28): 'Our Gang'
Spanky (US 32): 'Our Gang', McComas
Spare the Rod (GB 61): Bulloch
Sparrows (US 26): Butts, O'Donnell, Jones B., Berlinger, Jewell
Spartak / *Spartacus* (SU 26): Lyudvinski
Spasyonnoye pokoleniye / *The saved generation* (SU 59): Tokaryoff
Special Agent (US 49): Hunt
Special Delivery (US 27): Jewell, Winslow D.
Special Friendships (64 FR) − *see* Amitiés particulières
Special Kind of Love, A (78 US) − *see* Special Olympics
Special Olympics (US 78): Parry
Specijalno vaspitanje / *Special education* (YU 77): Štimac
Speed Demon, The (US 11): Pickford
Speed Demon, The (US 32): Ernest
Speeding Venus, The (US 26): Fox J.
Speed in the Gay Nineties (US 32): Watson D.
Speed Mad (US 25): Fox J.
Speed Maniac, The (US 19): Stone
Speed the Swede (US 23): Condon
Speed to Spare (US 20): Morrison E.
Spellbound (US 45): Bates, Infuhr
Spell of the Circus (US 31, srl): Nelson B.
Spezialist für alles / *General specialist* (GE 36): Teetzmann
Spider, The (US 31): McComas
Spider and the Fly, The (GB 49): Spenser J.
Spider and the Rose, The (US 23): Headrick
Spider Woman, The (US 44): Infuhr
Spielplatz / *Playground* (AT 66): Koester
'Spin and Marty' (US 55-58, TVS): Considine, Stollery
Spione / *Spies* (GE 27): Stark-Gstettenbaur
Spirit Chaser, The (85 AU) − *see* Frog Dreaming
Spirit of Audubon, The (US 15): Benham
Spirit of Christmas, The (US 13): Stewart G.
Spirit of Culver (US 39): Moran, Reynolds, Billings G.
Spirit of the USA, The (US 24): House N.
Splendid Crime, The (US 25): McBan
Splendid Road, The (US 25): McBan
Split Image (US 82): Scribner
Spomen / *Memory* (BG 73): Arshinkov
Spook Spoofing (US 28): 'Our Gang'
Spooky Hooky (US 36): 'Our Gang'
Sporting Blood (US 31): Jackson E.
Sporting Chance (US 31): Jackson E.
Sporting Instinct, The (GB 22): Brantford

Sporting Lover, The (US 26): Fox J.
Sport of Kings (US 47): Dennis
Spotkania w mroku / *Twilight encounter* (PL/DD 60): Halicz
Spotlight Scandals (US 43): Brown K., Lenhart
Spot Marks the X (US 86): Oliver B.
Spots Before Your Eyes (US 40): Blake, Tyler L.
Spriditis / *Tom Thumb* (SU 85): Neilands
Spring and Port Wine (GB 70): Jones L.
Springfield Rifle (US 52): Chapin M.
Spring Parade (US 40): Brown K., Lenhart
Sprucin' Up (US 35): 'Our Gang'
Sprung ins Nichts, Der / *Leap into the void* (GE 31): Lohmeyer
Spy, The (US 31): Durand, Frederick, Jewell
Square Shoulders (US 29): Coghlan, DeLacy, Reisner
Squaw Man, The (US 18): Moore P.
Squaw Man, The (US 31): Moore D.
Squealer, The (US 30): Lee D.
Sreča na vrvici / *Luck on the leash* (YU 77): Gruden
Srečno, Kekec! / *Good luck, Kekec!* (YU 64): Gjurin
Sredni Vashtar (US 42): Kidd R.
Sredni Vashtar (GB 76): Garcha
Sredni Vashtar (GB 81): Puttnam
Stackars Ferdinand / *Poor Ferdinand* (SE 41): Bernhard
Stackars miljonärer / *Poor millionaires* (SE 36): Hallberg
Stadtpark / *City park* (AT 51): Czeike
Stærkere end dynamit / *Stronger than dynamite* (DK 13): Kaulbach
Staff of Age, The (US 12): Moore J.
Stagecoach to Denver (US 46): Blake, Hyatt
Stage Fright (US 23): 'Our Gang'
Stage-Struck Lizzie (US 11): Boss
Stalemate (GB 77): Garcha
Stalking Moon, The (US 68): Clay
Stamboul (GB 31): Pavitt
Stand By Me (US 86): Phoenix R., Wheaton, Feldman, O'Connell
Stand Up and Cheer (US 34): Beckett
Stanley and Livingstone (US 39): Watson Bl., Kibrick L.
Stanno tutti bene / *Everyone's fine* (IT 90): Cascio
Star Boarder, The (US 14): Griffith
Star Boarder, The (US 20): Marion D.
Staretsat / *The old man* (BG 70): Arshinkov
Starfish, The (GB 52): Finzi C. and N.
Star for a Night (US 36): Moore D., Bupp S.
Starik Khottabich / *Old Khottabich* (SU 56): Litvinov
Star Maker, The (US 39): Hickman Dl., Collins
Starozhil / *The old-timer* (SU 61): Perevalov, Arkhipov
Stars in My Crown (US 49): Stockwell, Moss J.
Star Witness, The (US 31): Ernest, Moore D.
State of the Union (US 48): Nokes
Stawiam na Tolka Banana / *My money's on Tolek Banana* (PL 72, TVS): Łobodzinski, Gołębiewski
Staying Together (US 84): Kiger
Stazione Termini / *Termini Station* (IT/US 52): Beymer
Steack trop cuit, Un / *An overdone steak* (FR 60): Juross
Steadfast Heart, The (US 23): Depew, Devine
Steel Against the Sky (US 41): Dawson
Steeler and the Pittsburgh Kid, The (US 81): Thomas H.
Steiner - das eiserne Kreuz (77 GB/DE) − see Cross of Iron

Steklyanni zavtrak / *Glass for breakfast* (SU 35): Makutonin
Stella Dallas (US 25): Hall N., Miller W., Murphy J. and M., Watson C.
Stella Dallas (US 37): Butler, Jones D.
Stepchild (US 47): Ivo
Step Down to Terror (US 59): Kelman
Stepfather 2, The (US 89): Brandis
Stephanie (DE 58): Finkbeiner
Stephen Steps Out (US 23): Fairbanks, Moore P.
Steppa, La / *The steppe* (IT/FR 62): Spallone
Steptoe and Son Ride Again (GB 73): Fletcher, Pender
Stigma (US 23): Headrick
'Stig of the Dump' (GB 81, TVS): Warnock G.
Stihove (72 BG) − see Na zazoryavane
Stille Nacht, heilge Nacht / *Silent night, holy night* (NL 25): Klein H.
Stimme der Sehnsucht, Die / *The voice of longing* (DE 56): Ande
Sting 'Em Sweet (US 22): Morgan
Sting of Stings, The (US 27): Bennett M.
Stiny horkeho leta / *Shadows of a hot summer* (CS 77): Lieschke
Stitch in Time, A (GB 63): Lester
Stjaalne ansigt, Det / *The steel face* (DK 15): Schønberg
Stock Car (GB 55): Hines
Stolen Airliner, The (GB 55): Edmonds
Stolen Bride, The (US 27): Murphy M.
Stolen Child, The (US 23): Roubert
Stolen Jools, The (US 33): Hoskins
Stolen Nickel, The (US 12): Boss, Tannura
Stolen Plans, The (GB 52): Secretan
Stolen Triumph, The (US 16): Steuart
Stone Boy, The (US 84): Presson
Stone Fox, The (US 87): Cramer
Stopover (53 US) − see All I Desire
Stora äventyret, Det / *The great adventure* (SE 53): Norborg, Sucksdorff
Store dag, Den / *The big day* (DK 30): Fønss
Store forventninger / *Great expectations* (DK 22): Herzberg
Stork Bites Man (US 47): Jenkins
Stork Pays Off, The (US 41): Larson, Mummert
Storm Boy (AU 76): Rowe
Storm Center (US 56): Coughlin
Storm Fear (US 55): Stollery
Storming the Trenches (US 16): Griffith, Butterworth F.
Storm över Tjurö / *Storm on Tjurö* (SE 54): Dam
Story of Alexander Graham Bell, The (US 39): Watson Bs.
Story of David, A (GB 60): O'Sullivan
Story of Dr Wassell, The (US 44): Severn B., Nokes
Story of Louis Pasteur, The (US 35): Moore D.
Story of the Indian Ledge, The (US 11): Boss
Story of Three Loves, The (US 52): Nelson R., Olsen L.J.
Støv for alle pengene / *All gold is dust* (DK 63): Schmidt J.P.
Støv på hjernen / *Dust on the brain* (DK 61): Schmidt J.P.
Stowaway, The (US 15): Carr J. and S.
Stowaway in the Sky (60 FR) − see Voyage en ballon
Straight from the Heart (US 35): Cosbey, Ernest, Haines
Straight from the Shoulder (US 36): Holt D.
Strandgut / *Flotsam* (GE 24): Pottier
Strange Adventures of Mr Smith, The (GB 37): Singer
Strange Affair of Adelaide Harris, The (GB 79): Harris J.

Lech Rzegocki

Gustl Stark-Gstettenbaur

Josef Šlosar

Eric Shea in Ace Eli

Claus Detlev Sierck (l.) and Eberhard Itzenplitz

Master Sajjid in Son of India

Puneet Sira

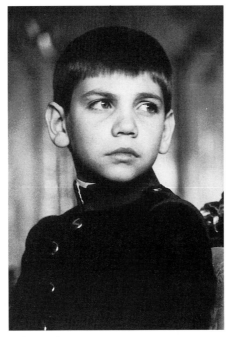

Gábor Svidrony

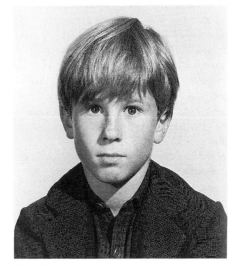

Kevin Tate

Strange Affair of Uncle Harry, The (US 45): Gray B.
Strange Bargain (US 49): Chapin M.
Strange Boarder, The (US 20): Rogers J.
Strange Companions (US 80): Sharrett M.
Strange Death of Adolph Hitler, The (US 43): Bates, Rodin M.
Strange Homecoming (US 74): Garrett
Strange Interlude (US 32): Alexander T.
Strange Interlude (US 88): Steele J.
Strange Love of Martha Ivers, The (US 46): Hickman Dl., Kuhn
Stranger, The (27 US) — see Cherokee Kid
Stranger on the Prowl (52 IT/US) — see Imbarco a mezzanotte
Stranger's Hand, The (53 IT/GB) — see Mano dello straniero
Stranger's Return, The (US 33): Alexander T.
Strangers When We Meet (US 60): Ferrell
Stranger Than Fiction (US 21): Barry W.
Strange Wives (US 34): Jones D., Phelps
Strano appuntamento /Strange rendezvous (IT 50): Staiola
Strano viaggio di Pim Popò, Lo /Pim Popo's strange journey
    (IT 20): Capelli
Strathmore (24 US) — see Flames of Desire
Straw Man, The (US 15): Stone
Street Beautiful, The (US 12): Tansey R.
Street of Illusion (US 28): Watson C.
Street of Memories (US 40): Beckett
Street of Missing Men (US 39): Ryan
Street of Seven Stars, The (US 18): Carr S.
Street of Sin, The (US 28): Haig
Street of Sinners (US 57): Halpin
Street Singers (US 13): Connelly
Streets of New York (US 39): Spellman
Streets of San Francisco (US 49): Gray G.
Street Song (GB 35): Singer
Street Urchin, The (US 16): Messinger
Streghe, Le /The witches (IT/FR 66): Lester
Streit um den Knaben Jo /The fight over young Jo (GE 37):
    Sierck, Itzenplitz
Strength of the Weak, The (14 GB) — see Unfit
Střevicky /The shoes (CS 62): Koblic
Strich durch die Rechnung /The account settled (GE 32): Wenkhaus
Strictly Dynamite (US 34): Searl
Strictly for the Birds (GB 63): Baulch
Strictly Modern (US 30): Bennett M.
Stříbrný favorit (60 CS) — see Třinactileti
Strike Up the Band (US 40): Nunn
Strip, The (US 51): Rettig
Strip, Strip, Hooray! (GB 32): Pavitt, Bartholomew
Strogaya igra /Hard play (SU 63): Burlyayev K.
Stroker Ace (US 83): Guffey
Strom, Der /The river (GE 42): Möller
Strong Boy (US 29): Scott D.
Strong Man, The (US 26): Haig
Struwwelpeter (DE 55): Hack
Stuchis v lyubuyu dver /Knock at any door (SU 58): Yeronin
Student ging vorbei, Ein /The passing of a student (DE 60): Hehn
Student Prince in Old Heidelberg, The (US 27): DeLacy
Studujeme za školou /We study for the school (CS 39): Salač
Stuff Heroes Are Made Of, The (US 11): Pickford

Stunde Null /Zero hour (DE 77): Henties
Stung (US 22): Jones J.
Stupéfiants /Narcotics (FR 32): Mercanton
Stützen der Gesellschaft /Pillars of society (GE 35): Teetzmann
Štvaní lidé /Hunted men (CS/AT/GE 32): Fehér H.
Successful Adventure, A (US 18): Steuart
Successful Failure (US 34): Breakston
Success Is the Best Revenge (FR/GB 84): Skol
Success of Selfishness, The (US 14): Benham
Suche nach dem wunderbunte Vögelchen, Die /Quest for the little
    many-coloured bird (DD 63): Mende
Suchkind 312 /Missing child No. 312 (DE 55): Haar
Such Women Are Dangerous (US 34): Scott D.
Suçlu çocuklar /Guilty children (TR 65): Utku
Suda priletayut lebedi /Swans come here (SU 75): Mambetov
Sudba barabanshchika /A drummer-boy's fate (SU 55):
    Yasinski, Burlyayev B.
Sudba cheloveka /A man's destiny (SU 59): Boriskin
Sudden Jim (US 17): Stone
Suddenly (US 54): Charney
Sudden Money (US 39): Bupp S., Lee B.
Sudden Terror (70 GB) — see Eyewitness
Sud sumashchedshikh /Judgment of the mad (SU 61): Burlyayev K.
Sühne der Martha Rex, Die /The atonement of Martha Rex
    (GE 19): Herzberg
Suicide's Wife, The (US 79): Lookinland T.
Suivez cet homme /Follow that man (FR 52): Fourcade,
    Maurin Y.-M.
Sullivans, The (US 44): Calkins, Cummings, Driscoll, Swan B.,
    Chapin M., Larson, Rodin M.
Sullivan's Travels (US 42): Winkler
Summer at Grandpa's (84 TW) — see Dongdong de Jiaqi
Summer Holiday (US 47): Jenkins
Summer Love (US 58): Winslow G.
Summer Madness (GB/US 55): Autiero
Summer Magic (US 62): Hodges E.
Summer Saps (US 29): Bailey Sd.
Summer Stock (US 50): Chapin M., Infuhr
Summertime (55 GB/US) — see Summer Madness
Summer to Remember, A (60 SU) — see Seryozha
Summertree (US 71): Calloway
Sun Comes Up, The (US 49): Jarman, Hickman Dw., Infuhr
Sunday Calm (US 23): 'Our Gang'
Sunday Dinner for a Soldier (US 44): Cummings, Driscoll
Sündenbock, Der /The scapegoat (GE 40): Rohringer
Sündige Grenze /Frontier of sin (DE 51): Jansen
Sun Down Limited, The (US 24): 'Our Gang'
Sun Never Sets, The (US 39): Hurlic
Sunnyside Up (US 29): Cooper Ja., Ernest
Sunset Blvd. (US 50): Ivo
Sunset Gun, The (US 12): Boss
Sunshine (US 20): Roubert
Sunshine of Paradise Alley (US 27): Janney, Nelson B., Holmes L.
Sun Valley Cyclone (US 46): Blake
Sun Valley Serenade (US 41): Gray G., Madore
Suomisen Ollin tempaus /Olli Suominen's escapade (FI 42): Pöysti
Suomisen perhe /The Suominens (FI 41): Pöysti

Suomisen taiteilijat / *The Suominen artistes* (FI 43): Pöysti
Super-Sleuth (US 37): Albright
Supersonic Saucer (GB 56): Edmonds
Superstition (US 82): Jacoby Bl.
Supply and Demand (US 22): Jones J.
Su precio unos dolares / *His price a few dollars* (MX 64): Bravo J.
Sure Fire Flint (US 22): Griffin
Sur le tas de sable / *On the sand-heap* (FR 31): Mercanton
Surprised Parties (US 42): 'Our Gang', Tyler L.
'Survival Guides' (US 84, TVS): Call
Surviving (US 85): Phoenix R.
Suspect, The (US 16): Connelly
Suspect, The (US 45): Cook T.
Süsse Zeit mit Kalimagdora, Die (68 DE/CS) − *see* Sladký čas
    Kalimagdory
Suton (82 US/YU) − *see* Twilight Time
Sutter's Gold (US 36): Bupp S. and T., Cosbey, Jones D., Watson D.
Svarta rosor / *Black roses* (SE 32): Winther
Svědomi / *Conscience* (CS 48): Prokeš, Jandl
Svensson ordnar allt / *Leave it to Svensson* (SE 38): Winther
Svezhi veter / *Fresh wind* (SU 26): Lyudvinski, Chernishoff
Svirachat (66 US/BG) − *see* Pied Piper
Svoya golova na plechakh / *A mind of one's own* (SU 60): Krivchenkov
S.W.A.L.K. (GB 70): Lester, Wild, Brockwell
Swallows and Amazons (GB 74): West S., Grendon
Swamp, The (US 21): Lee F.
Swamp Fire (US 46): Chapin M.
Swan, The (US 25): Depew
Swan, The (US 56): Cook C., Parks
Swanee River (US 39): Beard, Billings G.
Swarm, The (US 78): Juttner, Petersen Chr.
Swarm in May, A (GB 82): Hicks, McFarquhar
Swedish Love Story, A (70 SE) − *see* Kärlekshistoria
Sweeney Todd, the Demon Barber of Fleet Street (GB 36): Singer
Sweet and Lowdown (US 44): Dawson, McKim H., Rodin M., Swan
Sweethearts (US 38): Kilburn
Sweetie (US 29): Winslow D.
Sweet Revenge (US 09): Harron
Swell-Head (US 35): Moore D.
Świadectwo urodzenia / *Birth certificate* (PL 61): Hryniewicz, Mincer
Swift Lover, A (29 US) − *see* Gun Law
Swing High (US 30): Bennett M.
Swing it, fröken! / *Swing it, Miss!* (SE 56): Almgren
Swing it, magistern! / *Swing it, Sir!* (SE 40): Hjelm, Olsson
Swing Your Lady (US 37): Bupp T. and S.
Swing You Swingers! (US 39): Nichols
Swiss Family Robinson (US 40): Kilburn
Swiss Family Robinson (GB 60): Corcoran
'Swiss Family Robinson, The' (US 75, TVS): Olson
Sword in the Stone, The (US 63): Sorensen
Sylvia (US 64): Padilla
Symphonie des brigands, La (36 GB/FR) − *see* Robber Symphony
Symphonie eines Lebens / *Symphony of a life* (GE 42): Rohringer
Symphonie pastorale, La / *Pastoral symphony* (FR 46): Demorget
Symphony of Living (US 35): Lee L.
Symphony of Six Million (US 32): Lee L.
Syncopation (US 42): Bupp S.

Syndicat des fessés, Le / *The spanked boys' union* (FR 20): Touzé
Synnöve Solbakken (SE 19): Brunius
Synnöve Solbakken (SE 34): Granberg L.
Synnöve Solbakken (SE 57): Nilsson
Syova lechit druga / *Syova cures his friend* (SU 62): Rodionov
Szakadék / *The abyss* (HU 55): Csögör, Weiser A. and G.
141 perc a befejezetlen mondatból / *Unfinished sentence of 141 minutes*
    (HU 74): Elistratov
Szaleństwo Majki Skowron / *Majek Skowron's madness* (PL 75): Sikora
Szamárköhögés / *Whooping cough* (HU 87): Tóth M.
Szánkó, A / *The sledge* (HU 55): Weiser A. and G.
Szatan z siódmej klasy / *Seventh grade Satan* (PL 60): Halicz
Szerelmi álmok / *Dreams of love* (HU/SU 70): Kovács

Tabaré (MX 46): Pastor
Table for Five (US 83): Kiger
Tacuara y Chamorro (AR 67): Avalos, Di Nueci
Tadbir / *Endeavour* (IN 45): Kapoor S.
Tadjerobeh / *Experience* (IR 73): Yarmohamadi
Tad's Swimming Hole (US 18): Butterworth E.
Taffy and the Jungle Hunter (US 64): Padilla
Tåg til Himlen / *Train to Heaven* (SE 89): López C.
Taihen na otome / *Virgin extraordinary* (JP 33): 'Tokkan-Kozo'
Tail Spin (US 39): Kibrick L.
Taina dvukh okeanov / *The mystery of two oceans* (SU 55-56): Bristol
Taina gornovo ozera / *Mystery of the mountain lake* (SU 54): Mkrtchiyan
Taina Vip / *The Vip mystery* (SU 59): Fisenko, Gusev V.
Taini mudrovo ribolova / *Secrets of a wise fisherman* (SU 57): Siluyanov
Taiyo ni kakeru hashi (74 GB) − *see* Paper Tiger
Tajemnica starego szybu / *Secret of the old pit* (PL 55): Bustamante
Tajemství ocelového města / *Secret of Steel City* (CS 78): Potměšil
Take It From Me (US 26): Billings E.
Take Me Home (US 28): Scott D.
Take Me to Town (US 53): Aaker L.
Take My Life (GB 47): Wallbridge
Take One False Step (US 49): Ivo
Taking a Chance (US 28): Butts, Watson Bl.
Tak nachinalas legenda / *Birth of a legend* (SU 76): Orloff
Takoi bolshoi malchik / *Such a big boy* (SU 67): Zharkov
Tale of a Dog (US 44): 'Our Gang', Hickman C.
Tale of a Tooth (AU 56): Taylor
Tale of Five Cities, A (GB 51): Staiola
Tale of Old Tucson, A (US 14): Boss
Tale of Two Cities, A (US 11): Casey
Tale of Two Cities, A (US 35): Haines
Taler der Tante Sidonie, Die / *Aunt Sidonie's thalers* (GE 35):
    Brackmann
Tales of Manhattan (US 42): Hickman C.
Tales of Robin Hood (US 51): Stollery
Talisman (BG 78): Tsvetkov
Talk About a Stranger (US 52): Gray B.
Tall, Dark and Handsome (US 41): Bates
Tall in the Saddle (US 44): Samarzich
Tall Story (US 60): Phillips P.
Tall Stranger, The (US 57): Phillips P.
Tall T, The (US 56): Olsen C.
Tall Tale (US 94): Stahl

Tall Target, The (US 51): Mora

Tal vez mañana /*Perhaps tomorrow* (ES 58): Nevola

Tamandra, the Gypsy (US 13): Johnson R.

Tambien de dolor se canta /*There are sad songs too* (MX 50): Calpe, Cardona II

Tambor de Tacuarí, El /*The drummer of Tacuarí* (AR 48): Barbieri

Tambu-Lambu (SU 57): Perevalov, Trusov

Tamburino sardo, Il /*The Sardinian drummer-boy* (IT 15): Petrungaro, Roveri

Tamburino sardo, Il (51 IT) − *see* Altri tempi

Tamburino sardo, Il (84 IT) − *see* Cuore

Tammy and the Millionaire (US 67): Quinn T.

Tammy Tell Me True (US 61): Mumy

Tampon du colonel, Le /*The colonel's batman* (FR 35): Bara

Tangewala /*Horse-cart driver* (IN 72): Mehmood

Tangled Threads (US 19): Alexander B.

Tango Cavalier (US 24): Quinn B.

Tanhai /*Solitude* (IN 72): Mehmood

Tannenberg (GE 32): Klicks

Ta' Pelle med /*Take Pelle along* (DK 52): Holmberg

Tapfere Schulschwanzer, Der /*The brave truant* (DD 67): Kallenbach

Taps (US 81): Ward B.

Taqtwar (PK 88): Jamshid

Taralezhite se razhdat bez bodli /*Hedgehogs aren't born prickly* (BG 71): Arshinkov, Djambazov, Petrov

Tarantulas: the Deadly Cargo (US 77): Laborteaux M.

Taras Shevchenko (SU 26): Lyudvinski

Tarnished Angels, The (US 57): Olsen C.

'Tarzan' (US 66-68, TVS): Padilla

Tarzan and the Amazons (US 45): Sheffield J.

Tarzan and the Great River (US/CH 67): Padilla

Tarzan and the Huntress (US 47): Sheffield J., Tauzin

Tarzan and the Jungle Boy (US/CH 67): Bond S.

Tarzan and the Leopard Woman (US 45): Sheffield J., Cook T.

Tarzan and the Trappers (US 58): Sorensen

Tarzan and the Valley of Gold (US/CH 65): Padilla

Tarzan Finds a Son! (US 39): Sheffield J.

Tarzan Goes to India (GB/US/CH 62): 'Jai'

Tarzan of the Apes (US 18): Griffith

Tarzan's Deadly Silence (US 67): Padilla

Tarzan's Desert Mystery (US 43): Sheffield J.

Tarzan's Fight for Life (US 58): Sorensen

Tarzan '65/'66 (65 US/CH) − *see* Tarzan and the Valley of Gold

Tarzan's Jungle Rebellion (US 67): Padilla

Tarzan's New York Adventure (US 42): Sheffield J.

Tarzan's Savage Fury (US 52): Carlton

Tarzan's Secret Treasure (US 41): Sheffield J., Hickman C.

Tarzan's Three Challenges (US 63): Der

Tarzan the Mighty (US 28, srl): Nelson B.

Tarzan Triumphs (US 43): Sheffield J.

Taste of Melon, A (US 64): Mobley, Mumy

Tat des Anderen, Die /*Another's act* (DE 50): Bürger

Tatli günler /*Sweet days* (TR 69): Dönmez

Tatli rüyalar /*Sweet dreams* (TR 70): Inanoglu

Tato, sežeň štěně! /*Dad, buy me a puppy!* (CS 63): Smyczek

Tattered Dress, The (US 57): Herbert

Tattle Battle, The (US 13): Clark R.

Tatul /*Thornapple* (BG 72): Petrov

Taxi 13 (US 28): Watson C., D., H. and Bl.

Taxi 13 (SE 54): Dam

Tažni ptáci /*Birds of passage* (CS 61): Kříž

Teacher and the Miracle, The (57 IT/ES) − *see* Maestro

Teacher's Beau (US 35): 'Our Gang'

Teacher's Pet (US 30): 'Our Gang'

Teasing Grandpa (GB 01): Williamson A. and C.

Techot Volga /*The Volga flows on* (SU 62): Kekish

Teddy Tetzlaff and Earl Cooper, Speed Kings (US 13): Jacobs

Ted zas my /*Here we are again* (CS 39): Salač

Teiso mondo /*Questions of chastity* (JP 35): Hayama

Telefteo psema, To /*The last lie* (GR 58): Kailas

Telephone Operator, The (US 38): Cosbey, Kaye

Television (GE 31): Lohmeyer

Teljes gözzel /*Full steam ahead* (HU 51): Horváth L.

Telling Whoppers (US 26): 'Our Gang'

Tell Me My Name (US 77): McKeon D.

Temple of Dawn, The (US 20): Moore M.

Temple of Moloch, The (US 14): Boss

Temple of Venus, The (US 23): McBan, Wilkinson

Temps de vivre, Le /*A time to live* (FR 68): Damain

Ten /*Shadow* (SU 61): Nazarov S.

Ten Cent Adventure, A (US 15): Stone

Ten Cents a Dance (US 31): Shuford

Ten Commandments, The (US 23): Moore P.

Ten Commandments, The (US 56): Mazzola

Ten Commandments, The (88 PL) − *see* Dekalog

Tender Mercies (US 82): Hubbard

Tender Warrior (US 71): Lee C.

Tender Years, The (US 47): Lyon

Tendresse, La /*Tenderness* (FR 30): Bara

Tengoku to jigoku /*High and low* (JP 63): Egi, Sada, Shimazu

Ten okrutny, nikczemny chłopiec /*That cruel, disgusting boy* (PL 72): Mosior, Szczerkowski, Izdebski, Samosionek

Tension at Table Rock (US 56): Chapin B.

Tentata, La /*A woman tempted* (IT 18): Visca

Tenth Avenue Angel (US 47): Tyler D.

Tenth Avenue Kid (US 38): Ryan

Ten Years Old (US 27): 'Our Gang', Black B.

Te o tsunagu kora /*Hand in hand* (JP 62): Morihara

Terminator 2: Judgment Day (US 91): Furlong E.

Terms of Endearment (US 84): Fox H.

Terra /*Earth* (IT 20): Casarotti

Terra trema, La /*The earth shakes* (IT 47): 'Alfio'

Terre promise, La /*The promised land* (FR 25): Guichard, Rauzéna

Terror, The (US 28): Darro

Terror Abroad (US 33): Janney

Terror and the Terrier, The (GB 10): Miller F.

Terrorist (ZA 76): Knox

Terror Mountain (US 28): Darro

Terror out of the Sky (US 76): Eisenmann

Terrors (GB 30): Smith E., G. and R.

Terry on the Fence (GB 85): McNicholl

Tesoro de la Isla de Pinos, El /*Treasure on the Isle of Pines* (MX/CU 55): Calpe, Perez

Tesoro del Bengala, Il /*The treasure of Bengal* (IT 54): Poujouly

Testament (US 83): Harris R., Haas L.
Testament d'Orphée, Le / The testament of Orpheus (FR 59): Léaud
Testamento di Maciste, Il / Maciste's testament (IT 20): Allen W.
Testing Block, The (US 20): Headrick
Test of Donald Norton, The (US 26): Moore M.
Test of Friendship, The (US 08): Harron
Test Pilot (US 38): Spellman, Tucker T.
Tête folle / Crazy head (FR 60): Morat
Tettes ismeretlen, A / Danse macabre (HU 58): Csógör, Weiser A.
Teufel vom Mühlenberg, Der / The devil of Mill Hill (DD 54):
    Rettschlag
Texan, The (US 30): Nelson B.
Texas Kid, The (US 19): Eason
Texas Pioneers (US 32): Shuford
Texas Rangers, The (US 36): Bartlett
Texas Streak, The (US 26): Murphy J.
Texas Terrors (US 35): Nelson B.
Texas Terrors (US 40): McKim S.
Texas Tornado, The (US 28): Darro
'Texas Wheelers, The' (US 74, TVS): Becker
Tex Rides with the Boy Scouts (US 37): Bupp T.
Thank You (US 25): Murphy M.
Thank You, Jeeves! (US 36): Reynolds
That Certain Feeling (US 56): Mathers
That Certain Summer (US 72): Jacoby S.
That Lady (GB 55): Shine
That'll Be the Day (GB 73): Puttnam
That Model from Paris (US 26): Holmes L.
That Night (US 57): Brodrick
That Night With You (US 45): Infuhr
That Old Gang of Mine (US 26): Brown T.
That Others May Live (47 PL) — see Ulica Graniczna
That's My Boy (US 32): Haig
That Something (US 21): Griffith
Tha zisso gia sena / I'll live for you (GR 65): Kailas
Théâtre de la famille Roulotte / The caravan family theatre
    (FR c.29): Barty
Theerthayathra / Pilgrimage (IN 72): Satyajit
Their First Misunderstanding (US 11): Pickford
Their Mad Moment (US 31): Janney
Their Mutual Child (US 20): Moore P.
Thelma (US 22): DeLacy
Thelo na zissis manula / I want you to live, Mummy (GR 57):
    Kalatzopoulos
Them Nice Americans (GB 58): Gilmore
Theodor im Fussballtor, Der / Theodore the goalie (DE 50): Bürger
There Ain't No Santa Claus (US 26): Bennett M.
There's Magic in Music (41 US) — see Hard-Boiled Canary
There's No Business Like Show Business (US 54): Chapin B., Clark B.2
There's No Place Like Home (US 16): Short
There's One Born Every Minute (US 42): Switzer
There Was a War When I Was a Child (80 JP) — see Kodomo no koro
    senso na atta
There You Are! (US 26): Billings E.
These Wilder Years (US 56): Herbert, Washbrook
They Asked For It (US 39): Billings G., Bupp T.
They Call Me MISTER Tibbs! (US 70): Spell G.

They Came by Night (GB 40): Tyler G.
They Live By Night (US 48): Infuhr, Moss J.
They Made Me a Criminal (US 39): Sinclair
They Met Again (US 41): Tyler L.
They Shall Have Music (US 39): Reynolds, Kilburn, Kelly T.
Thiassos, O / The travelling players (GR 75): Koutiris
Thibault, Les / The Thibaults (FR 72, srl): Erimitchoi
Thief of Bagdad, The (US 24): McBan
Thief of Bagdad, The (GB 40): Sabu
Thief or Angel (US 18): Butterworth E.
Thiela se pediki kardia / Storm in a child's heart (GR 65): Kailas
Things Are Looking Up (GB 35): Henderson D.
Third Alarm, The (US 22): Lee F.
Third Alarm, The (US 30): Billings G.
Third Generation, The (US 20): Redden
Third Party, The (US 15): Connelly
Third Reich (GB 82): McGrath
Thirst (US 17): Jacobs
Thirteen Ghosts (US 60): Herbert
13 Hours by Air (US 36): Bartlett
Thirteenth Hour, The (US 47): Dennis
Thirteen Women (US 32): Albright
This Boy's Life (US 93): DiCaprio
This England (GB 41): McDowall
This Freedom (GB 23): Brantford
This Green Hell (GB 36): Singer
This Gun for Hire (US 42): Jones D., Winkler
This Is My Love (US 54): Mathers
This Is the Life (US 35): McKim S.
This Is the Life (US 43): Nichols
This Love of Ours (US 45): Miles P. (Perreau), Kuhn, Tyler L.
This Man Must Die (69 FR/IT) — see Que la bête meure!
This Property Is Condemned (US 66): Provost
This Side of Heaven (US 34): Moore D.
This Special Friendship (64 FR) — see Amitiés particulières
This Woman is Mine (US 41): Binyon
Thokar / Kick (IN 74): Mehmood
Thoroughbreds Don't Cry (US 37): Sinclair
Those Clever Kid Comedies (US 14): Clark A.
Those Country Kids (US 14): Griffith, Jacobs
Those Terrible Twins (AU 25): Canstell, Griffen
Those Troublesome Boys (GB 01): Williamson A. and C.
Those We Love (US 32): Conlon
Those Were the Days (GB 34): Singer
Those Without Sin (US 17): Jacobs
Thousand Clowns, A (US 65): Gordon Ba.
Threads of Destiny (US 14): Thaw
Three Bags Full (GB 49, srl): Hannaford
Three Cheers for Love (US 36): Hickman Dl., Lee B.
Three Days and a Child (66 IL) — see Shlosha yamin ve yeled
Three Days to Live (29 US) — see Red Sword
Three Eyes (US 82): Hathaway
Three Faces East (US 25): Noisom
Three Faces West (US 40): Bupp S.
Three for the Road (US 75): Garrett
Three Kids and a Queen (US 35): Burrud
Three Little Vagabonds (GB 13): Royston R.

Three Little Words (US 50): Gray B.
Three Live Ghosts (US 29): Cooper Ja.
Three Lives of Thomasina, The (GB/US 63): Winter, Gilmore, Garber
Three Married Men (US 36): Bartlett
Three Maxims, The (GB 36): Snelling
Three Men in a Tub (US 38): 'Our Gang', Tucker J.
Three Men in White (US 44): Cummings
'Three Mesquiteers' series (US 37-40): McKim S.
Three Miles Up (US 27): Jones B.
3 Ninja Kids (US 92): Slade, Treanor
3 Ninjas Kick Back (US 93): Slade
Three o'Clock in the Morning (US 23): Griffin
Three of a Kind (32 GB) – see Love on the Spot
Three of a Kind (US 44): Henry R.
Three on a Match (US 32): Darro, Phelps
Three's a Crowd (US 27): Butterworth J., Young
Three Smart Boys (US 37): 'Our Gang'
Three Smart Guys (US 43): 'Our Gang'
3:10 to Yuma (US 57): Curtis
Three Weeks (US 24): Sabiston
Three Who Loved (US 31): Moore D.
Three Wise Fools (US 46): Bates, Gray G.
Thrill Hunter, The (US 26): Darro
Through a Glass Window (US 22): Hamrick
Through Eyes of Men (US 20): Alexander B.
Through the Back Door (US 21): Wilkinson
Through the Magic Pyramid (US 81): Barnes C.
Through the Toils (US 19): Carr T.
Throwback, The (US 35): Nelson B.
Thunder (US 29): Albright
Thunderbolt, The (US 19): Eason
Thunderbolt (US 36): Nelson B.
Thunderhead Son of Flicka (US 45): McDowall
Thundering Fleas (US 26): 'Our Gang'
Thunder in the East (US 52): Cavell
Thunder Mountain (US 25): Jones B.
Thunder over the Prairie (US 41): Mummert
Thunder Rock (GB 42): Wallbridge
Thunder Trail (US 37): Lee B., Reynolds
Tian lun / Family relations (CN 35): Li
Ticklish Affair, A (US 63): Mumy, Robbins, Russell B.
Tides of Barnegat, The (US 17): Jacobs
Tierarzt Dr Vlimmen / Dr Vlimmen the vet (DE 56): Haar
Tierna infancia, La / Tender childhood (MX 65): Bravo J.
Tiger Bay (GB 59): Hammond B.
Tigers Don't Cry (ZA 76): Knox
Tiger Town (US 83): Henry J.
Tiger Walks, A (US 64): Corcoran
Tigress, The (US 15): Connelly
Tigress, The (US 27): DeLacy
Tigurcheto / Little tiger (BG 72): Vasilev V.
Tijera de oro, La / Golden scissors (MX 58): Jiménez Pons R.
Tiko and the Shark (62 IT/FR/US) – see Ti-Koyo e il suo pescecane
Ti koito si na nebeto / Thou which art in Heaven (BG 89): Kovachev B.
Ti-Koyo e il suo pescecane / Ti-Koyo and his shark (IT/FR/US 62): Pouira
Tilaï (BF/CH/FR 90): Ouedraogo

Till I Come Back To You (US 18): Butterworth F., Stone
Tillie and Gus (US 33): Leroy
Tillie's Punctured Romance (US 14): Griffith, Berlinger
Tillie's Punctured Romance (US 28): Bennett M.
Tillie the Toiler (US 40): Bartlett
Till the End of Time (US 46): Infuhr, Tyler D.
Till We Meet Again (US 36): Ernest
Tilly the Tomboy Buys Linoleum (GB 10): Potter
Ti lovis / You are hunting (YU 61): Gjurin
Time After Time (US 79): Feldman
Time Bandits (GB 81): Warnock C.
Time Lock (GB 57): Winter
Time of Your Life, The (US 48): Rees
Time Out for Lessons (US 39): 'Our Gang'
Time Out for Romance (US 37): Bartlett, Watson H.
Time to Live, A (US 85): Haim
Time Trouble (GB 85): Carney
Timm Thaler (DE 75, srl): Ohrner
'Timmy and Lassie' (57-64 US, TVS) – see 'Lassie'
Timothy's Quest (US 22): Depew
Timothy's Quest (US 36): Moore D., Bartlett
Tim Tyler's Luck (US 37, srl): Thomas F.
Timur i yevo komanda / Timur and his gang (SU 40): Shchipachev, Seleznyoff V., Smirnoff
Tin Drum, The (79 DE/FR) – see Blechtrommel
Tingujt e luftës / Sounds of war (AL 76): Goxhi
Tinko (DD 57): Reichhoff
Tin Soldier and the Doll, The (US 14): Hauck
Tin Star, The (US 57): Ray M.
Tiny Troubles (US 39): 'Our Gang'
Tiptoes (GB 27): Cardiff
Tired Business Men (US 27): 'Our Gang', Butts
Tire Trouble (US 24): 'Our Gang'
Tirez sur le pianiste / Shoot the pianist (FR 60): Kanayan
Tiro al aire / Head in the clouds (AR 80): Ferrario
Tis niktas ta kamomata / What happened in the night (GR 57): Kalatzopoulos
Titi premier, roi des gosses / Titi the First, King of the Kids (FR 26): Guichard
Title Cure, The (US 13): Boss
Tjocka släkten / Close relatives (SE 35): Winther
Tjorven, Båtsman och Moses / Tjorven, Boatman and Moses (SE 64): Lindholm, Ulvskog
Tjorven och Mysak / Tjorven and Mysak (SE 66): Lindholm
Tjorven och Skrållan / Tjorven and Young Yeller (SE 65): Lindholm, Ulvskog
Tko pjeva zlo ne misli / You can't go wrong with a song (YU 71): Zganec
Több, mint jatek / More than a game (HU 56): Koletar, Benkö, Weiser A. and G.
To Be or Not To Be (US 42): Caldwell
Tobor the Great (US 54): Chapin B.
To byl ceský muzikant / It was a Czech musician (CS 40): Jedlička A. and V.
Toby Tyler (23 US) – see Circus Days
Toby Tyler (US 60): Corcoran
To Cherish and Protect (US 15): Connelly

Töchter Ihrer Excellenz, Die / *Your Excellency's daughters* (GE 34): Schaufuss

Toda-ke no kyodai / *Siblings from the Toda family* (JP 41): Hayama

Today We Live (US 33): Alexander T.

Todesleiter, Die / *The ladder of death* (GE 21): Patatà

To Each His Own (US 46): Gray B. and G.

Toggle (GB 67): Kemp A.

To Hear a Rainbow Sing (US 74): Kerwin

To Hell and Back (US 55): Gebert

To Him That Hath (US 18): Jackson C.

Toilers, The (GB 19): Barker E.

To Kill a Mockingbird (US 62): Alford

Tokkan kozo / *Naughty boy* (JP 29): 'Tokkan-Kozo'

Tokyo na yado / *An inn in Tokyo* (JP 35): 'Tokkan-Kozo'

Tokyo no gassho / *Tokyo chorus* (JP 31): Sugawara

Told at Twilight (US 17): Morrison E.

Toll Gate, The (US 20): Headrick

Tom and His Pals (US 26): Darro

Tomb of Ligeia, The (GB 64): Gilmore

Tomboy, The (US 21): Wilkinson

Tomboy (US 40): Moran

Tom Brown of Culver (US 32): Wain

Tom Brown's Schooldays (GB 16): Coleman J., Barker E.

Tom Brown's Schooldays (US 40): Lydon

Tom Brown's Schooldays (GB 50): Davies J. H., Charlesworth, Dearman

Tomka dhe shokët e tij / *Tommy and his friends* (AL 77): Zhegu, Mosho, Mustafaraj

Tommy's Atonement (US 13): Johnson C.

Tommy's Geography Lesson (US 11): Boss

Tommy's Money Scheme (GB 14): Desmond

Tommy's Tramp (US 14): Harris B.

Tommy Tricker and the Stamp Traveller (CA/CN 88): Evans L., Rogers A.

Tomodachi / *Friends* (JP 40): Yokoyama

Tomorrow and Tomorrow (US 32): Alexander T., Tucker J.

Tomorrow at Ten (GB 62): Bishop

Tomorrow Is Another Day (US 51): Hyatt

Tomorrow's Love (US 25): O'Donnell

Tomorrow's Warrior (81 CY) − *see* Avrianos polemistis

Tomorrow's Youth (US 35): Moore D., Samarzich

Tomorrow, the World (US 44): Homeier, Wissler

Tom Pouce / *Tom Thumb* (FR 10): Mary

Tom Sawyer (US 17): Pickford, Collier

Tom Sawyer (US 30): Coogan J., Durkin, Searl

Tom Sawyer (SU 36): Kulchitski, Katsovich

Tom Sawyer (37 US) − *see* Adventures of Tom Sawyer

Tom Sawyer (68 MX) − *see* Aventuras de Juliancito

Tom Sawyer (US 72, srl): Albee, Tyler J.

Tom Sawyer (US 73): Whitaker, East

Tom Sawyer (81 SU) − *see* Priklyucheniya Tomi Soyera

Tom Sawyer, Detective (US 38): Cook B., O'Connor

Tom's Gang (US 27): Darro

Tom Thumb (58 MX) − *see* Pulgarcito

Tom Thumb (85 SU) − *see* Spriditis

Tom Tilling's Baby (US 12): Casey

Tongues of Flame (US 24): Devine

Tonio Kröger (DE/FR 64): Carrière

Tony, tobě přeskočilo / *Tony, you're crazy* (CS 68): Filip J.

Too Busy to Work (US 40): Mahan

Toofani toli / *Stormy group* (IN 37): Apte

Toofan Mail (IN 34): Apte

Too Good to Be True (US 88): Harris N. P.

Too Many Parents (US 36): Bailey Sd., Ernest, Lee B., Phelps, Reynolds, Scott D., Switzer, Van Atta

Too Many Winners (US 47): Gray G.

Too Much Wife (US 22): Fox J.

Toote khilone / *Broken toys* (IN 54): Kapoor Ro.

Too Young to Kiss (US 51): Infuhr

Topaze (US 33): Searl

Topio stin omikhli / *Landscape in the mist* (GR/FR/IT 88): Zeke

To Please One Woman (US 20): Griffith

Topo, El / *The mouse* (MX 71): Jodorovsky

Top of New York, The (US 22): Moore P.

Top o' the Morning (US 49): Hunt

Torch Singer, The (US 33): Leroy

Tordensköld går i land / *Tordensköld comes ashore* (DK 42): Fagerlund

Törichte Jungfrau, Die / *The foolish virgin* (GE 35): Brackmann

Tornado, The (US 24): Morgan

Torrents (FR 46): Gervais

To the Highest Bidder (US 18): Carr S.

To the Last Man (US 33): Ward, Watson D.

To the Rescue (GB 52): Edmonds

Totò e Marcelino / *Toto and Marcelino* (IT/FR 58): Calvo

Toto le héros / *Toto the hero* (BE/FR/GE 91): Godet

Totò y Pablito (58 IT/FR) − *see* Totò e Marcelino

Tottisalmen perillinen / *The heir of Tottisalmi* (FI 40): Hämäläinen

Totville Eye, The (US 12): Boss

Touben nuhai / *Boat people* (HK 82): Wu

Touch of a Child's Hand, The (US 10): Melford

Touch of Larceny, A (GB 59): Stephens M.

Toughest Man in Arizona (US 52): Hyatt

Tough Guy, The (US 26): Butts

Tough Guy (US 36): Cooper Ja.

Tough Luck (US 19): Morrison E.

Tough Winter, A (US 22): Cobb

Tough Winter, A (US 30): 'Our Gang'

Touha / *Desire* (CS 58): Jakeš

Tour de France de deux enfants, Le / *Two children's journey round France* (FR 23): Legeay, Willy

Tourments / *Torments* (FR 53): Urbain, Chapeland

Tournament Tempo (46 US) − *see* Gay Blades

Tournoi dans la cité, Le / *Tournament in the city* (FR 28): Mock

Toute sa vie / *All life long* (FR 30): Mercanton

Tovarich (US 37): Bupp T., Tucker J., Watson D.

Toward the Unknown (US 56): Provost

Towering Inferno, The (US 74): Lookinland M.

Tower of Lies, The (US 25): Noisom

Tower of London (US 39): Sinclair, Herbert-Bond, Dunagan

Tower of London (US 62): Losby, Martin E.

Town That Forgot God, The (US 22): Grauer

Toy, The (US 82): Schwartz S.

Toy Cart (IN 32): Kapoor Ra.

Toy Tiger (US 56): Hovey, Bernard, Mora

Track the Man Down (GB 55): Pike J.
Trading His Mother (US 11): Boss
Traffic in Hearts (US 24): Marion D.
Tragédie impériale, La / The imperial tragedy (FR 37): Claudio
Tragic Symphony (47 US) — see Song of My Heart
Trail Blazers, The (US 53): Hyatt
Trail of Chance, The (US 16): Clark A.
Trail of '98, The (US 29): Downs
Trail of the Horse Thieves (US 29): Darro
Trail of the Lonesome Pine, The (US 36): McFarland, Ernest
Trail of the Rustlers (US 50): Ivo
Trail to Gunsight (US 44): Henry R.
Trail to Laredo (US 48): Ivo
Traje blanco, Un / A white suit (ES 56): Gil, Rodriguez M.A.
Trapp-Familie, Die / The Trapp family (DE 56): Ande
Trapp-Familie in Amerika, Die / The Trapps in America (DE 58): Ande
Traqué, Le / Hunted man (FR/US 50): Maurin Y.-M.
Träume sind Schäume / Dreams are only bubbles (GE 38): Kieling
Travail / Labour (FR 19, srl): Haziza
Traveling Saleswoman, The (US 50): Infuhr
'Travels of Jaimie McPheeters, The' (US 63-64, TVS): Russell K.
Travels of Jaimie McPheeters, The (64 US) — see Guns of Diablo
Travesuras de Morucha, Las / Morucha's pranks (ES 62): Juan José
Trav, hopp och kärlek / Trot, hop and love (SE 45): Lindgren H.
Treasure at the Mill (GB 57): Palmer
Treasure in the Haunted House (US 64): McGreevey, Mobley, Mumy
Treasure Island (US 12): Rothermel
Treasure Island (US 17): Carpenter, Messinger, Perl, Sargent
Treasure Island (US 34): Cooper Ja.
Treasure Island (GB/US 50): Driscoll
Treasure Island (GB 58, srl): Palmer
Treasure Island (GB/FR/DE/ES 71): Burfield
Treasure Island (71 SU) — see Ostrov Sokrovishch
Treasure Island (86-89 FR/US) — see Ile au trésor
Treasure Island (US 90): Bale
Treasure Island -- the Musical (GB 83): Eady
Treasure of Lost Canyon, The (US 51): Ivo
Treasure of Matecumbe, The (US 76): Doran, Attmore
Treasure of the Sierra Madre, The (US 48): Blake
Tredici uomini e un cannone / Thirteen men and a cannon (IT 36): Brambilla
Tree Grows in Brooklyn, A (US 45): Donaldson T.
Tre engle og fem løver / Three angels, five lions (DK 82): Nezer
Tree of Knowledge, The (81 DK) — see Kundskabens træ
Trenadeset dni / Thirteen days (BG 64): Alurkov
30 ans, ou la vie d'un joueur / 30 years: a gambler's life (BE 12): Mertens
Tres mosqueteros de Dios, Los / God's three musketeers (MX 66): Bravo J.
Trésor de Cantenac, Le / The treasure of Cantenac (FR 49): Urbain
Trespasser, The (US 29): Albright
Treue Husar, Der / The faithful hussar (DE 54): Kaiser
Tribunal de justicia / Police court (MX 44): Fernandez, Roche
Tribute to Mother, A (US 15): Clark A.
Triflers, The (US 20): Alexander B.
Trifling with Honor (US 23): Messinger
Trigger, Jr. (US 50): Miles P.
Trigger Smith (US 39): Clark B.l
Trigger Trail (US 44): Henry R.

Trigger Trio, The (US 37): McKim S.
Trilogia di Maciste, La / The Maciste trilogy (IT 20): Allen W.
Třinactileti / Thirteen-year-olds (CS 60): Kauzlarič
Trio (GB 50): Hannaford
Trio Angelos (CS 63): Poláček
Trip to Paris, A (US 38): Kibrick S., Mahan
Trique, gamin de Paris / Trique, the Paris urchin (FR 60): Martaguet M.
Trishna / Insatiable desire (IN 78): Rajoo
Trishul / The trident (IN 78): Rajoo
Triumph (US 24): Billings E.
Triumph of the Rat (GB 26): Brantford
Trizhdi voskreshi / Thrice resurrected (SU 60): Krivchenkov
Tři zlaté vlasy děda Vševěda / Grandpa Knowall's three golden hairs (CS 63): Hádl
Trocadéro, bleu citron / Trocadero blue and yellow (FR 78): Melet
Troen, der frelser / Troen the saviour (DK 16): Heimann
Trois enfants dans la désordre / Three kids in chaos (FR 66): Maurin J.-F.
Trois tambours, Les / The three drummer-boys (FR 39): Brécourt, Buquet, Rétaux
Trois télégrammes / Three telegrams (FR 50): Gervais, Chapeland, Fourcade, Maurin Y.-M.
Troll (US 85): Hathaway
Trollsländar / Dragonflies (SE 20): Brunius
Tropic Madness (US 28): Durand
Trotting Through Turkey (US 20): Morrison E.
Trouble (US 22): Coogan J.
Trouble Buster, The (US 25): Black B.
Trouble for Two (US 36): Holt D.
Troubles Through Billets (42 US) — see Blondie for Victory
Trouble with Harry, The (US 56): Mathers
Trouble with 2B, The (GB 72): Brassett
Trouwe kameraden / Faithful comrades (NL 48): Koridon
Troye / The threesome (SU 27): Krestinski
Trudniye deti / Difficult children (SU 63): Biryukoff, Kekish
Trudnoye shchastiye / Difficult happiness (SU 58): Ashurov
True Blue (US 18): Carpenter
True Tilda (GB 20): Craig
True to Life (US 43): Winkler
Trumpin' Trouble (US 26): Winslow D.
Trust Your Wife (US 21): Barry W.
Truthful Sex, The (US 26): Schaeffer
Truxton King (US 23): Moore M.
Tschetan der Indianerjunge / Chetan, Indian boy (DE 72): Bowakow
Tsimu qu / Song of a loving mother (CN 37): Li
Tsubasa no gaika / Song of victory (JP 42): Sugi
Tsuigeki sanjuki / Attack by 30 soldiers (JP 54): Yamate
Tsumayo bara no yoni / Wife! Be like a rose (JP 35): Ito K.
Tsuzurikata kyodai / Brother and sister love writing (JP 58): Zushi
Tsuzurikata kyositsu / Composition class (JP 38): Kodaka
Tsvet granata (74 SU) — see Nran gouyne
Tsvetniye sni / Dreams in colour (SU 63): Klimov, Semyonov Vo.
Tucson Raiders (US 44): Blake
Tudor Rose (GB 36): Tester, Singer
Tulak Macoun / Macoun the tramp (CS 39): Salač
Tulipää / Flame-head (FI 80): Karskela, Railo, Suonsuu
Tullemands frieri / Tullemand's courtship (DK 10): Voigt
Tumbleweeds (US 25): Murphy J.

Tumbling River (US 27): Billings E.

Tumbhri kasam /*Swear by you* (IN 78): Rajoo

Tunco Maclovio, El /*That swine Maclovio* (MX 70): Bravo J.

Tunnel, The (GB 35): Fitzpatrick P.

Tuofeng shang de ai /*Camel love* (CN 85): Fang

Ture Sventon, privatdetektiv /*Ture Sventon, private detective* (NO/SE 72): Malmsjö

Turmoil, The (US 23): Messinger

Turmoil (36 US) — *see* Sins of Man

Turning Point, The (US 20): Moore P.

Turn in the Road, The (US 18): Alexander B.

Turn of the Road, The (US 15): Connelly

Turn of the Tide (GB 35): Blomfield

Tursi su suprug za mama /*Finding Mummy a husband* (BG 84): Prahov

Túsztörténet /*Stand off* (HU 89): Svidrony

Tuttles of Tahiti, The (US 42): Cook T., Infuhr

Tu vida entre mis manos /*Your life in my hands* (MX 54): Perez

Tüz, A /*The fire* (HU 17): Lubinsky, Szécsi

Tüzgömbök /*Balls of fire* (HU 75): Szücs

Två år i varje klass /*Two years in each class* (SE 38): Bernhard

Tvoyi druzya /*Your friends* (SU 60): Rodin S.

Twarz aniola /*Angel face* (PL 70): Dudek, Izdebski

Twee vorstinnen en een Vorst /*Two princesses and a prince* (BE 81): Clerckx

Twelve Desperate Hours (56 GB) — *see* Extra Day

Twenty Minutes of Love (US 14): Griffith

Twilight Time (US/YU 82): Nash D.

Twilight Zone the Movie (US 83): Licht

Twinky (GB 69): Kemp A.

Twist Oliver /*Oliver Twist* (HU 19): Lubinsky

'Twixt Love and Ambition (US 12): Johnson R.

Two Brides, The (US 19): Tansey S.

Two-Cent Mystery, The (US 15): Benham

Two Fisted (US 35): Lee B.

Two-Fisted Justice (US 31): Nelson B.

Two Gun Caballero (US 31): Nelson B.

Two-Gun Man, The (US 26): Butts

Two-Gun Man from Harlem (US 38): Beard

Two-Gun Troubadour (US 39): Lenhart

Two Hearts in Harmony (GB 35): Baxter

Two in a Crowd (US 36): Burrud, Watson Bl.

Two Kinds of Love (US 20): Eason

Two Little Bears, The (US 61): Carter, Patrick

Two Little Imps Doing Their Bit (US 17): Lee F., Messinger

Two Little Vagabonds (GB 03): Carrington

Two Little Vagabonds (US 14): Clark R.

Two Little Vagabonds, The (24 FR) — *see* Deux gosses

Two Living, One Dead (GB/SE 61): Moulder-Brown

Two Loves (US 61): Roberts A.

Two Merchants, The (US 13): Boss

Two-Minute Warning (US 76): Savage B.

Two Mothers (US 16): Griffith

Two Naughty Boys (GB 09): Williamson S. and T.

Two Naughty Boys Sprinkling the Spoons (GB 1898): Williamson A. and C.

Two Naughty Boys Teasing the Cobbler (GB 1898): Williamson A. and C.

Two Naughty Boys Upsetting the Spoons (GB 1898): Williamson A. and C.

Two of Us, The (67 FR) — *see* Vieil homme et l'enfant

Two Plus Two (US 82): Barnes C.

Two Too Young (US 36): 'Our Gang'

Two Wagons - Both Covered (US 23): Billings E.

Two Waifs (US 16): Stone

Two Weeks - with Love (US 50): Gray G., Rettig

Two Wise Maids (US 37): Searl

Two Years Before the Mast (US 44): Hickman Dl.

Tyag /*The sacrifice* (IN 75): Satyajit

Tyoplaya kompaniya /*The Hot Gang* (SU 24): Konstantinov, Zimin

Tyrant of Red Gulch (US 28): Darro

Tystnaden /*The silence* (SE 63): Lindström J.

Überlistet /*Outwitted* (GE 15): Zilzer

Ucieczka /*Escape* (PL 79): Hudziec

Udivitelnoye voskresene (58 CS/SU) — *see* V šest ráno na letišti

Uheldig jæger, En /*An unlucky hunter* (DK 10): Voigt

Uilenspiegel leeft nog /*Eulenspiegel lives!* (BE 36): Bruyninckx, Buyl

Ujala hi ujala /*Light, more light* (IN 74): Mehmood

Ukigusa /*Floating weeds* (JP 34): Shimazu

Ukigusa monogatari /*Story of floating weeds* (JP 34): 'Tokkan-Kozo'

Ukjent mann /*Unknown man* (DK 52): Henning-Jensen

Ukradena vzducholod /*The stolen airship* (CS 66): Bor, Pospišil

Ulica Graniczna /*Border Street* (PL 47): Złotnicki, Kruk

Ulice zpiva /*The street is singing* (CS 39): Salač

Ulička v ráji /*Little road to paradise* (CS/AT 36): Jedlička V.

Uljhan /*Confusion* (IN 75): Rajoo

Ultima avventura, L' /*The final adventure* (IT 31): Locchi

Ultima escuadrilla, La /*The last flight* (BR 51): Barbieri

Ultima neve di primavera, L' /*The last snow of spring* (IT 73): Cestiè

Ultimi della strada, Gli /*Lowest of the low* (IT 40): Artese, Locchi

Umarete wa mita keredo... /*I was born, but...* (JP 32): 'Tokkan-Kozo', Sugawara

Um ein Königskind /*The royal child* (AT 24): Lubinsky

Umi no koshinkyoku /*A march at sea* (JP 30): 'Tokkan-Kozo'

Um Recht und Ehre /*For right and honour* (GE 25): Pottier

U nas pervoklassnik /*Our first-class boy* (SU 61): Titov

Unchained (US 54): Considine

Uncle, The (GB 64): Duncan, Moulder-Brown

Uncle Buck (US 89): Culkin M.

Uncle Dick's Darling (GB 20): Craig

Uncle Hiram's List (US 11): Boss

Uncle Joe Shannon (US 78): McKeon D.

Uncle Sam of Freedom Ridge (US 20): Tansey S.

Uncle Silas (GB 47): Netscher

Uncle Tom's Cabin (US 10): Roubert

Uncle Tom's Cabin (US 18): Boardman, Carnahan

Uncle Tom's Cabin (US 27): Beard

Uncle Tom's Uncle (US 26): 'Our Gang', Butts, Durand

Uncommon Valor (US 83): Oliver B.

Unconquered (US 17): Jacobs

Under Age (US 41): Roy

Under California Stars (US 48): Chapin M.

Underdog, The (US 43): Larson, Binyon

Valor civile /*Civil courage* (IT 16): Roveri

Valparaiso mi amor /*Valparaiso my love* (CL 70): Alvarez, Rojo

Valurile Dunarii /*Waves of the Danube* (RO 60): Bodianu

Vampire, The (US 57): Mora (Morrow)

Vampires, Les /*The vampires* (FR 15, srl): Poyen

Vändkorset /*Crossroads* (SE 44): Nyström

Vang vir my 'n droom /*Catch me a dream* (ZA 75): Hopley

Vanishing Legion, The (US 31, srl): Darro

Vanishing Pioneer, The (US 28): Holt T.

Vanishing Virginian, The (US 41): Beckett, Jones D., Bates

Vanishing West, The (US 28, srl): Bennett M.

Vanity Fair (US 15): Steuart

Vanka (SU 60): Barsov

Vanka i mstitel /*Vanka and the avenger* (SU 28): Nolman

Vanka - yuni pioner /*Vanka, Young Pioneer* (SU 24): Konstantinov

Vanquished, The (US 53): Mora (Morrow)

Våran pojke /*Our boy* (SE 36): Granberg L. and O.

Vårat gäng /*Our gang* (SE 42): Hjelm

Varázsló, A /*The magician* (HU 69): Kovács, Laluja

Vardag i varuhuset /*Every day at the big store* (SE 37): Olsson

Vargtimmen /*Hour of the wolf* (SE 68): Rundquist

Vår Herre luggar Johansson /*The Almighty gives Johansson
   an earful* (SE 44): Lindgren H.

Varsity Show (US 37): McFarland

Varuj...! /*Look out!* (CS 47): Garvolt

Varya - kapitan /*Captain Varya* (SU 39): Seleznyov

Vasantha Maaligai (IN 72): Ramu

Vasco, the Vampire (US 14): Roubert

Vasek Trubachoff i yevo tovarishchi /*Vasek Trubachoff and his mates*
   (SU 55): Vishnev, Devkin

Vasili i Vasilissa /*Vasili and Vasilissa* (SU 81): Bobrovski

Västkustens hjältar /*Heroes of the West Coast* (SE 40): Bernhard

Vasya - reformator /*Vasya the reformer* (SU 26): Lyudvinski

Vas-y, maman /*Go on, Mum* (FR 78): Constantini

Vater braucht eine Frau /*Father needs a wife* (DE 52): Grimm

Vater, unser bestes Stück /*Father, the family treasure* (DE 57): Kaiser

Vaxdocken /*The wax doll* (SE 62): Axberg R.

Vecchia guardia /*The old guard* (IT 35): Brambilla

Veda /*Farewell* (TR 73): Inanoğlu

Veer Babruwahan (IN 50): Kapoor S.

Veldt, The (US 79): Bateman

Veliki i mali /*Big and small* (YU 56): Ivković

Velvet Glove, The (GB 77, srl): Sira

Velvet Fingers (US 20): Carr T.

Vena d'oro, La /*The vein of gold* (IT 55): Girotti

Vendelínův očistec a ráj /*Vendelin's purgatory and paradise* (CS 30):
   Pražský

Vendetta di Ursus, La /*The vengeance of Ursus* (IT 61): Chevalier

Venditore di palloncini, Il /*The balloon-seller* (IT 74): Cestiè, Valsecchi

Venenosa, La (FR 28): Mock

Vengeance (US 18): Jackson C.

Vengeance (US 30): Albright

Venoušek a Stazička /*Little Vaclav and little Anastasia* (CS 22): Branald

Venoušek a Stazička (CS 39): Salač

Vénus (FR 28): Mercanton

Venus and Adonis (US 13): Clark R.

Venus fra Vestø /*Vestø Venus* (DK 62): Schmidt J.P.

Venus Peter (GB 88): Strachan

Vera, Nadezhda, Lyuboff /*Faith, Hope and Charity* (SU 84): Bobrovski

Verden til forskel /*A world of difference* (DK 89): Kozlowski

Vergiss mein nicht /*Forget me not* (GE 35): Bosse

Verliebte Leute /*People in love* (AT 54): Friedl

Verlorene Ball, Der /*The lost ball* (DD 59): Schappo

Verloren paradijs, Het /*Lost paradise* (BE 78): Windross

Vermilion O'Toole (53 US) – *see* Take Me To Town

Verniye serdtsa /*True hearts* (SU 59): Maltsev, Siluyanov

Veronica (RO 73): Vîlcu

Veronico Cruz (AR/GB 87): Morales

Verraad van de Zwarte Ridder, Het /*Treachery of the Black Knight*
   (NL 62): van der Linden C.

Verrückte Familie, Eine (57 DE) – *see* Heute blau und morgen blau

Verschleierte Maja, Die /*The hidden Maja* (DE 51): Lödel

Verschwender, Der /*The spendthrift* (AT 52): Friedl

Versunkene Welten /*Sunken worlds* (AT 22): Lubinsky

Vertiges /*Vertigo* (FR 46): Rob

Veruntreute Himmel /*Heaven embezzled* (DE 58): Kratz

Verwehte Spuren /*Lost traces* (GE 38): Sierck

Very Idea, The (US 29): Watson Bl.

Very Thought of You, The (US 44): Madore

Veselý soubor /*The merry band* (CS 51): Mikulič

Vesenni potok /*Springtime stream* (SU 40): But

Vesna /*Spring* (SU 70): Laanemets

Vestens børn /*Children of the West* (DK 17): Jensen S.C.

Vesterhavsdrenge /*North Sea boys* (DK 50): Henning-Jensen

Vesyoliye artisti /*Merry artistes* (SU 38): Tumalaryants

Vesyoliye istori /*Merry tales* (SU 62): Kislaryoff, Kekish

Veter /*The wind* (SU 58): Krivchenkov

Vetter aus Dingsda, Der /*The cousin from Thingummy* (DE 53): Jansen

Via del peccato, La /*Street of sin* (IT 24): Palermi

Viaggio di Maciste, Il /*Maciste's journey* (IT 20): Allen W.

Vice Versa (GB 81): Spurrier

Vicious Years, The (US 50): Tamblyn

Victim, The (US 17): Benham

Victimas del pecado /*Victims of sin* (MX 50): Perez

Victors, The (GB 63): Flateau

Vie devant soi, La /*His life before him* (FR 77): Ben Youb

Vie en rose, La /*Rose-coloured life* (FR 47): Lecointe, Martaguet C.

Vie est un long fleuve tranquille, La /*Life is a long quiet river*
   (FR 88): Magimel

Vieil homme et l'enfant, Le /*The old man and the child* (FR 67): Cohen

Viennese Choir Boy, The (62 US) – *see* Almost Angels

Viennese Nights (US 30): Frederick

Vierge du rocher, La /*The Virgin of the Rock* (FR 33): Bara

View from Pompey's Head, The (US 55): Herbert

Vi gå landsvägen /*We take the high road* (SE 37): Olsson

Vigilantes of Boomtown (US 47): Blake

Vigilantes of Dodge City (US 44): Blake

Vigil in the Night (US 39): Nichols, Tucker T.

Vi hemslavinnor /*We domestic slaves* (SE 42): Hjelm

Vi kunne ha' det så rart /*We could have it so good* (DK 42):
   Fagerlund, Steen-Hansen

Vildfåglar /*Wild birds* (SE 55): Nilsson

Villa Borghese (IT 53): Girotti

Village, The (53 CH/GB) – *see* Unser Dorf

Village Blacksmith, The (US 21): Griffith, Moore P.
Village of the Damned, The (GB 60): Stephens M.
Village of the Giants (US 65): Howard R.
Villain Still Pursued Her, The (US 40): Bupp S.
Ville des pirates, La / The town of pirates (FR/PT 83): Poupaud
Villervalle i Söderhavet / South Sea Muddles (SE 63): Grönros
Vinden från väster / Wind from the West (SE 42): Nyberg
Vindicated (US 26): Holmes L.
Violent Journey, A (64 US) − see Fool Killer
Violent Saturday (US 55): Chapin B., Corcoran
Violettes impériales / Imperial violets (FR 23): Guichard
Violons du bal, Les / Ballroom violins (FR 74): Drach
Vi på Saltkråkan / Us from Saltkråkan (SE 64): Ulvskog, Lindholm
Vi på Solgläntan / Us from Solgläntan (SE 39): Hjelm
Vi på Vallberga / Us from Vallberga (SE 44): Nyström
Virgen que forjo una patria / The virgin who created a country (MX 42): Pastor
Virginia City (US 40): Jones D.
Virginian, The (US 29): Butts, Winslow D.
Virginian, The (US 46): Rodin M.
Virgin Spring (59 SE) − see Jungfrukällan
Virtuous Wives (US 18): Carr T.
Visages d'enfants / Children's faces (FR 23): Forest
Vishwas / The faith (IN 69): Mehmood
Visiteur, Le / The visitor (FR 46): Krebs, Tabary
Visit to a Chief's Son (US 74): Hogdon
Vi som går koksvägen / We go via the kitchen (SE 32): Granberg L. and O.
Vita katten, Den / The white cat (SE 50): Blitz
Vítězna křidla / Wings of victory (CS 51): Mikulič, Prokeš
Viva il cinema! / Long live the cinema! (IT 52): Cerusico
Viva Knievel! (US 76): Olson
Viva la Muerte / Long live Death (FR/TN 71): Chaouch
Viva Villa! (US 34): Durand
Vive la France! (US 18): Lee F.
Vive la Nation! (39 FR) − see Trois tambours
Vivir mañana / Live tomorrow (ES 83): Sanz
V kogtyakh sovetskoi vlasti / In the grip of Soviet power (SU 26): Lyudvinski
Vkus khalvi / The taste of halva (SU 75): Musin
Vlakas me patenda, Enas / A patent fool (GR 63): Kailas
Vlak do stanice Nebe / The train to Heaven Station (CS 72): Vavruša
Vlak u snijegu / The snowbound train (YU 76): Štimac
Vliegen zonder vleugels (76 NL) − see Peter en de vliegende autobus
V lyudyakh / Out in the world (SU 38): Lyarski
Vocation suspendue, La / Suspended vocation (FR 77): Schulmann
Voce del silenzio, La / The voice of silence (IT/FR 52): Girotti
Voglio vivere cosi / That's the way to live (IT 41): Barbetti
Voice of Destiny, The (US 18): Morrison E.
Voile bleu, Le / The blue veil (FR 42): François, Geffroy
Voina i mir / War and peace (SU 66): Yermilov
Vojnik / The soldier (YU/US 65): McIntosh
Volchi khutor / Village of wolves (SU 31): Lyudvinski
Volejte Martina / Call for Martin (CS 65): Smyczek
Volnitsa / Free woman (SU 55): Merkulov
Volshebnoye zerno / The magic seed (SU 41): Tumalaryants
Voltati Eugenio / Turn round, Eugenio (IT 81): Bonelli

Volt egyszer egy család / Once there was a family (HU 72): Ruttkai
Volvo (PL 67): Izdebski
Volzhskiye buntari / Volga rebels (SU 26): Zavyaloff
Von Liebe reden wir später / We'll talk about love later (DE 53): Condrus
Vor Liebe wird gewarnt / A warning of love (GE 37): Eugens
Voyage en Amérique, Le / Journey to America (FR 51): Fourcade
Voyage en ballon / Journey by balloon (FR 60): Lamorisse
Voyage Round My Father, A (GB 82): Cox A.
'Voyagers' (US 82, TVS): Peluce
Voyage-surprise / Mystery trip (FR 46): Simon
Vozdushnaya pochta / Air mail (SU 39): Shekhtman
Vozdushnoye priklyucheniye / Aerial adventure (SU 37): Tumalaryants
Vozvrashcheniye / The return (SU 40): Tumalaryants
Vreditel / The damager (SU 29): Pankratov
Vrijbuiters van het woud / Robbers of the forest (NL 65): van der Linden C.
V šest ráno na letišti / 6 a.m. at the airport (CS/SU 58): Sedláček, Siluyanov
V stepi / In the steppes (SU 50): Yeliseyev
Vstupleniye / A beginning (SU 62): Tokaryoff, Burlyayev K.
Vuk samotnjak / The lone wolf (YU 72): Štimac
Vulcano / Volcano (IT 49): Staiola
Vultures and Doves (US 12): Casey
Vyaternata melnica / The windmill (BG 60): Alurkov
Vyaturut na puteshestviyata / The wind of travel (BG 72): Arshinkov
Vzlomshchik / Burglar (SU 87): Elikomov
Vzorný kinematograf Haška Jaroslava / Jaroslav Hašek's model cinema (CS 56): Bejval, Postránecký, Pucholt
Vzrosliye deti / Grown-up children (SU 61): Rodionov

Wacky Zoo of Morgan City, The (US 70): Wixted
Wagons Roll at Night, The (US 41): Phelps, Winkler
Wagons West (US 52): Chapin M.
Wagon Wheels (US 34): Lee B.
Wagon Wheels (43 US) − see American Empire
Wagon Wheels Westward (US 45): Blake
Waif, The (US 15): Roubert
Waif of the Sea, A (US 12): Clark R.
Waif of the Wilderness (US 29): Nelson B.
Wait Till the Sun Shines, Nellie (US 52): Mazzola
Wait Until Spring, Bandini (BE/FR/IT/US 90): Vincent
Wakacje z duchami / Haunted holidays (PL 70, srl): Dymek E., Gołębiewski, Mosior
Wakai Tokyo no yane no shita / Under the roof of young Japan (JP 63): Ota
'Waldheimat' / My forest homeland (AT/DE 83, TVS): Gauster
Waldo's Last Stand (US 40): 'Our Gang'
Waldrausch / Forest murmurs (GE 39): Schmidhofer
Walkabout (AU 70): John
Walking Tall (US 73): Garrett
Walking Tall, Part 2 (75 US) − see Part 2 Walking Tall
Walking Tall the Final Chapter (US 77): Garrett
Walk Proud (US 79): Gomez P.
Walk Right In (US 24): Black B.
Walk the Proud Land (US 56): Mazzola
Wall, The (83 FR) − see Mur, Le
Walls of Jericho, The (US 18): Jones J.

Keith Skinner in Mademoiselle

Jaime Tejeda

Kambar Valiyev

Kit Wain

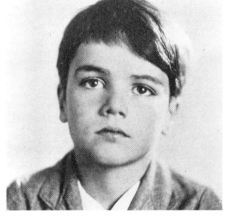

Christos Zannides

Bobby Young

Andrei Zikov in Patsani

Wall Street (US 29): Frederick

Waltzes from Vienna (GB 34): Singer

Waltz Me Around (US 20): Morrison E.

Wanderer of the Wasteland (US 45): Cook T., McKim H.

Wandering Footsteps (US 25): Darro

Wandering Jew, The (GB 23): Dear

Wanderlust (US 30): Watson Bl.

Wan jia denghuo /Myriads of lights (CN 48): Wang L.

Wanters, The (US 23): Headrick

War Against Mrs Hadley, The (US 42): Switzer

War and Peace (US/IT 56): Barrett

War and Peace (66 SU) – see Voina i mir

War Between Men and Women, The (US 72): Drier

War Dogs (US 42): Lee B.

War Feathers (US 26): 'Our Gang'

War Game, The (GB 62): Ellis I.

War Lord, The (US 65): Jensen J.

Warming Up (US 28): Schaeffer

Warned Off (GB 28): Pavitt

War of the Buttons (GB/FR 93): Fitzgerald G., Coffey J., Cunningham

Warrior Strain, The (GB 19): Wood S.

Was eine Frau im Frühling träumt /A woman's dreams in Spring
    (DE 58): Kaiser

Washee Ironee (US 34): 'Our Gang', Jones D.

Washington Story (US 52): Corcoran

Was kostet der Sieg? /What price victory? (AT 81): Bauer A.
    and A., Vogel N.

Was sagt Onkel Emil dazu /What does Uncle Emil say? (GE 32):
    Lohmeyer, Schaufuss

Was She Guilty? (20 NL/GB) – see Zooals ik ben

Wasted Lives (US 23): DeLacy

Wastrel, The (60 IT) – see Relitto

Wataridori itsu mata kaeru /When will the migrant bird return?
    (JP 62): Shimazu

Watashi no Papasan Mama ga suki /Daddy loves Mummy (JP 31):
    'Tokkan-Kozo'

Watch on the Rhine (US 43): Roberts E.

Wat eeuwig blijft /What remains for ever (NL/GB 20): Doxat-Pratt

Water Babies, The (GB/PL 77): Pender

Waterfront (GB 50): Netscher

Waterfront Lady (US 35): Albright

Waterloo Bridge (US 40): Winkler

'Waterloo Station' (AU 82, TVS): Smith P.

Way Back Home (US 31): Darro

Way Down Cellar (US 67): Patrick

Way Down South (US 39): Beard, Breen

Way of All Flesh, The (US 27): DeLacy, McBan

Way of All Flesh, The (US 40): Bupp T., Hickman Dl., West J.

Way of All Men, The (US 30): Janney

Way of the Strong, The (US 19): Redden

Way of the West, The (US 34): Nelson B.

Way to a Man's Heart, The (US 18): Steuart

Way to Heaven, The (US 14): Harris B.

Way West, The (US 67): Arngrim

Weapon, The (GB 56): Whiteley, Hines

We Are Not Alone (US 39): Scott D., Severn R.

Weather Wizards (US 38): Winkler

Wechma /Traces (MA 70): Dadda

Wedding Group (GB 36): Blomfield

Wedding Pumps (US 22): Morgan

Wedding Worries (US 41): 'Our Gang'

Wednesday's Child (US 34): Durand, Thomas F.

Week-End With Father (US 51): Hunt, Rettig,

Week in a Balloon, A (US 72): Drier

Wee Willie Winkie (US 37): Scott D.

Weib des Pharao, Das /Pharaoh's wife (GE 21): Pottier

Wei haizimen zhufu /Bless the children (CN 53): Wang L.

Weird Science (US 85): Hall A.M.

Weisse Dämon, Der /The white demon (GE 32): Schaufuss

Weisse Hölle vom Piz Palü, Die /The white hell of Piz Palu
    (GE 35, sound version): Teetzmann

Weisse Teufel, Der /The white devil (GE 30): Burns, Rive

Welcome Children (US 21): Griffith

Welcome Danger (US 29): Haig

Welcome Home, Johnny Bristol (US 71): Michenaud

Welcome to Hard Times (US 66): Shea M.

Well of Love (US 71): Kelly S.

Wells Fargo (US 37): Beckett, Butler, Cosbey, Tucker J.

Wells Fargo Gunmaster (US 51): Chapin M.

Welt in jenem Sommer, Die /The world that summer (DE 80):
    Schwarzbauer

Wênd Kûuni /Gift of God (BF 82): Yanogo

Wenn der Vater mit dem Sohne /Fathers and sons (DE 55): Grimm

Wenn die Glocken hell erklingen /When the bells ring brightly
    (AT 59): Ande

Wenn ein Mädel Hochzeit macht /When a girl gets married
    (GE 34): Richter

Wenn süss das Mondlicht auf den Hügeln schläft /When the sweet
    moonlight sleeps upon the hills (DE 69): Eser

We're All Gamblers (US 27): Searl

We're Only Human (US 35): Watson D.

Werewolf, The (US 56): Charney

Western Caravans (US 39): McKim S.

Westerners, The (US 19): Lee F.

Western Frontier (US 35): Henry R.

Western Prince Charming, A (US 12): Tansey R.

West of Cimarron (US 41): Hickman C.

West of El Dorado (US 49): Infuhr

West of Zanzibar (GB 54): Simons W.

West Point of the Air (US 35): Cosbey

West Point Widow (US 41): Winkler

Westward Ho (US 35): Jones D.

Westward Ho the Wagons (US 56): Stollery

We Who Are About To Die (US 36): Bupp S.

Whacko! (59 GB) – see Bottoms Up

What About Bob? (US 91): Korsmo

What a Life (US 39): Bartlett

What a Man! (GB 37): Singer

What Every Girl Should Know (US 27): Gordon Bo., House N., McBan

What Fools Men (US 25): Billings E.

What Happened to Mary (US 12-13): Boss

What Love Forgives (US 19): Connelly

What Money Can't Buy (US 17): Alexander B.

What Next? (GB 74): Robinson P.

What's a Fixer For (39 US) — *see* Fixer Dugan

What's Eating Gilbert Grape (US 93): DiCaprio

What's Your Hurry? (US 20): Fox J.

What the Firelight Showed (GB 14): Desmond

What the Moon Saw (AU 88): Shephard

What the Peeper Saw (71 GB) — *see* Night Hair Child

Wheel of Fortune (US 23): DeLacy

When a Dog Loves (US 27): McBan

When a Feller Needs a Friend (US 19): Carr J. and S.

When a Feller Needs a Friend (US 32): Cooper Ja., Haines, Moore D., Shuford

When a Feller's Nose Is Out of Joint (US 15, 'Sonny Jim'): Connelly

When a Man's a Man (US 24): Fox J.

When a Man's a Man (US 35): Butler

When Bobby Broke His Arm (US 17): Connelly

When Bobby Forgot (US 13): Casey

When Dolly Died (US 13): Roubert

When Every Day Was the Fourth of July (US 78): Petersen Chr., Drier, Shea E.

When Father Was Away on Business (85 YU) — *see* Otac na službenom putu

When Hearts Were Trumps (US 15): Butterworth F.

When I Grow Up (US 51): Driscoll, Hyatt

When Love Comes (US 22): Messinger

When Scouting Won (GB 30): Chant, Purnell

When the Bough Breaks (GB 47): Malone

When the Circus Came to Town (US 13): Clark R.

'When the Hurricanes' films (GB 13-14): Royston R.

When the Law Rides (US 28): Darro

When the Minstrels Came to Town (US 16): Butterworth F.

When the Whales Came (GB 89): Rennie

When the Wind Blows (US 20): Morrison E.

When the Wind Blows (US 30): 'Our Gang'

When Tomorrow Comes (US 39): Billings G., Bupp S. and T., Kuhn, Watson D.

When We Were in Our Teens (US 10): Pickford

When Wolves Cry (69 FR/IT) — *see* Arbre de Noël

When You and I Were Young (US 13): Butterworth F.

When You're in Love (US 37): Beckett

Where Are Your Children (US 43): Gray G.

Where Danger Lives (US 50): Stollery

Where No Vultures Fly (GB 51): Simons W.

Where's Johnny? (GB 74): Boal

Where's Willie? (US 78): Gilpin M.

Where the Children Are? (US 85): Cross

Where the Rainbow Ends (GB 21): Chinn, Grey

Where the Red Fern Grows (US 74): Petersen S.

Where the River Runs Black (US 86): Rabelo

Where the Trail Divides (US 14): Short

Which Shall It Be? (US 15): Benham

While America Sleeps (US 39): Winkler

While Justice Waits (US 22): Lee F.

While the Devil Laughs (US 21): Watson C.

Whiphand, The (US 20): Alexander B.

Whirlpool (GB 59): Palmer

Whirlwind (US 51): Ivo

Whirlwind Kids, The (GB 14): Royston R.

Whispering Smith (US 26): Coghlan

Whispering Smith (US 49): Gray G.

Whistle, The (US 21): Stone, Headrick

Whistling in the Dark (US 41): Tyler L.

White and Black Snowball, The (US 15, 'Sonny Jim'): Connelly

White and Unmarried (US 21): Beck, Stone

White Angel, The (US 36): Mauch Bl. and Bo.

White Bottle, The (US 20): Carr T.

White Circle, The (US 20): Barry W.

White Cliffs of Dover, The (US 44): McDowall

White Corridors (GB 51): Inglis

White Cradle Inn (GB 47): McKeag

White Dog (US 83): Oliver B.

White Fang (74 IT) — *see* Ritorno di Zanna Bianca

White Heather, The (US 19): Alexander B.

White Line, The (49 IT) — *see* Cuori senza frontiere

White Mane (53 FR) — *see* Crin blanc

White Mischief (GB 87): Mahinda

White Roses (US 10): Pickford

White Sheep, The (US 24): Daniels M.

White Shoulders (US 22): Headrick

White Water Summer (US 85): Astin S.

Whiz Kid and the Mystery at Riverton, The (US 74): O'Brien C., Shea E.

'Whiz Kids' (US 83, TVS): Laborteaux M., Porter T.

Whoever Slew Auntie Roo? (GB 71): Lester, Beaumont R.

Who Killed 'Doc' Robbin? (US 48): Olsen L.J., Belding, Miles P. (Perreau), Gray B.

Who Killed the Cat? (GB 66): Phillips G.

Whom the Gods Destroy (US 34): Beckett

Whom the Gods Love (GB 36): Fitzpatrick P.

Who Will Love My Children? (US 83): Kiger, Yothers

Why America Will Win (US 18): Fox J.

Why Did You Pick on Me? (80 IT) — *see* Chissà perche... capitano tutto a me

Why Do We Live? (US 23): DeLacy

Why Go Home? (US 20): Morrison E.

Why Women Remarry (US 23): Marion F.

Why Would I Lie? (US 80): Swann

Wicked (US 31): Cosbey

Wicked Woman, A (US 34): Searl, Billings G.

'Wickie' (DE 75, TVS): Halm

Wide-Open Town, A (US 22): Connelly, Devine

Widow (US 76): Olson

Wie kommen die Löcher in den Käse? / *How do the holes get into the cheese?* (GE 32): Löhr A.

Wien, du Stadt der Lieder / *Vienna, city of song* (GE 30): Stark-Gstettenbaur

Wienerbarnet / *Child of Vienna* (DK 24): Herzberg

Wien tanzt / *Vienna dances* (AT 51): Czeike

Wierook en tranen / *Frankincense and tears* (NL 77): Brouwers

Wie sagen wir es unseren Kindern? / *How do we tell our children?* (GE 45): Neie

Wie sag's ich meinem Kinde / *How do I tell my child?* (DE 70): Halm

Wie schön, dass es Dich gibt / *Thank God for you* (AT 57): Kratz

Wife vs. Secretary (US 36): Jones D.

Wiggle Your Ears (US 29): 'Our Gang'

Wig-Wag (US 11): Casey

Wigwam, De / *The wigwam* (NL 11): Ivens

Wild and Woolly (US 37): Scott D.,Searl, Switzer

Wild Beauty (US 46): Henry R.

Wildcat of Terror (US 41): Winkler

Wildcat of Tucson, The (US 41): Winkler

Wild Child, The (69 FR) — *see* Enfant sauvage

Wild Children (77 HK) — *see* Yeh hai chi

Wild Country, The (US 69): Howard C. and R.

Wilderer, Der / *The poacher* (GE 25): Peterhans

Wilderer vom Silberwald, Der / *The poacher of Silver Forest*
  (DE 57): Kratz

Wild Geese, The (GB/CH 77): Spurrier

Wild Girl (US 32): Watson D.

Wild Heritage (US 58): Winslow G.

Wild Horse Ambush (US 52): Chapin M.

Wild Money (US 37): Lee B.

Wildness of Youth (US 22): Connelly

Wild North, The (US 51): Mora

Wild Pony, The (83 CA) — *see* Wild Stallion

Wild Poses (US 33): 'Our Gang'

Wild Stallion (US 52): Lindgren O.

Wild Stallion, The (53 FR) — *see* Crin Blanc

Wild Stallion, The (CA 83): Byrne

Wild Sumac (US 17): Stone

Wild to Go (US 26): Darro

Wild West (US 46): Henry R.

Wild West Romance (US 28): Butts

Wilhelm Tell (GE 23): Peterhans

Willi (DE 69): Reichert

William Comes to Town (GB 48): Graham, Roper, Weske, Hannaford

Willie and the Yank (US 66): Russell K.

Willie Minds the Dog (US 13): Jacobs

Will Penny (US 67): Francis

'Willy' series (FR 12-14): Sanders

Willy Wonka and the Chocolate Factory (US 71): Ostrum

Wilson (US 44): Sheffield J.

Winchester '73 (US 50): Olsen L.J.

Wind, The (US 28): Janney, Schaeffer

Wind and the Lion, The (US 75): Harrison S.

Windfall (GB 55): Pike J.

Window, The (US 49): Driscoll

Winds of Jarrah, The (AU 83): Kounnas, Minty

Winged Hoofs (US 28): House N.

Wings (US 27): Haig

Wings for the Eagle (US 42): Bupp S., Winkler

Wings of Mystery (GB 63): Scott H.

Wings of the Morning (GB 36): Frost, Hepworth J.

Wings over Honolulu (US 37): Hurlic

Winking Parson, The (US 12): Boss

'Winners, The' (US 77, TVS): Gomez P.

Winner Take All (US 32): Moore D.

Winnie's Dance (US 11): Boss

Winnie the Pooh and the Blustery Day (US 68): Howard C.

'Winnie Winkle' series (US 26): Janney

Winning Grandma (US 18): Morrison E.

Winning of Barbara Worth, The (US 26): Shuford

Winning Ticket, The (US 35): Haines, Watson Bl.

Winslow Boy, The (GB 48): North N.

Winter of Three-Hairs, The (49 CN) — *see* San-Mao liulang ji

Wiosna zasadzimy kwiaty / *We'll plant flowers in the Spring*
  (PL 70): Samosionek

Wirtin zum weissen Rössl, Die / *The landlady of the White Horse*
  (GE 43): Rohringer

Wise Son, A (25 US) — *see* Wandering Footsteps

Within the Enemy's Lines (US 13): Boss

Without Benefit of Clergy (US 21): DeLacy

Without Children (US 34): Moore D.

Witness, The (GB 59): Stephens M.

Witness (US 85): Haas L.

Witness in the Dark (GB 59): Hines, O'Sullivan

Witte, De / *Whitey* (BE 34): Bruyninckx, Buyl

Witte van Sichem, De / *Whitey from Sichem* (BE 79): Clerckx

Wittgenstein (GB 93): Chassay

Wives of Men (US 18): Jackson C.

Wizard, The (US 90): Savage F.

Wizard of Baghdad, The (US 60): Burns M.

Wizard of Loneliness, The (US 88): Haas

Wizard of the Saddle (US 28): Barton

Wo die alten Wälder rauschen / *Where the old forests rustle*
  (DE 56): Finkbeiner

Wolf in Cheap Clothing, A (US 27): Madden

Wolga-Wolga / *Volga Volga!* (GE 28): Stark-Gstettenbaur

Woman Between, The (US 31): Albright

Woman Doctor (US 39): Jones D., Samarzich

Woman from Hell, The (US 29): Holmes L.

Woman He Loved, The (US 22): Guerin

Womanhood, the Glory of the Nation (US 17): Connelly

Woman I Love, The (US 37): Albright

Woman in His House, The (US 20): Headrick

Woman in the Window, The (US 44): Blake, McFarland

Woman Michael Married, The (US 19): Coffey C.

Woman Named Lou, A (US 25): Holmes L.

Woman Obsessed (US 59): Holmes D.

Woman of Paris, A (US 23): Coghlan

Woman of Pleasure, A (US 19): Barry W.

Woman of the Year (US 41): Larson

Woman on the Jury, The (US 24): Billings E.

Woman's Face, A (US 41): Nichols, Gray G.

Woman's Face, A (38 SE) — *see* Kvinnas ansikte

Woman's Fool, A (US 18): Clark R.

Woman's Temptation, A (US 59): Pike J.

Woman's Weapons (US 18): Moore P.

Woman to Woman (GB/US 29): Billings G.

Woman Under the Influence, A (US 74): Laborteaux M.

Woman Who Dared, The (US 16): Lee F.

Woman Who Gave, The (US 18): Thaw

Woman Who Obeyed, The (GB 23): Dear

Woman Who Understood, A (US 20): Butterworth J., Boardman

Woman Wise (US 37): Bupp S.

Women and Gold (US 24): Darro

Women Love Diamonds (US 27): Bennett M., Butts

Wonder Bar (US 34): Jones D.

Wonderful Nights with Peter Kinema (GB 14): Royston G.

Wonderful World of the Brothers Grimm, The (US 62):
Russell B.
Wonder Kid, The (GB 51): Henrey
Wonder of Women (US 29): Albright, Winslow D.
Wooden Gun, The (IL/US 79) − see Rové huliet
Wooden Soldier, The (US 28): Janney
World Accuses, The (US 35): Moore D.
World and Its Woman, The (US 19): Marion F.
World Changes, The (US 33): Rooney, Searl
World Gone Mad, The (US 33): Phelps
World That Summer, The (80 DE) − see Welt in jenem Sommer
World War in Kidland, The (US 16): Monahan
World War III (US 82): Peluce
Wo zhi liu san tsi lei /Lonely cried three times (CN 87): Fang
Wrecker, The (US 33): Albright
Wreck of the Hesperus, The (US 27): Shuford
Writing on the Wall, The (US 15): Connelly
Written on the Wind (US 56): Corcoran
Wrongdoers, The (US 25): Brown T.
Wrong Guys (US 88): Brandis
Wunder des Fliegens /The marvel of flight (GE 35): Ohlsen
Wuthering Heights (US 39): Downing R., Scott D.
Wyoming (US 40): Watson Bs.
Wyoming Wildcat, The (US 25): Darro
Wyrok /Sentence (PL 61): Roman

Xenophon, a Story of the Circus (US 12): Casey
X-15 (US 61): Livingston S.
Xiao peng yu /Little friends (CN 25): Zheng
X-Ray (US 81): Jacoby Bl.
X - the Unknown (GB 56): Brooke, Hines
Xtro (GB 82): Nash S.

Yaaba /Granny (BF 88): Ouedraogo
Yaadgaar /Remembrance (IN 70): Mehmood
Ya budu tantsevat! /I shall dance! (SU 62): Aliyev
Yakov Sverdloff (SU 40): Smirnoff
Ya kupil papu /I bought a Daddy (SU 62): Zagorski, Semyonov Vo.
Yale vs Harvard (US 27): 'Our Gang', Parrish
Yan Bibiyan (BG 84): Donchev
Yanco (MX 61): Ancona
Yank at Eton, A (US 42): Kilburn, Madore
Yankee Clipper, The (US 27): Coghlan
Yankee Doodle Dandy (US 42): Croft
Yan yang tian /Bright sunny skies (CN 48): Wang L.
Yara /The wound (TR 68): Utku
Yarn of the 'Nancy Bell', The (US 11): Boss
Ya tengo a mi hijo /At last I hold my son (MX 46): Bohigas
Yearling, The (US 46): Jarman, Gift
Yeh hai chi /Wild children (HK 77): Wong
Yellow Balloon, The (GB 52): Ray A.
Yellow Dog, The (US 18): Griffith
Yellow Earth (84 CN) − see Huang tudi
Yellow Sands (GB 38): McDowall
Yellow Ticket, The (US 18): Jackson C.
Ye Olde Minstrels (US 41): 'Our Gang'
Yesterday's Hero (GB 79): Medford

Yevdokiya (SU 61): Barsov
Yevreiskoye shchaste /Jewish luck (SU 25): Epstein
Yoake mae /Before dawn (JP 53): Kato
Yo fui una usurpadora /I was a usurpatress (MX 46): Roche
Yo-ho-ho (BG 81): Chuchkov
Yol (CH 82): Çelik
Yometori konki kurabe /Wives need patience (JP 30):
'Tokkan-Kozo'
Yo soy charro de levita /Rough but respectable (MX 49): Perez
You Are Guilty (US 23): Griffin
You Are Not Alone (78 DK) − see Du er ikke alene
You Belong to Me (US 30): Holt D.
You Came Along (US 45): Larson
You Can't Beat the Law (US 43): Larson
You Can't Buy Everything (US 34): Alexander T.
You Can't Cheat an Honest Man (US 39): Watson D.
You Can't Get Away With It (US 23): Black B.
You Gotta Start Somewhere (US 77): Gomez P.
You Live and Learn (GB 37): Fitzpatrick P.
You Never Know (US 22): Watson C.
Young America (19 US) − see Heart of Youth
Young America (US 32): Conlon
Young America (US 42): Hickman Dl., Binyon
Young and Innocent (GB 37): Baxter, Fitzpatrick P.
Young and the Brave, The (US 63): Padilla
Young and the Damned, The (50 MX) − see Olvidados
Young Aphrodites (62 GR) − see Mikres Afrodites
Young As You Feel (US 40): Mahan
Young Bess (US 53): Thompson R.
Youngblood Hawke (US 63): Cardi
Young Dr Kildare (US 38): Watson Bs.
Young Donovan's Kid (US 31): Cooper Ja.
Younger Generation, The (US 29): Janney
Youngest Profession, The (US 43): Beckett
Youngest Spy, The (62 SU) − see Ivanovo detstvo
Young Guns II (US 90): Getty
Young Harry Houdini (US 86): Wheaton
Young In Heart, The (US 38): Bupp S., Kuhn
Young Jacobites, The (GB 59, srl): Bulloch, Hines, Pike J.
Young James Bond (72 IN) − see Do bachche dus haath
Young Joe, the Forgotten Kennedy (US 77): Kerwin
Young King, The (23 US) − see Long Live the King
Young Magician, The (CA/PL 86): Jedwab
Young Man of Music (50 US) − see Young Man with a Horn
Young Man with a Horn (US 50): Lindgren O.
Young Man with Ideas (US 51): Diamond
Young Mr Lincoln (US 39): Jones D., Watson Bl.
Young Mr Pitt, The (GB 42): Tyler G.
Young Mother Hubbard (US 17): McDermott
Young People (US 40): Anderson Bb. Hickman Dl.
'Young Pimple' films (GB 14): Collet
Young Rajah, The (US 22): Moore M. and P.
Young Sherlock Holmes and the Pyramid of Fear (GB 85):
Cox A.
Young Sherlocks (US 22): 'Our Gang'
Young Sinners (US 31): Butts
Young Sleuths, The (US 16): Butterworth F.

Young Tom Edison (US 40): Hurlic
Young Whirlwind (US 28): Barton
Your Cheatin' Heart (US 64): Tate
You're Gonna Love It Here (US 78): Barnes C.
You're My Everything (US 49): Nokes
You're Only Young Once (US 38): Beckett
You're Pinched (US 20): Morrison E.
You're the One (US 41): Hickman C., Madore
Your Own Back Yard (US 25): 'Our Gang'
Yours, Mine and Ours (US 68): Shea C. and E., Vogel
You Said a Hatful (US 34): Bond T.
You Said a Mouthful (US 32): Hoskins
Youthful Affair, A (US 18): Connelly
Youthful Knight, A (US 13): Boss
You Will Remember (GB 40): McDowall
Yuma (US 71): Alejandro
Yume to shiriseba / If I knew it was a dream (JP 52): Shitara
Yumurcak / The kid (TR 69): Inanoğlu
Yumurcak köprüalti çocuğu / The kid from under the bridge (TR 70): Inanoğlu
Yunga so shkhuni 'Kolumb' / The boy from the schooner 'Columbus' (SU 63): Kislenko
Yuniye kommunari / Young communards (SU 38): Tirtov
Yu qing sao / Jade love (TW 84): Lin
Yurei ga shindara / If the ghost died (JP 36): Yokoyama
Yuvana dön baba / Come home, Daddy (TR 68): Dönmez

Zabijcie czarna owcę / Kill the black sheep (PL 71): Passendorfer
Za edna troika / Getting a third (BG 83): Tsvetkov
Zaganella e il cavaliere / Zaganella and the cavalier (IT 32): Locchi
Zakon druzhbi / The law of friendship (SU 31): Tulubev
Žalobníci / Sneaks (CS 60): Hašler
Zamba (US 49): Bridges B.
Zamin ka chand / Moon on earth (IN 37): Apte
Zamri umi voskresni / Freeze, die, come to life (SU 89): Nazarov P.
Zander the Great (US 25): Watson H.
Zappa (DK 83): Hoff, Tønsberg
Zardoz (IE 74): Boorman
Zare navstrechu / Greeting the dawn (SU 59): Mazayev, Boriskin, Bristol, Koval
Zarewitsch, Der / The Tsarevich (GE 33): Schaufuss
Zärtlichen Verwandten, Die / The tender kinsfolk (GE 30): Stark-Gstettenbaur
Zärtliches Geheimnis / Tender secret (DE 56): Ande
Za stenoi / Beyond the wall (SU 28): Lyudvinski, Chernishoff
Za trnkovym keřem / Behind the sloe-bush (CS 80): Holý
Za vlast Sovetov / For the power of the Soviets (SU 56): Maltsev
Zavorra umana / Human dregs (IT 20): Casarotti
Z biegiem lat, z biegiem dni / As days and years pass (PL 80): Hudziec
Zdravstvuite, deti! / Hello, children! (SU 62): Ashurov, Zharkov,
Zebra in the Kitchen (US 65): North J.
Zebry / Zebras (PL 64): Izdebski
Zeemansvrouwen / Sailors' wives (NL 30): Klein H.
Zeit mit dir, Die / The time with you (DE 48): Bürger

Zelená knížka / The green book (CS 48): Krčka, Mikulič, Jandl
Zelyoni Dol / Green Dol (SU 54): Podmasterev
Zelyoni furgon / The green carriage (SU 59): Kolokoltsev
Zelyoni patrul / The green patrol (SU 61): Guskoff, Kislaryoff
Zenbu seishin ijo ari / Everyone's mad (JP 29): 'Tokkan-Kozo'
Zenobia (US 39): Hurlic
Zerkalo / Mirror (SU 74): Daniltsev, Yankovski
Zéro de conduite / Nought for conduct (FR 32): de Bédarieux, Golstein, Lefebvre L., Pruchon
Zero Hour (US 57): Ferrell
Zew morza / Call of the sea (PL 27): Fijewski
Zhil-bil malchik / Once there was a little boy (SU 60): Basalin
Zhiviye geroyi / Living heroes (SU 59): Narkis, Buyzis, Malashazhkas
Ziel in den Wolken / Target in the clouds (GE 38): Eugens
Zimbo ka beta / Son of Zimbo (IN 64): Sachin
Zimmermädchen...dreimal klingen / Ring three times for chambermaid (GE 33): Klicks
Zimovanje u Jakobsfeldu / Winter in Jakobsfeld (YU 75): Štimac, Goncić
Zindagi zindagi (IN 72): Tito
Zindy, el niño de los pantanos / Zindy, child of the swamps (MX 72): Coster A.
Zip! Boom! Bang! (US 29): Watson D.
Žirafa v okně / A giraffe at the window (CS 68): Masner
Zirkus Renz / The Renz Circus (GE 43): Möller
Zláti úhoři / The golden eels (CS 79): Mikuláš
Zle pondělí / Black Monday (CS 60): Maxián, Smyczek
Złota mahmudia / The golden mahmudia (PL 86): Węgrzyniak
Zmory / Nightmares (PL 78): Hudziec
Żolnierz zwycięstwa / Soldier of victory (PL 53): Wargin
Zolotiye yabloki / Golden apples (SU 54): Bristol
Zolotoi dom / The golden house (SU 59): Semyonov B.
Zolotoi myod / Golden honey (SU 28): Litkin, Zavyaloff
Zonnetje / Sonny (NL/GB 20): Doxat-Pratt
Zooals ik ben / Just as I am (GB/NL 20): Doxat-Pratt
Zoo in Budapest (US 33): Albright
Zouzou (FR 34): Grave
Zpívající pudřenka / The musical powder-compact (CS 59): Maxián, Smyczek
Zub akuli / The shark's tooth (SU 59): Choloyev
Zug fährt ab, Ein / A train is leaving (GE 42): Eugens
Zum Teufel mit der Penne / Damn the dosshouse (68 DE): 'Heintje'
Zürcher Verlobung / Zürich engagement (DE 57): Kaiser
Zur Chronik von Grieshuus / The Grey House chronicles (GE 25): Peterhans
Zuster Brown / Nurse Brown (NL/GB 21): Doxat-Pratt
Zvonyat, otkroite dver / Go and answer the door! (SU 66): Kosikh
Zvyozdni malchik / The Star Boy (SU 57): Guskoff
Zvyozdochka / Little star (SU 62): Ilnitski, Kislenko
Zwei Kinder / Two children (GE 24): Pottier
Zwischen den Eltern / Between the parents (GE 38): Dann
Zwischen Himmel und Erde / Between heaven and earth (GE 42): Möller
Zwischen Mond und Sonne / Between moon and sun (DE 81): Spree
Zwölfjährige Kriegsheld, Der / The 12-year-old war hero (GE 15): Reinwald

Bibliography

Besides the film yearbooks and trade periodicals of various countries, I have been most indebted to:

The American Film Institute's catalogues of 1910-1929 and the 1960s.

Alfred Bauer's *Deutscher Spielfilm-Almanach*.

Bianco e Nero's *Filmlexicon degli Autore e delle Opere*.

Raymond Chirat's *Catalogues des Films Français*.

Gabe Essoe's *Tarzan of the Movies*.

Emilio García Riera's *Historia documental del cine Mexicano*.

Denis Gifford's *British Film Catalogue, 1895-1985*.

Johan Glenzdorf's *Internationales Film-Lexikon* (1960).

Arnold Hending's *Alverdens Barnestjerner* (Denmark 1949).

Piet Hein Honig and Hanns-Georg Rodek's *100001*.

Ephraim Katz's *International Film Encyclopedia*.

Kürschner's *Biographisches Theater-Handbuch* (1956, ed. Dr Herbert A. Frenzel and Prof. Dr Hans Joachim Moser).

Richard Lamparski's *Whatever Became Of . . .?* series.

Gerhard Lamprecht's *Deutsche Stummfilme*.

Einar Lauritzen and Gunnar Lundquist: *American Film Index, 1908-1915* and *1916-1920*.

Leonard Maltin and Richard W. Bann: *Our Gang – the Life and Times of the Little Rascals*.

Dr Kurt Mühsam and Egon Jacobson: *Lexicon des Filmes* (1926).

Jay Robert Nash and Stanley Ralph Ross: *The Motion Picture Guide*.

Francesco Savio's *Ma l'amore, no* (Italian films of the 1930s).

Jukka Sihvonen's *Kuviteltuja Lapsi*.

William T. Stewart, Arthur F. McClure and Ken D. Jones: *International Film Necrology*.

Sven G. Winquist and Torsten Jungstedt: *Svenska Filmskådespelar-Lexicon* (1973).

General Index

(Boy actors with featured entries in the book are in bold print, as are the pages of their main reference. Illustrations are indicated by an asterisk.)

Aaker, Dee, 241, 399
Aaker, Lee, 241*
Aapeli, 283
Aassen, John, 135*
Abbas, Khwaja Ahmad, 256
Abbott and Costello, 172, 198
Abe, Tetsue, 399
Abel, Al, 340
Abel, Walter, 129*
Abélard, Anatole, see **Mary, Anatole 'Bébé', 25**
Aber, Nestor, 399
Achard, Marcel, 198
Ackles, David, 399
Acord, Art, 59
Adames, John, 399
Adams, Brandon, 399
Adams, Robert, 96*
Adel, Léo, 399
Adeyev, Viktor, 399
Adiarte, Patrick, 240
Adrien, le petit, 399
Afravian, Adnan, 399
Agdamov, Ravshan, 399
Agensø, Anders, 358
Ageyev, Volodya, 399
Åhlin, Margita, 396
Ahromi, Hassan Haydari, 399
'Ahui', 399
Aidinyan, A., 399
Airey, Paul, 399
Åkerblom, Johan, 399
Akim, Filiz, 356
Akimovich, Lenya, 399
Akopyan, M., 399
Alankar, Master, 338
Albee, Josh, 399
Albert, Edward, Jr., 399, 437*
Albertini, Luciano, 38
Albright, Wally, 123, 131*, 138-9*
Alejandro, Miguel, 320*
Aleksandrov, Borya, 399
Aleksanian, M., 399
Aleksei, Tsarevich, 150, 394

Alekseyev, Igor, 399
Alexander, Ben, 32, 34, 49-51*, 52*, 437*
Alexander, Louis, 399
Alexander, Tad, 113*
Alexandersson, Gösta, 40*, 317
'Alfalfa', see **Switzer, Carl, 145**
Alfaro, Angel Diaz, 399
'Alfio', 206*
Alford, Philip, 276*
Alice (chimpanzee), 359*
Aliyev, Ibrahim, 399
Allen, Chad, 399
Allen, Chet, 212
Allen, Phillip R., 344*
Allen, Willi, 42
Allen, Woody, 342
Alleney, Ali, 399
Alleney, Tamba, 399
Allwin, Pernilla, 381
Almgren, Sven, 399
Alonso, José Luis, 399, 437*
Alonso, Pablo, 261, 399
Alonso, Tito, 399
Altman, Robert, 203, 208, 212, 225
Alurkov, Georgi, 299
Alurkov, Yanush, 299*
Alvarez, Pedro, 399
Alvina, Anicée, 305
Amazan, Claude, 327
Ambas, Genevieve, 330
Amis, Martin, 360
Ammon, Bernard, 399
Amo, Antonio del, 261
Ancona, Ricardo, 399, 437*
Anda, Raoul de, Jr., 210-11
Ande, Michael, 248-9*
Anderiesen, Hansje, 399
Andersen, Hans, 203, 230
Andersen, Mads Bugge, 399
Andersen, Poul, 399
Anderson, Bobby, 187*
Anderson, Lindsay, 94, 305
Anderson, Michael, Jr., 400

Anderson, Robert, 187
Andersson, Bibi, 317
Andersson, Erik, 400
Ando, Kazuhito, 352
Andor, Paul, see **Zilzer, Wolfgang, 17**
Andreas, Dimitri, 370
Andresen, Björn, 308-9*, 338
Andropov, Yuri, ix
Andrusco, Richie, 400
Angeletti, Marietto, 288*
Angeletti, Ruggero, 400
'Angelito', see **Gomez, Angel, 288**
'Angelo', see **Maggio, Angelo, 219**
Anger, Kenneth, 14, 168
Angst, Pavol, 400
Annichiarico, Vito, 400
Annis, Francesca, 374
Antín, Manuel, 308
Aoki, Tomihiro, 194-5
Aoki, Tomio 'Tokkan-Kozo', 118-19*, 124, 194
Aouini, Amor, 400
Apte, Ram, 154
Aravind, Master, 400
Archibald, Stephen, 342*
Arco, Nino del, 325*
Arden, Curtis, 400
Arglen, George, 200, 400
Arifi, Krenar, 400
Arkhipov, Tolya, 400
Arkin, Alan, 320
Armetta, Henry, 133*
Armstrong, Billy, 81
Arngrim, Stefan, 400
'Arnold', 38
Aronen, Ossi, 284
Arpagäus, Stefan, 225, 369
Arrabal, Fernando, 320
Arshinkov, Ivan, 340-1*
Artemus Boys, 400
Artese, Mario, 114
Arthur, George K., 90
Asahara, Nobutaka, 400

Berestowski, Wadim, 227, 269, 282, 319
Bergman, Ingmar, 168, 292, 317, 329, 381-2
Bergman, Ingrid, 179, 340
Bergman, Johan, 401
Bergner, Elisabeth, 68, 115, 184, 314
Berkeley, Busby, 152
Berkeley, Lady Molly, 228
Berle, Milton, see **Berlinger, Milton, 36**
Berlinger, Milton, 36
Bernard, Butch, 401
Berneis, Benno, 43
Berneis, Peter, see **Eysoldt, Peter, 43**
Bernhard, Göran, 179
Bernhardt, Sarah, 29, 97
Berri, Claude, 321
Bertolucci, Bernardo, 347
Best, Marc, viii, 6, 179, 257
Betanco, Antonio J., 376
Bettles, Robert, 237, 341
Beymer, Richard, 192, 398, 401
Bhattacharjee, Bibhu, 255
Bhattacharya, Niren, 401
Bhattarak, Param, 401
Bibhu, Master, see **Bhattacharjee, Bibhu, 255**
Bichkoff, Yura, 401
'Big Boy', see **Sabiston, Malcolm, 119**
Bigelow, Mabel, 106
Bill, Tony, 348
Billings, Elmo, 54*
Billings, George, 142
Billings, George A., 142
Billingsley, Peter, 386*
Binger, Maurits, 59, 72
Binyon, Claude and Hugh, 174
Binyon, Conrad, 174*
Birkin, Andrew, 364
Birkin, Jane, 364
Biru, Banyu, 401
Biryukoff, Gena, 401
Bishop, Piers, 401
Bisset, Jacqueline, 318
Bjerg, Peter, 358
Bjørnsson, Fredbjørn, 401
Black, Buck, 84*
Black, Jeremy, 401
Blackton, Charles Stuart, 401
Blain, Gérard, 333
Blake, Bobby, 168, 185-6*
Blanch, Jaime, 401
Blankenship, Harold, 401
Blasetti, Alessandro, 206, 215
Blawut, Jacek, 401
Bleger, Lucas, 401
Blier, Bertrand, 346
Blitz, Peter, 209
Blomfield, Derek, 100
Blusch, Walter, 401

Boal, Raymond, 401
Boardman, True, Jr., 40-1*
Boardman, True, Sr., 41
Boardman, Virginia True (Virginia Eames), 41
Bobikin, Tolya, 401
Bobrovski, Seryozha, 376*
Bocancea, Ionel, 328, 401
Bock, Raoul de, 401
Boda, Benjamin, 401
Bodianu, Ion, 401
Bødker, Cecil, 371
'Bodo', 401
Bodurov, Raiko, 299
Boer-van Rijk, Esther de, 59
Bogarde, Dirk, 212, 308
Bogart, Humphrey, 215
Bohigas, Fernandito, 401
Bohm, Hark, 337-8
Bohm, Marquard, 337
Böhme, Matthias and Wolfgang, 401
Bois, Curt, 18-19*
Boitot, Pascal and Patrick, 401
Bollner, Michael, 320
Bolme, Thomas, 401
Bond, James III, 401
Bond, Steve, 175, 231, 298-9
Bond, Tommy, 125, 153*, 158, 168
Bonelli, Francesco, 369-70
Bonnefous, Jean-Pierre, 401
Bonsall, Brian, 401
Boonthavee, Kampoon, 384
Boorman, Charley, 363
Boorman, John, 363
Bor, Hanuš, 286
Borg, Björn, 363
Borgnine, Ernest, 167, 317
Borisevich, Ye., 401
Boriskin, Pavlik, 401
Borowczyk, Walerian, 362
Borsi, József, 401
Borzunoff, Alyosha, 401
Boss, Frances and Matilda, 14
Boss, Yale, 5, 14-15*, 21
Bosse, Peter, 171, 174*, 179
Bosselmann, Lutz, 307*
Bostan, Elisabeta, 328, 368
Bosworth, Hobart, 30
Botha, Louwtjie, 401
'Bouboule', 37, 63
Boudreaux, Joseph, 401
Boudwin, Jimsy, 402
Boughedir, Selim, 402
Bourget, Paul, 40
Bourvil (André Raimbourg), 318
'Bout de Zan' (René Poyen), 26, **36-7***
Bowakow, Dschingis, 337-8*
Bowery Boys, The, 271

Bowie, David, 188
Bowyer, Ivor, 402
Boyd, Jimmy, 211
Bracken, Eddie, 398
Brackmann, Günther, 402
Bradbury, Ray, 389
Braden, Christopher, 402
Bradford, Jesse, 402
Bradley, Dai, see **Bradley, David, 301**
Bradley, David, 301*, 306, 389
Bradman, Don, 376
Brambilla, Franco, 402
Branagh, Kenneth, 394
Branald, Adolf, 45*, 64
Branald, Karel, see **Branald, Adolf, 45**
Branald, Richard, 45
Brandis, Jonathan, 394, 402
Brando, Marlon, 395
Brandt, Bert, 219
Brantford, Bert and Aggie, 48
Brantford, Mickey, 48*
Brassard, Georgie, 402
Brassett, Stephen, 402
Bratkauskas, Dainius, 345*
Brauer, Charles, see **Knetschke, Charly, 193**
Braun, Hermann, 95
Bravo, Danny, 271
Bravo, Juliancito, 307
Bray, Richard, 402
Brazier, Ben, 389, 402
Brazzi, Rossano, 273
Breakston, George, 95-6*, 301-2, 306
Brecht, Bertolt, 19, 90, 227, 281
Brécourt, Jacques, 402
Breen, Bobby, 133, 143, 153-4*, 194
Brenner, Hansl, 210*
Brent, Eve, 270
Breuer, Siegfried, 226
Brick, Mustapha, 282
Bridges, Beau, 229
Bridges, Jeff, Lloyd and Todd, 229
Brignoli, Omar, 402
Brignone, Guido, 109
Brimley, Wilford, 393
Bringmann, Peter F., 338
Bristol, Igor, 402
Britten, Benjamin, 229, 359
Brittenden, Tony, 332
Brockwell, Gladys, 52*
Brockwell, Leonard, 402
Brodie, Kevin, 294-5
Brodie, Steve, 294
Brodrick, Malcolm, 249-50*
Bronson, Charles, 319
Brook, Peter, 267, 362
Brooke, Michael, Jr., 402
Brooks, Louise, 65

530

534

Flateau, Léon and Serge, 286-7
Flensmark, Steen, 262*
Fletcher, Dexter, 85, **358-60***
Fletcher, Steve, 358
Fletcher-Cook, Graham, 358
Flipper (dolphin), 265
Flohr, Norbert, 406
Florath, Albert, 90, 127
Flynn, Errol, 1, 167
Foamete, Sanda, 328
Fog, Tobias, 395
'Foghorn', *see* **Winslow, George, 257**
Fogiel, Henryk, 461*
Fomchenko, Igor, 406
Fonda, Peter, 380
Fong, Allen, 384
Fønss, Mogens, 406
Fønss, Olaf, 53
Foote, David, 246
Ford, Aleksander, 87
Ford, Glenn, 304*
Ford, Harrison, 381, 398
Ford, John, 33, 71, 130, 133
Foreman, Carl, 287
Forest, Jean, 3, 44*, **54-5***, 97
Forlong, James, 406
Forman, Miloš, 237, 387
Formato, Domenico, 406
Formby, George, 398, 406
Forst, Willi, 89*
Forte, Fabrizio, 383
Fortunato, Pasquale, 406
Fossey, Brigitte, 220, 261
Foster, Flora, 18
Foster, Jodie, 329
Foster, Norman, 134*
Foster, Richard R., 406
Fourcade, Christian, 85, **233***
Fox, Edward, 212
Fox, Huckleberry, 394*
Fox, Johnny, Jr., 42-3*, 49, 54
Fox, William (b. 1911), 212
Fox, William, 103, **212-13***
Fram (bear), 368
Frame, Philip, 330*
Frana, H., 406
France, Anatole, 54
Francey, Micheline, 177
Franchina, Sandro, 406
Francis (talking mule), 138
Francis, Jon, 406
Francis, Kay, 104
Francis, Marie, 58
François, Michel, 164-5*, 177
Franju, Georges, 255-6
Frank, Jeffrey, 364-5, 461*
Franklin, Benjamin, 17

Franklin, Chester and Sidney, 5, 22, 35, 42, 44, 51, 91
Frątczak, Jozef, 406
Frayne, Stephen, 406
Freda, Riccardo, 183
Freddy-Karl, Serge, 407
Frederick, Freddie Burke, 109-10*
Frederick, Pauline, 109
Freimanis, Aivars, 382
Freitas, Ruben and Marco de, 407
Frend, Charles, 374
Frerichs, Christian, 407
Fresnay, Pierre, 177, 198, 242
Frezza, Giovanni, 407
Friedl, Fritz von, 226-7*
Friedl, Fritz von, Sr., 226
Friedrikh, Vitya, 407
Fritsch, Willy, 305
'Froggy', *see* **Laughlin, Billy, 180**
Frost, Philip, 407
'Frugolino', *see* **Roveri, Ermanno, 21**
Frye, Soleil Moon, 373
Fryk, Tomas, 362-3*
Fučik, Julius, 356
Fuehrer, Bobby, 7, 407
Fuller, Brook, 330*
Fuller, Jean, 407
Furlong, Edward, 407
Furlong, Kirby, 407
Furrh, Chris, 267

Gabin, Jean, 26, 144, 315
Gable, Clark, 154, 288
Gábor, Pál, 373
Gabriel, Vasso, 282
Gabriëlse, Bart, 407
Gabrovski, Slavyan, 407
Gaete, Emilio, 407
Gagnon, Jacques, 326*
Gaillard, Jimmy, 74*
Gainsborough, Michael, 168
Gajer, Václav, 377
Gale, Jože, 221
Galle, Gianluca, 407
Gallico, Paul, 228
Galo, Igor, 407
Gaman, Tom, 407, 461*
Gamba, Pierino, 204
Gambard (director), 25-6
Gamble, Mason, 407
Gance, Abel, 28, 39-40
Ganev, Dimiter, 367-8*
Ganguly, Rajiv, 407
Ganichev, Tolya, 407
Gans, Ronald, 298
Garber, Matthew, 407
Garbo, Greta, 79*, 127

Garcha, Kiran, 407
Garcia, Lolo, 407
García Lorca, Federico, 245
García Riera, Emilio, 163, 177
Gardner, Ava, 215
Gardner, Herb, 276
Garfield, John, 216*
Garfield, Leon, 371
Gargan, William, 116*, 198*
Gariazzo, Mario, 343
Garland, Judy, 102, 120, 125, 275, 298, 350
Garlick, Stephen, 407
Garner, Peggy Ann, 249
Garrett, Leif, 338*, 355
Garrison, David, 373
Garson, Greer, 184, 213*
Garvolt, Jaromír, 407
Gašević, Boško, 407
Gauster, Harald, 407
Gavrilov, Tolya, 407
Gazdag, Gyula, 395
Ge Zuozhi, 130-1*
Gebert, Gordon, 228*, 359
Geckler, Per, 262, 407
Géczy, István, 407
Geeson, Judy, 374
Geffroy, Henri-Charles, 140
Geffroy, Jean-Pierre, 140-1*, 144*, 155
Gélin, Daniel, 36, 325
Gélin, Xavier, 297
Gemini, Marco, 407
Gencel, Jacky, 228-9*
Genevois, Emile, 84-5*
Genevois, Simone, 3, 25
'Gennariello', *see* **Notari, Eduardo, 20**
Georgadze, Dato, 407
George VI, King, 213
George, Heinrich, 95
George, Jean, 309
George, Susan, 374
Gerritsen, Liza, 41
Gertler, Viktor, 238
Gerulaitis, Vitas, 319
Gervais, Gérard, 407
Geschonneck, Erwin, 343
Getty, Balthazar, 267, 407
Geula, Jack, 407
Gévai, G. Simon, 407
Gharbi, Ahmed, 407
Giai, Henri, 407
Giannozzi, Simone, 309
Gibson, Colin, 407
Gibson, Hoot, 122, 149
Gift, Donn, 186
Gil, Miguelito, 282-3*
Gilbert, Lewis, 257, 305, 374, 398
Gilling, John, 13

Hämäläinen, Raino, 148-9*
Hamilton, Lloyd, 106
Hammerstein, Oscar, 29
Hammond, Brian, 408
Hammond, Nicholas, 284
Hamrick, Burwell, 27-8
Hamshere, Keith, 273, 408
Handzlik, Jan, 408
Hanke, Jochen and Jürgen, 408
Hanley, Thomas, 408
Hannaford, David, 110, 225, **235-6*,**
    241, 386
Hannaford, Mark, 235
Hann-Byrd, Adam, 408
Hardy, Thomas (novelist), 392
Hardy, Capt. Thomas M., 71
Harkányi, Endre, 231, 408
Harlan, Veit, 127
Harper, Tommy, 408
Harper, Valerie, 373
Harris, Buddy, 408
Harris, Neil Patrick, 408
Harris, Richard, 333
Harris, Ross, 374
Harrison, Andrew, 408
Harrison, Simon, 408
Harron, Bobby, 10*
Harron, Johnnie, 10
Hart, William S., 20, 51
Hartleben, Dale, 408
Hartleben, Jerry, 408
Hartley, L.P., 314
Harvey, Anthony, 398, 408
Hašler, Karel, 408
Hathaway, Noah, 389-90, 393
Hauck, Roy, 5, **17**
Haudepin, Didier, 293*
Haudepin, Sabine, 293
Hauff, Wilhelm, 244
Havelock-Allan, Anthony, 228
Hawke, Ethan, 380, 408
Hawkes, Ian, 408
Hawkins, Jimmy, 231
Hawkins, Timmy, 231
Hawks, Howard, 178
Hawley, Andrew, 408
Hawtrey, Sir Charles, 17, 103
Hay, Will, 1, 111*, 133
Hayama, Masao, 137*, 157*
Hayes, Dirkie, *see* **Uys, Wynand, 334**
Haziza, Fabien, 28*
Haziza, Gilberte, 28
Headrick, Richard, 77*, 189
Hebert, Chris, 408
Heermann, Victor, 10
Hegedüs, Tommy, 409
Heggie, O.P., 104*

Hehn, Albert, 305
Hehn, Sascha, 305-6*
Heimann, Kai, 47
'Heintje' (Hein Simons), 310*
Hellbom, Olle, 319, 340, 367
Hemingway, Ernest, 216
Hemmings, David, 229*, 296, 374
Hemmings, Nolan, 229
Hen, Jozef, 269
Henderson, Dick, Jr., 409
Henderson, Simon, 409
Hénin, Georges, 40, 409
Hennig, Mike, 409
Henning-Jensen, Bjarne and Astrid, 239, 267
Henning-Jensen, Lars, 239
Henrey, Bobby, 215*
Henrey, Mrs Robert, 215
Henry, Justin, 386-7*
Henry, Mike, 298, 316
Henry, O. (William S. Porter), 361
Henry, Robert 'Buzzy', 67, **176-7*,** 198, 258
Henties, Torsten, 409
Hepburn, Katharine, 121, 270
Hepworth, Cecil, 17, 28
Hepworth, Henry, 103, 409
Hepworth, John, 103, 409
Hepworth, Ronnie, 103*, 164
Herbert, Charles, 277*
Herbert-Bond, John, 409
Herdt, Robbe de, 348
Herranz, Miguel Angel, 409
Herrmann, Lars, 365
Hershewe, Michael, 372*
Herzberg, Martin, 38, **47-8*,** 68, 136, 161
Heskiya, Zacco, 385
Heston, Charlton, 216, 288, 394
Heuzé, André (b. 1880), 62
Heuzé, André, 62*
Hickman, Cordell, 168, 169
Hickman, Darryl, 133, **169-70*,** 378
Hickman, Dwayne, 170, 409
Hicks, Oliver, 388-9*
Hicks, Tommy, 85
Hidalgo, Luis Maria, 409
Higgins, Jamie, 409
Higgins, Joel, 380
Hill, Terence, *see* **Girotti, Mario, 211**
Hill, Trevor, 409
Hillbillies, The, 185
Hiller, Arthur, 343
Hillien, Hervé, 409
Hines, Barry, 301
Hines, Frazer, 248
Hinson, Hall, 396
Hinton, Darby, 461*
Hintsch, Gyuri, 409
Hinz, Werner, 333

Hirabayishi, Kiyoshi, 409
Hirst, Stephen, 409
Hitchcock, Alfred, 91, 127, 303
Hitler, Adolf, 88, 171, 227
Hjelm, Kaj, 157-8*
Hodges, Eddie, 264*
Hodges, Greg, 409
Hodges, Hal, 409
Hoff, Morten, 409
Hoffman, Dustin, 221
Hoffmann, E.T.A., 238
Hoffmann, Günter, 249, 251
Hoffmann, Ilse, 367
Hoffmann, Kurt, 219
Hogdon, John Philip, 409
Holden, Peter, 409
Holden, William, 199*, 379
Holliday, Polly, 394
Holm, Barnaby, 364, 409
Holm, Ian, 364
Holmberg, Dagfinn, 409
Holmes, Denis (b. 1921), 285
Holmes, Dennis, 285
Holmes, John, 374-5*
Holmes, Leon, 60-1*, 136
Holt, David, 151*
Holt, Tim, 398, 409
Holý, Tomáš, 377*
Homeier, Skippy, 398, 409
Homolka, Oscar, 91
Honegger, Arthur, 212
Hook, Harry, 267
Hooks, Eric and Robert, 324, 409
Hooks, Kevin, 324
Hope, Bob, 146, 190
Hopson, Nicholas, 409
Hörbiger, Attila, 220*
Horneff, Wil, 409
Horváth László, 231-2*, 346
Hoskins, Allen 'Farina', 99-100*, 132, 135,
    160, 175
Hoskins, Bob, 359
Hoskins, Jannie, 100
Hough, John, 302
Hould, Ra, *see* **Sinclair, Ronald, 125**
House, Chandler, 47, 409
House, Donald, Dorothy and Jimmy, 47
House, Newton ('actor and cattleman'), 47
House, Newton, 47
Hovey, Tim, 253-4*
Howard, Clint, 304, 409
Howard, Rance and Jean, 304
Howard, Ronny, 172, **304-5*,** 358
Howard, Trevor, 246
Hrušecký, A., 409
Hryniewicz, Henryk, 409
Hubbard, Allan, 409, 461*

Pickford, Mary (Gladys Smith), 10, 13, 27, 32*, 35, 49, 52, 86, 92, 115
Pidgeon, Walter, 184
Pierreux, Jacqueline, 245
Piesis, Gunars, 382
Pike, John, 251*
Pike, Peter, 417
Pilagaonkar, Sharad, 320
Pilbeam, Nova, 97, 154
'Pim', 417
Pintauro, Danny, 417
Pipoly, Daniel, 267
'Pique-Puce', see **Poyen, René, 36**
Pirev, Erik, 417
'Pitusin', see **Hurtado, Alfredo, 82**
Pius XI, Pope, 66
Piwowarski, Radosław, 385
Plata, Manitas de, 317
Pleasence, Donald, 261
Pleva, Josef Václav, 308
Podmasterev, Seryozha, 417
Poe, Edgar Allan, 164
Poggio, Andres, 417
Pogorelski, Antoni, 382
Pogosian, A., 417
Pojani, Rauf, 327*
Poláček, Palko, 417
Polák, Jiří, 416, 497*
Polimeno, Santo, 417
Pollak, Kay, 363
Pollard, Snub, 57, 82
Polletin, Katia, 225
Pollock, Dee, 417
Pollock, Muriel, 184
Pomaski, Janusz, 417
Pomeranc, Max, 417
Ponce, Danny, 373, 385
'Poncianito', see **Perez, Ismael, 225**
Popescu, Dan, 417
Poplavets, Vanya, 417
Popoff, Sasha, 417
Porath, Ove, 417
Porro, Luca, 417
Porter, Gene Stratton, 41
Porter, Todd, 417
Porter, William, Jr., 417
Pospišil, Miša, 417
Postránecký, Václav, 241
Potměšil, Jan, 360
Potter, Bertie, 417
Pottier, Jeannette, 68
Pottier, Waldemar, 3, 68-9*
Potts, Danny, 417
Pouira, Denis, 417
Poujouly, Georges, 220-1*, 241, 245*, 315
Poupaud, Melvil, 417
Powell, Clive, 497*

Powell, Dick, 71
Powell, Michael, 111, 374
Powell, William, 128
Power, Tyrone, 58, 116
Poyen, René 'Bout de Zan', 3, 26, 36-7*
Pöysti, Lasse, 417
Prahov, Veselin, 397*
Pražský, Beda, 64*
Pražsky, Přemysl, 64
Prela, Kol, 417
Presley, Elvis, 73, 291-2
Presson, Jason, 380, 417
Price, Peter Edward, 219*
Prokeš, Jan, 192*
Prokopchuk, Dima, 417
Pronin, Vasili, 193
Provost, Jon, 230, 279-80*
Prowse, Heydon, 417
Pruchon, Gilbert, 94, 417
Ptichkin, Tolya, 417
Pucholt, Vladimir, 237*
'Pudge', see **Donaldson, Ted, 184**
Puente, Diego, 417
Puff, Henri, 321
'Pulgarcito', see **Quezadas, Cesareo, 290**
Pulvirenti, Orazio, 417
Pupko, Sasha, 417
Purcell, Emma, 11
Purnell, Frankie, 417
Puro, Teuvo and Sirkka, 35
Putten, Herbert van, 417
Puttnam, David, 359
Puttnam, Sacha, 417

Quan, Ke Huy, 387
Quezadas, Cesareo, 290*
Quine, Richard, 398
Quinn, Bill, 417
Quinn, Teddy, 417

Rabagliati, Alberto, 51
Rabelo, Alessandro, 417
Rabinowicz, David, 369
Racine, Jean, 245
Radcliffe, Violet, 5, 34, 44
Radenković, Vladimir, 417
Radetsky, Hansi, 417
Radhakrishnan, President, 320
Radonjić, Dragan, 417
Radványi, Géza, 231
Rae, John, 274, 389
Raffoul, François, 417
Raft, George, 106-7, 215
Ragó, Iván, 417
Rahmin, Rahman, 417
Railo, Tuomo, 417
Raitt, Bonnie, 248

Rajoo, Master, 362
Rakitin, Sasha, 417
Rameau, Jean Philippe, 177
Ramon, Bernice, 76
Ramon, Laon, see **Janney, Leon, 76**
Ramos da Silva, Fernando, 368-9*
Ramu, Master, 342
Randall, Ethan, 417
Rangno, Terry, 268*
Rao, Visweswara, 417
Rasp, Fritz, 80*, 193
Rathmann, Harald, 417
Ratiani, Gogi, 93-4*
Rau, Brigitte, 158
Raum, Warren, 417
Rauzéna, Fernand, 35
Rauzéna, Jean, 35-6*
Rawlings, Marjorie Kinnan, 189
Ray, Andrew, 213-14*
Ray, Michel, 248*, 272
Ray, Robin and Ted, 213
Ray, Satyajit, 250
Raye, Helen, 296
Raymond, Gene, see Gion, Raymond, 398, 417
Raymond, Ray, 14
Raynor, Etta, 34
Reboul, Nicolas, 417
Reck, Günther, 417
Redden, Arthur, 36
Redford, Robert, 186
Redgrave, Michael, 181, 240, 284
Redlin, Dwayne, 417
Reed, Carol, 97, 215
Reed, Oliver, 336
Rees, Lanny, 186-7*
Reeves, Breezy, Jr., see **Eason, Breezy, Jr., 67**
Reggiani, Serge, 217*
Reichert, Dirk, 417
Reichhoff, Max, 417
Reid, Mrs Wallace, 64*
Reiner, Rob, 381, 390
Reinhardt, Max, 101, 168
Reinwald, Grete and Hanni, 14
Reinwald, Otto, 14*
Reisner, Charles, 89
Reisner, Dean, 89
Réjane (Gabrielle-Charlotte Réju), 97
Relja, Mate, 307
Renard, Jules, 62
Renaud, Madeleine, 164
Renč, Filip, 356*
Renfro, Brad, 417
Rennie, Max, 389, 418
Rennie, Michael, 207
Reno, Bud, 372
Reno, Kelly, 198, 341, 364, 372-3*
Rentschler, Mickey, 118*, 136*